Fundamental Perspectives
on International Law

SECOND EDITION

William R. Slomanson
Professor of International Law
Western State University — San Diego

West Publishing Company

Minneapolis/Saint Paul   New York   Los Angeles   San Francisco

PHOTO CREDITS

61 United Nations/Photo by T. Chen; **142** European Community Delegation, Washington D.C.; **223** The Lyndon Baines Johnson Library; **253** left, American Petroleum Institute; right, American Mining Congress; **298** Consolidated News; **303** Official U.S. Air Force Photo; **365** United Nations; **366** United Nations; **385** U.S. Department of the Army; **495** National Archive; **536** AP/Wide World Photos.

PROJECT MANAGEMENT	Labrecque Publishing Services
COPYEDITING	Mark Woodworth
PAGE COMPOSITION	Tory McLearn
PROOFREADING	Lisa Auer
COVER IMAGE	Ralph Mercer/Tony Stone Images

WEST'S COMMITMENT TO THE ENVIRONMENT

In 1906, West Publishing Company began recycling materials left over from the production of books. This began a tradition of efficient and responsible use of resources. Today, up to 95 percent of our legal books are printed on recycled, acid-free stock. West also recycles nearly 22 million pounds of scrap paper annually—the equivalent of 181,717 trees. Since the 1960s, West has devised ways to capture and recycle waste inks, solvents, oils, and vapors created in the printing process. We also recycle plastics of all kinds, wood, glass, corrugated cardboard, and batteries, and have eliminated the use of Styrofoam book packaging. We at West are proud of the longevity and the scope of our commitment to the environment.

Production, Prepress, Printing and Binding by West Publishing Company.

 Text Is Printed on 10% Post Consumer Recycled Paper

British Library Cataloguing-in Publication Data. A catalogue record for this book is available from the British Library.

COPYRIGHT ©1990   By WEST PUBLISHING COMPANY
COPYRIGHT ©1995   By WEST PUBLISHING COMPANY
                    610 Opperman Drive
                    P.O. Box 64526
                    St. Paul, MN 55164-0526

Library of Congress Cataloging-in-Publication Data

Slomanson, William R.
   Fundamental Perspectives on International Law/William R. Slomanson.—2nd ed.
      p. cm.
   Includes bibliographical references and index.
    ISBN 0-314-06399-4 (hard: alk. paper)
    1. International law. I. Title.
JX3091.S56   1996
341—dc20   95-30466
                                                        CIP

Dedication

Otra vez para LAMPC
Las luces de mi vida

SUMMARY OF CONTENTS

TABLE OF CONTENTS

TABLE OF CASES

Principal case names are in italic type whereas names of cases cited or discussed in the text are in roman type. Page numbers in italics reference case texts and selected quotations. Case names cited in principal cases and within other quoted materials are not included in this table.

TABLE OF TREATIES/RESOLUTIONS/ MISCELLANEOUS INSTRUMENTS

This index contains treaties, resolutions, and miscellaneous agreements. The various provisions of the UN Charter are not included in this Table. Relevant provisions of the Charter are indexed in the subject index (p. 641) and set forth in Appendix A (p. 607).

Abbreviations: CSCE—Conference on Security and Cooperation in Europe; ICJ—International Court of Justice; IL—International Law; LON—League of Nations; NAFTA—North American Free Trade Agreement; NIEO—New International Economic Order; OAS—Organization of American States; UNGARES—United Nations General Assembly Resolution; UNSCRES—United Nations Security Council Resolution.

PREFACE

This is a fascinating time to study International Law. The end of the Cold War spawned new problems, including a breakdown of State sovereignty. Scores of States began to redefine themselves. The Soviet Union no longer exists, having broken up into a dozen new State entities. One of the independent States of Eastern Europe—Yugoslavia—disintegrated into five more States. One of these five—Bosnia—has further splintered into smaller entities. Ethnic cleansing and renewed pre–Cold War hostilities are increasingly commonplace. Access to these events is now facilitated by an *international* information superhighway linking public/private, urban/rural, and local/regional communities throughout the world. This book explores the dynamics of these contemporary developments connecting the past and future of International Law.

Several categories of texts are available for the introductory course in International Law. A *casebook* is essentially a collection of edited judicial opinions. But in this particular discipline, the applicable law consists of much more than cases and statutes. A *treatise* is a descriptive statement of principles that form the content of International Law. It does not contain the original text of the prominent international cases. Instead, the treatise presents legal norms in a descriptive or narrative format. It offers no questions or exercises to test application. By contrast, *Fundamental Perspectives on International Law* is a composite of the above teaching tools. It is designed for both undergraduate courses in International Law and for law school courses—where the instructor prefers a blend of cases, narrative commentary, and problems. The contents of this book are designed to integrate the most useful features of the various academic approaches, to introduce the essential doctrines of International Law, and to encourage classroom interaction.

The presentation of this course in a one-volume text requires some difficult choices about content. One must synthesize centuries of writings, from a variety of perspectives, to develop a contemporary snapshot. This is a particularly daunting task, given the many instances where State practice has not produced a focused picture of the content of International Law.

The Second Edition shares some important pedagogical features with the First. Professors are steadily incorporating more economics, history, and political science into their International Law courses—so that the well-rounded student can more fully appreciate content and evolution. This edition thus provides more depth in terms of the nonlegal component of International Law because, unlike national law, there is no dominant legislative, executive, or judicial branch for controlling State conduct. This textbook has also retained its "foreign flavor." It incorporates more perspectives than those embraced by just one nation of the nearly 200 members of the community of nations. Its goal is to synthesize the salient features of a discipline spawned by diverse legal systems, radically different cultures, numerous political variables, and centuries of evolution.

Changes in Second Edition

This Second Edition of *Fundamental Perspectives on International Law* is a substantial revision. It presents a familiar but modified chapter structure. The specific changes include:

- A new chapter on International Environmental Law;

- Chapters that now treat *separately* States/organizations, individuals/human rights, and jurisdiction/sovereignty;

- New sections on the history of International Law, the influence of religion, International Relations, changes in State status, corporate nationality, alternative dispute resolution, the International Criminal Court, humanitarian intervention, Laws of War, State terrorism, US human rights perspectives, international environmental standards, and the World Trade Organization;

- Additional perspectives on the sources of International Law, the work of key international organizations, sovereignty, dispute resolution, force, human rights, the environment, and International Economic Relations;

- More original documents and interdisciplinary materials incorporating history, political science, religion, economics, military strategies, and international relations—to illustrate the significant impact of *non*legal variables on the creation and evolution of international legal principles;

- Many new tables ("Exhibits") to facilitate quick access to course content and to present certain categories of information in a convenient graphic format;

- Many new and different cases, excerpts, and related questions to encourage student review and comprehension;

- New problems based on actual events, for applying the textual materials to contemporary issues in International Law;

- The placement of role-playing problems, a chapter summary, and a chapter bibliography near the end of each chapter to streamline the text;

- A glossary to promote student synopsis of textual content;

- A revised research guide, in an appendix that includes on-line computerized sources;

- An appendix on career opportunities.

Chapter Organization

Given the scope of inter-edition developments, there was a need to reorganize some of the contents into separate chapters, while combining certain sections with others for ease of presentation and comprehension. The opening definitional chapter emphasizes the sources of International Law, the impact of other disciplines, and the relation between national and international legal paradigms. The next building block contains Chapters 2 through 4 on States, organizations, and individuals/corporations. The following unit consists of Chapters 5 through 10 on the often interrelated themes of jurisdiction, sovereignty, diplomacy, treaties, and dispute resolution. The remaining module consists of Chapters 11 through 13 on the cross-cutting themes of international human rights, environment, and economic relations.

Supplemental Materials

The Instructor's Manual provides an analysis of all problems contained in the text, as well as other supporting information including tests and further reference material. Periodic teacher's updates, between editions, analyze key developments affecting the ebb and flow of International Law's ever-changing contours.

Acknowledgments

The author thanks the following individuals and institutions contributing to the evolution of this Second Edition: Brian Andenoro, for his research assistance; Western State University, for its continuing academic support; and the following colleagues and reviewers at other schools, who provided many useful suggestions that enriched this new edition:

L. Jerold Adams
Central Missouri State University

Nozar Alaolmolki
Hiram College, Ohio

Thomas Boudreau
Syracuse University

John King Gamble
Penn State University, Erie Campus

Karen Greenstreet
Marquette University, Wisconsin

Forest Grieves
University of Montana

Clinton G. Hewan
Northern Kentucky University

R. St. J. Macdonald
University of Toronto

Gerard F. Rutan
Western Washington University

William P. Statsky
San Diego, California

Dimitris Stevis
Colorado State University

Robert E. Williams
Pepperdine University, California

Finally, I thank the following individuals at West Publishing Company: Elizabeth Hannan, the project editor for this edition—whose encouragement played a key role in the very substantial revision of this book; Patty Bryant, Development Editor; Jean Amundsen, Production Editor; and Amelia Jacobson, Promotion Manager.

William R. Slomanson
San Diego, California

CHAPTER ONE

What Is International Law?

CHAPTER OUTLINE

■ INTRODUCTION

This first chapter opens with one of the most practical yet understated questions: Why *should* one study the discipline of International Law? It closes with an assessment of how *International* Law differs from "law" in the more orthodox context of *national* law. The basic substance of this chapter provides a sense of what International Law is, the developmental role of related fields, and the integral relationship between national and International Law.

These materials will thus serve as the cornerstone for studying and digesting ensuing chapters. They present the affiliated elements and corollaries of International Law. You may thus launch your study of this fascinating and provocative subject, outfitted with a working knowledge of the fundamental building blocks provided in this first chapter.

■ 1.1 WHY STUDY INTERNATIONAL LAW?

One may begin the study of International Law by considering the alternative—a nation or planet wherein leaders decide to totally disregard International Law. This scenario is not limited to the Dark Ages. That was the comparatively uncivilized period between the thousand–year Pax Romana and the medieval Renaissance's rekindling of the need for international cooperation.

A similar void reappeared more recently, during the 1966–1976 Cultural Revolution in the People's Republic of China. Courses on international law were cancelled. The teachers were summarily dismissed and sent elsewhere for reeducation. The Chinese government made no apologies about its distrust of International Law.[1] As one Chinese writer characterized the state of affairs, "in the Western capitalist world, suppression of the weak by the strong and the eating of small fish by big fish are not only tacitly condoned by bourgeois international law but also are cloaked with a mantle of legality."[2]

When the Cultural Revolution ended in 1976, China's leaders decided that China must participate in the quest for world peace, notwithstanding competitive ideologies within the community of nations. In a 1982 review of the government's new and more liberal policies, the president of the Chinese Society of International Law in Beijing announced that the People's Republic of China had ultimately abandoned its parochial view of International Law. Any historical tendency to remain aloof, or sequestered from the society of nations, was thus supplanted by China's recognition that its isolation was counterproductive to its national interests. His perspective was succinctly worded as follows:

> China's international lawyers must begin to work diligently to rebuild her science of international law which serves to promote world peace and truly represents the interests of the people the world over. . . .
>
> We need to make an intensive study of not only the theory of international law, but the different realms and branches of international law as well to facilitate China's international activities and her legislative work. While doing scientific research in this field, we also have the responsibility to train a new generation of specialists and scholars in international law.[3]

The study of International Law also serves a variety of interdisciplinary purposes. Many individuals mistakenly perceive it as falling within the exclusive dominion of the law schools. There are of course many career opportunities for lawyers in this discipline.[4] Yet the academic value of studying International Law is not limited to law students. Professor Chris Okeke of Nigeria suggests the following list of course objectives for international legal education in his country, where law is an undergraduate major (as it is in many nations of the world):

> (i) To expose the students to a clear understanding of the fact of inter-dependence that . . . states and other subjects of International Law, do not live in isolation, but rather must necessarily be interdependent; (ii) To teach the students to appreciate the universal principles and rules designed to ensure normal relations . . . irrespective of the differences in their economic, political and social systems; (iii) To educate the students in the spirit of humanism, democracy and respect for the sovereignty of all nations and peoples; (iv) To make the students to be constantly aware of the need to fight for the extermination of the rem-

nants (traces) of colonialism and all forms of racial and national oppression.[5]

Studying the doctrinal aspects of International Law as a student provides a window of opportunity for the future decision-maker. He or she may one day pursue concessions from a position of strength, without losing sight of this particular legal system's checks and balances. Winning a war, for example, does not necessarily resolve an international dispute. It temporarily provides the victor with the opportunity to exact concessions from the vanquished. If those concessions are unacceptable—as perceived by Germany under the Treaty of Versailles at the close of the first of the two World Wars—then the parties are not truly at peace. International Law thus embraces the essentials of transnational dispute resolution as an alternative to war and the various forms of low-intensity conflict.

The student of this subject will become acutely aware of the importance of the nonjudicial processes that are essential linchpins of the international legal system. As seen later in this introductory chapter, most of what is referred to as "International Law" is not found in case law or enforceable by international courts. The enforcement mechanisms in this particular branch of law have weaknesses, when compared to similar institutions in its member nations. Contemporary governments cannot operate their domestic institutions free of external constraints, however. As discussed earlier in this section, it took only one decade for the People's Republic of China to learn this lesson.

The materials in this text will reveal that resolving international conflict is not limited to the actions of presidents or prime ministers and diplomats, international organizations such as the United Nations, or judicial processes. Nongovernmental organizations such as the Red Cross or Amnesty International, journalists, military decision-makers, and many others play significant roles in the analysis and development of the events and conditions affecting international relations. How they respond to crises influences how nations behave. Therefore, they must understand the content of International Law and its varied applications.

Business interests are often directly affected by applications of International Law. Economic sanctions, for example, require a response in the corporate sphere of influence. In 1986, President Reagan ordered United States oil companies and civilians to leave Libya as a result of terrorist activity linked to the Libyan government. That decision affected Libya's ability to replace the US technical know-how and any export, shipping, and import infrastructure formerly operated by US enterprises. It also impacted the long-term operations of US interests in that region and limited access to Libyan oil. The subsequent decision of the Libyan government to ignore the United Nations Security Council has not improved Libya's posture in the global economy. Libya refused to release the terrorists allegedly responsible for the bombing of Pan Am flight 103 over Lockerbie, Scotland—further isolating it from the world community and the modern wave of economic integration.

International Law is thus a relevant factor in the decision making of those who influence national behavior. Nations can no longer function in a vacuum. Without customary expectations and treaty commitments, States could not conduct their international relations with the degree of certainty necessary for an ordered society. The demise of the medieval feudal systems demonstrated the need for a system of States that would function as a community of nations bound by commonly accepted norms of conduct—now referred to as International Law.

Contemporary support for the study of International Law is provided by UN General Assembly Resolution 45/40, declaring this to be the UN Decade of International Law (1990–1999). One of the main purposes of this endeavor is to encourage the teaching, study, dissemination, and wider acceptance of International Law. Thus, the UN seeks national support for the academic institutions offering courses in International Law, because education is the key to future success of the international legal system. The agenda of this global education program includes the following central theme:

> Special emphasis should be given to supporting academic and professional institutions already carrying out research and education in international law, as well as encouraging the establishment of such institutions where they might not exist, particularly in the developing countries. States are [thus] encouraged to contribute to the strengthening of the United Nations. . . .[6]

■ 1.2 PUBLIC INTERNATIONAL LAW DEFINED

The terms "nation," "State," and "country" are used interchangeably throughout this text. The terms "International Law," "Law of Nations," and "Public International Law" are used interchangeably unless otherwise distinguished.

Historical State-Driven Definition

International Law is traditionally defined as the body of rules which nations recognize as binding upon one another in their mutual relations. International jurists sometimes employ useful definitions of International Law in their opinions. The Permanent Court of International Justice (predecessor of the current world court) offered the following:

> International law governs relations between independent States. The rules of law binding upon States therefore emanate from their own free will as expressed in conventions [treaties] or by usages [customary state practice] generally accepted as expressing principles of law and established in order to regulate the relations between these co-existing independent communities or with a view to the achievement of common aims.[7]

As stated by Professor Luigi Condorelli of the University of Geneva, States may thus begin to apply a common practice which ultimately becomes the expected result in the international relations between all States—often referred to in the literature as *opinio juris*, meaning juridically mandatory. International Law does not necessarily consist of what States do. Rather, it is a blend of expectations and actual practice.[8] As expressed by the International Court of Justice (or ICJ, the judicial branch of the UN):

> Not only must the acts concerned amount to a settled practice, but they must also be such, or carried out in such a way, as to be evidence of a belief that this practice is rendered obligatory by the existence of a rule of law requiring it. . . . The States concerned must therefore feel that they are conforming to what amounts to a legal obligation. The frequency or even habitual character of the acts is not in itself enough [to constitute *opinio juris*].[9]

In addition to customary practice, the requisite expectations may also be derived from treaty participation or the adoption of UN resolutions. As stated in the ICJ case involving the alleged mining of Nicaraguan harbors by agents of the US, a General Assembly resolution may be evidence of *opinio juris*. The Court was referring to the Assembly's 1970 Resolution 2625(XXV) entitled Declaration on Principles of International Law concerning Friendly Relations and Co-operation among States in accordance with the Charter of the United Nations. The Court thus explained that "the adoption by States of this text affords an indication of their '*opinio juris*' as to customary international law on the question."[10]

Modern Definition/Other Actors

Contemporary International Law still governs the conduct of States. It is no longer limited to just States, however. It is also applicable to international organizations and, in limited circumstances, to individuals (as described in Chapter 4 of this book).

The proliferation of international organizations since World War II effectively meant that International Law could no longer be defined *solely* in terms of the practice of nations. Most international organizations are not able to define the contours of International Law independently of their national membership. Yet the increasing reliance of States on these organizations has thrust a degree of organizational vitality on these relatively new actors on the international scene (*see* § 3.1). State members may thus delegate certain sovereign powers to an international organization, which in turn requires its State members to observe the norms that the organization develops. For example, when the International Telecommunication Union allocates communication frequencies, its national members consent to be bound by its decisions.

Evidence of this expansion of International Law is available in contemporary studies defining its contours to include international organizations, individuals, and corporations. A representative study by the American Law Institute—a prominent group of private lawyers, government officials, and law teachers who are dedicated to the clarification and improvement of both domestic law and national performance in the field of International Law—thus provides as follows:

International Law . . . consists of rules and principles of general application dealing with the conduct of states and international organizations and with their relations *inter se* [among or between themselves], as well as some of their relations with persons, whether natural or juridical [corporations].[11]

Scope

A pervasive problem with defining the specific content of International Law is its constant ebb and flow, altered by influences (including State practice) and differences in interpretation. The periphery often shifts, leaving gray areas which are not distinctly sand or liquid. In certain areas of the law, it may be the standard of conduct at a *given* time because it is not static. Thus, it has been aptly described as evolving gradually in some cases and briskly in others. As expressed by one of the leading commentators writing for the US Department of State:

International law is, more or less, in a continual state of change and development. In certain of its aspects the evolution is gradual; in others it is avulsive. [W]hereas certain customs are recognized as obligatory, others are in retrogression and are recognized as nonobligatory, depending upon the subject matter and its status at a particular time.[12]

Certain publicists (specialists in International Law) adopt the view that this evolutionary process is so pervasive that International Law is not in fact a pre-existing body of rules. Instead, they assert that it is a process of authoritative decision making in which rules are constantly made and remade. These commentators do not question the existence of International Law. They question the utility of the traditional conception that this system is premised on inherited rules rather than acknowledging the undeniable impact of power. Thus, the "distinction between law and politics is artificial, even preposterous."[13] This particular perception links definition and content. Further detail about where one looks to ascertain the content of International Law is provided in § 1.4 (Sources of International Law).

The definitional perspective provided by this section will be more complete if the student recognizes three related themes regarding *universality, power,* and *process.*

First, *universality* of acceptance is not required for a norm to be incorporated into the body of International Law. If enough nations recognize a particular norm, by consistently using it in their international relations, that consensus will cause the norm to become a part of International Law. Given the sovereign nature of the State—both the governor and governed under International Law—a State that expressly rejects what others might term a "universal" rule is not bound by that "rule." Acquiescence may thus bind the same sovereign nation when it chooses not to tender an objection through diplomatic processes or treaty reservations.

One may argue that there should be a universal International Law which binds all nations, even when an objection *is* presented. The law would thus bind all subjects, much like domestic law binds all who are subject to its reach. It has thus been argued that violations of certain norms—including threats to peace, violations of fundamental human rights, and catastrophic risks to the environment—should fall into this category.[14] Whether this argument ultimately succeeds will depend on the degree to which the rather diverse global community of nations can approximate the homogeneity accomplished by members of the European Community. Its integrated institutions have been uniquely successful in achieving the perennial quest for stability and predictability in international relations.

The second theme affiliated with the definition of International Law is that no single nation, no matter how mighty, has the *power* to create or modify International Law. No statute of one nation can create global obligations. A bilateral treaty between two nations creates obligations *inter se,* for which one incurs an admissible claim under International Law if the other breaches its treaty commitments. Thus, International Law is not created, developed, or abolished by the demand of one country or a small group of countries. Its contours are determined by the common consent of many nations.

The third defining theme involves the general *process* or methodology for the evolution of International Law. Nations become bound by the norms of International Law, typically through their express or implicit consent. A nation is expressly bound, for example, by treaty commitments. A nation may also be bound implicitly, via the evolution of customary international practices to which it does not object. Both processes are described in subsequent materials on treaties and sources of International Law.

There are, of course, some wrinkles in the definitional fabric of International Law. Some commenta-

tors cautiously qualify the usual consensus-based definition to include "democratic" and "civilized" elements. Long before the demise of the Soviet Union, Moscow State University Professor Grigori Tunkin included the element that International Law consists of norms with a democratic character. He described it in his 1974 treatise as the "aggregate of norms which are created by agreement between states of different social systems, [which] reflect the concordant wills of states and have a generally *democratic* character. . . ."[15]

Some commentators add the qualification that International Law contains only those norms accepted by "civilized" nations. As stated by a British jurist sitting on the London Court of Appeal in 1977, "it is the sum of rules or usages which *civilised* States have agreed shall be binding upon them in their dealings with one another." This limitation finds support in the Statute of the International Court of Justice. Article 38.1.c provides that the Court may rely on "the general principles of law recognized by civilized nations." Of course, what constitutes "civilized" is subject to varied interpretations which are influenced by social, cultural, economic, and historical mores often seen through the lens of a particular observer.

■ 1.3 HISTORY OF INTERNATIONAL LAW

One can appreciate historical developments in International Law for several practical reasons. Most UN members (approaching 200, as opposed to the original fifty-one) did not exist in 1945. Thus, most members of the current international community suddenly became subject to the existing rules of International Law developed over the course of many centuries. Past developments thus provided an immediate link with the present for the new State or international organization with no comparable history.

Students of International Law should not fall victim to the modern penchant for ignoring the past. Although they are being educated in a very technical era which understandably emphasizes the present and the future, looking back prepares them for avoiding the trite but quite accurate adage that the leader who ignores history is thus condemned to repeat it. The following materials summarize (a) the development of International Law and (b) the schools of thought which shaped how we analyze and examine it.

Development

One could divide the history of Public International Law into three main periods: ancient, medieval, and modern.

Ancient International Law Recorded history indicates that people lived in parts of what is now the Middle East in roughly 25000 B.C. In approximately 4000 B.C., the area spawned two communities which were the cradle of modern civilization—the Egyptians and the Babylonians.

The process by which International Law first developed was spawned by ancient Egyptian and Indian practices. In approximately 3100 B.C., two Mesopotamian city-states concluded a treaty which governed their international relations. Egyptian pharaohs also entered into treaties with neighboring kings beginning in 1400 B.C. These agreements recognized sovereign rights over certain geographical areas, the extradition of refugees, and the exchange of what we now call ambassadors. The Hindus of 1100 B.C. urged humaneness in the conduct of war. Poisoned weapons were thus prohibited. While war in ancient India was not uncommon, victories there and in what is now China were not generally condoned because rulers were expected to aspire to higher glories than those attainable on the battlefield.

Around 800 B.C., the major Middle Eastern civilizations were inundated by a series of invasions. The most famous is that of Alexander the Great in approximately 300 B.C. He introduced the Greek language into the area, followed by the so-called Hellenic Age, which lasted some three hundred years.

The Greek city-states and their philosophers believed that there was a legal hierarchy of local and "higher" laws. Local laws governed the conduct of individuals within each city-state. The laws of the city-state were subordinate to codes such as the Customs of the Hellenes. Accepted practice under this code included protection for aliens via a consular official to represent their interests, diplomatic immunity for foreign agents, and the right of asylum in certain cases.

Ancient Chinese tradition did not embrace law in the sense it is understood in Western civilization. The need for a formalized legal order was perceived as the sign of a somewhat imperfect society. Never-theless, the Confucian influence provided for minimum order, the essentials of which authorized the use of force. The Confucian philosophy of 600 B.C. perceived the Chinese ruler as Heaven's descendent. He was thus considered superior to the rulers of other nations, thereby providing a sense of legitimacy for China's early conquests and domination of its Asian neighbors. Extraterritorial applications of this descendence were conducted under the guise of self-defense, humanitarian intervention, and reprisals or punitive expeditions against barbaric rulers who dared engage in unauthorized invasions against China.

The Romans ultimately conquered most of the Middle East by approximately 30 B.C. The Pax Romana (beginning in 31 B.C.) was a period of relative peace among the Roman, Greek, and "barbaric" city-States of that era. Rome fought incessantly, although those subservient to its control were free from war. Western civilization thus blossomed under Roman control. The ensuing thousand-year period effectively precluded attempts to reject the imposed use of internationally applicable norms. Roman law, for example, governed the rights of aliens—including development of the institution of the Praetor Pegreginus to settle legal disputes involving their interests. The Roman College of Fetiales negotiated treaties with non-Roman entities and decided legal matters associated with waging war against them.

Upon conquering the Greeks, Rome was also exposed to their notion of universality. These distant subjects of Rome's control—and even Rome itself—were then perceived as integrated elements of a unified "international" system.

Medieval International Law The medieval period in the development of International Law can be traced to a variety of developments in international relations. Charlemagne's coronation as Emperor of the West by Pope Leo III in A.D. 800 was a central feature. A new period in international relations followed—including the far-flung religious Crusades affecting Islamic interests, formation of codes such as the Law Merchant for medieval maritime dispute resolution, and the development of the concept of the "just war" by Thomas Aquinas, who was subsequently canonized as a saint by the Roman Catholic Church after he effectively linked the philosophy of Aristotle and the theology of Catholicism.

Islam had its own crusades around A.D. 700, much like those of Christianity. The Muslims conquered much of the Middle East. And, like the ancient Chinese, their Islamic theory was rather hostile to recognizing the possible equality of nations which were formed under the other unacceptable religious and cultural systems. Thus, such barbaric entities were not entitled to respect and integrity.

The Roman system of colonial administration was ultimately replaced with a feudal system during the so-called Dark Ages, however, thus eliminating the international personality of the State (or city-State) due to the effective merger of political authority and land tenure. Germanic and Viking influences thus impacted all of Europe where development of international norms had flourished. The ensuing fifteenth- and sixteenth-century intellectuals coined the term *Dark Ages* as the period of cultural squalor between antiquity and their Renaissance—their own self-serving term, pregnant with metaphors ironically designed to inspire admiration for what would become a period of intense international conflict.

The Catholic Church sought to rekindle some form of unification after the feudal, or virtually tribal, existence of "civilization" in the Dark Ages. Its leaders believed in some unifying central authority, which led to the pope's crowning of European monarchs in Rome. But the Protestant Reformation ultimately crushed the hopes of the Catholic Church to effectuate its version of international political stability. Thus, the feudal regions became sovereign in the sense now associated with statehood—but remained devoid of a community of nations in the modern sense described below. War among what may be perceived today as "micro-states" devolved into the so-called Thirty-Years' War from 1618 to 1648. The hopeless anarchy was epitomized by the 350 German "States" of that era. Each exercised absolute sovereignty within its particular feudal region.

The Dutch writer Hugo Grotius (1583–1645) was a major contributor to the development of modern International Law. He is often referred to as the "father of international law," although the term *International Law* was later coined by the English philosopher Jeremy Bentham in 1789. Grotius's fundamental contribution to the theory of International Law was *The Law of War and Peace*, published in 1625. It postulated a voluntary law of nations based on consent. Since his home nation (Holland) had just achieved independence after Europe's devastating Thirty-Years' War, Grotius developed support for the fundamental maxim that this new-found freedom from foreign domination necessitated an emphasis on the territorial sovereignty of each State. The transnational pretensions of the papacy and the Holy Roman Empire were thus supplanted by the postulate that States should be supreme in their respective spheres, subject to no external powers not expressly embraced by sovereign assent. Thus, the willingness to observe transnational norms should be expressly stated in treaties or implicitly drawn from customary State practice in international matters.

Modern International Law The so-called modern era of international relations originated in the 1648 Peace of Westphalia, spawned by unnecessary depletion of resources and general war-weariness. The evolution of an international body of customary norms was manifested in this series of treaties adopted by most European nations. These treaties effectively rekindled the notion of broader State sovereignty, unlike the local sovereignty of the previous medieval feudal period. This was the forerunner of the contemporary theme of collective self-defense found in treaties like the Organization of American States and the League of Nations. A representative passage provided that "each of the contracting parties . . . shall be held to defend and maintain all and each of the dispositions of this peace, against whomsoever it may be [broken] without distinction of religion."[16] The Westphalian treaties proved unstable, however. There was no international organization to maintain the peace. Any prospects for collective security gave way to the formation of alliances serving nationalistic rather than collegial interests.

The next major development in International Law was the Congress of Vienna in 1814–1815, initially designed to be an international organization for maintaining peace. Yet self-serving alliances later corrupted the possibility of world governance. One of the most infamous was the so-called Conference of Europe, which divided Africa for colonial purposes. Ironically, US President Monroe would announce his famous "Monroe Doctrine" seven years later, designed in part to prevent any similar action in the New World.

During the ensuing centuries, European powers became the most active and prominent members of the new "international" community, joined by the US in the late 1700s and Latin American nations after the turn of the century. The period between the 1648 Peace of Westphalia and the outbreak of World War I in 1914 gradually solidified the common perception of national sovereignty within the context of an international community of nations. Even non-European States catered to this western political ideal, effectively acquiescing in the development of Eurocentric notions of International Law.[17]

The final twentieth-century development was the collapse of the Soviet Union in the early 1990s. Along with its demise came the breakdown of statehood as originated in the 1648 Peace of Westphalia. This transformation of sovereignty has been evidenced by the now-defunct First World and Second World repression of nationalism, ethnic rivalries, and religious conflict. Ensuing developments are treated in subsequent sections of this book dealing with the ethnic dimension of International Law, the impact of religion, and the thriving danger of post–Cold War nationalism that has dispelled any hope for a Pax Americana.

The analyses of modern States and international organization are addressed in Chapters 2 and 3 of this book.

Schools

Several schools of thought developed for classifying the essence and development of Public International Law. The major colleges within this theoretical university include the schools of Natural Law, Positivism, and Eclectics.

Natural Law, typically attributed to eighteenth-century European jurists, actually dates from the time of the ancient Greeks in approximately 500 B.C. Good law must be in harmony with or reflect the essential nature of all peoples. Medieval disciples of this particular school of thought perceived the essential order of International Law as being premised on the expectations that God or nature has injected into the essence of life. Such laws are immutable, existing even in the absence of a divine being. A properly functioning international legal order must thereby incorporate only those principles of justice rooted in the natural reasoning process. The Catholic Church's Thomas Aquinas (mentioned above) contributed to this development by linking the philosophy of Aristotle and the theology of Catholicism.

This was the prevalent theory in medieval times, when fewer international obligations were established by written treaties (or positive rules). The current momentum in favor of the Natural Law underpinnings of International Law is likely a product of the Nazi horrors perpetrated during the Holocaust, which was preceded by positive law expressed in treaties like the one wherein Hitler and Stalin expressly divided parts of Europe.

The Positivism school is a by-product of the Protestant Reformation. It portrays consent as being the underlying basis for the development of International Law. No claimed international legal norm applies, no matter how staunchly ingrained in reason or morality, unless it is the product of consensual decision making among members of the international community. International Law process cannot exist independently of mutual consent, which is in turn based on customary practice, treaties, or other expressions of national consent. As the contemporary notion of "State" gradually developed its legal and political primacy, there was a predictable shift from Natural Law to Positivism as the underlying premise for defining the essence of International Law.

One criticism of this school of thought may be the absence of any yardstick for judging the morality of State conduct. There have been contemporary attacks on this school as being too rigid in terms of its consent requirement for International Law. As stated by Professor T.W. Bennett of the University of Cape Town, regarding the imposition of English law on tropical Africa:

> during the late nineteenth and early twentieth centuries, western legal thought was heavily influenced by positivism, a philosophy which has had a long-lasting and generally a malign[ing] effect on customary law. Positivism . . . provided a series of assumptions about the relationship of law and society which have been responsible for the distinctly 'legalistic' attitude that has characterized much subsequent work on the subject.[18]

Some contemporary writers thus recommend a return to a former era wherein Natural Law was the prevalent theory for explaining legal process in both the domestic and International Law contexts. Positivists believe in virtually complete freedom of contract. Naturalists, on the other hand, profess that States do not enjoy the complete freedom to establish their contractual (treaty) relations. Certain norms are too deeply rooted to tolerate extinction (addressed in § 1.4 of this text on *Jus Cogens*).[19]

The so-called Eclectic school occupies something of a middle ground, positioned somewhere between Natural Law and Positivism. Eclectic centrists ("Grotians") assert a historical continuum resulting in progressive international legal development—balanced on shifting emphases rather than polarized choices between "nature" versus "consent" choices. Babylonia (now Iraq) had its written Code of Hammurabi, based on Natural Law principles. The medieval Magna Charta provided for certain natural rights linking morals and law.[20] Public International Law should thus be seen as a merger of both naturalists' morality and the positivists' common assent of sovereign nations. This was one of the teachings of the above-mentioned Dutch writer Grotius. The international legal system is, under this view, necessarily premised on the combined applications of Natural Law and the common consent of nations. Writers of the French and American Revolutions urged this premise as the basis for both national and international order.[21]

One criticism of the Eclectic school is that its proponents have been too subjective or arbitrary in defining their brightline divisions between the morality and consent postulates for the other schools.

■ 1.4 SOURCES OF INTERNATIONAL LAW

Introduction

The word *sources* is one of the most common and misunderstood terms in the jargon of International Law. There is a confusing distinction between what the law is and where it may be found. A "source" of International Law, as used in this context, is *where* one may find the substantive content of International Law. Decision-makers or researchers typically look to the sources of this branch of law to find the relevant rule to apply to the issue at hand. In this sense, a source is not part of the substance of International Law. It is a process for ascertaining its content.

The international community has agreed to the following list of sources for ascertaining the content of International Law. This agreement is found in Article 38.1 of the Statute of the International Court of Justice (ICJ):

> The Court, whose function is to decide in accordance with international law such disputes as are submitted to it, shall apply: a. international conventions, whether general or particular, establishing rules expressly recognized by the contesting states; b. international custom, as evidence of a general practice accepted as law; c. the general principles of law recognized by civilized nations; d. . . . judicial decisions and the teachings of the most highly qualified publicists of the various nations, as subsidiary means for the determination of rules of law.

This statutory provision was extracted from Article 38 of the prior Statute, unanimously adopted by the First Assembly of the League of Nations in 1920 for the predecessor world court—the Permanent Court of International Justice (PCIJ). This first world court used the same source list from 1920 until its judges fled from Holland during World War II. The PCIJ's Article 38 descended from the common practice of other tribunals which had used these same sources for finding evidence of the substantive content of International Law. As later stated by the UN Secretary-General in 1949, the codification of this facet of International Law has been successfully accomplished by the definition of the sources in Article 38, which "has been repeatedly treated as authoritative by international arbitral tribunals."[22]

Not all nations use the identical list. The result is typically the same, however. The common statement of sources recommended for use in the United States, for example, is categorized somewhat differently. The Washington, D.C. American Law Institute has published a number of restatements of the law—a blend of what is and what should be the law in a particular field. Under § 102 of the Foreign Relations Law of the United States, published in 1987, the *sources* of International Law are customary law, international agreement, and general principles "common to the major legal systems of the world." Under § 103, the following are *evidence* of whether a rule has become International Law: decisions of international judicial and arbitral tribunals; decisions of national tribunals; the writings of scholars;

and State pronouncements which are not seriously challenged by other States.

General Assembly resolutions are a "secondary" evidence (similar to Article 38's "subsidiary" sources). That is because, unlike the pronouncements of States, Comment *c.* to § 103 provides that international organizations "generally have no authority to make law, and their determinations of [what is] law ordinarily have no special weight." These resolutions are thus secondary evidence of International Law because such declaratory pronouncements provide evidence of what the voting States consider the law to be. Unlike special lawmaking resolutions, which are occasionally intended to structure the conduct of members of an international organization, general pronouncements are not legally binding on member nations.

Ambiguity of the Term "Source" The term *source* is confusing, for several reasons. One reason is its distinctive application in the national versus international context. Sources of "the law" are more conveniently illustrated in the national law context. A nation's legislative acts, executive decrees, and judicial pronouncements are the essential sources of national law—they bind individual and corporate members of that nation, who must obey such pronouncements as soon as they are made. There is no comparable authority in International Law, a branch of the law that is premised on State consent (*see* § 1.8). In the international context, the term *source* means evidence of whether States have consented to certain rules, such as those that are incorporated into the fabric of International Law through long-term usage. In this context, decision-makers look to the above-listed sources of International Law for tangible proof of what rules States have consented to as binding in their international relations. A particular rule is an existing practice, such as a long-term custom, that has acquired international recognition because many States have followed that practice. The rule is the actual content of the law. Where it is found, for example in the protracted customary practice of States, is the source of that rule.

Another reason for the difficulty in determining whether the required national consensus exists is that International Law is not stagnant. The "rules" have a certain ambulatory quality, as they ebb and flow to reflect the political and social evolution of various regions of the world. It is sometimes difficult to establish clear evidence that there is an internationally accepted rule which applies to a pending problem. Absent such proof, the decision-maker

cannot automatically apply a proposed rule asserted by one of the parties to a dispute. Nations, international organizations, domestic or international courts, and arbitrators must therefore examine the established sources of International Law for confirmation of the requisite state consensus. The London Court of Appeal articulated this forensic process with the following pronouncement:

> rules of international law, whether they be part of our law or a source of our law, must be in some sense 'proved,' and they are not proved in English courts by expert evidence like [testimony about the] foreign law [of another nation]: they are 'proved' by taking judicial notice of international treaties and conventions, authoritative text-books, practice and judicial decisions of other courts in other countries which show that they have attained the position of general acceptance by civilised nations. . . . But if none moved, old rules would never die and new rules [would] never come into being. Some move must be made by states, or their tribunals, or jurists, to prevent petrifaction of the living law.[23]

Whether Article 38 is complete poses another problem in assessing its utility. Scholars have debated the completeness of the ICJ's list of sources.[24] While many agree with the completeness of this list, some commentators assert that there are other sources. Such sources have been characterized as being implicitly included in (or, alternatively, applied independently of) the listed sources. One example is UN resolutions.

Critics of Article 38 The 1944 wartime Report of the Informal Inter-Allied Committee on the Future of the "Permanent" Court of International Justice thus stated that "although the wording of this provision is open to certain criticisms, it has worked well in practice and its retention is recommended." Some critics question whether this aging articulation of the sources of International Law has continuing vitality. Some Western, Russian, and Chinese scholars have articulated forceful counterarguments. The former University of Chicago Professor Morton Kaplan and former US Attorney General Nicholas Katzenbach argued in their book on the political foundations of International Law that this list of sources became "stereotyped." It failed to clarify a method and technique for either supporting or refuting the changing nature of the listed sources. The literature from the former Soviet Union questioned what commentators characterized as the "imperfect formulation" of Article 38 of the Statute of the International Court. As stated by the prominent Russian writer Professor Grigori Tunkin of Moscow State University, a "practice" might not be a *general* practice within the meaning of this Article, although it is recognized as a legally binding rule between two nations or within a particular region of the world. Chinese scholars perceive the Article 38 list as Western-derived sources reflecting the external policy of the ruling classes of the countries that created it. In the words of one such critic, Article 38 is a circumlocution around terminology which avoids touching on the deeper social causes of International Law. These substantive "sources of bourgeois international law are the external policy of the bourgeoisie which is also the will of the ruling class of those big capitalist powers."[25]

Scholars in "Third World" nations embrace this latter perception regarding the Eurocentric rules of International Law. Their States were colonized long ago by the dominant States which cultivated these rules prior to the independence movement of the 1960s (further addressed in § 2.3 on Self-Determination). Their continuing acquiescence would perpetuate a process which would limit their ability to pursue radical changes, now that they have achieved their independence from the nations which created the modern core of International Law. Such States now seek changes in related economic structures, including the Western-derived rules regarding compensation for nationalization and the perceived inequitable distribution of global wealth.

Hierarchy Among Sources? The sequential arrangement of the sources within the ICJ Statute suggests an implicit hierarchy. The first layer of this ordering is that treaties, customs, and general principles are primary sources. Judicial decisions and scholarly writings are expressly designated as the "subsidiary" sources for determining the content of International Law (*see* Art. 38.d above, last phrase).

A rule derived from one of those sources may somehow differ from the rule provided by another source. An example would be a rule drawn from a bilateral treaty between only two nations, as opposed to a contradictory rule implicit in a more universal customary practice. The local treaty may not relieve the contracting nations from compliance with a widely accepted customary practice. Hitler and Stalin agreed to divide Europe, for example. Their secret treaty conflicted with the customary rule that such aggression violates the prohibition against waging wars which violate territorial sovereignty.

Some commentators further rank the comparative importance of even the first part of the statutory list of sources. Custom is thus considered both at the top and also as the effective basis for other sources. Professor Benedetto Conforti of the University of Rome thus asserts that

> Customary rules properly are placed at the top of the hierarchy of international norms. Included as a special category of customary rules, are general principles of law common to all domestic systems. Custom thus is both the highest source of international norms, and the only source of general rules. Treaties are second in ranking. Their obligatory character [itself] rests on a customary rule, *pacta sunt servanda* [good faith performance], and their entire existence is regulated by a series of customary rules known as the law of treaties. Third in the hierarchy are sources provided by agreements, including, most importantly, acts of international organizations.[26]

Yet other commentators characterize treaties as the most fundamental source. Professor Rudolf Bernhardt of Frankfurt University recognizes that custom is often superseded by treaties. His succinct and informative perspective is as follows:

> normal customary law . . . can as such be superseded by regional as well as universal treaties. States are in general free to conclude treaties which depart from customary law. This happens every day. Treaties on economic relations between certain States, double taxation agreements, defence alliances and human rights treaties all change the legal relations between the participating States, impose additional and different obligations, limit the existing freedom and sovereign rights of the States concerned, and [thereby] change the applicable norms. In this context, treaties have a "higher" rank than customary law.[27]

The possibility of an explicit hierarchy of sources was considered by the drafters of the predecessor Article 38 (adopted virtually intact in the current Statute of the ICJ). In 1920, the Committee of Jurists initially included a provision that the listed sources were to be considered *en ordre successif*—in successive order. It remains unclear, however, whether this phrase actually evinces an intent to create a hierarchy. These words were deleted at the First Assembly of the League of Nations. The League's records do not indicate whether this deletion meant that application of a hierarchy was either *not* intended or so unnecessary as to render these words surplusage in any Article 38 restatement of the sources of International Law. It may also be argued that the only reason for considering the (deleted) phrase *en ordre successif* was that preceding sources are easier for obtaining evidence of the content of International Law than those which follow. A treaty is more convenient than a custom; a custom is easier than a general principle; and so on.[28]

This section of the book now explores the essential meaning and effect of the listed (and other) sources of International Law.

Custom

The customary practice of nations is the oldest source of International Law. A continuous practice of States in their international relations, accepted by many nations, qualifies as such a custom. This particular source in Article 38.1(b) of the ICJ Statute has a rich and diverse history dating back to Roman times.[29] It is a key source, even today, for ascertaining the actual content of International Law—because many international obligations are not expressed in treaties.

A decision-maker's attempt to determine whether a particular custom is "binding" is fraught with obstacles. International custom is thus described by Professor Grigori Tunkin of Moscow State University as one of the most important and, at the same time, one of the most complex theoretical problems of International Law. It is therefore "natural that the question of customary norms of international law has been the object of constant attention of [the] specialists for a century."[30] This complexity has evolved from the dual process of determining both *where* to find evidence of the custom's existence and *when* it becomes obligatory.

There is often a continuum whereby a mere usage among a few nations ultimately ripens into an obligatory custom to be applied by all—on either a regional or a global basis. A common problem with proving the existence of a custom is determining whether a particular practice by some States is so recognized that it has matured into a binding custom applicable to all. It then becomes necessary to research the actual practice of States to determine whether enough of them expect that practice to be applied by their respective decision-makers.

Professor Ian Brownlie of Oxford University conveniently assembles the four elements for determining the existence of an international custom: (1) duration or passage of time; (2) substantial uniformity or consistency of usage by the affected nations; (3) generality of the practice, or degree of abstention; and (4) *opinio juris et necessitatis*, or international consensus about, and recognition of, the particular custom as binding.[31]

The fourth element is probably the most important, and often the most difficult to establish. The ICJ opinion in the 1969 *North Sea Continental Shelf Case* provides an authoritative analysis of international consensus in this context. That case dealt with whether the UN's 1958 Convention on the Continental Shelf, containing an equidistance principle for allocating resources within the area containing a continental shelf, codified a customary rule which would bind nations not parties to that Convention. The Court thus stated that in order for *opinio juris* to render such a custom binding:

> Not only must the acts concerned amount to a settled practice, but they must also be such . . . as to be evidence of a belief that this practice is rendered obligatory by the existence of a rule of law requiring it. . . . The States concerned must therefore feel that they are conforming to what amounts to a legal obligation. . . . There are [otherwise] many international acts, eg, in the field of ceremonial [behaviour] and protocol, which are performed almost invariably, but which are motivated only by considerations of courtesy, convenience, or tradition, and not by any sense of legal duty.[32]

Regional/Universality of Custom Regional customs used by only some nations may differ from international customs practiced by many other nations. Both categories of custom may be binding. In a 1950 ICJ opinion, for example, Colombia claimed that "American International Law" required

Peru to recognize Colombia's grant of asylum in the Latin American region, although diplomatic asylum was not recognized by customary practice elsewhere in the world. While the Court disagreed in this particular case (a decision for which is was harshly criticized, especially in African nations), it tacitly approved the potential application of regional practices where they could be proven to exist.

This dispute arose when Peru alleged that the Colombian embassy improperly granted asylum to a Peruvian national seeking to overthrow Peru's government. The ICJ thus explored the possibility that there might be a regional custom, as claimed by Colombia, that bound the parties to this dispute. The Court's formula was as follows:

> The Party which relies on custom . . . must prove that this custom is established in such a manner that it has become binding on the other Party . . . [and] that the [claimed right of asylum] . . . is in accordance with a constant and uniform usage, practised by the States in question, and that this usage is the expression of a right appertaining to the State granting asylum [Colombia] and a duty incumbent on the territorial State [Peru]. . . .[33]

Some commentators contend, however, that *universality* of practice is required for a custom to be binding under International Law.[34] This "require-

ment" has been advocated in socialist nations where International Law is not considered a part of the legal hierarchy of laws. The problem with this position is that universality is rarely achieved in an international system composed of many diverse nations. International custom gradually evolves through compromise and consistency of application. Professor James Hsiung of New York University, writing on Chinese recognition practice, notes the dissent. The practice of States is not the ultimate basis of International Law. It is, instead, substantive evidence of a general consensus or acceptable expectation. Dissent or change of consensus is therefore an indicator that a certain norm is not supported by universal consensus. It is, of course, impossible to measure precisely how strong a dissent must be before an existing norm is changed, or precisely when a rejected norm ceases to exist. Dissent, or change of consensus, if supported by a growing number of states, may thus bring about a new norm or revision, or at least indicate a possible trend toward change.[35]

Custom Applied The following case illustrates how decision-makers determine whether a supposed custom actually exists; and if so, whether it has been sufficiently acknowledged by the international community to be binding:

THE PAQUETE HABANA & THE LOLA

Supreme Court of the United States, 1900
75 U.S. 677, 20 S.Ct. 290, 44 L.Ed. 320

[Author's Note: The American press attributed the sinking of the USS Maine, *at anchor in Cuba's Havana Harbor, to a bomb planted aboard it by Spanish forces. During the ensuing Spanish-American War of 1898, US vessels patrolled Cuban waters to prevent activities that might aid Spain in its war efforts. The US Navy thus seized two coastal fishing vessels near the coast of Cuba. One was the* Paquete Habana. *The other was the* Lola.

The "prize courts" of nations at war typically determine the lawfulness of military seizures of foreign vessels. A prize is a captured enemy or neutral vessel suspected of carrying materials to aid the enemy. The trial judge examined US domestic law, to determine the validity of the seizure based on presidential execu-

tive decrees regarding the Law of Prize. That judge then addressed whether any exceptions authorized the return of the vessel and its fishing cargo to the owner, and to the crew members who were entitled to a percentage of the catch. The lower court's decision upheld the seizure of these coastal fishing vessels. In the appellate opinion by the US Supreme Court, the majority opinion surveyed how other nations customarily answer such questions when the seizure allegedly violates the law of nations.[36]

[Opinion:] Justice Gray delivered the majority opinion of the Court:

These are two appeals from decrees of the district court of the United States for the southern district of Florida condemning two fishing vessels and their cargoes as prize of war.

Each vessel was a fishing smack, running in and out of Havana, and regularly engaged in fishing on the coast of Cuba; sailed under the Spanish flag; was owned by a Spanish subject of Cuban birth, living in the city of Havana; was commanded by a subject of Spain, also residing in Havana; and her master and crew had no interest in the vessel, but were entitled to shares, amounting in all to two thirds, of her catch, the other third belonging to her owner. Her cargo consisted of fresh fish, caught by her crew from the sea, put on board as they were caught, and kept and sold alive. Until stopped by the blockading squadron she had no knowledge of the existence of the war or of any blockade. She had no arms or ammunition on board, and made no attempt to run the blockade after she knew of its existence, nor any resistance at the time of the capture.

Both the fishing vessels were brought by their captors into Key West. A libel [meaning the plaintiff's complaint asking] for the condemnation of each vessel and her cargo as prize of war [permitting the capture at sea of enemy property] was there filed on April 27, 1898; a claim was interposed by her master on behalf of himself and the other members of the crew, and of her owner; evidence was taken, showing the facts above stated; and on May 30, 1898, a final decree of condemnation and sale was entered, "the court not being satisfied that, as a matter of law, without any ordinance, treaty, or proclamation, fishing vessels of this class are exempt from seizure."

We are then brought to the consideration of the question whether, upon the facts appearing in these records, the fishing smacks were subject to capture by the armed vessels of the United States during the recent war with Spain.

By an ancient usage among civilized nations, beginning centuries ago, and gradually ripening into a rule of international law, coast fishing vessels, pursuing their vocation of catching and bringing in fresh fish, have been recognized as exempt, with their cargoes and crews, from capture as prize of war.

This doctrine, however, has been earnestly contested at the bar; and no complete collection of the instances illustrating it is to be found, so far as we are aware, in a single published work, although many are referred to and discussed by the writers on international law.

It is therefore worth the while to trace the history of the rule, from the earliest accessible sources, through the increasing recognition of it, with occasional setbacks, to what we may now justly consider as its final establishment in our own country and generally throughout the civilized world.

[*The Court next discussed the history of the claimed custom exempting coastal fishers from capture. This analysis commenced with King Henry IV's orders to his admirals in 1403 and then examined the relevant practices of France, Holland, Prussia, and the US.*]

Since the English orders in [the] council of 1806 and 1810 . . . in favor of fishing vessels employed in catching and bringing to market fresh fish, no instance has been found in which the exemption from capture of private coast fishing vessels honestly pursuing their peaceful industry has been denied by England or by any other nation. And the Empire of Japan (the last state admitted into the rank of civilized nations), by an ordinance promulgated at the beginning of its war with China in August, 1894, established prize courts, and ordained that "the following enemy's vessels are exempt from detention," including in the exemption "boats engaged in coast fisheries," as well as "ships engaged exclusively on a voyage of scientific discovery, philanthropy, or religious mission." Takahashi, International Law, 11, 178.

International law is part of our law, and must be ascertained and administered by the courts of justice of appropriate jurisdiction as often as questions of right depending upon it are duly presented for their determination. For this purpose, where there is no treaty and no controlling executive or legislative act or judicial decision, resort must be had to the customs and usages of civilized nations, and, as evidence of these, to the works of jurists and commentators who by years of labor, research, and experience have made themselves peculiarly well acquainted with the subjects of which they treat. Such works are resorted to by judicial tribunals, not for the speculations of their authors concerning what the law ought to be, but for trustworthy evidence of what the law really is.

This review of the precedents and authorities on the subject appears to us abundantly to demonstrate that at the present day, by the general consent of the civilized nations of the world, and independently of any express treaty or other public act, it is an established rule of international law, founded on considerations of humanity to a poor and industrious order of men, and of the mutual convenience of belligerent states, that coast fishing vessels, with their implements and supplies, cargoes and crews, unarmed and honestly pursuing their peaceful calling of catching and bringing in fresh fish, are exempt from capture as prize of war.

The exemption, of course, does not apply to coast fishermen or their vessels if employed for a warlike purpose, or in such a way as to give aid or information to the enemy; nor when military or naval operations create a necessity to which all private interests must give way.

On April 26, 1898, the [US] President issued another proclamation which, after reciting the existence of the war as declared by Congress, contained this further recital: "It being desirable that such war should be conducted upon principles in harmony with the present views of nations and sanctioned by their recent practice." This recital was followed by specific declarations of certain rules for the conduct of the war by sea, [although] making no mention of fishing vessels. 30 Stat. at L. 1770. But the proclamation clearly manifests the general policy of the government to conduct the war in accordance with the principles of international law sanctioned by the recent practice of nations.

[*The case then summarized the US admiral's argument in support of his seizure of the* Paquete Habana *and the* Lola. *The sailors of the two seized vessels were members of the naval military reserves of Spain and were capable artillerymen. The majority of the Court concentrated, however, on the existence of a general custom against the capture of such vessels.*]

The two vessels and their cargoes were condemned by the district court as prize of war; the vessels were sold under its decrees; and it does not appear what became of the fresh fish of which their cargoes consisted.

Upon the facts proved in either case [involving the vessels *Paquete Habana* and *Lola*], it is the duty of this court, sitting as the highest prize court of the

United States, and administering the law of nations, to declare and adjudge that the capture was unlawful and without probable cause; and it is therefore, in each case—

Ordered, that the decree of the District Court be reversed, and the proceeds of the sale of the vessel, together with the proceeds of any sale of her cargo, be restored to the claimant, with damages and costs.

[*The relevant portion of the dissenting opinion of three of the Supreme Court justices who heard this case follows below. They would have affirmed the seizure under the US Law of Prize. Under their view, the custom relied on by the majority was not binding on the US because the President could decide against using the international rules of war at any time. Further, it was not as clear to them that this custom had achieved the degree of international recognition accorded it by the majority of the judges in this case.*]

[We are] unable to conclude that there is any such established international rule, or that this court can properly revise action which must be treated as having been taken in the ordinary exercise of discretion in the conduct of war.

It cannot be maintained "that modern usage constitutes a rule which acts directly upon the thing itself by its own force, and not through the sovereign power" [quoting from *Brown* below]. That position was disallowed in *Brown v. United States*, and Chief Justice Marshall said:

This usage is a guide which the sovereign follows or abandons at his will. The rule, like other precepts of morality, of humanity, and even of wisdom, is addressed to the judgment of the sovereign; and although it cannot be disregarded by him without obloquy, yet it may be disregarded. The rule is in its nature flexible. It is subject to infinite modification. It is not an immutable rule of law, but depends on political considerations which may continually vary.

■ NOTES & QUESTIONS

The *Paquete Habana* case analyzed four issues relating to principles of customary International Law. How did the Court answer the following questions:

1. Is International Law a part of the law of the United States?

2. If so, what international custom was applied to this dispute?

3. How did the decision-maker (a court in this instance) determine the existence of that custom? What sources did the Court consult to answer the basic issue?

4. The dissenting members of the Court minimized the impact of customary practice, based on

what the US President may say in future executive orders about the applicability of International Law to the conduct of naval blockades. Which was more credible—the majority or the dissenting opinion?

Jus Cogens As private individuals can be barred from enjoying the benefits of an illegal contract under national law, nations should not be able to enter into agreements which violate customary international expectations. But universality would seem to be required whereby no nation could so deviate from that norm. This degree of consensus is, of course, difficult to prove. This dilemma lies at the heart of an expanding doctrine known as *jus cogens*—the Latin term for compulsory law.[37]

A certain polarity exists between *jus cogens* and the notion of absolute State sovereignty. The former term is derived from the Natural Law concept that certain norms exist from which no State may ever deviate. Such norms, assuming their existence, would not depend solely on the consent of States for their binding force. State sovereignty, on the other hand, could be characterized via the Positive Law conception that States are free to do as they wish. If all States agree that torture is an acceptable police tactic, then no Natural Law or divinity-based norm could preclude torture as a valid customary practice condoned by the agreement of the community of nations. This tension between *jus cogens* and State sovereignty has thus limited any widespread agreement that any such norm exists, which would preclude even universal nullification.

The 1969 Vienna Convention on the Law of Treaties, the UN International Law Commission's (ILC) 1976 Report of its Draft Articles on State Responsibility, and the 1986 Vienna Convention on the Law of Treaties between States and International Organizations all contain provisions concerning *jus cogens*. This doctrine espouses the Natural Law belief that there are certain peremptory norms of International Law from which no State or organization of States may deviate. A particular custom may be so staunchly ingrained in International Law that no other competing obligation may be undertaken—or continue—which vitiates the effect of that customary practice. Thus, under Article 53 of the Vienna Convention on State treaties and the Vienna Convention on treaties with international organizations, a peremptory norm of general international law is a norm accepted and recognized by the international community of States "from which no derogation is permitted and which can be modi-

fied only by a subsequent norm of general international law having the same character."[38]

There is little international support for identifying norms as being *jus cogens*. The unanswered question is *which* norms are "peremptory"? The classic example, almost grudgingly applied by the UN's judicial organ (the ICJ), has been the fundamental Charter norm which is the Article 2.4 prohibition on the aggressive use of force. In 1969, for example, the ICJ chose not to adopt *jus cogens* in its judicial reasoning when analyzing a use of force issue. By 1986, however, the same Court thoroughly embraced this theme as recommended by the UN's International Law Commission. The Court then characterized the prohibition on the aggressive use of force as a "conspicuous example of a rule in international law having the character of *jus cogens*."[39]

One of the pervasive barriers to linking *jus cogens* to other norms is the general lack of legislative power in the international community, where the governed nations are not authoritatively governed by a hierarchical higher power. Absent this refinement in the international legal process, one may fairly question the practical utility of a doctrine supposing the degree of universal adherence required for this "higher law" to apply. *Jus cogens* may ultimately be a good testing ground for whether the Natural Law school (described in § 1.3) can actually supplant the Positivist school focus on national consensus as the underlying basis for ordering international relations.

Treaties

Article 1(a) of the 1969 Vienna Convention on the Law of Treaties provides that a treaty is "an international agreement concluded between States in written form and governed by international law, whether embodied in a single instrument or in two or more related instruments and whatever its particular designation."

Treaties are the first source listed above in Article 38.1(a) of the Statute of the International Court of Justice. Historically, however, they have been less prominent in international law-making. A treaty is binding not in and of itself, but rather due to the customary rules or mutual expectations that it codifies. Nor does it bind nations which have not ratified it, although the customs it codifies may be binding as a matter of customary International Law.

Treaties are the most convenient source for quickly obtaining reliable evidence of international consensus. A multilateral treaty, ratified by many nations, is convenient proof of the existence of an international rule which embodies rights and obligations accepted by the parties to that treaty. When the participating countries intend to modify or create a new rule to bind all of them, their treaty adds to the substantive content of International Law and is thus one of its sources.

Regional treaties are not typically intended to have universal applicability. They are useful sources of International Law, however, when they contain rules intended to bind certain nations within a particular geographical region. The Charter of the Organization of American States (OAS), for example, provides that all international disputes which may arise between American States shall be submitted to the peaceful procedures set forth in the OAS Charter, "*before* being referred to the Security Council of the United Nations."[40] The member nations in the "American" region of the world have thus agreed to resolve their disputes with each other by first resorting to OAS regional agencies, rather than starting the resolution process by direct resort to the UN Security Council. While the UN Charter encourages such regionalism, this local treaty *requires* its members to seek an OAS solution first. Each OAS member thus incurred an obligation to seek redress in a regional forum before resorting to a universal forum. Conversely, a non-OAS nation from outside of the region is free to initiate its claim at the UN or in any other forum of its choosing.

Treaty/Custom Relation Multilateral treaties may provide evidence of international consensus, even when they are not universally adopted. One example is the UN Law of the Sea Treaty, which entered into force in November 1994. It is the best evidence of the respective rights and obligations of the parties who have accepted it. When enough nations have ratified such a treaty, it is the best source for resolving a law of the sea issue because it binds the ratifying parties.

Such treaties may also bind nonparties as a matter of customary International Law—if it codifies the general practice of most nations. A rule thus stated, initially in a treaty, may pass into the body of

customary International Law. This process was confirmed by the ICJ in its statement that a treaty may have

> generated a rule which, while only conventional or contractual in its origin [between the adopting parties], has since passed into the general *corpus* of international law, and is now accepted as such by the *opinio juris*, so as to have become binding even for countries which have never, and do not, become parties to the Convention. There is no doubt that this process is a perfectly possible one and does from time to time occur: it constitutes indeed one of the recognized methods by which new rules of customary international law may be formed.[41]

General Principles

National and international decision-makers may borrow principles from the internal law of individual nations, when resorting to the other sources of International Law does not produce an applicable rule. Treaties and customs are the typical sources for ascertaining the content of International Law. Yet they do not always provide a precise answer. The ICJ Statute appearing at the beginning of this section thus includes "the general principles of law recognized by civilized nations." The judges of the ICJ, and other decision-makers who so choose, may thus import principles from the internal jurisprudence of nations. General principles applied in virtually all national legal systems in the world have thus been incorporated into the body of International Law.

Why is this source of International Law needed? "General principles of law recognised by civilized nations" was inserted into both the PCIJ and ICJ Statutes (*see* Article 38 above) as a gap-filler. In any legal system, situations arise where the decision-maker realizes that there is no law covering the precise issue. It is in this situation that a judge will, by analogy, deduce a rule essentially drawn from his or her own legal system. Such principles may emanate from notions of justice, equity, or public policy. There is no supreme executive, legislative, or judiciary independent of the State's consent to be bound. Given the comparatively primitive development of the international legal system in relation to the needs with which it is faced, there are fewer decided cases than in many national legal systems.[42]

The precise contours of the "general principles" source is unclear. The drafters of Article 38.1(c) were themselves uncertain about the precise significance of the general principles source. Some scholars profess that only *International Law* principles may be drawn from national legal systems when, for example, the ICJ has not ruled on the precise point of law. Others perceive the general principles source as sufficiently broad to fill the interstitial gaps in International Law doctrine. Russian scholars interpret it to include general principles of both national and International Law. Chinese scholars disagree. This source should be interpreted to refer only to the principles of *national* law which are generally applied by many nations.[43]

Members of the committee of jurists who drafted the "general principles" provision for use by the two world courts likely recognized that there would be problems with applying this source. They probably wanted some ambiguity, to provide sufficient flexibility for establishing and refining international jurisprudence via resort to "general principles" found in national practice—even when a useful principle had not yet ripened into one used by all nations.

Thus, there are many conflicts about the precise nature of "general principles" as a source. None is more conspicuous than the scholarly debate about whether, following treaties and custom in the above statutory listing, general principles are only a *subsidiary* source of International Law. Others take the position that general principles are the embodiment of the highest principles, likened to a super-constitution of International Law.[44]

Both world courts have affirmed this source as an established and pragmatic basis for drawing certain principles from national jurisprudence to answer questions arising under International Law. In an often-quoted statement from a 1937 PCIJ case, Judge Anzilotti commented on the commonly applied equitable principle that a nonperforming nation cannot take advantage of another's nonperformance. He was thus convinced that this general principle was "so just, so equitable, so universally recognized, that it must be applied in international relations" as one of those general principles of law recognized by civilized nations under Article 38 of its Statute.[45]

The propriety of using national legal principles in international adjudication was reaffirmed by the majority opinion of the judges in a 1970 ICJ case dealing with the general principle of judicial independence from other branches of domestic government. The Court thus recognized the general principle of judicial independence, despite the existence of differences in degree between various legal systems, that "may be considered as a universally recognized principle in most of the municipal [national] and international legal systems of the world."[46]

Good faith is also a "general principle" which has surfaced on numerous occasions involving international disputes. This doctrine is enshrined in Article 2.2 of the UN Charter, requiring that members "shall fulfil in good faith the obligations assumed by them in the present Charter." Article 26 of the Vienna Convention on the Law of Treaties, and the Vienna Conventions on the Law of Treaties between States and International Organizations or between two International Organizations, all provide that every "treaty in force is binding upon the parties to it and must be performed by them in good faith." Good faith has thus enjoyed more unqualified acceptance than any other theme in International Law over a period of many centuries.[47]

Nonjudicial Application of General Principles

Near unanimity is probably necessary to prove the requisite international consensus for incorporating a "general principle" into International Law—thus limiting its utility outside of the judicial context, where the parties have already agreed to comply with the decision of the tribunal to which they have agreed to submit their dispute. The historical lack of unanimity in the community of nations has therefore committed this particular source to a lesser role in the work of other international decision-makers.

A classic example of the problem with applying a supposed general principle of law, outside of the judicial context, is found in the exchange of diplomatic correspondence between Mexico and the United States in 1938.[48] While the United States claimed that international custom prohibited Mexico's expropriation of property owned by US citizens without compensation, both nations professed their own convenient applications of the general principles of "reason, equity, and justice."

Mexico had expropriated farm land and oil properties without reimbursing the US owners. The US government wanted Mexico to compensate them for these seizures. US Secretary of State Cordell Hull sent the following communiqué to the Mexican ambassador to the United States. Hull thereby generated an exchange of letters which would be a useful source for determining what these two countries considered to be the "general principle" governing expropriations:

> If it were permissible for a government to take the private property of the citizens of other countries and pay for it as and when, in the judgment of that government, its economic circumstances and its local legislation may perhaps permit, the safeguards which the constitutions of most countries and established international law have sought to provide would be illusory. Governments would be free to take property far beyond their ability or willingness to pay, and the owners thereof would be without recourse. We cannot question the right of a foreign government to treat its own nationals in this fashion if it so desires. This is a matter of domestic concern. But we cannot admit that a foreign government may take the property of American nationals in disregard of the rule of [required] compensation under international law. Nor can we admit that any government unilaterally and through its municipal legislation can, as in this instant case, nullify this universally accepted principle of international law, based as it is on reason, equity and justice.

This was the obvious position that one would expect an aggrieved nation to take under the circumstances. Secretary Hull's argument thus presented what *was* a clear consensus or principle prior to World War I. Mexico took a different position, however, raising doubts about whether that previous international consensus (requiring "prompt and adequate" compensation for the expropriation of alien property) continued to exist. Mexico's Minister of Foreign Affairs responded to Hull's application of the general principles of "reason, equity and justice" with the following diplomatic communiqué. The Mexican minister therein denied the existence of a general principle of law requiring compensation under the circumstances:

> My Government [Mexico] maintains . . . that there is in international law no rule universally accepted in theory nor carried out in practice, which makes obligatory the payment of immediate compensation nor even of deferred compensation, for expropriations of a general

and impersonal character like those which Mexico has carried out for the purpose of redistribution of the land. . . . As has been stated above, there does not exist in international law any principle [that is] universally accepted by countries, nor by the writers of treatises on this subject, that would render obligatory the giving of adequate compensation for expropriations of a general and impersonal character. Nevertheless Mexico admits, in obedience to her own laws, that she is indeed under obligation to indemnify in an adequate manner; but the doctrine which she maintains on the subject, which is based on the most authoritative opinions of writers of treatises on international law, is that the time and manner of such payment must be determined by her own laws.

Secretary Hull responded with an assessment of what the US perceived to be the practice generally followed under the national constitutions of most nations. Hull's communiqué countered as follows:

> The Government of the United States merely adverts to a self-evident fact when it notes that the applicable precedents and recognized authorities on international law support its declaration that, under every rule of law and equity, no government is entitled to expropriate private property, for whatever purpose, without provision for prompt, adequate, and effective payment therefor. In addition, clauses appearing in the constitutions of almost all nations today, and in particular in the constitutions of the American republics, embody the principle of just compensation. These, in themselves, are declaratory of the like principle in the law of nations. . . .

Mexico's foreign affairs minister, not wishing this statement to remain undeflected, responded to Hull's communiqué on the principles applied by the constitutions of the American republics with Mexico's following assertion:

> This attitude of Mexico is not, as Your Excellency's Government affirms, either unusual or subversive. Numerous nations, in reorganizing their economy, have been under the necessity of modifying their legislation in such manner that the expropriation of individual interests

nevertheless does not call for immediate compensation and, in many cases, not even subsequent compensation; because such acts are inspired by legitimate causes and the aspirations of social justice, they have not been considered unusual or contrary to international law. As my Government stated . . . it is indispensable, in speaking of expropriations, to distinguish between those which are the result of a modification of the juridical organization and which affect equally all the inhabitants of the country, and those others decreed in specific cases and which affect interests known in advance and individually determined.

Mexico and the US ultimately negotiated a settlement of this compensation dispute. The quoted diplomatic correspondence demonstrates some of the difficulties with applying general principles of *national* law as a source for resolving a dispute having *international* law implications (State responsibility for injury to aliens, as discussed in Chapter 2 of this book). Parties to such international disputes are going to choose the general principle from their internal law that best serves their respective interests. Mexico and the US had posed mutually exclusive views on what each country perceived to be the applicable "general principle" governing compensation for the taking of foreign property.

■ NOTES & QUESTIONS

1. What was the "general principle" proposed by the US?

2. What was Mexico's response to the US argument?

3. Which ambassador made the better argument?

Judicial Decisions

Under Article 38 of the ICJ Statute above, judicial decisions are "subsidiary" sources for determining the content of International Law. This source refers to the case opinions of the courts within various nations. These tribunals operate as the judicial organs of their respective States. When a particular issue arising under International Law is decided the same way by the courts of various nations, an international tribunal will consider such consistent applications as evidence of State consensus about the proper resolution of that issue. As stated by Professor Hersch Lauterpacht of England, the "decisions within any particular State, when endowed with sufficient uniformity and authority, may be regarded as expressing the *opinio juris*" or an expression of what that State expects from others in its international relations.[49]

This source is "subsidiary" because a judge's decision does not *make* law. Rather, it declares the appropriate result which is based on the previously existing law. This is particularly true in civil law countries, where judges have less discretion than that of their common law counterparts when interpreting the law. Many civil law judges thus consider the common law judicial process to be one of judicial legislation, due to the comparative latitude enjoyed by common law judges. In the United States, for example, the development of the federal law of admiralty was delegated by the Congress to federal judges.

Judicial pronouncements by the courts of one nation cannot directly create or modify International Law. At best, they can be incomplete evidence of a rule which the courts of one member of the community of nations have implicitly adopted. A national court deciding a matter of International Law often draws on the decisions of courts from other nations or from international tribunals. Such decisions can be used to establish that there is an international consensus about the particular point to be decided. The US Supreme Court, for example, made an ambitious statement in 1815 about the utility of such judicial decisions. Its members were trying to resolve a commercial dispute concerning the government's seizure of sugar belonging to a citizen of another country during time of war. The Court stated as follows:

> The law of nations is the great source from which we derive those rules [about the ownership of seized enemy property] which are recognized by all civilized and commercial states throughout Europe and America. This law is in part unwritten, and in part conventional

[meaning the subject of a treaty]. To ascertain that which is unwritten, we resort to the . . . decisions of the Courts of every country, so far as they are founded upon a law common to every country, [which] will be received not as authority, but with respect. The decisions of the Courts of every country show how the law of nations, in the given case, is understood in that country, and will be considered in adopting the rule which is to prevail in this [case in which we seek evidence of the applicable international rule].[50]

Ironically, the "judicial decisions" source has evolved (since the just-quoted 1815 case) to the point where it has been characterized by some as the most important factor in the progressive development of International Law. Many scholars thus characterize judicial decisions as being entitled to greater significance than the secondary status provided by the Statute of the ICJ. As stated by the Court's President, decisions of international tribunals thus "exercise considerable influence as an impartial and well-considered statement of the law by jurists of authority made in light of actual problems which arise before them."[51]

The impact of judicial decisions is not limited to those of international courts. Numerous cases decided by national courts arise wherein local tribunals (including arbitrations) decide issues arising under International Law. State decision-makers thus contribute to the body of evidence on the content of International Law. Given the increasing frequency with which such decisions are rendered, collections of reliable cases and arbitral decisions are thus available for ascertaining the content of International Law via resort to these national judicial processes. Some of the classics include *International Law Reports* (Grotius Publications, Cambridge, Eng.) and *International Legal Materials* (American Society of International Law, Wash., D.C.). Similar resources are discussed in Appendix B, Exhibit B.4, of this book on research in International Law.

Impact of ICJ Opinions The ICJ is ostensibly fettered with a significant limitation not found in the national law of many UN members. Under Article 38.1(d), judicial decisions are sources of the law "[s]ubject to the provisions of Article 59." Article 59 of the ICJ Statute provides that the "decision of the

Court has no binding force except as between the parties and in respect of that particular case."

As stated by the PCIJ in 1926, the reason for this statutory limitation "is simply to prevent legal principles accepted by the Court in a particular case from being binding on other States or in other disputes."[52] Put another way, State sovereignty is the culprit responsible for this limitation which is not applied in most national courts. The drafters of this provision, first applicable to the PCIJ and now to the ICJ, recognized that this limit would encourage more States to submit their disputes to a distant tribunal in Holland. A bad result in one case would not haunt them in later disputes with other parties.

In contemporary practice, however, the ICJ has reapplied certain principles relied on in its earlier cases. As its case precedent has expanded, a number of its prior opinions have been the basis for resolving issues resurfacing in subsequent cases. Perusing current ICJ opinions reveals that the current world court has not been satisfied with the apparent Article 59 role of deciding today, only to have its opinion disregarded tomorrow. Otherwise, there would be little consistency in its decision-making process and less respect for its ability to participate in the progressive development of International Law.

Scholarly Writings

Article 38.1(d) authorizes the use of "the teachings of the most highly qualified publicists of the various nations, as subsidiary means for the determination of rules of law." Using the analyses of influential "publicists" is another authorized method for ascertaining the underlying content of International Law. A publicist is a highly qualified scholar who has written on the subject of International Law.

As a practical matter, one who is researching or deciding an International Law question often begins with academic writings for preliminary insight. Scholarly treatises have been helpful to international tribunals, as illustrated in the following passage in an opinion by the PCIJ. The Court was considering the circumstances under which an individual could be prosecuted for a crime committed in international waters. The Court began its analysis by stating that "as regards teachings of publicists . . . it is no doubt true that all or nearly all writers teach that ships on the high seas are subject exclusively to the jurisdiction of the State whose flag they fly."[53] This passage illustrates the potential impact which legal writers have made on the progressive development of International Law. The judges in this case, for example, incorporated the scholars' analyses of the jurisdictional issue to achieve a result which was consistent with International Law.

Scholarly writers serve a related purpose. Their commentaries trace historical and contemporary developments in the practice of States and the decisional law of their courts. Writers thereby publicize relevant developments. Professor Karol Wolfke of Poland therefore characterizes scholarly writings as essential instruments for analyzing disputed facts and judicial results as evidence of customary rules, as well as identifying trends in their evolution. Thus, in addition to "attracting attention to international practice and appraising it, the writers indirectly influence its further evolution, that is, the development of custom."[54]

The use of scholarly writings for determining the content of International Law is inherently limited. One reason is that scholarly writings often contain the author's perspective on what International Law *should* be, rather than what it *is*. This admonition was eloquently stated in an English appeals court opinion:

> The views expressed by learned writers on international law have done in the past, and will do in the future, valuable service in helping to create the opinion by which the range of the consensus of civilized nations is enlarged. But in many instances their pronouncements must be regarded rather as the embodiments of their views as to what ought to be, from an ethical standpoint, the conduct of nations . . . [rather] than the enunciation of a rule or practice so universally approved or assented to as to be fairly termed . . . "law."[55]

Given this court's admonition, one might characterize scholarly analysis as a behind-the-scenes "source" which applies in a very peripheral sense. The teacher's role, through scholarly writing, is limited to providing insight into evidence of the law's content—and not a primary law-making source for establishing the *opinio juris*, or State expectations based on the actual rules they use in their relations with other States. Publicists thus write *about* the rules and may influence the rule-making process. But they can never *make* the rules in the sense accomplished by custom, treaties, and general principles.

General Assembly Resolutions

Article 38 of the above ICJ Statute should not be regarded as the exclusive list of sources of International Law. Resolutions of international organizations may also play a role in ascertaining the law's substantive content. There has been a vast proliferation of international organizations in the more than half-century since the initial version of Article 38 was prepared for use by the PCIJ. UN General Assembly resolutions, for example, are the most universal category of resolutions by international organizations. International organizations have certain legal power on an international level (as described in Chapter 3 on International Organizations). They have not yet attained the same degree of law-making power as the State, which is still the essential "person" able to create rights and duties through treaties and customary practices which shape the development of International Law.

The strongest argument against characterizing General Assembly resolutions as normative or rule-making may be drawn from the language of the UN Charter itself. The Assembly's expressed role is to make recommendations. Under Article 10, for example, it "may discuss any questions or any matters within the scope of the present Charter, and . . . may make recommendations to the Members of the United Nations or to the Security Council. . . ." Under Article 11, it "may consider the general principles of cooperation in the maintenance of international peace and security . . . and may make recommendations with regard to such principles to the Members or the Security Council or both. . . ." Other General Assembly responsibilities include the promotion of international economic and social cooperation under Chapters IX and X of the Charter.

The former Legal Counsel of the United Nations has thus characterized General Assembly resolutions as nonbinding. Under his analysis:

> The General Assembly's authority is limited to the adoption of resolutions. These are mere recommendations having no legally binding force for member states. Solemn declarations adopted either unanimously or by consensus have no different status, although their moral and political impact will be an important factor in guiding national policies. Declarations frequently contain references to existing rules of international law. They do not create, but merely restate and endorse them. Other

principles contained in such declarations may appear to be new statements of legal rules. But the mere fact that they are adopted does not confer on them any specific and automatic authority. The most one could say is that overwhelming (or even unanimous) approval is an indication of *opino juris sive necessitatis* [the consensus of States regarding what binds them in International Law]; but this does not create law without any concomitant practice, and that practice will not be brought about until states modify their national policies and legislation. It may arise, however, through the mere repetition of principles in subsequent resolutions to which states give their approval. The General Assembly, through its solemn declarations, can therefore give an important impetus to the emergence of new rules, despite the fact that the adoption of declarations per se does not give them the quality of binding norms.[56]

Some commentators have nevertheless asserted that the UN General Assembly's resolutions *are* sources of International Law which can bind member nations through their normative effect. The following provides an example: Nations should control the operations of their multinational corporations, pursuant to the directives contained in General Assembly resolutions. While such resolutions are recommendations, they are also evidence of the customary practice of many States. One commentator thus asserts that "the liberal interpretation of 'recommendations' holds that the process of voting for resolutions is . . . capable of creating customary norms of international law."

UN resolutions may thus be useful source material when restating international norms professed by a sufficient number of countries. Examples include the unanimous affirmation of the principles contained in the Charter of the Nuremberg Tribunal punishing Nazi war criminals and the unanimous resolution producing the Genocide Convention. These particular General Assembly resolutions expressed the opinions of *all* UN members that they would henceforth recognize global prohibitions against such State conduct.[57]

Language from several passages of the International Court of Justice (ICJ) lend credence to the claim that at least some General Assembly resolu-

tions may be binding. In the *Expenses* case, involving the obligation of member nations to contribute to UN expenses, the Court commented that "Article 18 deals with the '*decisions*' of the General Assembly 'on important questions.' These 'decisions' . . . have dispositive force and effect . . . includ[ing] suspension of rights and privileges of membership, expulsion of Members and 'budgetary questions.'" In the *Namibia* case, dealing with South Africa's failure to comply with its trust obligations regarding the former South West Africa, the ICJ stated that it would not be correct to assume that, because the General Assembly is in principle vested with recommendatory powers, "it is debarred from adopting . . . resolutions which make determinations or have operative design." And in the separate opinion of the prominent British ICJ judge, Sir Hersch Lauterpacht, in the *South West Africa Voting Procedure* case: "A Resolution recommending . . . a specific course of action creates *some* legal obligation which . . . is nevertheless a legal obligation and constitutes a measure of supervision."[58]

Today, however, there is no definite consensus about the utility of organizational resolutions as a source of International Law. The fundamental question is: What *weight* do these resolutions deserve? Professor Anthony D'Amato of Northwestern University characterizes this question as a serious problem regarding the appropriate weight to give to recommendations of the Security Council or General Assembly. He notes that although books have been written about this subject, "there has been no consensus. Therefore, International law would surely be a much easier subject to study and master if U.N. resolutions could be treated as definitive statements of rules of international law."[59]

One drawback is that, unlike the typical situation within a member State of the UN, there is no similar legislature on the international level. General Assembly resolutions are thus binding only in the limited circumstances where they happen to incorporate existing International Law or are designed to cause States to conform their practices to existing expectations.

Much confusion has been generated by General Assembly resolutions purporting to create legal norms without recourse to the treaty process for accomplishing this result. One example is the 1946 "Nuremberg Principles," whereby the Assembly affirmed the Nuremberg trial process and judgments in a unanimous resolution. The same session also unanimously adopted the "Genocide Convention," characterizing genocide as an international crime. Although the UN Charter does not provide the General Assembly with express authority to "declare" such matters, the Assembly has continued to do so without significant scrutiny. Professor Oscar Schachter of Columbia University thus questions the apparent assumption that such resolutions are entitled to legal validity because a vote for a resolution may not be intended to signify agreement on the legal validity of the asserted norm. In his words, there is evidence that governments do not always have that intent when they either vote for a resolution or fail to object to it. They may fairly assume that since Assembly resolutions are recommendations, "their vote should mean no more than that. They may cast their vote solely on political grounds in the belief that a resolution of the General Assembly is entirely a political matter without legal effect."[60]

Thus, it is easy to overlook the association between resolutions and subsequent treaties based on those resolutions. Often, a General Assembly resolution, responding to an *ad hoc* situation, precedes the convening of a multilateral convention which later produces a treaty to codify State expectations. Then, the matter contained in the later treaty is more clearly a source of International Law than when the same matter was expressed in the prior resolution.

Although most General Assembly resolutions reflect only a political view of the situation at hand, the ICJ has recognized that certain resolutions may include the missing element of *opinio juris* (binding expectations recognized and practiced by State members). The Court is thus willing to rely on sources not found in the Court's Article 38 list of sources. In the 1986 *Nicaragua Case*, for example, the Court considered the Assembly's Declaration on Principles of International Law concerning Friendly Relations and Cooperation among States in accordance with the Charter of the United Nations as binding in the sense that it expressed the *opinio juris* of all UN members. In this limited sense, then, the General Assembly's Declaration on Principles of International Law was effectively characterized as a source of International Law.[61]

Security Council Resolutions Security Council resolutions are not normative or rule-making. They react to violations of existing International Law principles, which are carefully delineated in the Council's actions. These resolutions may be declarative of typically clear-cut rules which have been dishonored—requiring the Council to deal with breaches on a case-by-case basis.

■ 1.5 PRIVATE INTERNATIONAL LAW

While the contemporary line between "public" and "private" International Law is blurred, there remains a functional distinction between their respective applications. *Public* International Law refers to the practices of States which they consider binding in their mutual relations. *Private* International Law refers to resolution mechanisms for disputes involving non-State entities, such as individuals or corporations. The essential distinction is legal relations between States (public law) versus those between individuals and/or corporations (private law).

The historical derivation of both categories of International Law was closely enmeshed. Since the seventeenth century, the term *jus gentium,* or law of nations, has been used to refer to the public sector of International Law. The Romans used the same Latin phrase, however, to describe the body of law governing disputes between Roman citizens and foreigners. It was then used to describe what we would now call private International Law.

French and Italian scholars of the twelfth century developed related principles which are now referred to as "Conflict of Laws" principles for resolving transnational disputes between private individuals (as opposed to international disputes between nations). This field deals with the territorial reach of national laws, and is a part of the body of each nation's rules which deals with transnational disputes between individuals or corporations.[62] The terms "private International Law" and "conflict of laws" may be used interchangeably.

The public/private gap has narrowed over time, particularly since the end of World War II. Today, much of public International Law applies to individuals and corporations—as illustrated in Chapters 3 and 4 of this book. And much of private International Law applies to public entities such as State corporations engaged in international trade—as addressed in various chapters including Chapter 13 on International Economic Relations.

A number of model international treaties have been drafted for disputes involving individuals from nations with different laws on the same subject.

Diverse subjects, covering a multitude of private interests, are covered by these model treaties. Some examples are the 1971 Hague Convention on the Law Applicable to Road Traffic Accidents, the 1973 Hague Convention on the Law Applicable to Product Liability, the 1980 UN Convention on Contracts for the International Sale of Goods (CISG), the 1988 Hague Convention on the Law Applicable to Succession to the Estates of Deceased Persons, and the 1988 UN Convention on International Bills of Exchange and International Promissory Notes.

Just how do such treaties operate in the private sphere, as opposed to the public sphere involving legal relations directly between nations? An oral contract between private corporations, for example, may be legally enforceable under the law of Nation X but not the law of Nation Y. Under X law, an oral contract over $500 may be used to prove the existence of a contract, although it is based on an oral agreement. Under the law of Y, no (oral) contract for an amount over $500 can be enforced unless it is made in writing. Assume that both nations have ratified the above UN Sales treaty, to facilitate international contracts between the exporters and importers of both nations, as well as to encourage dispute resolution. Article 11 of the CISG Convention provides that a "contract of sale need not be concluded in or evidenced by writing. . . . It may be proved by any means, including witnesses." The oral contract is thus enforceable by the testimony of witnesses, in the courts of both X *and* Y, as evidence to prove the existence of the contract and its breach. The CISG treaty commitments by nations X and Y therefore provide a predictable result for the enforceability of contracts by private traders in both nations. The result no longer depends on the particular nation wherein the plaintiff chooses to sue or arbitrate to enforce the oral contract.

Feminist Perspective

A State actor incurs international liability for gender discrimination only in the rare instance where the perpetrator's objectives include official crimes against women as such. A clear example of State responsibility, in the context of discrimination against women, would be the Bosnian Serb tactic of encouraging the rape of Muslim (and other) women as a method for driving Muslims out of a particular area of Bosnia. This tactic was allegedly a military strategy for facilitating "ethnic cleansing," in order to gain more territory in Bosnia-Herzegovina. The Serbs have allegedly engaged in this heinous tactic, knowing that these women would never consider attesting to the fact of such atrocities because of their religious and cultural convictions.

The "public/private" International Law dichotomy has been characterized by certain legal theorists—particularly when analyzing "Third World" scenarios—as perpetuating a disengagement of the State from many historical, economic, and political realities. They believe that one critical disparity should be incorporated into analyses of the "State" as the primary actor in International Law. Human rights law is designed to guarantee freedom and equality of the individual on the *international* level—in the same manner that liberal theory is designed to guarantee the rights of liberty and equality of the individual on the *national* level. Neither of these legal paradigms sufficiently distinguishes between individuals based on gender, however.

Those concerned with their descriptions of the global history of gender discrimination may object to traditional International Law theory. It purports to focus on protecting the rights of the "individual" without accommodating the need to incorporate the disparate treatment of women in the dialogue. The problems of women have been acknowledged, yet theorists have never assumed the parallel responsibility of International Law to protect this class of persons due to the varied layers of inequality faced by women throughout the globe. As asserted in a 1993 study by the American Society of International Law:

> international law depends on an ambiguous definition of the state which includes [the elements of] territory, population, and government. The indeterminate nature of this definition means that women's unequal participation in the habitation, ownership, and use of territory and other material sources; women's primary role in the reproduction of population; and their absence from government is left unrecognized in international law. This [indifference] in turn ensures that male control of these processes at a national and global level remains undisturbed by international regulation.[63]

Until this feminist perspective is more fully probed, International Law concerns will continue to focus on the general protections accorded by treaty and UN resolutions (*see* § 11.2, on International Bill of Rights). It is non-State actors who typically batter or harass women. The responsible individuals normally incur no liability under International Law. Their liability is limited to national law, to the degree it protects women from abuse. It has only been "domestic" law that governs the liability of such non-State actors. The extent to which international society must play some greater role is not yet perceived by most theorists as being within the province of public International Law—dealing primarily with *State* responsibility, rather than that of abusers who are answerable to the degree that *national* law provides protection.

■ 1.6   INTERNATIONAL RELATIONS COMPARED

The disciplines of International Law and International Relations share the common feature of examining how States behave. There are distinctions, of course. One difference is that a professor of International Relations does not have to defend the tangibility of its existence. Given the obvious fact that nations engage in mutual relations, the study of International *Relations* may thus focus on its basic mission of assessing the variables affecting good and bad relations. One who professes International *Law* theory, on the other hand, must begin with a preliminary defense of its comparatively elusive existence. This justification is dictated by differences between national and international enforcement mechanisms (as discussed in § 1.8 on the national law versus International Law relationship and § 1.9 on whether International Law is really law).

Virtually every International Law coursebook begins with a study of the sources of International Law. Those who undertake only a skin-deep analysis of this field of law easily overlook its tangible impact. Their skepticism is based on the mistaken assumption that States act only in their own best interests—without any earnest regard for the external legal controls imposed by International Law. The excesses of certain national members of both the League of Nations and the United Nations are cited as the typical examples. As characterized by Professor Louis Henkin, former President of the

American Society of International Law, advocates of International Law have had to constantly defend its existence and relevance to world events. He is careful to add, however, what the so-called realists or pragmatists do not seem to recognize: "*almost all nations observe almost all principles of international law and almost all of their obligations almost all of the time.*" [64]

Having previously defined International Law and its sources, this section of your coursebook now examines the parallel discipline of International Relations. The first step is to trace the development of the contemporary field of International Relations—followed by a snapshot of some alternative dimensions related to the Cold War and its demise.

Evolution

International Relations is studied primarily in undergraduate curriculums. It is taught as one or more courses in the political science departments of most universities—or in the history or philosophy departments at others. An increasing number of universities offer a graduate degree in this field. Representative components of an International Relations course or major include: International Relations Theory; American or English Comparative Foreign Policy Analysis; Arms Control (or Disarmament); International Law (or a related title); Comparative Politics; Regional Studies; International Development; Peace Studies (or Conflict Resolution).

International Relations, as a distinct field of study, emerged early in the twentieth century. Post–World War I teachers, scholars, and diplomats recognized the need for the study of International Relations, premised on the platitude that history should not repeat itself.

International Relations soon underwent a great transformation, however, due to the harsh reality of the events leading to World War II. Political science "realists" thus perceived International Law as only a peripheral variable in the actual State practice of International Relations. While both disciplines analyzed State behavior, law was characterized as being too abstract and inflexible to adjust to the political reality of International Relations as actually practiced "in the trenches." As summarized by Professor Anne-Marie Burley of the University of Chicago:

> The discipline of international relations
> was born after World War I in a haze of

aspirations for the future of world government. These were quickly dimmed by World War II. The fledgling discipline was thus weaned on Political Realism . . . [by] seasoned observers of the interwar period [who] reacted against Wilsonian liberal internationalism, which presumed that the combination of democracy and international organization [the League of Nations] could vanquish war and power politics. They believed instead in the polarity of law and power . . . [because] states in the international realm were champions only of their own national interest. . . . The only relevant laws were the 'laws of politics,' and politics was a 'struggle for power.'[65]

Commencing in the late 1970s, however, International Relations theory shifted. Its analysts acknowledged the contributions made by International Law and international organizations, perceived as facilitating positive State behavior in collaborative ways. Rather than shackling State behavior by attempting to impose controls, international institutions were perceived as facilitating cooperation. International legal control was recognized as actually assisting governments in their pursuit of desirable interests—not as a doctrinal paradigm used only when convenient in suitable instances.[66]

Alternative Dimensions

Numerous seams are visible in the fabric of International Relations, most beyond the scope of this introductory book on International Law. The selections immediately below provide a window into two relevant features of International Relations: proletarian internationalism and the ethnic dimension of International Relations.

Proletarian internationalism has long been endorsed by socialist nations. One who studies post–Cold War International Relations should not make the mistake of discounting the impact of communism on this discipline. It was the Soviet Union, not communism, that withered away. World attention focused on South Africa in 1994, for example, when a new communist leader (Nelson Mandela) took power—thus supplanting a long period of race-based rule. While nations like the United States were quite supportive of the free elections there, one wonders how the US would have responded if the

Cold War against the sinister "communist threat" were still a political fact of international life.

Marx believed that socialism would ultimately spread to the capitalist or market-oriented industrialized nations. Yet its actual achievements, particularly with the demise of the Soviet Union, were at best disappointing. Soviet leaders had already denounced the primary architect of twentieth century communism—Joseph Stalin. Subsequent rifts among communist nations were thus predictable.

There are a number of factors which adversely influenced international relations among the Soviet-bloc nations after World War II. Communists typically took power in nations which were not ready for the full-scale communism that Marx advocated—a society free of class distinctions which had been perpetrated by market-oriented capitalism. Leaders within the various socialist nations tended to interpret communism in different ways, while often defending the chosen interpretation to best fit their particular nation's circumstances. Tito's Yugoslavia deviated from the pedagogical path, permitting some forms of capitalist ventures. Khrushchev of the USSR—who promised to bury capitalism—tolerated political and economic variations from the classic party line during the Eastern European struggle in the journey toward worldwide communism. He too was denounced because his reforms (including relaxation of the Stalinist mass terror approach) threatened a bureaucratic establishment which was less inclined to be conciliatory in Moscow's foreign relations. The Soviets had lost a crucial facet of the Cold War, when President Kennedy threatened to go to war if Khrushchev did not pull Russian missiles out of Cuba in 1962. This "loss" was almost immediately followed by the Americanization of Vietnam, much closer to the geopolitical center of communism.

A classic example of the elitist backlash to Khrushchev's peaceful coexistence policies appeared just four years after his forced retirement. The 1968 Warsaw Pact interference in Czechoslovakia was perceived among the Soviet-bloc nations as an exercise in raw power politics, rather than a constructive step in the orderly progression toward worldwide communism. Capitalist liberal democracies, on the other hand, had not fought among their own ranks for many decades. Capitalist nations, instead, tended to find other ways for resolving their international disputes—quite unlike the carnage perpetrated in the former Yugoslavia in the 1990s.[67]

Events in the former Yugoslavia in the 1990s also exposed the previously suppressed ethnic dimension of International Relations. The end of the Cold War did not end international rivalry. The demise of the Soviet Union did, however, unmask repressed ethnic conflicts—never resolved under the Soviet Union's totalitarian control of international affairs.

The respective anti-Soviet and anti-American dimensions of First World and Second World global relations masked other hostilities which eventually surfaced with a vengeance in the form of "ethnic cleansing" (the 1990s euphemism for genocide). Many Third World regimes had been neither democratic nor communistic. The respective label-makers could rationalize virtually any authoritarianism, or otherwise unacceptable democratic tendency, based on the convenient test of politics which were either "anti-American" or "anti-Soviet." They thus employed this litmus test of political stability and affinity for both the First World and Second World. Both sides in the Cold War thus perceived Third World nations as either good or bad, without regard to ethnonationalism. The negative features of nationalism based on ethnicity "surfaced" with unexpected fury in nations like the unified Germany and former Yugoslavia only after the end of the Cold War.

International communism may now be viewed in International Relations theory as an artificial interlude in the complex geopolitics which froze the normal growth of nationalist aspirations during the Cold War. As succinctly articulated by the editor of the *Journal of Political Science*, Professor Martin Slann of Clemson University:

> Soviet disintegration . . . is not only a question of fifteen or possibly more republics [including five *additional* nations subsequently spawned by the breakup of Yugoslavia] establishing themselves as sovereign or of some of them combining in some sort of federated system [such as the Community of Independent States]; within many of the republics themselves there are ethnic and religious minorities who see no reason why they should be prevented from pursuing their own national destinies. Some of them will almost certainly do so. And many of them [have] do[ne] so at the expense of their neighbors.[68]

A number of human rights abuses addressed in Chapter 11 of this book have been spawned by this ethnic dimension of International Relations. Ethnic conflict was effectively "placed on the back burner" until the end of the Cold War and the ensuing breakdown in national sovereignty addressed in Chapter 2 on States in International Law.

■ 1.7 RELIGION/CULTURE/ COMPARATIVE LAW

This section of the text briefly summarizes other disciplines which have influenced the development of International Law. They are typically overlooked in legal studies. Each is nevertheless a lens through which members of the diverse spectrum of nations view the precise nature of the generally worded norms which bind the community of nations.

Religion

The influence of religion was implied in this chapter's § 1.3 on the "History of International Law." Christianity, for example, was the filter used to retain those portions of Roman law imported into modern legal systems. This section of the book more directly addresses the impact of religion on developments in International Law.

Historical Affiliation There has long been an affiliation between religion and International Law— spawning both positive and negative results.

They have, at times, drawn guidance from one other. Each has also contributed to a mutual and progressive development over the centuries—although characterized by some as a somewhat symbiotic or even nonexistent relationship. Exhibit 1.1 illustrates the ostensible tether between these two institutions.

The Vatican City-State Vatican City is the site of the Apostolic (or Holy) See—the central government of the Roman Catholic Church. Its Head of State, the pope, exercises a unique spiritual reign over the world's Catholics. The premises of this tiny State are located near Rome, based on a 1929 treaty with Italy.

The Vatican city-State is the only religious entity which has achieved governmental recognition as a sovereign State. It has also maintained the longest tradition of diplomatic initiatives of any sovereign entity. Since the time of the Emperor Constantine in the fourth century A.D., the pope has received numerous foreign delegates. The Vatican currently maintains diplomatic relations with more than 120 nations. It finally established diplomatic ties with Israel in 1993, nearly a half-century after Israel achieved statehood.[69]

Some of the prominent developments in Vatican history include its role in encouraging the medieval crusades; dividing the Atlantic between Spain and Portugal in 1493; the 1867 US Congressional withdrawal of funding for a US delegation to the "Papal States"; President Franklin Roosevelt's sending a personal representative to the pope on the eve of the outbreak of World War II; criticism for effectively acquiescing in the Nazi takeover of Europe; and President Reagan's rekindling of the Vatican/US relationship in 1984 resulting in the opening of the Vatican embassy in Washington, D.C.

The contemporary Vatican function has generally been to mediate international crises and to facilitate the maintenance of peace and global order. In 1965, for example, the Vatican embassy negotiated a cease-fire in the Dominican Republic conflict involving the departure of US troops from the Republic. In 1990, Panama's leader, Manuel Noriega, sought refuge in Panama's Vatican embassy. The Vatican's role promoted Noriega's surrender to troops who had surrounded the embassy shortly after the US invasion of Panama. The Holy See (Vatican) achieved worldwide attention in 1994, during the UN Conference on Population in Cairo, Egypt. The Pope consolidated forces with States such as Iran and Libya to avert a multilateral approach which might include abortion as a means for limiting the world's population.

The following excerpt is from Professor James Nafziger of Willamette University (Oregon). It succinctly depicts the intriguing parallels between religion and International Law, with a focus on modern conflict:

EXHIBIT 1.1 Influence of Religion on International Law

485 B.C.: Babylonia	Biblical Book of Esther: "And in every province, and in every city, whithersoever the king's commandment and his decree came, . . . many of the people of the land became Jews; for fear of the Jews fell upon them." (In December 1993, the Vatican finally recognized the State of Israel—forty-four years after Israel was admitted to the UN as a member State.)
October 27, 1553: City-state of Geneva	Civil authorities/the Inquisition execute Spanish physician for unorthodox beliefs about immortality of Jesus. Dr. Michael Servetus characterized Jesus as "Son of Eternal God," contrary to Church's teaching that Jesus is "Eternal Son of God."
1625: Paris, France	Hugo Grotius's Prologue to *The Law of War and Peace* (seminal work earning him title of Father of modern International Law): "Throughout the Christian world I observed a lack of restraint in relation to war . . . and that when arms have once been taken up there is no longer any respect for law, divine or human. . . ."
1849: London, England	Henry David Thoreau publishes *On the Duty of Civil Disobedience* (a cornerstone of Quaker philosophy): "If a thousand men were not to pay their tax-bills this year, that would not be [as] violent and bloody [a] measure, as it would be to pay them, and enable the State to commit violence and shed innocent blood."
January 1, 1961: Moscow, Russia	Article 227 of the Criminal Code amended: "Organizing or directing a group, whose activity . . . carried on with the appearance of preaching religious beliefs and performing religious ceremonies, is related to causing harm to the health of the citizens . . . shall be punished by deprivation of freedom for . . . up to five years or by exile. . . ."

EXHIBIT 1.1 *(continued)*

Summer 1986: Egypt	Fundamentalist Muslim leader Umar al Talmasani—the predominant US attitude exports both Christianity, the traditional rival of Islam, and secularism, the modern rival of Islam. US foreign policy is "motivated by several factors, but the most important . . . [is] religious fanaticism . . . a continuation of the crusader invasion of a thousand years ago."
February 14, 1989: Tehran, Iran	Government leader Ayatollah Khomeini decrees British author Salman Rushdie must be killed because *The Satanic Verses* blasphemes Islam. (Fifth anniversary of decree: Iran will never rescind decree because "repentance in such a case is a matter solely concerning divine mercy in afterlife." The West's continued support for Rushdie = insult to Islam and Iran.)
January 13, 1993: Baghdad, Iraq	Saddam Hussein: "Another battle has started. Another holy war ordained so that we can attain another great victory for . . . the Iraqi people." President Bush tells US soldiers: "You are doing the Lord's work."
December 8, 1993: London, England	Prince Charles proclaims intent to become king, leaving Britain to ponder the prospect of a divorced king becoming head of the Church of England. (The British monarch automatically becomes the supreme governor of the Church and must pledge to uphold the Anglican faith—during the coronation ceremony.)
January 13, 1994: Rome, Italy	The pope calls for ending the war in Bosnia via humanitarian intervention, declaring that per moral teachings of the church: "all military aggression is judged to be morally wrong. Legitimate defense, by contrast, is viewed as admissible and sometimes obligatory. The history of our century has confirmed this teaching numerous times."
June 17, 1994: Dhaka, Bangladesh	2,000 Muslim fundamentalists march through the streets of Dhaka to demand the execution of author Taslima Nasreen. A local court ordered her arrest based on charges disclosing her writings which call for changes in Islamic laws to provide equal rights to women.

The Functions of Religion in the International Legal System

THE INFLUENCE OF RELIGION ON THE DEVELOPMENT OF INTERNATIONAL LAW

Professor James Nafziger[70]*
Willamette University College of Law

Religion and international law often appear to be congruent. They share elements of ritual, authority and universality that 'connect the legal order of any given legal society with that society's beliefs in an ultimate transcendent reality.' There is, too, a certain sanctity to any body of law, just as there is an authoritative and often constitutive structure in religion. Judaism is based on a Covenant. In Martin Buber's terminology of I and Thou, both religion and international law are essentially dialogue; both seek to prove orientation of knowledge and a greater realization of life. In a sense, the whole concept and

*© 1991 by Kluwer Academic Publishers. Reprinted with permission from Kluwer Academic Publishers, Dordrecht, the Netherlands. Footnotes omitted.

practice of global order presupposes a moral and teleological viewpoint that is essentially religious. United Nations Secretary General Javier Perez de Cuellar has referred to the UN Charter as 'my religion.' . . . As ethical systems, both law and religion address the global order in a profound manner; both are concerned with the manner in which we accept and organize the world and universe around us.

Sometimes, however, religion and positive international law are not congruent. They may even be in conflict. For example, prohibitions on whaling by national and international agencies, for the best of environmental reasons, may conflict with indigenous religious practices. Prescriptions to protect the rights of women, such as those that were developed and codified in the Convention on the Elimination of Discrimination of All Forms of Discrimination Against Women, have been rejected by some Islamic traditions. . . . [T]he Iranian invasion and occupation of the United States Embassy in Tehran [may be described] as a religious act designed, in accordance with a higher, revolutionary law 'to profane a place traditionally considered by treaties, international law, and custom to be inviolable. . . .'

Occasionally, when international law and religion conflict, the world community must 'just say no' to religion—whether viewed as the opiate of the masses or not. In today's threatened environment, it is simply unacceptable to interpret the Biblical injunction literally to '[b]e fruitful, and multiply and replenish the earth and subdue it: and have domain over the fish of the sea, and over the fowl of the air, and over every living thing that moveth upon earth.' . . .

Of course, conflict between religion and international law may sometimes be more apparent than real. Political and institutional factors, rather than genuine religious differences, may best explain theo-cratic defiance of international law that is expressed in religious terms. . . . Experts note that much of the tension between militant religiosity in the Third World and liberal, modernizing authority manifests not so much any real doctrinal differences as political claims by religious institutions (for example, by Shiite Muslims in Iran and the Afghan Mujahedeen) for recognition, full dignity, and equality—three values that many modern political and legal systems do not readily concede to religious forces.

In view of the discrepancies between religion and international law, it may be well to conclude that they are dimensions of each other; they are not so much congruent or united as they are related in a dialectical interdependence; they 'stand or fall together.' . . .

Integration of law and religion can, of course, result by definition whenever religious institutions or ideas are deliberately made the subject of international prescription. Examples include the Lateran Treaty between Italy and the Vatican . . . and the recognition of the Vatican as a state. 'Right to life' provisions in human rights instruments that are intended or interpreted to prohibit abortion have religious foundations. An extraordinarily inflammatory issue was the [1975] 'Zionism is racism' resolution of the United Nations General Assembly. . . .

Several global instruments articulate a fundamental freedom of thought, conscience and religion . . . [including the Universal Declaration of Human Rights, the International Covenant on Civil and Political Rights] and the Declaration on the Elimination of All Forms of Intolerance and Discrimination Based on Religion or Belief. . . . These provisions highlight the topic of religion's role in the international legal system, but do not reflect the positive functions of religion [even] when it is not deliberately made the subject of international prescription. . . .

Islamic Fundamentalist Conflict The collapse of the Soviet Union effectively unleashed what the Cold War seemed to repress for the four decades since World War II—vintage religious rivalries. Post-war political order was essentially maintained by the NATO/Warsaw Pact paradigm. Then came the subsequent breakdown in statehood, as perceived in Westphalian terms (see § 1.3, on the 1648 Peace of Westphalia). There are other unification models in the current global order, however.

A number of Western commentators have replaced the former Evil Empire with a new demon, often characterized or mischaracterized in Western writings as "religious fundamentalism." The US post–Gulf War policy of respecting Iraq's borders, for example, is perceived by a number of Muslims as effectively neglecting ethnic Kurdish and religious Shiite claims to autonomy in and around Iraq. Freezing its borders, via no-fly zones and the like, has arguably maintained the old world order, rather than establishing a new one. As stated in a comprehensive study of what Western writers have called the fundamentalist post–Cold War "insurgence":

> Fundamentalists are boundary-setters: they excel in marking themselves off from others by distinctive dress, customs, and conduct. But they are also, in most cases, eager to expand their borders by attracting outsiders who will honor fundamentalist norms, or by requiring that nonfundamentalists observe fundamentalist codes. The state is the final arbiter of disputes within its borders. In cases in which the state is "fundamentalist" (e.g., Iran, Sudan) or has been influenced by fundamentalist sociopolitical agendas (Pakistan, India, Egypt, Israel), the fundamentalism of the enclave is encouraged or even empowered to spill over its natural boundaries and permeate the larger society.[71]

A novel feature of the contemporary "fundamentalist struggle" involves what the West would describe as terrorist reactions to modern threats to essential fundamentalist doctrine. In March 1994, for example, suspected Muslim fundamentalists murdered two young schoolgirls in Algiers because they were unveiled. This action marked the bloody enforcement of a February 1994 vow, undertaken in the name of religion. Muslim women who do not cover their heads in public have thus joined a growing list of targets, including the Algerian army, police, secularist intellectuals, artists, journalists, and certain unsympathetic foreigners.

There has been a historic tendency of religious leaders to participate in cross-border power struggles, since the time of the medieval crusades. The degree of such participation is becoming more direct. A number of Muslim nations supported the Afghan Mujahedeen for fourteen years, during its struggle to disengage occupying Soviet troops. The rival factions within Afghanistan are tearing it apart, however, with political power struggles conducted in the name of Islam. If this scenario remains unchecked, religious violence could far surpass that done by the Inquisition and the crusades of the Roman Catholic Church in the medieval era. The destruction of religious icons could cost Afghanistan its predominant Islamic architectural heritage. Mosques have been special targets of violence, because people use them as safe havens from battles fought by rival factions of the Mujahedeen. The famous Blue Mosque in Kabul was filled with women and children when it was bombed in March 1994 by air. The traditional acquiescence in the use of mosques as sanctuaries has apparently been forsaken by rival religious groups. Even the Soviet regime never dared to break that tradition.

Culture

Overlooking *cultural* differences in private relationships sows the seeds of mistrust. It is no different in International Relations. Thus, one should not isolate "culture" and "International Relations" as completely distinct disciplines, or, alternatively, disregard one when studying the other.

Rather than a thin veneer, stripped away by the dictates of international conflict, culture presents a powerful unifying undercurrent which does not disappear with a stroke of power politics. Civilization antedated the medieval notion of statehood. Civilization's web of interrelational social structures will postdate the current onslaught on State sovereignty of the post–Cold War period. There has been resilient pressure to move away from bigger organizational units (for example, the Soviet Union) to smaller entities (including the post-Soviet breakup of the former Yugoslavia). Thus, international studies must contain a cultural component—probably more so now than at any time in the past.

Two layers of cultural differences adversely affect international communication. The first is the comparatively minor irritant associated with failing to appreciate some cultural difference, in a way that tends to undermine relationships. This recurring problem usually surfaces when two nations possess unequal bargaining power. The conduct of the stronger nation's representative is unaware of or ignores such differences. There is a protocol misstep spawned by communication gaps in intercultural relations. For example, during President Clinton's first official dinner function in a foreign nation in July 1993, he unexpectedly invited a translator to stand between himself and South Korea's President Kim, who was seated near the lectern. This event would have no cultural significance in the US. In Korea, however, it is an insult for anyone to stand between two heads of state. Strictly observed rules of etiquette apply in Korea, even between family members in *private* dinner settings. Further, there had been an agreement that each president would deliver post-dinner remarks in their native tongues, without the aid of an interpreter. The invitation to the translator was thus another form of cultural faux pas, although there were no *perceptible* consequences.

The more significant and often invidious form of cultural difference arises when an agreement is reached but applied very differently by the parties to that agreement. What often appears perfectly clear to both sides, when formulated in abstract principles, is very different when subsequently interpreted. Diplomacy, the subject of another chapter in this book, thus has a cultural dimension worth briefly considering at this point.

Intelligent diplomacy requires the representatives to take account of cultural differences because they should be seeking a lasting result which will be satisfying to all participants. It is no secret that one should attempt to negotiate from a position of strength. Yet the stronger nation's culture has rarely been exported, even when virtually forced on those who have been defeated in war or negotiated disputes. Raw power politics, although a fact of international life, does not ultimately succeed as well as attempting to accommodate the cultural values of the opponent in modern International Relations. As stated by Professor Frank Ninkovich of St. John's University in New York:

> Although diplomacy functions within cultural and intercultural contexts, historians of diplomacy have traditionally slighted cultural explanations of foreign policy in favor of tried and true concepts of power and interest . . . [but] insightful statesmen have always recognized that diplomacy also requires reckoning with cultural values which, because of their crucial role in shaping perceptions, are more significant than either ideological beliefs or abstract ideals. In one way or another, nearly all the major U.S. statesmen of the twentieth century took cultural factors into account as part of their approach to diplomacy; indeed, culture played a prominent and often decisive role in their decision-making.[72]

The cultural aspects of international relations have not been sufficiently considered by published studies. Anthropologists have admittedly failed to explore, in any depth, the relation between culture and many facets of what is governed by international norms. For example, Europe has been repeatedly ravaged by the scourges of war, more so than in any other region of the world. To what extent was the European concept of "State" the product of cultural biases favoring the waging of war on a grander scale than in any previous tribal era? Is warfare a cultural universal or, alternatively, is it a less prominent feature of certain societies?[73]

Culture and the modern "law" of human rights are also at odds. There is a serious issue regarding the universality of human rights norms, particularly those expressed in documents before the global decolonization of the 1960s. The 1948 Universal Declaration of Human Rights contains sweeping, all-inclusive language providing "universal" guarantees which have not been recognized in all cultures. The Universal Declaration has been attacked by Muslim fundamentalists as culture-bound, due to its Western derived values. Female circumcision, for example, is abhorred by Western culture as a gross violation of women's basic human rights. Yet it is a culturally accepted practice in Muslim and certain African nations. Thus, the entire Western-derived International Bill of Rights, promulgated through the auspices of the UN, has been interpreted to apply in a more limited way in these cultures. A Muslim scholar would seriously question the universality of overly broad, culturally insensitive "rights" which other nations have sought to impose through international political and legal processes.

Comparative Law

International Law is typically analyzed in terms of its universal applicability. Students must recognize, however, that the mutual expectations of State members of the international community cannot be objectively divorced from their own distinct legal systems. Earlier in this text, you studied the theme that general principles of law, drawn from various national legal systems, may be used by an international decision-maker as a gap-filler for determining what norms are considered mutually binding in international relations. There are, of course, different national legal systems from which these international norms are extractable. This endeavor therefore touches upon the related field of Comparative Law.

What is Comparative Law? Different legal systems—both national and international—draw from one another's experiences. It has been succinctly described in the leading American casebook as follows:

As a practical subject Comparative Law is a study of the legal borrowings or transplants that can and should be made; Comparative Law as an academic discipline . . . is . . . an investigation into the legal transplants that have occurred: how, when, why and from which systems they have been made; the circumstances in which they have succeeded or failed; and the impact on them of their new environment.[74]

The formal study of this comparative process began in Paris in 1900, when French scholars founded the International Congress for Comparative Law. This particular field of law still occupies a rather modest place in law school curriculums, however.[75]

Just as well-rounded students should consider the impact of religion and culture on International Law, they should also consider the influence of Comparative Law. There are many diverse legal traditions throughout the globe. National representatives in any international context—be they diplomats at the UN and multilateral conferences, or judges and arbitrators deciding international disputes—are far more likely to reach a workable result if they recognize that each representative's home-State law provides the lens through which he or she will perceive the international legal process. The different legal traditions within the same region of the world affect problem-solving strategies. For example, Western legal culture in Europe contains two major systems: the Civil Law (based on French law) and the Common Law (based on English law). The former is derived from Napoleon's Civil Code of 1804. The latter has its roots in earlier medieval judicial practice.[76]

Assume that a Civil Law lawyer and a Common Law lawyer are contemplating a private business agreement, or are negotiating on behalf of their respective governments at an international conference. Each should come to the bargaining table prepared to address the question of how disputes will be resolved, and under what terms. They must be aware of the different legal cultures potentially affecting the particular negotiation. If they are negotiating a business contract, they will incorporate a dispute resolution clause. They know that there will be no jury for resolving disputes in the Civil Law tradition. The Common Law judge will not be able to ask questions of witnesses. If there is a question of contractual interpretation, the Common Law judge

will be less constrained by applicable legislation than the Civil Law judge. There are different standards for satisfying the burdens of proof at trial. One of the most difficult phases in the development of the 1994 Rules of Procedure and Evidence for the UN's "Bosnian" War Crimes Tribunal was determining the extent to which the respective Common Law or Civil Law traditions would be utilized.[77]

■ 1.8 NATIONAL/INTERNATIONAL LAW NEXUS

The internal law of each nation governs the relations among individuals, corporate entities, institutions, and the government within that nation's borders. This section of the text addresses the relationship between a nation's internal law and International Law.

Scholars have traditionally used the term "municipal law" to distinguish the internal law of a nation and International Law. But the term "municipal" is ambiguous. Under US law, for example, a number of states of the United States have "Municipal Courts." Further, that term is not very descriptive of its international context. Thus, a national/international distinction is used in this text. The term "national" will therefore be used synonymously with the terms employed by various writers such as: domestic, internal, local, and municipal law. The commonly used term "domestic law" is avoided, due to its arguably sexist connotations asserted by certain writers.[78]

Monist/Dualist Debate

Scholars have debated the theoretical relationship between national and International Law for many decades. This controversy is typically described in terms of the "monist" versus "dualist" controversy.

Monist Approach

The Monist perspective is that the law of nations and the law of each nation form a unified and universal legal order transcending national borders. Their theory describes International Law as inherently woven into the legal system of every nation. One supporting argument is that nations do not reject International Law in principle—although they may have reservations about certain parts. Because so many national leaders have acknowledged the existence of International Law, it may be characterized as a part of human existence that is not restricted by national borders.

National courts routinely apply International Law when they are directed to do so by their national legislatures or constitutions. International Law therein manifests its Natural Law roots (*see* § 1.3). Otherwise, there would be legal anarchy in the absence of its foundational norms of behavior. International Law is thus an integral part of all local legal systems.

The position of the UN's International Court of Justice is unmistakably clear—national law can never prevail in the event of a conflict with International Law. As stated by the Court in the 1988 case where the US attempted to close the PLO Mission at the UN under antiterrorist legislation:

> It would be sufficient to recall the fundamental principle of international law that international law prevails over domestic [national] law [of the US]. This principle was endorsed by [US] judicial decision as long ago as the arbitral award of 14 September 1872 in the *Alabama* case between Great Britain and the United States, and has frequently been recalled since, for example in the case concerning the *Greco-Bulgarian "Communities"* in which the Permanent Court of International Justice laid it down that it is a generally accepted principle of international law that in the relations between Powers who are contracting Parties to a treaty, the provisions of municipal law cannot prevail over those of the treaty.[79]

What are some contemporary examples of circumstances where a nation has expressly incorporated some feature of International Law into its national law? In 1973, Canada merged the 1951 UN Convention Relating to the Status of Refugees definition of refugees (persecution based on "race, religion, nationality, etc.") into its national laws. Canada has since produced a rich vein of judicial case law literature interpreting the rights of refugees under this international definition. In 1993, a California state court overruled a State Board of Prisons policy that barred foreign-born inmates from serving indeterminate sentences in their home countries. This incarceration policy conflicted with the Strasbourg Convention on Transfers of Sentenced Prisoners. The California policy thus violated the US

Constitution's Supremacy Clause barring individual states of the US from undertaking policies which violate the federal government's treaty commitments. The French Constitution provides that treaties are "laws" which must be applied within the French legal system. Article 25 of the former West German Constitution provided that the "generally accepted rules of international law are binding upon the state power [to act] and upon every citizen." International Law is therein controlling because there can be no conflict with internal law.

The foremost proponent of the monist approach was probably the Austrian Professor Hans Kelsen. His articulation was that national and International Law have always been a part of the same basic system of universal norms. In an earlier era, these norms provided the basis for a system which came to be known as International Law. The same behavioral norms also drove national legal orders too. States, through the individuals who served as their agents, were expected to behave as people behave. International Law did not need to establish its primacy in relation to national law—these legal systems were characterized as interdependent rather than hierarchical.[80]

Dualist Approach

Dualists reject the monist perception of International Law as articulating an unrealistic assessment of national legal systems. They argue that International Law and national law are two quite distinct systems. Each nation retains the sovereign power to integrate or isolate the norms of International Law. National and International Law are not necessarily parts of a unified whole.

Why is International Law *not* an integrated legal system, since national and International Law both set standards of behavior for individuals and States? The quintessential feature of State sovereignty is consent. The paradigm effectively created by the 1648 Peace of Westphalia ultimately preached an immutable dogma: no State may be bound without giving its consent. When a nation actively decides to incorporate International Law into its national law, only then is International Law the law of that land. As discussed earlier in this chapter, decision-makers typically examine international customs or treaties to ascertain whether their expressed consent exists. Just as general principles of national law may be incorporated into International Law, International

Law *may* be similarly integrated into a State's national law. Until this occurs, however, International Law is more of a common goal or standard of achievement for that State and the international legal community.

A judge must therefore apply his or her national law, such as executive and legislative directives, even if to do so violates International Law. As illustrated in an opinion of the English Court of Appeals, International Law has no validity except insofar as its principles are accepted and adopted by England's internal law. Its courts must therefore acknowledge the existence of the rules which other nations may accept as binding among themselves. When determining issues arising under International Law, decision-makers "seek to ascertain what the relevant rule is, and having found it they will treat it as incorporated into the domestic law, so far as it is not inconsistent with rules enacted by statutes or finally declared by their tribunals."[81] In a similar instance, a US court declared that international practice is law only insofar as the legislature allows the courts to apply it. International Law thus bends to the will of the Congress because courts can annul legislation only when it is unconstitutional under national law. Judges therefore have the duty to enforce national legislation. Thus, an "act [congressional legislation] may contravene recognized principles of international comity, but that affords no more basis for judicial disregard of it than it does for executive disregard of it."[82]

Another dualist example involves the US prosecution of Nazi war crimes defendants. Australia, Canada, and Great Britain have passed special legislation which authorizes the trial of former Nazi suspects for war crimes. US law does not provide for prosecuting crimes against humanity, however. The violation of International Law via the waging of "war crimes against humanity" was an essential underpinning of the Allied post-war Nuremberg (and Tokyo) Charter. The Nuremberg principles were expressly approved by a UN General Assembly resolution. Yet this component of International Law has not been incorporated into US law. As a result, the US has been prosecuting these individuals on the basis that they lied on their passport applications regarding their whereabouts and working circumstances during the war. This scenario provides some practical proof for the dualist view of the derivative nature of International Law—which can only be utilized in national courts on the bases expressly recognized by national law.

"Equal Footing"

In practice, the monism/dualism distinction is rendered meaningless when a nation fails to observe International Law. Under the internal law of certain nations, International Law is characterized as being on "equal footing" with other national laws. This supposed parity often results in International Law's being subordinated to national law, however. In the US, for example, the Supreme Court long ago stated that "International law is a part of our law." This may suggest a monist flavor in the US application of International Law. The same court subsequently determined, however, that national legislation and treaties are *both* a part of US law. The last in time thus prevails. A later federal statute thus supersedes an earlier conflicting treaty. Further, the US Constitution *always* prevails when it conflicts with International Law. Timing is irrelevant. This approach thus incorporates the dualist conception, whereunder International Law is law but subject to modification by legal decision-makers.

Assume, for example, that the US enters into a treaty with Mexico. It allows all Mexican workers to enter the United States for the limited purpose of temporary working visits, without any other restrictions (similar to the 1951–1964 "Bracero Program" from an earlier era in US/Mexican labor relations). Prior immigration legislation does not authorize temporary work permits for the foreign laborers from any country. The subsequent treaty would effectively override the conflicting immigration legislation. The citizens of Mexico (only) may thereunder freely enter the US to work and return home after a specified period of time.

Assume further that Congress enacts a new immigration statute *after* entering into the above worker treaty favoring Mexican workers. This new legislation now restricts *all* foreign workers from entering the US—unless they otherwise qualify for immigration status. Under general US law, the post-treaty legislation supersedes the prior treaty obligation which had authorized Mexican workers to temporarily enter into the US to work. The so-called "equal weight" of the more liberal treaty and the more restrictive immigration statute triggers the last-in-time rule. This is another application of the dualist theory. International Law requires that the US continue to perform its continuing external treaty obligation to accept the Mexican workers. This treaty is at best equal, and of course less than equal, when in conflict with the subsequent legislative restriction. Further, under US (and Mexican) law, the national constitution always prevails in the event of a conflict with International Law.

Even in dualist legal systems, however, a nation may not assert its internal law in defense of its breach of International Law. As stated in the UN International Law Commission's 1949 Draft Declaration on the Rights and Duties of States, every nation must carry out its obligations arising from treaties and other sources of International Law in good faith. Thus, a nation "may not invoke provisions in its constitution or its [other internal] laws as an excuse for failure to perform this duty." And as stated by the Permanent Court of International Justice in 1931, "a State cannot adduce as against another State its own Constitution with a view to evading obligations incumbent upon it under international law or treaties in force."[83]

International Law "Applied" Who actually *applies* International Law? One may conjure the notion of fifteen robed judges ceremoniously sitting in the ICJ's Peace Palace in the Netherlands, determining the great international legal issues of the day. That Court's docket, just barely into double figures in recent years, illustrates that the bulk of judicial decision-making about international legal issues is primarily done elsewhere. Diplomats, presidents, treaty-drafters, and other public servants have occasion to determine the "what, how, and when" of applying International Law. But it is the judges and arbitrators of the world's *national* legal systems who

make International Law decisions on a day-to-day basis.

Your study of International Law would be incomplete without a sensible grasp of the fact that the day-to-day application of International Law occurs within the national legal systems of the world. The "legal" aspect of International Law is routinely determined by what Professor Benedetto Conforti of the University of Rome calls "Domestic Legal Operators." His useful perspective is as follows:

> Only through what we could term "domestic legal operators" can we describe the binding character of international law or, better still, its ability to be implemented in a concrete and stable fashion. "Domestic legal operators" are those charged by the State community to apply and enforce law and [thus] include judges, first and foremost. In every State system we find more or less similar provisions holding that actions must comply with international law as well as [with] municipal law. This being so, compliance with international law relies not so much on enforcement mechanisms available at the international level, but rather on the resolve of domestic legal operators such as public servants and judges to use to their limits the mechanisms provided by municipal law to ensure compliance with international norms [which are] . . . lacking in judicial and coercive enforcement procedures at the international level. . . .[84]

Can a national judge ignore the command of an applicable judgment of the judges of the International Court of Justice? This issue was considered in the following US court decision:

COMMITTEE OF U.S. CITIZENS LIVING IN NICARAGUA v. REAGAN

United States Court of Appeals
District of Columbia Circuit, 1988
859 Fed.Rptr.2d 929

[Author's Note: In 1984, Nicaragua obtained a judgment against the US in the International Court of Justice, based on US activities in Nicaragua designed to overthrow the "Sandinista" government (the political party so named in honor of Augusto Sandino, who led a peasant-guerilla army against US Marines in 1927–1933). The US attempted to withdraw from

this prior ICJ case. The judges nevertheless proceeded with that case (after the US purportedly withdrew) because the US had previously submitted to the ICJ's jurisdiction.

Various organizations, and certain US citizens living in Nicaragua, later sued President Reagan in his capacity as the US President. In this 1988 case filed in

Washington, D.C., the plaintiffs pleaded with the judicial branch of the federal government to issue an injunction that would bar the continued US funding of the Nicaraguan "Contras." They argued that the congressional funding legislation, signed by the president, ignored the prior ICJ judgment prohibiting further US activities which would continue to violate the territorial sovereignty of Nicaragua. The plaintiffs alleged that the Contra funding violated the federal Administrative Procedure Act, the Fifth Amendment, the United Nations Charter, and customary International Law. The case was dismissed by the federal trial judge and the plaintiffs appealed.

The Court of Appeals held that the UN Charter requirement, whereby member nations must honor ICJ judgments, does not confer rights on private individuals (including these plaintiffs) whereby they may force their own country to comply with an ICJ judgment. The appellate court decided that only an aggrieved nation may seek such relief—in an international forum—to force the US to comply with the previous judgment of the international court.]

[*Opinion:*] Appellants Have No Basis in Domestic Law for Enforcing the ICJ Judgment

1. The status of international law in the United States' domestic legal order

Appellants argue that the United States' decision to disregard the ICJ judgment and to continue funding the Contras violates three types of international law. First, contravention of the ICJ judgment is said to violate part of a United States treaty, namely Article 94 of the UN Charter. That article provides that "[e]ach Member of the United Nations undertakes to comply with the decision of the International Court of Justice in any case to which it is a party." Second, disregard of the ICJ judgment allegedly violates principles of customary international law. One such principle holds that treaties in force shall be observed. Appellants contend that another such principle requires parties to ICJ decisions to adhere to those decisions. Third, the United States may have violated peremptory norms of international law. Such norms, often referred to as jus cogens (or "compelling law"), enjoy the highest status in international law and prevail over both customary international law and treaties. Appellants . . . contend that the obligation of parties to an ICJ judgment to obey that judgment is not merely a customary rule but actually a peremptory norm of international law.

For purposes of the present lawsuit, the key question is not simply whether the United States has violated any of these three legal norms but whether such violations can be remedied by an American court or whether they can only be redressed on an international level. In short, do violations of international law have domestic legal consequences? The answer largely depends on what form the "violation" takes. Here, the alleged violation is the law that Congress enacted and that the President signed, appropriating funds for the Contras. When our government's two political branches, acting together, contravene an international legal norm, does this court have any authority to remedy the violation? The answer is "no" if the type of international obligation that Congress and the President violate is either a treaty or a rule of customary international law. If, on the other hand, Congress and the President violate a peremptory norm (or jus cogens), the domestic legal consequences are unclear. We need not resolve this uncertainty, however, for we find that the principles appellants characterize as peremptory norms of international law are not recognized as such by the community of nations. Thus, as we explain below in greater detail, none of the claims that appellants derive from violations of international law can succeed in this court.

2. The effect of subsequent statutes upon prior inconsistent treaties

Although appellants' complaint alleges that Congress' funding of the Contras violates Article 94 of the UN Charter appellants seem to concede here that such a claim is unavailing. They acknowledge, as they must, that "[o]rdinarily, treaty obligations may be overridden by subsequent inconsistent statutes." Brief for Appellants at 32.

. . .

At this stage of the present case, however, the key question is not whether Congress intended to abrogate Article 94. Since appellants allege that Congress has breached Article 94, we must determine whether such a claim could ever prevail. The claim could succeed only if appellants could prove that a prior treaty—the UN Charter—preempts a subsequent statute, namely the legislation that funds the Contras. It is precisely that argument that the precedents of the Supreme Court and of this court foreclose. We therefore hold that appellants' claims based on treaty violations must fail.

Our conclusion, of course, speaks not at all to whether the United States has upheld its treaty obligations under international law. As the Supreme Court said in the *Head Money Cases*, a treaty "depends for the enforcement of its provisions on the interest and honor of the governments which are parties to it. If these fail, its infraction becomes the subject of international negotiations and reclamations . . . [but] with all this the judicial courts [within a nation that is a treaty party can] have nothing to do and can give no redress." 112 U.S. at 598, 5 S.Ct. at 253. This conclusion reflects the United States' adoption of a partly "dualist"—rather than strictly "monist"—view of international and domestic law. "[D]ualists view international law as a discrete legal system [which] . . . operates wholly on an inter-nation plane." Henkin, The Constitution and United States Sovereignty: A Century of Chinese Exclusion and Its Progeny, 100 Harv. L. Rev. 853, 864 (1987).

. . .

Given that dualist jurisprudence, we cannot find—as a matter of domestic law—that congressional enactments violate prior treaties [i.e., the US has not generally adopted the monist approach].

. . .

The second paragraph of Article 94 provides that, [i]f any party to a case fails to perform the obligations incumbent upon it under a judgment rendered by the [ICJ], the other party may have recourse to the Security Council, which may, if it deems necessary, make recommendations or decide upon measures to be taken to give effect to the judgment. U.N. Charter art. 94, para. 2. Because only nations can be parties before the ICJ, appellants are not "parties" within the meaning of this paragraph. Clearly, this clause does not contemplate that individuals having no relationship to the ICJ case should enjoy a private right to enforce the ICJ's decision. Our interpretation of Article 94 is buttressed by a related provision in the Statute of the ICJ, which is incorporated by reference in the U.N. Charter. See U.N. Charter art. 92. The Statute provides that "[t]he decision of the Court has no binding force except between the parties and in respect of th[e] particular case." Statute of the International Court of Justice, June 26, 1945, art. 59 (hereinafter "ICJ Statute"). Taken together, these Charter clauses make clear that the purpose of establishing the ICJ was to resolve disputes between national governments. We find in these clauses no intent to vest citizens who reside in a U.N. member nation with authority to enforce an ICJ decision against their own government. The words of Article 94 "do not by their terms confer rights upon individual citizens; they call upon governments to take certain action." *Diggs v. Richardson*, 555 F.2d at 851. We conclude that appellants' attempt to enjoin funding of the Contras based on a violation of Article 94 would fail even if Congress' abrogation of treaties were cognizable in domestic courts.

3. Customary international law and subsequent inconsistent statutes

. . .

The question is whether such a violation is cognizable by domestic courts. Once again, the United States' rejection of a purely "monist" view of the international and domestic legal orders shapes our analysis. Statutes inconsistent with principles of customary international law may well lead to international law violations. But within the domestic legal realm, that inconsistent statute simply modifies or supersedes customary international law to the extent of the inconsistency.

. . .

As with their refusal to take notice of statutory abrogation of treaties, the courts' disregard of statutory breaches of customary international law is not necessarily required by the Constitution. In Professor Henkin's view, "[t]he framers of the Constitution respected the law of nations, and it is plausible that they expected the political branches as well as the courts to give effect to that law. Other countries [applying the monist approach] . . . give effect to international law over domestic legislation." Henkin, United States Sovereignty, 100 Harv.L.Rev. at 877 (footnotes omitted) (citing constitutions of West Germany, Italy, and Greece). Nonetheless, the law in this court remains clear: no enactment of Congress can be challenged on the ground that it violates customary international law. Those of appellants' claims that are predicated on this theory of illegality cannot succeed.

4. Peremptory norms of international law (jus cogens)

Appellants argue that the rule requiring parties who have submitted to an international court to abide by its judgment is not only a principle of customary international law but has become a form of jus cogens. Because such peremptory norms are nonderogable and enjoy the highest status within international law, appellants conclude that these norms are absolutely binding upon our government as a matter of domestic law as well.

. . .

We need not decide whether an ICJ judgment would restrict Congress' foreign affairs power if that judgment were in fact a peremptory norm of international law. ICJ judgments simply do not meet the Vienna Convention's—or any other authority's—definition of jus cogens.

. . .

Our conclusion is strengthened when we consider those few norms that arguably do meet the stringent criteria for jus cogens. The recently revised Restatement [of Foreign Relations Law of the US]

acknowledges two categories of such norms: "the principles of the United Nations Charter prohibiting the use of force," and fundamental human rights law that prohibits genocide, slavery, murder, torture, prolonged arbitrary detention, and racial discrimination. But see Restatement § 331 comment e (doctrine of jus cogens is of such "uncertain scope" that a "domestic court should not on its own authority refuse to give effect to an agreement on the ground that it violates a peremptory norm").

. . .

We think it clear, however, that the harm that results when a government disregards or contravenes an ICJ judgment does not generate the level of universal disapprobation aroused by torture, slavery, summary execution, or genocide. . . . In sum, appellants' attempt to enjoin funding of the Contras on the ground that it violates a peremptory norm of international law by contravening an ICJ judgment is unavailing. The ICJ judgment does not represent such a peremptory norm.

■ NOTES & QUESTIONS

The materials in other chapters in this book, especially Chapter 8 on treaties, will demonstrate that the UN Charter is not "self-executing." Thus, it does not create immediately binding obligations for the UN's member States. The Charter is, instead, a standard of achievement—a goal toward which nations are expected to aspire. If the *US Citizens* court

had recognized this status, the court would likely have relied on it to avoid an extensive discussion of Charter Article 94 (regarding compliance with ICJ decisions). Yet the court accurately raises the issue, without deciding it, that such noncompliance might one day be characterizable as *jus cogens*. Would such recognition of a member's obligation to apply ICJ judgments signal adoption of the dualist view of International Law?

■ 1.9   IS INTERNATIONAL LAW REALLY LAW?

The following conversation has likely occurred on a number of occasions, after the news of a serious breach of the "law" saturates front-page headlines. The following words may have been uttered on the following occasions: during either of the twentieth century's World Wars, after the facts of the Holocaust were exposed to world view, while Iran was holding American and Canadian diplomats hostage for 444 days, or when Saddam Hussein's forces torched more than 600 oil wells upon Iraq's flight from Kuwait:

Of course, International Law isn't really law. Those who purport to be international lawyers, and the ivory-tower professors who teach and write on this subject, have a vested interest in trying to convince their clients and students that International Law is something more than a myopic fantasy. The evidence is all around us: if International Law were *really* law, Hitler, Khomeini, and Hussein would have been stopped in their tracks! International Law, if it is 'law' at all, is thus quite primitive—because it lacks the essential powers of enforcement. Like God, one may refer to International Law with great reverence while harboring doubts about its very existence!

A 1990 editorial appearing in a national magazine echoed these sentiments by describing the term "International Law" as self-canceling. In a prominent reporter's words, the term *International Law* "is virtually an oxymoron. Law without a sword is mere words: lacking an enforcement mechanism . . . [it is] merely admonition or aspiration . . . [and to be effective it] must be backed by coercion legitimized by a political process. The 'international community' has no such process."[85]

The superficial appeal of such arguments must be dissected before one can seriously proceed to study the field of International Law. There would be little sense in taking this course, or specializing in International Law or a related discipline, if the tangibility of this branch of law could not be authoritatively illustrated and its reality ably defended.

International Law *is* primitive in the sense that it lacks the same legislative, executive, and judicial enforcement mechanisms which are available in most national legal systems. Under the terms of the UN Charter itself, the General Assembly makes recommendations as opposed to making law. Customary international practice and normative treaties are the essential law-makers in the international legal system (*see* § 1.4 on "Sources of International Law"). As will be seen in the later chapters of this text, the UN Secretary-General does not have the power to intervene in any conflict beyond that which is expressly provided by the disputing parties or the veto-ridden Security Council. Further, the International Court of Justice cannot exercise jurisdiction in a case where the defendant nation has not consented to the proceedings.

Critics of the international legal system thus claim that International Law is not "law," premised on an assumption that anything less than full and immediate enforcement power renders a legal system inherently impotent. These "realists" thus chastise the international legal system as being crude, in relation to the available enforcement powers in *national* legal systems. Their perspective does not adequately embrace a critical distinction: that national law governs the relationship between the State and the individual—as opposed to International Law, which governs relations between States. The limita-

tions of the international legal system render it comparatively "weak" in the judgment of these critics.

The response to this critique is that International Law's inherent enforcement limitations have been instituted by the States themselves. They are both the governors, and the governed, in a system *designed* to temper the availability of enforcement measures with respect for national sovereignty. As articulated by one of the most prominent US Supreme Court Chief Justices, who effectively described the Westphalian model of the modern nation-State: "The jurisdiction of the nation within its own territory is necessarily exclusive and absolute. It is susceptible of no limitation not imposed by itself. Any restriction upon it, deriving vitality from an *external* source, would imply a diminution in sovereignty. . . ."[86]

Some analysts nevertheless perceive this state of affairs as rendering International Law either nonexistent, ineffectual, or both. One should distinguish between law and its enforcement mechanisms, however. Prior to the Iranian hostage crisis of 1979–1980, for example, States had observed the institution of diplomatic immunity for two millenniums. It made little sense, even for nations at war, to "shoot the messenger." Iran concededly ignored UN Security Council resolutions and a judgment of the ICJ, each calling for the release of the hostages. Yet it would be a mistake to say that, lacking an efficient enforcement mechanism in that instance, International Law does not exist. Iran was totally isolated in terms of the international response to its egregious breach of diplomatic immunity. No nation adversely reacted when the US froze billions of dollars of Iranian assets in the US as a means of pressuring Iran to comply with International Law. And in the previous generation, a number of Hitler's henchmen paid with their lives for their roles in waging Germany's aggressive war—as a result of the work of the Allied Nuremberg War Crimes Tribunal.

The following materials present some refreshing perspectives on why International Law is "law," notwithstanding the intrinsic problems of enforcement and the actions of a few national leaders who believe that "might makes right."

Of Traffic Lights and International Law

One can not appreciate why International Law works, without first comprehending "law" as generating behavior which the particular society deems acceptable, and in spite of the indifference of certain scofflaws. Drawing upon a familiar scenario will help make this point.[87] Consider the busy intersection with its host of traffic signals. Motorists generally conform to those directions by proceeding only when the light is green and stopping when the light is red. Observing this routine behavior triggers the following question: *Why* do most motorists observe the commands emitted from the directional commands?

Conforming behavior does not necessarily result from the fear of punishment—police officers are not present at most intersections. The motorists at the intersection observe the law due to their common desire to proceed safely. Otherwise, there would be only chaos as each driver attempted to reach his or her respective destination. If most of them did not observe the traffic laws, there would be numerous collisions. These incidents would defeat the common goal of interacting, while possibly delaying the progress of some of the drivers. But observance of the law enables them to arrive at their destinations—even if they do not arrive on time. The few scofflaws are unlikely to ignore the traffic lights without at least minor (and in some cases major) consequences.

The international system is able to similarly maintain an astonishing level of order between nations (motorists) due to the common interest which they share in observing the fundamental expectations of global harmony (limiting serious collisions). While some States may occasionally ignore the norms of accepted behavior (such as military aggressors), the community of nations has nevertheless imposed a legal framework for establishing mutual

expectations (*see* § 1.2 on *opinio juris*). Most of these "drivers" in the international legal system engage in consistent and predictable behavior which does not offend the shared sense of global order.

The national decision to voluntarily observe International Law is premised on self-interest and the same cognitive survival instinct observable at traffic and international intersections. Self-interested States thus recognize that it is in their best interest to comply with the mutual expectations of International Law. Like most motorists who observe almost all traffic laws almost all of the time, national interests are served best by a prevailing order in both national and International Law.

While the above traffic light analogy is not flawless, it does exemplify the analogous operation of International Law as a cog in the wheel of international relations. One may thus avoid the all-too-common misperception that the legitimacy of governance depends primarily on coercive enforcement rather than commonly shared values. Hence, observance of the "law" does not have to be equated to the available degree of military or economic enforcement. States observe International Law, in most instances, without a UN standing army and without the comparable governmental institutions which are the benchmarks of national law.

Reciprocal Entitlement

Professor Anthony D'Amato of Northwestern University addresses the question of whether International Law is really law in terms of "reciprocal entitlement." The excerpt below, published in 1985, provides significant insight into the international legal process years later:

IS INTERNATIONAL LAW REALLY "LAW"?*

by Professor Anthony D'Amato
79 Northwestern Univ. L. Rev. 1306–1307 (1985)

. . .

Yet we might briefly consider the perspective of a new nation (perhaps a nation that has just received its independence from a colonial power).

Our new nation receives at its birth a host of entitlements. It has not chosen nor selected any of these entitlements; instead they are . . . thrust upon the new nation. The first entitlement is of fundamental importance: the entitlement of statehood, which means in the international system, that our

---

*Reprinted by special permission of the Northwestern University School of Law, Northwestern University Law Review.

new nation is a geographic entity entitled to exert its own legal jurisdiction in the area within its boundaries and to claim the inviolability of those boundaries against all other states. The legal sanctity of its borders signifies that our new state is a state in a community of states, and not merely a gang of thieves subject to the untrammelled degradations of other neighboring gangs. . . . Without such boundaries, the entity is hardly a "state." Yet, the boundaries are boundaries only by virtue of their recognition by all other states in the system.

. . .

Our new state might, therefore, look upon the International Law of the sanctity of its boundaries as a gift of a valuable entitlement. But the entitlement carries with it reciprocal duties, so that it is not necessarily [just] a gift. . . . Obviously, we cannot know, a priori, whether a new state likes or dislikes any particular entitlement. And that is indeed the point:

the new entitlements that accrue to the new state at its birth are those that the international system has imposed upon the new state. If pressed to make a judgment whether the host of entitlements as a whole are a blessing or a curse, we would conclude that, on the whole, the system of entitlements is beneficial to the new nation. This conclusion follows from the simple observation that international entitlements did not descend from God, but rather they evolved slowly over time to serve the collective self-interest of all the states. It is unlikely, therefore, that a system of rules that serves the collective self-interest would be inimical to the individual interests of any state. Nevertheless, it is possible that *some* of the entitlements would be contrary to the interest of our new nation. If so, there is nothing our new nation can do about it. The list of entitlements is a given; they are thrust upon our new nation without its initial consent.

■ SUMMARY

1. International Law consists of rules governing the conduct of States and international organizations. Individuals and corporations may be subject to International Law in certain instances.

2. A customary practice may be incorporated into International Law if it is understood as being obligatory in international relations.

3. The scope of International Law is sometimes unclear because it is not static. State practices vary vis-a-vis each other. What one State does in its own International Relations varies from time to time.

4. Universality of acceptance is not required for a norm to be incorporated into International Law. Conversely, no single nation or small group of nations can independently alter global expectations.

5. The history of Public International Law is divided into three main periods: ancient, medieval, and contemporary.

6. The theoretical schools of thought for classifying International Law focus on Natural Law—based on immutable norms inherent in any ordered system of law; Positive Law—based solely on the expressed consent of nations; and Eclectics—a blend of maxims drawn from various schools of thought including Natural and Positive Law.

7. A State's legislation, executive decrees, and judicial opinions are sources for ascertaining the content of the law of that State. One must use a different paradigm when seeking sources as evidence of the content of International Law, due to the absence of the same authoritative branches of government which could so limit State sovereignty.

8. International decision-makers typically draw from five commonly recognized sources which appear in the Statute of the International Court of Justice: (a) treaties; (b) international customs; (c) relevant general principles of law used by nations in resolving their internal disputes; (d) the "subsidiary" source of judicial and arbitral decisions by national and international tribunals; and (e) the scholarly writings of experts in International Law. Another source might be a unanimous resolution of the UN General Assembly which is intended to create or modify the practice of its State members.

9. The ebb and flow of international consensus often makes it difficult to establish unchallenged evidence of what is International Law, even when using these recognized sources.

10. Private International Law refers to resolution mechanisms for disputes involving non-State entities, such as individuals or corporations.

11. The feminist perspective is that the public/private International Law distinction is harmful because it is imperfect and unrealistic. It has failed to properly govern the conduct of non-State

abusers, who have historically been governed only by national laws.

12. International Relations study emerged as a distinct discipline after World War I. Liberal democratic theory embraced the hope that the League of Nations would put an end to war. The harsh reality of the events leading to World War II convinced political science "realists" that the companion discipline of International Law had only a peripheral variable in the actual State practice of International Relations.

13. More recently, International Relations theory acknowledges the contributions made by International Law and international organizations because they facilitate positive State behavior in collaborative ways.

14. Religion and International Law share elements of ritual, authority, and universality. Sometimes these disciplines conflict. Environmental prohibitions on whaling may conflict with indigenous religious practices. International protection of the rights of women are rejected by certain Islamic traditions.

15. Diplomacy requires the recognition of cultural values which, because of their crucial role in shaping perceptions, are more significant than either ideological beliefs or abstract ideals.

16. The mutual expectations of members of the international community cannot be divorced from their respective legal systems. Each may contain different norms which may be extracted for use in international legal transactions and when negotiating international rules—such as those used in the 1994 rules of procedure and evidence for war crimes in the former Yugoslavia.

17. Monists and dualists debate the theoretical relationship between national and International Law. Monists assert that International Law and the law of each nation form a unified, universal legal system. Dualists argue that International Law and national law are distinct legal systems. The State retains the essential sovereign power to integrate or ignore the norms of International Law.

18. Some States expressly integrate international law into their national legal systems. In most, however, International Law has no validity unless its principles are expressly incorporated into national law. There, the constitution prevails in all cases of conflict. Treaties and national legislation have parity. The last in time is thus controlling (US). Alter-

natively, treaties always govern when in conflict with national legislation (Mexico).

19. A State may not assert its internal (national) law as a defense to a breach of International Law. It is liable for a breach of this "external" source of law, even when national law is interpreted to compel the violation.

20. Some observers perceive International Law as weak and incapable of enforcement, asserting that the viability or very existence of law directly depends on the availability of enforcement mechanisms like those available under national law.

21. International Law is primitive, when compared with the enforcement mechanisms found in national legal systems. Yet the concept of national sovereignty restricts the ways in which International Law is effectively enforced.

22. Most nations routinely observe International Law because it is in their best interests to do so, much like motorists observe traffic signals at busy intersections. One supporting rationale for this observance of International Law is that all nations thus enjoy reciprocal entitlements—such as their mutually recognized rights and duties respecting sovereignty.

■ PROBLEMS

Problem 1.1 *(at end of § 1.2)*: A member of the class will serve as the blackboard recorder. Another class member will begin this exercise by articulating his/her version of the definition of "International Law." Others may then suggest any modifications which would more fully or more accurately complete the definition.

Problem 1.2 *(within § 1.4 after n.28)*: Assume that India becomes a party to a treaty with several other countries within its region of the world. Customary International Law does not prevent a country from nationalizing the property of either its own citizens or foreign citizens. However, the nationalizing country must compensate foreign citizens and corporations for the expropriated assets. Under the new treaty now ratified by India, the national parties have agreed that such compensation is no longer necessary. The "Western-derived rule of International Law requiring prompt, adequate, and effective compensation is henceforth abrogated." This international agreement therefore contains a new rule which is contrary to the traditional practice of many countries throughout the world.

India then decides to nationalize a chemical plant belonging to a multinational corporation based in the US, a country which is not a party to this regional treaty. The US claims that it is entitled to prompt, adequate, and effective compensation—asserting that customary International Law controls this dispute. India responds that the US is effectively bound by the local treaty because a number of countries in the region have now adopted the new "no-compensation" rule.

Assume that this dispute is submitted to the ICJ for resolution. You are one of the ICJ judges. You and your colleagues have to decide *which conflicting source*—the custom or the new treaty—governs the dispute between India and the US; and, *which source* of International Law—the custom or the treaty—is entitled to *more weight*. Your specific task is to examine Article 38.1 of the ICJ Statute to find out whether it provides guidance for your ruling on this preliminary matter.

Problem 1.3 *(end of § 1.4)*: D-Squad is a special unit within the police force of State X. X is a Latin American nation whose typical, although unofficial, policy is to torture any citizen who is suspected of "civil disobedience." A treaty known as the Convention Against Torture and Other Cruel, Inhuman, or Degrading Treatment or Punishment was adopted by the UN General Assembly as Resolution No. 39/46 (1984). It entered into force (under its own terms) when twenty nations ratified it (1987). X was not one of those nations. The UN consisted of approximately 175 nations, including State X, at the time of the D-Squad acts and the effective date of the Torture Convention. Neither State emergency nor superior orders to individual perpetrators are defenses to violations of this treaty. It applies to the conduct of States within their borders as a means for protecting individual citizens from their own governments when torture is used as an official or unofficial policy.

While X is not a party to this treaty, there are other treaties prohibiting torture—including the American Convention on Human Rights and the Inter-American Convention to Prevent and Punish Torture—which have not yet been accepted by a number of nations in the Western Hemisphere.

The "Committee Against Torture" is an administrative agency established by the above Torture Convention to monitor compliance with its antitorture provisions. Members of D-Squad engaged in activities in 1990 which clearly fit within the Convention's definition of torture. The Committee is conducting a hearing in which its representative is presenting evidence to the treaty's Torture Committee about whether or not X's *de facto* torture policy (not official but a "fact of life" in State X) violates International Law.

- The Committee representative will now present the first phase of the potential case against State X—specifically, what sources of International Law, if any, are applicable to this dispute?

- A student who represents the government of State X (which denies the existence of a torture policy) will respond to the Torture Committee representative's presentation of the case against State X.

Problem 1.4 *(§ 1.8 after n.83)*: Israel and the PLO enter into a "Gaza Autonomy Taxation" treaty in 1995. Under its terms, Israel will retain the right to exact an income tax from all Gaza workers until the year 2005—when a new State called Palestine will have the exclusive right to tax Gaza's workers. The agreed-upon use of the revenue derived from this taxation treaty will be to create funds for implementing the security of Gaza. The income tax money is earmarked for use as payment for the police force that will keep the peace in Gaza. Until the 1995–2005 transition period is over, Israel has the exclusive fiscal responsibility to pay for the Gaza police force. After that, Palestine will assume the obligation to pay for the police force, as well as the right to tax Gaza residents, who will benefit from the security provided by that force.

In the year 2000, a right-wing group within the P.L.O. decides to conduct a terrorist campaign in Gaza, with the objective of driving Israel out of Gaza before the end of the transition period in 2005. The Israeli Knesset (parliament) responds to the terrorist campaign by enacting emergency legislation extending Israel's ability to collect and retain tax revenues derived from Gaza for an indefinite period, pending the parliament's determination of when Gaza will be at least as secure as in the period leading up to the joint ratification of the 1995 tax treaty.

A Knesset representative advises her Palestinian counterpart that "Palestine" may never be able to collect Gaza's income taxes under the 1995 treaty. It appears that Gaza will not be secure enough, until sometime well into the twenty-first century, for Israel to actually surrender this taxing power to Palestine. Under International Law, Israel has a duty to perform its treaty obligations in good faith (as discussed in this textbook's treaty chapter). Assume that Israel has never addressed the question of whether its internal law or International Law would govern this potential "tax" treaty dispute with Palestinian authorities.

Two students will play the roles of the Israeli and Palestinian representatives. What arguments would each make on the question of whether it is Israel's emergency legislation or International Law which governs this dispute?

Problem 1.5 *(end of § 1.8)*: A panel of students will present their perspectives on the following questions:

1. Does the US follow the monist view regarding the incorporation of International Law into national law?

2. The UN Charter is not a binding treaty creating immediate obligations. Could a US court nevertheless be bound to follow ICJ judgments under some source in International Law other than a treaty? *US Citizens* suggests a potential basis for requiring the US to so comply. Put another way, what would it take for the ICJ judgment to rise to a level of observance whereby post-Charter treaties and national legislation could not override the UN Charter Article 94 provision "requiring" national compliance with ICJ judgments? Is that basis for binding a nation to follow ICJ judgments currently in force?

3. Why would the plaintiffs in *US Citizens* be unable to obtain a remedy, even if they *were* able to establish that the US *must* observe all ICJ judgments?

Problem 1.6 *(end of § 1.9)*: The Serbian post–Cold War advances in Bosnia-Herzegovina triggered a great deal of international frustration. Various rules of International Law, particularly the prohibition on violating territorial sovereignty, were ignored by the Serbs. The UN, NATO, and the US seemed powerless to act. The US and other NATO members stated that they merely wanted to carefully weigh the timing and degree of responsive action during a period when democracy and capitalism had not been staunchly incorporated into the various Yugoslavian territories involved in the Bosnia conflict. (England similarly appeased Hitler at the outset of a long war, by its cautious response to German territorial advances taken in violation of the territorial sovereignty of various States in Europe.) With the possible exception of Moscow, there was no international outcry when an embargo was launched against the entire area by the international community, and when NATO aircraft proceeded to bomb a few Serbian positions in Bosnia.

Many skeptics concluded that International Law is not "law." They viewed the international response to Serbian aggression as being strangled by political concerns—including the potential Russian reaction to any US/European measures against its traditional Serbian ally. Did they correctly equate cautious enforcement measures with the absence of any law to govern this war? Did the Bosnian scenario expose the political reality that expressions of caution by the international community are no more than a disguise for the fact that there is no applicable law to govern the relations between States?

Two students (or groups) will debate whether International Law is really law and whether swift and effective enforcement measures against scofflaws is the only genuine benchmark of any legal system.

■ BIBLIOGRAPHY

§ 1.1 Why Study International Law:

W. Bishop, *Foreword to the Student: Why Study International Law?*, in *International Law: Cases and Materials* xiii (3rd ed. Boston: Little, Brown and Co., 1971)

Falk, *A New Paradigm for International Legal Studies: Prospects and Proposals*, in R. Falk, et al., *International Law: A Contemporary Perspective* 651 (Dobbs Ferry, NY: Transnat'l, 1985)

M. Janis, *Careers in International Law* (Chicago: Amer. Bar Ass'n, 1993)

§ 1.2 Public International Law Defined:

R. Bledsoe & B. Boczek, *The International Law Dictionary* (Santa Barbara, CA: ABC-Clio, 1987)

J. Grant, et al. (ed.), *Parry and Grant Encyclopedic Dictionary of International Law* (2nd print. New York: Oceana, 1988)

L. Henkin, et al., *The Nature of International Law*, ch. 1, in *International Law, Cases and Materials* 1 (3rd ed. St. Paul: West, 1993)

M. Janis, *The Nature of International Law*, ch. 1, *An Introduction to International Law* 1 (2d ed. Boston: Little, Brown & Co., 1993)

M. Kaplan & N. Katzenbach, ch. 3, *The Theoretical Framework of International Law*, in *The Political Foundations of International Law* 56 (New York: John Wiley & Sons, 1961)

O. Schachter, *The Nature and Reality of International Law*, ch. 1, in *International Law in Theory and Practice* 1 (Dordrecht, Neth.; Boston: Martinus Nijhoff, 1991)

B. Weston, et al., *The International Legal Process*, ch. 1, in *International Law and World Order* 1 (2d ed. St. Paul: West, 1990)

§ 1.3 History of International Law:

B. Chimni, *International Law and World Order: A Critique of Contemporary Approaches* (New Delhi: Sage Pub., 1993)

Kennedy, *A New Stream of International Law Scholarship*, 7 *Wisconsin International Law Journal* 1 (1988)

Historical Evolution of the International Community, ch. 2 (1868–1918) & ch. 3 (1918–present) in A. Cassese, *International Law in a Divided World* 34 & 55 (New York: Oxford Univ. Press, 1988)

§ 1.4 Sources of International Law:

M. Akehurst, *The Hierarchy of Sources of International Law*, 47 *British Yearbook International Law* 273 (1975)

D. Harris, *The Sources of International Law*, ch. 2, in *Cases and Materials on International Law* 23 (4th ed. London: Street & Maxwell, 1991)

M. Nash, *Contemporary Practice of the United States Relating to International Law*, 88 *American Journal of International Law* 312 (1994)

E. McWhinney, *United Nations Law Making: Cultural and Ideological Relativism and International Law Making for an Era of Transition* (New York: Holmes & Meier, 1984)

C. Parry, *The Sources and Evidences of International Law* (Manchester, Eng.: Manchester Univ. Press, 1965)

S. Rosenne, *Practice and Methods of International Law* (New York: Oceana, 1984)

Sources of International Law, 19 Thesaurus Acroasium— Summer 1991 (Thessaloniki, Greece: Inst. Int'l Pub. L., 1992)

§ 1.5 Private International Law:

Charlesworth, Chinkin, & Wright, *Feminist Approaches to International Law*, 85 *American Journal of International Law* 613 (1991)

P. North & J. Fawcett, *Chesire and North's Private International Law* (12th ed. London: Butterworths, 1992)

§ 1.6 International Relations Compared:

G. Maris, *The Relevance of International Law within International Politics*, ch. 12, in *International Law: An Introduction* 363 (Lanham, MD: Univ. Press of America, 1984)

W. McWilliams & H. Piotrowski, *The World Since 1945: A History of International Relations* (3rd ed. Boulder, CO: Lynne Reinner, 1993)

Powell, *Absolute and Relative Gains in International Relations Theory*, 85 *American Political Science Review* 1303 (1991)

C. Sjolander & W. Cox, *Beyond Positivism: Critical Reflections on International Relations* (Boulder, CO: Lynne Reinner, 1994)

§ 1.7 Religion, Culture, Comparative Law:

M. Glendon, M. Gordon & C. Osakwe, *Comparative Legal Traditions: Text, Materials and Cases on the Civil and Common Law Traditions* (2nd ed., St. Paul: West, 1994)

B. Grossfeld, *Religion and Law*, ch. 14, in *The Strength and Weaknesses of Comparative Law* 107 (Oxford, Eng.: Oxford Univ. Press, 1990) (Weir translation)

D. Johnston & C. Sampson, *Religion, The Missing Dimension of Statecraft* (Oxford, Eng.: Oxford Univ. Press, 1994)

J. Plano & R. Olton, *The International Relations Dictionary* (4th ed. Oxford, Eng.: ABC-CLIO, 1988)

Purvis, *Critical Legal Studies in Public International Law*, 32 *Harvard International Law Journal* 81 (1991)

T. Reynolds, *Socialist Legal Systems: Reflections on Their Emergence and Demise*, 20 *International Journal of Legal Information* 215 (1992)

C. Varga (ed.), *Comparative Legal Cultures* (New York: NYU Press, 1992)

§ 1.8 National/International Law Nexus:

I. Brownlie, *The Relation of Municipal and International Law*, ch. II, in *Principles of Public International Law* 32 (4th ed. Oxford, Eng.: Oxford Univ. Press, 1990)

T. Frank & M. Glennon, *The Law of Nations as Incorporated into United States Law*, ch. 2, in *Foreign Relations and National Security Law* 108 (2nd ed. St. Paul: West, 1993)

R. Jennings & A. Watts, *Relation Between International and Municipal Law*, in I *Oppenheim's International Law* (Part 1) 52 (9th ed. Essex, Eng.: Longman, 1993)

Kratochwil, *The Role of Domestic Courts as Agencies of the International Legal Order*, in R. Falk, et al., *International Law: A Contemporary Perspective* 236 (Dobbs Ferry, NY: Transnat'l, 1985)

Sik, *International Law in the Municipal Legal Order of Asian States: Virgin Land*, R. Macdonald (ed.), *Essays in Honour of Wang Tieya* 737 (Dordrecht, Neth.; Boston: Martinus Nijhoff, 1994)

§ 1.9 Is International Law Really Law?:

Bierzanek, *Some Remarks on "Soft" International Law*, 17 *Polish Yearbook International Law* 21 (1988)

Falk, *International Jurisdiction: Horizontal and Vertical Conceptions of Legal Order*, 32 *Temple Law Quarterly* 295 (1959)

Georgiev, *Politics or Rule of Law: Deconstruction and Legitimacy in International Law*, 4 *European Journal of International Law* 1 (1993)

Niou & Ordeshook, *Stability in Anarchic International Systems*, 84 *American Political Science Review* 1207 (1990)

■ ENDNOTES

1. *See* Wang, *Teaching and Research of International Law in Present Day China*, 22 Colum. J. Transnat'l L. 77 (1983).

2. Chiu, *Communist China's Attitude toward International Law*, 60 Amer. J. Int'l L. 245, 250 (1966) (quoting Chinese-language source).

3. Huan, *Forward* to First Edition, *Chinese Yearbook of International Law* 4 (Taipei: Inst. Int'l Relations, 1983).

4. *See Postscript, International Law as a Career* 233 in A. D'Amato, *International Law: Process and Prospect* 233 (Dobbs Ferry, NY: Transnat'l Pub., 1987).

5. C. Okeke, *The Theory and Practice of International Law in Nigeria* 277–78 (Enugu, Nigeria: Fourth Dimension Pub., 1986).

6. U.N.G.A. Res. 45/40, reprinted in Schaff, *United Nations Decade of International Law*, 19 Int'l J. Legal Info. 130, 133–134 (1991).

7. *The SS Lotus* (France v. Turkey), 1927 P.C.I.J., Series A, No. 10, 18. A panel of US jurists, dealing with Nazi Germany's wrongful confiscation of a Swiss citizen's property in 1938, classically characterized International Law as "the relationship among nations rather than among individuals. 'It is termed the Law of Nations or International Law because it is relative to States or Political Societies and not necessarily to individuals, although citizens or subjects of the earth are greatly affected by it.'" Dreyfus v. Von Finck, 534 F.2d 24, 30 (2d Cir. 1976), *cert. den'd*, 429 U.S. 825 (1976), *disavowed on other grounds*, Filartiga v. Pena-Irala, 630 F.2d 876 (2d Cir. 1980).

8. The concept, development, and usage is analyzed by Professor Condorelli in M. Bedjaoui (ed.), *Custom*, ch. 7, *International Law: Achievements and Prospects* 179, 187–192 (Paris: UNESCO, 1991).

9. North Sea Continental Shelf Cases (Fed. Rep. Germany v. Denmark/Netherlands), 1969 I.C.J. Rep. 4, 44.

10. Case Concerning Military and Paramilitary Activities (Nicaragua v. U.S.), 1986 I.C.J. Rep. 101 [hereinafter *Nicaragua* case].

11. 1 *Restatement of the Foreign Relations Law of the United States* § 101, 22 (3rd ed. St. Paul: Amer. Law Inst., 1987).

12. 1 M. Whiteman, *Digest of International Law* 1 (Wash., DC: US Dep't State, 1963).

13. *See, e.g.,* M. McDougal & W. Reisman, *International Law as a Process of Authoritative Decision*, ch. 1 § 1,

in *International Law in Contemporary Perspective* 4 (Mineola, NY: Foundation Press, 1981).

14. Charney, *Universal International Law*, 87 Amer. J. Int'l L. 529 (Oct. 1993).

15. G. Tunkin, *Theory of International Law* 251 (Cambridge, MA: Harv. Univ. Press, 1974) (emphasis supplied).

16. Treaties of Osnabruck and Munster, set forth in *Fenwick treatise*, p.15 n.33 (cited in note 17 below).

17. On the historical development of International Law, *see*: A. Nussbaum, *A Concise History of the Law of Nations* (New York: MacMillan, rev. ed. 1953) (Mesopotamian treaty); Nanda, *International Law in Ancient Hindu India*, ch. 3, in M. Janis (ed.), *The Influence of Religion on the Development of International Law* 51, 54 (Dordrecht, Neth.; Boston: Martinus Nijhoff, 1991) (Hindu disapproval of war); *A Brief History of Public International Law*, ch. 15, in E. Paras, *International Law and World Organizations* 389 (4th rev. ed. Manila: Rex Book Store, 1985) (Greek city-State legal hierarchy); Chen, *The Confucian View of World Order*, ch. 2, in M. Janis (ed.), *The Influence of Religion on the Development of International Law* 31, 37 (Dordrecht, Neth.; Boston: Martinus Nijhoff, 1991) (divinity basis for Chinese reprisals); *see The Fetiales*, ch. 1, in C. Watson, *International Law in Archaic Rome* 1 (Baltimore: Johns Hopkins Univ. Press, 1993) (Roman college on legality of war); *The Historical Background of International Law*, ch. 1, in C. Fenwick, *International Law* 9 (4th ed. New York: Appleton-Century-Crofts, 1965) (Greek universality introduced to Romans); Baskin & Feldman, *The Role of Hugo Grotius in the Formation and Development of the International Law Science*, 1982 Soviet Yearbk. Int'l L. 275 (1983) (English trans.) ("father of International Law"); Lauterpacht, *The Grotian Tradition in International Law*, 23 Brit. Yearbk. Int'l Law 1 (1946) (derivation of term "International Law"); *Historical Evolution of the International Community: The Former Setting* (1648–1918), ch. 2, in A. Cassese, *International Law in a Divided World* 34 (Oxford, Eng.: Clarendon Press, 1986) (European ascendancy).

18. T. Bennett, *A Sourcebook of African Customary Law for Southern Africa* 2 (Cape Town: Juta & Co., 1991).

19. *See, e.g.,* Kunz, *Natural-Law Thinking in the Modern Science of International Law*, 55 Amer. J. Int'l L. 951 (1961) & *Natural Law vs. Positivism*, in G. Danilenko, *Law-Making in the International Community* 214–219 (Dordrecht, Neth.; Boston: Martinus Nijhoff, 1992).

20. Y. Danesh-Khoshboo, *The Civilization of Law: The Laws of Hammurabi and Magna Carta—Documents with Commentary* (Berrien Spring, MI: Vande Vere Pub., 1991).

21. *See* Schwarzenberger, *The Grotius Factor in International Law and Relations: A Functional Approach*, ch. 12, in H. Bull, B. Kingsbury & A. Roberts (ed.), *Hugo*

Grotius and International Relations 301 (Oxford, Eng.: Oxford Univ. Press, 1992).

22. *Survey of International Law in Relation to the Work of Codification of the International Law Commission*, Sec.-Gen. Memo. A/CN.4/Rev.1., p.22 (1949).

23. Trendtex Trading Corp. v. Central Bank of Nigeria, 1 All English Rep. 881, 902–03 (1977).

24. *See, e.g.*, I. Brownlie, *Principles of Public International Law* 3 (4th ed. Oxford, Eng.: Oxford Univ. Press, 1990) [hereinafter *Brownlie treatise*]; M. Akehurst, *A Modern Introduction to International Law* 23 (6th ed. London: Allen & Unwin, 1987); J. Brierly, *The Law of Nations* 56 (Waldock 6th ed. Oxford, Eng.: Clarendon Press, 1976). *But see* G. Maris, *International Law: An Introduction* 44 (New York: Univ. Press of Amer., 1984) (amidst chaos, there is no set rule of sources).

25. **Allied Report**: Cmd. Doc. 6531 (1944, p.36); **Western criticism**: M. Kaplan & N. Katzenbach, *The Political Foundations of International Law* 231–36 (New York: John Wiley & Sons, 1961); **Soviet criticism**: G. Tunkin, *Theory of International Law* 118 (Cambridge, MA: Harv. Univ. Press, 1974) [hereinafter *Tunkin treatise*]; **Chinese criticism**: Chiu, *Communist China's Attitude Toward International Law*, 60 *Amer. J. Int'l L.* 245, 257 (1966), quoting Ying T'ao, *Recognize the True Face of Bourgeois International Law from a Few Basic Concepts*, in *Studies in International Problems* 46–47 (1960) (Chinese-language periodical criticism).

26. *The Hierarchy of International Norms*, in B. Conforti, *International Law and the Role of Domestic Legal Systems* 115–16 (Dordrecht, Neth.; Boston: Martinus Nijhoff, 1993) (Provost translation).

27. Bernhardt, *Hierarchy Among the Sources of International Law?*, in D. Constantopoulos (ed.), *Sources of International Law*, XIX Thesaurus Acrosium 209 (Thessaloniki, Greece: Inst. Pub. Int'l Law, 1992).

28. *See* Akehurst, *The Hierarchy of the Sources of International Law*, 47 *British Yearbk. Int'l L.* 273, 274 (1974).

29. *See The Elements of International Custom*, ch. 1, in K. Wolfke, *Custom in Present International Law* 1 (2d rev. ed. Dordrecht, Neth.; Boston: Martinus Nijhoff, 1993).

30. *Tunkin treatise*, 113–14 (cited in note 25).

31. *Brownlie treatise*, 5–7 (cited in note 24).

32. 1969 I.C.J. Rep. 3, 44.

33. Asylum Case (Colombia v. Peru), 1950 I.C.J. Rep. 266, 276.

34. *See, e.g.*, Danilenko, *Customary Rule Formation in Contemporary International Law*, 1982 *Soviet Yearbk. Int'l L.* 169, 170 (1983) (English translation).

35. Hsiung, *China's Recognition Practice and International Law*, in J. Cohen, *China's Practice of International Law: Some Case Studies* 14, 17 (Cambridge, MA: Harv. Univ. Press, 1972).

36. The classic restatement of this feature of International Law was undertaken by Holland's Professor Verzijl.

The latest compilation of his work is contained in W. Heere & J. Offerhaus, IX-C *The Law of Maritime Prize* (Dordrecht, Neth.; Boston: Martinus Nijhoff, 1991).

37. A comprehensive analysis, commencing with the Peace of Westphalia, is provided in L. Hannikainen, *Peremptory Norms (Jus Cogens) in International Law* (Helsinki: Finnish Lawyers' Pub. Co., 1988).

38. 1969 Convention, 155 UN Treaty Series 331; 1986 Convention, UN Doc. A/Conf. 129/15; *see also* Draft Article 18(2) in S. Rosenne, *The International Law Commission's Draft Articles on State Responsibility* (Dordrecht, Neth.; Boston: Martinus Nijhoff, 1991).

39. **1969 case:** No. Sea Continental Shelf, 1969 I.C.J. Rep. 3, 42; **1986 case:** Nicaragua v. U.S., 1986 I.C.J. Rep. 14, 100.

40. Article 20, 2 U.S. Treaties 2394, 119 U.N.T.S. 3 (emphasis supplied).

41. North Sea Continental Shelf Case, 1969 I.C.J. Rep. 3, 41–42.

42. An excellent analysis of this problem is available in M. Shaw, *International Law* 84 (3d ed. Cambridge, Eng.: Grotius Pub., 1991) (regarding utility of "general principles" source).

43. *See § 12 General principles of law*, in R. Jennings & A. Watts, I *Oppenheim's International Law* (Part 1) 37, n.2 (9th ed. Essex, Eng.: Longman, 1992) (scholarly disagreement) [hereinafter *Jennings treatise*]. *Compare* Russian position in *Tunkin treatise*, 190–203 (cited in note 25) *with* Chiu, *Chinese Attitudes Toward International Law in the Post-Mao Era, 1978–1987*, 21 *Int'l Lawyer* 1127, 1140–41 (1987).

44. The various positions are presented in the classic treatise B. Cheng, *General Principles of Law as Applied by International Courts and Tribunals* 5 (1987 reprint of orig. 1953 ed. London: Grotius Pub., 1987).

45. Diversion of Water from the Meuse, P.C.I.J. Series A/B, No. 70, p.25 (1937). On "equity" as a separate source of International Law, *see The Incorporation of Equity as a General Principle of International Law*, ch. V, in C. Rossi, *Equity and International Law* 87 (Irvington, NY: Transnat'l Pub., 1993).

46. Barcelona Traction Case, 1970 I.C.J. Rep. 3, 33.

47. Its historical development is available in *Good Faith in the Doctrine of Public International Law*, ch. 5, in J. O'Conner, *Good Faith in International Law* 45 (Aldershot, Eng.: Dartmouth, 1991).

48. 3 G. Hackworth, *Digest of International Law* 655–61 (Wash., DC: US Gov't Print. Off., 1942).

49. H. Lauterpacht, *The Development of International Law by the International Court* 20 (rev. ed. London: Stevens & Sons, 1958).

50. Thirty Hogsheds of Sugar v. Boyle, 13 U.S. (9 Cranch) 191, 3 L.Ed. 701, 703 (1815).

51. *Jennings treatise*, 41 (cited in note 43 above).

52. Case Concerning the Factory at Chorzow (Germany v. Poland), 1926–29 P.C.I.J., ser. A, No. 7, 19 (Judgment of May 25, 1926).

53. The SS Lotus (France v. Turkey), 1927 P.C.I.J., ser. A, No. 10, p.26.

54. K. Wolfke, *Custom in Present International Law* 77 (2nd rev. ed. Dordrecht, Neth.; Boston: Martinus Nijhoff, 1993).

55. West Rand Central Gold Mining Co. v. The King, 2 King's Bench 391 (1905).

56. Suy, *Innovations in International Law-Making Processes*, in R. McDonald, et al. (ed.), *The International Law and Policy of Human Welfare* (Alphen aan den Rijn, Neth.: Sitjhoff & Noordhoff, 1978).

57. *See* Bergman, *The Norm-Creating Effect of a General Assembly Resolution on Transnational Corporations*, in F. Snyder & S. Sathirathai (ed.), *Third World Attitudes toward International Law: An Introduction* 231 (Dordrecht, Neth.; Boston: Martinus Nijhoff, 1987) (some resolutions are "norm-creating" sources); O. Asamoah, *The Legal Significance of the Declarations of the General Assembly of the United Nations* (The Hague: Martinus Nijhoff, 1966) (resolutions as sources when restating customary practice).

58. **Certain Expenses of the United Nations:** 1962 I.C.J. Rep. 151, p.163; **Legal Consequences for States of the Continued Presence of South Africa in Namibia (South West Africa) Notwithstanding Security Council Resolution 276 (1970):** 1971 I.C.J. Rep. 16, p.50; **South West Africa Voting Procedure:** 1955 I.C.J. Rep. 67, p.118.

59. A. D'Amato, *International Law: Process and Prospect* 75–76 (Dobbs Ferry, NY: Transnat'l Pub., 1987).

60. O. Schachter, *Resolutions and Political Texts*, ch. VI, in *International Law in Theory and Practice* 88 (Dordrecht, Neth.; Boston: Martinus Nijhoff, 1991).

61. *See Nicaragua* case, p.99–100 & 188 (cited in note 10 above).

62. McDougal, *"Private" International Law: Jus Gentium Versus Choice of Law Rules or Approaches*, 38 *Amer. J. Comp. L.* 521 (1990).

63. Wright, *Economic Rights, Social Justice and the State: A Feminist Reappraisal*, in D. Dallmeyer, *Reconceiving Reality: Woman and International Law* 117, 135–36 (Wash., DC: Amer. Soc. Int'l L., 1993).

64. *See* L. Henkin, *How Nations Behave: Law and Foreign Policy*, in Preface (1st ed. New York: Columbia Univ. Press, 1968); *quote*: 2d ed. (1979), p.47.

65. Burley, *International Law and International Relations Theory: A Dual Agenda*, 87 *Amer. J. Int'l L.* 205, 207 (1993).

66. *See, e.g.,* R. Keohane, *After Hegemony: Cooperation and Discord in the World Political Economy* 246 (Princeton: Princeton Univ. Press, 1984).

67. A very useful primer on International Relations between Communist nations is available in L. Holmes, *Politics in the Communist World* (Oxford, Eng.: Oxford Univ. Press, 1986).

68. Slann, *Introduction: Ethnonationalism and the New World Order of International Relations*, ch. 1, in B. Schechterman & M. Slann (ed.), *The Ethnic Dimension in International Relations* 3 (Westport, CT: Praeger, 1993).

69. Filteau, *U.S., Vatican Relations Gradually Improving*, in the *Catholic Standard and Times Newspaper*, June 21, 1990, p.20.

70. Essay No. 8, in M. Janis (ed.), *The Influence of Religion on the Development of International Law* 147, p.151–53 (Dordrecht, Neth.; Boston: Martinus Nijhoff, 1991) (footnotes omitted).

71. M. Marty & R. Appleby (ed.), *Introduction* to *Fundamentalisms and the State* 4 (Chicago: Univ. of Chicago Press, 1993).

72. Ninkovich, *Culture in U.S. Foreign Policy since 1900*, ch. 8, in J. Chay (ed.), *Culture and International Relations* 103 (New York: Preager, 1990) [hereinafter *Chay treatise*].

73. *See, e.g.*, Wallace, *Is War a Cultural Universal? Anthropological Perspectives on the Causes of Warfare in Human Societies*, ch. 2, in *Chay treatise*, p.21 (cited in note 72).

74. R. Schlesinger, et al., *Comparative Law: Cases—Text—Materials* 309 (5th ed. Mineola, NY: Foundation Press, 1988) [hereinafter *Schlesinger treatise*].

75. *See The Concept of Comparative Law*, ch. 1, in K. Zweigert & H. Kotz, *An Introduction to Comparative Law* (2d rev. ed. Oxford, Eng.: Oxford Univ. Press, 1992).

76. *See generally Common Law and Civil Law—Comparison of Methods and Sources*, in *Schlesinger treatise*, p.229 (cited in note 74).

77. *See* International Tribunal for the Prosecution of Persons Responsible for Serious Violations of International Humanitarian Law Committed in the Territory of the Former Yugoslavia since 1991: *Rules of Procedure and Evidence*, 33 *Int'l Legal Mat'ls* 484 (1994).

78. *See* § 1.5 of this book, *Feminist Perspective*.

79. Applicability of the Obligation to Arbitrate Under Section 21 of the United Nations Headquarters Agreement of 26 June 1947, 1988 I.C.J. Rep. 12, para. 57.

80. Hans Kelsen, *General Theory of Law and the State* 363–80 (Cambridge, MA: Harv. Univ. Press, 1945).

81. Chung Chi Cheung v. Regina, 1939 Court of Appeals 160 (1939).

82. Schroeder v. Bissell, 5 Fed.2d 838 (D.C. Conn. 1925).

83. **ILC quote:** 1949 *Yearbook of the International Law Commission* 286, 289 (1949); **PCIJ quote:** Polish Nationals in Danzig, 1931 P.C.I.J. Rep., ser. A/B, no. 44, p.24.

84. B. Conforti, *International Law and the Role of Domestic Legal Systems* 8–9 (Dordrecht, Neth.; Boston, MA: Martinus Nijhoff, 1993) (Provost translation).

85. Will, *The Perils of 'Legality,'* in *Newsweek*, 66 (Sept. 10, 1990).

86. The Schooner Exchange v. McFadden, 136 U.S. (7 Cranch) 116, 136 (1812) (Marshall, C.J.) (emphasis supplied).

87. Political science Professor Richard Thurston of Saint Peter's College (New Jersey) inspired the development of this useful analogy.

CHAPTER TWO

States in International Law

INTRODUCTION

Different categories of international "actors" exist. These are the entities and individuals whose conduct is governed by International Law. These actors thus possess international legal personality—the legal capacity that carries with it certain entitlements and obligations arising under International Law.

The "persons" with this legal personality include States, international organizations, nongovernmental organizations, and to some extent private individuals and corporations within a State. This chapter focuses on *States*—an often used and misused term.

After setting the fundamental building block of State legal capacity, this chapter then surveys an unprecedented alteration in the infrastructure of International Law—caused by the vast increase in the number of State actors. This phenomenon was caused by events including the post–World War II decolonization and the breakdown of States, exemplified by events occurring since the demise of the Cold War.

The related topics include recognition, a cardinal feature of international relations (arguably providing the spark that ignited the "Bosnian War"). The student of International Law must also appreciate the resulting rights and duties associated with achieving statehood, as well as State immunity from resolving certain disputes judicially.

2.1 LEGAL PERSONALITY OF THE STATE

The legal "capacity" or "personality" of the State is a central feature of its status in International Law. Individuals and corporate entities within a nation have rights and duties arising under that nation's internal laws. For example, they may petition the appropriate governmental institution for relief, when their rights have been adversely impacted by conduct of another individual or by the government itself. They thus have rights, and obligations vis-a-vis one another, that protect them and cause them to incur reciprocal duties arising under *national* law. They do not enjoy any like status under International Law, however. Recalling the materials from Chapter 1, it is the State that has rights and duties arising under International Law. Decision-makers often refer to such State entitlements and responsibilities as arising "on the *international* plane" or "at the *international* level."

The State is but one of the modern actors under International Law addressed in this book (which also analyzes international and nongovernmental organizations, individuals, and multinational corporations). While there are contemporary pressures to break away from the concept of "State," as it has been understood via the Western-derived notion developed by the European powers after the 1648 Peace of Westphalia, the fundamental player on the international scene is still the State. As described by UN Secretary-General Boutros-Ghali in his 1992 Report to the General Assembly: "This wider mission [of making the UN stronger and more efficient] . . . will demand the concerted attention and effort of individual States, or regional and nongovernmental organizations and of all of the United Nations system . . . [and the] foundation-stone of this work is and must remain the State. Respect for its fundamental sovereignty and integrity are crucial to any common international progress."[1]

This view of the State as the primary international actor is not new. More than a generation ago, one of the most prominent International Law scholars articulated the continuing dominance of the State as the major component of the international system. Professor Wolfgang Friedmann of Columbia University therein acknowledged this somewhat daunting phenomenon as follows: "It is by virtue of their law-making power and monopoly that states enter into bilateral and multilateral compacts, that wars can be started or terminated, that individuals can be punished or extradited . . . and [could be] eventually superseded only if national entities were absorbed in[to] a world state. . . ."[2]

The following materials thus address two preliminary questions: What does the term "State" mean? Under what conditions does an entity become a "State" (that is, what are the elements of statehood)? What is the relationship between a "state" (within a group of associated "states") and some larger national entity under International Law?

"State"

Like many other legal terms, the commonly used word *State* means different things to different people. A State is typically defined as being a group of societies within a readily-defined geographical area, united to ensure their mutual welfare and security. Commentators have debated the appropriate no-

menclature for describing the entity that is the subject of International Law. This particular difference of opinion often dwells on the proper usage of "nation" v. "State."[3]

The terms *State, nation, nation-state, community, country, people, government,* and *sovereign* have all been used interchangeably. They have distinct meanings, however. The following words in the Preamble to the UN Charter (emphasis supplied by the author) provide a convenient example of such usages: "We the *peoples* of the United *Nations* . . . [h]ave resolved to combine our efforts . . . [through] our respective *Governments.* . . ." Keeping in mind that there are subtle differences among these terms will unmask important distinctions that heads of State, diplomats, speakers, and writers do not always express to their respective audiences. While there is some overlap, reading the following definitions will at least generate some caution when one is attempting to digest the discourses on International Law found in various speeches, news reports, and texts:

- STATE —"a person of international law [which] should possess the following qualifications: (a) a permanent population; (b) a defined territory; (c) government; and (d) capacity to enter into relations with other States."

- NATION—"a practical association of human individuals who consider themselves to be a nation (on the basis of a shared religion, history, language or any other common feature)."

- NATION-STATE—the joinder of two terms, typically referring to a specific geographic area constituting a sovereign entity and possibly containing more than one group of nationals (individual citizens) based on shared religion, history, or language.

- COMMUNITY—"a group of persons living in a given country or locality, having race, religion, language and traditions of their own, and united by the identity of such . . . in a sentiment of solidarity. . . ."

- COUNTRY—the territorial element of the term *State*, with attendant borders that define its land mass.

- PEOPLE —"the permanently residing population of a territory with an internationally legal status (state, mandate territory, etc.)."

- GOVERNMENT—in International Law, the political group or entity responsible for engaging in foreign relations, which is the "true and lawful government of the state . . . which ought to exercise sovereignty, but which may be deprived of this right by a government *de facto.*"

- SOVEREIGN —occasional synonym for State or nation, although it actually describes "the evolving relationship between state and civil society, between political authority and the community . . . [being] as both an idea and an institution integral to the structure of Western thought . . . and to a geopolitical discourse in which territory is sharply demarcated and exclusively controlled."[4]

Statehood

Not all entities called a "state," and not all entities desiring recognition as a "State," may lay claim to that status under International Law. When *is* an entity entitled to statehood in the international sense of the word?

Four general elements are needed to vest an entity with the desired "international legal personality," or rights and duties identified with statehood arising under International Law. Under the 1933 Montevideo Inter-American Convention on the Rights and Duties of States, a "State as a person of international law should possess the following qualifications: *(a)* a permanent population; *(b)* a defined territory; *(c)* government; and *(d)* capacity to enter into relations with other States."[5] The simultaneous occurrence of these elements identifies a sovereign entity possessing international personality.

These legal criteria for statehood have been widely adopted. The extent of their acceptance, however, has not been matched by any simplicity of application. One reason for this complexity is that the absence of one or more of these statehood elements, over a period of time, does not necessarily deprive a State of its international personality. Analytical problems most often arise when: (1) larger States break up into smaller ones—as in the former Yugoslavia after the demise of the Soviet Union; (2) one part of a nation attempts to secede—as in the

American Civil War of the 1860s and Quebec's possible secession from Canada; and (3) a foreign power exercises *de facto* control over another state—for example, Nazi Germany's expansion in Europe and South Africa's long and illegal dominion of the Trust Territory of what is now Namibia.

Population Element The "permanent population" element is probably the least important of these elements of statehood. Neither a minimum population nor an express grant of nationality to the inhabitants is required for qualification as a state.[6] Nor does the absence of part of the population over a period of time prevent the existence of statehood. The nomadic tribes on the Kenya-Ethiopia border, for example, have been an ambulatory element of each nation's population for centuries. The transient nature of this significant component of each State's population has not diminished the existence of either bordering State.

Territorial Element Deficiencies with the other elements of statehood—defined territory and a government engaging in foreign relations—have posed more serious problems. The territorial element of Statehood has been blurred by mutually exclusive claims to the same territory by different nations. A classic example is the former Arab-Israeli territorial conflict, which had its roots in the United Nations plan to partition Palestine to create a Jewish state. This plan, devised in 1947 to divide Palestine into an Arab state and a Jewish state, was not implemented due to the Middle East War that erupted in 1948. Israel was able to expand its territory beyond that provided for by the UN plan, displacing millions of Arabs.

Professor Philip Jessup of Columbia University (who represented the United States in the UN Security Council in 1948 and later became a judge of the International Court of Justice) used the following illustration to demonstrate why *Israel* nevertheless satisfied the doctrinal elements of statehood as early as 1948:

ON THE CONDITION OF STATEHOOD

3 U.N. Security Council Official Records
383rd Meeting, at 9–12 (1948)

Over a year ago the United States gave its support to the principles of the majority plan proposed by the United Nations Special Committee on Palestine. That plan envisaged the creation of both a Jewish State and an Arab State in Palestine. We gave our support to the resolution of 29 November 1947 by which the General Assembly recommended a plan for the future government of Palestine involving, as one of its elements, the establishment of a Jewish State in part of Palestine.

. . .

The Security Council now has before it the application of the Provisional Government of Israel for membership [in the UN].

The consideration of the application requires an examination of . . . the question of whether Israel is a State duly qualified for membership. Article 4 of the Charter of the United Nations specifies the following:

"Membership in the United Nations is open to peace-loving States which accept the obligations contained in the present Charter and, in the judgment of the Organization, are able and willing to carry out these obligations."

. . .

The first question which may be raised in analyzing Article 4 of the Charter and its applicability to the membership of the State of Israel, is the question of whether Israel is a State, as that term is used in Article 4 of the Charter. It is common knowledge that, while there are traditional definitions of a State in international law, the term has been used in many different ways. We are all aware that, under the traditional definition of a State in international law, all the great writers have pointed to four qualifications: first, there must be a people; second, there must be a territory; third, there must be a government; and, fourth, there must be capacity to enter into relations with other States of the world.

In so far as the question of capacity to enter into relations with other States of the world is concerned, learned academic arguments can be and have been made to the effect that we already have, among the Members of the United Nations, some political entities which do not possess full sovereign freedom to form their own international policy, which traditionally has been considered characteristic of a State. We know, however, that neither at San Francisco nor subsequently has the United Nations considered that complete freedom to frame and manage one's own foreign policy was an essential requisite of United Nations membership.

I do not dwell upon this point because . . . Israel is free and unhampered. On this point, I believe that there would be unanimity that Israel exercises complete independence of judgment and of will in forming and in executing its foreign policy. The reason for which I mention the qualification of this aspect of the traditional definition of a State is to underline the point that the term "State," as used and applied in Article 4 of the Charter of the United Nations, may not be wholly identical with the term "State" as it is used and defined in classic textbooks of international law.

When we look at the other classic attributes of a State, we find insistence that it must also have a Government. No one doubts that Israel has a Government. I think the world has been particularly impressed with the way in which the people of Israel have organized their government and have established a firm system of administration and of law-making under the most difficult conditions. Although, pending their scheduled elections, they still modestly and appropriately call themselves the Provisional Government of Israel, they have a legislative body which makes laws, they have a judiciary which interprets and applies those laws, and they have an executive which carries out the laws and which has at its disposal a considerable force responsive to its will.

According to the same classic definition, we are told that a State must have a people and a territory. Nobody questions the fact that the State of Israel has a people. It is an extremely homogeneous people, a people full of loyalty and of enthusiastic devotion to the State of Israel.

The argument seems chiefly to arise in connection with territory. One does not find in the general classic treatment of this subject any insistence that the territory of a State must be exactly fixed by definite frontiers. We all know that, historically, many States have begun their existence with their frontiers unsettled. Let me take as one example my own country, the United States of America. Like the State of Israel in its origin, it had certain territory along the seacoast. It had various indeterminate claims to an extended territory westward. But, in the case of the United States, that land had not even been explored, and no one knew just where the American claims ended and where French and British and Spanish claims began. To the North, the exact delimitation of the frontier with the territories of Great Britain was not settled until many years later.

And yet, I maintain that, in the light of history and in the light of the practice and acceptance by other States, the existence of the United States of America was not in question before its final boundaries were determined.

The formulae in the classic treatises somewhat vary, one from the other, but both reason and history demonstrate that the concept of territory does not necessarily include precise delimitation of the boundaries of that territory. The reason for the rule that one of the necessary attributes of a State is that it shall possess territory is that one cannot contemplate a State as a kind of disembodied spirit. Historically, the concept is one of insistence that there must be some portion of the earth's surface which its people inhabit and over which its Government exercises authority.

Government Element The "government" element of statehood is problematic when separate entities, operating in different regions within a State, claim that each is the legitimate government of the entire territory of that State. Modern examples include Nationalist and Communist China, North and South Korea, and the two Vietnamese governments of the 1960s and 1970s. In each of these cases, separate entities possessing administrative, legislative, and executive systems claimed the exclusive right to govern the entire State. External interference by other States contributed to the rigidity that caused each government to adopt and maintain inflexible postures.

Another example of this lack of governance arises in the awkward situation where a State should be maintaining political order, yet a civil war or external threat has tempered its ability to actually "lead the way." The "Finland" of 1917, shortly after achieving independence from what was destined to become a strong centralized Soviet Union, is a classic example. In a territorial dispute with Russia regarding some islands off Finland's coast, the League of Nations appointed some jurists who considered the issue of *when* Finland attained statehood after the territory's independence. The fundamental requirement was that Finland, in fact, had to have an effective government. In the succinct description of these jurists:

the conditions required for the formation of a sovereign State did not exist. In the midst of revolution and anarchy, certain elements essential to the existence of a State . . . were lacking for a fairly considerable period. Political and social life was disorganized; the [civil] authorities were not strong enough to assert themselves; civil war was rife; further, . . . the Government had been chased from the capital and forcibly prevented from carrying out its duties; the armed camps and the police were divided into two opposing forces, and Russian troops, and after a time Germans also, took part in the civil war. . . . It is therefore difficult to say at what exact date the Finnish Republic, in the legal sense of the term, actually became a definitely constituted sovereign State. This certainly did not take place until a stable political organization had been created, and until the public authorities [of Finland] had become strong enough to assert themselves throughout the territories of the State without the assistance of foreign troops.

Foreign Relations Element The decisive criterion for statehood is the above Montevideo Convention attribute requiring the "capacity to enter into relations with other states." Under International Law, a State must function independently of any external authority—other than that imposed by International Law. Not all entities referred to as States possess this capacity.

A State may appear to possess the characteristics of a sovereign entity without actually being in control of its populace and territory. Foreign relations responsibilities may be entrusted, legally, to another State. Certain dependent States may be controlled by other more established States. The governmental functions of such "mandated" (League of Nations) or "trust" territories (United Nations) have been exercised under the auspices of the League and the UN—discussed in Chapter 3 on the UN Trusteeship Council.

There is also the matter of *which* government within a State is "the" government for purposes of International Law. Only a *national* government has the capacity to engage in international relations, not one of its component states or provinces. For example, the State of California is not a "State" under International Law. It does not engage in the type of relations that fall with the realm of International Law. This limitation may seem surprising, given the following facts. Until the early 1990s, when its defense industry was adversely affected by military cutbacks, California had the world's seventh-largest economy. Its legislature declared in State Senate Bill 1909 that the expansion of international trade was vital to the overall growth of California's economy. California thus established the California Trade and Commerce Agency in 1993, because "current state efforts to develop relations with foreign countries are insufficient for effective coordination and mobilization of the resources necessary to promote economic growth and trade." Its more than thirty-million-person population and geographic size dwarf many nations of the world.

Only the national government of the US engages in the kind of foreign relations that are the concern of International Law. Thus, no state of the United States may enter into a treaty—a limitation expressly recognized even under national law. Nor may the states located on the world's second-longest international border (some 2,000 miles with Mexico) impose either import or export duties on goods from Mexico or other nations—without the consent of Congress or unless absolutely necessary for inspection purposes.[7]

Under the internal law of some nations, the national government may even dismiss the state governments of lesser political entities within the country. In December 1992, for example, India's federal government dealt with Hindu militants by disbanding the state governments of three of its northern states. The New Delhi national government thus instituted its own rule in those states. A week before, a fourth state government was similarly ousted from power—after rampaging mobs of Hindu militants razed a sixteenth century mosque in the town of Ayodhya. This incident is the concern of national rather than International Law. It would be quite a different matter, however, if the national government of South Africa ousted the government of Lesotho, which is totally contained within South Africa's borders. Lesotho is slightly larger than the small US state of Maryland, while South Africa is about twice the size of Texas. But Lesotho gained its independence (from Great Britain) in 1966, the year it gained admission into the UN as a member nation. South Africa would thereby violate the territorial sovereignty of Lesotho if the government in Johannesburg suddenly decided to oust the government of Lesotho.

■ 2.2 CHANGING INFRASTRUCTURE

Earlier sections of this book introduced the fundamentals of International Law development, change, and application. This section presents a significant variable. A dramatic change has occurred in the makeup of the community of nations in a comparatively short period of time. The contemporary rules of modern International Law were developed over a span of approximately three centuries, and, by a comparatively homogenous group of nations with similar perspectives. The symmetry among the principal actors—the States that were initially the only infrastructure for International Law in the period immediately after World War II—has dissipated.

In 1945, the sovereign nations of the world gathered at San Francisco to develop an agreement to set the basic parameters for future international relations. Those fifty nations incorporated what they deemed to be the appropriate political, social, economic, and humanitarian purposes into their agreement, called the United Nations Charter.

Since then, the community of nations has nearly quadrupled in size to approximately 190 States, most of whom are UN members. The "charter" members no longer exercise the degree of control they enjoyed at its inception, when five of them were able to "call the shots" as the permanent, nonrotating members of the Security Council. These members were China (now the mainland People's Republic), the Soviet Union (now Russia), Great Britain, France, and the United States.

To better understand the nature of contemporary international legal process, one must acknowledge the drastic change wrought by the increase in this infrastructure of the International Law system. The major contributor was the decolonization of the 1960s. Another factor was the demise of the Soviet Union in the 1990s. These were not mere changes in numbers. The most influential participants in the conduct of world affairs just after World War II were nations with comparatively homogenous economic, political, and cultural outlooks. Most were in the Western Hemisphere or directly aligned with Western nations. A number of them had one or more colonies throughout the world at that time.

EXHIBIT 2.1 Renovated State Infrastructure Since 1945

UN MEMBERS	AMERICAS		EUROPE		ASIA/OCEANA		AFRICA	
1945 Original Members	Argentina Bolivia Brazil Canada Chile Colombia Costa Rica Cuba Dominican Republic Ecuador El Salvador	Guatemala Haiti Honduras Mexico Nicaragua Panama Paraguay Peru United States Uruguay Venezuela	Belgium Belorussia (Belarus) Czecho- slovakia —split '93 Denmark France Greece Luxembourg Netherlands Norway Poland Turkey	Ukraine U.S.S.R.: —until '91 —now the Russian Federation United Kingdom Yugoslavia: —split '92 now Serbia Montenegro -expelled from UN	Australia China: —Taiwan until '71 —P.R.C. now seated India Iran Iraq Lebanon New Zealand Philippines Saudi Arabia Syria		Egypt Ethiopia Liberia South Africa	
1945–1965	Jamaica Trinidad & Tobago		Albania Austria Bulgaria Finland Hungary Iceland Ireland Italy Malta Portugal Romania Spain Sweden		Afghanistan Burma Cambodia (Kampuchea) Cyprus Indonesia Israel Japan Jordan Kuwait Laos Malaysia Maldives Mongolia Nepal Pakistan Singapore Sri Lanka Thailand Yemen	Algeria Benin Burkina Burundi Cameroon Central African Republic Chad Congo Gabon The Gambia Ghana Guinea Ivory Coast Kenya Libya Madagascar Malawi Mali Mauritania Morocco Niger	Nigeria Rwanda Senegal Sierra Leone Somalia Sudan Tanzanania: Tang./Zanz. —merge '64 Tanganyika: until '61 Togo Tunisia Uganda United Arab Republic: Egypt/ Syria brief merger Zaire Zambia Zanzibar: —until '63

EXHIBIT 2.1   *(continued)*

UN MEMBERS	AMERICAS	EUROPE	ASIA/OCEANA	AFRICA
1965–1985	Antigua & Barbuda The Bahamas Barbados Belize (formerly Brit. Honduras) Dominica Grenada Guyana Saint Kitts and Nevis Saint Lucia Saint Vincent and the Grenadines Suriname	Federal Republic of Germany: –until '90 –now Germany German Democratic Republic: –until '90 –now Germany	Bahrain Bangladesh Bhutan Brunel Fiji Oman Papua New Guinea Qatar Solomon Islands United Arab Emirates Vanuatu Vietnam Western Samoa Yemen	Angola Botswana Cape Verde Comoros Djibouti Equatorial Guinea Guinea Bisseau Lesotho Mauritius Mozambique Sao Tome and Principe Seychelles Swaziland Zimbabwe
1985–1995		Andorra Armenia Azerbaijan Bosnia and Herzegovina Croatia Czech Republic Estonia Germany: including East/West Berlin Georgia Latvia Liechtenstein Lithuania Macedonia Moldova Monaco San Marino Slovakia Slovenia	Kazakhstan Kyrgystan Marshall Islands Micronesia North Korea South Korea Tazikistan Turkmenistan Uzbekistan	Eritrea Namibia

NON-UN MEMBERS   Kiribati (formerly Gilbert Islands), Nauru, New Caldonia, Niue[a], Palau[b], Serbia and Montenegro[c], Switzerland[d], Taiwan, Tonga, Holy See (Vatican City), Western Sahara (sovereignty unresolved), Gaza/West Bank (PLO[d])

[a] = free association with New Zealand / [b] = UN Trust territory / [c] = remainder of former Yugoslavia / [d] = UN Observer Status. Table does not include territorial possessions

Today, most of those colonies are independent nations that became members of the United Nations. Admission to that body, which was flooded with applications in the 1960s after independence from the original colonizing members of the UN, provided a significant validation for these new admittees. The hoisting of their new national flags at the UN, and in nations where they could afford to maintain embassies or consulates, signalled yet another "new world order" (a rather trite term invoked by world leaders for several centuries).

Significant differences exist within today's community of nations. The diversion from the colonization of an earlier era did little to improve the economic, military, and political vitality of these new members of the world community. That community now consists of radically different cultures, ideologies, and economic perspectives. This is one of

New States receive one form of international recognition through admission to the UN. Here, the flags of Bangladesh, Grenada, and Guinea-Bisseau are raised for the first time at the UN Headquarters in New York City on September 18, 1974—one day after their admission as UN member-States.

the underlying reasons why, during the Reagan years, the US began to withdraw from various UN organs—including the International Court of Justice and the Economic and Social Council—due to the declining clout exercisable by the host country over UN affairs. The progressive development of International Law is of course affected by these differences. A comparison of Western European and Asian-African attitudes, for example, readily illustrates that the State structure of the international community is not as homogenous as it was during the centuries when its norms were being cultivated by a much smaller group of more similarly oriented nations.

Many writers thus characterize modern International Law as having its essential roots in European culture (*see* § 1.3 on the "History of International Law"). As stated by Professor J.H. Verzijl of Holland in 1955, "there is one truth that is not open to denial or even to doubt, namely, that the actual body of international law, as it stands today, is not only the product of the conscious activity of the European mind, but has also drawn its vital essence from a common source of European beliefs, and in both of these aspects it is mainly of Western European origin."[8]

This European essence of International Law was exemplified by the meetings of European nations in the nineteenth century. The 1815 Congress of Vienna, as one example, established the so-called Concert of Europe. That group of nations exercised what its members believed to be their manifest right to deny the *de jure* existence of certain nations, without regard to their obvious *de facto* existence. The Berlin Congress of 1885, commonly referred to as the West Africa Conference, decided that the African continent was sufficiently uncivilized—thus warranting its colonization in the best interests of all nations. In a valiant gesture, that Conference of European powers deemed slavery abolished. Their real reason, however, was "prompted by [a] shortage of workforce[s] on the Western Coast of Africa, depopulated by the three-centuries-long export trade of slave labor to North and South America."[9]

Predictably, the western-derived basis for International Law has been criticized by modern scholars from both Western and non-Western nations.[10] Professor George Alexandrowicz of Queen's University in Ireland characterized this "European essence" of International Law as being unacceptably ethnocentric. In his words, "Asian States, who for centuries had been considered members of the family of nations, found themselves in an *ad hoc* created legal vacuum which reduced them from the status of international personality [statehood] to the status of candidates competing for such personality."[11]

One result of the post–World War II induction of former colonies into the community of nations was their irrepressible consensus that colonial rule was a form of aggression to be challenged with force, if necessary, as an act of self-defense. However, the language of the UN Charter, drafted by the former colonial powers, permitted the use of force in self-defense only if an "armed" attack occurred against a UN member.[12] Some have thus perceived this Charter provision as another ethnocentric limitation of International Law, imposed by the colonial powers as a new means of maintaining the status quo after the decolonization movement of the 1960s.

The economic perspectives of these new States (former colonies) has affected the underlying structure of International Law. These lesser developed States want to redistribute the global resources, to improve the living conditions of their peoples, and to obtain greater equality under International Law. During the 1974–1982 UN Law of the Sea Treaty negotiations, for example, the less powerful nations of the world established, in principle, one of their economic goals. This treaty calls for "the equitable sharing of financial and other economic benefits" derived from an area encompassing about 90 percent of the natural resources of the oceans (further discussed in Chapter 6 on the "Range of Sovereignty"). The economically dominant nations disagree with the principle of an equitable distribution of ocean resources. The US, for example, refused to sign the treaty when finally completed and acceptable in principle to most nations of the ("Third") world. The Reagan administration feared that this redistribution theme would unfairly deprive the US of technical know-how and the freedom to exploit

global oceanic resources. The more established members of the world community have spent a great deal of money on ocean fishing and mining development since World War II. Under the traditional application of International Law, wealthier nations are not required to share their economic gains from such activities with lesser developed nations. Otherwise, freedom of the seas would not remain as one of the basic canons of International Law.

This underlying difference in economic perspectives of the more developed and lesser developed States is expressed in the so-called New International Economic Order (NIEO). For example, International Law has traditionally prohibited a governmental taking of the property of a foreign citizen or business entity without compensation. The developed nations have historically claimed a right to "prompt, adequate, and effective" compensation when foreign nations have taken the property of their nationals or corporations under their indisputable sovereign power of nationalization. But in 1974, the so-called Group of 77 (G-77) nations declared the desirability of injecting an NIEO into contemporary nationalization practice. The UN General Assembly then announced the Declaration on the Establishment of a New International Economic Order and the Charter of Economic Rights and Duties of States.[13]

The so-called "G-77" (or Group of 77, now some 120 strong) thereby professed two essential propositions in its 1974 declarations. First, the "greatest and most significant achievement during the last decades has been the independence from colonial and alien domination of a large number of peoples and nations which has enabled them [G-77] to become members of the community. . . ." Second, the essential orders contained in the NIEO's "new order" include (1) the regulation and supervision of the activities of transnational corporations to ensure the national sovereignty of the countries wherein they operate; and (2) the "active assistance to developing countries by the whole international community, free of any political or military conditions." Thus, the colonial requirement of "prompt, adequate, and effective" compensation is no longer consistent with what the international standard *should* be. Third World States seek the freedom to use their own national laws as the yardstick for resolving whether compensation is required under the circumstances of each case. And, *if* compensation is required under the nationalizing State's internal law (rather than International Law), that nation should be free to determine the extent of compensation without external pressures from wealthy nations. The lesser developed members of the UN maintain that this legal domination should cease—to avoid International Law providing the compensation yardstick, rather than internal law.

These Third World nations now constitute the majority of nations in the UN. They do not, however, control global resources. Such nations need to obtain credit from the more powerful nations, to encourage investment by the economically powerful nations, and to expand the lesser developed export markets. World leaders thus met in Copenhagen in March 1995 at a UN summit—designed to alleviate the absolute poverty affecting more than one billion of the earth's inhabitants—but producing no concrete solutions. This economic tension now affects international relations in both direct and subtle ways to be explored elsewhere (including Chapter 13 on International Economic Relations).

■ 2.3   CHANGES IN STATE STATUS

Once a State has achieved international personality under International Law, its condition may change in a variety of ways. Examples just from the 1990s will illustrate the variety of possible status changes:

■ Two States may join together—East and West Germany joined to become Germany in 1990;

■ One State may peacefully separate into two States—in 1993, Czechoslovakia separated into the new States of The Czech Republic and Slovakia;

■ Groups within a State may secede from it to create their own State—Bosnia-Herzegovina, Croatia, Macedonia, and Slovenia, seceded from the former Yugoslavia during a two-year period beginning in 1992;

■ A State may cease to exist—Kuwait would have been absorbed into Iraq absent the international response to Iraq's 1990 invasion of Kuwait;

■ A former colony may become a part of another State, and then achieve independence—Eritrea thus became a State in 1993.

This section addresses the effect of those changes in status which are particularly important in current world affairs: "succession," "secession," and "self-determination" (which has become a variant of the succession/secession models). Each of these paradigms, associated with the acquisition of international personality, will now be summarized.

Succession

What happens when two States merge, or when one State splits into two or more States—thus becoming a new State or States? These entities acquire international personality or statehood. But how are their previous international obligations affected by the change?

"Succession" refers to the circumstance where one or more States takes the place of another State. Under Article 2 of both the 1978 Vienna Convention on Succession of States in Respect of Treaties and the 1983 Vienna Convention on Succession of States in Respect of State Property, Archives, and Debts, the term *succession* of States "means the replacement of one State by another in the responsibility for the international relations of the territory."[14]

Succession occurs in a variety of circumstances, including breakups and mergers. Contemporary examples include the 1993 split of Czechoslovakia into two States—the Czech Republic and Slovakia. These republics, in their respective territories, thus succeeded to the territory formerly occupied by the State of Czechoslovakia. This split was referred to as the "velvet divorce" due to the bloodless nature of this particular State's separation into two distinct States. Atypically, the breakup was not spawned by civil war or external pressure.

The converse situation is a merger, exemplified by the 1990 merger of the three territories of the Federal Republic of (West) Germany, the (East) German Democratic Republic, and the City of Berlin. The legal status of Berlin was never fully resolved, although all issues were laid to rest by the multiparty treaty merging Berlin into the new integrated State of "Germany." This merger was fully agreed to by all the nations having a territorial interest—East Germany, West Germany, France, the (former) Soviet Union, the United Kingdom, and the United States.[15] These entities thereby succeeded to the territory that was once two sovereign States and a special zone, each losing its formerly distinct international legal personality in the process.

Succession may also occur when a State, or a portion of it, is first occupied and then administered by another State. Nazi Germany's puppet State, referred to as Vichy State, ruled in the southern part of France from 1940 to 1942. It subsequently continued a shadowy existence for two more years, before fleeing to Germany in 1944. In 1992, French intellectuals called upon French President Mitterand to break a historical taboo by formally acknowledging that the Vichy regime persecuted French Jews—after a French court dropped charges of crimes against humanity involving a former Vichy police official. Mitterand responded that "the French state was Vichy and not the [French] republic." He thus sidestepped France's complicity in war crimes by characterizing the Vichy government as an entity separate from the French Republic to the north.

Succession can also result from independence and partition. Modern-day India is an example of both. In 1947, the territory of India thus achieved full independence from its mandate status. The new State of India replaced the former territory of the same name, which had been placed under British control by a League of Nations process in 1922. But the Indian territory was simultaneously split into two distinct States—India and Pakistan. This partition of the former territory of India thereby established two new international States, each with its own international legal personality.

While there are many other succession scenarios,[16] a pervasive legal question lingers about the *effect* of succession under International Law. Specifically, what effect does succession have on the former State's preexisting (1) treaties, (2) its property/debts, and (3) the nationality of its citizens?

(1) Does the successor State take over the treaty obligations of the succeeded State? The historical view is that a new State commences its career with a clean slate. But global (and even interregional) perspectives are by no means uniform. When the original thirteen colonies obtained their independence from Great Britain in 1776, the newly formed "United States" began its existence with a clean slate—free from the obligations incurred by any prior treaties regarding the territory occupied by these colonies. The former Spanish colonies of South America likewise began their statehood with a clean slate. Yet when Colombia separated from

Spain in 1823, the US took the position that Colombia remained bound by Spain's prior treaty commitments on behalf of the territory of Colombia. Then in 1840, when the Texas territory gained independence from Mexico, the US likewise declared that all US treaty commitments with Mexico regarding Texas remained in effect.[17]

Today, there is no general rule of State succession to prior *bilateral* treaty obligations which are purely "political," as opposed to those which are less political in nature. Political treaties include the international alliances and neutrality arrangements of the predecessor State. Such treaties cease to exist when the State which concluded them ceases to exist. They assume the existence of the contracting State and are thus dependent on its continued existence. Although there is some disagreement, nonpolitical treaties concluded by an extinct predecessor State, such as those involving commerce and extradition, likewise do not survive the extinction of the predecessor State. Yet the same treaties are likely to survive the succession, where two or more States agree to unify. Thus, when Nazi Germany absorbed Austria into Germany, the commerce treaties of the former State of Austria would not bind the successor German State. Yet commerce treaties of the former East and West Germanies *would* bind today's successor State of unified Germany.

Multilateral treaties ratified by the predecessor State, containing norms that have been adopted by many nations, survive succession. Thus, the successor State cannot claim a "clean slate" to avoid humanitarian treatment of the citizens of the predecessor State, when such treatment is the subject of a multilateral treaty to which only the predecessor is a party. This liability of the new or succeeding State is already rooted in norms of customary International Law that exist independently of the treaty, even where the succeeding State has not become a treaty party to that multilateral treaty.[18]

(2) Does the successor State take over the property and debts of the succeeded State? The property *and* the debts of an extinct State normally become the property of the successor State. The common scenario involves the public international debts of an extinct State. The successor State is expected to thus absorb both the benefits and the burdens sustained by the former State.

An exception is often claimed when the debts of the succeeded State are contrary to the basic political interests of the successor State. In this instance, international arbitrators have adopted the view that a successor State cannot be expected to succeed to such debts when they are repugnant to the fundamental interests of the succeeding State. When Yugoslavia reclaimed the territory of the "Independent Croatian State," an unrecognized puppet regime established on Yugoslavian territory during World War II, the successor State of Yugoslavia did not have to assume the debts of the former unrecognized fascist administration.[19]

The 1983 Vienna Convention on Succession of States in Respect of State Property, Archives and Debts addresses the matter, although it has not yet received sufficient ratifications to enter into force. The successor State is entitled to the property of the former State. Succession does not extinguish obligations, however, that are owed by the former State to public or private creditors. The Succession treaty thus provides that succession "does not as such affect the rights . . . of creditors."[20]

(3) Must the successor State provide its citizenship to the citizens of the succeeded State? When a State ceases to exist, so does the citizenship that it has previously conferred on its inhabitants. The former citizens of the extinct State must then look to the internal law of the successor State for new citizenship. This is generally a matter of internal rather than International Law. Yet international practice at least suggests that the new State confer its citizenship on those who were citizens of the succeeded State, based on their habitual residence. On the other hand, the new State may not *force* its citizenship on individuals within what has become a subjugated State. This would preclude Israel, for example, from imposing its citizenship on people within the so-called occupied territories it has acquired as a result of various wars.[21]

Succession of Governments Unlike the possible avoidance of obligations when a new state comes into existence, a new *government* may not claim a "clean slate." Otherwise, the stability of international relations would be significantly undermined if questions of succession to obligations arose every time that a new government assumed power.

International Law theory provides further support for the view that new governments cannot avoid international obligations because a "government" is not an international person—as described in § 2.1 of this book on the "Legal Personality of the State."

Secession

While *succession* involves the takeover of another State's territory, *secession* is the separation of a State. Questions of continuing obligations after secession would have arisen, for example, had the South won the American Civil War of the 1860s. Modern examples of secession arose in India and Yugoslavia. When Great Britain's mandate over India ended in 1947 (during a general British withdrawal from Asia), Pakistan was created by partitioning India's northwest territory from India. This partitioned State was intended to be a Muslim enclave, as orchestrated by the All-India Muslim League. Then in 1971, Bangladesh separated from Pakistan. This secession was rooted in Pakistan's attempt to base its national identity on religious grounds. In Yugoslavia, conflicts previously suppressed by the Cold War erupted in the 1990s. After the breakup of the Soviet Union, ethnic conflict and resurging nationalism spawned the breakup of the former Yugoslavia into five separate States.

There have been many secessionist or separatist movements around the globe even since the end of the Cold War. Prominent examples *just* in the former Soviet Union (which had already separated into fifteen independent States in 1991) include the following:

- **CRIMEAN PENINSULA** (February 1994)—the Black Sea's Crimean peninsula, adjacent to both Russia and Ukraine. The "Republic of Crimea" votes to separate from Ukraine (as also declared in May 1992), elects a president, and begins to advocate a union with Russia. Sixty-five percent of the peninsula, which was part of Russia until 1954, consists of ethnic Russians. Ukraine's parliament responds with its own vote, warning Crimea that it cannot engage in its own foreign relations independently of Ukraine.

- **GEORGIA** (January 1994)—Abkhazian separatists join with the Georgia government to request a UN peacekeeping force. Abkhazian is a Black Sea province seeking independence from Georgia. Some 200,000 refugees may return to Abkhazian after fleeing during fighting between separatists and the Georgian government.

■ AZERBAIJAN (September 1993)—The presidents of Armenia and Azerbaijan meet in an effort to halt the fighting in Nagorno-Karabakh, a mountainous region of Azerbaijan. More than 15,000 people have been killed, where Christian Armenians have sought independence from Muslim Azerbaijan since 1988.

The contemporary rash of such secessionist movements may thus be regarded as a rather dangerous phenomenon. As aptly characterized by Philosophy Professor Allen Buchanan of the University of Arizona:

[if] each ethnic group, each 'people,' is entitled to its own state, then it [secession movements] is a recipe for virtually limitless upheaval, an exhortation to break apart the vast majority of existing states, given that most [States] if not all began as empires and include a plurality of ethnic groups or peoples within their present boundaries.

. . . Secession can shatter old alliances . . . tip balances of power, create refugee populations, and disrupt international commerce. It can also result in a great loss of human life. And regardless of whether it acts or refrains from acting, each state takes a stand on each secessionist movement—if only by recognizing or not recognizing the independence of the seceding group.[22]

Prior to the end of World War II, international practice clearly supported the rule that a new State (seceding from another) could begin its existence without any restraints imposed by the treaty commitments of the State from which it seceded—other than those treaties directly governing the very existence of the new State. (After secession, the State from which another has seceded continues to be bound by its own existing treaty commitments that do not depend on the continued existence of the State that has seceded.)

Since World War II, the unequivocal rule—authorizing a fresh start for seceding States—became somewhat equivocal. New States which have seceded from others still enjoy a "clean slate," but not as to those treaties creating law intended to bind all States. Humanitarian treaties are the prime example. These normally codify existing customary practice. Thus when Pakistan separated from India in 1947, it acknowledged a continuing obligation to remain a party to the 1921 Convention for the Suppression of Traffic in Women and Children. Pakistan's recognition of this obligation was specifically premised on India's acceptance of the 1921 treaty (when the Pakistani territory was still a part of India.)[23]

Self-Determination

Succession, secession, and self-determination must be distinguished in order to place the latter concept into its proper context. *Succession* involves one State taking over another State's territory. State A is taken over by State B, for example, triggering questions of the extent to which B must assume the obligations of former State A. *Secession* refers to the separation of a State. State A splits away from State B, effectively taking with A some portion of B's territory. State A normally begins its existence with a clean slate—except for those State B obligations that are universal, such as the requirement to observe fundamental human rights. *Self-determination* means the "right" to choose self-governance or some related form of autonomy. The people of State A acquire the right to govern themselves—free of State B's domination.

Self-determination is the international norm that recognizes the right of colonies and territories, or of a particular group of people within a State, to effectively govern themselves. A hundred years ago, this book would be speaking only in terms of entire colonies or subjugated territories as the exclusive possessors of a right to self-determination. As a result of post–World War II decolonization, however, this "right" together with its qualifying criteria and attributes also belongs to groups of people within a State.

Contemporary examples of claims that self-determination has been denied include those of the Palestinians and Russia's Chechens. The Palestinians living in several nations of the Middle East have claimed the right of self-determination over "Palestine" since the UN Partition plan of 1947—which would have created a Palestinian State (in addition to Israel). The struggle of the inhabitants of Russia's predominantly Muslim region of Chechnya for full autonomy dates back to A.D. 965. During World War II, Stalin deported thousands of area inhabitants to Central Asia. In December 1994, a remarkable 40-mile human chain of 100,000 people protested Russia's continuing military assault on Chechnya.

The original *raison d'etre* of self-determination analysis was the decolonization of *States*. One of the classic examples was the situation in Namibia—

formerly called South West Africa when it was controlled by South Africa, originating with a League of Nations mandate. South Africa refused to comply with various UN resolutions demanding that South Africa relinquish its control of South West Africa. Ultimately, after seventy-four years of domination and a blistering decision from the International Court of Justice (ICJ),[24] South West Africa finally achieved its own sovereign identity and was admitted to the UN as the nation of Namibia in 1990. The general achievement of the self-determination of colonized territories is graphically illustrated in Exhibit 2.1 (see § 2.2)—which depicts the increased number of States that were former colonies prior to the 1960s.

Another contemporary example of self-determination arose in the context of the Baltic States that were overtaken by the Soviet Union in the 1940s. In February 1991, Estonians, Latvians, and Lithuanians voted to set themselves free from this domination by the Soviet Union. The takeover of the Baltic States remained unrecognized by many other States in spite of de facto Soviet control of the Baltics. Soviet President Gorbachev declared these votes "illegal" and dispatched orders to Soviet troops to increase army patrols in order to "maintain the civil order." After twenty deaths—and the European Union's withholding of $1 billion in food aid to the Soviet Union to protest the Soviet handling of the Balkans—the Kremlin withdrew its special troops in an effort to diffuse the confrontation over the Baltic right of self-determination. The European Community (now European Union) soon recognized the three Baltic States as independent States. In an official statement, the Community noted that it "warmly welcome[d] the restoration of sovereignty and independence of the Baltic states which they lost in 1940 [when Stalin annexed them into the Soviet Union]."

Self-determination concerns can also arise in the context of territories belonging to a State. In 1992, for example, the Canadian government signed an accord with Eskimo leaders that would create a native-run territory in Canada's Northwest Territories, to be called Nunavut. The agreement calls for the establishment of Nunavut, with the Nunavut government gradually assuming greater power in that portion of Canada. The Arctic Eskimos ratified a land claim agreement via a referendum, which would in turn result in the Canadian government's passing legislation establishing Nunavut in 1999.

The contemporary rallying point has become the self-determination of peoples. This term is typically used in state status dialogue to refer to a group within a State which seeks to establish its own identity. This may result in the creation of a separate State, although there are other alternatives, as will be seen in the ICJ's Western Sahara case presented below.

While some authors assert that the norm of self-determination was incorporated into International Law as early as the 1941 predecessor of the UN Charter,[25] it is actually the Charter that served as the explicit starting point for the development of the law of self-determination as expressed in Article 1.2 of the Charter. One of the UN's essential purposes is "respect for the principle of equal rights and self-determination of peoples. . . ." The Charter's self-determination cornerstone, however, is the Article 73 Declaration Regarding Non-Self-Governing Territories:

> Members of the United Nations which have or [will] assume responsibilities for the administration of territories whose peoples have not yet attained a full measure of self-government recognize the principle that the interests of the inhabitants of these territories are paramount, and [UN Members thus] accept as a sacred trust the obligation to promote to the utmost . . . the well-being of the inhabitants of these territories. . . .

A very sensitive UN document on the nature of self-determination came years later, in the midst of the movement to decolonize the many territories controlled by the original members. In Resolution 1514(XV) of 1960, the General Assembly proclaimed over objections by Western nations that the "subjection of peoples to alien subjugation . . . constitutes a denial of fundamental human rights, is contrary to the Charter of the United Nations . . . [because all] peoples have the right to self-determination . . . [and any inadequacy] of political, economic, social or educational preparedness should never serve as a pretext for delaying independence."

As the decolonization movement of the 1960s shifted from rhetoric to reality, the right of self-determination was further refined in other UN-sponsored documents. These were utilized by the so-called "Third World" nations as a mechanism for corroborating the parameters of this right. The colonial powers had previously abstained from endorsing Resolution 1514. They characterized it as a mere political claim designed to embarrass the colonial powers, on the alleged basis of a disparity between their discourse and practice in the areas of sovereign equality and human rights.

Article 1.1 of both the 1966 International Covenant on Civil and Political Rights and the 1966 International Covenant on Economic, Social and Cultural Rights was the next building block in the UN development of the law of self-determination. It thus provided as follows: "All peoples have the right of self-determination. By virtue of that right they freely determine their political status and freely pursue their economic, social and cultural development." While the General Assembly approved these covenants with near unanimity, certain Western powers maintained their reservations about this "right" of self-determination.

The General Assembly's 1970 Friendly Relations Declaration 2625(XXV) on self-determination further elaborated that every State has the duty to promote "realization of the principle of equal rights and self-determination of *peoples*." This document exemplified the shift in self-determination from "States" to "peoples." The 1970 Declaration drew no general objections, as is the case with UN Declarations that are by their very nature unanimously agreed-upon statements (unlike resolutions adopted by a majority of States).[26]

Now that the UN's diplomatic endeavor pointed in the direction of a State practice favoring the right of self-determination, the International Court of Justice was ready to assess the parameters of this right—as done in the following 1975 case.

The legal controversy addressed in this opinion, essentially between Spain and Morocco, began in the General Assembly where it had lingered from 1966 to 1974. Western Sahara was a Spanish protectorate since 1912. Like Mauritania, Morocco acknowledged the applicability of the principle of self-determination. Neither country abandoned their respective claims to Western Sahara. This particular phase of the controversy surfaced when Morocco directly presented its legal claim to Spanish authorities in 1974.

Due to the inertia with implementing prior resolutions on Western Sahara, the UN General Assembly requested this advisory opinion from the ICJ. Members of the Assembly thus hoped to advance the right of Western Sahara's peoples to self-determination. The General Assembly had previously resolved that the inhabitants possessed a right to self-determination, specifically finding that there should be a referendum conducted so that they could vote to determine the status of Western Sahara.

The general right to self-determination was being politically foiled by the maintenance of the colonial status of Western Sahara—also referred to as Spanish Sahara under Spain's claim via colonization of the territory (in 1884) long before this particular dispute arose. After it became a member of the UN in 1960, Mauritania claimed Western Sahara as a part of its national territory. At the time of this case, Mauritania was prepared to acquiesce in the will of the peoples of Western Sahara. It did not wish to confront Spain with a direct legal claim—unlike Morocco, which was far more possessive.

The possibility of submitting this case to the Court was then pressed in the General Assembly by Morocco "in order to guide the United Nations towards a final solution of the problem of Western Sahara. . . ." Spain's position was that a judicial decision was unnecessary and impractical, given the preexisting UN resolution calling for a referendum (which would effectively maintain the status quo). As this was an "advisory" opinion of the Court, there was no national defendant available to submit to the jurisdiction of the ICJ. The disclosed purpose of the opinion was to provide guidance to the General Assembly. The real purpose was to provide an authoritative analysis to demonstrate the absence of any genuine legal claim that could hinder the right of the Western Sahara inhabitants to self-determination. The ICJ's opinion nevertheless defined and confirmed the parameters of self-determination as it exists since the decolonization of the rest of Africa.

The Court's basic task was to determine the presence of any legal claims to this territory by the various nations involved—claims that would interfere with the inhabitants' right to exercise their right to self-determination. The General Assembly believed that a judicial resolution of the "territorial rights" versus the "right to self-determination" in Western Sahara would promote stability and harmony in the north-west region of the African continent:

WESTERN SAHARA

International Court of Justice, 1975
14 Int'l Legal Mat'ls 1355 (1975)*

[Author's Note: The numbered paragraphs are those of the Court.]

[*Opinion.*]   . . .

52. Extensive argument and divergent views have been presented to the Court as to how, and in what form, the principles of decolonization apply in this instance, in the light of the various General Assembly resolutions on decolonization in general and on decolonization of the territory of Western Sahara in particular.

. . .

55. The principle of self-determination as a right of peoples, and its application for the purpose of bringing all colonial situations to a speedy end, were enunciated in the Declaration on the Granting of Independence to Colonial Countries and Peoples, General Assembly resolution 1514 (XV). In this resolution the General Assembly proclaims 'the necessity of bringing to a speedy and unconditional end colonialism in all its forms and manifestations.' . . . To this end the resolution provides inter alia:

2. All peoples have the right to self-determination; by virtue of that right they freely determine their political status and freely pursue their economic, social and cultural development.

. . .

5. Immediate steps shall be taken, in Trust and Non-Self-Governing Territories or all other territories which have not yet attained independence, to transfer all powers to the peoples of those territories, without any conditions or reservations, in accordance with their freely expressed will and desire, without any distinction as to race, creed or colour, in order to enable them to enjoy complete independence and freedom.

The above provisions, in particular paragraph 2, thus confirm and emphasize that the application of the right of self-determination requires a free and genuine expression of the will of the peoples concerned.

. . .

57. General Assembly resolution 1514 (XV) provided the basis for the process of decolonization which has resulted since 1960 in the creation of many States which are today Members of the United Nations. It is complemented in certain of its aspects by General Assembly resolution 1541 (XV), which has been invoked in the present proceedings. The latter resolution contemplates for non-self-governing territories more than one possibility, namely:

(a) emergence as a sovereign independent State;
(b) free association with an independent State; or
(c) integration with an independent State.

At the same time, certain of its provisions give effect to the essential feature of the right of self-determination as established in resolution 1514 (XV). Thus principle VII of resolution 1541 (XV) declares that: 'Free association should be the result of a free and voluntary choice by the peoples of the territory concerned expressed through informed and democratic processes.' Again, principle IX of resolution 1541 (XV) declares [in part] that:

(b) The integration should be the result of the freely expressed wishes of the territory's peoples acting with full knowledge of the change in their status, their wishes having been expressed through informed and democratic processes, impartially conducted and based on universal adult suffrage. The United Nations could, when it deems it necessary, supervise these processes.

58. General Assembly resolution 2625 (XXV), 'Declaration on Principles of International Law concerning Friendly Relations and Co-operation among States in accordance with the Charter of the United Nations,'—to which reference was also made in the proceedings—mentions other possibilities besides independence, association or integration. But in doing so it reiterates the basic need to take account of the wishes of the people concerned:

> The establishment of a sovereign and independent State, the free association or integration with an independent State or the emergence into any other political status freely determined by a people constitute modes of implementing the right of self-determination by that people.

Resolution 2625 (XXV) further provides that:

> Every State has the duty to promote, through joint and separate action, realization of the principle of equal rights and self-determination of peoples in accordance with the provisions of the Charter, and to render assistance to the United Nations in carrying out the responsibilities entrusted to it by the Charter regarding the implementation of the principle.

. . .

60. Having set out the basic principles governing the decolonization policy of the General Assembly, the Court now turns to those resolutions which bear specifically on the decolonization of Western Sahara. . . . In particular it is pertinent to compare the different ways in which the General Assembly resolutions adopted from 1966 to 1969 dealt with the questions of . . . Western Sahara.

61. In 1966, in the Special Committee on the Situation with regard to the Implementation of the Declaration on the Granting of Independence to Colonial Countries and Peoples, Spain expressed itself in favour of the decolonization of Western Sahara through the exercise by the population of the territory of their right to self-determination. At that time this suggestion received the support of Mauritania and the assent of Morocco [and thus, *all three* States which had asserted territorial claims to Western Sahara].

. . .

In the case of Western Sahara, the resolution:

4. Invites the administering Power to determine at the earliest possible date, in conformity with the aspirations of the indigenous people of Spanish Sahara and in consultation with the Governments of Mauritania and Morocco and any other interested party, the procedures for the holding of a referendum under United Nations auspices with a view to enabling the indigenous population of the Territory to exercise freely its right to self-determination. . . .

In respect of this territory the resolution also set out conditions designed to ensure the free expression of the will of the people, including the provision by the administering Power of facilities to a United Nations mission so that it may be able to participate actively in the organization and holding of the referendum.

. . .

64. In subsequent years [since the U.N.'s initial 1966 Western Sahara resolution], the General Assembly maintained its approach to the question of Western Sahara, and reiterated in more pressing terms the need to consult the wishes of the people of the territory as to their political future. Indeed resolution 2983 (XXVII) of 1972 expressly reaffirms 'the responsibility of the United Nations in all consultations intended to lead to the free expression of the wishes of the people.' Resolution 3162 (XXVIII) of 1973, while deploring the fact that the United Nations mission whose active participation in the organization and holding of the referendum had been recommended since 1966 had not yet been able to visit the territory, reaffirms the General Assembly's:

> attachment to the principle of self-determination and its concern to see that principle applied with a framework that will guarantee the inhabitants of the Sahara under Spanish domination free and authentic expression of their wishes, in accordance with the relevant United Nations resolutions on the subject.

65. All these resolutions from 1966 to 1973 were adopted in the face of reminders by Morocco and

Mauritania of their respective claims that Western Sahara constituted an integral part of their territory. At the same time Morocco and Mauritania assented to the holding of a referendum. These States, among others, alleging that the recommendations of the General Assembly were being disregarded by Spain, emphasized the need for the referendum to be held in satisfactory conditions and under the supervision of the United Nations.

. . .

70. In short, the decolonization process to be accelerated which is envisaged by the General Assembly in this provision is one which will respect the right of the population of Western Sahara to determine their future political status by their own freely expressed will. This right is not affected by the present request for an advisory opinion, nor by resolution 3292 (XXIX); on the contrary, it is expressly reaffirmed in that resolution. The right of that population to self-determination constitutes therefore a basic assumption of the questions put to the Court.

71. . . . The right of self-determination leaves the General Assembly a measure of discretion with respect to the forms and procedures by which that right is to be realized.

. . .

162. The materials and information presented to the Court show the existence, at the time of Spanish colonization, of legal ties of allegiance between the Sultan of Morocco and some of the tribes living in the territory of Western Sahara. They equally show the existence of rights, including some rights relating to the land, which constituted legal ties between the Mauritanian entity, as understood by the Court, and the territory of Western Sahara. [These ties would thus defeat Spain's right to the territory.] On the other hand, the Court's conclusion is that the materials and information presented to it do not establish any tie of territorial sovereignty between the territory of Western Sahara and the Kingdom of Morocco or the Mauritanian entity. Thus the Court has not found legal ties of such a nature as might affect the application of resolution 1514 (XV) in the decolonization of Western Sahara and, in particular, of the principle of self-determination through the free and genuine expression of the will of the peoples of the Territory.

. . .

(Signed) Manfred LACHS, President [of the Court].

■ NOTES & QUESTIONS

1. The Court basically decided that neither Morocco nor Mauritania had legal ties that would jeopardize Western Sahara's right to self-determination. Spain could not claim the area, given the various UN directives for implementing the objective of decolonization—beginning with Resolution 1514. In another portion of the opinion, the Court decided that Spain could *not* claim the condition precedent to legal title because the area now referred to as Western Sahara was *terra nullius*—belonging to no one). (This theme is addressed Chapter 6 on the "Range of Sovereignty.") What did *Western Sahara* do—if anything—to aid in the progressive development of the international right of self-determination?

2. How did the Court define "self-determination"? Are there implementing options other than the establishment of a new State?

3. The Western Sahara was a Spanish protectorate from 1912 to 1976. After this case was considered by the Court in 1975, Western Sahara was partitioned between Mauritania and Morocco. Based on an agreement in 1975, the Spanish army departed in 1976. Morocco and Mauritania took over this territory. An indigenous liberation movement protested the 1975 partition agreement, however. In 1979, Mauritania thus ceded its portion of Western Sahara, and Moroccan troops took over. There has been no referendum of the inhabitants. Control over the territory remains politically unsettled, due to hostilities between the Moroccan government and the liberation front. A UN-administered cease-fire between independence-oriented guerrillas and territorial authorities has been in effect since September 1991.

4. Many of Africa's new States, former colonies of western powers, have either become "failed" States (e.g., Somalia) or are in jeopardy of acquiring this posture (e.g., Rwanda). Further, Africa is no

longer viable Cold War turf—where the two super-powers might have rescued and utilized such failing States as pawns in their political and military strategies. Colonialism provided a certain degree of order which has evaporated in a number of former colonies a generation later. The UN has not been the talismanic substitute for that order. Did self-determination thus achieve *only* a proliferation of new States, or did it result in something more for the inhabitants?

■ 2.4   RECOGNITION

The materials in this section deal primarily with recognition by States. Collective recognition by groups of States or international organizations of States is presented near the end of this section.

Recognition By States

Introduction The term *recognition* refers to several categories of decisions. The three most common decisions are analyzed in this section of the text. The first type is State recognition of another *State*, exemplified by the State practice of initiating international relations with another State. State A decides to recognize State B. State A then expresses its willingness to engage in foreign relations with the newly recognized State B. There has been a vast increase in the number of States, particularly since World War II and since the demise of the Cold War (*see* Exhibit 2.1 in § 2.2). This is the level at which most recognition decisions have taken place in the last fifty years.

A second category of recognition decision materializes when State A decides to continue relations with the new *government* of State B. Assuming that State B has not changed status (*see* § 2.3), its change of governments may trigger a host of political concerns in State A. State A may thus decide to officially recognize, or refuse to recognize, the new government of State B. One of the prominent examples has been the continued US refusal to recognize the Castro regime that overthrew the prior government of Cuba in 1959.

A third form of recognition arises when a State recognizes a state of *belligerency* in another State. Belligerents typically seek to overthrow the government of their State. State A may wish to recognize a belligerent force which is operating within State B. State A might overtly or covertly support the forces in State B. Alternatively, State A or its citizens may be indirectly involved with both sides, due to business or other contacts with B. Recognition may then give rise to a neutrality obligation on the part of State A, which is not supposed to act in a way that will adversely affect the territorial sovereignty of State B, whose government may be in the midst of fighting the belligerents.

In 1981, for example, Mexico and France officially recognized a leftist guerilla movement that had fought for several years against the Colombian Government. By recognizing this national liberation front as a "representative political force in Colombia," those nations also recognized the rebels' right to participate in negotiations to end the Colombian civil war. Then in 1992, the Colombian rebels were invited to Mexico City, where they signed a cease-fire agreement with Colombian leaders.

Writers and jurists have described recognition as one of the most chaotic and theoretically confusing topics in International Law. It is certainly one of the most sensitive and controversial.[27] These descriptions are unfortunately quite accurate: Recognition of another State, or an entity within it, typically involves a mixture of political, military, and international considerations described below. The materials that follow thus provide further details on the conditions for State recognition or involvement with one of the above entities.

Recognition of States Argentina's former Judge of the International Court of Justice aptly defines recognition of a new State as "a unilateral act whereby one or more States admit, whether expressly or tacitly, that they regard the . . . political entity as a State; consequently, they also admit that the . . . entity is an international legal personality, and as such is capable of acquiring international rights and contracting international obligations."[28]

Recognition is a significant political goal for new states. Their leaders desire equality of status with the other members of the community of nations. Recognition is one manifestation of that goal. Statehood permits new States to participate in the global conduct of international relations. Recognition is a minimum requirement that, much like needing "two jacks or better to open" in a poker hand, elevates a new State player to an enhanced position that increases the likelihood of successful participation in the game. Russia, for example, was keenly interested in the international recognition of its new republic—formed as a new commonwealth after a forty-year Cold War that stagnated its economy and shattered its relations with many other countries of the world. The US thus recognized Russia (and a number of other members of the former Soviet Union) almost immediately after creation of the Commonwealth of Independent States in 1991. The US delayed recognition of Ukraine, on the other hand, until it was clear that Ukraine would be able to function in harmony with the same Russia that had dominated Ukraine for nearly 600 years.

A new State may be recognized almost immediately, or in some cases, years after it is formed. The very existence of the German Democratic Republic (formerly East Germany) was considered a breach of the Soviet Union's duties under its World War II treaties with the Allied powers regarding the administration of German territory immediately after the war. It was obviously a "State" in terms of its *de facto* qualification for Statehood (*see* § 2.1 on Legal Personality of the State). Many Western nations did not recognize East Germany's *de jure* existence, however, until 1973. A series of unilateral recognitions cured what they had initially perceived as an illegal State.

There may also be delayed *de jure* recognition of a *de jure* State recognized by many other States. The Vatican did not recognize the State of Israel until 1994, forty-five years after Israel was admitted to the UN as a member State. The Vatican's recognition, not undertaken until after the Israel/PLO accords of 1993, was premised on many centuries of distrust between Catholics and Jews. The week before, Israel's largest-selling newspaper (*Yedioth Ahronoth*) stated that: "The Catholic Church is one of the most conservative, oppressive, corrupt organizations in all human history. . . . The reconciliation can be done only if the Catholic Church and the one who heads it fall on their knees and ask forgiveness from the souls of the millions of tortured who went to heaven in black smoke, under the blessing of the Holy See." This news account was referring to the Catholic Church's Inquisition of the Middle Ages and the World War II Holocaust—whereby many Israelis believe that the Catholic Church either did absolutely nothing to halt (or even clandestinely supported) Nazi Germany's appalling treatment of Jews.

De jure recognition may be prematurely granted. The European Community (now European Union, or "EU") recognized Slovenia and Croatia, for example, approximately six months after their vote of independence from the former Yugoslavia—an arguably premature decision that many consider to be the spark which fuelled the fires between ethnic rivals in the former Yugoslavia. Further, recognition of Bosnia-Herzegovina was apparently premature. The Russian newspaper *Pravda* reported in its February 27, 1993 issue that the "international carnage has been largely caused by the hasty recognition [by countries including Russia] of the independence of the unstable state of Bosnia and Herzegovina." This perspective is based on the fact that Bosnia-Herzegovina was not in control of its territory during the flurry of international recognitions descending on it shortly after its secession from the former Yugoslavia.

The Yugoslavian government in Belgrade immediately protested that the European Union's premature recognition of former territories of Yugoslavia violated International Law. Belgrade claimed that the virtually immediate international recognition thus violated its territorial sovereignty over the secessionists. In the case of Bosnia-Herzegovina, the EU has yet to expressly state that it has met the EU's 1991 Recognition Guidelines (*see* Collective Recognition below). One can readily argue that there was no *de facto* basis for recognition by other countries of Bosnia-Herzegovina, given the lack of control exercised over the territory and populace by the new Bosnian government. Yet the political nature of recognition decisions counsels that Yugoslavia's claim of premature recognition did not trigger any State responsibility for harm to Yugoslavia.

National decisions about the recognition of new States have thus been granted or denied for a variety of reasons. Since the recognizing State is usually satisfied that the legal elements of statehood are present, the essential decision of whether to recognize another State has been traditionally quite political in nature. Considerations in past recognition decisions have included: (1) whether the new State has been recognized by other members of the international community; (2) ethnocentric motives stemming from the perceived inferiority of certain nations— effectively limiting the recognition of new States from outside the European community for a number of centuries; (3) the need to appease certain domains—as when England recognized the nineteenth century Barbary Coast, whose pirates were stealing British ships and cargoes; (4) humanitarian motives—many states refused to recognize Southern Rhodesia because of its internal racial policies; and (5) commercial and military motives.[29] For example, Cuba achieved its independence as a result of the Spanish-American War. The US then conditioned its 1903 recognition of Cuba on the demand that Cuba lease the Guantanamo Naval Base to the US for 99 years. This base has been quite important to the political, military, and security interests of the US ever since (for example, the 1962 Cuban Missile Crisis and the 1994 Haitian "invasion" staging area for US troops).

Two theories of recognition have been consistently articulated in recognition discourses: the "constitutive" theory and the "declaratory" theory. Under the constitutive perception of the role of recognition, members of the community of nations *must* recognize a new State in order to constitute or establish its *de jure* international legal personality. The declaratory view, on the other hand, is that recognition by other States is *not* required for the new State to be considered a legitimate entity. Recognition merely declares or acknowledges the existing fact of statehood.

Although the constitutive theory is still advocated by some States and scholars (requiring sufficient recognition for *de jure* statehood),[30] recognition is not required generally as a condition for statehood under International Law. A new State's satisfaction of the basic elements of statehood are sufficient (*see* § 2.1), such that questions of recognition are only a matter of political decision-making at the international level. States thus have no duty to recognize a new State merely because it possesses all the factual attributes of statehood. Formal recognition is a matter of discretion, considered by most States and a majority of writers to be a political act with certain legal consequences that are discussed below. The former Yugoslavia, for example, is as much a State as is its former region that is now called Bosnia-Herzegovina. The decision of many nations not to recognize the Yugoslavian "rump" State is not a breach of any international obligation to formally recognize an existing entity so as to qualify it for statehood.

The prevailing declaratory theory is manifested in regional treaties that specifically negate recognition as an element of the definition of statehood. Less powerful States do not want recognition decisions to influence their political goals and those of new States. They do not want larger states to use recognition as a ploy to exact political concessions. Under Article 12 of the Charter of the Organization of American States, for example:

> The political existence of the State is independent of recognition by other States. Even before being recognized, the State has the right to defend its integrity and independence, to provide for its prosperity, and consequently to organize itself as it sees fit. . . . The exercise of these rights is limited only by the exercise of rights of other States in accordance with international law.

Recognition of Governments The recognition of a new State may, effectively, recognize the government in control of that State. States may also recognize the new *government* of an existing State. It is common practice to reconsider recognition when the government of an existing State changes. This situation typically occurs when there has been an unconstitutional change in government, such as a coup d'etat in a former republic.

As with recognition decisions involving new States, recognition of new governments may be lawfully withheld or withdrawn in most States. Recognizing States are often concerned about whether the populace under a new government has actually acquiesced in the change. In addition, a sudden change in the form of government can present significant economic, political, and military concern to other states. Many states did not recognize the Hanoi-installed Kampuchea government that took power in Cambodia in 1975 while Prince Sihanouk's UN-recognized government was in exile. The US did not recognize the government imposed by the 1991 military coup in Haiti, after the prior democratic election of a Haitian leader acceptable to the US After eighteen months, only the Vatican recognized the new Haiti government, arguably premised on the Catholic Church's distaste for the ousted but democratically elected Aristide—a former Catholic priest.

A number of new governments have reacted adversely to renewed recognition decisions. Their concern is that large and economically dominant States *reconsider* recognition as a device for exacting new concessions from small States. While the recognizing State may be merely seeking assurances that prior international obligations will continue to be performed, they may also exact other less desirable concessions. If the new government is hostile to the recognizing State, the latter might break diplomatic relations, impose economic sanctions, or build up its military presence in or near the territory of the unrecognized government.

The "Estrada Doctrine" is the response to such uses of recognition by powerful nations. This doctrine was named after Genaro Estrada, Mexico's Secretary of Foreign Relations, who introduced it in 1930. Estrada complained that a revolutionary change in government does *not* permit other countries to reconsider whether the new revolutionary government should be recognized.[31] By adopting the Estrada Doctrine, a number of Latin American nations have thus argued that larger developed nations have misused their power of recognition to undermine new governments—with significant costs to the peoples of the affected countries. New governments perceive this renewed occasion for recognition as a device for treading on their sovereign right to conduct internal and foreign affairs as they deem appropriate. *How* the new government came into existence is not a matter for external recognition decisions by other States.

On the other hand, recognizing governments may profess a rather principled question about a new government that has usurped democratic processes via its violent overthrow of a former government. In Haiti, for example, the democratically elected leader was overthrown by a military coup in 1991. The rebel leaders in Rwanda massacred hundreds of thousands of people in 1994, when they seized power from the former government. There was a mass exodus of refugees, fleeing for their lives due to the indiscriminate machete attacks by rebel forces in Rwanda. States with more democratic and less violent traditions thus tend to avoid international relations with "cutthroat" regimes.

Recognizing States are beginning to assert the arguable claim that there is an emerging international right to a democratic form of government. The 1991 EU Guidelines on Recognition refer to democracy as a factor in such decisions; a 1992 Organization of American States resolution demanded Haiti's return to democracy; and scholarly studies all point in this direction.[32] When there has been a bloody violation of that perceived right, via the violent overthrow of a prior democratic government, the failure to reconsider recognition may raise moral questions. To what degree does the international community of nations, by turning its head the other way, acquiesce in the continued operation of a new government which is carrying out mass executions of innocent civilians?

If recognition is a matter for political decision-makers, then what is the *legal* impact of recognition? A new government can face difficult legal barriers when it is not recognized by a particular country or the community of nations. An unrecognized government may not be able to effectively represent its interests elsewhere. For example, the unrecognized government and its citizens usually do not have access to the courts of the nonrecognizing State and must endure any fiscal or political consequences of nonrecognition.[33] A classic illustration of these consequences appears in the following case:

BANK OF CHINA V. WELLS FARGO BANK & UNION TRUST CO.

United States Federal District Court
Northern District of California, 1952
104 Fed.Supp. 59

[*Author's Note: The government-directed Bank of China at Shanghai deposited money into a US bank in San Francisco (Wells Fargo). Mao Tse-Tung subsequently overthrew the government of China in 1949. Wells Fargo then received conflicting demands to the ownership of the deposited money—from what were then the two "Banks of China." One demand was made by the new Chinese mainland's People's Republic* of China as the alleged successor to the government of all of China. The other claimant was the ousted Nationalist Chinese government seated in Formosa (now called Taiwan).

President Truman announced that the US recognized the Nationalist government in Formosa as the de jure *or legitimate government for all of China, referring to both Taiwan and mainland China. Judge*

Goodman of the federal court in San Francisco, however, had to resolve which Bank of China would receive the nearly $800,000 deposited with the Wells Fargo Bank prior to Mao's revolutionary takeover of China. The judge held in favor of the Nationalist Government. He explored the possibility of making this decision on several grounds, including statehood, which entity more clearly represented the Chinese people, equitable division of the deposit, and whether recognition by the US executive branch would legally foreclose his ability to decide in favor of either government.

Judge Goodman's decision was reversed for reasons unrelated to this portion of the case. His case footnotes are omitted.]

[*Opinion.*]   . . .

The issue before the Court has therefore been reduced to a comparatively narrow one. . . . Which Bank of China is legally entitled to the funds deposited with the defendant Bank?

The controlling corporate authority of the Bank of China is effectively vested in the Government of China by virtue of its majority stock ownership, its dominant voice in the managing directorate, and the supervisory powers accorded by the Articles of Association to the Minister of Finance. A determination of what government, if any, should be recognized by this court as now entitled to exercise this corporate authority over the deposit in suit, will govern the disposition of these causes.

The issue thus posed focuses attention at the outset on the fact that of the two governments asserting corporate authority, one is recognized by the United States [Nationalist China] while the other is not [People's Republic of China]. If this fact, per se, is determinative, the issue is resolved. If whenever this court is called upon to determine whether there is a government justly entitled to act on behalf of a foreign state in respect to a particular matter, the court is bound to say, without regard to the facts before it, that the government recognized by our executive is that government, then nothing more need be said here. To permit this expression of executive policy to usurp entirely the judicial judgment would relieve the court of a burdensome duty, but it is doubtful that the ends of justice would thus be met. It has been argued that such is the accepted practice. But the authorities do not support this view.

There is, of course, the long line of New York decisions arising out of the nationalization of Russian corporations by the Soviet Government at a time when it was unrecognized by the United States.

In those decisions, the New York courts stated time and again that no effect would be given to the acts of the unrecognized Soviet Government, in so far as property situated in this country was concerned. . . . Such decisions do not bar the way to giving effect to acts of non-recognized governments [however] even in respect to property within our borders, if justice so requires.

Some more recent decisions of the federal courts, involving Soviet nationalization of corporations of the Baltic states, give great weight to the executive policy of non-recognition. But it cannot be said that these decisions establish an all-embracing rule that no extra-territorial effect may ever be given the acts of an unrecognized government.

The [New York] decisions just set forth, as well as others in this field, reveal no rule of law obliging the courts to give conclusive effect to the acts of a recognized government to the exclusion of all consideration of the acts of an opposing unrecognized government. Nor does it appear that such a sweeping rule would be a sound one.

. . .

This is not to suggest that the courts should regard executive policy in respect to recognition and non-recognition of foreign governments as meaningless or of little consequence. In any particular situation, executive policy may be crucial, as indeed it appears to be in the present case. But, it is a fact which properly should be considered and weighed along with the other facts before the court.

Turning to the record in this case, it appears that two governments are governments in fact of portions of the territory of the State of China. The "Peoples" Government has supplanted the "Nationalist" Government in dominion over the entire Chinese Mainland with an area of more than 3,700,000 square miles, and a population of more than 460,000,000. The "Nationalist" Government controls one of the 35 provinces of China, the Island of Formosa, which has an area of 13,885 square miles and a population in excess of 6,000,000. It is obvious that the "Peoples" Government is now the government in fact of by far the greater part of the territory of the Chinese State. Nevertheless the "Nationalist" Government controls substantial territory, exceeding in area that of either Belgium or the Netherlands, and in population that of Denmark or Switzerland.

Each government, in its respective sphere, functions effectively. Each is recognized by a significant number of the nations of the world. Each maintains normal diplomatic intercourse with those nations which extend recognition. This has been the status quo for more than two years.

Each government is in a position to exercise corporate authority in behalf of the Bank of China. That is, each government is capable of utilizing the corporate structure and certain corporate assets to promote the corporate purposes. The Bank of China was chartered primarily to facilitate Chinese international commercial activities. . . . Each government is in a position to act through the corporate structure of the Bank of China to carry on these international functions in the areas abroad where such Government is recognized and these domestic functions within the territory such Government controls. Each government is in fact doing so. The Bank of China, as controlled by the Nationalist Government, continues to function on the Island of Formosa and through its foreign branches in the United States, Cuba, Australia, Japan, Indo China, and elsewhere where the Nationalist Government is recognized.

The Peoples Government as successor in fact to the Nationalist Government on the Chinese Mainland is exercising the prerogatives of the Government in respect to the Bank of China there. The Peoples Government has not nationalized the Bank of China, nor confiscated its assets, nor denied the rights of private stockholders. It exercises the authority vested in the Government of China as majority stockholder. The Bank of China continues to function in accordance with its Articles of Association under the guidance of the appointees of the Peoples Government and the majority of the directors previously elected by private stockholders on the Chinese Mainland and through branches in London, Hong Kong, Singapore, Penang, Kuala Lumpur, Batavia, Calcutta, Bombay, Karachi, Chittagong, and Rangoon.

The Nationalist and Peoples Governments have [each] maintained and strengthened their positions. Our national policy toward these governments is now definite. We have taken a stand adverse to the aims and ambitions of the [mainland] Peoples Government. The armed forces of that Government are now engaged in conflict with our forces in Korea.

We recognize only the Nationalist Government [located on Formosa] as the representative of the State of China, and are actively assisting in developing its military forces in Formosa. The Bank of China now operates as two corporate entities, each performing within the area of its operations the functions bestowed upon the Bank of China by its Articles of Association. Each Bank of China is in a position to employ the deposit in suit for corporate purposes.

From a practical standpoint, neither of the rival Banks of China is a true embodiment of the corporate entity which made the deposit in the Wells Fargo Bank. The present Nationalist Bank of China is more nearly equivalent in the sense of continuity of management. The Peoples Bank is more representative in ability to deal with the greater number of private stockholders and established depositors and creditors. Were the Court to adopt a strictly pragmatic approach, it might attempt a division of the deposit between these two banks in the degree that each now exercises the functions of the Bank of China. Or the Court might award the entire deposit to the bank it deems to be the closest counterpart of the corporation contemplated by the Articles of Association.

. . . Such a course would ultimately entail determining which bank best serves the corporate interests of the State of China. That determination could not be made, while the State, itself, remains divided, except by an excursion into the realm of political philosophy. . . . Here, there co-exist two governments, in fact, each attempting to further, in its own way, the interests of the State of China, in the Bank of China. It is not a proper function of a domestic court of the United States to attempt to judge which government best represents the interests of the Chinese State in the Bank of China. In this situation, the Court should justly accept, as the representative of the Chinese State, that government which our executive deems best able to further the mutual interests of China and the United States.

Since the Court is of the opinion that it should recognize the Nationalist Government of China as legally entitled to exercise the controlling corporate authority of the Bank of China in respect to the deposit in suit, the motion for [the bank deposit] in favor of the Bank of China, as controlled by the Nationalist Government, is granted.

■ NOTES & QUESTIONS

1. Assume that you are an appellate judge reviewing Judge Goodman's decision in the *Bank of China* case. On the basis of statehood, could you decide which government—the Nationalist Chinese or the Communist Chinese—should receive the deposited money?

2. What were the practical effects of the President's recognition decision?

Recognition of Belligerency A somewhat ill-defined situation referred to as a "belligerency" within a State may yield yet another basis for a recognition decision not directly involving statehood. The belligerent group, while not a State, may nevertheless achieve a degree of legal personality under International Law. Revolutionary groups that attempt to seize power in their own country—or a portion of it—may be recognized. The recognition may come initially from the existing government in the State of the belligerency or (as is typical) externally from a foreign State.

The recognition of belligerency normally confers certain rights upon the belligerent entity, as well as the government that opposes the belligerents. As stated by the US Supreme Court, these rights include the "rights of blockade, visitation, search and seizure of contraband articles on the high seas, and abandonment of claims for reparation on account of damages suffered by our citizens from the prevalence of warfare."[34] By blockading the South's Confederate ports, for example, the Union government in the northern states, in effect, recognized that a state of belligerency existed between itself and the Confederacy.

When *another* country is not a party to a dispute between the belligerent forces and the forces of the regular government, it is expected to remain neutral until the belligerency is resolved. England recognized the Confederate States of the United States as "belligerents" when the Civil War between the Northern and the Southern states of the US began in 1861. England did not, however, remain neutral as required under International Law: Ships for the Confederate South were built in British ports and prepared for war with the Union forces in the US. As a result, the Treaty of Washington of 1871 established the *Alabama Claims* international arbitration. Two years later, England paid over $15 million to the US as a consequence of the damages done by five vessels made in England for the belligerent Confederate forces. Ironically, Russian vessels paid port calls to New York and San Francisco in 1863, perceived by many observers as a tacit message that Russia then supported the Union in its quest to defeat the Confederacy. The difference between Czarist Russia and England was that Russia took no active role in aiding the Union during the Civil War.

The essential elements of the duty of neutrality are that the neutral State: (1) not take sides to assist either the belligerent or the regular government; (2) not allow its territory to be used as a base for hostilities by the belligerent forces; (3) acquiesce in restrictions imposed by the parties to the dispute if it wishes to remain entitled to respect of neutral State rights; (4) declare any change in status, as when it decides to side with the belligerency or the regular government; and (5) must accept State responsibility under International Law (*see* § 2.5) for any violation of its duty of neutrality.[35]

This customary practice developed prior to the effective date of the UN Charter. The Charter prohibits the use of force in international relations—an obligation that is also applicable to neutral States. To preserve the appearance of neutrality, a State considering involvement or intervention *should* thus await the direction of the UN Security Council. Intervening States (that have not declared war) should thus act in ways that will not strain the neutrality requirement.

A good example of a State's attempt to intervene, while appearing to preserve its neutrality, occurred in 1994 when France announced its intent to conduct a military intervention in Rwanda (a former Belgian colony). There had been a low-intensity conflict between the Rwandan government and the rebel Rwandan Patriotic Front since 1990. The intensity increased in 1994, when the outbreak of civil war caused civilian casualties in the hundreds of thousands, as well as producing a mass exodus driven by indiscriminate machete attacks on the populace. France advised the rebels that it would intervene, for the exclusive humanitarian purpose of ending these massacres. The French Foreign Minister stated in early June 1994: "I want to underline the fact that we are making great efforts to convince the RPF [rebel forces] that this operation is not aimed against them."

The rebels feared that France's intervention would thwart their interim successes in trying to overthrow the Rwandan government and its army. The French Foreign Minister thus assured all concerned that France would not proceed with its intervention, absent authority to do so by the UN Security Council (which was ultimately provided in late June). France's caution also served the neutrality interests of Zaire—the "jumping off" point for the departure of French troops to Rwanda. The UN ultimately established a Rwanda peacekeeping force to protect the populace from tribal warfare.

Collective Recognition

While *State* practice is normally emphasized in recognition discourses, an international organization or group of States may decide to extend (or withhold) collective recognition. Article 1(2) of the League of Nations Covenant, for example, provided for a form of collective recognition—permitting admission to this world body only if applicants expressed a commitment to observing international obligations. Thus, a State or other territory could attain membership "if its admission is agreed to by two-thirds of the Assembly, provided it shall give effective guarantees of its sincere intention to observe international obligations, and shall accept . . . regulations . . . in regard to its military, naval, and air forces and armaments." This article thus provided League members with a convenient basis for refusing to officially recognize or approve of the creation of new States by succession or unacceptable breaches of territorial sovereignty by aggressor States. As noted by the prominent Finnish statesman Erich in 1926, if the League of Nations did not succeed

> in repelling an aggression or in preventing an occupation . . . of the territory of a Member, the other Members must not recognize that *de facto* change as final and valid *de jure*. If one of the direct consequences of that unlawful aggression has been the establishment of a new State, the Members of the League of Nations should . . . refuse to recognize that new State the existence of which is conflicting with the supreme values [of the League]. . . .[36]

The United Nations does not collectively recognize States. The UN Charter contains prohibitions against force, as did the League Charter. Unlike the League, however, mere admission into the UN should not be regarded as an act of collective recognition. Many thought it unwise to imply recognition from mere admission into this second-generation world body. The Cold War quickly revealed that the brass ring of universality was more difficult to grasp than contemplated by League of Nations members. In 1950, the Secretary-General expressly stated that the UN "does not possess any authority to recognize either a new State or a new government of an existing State. To establish the rule of collective recognition by the United Nations, would require either an amendment to the Charter or a treaty to which all members would adhere."[37]

No such treaty ever materialized. There was a remarkable post-war influx of States onto the international scene (*see* Exhibit 2.1 in § 2.2). The variousness of their backgrounds suggests that any attempt to qualify admission with the acceptance of conditions of recognition would again result in another form of Cold War—thereby defeating the underlying UN purpose of bringing the world community together in one place, so as to diffuse conflicts and cultivate other essentials within the Charter's mandate.

The European Union or EU (formerly European Economic Community, EEC, and EC) has taken the leading role in developing recognition criteria. Its recognition requirements are comparatively objective—States have never been very lucid about their subjective criteria for recognizing other States. In 1991, the EU promulgated its Guidelines on the Recognition of New States in Eastern Europe and in the Soviet Union. This announcement was expressly linked with its commitment to the law of self-determination of States (*see* § 2.3 on Changes in State Status). The EU and its member States thus adopted the following five criteria that States seeking recognition must satisfy:

1. Respect for UN Charter provisions and its European counterpart (Conference on Security and Co-operation in Europe);

2. Guarantees for ethnic and national minorities;

3. Respect for the inviolability of all frontiers, which can be changed only by peaceful means and common agreement;

4. Acceptance of international commitments regarding disarmament and nuclear nonproliferation; and

5. Arbitration or like resolution of all disputes regarding succession and regional disputes.[38]

The EU will thus withhold recognition from States, territories, or colonies resulting from international aggression. Recognition will not be given to States that violate territorial sovereignty or fail to observe international human rights guarantees. The US heartily supported this new objective approach in the development of the international law of recognition.[39]

■ 2.5 STATE RESPONSIBILITY

Prior sections of this text defined International Law, the various influences that shape it, the State as the principal actor in its development, and its changing infrastructure due to the phenomenal increase in the number of States since 1945. This section briefly addresses another introductory matter: State responsibility under International Law. Once statehood is acquired, a State incurs immediate obligations associated with its international status. It is required to make reparations for any international wrongdoing because it has achieved *de facto* statehood. This requirement is of course immutable once status as a *de jure* State entity has been confirmed via recognition. Otherwise, States would not be equal sovereigns under International Law. World order could not tolerate only *some* States accepting responsibility for their wrongdoing that violates International Law.

Prior to delving into the specific content of International Law in subsequent chapters, it will be useful to consider the general consequences of a State's wrongful conduct. When a State commits a wrongful act against another State, its breach of International Law activates the requirement that it make reparations for that harm. Law students study the law of torts, contracts, and criminal law in their first year of law school. They learn to appreciate the underlying bases for determining what constitutes a breach of the law and how the resulting harm is remedied. Assuming that a State has committed some wrong through its active or passive conduct, International Law is similarly concerned with demanding State responsibility accompanied by some remedy.

Three fundamental elements establish State responsibility under International Law: (1) the existence of a legal obligation recognized by International Law; (2) an act or omission that violates that obligation; and (3) some loss or articulable damage caused by the breach of the obligation.[40]

These elements are drawn from a variety of sources, including various judicial and arbitral awards. In 1928, the quintessential articulation by the Permanent Court of International Justice was that "it is a principle of international law, and even a greater conception of [all] law, that any breach of an engagement [responsibility to another State] involves an obligation to make reparation."[41] In this particular instance, Germany was suing Poland in the former world court. While there is generally a sovereign right of expropriation, Germany sought reparations for Poland's breach of its *treaty* obligation not to expropriate a German factory once built in Poland.

The 1990 *Rainbow Warrior* arbitration reaffirmed that "the legal consequences of a breach of a treaty, including the determination of the circumstances that may exclude wrongfulness . . . and the appropriate remedies for breach, are subjects that belong to the customary law of state responsibility."[42] In 1985, French agents had destroyed the Greenpeace vessel *Rainbow Warrior* in a New Zealand harbor, after a Greenpeace protest about French nuclear testing in the South Pacific. A member of the Greenpeace crew was killed by a French agent. In 1986, the UN Secretary-General ruled that France had thus incurred State responsibility for the acts of its agents. France was then supposed to transfer the responsible French agents to its base in the Pacific, where they would stay for at least three years. They were clandestinely repatriated to France, however, without New Zealand's consent.

The above elements of State responsibility apply without regard to how one might characterize the obligation or the nature of the breach. The obligation may have been established by treaty or by customary International Law. The breach may be classified as either civil or criminal in nature. There is a persistent question, however, about whether the mere fact of some resulting harm is enough to trigger State responsibility; put another way, is some finding of fault or intent on the part of a State's agents required for State responsibility?

The ICJ's 1949 *Corfu Channel* opinion suggests that fault is required. Great Britain had sued Albania when British naval vessels hit mines recently laid in an international strait in Albanian. Albania denied any knowledge of the presence of those mines—notwithstanding rather suspicious circumstances. The Court stated that "it cannot be concluded . . . that that state [Albania] necessarily knew, or ought to have known, of any unlawful act perpetrated therein, nor yet that it necessarily knew, or should have known, the authors [of the act of mine laying in the strait]."[43] Professor Malcolm Shaw of the University of Leicester in England points out, however, that this lone passage from the Court is *not* tantamount to its general adoption of a fault requirement that would thereby limit State responsibility. While judicial and academic opinions are divided on this matter, most tend to agree on the existence of a strict liability standard—meaning that the State's fault, intent, or knowledge are *not* conditions for State responsibility. Thus it is not just heinous criminal activity that triggers State responsibility in International Law.[44] A State can be liable if it either fails to act or is unaware of floating mines in its territorial waters through which foreign vessels routinely navigate.

This important area of the law is by no means simple to articulate by codifying it in a draft/model treaty or resolution. Three international drafting commissions have attempted to restate the law of State responsibility. From 1924 to 1930, a Committee of Experts working with the League of Nations presented the first phase in this lengthy endeavor. Its draft articles were limited to the responsibility of States for injuries *within* their territories to either foreign citizens or their property (a theme that is further addressed in Chapter 13 on "International Economic Relations"). The 1949–1961 second phase, conducted under the auspices of the UN, attempted to codify State responsibility with roughly the same parameters. From 1963 to date, the third wave of attempts to codify the law of State responsibility has crested at the UN Charter. The drafters for this phase have broadened their efforts to cover State responsibility for all topics within the Charter's reach. The comparative length of this third phase is attributable to the concurrent change in the infrastructure of the UN's component States, which likewise began in the early 1960s (*see* Exhibit 2.1 in § 2.2).

Even today, the model law of State responsibility is couched in only the most general of terms—despite more than seventy years of laborious efforts to produce an acceptable draft for an international conference. Article 1 (of the thirty-five drafted thus far) almost bashfully provides as follows: "The international responsibility of a State which . . . arises from an intentionally wrongful act committed by that State, entails legal consequences. . . ." Article 3 adds that "the rules of customary international law shall continue to govern the legal consequences of an internationally wrongful act of a State not set out in the provisions of the present Part [of the draft codification]." Article 5 states that the legal consequences of State responsibility are subject "to the provisions and procedures of the Charter of the United Nations relating to the maintenance of peace and international security."[45] There remains much to be done.

The most specific application of the law of State responsibility involves injuries to aliens—foreign individuals and corporations harmed by government action on a discriminatory basis differing from the treatment of local citizens. This facet of State responsibility is addressed in Chapter 13 on "International Economic Relations."

■ 2.6 SOVEREIGN IMMUNITY

Prior sections of this book addressed the elements of statehood, the rights and obligations incurred when there is a change in State status, and the responsibility acquired when an entity achieves international legal personality by becoming a State. This section introduces an important adjunct to State status—that is, although a State may be responsible for certain conduct, the State's status as a sovereign entity may shield it from having to respond to suits against it in the courts of another country. Sovereign immunity means, essentially, that one State cannot claim jurisdiction over another State in its courts. State A ought not to be subjected to the ordinary judicial processes of the courts in State B.

This attribute of sovereignty is premised on one of the building blocks of International Law: All States are entitled to equality. The expression of this equality is often found in the constitutive documents of international organizations. Article 2.1 of the UN Charter provides that "The Organization is based on the principle of the sovereign equality of all its Members." Article 6 of the Charter of the Organization of American States provides that "States are juridically [legally] equal, enjoy equal rights and equal capacity to exercise these rights. . . ."

The scope of the sovereign's immunity includes States, heads of State, and (since World War II) State agencies conducting State business. Until then, State practice generally employed the "absolute" theory of sovereign immunity. The classic restatement of that theory, relied on by scholars in a number of nations, was that of Chief Justice Marshall of the US Supreme Court in 1812. France had confiscated a private vessel belonging to a US civilian crew, converting it into a French war vessel. When it subsequently entered a US port, former crew members claimed that this ship still belonged to them; they were the rightful owners of the converted French vessel. Thus, they arranged for its seizure, pending a judicial decision about the rightful ownership. The US government injected its views into the proceedings, raising the issue of whether France—through its military vessel—enjoyed sovereign immunity from suit in courts of the US. As Chief Justice Marshall succinctly noted, States *and their rulers* are immune from arrest or involvement in litigation in courts of other States. In Marshall's words:

> This full and absolute territorial jurisdiction being alike the attribute of every sovereign . . . would not seem to contemplate foreign sovereigns or their sovereign rights as its objects. One sovereign being in no respect amenable to another, and being bound by obligations of the highest character not to degrade the dignity of his nation, . . . can be supposed to enter a foreign territory . . . in the confidence that the immunities belonging to his independent sovereign station . . . will be extended to him.
>
> This perfect equality and absolute independence of sovereigns, and this common interest impelling them to mutual intercourse, and an interchange of good offices with each other, has given rise to a class of cases in which every sovereign is understood to waive the exercise of a part of that [otherwise] complete exclusive territorial jurisdiction, which has been stated to be the attribute of every nation.
>
> 1st. One of these [attributes] is admitted to be the exemption of the person of the sovereign from arrest or detention within a foreign territory. . . . A foreign sovereign is not understood as intending to subject himself to a jurisdiction incompatible with his dignity, and

the dignity of his nation, and it is to avoid this subjection that the license [to enter another nation without fear of seizure arrest] has been obtained.[46]

The scope of sovereign immunity also depends on what entities are embraced within the term *State.* There is a distinction between heads of State and agencies of a State. Absolute immunity is almost universally recognized for heads of State regarding their public and private acts while they are in a foreign State. In the famous case of *Mighell v. Sultan of Johore* of 1893, England extended sovereign immunity to a foreign head of State who was sued in England for breach of his promise to marry. The case against the sultan was thus dismissed.[47]

One aberration in contemporary practice is the case of Manual Noriega, Panama's former head of State. In 1989, the US invaded Panama, waited for him outside of the Vatican embassy there, seized him when he exited, and then returned him to the US where he stood trial on drug trafficking charges. This was perhaps the first time, since Roman leaders brought back captured foreign leaders in chains two thousand years ago, that a foreign ruler was captured abroad and returned for trial in the territory of the captors. The US relied on various legalities, including a state of war (commenced by the US invasion) and self-defense—premised on the danger that Noriega's dictatorship posed for US security interests in Panama. It was also labeled as a "gross violation" of International Law by the former president of the American Society of International Law.[48] This is likely the lone incident marring the almost universal application of the absolute theory of sovereign immunity for foreign Heads of State.

Examples of the continued application of sovereign immunity for heads of State include the Bosnian Serb leader Karadzic. In 1993, he was granted a visa by the US to travel to the UN. Although he stands accused of war crimes in Bosnia, he was assured immunity from arrest for those crimes while in the US to attend UN peace talks.

Sovereign immunity does not continue, however, for *former* rulers. While they normally are not sued just because they are no longer heads of State, a suit in foreign courts is nevertheless possible. The former Shah of Iran was served with a multibillion-dollar lawsuit in 1979, when he checked into a New York hospital. This suit was dismissed on other grounds (*see* § 9.8 on Act of State). Deposed Philippine

President Marcos was sued on numerous occasions after his 1986 departure from the Philippines. In the US, he could not claim sovereign immunity—for he was no longer the head of State, and the US government strongly supported Marco's successor in the Philippine government. Thus, the successor government of the Philippines agreed that the suits against Marcos could proceed in the courts of the US—effectively waiving whatever sovereign immunity Marcos might have enjoyed in the absence of this waiver.

The scope of sovereign immunity is not as clear in the case of State *agencies*. Commerce ministries, for example, are entitled to sovereign immunity in some countries. But as noted by Professor Ian Brownlie of Oxford University, "the principles on which courts act are still unsettled."[49] The essential question is the degree to which a commercial entity, operated by a foreign government, is entitled to immunity from suit in another State. This question has been answered in a variety of ways. How it is answered depends on whether the nation where suit is brought applies the historical rule of "absolute" sovereign immunity or the contemporary rule of "restrictive" sovereign immunity. The twentieth century proliferation of government-operated businesses has generated diverse opinions on whether a sovereign State and its agencies should *always* retain the historical protection from suit in another State.

Assume that a merchant vessel is owned and operated by a company that is a public agency of the Liberian government. This vessel arrives at its destination in State X with damaged merchandise. A privately owned Liberian vessel would be subject to a lawsuit authorizing seizure of the ship and keeping it in the State X port for longer than scheduled. If the vessel is publically operated by the State of Liberia, however, the *absolute* theory of sovereign immunity would bar the suit. Because the government of Liberia operates the ship, Liberia and its vessel would be immune from suit in the courts of State X. The advancement of the economic welfare of the Liberian people is no less a public purpose than the operation of a Liberian naval vessel that is visiting the same port in State X.

Under the modern *restrictive* theory of sovereign immunity, most States no longer extend Justice Marshall's *Schooner Exchange* rule of absolute immunity to government-owned or -operated merchant vessels. Military vessels still enjoy absolute immunity from seizure in foreign ports (and elsewhere under International Law as discussed in Chapter 6 on the Range of Sovereignty). But civilian vessels being operated by a State in its capacity as a trader competing with other private merchants would *not* be entitled to sovereign immunity under the restrictive application of sovereign immunity practice. This newer approach to sovereign immunity thus restricts the scope of available immunity when the State stands in the shoes of a private trader—doing what any trader could do, rather than doing only what a sovereign can do.

In other contexts, some States still apply the absolute theory of sovereign immunity when the activity is more closely associated with the political objectives of the State. The following case from Poland is an example. A woman named Aldona was a typist employed by the weekly magazine *Voice of England*. This magazine was published in Kracow, Poland, by the British Foreign Office of the British government. Aldona was dismissed from her job. She was not paid the remainder of the salary due under her contract with the magazine. She sued Great Britain in a Polish court for the breach of her contract by the English agency which published the magazine. The Polish courts dismissed her case because the defendant was a foreign sovereign. Aldona asserted that this dispute involved a mere contract of employment between a private person and a commercial magazine that was a profit-making enterprise—published by an agency of the British government for diplomatic and other political purposes.

Aldona's unsuccessful argument was that publishing a magazine should be characterized as economic rather than diplomatic activity. Her lawyer argued that if Great Britain's magazine could avoid paying her, on the basis of a dismissal on grounds of sovereign immunity, the contractual obligations of the British government in Poland would be meaningless. The Polish court first assessed reciprocity concerns. Absent a dismissal in this case, any subsequent suit against a Polish governmental entity in Great Britain would likely convince a British judge to allow a suit to proceed.

The Polish court also noted that while the English magazine was a commercial entity, in the sense of selling magazines for a profit, its underlying purpose was (unoffensive) political activity on the part of England. The Polish Supreme Court also tied up an important loose end—the plaintiff's remedy was not in the courts, but rather through diplomatic negotiations on her behalf. Thus, under the Polish Supreme Court's analysis:

> Polish Courts were unable, given the principle of reciprocity, to accept for deliberation the claim submitted by Aldona S., even if it concerned a commercial enterprise on behalf of the British authorities. However, such is really not the case, for the [lower Polish] Court of Appeal held that the publishing house of "Voice of England" is not a commercial enterprise. The objection of the plaintiff that this does not concern diplomatic but [rather] economic activity cannot be admitted as valid, for although the activity may not be diplomatic, it is political by its content, and economic only by its form. . . .
>
> Finally, the last objection of the plaintiff, that refusal of legal protection would render the obligations of the British Foreign Office as a publisher of a magazine in the territory of our State incomplete and unreal, is also unfounded, for, if the plaintiff does not wish to seek justice before English courts, she may take advantage of general international usage in connection with immunity from jurisdiction, and approach the [English] Ministry of Foreign Affairs, which is obliged to take up the matter with the [Polish] Ministry of Foreign Affairs of a foreign country with a view to obtain satisfaction for a just claim. This approach frequently produces speedier results than court procedure.[50]

Most States currently apply some form of the restrictive standard for resolving sovereign immunity questions. Certain States such as the People's Republic of China still adhere to the absolute immunity theory in *all* cases.[51] Western States typically restrict a foreign sovereign's immunity from suit depending on the circumstances. Major distinctions are made between state conduct which is (1) sovereign versus private; (2) public versus private; (3) commercial versus noncommercial; or (4) political versus trade-related. These enumerated distinctions are easily stated but difficult to apply. Consider the following Austrian Supreme Court case.

The plaintiff was an Austrian citizen whose automobile was damaged in a collision with a car owned by the US government in Austria. The driver of the US car was delivering mail to the US embassy. The lawyer for the US claimed sovereign immunity from suit in the Austrian courts, premised on the underlying purpose of the trip. Both the lower court and the Austrian Supreme Court allowed the case to proceed, however. It was the act of driving itself, rather than its underlying purpose, that would shape the scope of sovereign immunity. Any qualified driver can drive a car on an Austrian highway. Negligence on the highway, not the underlying purpose of delivering US government mail, therefore vitiated sovereign immunity for the US in the Austrian courts. As stated by the Austrian Supreme Court:

> Thus, we must always look at the act itself which is performed by State organs, and not at its motive or purpose. We must always investigate the act of the State from which the claim is derived. Whether an act is of a private or sovereign nature must always be deduced from the nature of the legal transaction . . . the action taken or the legal relationship arising [as from the collision on an Austrian highway].
>
> . . .
>
> [T]he act from which the plaintiff derives his claim for damages against the defendant is not the collection of mail but the operation of a motor car . . . and action as a road user. By operating a motor car and using the public roads the defendant moves in spheres in which private individuals also move.[52]

■ NOTES & QUESTIONS

1. Reciprocity among States was described by the *Aldona S.* court as the "most essential" principle in international relations. Does that statement mean that the court would apply absolute immunity to even a relatively innocuous commercial contract, regardless of the circumstances, when the defendant is a foreign sovereign?

2. Aldona could not use the courts of Poland to recover her wages. Was she without a remedy? If she had another remedy, would it be better than a judgment for money damages payable to Aldona?

3. In the Austrian collision case, the court referred to the distinction between "private and sovereign acts." Was the delivery of mail to the US embassy in Austria thus a private or a sovereign act of the US government?

4. Does the emphasis on "the nature of the act" refer to the collection and delivery of embassy mail or the driving of a car on an Austrian highway?

Today, most sovereign immunity questions involve acts of some State agency that is doing business in a foreign country. The most dramatic case in point in the US is presented in the case which appears immediately below. When reading it, consider whether sovereign immunity should be discarded as a vintage anachronism—held over from an era when States did not do business to the extent that they do today—or alternatively, whether it still serves a very utilitarian purpose in international relations.

The Nelsons, a married couple, filed this action against the Kingdom of Saudi Arabia, a Saudi hospital, and the hospital's purchasing agent in the United States. They alleged that the husband suffered personal injuries as a result of the Saudi government's unlawful detention, torture, and failure to warn him of the possibility of severe retaliatory action if he attempted to report on-the-job hazards. The Nelsons asserted jurisdiction under the US Foreign Sovereign Immunities Act of 1976, 28 United States Code § 1605(a)(2)—or FSIA. That legislation authorizes a US court to hear a case "based upon a *commercial* activity carried on *in* the United States by the foreign state."

The federal trial court dismissed the Nelsons' claim for lack of subject-matter jurisdiction—ruling that the US courts did not have the power to hear this case against Saudi Arabia and its agents because the torture and detention were not "commercial" activities within the meaning of the FSIA. The intermediate appellate court reversed, concluding that Mr. Nelson's recruitment and hiring were "commercial activities" of Saudi Arabia, thereby authorizing the prosecution of the Nelsons' court action because Saudi Arabia and its agents were conducting "commercial" activity as envisioned by Congress under its FSIA.

The Supreme Court reversed the intermediate court of appeals, thus reinstating the trial court's dismissal of this case. None of these courts was ruling on the merits of the Nelson case—they were merely determining *whether* such a case could even be presented in US courts (for a subsequent trial regarding liability and damages). The dismissal of such cases does not absolve the defendant of liability for State responsibility (*see* § 2.5). Rather, a judge is not the appropriate decision-maker. Reparations are usually the subject of diplomatic negotiations.

The law of sovereign immunity is not uniformly perceived by the various legal systems of the world, nor necessarily even by American judges. In this case alone, the trial, intermediate appellate, and Supreme Courts all differed on whether Saudi Arabia's sovereign immunity was waived by its recruiting and training of employees in the US. At the Supreme Court level, the justices were intensely divided on the question of whether this claim should be dismissed on the "technical" basis that the FSIA required the requisite degree of "commercial activity" for the Nelsons to be able to sue Saudi Arabia in the courts of the US. Only five of the nine justices agreed with the entire opinion of the majority (written by Justice Souter). One of the nine justices agreed with most but not all of the opinion. Two of them concurred with the result, but disagreed with some of the reasoning. Four justices concurred in part and dissented in part:

SAUDI ARABIA v. NELSON

Supreme Court of the United States, 1993
___ U.S. ___, 113 S.Ct. 1471, 123 L.Ed. 47

[Author's Note: The term "petitioner" refers to Saudi Arabia—the defendant in the courts below but the petitioner seeking reversal in the Supreme Court.

The term "respondents" refers to the Nelsons—the plaintiffs below, and now responding to the Saudi attempt to reverse the Court of Appeals directive that the trial judge should proceed with this case. Citations have been deleted.]

[*Opinion.*] Justice SOUTER delivered the [majority] opinion of the Court.

The Foreign Sovereign Immunities Act of 1976 [generally] entitles foreign states to immunity from the jurisdiction of courts in the United States, subject to certain enumerated exceptions. One [exception] is that a foreign state shall not be immune in any case "in which the action is based upon a commercial activity carried on in the United States by the foreign state." We hold that respondents' action alleging personal injury resulting from unlawful detention and torture by the Saudi Government is not "based upon a commercial activity" within the meaning of the Act, which consequently confers no jurisdiction over respondents' suit.

I

. . . Petitioner Kingdom of Saudi Arabia owns and operates petitioner King Faisal Specialist Hospital in Riyadh [Saudi Arabia], as well as petitioner Royspec Purchasing Services, the Hospital's corporate purchasing agent in the United States. The Hospital Corporation of America, Ltd. (HCA), an independent corporation existing under the laws of the Cayman Islands, recruits Americans for employment at the [Saudi] Hospital. . . .

In its recruitment effort, HCA placed an advertisement in a trade periodical seeking applications for a position as a monitoring systems engineer at the Hospital. The advertisement drew the attention of respondent Scott Nelson . . . while Nelson was in the United States. After interviewing for the position in Saudi Arabia, Nelson returned to the United States, where he signed an employment contract with the Hospital, satisfied personnel processing requirements, and attended an orientation session that HCA conducted for Hospital employees. In the course of that program, HCA identified Royspec [hospital's agent in US] as the point of contact in the United States for family members who might wish to reach Nelson in an emergency.

In December 1983, Nelson went to Saudi Arabia and began work at the Hospital, monitoring all "facilities, equipment, utilities and maintenance systems to insure the safety of patients, hospital staff, and others." He . . . discovered safety defects in the Hospital's oxygen and nitrous oxide lines that posed fire hazards and otherwise endangered patients' lives. Over a period of several months, Nelson re-peatedly advised Hospital officials of the safety defects and reported the defects to a Saudi Government commission as well. Hospital officials instructed Nelson to ignore the problems.

The Hospital's response to Nelson's reports changed, however, on September 27, 1984, when certain Hospital employees summoned him to the Hospital's security office where agents of the Saudi Government arrested him. The agents transported Nelson to a jail cell, in which they "shackled, tortured and bea[t]" him, and kept him four days without food. Although Nelson did not understand Arabic, Government agents forced him to sign a statement written in that language, the content of which he did not know; a Hospital employee who was supposed to act as Nelson's interpreter advised him to sign "anything" the agents gave him to avoid further beatings. Two days later, Government agents transferred Nelson to the Al Sijan Prison "to await trial on unknown charges."

At the Prison, Nelson was confined in an overcrowded cell area infested with rats, where he had to fight other prisoners for food and from which he was taken only once a week for fresh air and exercise. Although police interrogators repeatedly questioned him in Arabic, Nelson did not learn the nature of the charges, if any, against him. For several days, the Saudi Government failed to advise Nelson's family of his whereabouts, though a Saudi official eventually told Nelson's wife, respondent Vivian Nelson, that he could arrange for her husband's release if she provided sexual favors.

Although officials from the United States Embassy visited Nelson twice during his detention, they concluded that his allegations of Saudi mistreatment were "not credible" and made no protest to Saudi authorities. It was only at the personal request of a United States Senator that the Saudi Government released Nelson, 39 days after his arrest, on November 5, 1984. Seven days later, after failing to convince him to return to work at the Hospital, the Saudi Government allowed Nelson to leave the country.

. . .

II

The Foreign Sovereign Immunities Act "provides the sole basis for obtaining jurisdiction over a foreign state in the courts of this country." Under the Act, a foreign state is presumptively immune from the jurisdiction of United States courts; unless a specified exception applies, a federal court lacks subject-matter jurisdiction over a claim against a foreign state.

Only one such exception is said to apply here. The first clause of § 1605(a)(2) of the Act provides that a foreign state shall not be immune from the jurisdiction of United States courts in any case "in which the action is based upon a commercial activity carried on in the United States by the foreign state." The Act defines such activity as "commercial activity carried on by such state and having substantial contact with the United States," and provides that a commercial activity may be "either a regular course of commercial conduct or a particular commercial transaction or act," the "commercial character of [which] shall be determined by reference to" its "nature," rather than its "purpose."

There is no dispute here that Saudi Arabia, the Hospital, and Royspec all qualify as "foreign state[s]" within the meaning of the Act. 28 U.S.C. §§ 1603(a), (b) (term "foreign state" includes "an agency or instrumentality of a foreign state"). For there to be jurisdiction in this case, therefore, the Nelsons' action must be "based upon" some "commercial activity" by petitioners that had "substantial contact" with the United States within the meaning of the Act. Because we conclude that the suit is not based upon any commercial activity by petitioners, we need not reach the issue of substantial contact with the United States. . . .

[*The Court's footnote here concludes that "where a claim rests entirely upon activities sovereign in character, as here, jurisdiction will not exist . . . regardless of any connection the sovereign acts may have with commercial activity."*]

. . .

Petitioners' tortious conduct itself fails to qualify as "commercial activity" within the meaning of the Act, although the [FSI] Act is too "'obtuse'" to be of much help in reaching that conclusion. We have seen already that the Act defines "commercial activity" as "either a regular course of commercial conduct or a particular commercial transaction or act," and provides that "[t]he commercial character of an activity shall be determined by reference to the nature of the course of conduct or particular transaction or act, rather than by reference to its purpose." If this is a definition, . . . it "leaves the critical term 'commercial' largely undefined." We do not, however, have the option to throw up our hands. The

term has to be given some interpretation, and congressional diffidence necessarily results in judicial responsibility to determine what a "commercial activity" is for purposes of the Act.

Under the restrictive [codified in the FSIA], as opposed to the "absolute," theory of foreign sovereign immunity, a state is immune from the jurisdiction of foreign courts as to its sovereign or public acts (*jure imperii*), but not as to those that are private or commercial in character (*jure gestionis*). We explained [in an earlier case] . . . that a state engages in commercial activity under the restrictive theory where it exercises "'only those powers that can also be exercised by private citizens,'" as distinct from those "'powers peculiar to sovereigns.'" Put differently, a foreign state engages in commercial activity for purposes of the restrictive theory only where it acts "in the manner of a private player within" the market.

We emphasized . . . that whether a state acts "in the manner of" a private party is a question of behavior, not motivation: "[B]ecause the Act provides that the commercial character of an act is to be determined by reference to its 'nature' rather than its 'purpose,' [and] the question is not whether the foreign government is acting with a profit motive or instead with the aim of fulfilling uniquely sovereign objectives. Rather, the issue is whether the particular actions that the foreign state performs (whatever the motive behind them) are the type of actions by which a private party engages in 'trade and traffic or commerce.'"

. . .

[T]he intentional conduct alleged here (the Saudi Government's wrongful arrest, imprisonment, and torture of Nelson) could not qualify as commercial under the restrictive theory. The conduct boils down to abuse of the power of its police by the Saudi Government, and however monstrous such abuse undoubtedly may be, a foreign state's exercise of the power of its police has long been understood for purposes of the restrictive theory as peculiarly sovereign in nature. Exercise of the powers of police and penal officers is not the sort of action by which private parties can engage in commerce. "[S]uch acts as legislation, or the expulsion of an alien, or a denial of justice, cannot be performed by an individual acting in his own name. They can be performed only by the state acting as such."

. . .

III

The Nelsons' action is not "based upon a commercial activity" within the meaning of the first clause of § 1605(a)(2) of the Act, and the judgment of the Court of Appeals is accordingly reversed [thereby reinstating the trial court dismissal of this case without hearing the merits of the claim].

It is so ordered.

Justice WHITE, with whom Justice BLACK-MUN joins, concurring in the judgment.

. . .

The majority concludes that petitioners enjoy sovereign immunity because respondents' action is not "based upon a commercial activity." I disagree. I nonetheless concur in the judgment because in my view the commercial conduct upon which respondents base their complaint was not "carried on in the United States."

. . .

Justice KENNEDY, with whom Justice BLACK-MUN and Justice STEVENS join . . . concurring in part and dissenting in part.

I join all of the Court's opinion except . . . where, with almost no explanation, the Court rules that, like the intentional tort claim, the claims based on negligent failure to warn are outside the subject-matter jurisdiction of the federal courts.

. . .

Omission of important information during employee recruiting is commercial activity as we have described it. It seems plain that recruiting employees is an activity undertaken by private hospitals in the normal course of business. Locating and hiring employees implicates no power unique to the sovereign. In explaining the terms and conditions of employment, including the risks and rewards of a particular job, a governmental entity acts in "the manner of a private player within" the commercial marketplace.

. . .

Justice STEVENS, diessenting [from dismissal of this case].

. . .

In this case, as Justice WHITE has demonstrated [concurring in the result but arguing that the Saudi conduct *was* a commercial activity under the FSIA], petitioner's operation of the hospital and its employment practices and disciplinary procedures are "commercial activities" within the meaning of the statute, and respondent's claim that he was punished for acts performed in the course of his employment was unquestionably "based upon" those activities. Thus, the first statutory condition is satisfied; petitioner is not entitled to immunity from the claims asserted by respondent.

Unlike Justice WHITE, however, I am . . . convinced that petitioner's commercial activities . . . have sufficient contact with the United States to justify the exercise of federal jurisdiction. Petitioner Royspec maintains an office in Maryland and purchases hospital supplies and equipment in this country. For nearly two decades the Hospital's American agent has maintained an office in the United States and regularly engaged in the recruitment of personnel in this country. Respondent himself was recruited in the United States and entered into his employment contract with the hospital in the United States. Before traveling to Saudi Arabia to assume his position at the hospital, respondent attended an orientation program in Tennessee. The position for which respondent was recruited and ultimately hired was that of a monitoring systems manager, a troubleshooter, and, taking respondent's allegations as true, it was precisely respondent's performance of those responsibilities that led to the hospital's retaliatory actions against him.

. . .

If the same activities had been performed by a private business, I have no doubt jurisdiction would be upheld [and that this case would thus be able to proceed]. And that, of course, should be a touchstone of our inquiry; for as Justice WHITE explains, when a foreign nation sheds its uniquely sovereign status and seeks out the benefits of the private marketplace, it must, like any private party, bear the burdens and responsibilities imposed by that marketplace. I would therefore affirm the judgment of the Court of Appeals [which, in reversing the trial court, would have allowed this case to proceed].

■ NOTES & QUESTIONS

1. Some US courts have considered the following argument for piercing the shield of sovereign immunity: A head of government or an agency of the State acts in a way that is "outside" or "beyond the scope of" duties associated with the exemplary conduct of government. Thus, the protective shield of sovereign immunity is no longer available. The court is already aware that the alleged conduct is beyond the scope of allowable governmental conduct—as with torture that violates International Law (*see jus cogens* in § 1.4). The courts tend to distinguish between heads of government versus a State or State agency when judicially addressing whether sovereign immunity remains available to "the defendant" in US courts. *Compare* Hilao v. Estate of Marcos, 25 F.3d 1467 (9th Cir. 1994)—no sovereign immunity because *head of State's* acts of torture, execution, and disappearances are obviously beyond scope of presidential authority—*with* Seiderman de Blake v. Argentina, 965 F.2d 699, 718 (9th Cir. 1992), *cert. den'd*, 113 S.Ct. 1812 (1993)—alleged acts of torture perpetrated by *State* as responsible defendant for actions of military agent cannot be considered in US courts due to State's sovereign immunity.

2. *Should* the courts distinguish between a *State* defendant (shielded by sovereign immunity) and an *individual* defendant who was the head of State (no sovereign immunity)—for the same conduct of torture and murder?

CONSTITUTIONAL COURT JUDGMENT ON SOVEREIGN IMMUNITY WITH REGARD TO MEASURES OF CONSTRAINT

Constitutional Court of Italy, 1994
33 Int'l Legal Mat'ls 596 (1994)*

[Author's Note: In 1925, an executive decree effectively dismissed court proceedings by a private plaintiff against Greece and an agency of the Soviet Union. In 1926, this decree was codified in Italian Law No. 1263 (mentioned in the following opinion). Its first article provided that there could be no attachment or seizure of property, including seagoing vessels, belonging to a foreign State unless authorized by the Italian government's Minister of Justice. The Minister's common practice was first to determine whether a potential defendant State accorded Italy sovereign immunity from suit in its courts; and second, not to authorize such suits against other States on the basis of reciprocity of treatment.

Italy adopted a new constitution in 1948. Article 24 provides the rights of "judicial protection," "equality" of treatment, and "reasonableness" to Italian citizens. The above Italian Law No. 1263 thus came under increased scrutiny in the Italian courts, due to its apparent conflict with the Italian Constitution. It was ultimately ruled unconstitutional by this court under the following facts. Two Italian companies (Condor & Filvem) had sold goods to some private Nigerian companies. The Nigerian government later suspended all payments of its foreign debts. This precluded the Nigerian companies from paying their debts to the private Italian companies.

The Italian plaintiffs filed suit in the Court of Pisa, Italy. They obtained the attachment of a vessel (seizure for potential sale if debt not paid) belonging to a Nigerian State agency. In 1987, a subsequent ministerial decree declared the lower court's attachment of the vessel ineffective, thus denying the plaintiffs' right to sell the vessel in Italy in payment of the debts. Notwithstanding Law No. 1263, the plaintiffs lodged an action against this ministerial decree in regional administrative tribunal in Lazio, Italy. In 1991, that tribunal submitted the question of whether the Minister's decree violated the Italian Constitution to the Italian Constitutional Court at its seat in Rome.]

[Opinion.]

The Facts

1. . . . . According to the restructuring plan adopted by the Nigerian Government with respect to debts incurred up to December 31, 1983, the Nigerian Central Bank issued to the [plaintiff] Italian companies formal promises of payment backed by a guarantee from the Nigerian Government. As these promises have not been honored, the creditors have

---

*Reprinted with permission of International Legal Materials. © American Society of International Law.

obtained from the President of the Court of Pisa the prejudgment attachment of a ship moored in Italy, which belongs to the National Shipping Company of Nigeria. The Court of Pisa then declared that such prejudgment attachment is ineffective as a result of the aforesaid [Italian] ministerial decree. After declaring that . . . the condition of reciprocity [between Italy and Nigeria] existed, this ministerial decree refused the authorization to execute the prejudgment attachment and the continuation of the procedure [i.e., the ability to "execute" the attachment order by selling the vessel to repay the Italian plaintiffs]. . . .

According to the [lower administrative] Tribunal that raised the issue before the present [Constitutional Court in Rome], the rule [ministerial decree] in question is in breach of:

(a) Article . . . 24 of the Constitution, because it restricts the individual right of defense by precluding satisfaction of a credit through measures of execution (on the ground that the public interest, whose right of protection is vested in the State, must be safeguarded), without providing for any compensation;

. . .

(c) again, in a different respect, Article 24 of the Constitution, because the right of defense is not being restricted on the basis of predetermined [ministerially defined] criteria that would apply to all citizens alike, but on the basis of an evaluation susceptible to discriminate according to elements different from the condition of each individual subject and concerning the international relations of the State; and

(d) finally, Article 41 of the Constitution, because the restriction on the right of defense before a court in commercial relations is prejudicial to free economic initiative [of the people of Italy], as it precludes the possibility for enterprises to obtain that foreign States fulfil the obligations that they have undertaken in the exercise of activities as private persons.

. . .

4. The President of the Council of Ministers, represented by the [Italian] State attorney, intervened in the proceedings. . . .

According to the State attorney [of Italy on behalf of the Nigerian Government], the State of Nigeria has nothing to do with the obligations undertaken by the Nigerian private parties, co-contractors of [with] the Italian companies. It has never assumed the role of a "private contracting party," nor has it ever entered into a private relationship with the aforesaid companies. . . . Since the Italian State [allegedly] has no jurisdiction over disputes concerning the aforesaid measure, the attachment requested by the companies in question can never be confirmed by a title for execution against the State of Nigeria.

. . .

The Law

1. The Regional Administrative Tribunal of Lazio raises doubts on the validity . . . of the only . . . article of the royal executive order No. 1621 of August 30, 1925, transformed into the law No. 1263 of July 15, 1926. According to this article, "there shall be no attachment, seizure or, in general, measures of execution against the movable or immovable property, vessels, funds, securities and any other assets belonging to a foreign State, without the authorization of the Minister of Justice," provided that the [foreign] State in question accords reciprocity, to be declared by ministerial decree.

. . . [T]here was a breach of the principles of equality and reasonableness with respect to the principle of judicial protection of rights. This argument leads coherently to affirm the absolute invalidity of the provision in question for conflict with the Constitution.

. . . [T]he promises of payment which, pursuant to the [Nigerian Government's] restructuring plan, have been issued by the Central Bank of Nigeria and the co-related guarantees issued by the Nigerian government are outside such domain [sovereign immunity]. These are private acts concluded *jure gestionis* [private acts] and are therefore subject to Italian jurisdiction.

. . .

3. The issue raised before the present Court is well founded.

. . . Not long ago, the restrictive nature of immunity from jurisdiction was different, according to the prevailing view among States, from the absolute character (at least in principle) of immunity from execution. Over the last thirty years, an opposite trend has progressively emerged, especially in European countries. As a result of it, today one cannot affirm any more the existence of an international customary rule that would absolutely forbid coercive measures [i.e., attachment or seizure] against the property of foreign States.

. . .

Interpreted in this way, restrictive (or functional) immunity . . . has been affirmed, for example, by [court opinions from France, Germany, Switzerland, The Netherlands, United Kingdom, Canada, South Africa, Pakistan, Singapore, and Australia].

. . .

The foreign policy interest of the Government [where the case is filed] to preserve good international relations and to preclude that such relations be prejudiced by coercive measures adopted in the Italian territory against the property of a foreign State, . . . could justify restrictions of the rule in question within a context of international law. . . . In the present context, in which the principle of restrictive immunity has been widely accepted, it is improbable that many States would react if their property in Italy were subject to coercive measures. They could not object, by appealing to legal considerations, if their property received in the Italian territory the same treatment that, in similar cases, Italian property would receive in their territories.

In addition, the practical application of the norm in question . . . shows that, instead of producing a well grounded and rigorous balance of interests under the circumstances of each individual case, it has ended up virtually reintroducing absolute immunity. At least since 1953, when the first decree certifying the existence of reciprocity (regarding Yugoslavia) was issued and published in the Official Gazette, the requests for authorization have almost invariably been rejected. The summary grounds given in support of the decrees of reciprocity often hide the intent to prohibit provisional measures or

execution for mere reasons of courtesy or of "quiet life." These reasons are completely out of proportion with the damage inflicted on the private individual concerned, the more so when the case in question relates to business credits, the timely satisfaction of which affects the financial stability of the company, or labor credits, which deserve special protection in consideration of their function of providing the worker with his or her means of subsistence.

6. After all, the executive power will not be deprived of the necessary means to avoid the application of coercive measures against the property of a foreign State . . . whenever it would regard such measures . . . as susceptible to provoke reactions that would prejudice the national interest.

In consideration of this eventuality, it will be possible, for example, that the Italian State intervene in a procedure for execution and offer to pay the creditor as a third party, as provided in Article 1180 of the Civil Code. Likewise, in a procedure for provisional measures, the Italian State may offer to the applicant . . . a guarantee for the payment of the debt, the existence of which, as due by the foreign State, will be verified by means of an ordinary procedure.

. . .

FOR THESE REASONS THE CONSTITUTIONAL COURT declares that the . . . article comprised in the royal executive order . . . [of] 1925 ("Measures of execution against the property of foreign States in the Kingdom of Italy"), transformed into the law . . . of July 15, 1926, is invalid under the Constitution in so far as it makes it necessary to obtain the authorization of the Minister of Justice for measures of protection or execution against the property belonging to a foreign State other than that which, pursuant to the generally recognized rules of international law, cannot be subject to coercive measures.

■ NOTES & QUESTIONS

1. The Italian Constitutional Court addressed a fading distinction in the law of sovereign immunity: Even where the State of filing relied on the "restrictive" theory, the defendant State could usually evade a civil suit attachment of its property by merely claiming that it was being used for a public

governmental purpose. The executive branch of State A—whose courts might otherwise allow an attachment of the property—would then consider whether A's international interests might preclude the State A court from permitting the sale of State B's property found in State A. In practice, "absolute" immunity had effectively crept back into Italy's law of "restrictive" immunity whenever the defendant State claimed a public purpose for the end use of the seized property. The Constitutional Court thus summarized the interim change in attitude that limited the availability of this argument, since arbitrary and undefined standards were applied merely because the property owner was a foreign State—thus denying the constitutionally required equality of treatment and reasonableness to Italian plaintiffs in their courts.

2. Were Italy's interests best served under prior law—when a government minister had to approve all attachments of foreign government-owned property—or alternatively, under current law whereby Italian judges are free to authorize such attachments on a case-by-case basis (with possible intervention into the suit by the Italian government on behalf of a foreign government)?

■ SUMMARY

1. States have rights and duties arising under International Law, often referred to as arising "on the *international* plane." States are thus comparable to persons who have rights and obligations under national law. Terms like "State" and "nation" have legally distinct meanings, although they are often used interchangeably.

2. A State possesses international personality, or capacity, if it has (a) a permanent population; (b) a defined territory; (c) a government; and (d) the capacity to enter into relations with other States.

3. The global community of nations has nearly quadrupled in size since 1945. The current majority is composed of many new States with distinctly different cultures and values—in comparison to the original membership. International Law, developed mostly by State practice, has thus been altered by this influx of new States with diverse perspectives.

4. This change in the infrastructure of the international legal system was triggered by the decolonization movement of the 1960s. Most existing States were once colonial territories of the original members of the UN.

5. Succession results from one State taking over another State's territory. Secession refers to the separation of a State into two or more States. Self-determination is the right of States and people within a State to choose self-governance or some related form of autonomy.

6. Unlike States, new *governments* may not claim a "clean slate" regarding preexisting treaties and international obligations.

7. Recognition may be granted individually by one State or collectively by a group of States. Entities that may be recognized are new States, new governments, and belligerencies.

8. Recognition is not *required* under International Law. States are generally free to exercise their discretion about whether or not to grant recognition. While the decision to recognize is a political one, it has certain legal consequences including access to the courts and assets located in the recognizing State.

9. Recognition is considered an element of statehood under the so-called *constitutive* theory of recognition. The *declarative* theory applied by most States, however, merely declares the recognizing State's statement of *de jure* status regarding the recognized State (which has already attained statehood on a *de facto* basis).

10. As a result of statehood, a State is responsible for its acts or omissions that cause damage to another State. While attempts to codify this facet of International Law have not been completed, there is no doubt about the general proposition that a State must make reparations to another State harmed by its wrongful conduct.

11. It is unsettled whether fault or negligence is required to trigger State responsibility. Most commentators assert that there is automatic liability for reparations, whether or not the responsible State realizes that it has harmed another State.

12. States, heads of State, and State agencies are generally immune from being sued in the courts of another State. This defense to a lawsuit is referred to as sovereign immunity.

13. There are two theories of sovereign immunity: "absolute" and "restrictive." The absolute theory provides total immunity from suit in other States regardless of the nature or purpose of the sovereign's acts. The restrictive theory withholds immunity for conduct that places the foreign sovereign on equal footing with private actors in the State where the suit is filed.

14. Under the US Foreign Sovereign Immunities Act (FSIA), Congress intended that the courts examine the nature of the specific act—rather than the foreign sovereign's underlying purpose for doing the

act. If the act can be done by a private individual, there is no immunity. If the act is sovereign in nature, immunity is granted to preclude suit when the foreign sovereign's acts are of a sufficiently political or sovereign character.

■ PROBLEMS

Problem 2.1 (*§ 2.1 after Jessup excerpt On Condition of Statehood*): The Jessup excerpt presents the argument in favor of Israel's condition of statehood. This problem deals with the related question of *Palestinian* statehood. The Palestine Liberation Organization (PLO) was created in 1964 to "liberate" Palestine from Israeli control. Its members include people who are citizens of various Arab States. They have lived together since ancient times, long before the Western nation-state model was incorporated into International Law.

In 1919, the Palestinian people were provisionally recognized as an independent State by the League of Nations, as well as in the 1922 Mandate for Palestine addressed to Great Britain. The UN's 1947 partition plan would have created a Palestinian State, but for the outbreak of war between Arab States and the new State of Israel. The drive for a Palestinian State gained momentum in the 1970s. The creation of the State of Palestine has international support only insofar as it would occupy the *additional* territories conquered by Israel in various Middle East wars in the 1960s and 1970s—but not that portion of "Palestine" that became the independent State of Israel in 1948. The PLO historically denied Israel's right to exist in what it considered as "Palestine," dating from biblical times. Palestinians thus characterize the UN partition plan of 1947 as a criminal act that denied them rights they believed were guaranteed to them by the 1919 recognition and 1922 League Mandate to Britain.

Led by Yasir Arafat, the PLO initially insisted that a Palestinian State should *replace* Israel because the Jewish state had no right to exist in its current location. The PLO later softened its position by recognizing Israel's right to exist (although some of its more militant members—Hamas—still disagree) and that the PLO should be given territory taken by Israel during various Middle East conflicts after the 1947 UN partition plan (UN Gen. Ass. Res. 181(II)). Israel's borders have not been fixed by international agreement with its neighbors. The PLO thus argues that Palestine's borders are not yet established.

In 1974, the PLO was invited to participate in the UN General Assembly's debate on the Palestine question, and in an effort to secure peace in the Middle East. [*See* G.A. Res. 3210, 29 UN GAOR Supp. (No. 108) at 3, UN Doc. A/RES/3210(XXIX) (1974), and G.A. Res. 3375, 30 UN GAOR Supp. (No. 27) at 3, UN Doc. A/RES/3375(XXX) (1975).] The PLO was then officially recognized by Austria, India, and the Soviet Union. It was also accorded nonvoting "observer" status in the UN General Assembly. Participation in the UN was previously limited to traditional States and less controversial nongovernmental organizations (such as the International Red Cross).

In 1987, the US Congress enacted legislation entitled the Anti-Terrorism Act. It was designed to close the PLO's UN Observer Mission in New York City. The basis for the desired closure was that the PLO's alleged terrorist activities could flow into the US through the PLO's observer mission at the UN. The US government subsequently filed a lawsuit in a US court under the antiterrorist law, seeking to close the mission.

The PLO responded from Algiers by proclaiming the existence of the new and independent "State of Palestine." This 1988 declaration includes the assertions that "the people of Palestine fashioned its national identity" and "the Palestinian people has not ceased its valiant defence of its homeland . . . [of Palestine, which] was subjected to a new kind of foreign occupation" when Israel took over. [*See* Palestine National Council Political Communiqué and Declaration of Independence, reprinted in 27 Int'l Legal Mat'ls 1660, 1668 (1988). It contains much of the history surrounding this conflict.] This Palestinian declaration of statehood was immediately recognized by the Soviet Union. As of 1988, then, the PLO claimed that the State of Palestine finally achieved *de facto* if not *de jure* existence as a State.

In 1989, the International Court of Justice ruled against the US on its unilateral attempt to close the PLO mission at the UN headquarters in New York City. The Reagan administration unsuccessfully argued that the antiterrorist legislation required closure "irrespective of any international legal obligations that the United States may have. . . ." The US noted that since the PLO was *not* a State, the space for its observer mission had been provided only as a mere courtesy—because the US was the host government for the UN's New York facilities. One basis for countering the US position materialized in mid-1988. Jordan's King Hussein severed all forms of legal and administrative ties between Jordan and the West Bank—where Jewish settlers were introduced by Israel, and which the PLO claims to be its territory.

The UN General Assembly adopted Resolution 43/177 in December 1988, whereby it recognized the new State of Palestine and accorded it observer-*state* status, thus augmenting the mere "observer" status the PLO achieved years before.

As of 1990, 114 States had recognized the newly proclaimed State of Palestine, some twenty States more than the 93 that recognized Israel.

Assume that the PLO is applying to the UN for full State membership. Did the PLO already satisfy any or all of the four traditional elements of statehood *before* the 1993–1994 Palestinian autonomy agreements? *After* the autonomy agreements?

Problem 2.2 (*§ 2.3 after Succession materials*): Assume that State A has just annexed the territory of State B. State A thus takes over State B's territory and all of B's State-owned property. State B owes a large war reparations debt to State C. State C and State A have always had quite hostile relations. State A claims that it is entitled to a "clean slate," whereby International Law would not require A to assume B's war debts. What arguments can be made for and against B's clean-slate contention? Does it matter whether B's war debt was treaty-based or merely imposed by State C as the victor after winning the war?

Problem 2.3 (*end of § 2.3*): Members of the Palestine Liberation Organization (PLO) inhabit various countries in the Middle East. Although Israel and the PLO began to implement an autonomy agreement as to Gaza and the City of Jericho in 1994, the UN partition plan of 1947 "created" a Palestinian State—much of which devolved to other States as a result of ensuing wars between Arab States and Israel. Two students (or groups) will debate the following questions: are Palestinians within the States of Israel, Jordan, Lebanon, and Syria entitled to: (1) secede; (2) succession; (3) self-determination?

Problem 2.4 (*end of § 2.3*): Europe's gypsies apparently began their westward exodus from India in the tenth century. They have been a migratory people with no territory, political clout, or formal organization. Their itinerant wandering is both the hallmark of their culture and their greatest conflict with structured societies. It is thus difficult to educate, tax, and count them in population census. The Nazis slaughtered numerous gypsies during World War II in a genocidal campaign to achieve racial purity. They have been driven from their homes by Bosnian Serbs and Croat military forces. Thousands thus fled to Italy and Germany in the 1990s, only to face attack by neo-Nazis and expulsion under strict immigration laws. Perhaps one million Spanish gypsies now roam throughout Spain and camp in makeshift villages, literally on the edge of civilization, outside of towns and on the fringes of Spain's larger cities.

Gypsies gathered in Seville, Spain in May 1994 for the first Gypsie Congress. This Congress was conducted under the auspices of the European Commission, the executive agency of the European Union (an organization discussed in Chapter 3). The Commission is trying to help Gypsies help themselves in the current violence against them in Europe's waves of ethnic violence that resurfaced after the demise of the Cold War.

Are Spain's gypsies entitled to self-determination? If so, how would that right be implemented?

Problem 2.5 (*end of § 2.4*): Under UN Security Council Resolution 777, the State of "Yugoslavia" ceased to exist. In 1992, the former Yugoslavia split into what are currently five States—Bosnia-Herzegovina, Croatia, Macedonia, Slovenia, and the so-called rump-State of Yugoslavia (consisting of Serbia and Montenegro).

Selection of the name "Republic of Macedonia" created a problem for this former Yugoslav territory, its neighbor Greece, and the European Union—or EU, consisting of twelve States including Greece. Greece was furious about the chosen name, due to Greece's concern about its own province named Macedonia. It was in this particular province that Alexander the Great resided during his famous conquests during the Roman era. The name thus generates emotional depths among the Greeks. Greece's northern province of Macedonia and the Republic of Macedonia share a common international border of approximately 300 kilometers. Greece fears that the Republic of Macedonia, by selecting that particular name, has territorial aspirations for taking over the Greek province of Macedonia. Greece thus refers to this area as "Skopje," the name of its capital city. The Secretary-

General suggested that Macedonia change its name to "New" Macedonia.

The EU did not immediately recognize Macedonia, a territory desperately seeking recognition from other States. The EU had recognized Slovenia and Croatia approximately six months after their votes of independence from the former Yugoslavia. Regarding Macedonia, however, the EU leadership expressed that "there are still important matters to be addressed before a similar step by the Community and its member States will be taken." This was a smokescreen designed to temporarily delay recognition due to Greece's continuing objections to the recognition of Macedonia by member States of the EU. The EU then promulgated its Recognition Guidelines (*see* text § 2.4) as the device for structuring mutually agreed upon succession, secession, and self-determination of the territories of the former Yugoslavia. All applicants for recognition must now comply with the EU requirements, including approval of the involvement of the UN Secretary-General, the Security Council, and the EU Conference on Yugoslavia for resolving conflicts.

The EU did not expressly recognize Macedonia. Instead, it determined that its member States "were willing to recognize that State as a sovereign and independent State . . . and under a name that can be accepted by all parties concerned [that is, Greece] . . . [while] member States look forward to establishing with the authorities in Skopje [Macedonia's capital] a fruitful cooperative relationship."

The US did not announce its intent to recognize Macedonia until February 1994, after six members of the European Union first recognized Macedonia as a State. The US had previously sent troops to "Macedonia" to help control the spread of the Yugoslavian conflict into other States, including Greece.

Questions: (1) Is Macedonia a recognized State? (2) What would Macedonia have to do in order to satisfy EU Guidelines for Recognition? (3) Did the EU member States essentially recognize Macedonia without recognizing its name? (4) *Should* a territory such as Macedonia be recognized by other States outside of the EU?

Problem 2.6 (§ *2.6 after* Nelson *case*): Assume that after the Supreme Court's *Nelson* opinion, the US senator who went to the aid of the Nelsons while the husband was confined in Saudi Arabia decides to help future litigants in another way. Senator Hawk proposes the following legislation to Congress, as an amendment to the 1976 Foreign Sovereign Immunities Act:

> Be it hereby enacted that, from this day forward, all courts in the United States will—in doubtful cases involving the "commercial nature of the act" or conduct complained of—grant sovereign immunity to democratic sovereigns, and deny it by proceeding with cases against authoritarian sovereigns.

Two students will debate the propriety of this proposed legislation, specifically addressing whether Congress should thereby give democratic regimes greater sovereign immunity that authoritarian regimes.

■ BIBLIOGRAPHY

§ 2.1 Legal Personality of the State:

J. Crawford, *The Creation of States in International Law* (Oxford, Eng.: Oxford Univ. Press, 1979)

R. Lapidoth & M. Hirsch (ed.), *The Arab-Israeli Conflict and its Resolution: Selected Documents* (Dordrecht, Neth.; Boston: Martinus Nijhoff, 1992)

Murswiek, *The Issue of a Right of Secession—Reconsidered,* in C. Tomuschat (ed.), *Modern Law of Self-Determination* 21 (Dordrecht, Neth.; Boston: Martinus Nijhoff, 1993)

A. Osiander, *The States System of Europe, 1640–1990: Peacemaking and the Conditions of International Stability* (Oxford, Eng.: Oxford Univ. Press, 1994)

§ 2.2 Changing Infrastructure:

Abi-Saab, *The Newly Independent States and the Rules of International Law,* 8 Howard Law Journal 95 (1962)

R. Anand, *Confrontation or Cooperation?: International Law and the Developing Countries* (New Delhi: Banyan, 1986)

A. Bozeman, *The Future of Law in a Multicultural World* (Princeton: Princeton Univ. Press, 1971)

A. Carty, *The Decay of International Law?: A Reappraisal of the Limits of Legal Imagination in International Affairs* (Dover, NH: Manchester Univ. Press, 1986)

W. Friedmann, *The Changing Structure of International Law* (New York: Columbia Univ. Press, 1964)

K. Ginther & W. Benedek (ed.), *New Perspectives and Conceptions of International Law: An Afro-European Dialogue* (Vienna: Springer-Verlag, 1983)

McWhinney, *The "New" Countries and the "New" International Law: The United Nations' Special Conference on Friendly Relations and Co-operation Among States,* 60 American Journal of International Law 1 (1966)

S. Sinha, *Treatment of Asian and African Peoples under International Law during the Past Four Centuries*, ch. 1, in *New Nations and the Law of Nations* 11 (Leiden, Neth.: A.W. Sijthoff, 1967)

§ 2.3 Changes in State Status:

Bernanzez, *Succession of States*, ch. 18, in M. Bedjaoui (ed.), *International Law: Achievements and Prospects* 381 (Dordrecht, Neth.; Boston: Martinus Nijhoff, 1991)

Degan, *Equity in Matters of State Succession*, ch. 14, in R. Macdonald, *Essays in Honour of Wang Tieya* 201 (Dordrecht, Neth.; Boston: Martinus Nijhoff, 1994)

Eide, *In Search of Constructive Alternatives to Secession*, in C. Tomuschat, *Modern Law of Self-Determination* 139 (Dordrecht, Neth.; Boston: Martinus Nijhoff, 1993)

Israel-Palestine Liberation Organization, *Agreement on the Gaza Strip and the Jericho Area*, 33 *International Legal Materials* 622 (1994)

R. Lapidoth & M. Hirsch (ed.), *The Arab-Israeli Conflict and Its Resolution: Selected Documents* (Dordrecht, Neth.; Boston: Martinus Nijhoff, 1992)

Nanda, *Self-Determination in International Law*, 66 *American Journal of International Law* 321 (1972)

S. Trifunovska (ed.), *Yugoslavia Through Documents from its Creation to its Dissolution* (Dordrecht, Neth.; Boston: Martinus Nijhoff, 1994)

N. Wallace-Bruce, *Claims to Statehood in International Law* (New York: Carlton Press, 1994)

I. Zartman (ed.), *Collapsed States: The Disintegration and Restoration of Legitimate Authority* (Boulder, CO: Lynne Reinner, 1994)

§ 2.4 Recognition:

Antonowicz, *On the Nature of Recognition of States in International Law*, 8 *Polish Yearbook of International Law* 217 (1976)

Chinkin, *The Law and Ethics of Recognition: Cambodia and Timor*, ch. 10, in P. Keal, *Ethics and Foreign Policy* 190 (St. Leonards, Australia: Allen & Unwin, 1992)

Kato, *Recognition in International Law: Some Thoughts on Traditional Theory, Attitudes of and Practice by African States*, 19 *Indian Journal of International Law* 299 (1970)

G. Knight & H. Chiu, *The Law of the War and Neutrality in Warfare at Sea*, ch. XV, in *The International Law of the Sea: Cases, Documents, and Readings* (London: Elsevier, 1991)

Ruda, *Recognition of States and Governments*, ch. 21 in M. Bedjaoui (ed.), *International Law: Achievements and Prospects* 449 (Dordrecht, Neth.; Boston: Martinus Nijhoff, 1991)

§ 2.5 State Responsibility:

W. Butler, *Control over Compliance with International Law* (Dordrecht, Neth.; Boston: Martinus Nijhoff, 1991)

State Responsibility, ch. 8, in R. Wallace, *International Law: A Student Introduction* 166 (2nd ed. London: Street & Maxwell, 1992)

Thesaurus Acroasium: Responsibility of States (Thessaloniki, Greece: Inst. Int'l Public Law & Int'l Relations, 1993)

J. Weiler, A. Cassese & M. Spinedi (ed.), *International Crimes of State: A Critical Analysis of the ILC's Draft Article 19 on State Responsibility* (Berlin: De Gruyter, 1989)

§ 2.6 Sovereign Immunity:

J. Dellapenna, *Suing Foreign Governments and Their Corporations* (Wash., DC: Bureau Nat'l Aff., 1988)

Donoghue, *Taking the "Sovereign" Out of the Foreign Sovereign Immunities Act: A Functional Approach to the Commercial Activity Exception*, 17 *Yale J. Int'l Law* 489 (1992)

C. Jenks, *International Immunities* (New York: Oceana, 1961)

OAS Inter-American Draft Convention on Jurisdictional Immunity of States, 22 *International Legal Materials* 292 (1983)

Sucharitkul, *Immunity of States*, ch. 16, in M. Bedjaoui (ed.), *International Law: Achievements and Prospects* 327 (Dordrecht, Neth.; Boston: Martinus Nijhoff, 1991)

US Foreign Sovereign Immunities Act of 1976, 15 *International Legal Materials* 1388 (1976)

■ ENDNOTES

1. B. Boutros-Ghali, *An Agenda for Peace: Preventative Diplomacy, Peacemaking and Peace-keeping* 9 (New York: UN, 1992).

2. W. Friedmann, *The Changing Structure of International Law* 214 (New York: Columbia Univ. Press, 1964).

3. *See* Rice, *Nation v. State—Judgment for Nation*, 44 *Amer. J. Int'l L.* 162 (1950); Brandon, *State v. Nation: Fresh Evidence Admitted*, 44 *Amer. J. Int'l L.* 577 (1950).

4. State: Article 1, 165 L.O.N. Treaty Series 19, 49 U.S. Stat. 3097. **Nation:** B. Driessen, *A Concept of Nation in International Law* 13 (The Hague, Neth.: T.M.C. Asser Inst., 1992) [hereinafter *Driessen*]. **Community:** Greco-Bulgarian Communities Case, 1930 P.C.I.J. Rep., ser. B, No. 17, p.33. **People:** Drusen, p.17. **Government:** J. Fox, *Dictionary of International & Comparative Law* 101 (New York: Oceana, 1992). **Sovereign:** J. Falk & J. Camilleri, *The End of Sovereignty?: The Politics of a Shrinking and Fragmenting World* 11 (Hants, Eng.: Edward Elgar Pub., 1992).

5. 165 L.O.N. Treaty Series 19, 49 U.S. Stat. 3097.

6. Gunter, *What Happened to the United Nations Ministate Problem?*, 71 *Amer. J. Int'l L.* 110 (1977) (no minimum population); Case Concerning Acquisition of Polish Nationality (Germany v. Poland), 1923 P.C.I.J., ser. B, No. 7, p.18 (Judgment of Sept. 15, 1923) (express grant not required).

7. **Treaties:** US Const., Art. I, § 10(1). **Duties:** Art. 1, § 10(2).

8. Verzijl, *Western European Influence on the Foundations of International Law*, 1 *Int'l Relations* 137 (1955).

9. E. Osmanczyk, *Encyclopedia of the United Nations and International Agreements* 95 (2nd ed. London: Taylor & Francis, 1990).

10. *See, e.g.*, Sastri, *International Law and Relations in Ancient India*, 1 *Indian Yearbk. Int'l Affairs* 97 (1952).

11. Alexandrowicz, *Mogul Sovereignty and the Law of Nations,* 4 *Indian Yearbk. Int'l Affairs* 317, 318 (1955).

12. **Colonial aggression basis for self-defense:** Anand, *Attitude of the Asian-African States toward Certain Problems of International Law*, 15 *Int'l & Comp. Law Q.* 55, 63–66 (1966). **"Armed" attack requirement:** UN Charter, Art. 51.

13. The declaration is reprinted in 13 *Int'l Legal Mat'ls* 715 (1974). The G-77 charter is reprinted in 14 *Int'l Legal Mat'ls* 251 (1975).

14. **1978 treaty:** UN Doc. A/Conf. 80/31. **1983 treaty:** UN Doc. A/Conf. 117/14 (neither yet in force).

15. *See* Treaty on the Final Settlement with Respect to Germany, 29 *Int'l Legal Mat'ls* 1186, 1188 (1990) ("united Germany shall comprise the territory of the [FRG, GDR,] . . . and the whole of Berlin").

16. *See* R. Jennings & A. Watts, 1 *Oppenheim's International Law* (Part I) §§ 60–70 (9th ed. Essex, Eng.: Longman, 1993) [hereinafter *Oppenheim treatise*].

17. **Colombia:** J. Moore, 5 *Digest of International Law* 341 (Wash.,
DC: US Gov't Printing Off., 1906). **Texas:** J. Moore, 3 *History and Digest of the International Arbitrations to Which the United States has been a Party* 3223 (Wash., DC: US Gov't Print. Off., 1898).

18. *Oppenheim treatise* (Part I), § 62, 211–13 (cited in note 16).

19. Regarding Dues for Reply Coupons Issued in Croatia, 23 *Int'l L. Rep.* 591 (1956).

20. See *1983 treaty*, Article 9 on property & Article 36 on debts (cited in note 14).

21. *Oppenheim treatise* (Part I), § 62, 218–19 (cited in note 16).

22. A. Buchanan, *Secession: The Morality of Political Divorce from Fort Sumter to Lithuania and Quebec* 2 (Boulder, CO: Westview Press, 1991).

23. Schachter, *The Development of International Law Through the Legal Opinions of the United Nations Secretariat*, XXV *British Yearbk. Int'l L.* 91, 107 (1948).

24. Namibia (South West Africa) Case, 1971 I.C.J. Rep. 55.

25. Laing, *The Norm of Self-Determination, 1941– 1991*, 22 *Calif. W. Int'l L.J.* 209 (1992).

26. **Res. 1514:** Declaration on the Granting of Independence to Colonial Countries and Peoples, UN G.A.O.R. 15th Sess., Supp. No. 16 (A/4884). **CPR Covenant:** 999 U.N.T.S. 171. **ESC Covenant:** 999 U.N.T.S. 3. **Reservations:** *see, e.g.*, United Kingdom, UN G.A.O.R. 21st Sess., Third Comm., 1496th Mtg. 16 Dec. 1966, p.10–11. **1970 Declaration:** UN G.A.O.R. 25th Sess., Supp. No. 8, p.121 (A/8028).

27. P. Chandra, *International Law* 28 (New Delhi: Vikas, 1985) (chaotic); D. O'Connell, *International Law* 127 (2nd ed. New York: Oceana, 1970) (confusing); J. Dugard, *Recognition and the United Nations* 28 (Cambridge, Eng.: Grotius, 1987) (controversial) [hereinafter *Recognition*].

28. Ruda, *Recognition of States and Governments*, ch. 21, in M. Bedjaoui (ed.), *International Law: Achievements and Prospects* 450 (Dordrecht, Neth.; Boston: Martinus Nijhoff, 1991).

29. McDowell, *Contemporary Practice of the United States Relating to International Law*, 71 *Amer. J. Int'l L.* 337 (1977) (recognition by other States); C. Fenwick, *International Law* 157–59 (4th ed. New York: Appleton-Century-Crofts, 1965) (ethnocentric motives); *see* The Helena, 4 Ch. Rob. 3 (1801) (English case on pirate treaties), reprinted in W. Bishop, *International Law, Cases and Materials* 301 (3rd ed. Boston: Little, Brown & Co., 1971); G. Von Glahn, *Law Among Nations* 87–88 (6th ed. New York: Macmillan, 1992) (commercial/military motives).

30. Two major treatises sparked this post-war debate about the nature of recognition and are still the classics. Compare H. Lauterpact, *Recognition in International Law* 63 (Cambridge, Eng.: Cambridge Univ. Press, 1947)— recognition is not primarily a manifestation of national policy but the fulfillment of an international duty—*with* T. Chen, *The International Law of Recognition* 61 (Green ed. London: Stevens, 1951)—recognition is merely declarative of the existing fact of statehood.

31. Genaro Estrada's statement is reprinted in 25 *Amer. J. Int'l L. Supp.* 203 (1931). A provocative response was published in Jessup, *The Estrada Doctrine*, 25 *Amer. J. Int'l Law* 719 (1930).

32. **EU Guidelines:** reprinted in 31 *Int'l Legal Mat'ls* 1485 (1992) [hereinafter *Guidelines*]. OAS Haiti resolution: 86 *Amer. J. Int'l L.* 667 (1992). **Scholars:** Franck, *The Emerging Right to Democratic Governance*, 86 *Amer. J. Int'l L.* 46 (1992).

33. *See* Brown, *The Legal Effects of Recognition*, 44 *Amer. J. Int'l L.* 617 (1950); Comment, *Effects in Private Litigation of Failure to Recognize New Foreign Governments*, 19 *Univ. Chicago L. Rev.* 73 (1951).

34. The Three Friends, 166 U.S. 1, 63, 17 S.Ct. 495, 502, 41 L.Ed. 897 (1897).

35. *Unilateral and Third Party Claims: Neutrality*, Section 13.4, in C. Chinkin, *Third Parties in International Law* 299 (Oxford, Eng.: Clarendon Press, 1993).

36. *See* English translation in *Collective Recognition and Non-Recognition Under the League of Nations*, ch. 3, in *Recognition* 28 (cited in note 27).

37. Memorandum on the Legal Aspects of the Problem of Representation in the United Nations, UN Doc. S/1466, Mar. 9, 1950.

38. *See Guidelines* note 32 above.

39. *See 2 Foreign Pol. Bulletin* 39, 42 (Nov./Dec. 1991) (testimony of Deputy Ass't of Dep't of State).

40. Whether damage is actually required is subject to some question. *See* Tanzi, *Is Damage a Distinct Condition for the Existence of an Internationally Wrongful Act?*, in M. Spinedi & B. Simma (ed.), *United Nations Codification of State Responsibility* (New York: Oceana, 1987).

41. Case Concerning the Factory at Chorzow, P.C.I.J. ser. A, No. 17, p.29 (1928).

42. Rainbow Warrior Arbitration, 82 Int'l L. Rep. 499, 551 (1991). *See* Secretary-General's opinion contained in 81 *Amer. J. Int'l L.* 325 (1987).

43. 1949 I.C.J. Rep. 4, 18.

44. *State Responsibility*, ch. 13, in M. Shaw, *International Law* 485–87 (3rd ed. Cambridge, Eng.: Grotius, 1991).

45. The various provisions, their genesis, and their development are discussed in S. Rosenne, *The International Law Commission's Draft Articles on State Responsibility* (Dordrecht, Neth.; Boston: Martinus Nijhoff, 1991).

46. Schooner Exchange v. M'Faddon, 11 U.S. (7 Cranch) 116, 3 L.Ed. 287 (1812).

47. 1 Queen's Bench 149 (1893), reported in All Eng. Rep. 1019 (1963).

48. Henkin, *The Invasion of Panama Under International Law: A Gross Violation*, 29 *Columbia J. Transnat'l L.* 293 (1991).

49. I. Brownlie, *Principles of Public International Law* 341 (4th ed. Oxford, Eng.: Clarendon Press, 1990); case law "confused and reveals no consistent principles," 341–42 (3rd ed., 1979).

50. Aldona S. v. United Kingdom, Supreme Court of Poland (1948),

reported in 90 Journal du Droit International 191 (1963).

51. Fienerman, *Sovereign Immunity in the Chinese Case and Its Implications for the Future of International Law*, in R. Macdonald, *Essays in Honour of Wang Tieya* 251 (Dordrecht, Neth.; Boston: Martinus Nijhoff, 1994).

52. Collision with Foreign Government Owned Motor Car, Supreme Court of Austria, reported in 40 Int'l L. Rep. 73 (1961).

CHAPTER THREE

International Organizations

CHAPTER OUTLINE

■ INTRODUCTION

Chapter 2 addressed the legal identity and characteristics of the *State*, the primary actor in international affairs. This chapter continues with a related building block—the attributes of the international *organization*, an actor with increasing influence in the global domain.

Important contrasts exist between the legal capacity or "personality" of States and international organizations. The diversity of States is manifested in a number of ways—politically, militarily, and economically. But each is a sovereign entity and all are thus equal under International Law. Each State may thus display the basic badge of statehood: sovereign power over persons and things within its bor-

ders. International organizations also differ in a number of ways, but each owes its existence to the decision of a group of States that created it. A major exception is the *non*governmental organization—an actor in International Law, but not beholden to a State or group of States for its existence.

After first outlining the legal essence of international organizations, and then classification paradigms, this chapter will focus on the key *global* organization—the United Nations—and the most prominent *regional* organization—the European Union. This chapter then summarizes the salient features of some other regional organizations that are essentially political or military in nature. Economic international organizations will be addressed in the Chapter 13 analysis of International Economic Relations.

Like the *State* immunity analysis in Chapter 2, this chapter closes with the *organizational* immunities of the UN and those of the regional organization that operates within the boundaries of its member States.

Upon completion of this third chapter, the student will be prepared to undertake the final preliminary building block of International Law: the status of the *individual* in International Law, and how it has changed dramatically in the comparatively brief period since World War II.

■ 3.1 LEGAL PERSONALITY OF ORGANIZATIONS

Introduction to International Organizations

What *is* an international organization? The typical organization is established by treaty among three or more States to fulfill some common objective. Canada, Mexico, and the United States, for example, formed a number of international organizations to implement the trade-related goals of the North American Free Trade Agreement (NAFTA) which became effective in 1994. An international organization may also be described as a formal and continuously operating institution established by agreement of the members that created it. This section of the book deals mostly with public international organizations, established by three or more States. § 3.2 will address several private or nongovernmental international organizations.

One might first draw a parallel between States and international organizations. The history of the modern State began with the 1648 Peace of Westphalia (see § 1.3). The idea of an international organization pursuing common objectives is not a novelty of the twentieth century. Peace and religion were early motivators. The Egyptian Pharaoh Ikhnaton envisioned an international theological order some fourteen centuries B.C. The Amphictyon League of the ancient Greek city-states organized themselves with a view toward lessening the brutality of war. The medieval poet Dante proposed a global super-State, operating under control of a central court of justice. Yet these were not organizations in the modern sense, and there were no permanent organizational institutions.

When the Industrial Revolution took hold in the 1800s, it is not surprising that international organization began to focus on economic matters. The oldest international organization, in terms of the above conception of that term, is the Organization of American States (OAS)—formed in 1890 to develop and address regional economic relations in the Western Hemisphere.

The term *international organization* consists of two words that are often a source of confusion for one who has not yet studied International Relations. Modern International Law has consisted primarily of the norms that are developed, practiced, and mutually agreeable to *States* in their international relations. This historical fact should not lead to the assumption that *only* governments are involved in international transactions. The term *international* may thus refer to *both* intergovernmental relations between State representatives *and* relations among individuals, corporations, and groups across the borders between two or more States. Negotiations between the respective US and South Korean departments of defense to pressure North Korea into authorizing full nuclear inspections is an international transaction between governments. A US company's sale of household goods to a South Korean importer for resale is an international transaction not directly involving the respective governments.

The term *organization* can be similarly confusing because of dual usage. International relations between individuals, corporations, or governments are "organized" to some degree. International organization may thus be perceived as a *process*. But administrative entities also exist that facilitate international trade, diplomacy, and conferences. These may be perceived as *institutions* designed to accomplish mutual objectives of the participants in different countries.

This chapter addresses the "international organization" in terms of the formal institution that provides a structure for accomplishing what are typically treaty-based objectives. These organizations serve the diverse needs of member States and citizens within those States—all of whom benefit by the existence of an international organization established to work toward defined objectives.[1] Institutions such as the UN's International Atomic Energy Agency and the worldwide General Agreement on Tariffs and Trade (GATT) thus serve as permanent international organizations, seeking to fulfill the mandate of the treaties entered into by the States that created these organizations. Yet they have very different objectives.

Prior to the end of World War I, public international organizations were not as ubiquitous as today. Some private organizations, such as the Hague Conferences of 1899 and 1907 and the International Red Cross, were created, to control the negative aspects of State war potential—but no public or intergovernmental organizations consisting of States and operating through permanent administrative organs. There had been a century of relative peace since the defeat of Napoleon. It then became evident that avoiding another global war would be of paramount interest to all States. Governmental leaders recognized the role of State responsibility for causing World War I. This was the greatest malfunction in State relations since the beginning of the Peace of Westphalia in 1648. The Westphalian model was also responsible for the modern conception of the State as the *only* actor in International Law. This conception had to change in order for the process of international organization to materialize. There was relatively little contact between sovereign States.

The post-Napoleon Congress of Vienna of 1814–1815 temporarily set the stage for developing rules of international diplomacy. This Congress brought the nations of Europe together in *peacetime* to try to create rules for preventing another decades-long war in Europe. Unfortunately, this goal was not realized because of a variety of factors including the following: friction created by a waning British Empire attempting to control its historical leadership position in Europe; the expansionist leanings of the "Holy Alliance" of Austria, Prussia, and Russia as well as the Islamic Ottoman Empire; and a number of regional wars that deflected the Vienna Conference idea of meetings at regular intervals to *prevent* war rather than merely dealing directly with its consequences.

There had to be a period of relative global peace before international organizations could effectively function as international actors. The 1919 postwar meeting of the victorious nations at Versailles, France (like the 1814 meeting of Napoleon's victors), was the real benchmark of modern international organization and regular intergovernmental collaboration. This was this body that brought the notion of a "League of Nations" to fruition. Economic and social questions were not totally ignored. Such matters, however, took a back seat until the 1945 UN drafting Conference at San Francisco. The League and the UN became the primary examples of intergovernmental organization. If swords were to be beaten into plowshares, then these twentieth century international organizations would have to address economic and social matters. They would also have to consider individual rights, which were long excluded from direct protection on the international plane (a major contribution of the European Union as discussed in § 3.4).

The following events have adversely affected the smooth functioning of the international system of States and organizations as a whole: the end of the Cold War; the increase in economic stagnation of "have-not" countries of the world; their understandable demands for development in spite of growing environmental concerns; contemporary threats to the fragile democracy in States of the former Soviet Union and elsewhere; the proliferation of ethnic rivalries *within* States and in various regions of the globe; and the financial and political problems international organizations face in maintaining peace on a global (UN) or regional (NATO) scale. Yet these impediments suggest a call for multilateral responses, as opposed to leaving things to the diplomacy of the various sovereign States. Statehood is undergoing significant changes, now that there is a far more diverse community of States than those in existence immediately after World War II, now that many States are failing or breaking down into smaller units (*see* §§ 2.2 and 2.3), and now that pervasive and very basic concerns with life on this planet transcend sovereign borders—especially problems with the environment and population growth.

The Ford Foundation, a US-based research and policy-making institution, has traditionally advocated increased reliance on international organization as the vehicle for effecting positive changes in the historical dilemma, by facilitating international cooperation in an era when the State is the primary international player. In a 1990 study on international organizations and law, the Ford Foundation thus articulated a shifting paradigm whereby international organizations and nongovernmental organizations both assume a greater role in the progressive development of international order. As asserted in the foundation's position paper regarding the resulting need of more effective international organizations:

> it is abundantly clear that no single nation now dominates our age. The United States, the architect of the postwar order, is no longer able to control events singlehandedly, if it ever could. Japan, the European Community, the newly industrializing countries . . . and the dominant nations in some regions have become influential international actors. . . . Partly as a consequence of this diffusion of power, international organizations face far different challenges now than they did forty years ago. The United Nations, Breton Woods institutions [establishing the International Monetary Fund], and the international trade system are all under strain.
>
> . . .
>
> Linking the fields of international organizations and international law to multilateral cooperation . . . suggests an underlying conviction that institutionalized global coopera-

tion is a necessity . . . [that] should be based in law and should include enforceable rights and obligations.[2]

Growth in International Organizations

There is a striking parallel in the growth of States and international organizations (IOs) since the close of World War II in 1945. The number of *States* increased dramatically, from fifty-one to nearly two hundred (*see* Exhibit 2.1 in § 2.2). There has been an equally spectacular growth in the number of *international organizations*, from several hundred to nearly five thousand. Exhibit 3.1 illustrates the dramatic growth in these organizations.

EXHIBIT 3.1 Twentieth Century Growth in International Organizations

Year	Governmental	Nongovernmental
1870	7	- - -
1909	37	178
1956	132	973
1960	154	1,255
1964	179	1,470
1968	229	1,899
1972	280	2,173
1976	252	2,502
1981	337	4,265
1984	365	4,615
1986	369	4,649
1988	309	4,518
1991	297	4,620
2000*	- - -	10,000

Source: Vol. 1, App. 5 to *1991–1992 Yearbook of International Organizations* 1667 (Brussels: Union of Int'l Assn's, 1992)

* = earlier estimates that may be overstated

Legal Capacity under International Law

An organization of States has legal capacity under International Law if it satisfies three essential elements. *First*, it must be a *permanent* association of State members with established objectives and administrative organs. The League of Nations, the predecessor of the United Nations, satisfied this prerequisite because its member States intended for it to function indefinitely. The League's peace objectives, and its organs geared toward achieving them, qualified it as an international organization. *Second*, an international organization must possess some power that is *distinct* from the sovereign power of its State members. Organs of the European Union can order a member State to act, over that State's objection, in matters defined by the Union's constitutive international treaties (as discussed in the Irish abortion case in § 3.4). *Third*, the association's powers must be exercisable on an *international* level, rather than solely under the national legal systems of its member States. It is a popular myth, for example, that the International Criminal Police Organization (Interpol) operates on an international level that allows its agents to track and arrest international fugitives. In fact, Interpol's agents cannot act without the express consent of the national police of any State wherein it maintains a presence. It does not possess any international police power to apprehend criminals.[3]

The presence of the above three elements vests an association of States with an international capacity distinct from its member States. Public international organizations thus possess a legal personality or capacity to exercise certain "governmental" powers in a manner similar to but different from those of their individual State members. When an organization's State members yield the requisite degree of sovereignty to the organization, it has truly international power—the capacity to engage in conduct otherwise reserved for States—such as the ability to conclude treaties with other organizations or individual States, and to perform certain acts or refrain from engaging in them.

The United Nations is a good example for illustrating an international organization's legal capacity, as demonstrated in the following case. In November 1947, UN General Assembly Resolution 181(II) partitioned the former British Mandate referred to as "Palestine" to create new Jewish and Arab States in that territory. This resolution was accepted by the Jewish community but rejected by Arab States in the Middle East. Shortly after Israel declared its statehood in May 1948, hostilities began in and around what is now the State of Israel. Two weeks later, UN Security Council Resolution 50 called for a cessation of hostilities. A Norwegian, Count Bernadotte, was appointed the UN Mediator in Palestine for the purpose of negotiating a settlement. He was killed while pursuing this objective in the Palestinian territory. General Assembly Resolution 194(III) of December 1948 "Expresses its deep appreciation of the progress achieved through the good offices of the late United Nations Mediator in promoting a peaceful adjustment of the future situation of Palestine, for which cause he sacrificed his life."[4] The issue for the International Court of Justice was whether or not the UN Charter gave the UN the legal capacity, as an international organization, to seek reparations from the responsible State or States that kill UN agents:

REPARATION FOR INJURIES SUFFERED IN THE SERVICE OF THE UNITED NATIONS

Advisory Opinion, International Court of Justice (1949)
1949 International Court of Justice Reports 174

[Author's Note: This is an International Court of Justice (ICJ) "Advisory Opinion." There is no State defendant—a process described further in § 9.4 on the operation of the Court. The UN had requested that the ICJ render its opinion on this issue arising under International Law. The specific issue was whether or not the UN had the legal right to sue for damages to the UN in its capacity as an international organization. In addition to the death of the UN's Mediator in Palestine, UN agents from various countries were being injured or killed while performing duties on behalf of the organization while trying to control various hostilities. Prior to the decision by this Court, only the victim's State of citizenship had the undisputed right to sue (and, with luck, establish State responsibility for harm to such individuals).

In 1947, the UN maintained that there was State responsibility for injury to aliens (UN employees) caused by Israel, Jordan, and Egypt. In three separate incidents, individuals working for the UN were killed. The UN claimed that the responsible States failed to protect its these foreign citizens from private criminal acts. In the case of Israel, for example, two UN employees in Palestine were shot while driving through the Jewish portion of Jerusalem. The UN sought compensation from Israel for the loss of their lives. Its claim was brought for Israel's "failure to exercise due diligence and to take all reasonable measures for the prevention of the assassination; liability of the [Israeli] government for actions committed by irregular forces in territory under the control of the Israel[i] authorities; and failure to take all measures required by international law and by the Security Council . . . to bring the culprits to justice." Israel refused to pay any compensation, claiming that only the State of the victim's nationality had the legal capacity to assert the State liability of Israel. (See account in 8 M. Whiteman, Digest of International Law 742 (Wash., DC: US Gov't Print. Off., 1967.)

The Court analyzed whether the proposed harm to the UN, in its legal capacity as an international organization, could be reconciled with or supplant the right to seek reparations by the State of the victim's nationality. Put another way, if a Norwegian citizen is killed while abroad, only Norway could seek reparations from the responsible State. Norway's ability to sue would be based on the theory that an injury to a Norwegian national is also an injury to Norway. Could the UN Charter be construed, however, as furnishing the UN with the legal personality to sue for wrongs done to the UN in its capacity as the employer of the deceased?]

[Opinion.] The questions asked of the Court relate to the "capacity to bring an international claim;" accordingly, we must begin by defining what is meant by that capacity, and consider the characteristics of the [UN] Organization, so as to

determine whether, in general, these characteristics do, or do not, include for the Organization a right to present an international claim [for injury to its agent].

Competence to bring an international claim is, for those possessing it, the capacity to resort to the customary methods recognized by international law for the establishment, the presentation and the settlement of claims. Among these methods may be mentioned protest, request for an enquiry, negotiation, and request for submission to an arbitral tribunal or to the Court in so far as this may be authorized by the Statute [of the ICJ].

This capacity certainly belongs to the State; a State can bring an international claim against another State. Such a claim takes the form of a claim between two political entities [i.e., States], equal in law, similar in form, and both the direct subjects of international law. It is dealt with by means of negotiation, and cannot, in the present state of the law as to international jurisdiction, be submitted to a tribunal, except with the consent of the States concerned.

. . .

But, in the international sphere, has the Organization such a nature as involves the capacity to bring an international claim? In order to answer this question, the Court must first enquire whether the Charter has given the Organization such a position that it possesses, in regard to its Members, rights which it is entitled to ask them to respect. In other words, does the Organization possess international personality?

. . .

The Charter has not been content to make the Organization created by it merely a centre "for harmonizing the actions of nations in the attainment of these common ends" (Article I, para. 4). It has equipped that centre with organs, and has given it special tasks. It has defined the position of the Members in relation to the Organization by requiring them to give it every assistance in any action undertaken by it (Article 2, para. 5), and to accept and carry out the decisions of the Security Council; by authorizing the General Assembly to make recommendations to the Members; by giving the Organization legal capacity and privileges and immunities in the territory of each of its Members; and by providing for the conclusion of agreements between the Organization and its Members. Practice—in particular the conclusion of conventions to which the

Organization is a party—has confirmed this character of the Organization, which occupies a position in certain respects in detachment from its Members, and which is under a duty to remind them, if need be, of certain obligations. . . . The "Convention on the Privileges and Immunities of the United Nations" of 1946 creates rights and duties between each of the signatories and the Organization (see, in particular, Section 35). It is difficult to see how such a convention could operate except upon the international plane and as between parties possessing international personality.

In the opinion of the Court, the Organization was intended to exercise and enjoy, and is in fact exercising and enjoying, functions and rights which can only be explained on the basis of the possession of a large measure of international personality and the capacity to operate upon an international plane. It is at present the supreme type of international organization, and it could not carry out the intentions of its founders if it was devoid of international personality. It must be acknowledged that its Members, by entrusting certain functions to it, with the attendant duties and responsibilities, have clothed it with the competence required to enable those functions to be effectively discharged.

Accordingly, the Court has come to the conclusion that the Organization is an international person. That is not the same thing as saying that it is a State, which it certainly is not, or that its legal personality and rights and duties are the same as those of a State. Still less is it the same thing as saying that it is a "super-State," whatever that expression may mean. It does not even imply that all its rights and duties must be upon the international plane, any more than all the rights and duties of a State must be upon that plane. What it does mean is that it is a subject of international law and capable of possessing international rights and duties, and that it has capacity to maintain its rights by bringing international claims.

The next question is whether the sum of the international rights of the Organization comprises the right to bring the kind of international claim described in the Request for this Opinion. That is a[n international organization's] claim against a State to obtain reparation in respect of the damage caused by the injury of an agent of the Organization in the course of the performance of his duties. Whereas a State possesses the totality of international rights and duties recognized by international law, the rights and duties of an entity such as the Organization must depend upon its purposes and functions as specified or implied in its constituent documents and developed in practice. The functions of the Organization are of such a character that they could not be effectively discharged if they involved the concurrent action, on the international plane, of fifty-eight or more Foreign Offices, and the Court concludes that the Members have endowed the Organization with capacity to bring international claims when necessitated by the discharge of its functions.

Having regard to its purposes and functions already referred to, the Organization may find it necessary, and has in fact found it necessary, to entrust its agents with important missions to be performed in disturbed parts of the world. Many missions, from their very nature, involve the agents in unusual dangers to which ordinary persons are not exposed. For the same reason, the injuries suffered by its agents in these circumstances will sometimes have occurred in such a manner that their national State would not be justified in bringing a claim for reparation on the ground of diplomatic protection, or, at any rate, would not feel disposed to do so. Both to ensure the efficient and independent performance of these missions and to afford effective support to its agents, the Organization must provide them with adequate protection.

The obligations entered into by States to enable the agents of the Organization to perform their duties are undertaken not in the interest of the agents, but in that of the Organization. When it claims redress for a breach of these obligations, the Organization is invoking its own right, the right that the obligations due to it should be respected. . . . In claiming reparation based on the injury suffered by its agent, the Organization does not represent the agent, but is asserting its own right, the right to secure respect for undertakings entered into towards the Organization.

. . .

The question of reconciling action [this right to sue that is claimed] by the Organization with the rights of a national State may arise in another way; that is to say, when the agent bears the nationality of the defendant State.

. . .

The action of the Organization is in fact based not upon the nationality of the victim but upon his status as agent of the Organization. Therefore it does not matter whether or not the State to which the claim is addressed regards him as its own national, because the question of nationality is not pertinent to the admissibility of the claim.

. . .

■ NOTES & QUESTIONS

1. Article 104 of the UN Charter (*see* Appendix A to this book) provides that the UN has the "capacity as may be necessary" to exercise its functions and to fulfill its purposes within the territory of each of its member States. What Charter gap was filled by the *Reparations* case?

2. Under Article 100 of the Charter, UN employees performing UN duties cannot "seek or receive instructions from any government or from any other authority external to the Organization." Assume that a UN agent—a citizen of Norway—is carrying out a mission on behalf of the UN in Norway. The *Reparations* case suggests reasons for conferring the protection of the UN on the injured individual, even though the UN employee is still entitled to similar protection by his or her home State. Why?

3. In December 1991, the body of UN Colonel John Higgins was returned to the UN from Leba-

non. While on a UN peacekeeping operation in 1989, he was kidnapped and later brutally murdered. In January 1991, five European Community (EC) truce observers were shot down in their helicopter by Serbian Yugoslavian military forces in Croatia. Of course, neither Lebanon nor what was then Yugoslavia claimed responsibility for the deaths of these agents while on peacekeeping missions for, respectively, the UN and the EC. It is precisely in this situation that these international organizations would hold the right, under the *Reparations* rationale, to seek redress from the responsible States.

4. In December 1992, Cambodia's Khmer Rouge freed eleven UN peacekeepers—who had been kidnapped and threatened with execution. As a belligerent entity (*see* § 2.4), the Khmer Rouge would bear responsibility under International Law for any harm that might have come to these UN peacekeepers.

As a result of the above advisory opinion in the *Reparations* case, the UN has the international legal capacity to sue for harm to one of its employees while acting on a UN mission. This right was successfully used in the following case. The UN's claim was broader in the following case than the basic right to sue established in the *Reparations* case. In this second case, below, the UN was suing one of its member States as a defendant in its own national courts. It was also suing a private shipping company—an entity without legal capacity to sue or be sued on the international plane. Further, the UN was seeking damages in the national courts of a member State. The defendant, the US, had specially designated the UN as an international organization, thus able to enjoy the legal capacity in the host country to function under US national law.[5]

The earlier *Reparations* case established the UN's right to sue a responsible State for wrongful conduct harming the UN in its capacity as an international organization that dispatches peacekeeping agents to various trouble spots. The following case affirmatively answers the fundamental question about whether the UN has the capacity to sue in a *commercial* context:

BALFOUR, GUTHRIE & CO. v. UNITED STATES

United States District Court
Northern District of California, 1950
90 Fed.Supp. 831

[Author's Note: In 1947, the United Nations International Children's Emergency Fund arranged for the shipment of powdered milk from ports on the US West Coast to Mediterranean ports. The ship that transported the milk was owned by the US government and operated by a US steamship company. The shipping contract between the UN agency and the US provided for the milk to be delivered to and distributed in Italy and Greece. One portion of the shipment never arrived. The other part arrived in damaged condition. The UN (and various shippers, including Balfour) sued the United States and a private US steamship company to recover for the loss of and damage to the milk.

The UN's complaint is referred to as a "libel," which is the plaintiff's statement of the case against the defendant in a maritime suit.]

[*Opinion.*] Whether the United Nations may maintain these proceedings against respondent American Pacific Steamship Company can be first and more easily answered.

The International Court of Justice has held [in the above *Reparation* case] that the United Nations is a legal entity separate and distinct from the member States. While it is not a state nor a super-State, it is an international person, clothed by its Members with the competence necessary to discharge its functions.

Article 104 of the Charter of the United Nations provides that "the Organization shall enjoy in the territory of each of its Members such legal capacity as may be necessary for the exercise of its functions and the fulfillment of its purposes." As a treaty ratified by the United States, the Charter is part of the supreme law of the land. No implemental legislation would appear to be necessary to endow the United Nations with legal capacity in the United States. But the President has removed any possible doubt by designating the United Nations as one of the organizations entitled to enjoy the privileges conferred by the International Organizations Immunities Act, [which] states that "international organizations shall, to the extent consistent with the instrument creating them, possess the capacity—(i) to contract; (ii) to acquire and dispose of real and personal property; (iii) to institute legal proceedings."

The capacity of the United Nations to maintain the libel [suit] against the American Pacific Steamship Company is completely consistent with its charter. The libel asserts rights flowing from a contract made by a specialized agency of the United Nations in the performance of its duties. The agency, the International Children's Emergency Fund, was created by resolution of the General Assembly of the United Nations on December 11, 1946. Its function is to promote child health generally and in particular to assist the governments of countries, that were the victims of aggression, to rehabilitate their children. The solution of international health problems is one of the responsibilities assumed by the United Nations in Article 55 of its Charter.

Whether the United Nations may sue the United States is a more difficult question. It is apparent that Article 104 of the Charter of the United Nations was never intended to provide a method for settling differences between the United Nations and its members. It is equally clear that the International Organizations Immunities Act does not amount to a waiver of the United States' sovereign immunity from suit. The precise question posed is whether the capacity to institute legal proceedings conferred on the United Nations by that [UN Immunities] Act includes the competence to sue the United States in cases in which the United States has consented to suits by other litigants.

The broad purpose of the International Organizations Immunities Act was to vitalize the status of international organizations of which the United States is a member and to facilitate their activities. A liberal interpretation of the Act is in harmony with this purpose.

The considerations which might prompt a restrictive interpretation are not persuasive. It is true that history has recorded few, if any, instances in which international entities have submitted their disputes to the courts of one of the disputing parties. But international organizations on a grand scale are a modern phenomena. The wide variety of activities in which they engage is likely to give rise to claims against their members that can most readily be disposed of in national courts. The present claim is such a claim. No political overtones surround it. No possible embarrassment to the United States in the conduct of its international affairs could result from such a decree as this court might enter. A claim for cargo loss and damage is clearly susceptible of judicial settlement. Particularly is this so in this litigation inasmuch as the United Nations' claim is one of several of the same nature arising out of the same transaction or occurrence.

International organizations, such as the United Nations and its agencies, of which the United States is a member, are not alien bodies. The interests of the United States are served when the United Nations' interests are protected. A prompt and equitable settlement of any claim it may have against the United States will be the settlement most advantageous to both parties. The courts of the United States afford a most appropriate forum for accomplishing such a settlement.

Finally, it cannot be denied that when the Congress conferred the privileges specified in the International Organizations Immunities Act, it neither explicitly nor implicitly limited the kind or type of legal proceedings that might be instituted by the United Nations. There appears to be no good reason for the judicial imposition of such limitations [thus permitting the UN to sue the US and the private shipping company in a court of the US].

■ 3.2 CLASSIFICATION OF ORGANIZATIONS

The goal of an international organization (IO) is to promote the mutually established objectives of its members. Its functions are executed by governmental, nongovernmental, or a mixture of such representatives. International organizations can be classified in a variety of ways. This section provides the essential insight into analyzing what an organization is, by characterizing who created it and what it is supposed to do.

Traditional Model

Professor D.W. Bowett of Cambridge University advocates the traditional paradigm of organizational classification by using a "functional" approach. International organizations are thus: (1) public or private; (2) administrative or political; (3) global or regional; (4) and, they either have, or do not have, supranational power.

This traditional model is a convenient but aging starting point for characterizing the power and purpose of the myriad of contemporary international organizations. The initial public-versus-private distinction refers to the establishment of "public" organizations by States through their intergovernmental cooperation.[6] *States* may enter into written treaties to create international trade or communications associations—with machinery for implementing the joint decisions of the member governments. Private international organizations are typically established by *private* non-State legal persons or private corporations rather than by government-representatives—hence, the term "*Non*-Governmental Organization" or NGO. These international organizations are not created by an international treaty between sovereign States. Examples include the International Chamber of Commerce and the International Committee of the Red Cross.

The administrative-versus-political distinction has been blurred by modern practice. Administrative international organizations tend to have goals that are far more limited than those of political organizations. The UN's International Telecommunications Union, for example, serves an administrative purpose not associated with maintaining or directing political order. Its delegates allocate radio frequencies, including those used for space communications. Political associations are marked by the intergovernmental establishment of military or political order. The fundamental purpose of the United Nations was originally to implement a system of collective security to discourage unilateral uses of military force. Yet the UN Charter also contains provisions regarding mandating certain organizations within it to work toward the improvement of social and economic matters—which might be categorized as administrative or political.

The global-versus-regional distinction is less useful than some of the other distinctions. The UN is the prime example of a "global" organization. Its impact, however, is arguably more regional than global. It is *not* a world government and often serves as a forum for debating regional problems. And not all regional organizations are in fact regional. The North Atlantic Treaty Organization (NATO) is often referred to in the press as a Western European association. Yet the geographical position of certain long-term members such as the United States, Canada, and Iceland makes it difficult to analyze its work as limited to Western Europe—especially now that NATO is opening up to former Warsaw Pact members of the now dissolved Soviet Union (discussed in § 3.5).

The final traditional distinction involves organizations with-versus-without supranational power over member States. One definitional problem is that many international organizations are "supranational" ("supra" meaning "above"), in the sense that they are associations of States with independent organs for implementing the goals of the participants. It would be incorrect, however, to characterize the UN as having supranational power. It cannot dispatch a peacekeeping force independently of the approval of the five permanent members of the Security Council—and traditionally not without the consent of the State or States where troops are to be stationed. In the European Union, on the other hand, the member States have ceded some of their sovereign powers to community organs that may, *and do*, require member States to act in ways that would not occur unilaterally (*see Open Door* case in § 3.4).

Expanded Classification Model

Although the subject of international organizations has been studied for some time, a new descriptive paradigm did not emerge until the period after the dramatic numerical increase of the 1970s and 1980s (*see* Exhibit 3.1 in § 3.1). The first cog in the more recent method for classifying IOs thus draws upon the "IGO/INGO" distinction—presented by Professor Clive Archer of Scotland's University of Aberdeen.[7] UN Economic and Social Council Resolution 288(x) of 1950 provided that every "international organization that is not created by means of international governmental agreements [treaties] shall be considered as a non-governmental international organization."

IGO thus refers to international governmental organization, while INGO refers to an international *non*governmental organization. The UN is a *global* IGO. Its membership consists of States throughout the world. The European Union is an IGO that operates on a primarily *regional* international level.

Examples of INGOs include Amnesty International (headquartered in London), the International Olympic Committee (headquartered in Lausanne, Switzerland), and the American Society of International Law (Washington, D.C.). Amnesty's members are individuals from all over the globe who are concerned about State observance of the international human rights norms described later in this book (*see* Chapter 11). Amnesty was not founded by a conference of governmental leaders, and no State "sends" representatives to its meetings. The Olympic Committee is a worldwide international organization promoting sports and competition through the ideal that State friendships will ultimately be enhanced. The American Society of International Law is composed of individual lawyers, judges, and professors from all over the world (most residing within the US). It conducts seminars in and outside of the US, and it is a professional association devoted to the study of International Law in a way that organizes professionals to promote and influence State observance of International Law.

Some IOs consist of both IGOs *and* INGOs. Governments and private corporations might jointly form an IO to deal with a particular problem. The Communication Satellite Corporation (COMSAT), for example, is a mix of both States (*with* international legal capacity) and nongovernmental corporations (*without* legal personality under International Law). They have combined to achieve various objectives involving the delivery of better worldwide communications.

The relationship between IGOs and INGOs may be symbiotic, whereby dissimilar organs exist in close association or in a union with each other to serve mutually beneficial interests. Certain INGOs, for example, possess a special status at the UN. The PLO, the International Committee for the Red Cross, and the American Society of International Law are examples because they have been accorded special "observer status" by different organs within this global international organization. When the General Assembly meets at the UN headquarters in New York City, for example, the PLO sends representatives to monitor the proceedings. Its representative may even sit in a special section of the General Assembly room. In this way, such INGOs may more directly participate in the work of the UN. While such INGOs are neither States nor IGOs, they enjoy some degree of legal personality on the international level through such involvements with the IGO known as the UN.

The Red Cross, a private international union, enjoys yet another symbiotic relationship with IGOs. It was the Red Cross that promoted the intergovernmental Geneva Conventions of 1864, 1906, 1929, and 1949 (*see* § 10.6). The Red Cross sometimes acts in ways that do not always draw the support of an individual State at war. The North Vietnamese were not particularly interested in Red Cross commentary on the degree of protection afforded US and South Vietnamese prisoners in North Vietnam. The essential 1949 Geneva Convention was characterized by the North Vietnamese as inapplicable to an "undeclared" war. The Red Cross pressed all States to reconvene at another Geneva Convention in 1977, which established added protections for prisoners in "undeclared" wars.[8] On the other hand, the Bosnian Serbs applauded the Red Cross assistance with the 1994 evacuation of thousands of Muslims and Croatians from the town of Prijefor in Bosnia. Although the objective was to save them from the Bosnian Serbs, this atypical Red Cross evacuation effectively helped the Serbs in promoting their goal of ethnic cleansing.

In addition to the IGO/INGO distinction above, the remaining cogs in the contemporary analysis of organizational classification are: regional/universal organizations, purpose, and structure.

Regarding "purpose," one might contrast the UN Charter with the North American Free Trade Agreement (NAFTA). The Charter's first Article contains statements of purpose that are rather broadly worded. Member States therein "agreed" that:

> The Purposes of the United Nations are:
> 1. To maintain international peace and security. . .;
> 2. To develop friendly relations among nations based on respect for the principle of equal rights and self-determination of peoples. . .;
> 3. To achieve international co-operation in solving international problems of an economic, social, cultural, or humanitarian character. . .;
> 4. To be a centre for harmonizing the actions of nations in the attainment of these common ends.

Courts and commentators have spent many years analyzing the scope of this very broad statement of purpose. It literally appears to "cover the universe," given its attention to peace, economic, social, and cultural objectives. The NAFTA, on the other hand, is more limited, more specific, and less ambiguous. The liberal democracies that are its members are unlikely to go to war against each other. While equality or social improvements and cultural exchanges will be facilitated by NAFTA, its essential objective is to reduce trade barriers for the economic benefit of its trading partners. NAFTA Article 102.1 thus provides that:

> The objectives of this Agreement . . . are to:
> (a) eliminate barriers to trade in, and facilitate the cross-border movement of, goods and services between the territories of the Parties;
> (b) promote conditions of fair competition in the free trade area; (c) increase substantially investment opportunities in the territories of the Parties; (d) provide adequate and effective protection and enforcement of intellectual

property rights [copyright, trademark, and patent protection] in each Party's territory; (e) create effective procedures for the implementation and application of this Agreement, for its joint administration and for the resolution of disputes; and (f) establish a framework for further trilateral, regional and multilateral cooperation to expand and enhance the benefits of this Agreement.

Functional Shift

Global and regional alliances are generally shifting from a political to an economic orientation. The Warsaw Pact, a prominent figure in international affairs until 1991, is military history. What States, one might ask, will be NATO's common enemy, particularly now that a number of its former Warsaw Pact foes are joining NATO's Partnership for Peace Program?

The Arab League is splintered. First, Egypt was expelled due to President Sadat's decision to enter into friendly treaty relations with Israel. The League virtually fell apart during the Persian Gulf War. Members who formerly advocated Israel's demise fought their Arab League ally in Iraq to, among other things, protect Israel from Iraqi attack. The PLO autonomy in Gaza and Jericho further confirms the lack of unity about conquering Israel—the traditional military and political foe of League members.

The Organization of African Unity (OAU) is likewise devoid of its traditional political purpose due to events occurring in the aftermath of the Cold War. South Africa's unwinding of apartheid and the presidency of Nelson Mandela inadvertently deprived the OAU of the one issue that united its otherwise fractious membership. The OAU is thus pursuing economic objectives to a much greater degree than in the past, now that these vestiges of colonialism have dissipated.

At least seventeen international common markets and free trade areas are at work to advance the *economic* objectives of member States throughout the globe. The major groupings will be covered in Chapter 13 on "International Economic Relations."

■ 3.3 UNITED NATIONS

This section of the text covers five central themes:

- Events preceding creation of the UN ("Historical Backdrop");

- The impact of politics in the UN process ("Law and Politics");

- The UN's major institutions ("UN Structure");

- Assessment of successes and failures ("UN Assessment"); and

- Proposed modifications ("UN Reform Studies").

Historical Backdrop

The League of Nations was the first structured and operational global international organization and the direct predecessor of the United Nations. The League of Peace, a private organization in the US, proposed a League of Nations in a 1914 newspaper editorial at the outset of World War I. Great Britain's League of Nations Society began to promote this ideal in 1916. The South African statesman who coauthored both the Covenant of the League of Nations and the UN Charter made a decisive suggestion in one of the proposals leading to its creation. He proposed that the peoples in the territories formerly belonging to Russia, Austria-Hungary, and Turkey create an international organization to resolve their territorial disputes. All States would thereby abide by the fundamental principle that resolutions by "the league of nations should be substituted for any policy of national annexation."[9]

US President Woodrow Wilson was a key proponent of the League's creation. Drawing on the 1917 "Recommendations of Havana" prepared by the American Institute of International Law meeting in Cuba, Wilson's famous 1918 "Fourteen Points" speech to the US Congress advocated a "general association of nations [that] must be formed under specific covenants for the purpose of affording mutual guarantees of political independence and territorial integrity to great and small states alike." His essential purpose was to avoid a second World War, so that the first one would be "the war to end all wars." World leaders reacted by expressing their hope that the League would be a means for avoiding repetition of the secret military alliances and mutual suspicions that permeated the international atmosphere. The fear of another war thus generated the creation of this organization to encourage open diplomacy and cooling-off periods whenever international tensions threatened peace. Wilson witnessed the realization of his "First Point"—the creation of an international organization dedicated to open "covenants of peace, openly arrived at, after which there shall be no private international understandings of any kind but diplomacy shall proceed always frankly and in public view."[10]

The 1919 League of Nations Covenant, part of the Treaty of Versailles, was ultimately signed by seventy-three States. Its twenty-six articles dealt with a variety of problems, although the central theme was how to control military aggression. It was a progressive development in international relations because it established a two-organ permanent diplomatic conference (a General Assembly and a Security Council). The League was thus a central location for conference diplomacy. Unfortunately, it never achieved universality in terms of State participation.

The dream that the League of Nations would maintain international peace and security failed the test of reality. The US Senate failed to ratify the League of Nations Covenant. The senators feared a diminution of US sovereignty should the nation participate. They believed that membership would, instead, draw the US into further wars—thus opting for isolationism. The US never became a member of the League, a significant blow to the organization's potential effectiveness. League membership consisted essentially of the war-torn European countries.

While the League of Nations enjoyed some successes during its twenty-year existence, its failures eroded global confidence in the ability of international organizations to maintain harmonious relations between States. The League was unable to control the offensive military objectives of its member States. By the time that the Soviet Union (USSR) finally joined the League in 1934, Brazil, Germany, and Japan had already withdrawn. The USSR later invaded Finland, Japan expanded into Manchuria, Germany annexed Austria into the Third Reich, and Italy invaded Ethiopia. A few League members reacted by an almost submissive form of economic sanctions—a brief boycott of Italian-made shoes. The global economic depression of the 1930s, together with US isolationism, the expulsion of the USSR (after it invaded Finland), and a somewhat xenophobic atmosphere, all contributed to the ultimate demise of the League of Nations.

In 1942, a number of League members met during World War II to assess whether the League should continue and decided that it should be replaced by another global international organization to pursue the ideal of collective security. The name "United Nations" was devised by US President Roosevelt and was first used in the "Declaration by United Nations" of January 1, 1942. Representatives of the twenty-six Allied nations therein pledged that their governments would continue their fight against the Axis powers.

The United Nations Charter was drawn up by the representatives of fifty allied countries during the UN Conference on International Organization, held in San Francisco from April through June of 1945. (Poland was not represented at the conference but later signed the Charter, thus becoming one of the original fifty-one member States.) They deliberated the various proposals worked out by representatives of China, the USSR, the United Kingdom, and the US—thus beginning to plan during their meetings in Scotland from August through October of 1944. The drafting conference in the summer of 1945 at San Francisco just preceded the August bombing of Japan, which effectively ended the war. The new "United Nations" was officially established on October 24, 1945. That day is now universally celebrated as United Nations Day.

The UN's membership has dramatically changed since its inception in 1945—growing from 51 to almost 190 States. Exhibit 2.1 illustrates this progression (see § 2.2). Exhibit 3.2 in this chapter provides a brief review of some of the other major UN developments since 1945, while Exhibit 3.3 gives a structural illustration of the United Nations system.

EXHIBIT 3.2 Selected Chronology of Major UN Events*

1945	UN Charter created and enters into force
1946	First General Assembly (GA) London/reconvenes in New York
1947	GA adopts plan to partition "Palestine" to create Arab/Jewish States
1948	GA adopts Universal Declaration on Human Rights (*see* text § 12.2)
1949	GA establishes office of High Commissioner for Refugees (*see* § 12.3)
1950	Soviet Union (SU) boycotts Security Council (SC) for failure to oust Nationalist China representative / SC establishes Korean action under control of U.S. (UN signed truce with North Korea in 1953)
1952	Over South Africa's objections, GA begins study of Apartheid (SC voluntary arms embargo against South Africa: 1963/mandatory: 1977)
1956	Hungary obtains SC resolution regarding SU invasion (unenforced)/GA establishes first independent UN force to handle Suez Canal crisis
1960	GA adopts Declaration on Granting Independence to colonies and peoples/GA: SU's Nikita Khrushchev Secretary-General abusing position
1962	SC attempts to negotiate solution to Cuban Missile Crisis
1963	World Food Program established by UN Food and Agricultural Organization
1967	SC adopts Resolution 242 calling for Israeli withdrawal from occupied territories after Six-Day War with Middle East Arab States
1968	GA approves Treaty on Non-Proliferation of Nuclear Weapons, calling for ratification (1993: North Korea announces intent not to renew)
1969	Convention on Elimination of All Forms of Discrimination effective
1971	GA expels Chinese Nationalist representative/seats PRC delegation
1972	Kurt Waldheim begins Secretary-General service 1972–1986 (later accused of Nazi-era war crimes)
1974	GA bars South African delegation from participating in GA operations/despite Western objections, GA calls for New Int'l Economic Order
1975	GA passes resolution equating Zionism with racism (revokes in 1991)
1984	Office for Emergency Operations in Africa created for famine relief

EXHIBIT 3.2 *(continued)*

1989	GA announces the U.N. Decade of International Law (*see* § 3.4)
1990	Numerous SC/GA resolutions regarding Persian Gulf War (*see* §11.6)
1991	End of Cold War signals improved atmosphere for SC peace efforts
1992	UN concludes most expensive peace operation in history (Cambodia $2 billion)*/SC bans former Yugoslavia from SC seat (GA may expel)
1993	US President's GA speech chides UN inability to fulfill agenda/promises US will pay past-due assessments *if* new funding formula developed/Secretary-General flees from attack by Somali residents/UN not key participant in Bosnia conflict/Russia's Yeltsin requests UN support for Russia to be guarantor of stability in former USSR/UN evacuates 700 refugees from Rwanda
1994	GA establishes Post of High Commissioner for Human Rights/US requests UN ban on worldwide arms sales to North Korea/SC authorizes French request for humanitarian intervention in Rwanda/UN establishes Rwanda peacekeeping operation/Bosnian Serbs isolate UN peacekeepers, making them virtual hostages

*Further UN peacekeeping operations are addressed in § 10.3.

Law and Politics

§ 1.9 of this text drew on the analogy that most drivers (States) obey the traffic signals (international norms), even in the absence of a police presence on each corner to enforce the law (i.e., no standing UN military force under the effective supervision of the Security Council). Those who traverse the various intersections in international relations thus pursue their distinct but mutual interests by observing most of the norms most of the time.

Professor Oscar Schachter of Columbia University uses a comparable metaphor to describe the "patterns and politics" of the United Nations legal order. He succinctly describes the various entities, discussed in this section of the text, as a series of metropolitan and smaller areas linked by various roads, highways, and paths—the infrastructure consisting of the concepts, principles, and processes of the UN legal order. This excerpt provides useful insight into the complex political processes of the UN and the ways in which they have affected the international legal order since its inception in 1945. When you read it, note how non-State actors, including other international organizations and individuals, play an increasingly greater role in the progressive development of International Law:

UNITED NATIONS LAW

by Professor Oscar Schachter
88 American Journal of International Law 1, 16–23 (1994)*

As the United Nations system approaches its fiftieth anniversary, there is good reason to take a fresh view of its contribution to legal order in the contemporary world. . . . A half century of law creation and application by the United Nations and its specialized agencies has produced a corpus juris [body of law] of impressive breadth and diversity. Not surprisingly, the greater part of this law is known only to those specially concerned with a particular area or subject. Indeed, no one can be expected to be knowledgeable in all, or even most, of the fields covered. Still, along with the diversity, common elements can be found to enable us to characterize the total product as a distinctive, multilayered legal order. This essay is an overview of its essential and interesting features. It aims particularly at informing the many nonspecialists in and outside the international law community who have reason to be interested in the process and substance of the legal contribution of the UN system.

. . .

An overview of the UN legal order reveals complex patterns. We see a multitude of specialized bodies of law, each with its distinctive features, many intricate and dense. They are fully accessible only to specialists, versed in doctrine and procedure that often seem arcane to outsiders. We might envisage them as separate communities, on a terrain that includes cities, towns, villages, hamlets. Extending this metaphor, we note that they are connected to each other by roads, highways and paths, that is, by concepts, principles and processes. The communities differ, of course, in size, influence and their linkages to each other.

Two areas of UN law that stand out in public interest are human rights and the law relating to peace and security (i.e., force, arms, etc.). They would be metropolises on our imaginary map. Human rights, in fact, could be likened to a metropolitan area, since it embraces a large core city and many connected towns and villages.

. . .

A second "metropolis" on our map is the law of peace and security. In contrast to human rights, the goal of peace and security has been the raison d'etre of the UN Charter. Under this head, we find the leading cases, the great dramas of the United Nations, the intense disputes about the interpretation and application of principles. This is the field of law in which the stakes are highest and the authority of the United Nations always on trial. Even though politics and national interests are rightly recognized as predominant, law has a role in almost every aspect of UN activity in this area.

. . .

The metropolis of peace and security law, like human rights, has its suburbs. One of the most important is the regulation and prohibition of armaments, especially weapons of mass destruction. The legal pattern in this area is predominantly made up of negotiated agreements, on a global or regional basis. It also embraces inspection to ascertain compliance with legal obligations such as those contained in the Treaty on the Non-Proliferation of Nuclear Weapons or Security Council decisions under chapter VII as, for example, applied to Iraq. Efforts to outlaw mass weapons or their use on the basis of existing principles of customary law or the Charter itself persist in UN bodies but lack support by the major powers concerned.

Still another suburb in the peace and security area comprises the law developed by the Security Council and, to some degree, the General Assembly in respect of peace keeping, peace enforcement, inspection and control. However, as 1993 drew to a close, the lack of resolve on the part of major powers, along with weaknesses within the UN operations, augured a retreat from peace enforcement and perhaps from consensual peace keeping. While the main legal principles are not likely to be abandoned, we can expect changes in legal arrangements bearing on rules of engagement, command and control, and perhaps criteria for UN interventions.

. . .

Not all the fields of law in the UN system are as large as those mentioned. Some would be only villages or hamlets on our metaphorical terrain. For example, the United Nations has generated and furthered an international treaty on enforcing maintenance obligations across national lines, a barely noticed legal instrument of great value to those entitled to support payments (in the main mothers and children). Another "village" is concerned with aid to victims of crimes and abuses of power, a continuing project that seeks to prevent and curtail such victimization through legal and practical means. . . .

All of these subjects are part of the "terrain" of UN law since they were generated by UN organs or applied by them. Our metaphorical map reminds us that these various legal communities are not entirely separate, that highways and byways provide linkages in the form of common principles and processes.

Without pressing the metaphor, we find interconnecting doctrine in the basic postulates of international law to which participants in the UN system, whatever the subject, profess adherence. States are regarded as the principal actors in creating and applying law. Their independence and formal equality are taken as axiomatic. The principles of territorial integrity and pacta *sunt servanda* [good faith performance of obligations], as well as the customary rules of diplomatic intercourse, are accepted in the UN system, as they are in general international law. Also accepted is the basic divide between the international and domestic domains, though, as indicated earlier, the line between them may change or blur in particular cases. All of these propositions are recognized as applicable to the legally relevant activities in the UN system. They are the connecting highways that run across the landscape and impart a degree of unity to the various activities.

These connecting highways—the concepts and principles of international law—are a conspicuous feature of UN debates. As the Secretary-General recently observed, "political discourse and the vocabulary of law mix cheerfully with one another . . . the dialectic between law and diplomacy is constantly at work." Perhaps it is not always "cheerful." The Secretary-General went on to say that "the United Nations shows, better than any other organization, the competition States engage in to try and impose a dominant language and control the juridical ideology it expresses." We are thus reminded that legal discourse is not divorced from political conflict. On the one hand, the concepts of international law provide a necessary code of communication, and therefore greatly facilitate the institutionalization of international society. On the other hand, international law is often relied upon by states to resist the transfer of their power to international authority. We have to look beyond international law itself to evaluate the likely consequences.

An overview of UN law reveals several other interesting characteristics of the UN system. I would begin with the characteristic modes of decision making in the UN system. These are essentially political processes, but they are shaped by the conditions of quasi-parliamentary procedures and the mandates of constituent instruments. What is perhaps most important in this respect is the central role of blocs and alliances in law creation and law application. State autonomy and equality are profoundly affected—

that is, reduced—by the requirements of group cohesion. To be sure, these are not ironclad requirements. A member of the "77" (i.e., about 150 developing states) or of the European group may cast an independent vote, but this is exceptional. Many groups coexist, some based on particular interests (for example, petroleum producers), others on regional or historical ties.

. . .

Still another characteristic of the UN system is its relative transparency and linkages to nonstate actors. This may surprise outsiders who feel excluded by its arcane language and somewhat elitist character. However, on a closer look at activities of legal significance, it becomes evident that member states are not the only participants, even if in a formal sense they are the designated players. In actuality most efforts directed to achieving new law or giving effect to existing law involve substantial participation by nonstate actors. Many enter as "experts" through governments or nongovernmental bodies. They are usually part of the "epistemic communities" that share and produce knowledge of particular subjects. They are necessary to informed decisions on seemingly technical questions. Although many are formally under governmental authority, their specialized expertise gives them a degree of independence and also raises the level of international cooperation.

A somewhat different role is played by groups and individuals outside governments who are dedicated to "causes" and take part indirectly in UN deliberations as "lobbyists" or "activists." Their influence varies with cause and case, but it would be a mistake to regard them in general as outsiders. I would guess that their actual role in the political and technical aspects of UN lawmaking is increasing. The communications revolution, the spread of democracy and the growth of transnational interest groups are factors that favor a larger role for nongovernmental bodies. . . .

As a final comment, I suggest an architectural metaphor. It views the UN legal order as a three-level structure:

On its ground floor, I place the actions of states—including the demands and goals of the governments and other organized groups in furtherance of their needs, wishes and expectations.

On the second level are the activities of a legal character—the formation and invoking of legal norms, and their application to particular situations.

On the third level, I would place the broad policy goals, aspirations and ideals that influence governments and the other actors.

Each of these levels exhibits its own values and processes. But there is continuous movement from level to level. The sphere of law in the middle level is influenced by the interests expressed below and the ideals and policy manifested above. The connec-

tions run both ways. Legal norms have an impact on the perceptions of interest and needs in the lower level and on the policies of the top level. This image helps us to see that the UN Legal Order is influenced by the multitude of demands and interests from below and by the ideals and principles on the higher level. It also reminds us that law exercises its influence in both directions, up and down.

Our metaphors may help to avoid a reductive conception of law in the UN system. To appreciate its achievement, we need to comprehend UN law in its full complexity and diversity. We may also envisage, as our metaphors suggest, the promise of continued legal developments responsive to practical needs and shared ideals.

EXHIBIT 3.3 United Nations Structure

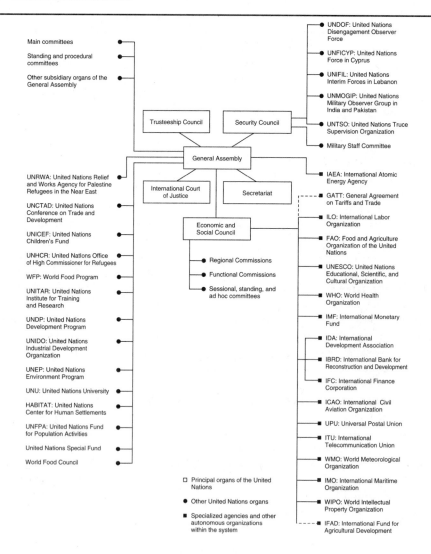

UN Structure

The six principal organs of the UN are: (1) General Assembly, (2) Security Council, (3) Economic and Social Council, (4) Trusteeship Council, (5) Secretariat, and (6) International Court of Justice (ICJ). Numerous other UN organs and specialized agencies also exist within the system, as depicted in Exhibit 3.3 above.

General Assembly The General Assembly (GA) is composed of all UN member States. The Assembly has various committees and commissions serving a variety of functions. Those functions include the making and consideration of reports on world events, the discussion of principles of international cooperation, the supervision of the UN's Trusteeship Council (discussed below), participation in selection of the judges of the ICJ, the approval of budgets and applications for membership, and the appointment of the UN Secretary-General.

Six major committees drive the work of the General Assembly—referred to as the "First Committee," and so on. After a committee reorganization prior to the opening of the 48th annual session in 1993, the traditional seven committees were reduced to six (with some renaming). The following inventory of the current Assembly committees suggests the structural arrangement of the day-to-day work of the Assembly: First Committee—*Disarmament and International Security;* Second Committee —*Economic and Financial;* Third Committee—*Social, Humanitarian and Cultural;* Fourth Committee—*Special Political and Decolonization;* Fifth Committee—*Administrative and Budgetary;* Sixth Committee—*Legal.*[11]

World leaders have often addressed the General Assembly on very sensitive problems in international relations. In 1960, Nikita Khrushchev spoke to the GA, accusing UN Secretary-General Dag Hammarskjold of abusing his position as head of this global organ. Khrushchev thus proposed that Hammarskjold be replaced by a three-person directorate so as to diffuse the power of the Secretary-General. It is unlikely that this criticism would have surfaced if the UN headquarters were located in Moscow, rather than New York. Yasir Arafat, the leader of the PLO who negotiated the Gaza/Jericho autonomy agreement of 1993, spoke to the GA in 1974. His objective was to seek UN assistance in consummating the dormant State of Palestine. The GA thus accorded special "observer status" to the PLO, whereby its representative could be present for all future meetings of the GA. In 1993, US President Clinton spoke in an effort to convince this body to reduce what he characterized as its overextended commitment to worldwide peacekeeping engagements. He also promised to pay US arrearages in assessed dues if the UN would develop a new funding formula for its national assessments (discussed below under "UN Reform Studies").

The GA is thus a global forum for the discussion of any matter within the scope of the UN Charter. Articles 10–17 of the Charter on the GA's functions and powers provide that it "may discuss," "may consider," "shall initiate studies and make recommendations," and "shall receive and consider annual and special reports." Malcolm Shaw, Professor of International Law at the University of Leicester in England, thus characterizes the General Assembly as "essentially a *debating chamber,* a forum for the exchange of ideas and the discussion of a wide-ranging category of problems."[12]

The General Assembly became more than a mere debate chamber in 1950 when its members recognized that the Security Council's power to act in sensitive cases would be vitiated by the veto power of the five permanent members of the Council. The Assembly thus adopted the Uniting for Peace Resolution. Its goal was to ensure a prompt response to threats to international peace when the Security Council would not, or could not, take action. The effect of this resolution, permitting the General Assembly to act in the absence of an express Charter authority to do so, is described in § 10.3 of this text.

The Assembly's specific Charter power is limited to the initiation of studies and the recommendation of peaceful courses of action by States or the UN Security Council. The Assembly's fundamental purpose is to promote international cooperation in political matters and to encourage the progressive development of International Law and its codification. Members of the Assembly therefore attempt to cooperate in the economic, social, cultural, educational, human rights, and health fields. During each annual session, they recommend measures for the peaceful adjustment of any situation deemed likely to impair friendly relations among nations.

The General Assembly is *not* a world legislature. It may pass resolutions, some of which ultimately become treaties. Other resolutions *may* indicate the degree of *opinio juris*—practices that States consider binding in their international relations (*see* § 1.4). The Assembly does not, however, have the power to enact legislation like a national legislature such as the US Congress, Mexican Parliament, or Japanese Diet. The underlying reason is that State members were unwilling to yield the requisite degree of sovereignty to an international organization that would allow it to make immediately enforceable laws. As succinctly stated by Professor Krzysztof Skubiszewski of the University of Pozman in Poland:

We know both from the reading of the UN Charter and the history of its drafting (the defeat of the Philippine proposal on this right presented at the [1945] Conference in San Francisco) that no power to make law for states has been conferred on the General Assembly or any other organ of the United Nations. For such power, whether comprising legislation by virtue of unanimous vote, or by majority decision with the guarantees of the system of contracting-out, or by majority decision binding for all, must always be based on an EXPLICIT AND UNEQUIVOCAL TREATY AUTHORIZATION.[13]

General Assembly special "observer status" is extended to selected international organizations such as national liberation movements. These organizations may thus attend meetings of the GA. Their representatives may be seated in a special chamber just off the main hall of the GA. Non-State actors may thereby participate in, and serve as resources for, the Assembly's State members. Nongovernmental observers, such as the Palestine Liberation Organization, often deal with governments on a *de facto* basis. This device provides greater access to the UN peace process. Private research institutions are also designated as nongovernmental observers of various UN organs operating under the GA. These include the Academic Council of the United Nations System (Brown University in Rhode Island) and the American Society of International Law (Tillar House, Washington, D.C.). These entities serve as think tanks for the pursuit of common objectives within the entire UN sphere of activities.

The General Assembly was effectively controlled by the UN until the late 1950s. After a paradigm shift associated with the induction of new independent States that were former colonies, the so-called "Third World" began to control the overall direction of the Assembly by the mid-1960s. The Assembly provides an unparlled form of recognition for these less powerful States. As aptly stated by Political Science Professor M.J. Peterson of Amherst University:

The egalitarian nature of the Assembly . . . makes it the favorite political organ of weak states . . . because it gives them an influence over decisions that they lack elsewhere in the international system. . . . The Third World Coalition . . . uses the Assembly more intensely than did the US-led coalition, but its relative lack of power has exposed more clearly the limits on Assembly control over outcomes in world politics.[14]

One of the resulting agenda shifts was the seventy-seven nation announcement of a New International Economic Order (*see* § 13.4). This program advocates an equitable redistribution of the world's wealth. The Assembly-driven Law of the Sea Treaty, referred to as LOST by the more powerful nations, became effective in November 1994. It illustrates one way in which this redistribution is to be accomplished. While economically powerful nations objected, the treaty text requires seagoing nations to contribute a portion of revenues they draw from mining and fishing the seas into an agency that, in turn, is supposed to repatriate a portion of these revenues to the less powerful nonseagoing States.

Security Council

(a) Purpose and Structure The Security Council (SC) is the UN organ with the primary responsibility for the maintenance of world peace. Under Article 39 of the Charter, the SC determines what constitutes a threat to peace and what measures shall be taken to maintain global peace and security. Under Article 47 of the Charter, the Council is responsible for submitting plans to UN members for establishing and maintaining a system to regulate armaments. Under Articles 41 and 42 of the Charter, the SC may decide what measures are to be employed to implement its decisions. The Council may order the complete or partial interruption of economic relations with States that violate international law. If the Council considers such sanctions inadequate, it may use air, sea, or land forces as necessary to maintain or restore international peace and security. The operations of multinational forces under

the control of the Council are described in § 10.3 of this book.

The Security Council consists of fifteen member States. The Council's size was purposely limited to ensure prompt and effective action by the UN, in contrast to the debating atmosphere of the *all*-member General Assembly. Nations could thus refer their disputes to the SC for resolution (as well as to the GA when it is in session). Unlike the Assembly, the Council functions continuously. A representative of each of the fifteen member States must be present at all times at UN Headquarters in New York City.

The Security Council's fifteen member States include five "permanent" members and ten "rotating" members periodically elected by the General Assembly. The five permanent members are China, France, Russia, the United Kingdom, and the United States. The "Russian" seat on the Council was formerly occupied by the Soviet Union until its demise in 1991. It is now occupied by Russia. The "China" seat has been occupied by the People's Republic of China since the Republic of China (Nationalist Chinese government) was ousted by UN action in 1971.

The makeup of the Security Council has always generated debates regarding its failure to reflect the composition of the General Assembly. The latter is a richly diverse body, consisting of States from every corner of the world, innumerable cultures, all political systems, and every form of economic development. Under the original Charter, however, five of the eleven SC members occupied permanent seats on the Council. Thus, any of the five could block Council action by the veto. None of the six rotating members could do so, absent a majority of votes to take action. In 1965, the UN altered the structure of the SC to increase the presence of less-powerful nations—many of which were former colonies of original UN members. The number of seats on the Council was increased from eleven to fifteen total members. The four new seats were designated as additional "rotating" seats, as opposed to "permanent" seats. A number of commentators viewed this as a minor concession in the struggle to improve the structure of the Council.

After the demise of the Soviet Union and the attendant Cold War with the US, Germany and Japan sought a change in their status from occasional rotating members to permanent members of the Security Council. This is essentially a US-backed program designed to increase the permanent five to seven. The British and French are opposed, as evinced by British Foreign Secretary Douglas Hurd's widely reported 1993 use of the old adage: "If it ain't broke, don't fix it." US Secretary of State Warren Christopher responded that the SC may not be broke; however, "It's time for some reorganizing." Ironically, the Japanese and German Constitutions contain limitations on their ability to participate in SC military actions.[15]

In the interim since 1945, the permanent membership on the Security Council has not reflected the diverse nature of the community of nations. Any status change on the Council should not ignore the less powerful but more populated States of Africa, Asia, and Latin America.

(b) The Veto Dilemma The League of Nations was plagued from the outset with its *unanimity* requirement for the League's Security Council to act. The United Nations Security Council voting procedure was initially perceived as an improvement that would facilitate its organizational power to respond quickly to State threats to peace. Nine of fifteen votes is thus one of two current conditions for Security Council action (changing from seven of eleven Council member votes in a 1965 "procedural" amendment adding four seats to the Council). The other condition is no veto by one of the five permanent members.

Ironically, the word "veto" is not contained in the UN Charter. Article 48 merely states that action "shall be taken by all the Members of the United Nations or by some of them, as the Security Council may determine." The Security Council Provisional Rules of Procedure contain the veto arrangements agreed upon at the 1945 UN drafting conference in San Francisco. The five major powers to emerge from World War II therein agreed that each would hold the right to veto SC action. Thus, mindful of both the US decision not to join the League of Nations and the Soviet Union's expulsion for invading Finland, none of the five permanent Council members could be drawn into an armed conflict that it did not want to enter.

National sovereignty was thus the essential culprit in what would soon become apparent with the advent of the "Cold War": The powerful States did not want to cede the requisite power to an international organization that it needed to effectively control threats to peace. There might be instances when a permanent SC member could clandestinely support the threatening State's action or, alternatively, remain too indifferent to risk involvement. National sovereignty concerns also thwarted materialization of the UN's Article 43 standing army, which would have functioned as an international police force. There would be little concern about this development, however, given the swift demise of the Council's power to act—buried in UN rules of procedure, rather than in the Charter itself. What, then, triggered the post-1945 veto dilemma, pitting the two most powerful World War II allies against one another, that would severely limit the UN's overall ability to respond to threats to peace?

The USSR temporarily boycotted SC meetings in 1950. The USSR had insisted that the People's Republic of China (communist mainland China) was the appropriate entity to occupy that seat in the Council, rather than the then-seated Republic of China (Nationalist government on Formosa supported by the UN—now referred to as Taiwan). This historic absence allowed the SC to vote in favor of UN involvement in the Korean Conflict, under the direction of a US military command. This would not have happened if the Soviet representative had been present for the vote (and possibly if the "China" seat had been occupied by mainland China, which came to the aid of North Korea during this 1950–1953 conflict). This event led to the infamous Cold War "veto" that continually paralyzed the SC's subsequent potential for fulfilling its mandate of maintaining international peace.

The permanent members' veto power has frequently rendered useless the Charter provisions for maintaining peace. This negative impact of superpower politics has been most evident when the holders of this veto power effectively bar international response to their *own* threats to international peace. Recent examples by each Council member, armed with the knowledge that it could block Security Council action via its potential veto, arguably include: the 1989 US invasion of Panama; France's involvement in the escape of the French agents responsible for the death of crew members on the Greenpeace vessel "Rainbow Warrior" in New Zealand in 1986; Great Britain's 1982 war with Argentina over the distant Falkland Islands just off Argentina's coast; the Soviet Union's takeover of Afghanistan in 1979; and any UN responsive action for the deaths of some 3,000 civilians in Beijing's Tienanmen Square during a demonstration for democracy in 1989.

Now that the Cold War has ended, is there a renewed opportunity for effective Security Council action uninhibited by the continued use of the veto? Focusing on 1992, the third-busiest year in Security Council history, one could argue that a virtual renaissance has flowered in its effective involvement in dealing with international matters—depicted in Exhibit 3.4.

EXHIBIT 3.4 Security Council 1992 Highlights

Open Meetings	129 (53 in 1991/69 in 1990/5 in 1959) First summit meeting of heads of State
Conflicts	Somalia Former Yugoslavia Iraq-Kuwait resolution implementation
Sanctions	Yugoslavia (May: expanded arms to total embargo) Somalia (January) Liberia (November) Libya (April for failing to produce terrorists)

EXHIBIT 3.4 *(continued)*

Peacekeeping (personnel)	Yugoslavia (22,000) Somalia (4,000) Mozambique approved (7,500 anticipated) Cambodia (20,000)
Renew Peacekeeping Operations	Angola Cyprus El Salvador Golan Heights
Membership Applications	Thirteen countries—mostly former Soviet Union Two meetings each application

Effective SC control of international conflict is arguably unlikely in the long run, without significant change (see UN Reform below). All members of the permanent five continue to have their own national sovereignty concerns, including the SC's avoiding any involvement in certain conflicts that they either support—overtly or covertly—or are not interested in pursuing from a national (rather than an international) perspective. Thus, the permanent five have all benefited from the veto, which has unfairly been attributed solely to the obstructionism of the former Soviet Union. Diverse political conflicts from all regions of the world could thus operate under the shadow of the more powerful nations in the global community that may use (or threaten to use) the veto to negate any UN involvement.

(c) Peacekeeping Operations The lack of effective UN involvement in various peacekeeping operations such as Bosnia and Somalia signal the lack of international commitment to reliance on the Security Council as a tool for facilitating an original ideal of the UN: "to save succeeding generations from the scourge of war." Although the frequency of the veto has declined in the aftermath of the Cold War, the circumstances giving rise to the underlying conflicts have not. There will be no effective international control of such conflicts until there is a genuine interest by State members of this global organization to integrate word and deed. In the words of UN Political Affairs Officer Anjali Patil in her book on the veto:

It really doesn't matter who enjoys the veto power in the Security Council; international peace and security cannot be maintained until all States accept the need to identify with the whole of humanity. We have struggled over the centuries for absolute peace but have not yet achieved it. While creating the United Nations has enabled us to avoid a [third] world war, we have yet to create a genuine international society.[16]

In January of 1992, world leaders conducted a summit-level meeting of the UN Security Council members in New York. This was the 3,046th meeting of the Council but the *first* meeting of the heads of State of this body since its inception. As then stated by Britain's SC President, on behalf of the Council to the heads of State at the close of this special meeting:

This meeting takes place at a time of momentous change. The ending of the Cold War has raised hopes for a safer, more equitable and more humane world. . . .

Last year, under authority of the United nations, the international community succeeded in enabling Kuwait to regain its sovereignty and territorial integrity, which it had lost as a result of Iraqi aggression.

The members of the Council also recognize that change, however welcome, has brought new risks for stability and security. Some of the most acute problems result from changes to State structures [*see* this text § 2.3]. . . .

The international community therefore faces new challenges in the search for peace. All Member States expect the United Nations to play a central role at this crucial stage. The members of the Council stress the importance of strengthening and improving the United Nations to increase its effectiveness."

Rather than themselves initiating just how this "strengthening and improvement" would happen, the Council's heads of State instead request that the UN Secretary-General assume this task. In his responsive work product entitled *Agenda for Peace*,[17] Boutros Boutros-Ghali made specific recommendations relevant to the Security Council in three general areas: (1) *preventative diplomacy*—formal fact-finding mandated by the SC; meeting "away" from the Council's New York headquarters notwithstanding this Charter requirement, so as to directly diffuse disputes by its presence; (2) *peacemaking*—mediation or negotiation by an individual designated by the SC; that the Council devise means for using financial institutions and other components of the UN system to insulate certain States from the economic consequences of potential economic sanctions under Article 41; that States undertake to make armed forces available to the Council, on a permanent basis, when it decides to tackle military action under Article 42; that the Council utilize peace-enforcement measures only in "clearly defined circumstances and with their terms of reference specified in advance;" (3) *peacekeeping*—that regional arrangements be undertaken in a manner that would effectively contribute to a deeper sense of participation, consensus, and democratization in international affairs.

The 1994 US reaction was interesting, to say the least. President Clinton signed a classified US Presidential Directive that one could characterize as responding to or defusing the UN Secretary-General's 1992 *Agenda for Peace* recommendations on peacekeeping operations. The Directive also modified the Bush administration's expansive UN policy and the unparalleled increase in UN peacekeeping operations after the SC's apparent renaissance during the Persian Gulf War. The following analysis could not be directly based on the President's classified document, although the US Department of State was able to provide a separate and more general analysis that summarizes the key elements of the announced US policy. The first paragraph addresses

the general US voting posture in future SC matters. The second paragraph provides some specifics about whether US troops can be committed to such actions:

We have determined that the United States should support international action when a threat exists to international or regional peace and security, such as international aggression, an urgent humanitarian disaster or interruption of established democracy or gross violation of human rights that is coupled with violence. In determining whether to support international action, the U.S. will consider whether operations have clear objectives, a defined scope, and an integrated politico-military strategy to achieve our objectives. An international "community of interests" should exist to support multilateral operations. For Chapter VI [presumably referring to Chapter VII] operations, a ceasefire should be in place. The availability of financial and human resources to carry out the strategy will be a critical factor in U.S. deliberations, as will the linkage of expected duration to clear objectives and realistic exit criteria for the operation.

The standards will be even more stringent when the U.S. considers deploying American forces to participate in peace operations. The U.S. will only participate in a peace operation when:

- It advances U.S. interests and the level of risk is acceptable;

- U.S. participation is necessary for the success of the operation;

- An integrated politico-military strategy exists to achieve our objectives;

- The personnel, funds, and resources are available to support the strategy;

- Command and control arrangements are satisfactory;

- Likely duration and exit conditions have been identified; and

- Domestic and Congressional support exists or can be marshaled.

We believe these factors are critical to the successful conduct of peace operations and to building public and Congressional support for U.S. involvement in those operations. As for command and control arrangements, the

President will never relinquish command over U.S. forces. However, the President will, on a case-by-case basis, consider placing appropriate U.S. forces under the operational control of a competent UN commander for specific UN operations authorized by the Security Council.[18]

How, and whether, the above proposals and refinements are implemented will depend on the degree to which post–Cold War politics and the continuing breakdown of States effectively recognize (or ignore) the required State infusion of sovereign power into this international organization. Otherwise, the UN will remain unable to effectively subdue the excesses of its scofflaws.

Economic and Social Council ECOSOC, headquartered in Paris, has a variety of functions under the UN Charter. Unlike the League of Nations, which was concerned primarily about military and political problems, the UN system has been more attentive to economic and social matters. The comparative UN priorities include the observance of human rights and the general welfare of the individual. ECOSOC thus conducts studies and issues reports on international economic, social, cultural, educational, and health matters. The results of these studies are forwarded to the General Assembly, to the State members of the United Nations, and to the UN's specialized agencies concerned with the promotion of human rights and fundamental freedoms for all people.

ECOSOC also prepares draft conventions for submission to the General Assembly and arranges international conferences on matters within its competence. Certain specialized agencies within the UN system work closely with this Council on issues affecting all economic and social matters. ECOSOC is the lead international agency, for example, that deals with illegal drug trafficking.[19]

When the US Reagan Administration began to shun participation in various UN agencies in the 1980s, an ECOSOC specialized agency was the first UN entity from which the US withdrew (1984). This was the UN Educational, Scientific, and Cultural Organization (UNESCO). The US maintains that the vast UN bureaucracy has produced much paperwork without tangible benefits, as discussed below under "UN Reform." In 1990, the US reaf-firmed its opposition to rejoining UNESCO. US Secretary of State James Baker's remarks provide telling insight into the US position, and also apparently on the UN in general: "Bluntly stated, UNESCO needs the United States as a member far more than the United States needs UNESCO." The US position was, essentially, that it could gain more leverage from nonmembership than from being just one of what was (at the time of withdrawal) 161 UN member States.

Trusteeship Council The Trusteeship Council (TC) is a distinct UN organ consisting of selected UN members and is responsible for the administration of territories that are incapable of self-government. Under Article 77 of the Charter, certain member States have supervised territories detached from enemy States, typically as a result of war. Under Article 73 of the Charter, supervising States accepting a "trust" territory must observe the principle that the interests of the inhabitants of these territories are paramount to any interests of the supervising State. The supervising State must therefore accept the obligation to promote the well-being of the inhabitants (*see* § 2.3 materials on Self-determination).

This "big brother" plan was devised to promote the political, economic, social, and educational advancement of the supervised territories not yet independent and capable of self-governance—at the close of World War II, when the UN Charter and its TC were created. Another goal was to help these territories achieve self-government through the progressive development of free political institutions. The US, for example, has administered the Trust Territory of the Pacific Islands since 1947. Portions of the population later developed their own forms of government and constitutions. In 1986, the UN's Trusteeship Council determined that the United States had satisfied its obligation to administer most of this territory. The United States then declared its obligations to be discharged. The Micronesia and Marshall Islands portion of this US trust territory later joined the UN as independent States.

The speed of this internationally supervised development has depended on the particular circumstances of each territory, its people, and their stage of political advancement. Most of the TC's work is completed, due to the success of the decolonization movement of the 1960s.

The leading example of a *breach* of this entire trust concept is the case of Namibia. This area was originally a League of Nations "Mandate," analogous to the League-generated British Mandate over Palestine. South Africa refused to yield to decades of UN pressure to release its trust territory of Namibia (formerly South West Africa). South Africa finally agreed to permit Namibia to govern itself in 1990, the year that it joined the UN as an independent State member.

There have been other alleged breaches of trust, or attempts by the governed territory to break free from the established State entrusted with the territory. Nauru, a tiny republic in the central Pacific Ocean, sued Australia in the International Court of Justice (ICJ) in 1989—alleging neglect by Australia's exploitation and removal of phosphates earlier in the twentieth century. Natives claimed that they were barred from seeking outside legal help to avoid such depletions during the Australian administration. In 1967, the UN General Assembly terminated the Trusteeship without making any reservation relating to Australia's administration of Nauru when it was under trusteeship. In 1992, the ICJ rejected Australia's contention that the UN's termination of the trusteeship barred the Court from hearing this breach of trust case. Eventually, the parties agreed to discontinue the case, which has been dismissed.[20]

One trust territory has unsuccessfully sued its administrative host to terminate the trust relationship. The overall Trust Territory of the Pacific Islands was reduced by the departure of Micronesia, the Marshall Islands, and the Commonwealth of the Northern Marianas—after the UN declared in 1986 that the US administration had been fulfilled as to these areas. The government of Palau then signed a "Compact of Free Association" with the US. This agreement was rejected by the people of Palau, however, in a series of UN-observed plebiscites. Thus, Palau remains under US-controlled UN trusteeship status. The US is concerned about an unacceptable provision in Palau's Constitution that declares that the islands are a "nuclear free nation."

In 1990, this remaining Trust Territory of the Pacific Islands—Palau—thus sued the US in a New York court in its bid for self-rule. The plaintiffs argued that continued UN trusteeship reneged on the lost promise of self-government. But any alteration of this trust relationship requires approval by the UN's Security Council, under Charter Article 83.

The US court dismissed this case, partially on the basis that US courts do not have the jurisdiction or power to hear cases to dissolve trust territory relationships—a power that is expressly reserved by the UN Charter to the Security Council in association with the Trusteeship Council.[21]

Although the TC may appear to be a relic of the 1945 Charter, in practice it may have some contemporary utility. A number of States are "failing," in the sense that they are experiencing difficulties in continued self-government. Famine, civil war, and economic deprivation are some of the contemporary causes. Liberia dissolved into chaos in 1990, when rival factions began to assert tribal rivalries—slaughtering tens of thousands in the crossfire. Similar events occurred in Rwanda in 1994. "Older" States from other regions of the world such as Afghanistan, Haiti, Mozambique, Somalia, and Zaire are bordering on the same fate. "Newer" States like Bosnia-Herzegovina and Azerbaijan are just one step further away from such failed status.

The daunting question is this: When should such States be declared temporary wards of the UN? One of many problems would be predictable reprisals of various local warlords in such a side-by-side relationship with the UN. Another problem is the deficit at the UN, caused by an increasing number of States that do not want to continue "throwing good money after bad." Bosnia mediator Britain's Lord Owen and the US's Cyrus Vance rejected this idea in the case of Bosnia. In 1992, the UN Secretary-General thus stated that the UN was "considering" this option. The alternative, however, is to idly observe such tragedy as it drags on indefinitely.

Secretariat The Secretariat administers all of the programs of the UN. Its approximately 26,500-person staff (Geneva, New York, Vienna, and some other sites) is headed by the UN Secretary-General, who is appointed by the General Assembly on recommendation of the Security Council. This individual is the chief administrative officer of the UN. He or she acts in that capacity when attending meetings of the various organs of the UN.

All employees of the Secretariat, including the Secretary-General, are expected to execute their duties independently of any national allegiances. Article 100 of the charter provides that in the "performance of their duties the Secretary-General and the staff shall not seek or receive instructions from any other authority external to the Organization.

They shall refrain from any action which might reflect on their position as international officials responsible only to the Organization." State members of the UN are thus expected to respect the exclusively international character and responsibilities of their citizens who join the UN staff.

A very important but obscure function of the office of the Secretary-General (SG) is preventative diplomacy. While the public has traditionally perceived the role of this office as rather titular, the SG has often undertaken quite perilous and even monumental negotiations to resolve international crises. The almost forgotten Article 99 of the UN Charter provides that the SG "may bring to the attention of the Security Council any matter which in his opinion may threaten the maintenance of international peace and security." In Boutros Boutros-Ghali's *Agenda for Peace*, requested by the heads of State at the first meeting of the Security Council in 1992, he aptly notes the increasing importance of this role. In his words:

> There is a long history of the utilization by the United Nations of distinguished statesmen to facilitate the processes of peace. . . . Frequently it is the Secretary-General himself who undertakes the task. While the mediator's effectiveness is enhanced by strong and evident support from the [Security] Council, the General Assembly and the relevant Member States acting in their national capacity, the good offices of the Secretary-General may at times be employed most effectively when conducted independently of the deliberative bodies.[22]

There is no clear theoretical framework, however, for a clear and consistent link between the SG's above Article 99 obligation to bring peace-threatening matters before the Security Council and the SG's ability to gather and evaluate conflict-prevention information. International courts are notorious for the same lack of facts when decisions are to be made, and their consequent need to fact-find during the proceedings (*see* § 9.4). This dilemma has also hampered various SGs, who have enjoyed varying degrees of success in carrying out their function as preventative problem solvers. This is a critical area in need of reform. The problem is succinctly stated by Professor of Peace Studies Thomas Boudreau of St. John's University in Collegeville, Minnesota:

Without a theoretical framework that justifies and clarifies a specific reform, each effort to improve the Secretary-General's ability to prevent conflict threatens to become a piecemeal "band-aid" solution. In short, there is a need to . . . define and develop a clear and consistent link between the Secretary-General's obligation under Article 99 and his ability to gather, ascertain, and evaluate information concerning conflict prevention. There seems to be a bankruptcy of ideas in the realm of information gathering by the United Nations. . . .[23]

International Court of Justice The ICJ is the UN's judicial organ. Unlike its predecessor, the Permanent Court of International Justice (which was *not* an organ of the League of Nations) the drafters of the 1945 UN Charter conceived this institution as a forum wherein international disputes could be resolved in the courtroom rather than on the battlefield.

It is headquartered at The Hague, in the Netherlands, and is generally viewed as not having fully lived up to the dream envisioned by its creators who drafted the relevant UN Charter provisions (*see* Appendix A of this text, Articles 92–96) and the associated Statute of the International Court of Justice. Once again, national sovereignty has been the culprit in undoing the 1945 vision of beating swords into plowshares. This dilemma, related problems, and proposals for its refurbishment are addressed in Chapter 9 of this text.

UN Assessment

Conflicting views abound regarding the UN's progress toward fulfilling its 1945 Charter objectives. This portion of the text summarizes the perspectives on whether the UN has played a significant role in discharging its Charter functions. Some commentators have asserted that it is only a place to let off steam, operating merely as a masquerade concealing the hegemony of its more powerful national members. The most accurate perception is one that carefully assesses both sides of the UN balance sheet. Although there have been pluses, many minuses can be attributed to the often-forgotten limitations imposed by State sovereignty.

Traditional Perceptions One perception is that the UN has lost nothing of its relevance. A contemporary International Law specialist, Arpad Prandler of Hungary, thus proclaims as follows:

> The Hungarian People's Republic, which in 1955 assumed the obligation to have respect for the Charter and implement its provisions, has taken a consistent stand . . . against concepts and suggestions which, though well-intentioned, have laid the blame on the Charter for both the failures of the World Organization and the negative tendencies for the international situation and which seek the cure for ills external to the Organization. . . . The aims and purposes of the Charter, namely the maintenance of international peace and security, the preservation and removal of threats to peace, the development of friendly relations among nations based on respect for the principle of equal rights and self-determination of peoples, and international cooperation in the economic, social and cultural fields are of unchanged significance and call for a fuller measure of implementation. . . . On the whole, the Organization . . . has stood the test of time.[24]

This perspective supports the view that the UN has at least managed to assist in repressing the military excesses and xenophobia that led to two World Wars in the twentieth century.

Another persistent view is that the UN has not—and cannot—accomplish its myopic goal of maintaining world peace. It is no stronger than the sum of its national parts.[25] Some who adhere to this assessment of the UN's performance are most willing to predict that—in the aftermath of the demise of the Soviet Union and the Cold War—only the resurrection of *US* interest can save a floundering UN. The US reliance on the UN to support the Bush administration's interests in Kuwait thus triggered an about-face. The Reagan administration had previously adopted the attitude that the UN needed the US more than the US needed the UN—signaling a US withdrawal from various UN agencies in the 1980s. Suddenly, however, the Bush administration could not cite International Law fast enough, and often enough, when the US was seeking Arab and global support for the rescue of Kuwait from the Iraqi annexation in 1990.

A third perspective is that the UN has enjoyed both successes and failures, but now faces a major crisis. In the 1986 opening statement to the Forty-first Annual General Assembly, UN Secretary-General Javier Perez de Cuellar of Peru stated that some nations have jeopardized the future of the UN. There was a "crisis of confidence" in the UN, he claimed, because some of its member States were refusing to pay their assessed contributions to the UN's annual administrative budget. The US, for example, did not pay all of its assessed dues during the 1980s. Although this refusal violates an international obligation to pay such dues,[26] who can possibly force any UN member State to make such payments? If such members continue to renege on this commitment, in their pursuit of political goals, the UN's ability to function will be in extreme peril unlike never before.

Another feature of this "mixed-bag" perception of UN performance is the comparative results in Kuwait and Yugoslavia. Security Council Resolution 687 was perhaps a more important milestone in UN history than the Persian Gulf War itself. This ceasefire resolution, among the many issued by the Council during and after the cessation of hostilities,[27] is a major break from prior resolutions—partially due to its breadth, but mostly due to its purported control over *future* State behavior. The Security Council ordered unprecedented and unparalleled controls on Iraq's future behavior in terms of observing international border delimitations, nonuse of chemical and nuclear weapons, sanctions, and required war reparations. The relevant paragraphs of the actual Resolution are reprinted below:

UNITED NATIONS SECURITY COUNCIL RESOLUTION 687

2981st Meeting, April 3, 1991

The Security Council,

. . .

Welcoming the restoration to Kuwait of its national sovereignty, independence, and territorial integrity and the return of its legitimate government,

. . .

2. *Demands* that Iraq and Kuwait respect the inviolability of the international boundary

. . .

4. *Decides* to guarantee the inviolability of the above-mentioned international boundary and to take as appropriate all necessary measures to that end in accordance with the Charter;

. . .

8. *Decides* that Iraq shall unconditionally accept the destruction, removal, or rendering harmless, under international supervision, of:

(a) all chemical and biological weapons and all stocks of agents. . .;

(b) all ballistic missiles with a range of greater than 150 kilometres and related major parts, and repair and production facilities;

. . .

14. *Takes note* that the actions to be taken by Iraq . . . represent steps towards the goal of establishing in the Middle East a zone free from weapons of mass destruction and all missiles for their delivery and the objective of a global ban on chemical weapons;

. . .

24. *Decides* that, in accordance with Resolution 661 (1990) and subsequent related resolutions and until a further decision is taken by the Council, all States shall continue to prevent the sale or supply . . . to Iraq by their nationals . . . of:

(a) arms and related *materiel* of all types. . . .

25. *Calls upon* all States and international organizations to act strictly in accordance with paragraph 24 above, notwithstanding the existence of any [prior] contracts, agreements, licenses, or any other arrangements;

. . .

30. *Decides that*, in furtherance of its commitment to facilitate the repatriation of all Kuwaiti and third party nationals, Iraq shall extend all necessary cooperation to the International Committee of the Red Cross. . .;

. . .

32. *Requires* Iraq to inform the Council that it will no commit or support any act of international terrorism. . .;

. . .

34. *Decides* to remain seized of the matter and to take such further steps as may be required for the implementation of this resolution and to secure peace and security in the area.

These portions of Resolution 687 provide the foremost statement of conditions ever made by the Security Council—due to their comprehensive nature and their purported control of future action by Iraq and all members of the international community. But for the Cold War veto described above, a similar resolution might have been issued in prior conflicts. This resolution thus signaled a zenith in the willingness of the Council to undertake its task of attempting to maintain global peace and security.

Adherence to this resolution was not as forthcoming as expected. Iraq chose to limit UN agents from conducting inspections of its war potential and seized certain agents during their UN-sanctioned visits. In spite of such problems with implementation, this resolution heralded what would appear to be the effective return of the Security Council from its Cold War hiatus.

Security Council Activism The Gulf War activism of the Security Council triggered the twin perceptions of the UN casting off the fetters of the Cold War, while simultaneously generating suspicion by those nations that might be the future objects of the hegemony of its more powerful members. Many "Third World" countries—as they were typically characterized during the Cold War—perceived the Gulf War and the Council's activism as providing the potential for a new form of control by the States that remained dominant after the Cold War. This concern is aptly articulated by Professor Yoshiro Matsui of Kyoto University as follows:

The Gulf War symbolizes the United Nations activism after the end of the Cold War. The Security Council adopted many resolutions under Chapter VII of the Charter [Action with Respect to Threats to the Peace] during and after the Gulf War, without being disturbed by the veto of its permanent Members, and this fact is highly appreciated . . . as illustrating a "rebirth" of the United Nations' collective security. . . .

But . . . there spreads a wide suspicion, especially among the nonaligned and developing countries, that this United Nations activism may be a Great Power hegemony in disguise, since they are the only possible targets of this activism. This suspicion seems to be reinforced by the fact that almost all the resolutions . . . have not specified the concrete article of the Charter as their basis [for Council actions against Iraq]. This ambiguous constitutionality . . . is not a happy one for the United Nations activism, and Member States have legitimate interests to see that the Security Council acts within the framework of the Charter which they have accepted.[28]

Professor Matsui attributes this suspicion to the inherently limited scope of available UN controls: neither the Charter, nor the Security Council, nor precedent give the Secretary-General authority to act in a military operation. The superpowers ensured their control of their own destiny in 1945, when the Charter emerged just short of providing such authority to the head of the UN. No State later chose to provide the *standing* military forces called for in Article 43 of the Charter—as opposed to the resulting *ad hoc* case-by-case basis whereby each nation must consent to provide supporting military forces.

Another facet of this concern about the constitutionality of the Security Council's activism is spawned by Article 2.7 of the UN Charter. It provides as follows:

Nothing contained in the present Charter shall authorize the United Nations to intervene in matters which are essentially within the domestic jurisdiction of any state or shall require the Members to submit such matters to settlement under the present Charter; but this principle shall not prejudice the application of enforcement measures under Chapter VII [Action with Respect to Threats to Peace].

Prior to the Gulf War, the long Cold War period had generated something other than the infamous veto—the restrictive application of Chapter VII.

Thus, it was historically difficult for the Security Council to take an "activist" role in maintaining international peace. With the weight of the world against Iraq's invasion of Kuwait, reminiscent of similar excesses of members of the now defunct League of Nations, the Council was able to assume a far more activist role no longer suppressed by a restrictive view of Article 2.7. Although Iraq might characterize Security Council intervention as injecting the organization into an internal matter regarding its "19th Province," its invasion of a UN member State set the stage for the subsequent activism, including Yugoslavia (humanitarian aid), Somalia (where force was used *first* by UN troops), and Rwanda (humanitarian relief).

The Security Council's activism was arguably reshelved during events unfolding in the former Yugoslavia beginning in 1992. Various regions of the former Yugoslavia voted for independence and were recognized, arguably prematurely (*see* § 2.4), by the international community. At the beginning of the "Gulf War" period, the first Security Council Resolution demanding Iraqi retraction from its invasion of strategically located and oil-rich Kuwait, came ten hours after the invasion. The Council never "took charge" in the less strategically located and resource-poor arena of Bosnia-Herzegovina. The Bosnian Serbs perpetrated a full-scale war, marked by the brutal infliction of extreme violations of humanitarian norms on the civilian population. There was clear evidence, in what became almost routine media reports, of the indiscriminate bombing of civilians, including an attack on a marketplace in Sarajevo that killed sixty-six people. The Serbs mistreated those in detention, ignored the basic international safeguards intended to protect civilians and medical facilities, and perpetrated a policy of "ethnic cleansing" that resulted in the disappearances or misplacement of hundreds of thousands of refugees on the basis of nationality and religion.

Unlike the Council's activism in the Iraq/Kuwait theater, there was a waning optimism about its continued role in maintaining peace. The Council engaged in a form of political "hot potato" regarding what entity should take charge of the international response to the Bosnia crisis. The Council authorized the use of force in three resolutions: (1) Resolution 770—"all necessary measures" *can* be "taken nationally or through regional agencies or arrangements" to deliver humanitarian assistance when needed in Bosnia-Herzegovina; (2) Resolution

816—States and regional groups *may* use necessary means that *they* may determine for enforcing no-fly zones established by the Council to contain this conflict; and (3) Resolution 836—UN member States "acting nationally or through regional organizations or arrangements" *may* use air power to protect UN peacekeepers on the ground in Bosnia (e.g., NATO bombing of Serb positions near Sarejevo in 1994). It seemed that the UN was now in search of a role.

The US feared ground-troop involvement in Bosnia, due to the fragile nature of its newly found relationship with Russia just after the Cold War. The Russian ties with the Serbs were too close for the US to risk extensive involvement. The NATO-based ultimatum that Serb guns withdraw from UN-designated "safe heavens" was the most effective tool for shifting political and military responsibility. The UN was simultaneously courting Russian membership, a convenient "regional arrangement" for finding peace and a face-saving device to "confront" Serb defiance of various UN directives. The UN would thereby exercise some degree of control via its plan to give NATO authority to order air strikes as needed to achieve political objectives.

The UN has achieved about as much success as can be expected from an international organization composed of totally autonomous States. It was never intended to be a supreme legislative body. Nor did its creators endow it with supranational powers to force its members to comply with the decisions of its organs—as evidenced by the lack of Charter language vesting the Secretary-General with effective control over military operations. Despite that, successes have been achieved in advancing human rights, resolving territorial disputes, promoting economic and social welfare programs, and developing draft treaties for State adoption. The eight-year-long UN process that produced the Law of the Sea Treaty is evidence of a significant success. Notwithstanding problems and reservations, the UN thus produced what will probably become the most comprehensive treaty that ever entered into force (*see* § 6.3).

While critics tend to focus on the limitations of the UN's politically sensitive bodies, such as the Security Council and the General Assembly, the UN has nevertheless operated over forty existing agencies pursuing programs to improve living conditions for millions of people (*see* Exhibit 3.3 on "UN Structure"). One result is that the UN can be credited with the global proliferation of human rights treaties in the last several decades, as discussed in Chapter 11 of this text.

Various UN agencies have also resolved a number of territorial disputes. The International Court of Justice has decided many boundary disputes. The UN Committee on the Peaceful Uses of Outer Space undertook the foundational work necessary to conclude the 1967 Treaty on Principles Governing the Activities of States in the Exploration and Use of Outer Space Including the Moon and Other Celestial Bodies. The space treaties produced at the UN[29] have thus provided a widely accepted paradigm for avoiding future territorial disputes and any militarization of space (*see* § 6.4).

UN economic and social welfare programs have eliminated diseases and generated hundreds of treaties dealing with narcotics, trade, slavery, atomic energy, road transportation, and famine relief efforts in Africa, among many others.[30]

Supposed Failures Three general failures are typically attributed to the UN: (1) it is unable to control the use of force among states; (2) it is no more than a debate chamber; and (3) it is an expensive paper mill without tangible benefits.

Has the UN in fact failed to control the use of force? The most fundamental norm in the UN Charter is found in Article 2.4. It codifies the agreement of the member nations to "refrain in their international relations from the threat or use of force against the territorial integrity or political independence of any state. . . ." But the UN does not control the military actions of its members. It *cannot* exercise greater power than that which is ceded to it by its member states. They, the States, have failed. One almost forgotten example is that the UN's original member States failed to provide a standing military force for immediate deployment in crisis.

Critics also routinely forget to incorporate Article 33 of the UN Charter into their analyses. This all but forgotten provision directs that the "parties to any dispute, the continuance of which is likely to endanger the maintenance of international peace and security, shall, first of all, seek a solution by negotiation . . . judicial settlement, resort to regional agencies or arrangements, or other peaceful means of their choice." Each nation is thus responsible for pursuing the Article 33 alternatives for maintaining good international relations. Contrary to popular belief, the UN cannot immediately step in to dissipate hostilities.

War and related hostilities are properly attributable to the UN's various State *members* for failing to control themselves, rather than to the UN itself for failing to control them. The UN has established some useful peacekeeping operations, as will be discussed in Chapter 10 on control of force by international organizations. But the UN members have failed to vest it with sufficient power and finances to control violations of the Charter's prohibition against the use or threat of force. Further, such operations cannot be conducted without the consent of the nations involved in the conflict. Thus, it is inaccurate to claim that the UN has failed, when in fact its member States never intended for it to be a supranational power that could act without case-by-case consent. Otherwise, the State members might have contributed the standing military forces envisioned in Article 43 of the Charter.

Other important reasons exist for blaming State *members* rather than the UN itself for its "failures." As discussed earlier in this section of the book, a single veto of any one of the five permanent members of the Security Council vitiates the possible use of an international military force to control threats to peace. Further, the General Assembly did not exercise its Charter-based power to expel violators of International Law from the UN until well after the historical Yugoslavia ceased to function. As a result of such inaction, the dream that the UN would enforce Charter norms has not been fully achieved. These limitations in the two major organs of the UN demonstrate that the original members did not create (nor do current members actually want) a powerful international organization. UN members want to retain the freedom to unilaterally preserve their sovereign powers to act, although they often pay lip service to general principles of peace with which no member would publicly disagree.

The "Turkish bath" criticism is that the UN has failed because it serves only as a place to let off steam. This characterization is somewhat accurate but definitely misleading. It was Jeanne Kirkpatrick, the former US chief delegate to the UN Security Council, who publicly referred to this body as a Turkish bath that cannot achieve its task of resolving international conflict. In 1986, UN General Assembly President Choudhury similarly stated that the Assembly needs to be strengthened because it "has been reduced to a mere debating body."[31]

Any UN inability to act or to achieve uniform compliance with international norms cannot be characterized as a complete failure. An undesirable function of the UN is to provide adversaries with an opportunity for global discourse. UN members thus meet both regularly and when there is a crisis. Without this debate forum, there would be no comparable opportunity for discussions that might bring the force of public opinion to bear on the conduct of certain nations. Distant events would receive little attention outside of a particular country or region before they might erupt into war. Access to the UN's political organs such as the General Assembly and the Security Council serves the national political agenda of establishing and maintaining dialogues on the issues that each nation considers important to preserve international peace.

The major powers structured this organization to conduct their affairs with a view toward their respective national interests. The permanent Security Council members effectively negated the possible impact that the UN might have had, if it had been given the requisite degree of power to actually beat swords into plowshares. Some commentators have thus asserted that the use or threatened use of the veto power has effectively resulted in a dictatorship within a democracy. The five permanent members "call all the shots," whether they will be fired, and at whom.

The third failure commonly attributed to the UN is the characterization that it is no more than a vast paper mill, existing to serve itself rather than its members. The UN is of course a very large business. It employs some 26,500 people throughout the world and generates over one billion pages of documents each year. Critics have thus argued that nations with comparatively large annual dues assessments are not obtaining a good return on their investments. Also, its six official languages require multiple translations and publication of the same information. Under Article 111 of the Charter, the five original languages included those of the permanent members of the Security Council—Chinese, French, Russian, and English (US and Great Britain). Spanish was initially included as an official language due to the large percentage of the world's population that speaks Spanish. Arabic was similarly added in 1977.

Financial Crisis In the mid-1980s, certain countries began to withdraw from various organs of the UN or to refuse to pay their full annual UN-assessed dues. The United States' 1986 assessment, for example, was approximately $200 million, or 25 percent, of the UN's total $800 million annual budget. By 1993, the US dues assessment was $374 million in arrears—which the president promised to pay only if the UN alters its funding formula to reflect growth in other national economies (such as Germany and Japan, which pay far less in annual dues). The US also pays 31.7 percent of the UN's peacekeeping costs, which is often larger than the annual budget category of UN-assessed US dues. In 1994, the combined US share of the UN's annual general budget and special peacekeeping costs was $1.334 billion.

The UN is owed much more, due to delayed payments from other countries. Secretary-General Boutros Boutros-Ghali announced in September 1993 that there had been an increase in operating costs—for 1992 versus 1993—from $1.4 billion up to $3.6 billion. The number of required peacekeepers would also rise from 80,000 to 100,000 individuals. As of the date of his announcement, only seven members had paid their dues in full. The UN will obviously reach the breaking point if members remain delinquent about paying their assessments.

The UN finally created an independent Inspector General in 1994. The creation of this new watchdog post helped to clear the way for the US to repay the $1 billion it owed the world body as of 1994. The US Congress was unwilling to pay arrearages in UN-assessed dues until this position was finalized by naming a German diplomat to probe mismanagement and waste. This international civil servant is also expected to placate national concerns about the inability to prosecute UN employees for their misconduct in office. The Inspector General is thus charged with the responsibility of ensuring strict financial oversight at the UN, as well as strengthening accountability in ways that should generate greater confidence in the UN's overall operations. There is the daunting question, however, of whether this measure is "too little, too late."

Some 80 percent of the UN's budget is paid by only fifteen nations, at a time when various UN agencies support a large number of staff in expensive cities such as Paris (UNESCO). It is thus understandable why traditional supporters like the US,

which pays 25 percent of the fixed annual budget, should demand more for its involvement—just as any private corporate structure would have to reorganize to meet the demands of its stockholders who perceive their stock as dwindling in value.

It is ironic that, in 1978, the US Department of State's legal advisor concluded that the US—and all member States—must pay their assessed obligations. In his words, "the General Assembly's adoption and apportionment of the Organization's expenses create a binding legal obligation on the part of State members to pay their assessed shares." This analysis was based on Article 17 of the UN Charter and the 1962 International Court of Justice case interpreting the Charter as requiring members to pay the organization's expenses as a matter of International Law. Certain UN members had then objected to the UN peacekeeping commitments in the former Belgian Congo and the Middle East, unsuccessfully claiming that the related expenditures were not "expenses of the Organization" within the meaning of the Charter.[32]

The UN is not the only international organization suffering from the spread of national delinquency in paying assessed shares of organizational budgets. A number of African nations have fallen behind in their payments to the Organization of African Unity (OAU). Given the concerns about the impact of this development on operational integrity, the OAU resolved that its member States must no longer threaten its continued operation in this manner. In 1990, the organization resolved to limit its annual budget ceiling to 10 percent above the amount expended in the previous year. Another remedial measure was to remind delinquent member States that they could not participate in organizational decision-making or present candidates for OAU posts.[33]

Certain US leaders have claimed that the UN bureaucracy does not produce tangible benefits, in addition to waste and mismanagement. Such claims could be characterized as examples of a nationalistic view that money should not be spent unless there is a self-evident return on the expenditure. Put another way, tangible benefits are a euphemism for being able to assert political control. US President Clinton's 1993 speech to the UN predicted more limited American involvement in the UN's various operations. The US pays *30 percent* of its overall costs, including special assessments *beyond* its annual assessed share of the UN's fixed yearly budget. The countries most involved in financing the UN have legitimate concerns about waste and mismanagement. A 1993 internal audit of one UN agency revealed budget irregularities, including payments that were "quite deplorable."

Some Western nations no longer deem participation in the UN as beneficial because they think the UN gives too much priority to "Third World" interests. This dissatisfaction with the UN is likely to continue now that the lesser developed countries constitute about three-fourths of the UN membership.

If powerful member States continue to use a cost-benefit analysis as the yardstick for deciding whether to participate in the UN, some other powerful nations are likely to limit or even terminate their participation. Their exit will signal the demise of the one global organization that has existed for the specific purpose of avoiding World War III. The UN image would continue to fade, possibly into irrelevance.

Control of Deadly Force   UN paralysis can also be deadly. Iraq has virtually mocked the UN with repeated violations of armistice agreements after the UN's US-led restoration of Kuwait's sovereignty. UN inspectors in Iraq were held captive while the UN negotiated their release. UN humanitarian relief was barred from entering Iraq, as were UN inspection teams that were supposed to have unfettered access to Iraq for the purpose of destroying its poison gas and nuclear weapons facilities. Khmer Rouge rebels in Cambodia seized six UN peacekeepers in 1992, claiming that they were agents of the Cambodian government sent to spy on rebel activities. In Africa, the Secretary-General was jeered and had to flee from rocks and garbage during his 1993 visits to Ethiopia and Somalia. In Bosnia, UN troops have stood idly by while Serbs bombed several of the UN-declared safe havens—prior to a relative period of peace enforced only by the threat of NATO air strikes on Serb artillery positions. Bosnia's Deputy Prime Minister Turajlic was murdered while under UN protection, riding with French troops.

UN rules of engagement permit returned fire only when a peacekeeper's life is in danger. The lone exception was briefly implemented after eighteen US soldiers were killed there in 1993, when irregular Somalian forces attacked a peacekeeping operation location in Mogadishu.

UN Reform Studies

The above analysis of the various UN organs referred to some of the contemporary suggestions for reforming the UN—including altering the number of permanent seats on the Security Council, increasing the Secretary-General's on-site fact-finding powers when conflicts arise (or are about to erupt), reducing the amount of paperwork generated by the Secretariat in the six official languages of the UN, and the Secretary-General's 1992 *Agenda for Peace* suggestions.[34]

Four other major studies have been made of contemporary UN reform, generated by different points on the political spectrum:

1. The 1980s reports of the Group of Intergovernmental Experts (UN);

2. The 1993 Ford Foundation report on more effective UN financing (private research corporation);

3. The 1993 report of the United States Commission on UN effectiveness (statutory entity created by the US Congress); and

4. A 1994 Ford Foundation report written by former senior UN officials.[35]

(1) During the 1980s, the UN General Assembly authorized a study of the UN for the purpose of exploring methods for improving its effectiveness. The 1986 report of the UN Group of Intergovernmental Experts from eighteen countries contained seventy-one recommendations—serving as their starting point for UN reform. These recommendations fall into several subdivisions. The first is streamlining the "intergovernmental" machinery of the UN Recommendation 1(e), for example, by greater coordination of the organization's numerous "conferences and meetings, in particular by staggering them throughout the year; this would ensure better utilization of conference facilities and established resources, limit the use of temporary personnel and reduce overtime." Another suggested improvement is to rearrange the structure of the Secretariat. Recommendation 15 would thus make a "substantial reduction in the number of staff members at all levels, but particularly in the higher echelons. . . ." In the overall area of personnel, Recommendation 50 is that the "Secretary-General should include in his annual reports to the General Assembly on personnel questions a [new and separate] section related to the ratings of the performance of staff and their promotion. The system of performance evaluation should be improved by introducing an element of comparison in the rating of staff."

This UN experts' self-study made a number of recommendations for improving the UN's planning and budget procedures. Recommendation 68 proposes a clear agreement among the UN's member States on the content of the UN's budget. The precise concern expressed by the experts' report is the following: "there is no clear linkage between priority setting and resource requirements either in the [periodic] medium term plan or in the [annual] programme budget. This has led to the fact that activities that are considered obsolete, of marginal usefulness or ineffective have not always been excluded from the programme budget."

(2) The 1993 Ford Foundation report, *Financing an Effective United Nations*, focused on two areas for improvement: the regular UN budget and peacekeeping. Regarding the annual UN budget, this group suggested that all members—particularly the larger contributors—pay their assessed dues *in full* and *on time*. Unlike the US presidential administrations of the 1980s and 1990s, this respected and independent US research institution did *not* favor the UN's scaling back of the US dues assessment. It said the US has much to gain from continued participation in a strong UN. Members should thus pay their dues in quarterly installments, rather than in an annual lump sum. Delays would be penalized with interest assessments. This budgetary change would greatly assist in operating the UN's Working Capital Fund, and help it anticipate such delays and facilitate responses on a more timely basis.

In the area of peacekeeping, the Ford Foundation assessment is that the international community should be prepared to accept increased peacekeeping costs in future years. The alternative of war and economic decline hold far greater disadvantages than allowing the world to slip into a chaotic series of uncontrolled conflicts. Finally, all member States with an above-average per capita gross national product should pay the same rate of peacekeeping assessments as their annual dues assessments. The US, for example, pays 30 percent of the costs of operating UN peacekeeping operations worldwide. Its fixed annual assessment is 25 percent of the UN's routine operations.

(3) The third of the four major studies on improving UN effectiveness is a report of the US Commission on the Effectiveness of the UN. In September 1993, this congressionally mandated study released its recommendations on the eve of the opening of the UN's 48th Session in New York—after a two-year study that included public hearings from across the US. This Commission, viewing the UN from a perspective that would benefit the US, made several novel recommendations.

Probably the most controversial is the suggested creation of a 5,000- to 10,000-member UN Rapid Deployment Force, composed of volunteers who are in turn volunteered by individual governments. This force would help to fill the vacuum left by the UN members' failure to provide a standing military force at the disposal of the UN under Article 43 of the Charter. UN headquarters would be equipped with state of the art communications gear appropriate for such a modern and rapidly deployable force to "put out fires." Thus, the UN should earmark special UN forces available to provide whatever logistical or tactical support is necessary to deal quickly with new conflicts.

This US Commission on the UN also recommended creation of an International Criminal Court to try international war criminals, terrorists, drug traffickers, and airline highjackers. The existence of such a Court would of course serve US interests. Saddam Hussein and various Bosnian Serbs might be thus triable in a way that would ameliorate public pressure on the US to do something when fundamental human rights are jeopardized in a theater that has little tactical significance for the US. Future "Noriegas" might not have to be captured during a US invasion of dubious legality. The UN actually later implemented this suggestion by its 1992 resolution creating an International Criminal Court (*see* § 9.5).

This US Commission on UN reform also recommended the creation of *another* international court—one dealing specifically with human rights. This would be a specialty court under the UN umbrella—in addition to the International Criminal Court. These courts would channel more international controls into the UN process, much like mutual international interests are served by the European Court of Human Rights in Strasbourg, France (*see* § 9.6).

The US Department of State should train more professionals in the handling of UN affairs of interest to the US. This recommendation finally admits, although indirectly, the extent to which the US attitude has typically been that "the UN needs the US more than the US needs the UN."

The US Commission's final recommendation urges that the US should take the lead in advancing reforms at the UN. The US could thereby actively engage in constructive multilateral diplomacy. As stated in the Commission's report of its findings, the American people do not want to be the "world's policeforce." They *would* accept a collective responsibility, however, to be part of an international "highway patrol."

Some of the US Commission members believe that the UN has done so poorly that it should not be given any added responsibilities in the twenty-first century. There is no question that the UN could be better managed. Yet the majority of Commission members believe that walking away would not improve global relations. Unlike an earlier era when the US Senate shunned the League of Nations, this contemporary report of US attitudes affirms that this is no time for isolationism.

(4) The 1994 Ford Foundation's independent report (the second on the same subject in two years) urged the UN to create a common headquarters for the General Assembly, the Secretariat, and the specialized agencies—as was originally contemplated by the UN drafters in 1945. All such agencies would thus be grouped in a common seat, rather than the current practice of spreading them all over the world. Geneva and Bonn were suggested as possible sites, although such a move might further diminish US support.

■ 3.4 EUROPEAN UNION

Introduction

The UN Charter recognizes the utility of autonomous international organizations in the various geographical regions of the world. Article 52(1) specifies that a State's membership in the UN does not preclude the simultaneous "existence of regional arrangements or agencies for dealing with such matters relating to the maintenance of international peace and security as are appropriate for regional action provided that such arrangements or agencies and their activities are consistent with the Purposes and Principles of the United Nations." This provision complements Article 33(1), whereby the State parties to any dispute "shall, first of all, seek a solution by negotiation . . .

[or] resort to regional agencies or arrangements, or other peaceful means of their own choice." Article 52(3) further requires that the UN Security Council encourage the settlement of local disputes through regional organizations.

Given the more regional concerns in the varied areas of the world, States developed a number of regional defense, economic, and political organizations. These entities have operated in harmony with the UN at the global level and with individual States at the regional level. These organizations have served a number of more specific needs not necessarily addressed in the UN Charter. That document had to be cast in rather broad and aspirational terms, providing general goals toward which nations could aspire in the aftermath of World War II.

This text is not designed for a separate course in international organization. Thus, many organizations cannot be covered if one is to learn the essentials in an introductory course dealing with International Relations. Some military and political organizations will be briefly profiled in the next section on "Other International Organizations." This section of the book, however, will focus on the European Union. It is probably the best example of how States have managed to integrate goals and results at the regional organizational level. Should this particular association of States continue to advance as rapidly as it has, since the 1957 inception of international integration on such a grand scale, then there is hope that Europe might overcome its reputation as being the most belligerent region in history.

Historical Backdrop

Long before the much-heralded European Union's Maastricht Treaty of 1992, the concept of an association of European States found political expression in both negative and positive ways. There were attempts to *impose* unity by Napoleon and Hitler. Napoleon sought to unite the Continent under French hegemony, until his military demise at the beginning of the nineteenth century. Hitler sought the subjugation of Europe under the dictatorship of Germany's Third Reich.

Peaceful attempts followed World War I. In 1923, Austria led the so-called Pan-European Movement. This unity movement called for the creation of a United States of Europe modeled on the success of the Swiss struggle for unity in 1648 (*see* § 1.3 on the Peace of Westphalia), as well as the interim solidarity evinced by the German Empire of 1871. In 1929, in speeches before the League of Nations Assembly in Geneva, French and German leaders proposed the creation of a European Union within the framework of the League of Nations.

These positive bids for peaceful unification were overcome by the dominant tide of nationalism and imperialism. The twentieth century's two "great wars" demonstrated the futility of the constant rivalry between European nations over many centuries. Europe's collapse, its political and economic exhaustion, and its outdated national structures signaled the need for a fresh start and a more radical approach to the reordering of Europe.[36]

The contemporary European Union is rooted in the creation of three communities. The first was the European Coal and Steel Community formed by the 1951 Treaty of Paris. The 1957 Treaty of Rome established the European Economic Community and the European Atomic Energy Community. The initial "community" goal was to create a common market (no internal tariff barriers) in coal and steel for the six member States of Belgium, France, West Germany, Italy, Luxembourg, and the Netherlands. This union would, it was hoped, secure peace by loosely integrating both the victorious and the vanquished European nations of prior world wars. Although France rejected the added aspiration of an international *defense* organization, the original six members built an economic community premised on free movement of workers, goods, and services. Mutually agreeable agricultural and commercial policies were adopted by the end of the 1970s.

In 1972, Denmark, Ireland, and Great Britain applied for membership. The admission of these States was accompanied by new agreements regarding social, regional, and environmental concerns. Plans for a European monetary system were launched in 1979, although there has yet to be a single currency. Some uniformity in monetary policies would ultimately enable the Community's member States to pursue common economic policies.

Greece, Spain, and Portugal joined in the 1980s, bringing the member-State total to twelve—while also bringing some disparity to the Community in terms of its members' respective stages of economic development. It was in this period that the Community began to grow in international stature, however. The Community, as an international or-ganization, possessed the legal capacity to conclude treaties on behalf of its member States. One example is the loose form of association with a number of Southern Mediterranean, African, and Caribbean/Pacific States under the four "Lome Conventions" concluded during the 1970s and 1980s.[37]

The Community's 1986 "Single Act" legislation was designed to formally establish a single market (similar to that enjoyed by the states of the United States) by 1992. One feature, yet to be actually realized, would have been a single currency—a key feature in promoting a true United States of Europe. The so-called "1992" program prompted the applications of Austria, Finland, Norway (voter-rejected in 1994), and Sweden (admitted in 1995), plus Cyprus, Malta, Sweden, Switzerland, and Turkey (not yet admitted)—all between 1987 and 1992. The twelve members also resolved to further strengthen their economic and political ties. (Under the "1992" legislation, the European Community is now referred to as the European Union.)[38]

The demise of the Soviet Union, the end of the Cold War associated with the former East/West struggle, the demolition of the Berlin Wall, and the unification of Germany have all signaled potential movement toward forging a greater European Union (EU) while integrating its eastern neighbors. Yet ethnic rivalries in Europe, the breakdown of sovereignty (*see* §§ 2.2–2.3), and the increasing influence of smaller commercial entities in the world market also suggest the possibility of an opposite result. Unless the EU is able to strengthen its internal structure and decision-making processes, it will never develop into the genuine union its members have now feverishly pursued for four decades. At this point in time, however, it is arguably the most advanced form of regional integration. The EU is the potential catalyst for uniting Europe in a way that could eliminate a number of barriers other than just trade. A summary of its essential institutions follows.

Community Law

The Treaty on European Union, or the so-called "Maastricht Treaty," was signed in Maastricht (a city in the Netherlands) in 1992. One objective was to amend all earlier treaties on varying Community subjects, in a way that would bring all of them under one umbrella treaty and eliminate any inconsistencies.

The objectives stated in the Maastricht Treaty are the primary features that define the anticipated future of this organization (Title I, Article B):

- "Creation of an area without [any] internal frontiers" (much like states of other federated unions such as the US);

- Social cohesion through an economic and monetary union, which will ultimately create a single currency (historically printed by each individual country);

- The further assertion of "its identity on the international scene, in particular through the implementation of a common foreign and security policy including the eventual framing of a common defence policy, which might in time lead to a common defense" (leaning towards the League of Nations and OAS Charter provisions providing that an attack upon one member of the international organization is an attack against all—a provision *not* employed in the UN Charter); and

- Strengthening the "protection of the rights and interests of the nationals of its Member States through the introduction of a citizenship of the Union" (facilitating even smoother international travel than currently permitted within the EU).

What makes *this* international organization different from the UN? Unlike the UN, the EU has a highly structured social, economic, and legal environment. The European Union was initially designed to integrate the European nations economically. Europe was crushed by World War II; its western nations had lost many of their colonies; and it needed to unite for it to compete with large powers like the United States to the west and the Soviet Union to the east. The economic unification of Europe thus began with the reduction of trade barriers within the Community and the establishment of a common economic policy in relation to nonmember nations.

Europe's economic integration has occurred in two key phases. The first was the *reduction* of trade barriers. The second phase, commonly referred to as "1992," was designed to *eliminate* trade barriers by 1992. Like the North American Free Trade Agreement (NAFTA)—the western hemisphere's "1994" —creating a trading environment with initially reduced and ultimately eliminated tariffs would bring about a single economic market in which all partici-

pating countries could compete. This would enable member States to access each other's markets more freely, while making it more difficult for nonmember countries. In such a market, the obstacles that would impede the movement of people, goods, services, or capital within the boundaries of the trading bloc would be first reduced and then eliminated. The EU's strategy was thus designed for the creation of one central bank, followed by one European currency for all member States. By contrast, there can never be a central bank for all UN members.

Another essential objective of this single market is the economic and political stability of Western (and maybe, one day, Eastern) Europe. Competitors within this Union will benefit because they will have larger markets, unimpeded by the usual customs inspections, tariffs, and other limitations on international business (*see* Chapter 13). The comprehensive Maastricht Treaty, containing all of the "1992" laws, will thus be the basic source of Community developments for decades to come. The "1992" rules have a significant impact on foreign business operations in Europe. The rules govern even minutiae such as the brands of ketchup to be used in US-owned fast-food restaurants in Paris, the angle of Ford headlights made in London, and the airing of "I Love Lucy" reruns in Amsterdam.

The Maastricht Treaty on European Union affirms a rich history of Community case law to protect the social and other fundamental human rights of the citizens of member States. The UN balance sheet, by comparison, has been rather poor. Its financial crisis may even be its demise. As discussed in Chapter 11 on "Human Rights", the relevant provisions of the UN Charter contain only hortatory language setting a standard for common achievement. UN resolutions are often just that—resolutions, without necessarily binding effect (*see* § 1.4). The EU treaty, on the other hand, confirms a degree of solidarity in "relations between the member States and between their peoples." This phrase (treaty Title I, Article A) echoes the degree to which the rights of the individual are directly incorporated into the future of this international organization. It also indicates that member States must occasionally do that which they would never do—but for membership in the EU.

An essential EU/UN difference is that institutions of the EU *are* equipped with the requisite degree of sovereignty to enable them to require member States to treat their citizens in ways that they would not otherwise consider under their own national laws. Unlike the UN, EU member States determined that entering into binding arrangements might have occasional short-term costs but long-range benefits.

The following case offers a dramatic illustration. 1992 was a stormy year in Ireland in terms of the very sensitive issue of abortion. Ireland's Constitution prohibits abortion, as a result of a referendum of its voters in 1983. It is also a crime, punishable by life imprisonment. A 1979 law had previously been enacted, making it unlawful to advocate or assist in the obtaining of an abortion in any manner. In similar ligation in 1992, a lower Irish court prohibited a raped fourteen-year-old girl from going abroad for the purpose of obtaining an abortion. After it became clear that she would commit suicide, the Irish Supreme Court overruled that opinion in a rather succinct one-sentence opinion. The European Court of Justice, seated in Luxembourg, had previously determined that it had no jurisdiction with regard to Ireland's national abortion law. Any

issues related to that law were characterized as "lying outside the scope of [European] Community Law." This decision did not address whether family planning counselors in Ireland could advise women about the option of traveling to England, where abortion is legal.

In the following case, the defendants' lawyer made one final attempt to resolve what they characterized as a "Community Law" issue. The defendants claimed that Ireland's judicial action, prohibiting abortion counseling, violated the European Human Rights Convention. In a companion case, some student newspapers were also charged with publishing information about pregnancy alternatives in violation of Irish laws. The resulting opinion of the European Court of Human Rights, seated in France, effectively reversed the Irish Supreme Court injunction against the various defendants. It is also a classic illustration of how an international organization can require a State to act in a way that is contrary to its national law:

CASE OF OPEN DOOR AND DUBLIN WELL WOMAN v. IRELAND
European Court of Human Rights, 1992*
No. 64/1991/316/387–388

[Author's Note: The Irish Supreme Court affirmed a lower Irish court order requiring defendants—Open Door Counselling, Ltd., Dublin Well Woman, Ltd., and certain individual defendants—to cease counseling on the availability of abortions outside of Ireland (resulting in the closure of defendant Open Door). They applied to the European Court of Human Rights (ECHR) for relief under the European Convention on Human Rights (European Convention) provisions—which protect freedom of expression and prevent disclosure of information received in confidence.

The ECHR did not rule directly on Ireland's constitutional ban on abortions. The majority of the Court's judges did rule, however, that preventing women from getting information on how to get abortions outside of Ireland violates the European Convention. This was a badly divided court: The overall opinion carried by a vote of fifteen to eight judges. Seven judges (of the twenty-three total) wrote their own separate opinions. The result nevertheless dictated that Ireland could no

longer use its own antiabortion laws to deprive its citizens of human rights guaranteed by the European Convention.

Note that the European Convention allows individuals (both individual and corporate) the right to participate as litigants. In the UN's International Court of Justice, only States may be parties in contentious litigation where the plaintiff State sues on behalf of its injured citizens—a role that Ireland would presumably be unwilling to undertake on the facts that follow. The Court's numbering of paragraphs is omitted.]

[Opinion.] The case was referred to the Court by the European Commission on Human Rights [and] . . . by the Government of Ireland. . . . It originated in two applications against Ireland lodged with the Commission . . . by Open Door Counselling Ltd, a company incorporated in Ireland; the second by another Irish company, Dublin Well Woman Centre Ltd., and one citizen of the United States of

*Reprinted with permission of Carl Heymanns Verlag, Cologne, Germany.

America, . . . and three Irish citizens, Ms Ann Downes, Mrs X and Ms Maeve Geraghty [two employed as trained counsellors for one of these companies and two in their capacity as women of child-bearing age residing in Ireland].

. . .

The applicants complained of an injunction imposed by the Irish courts on Open Door and Dublin Well Woman to restrain them from providing certain information to pregnant women concerning abortion facilities outside the jurisdiction of Ireland. . . .

. . .

On 19 December 1986 Mr Justice Hamilton, President of the High Court [lower Irish court], found that the activities of Open Door and Dublin Well Woman in counselling pregnant women . . . to travel abroad to obtain an abortion or to obtain further advice on abortion within a foreign jurisdiction were unlawful [under] . . . the Constitution of Ireland.

He confirmed that the Irish criminal law [thus] made it an offence to procure or attempt to procure an abortion. . . . Furthermore, Irish constitutional law also protected the right to life of the unborn from the moment of conception onwards.

An injunction was accordingly granted ". . . that the Defendants [Open Door and Dublin Well Woman] and each of them, their servants or agents, be perpetually restrained from counselling or assisting pregnant women within the jurisdiction of this court [Ireland] to obtain further advice on abortion or to obtain an abortion."

Open Door and Dublin Well Woman appealed against this decision to the [Irish] Supreme Court which in a unanimous judgment . . . rejected the appeal [thus affirming the lower court's injunction requiring the defendants to cease giving abortion information for the purpose of travel to Great Britain].

On the question of whether the above activity should be restrained as being contrary to the [Irish] Constitution, Mr Justice Finlay C.J. stated:

. . . the issue and the question of fact to be determined is: were they thus assisting in the destruction of life of the unborn?

I am satisfied beyond doubt that . . . the Defendants were assisting in the ultimate destruction of the life of the unborn by abortion.

. . .

[*In a companion case, an Irish antiabortion society applied to the lower Irish court to restrain the publication of information in student newspapers regarding abortion information. That court referred this and the Open Door/Well Woman matters to the European Court of Justice in Luxembourg for a determination of whether this issue fell within the ambit of Community Law. But on appeal of that reference, the Irish Supreme Court instead restrained the student publication from further publishing abortion counseling information. The dispositive statement from the Irish Supreme Court in the related newspaper case is provided by the ECHR in its* Open Door/Dublin Well Woman *decision.*]

I reject as unsound the contention that the activity involved in this case of publishing in the students' manuals the [Great Britain abortion clinic information] . . . can be distinguished from the activity condemned by this Court in [the Open Door counselling case]. . . . It is clearly the fact that such information is conveyed to pregnant women, and not the method of communication which creates the unconstitutional illegality. . . .

[*The ECHR now returns to its analysis of the* Open Door/Dublin Well Woman *defendants.*]

Section 16 of the Censorship of Publications Act 1929 . . . provides that:

It shall not be lawful for any person, otherwise than under and in accordance with a permit in writing granted to him under this section . . . to print or publish . . . any book or periodical publication (whether appearing on the register of prohibited publications or not) which advocates . . . the procurement of an abortion. . . .

. . .

In their applications lodged with the Commission . . . the applicants complained that the injunction[s] in question constituted an unjustified interference with their right to impart or receive information contrary to Article 10 of the [European Human Rights] Convention.

. . .

[*The Commission had then ruled that the Irish Supreme Court injunctions* did *violate the European Convention, thus triggering the ECHR's jurisdiction to hear this case. Its analysis continues with the* Open Door/Dublin Well Woman *defendants.*]

The applicants . . . invoked [Convention] Article 10 which provides:

1. Everyone has the right to freedom of expression. This right shall include freedom to hold opinions and to receive and impart information and ideas without interference by public authority and regardless of frontiers [within the Community].

2. The exercise of these freedoms . . . may be subject to such formalities, conditions, [and] restrictions . . . necessary in a democratic society . . . for preventing the disclosure of information received in confidence. . . .

In their submissions to the Court the [Irish] Government contested these claims and also contended that Article 10 should be interpreted against the background of Articles 2 . . . and 60 of the Convention the relevant parts of which state:

[2.]1. Everyone's right to life shall be protected by law.

. . .

60. Nothing in [the] Convention shall be construed as limiting or derogating from any of the human rights and fundamental freedoms which may be ensured under the laws of any High Contracting Party.

. . .

The Court cannot accept that the restrictions at issue pursued the aim of the prevention of crime since . . . neither the provision of the information in question nor the obtaining of an abortion outside the jurisdiction [i.e., in Great Britain] involved any criminal offence. However, it is evident that the protection afforded under Irish law to the right to life of the unborn is based on profound moral values concerning the nature of life . . . [which was] reflected in the stance of the majority of the Irish people against abortion as expressed in the 1983 referendum.

. . .

The Court [however] is not called upon to examine whether a right to abortion is guaranteed under the Convention or whether the foetus is encompassed by the right to life as contained in Article 2. . . .

The only issue to be addressed is whether the [Irish] restrictions on the freedom to impart and receive information contained in the relevant part of the [Irish court's] injunction are necessary in a democratic society for the legislative aim of protection of morals.

. . .

[T]he national authorities enjoy a wide margin of appreciation in matters of morals, particularly [when it] . . . touches on matters of belief concerning the nature of human life. . . .

However this power of appreciation is not unlimited. It is [thus] for the Court . . . to supervise whether a restriction [like this one] is compatible with the Convention.

. . .

In this context, it is appropriate to recall that freedom of expression is also applicable to "information" or "ideas" that offend, shock or disturb the State or any sector of the population. Such are the demands of that pluralism, tolerance and broadmindedness without which there is no "democratic society."

. . .

The [Irish] Government . . . [has] submitted that Article 10 should not be interpreted in such a manner as to limit, destroy or derogate from the right to life of the unborn which enjoys special protection under Irish law. . . . [T]he Court recalls [however] that the injunction . . . [and] the information that it sought to restrain was available from other sources. Accordingly, it is not the interpretation of Article 10 but the position of Ireland as regards the implementation of the [anti-abortion] law that makes possible the continuance of the current level of abortions obtained by Irish women abroad.

In light of the above, the Court concludes that the restraint imposed on the applicants from receiving or imparting information was disproportionate to the [governmental] aims pursued. Accordingly there has been a breach of Article 10.

■ NOTES & QUESTIONS

1. The Court held that Ireland violated Article 10 of the Convention and that it must pay damages to the defendant entities Open Door and Dublin Well Woman. These private corporations, and the individuals who were parties to this suit, were thus capable of personally enforcing their treaty rights provoked by Ireland's violations of the European Human Rights Convention. In the UN's International Court of Justice, only *States* may be parties to such enforcement proceedings (as discussed in Chapter 9 on the adjudication of international is-

sues). *Open Door* effectively means that an international organization may vary the traditional rules of International Law—which otherwise require a *State* to bring an action on behalf of its injured citizens against another State that is responsible for some alleged harm.

2. *Should* the European Union thus provide this protection to individuals? Put another way, what *is* the special protection afforded to individuals and corporations under "Community Law" that is not available to them at the UN under traditional principles of International Law?

European Union Institutions

This international organization of States is managed by a number of common institutions. Unlike the UN, there are not nearly as many individual agencies (*see* Exhibit 3.3 in § 3.3 showing *major* UN

agencies). Yet one may characterize the EU experience as not being as bogged down by a burdensome administrative superstructure. Exhibit 3.5 below summarizes the major EU institutions and their respective functions.

EXHIBIT 3.5 European Union Major Institutions (European Community = part of EU involved with policies derived from founding treaties and single market)

European Parliament Strasbourg, France (Committee meetings and partial sessions, Brussels, Belgium)	567 members directly elected by voters in EU countries; political driving force for initiatives and legislation; monitors day-to-day management via questions to *Commission* and *Council* (3,500 in 1992); establishes periodic commissions of inquiry and examines petitions from Community citizens
Secretariat (Luxembourg)	3,500 staff plus political group staffs
European Council	Heads of government and President of *Commission*; acts as guiding force via two meetings per year
Council of the European Union (Brussels; certain meetings, Luxembourg)	76 Ministers from member States (agricultural, employment, foreign, etc.); adopts major Community decisions based on *Commission* proposals; responsible for intergovernmental cooperation
European Commission (Headquarters in Brussels, plus staff in Luxembourg; 17,000 officials divided between 30 Directorates General)	17 members who propose Community legislation; primary guardian of Community treaties; executive body that ensures correct application of treaties; may initiate infringement proceedings against States/fines individuals and companies/refers matters to *Court of Justice;* administers budget and appropriations

EXHIBIT 3.5 *(continued)*

Economic and Social Committee (Brussels)	189 members representing employees, employers, farmers, consumers, etc.; coal and steel matters referred to *ECSC Consultative Committee* (96 other representatives of producers, workers, consumers, traders)
Committee of the Regions (Brussels)	189 members representing local and regional interests; must be consulted prior to the adoption of decisions involving a region
European Investment Bank (Luxembourg)	Raises funds to finance investments contributing to Community development; makes loans to less developed countries (especially Central and Eastern Europe)
European Court of Justice (Luxembourg)	13 judges and 6 advocates-general ensure that European treaties are interpreted and implemented per Community Law; judgments may be requested by member State, its courts, individual, company, or other Community institutions; ensures compatibility of any legal instrument with Community Law
Court of First Instance (Luxembourg)	12 judges, created in 1989, to deal mostly with actions brought by *individuals* (appeals may be lodged in Court of Justice)
European Court of Human Rights (Strasbourg, France)	23 judges adjudicate issues arising under actions within the Community allegedly in violation of the European Convention on Human Rights (*see, e.g., Open Door/Well Woman* case § 3.4)
Court of Auditors (Luxembourg)	12 members appointed by *Council* to ensure sound financial management, all Community revenue collected, lawful expenditures made
European Monetary Institution/Central Bank	Plan to administer single currency (ECU) [which failed to become part of "1992" legislation]

All institutions of the European Union have been affected by the dramatic events occurring between the third European elections of 1989 and the fourth round of elections in 1994. Members of those institutions face a different Europe that that of 1989, when communists were in power from Berlin to Vladivostok. Few people outside of the Netherlands had heard of Maastricht, and political union was not considered a reasonable priority.

The interim five years introduced the following astonishing events: the unification of Germany; the collapse of the Soviet Union—with the potential for adding more State members to the EU, which had just completed the processes of democratic elections and the movement toward market economies; the breakdown of sovereignty into smaller units—particularly in Europe; renewed conflict in the Balkans—an area with a significant role in the two great wars of the twentieth century; and the flareup of ethnic rivalries. These events suggest some of the reasons why so many member parliaments did not share the same degree of urgency about ratifying the various "European" treaties, including the great Maastricht Treaty (envisioning a single currency within the EU).

One critical feature for maintaining lasting peace in Europe may be the degree to which the EU and its eastern neighbors complete the process of integration. The EU is expected to quickly lower its various trade barriers, while its central and eastern "associates" are expected to open their national markets to the EU products in a somewhat more gradual fashion in terms of movement of persons, capital, and services. As Exhibit 3.5 demonstrates, virtually all of these major EU institutions will have a significant role to play in this particular segment of the planned integration of the greater part of Europe.[39]

The European Parliament in session at Strasbourg, France.

Yet the Parliament and the Council's heads of government will surely be cautious. They will be hesitant not only about full economic integration, because that would mean a single currency—something that failed to materialize as hoped by the drafters of the 1992 Maastricht Treaty. They will also be concerned with full, or more complete, *military* integration.

Expanding the EU to incorporate all States, including the eastern "associates," into other international organizations such as NATO will be no easy undertaking. Obvious problems have blocked NATO's adequately handling the Bosnia situation, which continually threatens the area's peace in the aftermath of the Cold War. But the EU (and even the UN) did not do much better. It was not until July 1994 that the EU was able to demonstrate any significant peacekeeping progress in Bosnia's then-two-year-old civil war. The EU took over the administration of Bosnia's city of Mostar, in an effort to demilitarize a city typically divided by Muslim-Croat rivalry. This event came only after a US-brokered agreement whereby a portion of the city was taken over by EU forces.

Full *political* integration would mean that members of a very diverse political spectrum would be willing to effectively become a super-State or federated Europe not unlike the federation of the states within the United States of America or the United States of Mexico. Further, Russia's path to democracy and a market economy is by no means clear or complete. Vladimir Zhirinovsky is the leader of the Liberal Democratic Party of Russia and a member of the Russian Parliament with a more significant following than western media reports. He is described as a "dangerous radical" in western terms but is rather popular to many Russians. He has threatened EU member Germany with nuclear attack if it "interferes" with Russian affairs. In his own words, as reported in the Moscow newspaper *Izvestia*'s foreign affairs section: If elected "I will not hesitate to use nuclear weapons."[40] He has also threatened the US over its ownership of Alaska, which he declares to have improperly deprived Russia of this valuable piece of what must ultimately become Russian property. Another threat to the current pursuit of full integration at this time is that EU leaders must take note of the 600-year rivalry between Ukraine and Russia, compounded by the fact that Russia does not have the former Soviet Union's monopoly on nuclear weapons.

If there is to be both a larger EU and a more complete integration of its members, its leaders will have to accommodate all of these very real concerns in a way that minimizes their disruptive impact on the perhaps impossible dream of full economic, military, and political integration resulting in a "Pax Europana."

■ 3.5   OTHER INTERNATIONAL ORGANIZATIONS

While the European Communities have received much global attention on the world stage in recent decades, a number of other international organizations are also influential international actors. Certain major economic organizations, including the General Agreement on Tariffs and Trade, the North American Free Trade Agreement, and the "Group of 77" will be covered in Chapter 13 of this text, on "International Economic Relations". The primary military and political international organizations are summarized in this section of the text. Those are as follows:

- North Atlantic Treaty Organization (NATO)

- Conference on Security and Cooperation in Europe (CSCE)

- Community of Independent States (CIS)

- Organization of American States (OAS)

- League of Arab States (Arab League)

- Organization of African Unity (OAU)

NATO

The North Atlantic Treaty Organization (NATO) is the world's major military defense organization. Its solidarity has occasionally waned, particularly when France withdrew in 1966.[41] France thereby expressed its concern that this regional international organization was effectively subject to US domination. (NATO has always depended a great deal on US military support.) In 1994, it was the US that proposed an eastward extension of NATO to incor-

porate former members of the Soviet Union—followed by the Clinton administration's advocating a cautious approach. The US thereby hoped to avoid Moscow's fear of encirclement (prior to Russia's 1994 decision to join NATO's Partnership for Peace Program, described below).

NATO is now a European intersection for Western powers (which formerly represented the Cold War interests of the United States in Europe) and the Eastern States from the now defunct Warsaw Pact (which represented the interests of the former Soviet Union). At the height of the Cold War, NATO members had more than two million military personnel deployed in Western Europe. The Warsaw Pact nations deployed about four million troops in Eastern Europe. In 1989, prior to the fall of the Soviet Union, US President George Bush pledged a reduction of US forces equivalent to a 10 percent cut in all NATO forces. This pledge was designed to encourage a like Soviet reduction in the Warsaw Pact forces in the States of Eastern Europe.

The demise of the Soviet Union and the Warsaw Pact in the early 1990s ultimately resulted in an association between former Warsaw Pact nations and those of NATO. In the NATO Secretary General's 1990 speech to the Supreme Soviet in Moscow, just before the Warsaw Pact was dissolved, Germany's Manfred Worner proposed an association as follows:

> This visit in itself symbolizes the dramatic changes of the past year. The Cold War now belongs to the past. A new Europe is emerging . . . [yet] age-old fears and suspicions cannot be banished overnight; but they can be overcome. Never before has Europe had such a tangible opportunity to overcome the cycle of war and peace that has so bedeviled its history.
>
> . . .
>
> I have come to Moscow today with a very simple message: we extend our hand of friendship to you. And I have come with a very direct offer: to cooperate with you. The time of confrontation is over. The hostility and mistrust of the past must be buried. We see your country, and all the other countries of the Warsaw Treaty Organization, no longer as adversaries but as partners in a common endeavor to build what you [might] call a Common European Home, erected on the

values of democracy, human freedoms, and partnership.

. . .

[The NATO Secretary General then proposes that out of the historical upheaval due to the demise of communism] the Soviet Union gains partners that will help in its great domestic task[s] of reform and renewal. Partners who will cooperate to ensure that the Soviet Union is an active and constructive part of the dynamic Europe of advanced industrial economies and technological interdependence of the 21st century. . . . Beyond confrontation we can address the immense global challenges of today and tomorrow: environmental degradation, drugs, terrorism, hunger, population, the proliferation of immensely destructive military technologies in the Third World. . . . The Alliance I have the honour to represent wants partners in the building of a new Europe. . . . Let us look to a common future, and work for it with trust and imagination.[42]

In June of 1994, Russia became the twenty-first State to sign the Partnership for Peace Program involving cooperation with NATO in joint military exercises, peacekeeping, and the exchange of military doctrine and weaponry. One week later, Russia's leader, Boris Yeltsin, signed an agreement with the European Union (EU) Commission President on economic matters—including the removal of quotas on Russian exports into EU countries.

One must of course distinguish between merely signing a Partnership for Peace agreement and full NATO membership. The "Partnership" is only a step in what has suddenly become a more complex process. Germany and the US are split on the issue of whether Russia should ultimately become a full-fledged member of NATO. Several months after Russia signed the NATO Partnership agreement—and one day after US troops finally withdrew from Berlin—Germany's defense minister proclaimed that allowing Russia to become a member would "blow NATO apart." Thus, vintage rivalries are still generating concern about European security—in a way that may preclude the full integration of all "European" States into this regional organization.

These developments are quite the opposite of the post–World War I western approach—which isolated Germany's Weimar Republic, deepened suspi-

cions in the entire region, bankrupted Germany, and created an atmosphere for Hitler's ascension to power. Neither development makes Russia a full-fledged "member" of NATO or the European Union. They do vouch for Russia's protection from attack—economically from EU countries, and militarily from NATO countries. These events provide no guarantees, but are at least symbolic of the new-found penchant for East-West cooperation. Russia should be less concerned about the entry of its Eastern European neighbors into a military organization like NATO.

With the demise of the Warsaw Pact, some commentators assert that NATO has become a relic of the Cold War. They perceive NATO as being rather ineffective in dealing with its local problems, such as containing the excesses of military forces in the former Yugoslavia. NATO, however, authorized the use of air strikes in 1993, under extensive international pressure to react to the Bosnian Serb attacks on civilian targets (when the UN itself did not adequately respond). NATO nevertheless awaited UN authorization for air strikes, before it made the unquestioned threat that it would bomb Serbian positions if the Serbs failed to retreat from UN-designated safe havens in Bosnia.

NATO vessels also carried out the UN embargo of the former Yugoslavia in the Adriatic commencing in 1993. Yet only a restricted amount of strategic material can reach that area by sea. Given this limited ability to quickly respond, top military officers endorsed plans for Rapid Reaction Forces, immediately deployable to handle regional trouble spots. This Force has not yet materialized, and was thus unavailable to deal with any of these conflicts.

CSCE

The Conference on Security and Cooperation in Europe (CSCE) is the other major regional international organization of Europe. It consists of fifty-three, mostly European, States. Its members also include Canada and the US. The CSCE has extended official "observer" status to Japan.

The CSCE roots date back to the mid-1950s when the Soviet Union initiated "European Security Conferences" attended by representatives of Eastern European States. These meetings resulted in creation of the Warsaw Treaty Organization as NATO's regional competitor. In the 1960s, the Warsaw Pact then initiated additional conferences seeking greater peace and security in Europe. Thanks to artful diplomacy by the Federal Republic of Germany in the field of East-West relations, the CSCE was born in 1972 just after conclusion of the first Strategic Arms Limitations Treaty between the US and the Soviet Union. The 1991 CSCE Madrid Conference produced the framework of the CSCE Parliament. The 1992 meeting of the CSCE Council of Ministers produced the Prague Document on the nonproliferation of nuclear weapons and limitations on arms transfers within Europe.[43]

There have been two defining moments in the CSCE process. The first major achievement was the so-called Helsinki Final Act of 1975 emphasizing concerns of regional security, economic matters, and humanitarian treatment. To ensure the equality of States—despite vast differences in economic, military, and political power—CSCE members resolved that its proceedings "shall take place outside military alliances." This has avoided a narrow NATO–versus–Warsaw Pact strategy for regional problem-solving. The CSCE functions somewhat like a remodeled UN, whereby diverse players on the European stage continually meet for purposes including the provision of "confidence building measures" regarding security and disarmament. The second major achievement of the CSCE process was the 1989 Concluding Document of Vienna. It contains a mandate for the Negotiation on Conventional Armed Forces (CFE) in Europe talks.

Another major contribution of the CSCE process was the 1990 Conventional Forces in Europe Treaty (CFE) Treaty of Paris.[44] A number of participating States (such as France) perceive the CSCE process as the genuine "European" alternative to resolving regional problems outside the assertedly US-dominated NATO process whose *raison d'etre* arguably vanished with the Warsaw Pact.

Yet another facet of the lasting importance of the CSCE process is its emphasis on human rights issues. Prior to the destruction of the Berlin Wall, for example, the US used the CSCE process as a vehicle for claiming that eastern CSCE States had failed to live up to its generous provisions, including the right to travel. Other specific provisions include freedom of religion and freedom from psychiatric abuse while in detention. The CSCE's Conference on the Human Dimension meets annually to exchange information about questionable State practices and unresolved human rights problems. In March 1995, Russia's president Boris Yeltsin agreed

to receive a permanent human rights mission from the CSCE to monitor events in Chechnya, the rebellious region consisting of mostly Muslims who seek independence.

Some limitations still hamper the CSCE process. Like the UN Charter, the CSCE 1975 Final Act is a political rather than legally binding document. It is not a treaty in the sense of creating immediate obligations, although some participants have argued that the 1975 Act resulted in some binding commitments by member States to at least continued participation in a Pan-European process.[45] This should not be surprising, given the historical diversity of its member States.

Another institutional weakness is that the CSCE has exhibited a rather "light" institutional structure. The follow-up conferences have generally been *ad hoc,* although the number of these specialized conferences has increased. It would be difficult, of course, to obtain any degree of progress without the continued willingness of delegates from Europe's participating CSCE States to meet at least periodically.[46] As a result, the CSCE has not been a "player" in the potential resolution of crises, such as that which occurred in Bosnia.

The CSCE finally developed some permanent administrative and political organs in the early 1990s. One of the foremost analysts of the CSCE process, Professor Arie Bloed of the University of Utrecht in Holland, characterizes the "new" and revitalized CSCE process as shifting to a cooperational mode from its earlier confrontational mode during the Cold War. As he describes it:

> nowadays one could speak of an "old" CSCE which existed until the end of the 1980s and a "new" CSCE since the beginning of the 1990s. To a great extent the "old" CSCE is characterized by a 'confrontational' approach by the participating States (in particular between the Western and East European States), whereas the emphasis in the "new" CSCE is on 'co-operation' between all CSCE States. This fundamental change is also clearly reflected in the institutionalization of the CSCE. The "old" CSCE consisted of only periodic follow-up meetings and *ad hoc* conferences on specific subjects; the "new" CSCE is characterized by the establishment of regularly

convening political organs and a number of small permanent administrative bodies.

. . . In spite of all the changes, however, at present the "Cold War origins" of the CSCE are still clearly visible in many respects and it may be expected that this will be the case in the foreseeable future as well.[47]

One by-product of this cooperation was the March 1995 Pact of Stability. It requires former East bloc States, wishing to join either the EU or NATO, to first settle any border disputes and ethnic conflicts. The Pact requires that these former Soviet bloc countries agree to permit the CSCE to be the watchdog agency for ensuring compliance. If this bargain eventually performs as designed, new Yugoslavia-like conflicts will be resolved before they can erupt—also advancing the objectives of democracy and peaceful international relations on the European continent.

CIS

The Community of Independent States (CIS) is roughly analogous to the former Soviet Union (SU). In 1991, seven of the fifteen States that would ultimately become UN members signed the Agreement Establishing the Commonwealth of Independent States. The accompanying document announced by the heads of State of Belarus, Russia, and Ukraine acknowledged the deadlocks plaguing the CIS from its inception, including "a profound economical and political crisis" and a "catastrophic drop in living standards." They nevertheless established the CIS with the following organizational objectives: "[pursuing] a policy of strengthening international peace and security. They undertake to discharge the international obligations incumbent on them under treaties and agreements entered into by the former Union of Soviet Socialist Republics, and are making provision for joint control over nuclear weapons and for their non-proliferation." These constitutive CIS documents thus contain guarantees of many of the same fundamental freedoms and human rights for individuals set forth in the UN Charter, the various CSCE statements on individual rights—and the specific objective of nonproliferation.

The companion Protocol contains the right of the other former States of the Soviet Union to accede to the CIS. This document, signed two weeks after the original CIS Declaration, contains the Alma Ata Declaration whereby former States of the SU commit to attaining the inviolability of existing territorial borders and "setting up lawfully constituted democratic States."[48] This document, which carefully submitted to the UN and thus its member States, expressed the regional solidarity favoring Russia as the entity to occupy the former seat held by the "SU" in the Security Council's permanent seat.

Some progress has been achieved in fostering CIS unity since its 1991 inception. Six members, facing bankruptcy, pledged to achieve a new economic union in 1993—a "ruble zone" that could lead to restoration of a common currency, in a region where the many new States would otherwise have to print and maintain their own money.

There have also been setbacks. Ukraine, the third largest nuclear power in the world, balked at yielding its nuclear weapons to Russia—the CIS partner that has threatened Ukrainian self-determination for some six hundred years. On the other hand, Ukraine elected a pro-Russian president in 1994. This result underscores the affection that many citizens still feel for the comparative predictability and security of the former Soviet Union. Russia's leader, Boris Yeltsin, delayed the scheduled elections of the Russian president for the disclosed reason of controlling any potential right-wing return to communism. Ruling by such decrees, however, was a prominent feature of Czarist Russia. Until new political infrastructure is solidly in place, CIS regional solidarity remains threatened by the lack of international organization necessary to keep totalitarian controls from resurfacing.

One might characterize Russia as being in roughly the same dominant position as the US in the latter's relations with other OAS members. During the February 1995 summit meeting of CIS leaders, there was no mention of Russia's attack on Chechnya—although many Russians and Russian military leaders have openly disagreed with Russia's handling of this province that is seeking to exercise its claimed right to self-determination.

OAS

The Organization of American States (OAS), headquartered in Washington, D.C., is composed of nearly all States of the Western Hemisphere. As a result of the 1962 Cuban Missile Crisis (see § 10.2), OAS members voted to suspend Cuba's participation because Cuba had "voluntarily placed itself outside of the inter-American system."[49]

The OAS is the world's oldest regional international association (other than the less formal entities discussed at the beginning of § 3.3 on the history of international organizations). In 1890, several nations created a bureau later known as the Pan American Union. It was subsequently incorporated into another entity called the Organization of American States in 1948.

Under Article 1 of its Charter, the OAS is a "regional agency" of the UN. These two international organizations are, however, quite distinct. The OAS is neither controlled by nor directly responsible to the UN. The loose association between these two organizations is an example of regionalism within a universal system. Arrangements like this were the preferred post–World War II apparatus for ensuring the coexistence of a new global organization and any regional groupings that might develop for the pursuit of regional concerns. The earlier League of Nations Covenant similarly provided that the League's creation would not affect the vitality of "regional undertakings like the Monroe Doctrine [US control of the Western Hemisphere to exclude external powers] for securing the maintenance of peace."[50]

Article 4 of the 1948 OAS Charter establishes the organization's essential purposes: "(a) To strengthen the peace and security of the continent; (b) To prevent possible causes of difficulties and to ensure the pacific settlement of disputes that may arise among the Member States; (c) To provide for common action on the part of those States in the event of aggression; (d) To seek the solution of political, juridical and economic problems that may arise among them; and (e) To promote, by cooperative action, their economic, social and cultural development."

The OAS has changed its functional orientation several times. It was a commercial international organization when its predecessor was formed in 1890, but its members adopted a nonintervention theme after World War I to discourage unilateral action by any OAS member in hemispheric affairs. To promote joint military responses to external threats, the OAS's 1947 Rio Treaty thus proclaimed that "an armed attack by any State against an American State shall be considered as an attack against all the American States."[51] Each member thereby promised to assist the others in repelling such attacks. While its members are still concerned with defense matters, its current emphasis is on the development of economic and political solidarity in the hemisphere. In 1987, for example, member nations began to pursue the possible economic reintegration of Cuba into the OAS.

The OAS promotes regional trade and economic improvement, pursuant to the so-called Alliance for Progress program it announced in the 1960s. The OAS Charter addresses nearly all facets of economic and political life in the region, drawing on the parallel provisions and organization found in the UN Charter. For example, it has both an organ of consultation similar to the UN Security Council and an international court similar to the UN's International Court of Justice (see § 9.6).

The claimed dominance of the US has been a traditional feature of the OAS's lack of a cohesive organization. In 1992, for example, the US provided $38 million of the annual $62 million OAS organizational budget. In 1994, Colombia's president was elected to the prestigious position of head of the OAS. Unfortunately for regional relations, this election was the first bid by Caribbean and Central American States to wrestle this position away from the South American States that have controlled it since its 1948 inception. US Secretary of State Warren Christopher spent a number of days prior to the election with other conference representatives. Costa Rica's president, the heir apparent to the OAU post, thus blamed the US for its meddling that allegedly cost Costa Rica the election.

The UN was not the only international organization seeking the restoration of Haiti's democratically elected president to power after the 1991 military coup. The OAS imposed an embargo on Haiti. In 1992, the US therefore seized an oil tanker bound for Haiti in violation of the embargo. This was the first time that an OAS embargo actually resulted in such action. On the other hand, one could ask whether this seizure could have been accomplished without the unyielding support of the US—the primary reason for the "UN" success during the Persian Gulf War.

Arab League

The League of Arab States is an international organization composed of twenty-one Middle Eastern states and the Palestine Liberation Organization (PLO). The League was established in 1945 to promote comprehensive cooperation among countries of Arabic language and culture.[52] It then established the Council of Arab Economic Unity in 1964 to promote an Arab Common Market and various other economic programs. The resulting institutions include the Arab Fund for Economic and Social Development for projects in Arab countries (1968), the Arab Bank for Economic Development in Africa (1973), and the Arab Monetary Fund (1976).

The primary goal of the League is political collaboration for preserving the independence and the State sovereignty of its members. The Council of the League deployed inter-League peacekeeping forces in Kuwait in 1961 and Lebanon in 1976. The latter effort eventually failed in 1989, however, when Syria refused League demands to withdraw its troops from Lebanon and Iraq (Syria's archenemy).

One of the League's long-term goals is to operate as a collective self-defense organization like NATO. Some States within the League question why the US unilaterally engaged in a missile strike against Iraq in 1993 (in response to a threat on the life of former President Bush) but would not readily engage in such tactics against the Bosnian Serbs although "armed" with the power to do so by both the UN and NATO.

The political solidarity of the League was adversely affected, however, by a number of events that occurred in the latter part of the twentieth century in relation to Israel. Under the Camp David Agreements of 1978, US President Jimmy Carter facilitated a series of meetings between Egypt's President Anwar Sadat and Israel's Prime Minister Menachem Begin at Camp David near Washington, D.C., leading to Egypt's establishing independent ties with Israel. Since this was contrary to League policy, Egypt was suspended from the League in 1979. Sadat was later assassinated. The 1991 Persian Gulf War further disintegrated Arab unity. Certain Arab members even went so far as to assist the US in protecting Israel from League member Iraq's missile attacks.

In 1993, the Israeli deportation of Muslim fundamentalists to Lebanon also helped rekindle the League's anti-Israel focus. The League sought worldwide support at the UN for the responsive Security Council resolution. Yet the evident lack of fervor in the private commentaries of Arab League representatives reflected a deep antipathy toward militant Arab fundamentalists. Many of them do not support the PLO's control of relations with Israel.

Now that the PLO has negotiated an autonomy agreement with Israel in the Gaza Strip and the City of Jericho, the League has less of an anti-Israel flavor. Yet the League's political cohesion remains in a state of flux due to worldwide claims that certain States within its membership have engaged in a systematic program of State terrorism to accomplish national goals.

OAU

The Organization of African Unity (OAU), more than any other international organization, is rooted in the Western-derived institutions of colonial rule and the perceived inferiority of nations on the African continent. The OAU's traditional goal has been African political unity in terms of self-determination. As succinctly described by Professor Gino Naldi of the University of East Anglia in England:

> Pan-Africanism has its origins in nineteenth-century America where the American Colonization Society for the Establishment of Free Men of Color of the United States was formed in 1816 in response to the alienation and exploitation of the Negroes with the purpose of repatriating freed slaves. This led to the founding of Liberia in West Africa [by freed slaves from the US] as a free and sovereign State in 1847. Nevertheless, the Pan-African movement, which gathered momentum at the turn of the century, continued to struggle for the end of the colonial system in Africa and called for the dismantling of the colonial boundaries agreed upon at the Congress of Berlin in 1885 [due to Africa's perceived inability to govern itself without European influence]. . . . But it was the post-Second World War era that provided the impetus for self-determination in Africa. The demand for political, economic and cultural self-determination became a flood that the colonial powers could not dam. The independence of Ghana on 6 March 1957 marked the beginning of a new dawn in Africa.[53]

The OAU was initially a political international organization, formally established in 1963 and headquartered in Ethiopia. It consists of most of the independent nations in Africa. The Republic of South Africa is the major exception. Now that white-rule and apartheid are no longer facts of political life in South Africa, the OAU is likely to integrate this State into its ranks. Morocco withdrew and Zaire suspended its membership when the

Western Sahara became an independent member in 1984—based on unresolved territorial claims (*see Western Sahara* case in § 2.3).

The OAU's current orientation is increasingly economic, premised on the 1991 treaty establishing the OAU's economic community.[54] It has played virtually no role in the events in the member States of Somalia, Liberia, and Mozambique—all of which were the objects of UN peacekeeping operations in the 1990s.

The fundamental purpose of the OAU has been the promotion of self-government and social progress throughout the African continent. Toward this end, the OAU has established a commission to mediate all disputes between African nations.[55] The OAU's distinctive political feature was its support for the black nationalist movements in southern Africa. The six so-called "Frontline Countries" are the bloc within the OAU that assisted the remaining colonial territories. The goal of the Frontline Countries was to assist specifically black South Africans who were subject to white minority rule under apartheid. These OAU internal institutions were dismantled just prior to Nelson Mandela's assumption of the presidency of South Africa in 1994. Another major goal, freeing South West Africa from South African rule—held in violation of numerous UN resolutions—was accomplished with the independence, renaming, and entry into the UN of the new renamed State of Namibia in 1990.

Global and regional international organizations with a primarily *economic* focus are covered in Chapter 13 of this book.

■ 3.6 ORGANIZATIONAL IMMUNITY

The concept of a State's immunity from being sued in the courts of another State was addressed in § 2.6 of this book. This section of the book raises a similar question: Are international organizations *also* entitled to immunity from being sued in the national courts of its member States?

Chapter 2 describes State sovereign immunity from suit in the courts of another State. Such immunity depends on whether the forum where the suit is filed follows the absolute or the restrictive approach to *sovereign* immunity. The answer to the question of *organizational* immunity is more complex, although the same rationale generally exists for shielding organizations from suits in their member States.

UN

The UN's physical facilities in the United States are inviolable. UN property and assets are immune from expropriation or any other form of seizure. Its agents and their personal baggage are immune from arrest or detention. Most States guarantee these protections by their participation in the Convention on the Privileges and Immunities of the United Nations. This immunity was adopted by the General Assembly in 1946 and by the United States in 1970. The UN thus enjoys the same immunity in the US that is enjoyed by foreign governments.[56]

Other Organizations

The scope of immunity for *other* international organizations is not as clear. The following case illustrates some of the reasons for insulating international organizations from such suits:

BROADBENT v. ORGANIZATION OF AMERICAN STATES

United States Court of Appeals
District of Columbia Circuit, 1980
628 Fed.Rptr.2d 27

[Author's Note: Broadbent and some co-workers lost their jobs at the General Secretariat of the Organization of American States (OAS). The plaintiffs in this case included US citizens, and foreign nationals residing in the US, who were employed at the OAS's permanent headquarters in Washington, D.C. They believed that they were wrongfully terminated.

They filed a complaint with an OAS administrative tribunal set up to resolve personnel disputes. This OAS tribunal decided that these employees should be reinstated, awarding a small amount of money damages in the event that the OAS Secretary General nevertheless denied their reinstatement. Plaintiffs then sued for $3 million in a federal court of the US—a completely *separate tribunal also located in Washington, D.C. They alleged that the OAS had improperly breached their employment contracts.*

The defendant OAS responded by seeking dismissal of their suit. The federal trial court dismissed their suit, at the trial court level, holding that the OAS was "absolutely" immune—under any circumstances—from such suits. The federal appellate court agreed that the OAS was entitled to organizational immunity. This higher court's view, however, was that "restrictive" immunity was the applicable standard to apply to an international organization, rather than the lower court's reliance on the absolute standard. Thus, both the trial and appellate courts achieved the same results by dismissing the case against the OAS. But they differed in terms of which standard was applicable—absolute or restrictive immunity. The latter immunity standard would thereby authorize future suits against international organizations in US courts if the circumstances were sufficiently "commercial."

Both the lower and appellate courts applied the Foreign Sovereign Immunities Act (FSIA) to the OAS, just as if it was a "State" within the meaning of the FSIA. If a foreign State would be entitled to immunity under the Act, so would an international organization like the OAS. Thus, the OAS was immune from suit. It was not conducting a "business" as a private trader when hiring and firing employees at the organization's Washington, D.C. headquarters.]

[*Opinion.*] Section 1605 of the FSIA provides that foreign states shall not be immune from the jurisdiction of American courts in any case based upon their commercial activity in the United States, with the commercial character of an activity determined by reference to its "nature" rather than to its "purpose." The conceptual difficulties involved in differentiating *jure gestionis* [acts by a private trader] from *jure imperii* [acts by a State] have led some commentators to declare the distinction unworkable. The restrictive immunity doctrine is designed to accommodate the legal interests of citizens doing business with foreign governments on the one hand, with the interests of foreign states in avoiding the embarrassment of defending the propriety of political acts before a foreign court.

In our view [the appellate court], the employment by a foreign state or international organization of internal administrative personnel—civil servants—is not properly characterized as "doing business." That view is supported by the legislative history of the FSIA, and the definition of "commer-

cial activity" in § 1603. The House [of Representatives] Report commented:

> Commercial activity.—Paragraph (c) of section 1603 defines the term "commercial activity" as including a broad spectrum of endeavor, from an individual commercial transaction or act to a regular course of commercial conduct. A "regular course of commercial conduct" includes the carrying on of a commercial enterprise such as a mineral extraction company, an airline or a state trading corporation. Certainly, if an activity is customarily carried on for profit, its commercial nature could readily be assumed. At the other end of the spectrum, a single contract, if of the same character as a contract which might be made by a private person, could constitute a "particular transaction or act."
>
> . . . By contrast, . . . an activity whose essential nature is public or governmental . . . would not itself constitute a commercial activity. . . . *Also public or governmental and not commercial in nature, would be the employment of diplomatic, civil service*, or military personnel, but not the employment of American citizens or third country nationals by the foreign state in the United States.

This report clearly marks employment of civil servants as noncommercial for purposes of restrictive immunity. The Committee Reports establish an exception from the general rule in the case of employment of American citizens or third country nationals by foreign states. The exception leaves foreign states free to conduct "governmental" matters through their own citizens. A comparable exception is not applicable to international organizations, because their civil servants are inevitably drawn from either American citizens or "third" country nations. In the case of international organizations, such an exception would swallow up the rule of immunity for civil service employment disputes.

The United States has accepted without qualification the principles that international organizations must be free to perform their functions and that no member state may take action to hinder the organization. The unique nature of the *international* civil service is relevant. International officials should be as free as possible, within the mandate granted by the member states, to perform their duties free from the peculiarities of national politics. The OAS charter, for example, imposes constraints on the organization's employment practices. Such constraints may not coincide with the employment policies pursued by its various member states. . . . An attempt by the courts of one nation to adjudicate the personnel claims of international civil servants would entangle those courts in the internal administration of those organizations. Denial of immunity opens the door to divided decisions of the courts of different member states passing judgment on the rules, regulations, and decisions of the international bodies. Undercutting uniformity in the application of staff rules or regulations would undermine the ability of the organization to function effectively.

We hold that the relationship of an international organization with its internal administrative staff is noncommercial, and, absent waiver, activities defining or arising out of that relationship may not be the basis of an action against—the organization—regardless of whether international organizations enjoy absolute or restrictive immunity.

The appellants were staff members of the General Secretariat of the OAS. Their appointments, terms of employment, salaries and allowances, and the termination of employment were governed by detailed "Staff Rules of the General Secretariat" promulgated by the OAS. The Staff Rules further establish an elaborate grievance procedure within the OAS, with ultimate appeal to the Administrative Tribunal of the OAS.

The Tribunal is competent to determine the lawfulness of an employee's termination of employment. If an employee has been wrongfully discharged, the Tribunal may order reinstatement. If reinstatement is ordered, the Tribunal may also establish an indemnity to be paid to the employee in the event the Secretary General exercises his authority to indemnify the employee rather than effect the reinstatement.

The employment disputes between the appellants and OAS were disputes concerning the internal administrative staff of the Organization. The internal administration of the OAS is a non-commercial activity shielded by the doctrine of immunity. There was no waiver, and accordingly the appellant's action had to be dismissed.

■ NOTES & QUESTIONS

§ 2.6 of this book analyzes the distinction between the "absolute" and "restrictive" immunity of *States*. (1) How did the *Broadbent* trial and appellate courts apply that distinction in very different ways to an *international organization*? (2) There was no difference in the end result. Why? (3) Would it have made a difference if there had been *no* administrative tribunal at the OAS to handle such terminations?

■ SUMMARY

1. Most international organizations are established by treaty between three or more States to fulfill some common objective. They serve the varied needs both of member States, and of citizens within those States, who may thus benefit by the existence of an international organization established to work toward defined objectives.

2. An international organization has legal capacity under International Law if it satisfies three essential requirements: (1) it must be a permanent association of State members with established objectives and administrative organs; (2) it must possess some power that is distinct from the sovereign power of its member States; and (3) the organization's powers must be exercisable on an international level, rather than solely within the national systems of its member States.

3. Certain organizations, such as the UN, have the legal capacity to bring a lawsuit in courts of its member States and to sue a member. Otherwise, the UN would not in fact have the ability to carry out its Charter functions.

4. The numbers and functions of international organizations have increased dramatically since the end of World War II, making classification more complex than in past eras.

5. Various classification schemes distinguish international organizations on the following bases: (1) public or private—put another way: governmental (created by treaty) or nongovernmental organizations; (2) administrative or political; (3) global or regional; (4) with or without the supranational power to require a member State to act in a certain way;

(5) purpose for existence—such as political, humanitarian, military, economic, and so on.

6. International organizations not created by treaty are referred to as international *non*governmental organizations, or NGOs. They fulfill an increasingly broad and complex scope of functions, sometimes in concert with *governmental* organizations (which consist only of States).

7. The UN structure consists of six principal organs: (1) General Assembly, (2) Security Council, (3) Economic and Social Council, (4) Trusteeship Council, (5) Secretariat, and (6) International Court of Justice. There are numerous other UN organs and specialized agencies within the system, as depicted in Exhibit 3.3.

8. The General Assembly consists of all member States. Its function is to make recommendations regarding any matter falling within the broad purposes of the United Nations.

9. The Security Council, consisting of five "permanent" and ten "rotating" members, is a smaller body that is charged with the responsibility of maintaining international peace and security. The Cold War veto thwarted the Council's objectives. States will have to determine whether or not to cede the requisite degree of sovereignty to the UN and its Security Council if this international organization is to actually maintain international peace.

10. The Economic and Social Council oversees the numerous Charter-based programs involving economic, social, and cultural facets of this global international organization.

11. The Trusteeship Council was devised to assist territories not capable of self-governance at the close of World War II. Very few trusts remain, largely due to the colonial independence movement of the 1960s and the fulfillment of their rights to self-determination.

12. The Secretariat, headed by the UN Secretary-General, is the large administrative staff that actually runs the UN and its various agencies at several locations throughout the world.

13. The International Court of Justice is the UN's judicial organ, located in the Netherlands. A primary role is to provide a forum for resolving disputes in the courtroom rather than on the battlefield.

14. Several major studies of UN reform were conducted in the 1980s and 1990s. Some recommendations have already been implemented, including the UN creation of an International Criminal Court. Most suggestions, however, await further scrutiny by UN member States. If not implemented, there is a serious question about the degree to which the UN can carry out its Charter mandate of maintaining international peace.

15. The UN is a global organization attempting to deal with a multitude of problems in a variety of cultures. Its primary emphasis has been the maintenance of peace. The European Union, by comparison, links a relatively homogenous group of States whose interests are primarily economic.

16. The ultimate goal of the 1992 Maastricht Treaty is to bond this region's nations by economic, military, and other political ties to fulfill the vintage dream of a Europe united and at peace.

17. The institutions of the EU operate in a highly structured social, economic, and legal environment. Thus, its achievements have provided a more successful model than the UN for integrating States in a way that is destined to maintain peace. It is far more difficult for the UN, due to its comparatively vast infrastructure of nations in many different stages of economic and social development.

18. The North Atlantic Treaty Organization (NATO) is the primary regional military organization in the world. It consists of most European nations, the US, and Canada. Some question the need for its existence after the demise of the Warsaw Pact, made up of former members of the Soviet Union. They are joining NATO's Partnership for Peace Program.

19. The Conference on Security and Cooperation in Europe (CSCE) is becoming a major political organization in Europe. It consists of far more member States than NATO—including France which defected from NATO in 1966. As its institutions mature, including the CSCE Parliament, which first met in 1992, it may obscure the need for other regional organizations dealing with the maintenance of peace and the regional security of Europe.

20. The Community of Independent States (CIS) is the contemporary international organization for States from the now defunct Soviet Union. The CIS was established partially to illustrate Eastern Europe's desire to ensure regional peace and security. This was the organization that facilitated the signing of the 1990 Conventional Forces in Europe arms reduction and nonproliferation treaty.

21. The Organization of American States (OAS) is the regional security agency of the States in the

Western Hemisphere. It is plagued with interregional rivalries and depends primarily for financial and military effectiveness on one member—the US.

22. The League of Arab States (Arab League) is similarly plagued with interregional differences in philosophy—many dealing with Israeli diplomacy. The Persian Gulf War and the signing of the Israel/PLO autonomy agreements have deprived the League of the initial reason for its existence—eliminating the State of Israel.

23. The Organization of African Unity (OAU) existed primarily to assault regional limitations on African self-determination. The dismantling of apartheid, Nelson Mandela's presidency of South Africa, and the achievement of statehood of Namibia in the 1990s effectively deprived this organization of any unifying political mission.

24. Many global and regional international organizations are retooling from a military/political perspective to one that is economic in scope.

25. The UN and its agents are absolutely immune from suit in member States including the US as host government.

26. The degree of organizational immunity depends on the internal law of member States. In the US, it appears that the analysis of international organizations is the same as for sovereign immunity. Whether there is immunity thus depends on whether the organization's conduct involves that of a governmental body or comparable to that of a private trader.

■ PROBLEMS

Problem 3.1 (*after* Reparations *case*): In September 1991, in the aftermath of the Persian Gulf War, a UN nuclear inspection team entered Iraq for the purpose of ensuring that it was not producing weapons of mass destruction. This inspection was to be conducted under a Security Council resolution requiring Iraq to divest itself of such weapons. Iraq seized forty-four team members, including citizens of several nations. The Security Council then approved Iraqi demands, which included that the inspectors list Iraq's secret nuclear-weapons program papers that they intended to take with them for further analysis. This minor Security Council concession (allowing Iraq to make some demand of the UN) may have saved the lives of the UN's inspectors. If they had been killed by Iraq, Iraq would

have State responsibility for reparations under International Law—to whom?

Problem 3.2 (*end of § 3.2*): In 1991, military leaders overthrew the democratically elected government of Haiti. The US considered this coup to be quite adverse to the hemispheric interests of other democratic nations in the Caribbean, as well as its own.

Assume that in January 1995, President Clinton announced that the US would undertake a "humanitarian intervention" in Haiti—as the president says—"to help the people of Haiti restore democracy." He refers to the French humanitarian intervention in Rwanda to assist inhabitants who were being massacred by rebel forces. Haiti's military government responds to the US announcement with its own statement that "North American imperialism will never prevent the people of Haiti from achieving their rightful role in hemispheric affairs, which have been dominated by the US since establishment of various international organizations including the Organization of American States (1890) and the UN (1945)."

The UN previously imposed an embargo on oil bound for Haiti. Assume further that the UN is unable to respond to *this* flare-up. The US has just vetoed a proposed UN Security Council resolution that would prohibit the US from acting unilaterally to invade Haiti. As covered in § 3.3, the veto of one of the "permanent five" could thus preclude Council action on this matter (e.g., from dispatching peacekeeping forces to Haiti). Further, Haiti's military leaders are unlikely to agree to a UN intervention that might threaten their continued control of Haiti's government.

In February 1995, assume also that there was a local response to the events in Haiti. The Organization of Central American States (OCAS) asked its members—consisting of States in Central America—to participate in a peace process. The organs of this international organization cannot act without the unanimous consent of all members of the OCAS. The dual goal of this conference will be to establish regional containment of the Haiti situation and to avoid a further confrontation between the US and Haiti. The OCAS is an independent international organization whose membership includes the US and Haiti. UN administrators have referred to this international organization as one of the UN's regional agencies. Under Article 33 of the UN

Charter, regional agencies may attempt to resolve threats to international peace.

The Inter-American Economic and Social Council is part of the infrastructure of the Organization of Central American States. Its fundamental purpose is to promote the economic and social welfare of the member States of the OCAS through better utilization of all natural resources within the region. It has thus made many recommendations to OCAS member States dealing with economic and social matters. To accomplish its purpose, Council members voted to conduct a research study of the effect of both the US and the new Haitian regime on the worsening of the economic and social well-being of this Caribbean nation. Council members believed that the economic scenario in Haiti would undoubtedly worsen as a result of social and military problems resulting from the US/Haitian confrontation. The Council study, not yet completed, will address these interrelated matters for the US and other OCAS members to consider what collective action might be taken to avert the further escalation of hostilities in this region.

What is the nature of the *OACS*—the international organization that is addressing this explosive situation? In other words, discuss the various ways in that one may classify this organization.

Problem 3.3 (*within Security Council materials after n.15*): The US has backed the addition of Germany and Japan as permanent members of the UN Security Council. Many other possible changes would arguably do a better job of making the Council "mirror" the Assembly by more accurately reflecting the factual composition of the community of nations. (1) Should Great Britain and France continue to occupy a permanent seat? (2) Alternatively, should one of these cede its seat to Germany, or could all three somehow rotate that "permanent" slot on the Council—as the "European" delegate? (3) Would Japan be entitled to the Asian permanent seat, given its economic superiority in global affairs? (4) Should China share this seat with India, given the latter's immense population that surpasses that of all Council members except China? (5) Should Germany, Japan, or any other nation be added as a permanent SC member—but *without* the right of veto, thus providing for an interim status on the Council? This would be permanent status without the attendant right of automatic veto now exercisable by the original five permanent members. (6) Would any of these changes *truly* influence, in a

positive way, the Security Council's ability to perform without diminishing its power to act? (7) Should there be some other change? (8) No change at all?

Class members will examine these various positions and resolve which would best suit the goals of (a) better representing the community of nations on the Security Council; and (b) better conducting the business of the Council under its Article 39 (or other) mandate(s).

Problem 3.4 (*end of Security Council materials in § 3.3 after n.18*): Which of the UN Secretary-General's *Agenda for Peace* proposals is most likely to be implemented? Do the 1994 US Presidential Directive factors conflict with the UN Secretary-General's proposals?

Problem 3.5 (*after Trusteeship Council materials in § 3.3*): The aftermath of the Cold War included the breakdown, if not splintering, of State sovereignty. For example, the Soviet Union broke down into a number of smaller States. One State under its influence, Yugoslavia, further split into five additional States.

One consequence of the realization of Statehood, especially by former colonies in Africa, has been the increasing frequency of what many have referred to as "failed States." These are States that have achieved independence but not sufficient economic and political stature to thrive. Warring tribes and ethnic groups are responsible for mass terror, executions, fleeing refugees, and economic hardship for the citizens of such countries.

Somalia is a classic example of the negative facets of statehood that have failed, or will fail, producing anarchy. UN efforts to provide humanitarian relief have resulted in mass looting, anti-UN actions, and anti-UN sentiment expressed by various segments of the populace. The UN Secretary-General fled for his life during a 1993 visit to Somalia during which he had hoped to bolster the spirit of the peacekeeping forces in Somalia.

Read Articles 75–85 of the UN Charter in Appendix A of this textbook. Reread the definition of statehood in § 2.1 of this textbook. Should the UN attempt to reestablish the Trusteeship system in Somalia, due to its apparent failure as a State? Would the UN's current financial problems (discussed in § 3.3) affect your decision?

Two students will now assume the roles of members of the UN's Trusteeship Council. They will debate (1) whether or not the UN should bring

Somalia "under its wings"; (2) what UN member State would administer such a Trust Territory (as proposed by the student advocating the creation of such a Trust; and (3) whether the Charter should be amended to delete the entire concept of trusteeship.

Problem 3.6 (*within Assessment of UN materials in § 3.3 after n.30*): Reread Security Council Resolution 687, quoted in the text. Then see Chapter VII in the UN Charter—set forth in Appendix A to this text, Articles 39–49. Consider the following 1974 statement in the General Assembly by Great Britain's representative (UN Gen. Ass. Records, 29th Sess., 2281st plenary meeting, 12 Nov. 1974, para. 55), speaking on the importance of continued adherence to Charter principles whenever State members fail to observe the rule of law in international affairs:

> this Organization is governed by the Charter. It cannot, consistently with itself and with the role it is designed to play in international affairs, disregard that Charter. We are either a law-abiding, law respecting body or we are nothing, a mere talking shop. If we put aside the Charter whenever its provisions may seem to a majority of us . . . to be inconvenient, then we lose all claim to authority and credence. In short, the Charter is and must be the constitutional foundation for all that we do. Respect for the Charter must permeate all our decisions.

Is Britain's Professor Matsui correct in his assertion that the Charter does not give the Secretary-General express authority to act in and conduct a military operation? Did the UN involvement in Kuwait thus violate the terms of UN Charter Article 2.7?

Problem 3.7 (*end of § 3.3*): Which of the UN Commission's proposals are most likely to improve the UN? Are these recommendations any more likely to succeed than those made by the 1993 Ford Foundation report? By the 1986 Report of the UN Experts?

■ BIBLIOGRAPHY

§ 3.1 Legal Personality of Organizations:

W. Feld, R. Jordan & L. Hurwitz, *International Organizations: A Comparative Approach* (3rd ed. Westport, CT: Praeger, 1994)

F. Kirgis, *International Organizations in Their Legal Setting* (2nd ed. St. Paul: West, 1993)

Legal Status of International Organizations and of Associated Persons and Premises, ch. 1, in F. Kirgis, *International Organizations in Their Legal Setting* 1 (2nd ed. St. Paul: West, 1993)

P. Menon, *The Law of Treaties between States and International Organizations* (Lewiston, NY: Edwin Mellon Press, 1992)

Moraweiecki, *Legal Regime of International Organization*, XV *Polish Yearbook International Law* 71 (1986)

§ 3.2 Classification of Organizations:

Essien, *International Organizations: A Selected Bibliography*, 10 *Fordham International Law Journal* 857 (Supplement, 1987)

Persons Other than States as Subjects of International Law, in R. Jennings & A. Watts, 1 *Oppenheim's International Law* (Part I) § 7, pp.18–22 (9th ed. Essex, Eng.: Longman, 1993)

§ 3.3 United Nations:
Generally—

M. Bertrand, *The Third World Organization* (Dordrecht, Neth.; Boston: Martinus Nijhoff, 1989)

G. Dirks, et al., *State of the United Nations, 1993: North-South Perspectives* (Providence, RI: Acad. Council on UN System, 1993)

Rene Dupuy, *The Development of the Role of the Security Council* (Dordrecht, Neth.: 1993)

L. Finklestein (ed.), *Politics in the United Nations System* (Durham, NC: Duke Univ. Press, 1988)

R. Gregg, *About Face?: The United States and the United Nations* (Boulder, CO: Lynne Reiner, 1993)

M. Rajan, *The Expanding Jurisdiction of the United Nations* (Bombay: N.M. Tripathi Ltd., 1982)

O. Schachter, *The Quasi-Judicial Role of the Security Council and the General Assembly*, 58 *American Journal of International Law* 961 (1964)

B. Sloan, *United Nations General Assembly Resolutions in Our Changing World* (Ardsley-on-Hudson, NY: Transnat'l, 1991)

L. Sohn, *Cases on United Nations Law* (2nd ed. Mineola, NY: Foundation Press, 1967)

K. Wellens (ed.), *Resolutions and Statements of the United Nations Security Council (1946–1992): A Thematic Guide* (2nd ed. Dordrecht, Neth.; Boston: Martinus Nijhoff, 1993)

R. Wells, *Peace by Pieces—United Nations Agencies and Their Roles: A Reader and Bibliography* (Metuchen, NJ: Scarecrow Press, 1991)

B. Williams, *State Security and the League of Nations* (Baltimore: John Hopkins Press, 1927)

Reform—

Y. Blum, *Eroding the United Nations Charter* (Dordrecht, Neth.; Boston: Martinus Nijhoff, 1993)

The Campaign for a New UN Charter (CNUNC) (Wash., DC: CNUNC, 1993)

H. Kelsen, *The Law of the United Nations: A Critical Analysis of Its Fundamental Problems* (New York: Praeger Press, 1950)

J. Mueller, *The Reform of the United Nations* (New York: Oceana, 1992) (two-volume collection of UN resolutions, reports, and documents from the *Annual Review of United Nations Affairs*)

§ 3.4 European Union:

European Union (Luxembourg: Office for Official Pub. Euro. Comm., 1994)

R. Folsom, *European Community Law* (St. Paul: West, 1992)

R. Keohane & S. Hoffman, *The New European Community: Decisionmaking and Institutional Change* (Boulder, CO: Westview Press, 1991)

W. Nicoll & T. Salmon, *Understanding the New European Community* (New York: Harvester/Wheatsheaf, 1994)

J. Steiner, *Textbook on EEC Law* (3rd ed. London: Blackstone Press, 1992)

A. Toth, *The Oxford Encyclopaedia of European Community Law* (Oxford, Eng.: Clarendon Press, 1990)

Treaty on the European Union (Luxembourg: Office of Official Pub. Euro. Comm., 1992)

§ 3.5 Other International Organizations:

S. Ali, *The International Organizations and World Order Dictionary* (Santa Barbara, CA: ABC-CLIO, 1992)

F. Kirgis, *International Organizations in Their Legal Setting* (2nd ed. St. Paul: West, 1993)

Lauwaars, *International Law: The Relationship between United Nations Law and the Law of Other International Organizations*, 82 *Michigan Law Review* 1604 (1984)

G. Naldi (ed.), *Documents of the Organization of African Unity* (London: Mansell, 1992)

O. Stoetzer, *The Organization of American States* (2nd ed. Westport, CT: Praeger, 1993)

§ 3.6 Organizational Immunity:

Comment, *United States Jurisdiction over Representatives to theUnited Nations, 63 Columbia Law Review 1066 (1963)*

Note, *How Much Immunity for International Organizations?*, 10 North Carolina Journal of International Law & Commercial Regulation 487 (1985)

■ ENDNOTES

1. The classic statement of these distinctions is provided in *Definitions and History*, ch. 1, in C. Archer, *International Organizations* (2nd ed. London: Routledge, 1992) [hereinafter *Archer treatise*].

2. *International Organizations and Law* 5–8 (New York: Ford Found., 1990).

3. **Capacity requirements:** *see International Organizations and Tribunals*, ch. XII, in I. Brownlie, *Principles of Public International Law*, 680–83 (4th ed. Oxford, Eng.: Clarendon Press, 1990) (especially authorities contained in fn. 8). **Capacity on national but not international level:** *see* Slomanson, *Civil Actions Against Interpol: A Field Compass*, 57 *Temple Law Quarterly* 553 (1984).

4. Further details on these resolutions and events are provided in R. Lapidoth & M. Hirsch (ed.), *The Arab-Israeli Conflict and Its Resolution: Selected Documents* (Dordrecht, Neth.; Boston: Martinus Nijhoff, 1992).

5. International Organizations Immunities Act, 59 Stat. 669, 22 U.S.C.A. §§ 288(a)–(f).

6. *See* Jacobson, Reisinger & Mathers, *National Entanglements in International Governmental Organizations*, 80 *Pol. Sci. Rev.* 141 (1986).

7. *Classification of International Organizations*, ch. 2, in *Archer treatise*, 38 (cited in note 1 above).

8. *Protocols Additional to the Geneva Conventions of 12 August 1949* (Geneva: Int'l Comm. Red Cross, 1977).

9. A succinct but authoritative history is available in *League of Nations*, E. Osmanczyk, *Encyclopedia of the United Nations and International Agreements* 511–16 (2d ed. London: Taylor & Francis, 1990) [hereinafter *1990 UN Encyclopedia*]. For a comprehensive study, *see* F. Walters, *A History of the League of Nations* (London: Oxford Univ. Press, 1952).

10. *See* Vol. 2 of *Selected Literary and Political Papers and Addresses of Woodrow Wilson* (New York: Grosset & Dunlap, 1952) for Wilson's "Fourteen Points" speech.

11. **Historical committee structure:** B. Finley, *The Structure of the United Nations General Assembly: Its Committees, Commissions, and Other Organisms: 1974–1980s* (White Plains, NY: Kraus Int'l, 1988). **1993 committee reorganization:** Schaff, *More Organizational Changes at the UN*, 22 *Int'l J. Legal Info.* 199 (1994).

12. M. Shaw, *International Law* 754 (3d ed. Cambridge, Eng.: Grotius, 1986) (emphasis supplied).

13. Skubiszewski, *The United Nations General Assembly and Its Power to Influence National Action*, in *Proceedings and Committee Reports of the American Branch of the International Law Association 1964 Annual Meeting* 153–54 (1964).

14. M.J. Peterson, *The General Assembly in World Politics* 2–3 (Boston: Unwin Hyman, 1990).

15. Article 9 of the Japanese Constitution bars the maintenance of "war potential." Articles 26 and 87(a) of the former "West" German Constitution banned the use of military forces for other than defensive purposes. Germany has sent troops to Somalia, while Japan has contributed financially to UN peacekeeping operations.

UN Peacekeeping Operations are discussed further in § 10.3.

16. *The UN Veto in World Affairs 1946–1990: A Complete Record and Case Histories of the Security Council's Veto* (Sarasota, FL: UNIFO Pub., 1992).

17. UN Doc. DPI/1247, reprinted in 31 *Int'l Legal Mat'ls* 953 (1992) [hereinafter *Agenda for Peace*]. A supplement was published in January 1995. *See* UN Doc. A/50/60, S/1995/1.

18. *Opening Statement of Dr. Edward Warner before the Senate Armed Services Subcommittee on Coalition Defense and Reinforcing Forces,* in *U.S. Department of Defense Statement on Peacekeeping,* 33 *Int'l Legal Mat'ls* 814 (1994). *See also* Scheffer, *U.S. Administration Policy on Reforming Multilateral Peace Operations,* 33 *Int'l Legal Mat'ls* 795 (1994) and *U.S. Department of State Statement on the Legal Authority for UN Peace Operations,* 33 *Int'l Legal Mat'ls* 821 (1994).

19. *See, e.g.,* ECOSOC, *Commission on Narcotic Drugs Report of the Thirty-Sixth Session* UN Doc. E/CN.7/1993/12/Rev.1, Supp. No. 9 (Vienna: UN, 1994).

20. **Termination does not bar subsequent proceedings:** Certain Phosphate Lands in Nauru (Nauru v. Australia), ICJ Communiqué No. 92/18 (Judgment on Preliminary Objections of June 26, 1992). **Dismissal as a result of settlement:** ICJ Communiqué No. 93/29 (Sept. 13, 1993) (whereby issues will never be publically adjudicated). A book-length treatment of this subject is available in C. Weeramantry, *Nauru: Environmental Damage under International Trusteeship* (Melbourne: Oxford Univ. Press, 1992).

21. Morgan Guarantee Trust v. Republic of Palau, 924 Fed.Rptr.2d 1237 (2nd Cir. 1991).

22. *Agenda for Peace* 21–22 (cited in note 17 above).

23. *Sheathing the Sword: The U.N. Secretary-General and the Prevention of International Conflict* 105-106 (New York: Greenwood Press, 1991).

24. Prandler, *The Unchanging Significance of the United Nations Charter and Some International Legal Aspects of its Application,* in H. Bokor-Szego (ed.), *Questions of International Law* 191, 192 (Dordrecht, Neth.; Boston: Martinus Nijhoff, 1986).

25. *See* Van Den Haag & Conrad, *The U.N. In or Out?: A Debate* (New York: Plenum Press, 1988); T. Franck, *Nation Against Nation: What Happened to the U.N. Dream and What the U.S. Can Do About It* (New York: Oxford Univ. Press, 1985).

26. *See* Nelson, *International Law and U.S. Withholding of Payments to International Organizations,* 80 *Amer. J. Int'l L.* 973 (1986).

27. A detailed account of all the relevant "Kuwait" resolutions, plus supporting national materials, is available in M. Weller (ed.), 3 *Iraq and Kuwait: The Hostilities*

and Their Aftermath (Cambridge, Eng.: Grotius, 1993) (third volume in series).

28. Matsui, *The Gulf War and the United Nations Security Council,* ch. 36 in R. Macdonald (ed.), *Essays in Honour of Wang Tieya* 511 (Dordrecht, Neth.; Boston: Martinus Nijhoff, 1994).

29. *See* Christol, *The Moon Treaty Enters into Force,* 79 *Amer. J. Int'l L.* 163 (1985).

30. An encyclopedic treatment of UN programs is available in the 1990 UN Encyclopedia (cited in note 9 above).

31. *N.Y. Times,* Sept. 17, 1986, p.3 (opening statement to Assembly's 41st session in New York).

32. **Legal Advisor:** Hansell, Memo. of Aug. 7, 1978, reprinted in *1979 Digest of United States Practice in International Law* 225, 226 (Wash., DC: US Gov't Print. Off., 1983). **Art. 17.2:** "The expenses of the Organization shall be borne by the Members as apportioned by the General Assembly. **ICJ case:** Certain Expenses of the United Nations, 1962 I.C.J. Rep. 168. An illustrative analysis of these points is available in Zoller, *The "Corporate Will" of the United Nations and the Rights of the Minority,* 81 *Amer. J. Int'l L.* 610 (1987).

33. *Resolution on Arrears of Contribution,* OAU Resolution 2 RADIC 660, reprinted in G. Naldi (ed.), *Documents of the Organization of African Unity* 45 (London: Mansell, 1992).

34. *See* note 17 above and accompanying text.

35. (1) *Report of the Group of High-level Intergovernmental Experts to Review the Efficiency of the Administrative and Financial Functioning of the United Nations,* Gen. Ass. Off. Records, 41st Sess., Supp. No. 49, Doc. No. A/41/49; (2) S. Ogata, et al., *Financing an Effective United Nations: A Report of the Independent Advisory Group on U.N. Financing* (New York: Ford Found., 1993); (3) J. Leach, et al., *Final Report of the United States Commission on Improving the Effectiveness of the United Nations* (Wash., DC: US Gov't Print. Off., 1993). (4) B. Urquhart & E. Childers, *Renewing the United Nations System* (New York: Ford Found., 1994).

36. *Introduction: Towards European Unification,* in *European Unification: The Origins and Growth of the European Community* 5–8 (Luxembourg: Office of Official Pub. Euro. Comm., 1986).

37. The 1975 "Lome I" Treaty and related documents are available in 14 *Int'l Legal Mat'ls* 595 (1975). The "Lome II" treaties are available in 19 *Int'l Legal Mat'ls* 327 (1980). The 1984 modifications are available in 24 *Int'l Legal Mat'ls* 571 (1985) ("Lome III" Final Act). The Protocol relating to the Community's association with Cyprus is reported in *Notice of Other Recent Developments,* 28 *Int'l Legal Mat'ls* 573, 574 (1989). The 1989 Lome IV agreement, joining sixty-nine States in an association with the Community, is reprinted in 29 *Int'l Legal Mat'ls* 783 (1990).

38. P. Fontaine, *A Brief History of European Integration*, ch. 1, in *Europe in Ten Easy Lessons* 5–6 (Luxembourg: Office of Off. Pub. Euro. Comm., 1992). *See also The History of the European Community*, ch. 1, in G. Berrmann, et al., *Cases and Materials on European Community Law* (St. Paul: West, 1993).

39. For an elaborate analysis of the negative aspects of European integration, *see* G. Harris, *The Dark Side of Europe* (2nd ed. New York: Columbia Univ. Press, 1994) (written by this member of the European Parliament's Secretariat).

40. *Izvestia, Personalities, Foreign Affairs*, Dec. 12, 1993, p.1.

41. An analysis of the French position is available in Stein & Carreau, *Law and Peaceful Change in a Subsystem: Withdrawal of France from NATO*, 62 *Amer. J. Int'l L.* 577 (1968). Albania withdrew from the Warsaw Pact in 1968 after the Soviet invasion of Czechoslovakia.

42. *A Common Europe—Partners in Stability: Speeches by the Secretary General of NATO*, reprinted in *Change and Continuity in the North Atlantic Alliance* 191, 191–95 (Brussels: NATO, 1990).

43. **Parliament:** *Final Resolution of the Madrid Conference Concerning the Establishment of the CSCE Parliamentary Assembly*, 30 *Int'l Legal Mat'ls* 1344 (1991). **Arms:** *Prague Document on Further Development of CSCE Institutions and Structures and Declaration on Non-Proliferation and Arms Transfers*, 31 *Int'l Legal Mat'ls* 978 (1992).

44. *See* S. Croft (ed.), *The Conventional Armed Forces in Europe Treaty: The Cold War Endgame* (Aldershot, Eng.: Dartmouth Pub., 1994).

45. *See, e.g.*, van Djik, *The Final Act of Helsinki—Basis for Pan-European System?*, 1980 *Netherlands Yearbook International Law* 110.

46. Additional CSCE details are available in A. Bloed, *From Helsinki to Vienna: Basic Documents of the Helsinki Process* (Dordrecht, Neth.; Boston: Martinus Nijhoff, 1990).

47. A. Bloed, *The Conference on Security and Co-operation in Europe: Analysis and Basic Documents* 2–3 (Dordrecht, Neth.; Boston: Martinus Nijhoff, 1990).

48. **Minsk Declaration:** UN Doc. A/46/771 (1991), reprinted in 31 *Int'l Legal Mat'ls* 138 (1992). **Policy Declaration:** 31 *Int'l Legal Mat'ls* 142 (1992). The various documents are reprinted in W. Butler, *Basic Legal Documents of the Russian Federation* (New York: Oceana, 1992).

49. Meeting of Consultation of Ministers of Foreign Affairs of Jan. 31, 1962, reported in 46 *US Dep't State Bull.* 281, No. 1182 (1962).

50. Article 21, League of Nations Covenant.

51. Article 3.1, Inter-American Treaty of Reciprocal Assistance, 21 *United Nations Treaty Series* 243, 62 U.S. Stat. 1681.

52. The text of the 1944 agreement is reprinted in 39 *Amer. J. Int'l L.* 266 (1945). A commentary is available in Khadduri, *The Arab League as a Regional Arrangement*, 40 *Amer. J. Int'l L.* 756 (1946).

53. *See* Elias, *The Commission of Mediation, Conciliation and Arbitration of the OAU*, XL *Brit. Yearbk. Int'l L.* 336 (1964).

54. *See* 30 *Int'l Legal Mat'ls* 1241 (1991).

55. G. Naldi, *The Organization of African Unity: An Analysis of its Role* 3 (London: Mansell, 1989).

56. **Convention:** 1 UN Treaty Series 15 (1946). **Resolution:** Gen. Ass. Res. 22A, 1 Gen. Ass. Off. Records, Supp. p.25, UN Doc. A/64 (1946). **US legislation:** International Organizations Immunities Act Section 2(b), 22 U.S.C.A. § 288 (1945) (1979 ed., 59 Stats. 669).

CHAPTER FOUR

Individuals and Corporations

■ INTRODUCTION

This is the final "preliminary" chapter. After surveying the meaning of the term *International Law* in the first chapter, the next two chapters launched an examination of the actors that shape its development—States and international organizations. This chapter adds another dimension to International Law—the role of the individual.

Since the dawn of the modern system of State dominance in International Law, in 1648 (*see* § 1.3 on the Peace of Westphalia), the State has been the primary actor in making, altering, and controlling the substance of International Law, to be studied in the following chapters. In the twentieth century, international organizations have played an increasingly important supporting role—particularly since the end of World War II.

The historical perspective was that the individual (meaning both natural persons and business entities such as corporations) played no direct role in shaping the development of this discipline. The first section of Chapter 4 explores a comparatively recent development—the international legal personality of the individual. The recognition of the individual as another actor in matters of International Law is probably most attributable to the complete and utter disregard of the individual by the State during the tenure of the Nazi regime's Third Reich.

The other sections of this chapter address nationality and its consequences, including statelessness, which is the absence of nationality. The prominent role of the multinational corporation in international affairs necessitates the discussion of corporate nationality and the attendant consequences requiring diplomatic representation.

The final section explores a very significant feature of the interplay between State and individual. That is the matter of State responsibility for injury to aliens and the evolving compensation rules for compensating individuals and corporations when their property is nationalized by the State.

■ 4.1 LEGAL PERSONALITY OF THE INDIVIDUAL

Soldier Jones Hypothetical

Assume that States X and Y share a common border. State X military intelligence indicates that State Y forces have been crossing into X from a small remote village in Y near the border. State Y villagers have been assisting State Y military forces by providing them with food and information about troop movements on the other side of the border in State X.

Jones is a soldier in the army of State X. His superior officer sends him into State Y on a secret mission called Operation Phoenix. The goal is to "neutralize" anyone who might help State Y forces cross into State X at the border village. Jones carries

out his orders and kills most of the civilian men, women, and children (all civilians) in the village. Some soldiers from State Y discover Jones in the act and pursue him to the Y coast near the village. Jones steals a yacht and escapes into international waters. His trail is traced in Exhibit 4.1.

EXHIBIT 4.1 Operation Phoenix

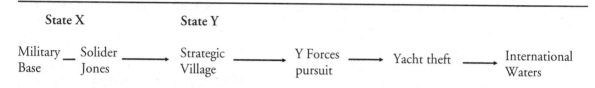

The remaining relatives of the slaughtered villagers want Soldier Jones and State X to pay for this brutal massacre. Operation Phoenix undoubtedly violated International Law. The State X military operation violated the territorial sovereignty of State Y. It would be futile, of course, for the relatives of the deceased villagers to personally go to State X to see its leaders, or to file suit in State X courts against Jones or the State X Army. It would be equally futile for them to file suits in State Y. Its courts would likely dismiss their suits on the basis of State X's having sovereign immunity in the courts of State Y (*see* § 2.6). A number of other limitations also preclude the *villagers* from pursuing a remedy from either Jones or State X. The relevant problems and remedies are discussed in this section's analysis of the following matters:

- Can the victims' relatives directly negotiate with State X for compensation?

- Can they pursue Jones and State X in an international tribunal?

- Has Jones—an individual—violated International Law?

Historically, States have been the sole subjects of International Law. They have created this body of rules that they deem binding in their relations with each other. Individuals and business entities have historically been the subjects of the national or internal law of the State. The laws of Morocco, for example, govern the conduct of a person living in Morocco or a corporation doing business there. If a private (nongovernmental) Moroccan corporation

wants to purchase metal from Germany, for example, it will have to consult the internal law of Morocco for any local import restrictions on German metal. For example, that corporation may not be able to import metal for the purpose of making automatic machine guns. A violation would subject the corporation and its directors or owners to punishment under the national law of Morocco.

Historical Lack of Individual's Capacity

An ancient theoretical dispute still ponders whether the individual—clearly a subject of *national* law—is also a subject of *International* Law. The English philosopher Jeremy Bentham, who coined the term "International Law" in his famous treatise of 1789, articulated the historical perspective that only the State could be its subject:

> transactions which may take place between individuals who are subjects of different states . . . are regulated by the internal laws, and decided upon by the internal tribunals, of the one or the other of these states. . . . There remain then the mutual transactions between sovereigns as such, for the subject of that branch of jurisprudence which may be properly and exclusively termed *international*.[1]

Bentham thus shared the perception that the individual was not a subject of International Law. In the "Soldier Jones Hypothetical" at the beginning of this section of the text, Jones would be theoretically unable to violate International Law because he is an individual rather than a State. Under International Law, only State X could incur responsibility for the slaughter of the Y villagers. Only States are the subjects of International Law and thus capable of breaching its obligations. Under Bentham's traditional view (and that of certain modern States), individuals and business entities lack the legal personality or capacity to incur responsibility because they are not considered subjects of *International* Law—only national law. The individual named Soldier Jones therefore violated the national law of State Y. His home State X violated International Law because its agent ordered him to undertake this mission. Jones himself was acting as an agent of State X. That State thus possesses the capacity to incur State responsibility as a legal "person" subject to the rules of International Law.

This perspective still prevails in a number of countries. The existence of a direct relationship between the individual and International Law is denied by Chinese and former Soviet scholars, for example. Chinese International Law texts published in the 1980s deny that individuals are the subjects of International Law.[2] A 1983 study by the East Asian Legal Studies Department of the University of Maryland corroborates the contemporary Chinese perspective that the sovereign quality of the State is inappropriately diminished by those who would subject State power to scrutiny by an individual under International Law. This study succinctly captures the attitude of the People's Republic of China as follows:

> Recognition of individual responsibility for personal acts under international law would . . . clash with Marxist principles regarding the class struggle in international relations. Moreover, the Chinese rejection of the concept of individuals as subject[s] of international law is an indisputable repudiation of the . . . conception of law which, by casting individuals in the role of international entities, attempted to circumvent the internal sovereign rule of the state. To the PRC, the only legitimate instrument to ensure the rights of individuals is the nation state.[3]

The traditional Soviet perception during the Cold War presented another alternative. The status of the individual can be acknowledged by International Law only to the extent that it is expressly recognized by the national law of the State. Otherwise, the United Nations Charter principles of State sovereignty and freedom from external intervention would be meaningless. The Soviet perspective was that even international organizations, heralding the human rights of the individual, could not circumvent the primacy of the State—for doing so would be tantamount to international interference in the internal affairs of the Soviet Union. With the advent of democratic institutions in the States of the former Soviet Union, one may anticipate some changes as their State practice evolves.

Modern Recognition of Individual Capacity

The above traditional paradigm was challenged in the twentieth century by other international jurists, as well as British and American scholars, who advocated the theory that the individual *is* a subject of International Law. They asserted that individuals enjoy international rights—particularly human rights—and that those rights must be defended not only by the traditional protector (the State) but directly by international organs possessing the legal power to interfere in the internal affairs of certain States. As argued by Professor Lung-chu Chen of New York University, authoritarian regimes have clung to the State-centered denial of individual status in International Law as a means of conveniently serving the totalitarian purposes of those States that govern without legitimate authority. Thus, they "will not tolerate their nationals complaining to other state elites or the larger community of mankind [for example, to international organizations such as the UN] about the deprivations within their particular communities."[4]

In the last half of the twentieth century, Western commentators began to seek international recognition of the individual as possessing rights and liabilities arising directly under International Law. One basis for this argument was the eighteenth century exception whereby individuals who committed certain types of crime were liable *as defendants* for violating the law of nations. Many jurists held that pirates were liable for their conduct directly under International Law—even when their conduct did not violate the law of the State where they were located, or the law of the State affected by their acts in international waters. Piracy was sufficiently heinous to be considered a crime against all nations. Individuals who committed this particular crime breached duties imposed upon them by International

Law. (*See* § 5.2 on the Universal principle of international criminal jurisdiction.)

In the nineteenth century, however, the notion of individual liability under International Law faded. Most jurists and commentators then characterized the rights and duties of International Law as applicable exclusively to States. Individuals had rights and obligations arising under national laws. They could thus breach *only* national laws.

The earlier view, recognizing that individuals could violate International Law (as well as national law) resurfaced as a result of Germany's Nazi regime in the twentieth century. Western scholars and jurists revived the theory that an individual could breach International Law—spawned directly by the 1946 Judgment at Nuremberg (and the companion war crimes trials in Tokyo). State practice then approved the trial of individuals for conduct that violated *only* International Law. German law, under Hitler's Third Reich, not only authorized genocide and related atrocities—it demanded it in many instances. The Nazis did not violate their State's laws. The resulting State denial of the dignity of the individual ultimately led France, England, the Soviet Union, and the United States to try the key Nazi war criminals as violators of *International* Law.

The liability of the Nazi defendants was based on the theory that there was a direct relationship between the individual and International Law. The defendants claimed that they had no obligations under International Law: Their only duty was to the Nazi State, which in turn, would bear any responsibility under International Law. The International Military Tribunal at Nuremberg disagreed in the following terms: "individuals have international duties which transcend the national obligations of obedience imposed by the individual State [to which they owe allegiance]. He who violates the laws of war cannot obtain immunity while acting in pursuance of the authority of the State if the State in authorizing action moves outside its competence under international law." (*See* § 9.5.) This trial generated an intense global interest in acknowledging the individual's liability under *International* Law, premised largely on the genocidal conduct of the Nazi defendants.

Plaintiff v. Defendant Distinction

Traditional doctrine espouses the following remedy for individual plaintiffs harmed by the action of a State—the decision of their home State to pursue a claim for harm done to them at the international level. It would thus fall within the province of State Y (the Soldier Jones case), rather than the individual relatives of the deceased Y villagers, to pursue a claim against State X for the acts of its military agents, making State X responsible under International Law. State Y was thus harmed because its villagers were harmed by the military agents of State X, including Jones, who went into State Y to execute Operation Phoenix. This type of State claim is considered distinct from the harm done to State Y's individual citizens—although the harm to State Y is derived from the harm to the individual villagers. The Permanent Court of International Justice thus characterized such claims as follows: "By taking up the case of one of its subjects and by resorting to diplomatic action or international judicial proceedings on his behalf, a state is in reality asserting its own rights—its right to ensure, in the person of its subjects, respect for the rules of international law."[5]

In the "Soldier Jones Hypothetical," Jones murdered State Y villagers in violation of the Geneva Conventions (*see* § 10.6) and arguably engaged in an act of piracy (*see* § 5.2). *Assuming* that these acts could be characterized as genocide or piracy, then Jones has violated International Law and would be directly punishable as an individual *defendant*. A relative of a deceased villager, however, would not have the capacity to be a *plaintiff* under International Law. None of the State Y villagers could be a party in an international tribunal. Only *States* or international organizations have the capacity to pursue claims in international proceedings (with the exception addressed in § 3.4 on the European Union). State Y would, in its discretion, have the international legal capacity to pursue a remedy against Soldier Jones and/or State Y. (If the circumstances warrant, an international organization might pursue a remedy on behalf of the deceased and the remaining State Y relatives.)

State Plaintiff Illustration

What are the practical consequences of the State consensus that individuals cannot directly pursue their own claims as plaintiffs under International Law? The State enjoys the virtually exclusive discretion regarding whether or not to pursue a remedy on the international level, such as lodging a diplomatic claim or instituting proceedings in an international tribunal. As articulated by the Permanent Court of International Justice: "Rights or interests of an individual the violation of which rights causes damage are always in a different plane to rights belonging to a State, which rights may also be infringed by the same act. The damage suffered by an individual is never, therefore, identical in kind with that which will be suffered by a State; it can only afford a convenient scale for the calculation of the reparation due the State [whose citizen has been harmed]."[6]

In the Soldier Jones hypothetical, State Y may thus initiate diplomatic communications with State X or adjudicate Y's claim against State X in an international tribunal. The relatives of the individual villagers cannot resort to these methods of dispute resolution. Further, any attempt by the State Y villagers to sue in the courts of either State X or State Y would likely result in dismissal under the sovereign immunity laws because Jones's conduct was "governmental" rather than "commercial" in nature (*see* § 2.6).

A major international tragedy in 1989 illustrates the application of this legal regime. Iran sued the US in the International Court of Justice for the 1988 destruction of an Iranian commercial airliner flying near a US naval vessel in the Persian Gulf. Under International Law, Iran's State status provided it with the ability to present its claim on this international level. The relatives of the Iranian citizens killed in the incident could not take such direct action against the US.

The Iranian relatives, of course, expected Iran to act on their behalf. Iran was harmed when its citizens were harmed, thus triggering Iran's discretion to pursue a remedy against the offending nation. Iran claimed that the death of the Iranians on the ill-fated flight, and the destruction of the Iranian aircraft, constituted unprovoked violations of the right to fly over international waters. Further, the surviving relatives of the Iranian victims would not be legally entitled to any recovery for the claimed breach of International Law. Any monetary compensation obtained by Iran for the destruction of the aircraft and the loss of life would belong to Iran. The victims' families would indirectly benefit only if Iran chose to give them that money. Many States do turn over such recoveries to the harmed individuals in these circumstances. But because of poor international relations, the US offer to provide compensation to the Iranian survivors was conditioned on the special requirement that all payments would go directly to the victims' families—rather than pass through the hands of the Iranian government.

Conclusions

The emergence of the individual (in addition to governments and international organizations) as possessing status in International Law is a distinct feature of modern International Law. Events occurring in Nazi Germany, coupled with the postwar pressure for decolonization and self–determination described in Chapter 3, undermined the traditional rule of State exclusivity as the primary actor on the international stage. Yet, the primacy of the State could nevertheless result in a future generation's decision to eliminate the capacity of both the individual and the international organization to function as international actors. As aptly described by Professor Antonio Cassese of the University of Florence in Italy, individuals and organizations could thus be characterized as the "ancillary" subjects of International Law. Under his description, "one may distinguish between *primary* and *secondary* subjects, the former embracing States, the latter encompassing individuals, as well as the other international subjects." While State practice currently supports a role for the individual on the international plane, State primacy could once again evolve into State *exclusivity* at the international level.[7]

■ 4.2 NATIONALITY/STATELESSNESS/ REFUGEES

An individual's nationality (also referred to as citizenship) is a bond between an individual and a State that establishes reciprocal rights and duties between them. This bond was once an automatic attribute of residence within the Roman Empire, except for the "barbarians" who did not reside within its territory. In A.D. 212, the Edict of Caracalla conferred Roman citizenship on all individuals who lived within the area controlled by the Empire. There were no distinctions regarding place of birth, parental citizenship, or whether one wanted to become a citizen or abandon citizenship.[8]

This section analyzes general citizenship rules, State competence in such matters, and related consequences for affected individuals. The four specific themes will be nationality, dual nationality, statelessness, and refugees.

Nationality

The bond known as "nationality" is a legal and political link between an individual or corporation and a State. In 1955, the International Court of Justice defined nationality of the individual as "a legal bond having as its basis a social fact of attachment, a genuine connection of existence, interests and sentiments, together with the existence of reciprocal rights and duties. It may be said . . . that the individual upon whom it is conferred . . . is in fact more closely connected with the population of the State conferring nationality than with that of any other State. . . ."[9]

Nationality establishes mutual expectations for both the State that confers it and the individual who acquires it. The State has the right, for example, to require its citizens to serve in its military forces. The State may also tax an individual or corporation for earnings accrued anywhere in the world. The individual is correlatively entitled to certain expectations based on his or her nationality. One of the most important of these rights is the State protection of the individual. This right means essentially that the home State assists its nationals when they are abroad and claim that they are being mistreated by another State or its agents. A US citizen who is mistreated by State X may seek the assistance of the US when he or she is suffering at the hands of a foreign State. Under International Law, such protection typically takes the form of diplomatic inquiries and protests on behalf of individuals harmed by State conduct that violates international expectations. In the *Nelson v. Saudi Arabia* case presented in § 2.6 of this text, Mrs. Nelson sought the aid of a US consular officer during the period that her husband disappeared into the Saudi Arabian jail system. He had reported dangerous working conditions at a local hospital where he was employed to do just that, and subsequently was arrested, detained, and tortured.

Nations have not always protected their citizens abroad. The concept of nationality was not introduced in mainland China, for example, until the mid-nineteenth century. Earlier, the Chinese government showed little interest in protecting its citizens abroad. The government's perspective was that choosing to live abroad was prima facie evidence of disloyalty. Residing among "barbarians" thus rendered Chinese citizens unworthy of the State's protection.[10]

Is nationality a matter of national or International Law? In 1923, the Permanent Court of International Justice responded that States were not limited in their nationality decisions. Exceptions include those situations where there was a treaty obligation to *confer* or the *inability* to confer nationality under the particular circumstances. In one of the leading cases, France conferred French nationality on residents of Tunis and Morocco, over a British protest on behalf of British citizens living in these territories. The Court was asked to decide whether this was a matter falling exclusively within France's nationality laws. The Court decided that this matter involved an issue arising under *International* Law—although the conferring of nationality was normally only a matter of the State's national law. In the Court's words: "nationality, is not, in principle, regulated by international law, [however] the right of a State to use its discretion is nevertheless restricted by obligations which it may have undertaken towards other States. In such a case, jurisdiction which, in principle, belongs solely to the State [conferring its nationality on residents of its territories], is limited by rules of international law."[11]

Under this judicial formulation, a State would be free to *deprive* its citizens of citizenship against their wishes. In 1915, the new Turkish government, fearing that Turkish Armenians were a dangerous "foreign element with cousins in the Russian army," deported them to Syria and other Middle Eastern areas. If the Turkish government had deprived them of their citizenship on the basis of their ethnic background, there may be no violation of International Law under the Court's 1923 formulation. (Subsequent refugee and statelessness treaties pose an impediment, as discussed below.) And in 1939, Stalin and Hitler signed a nonaggression treaty containing a secret protocol placing various nations, including Estonia, under Soviet influence. Stalin ordered the deportation of 60,000 Estonian nationalists to Siberia after taking away their Estonian citizenship. Under the PCIJ's 1923 approach, matters of nationality would fall exclusively within the jurisdiction of the Soviet Union because there was no nationality treaty between the Soviet Union and Estonia. Incidents like those involving the Armenians and Estonians stimulated international pressure to limit the total discretion exercisable by states in nationality matters. The results of such pressures are addressed below under the materials on statelessness.

Scholars are divided on the degree to which International Law plays a role in State nationality decisions. Some believe that International Law does not impose significant limitations on the national right to grant or withdraw citizenship. The International Law textbook that has been used at Russia's Moscow State University provides that the status of citizenship "is above all a national institution." This statement is qualified, however, by the following acknowledgment that there may be limits on State control of that institution: in "modern international law, principles and norms relating to questions of nationality are contained primarily in the United Nations Charter [and related international Human Rights documents]. . . ."[12] Some scholars have thus adopted the position that State nationality decisions are governed by both national *and* International Law, although the role of the latter is secondary and uncertain.

Western scholars disagree. They argue that International Law plays a *significant* role in nationality matters. Members of the International Law Institute of the Netherlands, for example, undertook a major study concluding that International Law limits the State in the application of its nationality laws. The head of the Department of International Law of the institute writes that "international agreements . . . have been instrumental in shaping the Netherlands law on nationality. The relevant provisions have been incorporated into or implemented by municipal [national] statutory law, thus accounting for the amendments which the 1892 [Netherlands] Nationality Act has undergone in the course of time."[13]

How is nationality acquired? Individual nationality (also referred to as citizenship) may be acquired in three ways: (1) passively, by parentage; (2) passively, by being born in a State that considers a child born there its citizen; and (3) actively, by naturalization of an individual who voluntarily changes allegiance from one State to another.

(1) Citizenship derived from parentage is a rule drawn from the ancient Roman law. The child's citizenship is that of the parents. This rule is referred to as *jus sanguinis*, or "blood rule" for establishing citizenship. A child born of Roman parents in any region of the world not under Roman control was nevertheless a Roman citizen. The *jus sanguinis* basis for acquiring nationality is used in Europe, Latin America, and many English-speaking countries.

(2) Many countries apply a nationality-by-birth rule. This is the rule known as *jus soli*, or "soil rule" for granting citizenship. In the Middle Ages, birth within certain European territories vested the new-

born with that nation's citizenship. Under its contemporary application, a child born in England—yet whose parents are Italian citizens—is an English citizen under the immigration and nationality laws of England. (This child would also be an Italian citizen because Italy follows the blood rule.)

Nationality determinations are often complicated by the simultaneous applicability of the laws of the country of parentage and the country of birth. Assume that a Japanese couple have a baby during a visit to the United States. Application of the parentage or *jus sanguinis* blood rule of Japan would make the baby a citizen of Japan. Application of the *jus soli* or soil rule of the US would make the baby a citizen of the US. This child is thus a citizen of both countries and may have to choose one of the two citizenships on attaining adult status.

There have been efforts to curtail the US application of the *jus soli* rule that confers US nationality upon birth in the US. The US Constitution provides that "All persons born or naturalized in the United States . . . are citizens of the United States. . . ."[14] The State of California's Governor Wilson proposed national legislation in 1993 that, if adopted by Congress, would create a federal constitutional amendment. That change in the national law of the US would repeal the guarantee that children of foreign nationals (including those that are *undocumented*) born on US soil are automatically US citizens. Foreign citizens who are legally in the US would not be affected.

(3) Individuals may actively (that is, intentionally) change their nationality through a process called naturalization. The national law of the country from which nationality is sought establishes its naturalization requirements. States with adjacent borders may have very different views about naturalization matters.

In Western Europe, French and German leaders sought to respectively close and open the door to immigrants in the same month. In June 1993, France's National Assembly overwhelmingly approved a tougher immigration law making it more difficult for foreign citizens to acquire French citizenship via marriage or residence with a family member in France. Immigration is one of France's most explosive social issues due to increasing crime, which the French press has attributed to "foreigners." Germany's Chancellor Helmut Kohl contemporaneously urged the German Parliament to make it easier to become a German citizen. Responding to pressure after fatal attacks on Turks in Solingen, Chancellor Kohl attempted to initiate a process that would change Germany's eighty-year-old nationality law, barring many life-long residents (including some who were *born* in Germany) from applying for German citizenship. Later that year, however, Germany introduced a tough immigration policy designed to halt the influx of immigrants triggered by the end of the Cold War. By one year later (1994), illegal immigration dropped by two-thirds and the number of individuals seeking political asylum dropped 72 percent.

Naturalization does not necessarily entitle an individual, however, to claim that he or she is a national of a particular country. Further, the relatively lax nationality laws of one State may be in conflict with the laws of another State. In 1955, the International Court of Justice addressed this recurring problem in the following case.

Nottebohm was a German citizen residing in Guatemala. He operated a successful business in both Guatemala and Germany before World War II. Guatemala's laws discriminated against foreign citizens and business entities that were nationals of countries with which it was at war. Thus, German citizens could not do business in Guatemala.

Just before Guatemala declared war against Germany, Nottebohm went to Liechtenstein and applied for citizenship. His purpose was to avoid the discriminatory laws against foreign citizens so that he could continue his lucrative business in Guatemala. There was no state of war between Guatemala and Liechtenstein. Liechtenstein waived its usual three-year waiting period for citizenship for Nottebohm. He immediately took an oath of allegiance and became a naturalized citizen of Liechtenstein and was then issued a passport prior to leaving for Guatemala. When Nottebohm attempted to return to Guatemala as a citizen of Liechtenstein, however, he was unable to reenter. His property in Guatemala was seized by the government. Guatemala still considered Nottebohm a German national and would not recognize Liechtenstein's grant of nationality.

In 1946, Liechtenstein first asserted its right to protect Nottebohm, whom it considered a naturalized citizen of Liechtenstein. In 1951, after unsuccessful negotiations with Guatemala, Liechtenstein instituted this suit in the International Court of Justice. Liechtenstein wanted to recover for damages to Nottebohm, caused by Guatemala's treatment of what Liechtenstein considered its citizen.

The opinion below addresses the requirements for the international recognition of citizenship conferred under national law. The legal question was whether Liechtenstein could present this claim on behalf of Nottebohm. The factual question was whether Guatemala had to recognize Nottebohm as a citizen of Liechtenstein. If not, Liechtenstein had no right to present this claim on behalf of an individual whom Guatemala still considered a German citizen:

NOTTEBOHM CASE (LIECHTENSTEIN v. GUATEMALA)

International Court of Justice (1955)
1955 International Court of Justice Reports 4

[*Opinion.*] [T]he Court must ascertain whether the nationality conferred on Nottebohm by Liechtenstein . . . bestows upon Liechtenstein a sufficient title to the exercise of protection in respect of Nottebohm as against Guatemala. In this connection, Counsel for Liechtenstein said: 'the essential question is whether Mr. Nottebohm, having acquired the nationality of Liechtenstein, that acquisition of nationality is one which must be recognized by other States.'

Guatemala expressly stated that it could not 'recognise that Mr. Nottebohm, a German subject habitually resident in Guatemala, has acquired the nationality of Liechtenstein without changing his habitual residence.' There is here an express denial by Guatemala of Nottebohm's Liechtenstein nationality.

The naturalization of Nottebohm was an act performed by Liechtenstein in the exercise of its domestic jurisdiction. The question to be decided is whether that act has the international effect here under consideration.

International arbitrators have given their preference to the real and effective nationality, that which accorded with the facts, that based on stronger factual ties between the person concerned and one of the States whose nationality is involved. Different factors are taken into consideration, and their importance will vary from one case to the next: the habitual residence of the individual concerned is an important factor, but there are other factors such as the centre of his interests, his family ties, his participation in public life, attachment shown by him for a given country and inculcated in his children, etc. [I]nternational law leaves it to each State to lay down the rules governing the grant of its own nationality. On the other hand, a State cannot claim that the rules it has laid down are entitled to recognition by another State unless it has acted in conformity with this general aim of making the legal bond of nationality accord with the individual's genuine connection with the State which assumes the defence of its citizens by means of protection as against other States.

According to the practice of States, to arbitral and judicial decisions and to the opinion of writers, nationality is a legal bond having as its basis a social fact of attachment, a genuine connection of existence, interests and sentiments, together with the existence of reciprocal rights and duties. It may be said to constitute the juridical connection of the fact that the individual upon whom it is conferred either directly by the law or as the result of an act of the authorities, is in fact more closely connected with the population of the State conferring nationality than with that of any other State. Conferred by a State, it only entitles that State to exercise protection vis-a-vis another State, if it constitutes a translation into juridical terms of the individual's connection with the State which has made him a national.

At the date when he applied for naturalization Nottebohm had been a German national from the time of his birth. His country had been at war for more than a month, and there is nothing to indicate that the application for naturalization then made by Nottebohm was motivated by any desire to dissociate himself from the Government of his country [Germany].

He had been settled in Guatemala for 34 years. He had carried on his activities there. It was the main seat of his interests. He returned there shortly after his naturalization, and it remained the centre of his interest and of his business activities. He stayed there until his removal as a result of war measures [passed by Guatemala] in 1943. He subsequently attempted to return there, and he now complains of Guatemala's refusal to admit him [now that he claims Liechtenstein rather than German nationality].

In contrast, his actual connections with Liechtenstein were extremely tenuous. No settled abode, no prolonged residence in the country at the time of his application for naturalization: the application indicates that he was paying a visit there and confirms the transient character of this visit by its request that the naturalization proceedings should initiated and concluded without delay. If Nottebohm went to Liechtenstein in 1946, this was because of the refusal of Guatemala to admit him. No indication is given of the grounds warranting the waiver of the condition of residence. There is no allegation of any economic interests or of any activities exercised or to be exercised in Liechtenstein, and no manifestation of any intention whatsoever to transfer all or some of his interests and his business activities to Liechtenstein.

These facts clearly establish, on the one hand, the absence of any bond of attachment between Nottebohm and Liechtenstein and, on the other hand, the existence of a long-standing and close connection between him and Guatemala, a link which his naturalization in no way weakened. That naturalization was not based on any real prior connection with Liechtenstein, nor did it in any way alter the manner of life of the person upon whom it was conferred in exceptional circumstances of speed and accommodation. In both respects, it was lacking in the genuineness requisite to an act of such importance, if it is to be entitled to be respected by a State in the position of Guatemala. It was granted without regard to the concept of nationality adopted in international relations.

Naturalization was asked for not so much for the purpose of obtaining a legal recognition of Nottebohm's membership in fact in the population of Liechtenstein, as it was to enable him to substitute for his status as a national of a belligerent State [Germany] that of a national of a neutral State [Liechtenstein], with the sole aim of thus coming within the protection of Liechtenstein.

Guatemala is under no obligation to recognise a nationality granted in such circumstances. Liechtenstein consequently is not entitled to extend its protection to Nottebohm *vis-a-vis* Guatemala.

■ NOTES

1. The ICJ thus dismissed Liechtenstein's claim filed on behalf of Nottebohm. He was a citizen of Liechtenstein under that country's internal *national* law. Under *International* Law, however, Liechtenstein could not confer its citizenship on Nottebohm under these circumstances and presumed that other countries like Guatemala would therefore have to recognize Nottebohm as a Liechtensteinian for the purpose of applying the citizenship laws of Guatemala. Guatemala properly continued to characterized Nottebohm as a citizen of Germany, and remained free to apply its discriminatory national laws against this citizen of a country with which Guatemala was at war.

2. The court never decided the merits of this claim regarding Guatemala's alleged mistreatment of Nottebohm—because he was not represented by a country with which he had the effective link of nationality. Liechtenstein therefore did not have the legal capacity to bring this particular claim. Only Germany possessed that right, which it did not invoke during or after the war.

3. The *Nottebohm* Court thus validated the following factors for international recognition of naturalization by another State: residence, center of interests, family ties, participation in public life, and attachment shown for a particular State.

Dual Nationality

A person is a dual national when he or she possesses the citizenship of more than one nation. This status of having multiple nationalities occurs when an individual (1) is born in a nation that observes the rule of *jus soli* (nationality by birth) and (2) simultaneously acquires the parents' citizenship because their home nation applies the rule of *jus sanguinis* (nationality by blood, that is, the nationality of the parents).

Dual nationality is also spawned by simultaneous recognition of the rules of both *jus sanguinis* and *jus soli*. Assume that a child is born in State X, where her parents are temporarily working. Their permanent home is in State Y. State X may apply the rules of both *jus sanguinis* and *jus soli* under these circumstances. Under State X's law, she is a citizen of State X because she was born in State X. X law may also recognize this child as a citizen of State Y because she was born of State Y parents. State X may require her to choose between State X and State Y citizenship, however, should she remain in X and achieve adult status.

Individuals occasionally face unusual burdens as a result of their dual nationality. A dual national may be subject to the nationality jurisdiction of two countries. Each nation may command that the same individual return to it, as when testimony is required (*see* § 5.2 on the nationality principle of international jurisdiction). Both nations may want to tax the income of such individuals or impress them into military service. An individual may not be able to predict which nation will provide them when they are harmed in a third nation (other than the nations of their dual nationality). In this instance, a famous international arbitration decision denied Italy the right to espouse a claim on behalf of an Italian citizen born of Italian parents. He was an Italian national under the law of Italy. He was Peruvian, however, by birth. The tribunal thus refused to recognize Italy's attempt to bring a claim on his behalf against Peru.[15] The international arbitrator in this case was unwilling to allow Italy to represent a national of Peru in a suit against Peru. As described earlier in this section, various attributes flow from the bond of nationality between a nation and its citizen who happens to be abroad. One of these attributes is that the individual's home nation may be expected to provide diplomatic protection in a dispute involving mistreatment of the individual by another nation that considers that person an alien. Here, Peru could not afford protection to an Italian national (who also happened to be a Peruvian national).

Some *multilateral* treaties have referred to dual citizenship, although they have done little to alleviate conflicting demands on individuals who are citizens of two nations. The 1930 Hague Convention on Certain Questions Relating to the Conflict of Nationality Laws was the first multilateral treaty addressing dual nationality. While it restates the basic nationality rules already discussed, none of its provisions resolves the dilemma posed for the individual dual national when two nations claim that person as their citizen. Under Article 3, for example, "a person having two or more nationalities may be regarded as its national by each of the States whose nationality he possesses." Thus, under this early treaty on dual nationality, each nation may apply its own law to the same individual. Some relief was available in the wording of the 1930 Hague Protocol Relating to Military Obligations in Certain Cases of Double Nationality. This treaty provides a model for avoiding competing military service claims in the case of dual nationals. It would have precluded dual military service for individuals who were dual nationals. It was not adopted by enough nations, however, to provide effective relief. The 1964 Paris Convention Concerning the Exchange of Information with Respect to Acquisition of Nationality is another multilateral treaty that was designed to assist dual nationals. While useful for the purpose of acquiring information, none of its provisions addresses inconsistent obligations for dual nationals.[16]

The most effective devices for avoiding inconsistent burdens are the various *bilateral* treaties that specifically address dual nationality problems. One classic burden arises when two states draft an individual into their armies. The Netherlands-Belgian Agreement of 1954, concerning the Military Service of Young Men Possessing Both Belgian and Netherlands Nationality, is a good illustration of international cooperation. It avoids the potential unfairness of having to serve in two armies just because an individual is a dual national. Military service for one nation automatically precludes military service obligations in another nation.[17]

Statelessness

The condition of statelessness is the lack of nationality in *any* State. Loss of one's original citizenship—typically conferred by birth or parentage—without obtaining a new citizenship renders the individual stateless. Such individuals cannot claim the citizenship of any State that might otherwise protect them. There is no State to come to the aid of an individual in need of diplomatic representation, due to the absence of the tie of nationality with any particular State.

During and after both world wars, numerous people became stateless. Many were refugees who lost their citizenship after fleeing from their native lands. They were not citizens of the State where they had found temporary refuge. Many fled certain Eastern European countries to avoid political persecution, only to find that they had been deprived of their original citizenship for doing so. Under the 1948 Hungarian Nationality Act, for example, the government of Hungary could "deprive of his Hungarian nationality a person who . . . on going abroad contravenes or evades the statutory provisions relating to the departure from the country." The 1951 Polish Nationality Act provided that a Polish citizen who resided abroad would be deprived of Polish nationality if the government determined that such an individual "left the territory of the Polish State unlawfully" or "refused to return to Poland at the summons of the competent authority."

The phenomenon of statelessness is not limited to the two world wars. Many of the refugees who fled Cuba in the 1960s and Vietnam in the 1970s, as a result of political persecution in those countries, lost their citizenship as a result of their decision to flee. They were thus stateless before they underwent any naturalization proceedings in the countries where they found temporary or permanent refuge.

The significance of statelessness is that individuals who acquire this status encounter great difficulty in traveling and obtaining work. The absence of identity documents such as birth certificates or passports often precludes such aliens from entering or working in most countries. The following case is a classic illustration of these difficulties. In 1957, the Supreme Court of British Columbia reviewed a deportation order made by Canadian immigration authorities regarding an individual named Hanna. He had sought residence in Canada and a waiver of compliance with its Immigration Act due to his statelessness. Judge Sullivan's account of Hanna's dilemma follows:

RE IMMIGRATION ACT AND HANNA

21 Western Weekly Reporter 400 (1957)*

[*Opinion.*] Hanna is a young man without a country—one of those unfortunate "stateless" persons of the world whose status is a matter of concern to humanitarians.

[He is] in the frustrating dilemma with which fate seems to have confronted him throughout his lifetime prior to his last arrival in Canada as ship-bound prisoner aboard a tramp motor-ship in her ceaseless meanderings from port to port throughout the world.

[The evidence was that] he was born at sea and that no known record of his birth is extant. The name of the vessel aboard which he was born, and particulars of her nationality or port of registry are unknown.

During his years of infancy and adolescence Hanna seems to have crossed and recrossed the international boundaries of Ethiopia, French Somaliland, British Somaliland and Eritrea without encountering difficulty with the immigration officials of those countries.

As he grew older Hanna seems to have encountered and had difficulty with the immigration officers of these adjacent countries, in none of which he could claim residence. He thereby learned that possession of a birth certificate is an indispensable requirement of modern society.

Almost three years ago, when he was in the port of Massaua, Eritrea, Hanna stowed away in an Italian tramp steamer in the hope of being carried in her to some country which would grant him asylum and right of residence. His plan met with frustration because upon arrival of such ship at any port he was immediately locked up and denied permission to land. After a year or more of such aimless wandering and imprisonment, Hanna escaped from the Italian vessel and concealed himself in the hold of the Norwegian motor-ship 'Gudvieg.' As a stowaway in such latter vessel he fared no better than before. He was [effectively] held prisoner aboard the 'Gudvieg' for more than 16 months and made three or more trips to Canada in her [prior to these proceedings].

From whatever angle one views it, so far as Hanna is concerned, this [Canadian] deportation order amounted to a sentence of imprisonment aboard The 'Gudvieg' for an indefinite term, and in my opinion and finding, no immigration officer has the legal right to exercise such drastic power.

■ NOTES

1. There is no record of what ultimately happened to Hanna. The judge in the *Hanna* case did *not* rule that Hanna could remain in Canada. Judge Sullivan merely ruled that Hanna could not be deported "as ordered" by immigration authorities. The immigration agency's order was, in effect, a decision that could have subjected Hanna to life imprisonment aboard the ship in which he arrived. The judge stated that no country had—or likely would—allow Hanna to leave that vessel.

2. In a similar deportation proceeding in the United States, a stateless seaman was detained at Ellis Island in New York Harbor for seven months. Like Hanna, he had been ordered deported without specifying a particular destination. The seaman instituted proceedings to modify this "pointless" deportation order. As in the Canadian *Hanna* case, the US judge acknowledged that a stateless seaman would be denied permission to land anywhere because there "is no other country that would take him without proper documents."[18] This seaman was thus permitted to work in New York and periodically report to US immigration officials.

3. In 1994, a federal court in California ordered the release of a Cuban citizen confined in federal prisons since 1985. He was one of the so-called Mariel Cubans, most likely released from a Cuban jail and sent off to the US to reduce Cuba's prison population. He appeared on US shores in 1980. He was initially ordered returned to Cuba. Cuba would take him back, and no longer considered him a Cuban citizen. No other country was willing to accept

him. For a total of fourteen years, he was subject to preventative detention. He was released from federal custody on grounds that his incarceration for such a long period was an excessive punishment. Then in September 1994, the same federal appellate court decided that it would reconsider its prior decision to release him—resulting in his remaining in custody. Barrera–Echavarria v. Rison (Warden), 21 Fed.Rptr.3d 314 (9th Cir. 1994), petition for rehearing *en banc* granted, 35 Fed.Rptr.3d 436 (9th Cir. 1994).

4. Like Hanna, a vessel at sea may be deemed "stateless." In March 1995, for example, a US Coast Guard airplane spotted a vessel on a routine patrol 600 miles south of the California–Mexico border. The vessel was not flying any flag, thus rendering identification from the air impossible. When the operator did not answer radio messages, a Coast Guard cutter then boarded it—finding ninety-five undocumented Asian immigrants. It was not illegal for that vessel to be in international waters (*see* § 6.3). But the failure to fly any flag, or respond to attempts to communicate with that vessel, rendered it "stateless" for the purpose of allowing this inspection. In 1994 alone, 1,168 Asian nationals were thus apprehended in their attempts to reach US shores.

International organizations have attempted to alleviate the problems caused by statelessness. In 1921, the League of Nations established the Office of the High Commissioner of Refugees in response primarily to people made stateless by the Russian Revolution of 1917. Members of the United Nations later established the UN Relief and Rehabilitation Administration to deal with the statelessness resulting from World War II. The UN Conference on the Elimination or Reduction of Future Statelessness has conducted a number of meetings to address this problem—without much success. The UN High Commissioner for Refugees currently deals with such matters.

Several treaties address, but have not resolved, the problem of statelessness. The goal of the 1930 Hague Protocol concerning Statelessness (discussed above) was to provide nationality to those deprived of citizenship as a result of political dissension or military conflict. This draft treaty never became effective because too few nations ratified its provisions, which prevented it from entering into force. The UN Convention on the Reduction of Statelessness entered into force in 1975. It obliges its signatories to grant their citizenship to stateless people who are willing recipients and found within their borders. It also removes the State discretion to deprive inhabitants of citizenship, except on grounds that are not associated with race, religion, and political beliefs. But there are only fifteen State members, hardly enough to signal a global commitment to the problem of statelessness.

Refugees

State treatment of international refugees is a problem that sometimes intersects with statelessness. This problem was originally spawned by the elimination of States and borders during the twentieth century's two World Wars. It has surfaced with increasing fury in the aftermath of the Cold War, in the former Yugoslavia and on the African Continent—including the stream of some one million refugees from Rwanda into Zaire and other African nations in 1994.

Refugee Conventions Shortly after World War II was over, it was evident that the wartime refugee problems did not cease with that war. Rather than spontaneous *ad hoc* agreements, the UN initiated a process leading to the 1951 Geneva Convention on the Status of Refugees and its 1967 Protocol. The basic 1951 Convention applies to refugees spawned by events occurring prior to 1951. The 1967 Protocol applies to all refugees.

These international refugee agreements do three things: they define *who* are refugees, determine their legal *status*, and provide the administrative and diplomatic *machinery* for implementing ameliorative treaty provisions.

Who are refugees under International Law? In Article 1.A.(2)., the 1951 Refugee Convention defines them as any person who:

> owing to [a] well-founded fear of being persecuted for reasons of race, religion, nationality, membership of a particular social group or political opinion, is outside the country of his nationality and is unable, or, owing to such fear, is unwilling to avail himself of the protection of that country; or who, not having a nationality and being outside the country of his former habitual residence as a result of

such events, is unable, or . . . unwilling to return to it.

What then is the refugee's legal status under International Law? One of the most important treaty protections is described in Article 33.1 of the 1951 Convention. A contracting party may not "return" an individual to his or her homeland if "his life or freedom would be threatened on account of his race, religion, nationality, membership of a particular social group or political opinion."

US Interpretation   The most famous case decided by any national court of a State party to the 1951 Refugee Convention has also been the most widely criticized. That is the following 1993 case, from the US Supreme Court, regarding Haitian refugees seeking asylum in the US. On September 30, 1991, a group of military leaders displaced the government of Jean-Bertrand Aristide, the first democratically elected president in Haitian history. All parties to the ensuing litigation (below) agreed that since this military coup, "hundreds of Haitians have been killed, tortured, detained without a warrant, or subjected to violence and the destruction of their property because of their political beliefs. Thousands have been forced into hiding."

Following the 1991 coup, the US Coast Guard suspended repatriations for a period of several weeks, and the US imposed economic sanctions on Haiti. In the meantime the Haitian exodus expanded dramatically. During the six months after October 1991, the Coast Guard interdicted over 34,000 Haitians. Because so many interdicted Haitians could not be safely processed on Coast Guard cutters, the Department of Defense established temporary facilities at the US Naval Base in Guantanamo, Cuba, to accommodate them during the screening process. In May 1992, the US Navy determined that no additional migrants could safely be accommodated at Guantanamo.

President Clinton then directed the Coast Guard to intercept vessels illegally transporting passengers from Haiti to the US, and to return those passengers to Haiti *without first determining* whether they may qualify as "refugees" under the 1951 UN Convention Relating to the Status of Refugees. The question presented in this case was whether such forced repatriation to Haiti violates the US Immigration and Nationality Act (INA) and Article 33 of the United Nations Protocol Relating to the Status of Refugees. The US Immigration Act was supposedly amended to codify the US treaty commitment under the 1951 Refugee Convention.

The treaty gap that triggered this litigation involved the term "returns" occurring on the high seas *before* entering US waters (or land)—rather than *after* arrival.[19] Put another way, does the French-language treaty term "refouler" broadly require a determination of refugee status for *all* "returns," or just those returns occurring *after* the asylum-seeker has arrived *within* the territory (or territorial waters) of a State that is a party to the 1951 Refugee Convention?

The federal trial court decided against the Haitians, thus confirming the legality of President Clinton's directive requiring returns to Haiti without making the "Article 33 Refugee Convention" determination. The federal Court of Appeals disagreed. Its judges did not accept the US government's argument that the treaty did not bar returns made prior to the refugee's arrival in the US or its territorial waters. This interim Court thus determined that the 1980 amendment to the INA had been intended to conform US immigration law to the provisions of the Refugee Convention. These judges read Article 33.1's "return" provision as "plainly" covering *all* refugees, regardless of their location when found and returned by the US Coast Guard. The US was engaged in the act of returning these refugees, thereby triggering the Article 33.1 requirement of determining whether these "returns" would subject the Haitians to death or other heinous mistreatment on the basis of their political beliefs.

Like the text and the history of the US law, the text and negotiating history of Article 33 of the United Nations Convention are both completely silent with respect to their applicability to returns that are undertaken *outside* territorial borders or waters. The "Respondents" (Haitians) argued that the 1967 Protocol's broad remedial goals prohibit a nation from repatriating refugees to their potential oppressors—whether or not the refugees are the objects of the US return *within* or *beyond* US territory.

The US Supreme Court majority decided, however, that in spite of the moral weight of this argument, Article 33 was not intended to have such *extraterritorial* effect. The treaty could not apply to a return ("refouler") occurring outside of US territorial waters, on the high seas between Haiti and the US.

The drafters of the 1951 Convention, and the parties to the companion Protocol—like the drafters of the conforming 1980 US immigration law amendment—apparently did *not* contemplate that any nation would ever gather fleeing refugees and then return them to the very country from which they so desperately sought to escape. This action clearly violated the "spirit" of Article 33. But the Supreme Court majority found that no treaty can impose uncontemplated extraterritorial obligations on those who ratify it, regardless of the general humanitarian intent of the treaty. Simply put, because the text of Article 33 said nothing about a signatory's "returns" *outside* of its territory, it therefore cannot prohibit such actions. The rather scathing dissent is presented below.

In the final paragraph of the Supreme Court majority's opinion, the judges presented their closing argument by quoting from the opinion of a lower court case with similar facts: "This case presents a painfully common situation in which desperate people, convinced that they can no longer remain in their homeland, take desperate measures to escape. Although the human crisis is compelling, there is no solution to be found in a *judicial* remedy" (implying the need for a diplomatic remedy or a treaty modification).

The following portion of the US Supreme Court's 1993 "Haiti" opinion is the dissent wherein Justice Blackmun agreed with the intermediate appellate court in this case. According to Justice Blackmun, the lower court's judges correctly interpreted the "refouler" (return) provision of the Refugee Convention as prohibiting President Clinton's Executive Order to the Coast Guard in violation of the treaty:

SALE v. HAITIAN CENTERS COUNCIL, INC.

Supreme Court of the United States, 1993
___ U.S. ___, 113 S.Ct. 2549, 125 L.Ed.2d 128

[*Opinion.*] Justice BLACKMUN, dissenting.

When, in 1968, the United States acceded to the United Nations Protocol Relating to the Status of Refugees, Jan. 31, 1967, it pledged not to "return ('*refouler*') a refugee in any manner whatsoever" to a place where he would face political persecution. In 1980, Congress amended our immigration law to reflect the Protocol's directives. Today's majority nevertheless decides that the forced repatriation of the Haitian refugees is perfectly legal, because the word "return" does not mean return, because the opposite of "within the United States" is not outside the United States, and because the official charged with controlling immigration has no role in enforcing an order to control immigration.

. . .

Article 33.1 of the Convention states categorically and without geographical limitation: "No Contracting State shall expel or return ('*refouler*') a refugee in any manner whatsoever to the frontiers of territories where his life or freedom would be threatened on account of his race, religion, nationality, membership of a particular social group or political opinion."

The terms are unambiguous. Vulnerable refugees shall not be returned. The language is clear, and the command is straightforward; that should be the end of the inquiry. Indeed, until litigation ensued, the Government consistently acknowledged that the Convention applied on the high seas.

The majority, however, has difficulty with the Treaty's use of the term "return ('*refouler*')." "Return," it claims, does not mean return, but instead has a distinctive legal meaning. For this proposition the Court relies almost entirely on the fact that *American* law makes a general distinction between *deportation* and *exclusion*. Without explanation, the majority asserts that in light of this distinction the word "return" as used in the Treaty somehow must refer only to "the exclusion of aliens who are . . . 'on the threshold of initial entry'" (citation omitted).

. . . The text of the Convention does not ban the "exclusion" of aliens who have reached some indeterminate "threshold"; it bans their "return." It is well settled that a treaty must first be construed according to its "ordinary meaning." Article 31.1 of the Vienna Convention on the Law of Treaties. The ordinary meaning of "return" is "to bring, send, or put (a person or thing) back to or in a former position." Webster's Third New International

Dictionary 1941 (1986). That describes precisely what petitioners [US government agencies] are doing to the Haitians. By dispensing with ordinary meaning at the outset, and by taking instead as its starting point the assumption that "return," as used in the Treaty, "has a legal meaning narrower than its common meaning," the majority leads itself astray.

The straightforward interpretation of the duty of nonreturn is strongly reinforced by the Convention's use of the French term "*refouler.*" The ordinary meaning of "refouler," as the majority concedes, is "[t]o repulse, . . .; to drive back, to repel." [French] *Dictionnaire Larousse* 631 (1981). Thus construed, Article 33.1 of the Convention reads: "No contracting state shall expel or [repulse, drive back, or repel] a refugee in any manner whatsoever to the frontiers of territories where his life or freedom would be threatened. . . ." That, of course, is exactly what the Government is doing. It thus is no surprise that when the French press has described the very policy challenged here, the term it has used is "*refouler.*" See, e.g., Le bourbier haitien, Le Monde, May 31-June 1, 1992 ("[L]es Etats-Unis ont decide de refouler directement les refugies recueillis par la garde cotiere." (The United States has decided [de refouler] directly the refugees picked up by the Coast Guard)

. . .

Article 33.1 is clear not only in what it says, but also in what it does not say: it does not include any geographical limitation. It limits only where a refugee may be sent "to", not where he may be sent from. This is not surprising, given that the aim of the provision is to protect refugees against persecution.

. . .

The Convention that the [US] Refugee Act embodies was enacted largely in response to the experience of Jewish refugees in Europe during the period of World War II. The tragic consequences of the world's indifference at that time are well known. The resulting ban on *refoulement*, as broad as the humanitarian purpose that inspired it, is easily applicable here, the Court's protestations of impotence and regret notwithstanding.

The refugees attempting to escape from Haiti do not claim a right of admission to this country. They do not even argue that the Government has no right to intercept their boats. They demand only that the United States, land of refugees and guardian of freedom, cease forcibly driving them back to detention, abuse, and death. That is a modest plea, vindicated by the Treaty and the statute. We should not close our ears to it.

I dissent [therefore, from the majority's holding which affirms the legality of President Clinton's Executive Order authorizing returns to Haiti without the required determination of refugee status under the 1951 Refugee Convention].

■ NOTES & QUESTIONS

1. Unfortunately, as the above 1993 Haitian case illustrates, no UN program or treaty has fully accomplished the goal of eradicating the problems identified in *Sale v. Haitian Centers Council, Inc.* The primary barrier is national distrust. Many countries share the concern about potential UN/treaty interference with nationality decisions that they would like to make on a case-by-case basis. Their view, effectively, is that the State's treatment of individuals remains a matter that should be exclusively within national jurisdiction. *Sale* arguably provided another illustration of the disdain shown by certain national courts for broad interpretations of their treaty commitments.

2. Justice Blackmun was not the only "dissenter." The majority's decision was chastised by the President of the American Society of International Law in the Society's Newsletter of Sept.–Oct. 1993. Society President Louis Henkin therein reacted as follows:

the Supreme Court has adopted an eccentric, highly implausible interpretation of a treaty. It has interpreted those treaties . . . not as other state parties would interpret them, not as an international tribunal would interpret them, [and] not as the U.S. Supreme Court would have interpreted them earlier in our history when the justices took the law of nations seriously, when they appeared to recognize that in such cases U.S. courts were sitting in effect as international tribunals [that is, prior to the establishment of the world courts by the League of Nations and the UN].

■ 4.3 CORPORATE NATIONALITY

Introduction

What is the nationality of a *corporation*? Like a natural person, a business entity also possesses nationality for purposes of International Law. While there are a variety of entities to which this section applies, the most common form is that of the corporation—a business entity typically formed for the purpose of limiting liability beyond that which is available to a natural person. This section will thus use the term "corporation" to refer collectively to all such institutions.

This section will also deal with the matter of the State's discretion not to present a claim on behalf of a corporation. A State's may have the right to present a claim on the international level through diplomatic endeavor or the pursuit of litigation in an international tribunal. As discussed in § 4.1 on the *individual's* international legal capacity, that right does not *obligate* a State to present such claims on an international level.

A corporation is considered a legal "person" under the national or internal law of most nations. *Where* it may claim citizenship presents problems, particularly in an age when so many corporations engage in international business transactions. A number of European nations treat a multinational corporation as a national of the country where its headquarters or home office is located. In the United States, a corporation is a US national if it is incorporated in one of the fifty states of the US.

§ 4.1 addressed the factual and legal bond of nationality between an individual and the State that has conferred its citizenship on that individual. There are also occasions when a corporation may need protection on the international level. A corporation may be taxed by more than one country, for example, each claiming that the corporation is a citizen of the respective countries.

State Discretion

By way of comparison to natural individuals, the State decision to protect corporations is not as readily exercised. One reason is that the genuineness of an *individual's* nationality link with a particular State is comparatively easy to establish (*see* § 4.2 on the *Nottebohm* case). The genuineness of a *corporation's* link with a particular country is a more complex question. Today's multinational enterprises are often owned by parent corporations—in turn, owned by numerous shareholders from various countries. When the enterprise is harmed, it is the individual shareholder-owners that are actually harmed. These investors sometimes seek the assistance of the States of their nationalities to help them obtain a remedy for the wrong done to the multinational enterprise.

A corporation from one nation may thus be the object of conduct giving rise to another nation's responsibility for discriminating against the corporation—solely because it is a foreign citizen. In a famous antitrust case decided by a national court in 1909, for example, Costa Rica nationalized the plaintiff US corporation's assets in Costa Rica. The apparent purpose of this taking of property was to conspire with another corporation in its attempt to monopolize the lucrative Central American banana trade.[20] Given the traditional requirements for nationalization discussed in the next section of this text, such conduct triggered Costa Rica's responsibility for a discriminatory taking of alien property in violation of customary international practice. As an alternative to suing in a US court, the plaintiff corporation could have requested that the US negotiate with the Costa Rican government for the return of its corporate property. This would have helped the individual investor recover their corporate assets abroad.

Proper State

Which country may present a claim on behalf of a corporation under International Law? Assume that Investco is a large multinational corporation located in Hong Kong. It is owned by shareholders from Brazil, France, Germany, South Africa, and the US. Investco's Hong Kong assets are nationalized in 1997, without any compensation, after the People's Republic of China assumes control of the territory. Under International Law, not all of these "shareholder" nations have the capacity to present a claim for compensation against China. In § 4.2, the International Court of Justice assessed the relevant nationality of Mr. Nottebohm to determine whether Liechtenstein's grant of nationality in fact generated the requisite ties to enable it to present his claim against Guatemala on the international level. A similar analysis is appropriate in the case of corporations. A tribunal would have to decide which of the various nations (in the Investco nationalization hypothetical) best represents the corporate personality of Investco. Under International Law, the appropriate State is normally the State where "Investco" is incorporated. There are exceptions, as will be discussed in the case below.

Assume that a Canadian corporation is nationalized, in a way that allegedly violates International Law. The individual shareholders are located throughout the world. The vast majority of them are Belgian citizens. Can they be diplomatically represented in international proceedings by Belgium? Would it be more reasonable to allow the State of the corporate headquarters, if located in yet another State, to present such claims (diplomatically or through judicial proceedings)? Should the international rule regarding who can represent a corporation be the same as the "genuine link" test from the *Nottebohm* case in § 4.2? Finally, does another country have the ability to present an international claim on behalf of a corporation when its home State (a) will not do so? (b) cannot do so because it has ceased to exist (a problem addressed in § 2.3 of this text)? All of these questions were addressed by the International Court of Justice in the following 1970 case.

Barcelona Traction was incorporated in Canada and operated a power company in Spain. It was declared bankrupt by a Spanish court that ordered the seizure of its assets. Belgium, England, Canada, and the US all tried to assist Barcelona Traction in resisting the seizure. Individual citizens in these countries owned the stock of the corporation. Its value would be decreased unfairly if the bankruptcy proceedings were inappropriately instituted. The shareholders believed that the Spanish authorities prematurely sought bankruptcy for some ulterior purpose.

Canada ultimately decided not to pursue the claim of the Canadian shareholders in this corporation. Belgian nationals owned the majority of stock in Barcelona Traction at the time of the bankruptcy. Belgium thus decided to prosecute this action in the ICJ against Spain.

The court dismissed the suit, ruling that Belgium could not represent Barcelona Traction. The corporation was a legal person separate from its stockholders, and its nationality was Canadian. The ICJ was unwilling to allow the nationality of the Belgian shareholders to serve as the basis for prosecuting this claim in an international tribunal. If the country of incorporation (Canada) is unwilling to pursue the claim, the State of the majority of the individual shareholders (Belgium) cannot—on that basis alone—represent the corporate interests. Selected portions of the ICJ's opinion now show the Court's reasons for generally vesting the State of incorporation with the exclusive right to represent a corporation in diplomatic or international judicial proceedings. The paragraph numbers are those of the ICJ:

BARCELONA TRACTION, LIGHT, AND POWER CO.

International Court of Justice
1970 International Court of Justice Reports (Second Phase) 3 (1970)

[*Opinion.*] 70. In allocating corporate entities to States for purposes of diplomatic protection, international law is based, but only to a limited extent, on an analogy with the rules governing the nationality of individuals. The traditional rule attributes the right of diplomatic protection of a corporate entity to the State under the laws of which it is incorporated and in whose territory it has its registered office. . . . However, in the particular field of the diplomatic protection of corporate entities, no absolute test of the 'genuine connection' has found general acceptance [as with *individuals* under the Court's *Nottebohm* case in § 4.2]. . . .

71. In the present case, [although 88 percent of the shares of Barcelona Traction were owned by Belgian nationals] it is not disputed that the company was incorporated in Canada and has its registered office in that country. The incorporation of the company under the law of Canada was an act of free choice. Not only did the founders of the company seek its incorporation under Canadian law but it has remained under that law for a period of over 50 years. It has maintained in Canada its registered office, its accounts and its share registers. Board meetings were held there for many years; it has been listed in the records of the Canadian tax authorities. Thus a close and permanent connection has been

established, fortified by the passage of over half a century. This connection is in no way weakened by the fact that the company engaged from the very outset in commercial activities outside Canada, for that was its declared object. Barcelona Traction's links with Canada are thus manifold.

72. Furthermore, the Canadian nationality of the company has received general recognition. Prior to the institution of proceedings before the Court, three other governments apart from that of Canada (those of the United Kingdom, the United States and Belgium) made representations concerning the treatment accorded to Barcelona Traction by the Spanish authorities. The United Kingdom Government intervened on behalf of bondholders and of shareholders. Several representations were also made by the United States Government, but not on behalf of the Barcelona Traction company as such.

. . .

75. The Canadian Government itself, which never appears to have doubted its right to intervene on the company's behalf, exercised the protection of Barcelona Traction by diplomatic representation for a number of years, in particular by its note of 27 March 1948, in which it alleged that a denial of justice had been committed in respect of the Barcelona Traction, Ebro and National Trust companies, and requested that the bankruptcy judgment be cancelled. . . .

76. In sum, the record shows that from 1948 onwards the Canadian Government made to the Spanish Government numerous representations which cannot be viewed otherwise than as the exercise of diplomatic protection in respect of the Barcelona Traction company. Therefore this was not a case where diplomatic protection was [totally] refused or remained in the sphere of fiction. It is also clear that over the whole period of its diplomatic activity the Canadian Government proceeded in full knowledge of the Belgian attitude and activity.

. . .

78. The Court would here observe that, within the limits prescribed by international law, a State may exercise diplomatic protection by whatever means and to whatever extent it thinks fit, for it is its own right that the State is asserting. Should the natural [individuals] or legal [corporate] persons on whose behalf it is acting consider that their rights

are not adequately protected, they have no remedy in international law. All they can do is to resort to municipal [internal] law, if means are available, with a view to furthering their cause or obtaining redress. . . . However, all these questions remain within the province of municipal law and do not affect the position internationally.

79. The State must be viewed as the sole judge to decide whether its protection will be granted, to what extent it is granted, and when it will cease. It retains in this respect a discretionary power the exercise of which may be determined by considerations of a political or other nature, unrelated to the particular case. Since the claim of the State is not identical with that of the individual or corporate person whose cause is espoused, the State enjoys complete freedom of action. Whatever the reasons for any change of attitude, the fact cannot in itself constitute a justification for the exercise of diplomatic protection by another government, unless there is some independent and otherwise valid ground for that.

. . .

88. It follows from what has already been stated above that, where it is a question of an unlawful act committed against a company representing foreign capital, the general rule of international law authorizes the national State of the company alone to make a claim.

. . .

96. The Court considers that the [unsuccessfully argued] adoption of the theory of diplomatic protection of shareholders as such, by opening the door to competing diplomatic claims, could create an atmosphere of confusion and insecurity in international economic relations. The danger would be all the greater inasmuch as the shares of companies whose activity is international are widely scattered and frequently change hands. It might perhaps be claimed that, if the right of protection belonging to the national States of the shareholders were considered as only secondary to that of the national State of the company, there would be less danger of difficulties of the kind contemplated. However, the Court must state that the essence of a secondary right is that it only comes into existence at the time when the original right ceases to exist [as when the

State of incorporation ceases to exist—as discussed in this text's § 2.3].

. . .

100. In the present case, it is clear from what has been said above that Barcelona Traction was never reduced to a position of impotence such that it could not have approached its national State, Canada, to ask for its diplomatic protection, and that, as far as appeared to the Court, there was nothing to prevent Canada from continuing to grant its diplomatic protection to Barcelona Traction if it had considered that it should do so.

■ NOTES & QUESTIONS

1. What general rule did the International Court of Justice use for determining which State could represent a multinational corporation in international (judicial or diplomatic) proceedings?

2. Are there any exceptions that would allow *another* State to present an international claim on behalf of a corporation?

3. The Court's language in this 1970 opinion solidly vests the State with the sole discretion to determine whether it will process a claim on the international level for a corporation or an *individual.* As will be seen in later materials, including Chapter 11 on human rights developments, a State that harms its *own* citizen cannot hide behind this discretion in order to avoid State responsibility under international human rights law.

■ 4.4   INJURY TO ALIENS

Introduction

There are various forms of State responsibility presented elsewhere in this book. State responsibility is a vast component of International Law, best handled by the somewhat scattered coverage of its diverse ingredients in relevant chapters.

§ 2.5 of the text dealt with the general theme of State responsibility in International Law. The general elements for this form of State liability are: (1) the existence of a State's legal obligation arising under International Law; (2) a State's act or omission that violates that obligation; and (3) some loss or articulable damage to another State caused by the breach of the obligation. As therein discussed, there have been numerous attempts to achieve consensus in articulating this facet of International Law—mostly without success.

A distinct mode of State responsibility is analyzed in Chapter 11 on Human Rights. As therein discussed, a State may be responsible for harm to *all* individuals within its borders—both citizens of the acting State, as well as foreign citizens. That form of State responsibility under International Law protects individuals from official State policies such as the genocide policy of Nazi Germany during World War II and South Africa's apartheid until the early 1990s.

This section of the book covers State responsibility for *injury to aliens*—a matter well suited for treatment in the chapter on individual and corporate personality in International Law. A State may be thus accountable for the acts of its agents harming aliens in a way that treats them differently from its own citizens.

Early commentators had some very practical reasons for establishing this category of State responsibility. The nationals of one state who have lived, traveled, or worked in another State have been abused and discriminated against throughout recorded history. One of the leading studies traces this historical phenomenon:

> Since ancient times foreigners have been regarded with suspicion, if not fear, either due to their nonconforming religious and social customs, their assumed inferiority, or because they were considered potential spies and agents of other nations. Thus, the Romans refused aliens the benefits of the *jus civile* [civil law], thirteenth-century England limited their recourse to the ordinary courts of justice [rather than all courts], and imperial Spain denied them trading rights in the New World.[21]

The development of the law of State responsibility for injury to aliens began approximately two centuries ago. One of the foremost commentators of the eighteenth century, Emerich de Vattel, wrote in his book on the *Law of Nations* that "[w]hoever ill-treats a [foreign] citizen injures the State, which must protect the citizen."[22] His articulation was adopted by many international tribunals and commentators as the rationale for recognizing State responsibility for injury to aliens. Avoiding the escalation of this type of discrimination, and its potential backlashes, became the practical goal of the law of State responsibility for injury to aliens.

This branch of State responsibility was drawn from the internal tort law as customarily applied by many States. Tort law governs civil wrongs by an *individual* for unreasonable conduct that harms another individual. If someone takes the property of another without justification, that person is liable under the internal tort law of many nations. Writers and jurists believed that a State should be similarly liable when its unreasonable acts or omissions harmed aliens. Such protection was necessary because national law typically insulated the State from the claims of its own citizens since "The King (meaning the State) can no wrong." When State X nationalized the property of a foreign citizen without compensation, that citizen's home State Y could therefore assert a case of State X's responsibility for the resulting harm to State Y (derived from the harm to its citizen) under International Law.

Codification Attempts

As long as the law of State responsibility for injury to aliens is not codified in a multilateral treaty, the friction between have and have-not nations will continue to impair international business and governmental relations. An express agreement would thus incorporate diverse national perspectives about the appropriate contours of State responsibility for injury to aliens. As stated in the International Law textbook currently used at Moscow State University in Russia, "codification is now an urgent task. Members of The League of Nations [just after World War I] sought to codify those norms of international law dealing with the responsibility of States for damage to the person or property of foreigners (which efforts served the interests of imperialist States)."[23]

Several attempts have been made to codify the law of State responsibility for injuries to foreign individuals and corporations. Each has produced a better understanding of the relationship of the individual and the State under International Law. The initial codification attempt was the 1929 draft Convention on Responsibility of States for Damage Done on Their Territory to the Person or Property of Foreigners. It was produced under the auspices of the Harvard Law School Research in International Law Project, compiled during the period between the two world wars. Another campaign to codify this branch of State responsibility surfaced in 1953, when members of the UN General Assembly decided that "it is desirable for the maintenance of peaceful relations between States that the principles of international law governing State responsibility be codified. . . ." This UN resolution resulted in the drafting of several reports on various facets of State responsibility. Those reports did not, however, generate a written multilateral agreement.[24]

One of the most extensive presentations of the law of State responsibility toward aliens was published in 1961. It is the Draft Convention on the International Responsibility of States for Injury to Aliens. The authors of this draft treaty were Harvard University Professors Louis Sohn and Marvin Baxter. Their work exemplifies the Western view that underdeveloped nations have a significant interest in importing foreign investment and technological assistance and can profit by the just treatment of foreign corporations and employees. The Sohn-Baxter perspective is that both developed and lesser-developed nations should encourage the fair and nondiscriminatory treatment of their citizens while abroad. The 1961 draft treaty does not incorporate the views of all commentators. It is an alternative, however, to the so-called "Third World" New International Economic Order (described below), under which a State *may* treat aliens differently than its own citizens in certain instances.[25]

Current UN efforts to codify State responsibility have not yet produced draft articles on this specific point.[26] This project, as it continues to develop, will hopefully contain draft treaty articles that may serve as a basis for greater international cooperation in finding more widely accepted norms. In the interim, these various restatements of State responsibility for injury to aliens are essentially academic undertakings that merely identify the problems.

Categories of Injury

What types of State conduct trigger responsibility for injury to aliens? While classification is no simple task, the customary violations may be listed as follows: (1) nonwealth injuries; (2) denial of justice, including what some writers characterize as separate subcategories of wrongful arrest/detention and lack of due diligence; (3) confiscation of property; and (4) deprivation of livelihood.

Nonwealth Injuries A State is responsible for injury to aliens when it is responsible for their deaths or physical injuries. This form of State responsibility evolved from the unreasonable acts or omissions of State agents adversely affecting a foreign citizen. A 1983 report by the Panel on the Law of State Responsibility of the American Society of International Law defined a "nonwealth injury" as follows:

> [It] is an injury inflicted by a State upon an alien either (1) directly through some act or omission causing physical or other personal injury to or the death of an alien, or (2) indirectly through some failure to act, including the failure under certain circumstances to prevent injury inflicted by another party, the failure to provide the injured alien with an effective remedy, or the failure to pursue, prosecute, and punish the responsible party.[27]

This category of harm is distinguished from the other types of State responsibility by its physical characteristics. While a nonwealth injury can have economic consequences, the harm is not directed at the victim's pocketbook. In October 1965, for example, Indonesian army forces conducted a campaign directed at Chinese nationals in Indonesia. Chinese citizens were beaten, arrested without cause, and murdered. Further, Indonesia's army issued permits allowing civilians to demonstrate for the purpose of persecuting Chinese nationals. The Chinese government sought and received assurances from Indonesia's central government that this violence would end. Had the Indonesian government refused the Chinese demands, it would have incurred further responsibility for physical nonwealth injuries to the Chinese nationals.

Denial of Justice: Discrimination Against Alien
A State's discriminatory application of its domestic laws to an alien is described as a "denial of justice." This is a somewhat "procedural" form of injury, rather than a physical harm. The standard procedures used (or not used) by the State are basically unfair because they do not affect local citizens in the same way.

There is no standard definition of this form of injury. National and international tribunals have nevertheless found a denial of justice in countless cases. There may be limitations, however. In Latin American States, a "denial of justice" occurs only when the State has *completely* refused access to its courts or the courts will not take the necessary steps to render a decision. The regional perspective is that there can never be a denial of justice based on the quality or unsatisfactory nature of the procedures used by the tribunal when it is deciding an alien's claim. If there is *some* access to some tribunal that at least decides the matter, a foreign citizen cannot complain about the quality of justice based on the use of different procedures than those in his or her own home state.[28]

Most nations adopt a broader interpretation of the term "denial of justice." A State can be responsible for injuring an alien when its tribunals do not provide adequate time or legal representation to prepare a defense. This must occur in a way that provides less protection than that afforded to the offending State's own citizens. Prohibiting communication with home State representatives or diplomats is an example. In a 1993 case in Saudi Arabia, the government did not allow either a US consular officer or the spouse access to a US citizen who was jailed and tortured for doing the job that he was hired to do by the government. (*See Nelson v. Saudi Arabia* case in § 2.6.) If local citizens are allowed to seek legal assistance, it is a denial of justice to withhold that right just because the prisoner is a foreign citizen.

Denial of Justice: International Minimum Standard? Another subcategory of denial of justice is the unreasonable arrest and detention of an alien. Incarceration is unlawful under International Law when it discriminates against aliens and unreasonably departs from generally accepted procedures. The arresting State is liable, for example, when it fails to give a reason for the arrest or detention of an alien defendant or when trial is delayed for an unreasonable time after arrest.

Can a State therefore incur liability for a denial of justice, when it treats foreign citizens in the same way that it treats its own citizens? A variation on the denial of justice theme thus arises when a State treats a foreign citizen in a substandard way, and then responds to a claim of mistreatment by defending on the basis of equal treatment of *all* individuals in the same circumstances. This problem triggers the daunting question of whether there is an "international minimum standard," below which no State may fall in its treatment of the individual. The comparatively poor treatment of individuals may not be discriminatory. Both foreign and local citizens may be subjected to the same type of treatment. If such a standard exists, however, then a State would not be able to use equality of treatment to justify its mistreatment of foreign and local citizens.

The historical maturation of such a standard has been retarded by economic and political differences between Western States and States in lesser developed regions of the world. What is probably the most definitive (and equally broad) statement defining the so-called international minimum standard was made by US Secretary of State Elihu Root in 1910:

Each country is bound to give to the nationals of another country in its territory the benefit of the same laws, the same administration, the same protection, and the same redress for injury which it gives to its own citizens, and neither more nor less: provided the protection which the country gives to its own citizens conforms to the established standard of civilization.

There is [however] a standard of justice very simple, very fundamental, and of such general acceptance by all civilized countries as to form a part of the international law of the world. The . . . system of law and administration shall conform to this general standard. If any country's system of law and administration does not conform to that standard, although the people of the country may be content to live under it, no other country can be compelled to accept it as furnishing a satisfactory measure of treatment of its citizens.[29]

The international minimum standard has thus been invoked in the following circumstances: The complaining State asserts that the responsible State departed from generally accepted standards of justice for the treatment of *any* individual—foreign or local. The responding State typically defends its action by reliance on the "national treatment" standard, set forth in the 1933 Montevideo Convention on Rights and Duties of States (ratified mostly by Latin American nations). Under this particular standard, a foreign citizen is entitled to no better treatment than the local citizens of the responding State. Equal treatment of local and foreign nationals precludes any international liability for injury to an alien. There is no clear consensus about the existence or scope of the international minimum standard of treatment—partially due to the comparative economic positions of the nations usually involved in these controversies.

The respective positions are illustrated in the following case, one of the few but more illustrative cases on the so-called international minimum standard. It did not involve a foreign citizen found in a different region of the world. It arose, instead, in the context of two States that shared the same border:

ROBERTS v. UNITED MEXICAN STATES

United States v. Mexico
General Claims Commission, 1926
4 Rep. Int'l Arb. Awards 77 (1974)

[Author's Note: Harry Roberts was a US citizen charged by Mexico with "assaulting a house." When he and several armed American companions gathered outside a house in Mexico, the owner called the Mexican police. After an exchange of small-weapons fire, the police arrested Roberts.

The Mexican Constitution provided that prisoners had to be brought to trial within twelve months of their arrest. Roberts was in a Mexican jail for nineteen months with no hearing. His conditions of incarcera-

tion were typical for Mexican prisons, but less adequate than such conditions in other countries such as the US.

After his release, Roberts obtained US assistance for presenting this case against Mexico. The respective countries had established international arbitration machinery (General Claims Commission) to handle such disputes. The US therein argued that Mexico was responsible for a denial of justice to its US citizen who was incarcerated in unenviable quarters in Mexico.

The relevant portion of the Commission's decision appears below.]

[*Opinion.*] This claim is presented by the United States of America in behalf of Harry Roberts, an American citizen who, it is alleged . . . was arbitrarily and illegally arrested by Mexican authorities, who held him prisoner for a long time in contravention of Mexican law and subjected him to cruel and inhumane treatment throughout the entire period of confinement.

. . .

It is alleged that there were undue delays in the prosecution of the trial of the accused which was not instituted within one year from the time of his arrest, as required by the Constitution of Mexico. These delays were brought to the notice of the Government of Mexico, but no corrective measures were taken. During the entire period of imprisonment, he was subject to rude and cruel treatment from which he suffered great physical pain and mental anguish.

. . .

The Commission is not called upon to reach a conclusion whether Roberts committed the crime with which he was charged. The determination of that question rested with the Mexican judiciary, and it is distinct from the question whether the Mexican authorities had just cause to arrest Roberts and to bring him to trial. Aliens of course are obliged to submit to proceedings properly instituted against them in conformity with local [national] laws.

. . .

In order to pass upon the complaint [alleging abuse of the international minimum standard of treatment] with reference to an excessive period of imprisonment, it is necessary to consider whether the proceedings instituted against Roberts while he was incarcerated exceeded reasonable limits within which an alien charged with crime may be held in custody pending the investigation of the charge against him. Clearly there is no definite standard prescribed by international law by which such limits may be fixed. Doubtless an examination of local laws fixing a minimum length of time within which a person charged with crime may be held without being brought to trial may be useful in determining whether detention has been unreasonable in a given case. The Mexican Constitution provides . . . that . . . a person accused of crime "must be judged

within four months if he is accused of a crime the maximum penalty for which may not exceed two years' imprisonment, and within one year if the maximum penalty is greater." From the judicial records presented by the Mexican Agent it clearly appears that there was a failure of compliance with this constitutional provision, since the proceedings were instituted on May 17, 1922, and that Roberts had not been brought to trial on December 16, 1923, the date when he was released.

. . .

There is evidence in the record that Roberts constantly requested the American Consul at Tampico to take steps to expedite the trial. Several communications were addressed by American diplomatic and consular officers in Mexico to Mexican authorities with a view to hastening the trial. It was the duty of the Mexican judge under . . . the Mexican Constitution to appoint counsel to act for Roberts from the time of the institution of the proceedings against him. The Commission is of the opinion that preliminary proceedings could have been completed before the lapse of a year after the arrest of Roberts.

. . .

With respect to this point of unreasonably long detention without trial, the Mexican Agency contended that Roberts was undoubtedly guilty of the crime for which he was arrested; that therefore had he been tried he would have been sentenced to serve a term of imprisonment, of more than nineteen months; and that, since, under Mexican law, the period of nineteen months would have been taken into account in fixing his sentence of imprisonment, it cannot properly be considered that he was illegally detained for an unreasonable period of time. The Commission must reject this contention, since the Commission is not called upon to pass upon the guilt or innocence of Roberts but to determine whether the detention of the accused was of such an unreasonable duration as to warrant an award of indemnity under the principles of international law. Having in mind particularly that Roberts was held for . . . [ninteen] months without trial in contravention of Mexican law [allowing only a twelve-month period to elapse without trial], the Commission holds that an indemnity is due on the ground of unreasonably long detention.

With respect to the charge of ill-treatment of Roberts, it appears from evidence submitted by the

American Agency that the jail in which he was kept was a room thirty-five feet long and twenty feet wide with stone walls, earthen floor, straw roof, a single window, a single door and no sanitary accommodations, all the prisoners depositing their excrement in a barrel kept in a corner of the room; that thirty or forty men were at times thrown together in this single room; that the prisoners were given no facilities to clean themselves; that the room contained no furniture except that which the prisoners were able to obtain by their own means; that they were afforded no opportunity to take physical exercise; and that the food given them was scarce, unclean and of the coarsest kind. The Mexican Agency did not present evidence disproving that such conditions existed in the jail. It was stated by the Agency that Roberts was accorded the same treatment as that given to all other persons, and with respect to the food Roberts received, it was observed in the answer that he was given "the food that was believed necessary, and within the [economic] means of the municipality."

. . .

But such equality is not the ultimate test of the propriety of the acts of authorities in the light of international law. That test is, broadly speaking, whether aliens are treated in accordance with ordinary [minimum] standards of civilization. We do not hesitate to say that the treatment of Roberts was such as to warrant an indemnity on the ground of cruel and inhumane imprisonment.

. . .

As has been stated, the Commission holds that damages may be assessed on two of the grounds asserted in the American memorial [stating the claim], namely, (1) excessively long imprisonment—with which the Mexican Government is clearly chargeable for a period of seven months, and (2) cruel and inhumane treatment suffered by Roberts in jail during nineteen months. After careful consideration of the facts of the case and of similar cases decided by international tribunals, the Commission is of the opinion that a total sum of $8,000.00 [in *1926* dollars] is a proper indemnity to be paid in satisfaction of this claim.

■ NOTES & QUESTIONS

1. On what basis did the United States allege that Mexico violated International Law? On what basis did Mexico maintain that it did *not* violate International Law? *See* text reference prior to *Roberts* regarding the "national treatment" provision in the Montevideo Convention.

2. This was no "compromise" verdict—a situation where a jury might hold for the plaintiff but award a nominal sum of damages. The $8,000 award was a significant sum of money in 1926—especially for the Mexico of that period to pay.

3. Did the Commission just impose US standards on Mexico, as opposed to "international" standards?

Denial of Justice: Lack of Due Diligence A State may incur responsibility under International Law, although the principal actor is *not* an agent of the State. The failure to exercise due diligence to protect a foreign citizen is wrongful if the unpunished act of a private individual is a crime under the laws of that State (or generally recognized as criminal conduct elsewhere in the principal legal systems of the world). Responsibility then arises under International Law if that State fails to apprehend or control the individual who has committed the crime against the foreign citizen.

Examples include the 1979 storming of the US embassy in Iran by Iranian citizens. Iran's leader de-

nied that his government had arranged for them to storm the embassy and take US and Canadian citizens hostage—because they were foreign citizens from unfavored nations. Iran nevertheless incurred State responsibility for failing to take any action to stop the crowds from stampeding the persons and property of these foreign citizens. A more common example of such State responsibility is the indifference of lower-echelon officials in circumstances where a local citizen would be given assistance. States are expected to respond to such officials who act, or fail to act, in a way that unreasonably affects an alien.

Confiscation of Property

Confiscation problems in International Law involve the State's right to nationalize, a limitation prohibiting confiscation, potential application of non-Western models, and the work of the Iran/US Claims Tribunal.

Right to Nationalize Both national and International Law concede the State's sovereign right to expropriate ("nationalize," "take," or "appropriate") property. This is a recognized incident of the State's status as a sovereign entity. The State possesses such power over persons and things within its borders, absent some treaty commitment *not* to nationalize foreign property. As succinctly stated by a modern Chinese scholar:

> Public international law regards nationalization as [a] lawful exercise of state power. This is because each state, being possessed of sovereignty, naturally has the right within its own territory to prescribe whatever economic and social system it chooses to establish. Speaking more concretely, each state has the exclusive right to regulate . . . conditions of acquisition, loss, and contents of ownership. Consequently, when one approaches this question from the standpoint of the principle of state sovereignty, one must recognize that states enjoy the right to adopt nationalization measures. Nationalization belongs to matters of national jurisdiction and therefore . . . neither the United Nations nor other states have a right to intervene [when another country nationalizes the property of its citizens].[30]

One should first distinguish the following situations when analyzing State responsibility in nationalization cases: (1) If State X takes property that belongs to citizens of State X and to foreign citizens, all affected individuals may have claims under the law of State X for compensation. Such rights normally arise only under the *national* laws of State X. (2) Alternatively, State X may take *only* property belonging to a foreign individual or corporation—but none belonging to its own citizens. As long as there is appropriate compensation for a taking, unrelated to the citizenship of the owner, State X does not incur any *international* responsibility. This is not considered an "injury to aliens" for the purpose of triggering State responsibility under International Law. (3) State X takes only the property of a foreign citizen and pays either no compensation, or inadequate compensation. This latter circumstance is the object of the law of State responsibility for injuring aliens via a confiscatory taking of property.

"Confiscation" Limitation If a State's taking of the property of a foreign citizen amounts to "confiscation," then there may be State responsibility in International Law. Under the traditional Western view, nationalizations must be undertaken for a "public" purpose and be accompanied by a "prompt, adequate, and effective" repayment for the property taken by the government.[31] There is no public purpose when government takes property that merely adds to the personal holdings of a dictator. Further, the mere provision of *some* compensation does not mean that the compensation is adequate. A nationalization thus violates International Law if the terms of the compensation granted to an alien are less favorable than the terms provided to the citizens of the nationalizing State—or the amount is below the fair market value of the property taken by the State.

The various standards for determining value are thus the subject of a great deal of controversy. Many States do not feel compelled to use any of them. Concepts like "fair market value," "replacement cost," or "book value" are rather indefinite terms, when applied by experienced accountants, let alone officials or mediators from different legal or social systems.

Nationalizations where compensation *is* paid often give rise to a claim of State responsibility. In such a case with major political undertones, Fidel Castro had just executed a revolutionary takeover of Cuba in 1959. The US subsequently imposed a quota on the amount of Cuban sugar importable into the US. Castro characterized this singular US sugar quota as an act of "aggression, [done] for political purposes." The Cuban government thus nationalized the sugar interests of US individuals and corporations, but not Cuban-owned sugar interests. Cuba was willing to pay for the nationalized sugar interests in its own government bonds—payable *twenty* years later at a rate of interest that was well below the fair market interest on similar bonds. This type of compensation was legal under the laws of Cuba. The US Department of State viewed this form of compensation as inadequate, however. The compensation was referred to as "manifestly in violation of those principles of international law which have long been accepted by the free countries of the West. It is in its essence discriminatory, arbitrary and confiscatory." Payment in long-term bonds at a low rate of interest was neither prompt nor adequate. The State Department further alleged that the overall purpose was specifically discriminatory because Cuba took the US property as a political response to the latter's import quota imposed on Cuban sugar.[32]

Non-Western Models A number of lesser-developed countries (LDC) have adopted the position that the more-developed countries (MDC), whose corporations operate within their borders, have unfairly profited from their long-term economic relationships. Foreign multinational corporations have thus been characterized as extracting enormous profits with little return for the local citizens. Thus, they do *not* perceive uncompensated nationalizations of foreign property as confiscatory violations of International Law. One supporting argument is that the MDCs have effectively deprived the LDC of their national sovereignty over natural resources through unacceptable business arrangements that unfairly take advantage of the LDCs. Huge profits, they argue, are thereby expatriated to the private shareholders of the MDCs' multinational corporations. Some of these profits should be injected into their sagging economies. Thus, an uncompensated nationalization returns only a fraction of what has been improperly taken from the LDC by one-sided business arrangements that effectively dilute natural sovereignty over disappearing natural resources with no tangible befits for the LDC.

Many LDCs responded to Western-derived compensation requirements with the premise stated in the UN General Assembly Resolution of 1962 on Permanent Sovereignty over Natural Resources. Its objective was to shift the paradigm of customary international practice developed while its drafters were still colonial territories. Thus, the standard for determining compensation for expropriations would be determined under the *national* law of the State taking such action, rather than under customary international practice. The Resolution therefore provides as follows: "the owner shall be paid appropriate compensation, in accordance with the rules in force in the State taking such measures . . . [and] the national jurisdiction of the State taking such measures shall be exhausted. However, upon agreement

by sovereign States . . . settlement of the dispute shall be made through arbitration or international adjudication. . . ."[33] The essential feature of this counterproposal to the western formulation is that national law would govern rather than International Law—as it had developed during many decades of State practice prior to this 1962 General Assembly resolution. A foreign individual or corporation would thus have to resort to the local remedies (if any) of the nationalizing State. That State would not have to engage in international adjudication absent its consent.

Should State X merely consider a complete nationalization of all foreign property in order to improve its economic balance sheet? This would be economic suicide for many States. To do so would frustrate the free flow of capital to a State whose leader suddenly nationalizes foreign property. Others would fear similar treatment in the future. The resulting lack of investment would retard the economic growth of State X.

The Latin American variation to the LDC perception of Western hegemony is the "Calvo Clause." It grew out of the local doctrine that no State's government should have to accept financial responsibility for civil insurrection resulting in mistreatment of foreign citizens at the hands of insurgents. The relevant adaption of this concept is that a State may impose conditions on foreign individuals and corporations doing business within its borders. A State may thus require that foreigners be treated on equal footing with local citizens. A foreign company doing business in a "Calvo Clause" country must relinquish its right under International Law to seek the diplomatic assistance of its home State when there has been a nationalization. As exemplified by Article 27.1 of the Mexican Constitution, foreigners must agree to "consider themselves as [Mexican] nationals in respect to such property, and bind themselves not to invoke the protection of their governments. . . ." This agreement thus waives any right to claim the assistance of a foreign government when the Mexican government has decided to nationalize foreign property.

In 1974, Asian and African States declared their alternative to the Western-derived customary State practice in nationalization cases—a New International Economic Order (NIEO). The NIEO is essentially an economic Bill of Rights for LDCs, designed to redistribute global wealth. International

Law has traditionally required prompt and adequate compensation. But this requirement was imposed by the more-developed countries, long before their colonies became independent after World War II (and particularly during the 1960s and 1970s). As stated by one of the leading Indian proponents of the NIEO, the LDCs therein adopted this "revolutionary position" as a necessity for injecting equitable considerations into an aging paradigm serving only colonial purposes. As stated by Professor S. Prakash Sinha of Pace University in New York, regarding the position thus advanced by "Third World" nations:

> They challenge some of the rules of international law as not consistent with their view of the new order and they point to the need for international law to reflect a consensus of the entire world community, including theirs, and promote the widest sharing of values. They criticise the system of international law as being a product of relations among imperialist States and of relations of an imperial character between imperialist States and colonial peoples. . . . Moved by the desire to cut inherited burdens, to free themselves from foreign control of their economies, and to obtain capital needed for their programmes of economic reconstruction, the newly independent States have resorted to expropriation of foreign interests. In their opinion, the validity of such expropriation is not a matter of international law.[34]

The traditional Western compensation formula —requiring "prompt, adequate and effective" compensation for State nationalizations of foreign property—has thus met strong resistance from the LDCs in various regions of the world. Their leaders do not believe that compensation is warranted in all cases, particularly when a multinational corporation has depleted natural resources and expatriated huge profits to more-developed countries. Lesser-developed countries thus view the traditional international norm as a vintage requirement that fails to reflect the expectations of most nations in today's economy. It fails to accommodate the interests of former colonies now trying to maintain their independence from the more-developed countries. Most of the lesser-developed countries (about three-fourths of all States) came into existence *after* World War II—and many in the 1960s. Thus, they argue

that they are not bound by the norms imposed by a few developed states in an earlier era.

Neither the traditional Western position nor the NIEO has been adopted in any multilateral treaty. The UN Law of the Sea Treaty, which became effective in 1994, contains a number of equitable redistribution provisions. But the MDCs have objected. The US did not even sign this treaty when it was opened for potential ratifications in 1982, instead waiting until the eve of its entering into force more than two decades later (*see* § 6.3).

Iran/US Claims Tribunal   One entity that could —but is unlikely to—develop a wider degree of global consensus on international expropriation norms is the Iran/US Claims Tribunal. The Iranian revolution, which led to the US hostages case (*see* § 7.4) and the treaty that freed them in 1980, presented a rich environment for the progressive unification of the various models for evaluating applicable law and compensation rules. In this instance, State takings were outspokenly anti-American, and done with utter disregard for any international norms. The Iranian government nationalized—or otherwise controlled—virtually all foreign property in all conceivable industries, with a view toward casting out the "US Demon." As part of the treaty agreement leading to release of the American hostages after 444 days in captivity, Iranian assets were made available to this Claims Tribunal for the purpose of satisfying claims against Iran, based on its relentless nationalization or related takings of US corporate interests (near the close of a long war wherein the US had quietly backed Iraq).

This tribunal is unlikely to break new ground, however. Its mandate, agreed to by negotiators for the US and Iran, is to decide all cases "on the basis of respect for law, applying such . . . rules and principles of commercial and international law as the Tribunal determines to be applicable. . . ."[35] The Tribunal has had the unenviable task of interpreting these "governing law" terms, but only in the several of the nearly five hundred cases it decided during its first ten years of existence. Most claimants avoided raising the issue of determining the precise international norms, perceiving the potential legal task as unproductively expensive due to its ambiguity and complexity. As stated by a practicing lawyer and one of the leading commentators on this issue: "In only a few cases has the issue been addressed, and in some of these, the awards suggest it was used more as a justification for achieving a result predetermined to be fair or equitable by the arbitrators than as a set of rules to be followed in reaching a reasoned decision based in law."[36]

Until a widely accepted treaty accomplishes a greater degree of international consensus, the debate about the appropriate compensation paradigm will continue to polarize the developed and developing States.

Deprivation of Livelihood

Another category of State responsibility for injury to aliens is the unreasonable deprivation of a foreign citizen's ability to enjoy a livelihood. The withdrawal of his or her ability to continue practicing a certain occupation is an unacceptable deprivation, if done for a discriminatory purpose.

The US Supreme Court case of *Asakura v. City of Seattle* is a useful illustration (and contained in § 8.1 on treaty classifications).[37] Under a treaty between Japan and the US, the citizens of both countries were entitled to enjoy equal employment rights with the citizens of each country. The city of Seattle subsequently passed a pawnbroker ordinance providing that "no such license shall be granted unless the applicant be a citizen of the United States." The Court determined that this ordinance "makes it impossible for aliens to carry on the business. It need not be considered whether the State, if it sees fit, may forbid and destroy business generally. Such a law would apply equally to aliens and citizens. . . ." The ordinance improperly discriminated against aliens in violation of the treaty specifically providing for equal treatment of Japanese citizens working in the US. If the court had ruled *against* the plaintiff Japanese pawnbroker who challenged the ordinance, the US would have incurred State responsibility for depriving foreign citizens of a livelihood during peacetime.

Conclusions

The preceding materials describe the fundamental categories and applications of the law of State responsibility for injury to aliens. Of course, not all States agree about their appropriate scope. Certain commentators zealously deny the very existence of this branch of International Law.

The various debates about the category of State responsibility covered in this section of the book are evidence of constant tension between two competing policies. One is the primacy of a State's territorial jurisdiction over persons and things within its territory. The opposing policy is the historical protection afforded to aliens by the external influence of International Law. The applicability of both policies often spawns a dilemma that pits them against one another. Professor Gerhard von Glahn of the University of Minnesota describes what is clearly the *Western* perception of the proper balance between these twin goals:

> Each state is the sole judge of the extent to which aliens enjoy civil privileges within its jurisdiction. But beyond those permissive grants, each alien, as a human being, may be said to be endowed with certain rights, both as to person and to property, that are his by virtue of his being. It is primarily in connection with those basic rights that a responsibility by the host state arises. It is in this sphere that claims originate and . . . may be advanced against the host state by the government to which the alien owes allegiance.[38]

This perspective emphasizes the existence of State territorial sovereignty. That sovereignty is not absolute, however. Another State or an international organization may thus raise questions about the treatment of a State's inhabitants under a law other than that of the acting State—that is, under the International Law of State responsibility for injury to aliens. The Western perspective embraces the primacy of International Law when a State treats a foreign citizen in a discriminatory manner. More powerful States, with multinational enterprises operating in distant lands, have much to gain from using this lens for viewing State responsibility.

Other States, typically those who have endured and/or prospered from a long-term relationship with foreign multinational corporations, disagree with this alleged hierarchy of International Law and national law. Traditionally, socialist States perceive the State as the centerpiece for all political, economic, and social existence. Customary International Law cannot, therefore, govern or define the relationship between the State and its inhabitants without the express consent of the State wherein the alleged responsibility arises. When viewed through this lens, the individual is seen as holding rights only insofar as the State permits. States whose natural resources have been depleted, during a protracted period of multinational operational control of the local economy, thus rallied in support of the two UN resolutions previously mentioned in this section of the book: (1) the UN General Assembly Resolution of 1962 on Permanent Sovereignty over Natural Resources, and (2) the UN General Assembly Resolution of 1974 on the New International Economic Order.[39]

A number of commentators from lesser developed States espouse a view that achieves the same national law-oriented result, although the method is quite different. They dispute the very existence of this branch of International Law. In the year before the UN's 1962 Natural Resources Resolution, the highly respected Judge Roy of the High Court of Calcutta, India, asserted that States have no *legal* responsibility to protect foreign citizens. He asserted that there is no more than a nonbinding *moral* obligation to prevent States from injuring alien inhabitants. Judge Roy's perspective is that Western nations conveniently advance the doctrine of State responsibility for injury to aliens to discourage nationalization of the property of their large corporations operating in other States. He views the various applications of this doctrinal approach, created by Western nations, as imperialist devices that are "shields against the liquidation of interests acquired [by those nations] and held by [their] abuse of international intercourse."[40]

One might restate Judge Roy's hypothesis as follows: Developed nations adopted the theory that all States are legally obligated not to injure aliens, including overpowering multinational corporations. This is merely a ploy to protect the uninhibited operation of these corporations based in wealthy nations. This branch of the "law" of State responsibility thus protects the superior economic position of "have" nations to maintain control of the "have not" nations. When the lesser-developed host nations reasonably react to what they perceive as economic domination—by nationalizing the property of foreign corporations only—they violate this supposed international standard.

Judge Roy's argument thus approves of discrimination against foreign multinational corporations. Under his view, the supposed nondiscrimination standard should not be applied to multinational corporations because many LDCs have no other practical recourse against this contemporary mode of economic imperialism. Relations between lesser-developed host nations and the corporations of more-developed nations will continue to either deteriorate or become mutually beneficial. The positive result would require that this branch of State responsibility ultimately reflect a true consensus rather than ignoring the relatively weak position of the resource-rich but technically-poor nation.

■ SUMMARY

1. The historical perspective was that the individual had no status (legal capacity) in International Law. Thus, an individual *claimant* could not pursue remedies for breaches of International Law at the international level. In certain cases such as piracy, however, an individual *defendant* could be punished under the law of nations for violations of its rules.

2. The policies of the Nazi regime, whereby the State totally disregarded any dignity of the individual, led to a post–World War revival of the status of the individual as a *defendant* who is legally capable of violating International Law.

3. The State has the discretion to pursue a remedy—through diplomacy or judicial action—on behalf of its citizens who are the objects of another State's actions that violate International Law. This discretion does not obligate the home State to prosecute such claims, however, leaving the individual to pursue remedies available under national law.

4. The State remains the primary actor in International Law, while individuals (and international organizations) occupy a somewhat ancillary role.

5. Nationality is normally a matter of national rather than International Law. States do not have to recognize one another's decisions that confer nationality, however. Many international decision-makers examine the extent of an individual's ties with the claimed country of nationality.

6. Nationality may be acquired in three ways: (1) by birth in a country that applies the soil rule of *jus soli*; (2) by being born of parents, anywhere in the world, when the parents' home country applies the *jus sanguinis* blood rule; and (3) by naturalization, whereby the applicant attains a new nationality that differs from his or her previous nationality.

7. One who possesses nationality in two or more countries is a dual national—who may thus be subjected to multiple conflicting obligations including double taxation and military service.

8. Statelessness is the condition whereby an individual has no nationality in any country. This renders the individual without a home country that

could otherwise provide international protection. Post–World War II statelessness treaties have attempted to ameliorate the plight of those so affected by the lack of State protection evidenced by nationality documents.

9. A refugee may or may not be stateless. The 1951 Refugee Convention (pre–1951 refugees) and its companion 1967 Protocol (*all* refugees) provide international protection for individuals who would be persecuted on being returned to their home State. There is some disagreement about the degree to which this treaty is applicable outside of the territory or territorial waters of States that have ratified this treaty.

10. Like individuals, corporations possess nationality entitling them to State protection via diplomatic representation or the institution of international judicial proceedings. While most or all of the shareholders might be located in one State, only the State of incorporation generally has the international capacity to represent a corporation.

11. The State of incorporation has the discretion to represent one of its corporations in international proceedings. This right is not an obligation. The State's decision not to represent a corporation thus requires an injured corporation to seek remedies (if any) under national rather than International Law.

12. The relevant international norms in this category of State responsibility grew out of concerns for foreign citizens who have been treated differently than local citizens in the State where they are residing.

13. The various methods of discrimination include: (1) nonwealth injuries; (2) denial of justice, including what some commentators characterize as the subcategories of wrongful arrest/detention and lack of due diligence; (3) confiscation of property; and (4) deprivation of livelihood.

14. The Western view emphasizes the primacy of customary international practice developed to ensure that *international* norms govern the relevant State conduct. The perspective of lesser developed States is that *national* law should govern.

15. A regional application of the lesser-developed nations' response to the traditional compensation requirements is the Latin American "Calvo Clause." A foreign enterprise waives its right to diplomatic protection from its home State when its directors believe that there has been discrimination. Such businesses are thus treated as local nationals, so as to avoid the potential application of any international norms regarding State responsibility for injuring aliens.

■ PROBLEMS

Problem 4.1 (*end of § 4.1*): Two Libyan military intelligence officers were apparently responsible for blowing up Pan Am flight 103 over Lockerbie, Scotland in 1989. All 270 passengers, from various countries of the world including England and the US, died very violent deaths. UN Security Council Resolution 731 of 1992 demanded the trial of these two suspects in the West. The Arab League negotiated with Libya's leader to turn over the suspects for trial outside of Libya. England and the US sought the extradition of these individuals from Libya for trial. Libya's leader (Colonel Ghadaffi) refused all of these demands/requests. Under International Law, who may seek remedies for the death of the passengers? Against whom?

Problem 4.2 (*after* Nottebohm *case in § 4.2*): In June 1989, the best-known dissident in the People's Republic of China entered the US Embassy in Beijing seeking diplomatic asylum. Fang Lizhi, a prominent astrophysicist and human rights advocate, remained there until June of 1990—refusing treatment for a heart ailment for fear of arrest. China's agreement to allow him to leave the US Embassy (without being arrested) for a new home in Great Britain signaled a thawing of Sino/US relations. The Chinese government acceded to US pressure to allow this dissident to leave China, possibly due to its desire to retain favorable trading status with the US.

Assume that Fang Lizhi is still residing in the US embassy in Beijing. He therein declares his intent to "defect" to either the US or Great Britain, now that his immediate family is assembled with him in the US embassy and ready to leave on short notice to any country that will take him. The US ambassador initially says that "the granting of asylum at this critical time might jeopardize the US negotiations with China on human rights issues." After conferring with the US Secretary of State and the British Foreign Minister, it is decided that Fang Lizhi should apply for British citizenship. He has never been in Great Britain. The British government is apparently willing to waive all citizenship requirements, including a waiting period of three years (as in *Nottebohm*). After one week, Great Britain issues Fang Lizhi a British passport, which is delivered to him in the US embassy in Beijing.

Assume also that (contrary to the actual facts in this case) the Chinese government protests and accuses the US and Great Britain of meddling in Chinese affairs. The PRC is *not* willing to allow Fang Lizhi to leave China. The Chinese government's Minister of Foreign Affairs advises all concerned that this dissident, engaging in anti-State conduct, will be arrested the moment that he departs the embassy because he remains a Chinese citizen.

What is Fang Lizhi's nationality? Must China recognize the British citizenship conferred on this individual under the *Nottebohm* case?

Problem 4.3 (*end of § 4.2 after the* Sale v. Haitian Council *case*): As Justice Blackmun stated regarding Jewish refugees during the World War II era: "The tragic consequences of the world's indifference at that time are well known." One example might be the following. Even prior to US entry into World War II, the fate of the Jewish citizens and some other minorities of Nazi Germany was well known—*see* M. Gilbert, *Auschwitz and the Allies* (New York: Holt, Rinehart & Winston, 1981). US families were willing and qualified to sponsor a number of Nazi Germany's Jewish children. In 1939, however, the US Congress defeated proposed legislation that would have rescued about twenty thousand such children from Nazi Germany. Why? This rescue would have exceeded the US immigration quota from Germany. *See A Brief History of Immigration to the United States* in T. Aleinkoff & D. Martin, *Immigration Process and Policy* 52 (St. Paul: West, 1985), describing this event as "what may be the cruelest single action in U.S. immigration history."

Beginning in 1994, daily newspaper accounts reported savage machete killings in Rwanda's civil war. Some one million Rwandans thus fled into Zaire and neighboring African nations. *Assume* that an organization like the Haitian Council is trying to save twenty thousand Rwandan orphans who are about to be expelled from Zaire. No one else is willing to take them. These children come from the "wrong" tribe. Thus, the successful rebel tribe leaders in Rwanda vow that such children will have no place in Rwanda's future if they return. The US embassy's ambassador to Zaire is thus approached by the Save the Rwanda Children Organization. Its representative presents a plan whereby willing and

qualified US citizens will take the Rwandan refugees from Zaire to the US. A part of this plan is an application to the US for asylum for these children, who are being discriminated against on the basis of "membership in a particular social group" (the wrong tribe whose leaders fought the successful rebels) under Article 33.1 of the Refugee Convention. After consultation with the US Department of State, the US embassy officer declines, on the basis that the US "does not have the capacity to become the haven for the world's refugees." The US refusal in Zaire thus means that those children will be returned from Zaire to Rwanda for likely extermination.

(1) Would the 1951 Refugee Convention affect the ability of the US to say no to this proposal, which will mean certain death for the children? (2) Blackmun's dissent in *Haitian Refugee Council* scolds the Supreme Court majority for its refusal to apply the 1951 Convention on an "extraterritorial" basis, that is, in the international waters between Haiti and the US. Could Blackmun's argument be extended to this hypothetical to require the US to receive the Rwandan refugee children?

Problem 4.4 (*§ 4.4 after "Confiscation of Property" subsection*): Reynolds–Guyana (RG) was a foreign-owned mining corporation that mined bauxite in Guyana for a number of decades. The parent company was a US corporation. Guyana is a former British colony which achieved its independence and statehood in 1966. RG's profits were substantial, although there was an enormous startup cost, including research and development.

In 1974, Guyana's government assessed an enormous "bauxite tax deficiency" against RG. The company immediately characterized this tax as fabricated for confiscatory purposes. Guyana's Prime Minister responded that RG would be fully nationalized by the end of 1974. A US agency (the Overseas Private Investment Corporation) advised RG not to pay the bauxite tax deficiency. This agency then negotiated the sale of RG's mining operations to a third party on terms acceptable to the government of Guyana.

Assume the following: (1) the majority of RG shareholders are US citizens who have become quite wealthy as a result of their stock investment in RG; (2) a 1973 Guyana law, passed on the eve of this 1974 controversy, provides that a "Calvo Clause" is presumed to be a part of every contract involving any foreign business operation in Guyana; (3) this

1973 law also contains a provision, similar to that contained in the Iran/US Claims Tribunal, stating that "any compensation dispute requires respect for the law, and the law to be applied to any nationalization is International Law."

Negotiators are now discussing whether Guyana has incurred State responsibility to compensate RG's parent corporation in the US for injuries suffered by the enormous bauxite tax deficiency. (There has been no sale to a third party, as occurred in the actual 1974 case.) Two students (or groups) will now debate the effect of assumptions (2) and (3) in the above paragraph.

■ BIBLIOGRAPHY

§ 4.1 Legal Personality of the Individual:

Grossman & Bradlow, *Conference on Changing Notions of Sovereignty and the Role of Private Actors in International Law: Are We Being Propelled Towards a People-Centered Transnational Legal Order?*, 9 *Amer. Univ. J. Int'l L. & Policy* 1 (1993)

R. Higgins, *Conceptual Thinking about the Individual in International Law*, in R. Falk, et al., *International Law: A Contemporary Perspective* 476 (Boulder, CO: Westview Press, 1985)

M. Janis, *Individuals and International Law*, ch. 8, in *An Introduction to International Law* 227 (2nd ed. Boston: Little, Brown & Co., 1993)

§ 4.2 Nationality/Statelessness/Refugees:

R. Donner, *The Regulation of Nationality in International Law* (2nd ed. Irvington-on-Hudson, NY: Transnat'l Pub., 1994)

J. Hathaway, *The Law of Refugee Status* (Toronto: Butterworths, 1991)

V. Nanda, *Refugee Law and Policy: International and U.S. Responses* (New York: Greenwood Press, 1989)

Refugees, ch. 4, in G. Naldi, *The Organization of African Unity: An Analysis of Its Role* 88 (London: Mansell, 1989)

H. Schermers, et al. (ed.), *Free Movement of Persons in Europe: Legal Problems and Experiences* (The Hague: Martinus Nijhoff, 1993)

§ 4.3 Corporate Nationality:

Charney, *Transnational Corporations and Developing Public International Law*, 1983 *Duke Law Journal* 748 (1983)

Rigaux, *Transnational Corporations*, ch. 5, in M. Bedjaoui (ed.), *International Law: Achievements and Prospects* 121 (Dordrecht, Neth.; Boston: Martinus Nijhoff, 1991)

I. Seidl-Hohenveldern, *Corporations in and Under International Law* (Cambridge, Eng.: 1987)

§ 4.4 Injury to Aliens:

Injury to the Persons and Property of Aliens on State Territory, ch. 23, in I. Brownlie, *Principles of Public International Law* (4th ed. Oxford, Eng.: Clarendon Press, 1990)

R. Jennings & A. Watts, *Property of Aliens: Expropriation* § 407 in 1 *Oppenheim's International Law* (Part II) 911 (Essex, Eng.: Longman, 1992).

McDougal, et al., *The Protection of Aliens from Discrimination and World Public Order: Responsibility of States Conjoined with Human Rights*, 70 *American Journal of International Law* 432 (1976)

A. Mouri, *The International Law of Expropriation as Reflected in the Work of the Iran/U.S. Claims Tribunal* (Dordrecht, Neth.; Boston: Martinus Nijhoff, 1994)

The Relevant Standard of Treatment, in M. Shaw, *International Law* 540 (3rd ed. Cambridge, Eng.: Grotius, 1991)

Responsibility for Injuries to Aliens, in H. Kindred, et al., *International Law: Chiefly as Interpreted and Applied in Canada* 540 (5th ed. Toronto: Edmond Montgomery Pub., 1993)

The Treatment of Foreign Nationals § 9.2, in M. Dixon, *Textbook*

on International Law 205 (2nd ed. London: Blackstone Press, 1993)

■ ENDNOTES

1. J. Bentham, *An Introduction to the Principles of Morals and Legislation* 296 (Dover, NH: Longwood Press, 1970) (Burns & Hart edition).

2. See Chiu, *Book Reviews and Notes*, 82 *Amer. J. Int'l L.* 892, at 894–95 (1988).

3. D. Salem, *The People's Republic of China, International Law and Arms Control* 13 (Baltimore: Univ. of Maryland, 1983).

4. Lung-chu Chen, *The Individual*, ch. 5 in *An Introduction to Contemporary International Law: A Policy Oriented Perspective* 76, 77 (New Haven, CT: Yale Univ. Press, 1989).

5. Mavrommatis Palestine Concessions case, P.C.I.J., ser. A, No. 2 (1924), reported in 2 Int'l L. Rep. 27. *See also* "rules creating individual rights and obligations . . . [are] enforceable by the national courts." Danzig Railway Officials case, P.C.I.J., ser. B, No. 15 (1928), reported in 4 Int'l L. Rep. 287.

6. Case Concerning the Factory at Chorzow (Germany v. Poland), 1928 P.C.I.J., ser. A, No. 17 (Judgment of Sept. 13, 1928).

7. See Cassese, *Individuals*, ch. 4, in M. Bedjaoui (ed.), *International Law: Process and Prospects* 114, 120 (Dordrecht, Neth.; Boston: Martinus Nijhoff, 1991).

8. E. Paras, *A Brief History of Conflict of Laws*, ch. 15, in *Philippine Conflict of Laws* 438 (7th ed. Manila: Rex Book Store, 1990).

9. Nottebohm Case (Liechtenstein v. Guatemala), 1955 I.C.J. Rep. 4.

10. *Determination of Chinese Nationality*, in 1 J. Cohen & H. Chiu, *People's China and International Law: A Documentary Study* 746 (Princeton: Princeton Univ. Press, 1974).

11. Nationality Decrees in Tunis and Morocco (Advisory Opinion), P.C.I.J., ser. B, No. 4 (1923), reported in 1 World Court Rep. 145.

12. G. Tunkin, *International Law* 338–339 (Moscow: Progress Publishers, 1982) (1986 English trans.).

13. Sik, *The Netherlands and the Law Concerning Nationality*, in 3 *International Law and the Netherlands* 3, 7 (Alphen aan den Rijn, Neth.: Sijthoff & Noordhoff, 1980).

14. US Const., Amend. XIV (1868). An analysis is available in Guendelsberger, *Access to Citizenship for Children Born Within the State to Foreign Parents*, 40 *Amer. J. Comp. L.* 379 (1992).

15. Canevaro Case (Italy v. Peru), 2 Rep. Int'l Arb. Awards 397 (1949).

16. **Convention:** Convention of 12 April 1930, 179 League of Nations Treaty Series 89 (1938). **Protocol:** Protocol of 12 April 1930, 178 League of Nations Treaty Series 227 (1937) (this series does not necessarily report treaties in chronological order). **1964 Paris Convention:** *see* Sik article, p.7 (cited in note 13 above).

17. Exchange of Notes at The Hague of 9 June 1954, 216 UN Treaty Series 121 (1955).

18. Staniszewski v. Watkins, 80 Fed.Supp. 132, 134 (So.Dist. N.Y., 1948).

19. *See generally*, Kahn, *Legal Problems Relating to Refugees and Displaced Persons*, in Hague Acad. Int'l L., 149 *Recueil des Cours* 287, 318 (1976).

20. Amer. Banana v. United Fruit, 213 U.S. 347, 29 S.Ct. 511, 53 L.Ed. 826 (1909).

21. F. Dawson & I. Head, *National Tribunals and the Rights of Aliens*, in 10 *International Law*, p.XI (Charlottesville, VA: Univ. Press of Va., 1971).

22. E. de Vattel, II *The Law of Nations* 136 (New York: Oceana, 1964) (translation of original 1758 edition).

23. Tunkin treatise, at 224 (cited in note 12 above).

24. **1929 draft:** *Responsibility of States*, 23 *Amer. J. Int'l L.* Special Supp. 131 (1929). **1953 attempt:** Gen. Ass. Res. 799 (VIII), Dec. 7, 1953, contained in G.A.O.R. (8th Session) Supp. (No. 17) at 52, UN Doc. A/2630.

25. The draft convention is reprinted in Sohn & Baxter, *Responsibility of States for Injuries to the Economic Interests of Aliens*, 55 *Amer. J. Int'l L.* 545, 548 (1961). The draft convention's principles were approved by the American Society of International Law's Panel on the Law of State Responsibility in 1980.

26. *See* S. Rosenne, *The International Law Commission's Draft Articles on State Responsibility: Part 1, Articles 1–35* (Dordrecht, Neth.; Boston: Martinus Nijhoff, 1991) *and* M. Spinedi & B. Simma (ed.), *United Nations Codification of State Responsibility* (New York: Oceana, 1987).

27. Yates, *State Responsibility for Nonwealth Injuries to Aliens in the Postwar Era*, in R. Lillich (Reporter), *International Law of State Responsibility for Injuries to Aliens* 213, 214 (Charlottesville, VA: Univ. Press of Va., 1983).

28. **Case examples:** The classic articulation is available in Lissitzyn, *The Meaning of the Term Denial of Justice in International Law*, 30 *Amer. J. Int'l L.* 632 (1936). **Latin America:** Puente, *The Concept of 'Denial of Justice' in Latin America*, 43 *Mich. L. Rev.* 383 (1944).

29. Root, *The Basis of Protection to Citizens Residing Abroad*, 4 *Proceedings of the American Society of International Law* 20–21 (Wash., DC: Amer. Soc. Int'l Law, 1910).

30. Li Hao-p'ei, *Nationalization and International Law*, in 1 *People's China and International Law: A Documentary Study* 719 (Princeton: Princeton Univ. Press, 1974).

31. This formulation appears in a diplomatic note exchanged between Mexico and the US in 1938. *See* § 1.4 of this text (General Principles) regarding this diplomatic exchange (and in the case cited in note 29 below) and 2 *Restatement (Third) of the Law of the Foreign Relations Law of the United States* § 712 (St. Paul: ALI Publishers, 1987) (containing extensive commentary and examples).

32. These facts and quotes are taken from Banco Nacional de Cuba v. Sabbatino, 376 U.S. 398, 84 S.Ct. 923, 11 L.Ed.2d 804 (1964).

33. Resolution 1803(XVII) is reproduced in 2 *Int'l Legal Matl's* 223 (1963).

34. Sinha, *Perspective of the Newly Independent States on the Binding Quality of International Law*, in F. Snyder & S. Sathirathai, *Third World Attitudes Toward International Law: An Introduction* 23, 29 (Dordrecht, Neth.; Boston: Martinus Nijhoff, 1987).

35. *Undertakings of the Government of the United States of America and the Government of the Islamic Republic of Iran with Respect to the Declaration of the Government of the Democratic and Popular Republic of Algeria*, Art. V, reproduced in 20 *Int'l Legal Mat'ls* 229, 232 (1981).

36. J. Westberg, *International Transactions and Claims Involving Government Parties: Case Law of the Iran–United States Claims Tribunal* 66 (Wash., DC: Int'l L. Inst., 1991).

37. 265 U.S. 332, 44 S.Ct. 515, 68 L.Ed. 1041 (1924).

38. G. von Glahn, *Law Among Nations: An Introduction to Public International Law* 251 (6th ed. New York: Macmillan, 1992).

39. *See* notes 33 & 34 of this chapter.

40. Roy, *Is the Law of Responsibility of States for Injuries to Aliens a Part of Universal International Law?*, 55 *Amer. J. Int'l L.* 863 (1961).

Extraterritorial Jurisdiction

■ INTRODUCTION

Prior chapters covered the essentials of International Law, including what it is and the "actors" who shape its contours. This chapter commences the analysis of the common problems in International Law—what they are and basic approaches to resolving them. The operational norms of International Law will be studied, first from the perspective of the State's ability to exercise its powers in an international or "extraterritorial" context.

This chapter focuses on the internationally recognized bases for the State's ability to exercise its sovereign powers—or jurisdiction—over events occurring beyond its own territory. This increasingly common feature of State jurisdiction should not nourish a system of sovereignty that becomes "permeable." Each State in the community of nations should render, and thus receive, equality and respect.

The final analytical section of this chapter covers extradition. One State should not encroach on another's sovereign boundaries by arresting a wanted criminal within another State. No State sent agents into Libya, for example, to seize the Libyan terrorists apparently responsible for bombing Pan Am flight 103 over Scotland in 1989—in spite of a UN resolution demanding their release for trial outside of Libya. The perceived benefits of invoking irregular alternatives to international extradition may yield exhilaration for the moment. Such a benefit, however, is not worth the ultimate costs to State sovereignty.

■ 5.1   DEFINITIONAL SETTING

The State's power to regulate the activities of its inhabitants, or those whose conduct has an effect within its boundaries, is often described in terms of "jurisdiction" and "sovereignty." Each of these terms has its own diverse meanings, depending on the context in which it is used. Although they are often used synonymously, there are some important distinctions between them.

Sovereignty exists when a State effectively governs its territory and populace (*see* § 2.1 on elements of statehood). The State thus has sovereign powers that it may use to control its inhabitants and sometimes even its citizens abroad. This is jurisdiction.

Sovereignty

The definition of sovereignty is the exclusive right of a State to govern the affairs of its inhabitants and to be free from external control. A sovereign State thus has the international capacity to exchange diplomats with other States, to engage in treaty-making, and to be immune from the jurisdiction of the courts of other States (when it is not acting as a private trader). State sovereignty exists when a State acts independently of the consent or control of any other State. The UN Trust Territories discussed in Chapter 3 are (or were) not sovereign entities. They are effectively supervised by another sovereign State until the trust relationship results in the territory's ability to independently govern its own inhabitants.

Under International Law, a foreign State cannot control people or institutions in another State if the latter actually possesses sovereignty. Regardless of legitimacy, a State is either a totally independent sovereign or, alternatively, controlled by another sovereign State due to its lack of sovereignty. Afghanistan, for example, emerged as a sovereign nation in 1709 after centuries of feudal conflict. It became a sovereign member of the United Nations in 1946. The 1979 Soviet invasion of Afghanistan violated the latter's sovereignty over its own territory. Soviet troops were introduced without the unclouded consent of Afghanistan's president, who was executed. Rebels claimed that the government of Afghanistan was a "puppet regime," effectively controlled by the Soviet Union. Afghanistan no longer retained the sovereign power to control its own territory. The Soviet Union began to withdraw its troops in 1988. With the demise of the Soviet Union in 1991, no external State exercised the sovereign supervision of Afghanistan's internal affairs. Once again, it became a sovereign State.

International theorists have often described State sovereignty in terms of a solid sphere—much like a billiard ball—whereby one nation cannot intrude into the internal affairs of another. When there is a clash between two or more such spheres of influence, the equality of sovereignty that is theoretically possessed by all States rigidly repels the other "billiard ball" on the international playing surface. Examples of what one might call "permeable" sovereignty occurred in 1989, when the US invaded Panama in order to remove its leader (General Noriega) for trial in the US, and in 1990, when US DEA agents arranged for the abduction of a Mexican doctor from Guadalajara for trial in the US. One can readily appreciate that the US actions in these cases were not designed to assert US sovereignty over these countries. A more limited purpose was intended in each instance: to further some specific US policy interests in the Western Hemisphere. These actions were quickly ended—unlike the Soviet Un-

ion's takeover of Afghanistan. The UN Charter prohibits the use of such force in international relations, however, on the basis of the sovereign equality and dignity of all members. The sovereign nature of Panama and Mexico were thus adversely impacted by these unilateral US actions, undertaken without the blessing of the Security Council (and thus distinguishable from US action in Haiti, which had that blessing).

Several historical events contributed to the emergence of the concept of State sovereignty (*see* § 1.3 on the History of International Law). One was the regional consolidation of autonomous feudal fiefdoms that existed for thousands of years in certain regions of the world. This vitiated the feudal power of numerous local rulers. A related development was the opposition to external intervention that arose in the Middle Ages. The leaders of the Holy Roman Empire, for example, attempted to expand its influence into Western Europe and the Middle East during their medieval crusades. To repel these invaders, the people of those areas sought to consolidate local territorial power into statewide sovereignty. This centralization of sovereign power led these societies to adopt the concept of State sovereignty to help repel foreign intruders.

The following description of sovereignty is ironic because it was made by a prominent commentator from the former Yugoslavia before its breakup and expulsion from the UN. Professor Branimir Jankovic of the Center for International Studies in Yugoslavia traces these roots of sovereignty. His perspective is as follows:

the idea of sovereignty originated when there appeared a growing opposition to feudal anarchy and to interference in the affairs of other states. The [emerging national] rulers of those times fought for their unlimited, sovereign authority, within their states as well as outside their borders. In this struggle to supersede the feudal retrogressive system and create a new social order, the idea of state sovereignty had a progressive significance. Although at first historically progressive, [sovereign] absolutism . . . was based upon an unlimited autocracy and brute force. It is in the ideology of absolutism that we find the roots of the theory of absolute sovereignty. . . . The sovereignty of a state means today its independence from external intervention. This is the supreme authority inherent in every independent state, limited only by the universally adopted and currently valid rules of international law. This supreme power extends within the borders of the national territory and is usually described as territorial sovereignty, or territorial jurisdiction of states.[1]

Jurisdiction

The term *jurisdiction* has several meanings. That terms includes the legal capacity of State X to (a) establish, (b) enforce, and (c) adjudicate rules of law within its boundaries. The State X legislature thus has the jurisdiction to enact laws governing conduct within X. The executive branch of State X has the power to enforce the State X laws against those within X who would break its rules. State X courts have the jurisdiction to adjudicate cases against civil and criminal defendants under the laws of State X.

As will be seen in Chapter 9 on arbitration and adjudication, international courts and arbitrators must likewise have jurisdiction to resolve claims. A crucial ingredient of the practice of the UN's International Court of Justice, for example, is whether the plaintiff State can establish jurisdiction over the "person" of the defendant State. As discussed later in this chapter, the power of a State to legislate and/or adjudicate matters involving some events occurring *outside* of that State involves the question of its "jurisdiction."

A preliminary but critically important limitation restricts jurisdiction in International Law. An unauthorized exercise of the sovereign power of State X in the territory of State Y constitutes what is referred to as X's "extraterritorial" jurisdiction in Y—generally characterized as violating International Law. The reason is that State Y possesses the right, based on its status as a sovereign entity, to be recognized as sharing equal rights and dignity with all other members of the community of nations. Thus, State X has the correlative obligation not to interfere with State Y's right to control the activities within its borders.

The interplay of sovereignty and jurisdiction often surfaces at the outset of virtually any inquiry of international magnitude. The preliminary jurisdictional questions analyzed in this chapter are then pursued in Chapter 6 on the "Range of Sovereignty". That closely related theme involves the degree to which one State may effectively exercise its

sovereignty outside of its territorial confines, based on acceptable State practice. Some questions thus explored in these two chapters are as follows: Will a State X court have the jurisdiction to apply its internal criminal law to an event occurring only partially in that State; or outside of, but aimed at State X; or on the high seas or in international airspace involving State X citizens or vessels and aircraft? To what extent does State X have the "jurisdiction" to control or regulate the use of airspace in the far reaches of the heavens; or in territorial waters beyond its territorial sea?

The exercise of a State's jurisdiction beyond its borders, where it does not possess territorial sovereignty, will be analyzed in terms of "extraterritorial" exercises of jurisdiction that may or may not violate International Law. The United States, for example, does not have the jurisdiction to send its drug enforcement agents into Mexico to apprehend a criminal. If it does so, it would violate International Law because any *de facto* exercise of its power conflicts with Mexico's exclusive *de jure* power over people and events in Mexico.

"Extraterritorial" Problem

Many States have, at one time or another, engaged in either overt or covert activity within the territory of another State. What constitutes acceptable State practice is a question of degree. The existence of an international diplomatic system, with a series of embassies and consulates, provides an acceptable level of such engagements (*see* Chapter 7). Arranging for the extraterritorial abduction of a foreign national for trial is quite another matter.

The US has been the object of much international attention, beginning essentially in the 1980s, due to its legislation and presidential orders that have been unmistakably "extraterritorial" in nature. A few examples will illustrate the degree to which a State's jurisdiction can leap outside of its territory or territorial waters. A 1984 US law criminalizes hostage taking outside of the US, when the hostages are US citizens or the conduct is designed to influence a US governmental organization to act in a particular way. A 1986 law serves as the basis for the US Coast Guard to board vessels, anywhere on the world's high seas, when the object of the search is to prevent drugs from flowing into the US. In 1993, a federal court in Washington, D.C. approved the application of the National Environmental Protection Act to conduct in Antarctica. In the same year, the US Supreme Court also approved (1) the US Drug Enforcement Administration's participation in the abduction of a Mexican national from Mexico for trial in the US; (2) the application of US antitrust law to London insurers engaged in a boycott affecting US insurers; and (3) the US Coast Guard's return of potential refugees on the high seas off Haiti.[2]

The US has reacted to objections to its extraterritorial jurisdiction by beginning to "legislate away" the criminal defendant's ability to raise this matter in defense—specifically providing that the court retains jurisdiction to proceed when to do so effectively condones an "extraterritorial" application of US law that is in violation of International Law. For example, an amendment to the US Maritime Drug Enforcement laws (Title 46 § 1903) now provides as follows:

> A claim of failure to comply with international law in the enforcement of this chapter may be invoked *solely* by a foreign nation [and not by the criminal defendant], and a failure to comply with international law shall not divest a court of jurisdiction or otherwise constitute a defense to any proceeding under this chapter.

The above examples involve the so-called "extraterritorial" application of national law to events occurring outside the State claiming to exercise valid jurisdiction. The exercise of such jurisdiction is in some cases more acceptable—in terms of international relations—than in others. Prior to assessing some of the more questionable State conduct later in this chapter, one must first consider the international norms that do empower the State to apply its laws to conduct occurring beyond its borders.

■ 5.2 FIVE JURISDICTIONAL PRINCIPLES

The term *international criminal law* appears frequently in analyses of this facet of the State's connection with the individual. It is an appealing description, but not particularly precise. The term is sometimes used to refer to the criminal aspects of *International* Law. This usage implies that internationally prescribed rules of criminal law exist along with limitations on their appropriate application. A treaty might, for example, prescribe the categories of crime that subject the of-

fender to extradition between State X and State Y when the laws of one (or both) of those States have been violated by the individual perpetrator. But this is only a procedural matter, as opposed to substantive rules of international criminal law that would govern the conduct of individuals throughout the world.

The more common usage of the term *international criminal law* involves applications of the *national* law of the various members of the community of nations. In this sense, the focus is the extent to which a State may pass laws and enforce them when some or all of the prohibited conduct occurs outside of its territory or territorial waters. Put another way, this is the international application of the national or internal criminal laws of that State. As succinctly explained by Professor Iain Cameron of Uppsala University in Sweden:

> a state can [thus] criminalize conduct which occurs outside its territory, and provide for prosecution of the actors should they come within its territory. A state's assertion of [its jurisdictional] competence in this way can be referred to as "extraterritorial criminal jurisdiction," although the actual prosecution and punishment of the offender is intraterritorial. All states apply their criminal law to events and conduct occurring outwith [without] their territories to a greater and lesser extent, and so all states apply rules which lay down the spatial scope of their criminal law and grant competence to their courts to try and punish people who have committed abroad [the] acts defined in their criminal codes as offences.[3]

In certain situations, a State may regulate or interfere with its own citizens' affairs anywhere in the world. Customary State practice thus recognizes jurisdictional competence, whereby a State may apply its criminal and civil laws to certain events occurring either in other States or outside of any State. This category of State jurisdiction arose in the context of criminal law enforcement. In 1935, a major study at the Harvard Law School traced the continuing need for exercising criminal jurisdiction in the international context. The Introductory Comment of the study explained it as follows:

> From its beginning, the international community of States has had to deal in a pragmatic

way with more or less troublesome problems of penal jurisdiction. In exercising such jurisdiction . . . States became increasingly aware of the overlappings and the gaps which produced conflicts [between two States wanting to prosecute the same criminal] and required cooperation. . . . In the 19th century, with the increasing facility of travel, transport and communication . . . the problems of conflict between the different national systems became progressively more acute.[4]

International practice produced five customary bases for legitimate State regulation of an individual's conduct, occurring either partially or wholly beyond its borders. They are presented in Exhibit 5.1.

EXHIBIT 5.1 State X International Jurisdictional Guide

Principle	Type Conduct For Which State May Prosecute
Territorial (Subjective)	• Defendant's conduct violates State X law • Conduct starts within State X • Completed within State X or outside
Territorial (Objective)	• Defendant's conduct violates State X law • Conduct starts outside State X • Completed or has "effect" within State X
Nationality	• Defendant's conduct violates State X law • Defendant is a citizen (national) of X • Conduct may start and end anywhere
Passive Personality	• Defendant's conduct violates State X law • Victim is a citizen (national) of X • Conduct may start and end anywhere

Protective	• Defendant's conduct violates State X law
	• Conduct may start and end outside State X
	  (Territorial must either start/end in X)
	  (Protective need not have "effect" in X)

Universality	• Defendant's conduct sufficiently heinous to violate the laws of all States • Conduct started and completed anywhere • All States may prosecute (not just X)

Territorial Principle

Under this principle, the State's jurisdictional authority is derived from the location of the defendant's act. That conduct typically starts and ends within the State that is prosecuting the defendant. The State may thereby punish individuals who commit crimes within its borders. Of all the jurisdictional principles, this application is the most widely accepted and the least disputed. This is only the starting point, however, because two other applications of the territorial principle have *international* applications—referred to as "subjective" and "objective" applications of this principle (discussed below).

The defendant may be a foreign citizen. A State has the jurisdictional power to prosecute violators of its laws, without regard to their nationality. Assume that State X is Italy. The criminal is a Swiss citizen who plots the overthrow of the Italian government. He is captured by the Italian police in Rome. Italy would have the territorial jurisdiction to prosecute and punish this defendant—although he or she is a foreign citizen. It does not matter whether the prohibited conduct began in Switzerland (ending in Italy) or began in Italy. As stated by Italy's Court of Cassation, in response to a Swiss defendant's attack on Italy's jurisdiction in such a case: There "is no rule of Italian public law or international law which exempts from punishment an alien who commits an act in Italy which constitutes a crime. . . . The crime of which the appellant [defendant] has been found guilty, is not less a crime because he is a Swiss national. . . ."[5]

Under International Law, State X *may* also exercise its sovereign powers over those whose extraterritorial conduct violates the laws of State X. The prior historical limitation—that a State could regulate *only* that conduct occurring within its geographical boundaries—no longer exists. Since the nineteenth century, improvements in travel and communication have greatly enhanced the criminal's ability to commit a crime (or parts of a crime) in more than one country. Thus, the unlawful conduct may occur partially inside and partially outside of State X under the "territorial" principle. When the conduct begins *inside* State X, and ends outside its territory, State X may rely on the so-called "*subjective*" application of the territorial principle of international criminal jurisdiction. When the conduct begins *outside* State X, and ends inside State X territory, State X may thereby rely on an "*objective*" application of the territorial principle of international criminal jurisdiction.

The so-called *subjective* form of territorial jurisdiction is used to justify legislation punishing criminal conduct that commences within a State and is then completed abroad. A State has the jurisdiction to punish the perpetrator of a crime thus consummated elsewhere, when the intent to commit the crime and the initial act in furtherance of the crime occurred within that State. Nineteenth century national legislation began to reflect this internationalization of criminal activity made possible by developments in technology and communication. As provided in the 1870 Spanish Law of Organization of the Judicial Power, for example, the "cognizance of crimes begun in Spain and consummated or frustrated in foreign countries falls to Spanish Courts and Judges. . . ."

The territorial principle has another potential application when a State's jurisdiction is based on activities occurring partially inside and partially outside of its borders. This is the so-called "objective" variation of the territorial principle. It is applied to conduct that, conversely, commences *outside* the prosecuting State and is completed within it. It is also referred to as the "effects doctrine." This facet of territorial jurisdiction is more easily abused, and thus subject to more limitations under International Law.

Certain crimes will justify the exercise of *territorial* jurisdiction when their effects are realized or felt within the State whose interests have been adversely affected. The leading international case on the "effects doctrine" was decided by the Permanent Court of International Justice (PCIJ) in the case below. Turkey arrested and prosecuted a French citizen for conduct that began and ended in international waters—as opposed to occurring within the territorial boundaries of some State's land or territorial seas. This is a significant case, because the finding that Turkish jurisdiction was authorized under International Law would mean that international jurists condoned State practice that based criminal jurisdiction on whether the "effects" of the defendant's conduct somehow appeared in the prosecuting State:

THE S.S. LOTUS (FRANCE v. TURKEY)

Permanent Court of International Justice, 1927
Permanent Court of International Justice Reports
Series A, No. 10 (1927)

[Author's Note: In 1923, the French mail steamer Lotus *was underway and headed for Constantinople. The* Lotus *collided with an outbound Turkish coal ship, the* Boz-Kourt, *in international waters far from Turkey. Eight Turkish seamen were killed when the* Lotus *hit the Turkish vessel. When the* Lotus *arrived in Turkey, Turkish authorities arrested and prosecuted the French ship's watch officer Lieutenant Demons (as well as the Turkish vessel's captain) for involuntary manslaughter. Defendant Demons' negligence allegedly*

cost the lives of Turkish citizens, as well as substantial property damage to the Turkish vessel.

France objected to Turkey's exercise of jurisdiction over the French citizen. The alleged criminal negligence did not occur on Turkish territory or in its territorial waters. After diplomatic protests, France and Turkey decided to submit the issue regarding France's objection to the PCIJ for resolution. The following portion of the court's opinion addresses whether International Law authorized Turkey to properly exercise its jurisdiction over conduct occurring on the high seas. France submitted that Turkey could not prosecute the French defendant for his conduct occurring outside of Turkey's territory or its territorial waters.

The PCIJ concluded that either France or Turkey could prosecute the French vessel's officer for involuntary manslaughter. (France could have done so under the Nationality Principle described later in this section.) Turkey was therefore authorized to prosecute Demons because the "effect" of his conduct was felt sufficiently within Turkey. The PCIJ herein confirmed the "objective" application of the territorial principle of State jurisdiction. Thus, Turkey did not violate International Law when it asserted its criminal jurisdiction in this high seas collision case outside of Turkish territory.]

[*Opinion.*] The violation, if any, of the principles of international law would have consisted in the taking of criminal proceedings against Lieutenant Demons. It is not therefore a question relating to any particular step in these proceedings [by Turkey] but of the very fact of the Turkish Courts exercising criminal jurisdiction. That is [because] the proceedings relate exclusively to the question whether Turkey has or has not, according to the principles of international law, jurisdiction to prosecute [France's citizen] in this case.

The prosecution was instituted in pursuance of [the following] Turkish legislation. . . . :

Any foreigner who . . . commits an offence abroad to the prejudice of Turkey or of a Turkish subject . . . shall be punished in accordance with the Turkish Penal Code provided that he is arrested in Turkey.

. . .

Now the first and foremost restriction imposed by international law upon a State is that . . . it may not exercise its power in any form in the territory of another State. In this sense, jurisdiction is certainly territorial; it cannot be exercised by a State outside its territory except by virtue of a permissive rule derived from international custom or from a convention.

It does not, however, follow that international law prohibits a State from exercising jurisdiction . . . [over] acts which have taken place abroad.

. . .

Such a view would only be tenable if international law contained a general prohibition to States to extend the application of their laws and the jurisdiction of their courts to persons, property and acts outside their territory. . . . But this is certainly not the case under international law as it stands at present. Far from laying down a general prohibition . . . it leaves them in this respect a wide measure of discretion.

. . .

[I]t is certain that the courts of many countries, even of countries which have given their criminal legislation a strictly territorial character, interpret criminal law in the sense that offences, the authors of which at the moment of commission are in the territory of another State, are nevertheless to be regarded as having been committed in the national territory [of the prosecuting State] if one of the constituent elements of the offence, *and more especially its effects,* have taken place there [emphasis supplied by author].

The offence for which Lieutenant Demons was prosecuted was an act—of negligence or imprudence—having its origin on board the [French ship] Lotus, whilst its effects made themselves felt on board the [Turkish ship] Boz-Kourt.

■ NOTES AND QUESTIONS

1. The PCIJ essentially held that Turkey could exercise its criminal jurisdiction over any "foreigner" who violated the quoted Turkish penal code provision by committing an offense abroad. On these facts, "abroad" included international waters—which belonged to no one, as opposed to conduct

within another State. The Court's articulation does not preclude the application of Turkish penal law to a *Turkish* citizen for his or her acts abroad that cause the same or similar effects within Turkey—such as the Turkish officer who also caused damage to the Turkish vessel. The Court approved the application of a "wide discretion" for Turkey to apply its laws to foreigners on the high seas. As will be seen in the next chapter, this development is also referred to as the ability of a State to exercise its jurisdiction based on the "law of the flag." A Turkish vessel may thus be legally characterized as a floating extension of the Turkish territory. Which form of the territorial principle did the Court thus approve in *Lotus*?

2. The Court further recognized the applicability of the "passive personality" principle to the French officer's conduct. The victims of his negligence were Turkish citizens, as was the vessel. This application will be addressed below.

Nationality Principle

Under this jurisdictional principle, a State may regulate the conduct of its own citizens, even when their acts occur entirely outside of that State (in limited circumstances). In 1992, US chess master Bobby Fischer defied a UN resolution imposing sanctions against the former Yugoslavia. No US citizen was permitted to travel to Yugoslavia, as a part of US compliance with that resolution. When Fischer defied the travel ban, the US Treasury Department issued him a letter warning him about the penalties for his refusal to comply. Although his conduct took place on foreign soil, the US could rely upon the nationality principle of jurisdiction to legitimize any ensuing prosecution for his acts.

Using the *Lotus* case as another example, France could have also prosecuted the French ship's officer for his negligence, which damaged the French ship. Such jurisdiction could have been exercised under the nationality principle because Lieutenant Demons was a French citizen.

This potential for the exercise of State jurisdiction is based on the legal bond between a State and its citizens. That link generates reciprocal rights and obligations. As previously analyzed in § 4.2, a State is expected to protect its citizens when they are abroad, for so long as they owe it their allegiance. Conversely, a citizen's status or conduct may touch on the interests of his or her home State, in a way that allows that State to request that the citizen return home. That State may also punish its citizen for certain conduct—for example, operating a public French vessel in a way that damages it in a collision at sea (based on the nationality link between France and its citizen).

The nationality principle is invoked less frequently than the territorial principle. One practical reason is that the territorial and nationality principles often overlap. France would not have to invoke the nationality principle to exercise its jurisdiction, should it want to prosecute Lieutenant Demons. The territorial principle would be conspicuously available because his negligence harmed a French vessel—an extension of France's territory on the high seas. In the *Lotus* case, Turkey did not claim that its criminal jurisdiction was based, in whole or in part on this principle, because the *Lotus's* watch officer was not a Turkish citizen.

Under the nationality principle, States enjoy relatively unfettered legal control over their citizens. A state's treatment of its own citizens is usually of no concern to other states.[6] The following case explains why—in addition to adding detail to the statement in the above *Lotus* case regarding the "wide discretion" available to States in exercising their jurisdiction based on the nationality principle, as follows:

BLACKMER v. UNITED STATES

Supreme Court of the United States, 1932
284 U.S. 421, 52 S.Ct. 252, 76 L.Ed. 375

[*Author's Note: This was a tax case arising out of the famous "Teapot Dome Scandal" during the administration of President Warren Harding in the 1920s. In litigation related to this scandal, the Supreme Court found that some high-ranking politicians had obtained oil leases through corrupt means. Blackmer, a US citizen, had some information needed by the*

US authorities to investigate them. He had moved to France, but had not relinquished his US citizenship.

A US consular officer in Paris served Blackmer with a notice to return to Washington to testify on behalf of the US government during criminal and civil investigations of the scandal. After Blackmer ignored this court order to return to the US, the trial judge found him in contempt of court for failing to appear. Blackmer then petitioned the US Supreme Court for relief from the lower court's contempt order and related fine. The following portion of the Supreme Court's opinion succinctly articulates the application of the nationality principle of jurisdiction requiring Blackmer's return.]

[*Opinion.*] While it appears that the petitioner moved his residence to France. . . , it is [also] undisputed that he was, and continued to be, a citizen of the United States. He continued to owe allegiance to the United States. By virtue of the obligations of citizenship, the United States retained its authority over him, and he was bound by its laws made applicable to him in a foreign country. Thus, although resident abroad, the petitioner remained subject to the taxing power of the United States. For disobedience to its laws through conduct abroad he was subject to punishment in courts of the United States.

. . .

While the legislation of the Congress . . . is construed to apply only within the territorial jurisdiction of the United States, the question of its application . . . is one of construction, not legislative power. Nor can it be doubted that the United States possesses the power inherent in sovereignty to require the return to this country of a citizen, resident elsewhere, whenever the public interest requires it, and to penalize him in the case of refusal.

Passive Personality Principle

Under the passive personality principle, jurisdiction is based on the nationality of the *victim* of a crime that occurs outside of the prosecuting State's territory. In contrast to the previously discussed principles: (a) the nationality principle relies on the nationality of the defendant; (b) the location of the defendant does not limit this basis for jurisdiction over someone who has harmed a citizen of the prosecuting State; and (c) the passive personality principle is probably the least used jurisdictional basis, given its potential for abuse.

An unlimited application of the passive personality principle would result in the prosecution of people who harm the citizens of the prosecuting State *anywhere in the world*. Although this principle is a recognized basis for exercising jurisdiction under international law,[7] it should not be used unless another principle is also applicable. In the *Lotus* case, for example, Turkey punished the conduct of a French citizen on the high seas. In addition to the territoriality principle ("effects" application), Turkey also relied on the passive personality principle to support its prosecution of the French ship's officer. His conduct harmed Turkish citizens and property interests. Because the French citizen's conduct took place outside of Turkey, the Permanent Court of International Justice cautiously acknowledged the theoretical availability of this jurisdictional principle—on these particular facts alone. International decision-makers have been far more cautious when the conduct complained of occurs *within* the territory of another State.

Some of the judges in the PCIJ's *Lotus* case expressed their belief that International Law does *not* permit assertions of jurisdiction exclusively on this basis. While Turkey had passive personality jurisdiction to prosecute the French watch officer, Judge Moore warned that jurisdiction based *solely* on the victim's citizenship would mean "that the citizen [victim] of one country, when he visits another country, takes with him for his 'protection' the law of his own country and subjects those with whom he comes into contact to the operation of that law. In this way an inhabitant of a great commercial city, in which foreigners congregate, may in the course of an hour unconsciously fall under the operation of a number of foreign criminal codes. . . ."[8]

Protective Principle

Under the protective principle, a State may exercise jurisdiction over certain criminal acts occurring outside its territory. Such acts must threaten the security, territorial integrity, or political independence of the State. The protective principle allows a State to prosecute its own citizens, as well as citizens of other States, for their conduct elsewhere.

The protective principle was first used in statutes of various Italian cities in the fifteenth century. It was widely used before the twentieth century in the numerous treaties dealing with criminal jurisdiction over aliens.[9] In modern applications, the perpetrator may choose not to enter the State whose laws have thus been violated. That State will then have to seek his or her extradition from a State where the offending individual is found.

The protective principle differs from the more familiar territorial principle because the effect of the criminal's conduct does *not* have to be felt within the territory of the offended State. In a US case thus distinguishing these two principles, a Canadian citizen made false statements while trying to obtain a visa from the US consulate in Montreal. The court noted that "the objective principle [requiring that the effects of the crime be directly felt within the territory] is quite distinct from the protective theory. Under the latter, all the elements of the crime occur in the foreign country and jurisdiction exists because these actions have a '*potentially* adverse effect' upon security or governmental functions . . . and there *need not be any actual effect* within the country as would be required under the objective territorial principle."[10]

Most states do not use this theory for exercising jurisdiction. In the leading treatise on international law as applied by Canada, for example, the contributors explain why. Their focus on the "security" theme underlying the protective principle points out its potential for abuse. They explain as follows:

> a state may exercise jurisdiction over acts committed abroad that prejudicial to its security, territorial integrity and political independence. For example, the types of crime covered could include treason, espionage, and counterfeiting of currency, postage stamps, seals, passports, and other public documents.
>
> Canada and other countries such as the United Kingdom have not favored this principle when unaccompanied by other [jurisdictional] factors such as nationality or other forms of allegiance tying the accused to the forum.[11]

Universality Principle

Certain crimes are deemed of "universal interest" because they are sufficiently heinous to be crimes against the entire community of nations. The perpetrators of these crimes are enemies of all mankind. Any nation where the perpetrator is found is expected to arrest the perpetrator, or alternatively, to extradite the criminal to a State that will prosecute. The universality principle has not been applied to civil (noncriminal) wrongs because they are not suf-

ficiently outrageous. Nor has this principle been applied, other than in the most shocking or morally degrading cases where it might be invoked as a matter of International Law.

There are several so-called "universal" crimes, including engaging in piracy (the earliest example of a universal crime), harming diplomats, hijacking aircraft, slave trading, engaging in certain wartime activities, and committing genocide. While some commentators may disagree with either the length or the completeness of this list, its moral accuracy cannot be contested.

This jurisdictional principle has been invoked when the other principles were not applicable. Piracy, for example, was (and is) usually committed on the high seas rather than within the territorial waters of any nation. The pirates often fled to distant lands or waters. Under the universal principle, however, all nations have the jurisdiction, as well as the duty, to apprehend pirates when they are present.[12]

The most prominent example of prosecution for a universal crime involved acts perpetrated during the Nazi Holocaust during World War II. In *Israel v. Eichmann,* Israel prosecuted Adolf Eichmann, Hitler's chief exterminator, under its Nazi Collaborators Punishment Law. That legislation and the ensuing prosecution was based on the application of *universal* jurisdiction because none of the other jurisdictional principles was available to Israel. The territorial principle could not apply because Israel did not become a State until 1948. The nationality principle was inapplicable, because Germany would have to be the prosecuting State. The passive personality principle did not apply since no victim could be a citizen of the State of Israel during the time that the conduct occurred. If there was no Israel then, the protective principle could not be invoked to protect its interests.

Eichmann, however, committed crimes constituting genocide (as described in Chapter 11 on Human Rights) against the citizens of various European States prior to Israel's existence. Eichmann was abducted from Argentina (where he had fled) by Israeli commandos, to stand trial in Israel. Argentina's territorial sovereignty was violated by Israel's abduction of Eichmann. The resulting prosecution was undertaken in Israel's capacity as a member of the community of nations. It nevertheless asserted its universal jurisdiction to prosecute Eichmann. In the opinion of Israel's Supreme Court:

The crimes defined in this [Israeli] law must be deemed to have always been international crimes, entailing individual criminal responsibility: customary international law is analogous to the Common Law and develops by analogy and by reference to general principles of law recognized by civilized nations; these crimes share the characteristics of crimes . . . which damage vital international interests, impair the foundations and security of the international community, violate universal moral values and humanitarian principles . . . and the principle of universal jurisdiction over "crimes against humanity" . . . similarly derives from a common vital interest in their suppression. The State prosecuting them acts as agent of the international community, administering international law.[13]

■ 5.3   EXTRADITION

Introduction

Section 5.2 covered the five jurisdictional bases for prosecuting criminals engaged in international activity, including acts outside of State X (or its territorial waters) that have an adverse effect within State X—exemplified by the *Lotus* case. The theoretical availability of jurisdiction is pointless, however, without the presence of the alleged criminal—so that State X law may be effectively enforced by punishing the offender. State X might try a criminal *in absentia* under its internal laws, where there is no treaty basis for obtaining the presence of the accused from State Y. There is no true "international criminal law" whereby criminal activity might be the subject of regional or global multilateral treaties. Instead, there are hundreds of bilateral treaties that list the mutually agreeable conditions for the signatories to surrender accused or convicted criminals to each other for conviction or punishment.

Extradition is the customary State practice for securing the presence of the criminal. Under this process, State X requests that State Y turn over an individual, located in State Y, who has committed a crime that violated the laws of State X. State X thereby requests the extradition through diplomatic channels. If State Y agrees to X's request, Y surrenders the accused to X authorities. This process has its origins in ancient civilization. The first recorded extradition treaty dates back to 1280 B.C., when an

Egyptian Pharaoh foiled an attempted invasion by the bordering Hittite nation. The ensuing peace treaty provided for the exchange of the activists, who had returned to their respective nations, seeking shelter after the unsuccessful invasion attempt.[14]

Utility

Extradition treaties are necessary because extradition is not automatically available. Under International Law, there is no duty to surrender a criminal to another nation. A citizen of Austria, for example, may commit a crime against his or her State and then flee to Germany. Germany may decide to honor—or ignore—Austria's request for the extradition of the Austrian criminal.

Some countries even prohibit or greatly limit extradition. The Honduran Constitution, for example, prohibits the extradition of Honduran citizens to the United States. Colombia and Slovenia's constitutions bar extradition of their own citizens to a foreign country. Thus in 1993, a Pennsylvania judge claiming Slovenian nationality fled from the US to Slovenia after being convicted of corruption—where he remains a fugitive and beyond the reach of US authorities. A related limitation is that—even when States X and Y have entered into such a treaty—the criminal may be located in State Z, which is not a party to the X-Y treaty.

The jurisdictional basis for extradition is thus found in a treaty or some national law of the extraditing State. It may not be implied from the lack of a prohibition against extradition. In 1936, the US Supreme Court acknowledged this principle of International Law in its following articulation:

> in the absence of a conventional or legislative provision, there is no authority vested in any department of the government to seize a fugitive criminal and surrender him to a foreign power. . . . There is no executive discretion to surrender him to a foreign government, unless that discretion is granted by law. It necessarily follows that as the legal authority does not exist save as it is given by act of Congress or by the terms of a treaty, it is not enough that statute or treaty does not deny the power to surrender. It must be found that [some] statute or treaty confers the power.[15]

When granted, extradition thus overcomes a major jurisdictional limitation that is closely linked to

State sovereignty. Extradition allows States to accomplish indirectly what they cannot do directly. Austria's police agents cannot enter Germany to apprehend criminals. Austria's objective of prosecuting them for their crimes is met, however, when Germany grants Austria's extradition requests. Extradition thus circumvents the limitation that Austria's territorial jurisdiction cannot extend beyond its borders into Germany. Extradition also accomplishes the international objective of facilitating international assistance for the apprehension of criminals. As classically stated in 1896 by the British jurist Lord Russell, "the law of extradition is . . . founded upon the broad principle that it is in the interest of civilised communities that crimes . . . should not go unpunished, and it is a part of the comity of nations that one State should afford to another every assistance towards bringing persons guilty of such crimes to justice."[16] The nation that honors a request for extradition today may want the requesting nation to return that favor tomorrow.

Extradition treaties typically list a mutually acceptable schedule of offenses subject to extradition. The crimes usually are major offenses against the law of both parties to the treaty. For example, Article II of the 1978 Treaty on Extradition Between the United States of America and Japan provides as follows:

> Extradition shall be granted in accordance with the provisions of this Treaty for any offense listed in the Schedule annexed to this Treaty . . . when such an offense is punishable by the laws of both Contracting Parties by death, by life imprisonment, or by deprivation of liberty for a period of more than one year; or for any other offense when such offense is punishable by the federal laws of the United States and by the laws of Japan by death, by life imprisonment, or by deprivation of liberty for a period of more than one year.[17]

The extraditable offenses in this treaty include murder, kidnapping, rape, bigamy, robbery, inciting riots, piracy, drug law violations, bribery, evasion of taxes, unfair business transactions, and violations of export/import laws.

"Irregular" Alternatives

States do not always depend on extradition treaties when seeking to prosecute certain individuals. They may expel or deport "wanted" individuals, without going through the process of extradition—or even when there is no extradition treaty. States have also engaged in kidnappings. Kidnapping a fugitive from the soil of another nation is an unfortunate alternative to extradition, however.[18]

One problem is that the laws of many nations do not provide a defense to the kidnapped individual in the ensuing criminal prosecution. The territorial sovereignty of the nation from which he or she was kidnapped has been violated. The violated State may protest. Under International Law, however, the resulting harm is to the State—rather than to the individual, who does not have the same legal capacity to use this violation of International Law for his or her criminal defense. In the *Eichmann* case (*see* § 5.2), Israel violated the territorial sovereignty of Argentina when its commandos went to Buenos Aires to capture and return Hitler's chief architect of the Holocaust for trial in Tel Aviv. He was not able to invoke this ground for any defense.

In the case of some of the more notorious defendants, few nations are likely to protest such abductions. Nor are many national courts prone to seriously consider the defense that the *way* in which these criminals are brought to justice requires their release. While Argentina's sovereignty was undoubtedly violated by Israel's kidnapping of Adolf Eichmann, his status as a key figure in Nazi Germany's "Final Solution" would not trigger many protests on behalf of Argentina.

In 1994, Carlos "the Jackal" was finally brought to justice in France. He is the world-famous terrorist who supposedly trained many European and Middle East terrorist organizations during the 1970s and 1980s. While having a medical operation in the Sudan, he was drugged and smuggled from the Sudan to Paris. While the Sudanese themselves may have arranged this kidnapping, his technical complaint about the method of capture and informal extradition were rejected by the French court. Alternatively, had French agents surreptitiously entered the Sudan without knowledge of the Sudanese, few nations would likely protest the violation of Sudan's territorial sovereignty.

Thus, if a crime or pattern of conduct is sufficiently heinous, State practice of course formally disapproves of such territorial violations—while informally characterizing the violation of territorial sovereignty defense as sufficiently technical to warrant proceeding with the criminal case. When the defendant is not so notorious, States are far more likely to risk international admonishment when they resort to this irregular means of "extradition."

An extradition treaty is designed to avoid the "necessity" of resorting to kidnapping and related devices. Such treaties can soothe international relations between two nations that have experienced adverse international relations over this very State conduct in the past. (Israel did not have such an agreement with Argentina in the Eichmann affair.) Put another way, if Mexico and the US are parties to a recent extradition treaty, should US agents be able to go into Mexico, arrange for the kidnapping of a Mexican citizen, and yet retain the sovereign jurisdiction to try him? To do so would only encourage aberrant State conduct that violates International Law. In one of the most (internationally) criticized cases ever decided by the US Supreme Court, the US effectively took the position that the *absence* of an express provision barring international kidnapping did not deprive the US courts of their jurisdiction to try the kidnapped individual.

In 1985, a US Drug Enforcement Administration (DEA) agent named Enrique Camerena was brutally tortured in Mexico for many hours. A Mexican doctor reportedly kept him alive so that Mexican drug lords could torture him—during one of the most sadistic murders in recorded history, and the first death of a US drug agent on Mexican soil. An individual convicted of conducting the torture was delivered by Mexican police, who pushed him through a fence onto the US side of the border in Texas.

Although there were earlier denials, President Bush conceded that a "system of rewards" was established to ensure the capture of this doctor—specifically, a $50,000 bounty ($20,000 actually paid by the DEA) and $6,000 per week in living expenses. A Mexican policeman was supposed to deliver the doctor to US authorities, but this arrangement fell through. Doctor Alvarez-Machain was then released from a Mexican jail. A private team of current and former US police officers assisted some Mexican nationals with kidnapping this doctor from his office in Guadalajara, Mexico, whereafter he "appeared" in a Los Angeles federal court to face criminal charges related to the Camerena murder. The Mexican government protested, demanding that Alvarez-Machain be released, due to what it characterized as a violation of the general principles of International Law on territorial sovereignty and jurisdiction.

In addition to claiming mistaken identity, his lawyers also defended the defendant doctor on the procedural ground that the way by which he appeared before the court was so outrageous that the US courts did not have jurisdiction to hold him for trial. Since the nineteenth century, the US courts have ruled that an individual criminal defendant may not obtain a dismissal based on how he or she was brought before the court—with the modern exception of conduct "shocking the conscience" of the court, which authorizes dismissals in these cases on the basis that they violate the basic tenets of "due process of law."

The US Government did not dispute the facts regarding the kidnapping. The federal trial judge in Los Angeles thus dismissed this case against the doctor, due to the "shocking" conduct of the US agents in violation of the laws of Mexico and the 1980 extradition treaty between the US and Mexico. In the words of the trial judge: "This court lacks jurisdiction to try this defendant." The intermediate Court of Appeals affirmed this dismissal—holding that the proper remedy was to release this Mexican national from US custody so that he could return to Mexico. The majority of the US Supreme Court's judges reversed, however, as set forth in the opinion that follows:

UNITED STATES v. HUMBERTO ALVAREZ-MACHAIN

Supreme Court of the United States, 1992
504 U.S. 655, 112 S.Ct. 2188, 119 L.Ed.2d 441

[*Opinion.*] THE CHIEF JUSTICE delivered the opinion of the Court.

The issue in this case is whether a criminal defendant, abducted to the United States from a nation with which it has an extradition treaty, thereby acquires a defense to the jurisdiction of this country's courts. We hold that he does not, and that he may be tried in federal district court for violations of the criminal law of the United States.

. . .

Respondent moved to dismiss the indictment, claiming that his abduction constituted outrageous governmental conduct, and that the District Court lacked jurisdiction to try him because he was abducted in violation of the extradition treaty between the United States and Mexico.

. . .

In the instant case, the Court of Appeals affirmed the district court's finding that the United States had authorized the abduction of respondent, and that letters from the Mexican government to the United States government served as an official protest of the Treaty violation. Therefore, the Court of Appeals ordered that the indictment against respondent be dismissed and that respondent be repatriated to Mexico. We granted certiorari, and now reverse [for purposes of authorizing further proceedings in the US].

. . .

In *Ker v. Illinois*, 119 U.S. 436, 7 S.Ct. 225, 30 L.Ed. 421 (1886) . . . [this court held] in line with "the highest authorities" that "such forcible abduction is no sufficient reason why the party should not answer when brought within the jurisdiction of the court which has the right to try him for such an offence, and presents no valid objection to his trial in such court."

. . .

The only differences between *Ker* and the present case are that *Ker* was decided on the premise that there was no governmental involvement in the abduction; and Peru, from which *Ker* was abducted, did not object to his prosecution. . . . Therefore, our first inquiry must be whether the abduction of respondent from Mexico violated the extradition treaty between the United States and Mexico. If we conclude that the Treaty does not prohibit respondent's abduction, the rule in Ker applies, and the court need not inquire as to how respondent came before it.

In construing a treaty, as in construing a statute, we first look to its terms to determine its meaning. The Treaty says nothing about the obligations of the United States and Mexico to refrain from forcible abductions of people from the territory of the other

nation, or the consequences under the Treaty if such an abduction occurs.

More critical to respondent's argument is Article 9 of the Treaty which provides: "1. Neither Contracting Party shall be bound to deliver up its own nationals, but the executive authority of the requested Party shall, if not prevented by the laws of that Party, have the power to deliver them up if, in its discretion, it be deemed proper to do so. "2. If extradition is not granted pursuant to paragraph 1 of this Article, the requested Party shall submit the case to its competent authorities for the purpose of prosecution, provided that Party has jurisdiction over the offense."

. . .

[But] Article 9 does not purport to specify the only way in which one country may gain custody of a national of the other country for the purposes of prosecution. . . .

The history of negotiation and practice under the Treaty also fails to show that abductions outside of the Treaty constitute a violation of the Treaty. As the [US] Solicitor General notes, the Mexican government was made aware, as early as 1906, of the *Ker* doctrine, and the United States' position that it applied to forcible abductions made outside of the terms of the United States-Mexico extradition treaty. Nonetheless, the current version of the Treaty, signed in 1978, does not attempt to establish a rule that would in any way curtail the effect of *Ker*. Moreover, although language which would grant individuals exactly the right sought by respondent [Doctor Alvarez] had been considered and drafted as early as 1935 by a prominent group of legal scholars sponsored by the faculty of Harvard Law School [*see* note 3 to this chapter], no such clause appears in the current treaty.

Thus, the language of the Treaty, in the context of its history, does not support the proposition that the Treaty prohibits abductions outside of its terms. The remaining question, therefore, is whether the Treaty should be interpreted so as to include an implied term prohibiting prosecution where the defendant's presence is obtained by means other than those established by the Treaty.

Respondent contends that the Treaty must be interpreted against the backdrop of customary international law, and that international abductions are "so clearly prohibited in international law" that there was no reason to include such a clause in the

Treaty itself. The international censure of international abductions is further evidenced, according to respondent [doctor], by the United Nations Charter and the Charter of the Organization of American States. Respondent does not argue that these sources of international law provide an independent basis for the right respondent asserts not to be tried in the United States, but rather that they should inform the interpretation of the Treaty terms.

. . .

In sum, to infer from this Treaty and its terms that it prohibits all means of gaining the presence of an individual outside of its terms goes beyond established precedent and practice . . . [and] to imply from the terms of this Treaty that it prohibits obtaining the presence of an individual by means outside of the procedures the Treaty establishes requires a much larger inferential leap, with only the most general of international law principles to support it. The general principles cited by respondent simply fail to persuade us that we should imply in the

United States-Mexico Extradition Treaty a term prohibiting international abductions.

Respondent [Alvarez] . . . may be correct that respondent's abduction was "shocking," and that it may be in violation of general international law principles. Mexico has protested the abduction of respondent through diplomatic notes, and the decision of whether respondent should be returned to Mexico, as a matter outside of the Treaty, is a matter for the Executive Branch. We conclude, however, that respondent's abduction was not in violation of the Extradition Treaty between the United States and Mexico, and therefore the rule of *Ker v. Illinois* is fully applicable to this case. The fact of respondent's forcible abduction does not therefore prohibit his trial in a court in the United States for violations of the criminal laws of the United States.

The judgment of the Court of Appeals is therefore reversed, and the case is remanded for further proceedings consistent with this opinion.

■ NOTES

1. Mexican (as well as some US and numerous Canadian) newspapers carried accounts of the extreme disappointment of the populace over this kidnapping of a Mexican citizen by agents of the US government for trial in the US. (Ironically, the North American Free Trade Agreement was enacted only two months after this decision.) Mexico and the US began to renegotiate the 1978 extradition treaty interpreted in this case. Doctor Alvarez-Machain was later released for lack of evidence. His US lawyer then filed a $20 million lawsuit against the US, based on the circumstances described in this case and allegations of torture by US agents related to the abduction. In the following year, Costa Rica's Supreme Court threw out the US/Costa Rican extradition treaty, on grounds that the *Alvarez-Machain* decision made a mockery of such treaties that are concluded with the US.

2. Professor Louis Henkin, President of the American Society of International Law and Professor Emeritus of International Law at Colombia University School of Law, bashed the Supreme Court's reasoning with his statement that "the Court might have considered whether U.S. courts should accept the fruits of such gross violations of international

law by United States officials. The Supreme Court . . . failed international law: It failed to take international law seriously or to help assure that the United States take it seriously."

Professor John Rogers of the University of Kentucky School of Law responded to Professor Henkin's Supreme Court bashing as "the kind of misreading that one might expect from a layperson. . . . There is a very respectable argument that permitting such a trial is perfectly consistent with United States obligations under customary international law, and that treaty has changed the customary rule." Professor Malvina Halberstam, of Yeshiva University Law School in New York, countered the outcry against the Supreme Court decision in *Alvarez-Machain* with her argument that "Commentators generally agree that the seizure of a person by agents of one state in the territory of another clearly violates international law. They also agree, however, that that does not deprive the court of jurisdiction over the person illegally seized."[19]

3. In a 1975 federal case from New York, the defendant—an Italian citizen living in Uruguay—moved to dismiss the indictment against him on facts similar to *Alvarez-Machain*. He was abducted from his home by Uruguay's police, turned over to Brazilian police, tortured, sedated, and flown to the

US—where he was immediately placed in the custody of the US Drug Enforcement Administration. He claimed that US officials participated in the abduction and torture. While the alleged conduct was not ultimately proven, the appellate court did rule on this potential defense as follows:

> we view due process as now requiring a court to divest itself of jurisdiction . . . where it has been acquired as the result of the government's *deliberate, unnecessary and unreasonable* invasion of the accused's constitutional rights. This conclusion represents but an extension of the well-recognized power of federal courts in the civil [case] context . . . to decline to exercise jurisdiction over a defendant whose presence has been secured by force or fraud.

US v. Toscanino, 500 F.2d 267, 275 (2nd Cir. 1974) (emphasis supplied). This approach has not been adopted in other federal circuits. It has been raised by defense counsel, however, as a much needed exception to the general rule: Defendants cannot rely on the circumstances of their arrest in another country, and the circumstances resulting in their appearance before a US court, to avoid prosecution.

4. Under a little-known Mexican statute, Mexican authorities may act as an extension of the US prosecutor's office in order to try cases in Mexico on the basis of evidence provided by US authorities. In 1993, California prosecutors in Santa Clara County sent materials to Zacatecas, Mexico, resulting in a forty-five-year sentence being imposed by the Mexican judge. A Mexican national had killed two people in California. This conviction was widely acclaimed in the US as providing a basis for "new" confidence in the Mexican legal system. From 1985 to 1992, San Diego prosecutors (in a city on the international border) obtained sixty-three of sixty-four attempted convictions under this Mexican statute based on this alternative US arrangement with Mexico—one that was never mentioned in *Alvarez-Machain* or related cases.

Now read the following case from the South African Supreme Court, dealing with precisely the same issue—but deciding that International Law *clearly* prohibited South African courts from exercising jurisdiction, when agents of the State had kidnapped a criminal defendant from Swaziland.

Ebrahim, the South African defendant in this case, had already completed a fifteen-year sentence in South Africa. In 1980, he subsequently left South Africa for Swaziland because he was a leading member of the African National Congress (ANC—President Nelson Mandela's political party). He was forcibly abducted from Swaziland in 1986 by unidentified persons and brought into the Republic of South Africa where he was formally arrested, tried, convicted of treason, and sentenced to twenty more years of imprisonment. Unlike the situation in *Alvarez-Machain*, where Mexico protested the US assertion of jurisdiction, Swaziland did not object to the kidnapping in this case—yet the Supreme Court nevertheless decided that the South African courts had no jurisdiction under the circumstances, resulting in the release of the defendant.

This appeal (decided fifteen months before *Alvarez-Machain*) raises the same question of whether a person abducted by State agents is amenable to the criminal jurisdiction of the courts of the State to which he is abducted. Ebrahim lost his jurisdictional plea in the lower court, as cited below.

The court first examined this problem via its historical antecedents, including the Roman and Dutch law. Contemporary South African law is still bound by the principles of Roman-Dutch law. Previous judicial decisions in which criminal jurisdiction had been "properly" exercised over abducted persons were discarded as a result of this case:

STATE v. EBRAHIM

Appellate Division for East/South-East Circuit, 1991
31 Int'l Legal Mat'ls 888 (1992)*

[*Opinion.*] Appellant argues that the abduction was a violation of the applicable rules of international law, that these rules are part of our law, and that the violation of these rules deprived the trial court of competence to hear the matter.

. . .

In *Nduli and Others v. Minister of Justice* [1978] this court decided that where the accused were abducted from Swaziland by members of the South African Police in breach of orders from their commanding officer, the South African state was not responsible and accordingly there was no violation of international law. Consequently the trial court was not deprived of its competence to try the accused. In that case, as in the present case, the accused were formally arrested in South Africa. In the present case, . . . the appellant was abducted from Swaziland to South Africa by persons who were not police but who acted under the authority of some state agency.

. . .

According to [Roman Law] Digest 2.1.20:
"Paul Edict book 1: One who administers justice beyond the limits of his territory may be disobeyed with impunity."

. . .

This limitation on the legal powers of Roman provincial governors and lawgivers is understandable and was unavoidable in the light of the great number of provinces comprising the Roman Empire in classical times, with their ethnic and cultural diversity, and their different legal systems which the politically pragmatic Romans allowed to remain largely in force in their conquered territories. Until late in the history of the Roman Empire certain provinces were controlled by the Senate and others by the Emperor. Intervention by one province in the domestic affairs of another was a source of potential conflict.

. . .

It is inconceivable that the Roman authorities would recognize a conviction and sentence, and allow them to stand, when they were the result of an abduction of a criminal from one province on the order or with the co-operation of the authority of another province. This would not only have been an approval of illegal conduct, and therefore a subversion of authority, but would also have threatened the internal inter-provincial peace of the Empire.

. . .

One of the foremost Roman-Dutch jurists was Johannes Voet (1647–1713), a Professor of Law in the University of Leiden. According to Voet in his Commentarius and Pandectas 48.3.2:

"So far however must the limits of jurisdiction be observed in seizing a person accused of crime that, if the judge or his representative pursues him when he has been caught in the judge's own area and has taken flight, he nevertheless cannot seize or pursue further than the point at which the accused has first crossed the boundaries of the pursuer. A judge is regarded as a private person in the area of another, and thus he would in making an arrest in that area be exercising an act of jurisdiction on another's ground, a thing which the laws do not allow."

. . .

From the repeated exposition and acceptance of the above rule in its different forms it is clear that the unlawful removal of a person from one jurisdiction to another was regarded as an abduction and as a serious breach of the law in Roman-Dutch law.

. . .

It is therefore clear that in Roman-Dutch law a court of one state had no jurisdiction to try a person abducted from another state by agents of the former state. The question must now be considered whether this principle is also part of our present law.

Our [English-based] common law is still substantially Roman-Dutch law as adjusted to local circumstances [in South Africa]. No South African statute grants or denies jurisdiction to our courts to try a person abducted from another state and brought into the Republic of South Africa.

. . .

Several fundamental legal principles are contained in these rules, namely the protection and promotion of human rights, good inter-state relations and a healthy administration of justice. The individual must be protected against illegal detention and abduction, the bounds of jurisdiction must not be exceeded, sovereignty must be respected, the legal process must be fair to those affected and abuse of law must be avoided in order to protect and promote the integrity of the administration of justice. This applies equally to the state. When the state is a party to a dispute, as for example in criminal cases, it must come to court with "clean hands". When the state itself is involved in an abduction across international borders, as in the present case, its hands are not clean.

Principles of this kind testify to a healthy legal system of high standard. Signs of this development appear increasingly in the municipal law of other countries. A telling example is that of United States v. Toscanino 500 F 2d 267, to which [defendant's counsel] Mr Mahomed referred us. The key question for decision in that [1974 US] case was formulated as follows:

"In an era marked by a sharp increase in kidnapping activities, both here and abroad . . .

we face the question as we must in the state of the pleadings, of whether a Federal Court must assume jurisdiction over the person of a defendant who is illegally apprehended abroad and forcibly abducted by Government agents to the United States for the purpose of facing criminal charges here."

The Court refused to follow the decisions of Ker v. Illinois 119 U.S. 342 (1888) and Frisbie v. Collins 342 U.S. 519 (1952) for the following reasons:

"Faced with a conflict between the two concepts of due process, the one being the restricted version found in Ker-Frisbie and the other the expanded and enlightened interpretation expressed in more recent decisions of the Supreme Court, we are persuaded that to the extent that the two are in conflict, the Ker-Frisbie version [whereby the offended State but not the abducted individual] must yield. Accordingly we view due process as now requiring a court to divest itself of jurisdiction over the person of a defendant where it has been acquired as the result of the Government's deliberate, unnecessary and unreasonable invasion of the accused's constitutional rights. This conclusion represents but an extension of the well-recognized power of federal courts in the civil context to decline to exercise jurisdiction over a defendant whose presence has been secured by force or fraud" (at 275).

. . .

It follows that, according to our common law, the trial court had no jurisdiction to hear the case against the appellant. Consequently his conviction and sentence cannot stand.

Avoiding Extradition

States do not honor extradition requests for a variety of reasons. The laws of the requesting State may be perceived as violating fundamental human rights. For example, Canada does not apply the death penalty in criminal cases. The US does. Canada initially refused extradition of a US citizen accused of the sex-torture slayings of thirteen people in 1985 in California. In 1991, a Canadian jet flew this individual to the US, after the Canadian Supreme Court restricted Canada's death penalty limitation on extradition—by interpreting the Canadian rule as inapplicable to non-Canadian citizens. In 1989, however, the European Court of Human Rights barred Great Britain from extraditing a West German citizen to the US—where he would face the death penalty.

Extradition treaties typically require that extraditable offenses be those that would violate the laws of both parties to the treaty. The conduct charged may violate the laws of both State X and State Y, but Y may prefer to try the accused. When Y's laws have *not* been violated, however, State practice varies on whether Y can refuse extradition and itself try the accused. Professor Prakash Chandra of Roorkee University in India comments on this contrast as follows: "Some jurists—Grotius, Vattel and Kent among them—hold that a state is bound to give up such fugitives but the majority . . . appear to deny such obligation. But mutual interests of states for the maintenance of law and order and the common desire to ensure that serious crimes do not go unpunished require that nations should cooperate with one another in surrendering fugitive criminals to the state in which the crime was committed."[20]

Another reason for refusing extradition is the so-called "political offense" exception to extradition. International treaties typically include some form of what might be characterized as an escape clause, in order to provide the requested State an opportunity to deny extradition. An all-too-familiar reason for the refusal is that the requested State clandestinely supports the acts of the individual charged with a crime in the requesting State. Extradition can thus be denied when the requested State characterizes the crime as a "political offense." In an amendment to the 1986 US/UK extradition treaty, for example, "extradition shall not occur if . . . the request for extradition has in fact been made with a view to try to punish him on account of . . . political opinions. . . ." US case law contains a relevant presumption: that Catholic citizens of Ireland will be mistreated when they are sent to certain British prisons—a basis for denying British requests for extradition when Irish nationals in the US are the object of a British extradition request. As concluded by a federal court in 1993:

> For the following reasons, and good cause appearing therefrom, the court grants Smyth the following presumption:
> (1) Catholic Irish nationals accused or found guilty of offenses against members of the security forces or prison officials are subjected systematically to retaliatory harm, physical intimidation and death in Northern Ireland.
> (2) Members of the security forces in Northern Ireland either participate directly or tacitly endorse these actions.[21]

The application of this political defense exception to extradition produced a useful breakthrough in the stormy political relationship between Taiwan and China. In 1994, China conceded that Taiwan could exclude certain hijackers from repatriation to China if a Taiwanese court finds that the hijacker acted out of political motives. In an fifteen-month period from April 1993 to August 1994, there had been twelve such aircraft hijackings from China by dissidents seeking asylum in Taiwan. China ultimately decided to recognize this defense, thus avoiding the closing off of this avenue of escape. As a result, China now recognizes the right of Taiwanese vessels to patrol the waters in the Taiwan Straits, as well as the jurisdiction of Taiwanese courts over such matters.

What *is* a political offense? This question is subject to much debate. The 1935 Draft Extradition Treaty produced by the Harvard Research in International Law project used this perennial definition: "the term 'political offense' includes treason, sedition and espionage, whether committed by one or more persons; it includes any offense connected with the activities of an organized group directed against the security or governmental system of the requesting State; and it does not exclude other offenses having a political objective." The commentary to this proposed article adds that no "satisfactory and generally acceptable definition of a political offense has been found yet, and such as have been given are of little practical value. . . ."[22] More than fifty years later, there is still no consensus on what constitutes a political crime for the purpose of standardizing this basis for avoiding extradition.[23]

State practice vests the decision about the "political" nature of the defendant's crime with the *requested* State who has custody of the offender. Interpretations always depend on the circumstances of the particular case. Under Article IV of the above US-Japan treaty, for example, extradition "shall not be granted . . . [w]hen the offense for which extradition is requested is a political offense or when it appears that the request for extradition is made with a view to prosecuting, trying or punishing the person sought for a political offense. If any question arises as to the application of this provision, the decision of the requested Party shall prevail." This typical "political offense" treaty exception is left purposefully vague. It therefore allows the requested party to determine unilaterally what constitutes a "political offense."

■ SUMMARY

1. Sovereignty is the right of a nation to govern the affairs of its inhabitants and to be free from external control. Jurisdiction refers to the three-part power of a State to enact laws prescribing certain criminal conduct, to apprehend offenders, and to try them for violations.

2. Five recognized bases for state jurisdiction are: (1) territorial principle, (2) nationality principle, (3) passive personality principle, (4) protective principle, and (5) universality principle.

3. Territorial jurisdiction is based on the location of the defendant's act. The two applications relevant to this course are the "subjective" principle (when the conduct commences within a State) and the "objective" principle (when the conduct commences outside but has the requisite "effects" within the prosecuting State).

4. Nationality jurisdiction is based on the nationality of the *defendant*. The passive personality principle, by comparison, is based on the nationality of the *victim*.

5. The protective principle authorizes a State to exercise jurisdiction over individuals for their criminal acts occurring outside its borders when those acts threaten the security, territorial integrity, or political independence of the state. The protective principle differs from the territorial principle in that the effects of the defendant's conduct do *not* have to be felt within the territory of the nation wishing to exercise its jurisdiction in the case.

6. The universality principle covers certain crimes that are considered to be against the entire community of nations. Any nation where the perpetrator of such a crime is found has the jurisdiction to arrest the criminal (who may be extradited). Such crimes include piracy, hijacking, and genocide.

7. Extradition is the process whereby one nation surrenders someone accused of a crime to another nation. It aids in the prosecution of criminals because one nation cannot enter another's territory to apprehend them. To do so depletes the sovereign equality of all nations.

8. Nations need not extradite an accused in the absence of a treaty. Extradition treaties typically list a mutually acceptable schedule of offenses, subjecting those who commit them to extradition.

9. International Law prohibits one nation from abducting a criminal defendant out of another nation. Authorities are divided as to whether the court of an abducting nation retains the jurisdiction to try kidnapped defendants.

10. Most extradition treaties contain an escape clause allowing the denial of extradition when a listed crime is a "political offense." The requested State has the discretion to deny extradition. There are no clearly adopted standards for the exercise of this discretion.

■ PROBLEMS

Problem 5.1 (*end of § 5.2*): In 1988, two Libyan citizens apparently planned and executed the bombing of Pan Am flight 103 over Lockerbie, Scotland (within the United Kingdom). All 259 people aboard met very violent deaths. Pan Am is a US corporation. There were both UK and US citizens aboard this ill-fated Pan Am flight.

The UK and the US indicted these individuals and demanded that Libya surrender them for trial—backed by a UN Security Council resolution demanding the same. (Libya said that it would cooperate, but only if former US President Ronald Reagan and former UK Prime Minister Margaret Thatcher be tried simultaneously for bombing Tripoli in 1986. That bombing was a reprisal for Libya's earlier bombing of a Berlin discotheque wherein a number of US soldiers died.)

On what bases may the UK and the US properly apply their criminal jurisdiction under the principles of "international criminal jurisdiction"?

Problem 5.2 (*after* State v. Ebrahim *case in §* 5.3): The US Supreme Court and the South African Supreme Court arrived at very different results on the issue of whether the abducting State's courts have the jurisdiction to proceed when the State is involved in the abduction of a defendant from foreign soil.

Assume that a South African citizen is abducted, through arrangements made by US agents, in order to stand trial in the US. South Africa protests, based on an extradition treaty between the two countries. South Africa and the US decide to resolve this matter in the International Court of Justice. The issue for the court is whether the US has the jurisdiction under International Law to proceed with the criminal case against the South African defendant.

Two students (or groups) will argue this matter before the class members, who will serve as the ICJ judges deciding the case based on those presentations.

■ BIBLIOGRAPHY

§ 5.1 Definitional Setting:

L. Henkin, *The Mythology of Sovereignty*, ch. 24, in R. Macdonald (ed.), *Essays in Honour of Wang Tieya* 351 (Dordrecht, Neth.; Boston: Martinus Nijhoff, 1994)

The Jurisdiction of States, ch. XII, in O. Schachter, *International Law in Theory and Practice 250* (Dordrecht, Neth.; Boston: Martinus Nijhoff, 1991

Lapidoth, *Sovereignty in Transition*, 45 *Journal of International Affairs* 2 (1992)

1 *Restatement of the Law: The Foreign Relations Law of the United States* §§ 401–404 (3rd ed. Wash., DC: American Law Institute, 1987)

§ 5.2 Five Jurisdictional Principles:

International Conflict of Laws, ch. 10, in M. Janis, *An Introduction to International Law* 321 (2nd ed. Boston: Little, Brown & Co., 1993)

Jurisdiction over Persons, ch. 9, in G. von Glahn, *Law Among Nations: An Introduction to Public International Law* 203 (6th rev. ed. New York: Macmillan, 1992)

C. Oliver, *The Jurisdiction (Competence) of States*, ch. 15, in M. Bedjaoui (ed.), *International Law: Achievements and Prospects* 307 (Dordrecht, Neth.; Boston: Martinus Nijhoff, 1991)

§ 5.3 Extradition:

M. Bassiouni, 2 *International Criminal Law* (Dobbs Ferry, NY: Transnat'l Pub., 1986)

Garcia-Mora, *Criminal Jurisdiction of a State over Fugitives Brought from a Foreign Country by Force or Fraud: A Comparative Study*, 32 *Indiana Law Journal* 427 (1957)

G. Gilbert, *Aspects of Extradition Law* (Dordrecht, Neth.; Boston: Martinus Nijhoff, 1991)

Gurule, *Terrorism, Territorial Sovereignty, and the Forcible Apprehension of International Criminals Abroad*, 17 *Hastings International & Comparative Law Review* 457 (1994)

■ ENDNOTES

1. B. Jankovic, *Public International Law* 115–117 (Dobbs Ferry, NY: Transnat'l Pub., 1983) (Pravo translation).

2. **Hostage law:** 18 U.S.C. § 1203. **Drug law:** 46 U.S.C. § 1901, et. seq. **Environmental case:** Environmental Defense Fund, Inc. v. Massey, 986 Fed.2d 528 (D.C. Cir. 1993). **Abduction case:** *see* text of US v. Alvarez-Machain case in § 5.3. **Antitrust case:** Hartford Fire Insur. Co. v. Merrett Underwriting Agency Management. Ltd., ___ U.S. ___, 113 S.Ct. 2891, 125 L.Ed.2d 612 (1993). **Refugee case:** *see* text of Sale v. Haitian Council case in § 4.2.

3. I. Cameron, *The Protective Principle of International Criminal Jurisdiction* 11–12 (Aldershot, Eng.: Dartmouth, 1994).

4. *The Research in International Law of the Harvard Law School, Jurisdiction with Respect to Crime*, 29 *Amer. J. Int'l L. Supp.* 443 (1935) [hereinafter *Harvard Research*].

5. Regarding Penati, Case No. 30, reported in 46 Annual Digest and Reports of Public Int'l L. Cases 74.

6. Human rights violations concern all States, however. Chapter 11 will thus explore the applicability of International Law to a State's treatment of its own citizens within its own borders.

7. *Harvard Research*, Art. 5 (cited in note 4 above).

8. The S.S. Lotus (France v. Turkey), P.C.I.J., ser. A, No. 10 (1927) (dissenting opinion of Judge Moore).

9. Beckett, *The Exercise of Criminal Jurisdiction over Foreigners*, 1925 *Brit. Yearbk. Int'l L.* 50.

10. US v. Pizzarusso, 388 Fed.2d 8 (2nd Cir. 1968), *cert. den'd* 392 U.S. 936, 88 S.Ct. 2306, 20 L.Ed.2d 1395 (1968) (emphasis supplied).

11. H. Kindred, et al., *International Law: Chiefly as Interpreted and Applied in Canada* 433 (5th ed. Toronto: Edmond Montgomery 1993).

12. *Symposium on Piracy in Contemporary National and International Law*, 21 *Calif. West. Int'l L.J.* 104 (1990).

13. Attorney-General of Israel v. Adolf Eichmann, Dist. Ct. of Jerusalem, reported in 36 *Int'l L. Rep.* 5, 15 (1968) (decided in 1961).

14. B. Yarnold, *International Fugitives: A New Role for the International Court of Justice* 11 (New York: Praeger, 1991).

15. Valentine v. United States ex rel. Neidecker, 299 U.S. Rep. 5, 9, 57 S.Ct. 100, 102, 81 L.Ed. 5 (1936).

16. Re Arton, 1 Queen's Bench 108, 111 (1896).

17. 31 U.S. Treaties 892 (1979), U.S. Treaties and Other International Agreements Series, No. 9625 (1980).

18. **Exclusion/deportation:** Evans, *Acquisition of Custody over the International Fugitive Offender—Alternatives to Extradition: A Survey of United States Practice*, 40 *Brit. Yearbk. Int'l L.* 77 (1964); **Force/fraud:** Glennon, *State-Sponsored Abduction: A Comment on United States v. Alvarez-Machain*, 86 *Amer. J. Int'l L.* 746 (1992).

19. **Henkin:** *Professor Henkin Replies*, Amer. Soc. Int'l L. Newsletter, p.6 (Jan.–Feb. 1993). **Rogers:** *Response to President's Notes on Alvarez-Machain*, Amer. Soc. Int'l L. Newsletter, p.6 (Jan.–Feb. 1993). **Halberstam:** *In Defense of the Supreme Court Decision in* Alvarez-Machain, 86 *Amer. J. Int'l L.* 736, 737.

20. P. Chandra, *International Law* 80 (New Delhi: Vikas Pub., 1985). *See also The Eisler Extradition Case*, 43

Amer. J. Int'l L. 487 (1949), a British case where the laws of Great Britain differed from those of the US.

21. In the Matter of the Requested Extradition of James Joseph Smyth, 826 Fed.Supp. 316, 323 (No. Dist. Cal. 1993).

22. *Draft Convention on Extradition, Harvard Research,* p.112–13 (cited in note 4 above).

23. C. Van Den Wijngaert, *The Political Offense Exception to Extradition: The Delicate Problem of Balancing the Right of the Individual and the Public International Order* (Deventer, Neth.:Kluwer,1980).

CHAPTER SIX

Range
of Sovereignty

Introduction

Chapter 2 introduced the fundamental concepts of statehood and sovereignty. Chapter 5 added the related theme that International Law limits the ability of one State to act within the territorial boundaries of another State. This chapter augments the sovereignty theme by illustrating the scope of exercisable sovereign powers in, over, and outside of the State.

In the case of land, the range of State sovereignty may be limited because some territories belong to no State, while some are incapable of ownership by any State. In certain instances, a State may control the waters off its coast with the same completeness of control that it exercises over its land boundaries. In other situations, a coastal State may exercise only a limited degree of control, to preserve its national interests. Continuing questions are raised about the

extent to which State sovereignty may be exercised in the airspace above the State, in the airspace over other States or international waters, and in outer space.

This chapter thus addresses one of the most critical national interests: Literally, how far may a State go in exercising its sovereign powers—without violating the rights of other States or the international community?

■ 6.1 CATEGORIES OF TERRITORY

Four types of territory emerged under the modern International Law spawned by State practice after the 1648 Peace of Westphalia discussed in Chapters 1 and 2:

- Territory owned by a sovereign State (sovereign territory);

- Territory not owned by any State due to its special status (trust territory);

- Territory capable of ownership, although not yet under sovereign control (*terra nullius*); and

- Territory that is not capable of ownership by any nation (*res communis*).

Sovereign Territory

One attribute of a State's sovereignty is the right to the exclusive control and ownership of its territory. Under International Law, the State is entitled to exercise sovereignty over the land located within its territorial frontiers. The extent of that sovereignty is typically limited by natural boundary lines. Oceans, mountains, and other natural frontiers usually provide geographical limits to a State's ability to control territory.

Trust Territory

A second category of land is not subject to the sovereignty of any State, due to its special status. These territories were the League of Nations "mandates" and the post–World War II United Nations "Trust Territories" (*see* § 3.3). No State, including the protecting State in whose care the territory has been placed, may lay claim to ownership or sovereign title over such territories. This special status is premised on the fact that these territories did/do not have the ability to control their own area due to a lack of a political infrastructure. The League and the UN thus placed them under the protection of established States, with the goal of ensuring that the populace therein would one day achieve national self-determination.

Terra Nullius

Certain territories were *capable* of being acquired, although no State (in the Westphalian sense of the word State) controlled them. These were referred to in an earlier colonial era as territories that were *terra nullius*. They were conveniently characterized as belonging to no one and thus capable of being legally acquired by the colonial European powers.

International Law, as it was shaped by those European States, provided that they were competent to characterize certain territories as *terra nullius*. In 1885, for example, the States attending the Conference of Berlin declared what was later deemed to be both immoral and illegal—that most of the African continent was *terra nullius* because the inhabitants of that continent were incapable of governing themselves. In a 1971 case before the International Court of Justice, South Africa argued that it was legally seized with the sovereign right to continue its control of Namibia (formerly South West Africa) because it was incapable of governing itself. The Court seized this opportunity to authoritatively declare that those European States "blundered" when they characterized Africa as *terra nullius* in the nineteenth century. As stated by the Court:

> African law illustrated . . . in the monstrous blunder committed by the authors of the Act of Berlin, the results of which have not yet disappeared from the African political scene. It was a monstrous blunder and a flagrant injus-

tice to consider Africa south of the Sahara as *terrae nullius*, to be shared out among the Powers for occupation and colonization, even when in the sixteenth century Victoria had written that Europeans could not obtain sovereignty over the Indies by occupation, for they were not *terrae nullius*.

> By one of fate's ironies, the declaration of the 1885 Berlin Congress which held the dark continent to be *terrae nullius* related to regions which had seen the rise and development of flourishing States and empires. One should be mindful of what Africa was before there fell upon it the two greatest plagues in the recorded history of mankind: the slave-trade, which ravaged Africa for centuries on an unprecedented scale, and colonialism, which exploited humanity and natural wealth to a relentless extreme. Before these terrible plagues overran their continent, the African peoples had founded states and even empires of a high level of civilization. . . .[1]

More than one State may attempt to control the activities of the people who inhabit areas that are supposedly *terra nullius*, thus raising the question of which State may legitimately claim territorial sovereignty because it is not controlled exclusively by either nation. In the famous 1928 *Palmas Island* arbitration, for example, the US and the Netherlands both claimed exclusive rights to an island located in the Philippine archipelago. The resulting arbitral opinion was a typical restatement of the imperialistic nature of the regime of *terra nullius* carried forward into twentieth century legal thought:

> Territorial sovereignty belongs always to one [State] . . . to the exclusion of all others. The fact [is] that the functions of a State can be performed by any State within a given zone . . . in those parts of the globe which, like the high seas or lands without a master, cannot or do not yet form the territory of a State. . . . In the exercise of territorial sovereignty there are necessarily gaps, intermittence in time and discontinuity in space. This phenomenon will be particularly noticeable in the case of colonial territories, partly uninhabited or as yet partly unsubdued.[2]

As a condition for establishing its right to claim sovereignty, a State must normally establish that the particular zone was in fact *terra nullius* and thereby available for occupation and the ensuing sovereign claim to title. The International Court of Justice's 1974 *Western Sahara* case analyzed this prerequisite in a dispute between Spain and Morocco over control of a portion of the Western Sahara desert. The Court confirmed the international expectation that mere occupation is not enough to justify a claim of sovereignty over an occupied area. It also must have been a *terra nullius* if the claimant State seeks exclusive sovereign control. The Court therein traced the history of the term:

> [The] expression "*terra nullius*" was a legal term of art employed in connection with "occupation" as one of the accepted legal methods of acquiring sovereignty over a territory . . . [and it] was a cardinal contention of a valid "occupation" that the territory should be *terra nullius*—a territory belonging to no-one—at the time of the act alleged to constitute the 'occupation'. . . . A determination that the Western Sahara was a '*terra nullius*' at the time of colonization by Spain would be possible only if it were established that at that time the territory belonged to no-one in the sense that it was then open to acquisition through the legal process of 'occupation.'[3]

Res Communis

The fourth general category of territory is territory incapable of ownership or control—typically referred to as *res communis*. It belongs to no one and must remain available for all to use. Under International Law, the entire community of nations must have unfettered access to such areas. These territories cannot be lawfully controlled by any State or group of States without the approval of the community of nations.

The clearest examples of *res communis* are the high seas and outer space, as discussed later in this chapter. It has been argued that Antarctica is a "land" area that is *res communis*. Article 4 of the 1959 Antarctic Treaty provides that States shall not recognize, dispute, or establish territorial claims there; and, no new claims may be asserted by parties to this treaty.

Some commentators have characterized Antarctica as *res communis*, because of the difficulty of occupying it due to harsh weather conditions. Some scholars have analogized Antarctica with the high seas, the deep sea bed, outer space, and even the Arctic, which has no land mass. Professor Emilio Sahurie of Chile disputes the "occupation" paradigm, however. He notes that even the high seas have been appropriated (as discussed later in this chapter). "Occupation" is becoming obsolete, with advances in modern technology. Thus, traditionalist scholars should acknowledge that only the moon and other celestial bodies are actually *res communis*. There is no territory on *earth* that is totally incapable of exploitation—a more accurate measure of sovereignty than "occupation."[4]

■ 6.2 SOVEREIGNTY OVER LAND

A State that has sovereignty over a territory normally possesses the exclusive right to the use of that territory. National sovereignty includes the right of a State to claim ownership or control of a territory, as well as the competence to exclude other nations from using it without consent.

State disputes over land ownership have existed for centuries.[5] Argentina's 1982 invasion of the Falkland Islands, for example, triggered the modern phase of its title dispute with England that began in 1833. Judges, arbitrators, and diplomats often have to rely on documents that are centuries old when resolving such disputes. In a 1953 case in the International Court of Justice, England and France each claimed the exclusive right to two islets within the English Channel. The ICJ analyzed a number of medieval treaties in an attempt to establish which State was entitled to this territory. The complexity of this analysis is illustrated by the Court's examination of the Treaty of Lambeth of 1217, the Treaty of Paris of 1259, the Treaty of Calais of 1360, and the Treaty of Troy of 1420. The ICJ also considered a papal declaration in 1500 that transferred the Channel Islands from the French Diocese of Coutances to the English Diocese of Winchester. Since none of these documents specifically mentioned the disputed islets, the Court granted title to England based on its acts of possession.[6]

The following material analyzes the general modes for establishing sovereign title. The historical approach is presented first, followed by contemporary criticisms of these modes.

Historical Approach

The historical or traditional methods for acquiring sovereignty over territory are as follows: occupation; conquest; cession; prescription; and accretion.

Occupation Exclusive occupation for an extended period of time has been the clearest basis for claiming valid ownership of territory. This mode of acquisition is referred to as an "original" claim to territory, as opposed to a "derived" basis for claiming sovereign title. In the latter instance, title may be expressly derived from a document, such as a treaty in which two or more States formally agree on exclusive or shared sovereignty over a particular territory.

During the previous colonization era, effective occupation required that the State occupy an area that was originally *terra nullius*—owned by no one but capable of ownership. The World Court has repeatedly stated that occupation is "legally an original means of peaceably acquiring sovereignty over territory . . . [however] it was a cardinal condition of a valid 'occupation' that the territory should be terra nullius—a territory belonging to no-one—at the time of the act alleged to constitute the 'occupation.'[7]

This method for establishing sovereign title was typically proven by initial "discovery"—the standard for initiating national claims to territory by occupation. The medieval perspective was that mere discovery, without actual possession, was sufficient to establish valid title. State practice in the later centuries of Europe's colonial expansion retreated from that view. After territory was discovered, there had to be at least some symbolic act signifying possession. State representatives had to plant a flag or create a more substantial tie, such as a settlement in the discovered territory. Thus, discovery coupled with such acts established a colorable title—one that was initiated but not necessarily perfected.

There is no general agreement about the effect of "discovery" on modern claims to State territory. Some countries hold that discovery generates legal rights. Others disagree. The US government, for example, claims that mere discovery yields *no* rights. When the US entered into a treaty with Russian in 1824, establishing the boundaries of Alaska, it declared that "dominion cannot be acquired but by a real occupation and possession, and an intention to establish it [by mere discovery] is by no means sufficient."[8] Under this view, some form of *occupation*

was thus necessary to claim legitimate sovereignty over territory. Thus, planting a US flag on the moon in 1969 did not establish any US sovereign rights or title to that territory.

The nineteenth century European powers, relying on discovery as a basis for initiating claims of exclusive land title, carefully provided for protecting their respective claims to the territories of the African Continent. The 1885 Berlin Conference, whereby well-established African tribes were deemed incapable of self-governance, echoed the international practice that any form of occupation should be immediately communicated to the other colonial powers. Formal notification to all signatories was thus designed to prevent or ameliorate problems of successive discoveries to the same territory.

Discovery was thus supposed to be followed by effective occupation. States generally agreed that they did not have to *physically* occupy the territory in question. They did have to conduct some activity, however, to demonstrate some form of actual governmental administration. The Europe-based Permanent Court of International Justice (PCIJ) confirmed this requirement in the 1933 Danish-Norwegian dispute over Eastern Greenland. The PCIJ declared that sovereign claims to territory often depend "upon continued display of authority, involv[ing] two elements each of which must be shown to exist: the intention and will to act as sovereign, and some actual exercise or display of such authority."[9] In this case, Denmark did not physically occupy the contested portion of Eastern Greenland. It did not establish settlements or send governmental officials to administer the area. Yet Denmark's title was successfully based on "the peaceful and continuous display of authority over the island." There was "effective" occupation during the several centuries that Denmark engaged in diplomatic exchanges with other governments concerning Eastern Greenland. These acts demonstrated an effective degree of occupation to support the Danish claim to sovereignty.

Conquest Another historical method for establishing title to territory is conquest. Nations often acquired territory by forcefully taking it. Israel conquered the West Bank of Jordan during its 1967 war with neighboring Arab nations. Germany annexed Austria in 1939. Japan annexed Korea in 1910. Belgium annexed the African Congo in 1908. The twentieth century development of rules prohibiting the use of force, however, outlawed this basis for *legitimately* claiming title to State territory (*see* § 10.2 on UN Charter Principles).

The 1945 UN Charter prohibits the use of force in international relations. After two World Wars, initiated by the expansionist territorial policies of a number of nations, the parties to the Charter effectively vitiated conquest as a basis for claiming title to property. Although there have been scofflaws, most States have observed this norm most of the time. When Israel successfully concluded several wars allegedly initiated by Arab countries, it claimed added territory by conquest—both as a reprisal and as a defense to further attack. The affected territories included the West Bank of Jordan, the Gaza Strip formerly belonging to Egypt, and the Golan Heights of Syria. The UN responded, in the cases of the West Bank and Gaza (and by implication the Golan Heights), with Resolution 242. This 1967 UN plea called for Israel to withdraw its forces "from territories occupied in the recent conflict." Israel withdrew from some of this territory in the mid-1970s and under the 1993/1994 Israeli peace accords with its neighbors—effectively rendering much of Resolution 242 moot. Whether Israel will give up the strategic Golan Heights occupied area is another question.

Cession The deeding of territory by one nation to another by international agreement is called cession. The grantee nation's right to claim title to the granted land is derived from an agreement of the two affected nations. In the 1928 *Island of Palmas Arbitration*, the Permanent Court of Arbitration (in the Netherlands) addressed the viability of transferring title by cession. The US unsuccessfully claimed sovereignty over an island in the Philippine archipelago based on the 1898 Treaty of Paris between Spain and the US. The Philippines proved that Spain did not have proper title to the Island of Palmas at the time it ceded its treaty rights to the US. Spain could not, therefore, cede more rights to the US than Spain itself possessed. The opinion generally addressed the way in which title by cession is established:

> [Titles] of acquisition of territorial sovereignty in present-day international law are either based on . . . occupation or conquest, or, like cession, presuppose that the ceding [grantor] and the cessionary [grantee] Power, or at least

one of them, have the faculty of effectively disposing of the ceded territory. . . . The title alleged by the United States of America . . . is that of cession, brought about by the Treaty of Paris, which cession transferred all rights of sovereignty which Spain may have possessed in the region indicated in Article III of the said Treaty and therefore also those concerning the Island of Palmas or Miangas.[10]

Cession has caused public resentment and smoldering hostility when it is forced on the granting State because it has lost a war. Germany, for example, was required to cede land to Poland after World War I. The ceded territory included more than one million ethnic Germans. For them, this change meant a drastic role reversal. The Polish government was suddenly confronted with a significant German minority in a region where power relationships had been quite different for more than a century. There may have been a legally sufficient transfer of title to this territory, but the German minority refused to consider themselves subject to Polish rule. Germany, in turn, refused to formally renounce the region, although it had been effectively forced to do so by the Treaty of Versailles. Poland was determined to create a homogenous society in this region, and there were lingering socioeconomic differences between the new "Polish" Germans and the other citizens of this new territory—formerly in Germany and now in Poland.[11]

Prescription State A may derive title to territory previously belonging to State B by occupying State B, or some part of it, without objection from State B. After a period of time (as yet undefined), the occupying State A may claim title to this former B territory by "prescription" if the original occupant (State B) does not effectively protest A's presence.

Prescription is not universally accepted as a method for acquiring sovereign title. Some nineteenth century jurists disputed the notion that prescription is recognized under International Law. They asserted that one State cannot legally claim title by merely usurping another's territory. Under this view, abandonment of disputed territory is an unacceptable legal fiction. The purported acquiescence in the prescriptive rights of the new occupant is merely a face-saving device. Most States do recognize prescription, however, as a valid basis for claiming sovereignty over territory. One practical reason is that ineffective or excessively delayed opposition to hostile occupation conveniently removes defects in sovereign claims to disputed territory.

Prescription is thus the usual mode for resolving long-term border disputes. The International Court of Justice addressed the underlying practicality of prescription when it resolved a sixty-year-old boundary dispute between France (on behalf of Cambodia) and Thailand (formerly Siam). Each claimed sovereign rights to the area surrounding a sacred temple on the Siamese-Cambodian border. In the 1962 *Case Concerning the Temple of Preah Vihear*, Thailand claimed title based on a 1904 treaty. It did not, however, rebuff Cambodia's occupation of the disputed area until it seized the temple, in 1954. The Court thus affirmed the utility of prescription as a device for acquiring title to property as follows:

> it appears to have amounted to a tacit recognition by Siam of the sovereignty of Cambodia . . . over [the Temple] Preah Vihear, through a failure to react in any way, on an occasion that called for a reaction in order to affirm or preserve title in the face of an obvious rival claim. . . . In general, when two countries establish a frontier between them, one of the primary objects is to establish stability and finality. This is impossible if the line so established can, at any moment . . . be called in question . . . indefinitely [because] finality would never be reached. . . .[12]

Accretion The other historical method for establishing sovereign title is accretion. A State's territory may be augmented by new formations of land gradually deposited from bodies of water. Examples include additions to territory by the formation of islands within a State's territorial waters or a natural change in the flow of an international river.

Sudden changes do not affect the boundary between two nations. The change must be gradual and imperceptible. The *Chamizal Arbitration* between the US and Mexico dealt with both types of change. One of the major boundaries between these two nations is the Rio Grande River. Treaties in 1848 and 1853 fixed this international boundary at a point farther north than that which existed at the time of the arbitration in 1911. In the interim period, the gradual southward movement of the Rio Grande exposed a tract of land that was formerly *within* the river. And in 1864, the river suddenly flooded. Both the gradual accretion and the sudden flood altered the course of the Rio Grande, producing a six-hundred-acre tract that became the subject of a territorial land dispute. The Mexican and US arbitrators thus described the impact of accretion, in this instance, as follows:

> [due to] the progressive movement of the river to the south, the American city of El Paso has been extending on the accretions formed by the action of the river on its north bank, while the Mexican city of Juarez to the south has suffered a corresponding loss of territory. . . . The contention on behalf of the United States of Mexico is that this dividing line was fixed, under those treaties, in a permanent and invariable manner, and consequently that the changes which have taken place in the river have not affected the boundary line which was established and marked in 1852.
>
> On behalf of the United States of America it is contended that . . . if the channel of the river changes by gradual accretion, the boundary follows the channel, and that it is only in a case of a sudden change of bed that the river ceases to be the boundary, which then remains in the abandoned bed of the river.[13]

The arbitrators resolved this US/Mexican dispute by dividing the tract in accordance with the usual international rules applicable to accretion. They decided that the US was entitled to sovereignty over that portion of the Chamizal Tract resulting from the *gradual* southward accretion of land prior to the 1864 flood. Mexico was entitled to the remaining acres exposed by the flood. In 1967, the US put an end to the matter by formally transferring this portion of the Chamizal Tract to Mexico.

New Modes of Territorial Acquisition

Title may now be acquired in ways other than those described above and developed in previous centuries. These newer methods include renunciation, joint decision, and adjudication.

Renunciation By renunciation, a nation relinquishes title to its territory. There is no transfer of title, unlike the "treaty cession" that formally transfers or cedes territorial sovereignty to a grantee nation. In 1947, Italy renounced title (obtained by conquest) to its territories in northern Africa. These

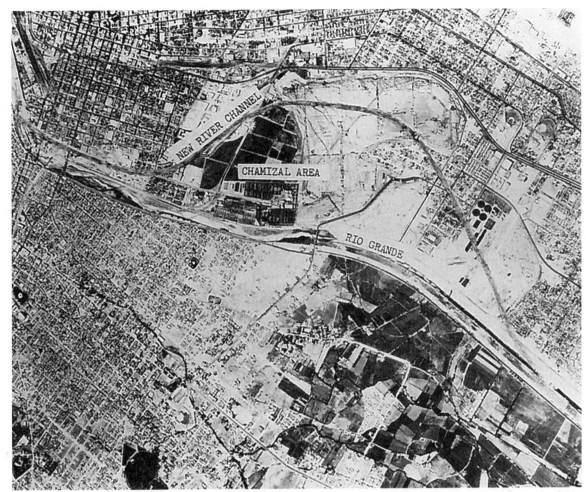

This photograph illustrates the disputed Chamizal Tract area adjacent to the Rio Grande River. The United States transfer of the remaining acres (exposed by the flood) to Mexico resolved this international dispute.

were involuntary renunciations orchestrated by the victorious Allied powers after Italy lost the war. A State may *voluntarily* relinquish its territorial sovereignty as well. This method of transferring sovereignty is sometimes referred to as "acquiescence," "estoppel," and even "prescription."

The distinction between renunciation and prescription is sometimes rather blurred. One difference is the need for occupation in order to establish prescription. None of these terms has been clearly defined or distinguished in International Law. Although there is a lack of precision in their application, they share a common denominator. A State may not assert a territorial claim in a manner that is inconsistent with its conduct.

In the 1968 *Rann of Kutch* arbitration, for example, Pakistan implicitly relinquished its title to an area on its common border with India. For over one hundred years, Pakistan's predecessor did not react to obvious assertions of sovereignty (by England and then India) in the disputed border area. The arbitrators thus determined that Pakistan had acquiesced in India's exercise of sovereignty over the disputed area. Pakistan could not reclaim this land after another State had peacefully occupied it for so long a period of time.[14]

Joint Decision A joint decision by the victors of war is a twentieth century device for transferring sovereignty over State territory. After each world war, victorious States claimed and exercised a right to dispose of certain property that the defeated States had obtained by forceful conquest.

After World War I, certain victors decided to jointly dispose of the territory of the losers. The Permanent Court of International Justice recognized this method for transferring sovereign territory in 1923. After World War II, the victorious nations felt compelled to impose security measures on the losing nations. One such measure was the joint decision of the Allies to reduce certain German frontiers. As a result, Germany was forced to yield its sovereignty over that territory.[15]

Adjudication Another method for legitimizing the transfer of sovereignty is adjudication. Title disputes to State territory are often examined by judges and arbitrators. Although many of them have classified adjudication as an independent mode for "acquiring" title to State territory, this is a misnomer. International tribunals have no more power than that granted to them by the sovereign States that create them. Adjudication is the result of an international agreement that authorizes a mutually acceptable tribunal to resolve a dispute between the participating States.

Title by adjudication is similar to a treaty cession from a grantor to a grantee State. In both instances, the participating States enter into an agreement about how they will fix a boundary line. By adjudication, the parties agree to establish sovereign rights after the tribunal examines the facts and renders its decision.

Criticisms of the Historical Approach

Contemporary scholars have criticized the historical modes for acquiring sovereignty over state territory. According to Professor Ian Brownlie of Oxford University, many "of the standard textbooks, and particularly those in English, classify the modes of acquisition in a stereotyped way which reflects the preoccupation of writers in the period before the First World War."[16] Some significant claims also arose (or resurfaced) after World War II. Professor Brownlie depicts some of the reasons why such claims will continue to adversely affect international relations in the following way: "The pressures of national sentiment, new forms of exploitation of barren and inaccessible areas, the strategic significance of barren and inaccessible areas previously neglected, and the pressure of population on resources, give good cause for a belief that territorial disputes will increase in significance. This is especially so in Africa and Asia, where the removal of foreign political domination has left the successor states with a long agenda of unsettled [sovereignty] problems, legal and political."[17]

Other criticisms of the historical modes of acquiring title are found in the so-called "Third World" attitudes about the development of International Law in the ethnocentric nations of the West. A number of States thus oppose the application of the long-established devices for validating sovereign title. These methods were developed long before many of the Third World nations became States. They seek a more significant role in the evolution of norms for determining contemporary territorial disputes. The historical bases for validating title plainly conflict with the contemporary perspectives of a growing number of such States. They oppose the conquest and cession bases for acquiring sovereign title. The legitimacy of conquest and treaties of cession, as viable methods for legally establishing sovereignty over territory, have been vitiated in this century by the development of League of Nations and UN norms prohibiting the use of force in international relations. Professor D.W. Greig of the Australian National University comments on this conflict:

> Whereas under *traditional* international law a cession [or treaty transferring sovereignty] imposed by force would be valid, the development of the twentieth century concept of the illegality of aggressive war would seem to cast doubts on the possibility that such a rule has survived. Indeed, prior to the Covenant of the League of Nations and to the Kellogg-Briand Pact [Renunciation of War] of 1928, a treaty of cession was not even necessary to validate a seizure of territory by force, for international law recognized annexation (or subjugation, or conquest, as it is variously termed) as a means of acquiring territory.[18]

Eastern scholars also criticize the traditional modes of acquiring sovereignty over territory for a related reason. The thrust of their objection is that Western countries have perpetuated an ethnocentric view of what is acceptable State practice. They hold Western writers and jurists responsible for perpetuating the historical view that certain territories did not contain "civilized" people. Western colonial powers characterized the inhabitants of Asia, Africa, and Latin America (before the mid-twentieth century) as inferior and uncivilized—thus generating ethnocentric norms for acquiring title to territory. Any occupation based on the concept of *terra nullius* is completely rejected by most non-European States, especially new States once subjected to the expansionist colonialism of the more developed States. Thus, there is no moral or ethical basis in modern International Law for control based on the convenient analysis of *terra nullius*. This device was used by the colonizing powers only to rationalize what the lesser developed States now characterize as immoral or criminal acts by their former oppressors.

The following excerpt from the Chinese periodical *Studies in International Problems* provides the Chinese perspective on the Western development of the modes for acquiring State territory. It addresses why the historical modes are unacceptable by Chinese standards. A key theme in this excerpt is the criticism of the Western concepts of "original" and "derivative" acquisition of sovereignty. Original acquisition as a basis for title to territory conveniently surfaced when the particular territory did not have a sufficiently powerful power controlling it. Derivative acquisition also perpetuated Western claims over territory even when it was previously owned by another social group of people or a "State," as analyzed immediately below:

A CRITICISM OF BOURGEOIS INTERNATIONAL LAW ON THE QUESTION OF STATE TERRITORY

Hsin Wu
KCWTYC (newspaper) No. 7:44–51 (1960)
Reprinted and translated in J. Cohen & H. Chiu
Vol. 1 *People's China and International Law* 323
Princeton University Press (1974)*

Bourgeois international law sums up the various methods by which imperialist countries have historically seized territory by classifying them. Methods of acquiring territory are divided into "*original acquisition*" and "*derivative acquisition*" according to the different owners of the annexed territory.

Methods of acquiring territory are divided into "*acquisition by means of treaty*" or "*acquisition not by means of treaty*" according to the different methods adopted at the time of annexation. All these methods of acquiring territories are given legal status, and beautiful legal terms are used to conceal the reactionary essence of these actions. Let us now strip off the legal covers to see what is meant by . . . [these Western terms].

"*Original Acquisition:*" According to the explanation of bourgeois international law, acquisition of land "*without an owner*" [terra nullius] is "original acquisition." What is land "without an owner"? Colonialists do not conceal the fact that this is not land which is entirely uninhabited, but merely land inhabited by what they do not regard as a "civilized people." They regard the vast lands in Asia, Africa, and Latin America as lands "without an owner," despite the fact that millions of owners live there and various nations exist there. They regard those people and nations as "barbarous" and "backward" and believe that they cannot be the owners of those lands. Thus, the lands should be occupied by "civilized" people and the acquisition of this territory by "civilized" countries is proper; it is a legitimate method of "original acquisition." In the words of the American scholar Hyde: "If the inhabitants of the territory concerned are an uncivilized or extremely backward people, deemed to be incapable of possessing a right of sovereignty, the conqueror may, in fact, choose to ignore their title, and proceed to occupy the land as though it were vacant." This statement shows how this authoritative American bourgeois scholar unabashedly defends aggressors. His reactionary theory is extremely absurd.

The inhabitants of so-called lands "without an owner" are by no means the kind of people whom colonialists and bourgeois scholars have described as barbarous, ignorant, willing to be slaves, and unable to exercise sovereignty. These descriptions are a great insult and defamation to these inhabitants. The true situation is that, whether it was in Asia, Africa, or Latin America, the indigenous inhabitants all had their own excellent cultures. Bourgeois

---

*Reprinted with permission of Princeton University Press. Footnotes omitted. Emphasis has been supplied by the author in certain passages.

scholars may consider Africa, for example, as the most barbarous land. But, everyone knows that the African people once had excellent civilizations in the Nile River region, the Congo River region and in Carthage. Long before their contact with Europeans, the Africans were experts in various handicraft skills and technology and were able to refine iron and other mineral ores. They could make various instruments of production, weapons, and furniture. In certain areas of Africa, national art already had reached a comparatively high standard. African folk literature was rich, colorful, and full of attraction. The allegation that they were willing to become slaves and were unable to exercise sovereignty is a lie inconsistent with history. . . . It was not that they were unable to exercise sovereignty but rather that they were prevented from exercising their sovereignty by colonialists' use of massacre and suppression.

It should be pointed out that there has been a change in the view of bourgeois international law concerning the methods of "original acquisition." At first, bourgeois scholars argued that "occupation" was one method of "original acquisition," that is, a state which "first discovered a land 'without an owner'" should be the owner of that piece of land. It was through this method of acquisition that Portugal and Spain, two of the earliest colonial powers, occupied a large number of colonies. Later, bourgeois scholars proposed the view of "effective occupation." . . . The theory of "occupation" did not meet the desire of the powerful imperialist countries that subsequently emerged, while "effective occupation" provides them with a legal basis for redistribution of the spoils.

"Derivative Acquisition:" Bourgeois international law holds that the difference between "derivative acquisition" and "original acquisition" is that the former does not refer to the method of acquiring territory without an owner but refers to the method of acquiring territory originally belonging to another state. The imperialist powers' plundering of foreign territory naturally would not be limited to [only] lands "without an owner." After lands "without an owner" were carved up, they naturally would plunder lands "with an owner." Lenin said: "When the whole world had been divided up, there was inevitably ushered in an era of monopoly ownership of colonies, and, consequently, of particularly intense struggle for the division and redivision of the world." There is no limitation on imperialism's ambition with respect to plundering territory.

. . .

Sometimes, imperialism nakedly uses the method of aggressive war forcibly to seize another state's territory; sometimes it uses camouflaged measures or various pretexts to force another state in fact to place its territory under imperialism's occupation. In order to prove the legality of the above-stated methods of seizing territory, bourgeois international law further classifies "derivative acquisition" into acquisition by means of treaty and acquisition not by means of treaty.

What are the methods of "derivative acquisition" *by means of treaty?* Bourgeois international law considers cession one of these methods. Every country has the right to cede its territory, and it has the right to acquire ceded territory. . . . In a discussion on the form of cession [by treaty], "Oppenheim's International Law" described the annexation of Korea in 1910 by Japanese imperialism and the annexation of the Congo in 1908 by Belgian colonialists as a method of acquiring ceded territory through *peaceable* negotiation. But everyone knows that Korea was forcibly occupied by Japanese bandits and the Congo was a victim of the colonial system. From these instances, we may clearly discern that countries which ceded their territories were all under compulsion and that they were either weak, small, or defeated countries. Countries which acquired ceded territories were all imperialist countries engaging in territorial expansion. Bourgeois international law writings have never been able to cite a single case in which an imperialist power ceded its territory to a weak or small country. Therefore, it can be said that cession of territory is a method of plundering the territories of weak and small or defeated countries used by imperialist countries through the use of war and threat of force. . . . Most outspoken on this point is the American scholar Hyde, who writes in his book "International Law, Chiefly as Interpreted and Applied by the United States": "The validity of a transfer of rights of sovereignty as set forth in a treaty of cession does not appear to be affected by the motives which have impelled the grantor to surrender them." Obviously, according to such an interpretation, it was legitimate for Japan to force the Manchu government of China to cede Taiwan and Penghu through the unequal Treaty of Shimonoseki of 1895, after the Sino-Japanese War. This is tantamount to saying that if a robber steals property by brandishing a dagger before an owner and by threatening his life forces him to put his fingerprint on a document indicating his consent, then the act of robbery becomes legal. Is that not absurd? No wonder bourgeois international law has sometimes been described as the law of bandits. There is no exaggeration in such a description.

Besides cession, bourgeois international law also considers *lease* as a method of "derivative acquisition" of territory by means of treaty. . . . In 1898 Germany *leased* Kiaochow Bay, Britain *leased* Wei-hai-wei, and France *leased* Kuang-chou Wan from China. These leases were acquired by concluding unequal treaties. These unequal treaties absolutely were not concluded through "peaceable negotiations" as described by bourgeois international law. As a matter of fact, lease of the above-mentioned Kiaochow Bay and other places was executed under threat of force. In November 1897 Germany sent four men-of-war to Kiaochow Bay to occupy Tsingtao on the ground that its missionaries had been killed. It was under these circumstances of armed occupation that the "Treaty of the Lease of Kiaochow" was concluded. The leases of Wei-hai-wei and Kowloon were also obtained under similar conditions. . . .

Bourgeois international law considers "conquest" a method of *acquiring territory where no treaty exists.* So-called conquest means that a state uses its armed forces for long-term occupation of the territory or a part of the territory of another state. Undoubtedly, this is a savage and aggressive act. Bourgeois international law, however, considers such a method of acquiring territory lawful, even though it does not go through the process of concluding a treaty. In analyzing the causes of war, "Oppenheim's International Law" states: "If . . . territory cannot be acquired by peaceable means, acquisition by conquest alone remains if International Law fails to provide means of peaceful change in accordance with justice." Charles Rousseau, Professor of International Law at the University of Paris, in his book "Principles Generaux du Droit International Public," held that conquest is a means of acquiring sovereignty over a certain territory. The British jurist Schwarzenberger held: "In the international society law is subordinate to the rule of force. If the whole State machinery [of the defeated State] has collapsed, conquest would permit acquisition of title to the territory of this State." According to these theories, colonial wars or other aggressive wars started by imperialist countries in order to annex territories of other countries are lawful. Thus, the Japanese seizure of China's three northeastern provinces, Italy's annexation of Ethiopia, and Fascist Germany's occupation of Poland, Czechoslovakia, and so forth were all lawful.

"Prescription" is also considered a method of "derivative acquisition" of territory not by means of treaty. According to the explanation of bourgeois international law, "prescription" means the acquisition by a state of title to a territory through prolonged occupation. Obviously, this recognizes imperialism's acquisition of legal title to a territory through prolonged occupation by force. "Oppenheim's International Law" held that "a State is considered to be the lawful owner even of those parts of its territory of which originally it took possession wrongfully and unlawfully, provided that the possessor has been in undisturbed possession for such a length of time as is necessary to create the general conviction that the present condition of things is in conformity with international order." This means that any country, regardless of its motive or the means it used—whether by way of annexation or aggression—as long as it has the power to be in prolonged occupation by force of the territory of another state, may consider its aggressive act as "lawful." History shows that colonialists in fact frequently used the concept of "prescription" to plunder the territory of other countries. Even recently, in certain countries, certain persons in power and bourgeois scholars have attempted to resort to the concept of "prescription" as a legal basis for putting certain territory of China's Tibet under the jurisdiction of another country.

In view of the foregoing, the "derivative acquisition" either by means of treaty or not by means of treaty mentioned by bourgeois international law is a general term which describes the various methods used by imperialist countries to plunder the territory of colonized countries and weak and small countries.

Modern Territorial Disputes

A number of pending territorial disputes have not been fully resolved. The less sensitive disputes are often submitted to the International Court of Justice. The disputes in Exhibit 6.1 are those that continue to threaten international stability. Certain entries suggest that the end of the Cold War has not diminished some hostilities that have taken many lives and interrupted the orderly progression toward a "new world order."

EXHIBIT 6.1 Selected Contemporary Territorial Disputes

Bosnia	*Area within former Yugoslavia under siege*
	1918 Yugoslav peoples create joint State
	1991 Croatia and Slovenia secede and arguably prematurely recognized by US, EC nations Macedonia secedes/Yugoslavia begins to breakdown/first of many ceasefire agreements/Bosnian Serbs battle Croats and Muslims
	1993 Serb Serajevo attack kills 66 civilians
	1994 UN peacekeepers continue to be killed Serbs napalm Bosnian village
Cordillera del Condor	*Fifty-mile stretch between Ecuador and Peru*
	1941 war over entire 1,000-mile common border/Ecuador later declares agreement void
	1981 bloody clashes rekindle hostilities
	1994 tension reignites military confrontation
Cyprus	*Greek-Turkish dispute split island in 1974*
	1878 treaty—under British administration
	1914 British annexation/1925 "Royal Colony"
	1960 Greece gives Cyprus independence and Cyprus becomes independent UN member
	1974 Turkish invasion of northern Cyprus
	1975 Turkey claims Cyprus is "self-governing" in northeast portion of Cyprus
	1983 Turkey proclaims Republic of North Cyprus/not recognized by UN or any other State
	1991 US President attempts to resolve dispute
Falkland Islands	*1982 war between Argentina and UK over control of archipelago near Argentine coast*
	1823 US announces Monroe Doctrine designed to keep foreign powers out of Latin America
	1833 UK occupies without protest by US Argentina claims as natural extension
	1965 Argentina, backed by many neighbors/UNGA, claims sovereignty in territorial waters
	1982 UNSC demands return to UK sovereignty; UK reverses prior decision and grants *full* UK citizenship to islanders; UK invades to restore its sovereign claim
	1984 Sovereignty talks result in deadlock
	1987 UK unilateral 150-mile fishing zone set
	1990 Restoration of diplomatic ties and lifting of UK fishing zone suspends resolution
Golan Heights	*Israeli occupied Syrian territory since 1967*
	1981 Israeli law claims sovereignty over Golan Heights/UNSC resolves that Israeli law "without international legal effect"

EXHIBIT 6.1   *(continued)*

Jerusalem	*Religious seat—Muslims, Jews and Catholics*

1917–1948 British occupation and League of Nations "Mandated" territory
1949 UN attempts place under permanent administration/Israel and Jordan only give provisional acceptance
1950 Israel proclaims as capitol of Israel
1967 Israel occupies whole city/UN objects
1993 Jerusalem *not* part of Arab/Israel accords
1994 Palestinian government declares itself in charge of all Islamic sites in Jerusalem/Jordan's King Hussein responds that Jordan will not yield its claim to that role/PLO wants city for Palestinian capital

Kurile Islands	*Archipelago between Hokkaido Island/Siberia*

1855 treaty ceded four islands to Japan
1945 Yalta agreement conceded to USSR
1986 Japanese renewed claim/proposed treaty
1991 Soviet official backs Japan's claim

Kuwait	*Iraq considers Kuwait its "19th province"*

1963 treaty resolution of boundary dispute
1990 Iraq invades Kuwait, triggering Persian Gulf War/UNSC resolves that Iraq must "restore territorial integrity of Kuwait"/Unofficial draft of this resolution calls on Iraq and Kuwait to accept unsettled boundary
1993 UN border commission completes boundaries

Nagorno-Karabakh (NK)	*Armenian enclave on border of Azerbaijan*

1923 became part of Armenia
1988 fighting begins over NK sovereignty
1992 Azerbaijan requests UN force to prevent flow of arms/troops into disputed region

Sevastopol	*1993 Russia decrees this city in Ukraine a "Russian" city*

Heightens tension over major Black Sea port/Ukraine claims ownership of former Soviet nuclear missiles
1954 Crimean peninsula between Ukraine/Russia transferred from Russia to Ukraine, marking 300th anniversary of their historical union
1991 Soviet Union collapses

EXHIBIT 6.1 *(continued)*

Spratly Islands   *Chain of 100 tiny atolls in South China Sea*

(subject to conflicting claims by China, the Philippines, Vietnam, Taiwan, Malaysia, and Brunei)

1988 Chinese capture six islands from Vietnamese in naval battle claiming numerous lives

1995 China establishes guard post on Mischief Reef in February/Filipino fisherman taken captive/the Philippines dispatches patrol boats and fighter planes (weakest military force of any State claiming area)

Taiwan   *China considers Taiwan China's 23rd province*

1867 US attempted to annex

1874 Japan attempted to annex

1885 France attempted to annex

1887 China declared a Chinese province

1897–1945 occupied by Japan

1949 Nationalists lose civil war to Communists/flee to Taiwan to establish government

1945–1971 Taiwan holds the UN "China" seat

1971–present: Mainland China occupies UN seat

1994 Taiwan artillery shells hit mainland/Chinese villagers hurt/Taiwan to pay

---

■ 6.3 SEA ZONES

Introduction

The widely heralded norm of "freedom of the seas" historically served the interests of the more powerful nations. Freedom of the seas thus authorized vessels from those nations to freely fish and navigate without limitation. Coastal States were thus precluded from interfering with a foreign vessel's activities and, effectively, the sovereignty of the nation whose flag it sailed under. With the dawn of the new system of State sovereignty heralded by the 1648 Peace of Westphalia (*see* § 1.3), European powers assumed that the ocean's resources were unlimited and that coastal States need not be concerned about events talking place in an area characterized as *res communis*—that is, open to all comers. As succinctly described by Professor Donat Pharand of the University of Ottawa:

> Beginning in the seventeenth century, the Law of the Sea was developed and maintained to accommodate the interests of the major maritime powers. They developed a legal regime which protected their colonial, commercial and military interests. That legal regime was characterized by two basic principles: the freedom of the seas and the sovereignty of the flag State. The expression "freedom of the seas" designated mainly two types of freedom, fishing and navigation. It was thought that biological resources of the sea were inexhaustible and that any State, having the necessary fishing capability, could simply go out and help itself without any restriction whatever. As for the sovereignty of the flag State, it meant that the country under whose flag the ship was sailing had exclusive jurisdiction over all activities aboard the ship. Certainly this was the case when the ship was on the high seas, that is beyond the traditional three-mile territorial sea. Aside from two exceptions covering slave trade and piracy, this principle of sovereignty of the flag State remained untouched. In a nutshell this represented the state of the law of the sea until after World War II.[19]

The end of World War II signaled many beginnings. One of these was the coastal State tendency to extend sovereignty into marine areas well beyond the traditional three-mile limit of the "Territorial" Sea. This narrow belt of ocean water remains sufficiently close to the State's land mass to be characterized—for jurisdictional purposes—as if it were land.

This expansion blurred the former distinction between the Territorial Sea and the High Sea. The Territorial Sea was previously thought to be the only marine area subject to the complete and exclusive control of any coastal State or international organization. The rest of the ocean was open to all under the norm known as "freedom of the seas." Other zones have been established that, while not yielding full sovereignty to the nearby coastal State, nevertheless protect certain treaty-based interests of the coastal State. All States, for example, have an important interest in guarding against illegal drug trafficking, immigration, and pollution—which know no boundaries. And a number of lesser developed States watched in dismay for some decades after the war, while the more developed States entered their general maritime regions to fish and exploit the nearby oceans, with technology that was unavailable to the coastal State.

As more nations began to extract resources from the sea, pressure mounted to limit the historical State expectation of freedom of the seas. The colonial period was in decline (see § 2.2). Thus, the new resource-rich but technology-poor coastal States expressed the view that freedom of the seas served the altered but ever-present colonial purposes of the larger and more economically powerful nations. This regime did not incorporate the interests of the new members of the international community—especially those coastal nations seeking to facilitate a more equitable distribution of the ocean's resources.

The UN sponsored various treaties that began to acknowledge limits on freedom of the seas, as well as to incorporate new coastal State perspectives regarding sea zones unheard of prior to World War II. Various UN-sponsored treaties began to codify such developments. The most important and comprehensive treaty entered into force in 1994.

1982 Law of the Sea Treaty

In November 1994, the most ambitious and comprehensive treaty of all times entered into force—the 1982 UN Convention on the Law of the Sea (also referred to as Law of the Sea Treaty, or LOST).[20] One-hundred seventeen nations originally "signed" this treaty in 1982, which is the first step toward multilateral codification of International Law. As discussed in Chapter 8, the next step in the usual treaty process is "ratification" by the individual States that previously signed it. After an agreed-on number of States ratify a treaty, then it enters into force. One of the final draft's 1982 provisions was that it would enter into force, thus codifying the International Law of maritime jurisdiction, one year after the sixtieth State (Guyana) so ratified the treaty (in 1993).

The final draft of the LOST was the result of the third multilateral treaty negotiation of the law of the sea undertaken in the twentieth century, consisting of numerous meetings of the national delegates from 1974 to 1982. The LOST has thus become *the* working document for all academics, practitioners, and decision-makers involved with the various sea regimes. This portion of the chapter addresses a comparatively new legal regime governing activities in the various sea zones. The LOST is the beacon for resolving virtually any issue involving exercises of State sovereignty in, on, or under the sea. Much of the LOST codifies prior State practice, while a number of provisions provided for progressive development that was finally acceptable to most nations of the world (fourteen years after the initial signing).

The major fishing and mining nations did not sign this treaty in 1982—making its acronym "LOST" annoyingly accurate. Nations including the US and Japan ultimately secured modifications, particularly of the deep seabed mining provisions, making it an agreement arrived at as a result of consensus rather than exhaustion. The executive branch of the US government ultimately signed the LOST in July 1994, prior to its submission to the US Senate for consent—which is required for treaty ratification (a process described in § 8.2). Other industrialized States that had similarly objected to the LOST are expected to follow the US lead.

This section of the book now explores the expanded range of State sovereignty in the following ocean-water areas, including the new sea zones expanding coastal State control over the oceans: (1) Internal Waters; (2) Territorial Sea; (3) High Seas; (4) Contiguous Zone; (5) Exclusive Economic Zone; (6) the Continental Shelf; and (7) the Deep Seabed.

Exhibit 6.2 depicts these zones at the outset, to illustrate the first major theme of this section: The coastal State may undertake certain activities

EXHIBIT 6.2 Sea Zones

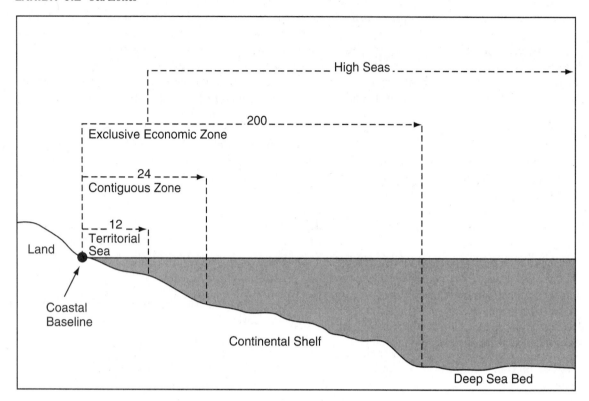

in ocean waters, including portions of the High Seas, to the exclusion of other States. This means that the exercise of State sovereignty is not limited to the land territory of the State. The degree to which the State may act in or control these various zones is limited, however. The further away from the coast that it desires to so act, the more likely that sovereign activity will affect the distinct rights of other States in these ocean waters—as governed by this new constitution of the oceans.

(1) Internal Waters

Article 8.1 of the LOST defines internal waters as the "waters on the landward side of the baseline of the territorial sea." As depicted in Exhibit 6.2, the coastal baseline is the point where the sea intersects with the coast. The baseline is the geographical yardstick for distinguishing internal water from the various sea zones that are the subject of this chapter.

As with its land and any inland fresh water areas, a State has the sovereign right to control its bays, rivers, and other internal waters that contain ocean waters. Like repelling foreign invaders from its soil, a State must monitor the military and commercial

activities of foreign (and local) vessels within its internal waters.

Two situations complicate the application of the exclusive jurisdiction of the coastal State over its internal waters. One is the problem of jurisdiction over events occurring on a foreign vessel while in port. The other situation involves conflicting rights in large coastal bays containing greater portions of open seas than the normal bay.

Ports For the purpose of separating a State's internal waters from the territorial waters off its coast, a port extends to the outermost permanent harbor facility forming an integral part of that harbor's system. A long entryway consisting of natural twists and turns is a part of the port. An artificial buoy area constructed outside of the mouth of that entryway, however, is not a part of the port.

Under International Law, each State has the absolute right to control the internal waters contained within its ports. State practice incorporates certain limitations on this right. When a foreign *warship* enters internal waters with permission, the port authorities do not board it, for mutual security reasons. Neither State wants to subject its military secrets to unnecessary scrutiny when its naval vessels enter a foreign port. Another limitation applies to *merchant* or other private vessels. They have the implied right to enter the internal waters of another State without express permission. They are routinely boarded for customs or immigration purposes, however.

The LOST does not cover the important jurisdictional problem associated with a member of a foreign crew who commits a crime while *in port* (as opposed to one committed on a ship passing through the Territorial Sea). When the vessel's sailors go ashore, they of course subject themselves to the laws or jurisdiction of the coastal State. When a crime is committed *on board* a foreign vessel in port, however, *either* the laws of the coastal or port State *or* the laws of the State to which the vessel is registered (the "flag State") might be applied.

The ancient rule was that any ship entering another nation's port became subject to the latter's complete control. Modern customary and treaty practice has altered that rule. In the case of crimes that do not affect the port's tranquility, the flag State—rather than the port State where the incident occurred—usually exercises primary jurisdiction to prosecute the criminal. That concession facilitates the smooth progress of international commerce and avoids undue interference in the ship's movements by the coastal State. But when the crime causes a *significant* intrusion on the port's tranquility, the perpetrator becomes subject to prosecution by the port State.

Not all States automatically cede jurisdiction over on-board crimes to the flag State. In some regions, all crimes occurring within the internal or territorial waters trigger the coastal nation's competence to prosecute foreign sailors (absent the usual treaty provision regarding *military* personnel). Under customary practice, the flag State is competent to act if the port State chooses not to prosecute. For example, one court in Argentina had to determine the question of Argentina's jurisdiction over a theft that occurred aboard an Argentine merchant vessel at anchor in the port of Rio de Janeiro, Brazil. The ship left the Brazilian port and returned to Argentina with the thief still aboard. The thief was prosecuted in the Argentine court system. His lawyer argued that Argentina had no jurisdiction because the crime occurred in Brazil. The court disagreed generally as follows:

> According to the rules of public international law . . . offences committed on board a private ship fall within the jurisdiction of the courts of the flag State if the ship is on the high seas, and fall within the jurisdiction of a foreign State only in the event that such offences have been committed while the ship is in the [internal or] territorial waters of that other State. . . . [The court then decided that Argentina nevertheless had jurisdiction because this] principle is not an absolute rule . . . for if the foreign State does not choose to exercise its right to institute proceedings because it considers that the act has not affected the community at large or the peace of the port (as maintained in French and Italian doctrine), the flag [State] may then assert full authority over the ship for the purpose of restoring order and discipline on board or protecting the rights of the passengers. . . .[21]

The rights of the port and flag States are not always left to judicial interpretation under customary International Law. The respective jurisdictional rights are often agreed to by treaty. Such treaties typically cede *primary* jurisdiction to the flag State. They frequently contain a "port tranquility" exception permitting the port State to prosecute foreign sailors in specified situations.

What type of criminal conduct activates the so-called "port tranquility" exception to the primary jurisdiction of the flag State? The US Supreme Court addressed this question in the following case—relied on by courts throughout the US on many subsequent occasions:

MALI v. KEEPER OF THE COMMON JAIL OF HUDSON COUNTY

Supreme Court of the United States, 1887
120 U.S. 1, 7 S.Ct. 385, 30 L.Ed. 565

[*Author's Note: Wildenhus and Fijens were Belgian sailors aboard a Belgian steamship anchored in the port of Jersey City, New Jersey. In a fight below decks, Wildenhus stabbed and killed Fijens. The Jersey City police learned about this incident and arrested Wildenhus. Several Belgian crew members witnessed this incident. They too were placed in the port jail as witnesses for the proceedings against Wildenhus.*

The treaty between Belgium and the US ceded "primary" jurisdiction over shipboard crimes to the respective flag States to which the vessels were registered. A Belgian consular official in New Jersey thus relied on this treaty to seek the release of the Belgian sailors to his custody. This foreign official was acting on behalf of Belgium, referring to himself as the "petitioner." The issue was whether the port tranquility doctrine should be applied to deprive the flag State (Belgium) of its primary jurisdiction under the treaty.

The first portion of the reported case is a factual account provided by the lawyers representing the US (on behalf of the prosecution by the state of New Jersey). In the latter portion of this opinion, the Chief Justice then delivered the Supreme Court's decision—agreeing with the lower courts that the treaty permitted New Jersey to prosecute the Belgian sailor under the circumstances. This particular homicide thus provided cause for invoking the port tranquility exception to Belgian jurisdiction over events occurring aboard its vessel.]

[*Opinion.*] This appeal brought up an application made to the Circuit Court of the United States for the District of New Jersey, by Charles Mali, the "Consul of His Majesty the King of the Belgians, for the States of New York and New Jersey, in the United States," for himself as such consul, "and in behalf of one Joseph Wildenhus, one Gionviennie Gobnbosich, and one John J. Ostenmeyer," for the release, upon a writ of habeas corpus, of Wildenhus, Gobnbosich, and Ostenmeyer from the custody of the keeper of the common jail of Hudson County, New Jersey, and their delivery to the consul, "to be dealt with according to the law of Belgium." The facts on which the application rested were thus stated in the petition [requested by Belgium]:

Second. That on or about the sixth day of October, 1886, on board the Belgian steamship Noordland, there occurred an affray between the said Joseph Wildenhus and one Fijens, wherein and whereby it is charged that the said Wildenhus stabbed with a knife and inflicted upon the said Fijens a mortal wound, of which he afterwards died.

. . .

Fifth. That at the time said affray occurred the said steamship Noordland was lying moored at the dock of the port of Jersey City, in said state of New Jersey.

. . .

Seventh. That said affray occurred in the presence of several witnesses all of whom were and still are of the crew of the said vessel, and that no other person or persons except those of the crew of said vessel were present or near by.

. . .

Article XI of a Convention between the United States and Belgium "concerning the rights, privileges, and immunities of consular officers" . . . is as follows:

The respective consuls-general, consuls, vice-consuls, and consular agents shall have exclusive charge of the internal order of the merchant vessels of their nation, and shall alone take cognizance of all differences which may arise, either at sea or in port, between the captains, officers, and crews, without exception, particularly with reference to the adjustment of wages and the execution of contracts. The local authorities shall not interfere, except when the disorder that has arisen is of such a nature as to disturb tranquility and public order on shore, or in the port, or when a person of the country or not belonging to the crew, shall be concerned therein.

In all other cases, the aforesaid authorities shall confine themselves to lending aid to the consuls and vice-consuls or consular agents, if they are requested by them to do so, in causing the arrest and imprisonment of any person whose name is inscribed on the crew list, whenever, for any cause, the said officers shall think proper.

The claim of the consul was, that, by the law of nations, and the provisions of this treaty, the offence with which Wildenhus was charged is "solely cognizable by the authority of the laws of the Kingdom of Belgium," and that the State of New Jersey was without jurisdiction in the premises. The Circuit Court refused to deliver the prisoners to the consul and remanded them to the custody of the jailer. To reverse that decision this appeal was taken.

[*Chief Justice Waite orally restated these facts and then delivered the essential opinion of the Court as follows:*]

. . . [T]he courts of the United States have power to issue writs of habeas corpus which shall extend to prisoners in jail when they are in "custody in violation of the Constitution or a law or treaty of the United States," and the question we have to consider is, whether these prisoners are held in violation of the provisions of the existing treaty between the United States and Belgium.

It is part of the law of civilized nations that when a merchant vessel of one country enters the ports of another for the purposes of trade, it subjects itself to the law of the place to which it goes, unless by treaty or otherwise the two countries have come to some different understanding or agreement; for, as was said by Chief Justice Marshall in *The Exchange* [case] "it would be obviously inconvenient and dangerous to society, and would subject the laws to continual infraction, and the government to degradation, if such . . . merchants did not owe temporary and local allegiance, and were not amenable to the jurisdiction of the country." And the English judges have uniformly recognized the rights of the courts of the country of which the port is part to punish crimes committed by one foreigner on another in a foreign merchant ship. As the owner has voluntarily taken his vessel for his own private purposes to a place within the dominion of a government other than his own, and from which he seeks protection during his stay, he owes that government such allegiance for the time being as is due for the protection to which he becomes entitled.

From experience, however, it was found long ago that it would be beneficial to commerce if the local government would abstain from interfering with the internal discipline of the ship, and the general regulation of the rights and duties of the officers and crew towards the vessel or among themselves. And so by comity it came to be generally understood among civilized nations that all matters of discipline and all things done on board which affected only the vessel or those belonging to her, and did not involve the peace or dignity of the country, or the tranquility of the port, should be left by the local government to be dealt with by the authorities of the nation to which the vessel belonged as the laws of that nation or the interests of its commerce should require. But if crimes are committed on board of a character to disturb the peace and tranquility of the country to which the vessel has been brought, the offenders have never by comity or usage been entitled to any exemption from the operation of the local laws for their punishment, if the local tribunals see fit to assert their authority. Such being the general public law on this subject, treaties and conventions have been entered into by nations having commercial intercourse, the purpose of which was to settle and define the rights and duties of the contracting parties with respect to each other in these particulars, and thus prevent the inconvenience that might arise from attempts to exercise conflicting jurisdictions.

Next came a form of convention which in terms gave the consuls authority to cause proper order to be maintained on board and to decide disputes between the officers and crew, but allowed the local authorities to interfere if the disorders taking place on board were of such a nature as to disturb the public tranquility, and that is substantially all there is in the convention with Belgium which we have now to consider. This treaty is the law which now governs the conduct of the United States and Belgium towards each other in this particular. Each nation has granted to the other such local jurisdiction within its own dominion as may be necessary to maintain order on board a merchant vessel, but has reserved to itself the right to interfere if the disorder on board is of a nature to disturb the public tranquillity.

The treaty is part of the supreme law of the United States, and has the same force and effect in New Jersey that it is entitled to elsewhere. If it gives the consul of Belgium exclusive jurisdiction over the offence which it is alleged has been committed within the territory of New Jersey, we see no reason why he may not enforce his rights under the treaty by writ of habeas corpus in any proper court of the United States. This being the case, the only important question left for our determination is whether the thing which has been done—the disorder that has arisen—on board this vessel is of a nature to disturb the public peace, or, as some writers term it, the "public repose" of the people who look to the state of New Jersey for their protection. If the thing done—"the disorder," as it is called in the treaty—is of a character to affect those on shore or in the port when it becomes known, the fact that only those on the ship saw it when it was done is a matter of no moment. Those who are not on the vessel pay no special attention to the mere disputes or quarrels of the seamen while on board, whether they occur under deck or above. Neither do they as a rule care for anything done on board which relates only to the discipline of the ship, or to the preservation of order and authority. Not so, however, with crimes which from their gravity awaken a public interest as soon as they become known, and especially those of a character which every civilized nation considers itself bound to provide a severe punishment for when committed within its own jurisdiction. In such cases inquiry is certain to be instituted at once to ascertain how or why the thing was done, and the popular excitement rises or falls as the news spreads and the facts became known. It is not alone the publicity of the act, or the noise and clamor which attends it, that fixes the nature of the crime, but the act itself. If that is of a character to awaken public interest when it becomes known, it is a "disorder" the nature of which is to affect the community at large, and consequently to invoke the power of the local government whose people have been disturbed by what was done. The very nature of such an act is to disturb the quiet of a peaceful community, and to create, in the language of the treaty, a "disorder" which will "disturb tranquillity and public order on shore or in the port." The principle which governs the whole matter is this: Disorders which disturb only the peace of the ship or those on board are to be dealt with exclusively by the sovereignty of the home of the ship, but those which disturb the public peace may be suppressed, and, if need be, the offenders punished by the proper authorizes of the local jurisdiction. It may not be easy at all times to determine to which of the two jurisdictions a particular act of disorder belongs. Much will undoubtedly depend on the attending circumstances of the particular case, but all must concede that felonious homicide is a subject for the local jurisdiction, and that if the proper authorities are proceeding with the case in a regular way, the consul has no right to interfere to prevent it.

The judgment of the Circuit Court is affirmed.

■ NOTES & QUESTIONS

1. What is the test for determining whether the port State or the flag State has jurisdiction when a crime has been committed aboard a vessel in port? Is the rule in *Mali* (Wildenhus) likely the following: If the port authorities find out about a crime, they may characterize it as offending the port's tranquility?

2. The elasticity of the term *port tranquility* raises questions about the degree of discretion the port authorities may exercise in deciding whether to prosecute. You are the Jersey City District Attorney. There is a nonlethal fistfight between two Belgian citizens below decks on a Belgian merchant vessel. Would it offend the civility or tranquility of New Jersey? Would a fistfight *on* the decks offend its port tranquility?

3. Would it be more appropriate to vest *exclusive* jurisdiction in the coastal State only (the old customary rule) *or* in the flag State *only* (no port tranquility doctrine)?

Bays. Most bays consist of only internal waters. Large bays with wide mouths present the question of whether they contain *only* internal water, or alternatively, whether they also contain territorial *and* international waters. This type of bay illustrates the natural tension between freedom of the high seas in international waters and the coastal State's need to control activities in a strategic bay penetrating deep into its coastline.

A classic illustration of this tension drew worldwide attention in 1986 when US warplanes were nearly shot down over the Gulf of Sidra in the large southern indentation of the Mediterranean Sea on Libya's coastline. Libya's leader, Muammar Qaddafi, had proclaimed the "Line of Death" across the mouth of this gulf, which is approximately three hundred miles across. At its deepest indentation on Libya's coastline, this gulf extends well over one hundred miles into Libya's coastline on the Mediterranean Sea. Libya considers the entire gulf to be internal waters subject to its exclusive control. The US warplanes were operating over the gulf on the premise that it contains international waters due to its immense width.

Article 10 of the LOST defines a bay as "a well marked indentation whose penetration . . . constitute[s] more than a mere curvature of the coast. An indentation . . . [must be] as large as, or larger than, that of a semicircle whose diameter is a line drawn across the mouth of that indentation." The mouth of a bay consists of its natural entrance points.

A coastal State may exercise complete sovereignty up to twelve nautical miles from its coast (as discussed in the section below on the "Territorial Sea"). In the case of a bay, if the Article 10 semicircle's diameter of the bay is *less* than twenty-four miles between each side of the mouth of the bay, its waters consist solely of internal waters. If the diameter is *greater* than twenty-four miles, the bay also contains High Seas in the center of the mouth *and* territorial waters up to twelve miles from the entire coastline that forms the land boundary of the bay.

The 1910 *North Atlantic Coast Fisheries* arbitration between England and the US addressed the significance of bays to the coastal State:

> [A]dmittedly the geographical character of a bay contains conditions which concern the interests of the territorial sovereign to a more intimate and important extent than do those [interests] connected with an open coast. Thus conditions of national security and integrity, of defense, of commerce and of industry are all vitally concerned with the control of the bays penetrating the national coast line. This interest varies, speaking generally, in proportion to the penetration inland of the bay. . . .[22]

Another type of bay is particularly important, in the sense described by this arbitration opinion—the *historic* bay. Such bays contain only *internal* waters (as opposed to the "territorial" waters discussed be-

low) although their mouths are wider than the twenty-four-mile limitation of the LOST. Over a long period of time, a State may claim exclusive sovereignty over a large bay that would also contain the other categories of ocean waters (depicted in Exhibit 6.2)—due to the greater than twenty-four-mile distance between its natural entrance points. If other States have not disputed such a claim, then they have acquiesced in the coastal State's treatment of the large historic bay as containing only internal waters.

One of the classic disputes involves the continuing US objection to Canada's claim that Hudson Bay is a "historic" bay consisting solely of internal waters. It is fifty miles wide at its mouth. As stated by the Canadian Minister of Northern Affairs and Natural Resources in 1957, "the waters of Hudson Bar are Canadian by historic title. . . . Canada regards as inland waters all the waters west of a line drawn across the entrance to Hudson Strait. . . ."[23] The US characterizes most of the Hudson Bay as *international* waters, however, on the basis that the US has consistently disputed Canada's claim that Hudson Bay contains primarily internal waters. The international status of this bay has not been resolved, since neither nation has a strong enough interest to resolve this dispute.

(2) Territorial Sea

States have historically disagreed about the dividing line between the High Seas and the Territorial Sea. Unilateral expansions of exclusive sovereignty over what some nations boldly characterized as their Territorial Seas crested during the fifteenth and sixteenth centuries. The range of national claims extended deep into what is now considered the High Seas. Denmark and Sweden claimed large portions of the globe's northern seas, and each claimed complete sovereignty over the entire Baltic Sea. England claimed the entire English Channel and much of the North Sea. The pope, as Head of the Holy See (or the Vatican State), ceded most of the Atlantic and Pacific oceans to Spain and Portugal in 1492. He viewed this concession as a natural adjunct of their rights in the trade routes to the New World.

These extravagant claims were opposed by other nations and abandoned by the beginning of the eighteenth century. International practice never confirmed the pope's authority to cede the right to the Atlantic and Pacific oceans. The sheer inability to control such vast maritime areas gave credibility to the "cannon shot" theory of coastal jurisdiction—a nation could claim only that adjacent sea belt that it could actually control with military power.

Under the LOST, the Territorial Sea extends outward twelve nautical miles from the national coastline. A coastal State thus exercises sovereignty over this portion of its territory, essentially to the same extent that it does so over its land mass. The range of sovereignty thus includes the air over the Territorial Sea belt adjacent to the coast, the seabed below, and the subsoil within it.

Under International Law, a State *must* exercise its sovereign power in this adjacent strip of water. The minimal expectation is that the coastal State will chart the waters this close to its coast to provide warning of navigational hazards. As stated by England's Judge McNair in a 1951 decision by the International Court of Justice:

> To every State whose land territory is at any place washed by the sea, international law attaches a corresponding portion of maritime territory consisting of what the law calls territorial waters. . . . No maritime States can refuse them. International law imposes upon a maritime State certain obligations and confers upon it certain rights arising out of the sovereignty which it exercises over its maritime territory. The possession of this territory is not optional, not dependent upon the will of the State, but compulsory.[24]

Numerous definitional undercurrents muddy the scope of the Territorial Sea, including the location of the "baseline," the "breadth" of the Territorial Sea, what constitutes "innocent" passage, and the extent to which there exists a right to pass through former straits containing international waters.

Baseline The Territorial Sea (TS) begins at the baseline (as depicted in Exhibit 6.3). The TS begins where the ocean's edge meets the coastline. Under Article 5 of the LOST, the "normal baseline for measuring the breadth of the territorial sea is the low-water line along the coast as marked on large-scale charts officially recognized by the coastal State." The baseline thus marks the inner boundary of the various coastal sea zones described in this chapter (*see* Exhibit 6.2).

The demarcations on the coastal State's official baseline charts do not mandate international recognition of its placement of the baseline. There are limitations. Under International Law, coastal baselines must follow the general direction of the coast. Unnatural land contours make it difficult, however, to establish indisputable baselines. Article 7.3 of the LOST therefore contains the general agreement that "the sea areas lying within the lines must be sufficiently closely linked to the land domain to be subject to the regime of internal waters." This general language does little to resolve the question of proper baseline placement for erratic coastlines.

The International Court of Justice set forth some of the guidelines for the international recognition of baselines in the 1951 *Anglo-Norwegian Fisheries* case. When Norway announced the location of its base lines after World War II, it included a substantial portion of common international fishing areas within its *internal* waters. Norway has many ramparts of rocks and small islets that interrupt the natural course of its coastline. Norway drew *straight* baselines connecting the rocks and islets off its coast, rather than using the traditional method of tracking the contour of its irregular coastline. By placing its baselines at the outer edge of these rock and islet configurations, Norway had claimed a greater share of the common fishing area than Great Britain was willing to recognize. A number of countries had fished in this area within the baselines suddenly established by Norway. British fishermen had operated off Norway's coast (*within* the straight baseline area set by Norway) since the early 1900s. The parties to this dispute had exchanged diplomatic correspondence about their mutual rights to these fishing grounds over a period of years. The ICJ thus delineated the general rules applicable to baseline placement for cases involving such unusual coastlines:

> The delimitation of sea areas has always an international aspect; it cannot be dependent merely upon the will of the coastal State as expressed in its municipal [internal] law. . . .
>
> It is the land which confers upon the coastal State a right to the waters off its coasts. It follows that while such a State must be allowed the latitude necessary in order to be able to adapt its delimitation to practical needs and local requirements, the drawing of baselines must not depart to any appreciable extent from the general direction of the coast.

EXHIBIT 6.3 Straight Baseline Method

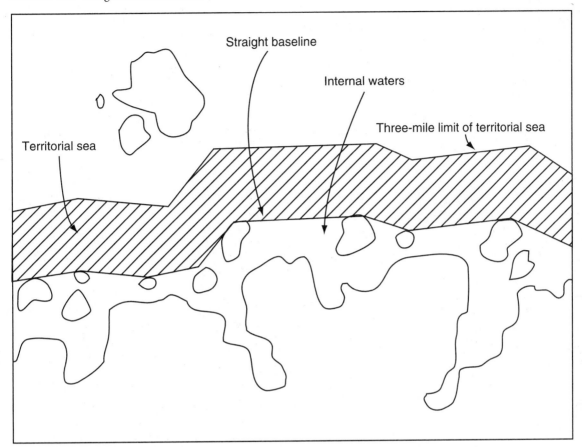

Another fundamental consideration . . . is the more or less close relationship existing between certain sea areas and the land formations which divide or surround them. The real question raised in the choice of baselines is in effect whether certain sea areas lying within these lines are sufficiently closely linked to the land domain to be subject to the regime of internal waters. This idea, which is at the basis for the determination of the rules relating to bays, should be liberally applied in the case of a coast, the geographical configuration of which is as irregular as that of Norway.

Finally, there is one consideration not to be overlooked, the scope of which extends beyond purely geographical factors: that of certain economic interest peculiar to a region, the reality and importance of which are clearly evidenced by a long usage. . . .

The majority of the ICJ's judges thereby approved Norway's straight baseline method in these unusual circumstances—because the resulting straight lines were sufficiently aligned with the general direction of the Norwegian coast. Although this method did not produce the usual replica of the coastal nation's coastline, it was acceptable in international practice. Exhibit 6.4 generally depicts the Court's description of the acceptable method Norway used to establish its baselines.

The International Court of Justice decided that a State with a highly irregular coastline, with many offshore rocks and islands, may draw a straight baseline joining the *outer* points of the islands near its coast. The inner edge of the Territorial Sea thus begins from this extended baseline.

Territorial Sea Breadth The breadth of the Territorial Sea has long been the subject of major international controversies. In 1492, for example, Spain

EXHIBIT 6.4 Bay/Baseline/Harbor/Island/Territorial
Sea Illustration

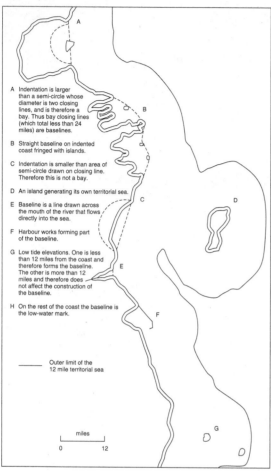

A   Indentation is larger
    than a semi-circle whose
    diameter is two closing
    lines, and is therefore a
    bay. Thus bay closing lines
    (which total less than 24
    miles) are baselines.

B   Straight baseline on indented
    coast fringed with islands.

C   Indentation is smaller than area of
    semi-circle drawn on closing line.
    Therefore this is not a bay.

D   An island generating its own territorial sea.

E   Baseline is a line drawn across
    the mouth of the river that flows
    directly into the sea.

F   Harbour works forming part
    of the baseline.

G   Low tide elevations. One is less
    than 12 miles from the coast and
    therefore forms the baseline.
    The other is more than 12
    miles and therefore does
    not affect the construction of
    the baseline.

H   On the rest of the coast the baseline is
    the low-water mark.

_____ Outer limit of the
        12 mile territorial sea

miles

0   12

Source: R. Churchill & A. Lowe, *The Law of the Sea* 39
(Manchester, Eng.: Manchester University Press, 1988)

claimed exclusive territorial sovereignty over the entire Pacific Ocean. Portugal similarly claimed the Indian Ocean and most of the Atlantic Ocean.[25] Claims to entire oceans, however, were never recognized under International Law. States recognized the existence of a much narrower belt of water subject to the coastal State's exclusive control. In 1702, the writings of an often-quoted Dutch judge analyzed how to measure the breadth of this particular coastal zone:

> Wherefore on the whole it seems a better rule that the control of the land [of its adjacent Territorial Sea] extends as far as a cannon will carry; for that is as far as we seem to have both

command and possession. I am speaking, however, of our own times, in which we have those engines of war; otherwise, I should have to say in general terms that the control of the land ends where the power of men's weapons ends; for it is this, as we have said, that guarantees possession.[26]

This often-cited passage reveals that the three-mile shooting range of the eighteenth century cannon established the width of the Territorial Sea. The coastal State could claim no more than it could control. Under this view, the maximum range of existing weapons was the yardstick for measuring the breadth of the Territorial Sea. Had this view persisted until the 1960s, the range of intercontinental missiles would make entire oceans the territorial waters of the launching nation.

After the American Revolutionary War, the United States claimed a Territorial Sea that extended from the outer tips of various capes on its eastern coast. It used a straight baseline method that did not generally conform to its coastline, and the resulting baselines were *not* a natural extension of the coastline (unlike Norway's straight baselines that connected the rocks and islets immediately adjacent to its coast [*see* reference in above *Anglo-Norwegian Fisheries* case]). The US Territorial Sea, contained within the lines drawn from cape to cape, purported to extend the exclusive jurisdiction far beyond three miles from its shores. Various nations objected to this departure from international practice. In 1793, Secretary of State Thomas Jefferson responded by suspending the reliance on this cape-to-cape baseline method. He formally advised England and France as follows:

> [The] President of the United States, thinking that, before it shall be finally decided to what distance from our seashores the territorial protection of the United States shall be exercised . . . finds it necessary in the meantime to fix provisionally on some distance for the present government of these questions. You are sensible that very different opinions and claims have been heretofore advanced on this subject. The greatest distance to which any respectable assent among nations has been at any time given, has been the extent of human sight, estimated at upwards of twenty miles, and the smallest distance . . . is the utmost range of a

cannon ball, usually stated at one sea league [three nautical miles]. Some intermediate distances have also been insisted on, and that of three sea leagues has some authority in its favor. The . . . President gives instructions to the officers acting under his authority to consider those heretofore given are restrained for the present to the distance of one sea league or three geographical miles from the seashores.[27]

Certain coastal States claimed Territorial Sea boundaries much wider than the customary limit. Most of these claims were made by lesser developed nations with significant fishing or seabed resources adjacent to their coasts but not the superior technology possessed by developed nations to take advantage of these resources. In 1952, for example, Chile, Ecuador, and Peru claimed a Territorial Sea of two hundred nautical miles from their coasts. In 1956, a number of other nations in the same region of the world attended the Meeting of the Inter-American Council of Jurists in Mexico City, which adopted the following principle: "The distance of three miles as the limit of territorial waters is insufficient, and does not constitute a general rule of international law. Therefore, the enlargement of the zone of the sea traditionally called 'territorial waters' is justified. Each State is competent to establish its territorial waters within reasonable limits, taking into account geographical, geological, and biological factors, as well as the economic needs of its population, and its security and defense." Such statements generated worldwide pressure to expand the historical three-mile limit.[28]

In 1958, under sponsorship of the United Nations, representatives of eighty-six nations gathered in Geneva, Switzerland, to pursue a global agreement about the breadth of the various sea zones. The Geneva Convention on the Territorial Sea and Contiguous Zone (1958 LOS Convention) expressly adopted the customary three-mile limit. However, many nations subsequently extended their Territorial Sea zones to twelve nautical miles. The 1982 Conference on the Law of the Sea (attended by 148 States) thus adopted this development in State practice. Under Article 3 of the LOST, every "State has the right to establish the breadth of its territorial sea up to a limit not exceeding 12 nautical miles. . . ."

Shortly after its independence, the US announced its adherence to the customary three-mile limit and retained that limit for two centuries. Although some 140 nations adopted a twelve-mile limit at the UN's 1982 Conference, the US rejected the entire convention (as discussed below under deep seabed mining analysis). In 1988, however, President Reagan unilaterally extended the US Territorial Sea from three to twelve miles in "accordance with international law, as reflected in the applicable provisions of the 1982 United Nations Convention on the Law of the Sea."[29]

This enlargement of territorial waters had two major effects upon the International Law of the Sea. First, it limited freedom of the seas because coastal States could regulate more activities due to the nine-mile *extension* of the Territorial Sea from three to twelve miles. That development also extended the existing rules of "innocent passage." Second, many straits through which ships pass from one part of the High Seas to another no longer contained international or High Seas. Ships in those waters suddenly became subject to regulation by the coastal States on either side of the strait. Both of these developments were addressed in the LOST as follows:

Innocent Passage One of the most tangible impacts of the change to a twelve-mile Territorial Sea was the extension of coastal State rules of "innocent passage" to passing vessels. Article 18.1 of the LOST Convention defines *passage* as "navigation through the territorial sea for the purpose of:

(a) traversing that sea without entering internal waters. . . or

(b) proceeding to or from internal waters. . . ."

But when is passage "*innocent?*" In 1986, two US naval vessels entered the Black Sea via the Turkish Straits. They were equipped with electronic sensors and sophisticated listening devices. Their disclosed purpose was to exercise what the US naval authorities characterized as their "right of innocent passage" through the territorial waters of the Soviet Union (SU). The SU placed all of its Black Fleet military vessels on combat alert. The SU protested this entry as unnecessarily provocative and a clear violation of the territorial sovereignty of the SU.

Under Article 19 of the LOST, "*innocent*" passage means passage that is "not prejudicial to the peace, good order, or security of the coastal State." Further, the passing vessel may not stop nor anchor, unless incidental to ordinary navigation or undertaken for the purpose of the authorized entry into a foreign port. A vessel may thus proceed to or from port, and render assistance to persons, ships, or aircraft needing emergency assistance.

Under Article 19 of the LOST, foreign vessels must determine and observe the regulations promulgated by coastal States to avoid a breach of the established innocent passage rules. Such regulations relating to customs, immigration, and sanitation protect the coastal nation's interests in its territorial waters. An oceanliner carrying passengers into another State's territorial waters must comply with local tax laws affecting its cargo, passport regulations affecting its passengers, and waste offloading requirements. Military vessels, when expressly permitted to enter a foreign port, normally give notice of their intended arrival at least several days in advance.[30]

The application of the "innocent passage" regime is nevertheless elastic and ill-defined. Nations sometimes disagree about whether certain conduct poses a threat. A "threat" can take many forms because it is viewed in the eyes of the coastal State beholder. On the other hand, a foreign military ship authorized to enter the territorial waters of another State could undertake military exercises upon arrival. Submarines might navigate below the surface in territorial waters, undetected by the coastal authorities. Foreign vessels can collect hydrographic information, conduct research, fish, or disseminate propaganda via radio signals. During the Cold War, Soviet "fishing" trawlers with elaborate electronic devices aboard hovered just outside of the US three-mile territorial water limits to gather information. There are, of course, other less conspicuous activities that can be labeled as threats by a coastal State.

Suppose that a private vessel called the *Greenpeace* distributes leaflets or displays signs against nuclear weapons to ships passing through the territorial waters of a major nuclear power. That State's coast guard vessel may stop the dissemination of such information because the activities of the *Greenpeace* are not considered innocent. The LOST provisions are ambiguous, but are at least a better option than no definition at all. Yet the ongoing political processes between certain States often contravene the spirit—if not the letter—of the LOST innocent passage regime. The above 1986 US naval entry into the Black Sea is a drastic illustration.

The coastal State's discretion to arbitrarily apply locally defined rules of innocent passage are limited by the LOST. Article 24 imposes a duty not to "impair" the innocent passage of foreign ships. The coastal State cannot impose requirements of navigation that effectively deny or restrict the right of innocent passage. Failure to publicize dangers to navigation in the State's official navigational charts, for example, would make Territorial Sea passage impractical and dangerous. Article 24 also prohibits coastal States from promulgating regulations that discriminate against the ships or cargo of a particular nation—or ships carrying cargo to or from certain nations. The Arab embargo of Israeli shipping and goods would breach this provision of the treaty (*see* § 8.4).

Strait Passage The second major effect of the LOST enlargement of the breadth of the Territorial Sea from three to twelve nautical miles involves certain strategic straits. A strait is a natural sea passage that connects two large maritime areas. The Strait of Hormuz, for example, connects the Persian Gulf and the Indian Ocean. The Strait of Gibraltar connects the Mediterranean Sea to the Atlantic Ocean.

When the navigable channel of such a strait is *greater* than twelve miles from each of the national coasts bordering on the strait, that strait still contains some international waters or "High Seas." Ships are entitled to unrestricted passage through the High Seas portion of such straits (as long as their activities are beyond the coastal State's control of its adjacent Contiguous Zone).

When the strait is *less* than twenty-four miles wide at its narrowest point, it contains only territorial waters. As a result of the LOST augmentation of coastal jurisdiction (from three to twelve nautical miles), approximately 116 such "international straits" formerly containing High Seas suddenly became Territorial Seas. Coastal States would, under customary State practice, appropriately apply their "innocent passage" rules to such waters. Under the LOST "strait passage" articles, however, the coastal State's innocent passage rules do *not* apply to these special straits. Military and commercial vessels alike may freely transit, just as if those special straits still contained slices of High Seas within them.

The Bering Strait between the former Soviet Union (Siberia) and Alaska provides a useful illustration. That strait is nineteen miles wide at its narrowest point. Ships pass through it when going between the Arctic and the northern Pacific oceans. The former Soviet Union claimed a twelve-mile Territorial Sea. Prior to 1988, the US three-mile Territorial Sea claim left a four-mile slice of High Seas at the narrowest point of passage. Military and commercial vessels could freely navigate in that strip of international waters in the middle of the strait. Now that the US has adopted a twelve-mile Territorial Sea, there are no High Seas left in that strait. All States would otherwise be subject to the "innocent passage" rules promulgated by Russia (on the eastern border of the strait and the US on its western border). At the narrowest point, the Bering Strait now contains only the *Territorial* Sea of both the US and Russia—normally delimited by an equidistance principle in the middle of the Bering Strait. Under the regime of "transit passage," proposed by the US to govern straits traditionally used for international navigation, all States could navigate the Bering Strait as if it still contained a slice of High Seas in the middle.

The LOST's "transit passage" provisions are designed to balance two competing national interests: the pre-1982 right to transit through straits containing some international waters—that is, high seas given only a three-mile limit—and the extension of the coastal State's jurisdiction over its Territorial Seas from three to twelve miles. Under Article 38.2, ships and aircraft *may* transit through such territorial-water straits formerly containing international waters "solely for the purpose of continuous and expeditious transit of the strait between one part of the high seas . . . and another part of the high seas. . . ." Thus, the coastal State or States may not impede such transit on the basis that the otherwise amorphous rules of innocent passage apply to these waters that would otherwise be territorial waters due to the narrowness of the strait.

Under LOST Article 42, the coastal State may of course promulgate rules ensuring transit passage that establish sea lanes and traffic separation schemes for safe navigation, as well as the prevention of pollution, fishing, and the offloading of persons and commodities. None of these reasonable limitations may be applied, however, in a way that impedes the right of transit through such territorial waters connecting the high seas.

Assume that the US and Russia agree to apply the above Article 38 transit passage provision of the LOST. A Chinese ship passing through the Bering Strait between the Arctic and northern Pacific oceans would not be subject to either the US or Russia's innocent passage rules when it passes through the otherwise exclusively territorial waters of the Bering Strait at its narrowest point. Neither coastal State could prohibit the foreign commercial vessel in these overlapping territorial waters—although the Chinese vessel would pass less than twelve miles from the coast of both the US (Alaska) and Russia (Siberia). As long as the Chinese vessel is merely passing through this strait, the US/Russia adoption of the transit passage provisions under Article 38 of the LOST would entitle that ship to pass freely through the strait as if it still contained High Seas.

(3) High Seas

The High Seas—or international waters—consist of that part of the ocean not subject to the complete territorial sovereignty of any State. The Article 86 LOST "High Seas" provisions apply to "all parts of the sea that are not included in the exclusive economic zone, in the Territorial Sea, or in the internal waters of a State."

The most fundamental division of all is the distinction between the coastal State's twelve-mile *Territorial Sea* and the *High Seas.* Two additional ocean-water zones (described below in some detail) overlap the coastal State's Territorial Sea and also contain a portion of the High Seas within them. These are the Contiguous Zone and the Exclusive Economic Zone. As depicted in Exhibit 6.2, the outer edge of the Territorial Sea zone marks the inner edge of the High Seas.

Freedom of the High Seas has long been a universal tenet of International Law. In 1927, the Permanent Court of International Justice reaffirmed the ancient principle that this freedom was virtually absolute. The court held that this liberty was subject to only those special limitations expressly recognized by State practice:

It is certainly true that—apart from certain special cases which are defined by international law [such as capturing pirates or exercising the right of self-defense]—vessels on the high seas are subject to no authority except that of the State whose flag they fly. In virtue of the principle of the freedom of the seas, that is to say, the absence of any territorial sovereignty upon the high seas, no State may exercise any kind of jurisdiction over foreign vessels upon them. Thus, if a war vessel, happening to be at the spot where a collision occurs between a vessel [from its own country] . . . and a foreign vessel, were to send on board the latter an officer to make investigations or to take evidence, such an act would undoubtedly be contrary to international law.[31]

The traditional doctrine of freedom of the seas was itself a limitation in that it restricted national attempts to unreasonably extend the range of exclusive coastal sovereignty into international waters. Such claims conflicted with the rights of all States to fish and to navigate over international trade routes. The Dutch judge, to whom the cannon-shot rule of territorial sovereignty is attributed, thus refused to recognize greater sovereignty than that recognized under International Law.[32]

Twentieth century technology has caused the free seas pendulum to swing in the opposite direction, however. Free accessibility to the High Seas has resulted in a depletion of the world's marine resources and a reevaluation of the international penchant for a *laissez faire* ocean policy. A Yale University professor and student succinctly provide the following chronology of the movement toward, and then away from, freedom of the seas in the following excerpt:

THE HYDROGEN BOMB TESTS IN PERSPECTIVE: LAWFUL MEASURES FOR SECURITY

Myers McDougal & Norbert Schlei
64 Yale Law Journal 648, 661–62 (1964)

The concept of "freedom of the seas" entered the law of nations as a reaction against broad claims to territorial sovereignty over vast sea areas put forward by Spain, Portugal, England, and other states in the sixteenth and seventeenth centuries. The object of these claims was to monopolize fisheries, and trade with areas thought particularly rich in resources. . . . No interference whatever with navigation was justified because effective occupation was impossible by the nature of the sea itself. The same principle was applicable to fisheries . . . for the additional reason that the resources of the sea were inexhaustible. . . . The claim of the Dutch to free navigation, on the other hand, could not possibly interfere with free use of the same resources by others. It is familiar history that common interest in navigation and fishing triumphed over monopoly, and that the great principle of "freedom of the seas" became in this sense universally accepted. . . . It has long been clear [however] that vast areas of the sea could in fact be occupied, in the sense that others could be effec-tively excluded by shore batteries, and by naval and air forces armed with modern weapons. Moreover, it is no longer possible to say that complete freedom of navigation and fishing cannot possibly interfere with free use of the seas by others. Modern vessels . . . throng trade routes which follow the shortest and safest track between ports, and collisions are not infrequent. Vessels similarly interfere with the navigation of others by trawling, dredging, or engaging in dangerous naval maneuvers and military exercises, and they discharge oil waste that fouls beaches and destroys marine life. Contemporary technology has demonstrated that the resources of the sea are by no means inexhaustible, and more than once the free use of dangerously efficient new methods has threatened to destroy valuable fishery resources forever. Manifold national interests of critical importance no longer cease at the shore or near it, and have come to affect not only pirates, invading military forces and smugglers, but innocent bypassers as well.

Freedom of the seas is no longer absolute. The 1958 UN LOS Conference delegates produced treaty language regarding the historical rule of complete freedom of the High Seas beyond what was then the three-mile Territorial Sea. Article 1 of the 1958 Convention on the High Seas[33] defined the High Seas as "all parts of the sea that are not included in the Territorial Sea or in the internal waters of a State." Article 2 added that the "high seas being open to all nations, no State may validly purport to subject any part of them to its sovereignty." Then the UN Conference pendulum swung in the other direction during the 1974–1982 LOST process: The Territorial Sea was quadrupled, the size of the Contiguous Zone was doubled, and a *200*-mile Exclusive Economic Zone was created.

The impact has been a "territorialization" of the oceans, once thought to belong to all. One result of the expansions and zone creation, described in the following materials, was the effective extension of the range of coastal sovereignty into nearly forty percent of the oceans. Further, the remainder of the High Seas are expected to come under control of an International Sea-bed Authority, which will regulate *all* resource-extraction activities in the far reaches of the oceans. Thus, the High Seas could hardly continue to be characterized as *res communis* (belonging to all), although the major powers have attempted to maintain some degree of their freedom via the special 1994 modification below on deep seabed mining. As aptly stated by Professor Francis Ngantcha in his book by the Geneva Institute of International Studies:

The Law of the Sea has traditionally been aimed at protecting the international community's interests over the inexhaustible uses of ocean space. To this end, the main pillar of the law has been freedom of the sea—with the implication that seagoing vehicles may freely roam the oceans. When much of the ocean space was considered *res communis*, this tenet was considered unquestionable.

The 'territorialization' of the ocean space, i.e. its division into zones of costal State sovereignty and/or jurisdiction, has put a stop to the 'old' system of 'free' global maritime communication and transportation. Consequently, the international networks of trade and commerce, naval mobility, overflight, etc. have come to depend upon the national maritime spaces of third States for purposes of passage.[34]

There is also the problem of the degree to which a coastal State may properly exercise jurisdiction in the High Seas, as a means of protecting itself against criminal activities that threaten its national interests. Chapter 5 of this book addressed such exercises of sovereignty via so-called "extraterritorial" jurisdiction based on the five principles of international criminal jurisdiction (*see* § 5.2). The increased drug trafficking problem, for example, threatens a coastal State's interests long before the drugs reach any of the law of the sea treaty zones.

Consider the following scenario, wherein US customs inspectors seized drugs and arrested the leader of an international drug smuggling ring just off the coast of Singapore:

UNITED STATES OF AMERICA v. LARSEN

United States Court of Appeals
Ninth Circuit, 1991
952 Fed.Rptr.2d 1099

[*Author's Note: The defendant was convicted of "aiding and abetting the knowing and intentional possession with intent to distribute marijuana" under federal controlled substances laws. The appellate court held that Congress intended that the following statute be applied outside of the US if necessary: "it shall be unlawful for any person knowingly or intentionally to manufacture, distribute, or dispense, or possess with intent to manufacture, distribute, or dispense, a controlled substance." US customs agents were thus authorized to seize a private vessel and arrest its crew in the High Seas near Singapore—thousands of miles* from the California forum where the defendant was brought to trial for his violation of this statute.]

[*Opinion.*] Before BROWNING, ALARCON and T.G. NELSON, Circuit Judges.

Charles Edward Larsen was convicted for his involvement in an international marijuana smuggling operation. . . . Larsen challenges the legality of his conviction on numerous grounds, including the court's extraterritorial application of 21 U.S.C. § 841(a)(1) [the controlled substances law serving as the basis for his arrest near Singapore]. We affirm.

Larsen's conviction was based on evidence which established that he, along with codefendants and numerous other individuals, conspired to import shipments of Southeast Asian marijuana into the United States from 1985 to 1987, and to distribute the marijuana in the United States. The profits from these ventures were concealed by a fictitious partnership created by the defendant and others. This partnership was used to purchase the shipping vessel intended to transport the marijuana. During some of the smuggling operations, Larsen served as captain of the vessel.

Under Count Eight, Larsen was convicted of aiding and abetting codefendant Walter Ulrich in the crime of knowing and intentional possession with intent to distribute marijuana in violation of 21 U.S.C. § 841(a)(1). The marijuana was seized by [US] customs inspectors from a ship on the high seas outside of Singapore. Larsen claims that the district court erred when it denied his motion to dismiss Count Eight because 21 U.S.C. § 841(a)(1) does not have extraterritorial jurisdiction. . . .

Congress is empowered to attach extraterritorial effect to its penal statutes so long as the statute does not violate the due process clause of the Fifth Amendment. There is a presumption against extraterritorial application when a statute is silent on the matter. However, this court has given extraterritorial effect to penal statutes when congressional intent to do so is clear. Since 21 U.S.C. § 841(a)(1) is silent about its extraterritorial application, we are "faced with finding the construction that Congress intended."

The [US] Supreme Court has explained that to limit the locus of some offenses "to the strictly territorial jurisdiction would be greatly to curtail the scope and usefulness of the statute and leave open a large immunity for frauds as easily committed by citizens on the high seas and in foreign countries as at home." Congressional intent to attach extraterritorial application "'may be inferred from the nature of the offenses and Congress' other legislative efforts to eliminate the type of crime involved.'"

Until now, the Ninth Circuit [where appeals from California federal trial courts are heard] has not applied this "intent of congress/nature of the offense test" to 21 U.S.C. § 841(a)(1); however, four other circuits have. They all held that Congress did intend the statute to have extraterritorial effect.

The Fifth Circuit held that Congress intended that 841(a)(1) have extraterritorial effect because it was a part of the Comprehensive Drug Abuse Prevention and Control Act of 1970, and the power to control illegal drug trafficking on the high seas was an essential incident to Congress' intent to halt drug abuse in the United States.

The Third Circuit held that Congressional intent to apply 841(a)(1) extraterritorially could be implied because "Congress undoubtedly intended to prohibit conspiracies to [distribute] controlled substances into the United States . . . as part of its continuing effort to contain the evils caused on American soil by foreign as well as domestic suppliers of illegal narcotics. . . . To deny such use of the criminal provisions 'would be greatly to curtail the scope and usefulness of the statute.'"

The First Circuit concluded that the district court had jurisdiction over a crime committed on the high seas in violation of 841(a)(1) because "[a] sovereign may exercise jurisdiction over acts done outside its geographical jurisdiction which are intended to produce detrimental effects within it."

The Second Circuit similarly held that "because section 841(a)(1) properly applies to schemes to distribute controlled substances within the United States," its extraterritorial application was proper.

Extraterritorial application of a drug possession/distribution statute comports with the reasoning behind the Supreme Court's *Bowman* decision, since such a statute is "not logically dependent on locality for the Government's jurisdiction, but [is] enacted because of the right of the government to defend itself against obstruction, or fraud wherever perpetrated" and "[i]t would be going too far to say that because Congress does not fix any locus it intended to exclude the high seas in respect of this crime" [citation omitted].

. . .

Larsen cites to a passing reference in *Hayes* which stated that Congress accepted the views of representatives from the Department of Justice and the DEA who testified that the Comprehensive Drug Abuse Prevention and Control Act of 1970 did not apply to American ships on the high seas. While the *Hayes* court acknowledged that some might conclude that § 841(a)(1) does not apply extraterritorially because of this Congressional testimony, the court nevertheless held that § 841(a)(1) did have extraterritorial application.

In affirming Larsen's conviction, we now join the First, Second, Third, and Fifth Circuit Courts in finding that 21 U.S.C. § 841(a)(1) has extraterritorial jurisdiction. We hold that Congress' intent [to apply this drug law to the High Seas] can be implied because illegal drug trafficking, which the statute is designed to prevent, regularly involves importation of drugs from international sources.

[CONVICTION] AFFIRMED.

■ NOTES & QUESTIONS

1. *Larsen* deals with something different than extracting resources from the High Seas. The US was prosecuting a US citizen for criminal conduct occurring on the High Seas. *Should* the US have such jurisdiction to apply its laws *anywhere* on the High Seas?

2. Assume that the drug seizure and Larsen's arrest occurred in one of the following sea zones: (a) Singapore's Exclusive Economic Zone; or (b) Singapore's Contiguous Zone; or (c) Singapore's Territorial Sea. Would the location of the arrest and seizure present greater concern to Singapore in one zone rather than another?

3. Would the US be violating any rights of the nation of Singapore if these events occurred in these various zones?

(4) Contiguous Zone

Coastal State sovereignty is *exclusive* in the Territorial Sea (TS) belt immediately adjacent to its land mass. A coastal State may also exercise *limited* jurisdiction in the Contiguous Zone (CZ) extending twenty-four nautical miles from its coast. As depicted in Exhibit 6.2, the outer edge of the TS is the midpoint of the CZ.

The coastal State's sovereign rights in its CZ allow it to enforce customs or immigration policies. Under Article 33.1 of the LOST, the activities of foreign States or their vessels in the CZ are subject to the coastal State's jurisdiction for the express purposes of enforcing "customs, fiscal, immigration, or sanitary laws."

Why *is* there a CZ? The CZ's proximity to the coastline requires a balance of international and coastal State rights to use or control adjacent coastal waters. A coastal State's enforcement of special maritime laws in this zone is not an unreasonable infringement of the international right to freely navigate through them. During the eighteenth and nineteenth centuries, State practice acknowledged the right to seize foreign and domestic vessels, and arrest their occupants, in international waters at some distance beyond the three-mile Territorial Sea. Coastal States were unwilling to ignore harmful or illegal activities occurring in this fringe area just beyond their Territorial Seas. Rumrunners, for example, would hover there without dropping anchor. They sought opportunities to enter the Territorial Sea or to turn over their contraband to smaller boats that could then offload at undisclosed locations ashore. This gave rise to the so-called "hovering laws" during the US Prohibition era of the 1920s, extending coastal jurisdiction for the limited purpose of fending off anticipated violations of the US liquor laws. The same concern exists today, given the extent of international drug traffic.

A number of early twentieth century developments impacted the creation and subsequent extensions of the CZ. The 1928 meeting of Stockholm's *Institut de Droit International* (Institute of International Law) was the first major attempt to assess the proper scope of such hovering laws. The 1929 Harvard Law School study of the *Law of Territorial Waters* stated that "navigation of the high sea is free to all States. On the high sea adjacent to the marginal [territorial] sea, however, a State may take such measures as may be necessary for the enforcement within its territory or territorial waters of its customs, navigation, sanitary or police laws or regulations, or for its immediate protection."[35] State practice had incorporated this theme into national laws governing the small fringe of water just beyond the traditional three-mile Territorial Sea. The League of Nations' 1930 Conference on the Law of the Sea did not reach any express agreement about the precise scope or breadth of the CZ. The participants did agree on one important matter: Unlike territorial waters where a coastal nation *must* exercise its sovereign control, a State had to expressly declare its claim to jurisdiction over a CZ. Under International Law, the CZ is *not* a necessary adjunct of the range of territorial sovereignty, as is the Territorial Sea zone.

This consensus placed the burden on coastal States to justify any extension of sovereignty beyond their Territorial Seas. Other States did not have to recognize unusual jurisdictional claims in areas beyond the historic three-mile Territorial Sea. A major difference was that a coastal State could not claim *exclusive* sovereignty over its CZ for all purposes. It could monitor and exclude hovering activities there. It could not limit passage that was otherwise unharmful to coastal State interests.

One problem with the 1958 UN Convention was the specific twelve-mile breadth of the Contiguous Zone. Its establishment may have been a step backward. The drafters' intent was to place a single limit on the diverse national interests claimed by coastal States in this zone. States that wanted jurisdiction over a larger sea zone, however, did not ratify this provision of the 1958 Convention. For example, they did not acquiesce in the prospect of their coast guard cutters idly standing by while contraband was being unloaded just outside the proposed twelve-mile Contiguous Zone.

The third twentieth century UN Law of the Sea Conference produced some answers to these problems through seaward extensions of sovereign control. As a result of negotiations from 1974 to 1982, the LOST delegates expanded the Territorial Sea to twelve miles from the coastal baseline, and the Contiguous Zone to twenty-four miles from that point. These new treaty extensions, essentially codifying State practice, resolved the debate over the proper breadth of the contiguous zone.

The 1958 Conference delegates began a process of expanding national jurisdiction over the High Seas that would resurface in the 1982 LOST in at least two ways. First, they expressly endorsed an expanded twelve-mile Contiguous Zone. That agreement codified the State practice that had already extended coastal jurisdiction in this zone. A number of States had claimed limited sovereign rights in such a zone for many decades before the 1958 conference. Second, the 1958 UN Law of the Sea representatives also extended coastal jurisdiction over their Continental Shelves "to where the depth of the superjacent waters admits of the exploitation of the natural resources. . . ." This provision effectively permitted coastal States to monopolize the marine resources in and over their Continental Shelves—a portion of which extends under the Contiguous Zone.[36]

(5) Exclusive Economic Zone

During the 1974–1982 negotiations, State representatives proposed a novel plan to accommodate the competing interests of all nations in the freedom of the High Seas and the coastal States' interest in preventing the depletion of natural resources in those seas. Customary State practice had condoned the regulation of economic conduct in the waters off national shorelines involving fishing, mining, security, and certain other State interests. These national interests were effectively codified by the 1982 LOST provisions expressly establishing a two-hundred-mile Exclusive Economic Zone starting at the coastal baseline. The "economic" zone overlaps the twenty-four mile Contiguous Zone and the twelve-mile Territorial Sea.

The Exclusive Economic Zone (EEZ) extends seaward up to 200 nautical miles from the coastal baseline, as depicted in Exhibit 6.2. Under Article 56 of the LOST, the coastal State enjoys sovereign rights in the EEZ for the purposes of "exploring and exploiting, conserving and managing the natural resources . . . of the waters superjacent to the sea-bed and its subsoil, and with regard to other activities for the economic exploitation and exploration of the zone, such as the production of energy from the water. . . ."

This comparatively new zone is a product of the tension between historical expectations of freedom of the seas and modern pressures to decentralize the exploitation of ocean resources by lesser developed nations. After World War II, the more developed nations used their superior technology to extract the rich fishing and mineral resources contained in the sea and the seabed. Many of these natural resources were located just beyond the Territorial Seas of the lesser developed nations who experienced a resulting depletion of these natural resources—virtually within sight but beyond their grasp. Even some developed nations were similarly concerned about protecting the resources off their own coasts from unlimited exploitation by certain developed nations.

The sovereignty equation does not preclude *all* activity in this portion of the High Seas that could be characterized as "economic." Although the coastal State enjoys some primary rights in this area, Article 58 provides that *all* States retain the right therein to navigate, overfly, lay submarine cables and pipelines "compatible with . . . this Convention."

These provisions thus authorize the *less* powerful coastal States to share in the wealth of natural resources near their shorelines. They have thus established licensing regimes for recapturing a percentage of the revenues derived when other States extract natural resources from the sea or the subsoil under the sea—up to 200 nautical miles from their coasts.

Some of the *more* powerful States have effectively extended this zone by augmenting it to accommodate what they characterize as special circumstances. In 1994, Canada enacted "emergency" legislation authorizing the arrest of violators of its new ban on catching the endangered "turbot" fish—in the Grand Banks area 220 miles off Newfoundland. In March 1995, Spanish and Portuguese fishing trawlers were either seized or threatened with capture. The European Union then engaged in diplomatic attempts to convince Canada to cease this interference with the recognized right to fish in international waters beyond the 200-mile EEZ.

How did the concept of an EEZ materialize? In 1974, a coalition of approximately half of the members of the UN made a significant statement about resource conservation and a more desirable method of distributing the wealth derived from global resources. They promulgated a novel plan calling for a redistribution of the world's wealth. The so-called "Group of 77" (or G-77) published its Declaration on the Establishment of a New International Economic Order and the Charter of Economic Rights and Duties of States (*see* § 13.4). This Group's specific objective was to impose restraints on certain nations and their transnational corporations. The G-77 claimed, for example, that US and Japanese corporations were depleting global ocean resources for the benefit of only a few nations. G-77 thus declared that such wealth should be shared equitably by the people of all nations. This group wanted to expand the national sovereignty of the economically underdeveloped countries, in or near the locations where these corporations operated, hoping to secure the active assistance of the entire international community.

That same year (1974) also marked the beginning of the new negotiations on the UN Conference on the Law of the Sea. G-77 therein sought international support for its stated goals while nurturing a solid majority in the UN Conference negotiations. Members of this Group pursued their "new deal" economic strategy by pressing for the need to change global ocean resource management. One result was the international adoption at the conclusion of the 1982 final draft of the Law of the Sea Treaty of the Exclusive Economic Zone described above.

Just before this conference began, G-77 member Kenya proposed adoption of an "Exclusive Economic Zone." Kenya's proposal was similar to the "patrimonial" sea plan put forth by several Latin-American nations attempting to extend their coastal sovereignty over a two-hundred-mile area from their coasts—similar in size to the 1946 US proclamation of the Continental Shelf Doctrine, with its attendant effect of extending US control over economic activities to approximately 200 miles from both its coasts. Most Latin American nations that supported the patrimonial sea concept did not pursue adoption of a two-hundred-mile *territorial* sea—as did Chile, Ecuador, and Peru in 1952. Those nations did not have Continental Shelves to support the exercise of territorial sovereignty like that claimed by the US.

The emergence of these developments was succinctly chronicled by Professor Louis Henkin of Columbia University:

> The drive to extend coastal-state jurisdiction has come particularly from Latin American states. Those rich in off-shore minerals have been reasonably content . . . especially with the extravagant interpretations that would give them the resources of the entire submerged landmass out to the ocean abyss. Some states, having little continental margin, have asked "compensation" in the form of rights in the deep sea-bed for many miles from their shores. . . . Within the general campaign of the poorer states for change in the international economic system and its law . . . mining and fishing states in Latin America have joined to propose a "patrimonial sea" of 200 miles in which the coastal state would have exclusive rights to all resources. A group of African states has also proposed such an "exclusive economic zone."[37]

After eight years of negotiating the EEZ, approximately 140 of the 161 countries represented at the Law of the Sea Conference voted to adopt it in principle by signing the 1982 final draft. Economically developed nations abstained from voting because they recognized that this EEZ would effectively "territorialize" a significant portion of the

High Seas where they were used to extracting its resources at will. Israel, Turkey, the US, and Venezuela thus rejected the treaty's "economic" changes—clinging to the aging paradigm of "freedom of the seas." The nations that either abstained from voting, or generally rejected the 1982 Convention, were not prepared to abandon the traditional rule of free exploitation of the seas beyond the Territorial Sea and Contiguous Zones.

Now that the LOST has entered into force (as of November 1994), coastal States expect to enjoy greater profits from their EEZs. They may—and do—charge licensing fees for taking fish or minerals from that zone. They may erect artificial islands or structures to harvest fish in the waters and minerals in the seabed of the EEZ. They may also conduct marine research and legitimately exclude other States from engaging in such activity.

Although the general concept of an EEZ is now firmly established in International Law, the vagueness of the 1982 Convention—typical of any multilateral treaty where a wide degree of consensus is sought—masks the continued disagreement about the respective rights of different States in the same EEZ. The difficulty in reaching any agreement over the eight-year negotiating period was partially overcome by the use of vague language, enabling all participants to claim that their varied objectives had been achieved. Under the above-quoted Article 56 of the 1982 LOST Convention, the coastal nation may exercise limited sovereignty in its EEZ to "explore," "exploit," "conserve," and "manage" the natural resources of the waters, seabed, and its subsoil. This language provides no objective yardstick, however, for measuring the *discretion* of the coastal State to exclude the activities of other states in its EEZ. For example, the coastal State may determine the "allowable catch" of fish to be taken by other States from its EEZ. This treaty language contains no concrete standard to define just what constitutes an allowable catch. Under Article 62, when a State fails to determine its allowable catch, or does not have the "capacity to harvest the entire allowable catch, it shall, through agreements . . . give other states access to the surplus of the allowable catch. . . ." This article thus requires the coastal State to provide for access to the surplus by other nations. Unfortunately, this provision means no more than an agreement to agree at a later time—without the benefit of guidelines to define specifically the non-coastal State's right of access to the surplus resources of the EEZ.

Two further problems limit the expansion of jurisdiction into the EEZ. First, the underlying purpose of equitably distributing global wealth will not be served by expanding coastal State rights in an EEZ without some correlative increase in the rights of *landlocked* States. They have no EEZ and thus no similar basis for developing their share of ocean resources. Under Article 70 of the LOST, their rights were implicitly resolved. Landlocked or "geographically disadvantaged States shall have the right to participate, on an equitable basis, in the exploitation of an appropriate part of the surplus of the living resources of the exclusive economic zones of coastal States of the same subregion or region, taking into account the relevant economic and geographical circumstances of all the States concerned." But this language does not require that landlocked states receive any greater rights than any other group of States. If Paraguay, a landlocked state, fishes in Argentina's EEZ, it must pay the same license fees as any other nation. How, then, would Paraguay obtain the Article 70 benefit of equitable participation in Argentina's surplus fish available for such geographically disadvantaged states?

The second problem with creation of the EEZ, and its attendant expansion of the range of coastal sovereignty, is that many States cannot claim an *exclusive* 200-mile EEZ because their respective shorelines are less than four hundred miles apart. Under Article 74 of the LOST, States with opposing or adjacent coastlines are expected to resolve any inconsistent claims to their respective EEZs "by agreement on the basis of international law . . . in order to achieve an equitable solution." A similar problem arises with delimitation in facing or adjacent Continental Shelves, a regime addressed below. Between 1969 and 1993, the International Court of Justice thus heard *six* cases wherein it was called upon to establish respective rights in such EEZs or Continental Shelves in various regions of the world. The Court has not been able to produce a uniform principle other than the rather vague notion of "equidistance"—a term meaning different things to different nations.[38]

In practice, some nations have established their respective rights to overlapping coastal zones by using an equidistance principle. Italy and what was the former Yugoslavia, for example, faced one another across the Adriatic Sea—which is only 100 miles across at many points. LOST Article 74 mandates an agreement to "achieve an equitable solution" to the geographic inability of both nations to claim the approximately 200-mile width of the Adriatic as their Exclusive Economic Zones. Under customary State practice, the Italian and (former) Yugoslavian EEZs would extend to a median line that is equidistant from both coasts. Italy and Yugoslavia would thus be entitled to comparable EEZs of some fifty nautical miles at certain points from their respective shores.

Article 59 of the 1982 LOS Convention says that conflicts over the control and the breadth of the EEZ are supposed to be resolved "on the basis of equity and in light of all the relevant circumstances, taking into account the respective importance of the interests involved to the parties as well as to the international community as a whole." This article is obviously vague. It does not define "equity," "relevant," or "interests." This vagueness is yet another illustration that consensus was achieved only through the use of broad terminology without clarity of application.

The approval, in principle, of the EEZ has nevertheless had the following impact upon the International Law of the Sea. Over one-third of all ocean space, containing 90 percent of global fishing resources, is now subject to the sovereignty of the coastal nations of the world. Now that the 1982 LOST has been adopted by enough countries for its entry into force, the G-77 have achieved one objective in their proposed New International Economic Order: an increase in the national sovereignty of many lesser-developed nations over global economic resources in the ocean waters near their shores but beyond both the Territorial Sea and the Contiguous Zone.

On the other hand, there is no evidence that international approval of the 1982 Convention's EEZ articles have helped or will actually help the poorer or underdeveloped States, as envisioned by the proponents of the EEZ. As stated by Professor Arvid Pardo, Malta's former ambassador to the United Nations and a LOST participant:

the Convention is grossly inequitable not only as between coastal States and landlocked and geographically disadvantaged States, but also as between coastal States themselves: only ten of these in fact obtain more than half of the area which the Convention places under na-

tional control [since so many nations separated by international waters are less than four hundred miles apart]. . . . It should be noted that adequate scientific capability, appropriate technology and substantial financial resources are required to effectively develop offshore resources, particularly mineral resources; thus, only wealthy countries and a few large developing countries such as China, Brazil, India and a few others have the means themselves to engage in significant offshore development. This could mean that marine areas under the jurisdiction of many small developing countries . . . could be exploited in practice predominantly for the benefit of technologically advanced countries with far-reaching political consequences.[39]

This perspective illustrates that comparatively wealthy and developed States are thus likely to continue extracting the usual benefits from their international ventures in the EEZs of other nations.

(6) Continental Shelf

Historical Development The US devised a novel approach for protecting its natural resources by being the first nation to claim the right to control the resources over its Continental Shelf (CS). In 1946, President Truman unilaterally announced a "fishing conservation zone" beyond the three-mile Territorial Sea. This conservation measure initiated the so-called Continental Shelf Doctrine whereby the US claimed limited jurisdiction over the continental shelf adjacent to its coasts—a distance of approximately two hundred nautical miles on both coasts.

Truman did not claim *exclusive* sovereignty in this area of the High Seas for the US. To preserve the rights to the fishing resources in the waters above the US Continental Shelf, he expanded coastal sovereignty for the limited purpose of controlling *economic* activity over the Continental Shelf. Other nations thus retained the right to pass freely through the High Seas over the shelf. They could not fish there, however, without obeying US coastal fishing regulations. The Continental Shelf Doctrine was later adopted by some other nations and was the central theme of the 1958 United Nations Convention on the Continental Shelf.[40]

Many States have a Continental Shelf that differs drastically from that of the US. Chile, Ecuador, and

Peru, for example, have shelves that extend out to only a few miles from their coastlines before dropping off to great depths—unlike the much broader US shelf. For this reason they took a more direct approach to preserving their economic resources in the High Seas near their coasts. In 1952, those three States simultaneously became the first nations to claim 200-mile-wide Territorial Seas. Unlike the US, they claimed *exclusive* territorial sovereignty in this 200-mile area adjacent to their coasts. They perceived little difference between their claim of exclusivity and Truman's Continental Shelf Doctrine for claiming sovereignty over a 200-mile fishing area adjacent to both US coasts.

LOST Treatment Article 76 of the 1982 LOST defines the CS as the coastal State's "sea-bed and subsoil of the submarine areas that extend beyond its territorial sea throughout the natural prolongation of its land territory. . . ." The range of the CS may vary from 200 nautical miles from the coastal baseline to 350 nautical miles, depending on the natural extension of the coastal State's underwater land mass—which often drops off to great depths relatively close to their coasts. The CS depicted in Exhibit 6.2 naturally slopes off without a sudden drop—as is the case with the US. There is no CS, to speak of, off coastal States such as Chile, Ecuador, and Peru. This is one reason why they opted to react to President Truman's 1946 CS announcement with their 1952 200-mile Territorial Sea claims.

What happens when two or more coastal States *share* the same CS? What are their respective rights regarding use of their shared CS? The International Court of Justice addressed this matter in its 1969 *North Sea Continental Shelf Cases* decision. Germany, Denmark, and the Netherlands disputed the respective CS delimitations in the North Sea, on each of their coasts—where there is no outer boundary to the CS. The Court stated that there was no obligatory method of delimitation, but that the parties should agree in accordance with equitable principles. Thus, delimitation is to be generally arranged "by agreement in accordance with equitable principles . . . in such a way as to leave as much as possible to each party all those parts of the continental shelf that constitute a natural prolongation of its land territory into and under the sea, without encroachment on the natural prolongation of the land territory of the other[s]. . . ."[41]

The 1982 LOST essentially codified the *North Seas Continental Shelf Cases* decision in Article 83.1. States with opposite or adjacent coasts must thereunder enter into an "agreement on the basis of international law." Unfortunately, this is merely an agreement to agree—but typical of multilateral conventions where consensus is achieved by the use of rather question-begging language with which no State could disagree.

(7) Deep Seabed

Historical Development Exploitation of marine life was the first of two major reasons for international interest in extending national sovereignty into the High Seas. The second reason was control of mineral exploitation in the seabed just beyond the Territorial Sea and Contiguous Zone. After World War II, the technology for deep seabed mining advanced quickly. Valuable ore deposits beyond the three-mile Territorial Sea became increasingly accessible and were thus extracted on a first-come, first-served basis. The coastal State could exercise exclusive sovereignty in the Territorial Sea, limited sovereignty in the Contiguous Zone, but no further control in the High Seas. Under International Law, the High Seas beyond these zones were *res communis*—belonging to no one and thus accessible by all. Many coastal States could not obtain, nor could they prevent other States from extracting, the mineral resources under these waters just beyond their sovereign control.

In 1970, the UN General Assembly proclaimed another legal category of territory designated as the "Common Heritage of Mankind" (CHM). In Resolution 2749, the Assembly thus attempted to institutionalize the CHM in areas beyond national jurisdiction (including the moon and other celestial bodies). Management, exploitation, and distribution of the resources of the ocean area beyond national control should be decided by the international community—rather than being left to the discretion of its individual States and their multinational corporations. To this end, the UN called for the convening of a new law of the sea conference to reflect this change in attitude by drafting articles to be negotiated by the international community.[42]

LOST Provisions The work of the ensuing conference then produced the most drastic revision of the historical conception of free seas. In the new regime of the 1982 Law of the Sea Treaty (LOST) on

Resources, on and below the seabed, are increasingly being exploited. *At the left*, a specially constructed barge lays a submarine pipeline in the North Sea (off the coast of Great Britain) to carry oil obtained from offshore drilling. *At the right*, samples of mineral deposits are dredged up from below the surface of the ocean floor.

resources in the deep sea bed, the Part XI (Articles 136–153) addressed what was called "The Area." It was essentially these provisions that delayed the treaty's entry into force for more than two decades. Developed nations had been profitably mining this area for two decades prior to the 1982 LOST final draft. (The 1994 modifications acceptable to major powers like the US will be addressed later in this section.)

Article 1 of the LOST defines "The Area" as the ocean floor and its subsoil "beyond the limits of national jurisdiction." Article 136 provides that "The Area and its resources are the common heritage of all mankind." This is the area under the oceans that does not otherwise fall within any of the zones described earlier in this section of the book. There are valuable minerals located in the High Seas, or the area beyond the Territorial, Contiguous, and Exclusive Economic Zones.

While no *State* may exercise its exclusive or limited jurisdiction within "The Area," an organization called the International Sea-bed Authority ("The Authority") is supposed to control virtually all aspects of deep seabed mining in The Area. Article 137.2 of the LOST contained an essential feature that drew objections from the major maritime powers: "All rights in the resources of the Area are vested in mankind as a whole, on whose behalf the [International Sea-bed] Authority shall act. These rights are not subject to alienation [sale or licensing by a national authority]. The minerals recovered from the Area, however, may only be alienated in accordance with this Part [XI] and the rules, regulations and procedures of the Authority."

Under the 1982 Convention, the ISBA consists of all national participants in the LOST. It is to be based in Jamaica and funded by assessed contributions from UN members. The ISBA is expected to organize and control all economic activities in "The Area." Mineral resources within it are beyond national jurisdiction (outside of the exclusive economic zone of 200 miles), and thus fall within "The Authority's" control.

The 1982 Convention confers several fundamental tasks upon "The Authority:"

- To ensure that mining activities within the Area are "carried out for the benefit of mankind as a whole . . . taking into particular consideration the interests and needs of developing States and of peoples who have not attained full independence. . . . The Authority shall provide for the equitable sharing of financial and other economic benefits derived from activities in the Area through any appropriate mechanism. . . ." (Article 140);

- To establish regulations and procedures that will accomplish the required equitable sharing of the profits derived from the mineral resources in the Area (Article 160);

- To take measures to acquire technology for itself and to encourage the "transfer to developing States of such technology and scientific knowledge so that all States Parties [to the Convention] benefit therefrom" (Article 144.1); and,

- To promote the "effective participation of developing States in activities in the Area. . . ." (Article 148).

These tasks will be accomplished by the Authority's operation of "The Enterprise," its mineral exploration and exploitation organ. The Enterprise will monitor the commercial production of all mineral resources in "The Area." It will be funded by "revenues [derived] by the Authority and the transfer of technology to the Enterprise" (Article 150d). The revenues derived from "The Enterprise" will be the royalty payments or profit shares of national or individual miners who extract minerals from seabeds in the area. The collection of these revenues and potential transfer of mining technology to "The Authority's Enterprise" are designed to circumvent what some 1982 Law of the Sea Conference delegates characterized as the monopolistic behavior of the larger developed nations. A small group within the community of nations possesses the requisite technology for mining these deep seabed resources. Under LOST Article 150g, however, the Enterprise will ensure the "enhancement of opportunities for

all . . . irrespective of their social and economic systems or geographical location, to participate in the development of the resources of the Area and the prevention of monopolization of activities in the Area."

In 1994, US Secretary of State Warren Christopher announced the US intent to sign the 1982 UN LOST. The US realized that the LOST would soon enter into force in November 1994, because the minimum number of ratifications (sixty) had already been deposited with the UN. This forthcoming event was a motivating factor for the July 1994 US signing (which is not the same thing as ratification—*see* § 8.2, on treaty formation). What was acceptable to approximately 160 States, as of 1994, would be hard for the "holdout" major seagoing powers to change unilaterally.

The primary basis for this US reversal of policy was based on the successful negotiation of a separate agreement entitled the "Agreement Relating to Implementation of Part XI of the United Nations Convention on the Law of the Sea." As articulated by Mr. Christopher for the *Congressional Record*, the US position was that the LOST Article XI provisions are "seriously flawed." Yet "it is imperative from the standpoint of our security and economic interests that the United States become a party to this Convention. . . . Its strategic importance cannot be overstated. . . . The result is a regime that is consistent with our free market principles and provides the United States with influence over decisions on deep seabed mining commensurate with our interests." Thus, the US intends to become a party to the LOST by ratifying the two agreements (1982 LOST and special 1994 Agreement) as if they were a single instrument.[43]

US corporations have a huge economic stake in the US's becoming a party to the LOST. The beneficiaries include the major telecommunications companies such as American Telephone and Telegraph. It has laid a great deal of cable throughout the oceans of the world, connecting many continents and foreign enterprises. This treaty ensures that AT&T will be allowed to continue to lay and maintain these ocean-floor cables. Offshore drilling companies will similarly benefit due to the effective removal of certain jurisdictional uncertainties. Oil companies and other shippers will enjoy the unrestricted passage of their oil tankers and cargo ships throughout the various sea zones of the 160 signatories. The Pentagon now supports this treaty as a basis for ensuring unimpeded warship passage, particularly within these straits that formerly contained High Seas—while currently containing Territorial Seas due to the modern expansions of coastal State jurisdiction in the world's oceans.

On the other hand, this constitution of the oceans suggests the creation of a new form of cartel—"The Enterprise." This entity would be responsible for the mandated sharing of technology, the degree of production control and pricing, and an infrastructure not unlike that of the Organization of Petroleum Exporting Countries responsible for worldwide price increases and production quotas—hardly a free-market enterprise.

The special 1994 Agreement removes a number of such objections tendered by the US and other major industrialized powers to the deep seabed mining provisions of the 1982 LOST. They objected to control of deep seabed mining resource allocation as unnecessarily excluding the input of the major powers within the International Sea-bed Authority. Also, they opposed mandatory technology transfer, production limitations, more onerous financial obligations for the private enterprises of the mining nations, and a subsidized international enterprise that could compete unfairly with existing commercial enterprises. These States that sought a more free market-oriented regime, whereunder their interests have flourished since World War II.

The 1994 Agreement specifically permits countries such as the US to block decisions on a basis that reflects its comparative economic interests in the Law of the Sea. For example, the US may now block the financial or budgetary decisions of the International Sea-bed Authority. This agency could otherwise decide to use revenues derived from "The Enterprise" to fund a liberation movement not in line with US interests. For parties to the 1994 special Agreement, the mandatory technology transfer provisions are supplanted by more cooperative arrangements or joint ventures involving procurement on the open market. Also, "The Enterprise" will not have to be financed by the developed States only. Like the General Agreement on Tariffs and Trade (GATT) discussed in Chapter 13 of this book, this seabed organization would not authorize the underwriting of certain national operations by subsidies taken out of royalties to be charged to only the mining nations. There is also a form of "grandfathering" provision allowing mining, already licensed under

US law to operate on the same favorable terms as those previously granted by "The Authority" to French, Japanese, Indian, and Chinese companies whose mine site claims have already been registered. To meet yet another objection with the wording of the Article XI provisions of the LOST, certain financial obligations otherwise imposed on mining nations at the exploration stage are eliminated under the special 1994 Agreement.

In a nutshell, the July 1994 special Agreement restructured Part XI of the 1982 LOST as a compromise geared toward achieving more universal participation in a global law of the sea. (There were 159 State parties to the LOST as of the 1994 US decision to join.) As stated in the August 1994 Report of the Section of International Law and Practice of the American Bar Association, recommending that the US sign (and ratify) the 1982 LOST, "new threats to United States security posed by the end of the Cold War and by the rise of new nations and regional powers [make] . . . it important to seek long-term stability of rules related to the oceans."[44]

For those nations that are otherwise parties to the 1982 LOS Convention, there is no specific timeframe for either The Enterprise's commencement of mineral production or The Authority's equitable distribution of the revenues generated by The Enterprise. The LOST does contain two related timetables. Upon ratification by a sufficient number of nations (that is, in 1994), The Authority will review the progress made toward these production and distribution goals every five years. There will be another international review conference fifteen years after the Authority begins its commercial production of minerals in "The Area" to monitor the Authority's progress toward exploration, exploitation, conservation, and distribution of the resources from the ocean areas beyond national control.

Two questions remain about the actual realization of this 1982 Convention's goals. First, how will an international organization actually redistribute global wealth in a way that satisfies the diverse interests of its State members? Second, absent specific decision-making procedures, just how will The Authority implement the goal of international exploitation of mineral resources for the benefit of all?

Individual conference participants have given mixed reviews of achievements by the 1982 LOST provisions. Tommy Koh, Singapore's ambassador to the United Nations and President of the Conference, described the Area/Authority provisions as a success. In his view, the delegates reconciled the competing interests of many diverse groups of nations. His positive assessment is articulated as follows:

the international community as a whole wished to promote the development of the seabed's resources as did those members of the international community which consume the metals extracted from the . . . nodules [in the ocean's floor]. The developing countries, as co-owners of the resource, wanted to share in the benefits of the exploitation of the resources and to participate in the exploitation. . . . A seabed miner will have to pay to the International Seabed Authority either a royalty payment or a combination of a royalty payment and a share of his profits. . . . Under the Convention, a seabed miner may be required . . . to sell his technology to the Authority. This obligation has caused great concern to the industrialised countries. It should be borne in mind, however, that the obligation [to transfer technology] cannot be invoked by the Authority unless the same or equivalent technology is unavailable in the open market. A contract study by the U.S. Department of the Interior indicates that there is a relatively large number of suppliers of ocean mining system components and design construction services. If this is true, then the precondition [requiring technology transfer to the Authority] cannot be met and the obligation can never be invoked.[45]

The perspective of Malta's ambassador to the UN Conference on the Law of the Sea is not as positive as that of Ambassador Koh's. Ambassador Pardo's contrary appraisal is as follows:

the Convention reflects primarily the highly acquisitive aspirations of many coastal States, particularly of those developed and developing States with long coastlines fronting on the open ocean and of mid-ocean archipelagic States. Perhaps as much as forty percent of ocean space, by far the most valuable in terms of economic uses and accessible resources, is placed under some form of national control [by adoption of the exclusive economic zone].

. . . Additionally, elaborate provision is made for [the Authority's] international management of the mineral resources of the seabed beyond national jurisdiction. Nevertheless, the approach of the Convention to problems of marine resource management appears seriously deficient in several respects. . . . [T]he common heritage regime established for the international seabed is a little short of disaster. The . . . competence of the Authority is limited strictly to the exploration and exploitation of mineral resources; the decision-making procedures . . . ranging, according to the nature of the question, from a two-thirds majority to a consensus, are such as to render unlikely appropriate and timely decisions on important questions. . . . Thus, there arises the unpleasant prospect of the establishment of new and expensive international organizations incapable of effectively performing the functions for which they were created. . . . It is a pity that this side of the Convention has not been developed in a practical way. Instead a truly historic opportunity to mold the legal framework governing human activities in the marine environment in such a way as to contribute effectively to the realization of a just and equitable international order in the seas . . . has been lost.[46]

The deep seabed mining provisions of the 1982 LOS Conference are ambitious and call for the international control of mining in the world's seabeds beyond the limits of national jurisdiction. The program outlined by these provisions has not yet been implemented. But the signing by approximately 160 nations, the LOST's 1994 entry into force, the anticipated US ratification, and a potential regime of compulsory dispute resolution are obviously rather positive developments.[47]

■ 6.4 AIR ZONES

This section of the chapter on the range of State sovereignty now turns to the distinct air zones and the degree to which a State's power may be exercised within them. The essential questions are as follows: (1) what are the State's rights and obligations in the airspace above its own territory? (2) in that of other States? (3) in air zones over international waters belonging to no one? (4) in outer space?

Domestic Airspace

Introduction A State has the sovereign right to control persons and things within its territory. Control of the land portion of State territory is addressed in §§ 6.1–6.2. This section addresses the analogous national power over airspace.

Few branches of International Law developed as rapidly as International Air Law. Prior to World War I, there were no norms to govern international flight. The military use of aircraft in World War I quickly changed this. Hostile aircraft could approach more swiftly than approaching armies or warships. Rapid advancements in the technology of air travel profoundly accelerated the need to establish norms to control national airspace. Almost immediately, States quickly claimed the right to include airspace within the definition of their "territory."

State practice also anticipated the impact of air travel on international trade. A 1942 commentary in the *American Journal of International Law* addressed the significance of commercial air travel for internal security and foreign competition:

> The unprecedentedly accelerated speed of change in the last thirty years has been such that, politically, air navigation has already passed through many of the phases which it took sea navigation centuries to span.
>
> As to air navigation, it may be observed that in 1910 the states were preoccupied only with guaranteeing the safety of their territory; the necessity of permitting other states to navigate freely to and over their territory was recognized to the fullest extent where this freedom did not affect the security of the state. The period 1910–1919 can thus be compared with that period in the history of shipping in which the adjacent seas were appropriated primarily to secure the land from invasion.
>
> In 1919 the first consideration was still the security of the states, but . . . some small clouds were already appearing on the horizon of the free sky. In the minds of some . . . the idea took shape to use the power of the state over the air to protect its own air navigation against foreign competition. As in shipping,

the pretensions to the appropriation of the sea and the power to restrict foreign sea commerce grew in proportion to the increase in the direct profits to be expected from them, so in aviation the pretensions to unrestricted sovereignty—not in doctrine but in practice—grew in proportion to the development of aviation during the period from 1919 to 1929.[48]

National legislation thus imposed various limitations on international air travel. It prohibited the unauthorized entry of aircraft. These laws restricted freedom of navigation, types of importable cargo, and conditions of passenger travel. States soon recognized the need to enter into international treaties for the purpose of establishing their mutual expectations.

1919 Paris Convention The vertical extension of the range of State sovereignty was first incorporated into the 1919 Paris Convention Relating to the Regulation of Aerial Navigation. Article 1 provided for the mutual recognition "that every Power [State] has complete and exclusive sovereignty over the air space above its territory." Under Article 15, each State party to this treaty could "make conditional on its prior authorisation the establishment of international airways and the creation and operation of regular international air navigation lines, with or without landing, on its territory."[49] As the degree of international commerce grew exponentially, the need became more evident that the international community should solidify its expectations via a comprehensive constitution of the air.

1944 Chicago Convention The next air treaty was the 1944 Chicago Convention on International Civil Aviation. It contains the contemporary principles of International Air Law. Most nations of the world are parties to this treaty. Its fundamental provisions and their applications are summarized below:

Article 1 The contracting States recognize that every State has complete and exclusive sovereignty over the airspace above its territory.

Article 2 For the purposes of this Convention the territory of a State shall be deemed to be the land areas and territorial waters adjacent thereto under the sovereignty . . . of such State.

These provisions codify the sovereign right to completely exclude air travel through the airspace above the State's land mass *and* above the territorial waters adjacent to its coastlines. France, for example, legally denied US President Ronald Reagan's request that US aircraft be allowed to fly over France and its territorial waters on a 1986 retaliatory bombing mission into Libya. US warplanes were thus required to fly a rather circuitous route around France's territorial air space and through the Straits of Gibraltar to gain access to Libya via the western entrance to the Mediterranean Sea.

In most instances, States encourage *commercial* flights through their airspace in order to maintain economic ties with other States. The Chicago Convention thus governs both the nonscheduled flights of private aircraft and the scheduled flights of commercial passenger and cargo air services. The key articles, their intended applications, and the essential provisions on military and other state aircraft are provided below:

Article 5 Each contracting State agrees that all aircraft of the other contracting States, being aircraft not engaged in scheduled international air services shall have the right . . . to make flights into or in transit non-stop across its territory and to make stops for non-traffic purposes without the necessity of obtaining prior permission, and subject to the right of the State flown over to require landing.

Article 6 No scheduled [commercial] international air service may be operated over or into the territory of a contracting State, except with the special permission or other authorization of that State. . . .

Private Aircraft Noncommercial private aircraft enjoy the general right to fly into or over state territory (Article 5 above). They may land for refueling and other purposes without prior permission. An English citizen thus may land to refuel his plane at a French airport while en route to Germany. That pilot must, however, file a flight plan at the flight's point of origin. France may alter the flight plan if it somehow interferes with any French regulation or security concerns. State practice is more restrictive in the case of *commercial* aircraft (Article 6 above). They may *not* fly over or land in the territory of an-

other country without advance routing or landing arrangements.

The International Civil Aviation Organization (ICAO) regulates international commercial aviation. Established by the State parties to the Chicago Convention, this international organization schedules air routes, cargo delivery, and passenger service. Under Article 44 of the Chicago Treaty, the ICAO promotes "the safe and orderly growth of international civil aviation throughout the world . . . [by] development of airways, airports, and air navigation facilities . . . [and avoidance of] economic waste caused by unreasonable competition."

The organization's member States are encouraged to use a neutral tribunal to resolve disputes involving the ICAO's administrative decisions. Article 84 provides that States may appeal such decisions "to an *ad hoc* arbitral tribunal agreed upon with the other parties to the dispute or to the Permanent Court of International Justice." In 1972, the PCIJ's successor tribunal—the International Court of Justice—decided that it would also review ICAO decisions.[50] The ICJ accepted another case in 1989, requesting the review of an ICAO decision that the United States was not legally responsible when one of its naval vessels shot down an Iranian commercial aircraft over the Persian Gulf. Iran filed a suit, asking the court to declare the ICAO's decision erroneous. The parties ultimately dismissed this suit in 1994 after a number of delays in its pleading phase.

The 1944 Chicago Convention did not resolve many of the problems associated with the actual scheduling of air services. The commercial airlines of the world thus formed a private organization called the International Air Transport Association (IATA), which has focused its work on achieving the Chicago Convention goal of avoiding "unreasonable competition." The IATA is essentially a cartel of private airlines attempting to avoid destructive or excessive competition among international airlines—an unusually competitive business. One IATA goal, for example, is to ensure that flights by competing airlines do not leave the same airport at the same time. Such competition would ultimately destroy one or more of the competitors.

Some airlines have claimed that there is, in fact, a great deal of *anti*competitive activity in international aviation. In 1983, for example, Laker Airways of England filed lawsuits in England and the US, claiming that various Belgian, British, and Dutch airlines (IATA members) conspired to bankrupt

Laker Airways because it offered very competitive air fares to the public. Members of the IATA allegedly perceived Laker's operations as a threat to the price structure established by their association. Laker thus claimed that during meetings of the IATA in 1977, the IATA airlines "agreed to set rates at a predatory level to drive Laker out of business." Laker also alleged that these international air carriers conspired to stop Laker from expanding its international air routes.[51]

Restrictive business practices in the international airlines industry are not limited to just private airline carriers. Many governments subsidize their government-owned or certain private international airlines, a practice that facilitates continuing operation and increases their share of the international market. These subsidies permit the favored airlines to charge lower fares or operate at a better profit margin, even when they charge the same or lower fares than their competitors. Subsidizing countries thereby create artificial economic barriers to normal market competition. They impose limitations, for example, on certain categories of importable cargo and on frequency of passenger aircraft entry into their airspaces. Similar barriers to international competition are addressed in § 13.3.

State Aircraft Public (as opposed to private) aircraft are operated by the military, customs, and police authorities. These flights are not generally governed by the 1944 Chicago Convention, although it does make certain limited provisions for such aircraft.

Article 3
(a) This convention shall be applicable only to civil aircraft, and shall not be applicable to state aircraft.
(b) Aircraft used in military, customs and police services shall be deemed to be state aircraft. [However,]
(c) No state aircraft . . . shall fly over the territory of another State or land thereon without authorization by special agreement.

Unlike *non*scheduled private aircraft, government aircraft cannot enter another State's national airspace without the express prior agreement of the receiving State. These agreements are often made on a case-by-case basis, and otherwise by treaty arrangements between friendly countries. Before making an emergency landing in another State, a military pilot must seek permission to enter that State's airspace (or to land). Otherwise, one State could send its planes on a hostile mission under the pretext of a feigned emergency. Military flight agreements, such as those governing a State aircraft's entry into foreign airspace during joint military exercises, are normally made by formal agreements between affected States.

The following case is a classic illustration of the national and international concerns about the presence of foreign State aircraft over a State's territory—even when the plane has no weapons systems. This case further illustrates that more than one State can effectively violate International Law when a single plane makes an unauthorized entry into another State's airspace:

POWERS CASE

Union of Soviet Socialist Republics
Military Collegium of the Soviet Supreme Court, 1960
30 International Law Reports 69 (1966)*

[Author's Note: In 1960, the US authorized the flight of a U-2 military reconnaissance aircraft over the former Soviet Union. The U-2 was shot down, and the Soviet Union prosecuted its pilot for espionage. The following excerpts are from the military panel of the Soviet Supreme Court. In addition to noting the territorial sovereignty concerns, you should assess whether the Soviet Union was being overly technical about the threat posed by this unarmed aircraft in the upper periphery of its airspace where combat aircraft were unable to fly.]

*Reprinted with permission from Grotius Publications, Cambridge, England.

[*Opinion.*] On May 1, 1960, at 5 hours 36 minutes, Moscow time, a military unit of the Soviet anti-aircraft defence in the area of the city of Kirovabad, the Tajik S.S.R., at an altitude of 20,000 metres, unattainable for planes of the civil air fleet, spotted an unknown aircraft violating the State frontier of the U.S.S.R.

The military units of the Soviet anti-aircraft defence vigilantly followed the behaviour of the plane as it flew over major industrial centres and important objectives, and only when the intruder plane had penetrated 2,000 kilometres into Soviet territory and the evil purpose of the flight, fraught with disastrous consequences for world peace in an age of thermonuclear weapons, became absolutely obvious, a battery of ground-to-air missiles brought the aggressor plane down in the area of Sverdlovsk at 8 hours 53 minutes as ordered by the Soviet Government.

The pilot of the plane bailed out and was apprehended upon landing. On interrogation, he gave his name as Francis Gary Powers, citizen of the United States of America. Examination of the wreckage of the plane which had been brought down showed that it was of American make, specially designed for high altitude flights and fitted with various equipment for espionage reconnaissance tasks.

In April 1956, Powers was recruited by the Central Intelligence Agency of the United States for special intelligence missions in high-altitude aircraft.

After he had concluded a secret contract with the United States Central Intelligence Agency for a term of two years, Powers was allotted a high salary of 2,500 dollars a month for espionage activity. He underwent special training and was assigned to the intelligence air detachment under the code name of "Ten-Ten," stationed at the American-Turkish war base of Incirlik, near the town of Adana, in Turkey.

The Court has established that the detachment "Ten-Ten" is a special combination of the United States military and civilian intelligence designed for espionage against the Soviet Union with the help of reconnaissance planes sent into Soviet air space.

. . .

Having taken off from Peshawar airport in Pakistan, Powers flew over the territory of Afghanistan and for more than 2,000 kilometers over the Soviet Union in accordance with the established course. Besides Powers' testimony, this is confirmed by the American flight map discovered in the debris of the U-2 plane and submitted to the Court, bearing the route plotted out by Major Dulak, navigator of the detachment "Ten-Ten," and also notes and signs made by Powers, who marked down on this map several important defence objectives of the Soviet Union he had spotted from the plane.

Throughout the flight, to the very moment the plane was shot down, Powers switched on his special intelligence equipment, photographed important defence objectives and recorded signals of the country's anti-aircraft radar installations. The development of the rescued aerial photography films established that defendant Powers photographed from the U-2 plane industrial and military objectives of the Soviet Union—plants, depots, oil storage facilities, communication routes, railway bridges and stations, electric transmission lines, aerodromes, the location of troops and military equipment.

The numerous photos of the Soviet Union's territory, taken by defendant Powers from an altitude of 20,000 metres, in possession of the Military Collegium of the U.S.S.R. Supreme Court, make it possible to determine the nature of industrial establishments, the design of railway bridges, the number and type of aircraft on the airfields, the nature and purpose of military material.

Powers tape-recorded impulses of certain radar stations of the Soviet Union with a view of detecting the country's anti-aircraft defence system.

Powers himself admitted that he realized when intruding into the air space of the Soviet Union that he was violating the national sovereignty of the U.S.S.R. and flying over its territory on an espionage mission, whose main purpose consisted of detecting and marking down missile launching sites.

. . .

In considering the Powers case, the Military Collegium of the U.S.S.R. Supreme Court takes into account that the intrusion of the American military intelligence plane constitutes a criminal breach of a generally recognized principle of international law, which establishes the exclusive sovereignty of every State over the air space above its territory. This principle, laid down by the Paris Convention of October 13, 1919, for the regulation of aerial navigation, and several other subsequent international agreements, is proclaimed in the national legislations of different States, including the Soviet Union and the United States of America.

Violation of this sacred and immutable principle of international relations creates in the present conditions a direct menace to universal peace and international security.

At the present level of military technology, when certain States possess atomic and hydrogen weapons, as well as the means of delivering them quickly to targets, the flight of a military intelligence plane over Soviet territory could have directly preceded a military attack. This danger is the more possible in conditions when the United States of America, as stated by American generals, constantly keeps bomber patrols in the air, always ready to drop bombs on earlier marked-out targets of the Soviet Union.

Under these conditions the aggressive act of the United States of America, carried out on May 1 of this year by defendant Powers, created a threat to universal peace.

. . .

After that the American leaders—President Eisenhower, Vice-President Nixon and State Secretary Herter—admitted that spying flights over Soviet territory by American planes constitute part of the "calculated policy of the United States of America."

Thus, the leaders of the United States of America proclaimed the violation of the sovereignty of other States and espionage against them as the official State policy of America.

. . .

The Military Collegium of the Supreme Court of the Soviet Union has established that Powers could not have carried out the spy missions assigned to him without the use of the United States of America, for aggressive purposes, of the war bases and aerodromes on the territories of the States neighboring on the Soviet Union, including the territories of Turkey, Iran, Pakistan and Norway.

Powers' flight has proved that the Government of the United States of America, having bound Turkey, Iran, Pakistan, Norway and other States by bilateral military agreements, has established war bases and aerodromes on their territories for dangerous provocative actions, making these States accomplices in the aggression against the Soviet Union.

■ NOTES & QUESTIONS

What State or States violated Soviet airspace? Was the Soviet Union being overly technical about the threat posed by the unarmed US plane?

A number of unresolved problems linger in International Air Law, two of which are particularly sensitive. States have not agreed on the permissible degree of response to violations of national airspace. Nor have they agreed on the altitude that constitutes the upper limits of territorial airspace. The upper limit is important because it separates national airspace from outer space.

Excessive Force How much force may a State use to repel intruders? A number of military planes have purposefully or accidentally entered foreign airspace. A number of commercial aircraft have also encroached on territorial airspace. In some parts of the world, these unexpected intrusions are routinely ignored. In some cases, however, the intruder has been ordered to change course, escorted out of the offended State's territorial airspace, fired on as a warning, forced to land, or actually shot down.

During the decade after World War II, a number of incidents occurred in which deadly force was the response to *non*military aerial intrusions. In the major international incident of 1955, an Israeli commercial plane flew into Bulgarian airspace while en route from Austria to Israel. A Bulgarian military aircraft shot it down over Bulgaria, killing all fifty-eight passengers. Israel instituted proceedings in the International Court of Justice. The court decided, however, that it could not hear the case because Bulgaria had not consented to the court's jurisdiction to hear such cases.[52] Israel and Bulgaria ultimately negotiated a compensation agreement in 1963.

Unfortunately, some States still use deadly force to react to nonmilitary intrusions of their airspace. In 1983, for example, a Korean passenger jet flew over some Soviet islands after departing from Alaska en route to Korea. Eight Soviet military aircraft monitored the movement of the KAL flight 007, but their pilots claimed they had been unable to communicate with the Korean plane. After the airliner turned away from the Soviet mainland, and while in Soviet airspace, one of those Soviet jets shot it down. All 269 of the passengers and crew were killed. This incident generated a number of diplomatic protests, ICAO deliberations, and several meetings of the United Nations Security Council.[53] The KAL flight 007 incident demonstrates the importance that the former Soviet Union attributed to the presence of *any* nonscheduled aircraft in its national airspace.

Upper Limit The upper limit of territorial airspace has not been precisely established. While the 1944 Chicago Convention is the centerpiece of International Air Law, it does not define the extent or height of national airspace. Different States thus claim different legal limits.

As a practical matter, territorial airspace is limited to the *navigable* airspace over State territory and its adjacent Territorial Seas—twelve nautical miles from the coastline under the Law of the Sea Treaty, which entered into force in 1994. This is the limit used by most States when they characterize the extent of their territorial airspace. Navigable airspace is the highest altitude attainable by military aircraft not in orbit.

Airspace Abroad

The prior materials in this section of the book illustrate that each State obviously has the sovereign right to control its own airspace. What is not quite so obvious is the extent to which a State may exercise jurisdiction over events occurring in a foreign State's airspace or over international waters.

Chicago Convention The previously discussed 1944 Chicago Convention on International Civil Aviation is the fundamental treaty on International Air Law. Other international treaties were subsequently drafted to address the acceptable circumstances whereby a State could exercise jurisdiction over criminal offenses aboard its aircraft flying over international waters or in the airspace of another State. The need to expand jurisdiction over crimes aboard civil (nonmilitary) aircraft became apparent

as States realized the difficulty of prosecution due to voids in applicable jurisdictional principles.

A classic instance of this vacuum emerged in 1950, when a US passenger assaulted several US citizens aboard a plane registered to a US airline company—while it was flying over international waters outside of the US. The Chicago Convention vests jurisdiction in the State where an incident occurs. But this event took place *beyond* national airspace. The American prosecutor thus resorted to US internal law, which unfortunately did not apply to this conduct. Under US law, there had to be a statute that specifically made the passenger's conduct a criminal act. The only relevant statute made it a crime to assault passengers on "vessels" that were "on the high seas." The plane was not a vessel, within the meaning of the only applicable statute. Nor was the plane "on" the high seas.[54] The US was *unable* to prosecute this individual due to the absence of an applicable national law. The case was dismissed and the defendant was thus released from custody. The US Congress reacted by expanding this statute to include such offenses. This incident signaled the need for an international response. State representatives negotiated and then ratified a series of international treaties to fill the legal gap.

Tokyo Convention After World War II, the wartime concern about hostile flights was eclipsed by another problem. Airlines with large fleets of commercial aircraft were understandably concerned about their aircraft being subjected to the exclusive control of foreign nations while operating within foreign airspace. Within two decades after the war ended, the airline industry convinced their respective governments to negotiate the first multilateral air treaty containing *several* jurisdictional alternatives—the 1963 Tokyo Convention on Offences and Certain Other Acts Committed on Board Aircraft. It became effective in 1969 and has been ratified by most nations of the world.[55]

The Tokyo Convention established a framework for punishing individuals who commit violent crimes during international flights. This treaty emphasizes the jurisdiction of the aircraft's State of registration (often called the flag state), rather than that of the airspace of the State where the offense is committed. This treaty thus facilitated prosecution under jurisdictional principles not contemplated by the 1944 Chicago Convention, while effectively expanding the range of sovereignty now exercisable in the airspace above distant lands. Because States had the exclusive sovereign power over the airspace above them (Chicago Convention), they had the correlative right to yield this total control of their airspace for mutually acceptable purposes. Under Article 3 of the Tokyo Convention, the "State of registration of the aircraft is competent to exercise jurisdiction over offences and acts committed on board [and each participating State] shall take such measures as may be necessary to establish its jurisdiction as the State of registration over offences committed on board aircraft registered in such State."

Under Article 4 of the Tokyo Convention, a State that is *not* the State of registration cannot generally interfere on the basis that its otherwise applicable *territorial* criminal jurisdiction applies in its own airspace—*except* in the following specific cases:

(a) The offense has effect on the territory of such State;

(b) The offense has been committed by or against a national

or permanent resident of such State;

(c) The offense is against the security of such State. . . .

These exceptions essentially retained the common jurisdictional principles studied in § 5.2 of this book, as will be illustrated below. Assume that a Japanese airliner is flying in an easterly direction at 25,000 feet over Hawaii and it is en route to Canada. A German passenger assaults and kills a French citizen during the flight. All of these countries are parties to both the Chicago and the Tokyo conventions. Under the territorial principle of international criminal jurisdiction, the incident occurred "in" the US because the Japanese aircraft was flying within the navigable airspace of a state of the US. Under the 1944 Chicago Convention, the US has "complete and exclusive sovereignty over the airspace above its territory." Under Article 3 of the 1963 Tokyo Convention, however, Japan is the State of registration, or the flag State. Japan would thus be "competent to exercise jurisdiction over offences and acts committed on board [its airliner and should] take such measures as may be necessary to establish its jurisdiction." Since the US is a party to the Tokyo Convention, it will yield its territorial right to prosecute the German passenger to Japan. Japan will thus be obliged to prosecute this German citizen for the offense aboard the Japanese aircraft

(unless its accedes to a US request to have the perpetrator tried in the US).

Under Article 4 of the Tokyo Convention, States other than the State of registration should not interfere by exercising their criminal jurisdiction over the offender. While the US has territorial jurisdiction over the German passenger, it should assist Japan in the latter's efforts to prosecute him. If the plane lands in Hawaii, the US should grant Japan's extradition request.

There are significant exceptions to the treaty norm of ceding jurisdiction to the State of registration. Other States may prosecute the German citizen in four situations. First, another State may prosecute the German passenger if his crime has an effect in its territory. This exception draws from the "effects doctrine" authoritatively established by the Permanent Court of International Justice in the SS Lotus Case in 1927 (set forth in the text of § 5.2). The Tokyo Convention thus provides for applications of the territorial principle of international criminal jurisdiction. If the captain of the Japanese airliner has to alter course or altitude to respond to the incident, that action might violate navigational rules established for the safety of aircraft flying over Hawaii. The US could then request the plane to land and prosecute the German for various crimes against the United States—over Japan's objection. This is an example of the territorial principle of jurisdiction that remains available under the terms of the Tokyo Convention.

The second and third bases for States other than Japan—the State of the aircraft's registration—to exercise jurisdiction over the German citizen in the above hypothetical draw on the nationality and passive personality principles of criminal jurisdiction. Germany and France may prosecute the German passenger under Article 4b above: his "offense has been committed *by* or *against* a national or permanent resident of such State [that is a treaty party]." Germany may thus prosecute its German national under the nationality principle; and France may thus prosecute the German passenger for killing a French citizen under the passive personality principle.

The fourth exception to Japan's primary jurisdiction as the State of registration of the aircraft involves the protective principle of jurisdiction. The German passenger may thus be prosecuted outside of Japan if this "offense is against the security" of some other State. It is unlikely that the US would actually claim that its security was threatened by the killing of the French citizen, or alternatively, by the unusual maneuvers of the Japanese aircraft over Hawaii. Suppose, however, that the French citizen was working for the US Central Intelligence Agency and was carrying sensitive documents stolen by the German killer. In such a case, US security interests might support the exercise of US jurisdiction on these facts to prosecute the German citizen—under the "security exception" to Japan's usual primary jurisdiction exercisable because the conduct occurred aboard the Japanese aircraft.

These added jurisdictional bases for extending the range of State sovereignty have thus invoked all the typical bases for international criminal jurisdiction except for one—the universality principle discussed immediately below. The following treaty (Hague Convention) was needed because the above Tokyo Convention was never intended to combat unlawful interference with civil aviation. This is why the Tokyo Convention paid lip service to primary jurisdiction of the State of registration while retaining all of the usual criminal jurisdictional principles as express exceptions to the supposedly basic rule that flag State A would "have the first shot" at criminal conduct aboard State A's aircraft operating over State B.[56]

Hague Convention The 1970 Hague Convention for the Suppression of Unlawful Seizure of Aircraft added another jurisdictional alternative for prosecuting crimes on international flights. Its universal principle of jurisdiction provides that certain crimes are sufficiently heinous to be considered crimes against *all* States. Each State thus has the jurisdiction to capture and punish, or alternatively, to extradite the perpetrator of such crimes (*see* § 5.2 on the "Universal Principle"). The Hague Convention extends the universal principle of jurisdiction to aircraft hijackings. The related 1971 Montreal Sabotage Convention similarly establishes universal jurisdiction over those who bomb or sabotage (rather than merely seize) commercial aircraft.[57]

The terrorist bombing of Pan Am flight 103 over Lockerbie, Scotland in 1988 thus triggered the criminal liability of the Libyan individuals responsible for the resulting death of its 230 passengers. Libya had and still has the responsibility to thus prosecute these perpetrators or turn them over for trial in Scotland or the US, where they have been indicted. UN Security Council Resolution 731 of 1992 resolved that Libya must release them for trial. Libya responded with a suit in the International Court of Justice, claiming that the US and the UK had themselves breached the Montreal Convention. Libya presented the theory in this unresolved case that the US and the UK had rejected Libyan efforts to resolve this matter in good faith. Libya claims that the US and the UK allegedly threatened the use of force. It thus requested that the ICJ issue an order prohibiting those countries from acting in any way that would further threaten peaceful relations. Libya was presumably concerned that, like the 1986 US bombing of Tripoli in response to another terrorist incident, these nations might undertake a military mission to extract the Libyan agents allegedly responsible for the bombing of Pan Am flight 103.

The Court decided *not* to grant Libya's request for these measures pending the resolution of this matter between Libya and the US/UK. The essential stumbling block was that another UN organ, the Security Council, had already demanded that Libya turn over the terrorists for trial elsewhere under SC Resolution 731. The ICJ did not want to be in the awkward position of rendering an inunction against US/UK action under the existing norm of International Law that prohibits the use of force to resolve disputes. The Court avoided this dilemma by noting that Libya chose, instead, to base its request for relief on the Montreal Convention—which does *not* involve any issue involving reprisals or the responsive use of force by another State. This possibility was never contemplated under the terms or intended scope of the Montreal treaty. In the words of the ICJ's Judge Shahabuddeen (from Guyana):

> In this case, it happens that the decision which the Court is asked to give [in favor of Libya] is one which would directly conflict with a decision of the Security Council. . . . Yet, it is not the jurisdictional ground for today's Order [denying Libya's request that the US/UK not take any action involving the use of force until this case is resolved on its merits]. This [denial] results not from any collision between the competence of the Security Council and that of the Court, but from a collision between the obligations of Libya under the decision of the Security Council and any obligation it may have under the Montreal

Convention. The [UN] Charter says that the former [must] prevail.[58]

The fundamental theme of the Hague Convention is that all States must take the necessary steps to prosecute or extradite those who unlawfully seize commercial aircraft. This treaty is a direct response to the rash of international hijackings that began in the late 1960s. Too many nations clandestinely supported the political goals underlying those hijackings, seeking to publicize the political problems of the Middle East. These nations thus characterized brutal crimes aboard hijacked aircraft as "political conduct" rather than extraditable common crimes (see § 5.3 on this exception to extradition). They granted asylum to, or did not otherwise prosecute, the responsible hijackers. Consequently, there was a growing international desire to limit such asylum for what most States characterized as "universal" crimes.

The right or privilege of asylum is waning as a defense to punishment or extradition, in those instances where most nations would consider universal jurisdiction applicable. Cuba and the US, for example, concluded a bilateral extradition agreement in 1973. Its terms represented a significant departure from the earlier Cuban perspectives.[59] Cuba did not recognize hijacking as an essentially universal crime whenever its government was motivated by the anti-Western political goals of the hijacker. This 1973 agreement provides that if a particular air or sea hijacking offense is not punishable under the laws of the State in which the offenders arrive, each State will nevertheless be obliged to return them to the territory of the other party. The US/Cuban option of granting asylum, on the basis that a hijacking was a "political offense," was supposedly foreclosed by this agreement. Neither country may avoid the obligation to extradite the offender to the other nation under the terms of this agreement. The US nevertheless ignored its provisions after several Cuban aircraft were hijacked to the US in 1991 and 1992. The US policy of isolating Cuba has prompted various US presidential administrations to allow such hijackers to seek asylum in the US in spite of the 1973 agreement.

Some governments have invoked the convenient ploy of characterizing certain aircraft hijackings as "political" rather than common crimes. The 1970 Hague Convention neither addresses nor precludes this practice. Under the 1976 European Convention on the Suppression of Terrorism, offenses governed by the 1970 Hague Convention *cannot* be characterized as "political" offenses. This European treaty applies to only a handful of nations, however, who are parties to the Hague convention.[60]

The Hague Convention was nevertheless the first *multilateral* step toward establishing air hijacking as a universal crime. More than 140 nations are parties to this treaty, which permits the exercise of jurisdiction over international flights by States other than the state of registration. Under Article 4 of the Hague Convention, each "Contracting State shall take such measures as may be necessary to establish its jurisdiction over the offense . . . [and] shall likewise take such measures as may be necessary to establish . . . jurisdiction over the offense in the case where the alleged offender is present in its territory and it does not extradite him. . . ." Article 8 provides that the "offense shall be treated, for the purposes of extradition between Contracting States, as if it had been committed *not only* in the place in which it occurred *but also* in the territories of the States required to establish their jurisdiction in accordance with Article 4" (emphasis supplied by author).

Assume that the German terrorist (mentioned in the prior hypothetical scenario in this section of the book) forcefully takes control of a Japanese airliner over Hawaii. The hijacker causes it to land in Canada to refuel. The plane is then diverted to Libya. Libya does not comply with its treaty obligation to capture and prosecute the hijacker, who has committed a universal crime against all States under the Hague Convention. The terrorist then escapes to Lebanon. All of these nations are parties to the Hague Convention.

What States may thereby exercise jurisdiction over the German terrorist under the 1970 Hague Convention? Under Article 4, *each* of these State parties must take measures to ensure that jurisdiction is somehow established. In this case, Japan *could* exercise its jurisdiction over the terrorist—but only if Lebanon were convinced to surrender the terrorist to Japan. Japan is the State of registration of the aircraft with "territorial" jurisdiction over events occurring aboard it anywhere in the world.

Under Article 6, any State "in the territory of which the offender or the alleged offender is present, *shall* take him into custody or take other measures to ensure his presence." Canada or Lebanon would thus have the obligation to exercise jurisdiction in the case of such a "universal" crime. The Hague treaty requires them to take the necessary steps to prosecute or extradite the terrorist—either when the plane landed for refueling in Canada, or when it arrived at the final destination of Libya.

Since neither Canada nor Libya actually captured the hijacker, Lebanon would incur the ultimate obligation under the Hague Convention. Lebanon would be justified in treating the terrorist's act "as if it had been committed not only in the place in which it occurred but also in the territories of the States required to establish their jurisdiction" over this hijacking incident. Lebanon is thereby obligated to capture this terrorist upon arrival in its territory. Mere custody of the terrorist would give Lebanon the right (or obligation) to either try or extradite the hijacker to Japan, Canada, or the US. Parts of the crime occurred in their respective territorial airspaces.

Unfortunately, certain States have clandestinely supported hijacking incidents while appearing to satisfy their Hague Convention prosecution obligations. Under Article 7, a State that does not extradite a hijacker is "obliged, without exception whatsoever . . . to submit the case to its competent authorities for the purpose of prosecution." States that are sympathetic to the political cause of particular hijacker, however, have sometimes allowed the terrorist to "escape." Alternatively, they have conducted mock trials for the purpose of concluding that the terrorists were *not* guilty of hijacking charges in violation of the Hague Convention. In 1973, for example, an Italian court released the hijackers of an Israeli passenger plane and tried them *in absentia*. Cyprus released Arab terrorists who attacked an Israeli plane in Cyprus after they were sentenced to imprisonment. These States technically met their treaty obligation to "prosecute" terrorists who seize commercial aircraft.[61]

Outer Space

The actual exploration of outer space began in 1957 when the Soviets launched their Sputnik satellite. This was the first manmade object to orbit the earth. In 1961, the UN General Assembly thus resolved that international "law, including the Charter of the United Nations, applies to outer space and celestial bodies."[62]

The current status of outer space is analogous to the historical maritime concept of *res communis*. The High Seas are *res communis*, meaning that they are incapable of ownership and open to the peaceful use of all States (*see* § 6.3). Under International Law, space and the planets within it are governed by the same international regime. In 1967, the UN Treaty on Principles Governing the Activities of States in the Exploration and Use of Outer Space, Including the Moon and Other Celestial Bodies, established mutual State expectations about international relations in outer space. Under Article I of the Outer Space Treaty, as it is known, the "exploration and use of outer space . . . shall be carried out for the benefit and in the interests of all countries, irrespective of their degree of economic or scientific development, and shall be the province of all mankind."[63]

In the twenty-first century, people likely will inhabit space stations and other planets for extended periods of time, if not permanently. Will these societies in fact govern themselves in accordance with the peaceable norms of International Law developed on the Planet Earth? A number of critical questions that will have to be answered include the following:

1. Will interplanetary colonization result in "States" as we now know them?

2. Will the UN Charter's prohibition against the use of force actually be extended into space? Or be abandoned? Or be supplanted by some other regime?

3. Will the national entities on Earth—referred to as States—apply Earth-bound legal principles to the vast reaches of outer space? Alternatively, will various social groupings in space apply different paradigms that each planet or solar system considers appropriate for their independent galaxies separated by light years of travel?

4. Will the existence and discovery of another species of life make these questions irrelevant?

One must presume that, notwithstanding well-intentioned statements from the UN, nationalism and international tension will be exported into space. This presumption is evident in the following assessment of two US space specialists in 1986. Their view employs the typical Western perspective on the irreconcilable conflict in East-West relations:

Thus we see two distinct and dissonant sets of values at work in the modern social arena.
. . . These paradoxical, competing values are

important both within and among countries. Totalitarian states, of course, adhere to military techniques both for survival and as the firmest foundation for loyalty and respect. They adhere to the atavistic view that the only true respect is born of fear. . . . The modern scientific view says that human diversity and sovereignty demand liberty both within and among states and that world peace will never be achieved otherwise . . . [although] many states do not seem to have learned this lesson fully. And since military tactics are to take by force, fire is fought with fire. All sides risk the incendiary consequences, because the chosen countertactic is counterforce . . . [although] the countertactic is endless escalation, perhaps even conflagration.[64]

Several attempts have been made to define the principles for peaceably governing activities in the airspace far above the navigable airspace of the Earth. These principles constitute the expanding International Law of Outer Space. The basic documents are the following, chronicled in Exhibit 6.5 for ease of reference:

EXHIBIT 6.5 Outer Space Charter*

1958 UNGA Res. 1348(XIII)	Peaceful use of outer space and avoidance of national rivalries in outer space
1959 UNGA Res. 1472(XIV)	Freedom of space exploration
1961 UNGA Res. 1721(XIV)	Use for benefit of all mankind
1962 UNGA Declaration of Legal Principles Governing theActivities of States in the Exploration and Use of Outer Space (3 ILM 157)	General Assembly resolves to conclude a nuclear test ban treaty—did not specifically recognize military use of outer space
1963 Treaty Banning Nuclear Weapon Tests in Atmosphere, Outer Space and Under Water (2 ILM 883)	No nuclear explosions permitted in outer space
1963 UNGA Res. 1884(XVIII) Regarding Weapons of Mass Destruction (2 ILM 1192)	Seeks expressions of US and USSR not to station nuclear or other weapons of mass destruction in outer space
1967 UNGA Treaty on Principles Governing the Activities of States in the Exploration and Use of Outer Space, Including the Moon and Other Celestial Bodies (6 ILM 386)	Outer Space Treaty—the *Magna Charta* of outer space regime; no weapons of mass destruction allowed; no military bases or maneuvers in space, although use of military for science; implicit acceptance of conventional weapons

EXHIBIT 6.5 *(continued)*

1971 Convention on International Liability for Damage Caused by Space Objects (10 ILM 965)	Launching State liable for damage caused by falling space debris (Liability Convention)
1979 UNGA Moon Treaty (18 ILM 1434)	Clarifies ambiguities in 1967 Outer Space Treaty—moon thus subject to same demilitarization regime as other bodies "Peaceful purposes" remains undefined
Various Bilateral Treaties most prominent = SALT I and II (20 ILM 477; 26 ILM 232)	SALT Agreements between the US and former USSR providing for Strategic Arms Limitations

*ILM=International Legal Materials/UNGA=UN General Assembly

The essential features of the current international legal regime include Article III of the 1967 Outer Space Treaty—the Magna Charta of outer space. It provides that "activities in the exploration and use of outer space . . . [are governed by] international law, including the Charter of the United Nations, in the interest of maintaining international peace and security and promoting international co-operation and understanding." Thus, International Law decisively mandates free access to outer space, the moon, and other celestial bodies. Unlike exploration on the Planet Earth, national exploration of the other planets will *not* give rise to any sovereign rights. For example, the US landed on the moon in 1969. Under the 1967 Outer Space Treaty, it did not thereby acquire any sovereign rights. The US cannot own the moon, nor can it preclude other nations from gaining access to it. The universe may be thus explored for *scientific* purposes disassociated from any expansion of national sovereignty.

The Outer Space Treaty also demilitarizes outer space. Its national signatories "undertake not to place in orbit around the Earth any objects carrying nuclear weapons or any other kinds of weapons of mass destruction, install such weapons on celestial bodies, or station such weapons in outer space in any other manner . . . [because the] moon and other celestial bodies shall be used by all States Parties to the Treaty exclusively for peaceful purposes." The treaty does permit, however, a limited military presence in space. Article IV concurrently provides that the "use of *military* personnel for scientific research or for any other peaceful purposes shall *not* be prohibited" (emphasis supplied by author).

The demilitarization language in the 1967 Outer Space Treaty was drawn in part from the 1963 Nuclear Test Ban Treaty, whose original members were the United Kingdom, the former Soviet Union, and the US. Over 110 other nations are currently parties to the Nuclear Test Ban Treaty. Its principle provision in Article I of the Outer Space Treaty contains a promise that each member "undertakes to prohibit, to prevent, and not to carry out any nuclear weapon test explosion, or any other nuclear explosion, at any place under its jurisdiction or control. . . ."

This language, contained in both the Test Ban Treaty and the Outer Space Treaty, is nevertheless ambiguous. It is really a compromise to ensure the participation of the then-existing space powers in the Outer Space Treaty, which would not have approved a *total* ban on a military presence in space. This article was a basis for the former Soviet claim that the US would violate the Outer Space Treaty if it had implemented the proposed Strategic Defense Initiative announced by the Reagan administration in 1983. Under that proposal, the US once considered placing nuclear military installations in outer space to defensively neutralize Soviet weapons—and those of other countries—before they could reach the US.

The Outer Space Treaty also incorporates *non-military* concerns. It requires participants to assume full civil liability for their activities in outer space causing harm to any of Earth's inhabitants. Under Article VI, launching nations "bear international responsibility for national activities in outer space. . . ." This requirement inspired the creation of the 1971 Liability Convention, under which ratifying States have accepted automatic responsibility for damage caused by their spacecraft upon reentering Earth's atmosphere.

Under Article II of the 1971 Liability Convention, a "launching State shall be absolutely liable [even if its conduct is not negligent] to pay compensation for damage caused by its space object on the surface of the earth or to aircraft in flight." The launching State should provide advance notification of an anticipated breach of airspace caused by a falling object.

This convention was first applied in 1979, when Canada lodged a claim against the former Soviet Union alleging that the Soviet Union did not comply with its treaty obligation to notify Canada of a nuclear-powered satellite's potential reentry into Canadian airspace. Canada claimed that when the Cosmos 954 satellite fell, it deposited harmful radioactive debris in various parts of Canada's Northwestern Territories. Canada's claim was later resolved diplomatically.[65]

The research and exploration of outer space is "on hold" in the sense that there is no longer a space race between the two superpowers of the Cold War. Further, economic considerations make it difficult for the US to continue the massive planning that occurred immediately after the Russian Sputnik went into orbit in 1957—culminating in putting the first man on the moon in 1969. Yet other States are interested in pursuing the age-old dream of space travel. As aptly stated in 1992 by Peter Jankowitsch, Austria's Secretary of State for European Integration and Economic Development:

> The future will undoubtedly see an increasing number of countries active in space, further advances in space technology, and an increasing dependence on satellite services. As it was noted during a recent conference . . . [f]or the high-tech industry, space is a ticket to survival and a good cash flow. For the military, it's a threat[ening] environment to be overcome as well as an opportunity for enhanced surveillance . . . [and] warning time. For arms controllers, it is either the nightmare of the weaponization of a pristine arena, or the solution to verification problems which would obviate the need for on-site inspection and allow independent objective verification by the international community. For lawyers, it's another place to restrict and regulate.[66]

■ SUMMARY

1. There are four general types of territory: (1) territory owned by a sovereign State, (2) territory not owned by any State due to its special status, (3) territory capable of ownership but not yet under sovereign control, and (4) territory that is not capable of ownership by any State.

2. Certain territories are not subject to the sovereignty of any nation due to their special status. These were the League of Nations "mandates" and United Nations "trust" territories.

3. An area that is *terra nullius* belongs to no one but is capable of acquisition. In the event of a sovereignty dispute, a State can usually establish a legitimate claim by showing that the disputed territory was initially *terra nullius*.

4. Territories that are *res communis* belong to no one and must remain available for all to use. They are incapable of ownership or control by any sovereign State. It has been argued that Antarctica falls within this category, based primarily on the inability of States to effectively occupy it. The high seas and outer space are the best examples of *res communis*.

5. Five historical methods were used to acquire title to land: (1) occupation, (2) conquest, (3) cession, (4) prescription, and (5) accretion. *Occupation* must be "effective." When two States claim title to the same territory, the successful State usually establishes its title by actual possession. Modern prohibitions on the use of force have outlawed *conquest* as a legitimate basis for claiming sovereignty over a conquered territory. In a cession treaty, the grantor State cedes its title to the grantee State. Title by *prescription* occurs when another State's territory is occupied without a clear legal basis, but the supposed State owner does not protest the occupation for some period of time. *Accretion* may alter international boundaries by the gradual accumulation of land deposits. Sudden changes do not affect the boundary between two nations. The change must be gradual and imperceptible.

6. Title may also be established by renunciation, joint decision, and adjudication.

7. The historical methods for acquiring sovereignty over State territory have been criticized for ignoring the rights of the prior inhabitants of

territories that States conveniently characterized as "uncivilized."

8. Internal waters are the waters on the land side of the coastal baseline. The baseline is where the ocean meets the coast, separating internal waters from the Territorial Sea.

9. Some special problems with the regime of internal waters include crimes committed aboard a vessel in port—normally subject to the jurisdiction of the vessel's flag (home) State of registration. The port State may prosecute, however, when the crime sufficiently disturbs the port's tranquility. A bay is a well-marked indentation whose penetration is too deep to constitute a mere curvature of the coastline. Bays wider than twenty-four miles at their mouths normally contain international waters. They may be historic bays, instead, which contain most or only internal waters.

10. The Territorial Sea (TS) begins at the baseline, which marks the inner boundary of the various coastal sea zones described in this chapter. The TS extends out to twelve nautical miles from the coastal baseline. This portion of the ocean is subject to the *exclusive* sovereignty of the coastal State.

11. Two related problems with the Territorial Sea involve passage. The coastal State administers its rules of innocent passage in the TS zone. Under International Law, passage is innocent as long as it does not "prejudice the peace, good order, or security of the coastal State." A number of straits formerly containing international waters may be subject to the rules of innocent passage due to recent expansions of territorial jurisdiction. Under the Law of the Sea Treaty (LOST), which entered into force in 1994, many of these straits will be subject to a more liberal form of coastal jurisdiction referred to as "strait" passage. Ships will be authorized to pass through them as if they still contain High Seas.

12. The High Seas is that part of the ocean not subject to the *exclusive* territorial sovereignty of any nation. These waters are beyond the national sovereignty exercisable in a coastal State's Territorial, Contiguous, or Exclusive Economic Zones.

13. The LOST extended coastal State jurisdiction in the High Seas in several ways. It adopted a twenty-four-mile Contiguous Zone (formerly twelve). The coastal State may therein protect its interests in enforcing its laws governing matters such as immigration, customs, and drug control. The Continental Shelf (CS) regime of the LOST further permits coastal State control of resources in the CS,

in some cases from 200 to 350 nautical miles from the coast. There is also an Exclusive Economic Zone (EEZ) allowing State control over resources in the waters up to 200 nautical miles from shore. Other nations must thus pay fees for using the resources within the coastal State's EEZ. This provides some redistribution of the wealth within the EEZ to a coastal State lacking the technology to take advantage of its nearby resources.

14. The deep seabed beyond the EEZ is not subject to coastal control. Provisions of the 1982 LOST, objected to by the major maritime powers, provide that the oceans are otherwise subject to international control by the dormant International Sea-Bed Authority. When "The Authority" is operational, its task will be to supervise the equitable distribution of the world's ocean resources. Under a 1994 special agreement generated by the US and other major maritime powers, a number of the LOST provisions will not apply to those nations. Thus, they may ratify the LOST without subjecting themselves to the required technology transfer, sharing of revenues, and decision-making process that would otherwise disregard the pro rata interests of these maritime powers.

15. The lesser-developed nations of the world want to participate effectively in the exploration and exploitation of the natural resources adjacent to their coastlines, as well as throughout all of the oceans. The coastal State EEZ and the International Sea-Bed Authority are some treaty-based tools for accommodating the conflict between the historical rule of freedom of the seas and the modern penchant for an equitable distribution of ocean resources.

16. Airspace is included within the concept of "State territory." Under general principles of International Law, States enjoy exclusive sovereignty in the airspace above their territory. They may thus limit the entry of aircraft into their national airspace and may also restrict freedom of navigation—that is, the types of importable cargo, and the scope of passenger airlines operations within their territories.

17. Various treaties have impacted the original notion of exclusivity of sovereignty over national airspace. The 1944 Chicago Convention on International Civil Aviation contains the fundamental principles of International Air Law. Also, two international organizations regulate international commercial aviation. The *public* entity, whose membership consists of States, is the International Civil

Aviation Organization. The International Air Transport Association is a *private* entity, a cartel of commercial airlines designed to control destructive competition.

18. *State* aircraft are operated by the military, customs, or police authorities of a State. They cannot enter another country's national airspace without express prior consent, often the subject of some treaty arrangement.

19. As to private (nongovernment) aircraft, States have agreed to limit their absolute jurisdiction over their airspaces under various international treaties. Under the 1963 Tokyo Convention on Offences and Certain Other Acts Committed on Board Aircraft, the *State of registration* has primary jurisdiction or control over its own aircraft wherever they are operating. The 1970 Hague Convention for the Suppression of Unlawful Seizure of Aircraft provides for "universal" jurisdiction. Hijacking is thereby considered a crime against *all* nations, and each nation has the jurisdiction to capture and punish or to extradite aircraft hijackers. And certain treaties contain provisions that prohibit or limit the state practice of treating aircraft hijacking and other violent crimes as "political offenses" based on the motives of the offender. These treaties preclude excusing hijackers under the political offense exception to most extradition treaties.

20. Unexpected intrusions by a foreign commercial aircraft are often ignored. States may, however, order course changes, escort offending planes out of their airspace, fire warning shots, or force landings. During the Cold War, some nations considered *any* intrusion to be of major significance, thus warranting the most extreme measures to repel such flights—including those of *commercial* aircraft.

21. The fundamental outer space treaties of the space charter are the 1967 Outer Space Treaty and the 1963 Nuclear Test Ban Treaty. The Outer Space Treaty and the Nuclear Test Ban Treaty provide that outer space cannot be owned or claimed by any nation, is accessible to all nations, and shall be used for peaceful and scientific purposes. The language of these treaties extends existing principles of International Law into outer space. It is possible, however, that these norms will be ignored and replaced with a new regime—either constructive or destructive—as outer space activities develop in the twenty-first century.

■ PROBLEMS

Problem 6.1 (*end of § 6.2*): Assume the following facts: Iran (or its predecessor, Persia) has exercised sovereignty over the island of Qais in the Persian Gulf (near Iran's coastline) for five hundred years. Iran and Iraq are at war (sometime during their 1980–1988 war). Iraq's military forces seize Qais and refuse to return Qais to Iranian control. Iraq does not physically occupy Qais, but its military vessels prohibit Iran from gaining any access to Qais. Iran takes no action until fifteen years later, when it lodges a formal diplomatic protest with Iraq, disputing Iraq's current control of Qais. Iran insists that Qais remained under Iraq's historical territorial sovereignty.

Two students will act as representatives for Iran and Iraq. They will debate whether Qais is now legally owned by Iran or Iraq.

Problem 6.2 (*§ 6.3 under (2) Territorial Sea*): The US and the hypothetical nation of Estado are on the verge of a military confrontation. A sizeable US fleet is steaming towards Estado to engage in what some cantankerous senators have branded "gunboat diplomacy"—a show of force designed to illustrate the US decision to back up its political position with a show of military strength.

The US fleet crosses into what Estado has claimed to be its 200-nautical-mile "Territorial Sea" (announced in 1952). Estado has never announced a sovereign claim to any other sea zone. Estado claims exclusive sovereignty over all of Bahia Grande. This would be the first time that foreign vessels have ever entered Bahia Grande without Estado's permission.

The fleet continues to head directly for Estado's Port El Centro. The Port is located on the southern edge of Bahia Grande—a large bay on the northern border of Estado. Its east-west mouth is forty nautical miles wide. The Port's outer harbor facilities are on the coastal baseline twenty miles south from the mouth (or entrance points of the bay). These facilities are on a point of the bay's coastline that is equidistant from the entrance points forming the mouth of the Bahia Grande.

The US military forces passed through the center of the navigable channel of the bay—located in the middle of the mouth of the bay. The US armada pauses at a point that is fifteen miles from the outer edge of Port El Centro on the coastline and equidistant from the sides of the semicircular coastline forming the edges of Bahia Grande. This resting point is also five miles south of a line that could be drawn across the bay between its entrance points. All US military forces are operating in "Combat Readiness Alfa," the highest degree of preparation for actual combat. Various units in this task force have nuclear capabilities.

When the US forces come to rest in the bay, are they located in the *internal* waters of Estado or in *international* waters as defined by International Law?

Problem 6.3 (*§ 6.3 at end of (2) Territorial Sea*): A US Navy vessel and a US passenger ship are about to pass through an international strait between two coastal nations. The strait's natural width varies from fifteen to twenty-five nautical miles between the bordering coastal States. Each State has ratified the 1982 Convention on the Law of the Sea. The navigational officer (NO) does not know whether the two coastal States have ratified Articles 37–44 of the UN Convention on the Law of the Sea authorizing "strait passage." (The NO's petty officer is researching the ships' records, which will be subsequently reported to the captain.)

NO#1 is the navigational officer aboard the Navy vessel. NO#2 is the navigational officer aboard the passenger ship. Each NO will advise their respective captains (that is, the class) of the rights of each ship and the coastal States. The NOs will thus review the various rules of passage outlined in the materials in this section of the book—*(2) Territorial Sea.*

Problem 6.4 (*end of § 6.3*): Refer to Problem 6.2 above, wherein the US fleet steams into Estado's Bahia Grande. Assume that Bahia Grande is *not* a historic bay that contains only internal waters.

Refer to the Exhibit 6.2 Sea Zones chart at the beginning of this section of the book. Assume that Port El Centro's outer harbor facilities are located on that chart at the point marked "Coastal Baseline."

Apply the 1982 LOST principles—and any applicable customary International Law principles—to answer the following questions:

1. Did the US violate Estado's territorial waters when it crossed into Estado's 200-mile Territorial Sea?

2. What coastal zone did the US fleet first enter when it was en route to Estado?

3. Did the US fleet ever enter Estado's contiguous zone? If so, where?

4. Did the US fleet ever enter Estado's territorial waters? Where?

5. Where do Estado's internal waters meet its Territorial Sea?

Problem 6.5 (*end of § 6.3*): Assume that the US and a hypothetical nation called Estado enter into a treaty giving US corporations the right to establish business operations in Estado. Assume that a large multinational enterprise called Mineco is the US-based corporate parent for many worldwide subsidiary corporations. Mineco has established a foreign corporate subsidiary in Estado. None of Mineco's key management personnel are citizens of Estado, although all of Mineco's blue collar workers are Estado nationals.

Under the Estado/US licensing agreement, Mineco is solely responsible for all mining of "Wondore," a valuable ore found mainly in and near Estado. Wondore is used to create energy. US scientists are now exploring whether it can also serve as the energy alternative to oil. Under the licensing agreement with Estado, Mineco has the exclusive right to do all of the drilling in and near this resource-rich nation. There are vast reserves of Wondore in the seabed adjacent to Estado's shores—up to 300 nautical miles from its coastline. Mineco is now examining the viability of drilling under the ocean floor in a corridor that stretches from Estado to 300 nautical miles seaward from its coast.

Assume that Estado is a party to and has ratified the 1982 Law of the Sea Treaty, which entered into force in 1994. The US position is not relevant, because any rights involving mining in or near Estado waters will depend on Estado's position regarding the LOST. You should assume the following alternatives: (a) that Estado *is*, and alternatively, that (b) Estado *is not* a party to the special 1994 Agreement (prompted by the US to avoid the impact of the LOST's Part XI provisions regarding the mining of deep seabed resources). How does the new LOST affect Estado/Mineco's right to extract these minerals from the 300-mile corridor?

Problem 6.6 (*§ 6.4 after* Powers *Case*): The US and a neighbor in the Caribbean are engaged in what may turn out to be a hostile conflict. A US fleet containing US Marine and Naval forces is now steaming toward the hypothetical State of Estado. A US multinational corporation owns a satellite that is orbiting over Estado at an altitude of 22,500 miles. That corporation allows the US forces to use its satellite to monitor events occurring in Estado. This sophisticated satellite permits a monitor aboard the fleet command ship to count individual troops in Estado.

US fighter/bomber aircraft are launched in international waters and fly over Estado, after the satellite confirms that all Estado military aircraft are on the ground. Does the *presence* of the US satellite "over" Estado violate its airspace under the 1944 Chicago Convention or customary State practice?

Problem 6.7 (*§ 6.4 after n.61*): this problem builds on the US/Estado potential military confrontation use in prior Problems in the text.

A group of Estado extremists seizes a US commercial airliner while it is flying over Jamaica. There are eighty US citizens on board the aircraft. The hijackers divert the plane to Estado. While en route, they broadcast that their reason for seizing the aircraft is to bring world attention to the plight of Estado. They proclaim that their only way of dealing with US imperialism is to capture one of its aircraft and to bring the US hostages to Estado. They arrive in Estado and are hidden from public view. It is not clear whether Estado's government played a role in planning this hijacking.

The Estado hijackers are tried in one of Estado's "People's Tribunals" and found *not* guilty. Estado is a party to all of the multilateral treaties dealing with commercial international airflight described in this section of the book. Estado is not a party to any regional air treaty, such as the referenced European Convention.

Has Estado breached the air treaties to which it is a party? How?

Problem 6.8 (*end of § 6.4*): This problem continues with the US/Estado potential military confrontation in prior Problems in this section of the text. First, reread Problem 6.6 above.

Assume that Estado and the US are parties to all the treaties contained in § 6.4 on outer space. Could the *use* of the US satellite violate any of those treaties? How?

■ BIBLIOGRAPHY

§ 6.1/2 Categories of Territory/Sovereignty over Land:

Elliot, *Antarctica*, ch. 9, in P. Keat (ed.), *Ethics and Foreign Policy* 169 (St. Leonards, Aust.: Allen & Unwin, 1992)

Sovereignty over Territory, ch. 7, in M. Dixon & R. McCorquodale, *Cases and Materials on International Law* 225 (London: Blackstone Press, 1991)

Territory, ch. 5, in D. Harris, *Cases and Materials on International Law* 173 (4th ed. London: Street & Maxwell, 1991)

Y. Zoubir & D. Volman, *International Dimensions of the Western Sahara Conflict* (Westport, CT: Greenwood Pub., 1993)

§ 6.3 Sea Zones:

E. Brown, *International Law of the Sea* (Brookfield, VT: Ashgate Pub., 1994) (two volumes)

J. Charney & L. Alexander, *International Maritime Boundaries* (Dordrecht, Neth.; Boston: Martinus Nijhoff, 1991) (two volumes)

G. Knight & H. Chiu, *The International Law of the Sea: Cases, Documents, and Readings* (London: Elsevier, 1991)

Law of the Sea Forum: The 1994 Agreement on Implementation of the Seabed Provisions of the Convention on the Law of the Sea, 88 *American Journal of International Law* 687 (1994)

D. Pharand & U. Leanza, *The Continental Shelf and the Exclusive Economic Zone: Delimitation and Legal Regime* (Dordrecht, Neth.; Boston: Martinus Nijhoff, 1993)

The United Nations Convention on the Law of the Sea, 1982 and The Agreement Relating to the Implementation of Part XI of the Convention, 1994 (London: Simmonds & Hill, 1994) (introductory commentary and texts on disk)

F. Vicuna, *Exclusive Economic Zone: A Latin American Perspective* (Boulder, CO: Westview Press, 1984)

P. Yuan, *The United Nations Convention on the Law of the Sea from a Chinese Perspective*, 19 *Texas International Law Journal* 415 (1984)

§ 6.4 Air Zones:

K. Bockstiegel & M. Benko (ed.), *Space Law: Basic Legal Documents* (Dordrecht, Neth.; Boston: Martinus Nijhoff, 1990)

P. Dempsey, *Law and Foreign Policy in International Aviation* (Dobbs Ferry, NY: Transnational Publishers, 1987)

J. Fawcett, *Outer Space* (Oxford, Eng.: Oxford Univ. Press, 1985)

N. Jasentuliyana (ed.), *Space Law: Development and Scope* (Westport, CT: Praeger, 1992)

C. Johnsson, *International Aviation and the Politics of Regime Changes* (New York: St. Martin's Press, 1987)

Jurisdiction at Sea and in the Air, R. Jennings & A. Watts, 1 *Oppenheim's International Law* (Part I), § 141, p.479 (Essex, Eng.: Longman, 1993)

Kou Li (ed.), *World Wide Space Law Bibliography* (Montreal: McGill Univ.—De Daro Pub., 1978) (two volumes with annual supplements)

N. Matte (ed.), *Space Activities and Emerging International Law* (Montreal: McGill Univ., 1994)

■ ENDNOTES

1. Namibia (South West Africa) Case, 1971 I.C.J. Rep. 55.

2. U.S. v. The Netherlands, Permanent Court of Arbitration, No. XIX, 2 Rep. Int'l Arb. Awards 829 (1949).

3. 1975 I.C.J. Rep. 4 (and set forth in § 2.3 of this text).

4. **Antarctica** is **res communis**: Balch, *The Arctic and Antarctic Regions and the Law of Nations*, 4 *Amer. J. Int'l L.* 265 (1910). Not **res communis**: E. Sahurie, *The International Law of Antarctica* 420 (Dordrecht, Neth.; Boston: Martinus Nijhoff, 1992). **Treaty text:** *see* 54 *Amer. J. Int'l L.* 476 (Supp. 1960), 19 *Int'l Legal Mat'ls* 860 (1980).

5. Various descriptions are available in G. Goetz & P. Diehl, *Territorial Changes and International Conflict* (London: Routledge, 1992).

6. The Miniquiers and Ecrehos Case (France v. United Kingdom), 1953 I.C.J. Rep. 47 (1953).

7. Western Sahara Case (Spain v. Morocco), 1975 I.C.J. Rep. 3, citing Permanent Court of International Justice's Legal Status of Greenland case, P.C.I.J., ser. A/B, No. 53 (1933).

8. *See* G. von Glahn, *Title to Territory, Air, and Space*, ch. 14, in *Law Among Nations* 368 (6th ed. New York: Macmillan, 1992).

9. Status of East Greenland Case (cited in note 7 above).

10. 1928 Permanent Court of Arbitration No. XIX, 2 Rep. Int'l Arb. Awards 829 (1949).

11. *See* R. Blanke, *Orphans of Versailles: The West German Minority in Western Poland*, 1918–1939 (Lexington, KY: Univ. Press of Kentucky, 1993).

12. 1962 I.C.J. Rep. 6.

13. Award by the United States–Mexico International Boundary Commission Constituted by Treaty of June 24, 1911, 11 Rep. Int'l Arb. Awards 309 (1962).

14. *See* Summary of the Indo-Pakistan Western Boundary (Rann of Kutch) Case (India v. Pakistan), 1968 Int'l L. Rep. 2 (1976); excerpts reprinted in 7 *Int'l Legal Mat'ls* 635 (1968).

15. **PCIJ application:** Jaworzina Boundary Case, P.C.I.J., ser. B, No. 8 (1923). **Post-WWII application:** I. Brownlie, *International Law and the Use of Force by States* 408 (Oxford, Eng.: Oxford Univ. Press, 1963).

16. I. Brownlie, *Principles of Public International Law* 131 (4th ed. Oxford, Eng.: Clarendon Press, 1990) [hereinafter *Brownlie treatise*].

17. *Brownlie treatise*, p.127 (cited in note 16 above).

18. D. Greig, *International Law* 160 (2nd ed. London: Butterworths, 1976) (emphasis supplied).

19. Pharand, *The Law of the Sea: An Overview*, ch. 1, in D. Pharand & U. Leanza, *The Continental Shelf and the Exclusive Economic Zone: Delimitation and Legal Regime* 5 (Dordrecht, Neth.; Boston: Martinus Nijhoff, 1993).

20. UN Doc. A/CONF. 62/122 (1982), reprinted in 21 *Int'l Legal Mat'ls* 1261 (1983), and in H. Kindred et al., *International Law Chiefly as Interpreted and Applied in Canada: Documentary Supplement to Fifth Edition* 97–148 (5th ed. Toronto: Edmond Montgomery Pub., 1993).

21. Re Bianchi, Camara Nacional Especial [special chamber of the national court of] Argentina, 24 Int'l L. Rep. 173 (1961) (decided in 1957).

22. Tribunal of the Permanent Court of Arbitration, reprinted in Sen. Doc. No. 870, Vol. I, 61st Congress, 3rd Sess., p.64 (1912).

23. Excerpt from Canadian Parliamentary debate, reprinted in H. Kindred, et al., *International Law Chiefly as Interpreted and Applied in Canada* 665–66 (5th ed. Toronto: Edmond Montgomery Pub., 1993).

24. Anglo-Norwegian Fisheries Case (England v. Norway), 1951 I.C.J. Rep. 116, 160 (Judgment of Dec. 18, 1951).

25. *See* 2 *Yearbk. Int'l L. Comm'n* 36, UN Doc. A/CN.4/17 (1950) on the Vatican's proclamations granting these rights.

26. Bynkershoek, *De Dominio Dissertatio* [Possession of the Sea Dissertation], reprinted in *Classics of International Law*, ch. 2, 44 (Wash., DC: Carnegie Endowment for Int'l Peace, Magoffin translation 1923).

27. 1 J. Moore, *Digest of International Law* 702–703 (Wash., DC: US Gov't Print. Off., 1906).

28. **1952 declaration:** *see* U.S. Naval War College, 51 *Int'l Law Situation and Documents* 1956, p.265 (1957). **1956 declaration:** *see* U.S. Naval War College, 50 *Int'l Law Situation and Documents* 1955, p.244 (1957).

29. Presidential Proclamation on the Territorial Sea of the United States, 24 *Weekly Compilation of Presidential Documents* 1661 (1989), reprinted in 28 *Int'l Legal Mat'ls* 284 (1989).

30. Shortly after this incident, the US and the USSR decided that one another's commercial vessels could enter their respective ports and pass through territorial waters. Specified ports agree on, and a minimum of two-days' notice was required. This 1990 agreement expressly excluded "war vessels." *Agreement Regarding Certain Maritime Matters between the Government of the United States of America and the Government of the Union of Soviet Socialist Republics*, US Treaties and Other International Agreements Series No. 11453 (1990).

31. The SS Lotus (France v. Turkey), P.C.I.J., ser. No. 10 (1927) and set forth in § 5.2.

32. *See* text accompanying note 26 above.

33. 450 UN Treaty Series 82 (1963).

34. F. Ngantcha, *The Right of Innocent Passage and the Evolution of the International Law of the Sea: The Current Regime of 'Free' Navigation in Coastal Waters of Third States* 1 (London: Pinter, 1990).

35. *Harvard Research Draft*, Art. 20, reprinted in 23 *Amer. J. Int'l L.* 250 (1929).

36. **Expanded CZ:** Convention on the Territorial Sea and Contiguous Zone, Art. 24.2, 516 UN Treaty Series 205 (1964). **Shelf agreement:** Convention on the Continental Shelf, Art. 1, 499 UN Treaty Series 311 (1964).

37. Henkin, *Politics and the Changing Law of the Sea*, 89 *Pol. Sci. Quarterly* 56–57 (1974).

38. *See* L. Henkin, R. Pugh, O. Schachter & H. Smit, *International Law: Cases and Materials* 1283 n.1 (3rd ed. St. Paul: West, 1993).

39. Pardo, *The Convention on the Law of the Sea: A Preliminary Appraisal*, in F. Snyder & S. Sathirathai, *Third World Attitudes Toward International Law* 737, 741 & 747 n.32 (Dordrecht, Neth.; Boston: Martinus Nijhoff, 1987) [hereinafter *Third World Attitudes*].

40. **Truman's CS declaration:** 10 Fed. Register 12304, 59 Statutes at Large 884 (1945)—Presidential Proclamations 2667 & 2668.

1958 CS Convention: 400 UN Treaty Series 311 (1961).

41. 1969 I.C.J. Rep. 3, 53.

42. **CHM Resolution:** Gen. Ass. Reso. 2749(XXV), UN Gen. Ass. Off. Rec. (GAOR), 25th Sess., Supp. No. 28, p. 24, reprinted in 10 *Int'l Legal Mat'ls* 220 (1971). **Analysis:** Joyner, *Legal Implications of the Concept of the Common Heritage of Mankind*, 35 *Int'l & Comp. L.Q.* 190 (1986).

43. **1994 Agreement:** Annex I to Consultations of the Secretary-General on Outstanding Issues Relating to the Deep Seabed Mining Provisions of the United Nations Convention on the Law of the Sea, UN Doc. A/48/950 (1994) (revising UN Doc. SG/ LOS/CRP.1/Rev.1), reprinted in 33 *Int'l Legal Mat'ls* 1309 (1994). **Christopher quote:** *United States to Move Ahead with the Law of the Sea Convention*, 140 *Congressional Record–Senate*, 103 Cong., 2nd Sess. (June 30, 1994).

44. The author thanks Professor John Noyes of the International Section of the ABA for timely providing this Recommendation.

45. Koh, *Negotiating a New World Order for the Sea*, in *Third World Attitudes* 715, 725–26 (cited in note 39 above).

46. Pardo, *Third World Attitudes* 737, 741–44 (cited in note 39 above).

47. A thoughtful analysis of the LOST's dispute resolution mechanisms is available in Noyes, *Compulsory Third-Party Adjudication and the 1982 United Nations Convention on the Law of the Sea*, 4 *Connecticut J. Int'l L.* 675 (1989).

48. Goedhuis, *Civil Aviation After the War*, 36 *Amer. J. Int'l L.* 596, 605 (1942) (referring to World War I).

49. 11 League of Nations Treaty Series 173 (1922). The US was never a party to this first international air treaty.

50. Jurisdiction of the ICAO Council (India v. Pakistan), 1972 I.C.J. Rep. 46.

51. Laker Airways v. Sabena, 731 Fed.2d 909 (D.C. Cir. 1984). A history of the various English and American cases regarding Laker is available in 1 *Restatement of the Foreign Relations Law of the United States* 252–53 (3rd ed. Wash., DC: Amer. Law Inst., 1987).

52. Case Concerning the Aerial Incident of July 27, 1955 (Israel v. Bulgaria), 1957 I.C.J. Rep. 182.

53. A thoughtful analysis of this incident is provided in Fitzgerald, *The Use of Force Against Civil Aircraft: The Aftermath of the KAL Flight 007 Incident*, 22 *Canadian Yearbook Int'l L.* 291 (1984).

54. *See* U.S. v. Cordova, 89 Fed.Supp. 298 (E.D. N.Y. 1950).

55. 704 UN Treaty Series 219 (1969).

56. *See* Milde, *Law and Aviation Security*, in T. Masson-Zwaan & P. Mendes de Leon, *Air and Space Law: De Lege Ferenda, Essays in Honor of Henri A. Wassenbergh* 93 (Dordrecht, Neth.; Boston: Martinus Nijhoff, 1992) [hereinafter *Air and Space Law* treatise].

57. *Hague Suppression treaty:* 22 US Treaties and Other International Agreements Series No. 1641, T.I.A.S. Series No. 7192 (1971). *Montreal Sabotage treaty:* Convention for the Suppression of Unlawful Acts Against the Safety of Civil Aviation, 24 UN Treaty Series 564, US Treaties and Other International Acts Series No. 7570 (1971).

58. **Case:** Questions of Interpretation and Application of the 1971 Montreal Convention Arising from the Aerial Incident at Lockerbie (Libyan Arab Jamahiriya v. United Kingdom), Request for the Indication of Provisional Measures, reprinted in Official Documents, 86 *Amer. J. Int'l L.* 638 (1992). **Case quote:** *id.*, p.651 (Shahabuddeen, J., Separate Opinion).

59. Cuba–United States Memorandum of Understanding on the Hijacking of Aircraft and Vessels, reprinted in 12 *Int'l Legal Mat'ls* 370 (1973).

60. Reprinted in 15 *Int'l Legal Mat'ls* 1272 (1976).

61. These and similar examples are collected in Slomanson, *I.C.J. Damages: Tort Remedy for Failure to Punish or Extradite International Terrorists*, 5 *Calif. West. Int'l L.J.* 121 (1974).

62. Gen. Ass. Reso. 1721(XVI) of Dec. 20, 1961.

63. 610 UN Treaty Series 205 (1967).

64. G. Robinson & H. White, *Envoys of Mankind: A Declaration of First Principles for the Government of Space Societies* 30–31 (Wash., DC: Smithsonian Inst. Press, 1986), reprinted with the permission of the Smithsonian Institution.

65. The diplomatic exchanges between Canada and the former USSR are reproduced in 18 *Int'l Legal Mat'ls* 899 (1979).

66. Jankowitsch, *Legal Aspects of Military Space Activities*, in *Air and Space Law* treatise 143, 155 (cited in note 56 above).

Diplomatic Relations

■ INTRODUCTION

Diplomacy plays a significant role in the shaping of international legal developments. Kings, queens, and presidents rely on their diplomats to address the day-to-day crises resolved through quiet diplomacy. The UN Secretary-General, for example, does not merely preside over various UN meetings. Under Article 99 of the UN Charter, he or she "may bring to the attention of the Security Council any matter which in his opinion may threaten the maintenance of international peace and security."

This chapter depicts the working environment and some significant legal ramifications of the institution of the "diplomat." The preliminary analysis involves how diplomatic relations are initiated and broken. Once established, what is the nature of diplomatic and "consular" functions? A recurring theme is the legal effect of acts undertaken within an embassy or consular premises, when the laws of the host country differ. Also, there are many famous cases involving diplomatic asylum—but what are the relevant legal principles?

Newspaper stories typically deplore the situation whereby some diplomat has "once again" avoided civil or criminal prosecution, solely due to his or her status as a diplomat. What happens when that position is abused by conduct unbecoming a diplomat?

■ 7.1 FOREWORD TO INTERNATIONAL DIPLOMACY

Historical Development

For centuries, special envoys have represented the interests of their rulers in other regions of the world. A treatise, supposedly written in the third century B.C., described Greek practice around 800 B.C. There were three categories of what we now call diplomats, consuls, and couriers: those with ministerial rank, those with slightly lesser rank, and the mere conveyers of messages. The Greek city-states developed lasting rules of diplomatic exchanges, inaugurating an era that protected messengers who brought bad news from distant lands.[1]

Around A.D. 1500, permanent representatives called "ambassadors" were first established in Italy. This institution then flourished elsewhere in Western Europe, although other nations resisted it for several more centuries. As chronicled by M.S. Anderson, professor of international history at the London School of Economics, the environment was then quite conducive to this root from which modern diplomacy grew:

by the middle of the fifteenth century there were clearly taking root in Italy new diplomatic techniques and institutions. These formed the basis of a system of interstate relations recognizable as the direct ancestor of the one which exists today. . . . [M]ost of the Italian peninsula was divided between a fairly small number of relatively well-organized states. . . . These competed with one another intensely for power, for territory, [and] in the last analysis for survival. It was therefore essential for their rulers to watch closely each other's doings and to be as well informed as possible about each other's policies and ambitions. . . . In Italy it was therefore possible to raise day-to-day government to a high pitch of efficiency, to control the territory of these states effectively from a single centre, in a way which was still impracticable in France, Spain, or the growing Habsburg [dynasty in Hungary]. . . .

Fifteenth-century Italy, then, was in miniature what in the following hundred years most of western Europe and later the rest of the continent [and modern diplomacy] was to become.[2]

The 1814–1815 Vienna Congress focused on the norms for engaging in international diplomacy. Most European States thereby established the mutually acceptable institutions that governed their international relations. Diplomacy, previously considered a somewhat discredited activity, was finally perceived as a very positive institution. Preventative diplomacy was viewed as a vehicle that would not necessarily prevent war—but would serve the long-term interests of *both* the international community *and* individual States.

The drafters of the 1945 UN Charter included a provision that implicitly recognizes the importance of maintaining diplomatic ties. Should a State fail to carry out its peaceful membership obligations, Article 41 authorizes the Security Council to call on its members to sever or limit diplomatic relations with the offending State. This sanction was conceived as a technique for disrupting conduct constituting a threat to international peace. The target State would lose the benefit of trade, as well as other ties, with the remaining UN member States. In 1992, the UN thus imposed sanctions against Libya for its failure to surrender the two Libyans terrorists allegedly re-

sponsible for the bombing of Pan Am flight 103 over Lockerbie, Scotland in 1988. Those sanctions prohibited arms sales to Libya, commercial flights into that country, and the forced scaling back of its diplomatic missions throughout the world.

The respective 1961 and 1963 Vienna Conventions on Diplomatic and Consular Relations are the current encyclopedias of diplomatic practice, and form the core of this chapter.

Perceptions of Diplomatic Role

The essential role of the diplomat has not always been characterized in a uniform way. For example, diplomats are often thought of or treated as "spies." In Czarist Russia, government leaders feared that the presence of foreign ambassadors would be an invitation to spy on Russia. Allegations of espionage continued to plague international diplomacy during the Cold War. In 1985, the former Soviet Union (which now hosts a number of foreign diplomatic missions in Moscow) charged a group of US diplomatic personnel with spying. They were required to leave Russia. The US responded by ejecting a number of Soviet diplomats from the United Nations in New York City. Then in 1987, the US refused to occupy a newly constructed diplomatic complex in Moscow because the walls contained hidden listening devices. In 1994, the US expelled a diplomat identified as Russia's senior intelligence agent. France expelled four American diplomats in 1995 for their alleged industrial and political espionage. The CIA station in Paris supposedly stole secrets regarding France's nuclear arsenal and its anticipated trade posture to support US industry.

The Chinese have characterized the diplomat as a "fighter." During the 1966–1976 Cultural Revolution, the Chinese press often referred to diplomats in this context, as illustrated in the following excerpt:

The diplomatic personnel of great socialist China are proletarian diplomatic fighters. At any time and in any place, they . . . show a dauntless revolutionary spirit, a firm and correct political orientation, an unconquerable fighting will. They are capable of accomplishing all the missions of proletarian revolutionary diplomacy however complicated or perilous the situation. The proletarian fighters on the diplomatic front . . . can distinguish friends from enemies. They are most modest in their attitude toward [other] revolutionary people and countries; they respect them; they resolutely support their revolutionary struggles, displaying the proletarian internationalist spirit. They repudiate all manifestations of great-power chauvinism. They wage a firm, blow-for-blow struggle against the imperialists, modern revisionists and all reactionaries, and relentlessly rebuff their provocations.[3]

There are, of course, less dogmatic definitions of the role of the modern diplomat. Harold Nicolson, the famous twentieth century British diplomat and prolific writer, defined international diplomacy as "the application of intelligence and tact to the conduct of official relations between the governments of independent states." The historical nineteenth century European conception was that diplomacy is the art of negotiation or communication.[4]

Most contemporary commentators perceive diplomats as foreign-based emissaries who promote friendly relations. Their role includes maintaining the vigilance necessary to ensure that various legal relationships are observed. On the other hand, "realists" do not perceive diplomats as carrying out just their titular functions—guided by the norms of International Law. Indeed, the integrity of the international system is often sparked by periodic diplomatic protests over conduct that another State considers incompatible with existing law (as discussed in § 7.2 below).

During the emergence of the so-called "realist" period of the 1960s, former US Secretary of State Henry Morgenthau criticized any legalistic perception of modern diplomacy as myopically idealistic. He characterized diplomats as, in reality, practical manipulators of power relationships, rather than facilitators of International Law. Diplomats are thus perceived as negotiating on the basis of the respective strength of the States they represent. This role paralleled the Chinese view that the diplomat is a fighter. Morgenthau thus contended that international "politics, like all politics, is the struggle for power [and that the] means at the disposal of diplomacy are three: persuasion, compromise and threat of force." US President Nixon and Secretary of State Kissinger restated this theme as their justification for unpopular tactics utilized during the Vietnam War, specifically echoing Morgenthau's sentiment that "We must negotiate from a position of strength."

A closely related perspective is that, unlike the individual, the State itself is not endowed with any ethical responsibility in the conduct of its diplomatic persona. Under this view, there is no ultimate authority to which the State must answer. As adeptly articulated by Professor David Boucher of the Welsh University College of Swansea:

The state itself is [often] implicitly and explicitly personified. It, like individuals, has interests, and is motivated by the same psychological factors. The state as the creator and sustainer of morals internal to itself, is not itself constrained by a moral code in its relations with other states. The international sphere is *devoid* of the notions of justice and injustice because no ultimate authority exists to subordinate the individual states to it and create the conditions necessary for the emergence of morality.[5]

The contrary perspective of certain "idealists" is that State representatives have the moral and ethical obligation to solve problems in a way that benefits all of the immediate parties—and any other State or entity affected by international negotiations. The State, through its representatives, should not be using international relations as a device for improving its destiny at a significant cost to another State or the community of nations.

Former Canadian Prime Minister Lester Pearson advocated the "realist" theory that the character of diplomacy depends on the particular issue at hand. In his assessment of nuclear diplomacy, for example, he stressed that force must be recognized as the essential backdrop for successful control of the arms race. In his words: "Protection from these grim consequences of our own [nuclear] genius requires possession of overwhelming, destructive power" to avoid mutual destruction. Those States with nuclear powers must thus negotiate from a position of strength. This power theory is essentially echoed by the leading Soviet publicist, Professor Grigori Tunkin of Moscow State University. He characterizes diplomacy as the most important means of accomplishing a State's foreign policy. He defines diplomacy as the activity of "heads of states, of governments, of departments of foreign affairs, of special delegations and missions, and of diplomatic representations appertaining to the effectuation by peaceful means of the purposes and tasks of the foreign policy of a state."[6]

Any attempt to synthesize these varied definitions of diplomacy produces at least one conclusion—that diplomats often deal with each other from diverse political perspectives about the fundamental nature of their role. This starting point in a discourse on diplomacy provides some insight into why diplomatic negotiations deteriorate: The participants often pursue varying purposes from different moral, political, and sociological perspectives.

Diplomats must thus decide what particular methods are best suited to achieve their respective foreign policy objectives. To do this, they must first determine what those objectives are and what alternatives are available to accomplish them. Diplomats must be prepared, for example, to deal with different constitutional and social systems in the host State. A new ambassador cannot expect to achieve diplomatic goals without knowing what results can be realistically achieved. The ambassador must continue to assess the objectives of the host State, and the degree to which he or she can reasonably negotiate in favor of the home State. Next, the diplomat must gauge the extent to which the objectives of the sending and receiving State are compatible. Finally, the diplomat must employ means that are suitable to the pursuit of desired objectives.[7]

Altered Diplomatic Status

The technological innovations of the twentieth century changed diplomacy in two dramatic ways. First, they altered the *status* of the diplomat. Nineteenth century diplomats, serving far from the seat of their governments, had much wider discretion when reacting to problems at their outposts. Travel and communications were difficult and slow. An ambassador had to react to local crises without the benefit (or detriment) of any immediate directions from his government. Instantaneous communications and supersonic travel now limit the need to rely on such undirected judgment.

The scope of diplomacy itself was also changed. Summit diplomacy by heads of State has limited the role of ambassadors. Presidents, prime ministers, emperors, and sheikhs attend well-publicized conferences on major issues. They negotiate directly with each other and reach agreements on general principles. In 1992, the fifteen heads of State in the nations then serving on the UN Security Council met for the first time to discuss their respective interests in the operations of this UN body. In 1972, the first US president to visit the People's Republic of China (Richard Nixon) personally directed the establishment of more friendly international relations between these two powers.

The role of the diplomat in international relations—once the sole province of ambassadors—has been minimized, in comparison to that of his or her nineteenth century counterpart. In the US, for example, there has been an increasing tendency toward the centralization of foreign policy decisions at the White House.[8] Modern "shuttle diplomacy," typified by President Nixon's use of Secretary of State Henry Kissinger in Middle East and Vietnamese negotiations, further limited the degree of autonomy once enjoyed by US ambassadors.

Another twentieth century development significantly influenced the role of the diplomat: the modern aspects of international terrorism, wrought by speed of travel and new weapons technologies. Diplomats must sometimes conduct their affairs in the hostile shadow of intimidation from terrorist groups. A number of these obscure groups have been clandestinely supported by certain governments as a crude instrument for furthering their foreign policy interests. Diplomats at all levels of government have thus encountered the threat of assassination by those States or individual groups whose political philosophy differs from their own.

Examples are not limited to any particular region or target nation. Egypt's leader Anwar Sadat paid with his life for the 1978 Camp David Agreements, which he directly negotiated with Israel through President Carter's mediation. Egypt thereby became the first Arab State to directly negotiate with Israel. Sadat's murder was attributed to extremists within (and probably also outside) Egypt who feared that this would one day lead the way to friendly relations with Israel.[9] Selected examples of the unfortunate relationship between the terrorist and the diplomat (just from the 1990s) are provided in Exhibit 7.1.

EXHIBIT 7.1 Selected Terrorist Activities Involving Diplomats

1995 Rabat, Morroco	Suicide terrorist, protesting Russian war in Chechnya, explodes bomb inside Russian embassy in Morroco's capital city
1994 Bogota, Colombia	Ambassador to Honduras shot by three gunmen in politically motivated assassination in Bogota, Colombia/leftist guerrillas allegedly responsible for killing her during wave of terrorist events designed to stall government efforts to achieve stability
1994 Brazzaville, Congo	US evacuates embassy staff after ambassador's residence comes under automatic weapons fire
1993 Sarajevo, Bosnia-Herzegovina	First US diplomat arrives on job in flak jacket and helmet due to shelling; unable to immediately present credentials due to lack of place to physically locate mission
1993 Moscow, Russia	US marine shot while guarding the US embassy compound in Moscow. 400 embassy employees take shelter underground, during period when Russian authorities attempting to control "hardliners'" revolt against democratic reforms in former Soviet Union
1993 Geneva, Switzerland	Kurdish separatists shoot at Turkish embassy; attempt to storm Turkish consulates in Zurich and Geneva
1993 Marseilles, France	Ten people held hostage by Kurdish separatists in Turkish consulate
1993 Mogadishu, Somalia	French and Egyptian embassies attacked to protest continued presence of UN forces
1993 San'a, Yemen	US diplomat kidnapped for six days; responsible tribe demands back pay for Yemeni employees discharged from oil-pumping station operated by US company
1993 San Jose, Costa Rica	Heavily armed men storm Nicaraguan embassy, taking ambassador and nine others hostage to call attention to home political scenario
1992 New York/Ottawa	Iranian diplomatic missions invaded; burned by opponents of Tehran government's bombing of rebel camp in Iraq; hostages seized
1992 Tripoli, Libya	Libyan protestors attack embassies of UN Security Council States voting to impose sanctions for Libya's failure to turn over terrorists responsible for bombing civilian aircraft over Scotland (flowers placed at embassies of *abstaining* States)
1991 Beirut, Lebanon	Rocket-propelled grenade fired at US embassy on eve of Madrid Middle East peace talks

The student of diplomacy must also recognize that modern diplomacy has been used as both a sword and a plowshare. The 1994 US/North Korea energy aid agreement is a *positive* example of economic diplomacy. In 1993, North Korea announced its intent to withdraw from the Nuclear Nonproliferation Treaty (signed by 153 countries). It denied access to its nuclear-capable facilities to inspectors from the UN's International Atomic Energy Agency. The US, after preliminarily unsuccessful negotiations, threatened sanctions. The international community was concerned that North Korea's aging leader was unwilling to move beyond the Cold War era in order to cooperate in international controls on nuclear proliferation. Under the 1994 agreement, the US will provide $4 billion of energy aid—to assist North Korea's desperate economic situation and to dissuade the further development of its nuclear capability. This program is designed to provide economic assistance, vitiate North Korea's isolationism, and promote diplomatic and other ties.

The Arab boycott of Israeli goods could be described as one the *worst* examples of economic diplomacy. The Arab League's official forty-year policy has been to influence other States not to buy from, nor sell to, Israel—a scenario that should not survive the diplomatic breakthroughs beginning with the 1993 Israeli/PLO Washington Peace Accords. On the other hand, one might characterize efforts to tie diplomacy with human rights as a quite positive development in international diplomacy. The US (with less to lose than the smaller economic powers) is in a convenient position to exact human rights concessions from the People's Republic of China—in exchange for conferring most-favored-nation status in international trade.

The following materials address some other benchmarks of international diplomacy—the current operating functions of diplomats and consular officials; the regime applicable to acts undertaken within an embassy that have different legal results under host country law; the norms involving diplomatic asylum; and ways of dealing with a diplomat who has abused his or her immunity.

◼ 7.2 DIPLOMATIC AND CONSULAR FUNCTIONS

Systemic Overview

When two States agree to establish diplomatic relations, they exchange representatives who usually work in the respective capitals of each State. Under the 1961 Vienna Convention on Diplomatic Relations discussed below, such representatives have been referred to as "ambassador," "minister," and "head of mission." The terms *embassy* and *mission* are popular descriptions of the building where foreign officials undertake many of their diplomatic tasks. However, the term *embassy* is a technical one describing the function or position of the ambassador. The term *mission* is the actual process of maintaining permanent diplomatic offices in the host State. The term *premises* refers to the buildings and land used for the purposes of the foreign mission. A *charge d'affaires* is normally the second-ranking official in the delegation who takes charge of the mission and premises in the absence of the primary diplomat.

No State has established diplomatic offices in all other States of the world. Financial limitations have subjected many consulates and embassies to closure. The US maintains approximately 140 embassies abroad and hosts about 130 foreign embassies in Washington, D.C. The US also maintains over one hundred "consular posts" to deal with commercial matters throughout the world. Certain States can afford embassies in only a few places, however. Not all countries can afford such "luxuries." In 1993, the Philippines announced that it would close its consulates in a number of US cities. It also closed its embassies in Cuba, Jordan, Micronesia, Morocco, Peru, Poland, Romania, Senegal, and Sri Lanka.

The host State may also close (or withhold occupancy of) an embassy—without necessarily breaking diplomatic relations. The US closed Washington's Rwandan embassy in July of 1994, for example. The Rwandan diplomats were ordered to leave the US with only five days' notice. (The US also commenced the process for seeking removal of the Rwandan representative from the UN Security Council.) President Clinton explained that the US was not breaking formal ties with Rwanda. Instead, he was reducing relations to the lowest possible level. In President Clinton's words: "The US cannot allow representatives of a regime that supports genocidal massacres to remain on our soil." In 1990, the military government of Lebanon was no longer recognized by the US. Thus, in spite of claims emanating from "leaders" in Lebanon, the US refused to allow Lebanon's former representative to occupy the Lebanese embassy in Washington. And in 1992 and 1981, China downgraded the Beijing missions of France and the Netherlands, due to their respective sales of fighter planes and submarines to Taiwan.

The process of exchanging diplomats begins with an "accreditation." The State A host government must consent to the particular diplomat dispatched from State B. State B's agent typically presents his or her "credentials" to a representative of State A's head of State. During the failed 1991 coup by certain Russian military leaders against Mikhail Gorbachev, the ranking US diplomat refused to present his credentials to the coup's leaders. He was forced to leave Russia, but was hastily replaced by a new US ambassador who immediately presented his credentials to Gorbachev—as a show of US support for maintaining the democratic reforms sought by Gorbachev. The credential is thus a testimonial document, identifying the State B agent as State B's official representative. State A's consent is confirmed by an *agrément* indicating its approval of State B's diplomat.[10]

Certain States have arranged for *multiple* accreditations, whereby the diplomatic premises contains the several embassies of more than one foreign government. Conversely, there are some States that do not have any diplomatic presence—often relying on

EXHIBIT 7.2   Representative US Diplomatic Mission*

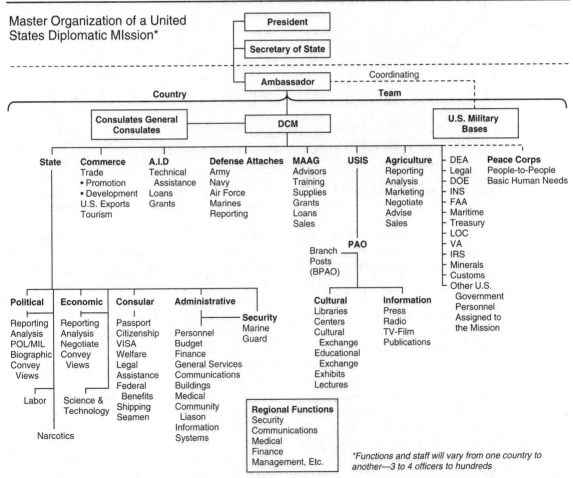

*Functions and staff will vary from one country to another—3 to 4 officers to hundreds

*Source: D. Mak & C. Kennedy, Appendix C, *American Ambassadors in a Troubled World* (Westport, CT: Greenwood Press, 1992). Printed with permission.

their United Nations mission to promote their diplomatic interests in New York or Geneva.

The *location* of the diplomatic premises occasionally signals some political aperture. Foreign missions are normally located in the capital city of the host State. For example, Massachusetts Avenue in Washington, D.C. is commonly referred to as "Embassy Row," due to the large number of foreign missions located on that street. And in Israel, most States have located their diplomatic premises in Tel Aviv. Unlike Israel, they do not recognize Jerusalem as the capital of Israel (so claimed since 1950). In an unusual break with international practice in 1993, the essentially Muslim State of Kyrgyzstan established its embassy in Jerusalem—a holy place for Muslims. The president of that former Soviet republic announced this decision during his visit to Jerusalem. Only El Salvador and Costa Rica had previously maintained embassies in Jerusalem (rather than Tel Aviv).

Diplomatic relations, once established, do not always proceed smoothly. An adverse development in the international relations between State A and State B may occur. A diplomat may act in a manner considered unacceptable to the host State. A diplomat may then be asked to leave—with or without specified reasons. Host State A declares that the particular diplomat is *persona non grata* (unwelcome), necessitating his or her return to sending State B. On the eve of the 1991 UN-imposed Iraqi departure date from Kuwait (and the ensuing Persian Gulf War), Iraq's ambassador was summoned to the US State Department in Washington to advise him that he must reduce the size of his diplomatic staff to four people who could travel no further than twenty-five miles from their embassy. The rest of the staff was thus ordered to leave the US—including the Iraqi ambassador himself. While the US did not then "break" diplomatic relations with Iraq, it did close the US embassy in Baghdad.

Not all States follow this customary practice of merely terminating a particular diplomat's welcome. Contrary to International Law, diplomats have been held captive or prohibited from exiting the host State. During its Cultural Revolution, the People's Republic of China withdrew the diplomatic status of a representative in the Indian embassy and forbade his departure until he was punished for the "crimes" with which he had been charged. In a similar episode during the same period, a Dutch chargé d'affaires in China was declared *persona non grata*.

Rather than facilitating his return to the Netherlands, China did not grant this officer an exit visa until after five months of confinement. In response to this episode, Chinese diplomats in the Netherlands remained secluded in their offices—to avoid having to testify about this affair to Dutch officials. China's actions violated both the customary practice of States and the fundamental diplomatic treaty discussed below. This incident illustrates how host States can readily interfere with the normal conduct of diplomatic relations.[11]

Suspension or termination of diplomatic relations is completely *discretionary* under State practice. International Law does *not* require a legal basis for such disruptions. States may suddenly refuse to deal with each other. The sending and host States may opt to recall their respective diplomatic agents. During the student demonstrations in Beijing in 1989, the US did not break diplomatic relations with China. The US did prepare its diplomats to leave Beijing for their safety—an action designed to demonstrate the US protest of the massacre of students seeking democratic reform in China.

Severing diplomatic ties does not necessarily cut off the continuing need to deal with each other—even when there are no "official" links. This unconventional diplomacy—when States and other entities without diplomatic relations must nevertheless talk to the "enemy"—is a worldwide phenomenon. This form of diplomatic exchange is the product of the need for communication between States or other entities publicly at war but privately seeking a reconciliation or some other mutually recognized objective.

One of the more common devices for this form of diplomacy is the use of the diplomatic corps of third parties that do enjoy good relations with both of the hostile States. Cuba and the US have had indirect dealings with each other ever since Fidel Castro assumed political power in 1959. The US broke diplomatic relations with Cuba. But the Swiss and former Czechoslovakian embassies in Havana exchanged information on behalf of the US and Cuban government for many years. The Cuban Interest Section of the former Czechoslovakian embassy in Washington, D.C., also acted as a go-between in such matters. In March 1995, an Iraqi court sentenced two Americans to an eight-year prison term because they strayed into Iraqi territory—during a visit with friends in the demilitarized zone between Kuwait and Iraq. The US and

Iraq had no *official* diplomatic ties. Poland had such ties with both countries. Its diplomats thus served as go-betweens to negotiate the release of the US citizens.

In 1979, the US recognized the government of the People's Republic of China as the political entity responsible for "China." The US nevertheless maintains relations with Taiwan, which is treated as a State and permitted access to US courts—unlike the People's Republic of China and the former Soviet Union when they were not recognized by the United States. Prior to 1993, when mainland China and Taiwan took the first steps to resolve forty years of political hostility, their proximity required unofficial communications on a regular basis—notwithstanding lack of diplomatic ties and their mutual nonrecognition. This novelty is succinctly described by the University of Leicester's Chair in International Politics, G.R. Berridge, as follows: "Intermediaries are valued by hostile states seeking some kind of accommodation when at least one of the parties regards the political price of direct talks as unacceptably high, or believes that the participation of a third party in any negotiation with its enemy will bring it material gain and additional security from any settlement."[12]

States undertake other forms of unconventional diplomacy when they do not recognize one another. Israel and the Palestine Liberation Organization secretly communicated for many years prior to their 1993 Washington peace accord. The United Kingdom and Sinn Fein (seeking independence for Northern Ireland) also communicated secretly prior to the 1994 announcement of their new working relationship. The clandestine methods for international communication include disguised embassies, ceremonial occasions such as the so-called "working funeral" when a prominent dignitary has died, special envoys including the diplomatic corps of third States, and joint commissions such as the US-Iran Claims Tribunal (*see* § 4.4 on Iran/US Claims Tribunal).

Basic Diplomatic Functions

1961 Vienna Convention The general functions of the diplomat are globally defined in the Vienna Convention on Diplomatic Relations provisions as follows. The diplomat thus:

(a) Represents the sending State in the receiving State;

(b) Protects the interests of the sending State and of its nationals, within the limits permitted by the receiving State's internal laws and International Law;

(c) Negotiates with the Government of the receiving State;

(d) Ascertains, by lawful means, conditions and developments in the receiving State, and reports them to the Government of the sending State; and

(e) Promotes friendly relations between the sending State and the receiving State by prodding the development of their economic, cultural, and scientific relations.[13]

The key members of State A's embassy staff are usually nationals of State A. They *may* be citizens of some other State, but only with the consent of the host (receiving) State B. This special provision helps to ensure that State A's diplomatic mission represents *only* the interests of State A. If a diplomat representing State A were a citizen of State B, for example, this hypothetical "A" diplomat would face constant conflicts of interest while trying to represent the interests of State A—and simultaneously representing the conflicting interests of his or her own State B. As discussed later in this section of the book, certain *consular* officials are routinely nationals of the *host* State (as opposed to the foreign/sending State that they represent in the host State).

Protecting the interests of State A includes assisting any A nationals who are present in host State B. The performance of this duty fulfills the State B responsibility to protect its nationals while they are in other countries (*see* § 4.2 on nationality). The diplomat may deal with a variety of problems confronting his or her fellow citizens, including making arrangements for a criminal defense or for the transfer of deceased individuals or their property between the host State and the home State.

The Vienna Convention addresses other important diplomatic details—including ascertaining and reporting conditions and developments in the host State to the sending State. Only "lawful means" may be used in this reporting process, however. Host States often claim that foreign diplomats overstep the bounds of the law in their reporting activity. When US embassy employees were being held hostage in Iran in 1979–1980, Iran accused the US of having used its embassy in Tehran to conduct espionage against the Iranian people through covert CIA activities since the 1950s.

Secret Diplomacy As important as what diplomats do is *how* they do it. For example, should diplomacy be conducted openly or in secret? President Woodrow Wilson's famous "Fourteen Points" speech to the US Congress in 1918 advocated "[o]pen covenants of peace, openly arrived at, after which there shall be no private international understandings of any kind but diplomacy shall proceed always frankly and in public view." Wilson was admonishing certain governments engaging in secret arrangements leading to World War I.

As similarly articulated by the skillful British diplomat and commentator Sir Harold Nicolson, international policy-making should never be undertaken in secret. Consider his durable remarks, regarding World War II, which have arguably retained their appeal to this day: "No system should ever again be tolerated which can commit men and women, without their knowledge or consent, to obligations which will entail upon them, either a breach of national good faith, or the sacrifice of their property and lives."[14]

The pendulum may be swinging in the other direction. In March 1986, US Secretary of State George Shultz complained that diplomats and heads of State *cannot* effectively conduct their affairs in public. Shultz felt that US Cold War relations with the former Soviet Union were becoming far less productive. Diplomatic exchanges about nuclear arms control were being conducted in public forums. He perceived the presence of the media as unduly influencing the effectiveness of these critical diplomatic efforts. Shultz thus called upon the leaders of both Cold War powers to engage in a more "quiet" diplomacy, conducted via private discussions rather than open conversations effectively directed at the public and the media rather than only the respective negotiators.

Those who favor policies arrived at secretly by the "experts" advocate that public scrutiny tends to minimize the advantage of swift decision making. This can result in the elimination of the element of surprise in political and military action. On the other hand, critics counter that any advantage associated with secrecy and surprise merely compound suspicion and thereby increase the probability of diplomatic miscalculation or even nuclear holocaust. US Secretary of State Warren Christopher thus received a rather blunt lecture regarding one form of secret diplomacy from the Chinese Communist Party's leader in 1994. After Christopher had met secretly with China's leading dissident while on a trade mission to Beijing, the Chinese leader claimed that the result of this secret meeting was that "public opinion flared up, and U.S. officials made accusations against China" that would not survive public scrutiny in any country. The Chinese reaction to the secret meeting with the Chinese dissident made it far more difficult for the US to achieve its diplomatic objective of exacting human rights concessions in exchange for the US's continuing China's favorable trade status.

International Law Do diplomats normally apply the rules of International Law while executing their roles as representatives of the State? Although the "idealists" expect diplomats to comply with these rules, many "realists" question whether this actually occurs in practice. At the 1983 Annual Meeting of the American Society of International Law in Washington, D.C., the panel on International Law and Diplomacy included Canada's ambassador to the United States. Ambassador Gottlieb aptly described the idealist perspective on the conduct of diplomacy:

> there were two [adverse] trends in the international environment influencing the conduct of diplomacy and its relationship to international law. The first related to the potential rise of international conflicts given the political and economic disparities both within and between states, the weakening of the superpower umbrella, the emergence of regional powers and of new centers of economic and political power, and the continuance of border disputes. . . . The other trend concerned the states' adoption of [both] economically defensive and aggressive policies in response to the world recession, the severe unemployment affecting major industrialized states and the external debt problems of developing countries. These trends exemplify the need to anchor the conduct of diplomacy in international law, as well as the need to develop this body of law. . . . [One] hope[s] that international law would keep pace with the demands imposed by these trends and that, in some cases, international law might even exceed the requirements placed on it.

This Canadian diplomat's perspective is one of cautious optimism. On the same occasion, however, the Venezuelan ambassador to the United States expressed his view that international law was *not* important in the conduct of diplomacy—which is controlled primarily by the will of governments rather than rules of law. Ambassador Perez-Chiriboga's "realist" perspective is summarized as follows:

> Regarding the application of international law to diplomatic functions, . . . this topic [should] be analyzed in light of article 3 of the Vienna Convention which defined diplomatic functions. It was the Ambassador's opinion that knowledge of international law was not important in representing and promoting friendly economic relations. On the other hand, he stated that such knowledge was necessary to negotiate, report and protect the interests of the sending state in the receiving state. The Ambassador noted that in his 25 years as a foreign service officer, knowledge of international law had been indispensable on only two occasions. The first case had occurred when he was Ambassador to the Netherlands and assisted in negotiating the limits of maritime and submaritime zones between Venezuela and the Netherlands Antilles. The other case had involved an anti-OPEC case brought in California while he was Ambassador to the United States.
>
> In conclusion, he stated that international law did play a[n effective] role in the practice of international diplomacy, but that not all steps taken in the conduct of diplomacy fell within the parameters of international law. Ambassador Perez-Chiriboga added that diplomacy was conditioned by the will of governments and that the role of international law in this field would increase [only] if governments respected international law.[15]

Basic Consular Functions

Consular officials are *not* usually diplomatic representatives. They are not normally accredited to the host State, although they are official agents of the sending State. Consular officers often conduct "diplomatic" negotiations in international trade matters, however.

One of the most sensitive consular functions is providing access to jailed nationals of the home State of local consular officials. Denial of access, or delays, often generate friction in international rela-

tions. In 1993, for example, the US protested to Israel due to Israel's treatment of three jailed Palestinian-Americans from Chicago. They were visiting relatives in the occupied West Bank—where they were arrested and confined without prompt access to either lawyers or US diplomatic officials. The resulting US protest occurred during the period when the US was attempting to bring Israel and the PLO together for the long-awaited peace accords (ultimately achieved in Washington several months later).

Historical Evolution Consular institutions have had a longer and more varied history than the (medieval Italian) diplomatic mission described above. The forerunner of the modern consul appeared almost as early as people began to trade. The Preamble to the 1963 Vienna Convention acknowledges that "consular relations have been established between peoples since ancient times." Used in this context, *peoples* is a term meaning pre-"State"—in the Westphalian sense of the word *State* (*see* § 1.3 on the History of International Law).

As succinctly described by Professor Luke Lee of American University in Washington, D.C.:

> the many political contributions of the Greek city-states . . . [include] the early development of the consular system; the *prostates* and the *proxenos* are considered forerunners of the modern consuls. The *prostates* were chosen by Greek colonists to live abroad to act as intermediaries in legal and political relations between the foreign (Greek) colony and the local government [of a distant land]. About the sixth century BC the Egyptians allowed Greek settlers . . . to select *prostates*, who administered Greek law to the Greeks. In the same period, similar institutions could be found in certain parts of India.
>
> During the first millennium BC, *proxenoi* were appointed in the Greek city-states to look after the interests of the appointing [city-]State. The *proxenos*, though more a political than commercial agent, has been likened to the modern honorary consul, and was [thus] chosen from the nationals of the receiving State.[16]

1963 Vienna Convention The 1963 Vienna Convention on Consular Relations contains the globally-defined consular functions.[17] Consular officials thus:

(a) protect the interests of the sending State and its nationals, within the limits permitted by International Law;

(b) further the development of commercial, economic, cultural and scientific relations—and otherwise promote friendly relations;

(c) ascertain conditions and developments in the commercial, economic, cultural, and scientific life of the receiving State—and report thereon to the government of the sending State and other interested persons;

(d) issue passports and travel documents to nationals of the sending State, and visas or appropriate documents to persons wishing to travel to the sending State;

(e) safeguard the interests of nationals, including minors and other persons lacking full capacity of the sending State;

(f) represent or arrange appropriate representation for nationals of the sending State before the tribunals and other authorities of the receiving State—where such nationals are unable to assume the defense of their own rights and interests—including the transmission of judicial documents or the taking of evidence for the courts of the sending State;

(g) exercise rights of supervision and inspection provided for in the laws and regulations of the sending State for vessels having the nationality of the foreign State—as well as aircraft registered in that State; and

(h) assist vessels and aircraft and their crews, or take statements regarding the voyage of a vessel, examining and stamping the ship's papers, or conduct investigations into any incidents that occurred during the voyage (see Mali case in § 6.3).

The 1967 European Convention on Consular Functions began with meetings of the Committee of Ministers of the Council of Europe in 1960. The UN process leading to the above 1963 Consular Convention was global in scope, and ultimately ratified by most countries of the world, including those in Europe. It was evident, however, that this global treaty would deal primarily with consular relations and privilege/immunity matters. The 1967 European Convention therefore concentrates on the specialized consular functions relevant to the on-going process of European integration.[18] It elaborates on the rather general Article 5 language of the 1961 Vienna Convention describing the functions summarized above.

In addition to these multilateral and regional treaties, many bilateral treaties address the distinctive consular functions of the respective States.

Consular officers prepare trade reports, gather information relevant to international trade, and investigate alleged infractions of commercial treaties in (or by) the host State. Consuls also supervise international shipping. Seagoing vessels must be registered to a particular country, and they must fly that country's flag. Consuls authenticate the registration papers of their home State's ships in the host State. Consuls help their home State's nationals resolve host-State customs and immigration problems. Consuls also provide needed services to fellow citizens who become ill or indigent while in the host State. They take charge of the estates of deceased home-State nationals and arrange for property distribution under the host State's laws. Unlike diplomats, consuls often directly assist their fellow nationals with personal problems that are not likely to have sensitive political repercussions.

States often appoint *honorary consuls* to assist in the promotion of their trade policies. These individuals are typically nationals of the *host* State who have expertise in host State business matters. The honorary consul is *not* a "representative" who can speak on behalf of the foreign State that he or she represents. On the other hand, "Consuls General" and "Consular Officers" serving within the premises of a sending State's diplomatic mission *are* considered diplomatic representatives. These officers are citizens of the sending State, rather than the host State. Their function is also more closely tied to the public interests of the State that they represent.

■ 7.3 EXTRATERRITORIALITY AND ASYLUM

Two important corollaries relate to diplomatic and consular functions: First, what is the effect of an act undertaken in a foreign embassy or consulate—when the consequences would be different in the host State where the building is located? Second, may a foreign State give diplomatic asylum within its embassy or consular premises—when to do so would offend the wishes of the host State?

Extraterritoriality Fiction

The special international status of embassies and consular premises has generated the question of whether they are, under International Law, a part of the host State or of the sending State. Both have been historically considered an extraterritorial extension of the sending State—once it establishes a diplomatic mission in the receiving State. This fiction would mean that acts done within an embassy or consulate would be governed by the law of the sending State, should those acts be contrary to host State law.

The historical basis for this legal fiction is derived from the practice of medieval "Christian" States. Their consuls exercised full civil and criminal jurisdiction over their fellow nationals who were located in *non*-Christian States. This exclusion from the jurisdiction of the local tribunals was rooted in the convenient legal fiction of "extraterritoriality." Foreign nationals could thus invoke the protection of the more favorable laws of their own home States—a form of extraterritorial jurisdiction (*see* § 5.1). The Sino-Russian Treaty of Nerchinsk of 1689 thus provided that criminals would be delivered to the consular officers of their own countries for prosecution. The Franco-US Consular Convention of 1788 similarly provided for consular jurisdiction over civil disputes between Frenchmen, when they were both in the US, and Americans, when both were in France. The Japanese-American Treaty of 1858 was a model for a number of similar pacts providing for this extraterritorial regime conferring special jurisdiction on consular officers in the host State.[19]

An increasing number of contemporary courts apply a pragmatic analysis of such immunity, effectively rejecting this historical fiction. The codification of diplomatic and consular immunity has vitiated the need for this extraterritoriality fiction. Egypt's consulate in London, for example, would have been historically characterized as being located on Egyptian soil. The contemporary approach is that the Egyptian consulate in London is, of course, located in England for *all* purposes. As the modern concern is limited to protecting diplomatic and consular premises, the need for the extraterritoriality fiction has eroded as an alternative for protecting nationals located in the host State. The following case illustrates both the historical fiction and the modern status of the sending State's diplomatic and consular premises:

RADWAN v. RADWAN

Family Division—London, England, 1972
3 All English Reports 967 (1972)*

[Author's Note: Mr. Radwan was an Egyptian national who entered into a polygamous marriage with an English woman. Their marriage was performed in the Egyptian Consulate in Paris.

Mr. Radwan subsequently moved to England. He entered the Egyptian consulate in London for the purpose of divorcing his English (second) wife via the Middle Eastern "talaq" procedure: In her absence, he orally decreed three times that they were divorced. This talaq procedure constituted a valid divorce under the laws of Egypt, but not under English law.

Several years later, the English wife filed her separate divorce suit in the English courts, anticipating that she would be entitled to a better divorce settlement under English law than under Egyptian law. Her English lawyer argued that the talaq divorce, while performed within the Egyptian consulate in London, was not entitled to recognition under English law. It could not be recognized as a divorce performed "outside of the British Isles."

Mr. Radwan, hoping to avoid an unfavorable English divorce decree, responded to his "wife's" suit in the English courts on the basis that he had already obtained a valid divorce—by performing the above-described talaq procedure in Egypt's consulate in London. Thus, he argued, his talaq divorce was effective because—under British law—it was effectively performed in Egyptian territory (that is, in Egypt's consulate in London). Judge Cummins's decision—in which he disagrees with Mr. Radwan—follows.]

[*Opinion.*] I have read the relevant sub-paragraph of the petition whereby the talaq divorce is pleaded. The husband put in evidence the affidavit of Mustapha Kamil Abdul Fata, Deputy Consul General of the Consulate General of the United Arab Republic of Egypt in Kensington Palace Gardens in London.

---

*Reprinted with Permission of Butterworth and Company, Ltd., London, England (court's footnotes omitted).

In it he swore [in his capacity as an expert on Egyptian law] as follows:

(1) The Egyptian Consulate in London is regarded as being Egyptian territory on Egyptian soil.

(2) The divorce . . . registered in Cairo . . . is valid and recognised by Egyptian law.

. . .

I also received the affidavit of Jamil Nasir, a person qualified in Egyptian law. In that affidavit he says that . . . under Egyptian law the Consulate General of the United Arab Republic in London is regarded as Egyptian territory. He does not give any reasons for that opinion, but I note that it corresponds with the [above-quoted] statement of the deputy consul of the Consulate General in London.

. . .

The facts are as follows. The husband was born in Cairo. He is and at all material times was a Mohammedan. He was and remains a subject of the United Arab Republic. . . . On 1st [of] April 1970 he entered the Egyptian Consulate in London; the procedure stated in the affidavit of the deputy consul of the Consulate General was followed. The husband three times declared the prescribed [talaq] form of divorce in the presence of two witnesses. All the steps were carried out in accordance with Egyptian law. After the prescribed 90 days the divorce was finalised in accordance with Egyptian law, and in accordance with that law it was no impediment to the efficacy of the proceedings that the wife knew nothing about it at all.

. . .

The question for my decision is whether by *English* law the Consulate General of the United Arab Republic is part of a country outside the British Isles within the meaning of the Recognition of Divorces and Legal Separations Act 1971. By that Act the relevant sections providing for recognition will have effect in respect of overseas divorces if they have been obtained by means of judicial or other proceedings *in any country outside the British Isles*, and it is necessary for the efficacy of the talaq divorce that it should have been obtained outside the British Isles by reason of the fact that at the material time the husband had acquired English domicil. [*Emphasis supplied by author.*]

Curiously, the question has not arisen for decision in England before, that is, the question whether the premises of an embassy or consulate are part of the territory of the sending state as compared to the territory of the receiving state.

I quote and adopt the observations of [legal commentator] Mr J E S Fawcett:

there are two popular myths about diplomats and their immunities which we must clear away: one is that an embassy is foreign territory, and the other is that a diplomat can incur no legal liabilities in the country in which he is serving. The first is a confusion between territory or property and jurisdiction over it, and it is important to clarify it for it has sometimes arisen over ships and aircraft. The building occupied by a foreign embassy and the land on which it stands are part of the territory of what we call the receiving state: it is therefore under the jurisdiction of that state. But the members of the mission and their activities in the embassy are primarily under the control and jurisdiction of the sending state. International law avoids conflict between these jurisdictions by laying down rules to cover the whole field of diplomatic relations. These rules have been embodied in the Vienna Convention [on Diplomatic Relations of] 1961, which may be taken as reflecting existing law and practice. This Convention, and that on Consular Relations drawn up in 1963, are among the first steps . . . in the successful codification of international law. The premises of a mission are inviolable, and the local authorities may enter them only with the consent of the head of the mission. But this does not make the premises foreign territory or take them out of the reach of the local law for many purposes: for example, a commercial transaction in an embassy may be governed by the local law, particularly tax law; marriages may be celebrated there only if conditions laid down by the local law are met; and a child born in it [the diplomatic premises] will, unless his father has diplomatic status, acquire the local nationality.

[*Judge Cummins then considered similar cases involving this issue arising in other countries. This is a good illustration of a decision-maker's resort to customary State practice as a basis for ascertaining the content of International Law.*]

FRANCE: *Nikitschenkoff Case:* The court was dealing with murderous assaults on the first secretary of the Russian embassy in the Russian embassy in Paris, and an argument was submitted that the place of the crime being the premises of the Russian embassy was a place situated outside the territory of France and not governed by French law. The decision was a decision under art 3 of the Code of Napoleon. The court said:

> [that] all those who live in the territory [France] are subject to [French] police and security laws; Whereas, admitting as exceptions to this rule of public law the immunity which, in certain cases, international law accords to the person of foreign diplomatic agents and the legal fiction in virtue of which the premises they occupy are deemed to be situated outside the territory of the sovereign to whom they are accredited; Whereas, nevertheless, this legal fiction cannot be extended but constitutes an exception to the rule of territorial jurisdiction . . . and is strictly limited to the ambassador or minister whose independence it is designed to protect and to those of his subordinates who are clothed with the same public character; Whereas the accused is not attached in any sense to the Russian Embassy but, as a foreigner residing for the time in France, was subject to French law; and whereas the place where the crime which he is charged with committing cannot, in so far as he is concerned, be regarded as outside the limits of [French] territory . . . the jurisdiction of the French judiciary [is] clearly established.

GERMANY: the *Afghan Embassy* case.
ITALY: [*citing several cases*].

In all these cases the court rejected the argument that diplomatic premises were not part of the territory of the receiving state. . . .

. . .

Although international conventions [treaties] do not have the force of law unless embodied in municipal legislation [of an individual state], they may in the field of international law be valuable as a guide to the rules of international law which this country as a signatory respects.

. . .

If it was the view of the high contracting parties [to the Vienna Convention] that the premises of missions were part of the territory of the sending state, that would undoubtedly be formulated [within the language of those treaties].

■ NOTES & QUESTIONS

1. In the initial phase of this stormy divorce, Judge Cummins thus ruled that Mr. Radwan did not legally divorce his English wife in a place "outside of" England—merely because he was in the Egyptian consulate. The talaq divorce procedure thus was performed *in* England, was ineffective under English law, and would not be recognized by England. Mr. Radwan was still married to his English wife under the laws of England. His purported divorce (in England) thus failed to bar his English wife from seeking her own divorce in the English courts. If the talaq procedure had *actually* occurred in Egypt, on the other hand, England would then have recognized the divorce.

2. The English wife was thus able to pursue her independent divorce proceedings in England. In the subsequent proceedings, the same Judge Cummins decided the related question of whether the "marriage" was governed by Egyptian or French law. The Radwan marriage (performed in the Egyptian consulate in Paris) and Mr. Radwan's talaq divorce (performed within the Egyptian consulate in London) were both recognized as valid under *Egyptian* law. But neither event took place in Egypt. Judge Cummins consistently ruled in Radwan No. 2 that the marriage occurred in France, *rather than in Egypt.* He noted that the extraterritoriality fiction regarding foreign consulates was not recognized under French law (nor English law, as he had decided in Radwan No. 1). The marriage undertaken in the Egyptian consulate in Paris was *also* void under host State (French) law. Radwan v. Radwan (No. 2), 3 All England Law Reports 1026 (1972).

3. The popular misconception is that embassies and consulates are "on" foreign soil. The Vienna Conventions are mentioned in the *Radwan* opinion because they effectively replaced the extraterritoriality fiction with an express protection for diplomatic

premises. Judge Cummins bases his opinion on what is *not* said in those treaties. How, then, does their silence on this matter support the proposition that "extraterritoriality" is a fiction no longer needed in International Law?

Diplomatic Asylum

Asylum is the protection from arrest or extradition typically given to a host-State political refugee by a foreign-State diplomat. During the 1989 Tienanmen Square demonstrations in the People's Republic of China, for instance, the US granted asylum to China's top dissident. He and his wife stayed in the US embassy in Beijing. Chinese authorities had ordered his arrest for treason, demanding that the US government surrender him to the local authorities waiting outside the US embassy in Beijing. At the same time, the Chinese sealed their international borders to prevent any clandestine escape attempts. (This particular incident is Problem 4.2 in § 4.6 of this book.)

Two other prominent asylum incidents involved the Vatican and the US. In the most recent of the two, the US had just invaded Panama in 1989. Its dictator, General Manuel Noriega, remained in hiding for five days. He then entered the Vatican embassy in Panama City, after evading US military personnel seeking to return him to the US for trial on drug trafficking charges. The Vatican diplomat initially refused to turn Noriega over to the invading US forces—which had surrounded the embassy with US troops, tanks, and helicopters to avoid any possible escape. After an agreement with US authorities, the Vatican decided to surrender Noriega to the US forces. After his immediate capture, he was returned to the US for trial. Whether the Vatican actually granted asylum became a moot issue. Noriega was able to obtain temporary refuge in the embassy until he could arrange a satisfactory bargain with the US

authorities. This was not the first time that the Vatican effectively granted asylum to someone wanted by US authorities. In 1866, Pope Pius XI granted diplomatic asylum to John Surratt, Jr., who had conspired with John Wilkes Booth to assassinate US President Lincoln. Ultimately, the pope surrendered Surratt to the US for prosecution.

Other sensational instances of asylum have generated the popular belief that individuals are *routinely* granted such refuge in foreign embassies. Political relations may be harmed, however, when asylum is granted. A classic case was that of Hungary's Cardinal Jozsef Mindszenty, who remained within the premises of the US embassy in Budapest, Hungary for fifteen years. He had been arrested for antigovernment activities in 1948, jailed in 1949, and freed for several days during a popular revolt in 1956. He then sought refuge in the US embassy. Although the US did not normally grant asylum, it considered this particular request a special case. Mindszenty remained in the embassy, under a grant of diplomatic asylum, from 1956 to 1971—when Hungary finally agreed to his safe passage to the Vatican.

In the leading international judicial opinion on diplomatic asylum, the International Court of Justice (ICJ) articulated the general principle that States do not *officially* recognize a right of asylum. Diplomatic asylum had been granted with some frequency, however, in Latin America. The following case presents a unique situation because the court failed to acknowledge the *regional* custom of granting asylum—a decision for which it was much criticized:

ASYLUM CASE

Colombia v. Peru
International Court of Justice, 1950
1950 I.C.J. Rep. 266

———

[Author's Note: Haya de la Torre was a Peruvian national who led an unsuccessful rebellion against Peru in 1948. When the Peruvian government issued a warrant for his arrest on criminal charges related to this political uprising, de la Torre went to the Colombian *embassy in Lima, Peru. He requested and was granted asylum by the Colombian ambassador on behalf of the government of Colombia. Colombia then requested permission from Peru for de la Torre's safe conduct*

*from the Colombian embassy, through Peru, and into
Colombia. Peru refused to give its permission, however.*

*Colombia thus brought this suit against Peru in the
ICJ, asking the Court to declare that Colombia had
properly granted asylum pursuant to regional State
practice. Colombia therefore wanted Peru to consent to
de la Torre's safe passage out of the Colombian embassy
and through Peru (into Colombia). Peru's lawyers responded that Colombia could not unilaterally grant
asylum over Peru's objection. De la Torre had committed a common crime, subjecting him to prosecution by
Peru, just like any other criminal. Colombia thus had
no right to characterize its own grant of asylum.]*

[*Opinion.*] In the case of diplomatic asylum, the
refugee is within the territory of the State where the
offence was committed. A decision to grant diplomatic asylum involves a derogation from the sovereignty of that State. It withdraws the offender from
the jurisdiction of the territorial State and constitutes an intervention in matters which are exclusively within the competence of that State [Peru].
Such a derogation from territorial sovereignty cannot be recognised unless its legal basis is established
in each particular case.

. . .

The Havana Convention on Asylum of 1928 . . .
lays down certain rules relating to diplomatic asylum, but does not contain any provision conferring
on the State granting asylum a unilateral competence to qualify the offence with definitive and
binding force for the territorial State. . . .

A competence of this kind is of an exceptional
character. It involves a derogation from the equal
rights of qualification which, in the absence of any
contrary rule, must be attributed to each of the
States concerned; it thus aggravates the derogation
from territorial sovereignty constituted by the exercise of asylum. Such a competence is not inherent in
the institution of diplomatic asylum. This institution would perhaps be more effective if a rule of
unilateral and definitive qualification were applied.
But such a rule is not essential to the exercise of
asylum.

. . .

The Colombian Government has finally invoked
"American international law in general" [to justify
its grant of asylum]. In addition to the rules arising
from agreements, . . . it has relied on an alleged re-

gional or local custom peculiar to Latin-American
States. The Party which relies on a custom of this
kind must prove that this custom is established in
such a manner that it has become binding on the
other Party, . . . that it is in accordance with a constant and uniform usage practised by the States in
question, and that this usage is the expression of a
right appertaining to the State granting asylum and
a duty incumbent on the territorial State. This follows from Article 38 of the Statute of the Court,
which refers to international custom "as evidence of
a general practice accepted as law."

. . .

[T]he Colombian Government has referred to a
large number of particular cases in which diplomatic
asylum was in fact granted and respected. But it has
not shown that the alleged rule of unilateral and definitive qualification was invoked or . . . that it was,
apart from conventional stipulations, exercised by
the States granting asylum as a right appertaining to
them and respected by the territorial States as a duty
incumbent on them and not merely for reasons of
political expediency. The facts brought to the
knowledge of the Court disclose so much uncertainty and contradiction, so much fluctuation and
discrepancy in the exercise of diplomatic asylum and
in the official views expressed on various occasions,
there has been so much inconsistency in the rapid
succession of conventions on asylum, ratified by
some States and rejected by others, and the practice
has been so much influenced by considerations of
political expediency in the various cases, that it is
not possible to discern in all this any constant and
uniform usage, accepted as [mutually-accepted] law,
with regard to the alleged rule of unilateral and definitive qualification of the offence.

The Court cannot therefore find that the Colombian Government has proved the existence of such a
custom. But even if it could be supposed that such a
custom existed between certain Latin-American
States only, it could not be invoked against Peru
which, far from having by its attitude adhered to it,
has, on the contrary, repudiated it by refraining
from ratifying the Montevideo Conventions of
1933 and 1939, which were the first to include
a rule concerning the qualification of the offence
[as "political" in nature] in matters of diplomatic
asylum.

. . .

Article 2 lays down in precise terms the conditions under which asylum shall be granted to [political] offenders by the territorial State . . . the essential justification for asylum being in the imminence or persistence of a danger for the person of the refugee. It was incumbent upon the Government of Colombia to submit proof of facts to show that [this] condition was fulfilled.

. . .

Asylum may be granted on humanitarian grounds . . . to protect political offenders against the violent and disorderly action of irresponsible sections of the population. It has not been contended that Haya de la Torre was in such a situation at the time when he sought refuge in the Colombian Embassy at Lima.

. . .

In principle, it is inconceivable that the Havana Convention could have intended the term "urgent cases" to include the danger of regular prosecution to which the citizens of any country lay themselves open by attacking the institutions of that country, nor can it be admitted that in referring to "the period of time strictly indispensable for the person who has sought asylum to ensure in some other way his safety," the Convention envisaged protection from the operation of regular legal proceedings. . . .

In principle, asylum cannot be opposed to the operation of justice. An exception to this rule can occur only if, in the guise of justice, arbitrary action is substituted for the rule of law. Such would be the case if the administration of justice were corrupted by measures clearly prompted by political aims. Asylum protects the political offender against any measures of a manifestly extra-legal character which a Government might take or attempt to take against its political opponents. The word "safety," which . . . determines the specific effect of asylum granted to political offenders, means that the refugee is protected against arbitrary action by the Government, and that he enjoys the benefits of the law. On the other hand, the safety which arises out of asylum cannot be construed as a protection against the regular application of the laws and against the jurisdiction of legally constituted tribunals. Protection thus understood would authorise the diplomatic agent to obstruct the application of the laws of the country whereas it is his duty to respect them; it would in fact become the equivalent of an immu-

nity, which was evidently not within the intentions of the draftsmen of the Havana Convention.

It has not been shown that the existence of a state of siege [in Peru] implied the subordination of justice to the executive authority, or that the suspension of certain constitutional guarantees entailed the abolition of judicial guarantees. . . .

The Court cannot admit that the States signatory to the Havana Convention intended to substitute for the practice of the Latin-American republics, in which considerations of courtesy, good-neighbourliness and political expediency have always held a prominent place, a legal system which would guarantee to their own nationals accused of political offences the privilege of evading national jurisdiction. Such a conception, moreover, would come into conflict with one of the most firmly established traditions of Latin-America, namely, nonintervention [for example, by Colombia into the internal affairs of another State—Peru].

. . .

[The court must] reject the argument that the Havana Convention was intended to afford a quite general protection of asylum to any person prosecuted for political offences, either in the course of revolutionary events or in the more or less troubled times that follow, for the sole reason that it must be assumed that such events interfere with the administration of justice. It is clear that the adoption of such a criterion would lead to foreign interference of a particularly offensive nature in the domestic affairs of States; besides which no confirmation of this criterion can be found in Latin-American practice, as this practice has been explained to the Court.

In thus expressing itself, the Court does not lose sight of the numerous cases of asylum which have been cited.

. . .

If these remarks tend to reduce considerably the value as precedents of the cases of asylum cited . . . they show none the less, that asylum as practised in Latin-America is an institution which, to a very great extent, owes its development to extra-legal factors. The good-neighbour relations between the republics, the different political interests of the Governments, have favoured the mutual recognition of asylum apart from any clearly defined juridical system. Even if the Havana Convention, in particular, represents an indisputable reaction against certain abuses in practice, it in no way tends to limit the practice of asylum as it may arise from agreements between interested Governments inspired by mutual feelings of toleration and goodwill.

. . .

■ NOTES

1. In the above case, the ICJ decided that Haya de la Torre's asylum should be terminated because Colombia could not properly grant it. Colombia's unilateral decision that de la Torre was engaged in "political activity," rather than a common crime against Peru, was not entitled to recognition by other countries (*see* § 5.3 on this distinction).

2. Although the ICJ ruled that this asylum was not *legally* valid, Peru's citizen was effectively sheltered anyway. Peru could not enter the Colombian embassy to force his surrender. Colombia, on the other hand, could not force Peru to grant de la Torre safe passage out of Peru. After this decision, Colombia and Peru ultimately negotiated an arrangement permitting de la Torre to leave Peru for Colombia.

3. Four years after this judgment, Peru ratified the Caracas Convention on Diplomatic Asylum. Article 2 therein provides that "every State has the right to grant asylum. . . ." Article 4 adds that it "shall rest with the State granting asylum to determine the nature of the offense [common crime versus political act] or the motives for the persecution." These provisions require treaty signatories to recognize unilateral grants of asylum, rather than depend on a distant court's interpretation or application of the *general* International Law that may differ from a *regional* State practice. *See* Comment, *Diplomatic Asylum in the United States and Latin America: A Comparative Analysis*, 13 *Brooklyn J. Int'l L.* 111 (1987).

4. The ICJ's judgment in the *Asylum Case* was criticized by many States—especially in Latin America where diplomatic asylum was a common regional practice. Commentators characterized the Court as suffering from the continuing influence of

The Court considers that there did not exist a danger constituting a case of urgency within the meaning of Article 2, paragraph 2, of the Havana Convention.

European judicial perspectives. A representative criticism by a Brazilian author is as follows:

[The various judicial pronouncements in the *Asylum Case*] received wide publicity and were the object of various learned papers; those written in Spain and Latin America were, with rare exception, highly critical of the stand taken by the International Court of Justice.

. . .

From a Latin American point of view, [the judgment] contains certain affirmations which simply went to prove that the Court was not qualified to pass judgment since it had examined a typical Latin American juridical institution [diplomatic asylum] *exclusively from a European and biased point of view.* . . . Just as the [reasoning] . . . of the International Court of Justice on the question of the international status of South-West Africa made most Afro-Asian States distrust the court, the Haya de la Torre case alienated most Latin American States, thus contributing to the atmosphere of ill-will which characterizes the relations of most States with the principal judicial organ of the United Nations [the ICJ].[20]

5. In the referenced *South-West Africa* case decided by the ICJ in the same year as the *Asylum Case*, the Court ruled that the Union of South Africa had no obligation to place South-West Africa (a former League "Mandate") under the UN Trusteeship system. As a result, this territory remained subject to domination by the white minority government of South Africa until independence forty years later (as the new State of Namibia). *See* International Status of South-West Africa, 1950 I.C.J. Rep. 128.

■ 7.4 IMMUNITIES AND ABUSE OF IMMUNITY

This section of the book addresses two themes that are an integral part of the International Law of Diplomacy: the extent to which the sending State and its representatives may invoke immunity from prosecution in the host State; and the pressure to seek a waiver of any immunities when a diplomat engages in conduct unbecoming his or her position.

Diplomatic and Consular Immunities

Evolution Many centuries ago, it was customary practice to protect the representatives of other governments. Without such rules, representatives could not perform their economic and political functions without fear of injury or death. Protective measures—now referred to as immunities—were created in order to limit the absolute power or jurisdiction of the host States wherein they served. The mutual interests of the sending and receiving States required the creation of special privileges and immunities from local laws. Diplomats were not subject to prosecution by host State authorities or private citizens—in either civil and criminal matters. This immunity thus allowed envoys to engage in international diplomacy without fear of arrest or time-consuming involvement in litigation unrelated to the reason for that presence in the home State.

Professor Ian Brownlie of Oxford University explains the rationale for diplomatic immunity with his formulation that the "essence of diplomatic relations is the exercise by the sending government of state functions on the territory of the receiving state by license [permission] of the latter. Having agreed to the establishment of diplomatic relations, the receiving [host] state must take steps to enable the sending state to benefit from the content of the license. The process of giving 'full faith and credit' to the license results in a body of 'privileges and immunities.'"[21]

This vintage device, now known as diplomatic immunity, has additional roots in the medieval State practice recognizing the need for safe passage through third States. In the fifteenth and sixteenth centuries, a ruler who hoped to defeat an alliance between two other rulers would literally select their emissary as the target. If King B hoped to frustrate an alliance between Kingdom A and Kingdom C, King B need only kill or imprison any intermediary who was passing through Kingdom B. The French envoys Rinco and Fregoso were murdered by Emperor Charles V. Spain's Ambassador Mendoza was imprisoned in France for four months while on a mission to England. Incidents such as these ultimately led to State recognition of diplomatic immunities and privileges.[22]

Due to continuing frustration with the practical rationale of "not shooting the messenger," a number of States began to codify their expectations about diplomatic immunity in their internal laws. England's Diplomatic Privileges Act of 1708, for example, was a direct result of the arrest and detention of the Russian ambassador and his coach by English authorities. The Act was designed "to prevent like insolences for the future."[23]

Consular immunity is more limited than that of diplomatic immunity. The diplomat, and his or her staff, are granted *full* immunity from the jurisdiction of the host State. Consular immunity accords a lesser degree of insulation from host-State arrest or civil litigation. Consular officers normally represent less sensitive interests than ambassadors and like diplomats. As restated by Stefan Sawicki in the Polish Yearbook of International Law, "members of the consulate enjoy the immunity only in relation to official acts considered as [an] expression of a sovereign State. . . ."[24] Unlike diplomats, not all conduct is shielded from the host State's jurisdiction.

Modern Efficacy The contemporary importance and continuing applicability of diplomatic and consular immunity is illustrated in the following passage from the 1980 *Hostage Case* (set forth later in this section of the book):

EXCERPT FROM IRANIAN HOSTAGE CASE

19 International Legal Materials 553 (1980)

In a course of lectures which he gave in 1937 at the Hague Academy of International Law on the subject of "Islam and *jus gentium*" [the law of nations], Professor Ahmed Rechid of the Istanbul law faculty gave the following account of the inviolability of the envoy in Muslim law:

'In Arabia, the person of the ambassador had always been regarded as sacred. Muhammad consecrated this inviolability. Never were ambassadors to Muhammad or to his successors molested. One day, the envoy of a foreign nation, at an audience granted to him by the Prophet, was so bold as to use insulting language. Muhammad said to him: 'If you were not an envoy I would have you put to death.' The author of the 'Siyer' which relates this incident draws from it the conclusion that there is an obligation to respect the person of ambassadors.'

Ahmed Rechid adds further on:

'The Prophet always treated the envoys of foreign nations with consideration and great affability. He used to shower gifts upon them and recommended his companions to follow his example, saying: 'Do the same as I.'

In a work entitled *International Law*, published by the Institute of State and Law of the Academy of Sciences of the USSR, the following is to be read on the conduct in the Middle Ages of the Arabs, the bearers of the Islamic faith:

'The Arab States, which played an important part in international relations in the Middle Ages (from the 7th century) had well-developed conceptions regarding the Law of Nations, closely linked with religious precepts.

The Arabs recognised the inviolability of Ambassadors and the need for the fulfillment of treaty obligations. They resorted to arbitration to settle international disputes and considered the observance of [such] definite rules of law necessary [even] in time of war....'

The contemporary rules of diplomatic immunity are contained in the Vienna Convention on Diplomatic Relations of 1961.[25] Its essential provisions, observed by the approximately 150 State parties, are as follows:

Article 22 1. The premises of the mission shall be inviolable. The agents of the receiving State may not enter them, except with the consent of the head of the mission. 2. The receiving State is under a special duty to take all appropriate steps to protect the premises of the mission against any intrusion or damage and to prevent any disturbance of the peace of the mission or impairment of its dignity. 3. The premises of the mission, their furnishings and other property thereon and the means of transport of the mission shall be immune from search, requisition, attachment [seizure resulting in custody and control by a court] or execution [sale of property to satisfy court judgment].

Article 24 The archives and documents of the mission shall be inviolable at any time and wherever they may be.

Article 27 1. The receiving State shall permit and protect free communication on the part of the mission for all official purposes. In communicating with the Government and the other missions and consulates of the sending State, wherever situated, the mission may employ all appropriate means, including diplomatic couriers and messages in code or cipher. However, the mission may install and use a wireless transmitter only with the consent of the receiving State. 2. The official correspondence of the mission shall be inviolable. Official correspondence means all correspondence relating to the mission and its functions. 3. The diplomatic bag shall not be opened or detained. . . . 5. The diplomatic courier, who shall be provided with an official document indicating his status and the number of packages

Although the receiving (host) State is obliged to protect the premises of the sending State's diplomatic mission, complete protection from terrorist attacks is impossible. This picture shows the former Soviet Embassy in Washington, D.C. in 1968, after a bomb exploded outside the window at the lower left.

constituting the diplomatic bag, shall be protected by the receiving State in the performance of his functions. He shall enjoy personal inviolability and shall not be liable to any form of arrest or detention.

Article 29 The person of a diplomatic agent shall be inviolable. He shall not be liable to any form of arrest or detention. The receiving State shall treat him with due respect and shall take all appropriate steps to prevent any attack on his person, freedom or dignity.

Article 30 1. The private residence of a diplomatic agent shall enjoy the same inviolability and protection as the premises of the mission. 2. His papers, correspondence and . . . his property, shall likewise enjoy inviolability.

Article 31 1. A diplomatic agent shall enjoy immunity from the criminal jurisdiction of the receiving State. He shall also enjoy immunity from its civil and administrative jurisdiction [regarding torts, contracts, and other legal matters].

A number of these provisions (also found in the 1963 Vienna Convention on *Consular* Relations[26]) were the subject of worldwide attention during the Iranian Hostage Crisis of 1979–1980. Their continuing vitality, notwithstanding 444 days of a diplomatic stalemate over the hostages, was illustrated by the fact that *no* State supported Iran's actions. The UN Security Council unanimously resolved that Iran must immediately release the US and Canadian diplomatic and consular personnel who were seized at the US embassy and various consular offices in Iran. This crisis, together with its international legal implications, is analyzed in the following case:

CASE CONCERNING UNITED STATES DIPLOMATIC AND CONSULAR STAFF IN TEHRAN

International Court of Justice, 1980
19 International Legal Materials 553 (1980)*

[*Author's Note: On November 4, 1979, the US embassy in Tehran, Iran, was overrun by several hundred of the 3,000 Iranians who had been demonstrating at the embassy gates. They seized diplomats, consuls, and marine personnel and then occupied the embassy premises. Two US consulates in other cities in Iran were also occupied and then closed on the following day. The embassy personnel in Tehran were physically threatened and denied any communication with either US officials or relatives.*

Several hundred thousand demonstrators converged on the US embassy premises on November 22, 1979. The Iranian government made no effort to intervene or to assist the hostages inside the building. While a few hostages were released, most were subsequently removed to unknown locations outside of the embassy premises.

The US instituted this suit against Iran in the International Court of Justice, alleging that Iran breached the Vienna Conventions on Diplomatic and Consular Relations, the Vienna Convention on the Prevention of Crimes against Internationally Protected Persons, and the 1955 US-Iran Treaty of Amity.

The position of the Iranian government is contained in correspondence it submitted to the court. Iran refused to send lawyers to represent Iran, to file any official papers, or to directly participate in these proceedings. The ICJ nevertheless considered Iran's correspondence and made preliminary reference to it as follows.]

[*Iranian Correspondence.*] The Government of the Islamic Republic of Iran . . . draws the attention of the Court to the deep-rootedness and the essential character of the Islamic Revolution of Iran, a revolution of a whole oppressed nation against its oppressors and their masters, the examination of whose numerous repercussions is essentially and directly a matter within the national sovereignty of Iran.

. . .

For this question [regarding detention of the diplomatic hostages] only represents a marginal and secondary aspect of an overall problem, one such that it cannot be studied separately, and which involves . . . more than 25 years of continual interference by the United States in the internal affairs of Iran, the shameless exploitation of our country, and numerous crimes perpetrated against the Iranian people, contrary to and in conflict with all international and humanitarian norms.

The problem involved in the conflict between Iran and the United States is thus not [merely] one of the interpretation and the application of the treaties upon which the American Application is based, but results from an overall situation containing much more fundamental and more complex elements. Consequently, the Court cannot examine the American Application divorced from its proper context, namely the whole political dossier of the relations between Iran and the United States over the last 25 years. This dossier includes . . . all the crimes perpetrated in Iran by the American Government, in particular the *coup d'etat* of 1953 stirred up and carried out by the CIA, the overthrow of the lawful national government of Dr. Mossadegh, the restoration [then] of the Shah and of his regime which was under the control of American interests, and all the social, economic, cultural and political consequences of the direct interventions in our internal affairs, as well as grave, flagrant and continuous violations of all international norms, committed by the United States in Iran.

[*Opinion of the Court. The paragraph numbers are those of the court.*]

22. The persons still held hostage in Iran include, according to the information furnished to the Court by the United States, at least 28 persons having the status, duly recognized by the Government of Iran, of "member of the diplomatic staff" within the meaning of the Vienna Convention of Diplomatic Relations of 1961; at least 20 persons having the status, similarly recognized, of "member of the administrative and technical staff" within the meaning of that Convention; and two other persons of United States nationality not possessing either diplomatic or consular status. Of the persons with the status of member of the diplomatic staff, four are members of the Consular Section of the Mission.

23. Allegations have been made by the Government of the United States of inhumane treatment of hostages; the militants and Iranian authorities have asserted that the hostages have been well treated, and have allowed special visits to the hostages by religious personalities and by representatives of the International Committee of the Red Cross. The specific allegations of ill-treatment have not however been refuted. Examples of such allegations, which are mentioned in some of the sworn declarations of hostages released in November 1979, are as follows: at the outset of the occupation of the Embassy some were paraded bound and blindfolded before hostile and chanting crowds; at least during the initial period of their captivity, hostages were kept bound, and frequently blindfolded, denied mail or any communication with their government or with each other, subjected to interrogation, threatened with weapons.

24. Those archives and documents of the United States Embassy which were not destroyed by the staff during the attack on 4 November have been ransacked by the militants. Documents purporting to come from this source have been disseminated by the militants and by the Government-controlled media.

. . .

36. . . . . [T]he seizure of the United States Embassy and Consulates and the detention of internationally protected persons as hostages cannot [despite Iran's written communication to the ICJ] be considered as something "secondary" or "marginal," having regard to the importance of the legal principles involved. It also referred to a statement of the Secretary-General of the United Nations, and to Security Council resolution 457 (1979), as evidencing the importance attached by the international community as a whole to the observance of those principles in the present case as well as its concern at the dangerous level of tension between Iran and the United States.

. . .

46. [The court *is* able to hear this case because the] United States' claims here in question concern alleged violations by Iran of its obligations under several articles of the Vienna Conventions of 1961 and 1963 with respect to the privileges and immunities of the personnel, the inviolability of the premises and archives, and the provision of facilities for the performance of the functions of the United States Embassy and Consulates in Iran. . . . By their very nature all these claims concern the interpretation or application of one or other of the two Vienna Conventions.

47. The occupation of the United States Embassy by militants on 4 November 1979 and the detention of its personnel as hostages was an event of a kind to provoke an immediate protest from any government, as it did from the United States Government, which despatched a special emissary to Iran to deliver a formal protest.

. . .

It is clear that on that date there existed a dispute arising out of the interpretation or application of the Vienna Conventions and thus one falling within the scope of the Protocols [which are a part of the Vienna Conventions on Diplomatic and Consular Relations *requiring* States to submit such disputes to the ICJ for resolution].

. . .

61. The conclusion just reached by the Court, that the initiation of the attack on the United States Embassy on 4 November 1979, and of the attacks on the Consulates at Tabriz and Shiraz the following day, cannot be considered as in itself imputable to the Iranian State does not mean that Iran is, in consequence, free of any responsibility in regard to those attacks; for its own conduct was in conflict with its international obligations. By a number of provisions of the Vienna Conventions of 1961 and 1963, Iran was placed under the most categorical obligations, as a receiving State, to take appropriate

steps to ensure the protection of the United States Embassy and Consulates, their staffs, their archives, their means of communication and the freedom of movement of the members of their staffs.

62. Thus, after solemnly proclaiming the inviolability of the premises of a diplomatic mission, Article 22 of the 1961 Convention continues in paragraph 2:

"The receiving State is under a special duty to take all appropriate steps to protect the premises of the mission against any intrusion or damage and to prevent any disturbance of the peace of the mission or impairment of its dignity." [Emphasis supplied by the Court.]

So, too, after proclaiming that the person of a diplomatic agent shall be inviolable, and that he shall not be liable to any form of arrest or detention, Article 29 provides:

"The receiving State shall treat him with due respect and *shall take all appropriate steps to prevent any attack on his person, freedom or dignity."* [Emphasis supplied by the Court.]

The obligation of a receiving State to protect the inviolability of the archives and documents of a diplomatic mission is laid down in Article 24, which specifically provides that they are to be "inviolable at any time and wherever they may be." Under Article 25 it is required to "accord full facilities for the performance of the functions of the mission," under Article 26 to "ensure to all members of the mission freedom of movement and travel in its territory," and under Article 27 to "permit and protect free communication on the part of the mission for all official purposes." Analogous provisions are to be found in the 1963 [Consular] Convention regarding the privileges and immunities of consular missions and their staffs (Art. 31, para. 3, Arts. 40, 33, 28, 34 and 35). In the view of the Court, the obligations of the Iranian Government here in question are not merely contractual obligations established by the Vienna Conventions of 1961 and 1963, but also obligations under general international law.

63. The facts set out in paragraphs 14 to 27 above establish to the satisfaction of the Court that on 4 November 1979 the Iranian Government failed altogether to take any "appropriate steps" to protect the premises, staff and archives of the United States' mission against attack by the mili-

tants, and to take any steps either to prevent this attack or to stop it before it reached its completion. They also show that on 5 November 1979 the Iranian Government similarly failed to take appropriate steps for the protection of the United States Consulates at Tabriz and Shiraz. In addition they show, in the opinion of the Court, that the failure of the Iranian Government to take such steps was due to more than mere negligence or lack of appropriate means.

. . .

77. . . . Paragraphs 1 and 3 of that Article [22] have also been infringed, and continue to be infringed, since they forbid agents of a receiving State to enter the premises of a mission without consent or to undertake any search, requisition, attachment or like measure on the premises. Secondly, they constitute continuing breaches of Article 29 of the same Convention which forbids any arrest or detention of a diplomatic agent and any attack on his person, freedom or dignity. Thirdly, the Iranian authorities are without doubt in continuing breach of the provisions of Articles 25, 26 and 27 of the 1961 Vienna Convention and of pertinent provisions of the 1963 Vienna Convention concerning facilities for the performance of functions, freedom of movement and communications for diplomatic and consular staff, as well as of Article 24 of the former Convention and Article 33 of the latter, which provide for the absolute inviolability of the archives and documents of diplomatic missions and consulates. This particular violation has been made manifest to the world by repeated statements by the militants occupying the Embassy, who claim to be in possession of documents from the archives, and by various government authorities, purporting to specify the contents thereof. Finally, the continued detention as hostages of the two private individuals of United States nationality entails a renewed breach of the obligations of Iran under Article 11, paragraph 4, of the 1955 Treaty of Amity, Economic Relations, and Consular Rights.

. . .

79. . . . [J]udicial authorities of the Islamic Republic of Iran and the Minister for Foreign Affairs have frequently voiced or associated themselves with, a threat first announced by the militants, of having some of the hostages submitted to trial

before a court or some other body. These threats may at present merely be acts in contemplation. But the Court considers it necessary here and now to stress that, if the intention to submit the hostages to any form of criminal trial or investigation were to be put into effect, that would constitute a grave breach by Iran of its obligations under Article 31, paragraph 1, of the 1961 Vienna Convention. This paragraph states in the most express terms: "A diplomatic agent shall enjoy immunity from the criminal jurisdiction of the receiving State." Again, if there were an attempt to compel the hostages to bear witness, a suggestion renewed at the time of the visit to Iran of the Secretary-General's Commission, Iran would without question be violating paragraph 2 of that same Article of the 1961 Vienna Convention which provides that: "A diplomatic agent is not obliged to give evidence as a witness."

. . .

83. In any case, *even if the alleged criminal activities of the United States in Iran could be considered as having been established*, the question would remain whether they could be regarded by the Court as constituting a justification of Iran's conduct and thus a defence to the United States' claims in the present case. The Court, however, is unable to accept that they can be so regarded. This is because diplomatic law itself provides the necessary means of defence against, and sanction for, illicit activities by members of diplomatic or consular missions. [Emphasis supplied by author.]

. . .

85. Thus, it is for the very purpose of providing a remedy for such possible abuses of diplomatic functions that Article 9 of the 1961 Convention on Diplomatic Relations stipulates:

"1. The receiving State may at any time and without having to explain its decision, notify the sending State that the head of the mission or any member of the diplomatic staff of the mission is *persona non grata* or that any other member of the staff of the mission is not acceptable. In any such case, the sending State shall, as appropriate, either recall the person concerned or terminate his functions with the mission. A person may be declared *non grata* or not acceptable before arriving in the territory of the receiving State.

2. If the sending State refuses or fails within a reasonable period to carry out its obligations under paragraph 1 of this Article, the receiving State may refuse to recognize the person concerned as a member of the mission."

87. . . . The Iranian Government did not, therefore, employ the remedies placed at its disposal by diplomatic law specifically for dealing with activities of the kind of which it now complains. Instead, it allowed a group of militants to attack and occupy the United States Embassy by force, and to seize the diplomatic and consular staff as hostages; instead, it has endorsed that action of those militants and has deliberately maintained their occupation of the Embassy and detention of its staff as a means of coercing the sending State. It has, at the same time, refused altogether to discuss this situation with representatives of the United States. The Court, therefore, can only conclude that Iran did not have recourse to the normal and efficacious means at its disposal, but [instead] resorted to coercive action against the United States Embassy and its staff.

■ NOTES & QUESTIONS

1. What rules of International Law were breached by Iran in the *Hostage Case*?

2. Assume that the US *was* responsible for the violations of International Law as asserted by Iran in the preliminary passage of this case (directly before the numbered paragraphs of the court's opinion). Do such violations justify Iran's kidnapping the hostages or taking over the embassy?

3. Would the ICJ rule differently if Iran were *not* a party to the Vienna Conventions on Diplomatic and Consular Relations?

General Perception There are many contemporary criticisms leveled at diplomatic immunity. Journalistic endeavors to sensationalize abuses of diplomatic immunity always revisit the question of its

Staff members from the US embassy in Tehran, Iran, pose for a group picture after their release from being held hostage for 444 days. They were seized when militant Iranian students overran the embassy in 1979, seeking the return of the former Shah of Iran who was deposed and then living in the US. *Abuse of Diplomatic Immunity*

underlying necessity. In the major book on the subject, two Washington, D.C. journalists presented their widely read criticism in the following introductory nutshell—which probably represents the perspective of most members of the lay public (as well as that of US Senator Jesse Helms, who subsequently proposed legislation on several occasions to curb such abuses). The journalist's reprimand is as follows:

> No president of the United States, judge, police officer, or celebrity is permitted to rape or rob without fear of criminal prosecution. Yet, we have officially labelled thirty-seven thousand visitors currently [1987] living in . . . [major] cities as *above and beyond the law.*
>
> Most of these given this *enormous exemption from civilized behavior* are not diplomats. They are the wives, children, drivers, and valets of ambassadors and ministers sent to this country to represent their nations. . . .

This *immunity is particularly bizarre* since it is not limited to incidents occurring in the course of "official duties" but rather serves as an absolute security blanket. . . .[27]

This perspective is not unique. Not all States observe the general international rule of diplomatic immunity from criminal prosecution. During the Cultural Revolution (1966–1976), representatives of the People's Republic of China "declared that diplomatic immunities were of bourgeois origin and that they had no place in a socialist society."[28]

Available Alternatives The above examples of moral indignation with diplomatic immunity do not appreciate that there are alternatives available to deal with such abuses—as suggested in the *Hostage Case* set forth above. The ICJ therein refers to the following remedies for abuse of immunity in its paragraph 86:

Even in the case of armed conflict or in the case of a breach in diplomatic relations those provisions require that both the inviolability of the members of a diplomatic mission and of the premises, property and archives of the mission must be respected by the receiving State. Naturally, the observance of this principle does not mean—and this the Applicant Government expressly acknowledges—that a diplomatic agent *caught in the act* of committing an assault or other offence may not, on occasion, be *briefly arrested* by the police of the receiving State *in order to prevent the commission* of the particular crime. [Emphasis supplied by author.]

One must of course acknowledge that the participation of more than 150 States in the Vienna Convention on Diplomatic Relations means that the systemic benefits have not been vitiated by the occasional costs. Assume that a State A diplomat commits a crime in host-State B. The interests of both States are better served if State B declares State A's offending ambassador *persona non grata* (*see* § 7.2). If State B were to arrest the State A diplomat, State B would risk reciprocal treatment—the authorities in State A might one day respond by arresting a State B diplomat or consular officer who commits a crime or civil wrong while working in State A.

Insurance is another alternative. State B citizens can thus be protected against certain consequences of diplomatic conduct through this risk-shifting device. A portion of the risk of having A's diplomats in State B is borne by State A, which has sent them to B. This insurance benefits State B nationals. While the State A diplomat is not thereby subject to suit in State B's courts, a State B insurer can thereby assume a portion of the risks associated with diplomatic negligence. B nationals would thus have a monetary remedy, like that available to them when they insure themselves against the conduct of *private* (nondiplomatic) individuals in State B. This convenient compromise permits the A diplomat to continue his or her duties without the inconvenient disruption of having to defend lawsuits in B's courts. The insurer will do this, instead, and the responsible diplomat does not fully "escape" liability. The US Department of State has promulgated standards regarding compulsory diplomatic insurance.[29]

"Waiver" of diplomatic immunity is an alternative for appropriate *criminal* cases. When an individual entitled to immunity under the Vienna Diplomatic or Consular Convention has allegedly committed a serious criminal offense, the host State might request that the sending State waive diplomatic immunity of its agent. There have been several attempts to pass US legislation whereby the US could automatically initiate proceedings in cases involving serious crimes. US Senator Jesse Helms has proposed a "Diplomatic Immunity Abuse Prevention Act" on several occasions—which may one day survive congressional scrutiny. Under its terms, a request for waiver would be initiated in all such cases by the US Secretary of State. In the interim, States are not precluded from requesting such waivers on an *ad hoc* basis when circumstances so warrant. The sending State could thus ensure the continuance of mutually beneficial relations if one of its diplomats committed a serious crime (which would violate the laws of both nations). Such waivers would not unjustly surprise any diplomatic representative who occupies that position due to his or her awareness of host State culture and general norms of conduct.

Diplomatic Bag Complaints about diplomatic immunity include the occasional problem with the so-called "diplomatic bag." Article 27.3 of the Vienna Convention on Diplomatic Relations provides that a "diplomatic bag shall not be opened or detained." The following excerpt from a French journal (Review of Public International Law) demonstrates the difficulties that can arise during the juxtaposition of treaty obligations and practical reality:

SEIZURE OF ARMS IN BAGGAGE OF DIPLOMAT IN TRANSIT

78 Revue Generale de Droit International Public 247 (1974)*

Five hand grenades, five revolvers, eight kilos of explosive devices, and 21 letter bombs not yet addressed, rifles and ammunition were discovered on the evening of October 23, 1972, by Dutch customs officers at the airport of Schiphol in the baggage of an Algerian diplomatic agent accredited to a South American nation which the Dutch Minister of Justice refused to identify. Aged 32, born in Jordan, but carrying an Algerian diplomatic passport, the diplomat, who was identified only by the initials II.R., came from Damascus via Frankfurt and was en route to Rio de Janeiro. He declared himself to be entirely ignorant of the contents of his baggage, explaining only he thought he was carrying documents delivered to him in Damascus and destined for an Algerian embassy in a South American republic, which he declined to identify further. He added nevertheless he had bought the rifles, which were found separately, for diplomatic colleagues. The Queen's prosecutor [of the Netherlands] did not institute judicial proceedings against the diplomat because in his judgment it had not at all been established that the diplomat was actually aware of the contents of his baggage. As a result the diplomat was authorized to continue his trip to South America, but his bags were retained for an investigation.

Following the discovery, the Israeli government—which was convinced the arms seized were to be used in organizing an attack upon its embassy in Brazil—requested an explanation from the Dutch government, because in its opinion the Algerian diplomat should have been held by the authorities at the airport "because diplomatic immunity applies only in the countries where diplomatic agents are accredited and not in the countries through which they are only in transit." One should have some reservations about this assertion which is contrary to established practice and is contradicted by Article 40 of the Vienna Convention of April 18, 1961, on Diplomatic Relations by whose terms a diplomatic agent in transit through the territory of a third state is given "inviolability and every other immunity necessary for his passage or return." But, inasmuch as the acts here were outside official functions, the immunity of agents in transit, already subject to strict limitations, obviously ceases in a case of flagrant offense.

The UN's International Law Commission has been working on draft provisions that would amend the status of the diplomatic courier and the diplomatic bag—via optional protocols to the Vienna Convention. The objective is to provide the State parties to the Vienna Convention on Diplomatic Relations an opportunity to place further restrictions on such immunity in a way that would better control potential abuse. The UN's Sixth Committee (Legal) is thus conducting informal consultations on the question whether the General Assembly should convene an international conference, for the purpose of creating draft articles on this sensitive topic.[30]

■ SUMMARY

1. International diplomacy is the conduct of relations between governments. Diplomatic relations are established through the mutual consent of both the sending and host States. Ambassadors represent the head of State of the sending State and normally reside in the national capital of the host State.

2. Modern modes of communication and transportation have altered the diplomatic role. Ambassadors no longer have the degree of autonomy exercised by their predecessors—who were often out of contact with their home States for lengthy periods of time. Further, heads of State now engage directly in international diplomacy.

---

*Translation provided with permission of Foundation Press, Mineola, New York. Reprinted with the permission of Editions A. Pedone, Paris, France.

3. The diplomat's duties include: (a) representing the sending State; (b) protecting the interests of the sending State; (c) negotiating with the host government; (d) reporting conditions in the host State to the sending State; and (e) promoting friendly relations.

4. Diplomacy is traditionally undertaken in private settings. Some world leaders have directed their diplomatic efforts toward a comparatively public audience during joint summit meetings. Foreign policy-making is appropriately debated in a public arena, but negotiations to implement national policies are often best handled by career diplomats in a private setting.

5. Consular officers are not necessarily diplomatic representatives. They may occasionally undertake diplomatic tasks by conducting their affairs from within the embassy premises rather than in a separate office in the host State. Consuls typically implement the trade policy of the sending state. Their immunities are not as broad as the "diplomat" who enjoys complete immunity from the jurisdiction of the host State. Consular immunity is extended only for those official acts that directly represent the interests of the sending State.

6. The "extraterritoriality fiction" was that foreign embassies and consulates are considered to be on "foreign" soil. This practice arose under customary State practice to validate certain activities occurring within these premises. The adoption of the Vienna Convention on Diplomatic Immunity (and its companion Consular Convention) eliminated the need to rely on this fiction—by expressly providing for the comprehensive protection of the premises, occupants, and diplomatic bag or pouch.

7. There is no general right of diplomatic asylum under International Law. Such a right may exist under regional practice or treaties, however. The UN's International Court of Justice has been criticized for not applying such regional practices to cases involving States in the affected region. A conflict may arise when one State's embassy grants asylum to a host State national accused of a crime. Although there is no *general* right of asylum, an impasse often occurs because the host State cannot legally enter the premises of the diplomatic mission to arrest the accused.

8. A State may suspend or completely terminate international relations with another State. Two States may recall their diplomats from the respective capitals, even when there is a continuing need to deal with one another. Some States have done so through the assistance of third States with a diplomatic presence in the two States that have broken formal diplomatic ties.

9. Immunity from the application of the host State's law permits diplomatic and consular representatives to carry out their functions without fear of arrest or involvement in litigation. The Vienna Conventions on diplomatic and consular immunities specifically provide for the inviolability of: (a) embassy and consulate premises; (b) the documents on these premises; (c) the diplomatic bag, wherever it is located; (d) the person of the diplomatic agent; and (e) his or her private residence.

10. When a diplomatic representative abuses the immunity conferred under International Law, the host State may declare that individual *persona non grata*, which results in his or her expulsion. Absent a waiver of the sending State, host State authorities may not arrest or try diplomatic representatives for their crimes or civil wrongs (for example, causing an automobile accident). Insurance may be available to protect adversely affected individuals in the host State.

■ PROBLEMS

Problem 7.1 (*end of § 7.3*): In 1992, Peru's ex-President Alan Garcia sought refuge in the Colombian embassy in Peru. This Peruvian president (from 1985 to 1990) was an outspoken opponent of his successor. Garcia had been in hiding since the new president dissolved the Peruvian Congress and temporarily closed the Peruvian courts. Colombia decided to grant Garcia diplomatic asylum. Colombia then began steps to process Garcia's orderly departure from Peru. Did Colombia violate International Law by granting diplomatic asylum to former President Garcia in 1992?

Problem 7.2 (*end of § 7.4*): The following hypothetical is adapted from actual events. Many of the applicable rules of International Law are set forth in the 1961 Vienna Convention on Diplomatic Relations and the 1980 *Hostage Case* (set forth in the text in § 7.4) in which the International Court of Justice interpreted that convention. Students will engage in diplomatic negotiations to achieve what they believe to be the best resolution under International Law. This exercise is designed to illustrate the rules of immunity and some of their practical limitations:

The Problem Rieferbaan's is a discotheque in Germany near a US military base. US soldiers often socialize at Reiferbaan's. Magenta is a State that has an embassy in Germany but no diplomatic relations with the US. Magenta's embassy is ten minutes from Rieferbaan's by car.

The first secretary of Magenta's diplomatic mission in Germany is Charge d'Affairs Mann. The leader of Mann's home State (Magenta) has directed Mann to openly criticize the United States and to take all steps necessary to publicize Magenta's belief that the US should pull its troops out of Western Europe. Magenta's leader directs Charge d'Affairs Mann to set off a bomb at the discotheque when it is crowded with US soldiers. Mann and the Magenta head of State communicate secretly via coded radio signals. Unknown to Mann, the Army Intelligence Office at the US military base (in conjunction with a government radio station in Germany) has broken Magenta's code for diplomatic transmissions. The US and German governments are thus fully aware of the terrorist plot. They want it to develop, however, to a point where Magenta cannot deny responsibility.

Charge d'Affairs Mann has assembled a group of armed anti-US "freedom fighters" at Magenta's embassy premises, and at various points between the embassy and Rieferbaan's. The Army Intelligence Office learns that there will be a very specific but innocuous message brought directly from Magenta's leader to Mann (at Magenta's embassy) in a diplomatic pouch from Magenta. It contains the signal to go ahead with the terrorist bombing at the Rieferbaan Disco. Magenta's diplomatic courier arrives at a German airport, is detained by US soldiers, and is then arrested by German police. The State of Magenta's official diplomatic pouch is seized and opened. The US soldiers and the German police thus intercept the message that would have resulted in the bombing of the discotheque and a massive loss of life.

German police later surround Magenta's embassy where the key "freedom fighters" are located. They advise Charge d'Affairs Mann by telephone that the plot has been discovered, and that the courier and pouch have been seized due to Magenta's "abuse of transit" via the diplomatic pouch brought into Germany. Everyone in the embassy is ordered to immediately come outside and cross the street onto "German soil."

Three students will act as diplomatic representatives. Student 1, Hans Smit, is a German career diplomat assigned to negotiate a successful conclusion to this crisis. Student 2 is Joanna Shultz, the US Ambassador to Germany. Student 3 will assume the role of Charge d'Affairs Mann, Magenta's ambassador to Germany.

Part One Hans Smit (student 1) and Joanna Shultz (student 2) confer at a government building in Germany near the Magenta embassy. They are trying to decide whether Charge d'Affairs Mann should be invited to join them. Germany, the US, and Magenta are parties to the Vienna Convention on Diplomatic Relations. Smit and Shultz should assess whether Mann can be characterized as having *waived* the treaty's immunity provisions. If Mann decides to confer with them outside of the Magenta embassy, they should further assess the possibility of revoking his diplomatic immunity to arrest him.

Part Two Assume that Smit and Shultz decide to invite Mann to negotiate but not to arrest him. Can Mann reasonably claim that Germany and the US have violated the Vienna Convention? What specific claims will Mann be able to assert?

Part Three The three ambassadors are discussing whether the "freedom fighters" in the Magenta embassy should be permitted to go freely from Germany to France, as they have requested. If Germany decides against this resolution, what can it do to the "freedom fighters"?

■ BIBLIOGRAPHY

§ 7.1 **Foreword to International Diplomacy:**

Chay, *Diplomatic History and International Relations*, ch. 3, in J. Chay (ed.), *Culture and International Relations* 34 (New York: Praeger, 1990)

R. Cohen, *Negotiating Across Cultures: Communication Obstacles in International Diplomacy* (Wash., DC: US Inst. Peace, 1991)

The Diplomatic Instrument, ch. 15, in Lung-Chu Chen, *An Introduction to Contemporary International Law: A Policy-Oriented Perspective* 253 (New Haven, CT: Yale Univ. Press, 1989)

J. Findling, *Dictionary of American Diplomatic History* (2nd ed. New York: Greenwood Press, 1989)

D. Mak & C. Kennedy, *American Ambassadors in a Troubled World: Interviews with Senior Diplomats* (Westport, CT: Greenwood Press, 1992)

K. Tomasevski, *Development Aid and Human Rights Revisited* (London: Pinter Pub., 1993)

§ 7.2 Diplomatic and Consular Functions:

L. Dembinski, *The Modern Law of Diplomacy: External Missions of States and International Organizations* (Dordrecht, Neth.; Boston: Martinus Nijhoff, 1988)

A. Kapur (ed.), *Diplomatic Ideas and Practices of Asian States* (Leiden, Neth.: E.J. Brill, 1990)

P. Kent & J. Pollard (ed.), *Papal Diplomacy in the Modern Age* (Westport, CT: Praeger, 1994)

A. Kremenyuk (ed.), *International Negotiation, Analysis, Approaches, Issues* (San Francisco: Jossey-Bass Pub., 1991)

L. Lee, *Consular Law and Practice* (Oxford, Eng.: Clarendon Press, 1991)

B. Murty, *The International Law of Diplomacy: The Diplomatic Instrument and the World Public Order* (New Haven, CT: New Haven Press/Martinus Nijhoff, 1989)

B. Sen, *A Diplomat's Handbook of International Law and Practice* (3rd ed. Dordrecht, Neth.; Boston: Martinus Nijhoff, 1988)

§ 7.3 Extraterritoriality and Asylum:

R. Jennings & A. Watts, *So-called Diplomatic Asylum*, § 495 in 2 *Oppenheim's International Law* 1082 (9th ed. Essex, Eng.: Longman, 1993)

Note, *Toward Codification of Diplomatic Asylum*, 8 *New York Univ. J. Int'l L.* (1976)

C. Ronning, *Diplomatic Asylum: Legal Norms and Political Reality in Latin American Relations* (The Hague, Neth.: Martinus Nijhoff, 1965)

§ 7.4 Immunities and Abuse of Immunity:

Brown, *State Practice Under the Vienna Convention* 37 *International & Comparative Law Quarterly* 53 (1988)

C. Lewis, *State and Diplomatic Immunity* (London: Lloyd's of London Press, 1985)

Shapiro, *Foreign Relations Law: Modern Developments in Diplomatic Immunity*, 1989 *Annual Survey American Law* 281 (New York: NYU, 1990)

Zeidman, *Abuse of the Diplomatic Bag: A Proposed Solution*, 11 *Cardozo Law Review* 427 (1989)

■ ENDNOTES

1. Regarding the ancient treatise, *see Diplomacy in Historical Perspective*, § 1.2, in B. Murty, *The International Law of Diplomacy: The Diplomatic Instrument and the World Public Order* 3 (New Haven, CT: New Haven Press/Martinus Nijhoff, 1989) [hereinafter *International Law of Diplomacy*].

2. M. Anderson, *The Rise of Modern Diplomacy* 1450–1919, p.2–3 (London: Longman, 1993).

3. Translation provided by Philippe Ardant, *Chinese Diplomatic Practice during the Cultural Revolution*, ch. 3, in *China's Practice of International Law: Some Case Studies* 92–93 (Cambridge, MA: Harv. Univ. Press, 1974) [hereinafter *Chinese Diplomatic Practice*].

4. **Nicolson:** Nicolson, *The "Old" and the "New" Diplomacy*, in R. Pfaltzgraff (ed.), *Politics and the International System* 425 (2nd ed., Philadelphia: Lippincott, 1972). **Other Europeans:** Garden, 1 *Traite Complet de Diplomatie ou Theorie Generale des Relations Exterieures des Puissances de L'Europe* 1 (Paris 1833) (diplomacy is the science or "art of negotiation"); C. Calvo, 1 *Dictionnaire de Droit International Public et Privie* 25 (Berlin 1885) (science of state relations, or simply the "art of communication").

5. **Morgenthau:** H. Morgenthau, *Politics Among Nations* 541 (3d ed. New York: Knopf, 1960) [hereinafter *Morganthau treatise*]. **Boucher:** Boucher, *Reconciling Ethics and Interests in the Person of the State: The International Dimension*, ch. 3, in P. Keal (ed.), *Ethics and Foreign Policy* 44, 46 (St. Leonards, Aust.: Allen & Unwin, 1992) (emphasis supplied).

6. L. Pearson, *Diplomacy in the Nuclear Age* 64 (Cambridge, MA: Harv. Univ. Press, 1959). G. Tunkin, *Theory of International Law* 273 (Cambridge, MA: Harv. Univ. Press, 1974).

7. *Morgenthau treatise*, p.539–40 (cited in note 5 above).

8. *See* Bacuss, *Diplomacy for the 70's: An Afterview and Appraisal*, 68 *Amer. Pol. Science Rev.* 736 (1974) (post–World War II tendency encouraged by all US presidents).

9. *See* N. Hevener (ed.), *Diplomacy in a Dangerous World: Protection for Diplomats under International Law* (Boulder, CO: Westview Press, 1986).

10. *See* Vienna Convention on Diplomatic Relations of 1961, Articles 1–5, 500 UN Treaty Series 95 (1964), reprinted in 18 *Int'l Legal Mat'ls* 149 (1979) [hereinafter *Diplomatic Convention*].

11. Accounts of these incidents are available in *Chinese Diplomatic Practice* p.100 (Raghunath Affair) & p.103 (Jongejans Affair) (cited in note 3 above).

12. **Taiwan relations:** Taiwan Relations Act of 1979, 22 US Code § 3303 (1986) (change of recognition status of Taiwan does not affect legal rights vested prior to recognition of the PRC). See § 2.4 of this book on the specific legal effects of nonrecognition. **Unconventional diplomacy:** G. Berridge, *Talking to the Enemy: How States without 'Diplomatic Relations' Communicate* 129 (New York: St. Martin's Press, 1994).

13. *Diplomatic Convention*, Art. 3 (cited in note 10 above).

14. **Wilson quote:** 2 *Selected Literary and Political Papers and Addresses of Woodrow Wilson* (New York: Grosset & Dunlap, 1927). **Nicolson quote:** reprinted in T. Couloumbis & J. Wolfe, Introduction to International Relations 161 (3rd ed. Englewood Cliffs, NJ: Prentice-Hall, 1986).

15. **Canadian perspective:** Panel, *International Law in International Diplomacy*, in *Proceedings of the 77th Annual Meeting* 99 (Wash., DC: *Amer. Soc. Int'l Law*, 1985). **Venezuelan Perspective:** *id.*, p.103.

16. *Historical Evolution*, ch. 1, in L. Lee, *Consular Law and Practice* 4 (Oxford, Eng.: Clarendon Press, 1991) [hereinafter *Consular treatise*].

17. 596 UN Treaty Series 261 (1967), Art. 5, reprinted in E. Osmanczyk, *Encyclopedia of the United Nations and International Agreements* 987 (2nd ed. New York: Taylor & Francis, 1990) [hereinafter *Consular Relations Convention*].

18. European Treaty Series No. 61, reprinted in *Consular treatise*, p.705 (cited in note 16 above).

19. *See Extraterritoriality* in *Consular treatise*, p.6–7 (cited in note 16 above).

20. G. Do Nascimento e Silva, *Diplomacy in International Law* 104–106 (Leiden, Neth.: Sijthoff, 1972). In the *South West Africa Cases* (Ethiopia and Liberia v. South Africa), 1966 I.C.J. Rep. 6, the ICJ held that the plaintiff States did *not* have a sufficient interest to represent the rights of persecuted natives in South Africa. The suit was thus dismissed, leaving those natives without an effective remedy.

21. I. Brownlie, *Principles of Public International Law* 348 (4th ed. Oxford, Eng.: Clarendon Press, 1990).

22. *Claims to Formal Bases of Capability*, ch. 7, in *International Law of Diplomacy* 333, 424–25 (cited in note 1 above).

23. *See* Empson v. Smith, 2 All England Rep. 881, 883 (1965) (discussing the Russian ambassador's detention).

24. XV *Polish Yearbk. Int'l L.* 119, 120 (1986).

25. *Diplomatic Convention* (cited in note 10 above).

26. *Consular Relations Convention* (cited in note 17 above).

27. C. Ashman & P. Trescott, *Is Diplomatic Immunity Really Necessary?*, Introduction to *Diplomatic Crime* 14–15 (New York: Knightsbridge Pub., 1988 paperback ed.) (emphasis supplied).

28. *See Chinese Diplomatic Practice*, p.94 (cited in note 3 above).

29. **Insurance scenario:** see Note, *Insuring Against Abuse of Diplomatic Immunity* 38 *Stanford L. Rev.* 1517 (1986). **US Dep't State standards:** Regulations on Compulsory Liability Insurance for Diplomatic Missions and Personnel, 22 Code of Fed. Regs. 151 (1980), reprinted in 18 *Int'l Legal Matl's* 871 (1979). **Federal statute:** 22 US Code § 254e.

30. *Report of the Secretary-General on United Nations Decade of International Law*, UN Doc. A/47/384, para.153, p.49 (Aug. 26, 1992).

CHAPTER EIGHT

Treaty System

CHAPTER OUTLINE

■ INTRODUCTION

States have established their respective rights and obligations through treaties for many centuries—first orally, and then in writing. The primary method of determining mutual expectations is the written treaty, currently governed on a global basis by the 1969 Vienna Convention on the Law of Treaties (effective 1980).

This chapter opens with the following question: "What *is* a treaty?" This first level of analysis is definitional, and accompanied by a very useful compass: a paradigm for classifying the various categories of treaties.

This chapter then proceeds to summarize the central themes in the international treaty process—formation, performance, termination, and suspension. Each facet of the treaty system has its own special standards, consisting of obligations that must be observed if international relations are to function smoothly.

Although this is a survey course in *International Law*, there is a global interest in the operation of the *US* treaty system, and how it varies from the international norm. One section of this chapter is thus devoted to US treaty practice.

The final section is a brief but comprehensive problem designed to review some important elements of treaty practice. It is based on a charged political context that was actually designed to drive a State out of existence. This problem will help set the stage for some of the trade measures covered in Chapter 13 on International Economic Relations.

■ 8.1   DEFINITION AND CLASSIFICATION

Definitional Contours

The word *treaty* means different things to different countries. Important distinctions in US law are analyzed later in this chapter. As the starting point, the UN International Law Commission (ILC—an organ of the General Assembly) studied and defined the word *treaty*. The ILC characterized it is a "generic term covering all forms of international agreement in writing concluded between states."[1] (The ILC study was not concerned with oral agreements.)

Some three dozen terms are typically used interchangeably with the term *treaty*. As a result, a major study of International Law at the Harvard Law School described treaty law as "confusing, often inconsistent, unscientific and in a perpetual state of flux." The legal distinctions among these various terms are minimal, however, in the sense that each synonym creates binding obligations under International Law. The above ILC study thus concluded that "judicial differences, in so far as they exist at all . . . lie almost exclusively in the method of conclusion and entry into force." Article 2.1 of the 1969

Vienna Convention on the Law of Treaties thus defined a treaty as "an international agreement concluded between states in written form and governed by international law, whether embodied in a single instrument or in two or more related instruments and whatever its particular designation."[2]

Other definitional preliminaries include the important theme that a treaty may be made not only by a State, the centerpiece of the international system, but also by an international organization. In 1991, for example, the International Monetary Fund signed an accord with the Soviet Union (on the eve of its demise) to establish a special association, whereby this international organization could advise the "Soviets" on economic and fiscal policy. The underlying agreement was made at the instance of the Group of Seven industrialized States who wanted to avoid marginalizing the Soviets and to help them make the transition to a market economy.

The 1969 Vienna Convention on the Law of Treaties deals only with *State* treaties, however. The drafters wanted to concentrate first on State treaty matters, thus saving the treaties of international organizations for another day. The 1986 "Vienna Convention on the Law of Treaties Between States and International Organizations or Between International Organizations" thus provides the *organizational* facet of international treaty law.[3]

Like other disputes, treaty disputes have adversely affected international relations on many occasions and in a variety of contexts. There have been interpretational problems with the formation, observation, and termination of treaties. The UN thus developed a code to govern international agreements—that is, a treaty on treaties. The ILC spent a number of years drafting the VCLT blueprint for resolving problems with the creation, observance, and cessation of treaties. The result of that commission's work was the 1969 Vienna Convention on the Law of Treaties (VCLT). It governs *written* treaties made *after* 1980—when the convention was ratified by the required minimum number of nations to become effective evidence of International Law. It provides the best insight into the treaty practice of States and thus forms the core of this chapter on the treaty system.

Analogy to Contract Law?

The study of any discipline should identify latent problems with the paradigm that is the core of this analysis. The core of this chapter is the application of the 1969 VCLT to the various disputes discussed in this chapter. The VCLT became "law," in the international sense, in 1980 when the requisite number of States ratified the final 1969 draft—produced after years of study and negotiation under auspices of the UN's International Law Commission. There remains the daunting question of whether international treaties are sufficiently analogous to contracts between private individuals. If not, there will always be inconsistencies with the VCLT's reliance on contractual analogies from the internal law of States.

The first major study of the Law of Treaties was the so-called Harvard Draft of 1935. It identified the treaty area of International Law as "confusing, often inconsistent, unscientific and in a perpetual state of flux." The drafters of the second twentieth century attempt to produce a global yardstick (that is, the VCLT) may have oversimplified treaty law—by adopting a relatively narrow "contract" approach to the broader underlying function of international agreements. Professor Andreas Gasis of the Hellenic Institute of International and Foreign Law in Greece raises this issue as follows:

> As is well known, man, when faced with a problem not previously encountered, frequently resorts to a familiar solution, derived from an analogous situation. . . . This practice is widespread in the realm of European Continental Law, where the more elaborated Civil Law of Roman origin has systematically been used as the root on to which new branches of law have been grafted. . . . This method, however, reflects a kind of imposed and contingent solution, not always successful, in the face of real changes in society, and slowly the new areas of law thus defined begin to operate autonomously and evolve in their own way.
>
> The . . . phenomenon has also appeared in the realm of international law, where there has been an attempt to codify a Law of Treaties in recent years. Thus, the relevant Vienna Convention on the Law of Treaties, 1969, taking a notoriously narrow "contract" view of Treaties, covers such subject matters as the "conclusion" of Treaties. . . . Hence, when reading the text . . . , one cannot escape the impression of being at the forefront of . . . [some species of] a Continental Civil Code governing private law contract, or . . . the common law

tradition [both of which govern contracts between *private* individuals rather than the *public* law embodied in international agreements involving States or international organizations].[4]

Some commentators have thus objected to the VCLT as being too doctrinal an approach—failing to acknowledge that an international treaty is something considerably different from the convenient analogy of the law of contracts governing private relationships between individuals (who often speak the same native language). Thus, it has been argued that a treaty should not be thought of as a "concluded" agreement expressing the complete intent of the parties making it. It is, instead, merely evidence of an underlying legislative purpose ascertained by international consensus, and only partially expressed in the terms of a treaty. The meaning associated with a particular treaty word often undergoes subsequent alteration, due to the lapse of time or a change in fashion. The nineteenth century writer Robert Phillimore opined that "due construction of the instrument may require a [k]nowledge of the antiquated as well as the present use of the words. . . ."[5]

Professor Gasis (quoted above) characterizes the "scientific" approach of the Vienna Convention as an attempt to standardize treaty language that bridges *distinct* cultures and legal traditions—but at the more than occasional cost of quashing the intended meaning of one or more parties to a treaty. The VCLT's objective standards are superimposed on the subjective intent of one or more State parties. While this approach may be perfectly reasonable for construing a contract within Country X, and between its private traders, it makes less sense in the international context where the written agreement is only one part of a larger understanding between Countries X, Y, and Z.[6]

The issue is whether the treaty portion of Public International Law and the State's internal law of private contracts are analogous. This matter has been effectively answered in the affirmative by the routine resort to the VCLT for resolving questions of treaty interpretation. One should nevertheless acknowledge that the twentieth century treaty/contract analogy is not without its critics.

Classifications

While many treaty classifications are possible, four general distinctions illustrate the fundamental nature of most treaties. They are thus distinguishable as follows: oral or written; bilateral or multilateral; lawmaking or contractual; and self-executing or declaration of intent.

Oral v. Written The Vienna Convention on the Law of Treaties was drafted in terms of "written" treaties. While most treaties are written, a State may also incur international obligations based on an oral agreement.

State representatives have often entered into oral agreements containing mutual obligations for their respective States. Denmark and Norway established Denmark's sovereignty over Eastern Greenland in a manner far less formal than a written treaty. The right to this vast area had been disputed since the 1819 termination of their union. In a recorded conversation in 1919, the Norwegian Minister of Foreign Affairs and a Danish diplomat agreed that Norway would not object to Danish control over all of Greenland—including the disputed portion of its eastern coast. The Permanent Court of International Justice thus held that this oral understanding resulted "in the settlement of this [sovereignty] question."[7] The Court accorded great weight to the context in which this particular conversation occurred. Although not as formal as a written treaty, this agreement was nevertheless binding on Norway. It was made between two diplomats, on a question falling within the negotiating authority each possessed on behalf of his respective State.

Bilateral v. Multilateral A *bilateral* treaty establishes mutual rights and obligations between two States. It normally affects just them and no others. Other States typically derive no benefits or duties from such a treaty. The States entering into this type of treaty do not intend to establish rules that contribute to the progressive development of International Law. For example, there are hundreds of bilateral extradition treaties, each listing the circumstances under which the two treaty parties agree to return criminals to the State requesting extradition.

There has been a significant proliferation of multilateral treaties in the twentieth century. Writing on the impact of the 1994 UN Convention on the Law of the Sea, Professor Louis Sohn of George

Washington University traces the phenomenal increase in multilateral treaty making, particularly since the end of World War II, in the following excerpt:

INTERNATIONAL LAW IMPLICATIONS OF THE 1994 AGREEMENT

Professor Louis B. Sohn

88 American Journal of International Law 696, 701–702 (1994)*

International lawyers have by now accepted the fact that rules for drafting and putting into force such [multilateral] agreements are flexible. . . .

This flexibility is due primarily to the tremendous increase in the last fifty years in the role being played by international institutions and multipartite diplomacy. Originally, evidence of the existence of a rule of international law could be found only in books written by eminent professors or in briefs prepared by practitioners in disputes involving international law. . . . The Hague Peace Conferences of 1899 and 1907 inaugurated a new approach: the contracting parties, acting on behalf of "the society of civilized nations," agreed on a number of lawmaking conventions . . . [regarding] "the principles of equity and right on which are based the security of States and the welfare of peoples . . . and the dictates of public conscience."

During the period of the League of Nations, while the 1930 Codification Conference [on treaty practice] did not prove successful, the number of multipartite treaties increased considerably. Professor Manley O. Hudson collected in the first eight volumes of *International Legislation,* covering the period 1918 to 1941, 610 international multipartite treaties of that period. Since the Second World War, the United Nations, acting not only through the International Law Commission, but also through its specialized agencies and special conferences . . . together with the increasing number of regional organizations and various groups of states dealing with specific topics of international law, has given birth to several thousands of multipartite agreements covering practically every conceivable subject [over *33,000* as of 1995].

Assume the following facts: Arthur lives in Argentina. He assaults one person while he is in Brazil and a different person while he is in Chile. Arthur then returns to his home in Argentina. Both Brazil and Chile want Argentina to extradite Arthur to their respective countries to prosecute him for the respective aggravated assaults. Argentina has an extradition treaty with Brazil requiring Argentina to extradite Arthur to Brazil—because aggravated assault is an extraditable offense under the Argentina-Brazil treaty. Argentina also has an extradition treaty with Chile, but the Argentina-Chile treaty does *not* require extradition for the crime of aggravated assault. Chile cannot invoke the benefits of the Argentina-Brazil bilateral treaty to obtain Arthur's extradition. The latter agreement was never intended to create a duty of extradition in favor of third States (such as Chile) that are not parties to the particular bilateral treaty.

A *multilateral* treaty is an international agreement among three or more States. Most of the military, political, and economic organizations discussed in Chapter 3 were created by multilateral treaties—expressing the mutual rights and duties of the member States and the competence of the particular organization created by their treaty.

Assume as follows: A Latin American treaty has been ratified by virtually all members of that region. It contains the obligation to extradite individuals who commit aggravated assault. The treaty negotiators met to establish uniform extradition standards; various States agreed on mutually acceptable treaty language requiring extradition for this particular crime; and nearly all Latin American States ratified this hypothetical treaty. This multilateral treaty *may* nevertheless contain obligations for third States, who have not ratified it, if the treaty codifies common State practice (see § 1.2 on customary International Law).[8]

Lawmaking v. Contractual Treaties may also be classified as either "lawmaking" or "contractual." A lawmaking treaty creates a *new* rule of International Law designed to modify existing State practice. The 1982 United Nations Law of the Sea Treaty contains a number of new rules governing jurisdiction over the oceans. Although it codifies (restates) some previously existing rules of customary International Law, this multilateral treaty contains some novel law*making* provisions. An International Sea-bed Authority would thus control the ways in which the ocean's resources are globally (re)distributed. And, so-called free "transit passage" would replace the otherwise applicable regime of restricted "innocent passage" through the territorial waters of coastal States (*see* § 6.3). These provisions would *change* prior State practice, which did not previously require either equitable redistribution of global resources or transit passage.

On the other hand, some treaties are merely "contractual." A treaty regulating the imports and exports of two or more States typically establishes only rights and obligations that are already available under common international practice. In one sense, the North American Free Trade Agreement (NAFTA) broke new ground by legally associating Canada, Mexico, and the US into a large free-trade area. Yet there was nothing novel, or law*making*, about their reduction of trade barriers, or entry into a form of common economic market. Many States had already done so. The NAFTA merely created an international contract establishing the respective rights and duties of the State parties, just like a private contract would do so between merchants engaged in cross-border transactions. The NAFTA did not attempt to establish new principles that should generally govern trade practices under International Law. The NAFTA deals only with the rights of the contracting States, and not the rights of the entire community of nations. In this sense, the NAFTA was not lawmaking. One should distinguish the new 1995 World Trade Organization (WTO) which replaces the established General Agreement on Tariffs and Trade process (described in § 13.3). The WTO process involved a law*making* treaty in terms of its new provisions designed to change the way in which nations generally resolve their international trade disputes.

Some commentators challenge the continuing vitality of the so-called "lawmaking" versus "contractual" distinction. The extensive development of treaties, typified by the 1899 and 1907 Hague process, resulted in a number of treaties containing new norms of International Law. These were designed to govern international society as a whole. In modern times, the distinction between the lawmaking and the merely contractual treaty tends to blur. Comparatively fewer masterpieces of legislation, in the lawmaking sense, are being created. International treaties now address mostly "contractual" matters between States, rather than creating fresh norms of international conduct that are suddenly applicable to all—on ratification by a large number of States. As succinctly recounted by French Professor Paul Reuter in his distinguished treatise on treaty law:

> The development of treaties during the second half of the nineteenth century prompted several new doctrinal distinctions. . . . [T]he expressions 'law-making treaties' and 'contractual treaties' came into use, the former referring to the treaties which first laid down general conventional rules governing [all of] international society. . . . It is [thus] important to make clear, when speaking of treaties as either [normative] 'legislation' or [mere] 'contracts', whether they are being viewed from a legal or sociological standpoint.[9]

Professor Reuter then proceeds to explain that the great collective instruments of modern society are no longer contracts or treaties, in the sense originally elicited by either term. From the sociological point of view, the private contract is well suited for application to private individuals. They are the relatively equal subjects of the private contract law of the one or two States involved in their transaction. Equal bargaining power is hardly the case in the community of nations, however. On the other hand, modern multilateral treaties are rarely lawmaking treaties that create new norms of International Law. They are usually cast in the most general of terms, so as to encourage greater participation. Thus, those terms do not purport to modify customary State practice.

Self-Executing v. Declaration of Intent A treaty may be further classified as "self-executing" when it imposes immediate obligations within the treaty itself; and, alternatively, as merely a declaration of intent when it contains general statements of principle setting a standard of achievement for all parties. A self-executing treaty requires *no further action* to impose binding obligations on its signatories. It is instantly incorporated into both International Law *and* the internal law of each treaty member by the express terms of the treaty. There is no need for additional executive or legislative action by the State parties to create immediately binding legal obligations. On the other hand, treaties declaring intent *require subsequent State action* before the parties incur any obligation to execute the express treaty requirements.

Most multilateral treaties are *not* self-executing. The State drafters who sign them intend that they be *only* statements of principle that do not impose *immediate* legal obligations. These treaties tend to articulate mutually agreeable goals or standards of achievement. Each participant must undertake some subsequent act under its internal law, however, to ripen the stated standards into a binding legal obligation to perform. If such treaties *were* self-executing, few States would participate. There is a vast difference in States' economic, cultural, political, and military ability to perform all desirable aspects of the major multilateral treaties. Participation by all, attainable on the basis of merely stating aspirational goals, thus accommodates the referenced differences while expressing common objectives with which no State could disagree in principle.

The United Nations Charter is the classic example of a treaty containing statements of principled goals, as opposed to immediately binding obligations. The following case illustrates why:

SEI FUJII v. STATE OF CALIFORNIA

Supreme Court of California, 1952
38 Cal.2d 718, 242 P.2d 617

[Author's Note: A Japanese citizen named Sei Fujii lived in California. He held title to his land but was ineligible for US citizenship under then-applicable naturalization laws (which were subsequently repealed). California's alien land law, at the time, prohibited alien ownership of land in the State. This law was enacted before the US became a party to the United Nations Charter in 1945.

Sei Fujii's land was taken by the state of California in 1948. He then sued the state, seeking a declaration that its prohibition against alien ownership of land conflicted with the UN Charter's provisions prohibiting racial discrimination.

A portion of the Court's opinion addressed the question of whether the UN Charter could be classified as "self-executing." If so, the Charter would be the type of treaty that imposes an immediate obligation on governmental entities within the US (including the California legislature) to extinguish any existing laws permitting discrimination on the basis of race. If not self-executing, then California could legally continue to so discriminate—although the US would have the moral responsibility to achieve the UN Charter's objective at some time in the future.

Justice Gibson delivered the opinion of the California Supreme Court, as set forth below. The Court's footnotes and citations are omitted. Emphasis within the opinion has been supplied by the author.]

[*Opinion.*] It is first contended that the land law has been invalidated and superseded by the provisions of the United Nations Charter pledging the member nations to promote the observance of human rights and fundamental freedoms without distinction as to race. Plaintiff relies on statements in the preamble and in articles 1, 55 and 56 of the charter [containing the pledge to achieve "human rights and fundamental freedoms for all without distinction as to race"].

It is not disputed that the charter is a treaty, and our federal Constitution provides that treaties made under the authority of the United States are part of the supreme law of the land and that the judges in every state are bound thereby (US Const., art. VI). *A treaty, however, does not automatically supersede local laws which are inconsistent with it unless the treaty provisions are self-executing.* In the words of Chief Justice Marshall [in an earlier US Supreme Court decision]: A treaty is "to be regarded in courts of justice as equivalent to an act of the Legislature, whenever it operates of itself, without the aid of any legislative provision."

In determining whether a treaty is self-executing courts look to the intent of the signatory parties as manifested by the language of the instrument, and, if the instrument is uncertain, recourse may be had to the circumstances surrounding its execution.

. . .

In order for a treaty provision to be operative without the aid of implementing legislation and to have the force and effect of a statute, *it must appear that the framers of the treaty intended to prescribe a rule that, standing alone, would be enforceable in the courts* [without further action by the parties to that treaty].

. . .

It is clear that the provisions of the preamble and of article 1 of the charter which are claimed to be in conflict with the alien land law are *not* self-executing. They state general purposes and objectives of the United Nations Organization and *do not purport to impose legal obligations* on the individual member nations or to create rights in private persons. It is equally clear that none of the other provisions relied on by plaintiff is self-executing. Article 55 declares that the United Nations "shall promote . . . universal respect for, and observance of, human rights and fundamental freedoms for all without distinction as to race, sex, language, or religion," and in Article 56, the member nations "*pledge themselves to take joint and separate action* in cooperation with the Organization for the achievement of the purposes set forth in Article 55." Although the member nations have obligated themselves to cooperate with the international organization in promoting respect for, and observance of, human rights, it is plain that *it was contemplated that future legislative action by the several nations would be required to accomplish the declared objectives*, and there is nothing to indicate that these provisions were intended to become rules of law for the courts of this country upon ratification of the charter.

The language used in articles 55 and 56 is *not* the type customarily employed in *treaties which have been held to be self-executing* and to create rights and duties in individuals.

. . .

It is significant to note that when the framers of the charter intended to make *certain* provisions effective without the aid of implementing legislation they employed language which is clear and definite and manifests that intention. For example, article 104 provides: "The Organization shall enjoy in the territory of each of its Members such legal capacity as may be necessary for the exercise of its functions and the fulfillment of its purposes." Article 105 provides: "1. The Organization shall enjoy in the territory of each of its Members such privileges and immunities as are necessary for the fulfillment of its purposes. 2. Representatives of the Members of the United Nations and officials of the Organization shall similarly enjoy such privileges and immunities as are necessary for the independent exercise of their functions in connection with the Organization." In *Curran v. City of New York,* these articles [in the UN Charter] were treated as being self-executory.

The provisions in the charter pledging cooperation in promoting observance of fundamental freedoms lack the mandatory quality and definiteness which would indicate an intent to create justiciable rights in private persons immediately upon ratification. Instead, they are framed as a promise of future action by the member nations. Secretary of State Stettinius, chairman of the United States delegation at the San Francisco Conference where the charter was drafted, stated in his report to President Truman that article 56 "pledges the various countries to cooperate with the organization by joint and separate action in the achievement of the economic and social objectives of the organization without infringing upon their right to order their national affairs according to their own best ability, in their own way, and in accordance with their own political and economic institutions and processes."

. . .

The humane and enlightened objectives of the United Nations Charter are, of course, entitled to respectful consideration by the courts and legislatures of every member nation, since that document expresses the universal desire of thinking men for peace and for equality of rights and opportunities. The charter represents a moral commitment of foremost importance, and we must not permit the spirit of our pledge to be compromised or disparaged in either our domestic or foreign affairs. We are satisfied, however, that the *charter provisions relied on by plaintiff were not intended to supersede existing domestic legislation*, and we cannot hold that they operate to invalidate the Alien Land Law.

The UN Charter was not generally intended to impose across-the-board obligations on the community of nations—with its varying degrees of development and financial ability to achieve the stated objectives. The essential distinction to be made is whether the States that ratified a particular treaty meant it to simply suggest standards of achievement, as opposed to immediate legal obligations enforceable by the individuals who would benefit from the treaty's objectives.

The following excerpt from a Supreme Court decision construes the effect of a bilateral treaty with Japan conflicting with a law enacted by a state within the US. In this instance, Japan and the US intended that their respective citizens would benefit from the treaty agreement. If the treaty were self-executing, a governmental entity within the US could not properly enact conflicting legislation.

ASAKURA v. CITY OF SEATTLE

Supreme Court of the United States, 1924
265 U.S. 332, 44 S.Ct. 515, 68 L.Ed. 1041

[Author's Note: The emphasis within certain passages has been supplied by the author.]

[*Opinion.*] Plaintiff in error is a subject of the Emperor of Japan, and, since 1904, has resided in Seattle, Washington. Since July, 1915, he has been engaged in business there as a pawnbroker. The city passed an ordinance, which took effect July 2, 1921, regulating the business of pawnbroker and repealing former ordinances on the same subject. It makes it unlawful for any person to engage in the business unless he shall have a license, and the ordinance provides "that no such license shall be granted unless the applicant be a citizen of the United States." Violations of the ordinance are punishable by fine or imprisonment or both. Plaintiff in error brought this suit in the Superior Court of King County, Washington, against the city, its Comptroller and its Chief of Police to restrain them from enforcing the ordinance against him. He attacked the ordinance on the ground that it violates the treaty between the United States and the Empire of Japan, proclaimed April 5, 1911. . . . It was shown that he had about $5,000 invested in his business, which would be broken up and destroyed by the enforcement of the ordinance. The Superior Court granted the relief prayed. On appeal, the Supreme Court of the State held the ordinance valid and reversed the decree.

. . .

Does the ordinance violate the treaty? Plaintiff in error invokes and relies upon the following provisions: "The citizens or subjects of each of the High Contracting Parties shall have liberty to enter, travel and reside in the territories of the other to carry on trade, wholesale and retail, to own or lease and occupy houses, manufactories, warehouses and shops, to employ agents of their choice, to lease land for residential and commercial purposes, and generally to do anything incident to or necessary for trade upon the same terms as native citizens or subjects, submitting themselves to the laws and regulations there established. . . . The citizens or subjects of each shall receive, in the territories of the other, the most constant protection, and security for their persons and property. . . ."

A treaty made under the authority of the United States "shall be the supreme Law of the Land; and the *Judges in every State shall be bound thereby*, any Thing in the Constitution or Laws of any State to the Contrary notwithstanding." Constitution, Art. VI, § 2.

The treaty-making power of the United States . . . extend[s] to all proper subjects of negotiation between our government and other nations. . . . The treaty [in this instance] was made to strengthen friendly relations between the two nations. As to the things covered by it, the provision quoted establishes the rule of equality between Japanese subjects while in this country and native citizens. Treaties for the protection of citizens of one country residing in the territory of another are numerous, and make for good understanding between nations. . . . *The rule of equality established by it cannot be rendered nugatory in any part of the United States by municipal ordinances or state laws* [unlike the treaty analyzed in the *Sei Fujii* case above, which did *not* impose immediate obligations]. It stands on the same footing of supremacy as do the provisions of the Constitution and laws of the United States. It [the US/Japan friendship treaty] *operates of itself without the aid of any legislation,* state or national; and it will be applied and given authoritative effect by the courts.

. . .

The purpose of the ordinance complained of is to regulate, not to prohibit, the business of pawnbroker. But it makes it impossible for aliens to carry on the business. It need not be considered whether the State, if it sees fit, may forbid and destroy the business generally [thus applying equally to all, regardless of race or citizenship]. Such a law would apply equally to aliens and citizens, and no question of conflict with the treaty would arise. The grievance here alleged is that plaintiff in error, *in violation of the treaty, is denied equal opportunity* [under the Seattle ordinance].

. . .

Decree reversed [so that the plaintiff Japanese citizen may continue to practice his profession as pawnbroker; and the defendant city must repeal its city ordinance, which violated the treaty].

■ NOTES & QUESTIONS

The Seattle pawnbroker ordinance in *Asakura* violated an international treaty. The California land statute in *Sei Fujii* did not. What was the difference?

■ 8.2 FORMATION/PERFORMANCE/ CESSATION

This section of the book deals with the overall treaty process—how a treaty is formed, expectations regarding its performance, and the circumstances whereby treaty obligations may be interrupted.

This section does not address all possible facets of the treaty process. The first limiting factor is the exclusion of international organizations. Although the analysis is quite similar to that of treaties involving States, it is not identical. While the UN's International Law Commission has compiled a draft treaty to govern interpretation of the treaties of international organizations (1986), this section's analysis focuses on the essentials regarding the treaty governing *State* treaties (1969). Unlike the 1986 draft organizational treaty, the State treaty has entered into force (1980).[10] The other limitation is that these materials cover the *multilateral* treaty process, typically addressing the major topics of International Law, rather than the bilateral process between two States. The latter category of treaties tends to cover narrower themes. These are often "contractual" treaties of interest to only the immediate parties—as opposed to law*making* treaties of interest to the community of nations.

Treaty Formation

The process of treaty formation includes a variety of consecutive phases. The essential steps are: negotiations, signature (or accession), ratification, reservations (if any), entry into force, and registration. The final formation problem addressed below is treaty "invalidity."

Negotiations The evolution of a multilateral treaty often begins when an international organ, such as the UN's International Law Commission or the General Assembly, decides to study some problem of wide concern. The UN General Assembly might then resolve that this particular problem should be the subject of an international conference. If State representatives reach a consensus, they typically begin the treaty process with preliminary negotiations. They will thus agree to activate an international conference. Maritime nations of the world first met in 1974, for example, to develop an International Law of the Sea. Their initial discussions expanded over the course of the next eight years, during which most nations of the world negotiated their respective positions on proper use of the oceans and their natural resources. These representatives drafted and redrafted a form of "constitution" that formed the final treaty text—satisfactory to most of the participants in principle (*see* § 6.3 on the Law of the Sea Treaty which entered into force in 1994).

The representatives at these conferences must possess the authority to negotiate on behalf of their respective States. Not unlike with diplomatic credentials, they are normally vested with what is referred to as "full powers" by the represented State. A document from his or her government is presented to a chair or conference committee, at the inception of the conference, vesting that agent with various powers: to negotiate, provisionally accept, and perform any act necessary for completing that initial phase of the treaty process on behalf of the represented State. Otherwise, the participants would not know whether *any* development or result is presumably acceptable to the governments that will one day have to decide whether to ratify the final draft of the negotiated treaty text.

The lack of this authority adversely affected international relations when a former US minister to Romania signed two bilateral treaties without the President's authority to do so. In one instance, the US minister improperly advised the President that he was signing a different treaty than the one he actually signed with Romania. As to the other agreement, he had *no* authority whatsoever to actually bind the US.[11] The US attempt to avoid its obligations under those treaties was of course resisted by Romania because the US had officially entered into these two agreements.

To ameliorate the effects of such complications, the claimed absence of such authority is now governed by Article 8 of the Vienna Convention on the Law of Treaties (VCLT). It provides that any "act relating to the conclusion of a treaty performed by a person who cannot be considered . . . as authorized to represent a State for that purpose is without legal effect unless afterwards confirmed by the competent authority of the State." This language theoretically creates the potential for abuse, whereby a State can enter into a treaty and subsequently disavow the authority of its representative. In practice, however, the representative's presentation of documentary powers at the inception of a conference notifies all participants of the extent of a particular delegate's powers—which in some cases may be limited by the dispatching government.

Signature   The next significant step in the treaty process is the "opening for signature." States and international organizations are thus invited to sign (ratify) the final treaty draft. This event signals that the negotiating States have agreed, in principle, to the general wording of the articles appearing in the text of the final draft of the treaty. Drawing from the example of the Vienna Convention on Diplomatic Relations discussed in Chapter 7, this stage was reached in 1969. The representatives concluded their drafting of this new "constitution" on diplomatic relations. In one sense, this was only the beginning. Article 81 of the VCLT provided as follows: "The present Convention shall be open for signature by all States Members of the United Nations . . . and by any other State invited by the General Assembly to become a party to the Convention . . . ." (until a particular date, at Austria's Federal Ministry for Foreign Affairs in Vienna—where negotiations took place—and, subsequently, at the UN in New York).

Alternatively, a State may "accede" to a treaty—as opposed to "signing" it. The State may thereby consent to be provisionally bound, in principle, like those States that have already signed the treaty. Alternatively, accession may express a State's willingness to immediately accept the treaty's obligations—without the necessity of ratification (discussed below). Accession is normally used by States that did not participate in the initial drafting process leading to the making of the treaty.

Ratification   In the next major stage of the treaty process, States must decide whether to accept or reject the rights and obligations in the final draft of the treaty. Unanimous and immediate consent of all States is possible, but quite atypical, for reasons addressed below in the discussion of the "Reservations" portion of this treaty process.

Acceptance of the treaty and the obligations it contains normally evolves through a two-stage process. The first stage is *provisional* acceptance of the treaty by the conference delegates. This stage expresses *their* consent (as opposed to that of the States represented) to the wording of the final draft. Unless otherwise specified, the signature of a representative on a multilateral treaty merely indicates that his or her State agrees, in principle, with the terms of the treaty.

Final acceptance is typically the next step at this stage. States may thus expresses their willingness to accept the treaty. This consent to be bound may occur in a variety of ways, including adoption (unanimous consent when the conference ends), signature of the representatives at the conference (but only if the treaty's express terms so provide), and "ratification."[12] Post-conference ratification is the typical mode for full acceptance of a treaty. Ratification means essentially that the conference delegate has submitted the provisionally accepted treaty text to the proper authority in his or her State for final approval—to be determined in accordance with that State's internal laws on treaty acceptance.

Sir Humphrey Waldock of Oxford University provides a useful explanation for the necessity of post-conference ratification by each potential State party:

> Ordinarily there are two stages in the making of a treaty: . . . [first,] signature . . . of the contracting states, and [second] its ratification by or on behalf of the heads of those states. There are good reasons why this second stage should be necessary before a treaty . . . becomes actually binding. In some states, for example, constitutional law vests the treaty-making power in some organ which cannot delegate it to the plenipotentiaries [treaty conference delegates], and yet cannot itself carry on negotiations with other states; for example, in the United States the power is vested in the President, but subject to the advice and consent of the Senate. But apart from such cases, the interests with which a treaty deals are often so complicated and important that it is reasonable that an opportunity for considering the treaty as a whole should be reserved. A democratic state must consult public opinion, and this can hardly take shape while the negotiations, which must be largely confidential, are going on. These being the reasons that render ratification necessary, it is clearly impossible, as is done by some writers, to specify the circumstances in which a refusal to ratify is justified and those in which it is not.[13]

Reservations A State's acceptance of the treaty is not necessarily an "all-or-nothing" proposition. States may tender reservations when they finally consent to the general terms of the final draft of the treaty that has been opened for signature. A reservation is a unilateral variation, submitted at the time of acceptance of the treaty. It purports to exclude or modify the legal effect of certain provisions as applied to that State. The State normally agrees with the text generally, but does not wish to become a party to the treaty on *all* terms. A State's provisional

acceptance at the drafting conference does not preclude it from tendering a subsequent reservation.

A reservation to a specific provision of the treaty permits a State to become a party, although its consent is conditional. Its reservation limits the application of some specific treaty provision to that State. If the reservation is acceptable to the other parties, it limits the scope of the reserving State's consent. Although *that* State is not then bound by the "objectionable" treaty provision, which is the subject of its reservation, it is bound by all *other* terms of the treaty.

In the case of a *bilateral* treaty between just two nations, reservations are normally not used. When the term "reservation" is used in this context, it identifies a new proposal that reopens the joint negotiations over what terms will be in the proposed treaty. Both States must agree on all terms of a bilateral treaty. In the case of a *multilateral* treaty, however, portions of the provisionally accepted conference draft usually undergo further scrutiny by the individual State parties. They may later limit the scope of the treaty, as it applies specifically to them.

Assume that the representatives of States A, B, C, and D provisionally accept the final text of a treaty at the conclusion of their drafting conference. They all express their agreement to be bound by the broadly worded principles stated in this hypothetical treaty. It is now open for signature (ratification). Thus, the terms of this treaty are *not* self-executing. No State is yet bound to perform the obligations specified in the treaty—until each has finally accepted it via individual State ratification. When State A's leaders later review this treaty for possible ratification, they decide to object to the application of one of the treaty clauses. State A will thus tender a reservation to that particular provision of the treaty. Assuming that A's reservation is compatible with the overall treaty principles, A is excused from performing that provision of the treaty. Assume that B, C, and D do *not* tender the same reservation when they ratify this treaty. Unlike State A, they *are* bound by this treaty clause although it does not apply to A. States B, C, and D must therefore perform the relevant obligation contained in that clause vis-a-vis one another. They do not have to perform, however, in their dealings with State A. That particular provision of the final draft treaty—the subject of A's reservation—is *not* effective between State A and any of the other parties to this treaty.

Why are reservations permitted? They encourage wider participation in multilateral treaties through a very practical compromise. Broad participation is better than limited participation by only those few States who might be willing to accept *all* terms of a draft treaty. For example, few States would agree to be sued in the International Court of Justice (ICJ) if they were unable to make reservations to the final draft treaty provision regarding the ICJ's competence to hear and decide cases. Article 36.6 of the UN's Statute of the ICJ provides that any disputes over the Court's jurisdiction—the power to hear the particular case—are to be determined by the Court itself. Nearly all States of the world are parties to this Statute—which is itself a treaty. The original UN members provisionally agreed, in principle, with the Statute's directive that the *Court* is to decide whether it can hear a particular case. Ironically, virtually all systems of law recognize the power of a court to determine its own power to hear a particular case that has been filed with the court. Many of those same States ultimately decided *not* to give their full consent to Article 36.6, however. Many of them tendered reservations to this treaty-based competence of the *ICJ* to decide its jurisdiction. Those States reserved the question of the Court's power to hear a case *for themselves*, rather than allowing the Court to decide its own jurisdiction pursuant to Article 36.6 of the ICJ Statute. States also had the option regarding whether or not to *unconditionally* submit to the jurisdiction of the Court in all cases; or, alternatively, to tender reservations that would limit the Court's competence to hear only certain types of cases when they were sued. There was a practical need for compromise in this particular treaty context. Without the possibility of such a treaty reservation, a number of major powers would not have recognized the Court's power to hear any international controversy. Reservations such as this one thus accommodate the special interests of certain States that would not otherwise participate in the overall process of international adjudication by the ICJ (*see* § 9.4).

It is not clear whether such conditional consent can be used in all treaties. The drafting conference negotiators may decide to insert a prohibition *against* reservations within the express language of a treaty. One of the most significant problems arises when a treaty says nothing about whether reserva-

tions are permitted. The classic example is the United Nations Genocide Convention. The general principles of this 1948 treaty were unanimously adopted by all UN members in the aftermath of the Holocaust in Nazi Germany. Many States, however, did not ultimately ratify the Genocide treaty. They were reluctant to accept it, without knowing what specific obligations it entailed. They faced the dilemma of their willingness to accept this treaty's obligations in general, yet fearing that the absence of a reservation provision might one day subject them to scrutiny under the Convention—on grounds that they had never contemplated.[14]

The following ICJ *Genocide Case* addresses this problem. In 1948, the UN General Assembly unanimously adopted the Convention on Genocide. As discussed in § 1.4 of this text, this resolution would not be a source of International Law. It could not directly bind the State members of the General Assembly without further action on their part via individual State ratifications. In 1950, the UN General Assembly requested an advisory opinion (noncontentious litigation and no defendant). The 1948 Convention had just entered into force, due to the deposit of the minimum number of ratifications by 1950. There was no provision on the very sensitive question of whether reservations were permitted. If reservations *were* generally authorized, States could theoretically exclude certain forms of genocide from their consent to be bound by this treaty.

Some parties to the Genocide Convention were understandably concerned about the possibility that subsequent ratifications might include reservations purporting to retain the sovereign power to act in ways that could be interpreted as genocide. The General Assembly wanted the ICJ to interpret the Genocide Convention for the purpose of determining whether a State might ratify the Convention, and at the same time, tender a limiting reservation to its broad terms.

The Court delivered a very general and abstract answer to this sensitive question. Noting the apparent divergence of State views on this question, the ICJ decided that this treaty *implicitly* contained the right to become a party—and simultaneously present a reservation—as long as it was "compatible" with the language and purpose of the treaty. The relevant portion of the opinion follows—unsigned by any member of the Court:

RESERVATIONS TO THE CONVENTION ON GENOCIDE

International Court of Justice, 1951
1951 International Court of Justice Reports 15

[Author's Note: The emphasis in certain passages has been supplied by the author.]

[*Opinion.*] [T]he precise determination of the conditions for participation in the [Genocide] Convention constitutes a permanent interest of direct concern to the United Nations which has not disappeared with the entry into force of the Convention.

. . .

It is well established that in its treaty relations a State cannot be bound without its consent, and that consequently no reservation [by one state] can be effective against any [other] State without its agreement thereto. It is also a generally recognized principle that a multilateral convention is the result of an agreement freely concluded upon its clauses and that consequently none of the contracting parties is entitled to frustrate or impair, by means of unilateral decisions or particular agreements, the purpose and *raison d'etre* of the convention. To this principle was linked the notion of the integrity of the convention as adopted, a notion which in its traditional concept involved the proposition that *no reservation was valid unless it was accepted by all* the contracting parties without exception, as would have been the case if it had been stated during the negotiations.

This concept, which is directly inspired by the notion of contract, is of undisputed value as a principle. However, as regards the Genocide Convention, it is *proper to refer to a variety of circumstances which would lead to a more flexible application of this principle.* Among these circumstances may be noted the clearly universal character of the United Nations under whose auspices the Convention was concluded, and the very wide degree of participation envisaged by Article XI of the [Genocide] Convention. Extensive participation in conventions of this type has already given rise to greater flexibility in the international practice concerning multilateral conventions. More general resort to reservations, very great allowance made for tacit assent to reservations, the existence of practices which go so far as to admit that the author of reservations which have been re-

jected by certain contracting parties is nevertheless to be regarded as a party to the convention in relation to those contracting parties that have accepted the reservations—all these factors are manifestations of a new need for flexibility in the operation of multilateral conventions.

It must also be pointed out that although the Genocide Convention was finally approved unanimously, it is nevertheless the result of a series of majority votes. The majority principle, while facilitating the conclusion of multilateral conventions, may also make it necessary for certain States to make reservations. This observation is confirmed by the great number of reservations which have been made of recent years to multilateral conventions.

In this state of international practice, it could certainly *not be inferred from the absence* of an article providing for reservations in a multilateral convention that the contracting States are *prohibited from making . . . reservations.* Account should also be taken of the fact that the absence of such an article or even the decision not to insert such an article can be explained by the desire not to invite a multiplicity of reservations. The character of a multilateral convention, its purpose, provisions, mode of preparation and adoption, are factors which must be considered in determining, in the absence of any express provision on the subject, the possibility of making reservations, as well as their validity and effect.

. . .

The Court recognizes that an understanding was reached within the General Assembly on the faculty [ability] to make reservations to the Genocide Convention and that it is permitted to conclude therefrom that States becoming parties to the Convention gave their assent thereto. It must now determine *what kind of reservations may be made* and what kind of objections may be taken to them.

The solution of these problems must be found in the special characteristics of the Genocide Convention. The origins and character of that Convention, the objects pursued by the General Assembly and the contracting parties . . . furnish elements of interpretation of the will of the General Assembly and the parties. The origins of the Convention show that it was the intention of the United Nations to condemn and punish genocide as "a crime under international law" involving a denial of the right of existence of entire human groups, a denial which shocks the conscience of mankind and results in great losses to humanity, and which is contrary to moral law and to the spirit and aims of the United Nations (Resolution 96(I) of the General Assembly, December 11th 1946). The first consequence arising from this conception is that the principles underlying the Convention are principles which are recognized by civilized nations as binding on States, even without conventional obligation. A second consequence is the universal character both of the condemnation of genocide and of the co-operation required "in order to liberate mankind from such an odious scourge" (Preamble to the Convention). The Genocide Convention was therefore intended by the General Assembly and by the contracting parties to be definitely universal in scope. It was in fact approved on December 9th, 1948, by a resolution which was unanimously adopted by fifty-six States.

The objects of such a convention must also be considered. The Convention was manifestly adopted for a purely humanitarian and civilizing purpose. It is indeed difficult to imagine a convention that might have this dual character to a greater degree, since its object on the one hand is to safeguard the very existence of certain human groups and on the other to confirm and endorse the most elementary principles of morality. In such a convention the contracting States do not have any interests of their own; they merely have, one and all, a common interest, namely, the accomplishment of those high purposes which are the *raison d'etre* of the convention. Consequently, in a convention of this type one cannot speak of individual advantages or disadvantages to States, or of the maintenance of a perfect contractual balance between rights and duties. The high ideals which inspired the Convention provide, by virtue of the common will of the parties, the foundation and measure of all its provisions.

The foregoing considerations, when applied to the question of reservations, and more particularly to the effects of objections to reservations, lead to the following conclusions.

The object and purpose of the Genocide Convention imply that it was the *intention of the General Assembly* and of the States which adopted it that *as many States as possible should participate*. The complete exclusion from the Convention of one or more States would not only restrict the scope of its application, but would detract from the authority of the moral and humanitarian principles which are its basis. It is inconceivable that the contracting parties readily contemplated that an objection to a minor reservation should produce such a result. But even less could the contracting parties have intended to sacrifice the very object of the Convention in favour of a vain desire to secure as many participants as possible. The object and purpose of the Convention thus limit both the freedom of making reservations and that of objecting to them. It follows that it is *the compatibility of a reservation with the object and purpose of the Convention* that must furnish the criterion for the attitude of a State in making the reservation on accession as well as for the appraisal by a State in objecting to the reservation. Such is the rule of conduct which must guide every State in the appraisal which it must make, individually and from its own standpoint, of the admissibility of any reservation.

Any other view would lead either to the acceptance of reservations which frustrate the purposes which the General Assembly and the contracting parties had in mind, or to recognition that the parties to the Convention have the power of excluding from it the author of a reservation, even a minor one, which may be quite compatible with those purposes.

It has nevertheless been argued [independently of these proceedings] that any State entitled to become a party to the Genocide Convention may do so while making any reservation it chooses by virtue of its sovereignty. The Court cannot share this view. It is obvious that so extreme an application of the idea of State sovereignty could lead to a complete disregard of the object and purpose of the Convention.

■ NOTES & QUESTIONS

What test did the International Court of Justice use to determine whether a reservation to a multilateral treaty is permissible?

Entry into Force The next major phase of the treaty process is "entry into force." The participants may have provisionally accepted the treaty's final draft language at the drafting conference, followed by final acceptance of the treaty by their individual ratifications. Unlike bilateral treaties, where only two States have to agree to achieve consent, multilateral treaties typically require some indicia of a sufficient degree of international consensus. An "entry into force" provision ensures that an agreed-upon minimum number of States ultimately ratify the treaty, thus enabling the characterization of that treaty as representing the content of International Law. On the other hand, nothing precludes certain parties or international organizations from claiming that a treaty, not yet entered into force, is nevertheless evidence of that which States already consider binding in their mutual relations. For example, no State would claim that the Genocide Convention's ratification by the minimum number of States was a condition precedent to the illegality of an official (Nazi) State policy of genocide. But the objectives of the Convention were to codify this customary expectation, while further defining the specific acts that would qualify as genocide (see § 11.1 on Human Rights).

The *manner* and *date* of entry into force is determined from the particular treaty's express provisions. Multilateral treaties normally enter into force when a minimum number of ratifications are deposited at some central location, such as the UN. The Genocide Convention, for example, did not enter into force until twenty States had deposited their ratifications with the UN Secretary-General. The 1982 UN Law of the Sea Convention (discussed in Chapter 6) did not enter into force until 1994—one year after the sixtieth State ratified it, pursuant to a concluding article in that treaty.

States that have not ratified it are normally not bound by the multilateral treaty once it has entered into force. They may be bound by its underlying norms if the treaty codifies the existing practice of most States (see § 1.4 on "Sources of International Law"). Those States may also subsequently consent to be bound by submitting their ratifications and any compatible reservations.

Registration Treaties must also be registered, meaning that they must be sent to the UN Secretariat or other appropriate international institution for dissemination to interested parties. This requirement approximates the filing of an important document such as a pleading filed with a court. Registration thus ensures that international agreements are public, as opposed to the secret treaties that led to World Wars I and II. Treaties are usually registered at the UN—or at the headquarters of the international organization most directly involved with the object of the particular treaty.

Publication is typical, but not necessarily required. (Treaties, both bilateral and multilateral, are published in the UN's publication entitled the *United Nations Treaty Series*.) Certain countries, especially those with the economic ability to do so, publish all of their treaties. While some government representatives might prefer to engage in "quiet" diplomacy and treaty negotiations, the product of their efforts must be subjected to public scrutiny. The US Congress therefore requires publication in the comprehensive United States Statutes at Large. Once published therein, those statutes "shall be legal evidence of laws . . . treaties, and international agreements other than treaties [that is, executive agreements]."[15]

A curious difference is observed in the League of Nations Covenant and the UN Charter—both requiring treaty registration. Article 18 of the Covenant contained an outright bar that voided the potential effects of any unregistered treaty. Secret treaties were thus characterized as void from the outset. UN Charter Article 102, on the other hand, provides that a party to an unregistered treaty may not "invoke that treaty or agreement before any organ of the United Nations." This does not "void" the treaty. It declares that the instrument cannot be used in any proceedings involving the UN, such as judicial proceedings in the International Court of Justice. In 1992, a London newspaper reported that presidential candidate Bill Clinton had struck a secret deal with the head of the European Community—whereunder a new world trade agreement (effective 1995) would be delayed until after his election. This report was denied. Hypothetically, such an agreement would be void under League practice, and unusable in *any* UN proceedings.

As a practical matter, many treaties are not registered (nor published). And to avoid the time and money inherent in the registration process, certain international organizations have narrowly construed the meaning of the word "treaty," a theme addressed in § 8.3 on the broad and narrow definitions of that term under US treaty law. Both of the Vienna Conventions—regarding the treaties of States and of international organizations—refer to this obligation to register treaties.[16]

Invalidity International agreements should be the product of a mutually beneficial decision to create rights and honor obligations. Unfortunately, a number of treaties have been imposed by one State on another as a result of their inherently unequal bargaining positions.

During the seventeenth and eighteenth centuries, writers first raised the question of whether treaties were valid in the absence of any real bargaining or negotiations. In 1646, the famous Dutch author Hugo Grotius distinguished between equal and unequal treaties. He described an unequal treaty as one that is forced on one nation by another and not the result of a fair exchange of rights and obligations. In 1758, the Swiss author E. de Vattel examined the problem of unequal treaties—concluding that States, as well as persons, should deal fairly with one another. The principle that individuals did not have the right to impose their wishes on others should apply with equal force to sovereign States. Vattel hypothesized that because States "are no less bound than individuals to respect justice, they should make their treaties equal, as far as possible."

Neither of these influential writers questioned the *legal validity* of such treaties. They presumed them to be legitimate. A bargained-for exchange was not considered a necessary prerequisite for a valid treaty between sovereign States. But as later stated by the American author H. Hallet in 1861, "the inequality in the . . . engagements of a treaty, does not, in general, render such engagements any the less binding upon the contracting parties."[17]

There are many examples of such unequal treaties. In 1807, Napoleon threatened to place the king of Spain on trial for treason unless the king surrendered his throne. Having no choice, King Ferdinand entered into an agreement with France containing no advantages for Spain. In the 1856 Treaty of Paris, Russia was prohibited from maintaining a naval fleet on the Black Sea (on its eastern border). The Treaty of Versailles ending World War I was signed by German delegates who had unsuccessfully objected to terms requiring that the responsible party (Germany) pay the other treaty parties (the victors) for their damages incurred during the war. In 1903, two US treaties illustrated unequal bargaining in treaty relations. The US condition for recognizing Cuba's independence from Spain was the Guantanamo Naval Base Treaty. The US thereby "acquired" the ninety-nine year lease for a military base that proved critical to US interests (for example, during the 1962 Cuban Missile Crisis and the 1994 Haitian "invasion"). The 1903 Panama Canal Treaty established US control over the Canal (until relinquished in 1977)—a former province of Colombia. Neither of these treaties was the product of intense negotiations. And just prior to World War II, Hitler threatened to bomb Czechoslovakia, forcing the creation of a treaty placing the Czechs under German "protection."[18]

In the twentieth century, several events led legal commentators to review the presumption that unequal treaties are valid. Professor Hungdah Chiu of the National Chengchi University in Taipei summarized them as follows:

> After the 1917 Bolshevik revolution in Russia, the Bolshevik government offered to abolish and later did abolish some former Tzarist treaties imposed upon China, Persia, and Turkey; and Soviet writers then began to discuss the question of the validity of those "coercive, predatory, and enslaving" treaties, although the term "unequal treaties" was not widely used after World War II. This early development in the Soviet Union, however, was generally ignored by Western scholars.

> In the 1920s, however, the problem of unequal treaties received world-wide attention when China demanded the abolition of some treaties that it termed unequal. Only then did some Western writers renew interest in the problem. Thus, in 1927, at the annual

meeting of the American Society of International Law, a session was devoted to the discussion of China's unequal treaties. With the abolition of what were presumed to be the last of China's unequal treaties in the early 1940s, Western scholars again lost interest in the subject.

With the emergence of many new states in Asia and Africa in the 1960s, the question of unequal treaties again began to attract worldwide attention. When the Draft Articles on the Law of Treaties prepared by the United Nations International Law Commission was sent to UN member states for comment, many states expressed concern about the question of unequal treaties.[19]

In the 1960s, many of the newly created nations of Africa and Asia advocated the proposition that unequal treaties were no longer acceptable under International Law. Their forum was the negotiations regarding the Vienna Convention on the Law of Treaties. One supporting argument was that Section 2.4 of the UN Charter requires all members to "refrain in their international relations from the threat or use of force . . . [which is] inconsistent with the purposes of the United Nations." If force is illegal, then coercion in the treaty process should invalidate the legality of a treaty.

The result of the VCLT negotiations was the incorporation of two articles applicable to treaties concluded after the effective date of the VCLT (January 27, 1980). Article 51 provides that the "expression of a State's consent to be bound by a treaty which has been *procured by the coercion of its representative* through acts or threats directed against him shall be without any legal effect" (emphasis supplied). Article 52 provides that a "treaty is void if its conclusion has been *procured by the threat or use of force in violation of the principles of international law* embodied in the Charter of the United Nations" (emphasis supplied). Although coerced treaties concluded prior to the VCLT were presumed valid by some writers, Articles 51 and 52 expressly negated that presumption for subsequent treaties. As stated by the International Court of Justice in 1973, there "can be little doubt, as is implied in the Charter of the United Nations and recognized in Article 52 of the Vienna Convention on the Law of Treaties, that under con-

temporary international law an agreement concluded under the threat or use of force is void."[20]

During the Vienna Conference negotiations, a number of Eastern communist bloc and African states advocated the view that Article 52's prohibition against force should expressly include economic, military, and political coercion. Their attempts to ban treaties procured through these categories of force were rebuffed by Western representatives. The Western position was that, given the difficulty of defining "force" in the treaty process, it would be too difficult to determine whether a treaty was invalid because it was allegedly signed as a result of such duress.

Article 52 of the VCLT therefore does not contain a specific definition of force. Instead, it generally prohibits the threat or use of force in violation of the principles of International Law embodied in the UN Charter. This language meant only that "the precise scope of the acts covered by this definition should be left to be determined in practice by interpretation of the relevant provisions of the [UN] Charter." Yet Article 2.4 of the Charter vaguely prohibits the use of force "against the territorial integrity or political independence of any state. . . ." The Vienna Convention Article 52 definition of force in the treaty process was left purposefully vague since it relied on the vague definition of force as expressed in the UN Charter.[21]

Some of the ambiguity about the scope of the term *force* was offset at the conclusion of the VCLT. The delegates adopted the separate Declaration on the Prohibition of Military, Political or Economic Coercion in the Conclusion of Treaties. They therein stated that the United Nations Conference on the Law of Treaties "*solemnly condemns* the threat or use of pressure in any form, whether military, political, or economic, by any State in order to coerce another State to perform any act relating to the conclusion of a treaty in violation of the principles of the sovereign equality of States and freedom of consent. . . ."[22] This Declaration was actually made independently of the VCLT, rather than being directly expressed in VCLT Article 52 prohibition. Excluding any prohibition against "economic" or "political" coercion from the *text* of Article 52 was a compromise—illustrating Western opposition to nonmilitary duress as a basis for invalidating a treaty. Because the VCLT itself defines coercion only by the reference to the "principles of international law embodied in the Charter of the United Nations," it is difficult to determine when a treaty would be void on the basis of duress in its creation.

Treaty Observance

Several parameters measure the degree to which a State has complied with its treaty obligations by performing "its end of the deal." The relevant themes in this part of § 8.2 are:

- Good faith performance of national treaty obligations;

- Changed circumstances justifying nonperformance;

- Express and implied consent to suspension or termination;

- Material breach by one party, justifying another's nonperformance;

- Impossibility of performance; and

- Conflict with a peremptory norm of International Law as a basis for treaty avoidance.

Good Faith Performance   Under Article 2.2 of the United Nations Charter, "Members . . . shall fulfil in good faith the obligations assumed by them in accordance with the present Charter." The universal character of this norm was aptly articulated by the former Dutch ambassador to the UN in 1967:

> The principle of good faith itself . . . extends beyond the scope of this article and is generally recognized as expressing a fundamental concept underlying the entire structure of the international public order. It applies to the observance and interpretation of treaties and even to the obligation not to frustrate the object of a treaty prior to its entry into force, as well as to the fulfillment of obligations arising from other sources of international law. Particularly in the context of the law of treaties the principle of good faith . . . clearly emerges as having a fundamental and universal nature.[23]

The inherent limitation on State conduct, after it has entered into a treaty relationship with another State or international organization, is that the State may not act in such a way as to frustrate the purpose of the treaty. Typically, nothing in the express terms of the instrument itself prohibits the contemplated action authorized under the State's *internal* law. Yet the State has incurred an obligation—under *International* Law—not to do anything that would deprive the other party or parties of their reasonable expectations under the treaty. A State may not, for example, pass subsequent internal legislation that creates an inconsistency with its obligations under a treaty. In a US/UK treaty delineating the fishing rights of US citizens in Canadian waters, the UK's post-treaty regulations limited those rights in a way not contemplated by the wording of the treaty. In the words of the arbitrators in this major case, these regulations had to be "drawn according to the principle of international law that treaty obligations are to be executed in perfect good faith, therefore excluding the right to legislate at will concerning the subject-matter of the treaty, and limiting the exercise of sovereignty of the States . . . to such acts as are consistent with the treaty. . . ."[24]

Various cases decided by the International Court of Justice illustrate some problems with *applying* this good faith performance standard. In the following cases, the ICJ dealt with what it perceived to be tardy claims that were not, under the circumstances, made in good faith. In the 1960 *Case Concerning the Arbitral Award Made by the King of Spain*, a bilateral treaty required Honduras and Nicaragua to arbitrate their boundary dispute. Spain's king was agreed upon as the arbitrator after the treaty-designated arbitrator failed to act. When the king decided this boundary dispute in 1906, neither country objected to his decision. Years later, Nicaragua challenged the validity of the award "[because the king] was not designated arbitrator in conformity with the provisions of the . . . Treaty [which] had elapsed before he agreed to act as arbitrator." Honduras responded that Nicaragua was acting in bad faith—it had waited too long to assert this potential bar to enforcement of the king's 1906 award. The ICJ held that Nicaragua could not, in good faith, raise such procedural problems so many years after the arbitration was complete and the treaty purpose fulfilled. In the words of the ICJ:

> Having failed to challenge the competency of the King as sole arbitrator before or during the course of the arbitration but, on the contrary, having invited him to make an award on the merits, Nicaragua was thereafter precluded

from contesting the regularity of the appointment.

All the relevant facts relating to that appointment were known to it when it participated in the arbitration. Each State party to the arbitration proceedings was entitled to place faith upon the deliberate conduct of the other State in the course of such proceedings. Nicaragua cannot be permitted to be placed in the position where, had the Award been satisfactory from its point of view, it could have accepted it, if not be free to disregard it as a nullity.

It would be contrary to the principle of good faith governing the relations between States were it [Nicaragua] permitted now to rely upon any irregularity in the appointment to invalidate the Award. Its conduct up to the moment the Award operated in my opinion so as to preclude it thereafter from doing so. . . .[25]

In a similar case, Cambodia and Siam (now Thailand) agreed to a boundary delimitation made by a Mixed Commission of Thai and Cambodian individuals. The Commission's work was completed in 1907. A subsequent dispute arose over an important religious site, situated at the border but not mentioned in surveys conducted by the Commission's officers. The Commission's surveys apparently placed the temple area within the territory comprising French Indochina (which included what is now Cambodia). The Commission members from Siam received copies of the surveys and did not object at the time of the Commission's finding. Years later, Thailand (formerly Siam) refused to cede authority over the area to Cambodia. In the 1960 proceedings before the ICJ, Thailand had two objections to the treaty-based boundary of 1907: The surveys were not actually the work of the treaty-designated commission, and they contained material errors in the placement of the Thai-Cambodian boundary. The ICJ rejected Thailand's claim for two reasons. It was not made in good faith due to the tardiness in asserting it; and Thailand had apparently acquiesced in the boundary line fixed by the Commission decades before its first objection. Both forms of conduct led to the Court's useful articulation regarding the importance of good faith treaty performance:

The primary foundation of this principle is the good faith that must prevail in international relations, inasmuch as inconsistency of conduct or opinion on the part of a State to the prejudice of another is incompatible with good faith. Again, I submit that such inconsistency is especially inadmissible when the dispute arises from bilateral treaty relations. A secondary basis of the principle is the necessity for security in contractual relationships. A State bound by a certain treaty to another State must rest in the security that a harmonious and undisturbed exercise of the rights of each party and a faithful discharge of reciprocal obligations denote a mutually satisfactory state of things which is permanent in character and is bound to last as long as the treaty is in force. A State cannot enjoy such a situation and at the same time live in fear that some day the other State may change its mind or its conduct and jeopardize or deny rights that for a long time it has never challenged. A continuous and uncontroverted fulfillment of a treaty is tantamount to a pledge, a security renewed day by day that the treaty rights, passiveness or any form of express or tacit acquiescence, other disputes have been decided against litigant States on the general basis of inconsistency between the claims of States and their previous acts.[26]

The lack of a precise definition of good faith treaty performance raises the question of whether it is in fact a general principle of International Law. Professor Charles Fenwick, former director of the Department of Legal Affairs of the Pan American Union, asserted the doubtful applicability of this so-called norm. He used treaties of peace—imposed by the victor on the vanquished—as his prime example that good faith was *not really expected* in treaty matters. When a vanquished State wanted to repudiate a treaty imposed on it by a victorious nation, the simple solution was another war. Given this fact of international life, he argued that "it is doubtful whether third states would have cast any reproach of bad faith against it [the repudiating State] for attempting to do so. Appearances could be saved, if [even] necessary, by finding other grounds of war, and then, if the outcome were successful, taking back what had been previously granted under duress. . . . Thus the faithful execution of treaties of peace was adjusted to shifts in the balance of power, and the principle of good faith was maintained while being indirectly undermined."[27]

Various organizations have attempted to articulate a standard for resolving questions about the precise content of the good faith yardstick—often referred to as *pacta sunt servanda.* The UN's International Law Commission (ILC)—an organ of the UN General Assembly—commenced its study of the *pacta sunt servanda* "norm" shortly after the UN was created. The ILC's initial work product was the Draft Declaration on the Rights and Duties of States. Article 13 provided that every "State has the duty to carry out in good faith its obligations arising from treaties . . . and it may not invoke provisions in its constitution or its [internal] laws as an excuse for failure to perform this duty."[28] This attempt to define good faith was *so* generally acceptable that it was virtually useless as a functional device for describing its content. Some Vienna Conference delegates even argued in favor of *disposing* of the term from international treaty law, due to their inability to satisfactorily define it.[29]

Consensus was finally achieved by the very general wording chosen for Article 26 of the VCLT. It provides that every treaty "is binding upon the parties to it and must be performed by them in good faith." That language is no more specific than any earlier attempt to define good faith. At a minimum, however, it is agreed that good faith performance of treaty obligations does not mean literal compliance to the maximum extent possible. Performance can be assessed only by reference to the circumstances of each particular case.

Change in Circumstances A treaty is no longer binding if there has been a fundamental change in circumstances. This concept is referred to in the international literature as the doctrine of *rebus sic stantibus.* While a treaty is a solemn contract between States, a party may invoke changed circumstances as an excuse for suspending or terminating that contract.

Defining this concept is as difficult as defining good faith. Commentators, diplomats, and jurists are unable to agree on the precise circumstances for properly invoking this basis for avoiding treaty obligations. This obstacle has not impeded either academic or judicial reference to the doctrine of *rebus sic stantibus,* however. The spectrum of views is that it is "clearly a reasonable doctrine which . . . international law should recognize," merely an "alleged

principle of international law," and "an unsuitable method for altering treaty obligations to accommodate changed conditions." Wang Yao-t'ien, a prolific Chinese scholar, viewed changed circumstances as a contrivance fashioned by capitalist States to abrogate treaties at will. In his 1958 treatise on trade treaties, he wrote that two States should *renegotiate* their treaty, rather than one of them purporting to unilaterally suspend or terminate treaty obligations. In his words: "There is a so-called doctrine of '*rebus sic stantibus*' in the works of bourgeois international law. . . . In international relations, sometimes it is necessary to revise or abrogate a treaty in the light of fundamental change of circumstances. However, capitalist states frequently use this principle as a pretext to justify their unilateral [abrogation] of treaties. Generally, the process should be: When a fundamental change of circumstances occurs, the contracting states should seek revision or reconclusion of the original treaty through diplomatic negotiation."[30]

Professor Oliver Lissitzyn of Columbia University in New York most accurately referred to the changed circumstances doctrine as a right with unsettled contours. In his words:

> After centuries of doctrinal discussion, the existence, scope and modalities of such a right remain controversial and perplexing. Its practical importance may at times be exaggerated; but nations dissatisfied with the *status quo* continue to regard it as a welcome device for escaping from burdensome treaties, while others fear it as a threat to stability and to their interests. Terminology has complicated the problem. Scholars, in efforts to define the asserted right and its scope or to provide a doctrinal basis for its modalities, have resorted to numerous technical labels drawn largely from municipal [national] legal systems. Governments, in asserting the right, have variously employed or refrained from employing such terms as *rebus sic stantibus.*[31]

Most theorists do not believe that changed circumstances permit a unilateral abrogation of treaty commitments. When circumstances beyond the control of the parties necessitate the alteration of a treaty commitment, the remedy is usually suspension or termination of the treaty—depending on the extent of the conditions that have changed. In practice, however, the State claiming changed circumstances may no longer want to fulfill its commitments because they are inconvenient or not as beneficial as anticipated.

During the 1960s, the drafters of the Vienna Convention on the Law of Treaties attempted to clarify the legal contours of the changed circumstances doctrine. The drafting committee's members articulated their concern as follows:

> Almost all modern jurists, however reluctantly, admit the existence in international law of the principle . . . commonly spoken of as the doctrine of *rebus sic stantibus.* . . . Most jurists, however, at the same time enter a strong *caveat* as to the need to confine the scope of the doctrine within narrow limits and to regulate strictly the conditions under which it may be invoked; for the risks to the security of treaties which this doctrine presents . . . [are] obvious. The circumstances of international life are always changing and it is easy to allege that the changes render the treaty inapplicable.[32]

The ultimate work product of the Vienna Convention on changed circumstances was Article 62. The essential provision (Art. 62.1) provides as follows:

A fundamental change in circumstances which has occurred with regard to those existing at the time of the conclusion of a treaty, and which was not foreseen by the parties, may not be invoked as a ground for terminating or withdrawing from the treaty unless:

(a) the existence of those circumstances constituted an essential basis of the consent of the parties to be bound by the treaty; and

(b) the effect of the change is radically to transform the extent of obligations still to be performed under the treaty.

The existence of the changed circumstances doctrine has been reluctantly conceded in international litigation. In 1929, the Permanent Court of International Justice grudgingly recognized its vitality. The Court refused to assess its contours, however, ultimately choosing not to apply it.[33] In the early 1970s, the International Court of Justice ruled against a State's asserting changed circumstances as a defense to its unilateral termination of a treaty. The case progressed through several phases. The segment dealing with changed circumstances is presented below. It echoes the sentiment of the VCLT commentators that renegotiation or judicial settlement is the acceptable alternative to unilateral termination:

FISHERIES JURISDICTION CASES

International Court of Justice, 1973
[1973] International Court of Justice Reports 49

[Author's Note:] Various nations have fished in the waters surrounding Iceland for centuries. After World War II, Iceland became concerned that these nations, using advanced technology, were rapidly depleting valuable fishing resources—Iceland's primary livelihood. In 1959, its parliament declared that "Iceland has an indisputable right to fishery limits of 12 miles (rather than 3), that recognition should be obtained of Iceland's right to the entire continental shelf area (about 50 miles) and that fishery limits of less than 12 miles [when the international norm was a three-mile territorial sea] from the base-lines around the country are out of the question."

In 1961, Iceland and England were engaged in a diplomatic Exchange of Notes that ultimately became a treaty. Iceland agreed to give England six months' no-tice of any further extension of Icelandic fisheries jurisdiction and to submit any fisheries disputes to the ICJ. In 1971, Iceland advised England of Iceland's intent to extend its fisheries jurisdiction again—this time to the entire continental shelf surrounding Iceland's shores. (The US had similarly created a 200-mile continental shelf zone in 1945.) England objected because a coastal state's ability to control fishing in international waters was well under the fifty-mile limit suddenly claimed by Iceland (when there was no Exclusive Economic Zone).

In 1972, the Althing (Iceland's parliament) adopted a resolution that the twelve-mile agreement of 1961 had to be repealed due to changed circumstances. England (and Germany) sued Iceland in the ICJ to preserve their fishing rights under the 1961 treaty. Although Iceland chose not to appear in the ICJ proceedings, it did provide the Court with a written defense: The technological circumstances had changed so drastically that Iceland was compelled to unilaterally abrogate its 1961 treaty with England. The court ruled (in Iceland's absence) that Iceland could not properly invoke changed circumstances. English ships were not thereby precluded from fishing within the fifty-mile area claimed by Iceland.

The portion of the opinion dealing with changed circumstances follows. The paragraph numbers are those of the Court. Emphasis have been supplied by the author at various points in the opinion.]

[*Opinion.*] 35. In his letter of 27 June 1972 to the Registrar [of the Court] the Minister for Foreign Affairs of Iceland refers to 'the changed circumstances resulting from the ever-increasing exploitation of the fishery resources in the seas surrounding Iceland.' Judicial notice should also be taken of other statements made on the subject in documents which Iceland has brought to the Court's attention. Thus, the resolution adopted by the Althing on 15 February 1972 contains the statement that 'owing to changed circumstances the Notes concerning fishery limits exchanged in 1961 are no longer applicable.'

36. In these statements the Government of Iceland is basing itself on the principle of termination of a treaty by reason of change of circumstances. International law admits that a fundamental change in the circumstances . . . [that] resulted in a radical transformation of the extent of the obligations imposed by it [the treaty], may, under certain conditions, afford the party affected a ground for invoking the termination or suspension of the treaty. This principle, and the conditions and exceptions to which it is subject, have been embodied in Article 62 of the Vienna Convention on the Law of Treaties, which may in many respects be considered as a codification of existing customary law on the subject of the termination of a treaty relationship on account of change of circumstances.

37. One of the basic requirements embodied in that Article is that the change of circumstances must have been a fundamental one. In this respect the Government of Iceland has, with regard to developments in fishing techniques, referred . . . to the increased exploitation of the fishery resources in the seas surrounding Iceland and to the danger of still further exploitation because of an increase in the catching capacity of fishing fleets. The Icelandic statements recall the exceptional dependence of that country on its fishing for its existence and economic development.

. . .

In this same connection, the resolution adopted by the Althing on 15 February 1972 had contained a paragraph in these terms:

That the Governments of the United Kingdom and the Federal Republic of Germany be again informed that because of the vital interests of the nation and owing to changed circumstances the Notes concerning fishery limits exchanged in 1961 are no longer applicable and that their provisions do not constitute an obligation for Iceland.

38. The invocation by Iceland of its 'vital interests,' which were not made the subject of an express reservation to the acceptance of the jurisdictional obligation under the 1961 Exchange of Notes, must be interpreted, in the context of . . . the traditional view that the changes of circumstances which must be regarded as fundamental or vital are those which imperil the existence or vital development of one of the parties.

39. The Applicant [England] for its part, has expressed before the Court the view that 'the danger of overfishing has not yet materialized', and made it clear, in its oral argument, that it was not to be understood as accepting the correctness of the claim by the Government of Iceland that the technical development of fishing equipment and modern fishing techniques had made it more pressing than before to take conservation measures in order to prevent overfishing in the waters around Iceland.

. . .

41. It should be observed in this connection that the exceptional importance of coastal fisheries to the Icelandic economy is expressly recognized in the 1961 Exchange of Notes, and the . . . point is not disputed.

42. Account must also be taken of the fact that the Applicant, in its contentions before the Court, expressed the opinion that if Iceland, as a coastal State specially dependent on coastal fisheries for its livelihood or economic development, asserts a need to procure the establishment of a special fisheries conservation regime (including such a regime under which it enjoys preferential rights) in the waters adjacent to its coast but beyond the exclusive fisheries

zone provided for by the 1961 Exchange of Notes, it can legitimately pursue that objective by collaboration and agreement with the other countries concerned, *but not by unilateral assumption of exclusive rights within those waters.* The exceptional dependence of Iceland on its fisheries and the principle of conservation of fish stocks having been recognized, the question remains as to whether Iceland is or is not competent unilaterally to assert an exclusive fisheries jurisdiction extending beyond the 12-mile limit. . . .

43. Moreover, in order that a change of circumstances may give rise to a ground for invoking the termination of a treaty it is also necessary that it *should have resulted in a radical transformation of the extent of the obligations still to be performed. The change must have increased the burden of the obligations to be executed to the extent of rendering the performance something essentially different from that originally undertaken.* In respect of the obligation with which the Court is here concerned, this condition is wholly unsatisfied; the change of circum-

stances alleged by Iceland cannot be said to have transformed radically the extent of the jurisdictional obligation which is imposed in the 1961 Exchange of Notes. The compromissory clause enabled either of the parties to submit to the Court any dispute between them relating to an extension of Icelandic fisheries jurisdiction in the waters above its continental shelf beyond the 12-mile limit. The present dispute is exactly of the character anticipated in the compromissory clause of the Exchange of Notes. Not only has the jurisdictional obligation not been radically transformed in its extent; it has remained precisely what it was in 1961.

44. The Applicant, in the oral proceedings, advanced the contention that the assertion of changed circumstances does not . . . release the State invoking them from its treaty obligation *unless* it has been *established, either by consent* of the other party *or by judicial or other settlement* between the parties, that the changed circumstances are of a kind which justifies release from existing treaty obligations.

Treaty Termination and Suspension

The inability to readily invoke the changed circumstances doctrine requires continued *performance* of a treaty. The materials that follow illustrate far more viable methods of treaty suspension or termination.

The stability of the treaty system is nourished by the State fulfillment of treaty commitments. International agreements normally remain in force until the contracting parties jointly decide to modify them. A State may, however, legitimately terminate or suspend its treaty obligations by internationally accepted means. The following materials address the traditional bases for terminating or suspending obligations arising under a treaty.

Express Consent A treaty can terminate by its own terms, in conformity with provisions originally inserted by the State parties. The expiration of a certain amount of time is a routine basis for termination. States typically enter into treaties of indefinite duration, however. Some States nevertheless prefer to limit their treaty commitments to a specified number of years. The People's Republic of China commonly makes treaties that will remain in force only for an explicit time frame. For example, the 1950 Sino-Soviet Treaty of Friendship, Alliance, and Mutual Assistance provided that the "present

treaty will be valid for thirty years. If neither of the contracting parties . . . desire[s] to renounce the treaty, it shall remain in force for another five years and will be extended in compliance with this rule."[34]

Treaties more typically contain provisions for *advance* notification of termination. The 1955 Sino-Indonesian Treaty on Dual Nationality provided that if "after the expiration of twenty years, one party requests its termination, it must so notify the other party one year in advance and in written form; and the present treaty shall be terminated one year after the tendering of such notification." The 1954 Mutual Defense Treaty between the United States and the Republic of China (Taiwan) provided that it would remain in force "indefinitely [although] either Party may terminate it one year after notice has been given to the other Party." In 1978, President Carter gave notice that he intended to terminate the treaty with Taiwan. That treaty was terminated by the US one year later, when he officially recognized the People's Republic of China (mainland China) as the *de jure* government of China.

A treaty may be terminated or suspended even when it does *not* contain revocation or notice provisions. The participants may simply repeal it (unanimously—in *another* multilateral treaty). The parties to an earlier treaty may expressly suspend or terminate it (or certain portions) in a later treaty. Under Article 58 of the Vienna Convention on the Law of Treaties, two (or more) nations may suspend a treaty as it relates to their mutual obligations to one another. Such a limited suspension may not be incompatible with the overall treaty, however. Under the 1982 Convention on the Law of the Sea, for example, there is a twelve-mile territorial sea zone. Australia and New Zealand may suspend that provision of the treaty as between themselves only. Each may decide to observe a three-mile territorial sea zone for *their* respective fishing vessels, while *other* State parties must observe the twelve-mile zone contained in the Law of the Sea treaty when entering Australian or New Zealand waters.

Implied Consent   The parties to an international agreement can disapprove it by *implication.* If a treaty is silent, termination or suspension can be implied from the circumstances of the parties' conduct. They may decide to enter into a subsequent agreement containing the same subject matter as the earlier treaty. If provisions in the second treaty conflict with the first, then the first is cancelled by implication.

Two treaty agreements, or the conflicting provisions within them, must of course be incompatible in order to imply termination of the earlier treaty. In a 1939 case in the Permanent Court of International Justice (PCIJ), a majority of the Court ruled that the two relevant agreements were compatible. Justice Anzilotti's dissent in that case succinctly stated the general requirements for implicit treaty abrogation: There "was no express abrogation [of the 1931 treaty]. But it is generally agreed that, beside express abrogation, there is also tacit abrogation resulting from the fact that the new provisions are incompatible with the previous provisions, or that the whole matter which formed the subject of these latter [understandings] is henceforth governed by the new provisions."[35]

Under Article 59(b) of the 1969 Vienna Convention on the Law of Treaties (VCLT), the parties may consent by implication to treaty termination when a subsequent treaty is "so far incompatible with the earlier one that the two treaties are not capable of being applied at the same time."

The other basis for implied consent to treaty termination is failure of compliance. A treaty can be negated by implication when all of the parties ignore it. The absence of objections constitutes an implied understanding that the treaty is no longer in force.

Material Breach   One party's treaty breach may allow the other(s) to consider the treaty as either suspended or terminated. The breach must be material. Under Article 60 of the VCLT, material breach of a *bilateral* treaty by one party permits the other party "to invoke the breach as a ground for terminating the treaty or suspending its operation in whole or in part." Material breach of a *multilateral* treaty similarly entitles "the other parties . . . to suspend the operation of the treaty . . . in the relations between themselves and the defaulting State [but not one another]. . . ." The clearest example of a material breach under Article 60 would be an outright repudiation of a treaty. The other party would then be authorized to suspend or terminate its obligations under that treaty.

In practice, it is often difficult to establish what constitutes a *material* breach, and, *which* party is actually responsible for the breach. In 1966, for example, North Vietnam claimed that South Vietnam had materially breached the Geneva Accords. That international agreement—agreed to by representatives of both governments—called for a cessation of hostilities in Vietnam, the reduction of military forces, and reunification through free elections.

The North Vietnamese claim of material breach by South Vietnam was based on the introduction of US military forces into the Southern portion of the country, in rapidly increasing numbers. The US justified South Vietnam's departure from the Geneva agreement on the basis of a material breach by North Vietnam. The US claimed the "substantial breach of an international agreement by one side [North Vietnamese aggression in South Vietnam] permits the other side to suspend performance of corresponding obligations under the agreement. South Vietnam was allegedly justified in refusing to implement the provisions of the Geneva Accords," which otherwise would have required it to limit expanded military involvements and to arrange unification elections. Specifically, the introduction of military personnel into the southern portion of the country "was justified by the international law principle that a material breach of an agreement by one party [North Vietnam] entitles the other [South Vietnam] at least to withhold compliance . . . until the defaulting party is prepared to honor its obliga-tion."[36] North Vietnam and South Vietnam thus accused each other of materially breaching their respective commitments under the Geneva Accords.

In a 1972 case in the International Court of Justice, Pakistan complained that India materially breached several aviation treaties. An Indian aircraft had been hijacked and diverted to Pakistan. India then revoked Pakistan's right to fly over Indian territory. For reasons unrelated to the merits of this case, the ICJ did not resolve whether India breached the aviation treaties when it refused to allow Pakistani aircraft in Indian airspace. It did find, however, that the Indian suspension of Pakistan's treaty rights to pass over Indian territory, and to land in India, constituted material breaches of their aviation treaty.[37]

Impossibility of Performance A party to a treaty may invoke impossibility of performance as a basis for suspending or terminating its obligations under that treaty. Article 61 of the VCLT provides that impossibility "results from the permanent disappearance or destruction of an object indispensable for the execution of the treaty." The drafters of the VCLT used the following examples: submergence of an island that is the object of a treaty relationship, the drying up of a river, and the destruction of a dam or hydroelectric installation indispensable for the execution of a treaty. The extinction of these objects would terminate (or temporarily suspend) rights and obligations arising under a treaty governing their use.[38]

Another instance of impossibility of performance is the destruction or extinction of a State that is a party to a treaty.[39] This scenario does not yield the option, however, to terminate treaty obligations merely because there has been a political change in the government or governing structure (*see* § 2.3 of this book).

A fundamental change that *radically* alters the nature of treaty obligations has been characterized by some jurists as impossibility of performance—presenting a fine-line distinction from the above "changed circumstances" analysis. Although there are similarities, the criteria employed for applying "impossibility" differ. Every impossibility of performance includes a changed circumstance; however, every changed circumstance does not include an impossibility of performance. The changed cir-cumstances doctrine may excuse *difficulty* of performance, while the impossibility of course excuses only performance that is totally *impossible*. The reasons for allowing a changed circumstances termination of a treaty include the rights both to maintain the legitimate expectations of the parties and to facilitate peaceful changes in international relations. The reason for impossibility of performance, however, is to exonerate one or both parties from treaty performance when the impossibility renders the treaty meaningless.[40]

Assume that Spain and Portugal establish their respective rights to fish in an area on either side of a boundary in the international waters near their coasts. They agree to regulate their own fishers on either side of the line separating Spain's area and Portugal's area. The purpose of the treaty is to maintain an equal distribution of the resources near their respective coasts. If the fish unexpectedly migrated into Portugal's area, the treaty would be suspended. The changed circumstance is that fish are *temporarily* unavailable in equal numbers to both Spain and Portugal. Spain's fishers would be permitted to fish in Portugal's area of the High Seas, due to the treaty's mutually agreed purpose of equitable distribution. The same fishing treaty would be terminated under the impossibility doctrine if all of the fish were *permanently* driven away by contamination of the treaty area. The treaty would be meaningless because the object of that agreement would no longer exist.[41]

Conflict with Peremptory Norm A treaty is void if it conflicts with a peremptory norm of International Law. The common descriptive term for such a norm is *jus cogens*, meaning a widely acknowledged law from which no State could deviate (see § 1.4 of this book). Article 53 of the Vienna Convention on the Law of Treaties (VCLT) defines this term as a norm that is "accepted and recognized by the international community of States as a whole as a norm from which no derogation is permitted and which can be modified only by a subsequent norm of general international law having the same character."

The VCLT does not define just what is it that constitutes a norm from which no derogation is permitted. A number of jurists thus deny the existence of *jus cogens* in International Law, because even the most generally accepted rules have not achieved universality. Professor Grigori Tunkin of Moscow State University explains that the "arguments of opponents of *jus cogens* can be reduced to the fact that such principles are possible only in a well-organized and effective legal system, and since international law is not such a system, the existence of principles of general international law having the character of *jus cogens* is impossible."[42]

One can make a reasonable argument, however, that *jus cogens* would render certain treaties void. When two States have entered into a treaty, in which they agree to invade another country, that agreement violates the most fundamental UN Charter article—which is the Section 2.4 prohibition on the use of force in international relations. Such a treaty violates an undisputable Charter norm. State A and State B could not legitimately circumvent the Article 2.4 prohibition against the use of force by merely signing a treaty to invade State C.

Limitations A State's ability to suspend or terminate its treaty commitments is limited. The severance of diplomatic or consular relations, for example, does not necessarily affect treaty rights and obligations. Article 2.3 of the Vienna Convention on Consular Relations (VCLT) provides that the "severance of *diplomatic* relations shall not *ipso facto* [automatically in and of itself] involve the severance of *consular* relations" (emphasis supplied). Article 45 of the VCLT expressly provides that a break in diplomatic relations does *not* alter the continuing obligation to honor treaty obligations that have nothing to do with diplomatic or consular matters. Therefore, war and other hostile relationships do not terminate all treaty obligations of parties to the conflict. States are expected to continue to perform their obligations under treaties like the Geneva Conventions of 1949 dealing with Red Cross assistance, the laws of war, and treatment of prisoners of war (*see* § 10.6).

Theory and practice, however, diverge in terms of the actual wartime performance of treaty obligations. Treaties are often suspended or terminated on grounds of impossibility and fundamental change of circumstances—or implicitly terminated by the failure (implied consent) of the parties to observe their mutual treaty commitments. The outbreak of war does not automatically terminate treaty obligation. The US war with Germany, for example, did not automatically terminate the 1923 US treaty obligation to transmit property of deceased individuals to

German citizens.[43] A *prolonged* state of war often presents problems with the performance of treaty requirements, such that continuing these obligations makes no sense.

■ 8.3 UNITED STATES TREATY PRACTICE

This section deals with two key elements of US treaty practice. The first is the significant distinction between the terms "treaty" and "executive agreement." Under International Law, all presidential executive agreements are treaties. Under US law, however, executive agreements are not necessarily treaties. The second major theme is how to resolve conflicts between a treaty or executive agreement and the US Constitution or a federal statute.

Treaty vs. Executive Agreement

As discussed in § 8.2, the term "treaty" is a generic word that supports the contemporary use of some three dozen synonyms for an international agreement. International Law does not distinguish between an agreement designated as a "treaty" and other agreements with different titles that also create international obligations. The manner of creation of an international obligation does not affect its binding nature under *International* Law.

Under the *internal* law of the US, the word "treaty" has a narrower meaning that has spawned scholarly debate and lawsuits between the legislative and executive branches of government (as when certain US senators sued President Carter in 1977 over his agreement relinquishing US control of the Panama Canal). The president makes all US treaty commitments. But the term "treaty" refers only to those international agreements made by the president *with the consent of the Senate*. The president may also enter into "executive agreements," which do not necessarily involve Senate approval.

The *treaty* versus *executive agreement* distinction was spawned by early US practice, under the so-called Treaty Clause in Article II of the US Constitution. It provides that the president "shall have the Power, by and with the Advice and Consent of the Senate, to make Treaties, provided two-thirds of the Senators present concur. . . ." During the Constitutional Convention of 1787, the House of Representatives was ultimately excluded from an express treaty-making role with the Senate, as originally proposed. After debating the matter, the delegates acknowledged the widespread feeling that diplomatic negotiations required a degree of secrecy possible only in the smaller senatorial body (of twenty-six senators from thirteen colonies). The fervor of this debate effectively overshadowed the importance of what remained in the final draft of the Constitution—which excluded the House and included the president.[44] Thus, the president has the express constitutional power to *make* treaties when the Senate gives its *consent.* Almost immediately, US presidents (without seeking the consent of the Senate) began to enter into "executive agreements." This form of international treaty-making is not a "treaty" under the Constitution.

How did this contrast arise? The US Constitution does not define "treaties." When it was adopted in 1787, its drafters apparently saw no need to define a concept that was then well known in international practice.[45] The Treaty Clause has not been interpreted by the judicial branch of the US government to mean that the president *must* have the Senate's advice and consent for *all* international agreements. The president may thus enter into executive agreements, which do not require Senate approval.

During the early development of relations between the executive and congressional branches of government, two factors influenced the Senate to acquiesce in executive agreements—which were treaties made *without* its advice and consent. First, the relationship between the president and the Senate had evolved in favor of such action. Second, the Senate had to support the president's general management of foreign relations. It had no constitutional authority to negotiate directly with foreign governments—unlike the president who is empowered to "make" treaties with other States (and now with international organizations).

Two types of executive agreement evolved. One is the *congressional*-executive agreement, whereby the president can request approval of an executive agreement by a joint resolution of both houses of Congress. Professor Louis Henkin of Columbia University presented the following explanation for the existence of this implied presidential power:

Neither Congresses nor Presidents nor courts have been troubled by these conceptual difficulties and differences [between *treaty* and *executive* agreements]. Whatever their theoretical merits, it is now widely accepted that the Congressional-Executive agreement is a complete [legitimate] alternative to a treaty: the President can seek approval of any agreement by joint resolution of both houses of Congress instead of two-thirds of the Senate only. Like a treaty, such an agreement is the law of the land, superseding inconsistent state laws as well as inconsistent provisions in earlier treaties, in other international agreements or acts of Congress.[46]

The other category of executive agreement is the *sole* executive agreement. While congressional approval for executive agreements is often sought, it has been completely avoided in some instances. The president has thus exercised the inherent power to incur an international obligation independently of the Senate (via Article II treaty) or both houses of Congress (via congressional-executive agreement). Professor Oliver Lissitzyn of Columbia University describes the historical, but troubled, development of the president's executive agreement power:

The making of executive agreements is thus a constitutional usage of long standing which apparently rests upon the President's vast but ill-defined powers in the fields of foreign relations and national defense. Neither the usage nor the decisions of courts, however, provide clear-cut guidance as to the *scope* of the treaty-making power and the scope of the executive agreement-making power are not mutually exclusive. What may be properly accomplished by executive agreement may also be accomplished by treaty. . . .

It is not believed that any attempt to delimit rigidly the scope of the executive agreement-making power is likely to be successful or to result in a correct portrayal or prediction of actual practice. Some writers, while refusing to regard the executive agreement-making power as co-extensive with the treaty-making power, wisely refrain from attempting to define the scope of the former. . . .

It may be proper, therefore, to regard the executive agreement-making power as extending to all the occasions on which an international agreement is believed by the Chief Executive to be necessary in the national interest, but on which resort to the treaty-making procedure is impracticable or likely to render ineffective an established national policy. The test here suggested is the only one that adequately accounts for the variety of situations in which the President, with or without the approval of Congress, has resorted to the executive-agreement procedure. It also accounts for the increasing frequency of resort to the executive-agreement method in recent years, with the growth of complexity in international affairs and of pressure of work in the Senate.[47]

The president has undertaken certain executive agreements either *before* or *after* seeking input from the legislative branch of the government. Some US international agreements have thus involved *prior* Senate or congressional approval, while others have been concluded with *subsequent* approval. Thus, the president's power in the field of foreign relations would be well-defined as ill-defined. *Why* a particular agreement falls within one of these three categories is probably best explained by congressional acquiescence in presidential discretion when exercising control over foreign affairs.

Exhibit 8.1 illustrates the historical comparison between "treaties," in the constitutional sense of requiring the Senate's advice and consent, and "executive agreements" undertaken via either the congressional or sole variation of that term. It is readily evident that the executive agreement has far surpassed the treaty in terms of how the president exercises his or her power as the maker of international agreements.

EXHIBIT 8.1   Executive Agreement/Treaty Comparison

Era	No. of Agreements	No. of Treaties
1789–1799	0	8
1800–1899	115	312
1900–1932	388	411
1933–1979	8,405	550
Totals	8,908	1,281

Source: Adapted from L. Margolis, *Executive Agreement and Presidential Power in Foreign Policy* 108 (New York: Praeger, 1985).

A clear articulation of the circumstances in which Senate approval of Article II treaties *must* be obtained has been quite elusive. The Senate expressed its concern about the increasing use of executive agreements when the subject, in its view, logically required Senate approval as a "treaty." From 1952 to 1957, Senator Bricker generated an intense debate over his proposed amendment to the Constitution's Treaty Clause. He advocated that *all* international agreements by the US should become effective *only through legislation* passed by both the House of Representatives and the Senate. If it had been successful, this constitutional amendment would have eliminated the president's ability to enter into *any* international agreement without express congressional approval. He or she would have thus been more of a negotiator than a maker of treaties.

Although the so-called Bricker Amendment failed, Congress did pass the Case Act in 1972. It requires the president to advise Congress (in writing) of *all* international agreements made without the consent of the Senate or without a joint resolution of Congress. If the president believes that public disclosure would prejudice national security, however, he or she may secretly enter into and then transmit a completed executive agreement to the Senate Committee on Foreign Relations and the House Committee on Foreign Affairs.[48]

The US Supreme Court has been occasionally called upon to define the scope of the president's executive agreement power. In a case growing out of President Carter's 1979 executive agreement with Iran—ending the hostage crisis and providing a basis for resolving business claims against Iran—the Court perceived that general power as follows: "In addition to congressional acquiescence in the President's power to settle [such] claims, prior cases of this Court have also recognized that the President does have *some* measure of power to enter into executive agreements without obtaining the advice and consent of the Senate."[49]

The difficulty in drawing a precise legal demarcation between the president's executive agreement power, and the required Senate consent under the US Constitution, is illustrated in the case that follows below. In 1968, President Johnson made an executive agreement with the Republic of the Philippines providing for the preferential employment of Filipino citizens at US military bases in the Philippines. Its purpose was to ensure the availability of suitable employees on those bases. The underlying rationale was that giving these jobs to local nationals would result in lower wage costs and less turnover in these positions, due to the comparatively limited availability of US citizens (typically military dependents) to remain in these positions on foreign military bases. To accomplish this goal, the president decided to establish conditions favoring foreign nationals as employees on those bases.

Three years later, Congress enacted a law *prohibiting* any employment discrimination against US citizens on US overseas military bases—unless a "treaty" expressly permitted such discrimination as necessary to the national interests of the US. Four more executive agreements followed, providing for preferential treatment of foreign citizens at various military bases overseas—*after* passage of the 1971 nondiscrimination legislation. However, none of them was submitted to the Senate for its advice and consent as arguably required by the 1971 law.

In 1978, several US citizens working at one of the US naval bases in the Philippines were notified that their jobs had been converted into "local" positions (pursuant to the discrimination authorized by executive agreement with the Philippines). This meant that they would be discharged from their employment with the US Navy, so that "local" Filipino citizens could obtain those "local" jobs. The plaintiffs sued the US government (in the name of Secretary of Defense Weinberger) for violating the 1971 antidiscrimination statute. The Rossis, and some others who had lost their jobs, thus sought reinstatement in their employment.

The Supreme Court had to interpret the "treaty exception" in Section 106 of the statute, which otherwise prohibited discrimination in the absence of a "treaty." Did this exception mean that discrimination against US citizens would be permitted *only* under a "treaty" in the constitutional sense of that term, which *requires* Senate consent to discriminate against US citizens abroad? Alternatively, did Congress intend to leave untouched the president's power to enter into an *executive agreement* permitting job discrimination? If the latter were the case, then an executive agreement would be deemed a "treaty" within the meaning of the federal nondiscrimination statute—and thus a "treaty exception" *had* in fact been properly invoked to authorize discrimination against US nationals at the US military base in the Philippines. In this sense, there would be no distinction between an "Article II treaty" and an executive agreement made only by the president without the Senate's consent.

The Supreme Court's task was to construe the federal statute, which provides as follows: "*Unless prohibited by treaty*, no person shall be discriminated against . . . in the employment of civilian personnel . . . in any foreign country because such person is a citizen of the United States or is a dependent of a member of the Armed Forces of the United States."

Justice Rehnquist's following opinion illustrates the difficulties with distinguishing between "treaties" and "executive agreements" in a very sensitive context with significant foreign policy ramifications:

WEINBERGER v. ROSSI

Supreme Court of the United States, 1982
456 U.S. 25, 102 S.Ct. 1510, 71 L.Ed.2d 715*

[*Opinion.*] Our task is to determine the meaning of the word "treaty" as Congress used it in this statute. Congress did not separately define the word, as it has done in other enactments. We must therefore ascertain as best we can whether Congress intended the word "treaty" to refer solely to [the Constitution's] Art. II, § 2, cl. 2, "Treaties"—those international agreements concluded by the President with

---

*The Court's citations and footnotes are omitted.

the advice and consent of the Senate—or whether Congress intended "treaty" to also include executive agreements such as the BLA [Base Labor Agreement permitting discrimination].

The word "treaty" has more than one meaning. Under principles of international law, the word ordinarily refers to an international agreement concluded between sovereigns, regardless of the manner in which the agreement is brought into force. Under the United States Constitution, of course, the word "treaty" has a far more restrictive meaning. Article II, § 2, cl. 2, of that instrument provides that the President "shall have Power, by and with the Advice and Consent of the Senate, to make Treaties, provided two thirds of the Senators present concur."

Congress has not been consistent in distinguishing between Art. II treaties and other forms of international agreements. For example, in the Case Act, 1 U. S. C. § 112b(a) [see analysis accompanying this text's note 48 above], Congress required the Secretary of State to "transmit to the Congress the text of any international agreement, other than a treaty, to which the United States is a party" no later than 60 days after "such agreement has entered into force." Similarly, Congress has explicitly referred to Art. II treaties in the Fishery Conservation and Management Act of 1976, 16 U. S. C. § 1801 and the Arms Control and Disarmament Act, 22 U. S. C. § 2551.

On the other hand, Congress has used "treaty" to refer only to international agreements *other than* Art. II treaties. In 39 U. S. C. § 407(a), for example, Congress authorized the Postal Service, with the consent of the President, to "negotiate and conclude postal treaties or conventions." A "treaty" which requires *only* the consent of *the President* is not an Art. II treaty. Thus it is not dispositive that Congress in § 106 used the term "treaty" without specifically including international agreements that are not Art. II treaties [emphasis supplied].

. . .

Thus, if Congress intended to limit the "treaty exception" in § 106 to Art. II treaties, it must have intended to repudiate these executive agreements that affect the hiring practices of the United States only at its military bases overseas. One would expect that Congress would be aware that executive agreements may represent a *quid pro quo* [bargained for exchange whereby] the host country grants the United States base rights in exchange for the preferential hiring of local nationals [of the host State].

. . .

At the time § 106 was enacted, there were in force 12 agreements in addition to the BLA providing for preferential hiring of local nationals on United States military bases overseas. Since the time of the enactment of § 106, four more such agreements have been concluded, and none of these were submitted to the Senate for its advice and consent. We think that some affirmative expression of congressional intent to abrogate the United States' international obligations is required in order to construe the word "treaty" in § 106 as meaning only Art. II treaties. We therefore turn to what legislative history is available in order to ascertain whether such an intent may fairly be attributed to Congress.

The legislative history seems to us to indicate that Congress was principally concerned with the financial hardship to American servicemen which resulted from discrimination against American citizens at overseas bases. As the Conference Committee Report explains:

"The purpose of [§ 106] is to correct a situation which exists at some foreign bases, primarily in Europe, where discrimination in favor of local nationals and against American dependents in employment has contributed to conditions of hardship for families of American enlisted men whose dependents are effectively prevented from obtaining employment."

The Conference Report, however, is entirely silent as to the scope of the "treaty" exception. Similarly, there is no mention of the 13 agreements that provided for preferential hiring of local nationals. Thus, the Conference Report provides no support whatsoever for the conclusion that Congress intended in some way to limit the President's use of international agreements that may discriminate against American citizens who seek employment at United States military bases overseas.

On the contrary, . . . Congress was not concerned with limiting the authority of the President to enter into executive agreements with the host country, but [Congress] with the ad hoc decision-making of military commanders overseas. In early 1971 [just before Congress passed § 106], Brig. Gen. Charles H. Phipps, Commanding General of the European Exchange System, issued a memorandum encouraging the recruitment and hiring of local nationals instead of United States citizens at the system's stores [on US military bases]. The hiring of local nationals, General Phipps reasoned, would result in lower wage costs and turnover rates. Senator Schweiker, a sponsor of § 106, [thus] complained of General Phipps' policy [of discriminating against US nationals on US military bases in Europe].

. . .

While the question is not free from doubt, we conclude that the "treaty" exception contained in § 106 extends to executive agreements as well as to Art. II treaties [thus characterizing these executive agreements as "treaties" for the purpose of authorizing discrimination against US nationals on foreign US military bases].

. . .

■ NOTES & QUESTIONS

1. The Supreme Court effectively "lent its hand" to the president's intentional discrimination against US citizens hoping to work on US military bases abroad. This meant that military dependents, typically spouses of enlisted personnel with a generally lower wage structure than that of military officers, would be unable to work—and, in many cases, therefore unable to accompany their military spouses during overseas assignments. The intermediate appellate court decision was thus overruled. *Rossi v. Brown*, 206 U.S.App.D.C. 148 (1980). Was *Weinberger v. Rossi* a *good* decision? Was it a *proper* decision under US treaty law?

2. The materials in this section suggest a two-part process for deciding whether the president's exercise of the executive agreement power transgresses any limits contained in the constitutional Treaty Clause or limiting congressional legislation (although *Rossi* did not interpret § 106 of the antidiscrimination statute as posing a bar to the president's powers in this particular instance). First, the president (through the appropriate federal agency) must determine whether his or her proposed executive agree-

ment falls within the parameters of the Treaty Clause—which may (or may not, per *Rossi*) require Senate consent. Second, the president must examine existing congressional legislation and attitudes to determine whether congressional approval should or must be obtained. As stated in the principle treatise on constitutional law in the US:

> The precise scope of the President's power to conclude international agreements without the consent of the Senate is unresolved. At one extreme, the proposition that the treaty is the exclusive medium for affecting foreign policy goals and, consequently, that executive agreements are *ultra vires* [unconstitutional] seems adequately refuted. . . .
>
> At the other extreme the notion that executive agreements know no constitutional bounds proves equally bankrupt. Executive agreements, no less than treaties, must probably be limited to appropriate subject matter. The more difficult question is whether there exist species of international accord that may take the form of a treaty, but not that of an executive agreement.*

Supreme Law of the Land

The question whether a treaty or executive agreement is the appropriate way to create an international agreement is one of *two* major problems in US treaty practice. The other involves conflicts among the US Constitution, federal statutes, and international treaties. Under International Law, a State may not rely on its internal law to avoid international obligations. In parts of Europe, Mexico, and certain other regions, treaties *must* take prece-

dence over their internal laws in the event of a conflict.[50] The internal laws of the US occasionally clash with, and may supersede, a prior international agreement. This portion of the book addresses the resolution of these conflicts under *US* law (as opposed to *International* Law where international obligations always take precedence over any conflicting State law).

The US Constitution does not provide a direct answer to the resolution of such conflicts. Article VI

Treaties and Executive Agreements, § 4–5 in L. Tribe, *American Constitutional Law* 225, pp. 228–29 (2nd ed. Mineola, NY: Foundation Press, 1988).

provides only that the "Constitution, and the Laws of the United States [federal statutes] which shall be made in Pursuance thereof and all Treaties made . . . shall be the supreme Law of the Land. . . ." This wording does not establish any relative hierarchy in the event of a conflict.

Conflict with Constitution The US Supreme Court has consistently held that the Constitution prevails when it conflicts with legislation or treaties. Both a federal statute *and* a treaty (executive agreement) were in conflict with the Constitution in the 1957 case of *Reid v. Covert.*[51] The Court held that civilian wives who had killed their military husbands on US bases in England and Japan could not be tried by a military courts-martial. The Supreme Court examined two sources of law to arrive at this conclusion. The Uniform Code of Military Justice (UCMJ) is federal legislation that provided for a courts-martial in this situation. Presidential executive agreements with those countries, governing crimes occurring on US bases abroad, incorporated these provisions of the Uniform Code—making them expressly applicable to military dependents. The court found that neither the Military Justice Code nor the executive agreements could deny the spouses' constitutional rights to indictment by a civilian grand jury and a jury trial by their peers. These rights contained in the US Constitution could not be withdrawn by either federal statute (UCMJ) or executive agreement (applying the UCMJ to military dependents abroad).

Treaty vs. Statute Treaties and federal statutes are on equal footing under Article VI of the Constitution. Each is therein referred to as the "supreme law of the land." Neither is superior to the other under the express terms of the Constitutional wording. The US Supreme Court applies the following rule: "The last in time prevails." As stated in the above *Reid* decision, the Court has "repeatedly taken the position that an Act of Congress . . . is on full parity with a treaty, and that when a statute which is subsequent in time is inconsistent with a treaty, the statute to the extent of conflict renders the treaty null."[52]

Under the internal law of the US, then, Congress may *denounce* treaties. In its comprehensive Anti-Apartheid Act of 1986, for example, Congress expressly repudiated a presidential executive agreement for air service with South Africa (prior to the im-

provement in international relations when the white minority government stepped down from power in 1993).[53]

Another related conflict may arise between international and internal law. The internal laws of the US may be incompatible with *customary* International Law—which is not necessarily expressed in a treaty. The practice of States is a major source of this category of International Law (*see* § 1.4). Courts in the US do not necessarily apply the "customary" branch of International Law. US courts must adhere to the will of the US Congress, as expressed in federal legislation. If Congress intended that a US statute violate the customary practice of States, then a US judge must follow the will of Congress.

US courts do not *blindly* apply internal law, however, when to do so would unnecessarily conflict with International Law. Judges thus presume, where possible, that Congress did *not* intend to violate International Law by a federal statute. This presumption is often used to interpret US legislation in a way that avoids violations of the customary practice of States. This presumption cannot be invoked, however, if Congress unmistakably intended to disregard some principle of customary international law. (*See, e.g., Larsen* case in § 6.3—involving the Congressional intent supporting the application of US legislation near the coast of Singapore).

The applicability of this presumption is explained in a 1925 Prohibition-era rum-running case as follows:

If we assume for the present that the national legislation has, by its terms, made the acts complained of a crime against the United States . . . then there is no discretion vested in the federal court, once it obtains jurisdiction, to decline enforcement [on the basis of a violation of International Law]. International practice is law only in so far as we adopt it, and like all common or statute law it bends to the will of the Congress . . . [because] it . . . follow[s] that in construing the terms and provisions of a statute it [the court] may . . . assume that such principles were on the national conscience and that the congressional act did not deliberately intend to infringe them. In other words, unless it unmistakably appears that a congressional act was intended to be in disregard of a principle of international comity, the presumption is that it was intended to be in conformity with it.[54]

Likewise, legislation by the individual political subdivisions within the federated system of the US government may not override the will of Congress. In the US Supreme Court case in point, the state of Missouri could not pass legislation that effectively controlled matters falling within the federal government's treaty power. Missouri could not purport to control the hunting laws regarding migratory birds en route from Canada through the US to Mexico and other countries. This is a matter that fell within the national treaty power, which thus took priority over the right of Missouri to control the people and things (migratory animals) temporarily within its boundaries.[55]

■ 8.4 ECONOMIC COERCION CASE STUDY

Introduction

Arab nations began their boycott of Israeli products shortly after World War II. The essential details are provided below. This scenario will be used to analyze and review materials contained in Chapter 8 on the treaty system. That arrangement may nevertheless serve as a useful basis for analyzing the nature and scope of international treaty commitments in a context adapted from this very real world scenario that, for forty years, held together as a vivid reminder of how the treaty system can be used for the most sensitive of political purposes—to drive a nation out of existence.

Several events have impacted the solidarity once enjoyed by the twenty-one member States of the Arab League (see § 3.5). Egypt broke ranks by its decision to meet with Israel—incident to the 1979 "Camp David" agreements (facilitated by US President Carter near Washington, D.C.). Kuwait had not been interested in the Arab boycott of Israeli goods for some time, particularly in the aftermath of the Persian Gulf War when it was rescued from the Iraqi conquest. That war pitted various Arab League members against Arab League member Iraq. The 1993 Washington Peace Accords between Yasir Arafat (PLO) and Prime Minister Rabin (Israel) presented an important breakthrough in terms of eradicating the Arab boycott of Israel—which had threatened international relations in the Middle East

for four decades. For the purpose of the following problem, assume that the Arab League boycott is still in existence and as tangible as it was before the 1993 Washington peace accords.

Essential Facts

Members of the Council of the Arab League of Nations drafted and unanimously approved the 1954 Unified Law on the Boycott of Israel. The Council was composed of State representatives from each State in the League. The Council was established to promote cooperation through periodic meetings of the foreign ministers of each Arab State. The Arab states thus agreed to prohibit the purchase of Israeli exports when they approved the Unified Law as follows:

> (1) All persons within the enacting country [in the Arab League] are forbidden to conclude any agreement or transaction, directly or indirectly with any person or organization (i) situated in Israel; (ii) affiliated with Israel through nationality; or (iii) working for or on behalf of Israel, regardless of the place of business or residence; and
> (2) Importation into the enacting country [adopting this boycott] is forbidden of all Israeli goods, including goods manufactured elsewhere [outside of Israel] containing ingredients or components of Israeli origin or manufacture.

All League members implemented the Unified Law adopted by the Council in 1954. Their national legislation contains only minor variations from the above terms. Saudi Arabia's version, for example, provides as follows:

Code of Regulation for the Boycott of Israel

1(a). All persons, whether natural or legal [meaning corporate entities], are prohibited from concluding, whether directly or through an intermediary, any covenant with any entities or persons resident in Israel, of Israeli nationality, or working for . . . Israel, wherever they may reside.

2.(a). The introduction or importation of Israeli goods, merchandise, and products of all kinds, or of financial documents or other negotiable instruments into the [Saudi] Kingdom is prohibited. . . .

In 1972, the Arab League announced a revision of the boycott law, called the General Principles for the Boycott of Israel. This version retained the broad language of the original agreement and supplemented it by imposing three specific categories of prohibitions. A *primary* boycott bars Arab states from exporting goods to, and importing goods from, Israel. A *secondary* boycott generally bans trade between league members and countries that trade with Israel. Israel's trading partners are thus placed on a blacklist that limits their ability to trade with nations in the Arab League.

A *tertiary* boycott further discourages trade with Israel. League members may not deal with companies that do any business with blacklisted countries: for example, a company contracted to supply buses to Saudi Arabia. When the Saudis learned that the seats were made by another firm located in a blacklisted country, they threatened to cancel the bus order. The bus manufacturer then substituted different seats made by a different firm *not* located in a blacklisted country. The Saudis decided that the contract was thus acceptable, and the buses were delivered to Saudi Arabia.[56]

The League's Unified Law further prohibits trade with persons "affiliated with Israel through nationality." Some States outside of the Arab League passed legislation to *punish compliance* with this boycott. Some commentators asserted further that this language is a euphemism for "persons of the Jewish faith." If so, the Arab boycott applies to all Jewish-owned businesses wherever they are located. League members reject this assertion. The above-quoted Saudi version of the Unified Law, for example, prohibits trade with persons "of Israeli nationality." The Saudi statute differs from the text of the Arab League's Uniform Law and is *not* susceptible to the argument that it conceals racism directed at *all* Jews, wherever they may reside. The Saudi law merely limits trade with Israeli citizens without regard to ethnic background or "affiliation with" Israel.[57]

The Arab boycott of Israel was a comparatively hostile form of nonmilitary pressure. Travelers in the Middle East were not surprised to see lists at airport customs booths listing Israeli-made goods, or goods from "offending" countries that dealt with Israel, whereby the traveler could not bring listed goods into the port of entry.

Boycotts are not, of course, unique to the Middle East. Economic boycotts and embargoes have been used by other countries as an alternative to military coercion. The US, for example, has participated in boycotts against Cuba, Iran, Nicaragua, North Korea, and Vietnam. The international boycott of South Africa was based, in part, on UN resolutions condemning apartheid.

Problem

Based upon the above facts and materials presented in this chapter, respond to the following questions. The section number(s) indicate which part of the chapter is most directly applicable to the particular question:

1. Is the Unified Law on the Boycott of Israel and its related General Principles a treaty? *See* § 8.1 on definitions.

2. There are several categories of treaties. How should this treaty be classified? *See* § 8.1 on classification and § 8.2 on formation/performance.

3. Assume that it is 1955—the year after passage of the Arab League's Unified Law. Saudi Arabia has just adopted the boycott agreement (the Unified Law), which prohibits trade with persons "affiliated with Israel through nationality." Saudi Arabia, however, submits a reservation to the League at the time it registers its consent to accept its obligations. The Saudi version of the Unified Law is a prohibition against trade with "persons of Israeli nationality who are residents of Israel." This language was carefully chosen to avoid any implication of *worldwide* discrimination against Jewish businesses.

Assume that the league's Unified Law is a treaty. Does Saudi Arabia's reservation permit it to become a party to the Unified Law? What test should be used to decide this question? *See* § 8.2 on formation.

4. Assume that the League's boycott agreement was not self-executing. Assume also that one of the States in the Arab League, State X, has a constitutional system like that of the United States. State X's leader must obtain the consent of X's legislative body to enter into certain treaties—but not all treaties. Would that leader be more likely to use an executive agreement or an Article II treaty to implement the boycott? *See* § 8.3 on "United States Treaty Practice".

5. Egypt was a member of the Arab League and a party to the original boycott agreement of 1954. Egypt terminated its participation in the boycott in 1979 (incident to the so-called Camp David agreement described in the background for this problem). Under International Law, did Egypt have a basis for terminating its boycott obligations? *See* § 8.2 on termination/suspension and § 8.2 on invalidity.

■ SUMMARY

1. Under International Law, the term *treaty* is a generic one, describing many forms of international agreements. Legal distinctions as to treaty names or designations relate primarily to the way in which the treaty is made. All such commitments are binding under International Law.

2. Uniform State expectations regarding treaty formation and observance are contained in the Vienna Convention on the Law of Treaties. It defines the term *treaty* as a "written" agreement between states that is governed by International Law.

3. Treaties may be classified as (a) oral or written, (b) bilateral or multilateral, (c) lawmaking or contractual, and (d) self-executing or statements of principle. The difference between a bilateral and multilateral treaty is the number of participants. Unlike law*making* treaties, contractual treaties are not intended to *create* rules of International Law. Self-executing treaties create immediate legal obligations. Some treaties contain only declarations of principle that merely set goals or standards of achievement for the participating States.

4. The treaty process consists of several essential stages: negotiations, ratifications, reservations, entry into force, and registration.

5. The negotiations will hopefully result in the production of a final treaty text—acceptable in principle to all conference delegates. Subsequent State acceptance typically involves a two-stage process. The first stage is provisional acceptance. This means that the final draft is acceptable, in principle, to the treaty drafting participants. The second stage is postconference ratification by each individual participant.

6. A reservation is a limitation on a State's acceptance of the obligations expressed in the final draft of a multilateral treaty. The reserving State expresses its general consent to be bound by the treaty, although its final acceptance is limited by the terms of the reservation. Other States that give their consent, without any reservation, are bound by all the terms of the final draft of the treaty.

7. A reservation must be *compatible* with the object and purpose of the treaty. By permitting reservations, member States thus encourage the widest participation for attaining the objectives of a multilateral treaty.

8. Various conditions may invalidate a treaty, including the use of force. "Invalidity" may also involve the distinction between so-called equal and unequal treaties. Unequal treaties are *imposed* on one of the parties. There is no fair exchange of treaty rights and obligations because one State *must* accept what the other State demands. Under the Vienna Convention on the Law of Treaties, a treaty is invalid when the threat or use of force violates "principles of international law embodied in the Charter of the United Nations." At the close of the Vienna Conference, the participants declared (in a separate document) that economic, military, and political coercion was specifically unacceptable. Not all States adhere to the more specific definition of force in the postconference Declaration.

9. US treaty practice distinguishes between treaties and executive agreements, both of which are equally binding under *International* Law. Under *US* law, the Constitution provides that the president cannot enter into a treaty without Senate approval. The president can nevertheless make an executive agreement without Senate consent. Presidents often obtain some form of congressional approval for such agreements, although none is sought in certain matters that are often not very sensitive exercises of this inherent power.

10. The US Constitution overrides conflicting federal statutes and international treaties. Statutes and treaties, on the other hand, are on equal footing. In the event of a conflict, the latest in time prevails. US courts presume that where the intent of Congress is unclear, its legislation is *not* designed to intentionally violate International Law. Where such intent *is* clear, however, US courts must apply subsequent federal legislation that violates an earlier treaty or customary International Law.

■ PROBLEMS

Problem 8.1 (*§ 8.1 after* Asakura *case*): Refer to the 1980 *Hostage Case* from the International Court of Justice and the 1961 Diplomatic Relations Convention provisions—both set forth in § 7.4 of the text. Answer the following questions, based on the materials in § 8.1:

(1) Did the Diplomatic Convention's referenced articles have to be "self-executing" for the US to claim that Iran breached that treaty?

(2) *Are* those provisions self-executing? Can this be answered by reading the given articles? Based on the *Sei Fujii* and *Asakura* cases, how would you resolve the question of whether the Diplomatic Relations treaty is self-executing?

Problem 8.2 (*§ 8.2 after* Reservations *case*): Article 17(2) of the 1969 Vienna Convention on the Law of Treaties (VCLT) states that when "it appears from the . . . object and purpose of the treaty that the *application* of the treaty *in its entirety* between all the parties is an *essential condition of the consent of each one to be bound* by the treaty, a reservation requires acceptance by *all* the parties" (emphasis supplied). VCLT Article 19(1)(a) provides that the legal effect of a reservation is that it "[m]odifies for the reserving state the provisions of the treaty to which the reservation relates to the extent of the reservation."

Assume the following facts: La Luce del Pueblo—meaning "Light of the People," or LLP—is an ultraradical group of citizens within a hypothetical Caribbean State called Hapha. Last September, Hapha's military leader placed the LLP in charge of guarding some kidnapped US citizens who were being held incommunicado during hostilities with the US. Without authority from the country's leader, some members of LLP decided to mistreat the US citizens. Several of them were beaten. One was brutally murdered. His body was then dumped on the steps of the US embassy in Hapha, where journalists had gathered to learn about the latest developments in the ongoing hostilities.

A number of foreign newspapers printed a picture of the body of the dead US citizen on the US embassy steps. Their news story about the beatings and execution assigned responsibility "to LLP, the zealous group of Hapha idealists who say that they resent the decades of the US dominance in hemispheric affairs." The newspaper account included LLP's statement to these journalists that "we plan, for the benefit of the People's Revolutionary Party (led by Hapha's military leader), to eliminate all US citizens in Hapha who hinder our progress." Subsequently, US citizens were randomly attacked and beaten in Hapha's restaurants and bars. Nationals from other countries were not harmed in these incidents. Hapha's leader denied any involvement with what he characterized as "an idealistic but irresponsible splinter group of radicals that will be dealt with *if found.*" Worldwide media attention now focused

on Hapha and its hostilities with the US on a daily basis.

Some US senators thus stated for the Congressional Record that "Hapha had added genocide to the long list of international obligations breached by Hapha in the last generation. Hapha has failed to adhere to the bilateral treaties between the two nations, to the wishes of the Organization of American States, and to the obvious norms of international behavior." Under the Genocide Convention, the killing of members of a particular ethnic group with the intent to destroy that group is genocide.

Under one of those US-Hapha treaties, murder is an extraditable offense. Last August, the US Department of State demanded that Hapha extradite those responsible for killing the US citizen, so that they could be tried—either in the US or in some international tribunal for the crime of genocide. Hapha refused this extradition request because "those who have killed the US citizen did not commit genocide."

Assume that Hapha, attempting to show its solidarity with the world community, chooses this point in time to become a party to the Genocide Convention. Hapha tenders its consent to the appropriate international authority. It also submits the following reservation: "Hapha hereby adopts the Genocide Convention as binding. Hapha reserves the sovereign right, however, to use *any* means at its disposal to eliminate US threats to Hapha's territorial integrity."

Is it possible for Hapha to tender this reservation to the Genocide Convention? Specifically, is this reservation permissible under the ICJ's *Reservations Case* and the Vienna Convention on the Law of Treaties?

Problem 8.3 (*§ 8.2 after n.22*): In 1980, the Vienna Convention on the Law of Treaties became effective when the minimum number of national ratifications were deposited with the UN. During the negotiating process, US hostages remained captive in the American embassy and other locations in Iran. The US and Iran had no direct diplomatic relations. Algeria assisted US President Jimmy Carter in negotiating a treaty with Iran to secure the liberation of those hostages. The hostages were released in exchange for the release of Iranian assets in the US frozen by Carter near the outset of the crisis. The US also agreed to return assets subject to its control belonging to the family of the former Shah of Iran. Various documents about that treaty and related matters are reprinted in 20 *International Legal Materials* 223–40 (1981). A criticism of the US Department of State's decision *not* to raise the question of force in that treaty process is presented in *Iranian Hostage Agreements*, in the Malawer book, p.27 (cited in note 19 of this chapter).

A very sensitive provision of this treaty required arbitration of any subsequent disputes related to the "Hostage Crisis." This provision precluded the hostages, their families, or any governmental entity from suing Iran in the US, the International Court of Justice, or anywhere else. President Carter's economic sanctions were not working; and he did not want to undertake further military action to retrieve the hostages from Iran after a failed rescue attempt in 1979. Instead, he entered into an executive agreement that resolved this crisis and guaranteed the safety of the hostages. Subsequent suits by several hostages were dismissed by US courts on the basis of the president's agreement not to permit suits against Iran spawned by the hostage crisis.

Assume that the US Senate is debating the propriety of President Carter's negotiations leading to the executive agreement between the US and Iran. The topic of this hypothetical Senate debate is *not* whether the Senate's advice and consent is necessary for the hostage release agreement with Iran. The Senate has decided that the US will not rely on any of its internal laws as a basis for avoiding this treaty's obligations to Iran. There will be no claim that the president exceeded his authority by failing to obtain the advice and consent of the Senate when he concluded the executive agreement with Iran. The Senate has chosen to debate, instead, whether it can avoid the US obligations under the treaty on the basis that the president had to enter into the hostage-release treaty under duress.

Senator Dove represents a number of the senators who do not wish to alter or negate the effect of the president's arrangement with Iran. They do not want to risk renewed hostilities or create the impression that America goes back on its obligations. Dove contends that "there was no physical or economic coercion that forced this powerful nation into President Carter's treaty. It was the *United States* that employed forceful tactics, rather than Iran, when Carter's military rescue mission failed."

Senator Hawk represents the opposing group of senators. She and her colleagues hope to refreeze Iranian money accounts and gold bullion, still within the US or controlled by private US businesses in foreign countries. She wants to renew the Hostage Case litigation in a separate phase in the International Court of Justice. (*See* § 7.4 of this book for excerpts from the ICJ case involving the Court's order that Iran free the US hostages.) Relying on Article 52 of the Vienna Convention on the Law of Treaties, Hawk believes that the ICJ should render an authoritative decision depicting the hostage treaty as invalid on the basis of duress.

Senator Hawk thus contends that "the Iranian treaty would never have seen the light of day if we were not forced into it by the hostage situation. Senator Dove's litmus test for validating the treaty is an imaginary bright line that separates military and nonmilitary coercion in all circumstances. The proper approach, in my opinion, is to invalidate the Iranian deal by distinguishing between *lawful* and *unlawful* coercion—rather than Senator Dove's approach, which isolates military duress [to invalidate the treaty] from nonmilitary duress [whereby the treaty would be unaffected]."

Make the following assumptions: (a) Iran is a party to the Vienna Convention on the Law of Treaties; (b) it did not make any reservations; (c) the hostages have been released, but the Iranian assets are still available for seizure; (d) the Carter hostage release agreement was made after the January 27, 1980 "start" date for the prospective applicability of the VCLT. Two students will present the arguments that Senators Dove and Hawk might use in their senate debate on the applicability of the VCLT. Can the US thus void its treaty obligations to Iran under President Carter's executive agreement?

Problem 8.4 (*§ 8.2 after* Fisheries Jurisdiction *cases*): The US and the hypothetical Latin American State of Estado entered into the 1953 Treaty of Friendship, Commerce, and Navigation (FCN). This general treaty initiated their international relationship and covered a number of details. In the relevant treaty clause, the US agreed that Estado could nationalize American business interests. In return, Estado was required to provide reasonable compensation—defined in the treaty as "the fair market value of all nationalized assets."

The US/Estado relationship turned sour in the 1990s. The government of Estado nationalized a major US corporation's property in Estado, with no compensation. Estado resisted the US claim of entitlement to compensation under the 1953 friendship treaty. Estado's Minister of State issued the following statement:

a fundamental change in circumstances has precluded the continued viability of the 1953 FCN Treaty. The 1974 United Nations Declaration on the Establishment of a New International Economic Order obviously necessitates termination of the compensation requirements of the outmoded US-Estado FCN Treaty [see § 4.4 of this text on the NIEO]. The changed circumstance is that our nation, so rich in natural resources, need no longer fall prey to another nation's multinational enterprises. The United States corporation has plundered untold billions of dollars in excessive profits from the very core of Estado, and all of the profits have been repatriated back into the United States—rather than benefiting the Estado economy. The content of International Law developed by powerful nations over the many centuries before Estado even existed. It is thus a self-perpetuating vehicle, used by countries like the United States, to justify its asserted right to compensation in the amount of the "fair market value" of nationalized property. Due to changed circumstances, Estado may reasonably justifiably its refusal to pay *any* compensation to a corporation that has already acquired much more than it could ever repay to Estado. As a showing of good faith on the part of my Government, Estado will not seek reimbursement in an international forum—settling instead for the fair market value of the nationalized assets, which is only a small fraction of what the United States enterprise has already taken from the people of Estado.

Can Estado properly invoke the doctrine of *rebus sic stantibus* to terminate its treaty obligation to repay fair market value for the nationalization of the US corporation?

Problem 8.5 (*end of § 8.2*): Refer to Problem 8.4 above. Estado later repealed *all* treaty commitments with the US, after the US senators widely condemned its nationalization of the US corporate property. Questions: (1) Is the US now required to perform its obligations under any treaty with Estado? (2) Does the US have any remedies under the Vienna Convention on the Law of Treaties?

■ BIBLIOGRAPHY

§ 8.1 Definition and Classification:

J. Grenville, *The Major International Treaties 1914–45: A History and Guide with Texts* (London: Methuen, 1987)

Nahlik, *On Codification of International Law*, XV *Polish Yearbook of International Law* 103 (1986)

M. Tuscano, *The History of Treaties and International Politics: The Documentary and Memoir Sources* (Baltimore: Johns Hopkins Univ. Press, 1966)

§ 8.2 Formation/Performance/Cessation:

Gamble, *Reservations to Multilateral Treaties: A Macroscopic View of State Practice*, 74 *American Journal of International Law* 372 (1980)

F. Horn, *Reservations and Interpretive Declarations to Multilateral Treaties* (The Hague, Neth.: T.M.C. Asser Inst. 1988)

A. McNair, *The Law of Treaties* (Oxford, Eng.: Clarendon Press, 1961)

Nahlik, *The Grounds of Invalidity and Termination of Treaties*, 65 *American Journal of International Law* 736 (1971)

Note, *Effect of Duress on Iranian Hostage Settlement Agreement*, 14 *Vanderbilt Journal of Transnational Law* 847 (1981)

S. Rosenne, *Breach of Treaty* (Cambridge, Eng.: Grotius, 1985)

S. Rosenne, *The Law of Treaties—A Guide to the Legislative History of the Vienna Convention* (Dobbs Ferry, NY: Oceana, 1970)

A. Vamvoukos, *Termination of Treaties in International Law: The Doctrines of Rebus Sic Stantibus and Desuetude* [Acquiescence] (Oxford, Eng.: Clarendon Press, 1985)

Wehberg, *Pacta Sunt Servanda*, 53 *American Journal of International Law* 775 (1975)

P. Wesley-Smith, *Unequal Treaty: 1898–1997* (rev. ed. Hong Kong: Oxford Univ. Press, 1984)

§ 8.3 United States Treaty Practice:

Glennon, *The Senate Role in Treaty Ratification*, 77 *American Journal of International Law* 257 (1983)

L. Henkin, *Foreign Affairs and the Constitution* (Mineola, NY: Foundation Press, 1972)

Surrency, *How the United States Perfects an International Agreement*, 85 *Law Library Journal* 343 (1993)

§ 8.4 Economic Coercion Case Study:

Areeda, *Remarks on the Arab Boycott*, 54 *Texas Law Review* 1432 (1976)

■ ENDNOTES

1. Comment (2) to Art. 2, Int'l L. Comm'n Commentary on the Vienna Convention on the Law of Treaties, in *Official Documents—United Nations Reports of the International Law Commission*, 61 *Amer. J. Int'l L.* 248, 287 (1967) [hereinafter *Commentaries*].

2. **Harvard study:** *Draft Convention on the Law of Treaties*, 29 *Amer. J. Int'l L.* 652, 712 (Supp., 1935). **Multiple terms:** A comprehensive table depicting these terms, with accompanying details, is available in Myers, *The Names and Scope of Treaties*, 51 *Amer. J. Int'l L.* 574, 576 (1957). **ILC study:** *Commentaries*, Comment (3) to Art. 2, p.288 (cited in note 1 above). **VCLT definition:** The text of this convention is reprinted in 63 *Amer. J. Int'l L.* 875 (1969) and 8 *Int'l Legal Mat'ls* 679 (1969) [hereinafter *VCLT*].

3. UN Gen. Ass. Doc. A/CONF.129/15 of March 20, 1986, reprinted in P. Menon, *The Law of Treaties Between States and International Organizations* 159 (Lewiston, NY: Edwin Mellon Press, 1992) [hereinafter *Organizational treaty*].

4. Gasis, Preface to E. Raftopoulos, *The Inadequacy of the Contractual Analogy in the Law of Treaties* XIII (Athens: Hellenic Inst. Int'l & Foreign Law, 1990) [hereinafter *Inadequacy of the Contractual Analogy*].

5. R. Phillimore, 2 *Commentaries Upon International Law* 99 (3rd ed. London: Butterworths, 1892).

6. *The Public Law View of Treaties in the 19th and the Early 20th Century*, ch. 5, in *Inadequacy of the Contractual Analogy* 151 (cited in note 4 above).

7. Status of Eastern Greenland (Denmark v. Norway) 1933 P.C.I.J., ser. A/B, No. 53.

8. The general rule against creation of third-party obligations is exhaustively examined in *States as Third Parties to Treaties: Formal Prescriptions*, ch. 2, in C. Chinkin, *Third Parties in International Law* 25 (Oxford, Eng.: Clarendon Press, 1993). Potential exceptions are also addressed in A. Verdross, *Volkerrecht* 143–44 (5th ed. Vienna: Springer Verlag, 1964). An English-language statement of the Verdross Position is provided in G.I. Tunkin, *Theory of International Law* 93 (Cambridge, MA: Harv. Univ. Press, 1974) (Butler translation from Russian language) [hereinafter *Tunkin treatise*].

9. P. Reuter, *Introduction to the Law of Treaties* 20 (2d ed. London: Pinter Pub., 1989) (Mico & Haggenmacher translation).

10. *See* text accompanying note 3 above.

11. An account of this event is provided in 4 G. Hackworth, *Digest of International Law* 467 (Wash., DC: US Gov't Print. Off., 1942).

12. *See Commentaries*, Articles 10–12, at 303–13 (*VCLT*, cited in note 1 above). These terms are defined in Articles 9–13 of the *final* text of the *VCLT*.

13. J.L. Brierly, *The Law of Nations* 319–20 (Waldock 6th ed. London: Oxford Univ. Press, 1963) [hereinafter *Brierly treatise*].

14. **Treaty:** Convention on the Prevention and Punishment of the Crime of Genocide of December 9, 1948, 78 UN Treaty Series 277 (1951). **Nonparties:** the US did not become a party until 1986, due to prior senatorial concern about the meaning and application of its various terms.

15. 1 US Code § 112.

16. **States:** *VCLT*, Art. 80.1 (cited in note 2 above). **Organizations:** *Organizational treaty*, Art. 81.1 (cited in note 3 above).

17. **Grotius:** 2 *De Jure Belli Ac Pacis* [The Law of War and Peace] 394 (Kelsey translation, Wash., DC: Carnegie Endowment for Int'l Peace, 1925). **E. de Vattel:** 3 *Le Droit de Gens ou Principes de la Loi Naturelle* [The Law of Nations or Principles of Natural Law] 165 (Wash., DC: Carnegie Endowment for Int'l Peace, 1916 reprint of 1758 treatise). **American author:** H. Halleck, *International Law* 196 (San Francisco: Bancroft, 1861).

18. **Treaty of Paris:** An account of this event and its related treaty validity problems is provided in the *Brierly treatise*, at 332–33 (cited in note 13 above). **Treaty of Versailles:** This treaty and its consequences are described in C. Fenwick, *International Law* 531–32 (4th ed. New York: Appleton, 1965) (Fenwick translation from the French) [hereinafter *Fenwick treatise*]. **Hitler treaty:** A detailed account of this event is provided in Von Glahn, *Law Among Nations* 581 (6th ed. New York: Macmillan, 1992).

19. Chiu, *Comparison of the Nationalist and Communist Chinese Views of Unequal Treaties*, in J. Cohen (ed.), *China's Practice of International Law: Some Case Studies* 241–42 (Cambridge, MA: Harv. Univ. Press, 1972) (footnotes omitted). A brief assessment and criticism of the Soviet writers on this subject is available in S. Malawer, *Soviets and Unequal Treaties*, in *Essays on International Law*, at 101 (Buffalo, NY: Hein, 1986) [hereinafter *Malawer book*].

20. Fisheries Jurisdiction (U.K. v. Iceland), 1973 I.C.J. Rep. 1, 14.

21. **Communist/African position:** An account of the varied perspectives of the participants is available in Kearney & Dalton, *The Treaty on Treaties*, 64 *Amer. J. Int'l L.* 495, 532–35 (1970) [hereinafter *Treaty on Treaties* article]. **"Force" left undefined:** *Commentaries*, Art. 49 [now Art. 52], Comment (3), p.407 (*VCLT* cited in note 1 above).

22. UN Doc. A/CONF. 39/26, contained in *Documents of the Conference*, p.285, May 22, 1969. The text is reprinted in 8 *Int'l Legal Mat'ls* 733 (1969).

23. Houben, *Principles of International Law Concerning Friendly Relations and Co-operation among States*, 61 *Amer. J. Int'l L.* 703, 725 (1967).

24. North Atlantic Coast Fisheries Arbitration, Permanent Court of Arbitration No. VII (1910), 11 *Royal Inst. Foreign Affairs* 167 (1932).

25. Honduras v. Nicaragua, 1960 I.C.J. Rep. 192 (Judgment of Nov. 18, 1960).

26. Case Concerning the Temple of Preah Vihear (Cambodia v. Thailand), 1962 I.C.J. Rep. 6 (Judgment of June 15, 1962).

27. *Fenwick treatise*, p.531 (footnote omitted) (cited in note 18 above).

28. *See Proposed Article 13, Report of the International Law Commission Covering Its First Session*, contained in UN GAOR, 4th Session, Supp. No. 10, Doc. A/925, p.8 (1949).

29. *See Treaty on Treaties*, pp.516–17 (cited in note 21 above). This proposal is therein reported by members of US Department of State participants in the VCLT.

30. **Spectrum of views:** The quoted characterizations are contained in the *Brierly treatise*, p.338 (cited in note 13 of this chapter) [clearly reasonable]; Briggs, *The Attorney General Invokes Rebus Sic Stantibus*, 36 *Amer. J. Int'l L.* 89, 93 (1942) [alleged principle]; M. Akehurst, *A Modern Introduction to International Law* 139 (6th ed. London: Allen & Unwin, 1987) [unsuitable]. **Chinese view:** This excerpt is from *International Trade Treaties and Agreements* (Peking: 1958) and is reprinted in 2 J. Cohen & H. Chiu (ed.), *People's China and International Law*, p.1257 (Princeton: Princeton Univ. Press, 1974) [hereinafter *People's China*].

31. Lissitzyn, *Treaties and Changed Circumstances (Rebus Sic Stantibus)*, 61 *Amer. J. Int'l L.* 895 (1967).

32. *Commentaries*, Art. 59 [now Art. 62], p.428–29 (cited in note 1 above).

33. *See* The Free Zones of Upper Savoy and the District of Gex (Switzerland v. France), 1929 P.C.I.J., ser. A, No. 22 & ser. A/B No. 46, 2 World Court Rep. 448 (1971).

34. Translation provided in 2 J. Cohen & H. Chiu, *People's China* 1166, 1167 (cited in note 30 above).

35. Electricity Company of Sopia and Bulgaria, (Belgium v. Bulgaria), 1939 P.C.I.J., ser. A/B, No. 77, p.64 [dissenting opinion of Judge Anzilotti].

36. The US government's brief is reprinted in US Department of State, *The Legality of United States Participation in the Defense of Viet-Nam*, 60 *Amer. J. Int'l L.* 565, 585 (first quote) and 577 (second quote) (1966). For additional detail, *see* American Society of International Law, The *Viet-Nam War and International Law* (Princeton: Princeton Univ. Press, 1968) (three volumes).

37. Appeal Relating to the Jurisdiction of the ICAO Council (India v. Pakistan), 1972 I.C.J. Rep. 46 (Judgment of Aug. 18, 1972).

38. *Commentaries*, Art. 58 [now Art. 61], Comment (2), p.427 (cited in note 1 above).

39. *See* the English case of West Rand Central Gold Mining Co. v. The King, [1905] King's Bench 391 [England] (treaty obligations favoring conquered State continue).

40. Lissitzyn, *Treaties and Changed Circumstances (Rebus Sic Stantibus)*, 61 *Amer. J. Int'l L.* 895 (1967).

41. *See* American Law Institute, *Restatement Second of the Foreign Relations Law of the United States*, § 153, Illustration 1 (St. Paul: West, 1965). (Unlike the prior *Restatement*, the new *Restatement Third* does not use illustrations in the replacement § 336.)

42. **Judicial denial:** *Commentaries*, Comment (1) to Art. 50 [now Art. 53], p.409 (cited in note 1 above). **Impossible:** *Tunkin treatise*, p.149 (cited in note 8 above).

43. Clark v. Allen, 331 U.S. 503, 67 S.Ct. 1431, 91 L.Ed. 1633 (1947).

44. The process is recounted in Bestor, *Advice from the Very Beginning, Consent when the End is Achieved* in L. Henkin, M. Glennon & W. Rogers, *Foreign Affairs and the U.S. Constitution* 6 (Ardsley-on-Hudson, NY: Transnat'l Pub.: 1990).

45. An analysis of the drafters' intent is available in Henkin, *International Concern and the Treaty Power of the United States*, 63 *Amer. J. Int'l L.* 272 (1969).

46. L. Henkin, *Foreign Affairs and the Constitution* 175 (Mineola NY: Foundation Press, 1972) (footnotes omitted).

47. Lissitzyn, *The Legal Status of Executive Agreement on Air Transportation*, 17 *J. Air L. & Comm.* 436, 439–42 (1950) (footnotes omitted).

48. The relevant section of the Case Act is contained in 1 US Code § 112b(a).

49. Dames & Moore v. Regan, 453 U.S. Rep. 654, 682, 101 S.Ct. 2972, 2988, 69 L.Ed.2d 918 (1981) (noting that the president's power to settle claims regarding international relations had been exercised for 200 years with congressional acquiescence) (emphasis supplied).

50. **Switzerland:** Librairie Hachette, S.A. v. Societe Cooperative, XXV *Annuaire Suisse de Droit International* 239 (1968). **Belgium:** Minister for Economic Affairs v. S.A. Fromagerie Franco-Suisse, 1972 *Common Market Law Rep.* 330. **Mexico:** Constitution, Art. 133.

51. 354 U.S. 1, 77 S.Ct. 1222, 1 L.Ed.2d 1148 (1957).

52. *Reid*, 354 U.S. 18, 77 S.Ct. 1231.

53. South African Airways v. Dole, 817 Fed.Rptr.2d 119 (D.C. Cir. 1987).

54. Schroeder v. Bissell, 5 Fed.2d 838 (D.C. Conn. 1925).

55. Missouri v. Holland, 252 U.S. 416, 40 S.Ct. 382, 64 L.Ed. 641 (1920).

56. *See* Doyle, *International Boycotts*, in V. Nanda, *The Law of Transnational Business Transactions* 13–14 (New York: Clark Boardman, 1984).

57. **Laws punishing compliance:** *see* Fenton, *United States Antiboycott Laws: An Assessment of Their Impact Ten Years after Adoption,* 10 *Hastings Int'l & Comp. L. Rev.* 211 (1987). **Arguable applicability to all persons of Jew**ish **faith:** 3 A. Lowenfeld, *International Economic Law: Trade for Political Ends* 314 (New York: Clark Boardman, 1983).

CHAPTER NINE

Arbitration
and Adjudication

CHAPTER OUTLINE

■ INTRODUCTION

Earlier chapters dealt with the resolution of international disputes by a variety of processes.
The initial definitional chapter and the chapter on States depicted various political, economic,
and military modes of dispute resolution. The chapter on international organizations covered certain
bodies that function to promote peaceable dispute
resolution—the UN Security Council being a prime
example. Chapters 7 and 8 also dealt with dispute
resolution, in both its positive and negative forms.
States routinely resort to diplomacy—and occasion-

ally less agreeable approaches—in the treaty process,
where unequal treaties have been forced on other
States to resolve disputes.

This chapter examines the arbitration and adjudication alternatives for resolving international disputes. The essential objective will be to develop a
sense of when, where, and why States are willing to
rely on some third party or entity to resolve their
disputes. For good reasons, private individuals and
enterprises typically opt for an arbitral method to resolve cross-border disputes involving international
trade.

After an overview of the international arbitration
and litigation models, the materials in this chapter
will proceed through the maze of global, regional,
and national court alternatives for resolving contemporary international problems.

■ 9.1 ARBITRATION/ADJUDICATION BLUEPRINT

Introduction

■ *Who* can pursue a remedy for a violation of International Law?

■ *Where* can a violation of international law be adjudicated?

■ *Should* it be arbitrated instead?

■ *What* are the *available institutions* involving
third-party dispute resolution as an alternative to
war?

■ *How feasible* is a litigious mode of dispute resolution in a case involving international relations between States? Between individuals? Between a

State and an international organization? In cases involving sensitive matters, as opposed to those of lesser importance to national interests?

Chapter VI of the UN Charter provides the usual starting point for any International Law or International Relations course dealing with peaceful settlement of international disputes. Under Article 33 of the UN Charter, the national parties to any dispute "shall, first of all, seek a solution by negotiation . . . arbitration, judicial settlement, resort to regional agencies or arrangements, or any other means of their own choice." Other provisions in the Charter then deal with continuing threats to international peace and the role of agencies such as the Security Council (as addressed in § 3.3 of this book on the UN).

One State's pursuit of *litigious* remedies against another State is typically complicated by developments in their international relations. The allegedly offending State will not readily admit its liability, even in the clearest of circumstances. In the case of a conspicuous breach, an apology or promise that the offending act will not be repeated may be unacceptable for political or security reasons. For example, the US never admitted international liability when an American U-2 reconnaissance aircraft violated Russian airspace in 1960. The plane was shot down two thousand meters within the Soviet border, but the pilot claimed that he had merely strayed off course (*see Powers* case in § 6.4). In 1983, the Soviet Union did not admit liability when a Russian pilot shot down a Korean commercial aircraft that strayed off course over Russian territory. Nearly three hundred civilian passengers and crew were killed in the name of territorial sovereignty. The Soviets claimed that warnings were given, and that this response to an intrusion of its airspace did not involve the use of "excessive force."

States are understandably reluctant to admit that they have breached International Law. National representatives must then consider whether it is practical to resolve disputes through arbitral or adjudicatory bodies. The litigation option has not been a viable alternative in situations involving *sensitive* disputes or open hostilities. The States involved must first consent to being sued in international tribunals (as analyzed in § 9.4 of this chapter). Unfortunately, the docket of the UN's International Court of Justice is the envy of most national judges, who are far busier in terms of their comparative volume of cases.

As discussed below, arbitration has been the preferable option for those disputes that are susceptible to resolution by more formal modes.

The common questions regarding the resolution of disputes by a "third party," that is, a person or entity *not* a party to the dispute, will be at the core of this chapter's analysis of litigation in International Law. Arbitration will be addressed at the outset, because more international disputes have been resolved through arbitral tribunals than by international courts. Judicial remedies follow.

The term *arbitration* is used here, in a generic sense, referring to a variety of modes of dispute resolution not involving a *judicial* body such as the UN's International Court of Justice, or its International Criminal Court. Further detail is provided about arbitration/adjudication distinctions in § 9.3 on arbitral classifications.

Arbitration: Historical Development

The small city-States of ancient Greece used arbitration as a method for resolving their disputes. A treaty in 445 B.C. grew out of the Peloponesian War between Athens and Sparta. These city-States agreed not to resort to war, as long as the other was willing to resolve a dispute via arbitration. A violation of this treaty subsequently resulted in a ten-year war, whereafter the parties once again agreed not to engage in war—and to submit their future disputes to arbitration.[1]

Modern international *commercial* law is based on the trade practices that developed in medieval Europe by merchants engaged in international trade. Their standard expectations were called the "Law Merchant." This body of law was created and developed by specialized tribunals in various Mediterranean ports—where private merchants resolved their domestic and international business disputes via a form of arbitration. The Law Merchant thus flourished in the twelfth century Italian city-States, later spreading to other commercial centers. The customary practices developed by these tribunals were ultimately incorporated into the commercial laws of many nations.

International arbitration had its own "Dark Ages," however, almost until the nineteenth century. The famous Jay Treaty (Convention of Amity) of 1794 between Great Britain and the United States established a regime whereby an equal number of British and American nationals were selected to serve on an arbitral commission. Its mandate was to settle matters arising out of the Revolutionary War that remained unsettled by British/American diplomacy.[2] The same two countries further encouraged the modern use of international arbitration in their 1871 Treaty of Washington Arbitration. The US claimed that Great Britain had violated the neutrality rules arising under customary international practice. Great Britain had aided the South during the American Civil War by building ships for the Confederate Navy. The arbitral tribunal thus ordered Great Britain to compensate the US for its ensuing loses. When Great Britain complied, there was a renewed interest in using inter-State arbitration to settle international disputes. The national practice of inserting arbitration clauses into treaties increased dramatically. Arbitration began to flourish, with the establishment of some 200 arbitral tribunals that would decide hundreds of cases.

Russia's Czar Nicholas then decided to invite State members of the international community to meet at the Netherlands city of The Hague. The national delegates thus attended the Hague Peace Conferences of 1899 and 1907. The resulting *1899* Hague Convention for the Pacific Settlement of International Disputes recognized arbitration as "the most effective and at the same time the most equitable means of settling disputes which diplomacy has failed to settle." The *1907* Convention for the Pacific Settlement of Disputes was the first multilateral treaty to provide that "International Arbitration has for its object the settlement of disputes between States by judges of their own choice and on the basis of respect for law." Before (and since) these Conventions, most of the arbitrators were not "judges" but heads of State, academics, national agencies, and politicians.[3] It was this Hague Conference process that produced the Permanent Court of Arbitration in 1907—still operable, but without a significant caseload for a half-century. This "Court" will be addressed later in this chapter.

Articles 12 and 13 of the Covenant of the League of Nations "mandated" that League members would not go to war if the subject of their dispute had already been submitted to arbitration. Three months were to elapse, *after* an award, before one State could resort to war against another. This Covenant also created the first "World Court"—the Permanent Court of International Justice (PCIJ) at The Hague. As a result, resort to international arbitration declined—from the PCIJ's inception in 1920

until after World War II. The number of treaties containing an arbitration clause, however, or alternatively requiring the State parties to resort to the PCIJ, continued to climb.[4]

With establishment of the second "World Court"—the International Court of Justice (ICJ) at The Hague in 1945—the State members of the international community once again envisioned the submission of legal disputes to a *permanently* constituted judicial body, as opposed to the *ad hoc* arbitrations typical of inter-State alternative dispute resolution. The foremost collection of data regarding international arbitrations has been compiled by Professor A.M. Stuyt of Nijmegan University in the Netherlands. His *Survey of International Arbitrations* lists nearly 180 inter-State arbitrations between 1900 and 1945. In the last half of this century, roughly the same period of years (1945–present) produced only 43 inter-State arbitrations.[5]

A growing class of international disputes has nevertheless been submitted to various permanent arbitral tribunals. While States generally moved away from *inter-State* arbitration, other forms of international arbitration involving private parties began to flourish, as described in § 9.3 below.

Adjudication: Historical Development

Before the twentieth century, international disputes were usually resolved by diplomatic negotiation, occasionally by arbitration, and often by war. Negotiations did not always subdue the use of force—which unfortunately remained the ultimate instrument of diplomacy. Arbitration was not a good vehicle for preventing the escalation of international disputes. If States chose arbitrators on an *ad hoc* basis, it was to handle a specific problem *after* the dispute arose. This would effectively permit the stronger State to dictate terms that were not a fully bargained-for exchange. Furthermore, States rarely consented to arbitrating their more sensitive problems in the absence of a forced compromise.

Some national leaders wanted a more durable dispute resolution alternative. The Latin American participants in the Hague Conferences proposed, and then implemented, a judicial response to the perennial problems with inter-State dispute resolution. They established the Central American Court of Justice in 1908, the first regional and international court. It ceased to function, however, in 1918. One reason was the forecast that the French conceived League of Nations and the Permanent Court of International Justice (PCIJ) would supplant any need for *regional* international courts. A global court would, it was hoped, shift the resolution of inter-State disputes from the battlefield to the courtroom. The States creating the PCIJ wanted it to play a role in the achievement of world peace through law. Some believed that this court would function as a judicial buffer between adversaries who would otherwise resolve their disputes in a military arena. Others anticipated that such a world court would be, at the very least, a neutral forum for settling certain disputes. A number of national leaders, including US President Woodrow Wilson, believed that an international court could positively influence national adherence to International Law.

The concept of a *world* (as opposed to *regional*) Court evolved through two phases, each commonly associated with a particular international organization: the former Permanent Court of International Justice (PCIJ) and the current International Court of Justice (ICJ). The PCIJ was *not* an organ of the League, however. A State desiring to use it would enter into a treaty with another State. Several hundred bilateral treaties among the various nations of the world conferred jurisdiction on the PCIJ. On the other hand, States who joined the UN are automatically members to the companion treaty—the Statute of the International Court of Justice. (While they are not *required* to use the ICJ, this involuntary nexus with the Court's Statute affirmed the judicial existence of the latter world court.)

The PCIJ was the first permanently constituted dispute resolution mechanism available to *all* nations of the world. In the case of States unwilling to actually litigate their differences, organs of the League of Nations could (and did) request "advisory" opinions from the PCIJ. The PCIJ thus had the power to theoretically apply International Law to situations where a potentially liable State was unwilling to appear in judicial proceedings as a defendant. From 1922 to 1940, the PCIJ heard twenty-nine cases between adversaries who litigated their cases in the court. It also rendered twenty-seven advisory opinions (a special form of "adjudication" analyzed in § 9.4).[6]

Two paradoxes contributed to the demise of the PCIJ. First, while this court was sponsored by the League of Nations, it was not an official organ of the League. Second, while US President Wilson played a fundamental role in developing international support for the League, the US did not join the League and never appeared as a litigant in the PCIJ. The Senate blocked US participation in the League. Due to the rampant post–World War I isolationist sentiment, senators feared *any* international alliances because any one of them might one day draw the US into a second world war.

The outbreak of World War II in 1939 destroyed the potential effectiveness of the PCIJ. The court conducted its last public sitting in that year—when most of the judges fled to Geneva to take advantage of Switzerland's wartime neutrality.

The dream of a global judicial body was not totally shattered by the abrupt reality of war. In 1943, the "Four Powers" (China, the Soviet Union, Great Britain, and the US) determined that another global international organization should replace the League of Nations. The possibility of another world court was also rekindled by Great Britain's invitation to a group of International Law experts who met in London. These experts agreed that another global court should be created. It would have to be a completely new court in order to diffuse the criticism of the earlier PCIJ—perceived by many States as a European institution designed by European jurists to dominate the legal affairs of other nations.

■ 9.2 ALTERNATIVE DISPUTE RESOLUTION

A variety of alternative dispute resolution (ADR) mechanisms are available in International Law that are less formal than either arbitration or court proceedings. These forms include the "diplomatic" means of settlement: negotiation, inquiry, mediation, conciliation, and minitrial. (By contrast, a judicial hearing in an international court would be the most formal method of peaceful dispute resolution.)

Disputes are an inevitable part of International Relations. The emergence of modern International Law in the seventeenth century (*see* Peace of Westphalia in § 1.3) was not accompanied by either a world government or a discontinuation of the use of force by the State members of the international community. As that community grew in size, there was less to share and there were more pressures on the ability to peaceably cohabit the planet—in terms of land mass, airspace, oceans, and natural resources. How to resolve the related disputes is the objective of these alternatives to war. Exhibit 9.1 depicts the

EXHIBIT 9.1 United Nations Directives on Alternative (Nonmilitary) Dispute Resolution

UN Charter Article 2.4	The most fundamental norm of the entire Charter: States shall "refrain in their international relations from the threat or use of force" to settle their disputes
UN Charter Article 2.3	States "shall settle their international disputes by peaceful means in such a manner that international peace and security . . . are not endangered"
UN Charter Article 33.1	"The parties to any dispute . . . shall, first of all, seek a solution by negotiation, enquiry, mediation, conciliation, arbitration, judicial settlement . . . or other peaceful means of their own choice"
1970 General Assembly Resolution 2625(XXV)	Regarding the application of Article 2.3: States "shall accordingly seek early and just settlement of their international disputes by negotiation, enquiry, mediation, conciliation. . . ."

relevant UN Charter-based dictates in the area of alternative dispute resolution.

Negotiation

The negotiation form of ADR differs from the other informal modes because its conduct is completely controlled by the immediate parties to an existing dispute. The negotiation of disputes is discussed generally in § 7.1 on diplomatic relations. Negotiations between States are normally conducted through diplomatic channels. The negotiations may be accomplished by heads of State, ambassadors, draft treaty conference participants (§ 8.2), respective foreign ministers, and other designated representatives.

The parties may also *consult* with one another in an attempt to avoid a dispute. The goal of consultation is to analyze and discuss a proposed course of action, potentially harmful to another State, before it occurs. This form of negotiation facilitates problem-solving before any adverse action has been taken. The acting State might thus alter its proposed action in a way that accomplishes its objectives, but with a less significant impact on the consulted State. After the 1982 Falkland Islands War between Argentina and Great Britain, these States hoped to avoid unnecessary confrontations due to the presence of their respective military forces in the same area. In 1990, they entered into an Interim Reciprocal Information and Consultation System. It provides that their consultation system will govern

"movements of units of their Armed Forces in Areas of the South West Atlantic. The aims of this [conciliation] system are to increase confidence between Argentina and the United Kingdom and to contribute to achieving a more normal situation in the region [including a direct communication link]."[7]

Inquiry

Unlike direct negotiations, the other ADR modes involve the assistance of a third party to resolve an international dispute.

An inquiry, for example, occurs when someone who is not a party to the dispute attempts to provide the disputing parties with an objective assessment. A continuing stalemate may lead to more confrontational modes for settling the contest. Thus, the presence of a third party may facilitate the injection of a more balanced approach to resolving the dispute before it erupts.

The term *inquiry* is commonly used in two senses. The broader connotation refers to the process itself—whereby a court, arbitral body, international organization, or individual tries to resolve a dispute between other States or entities. The narrower connotation of this term, as used in this section of the book, refers to some specific institutional arrangement (rather than arbitration or some other ADR mode) requiring an independent investigation of the underlying facts of the disputed issue.[8] The 1899 Hague Convention for the Pacific Settlement of International Disputes (*see* § 9.1) thus contains

358 FUNDAMENTAL PERSPECTIVES ON INTERNATIONAL LAW, Second Edition

six articles calling on States to establish commissions of inquiry for fact-finding in international disputes.

In the famous *Dogger Bank Inquiry*, a group of Russian war vessels were en route from the Baltic Sea to the Far East in 1904, in order to engage in the war with Japan. The Russian ships steamed directly into a fleet of Japanese fishing vessels (at the so-called Dogger Bank in the North Sea). The Russian fleet assumed that it was under attack by Japanese war vessels, which were reportedly in this area. It fired on the fishing vessels, sinking one, damaging others, and killing or wounding a number of Japanese civilian fisherman. England then made plans to intercept the Russian fleet. France intervened diplomatically, convincing the Russians and Japanese to establish a commission of inquiry under the Hague Convention paradigm. Five admirals from Russia, Japan, France, Austria-Hungary, and the United States spent two months hearing evidence from witnesses. The Commission found that the Russian admiral had no justification for opening fire—although the report was worded so as to not discredit the Russian admiral. Russia received the Commission's findings and decided to pay damages as a result of the conduct of this Russian squadron.[9]

Mediation

Mediation is another ADR device invoking the assistance of an "outsider" who is not a party to the dispute. Unlike the commission of inquiry, which is basically a fact-finding tool, the mediator is typically authorized to advance his or her own proposal for actually resolving the dispute. Nothing is binding about the mediator's role—otherwise he or she would be an arbitrator or judicial officer seized with the power to require a particular result. Thus, there is no prior commitment by the parties to accept the mediator's proposal.

The mediator makes his or her proposals informally, based on information supplied by the parties. The mediator does not undertake an independent investigation (as would a commission of inquiry). Where negotiations are deadlocked, the mediator can attempt to move the parties in the direction of at least considering his or her proposal. Such proceedings are normally informal and private, unlike an arbitration or judicial proceeding with formal procedures for taking evidence from witnesses in an open hearing. The Red Cross often acts in this capacity, in those conflicts where the parties are unlikely to negotiate face-to-face. Algeria served in the

capacity of mediator during the Iran/US Hostage Crisis in 1979–1980.

"Good offices" is a variant of the mediation technique. A third party communicates the statements of the disputing parties to one another. This is a useful technique when the dispute involves States that do not maintain diplomatic communications (*see* Systemic Overview in § 7.2). Good offices may also involve the "outsider" inviting the disputing parties to a settlement conference, or undertaking other steps to facilitate their communications. This theme was the focal point of the 1936 Inter-American Good Services and Mediation Treaty, as well as the 1948 American Treaty on Peaceful Settlement of Disputes (the "Bogota Treaty"). The UN Secretary-General has often used his position to facilitate inter-State settlement of disputes through the "good offices" of the UN.

Conciliation

The so-called "textbook" definition of conciliation was provided by the late Professor Clive Parry of Cambridge, England. It is the "process of settling a dispute by referring it to a commission of persons whose task it is to elucidate the facts and (usually after hearing the parties and [then] endeavoring to bring them to an agreement) to make a report containing proposals for a settlement, but not having the binding character of an [arbitral] award or [court] judgment."[10]

The conciliator is designated by the potential litigants, who may already be involved in a formal arbitral or judicial process, to help them reconcile their differences. Attempts to reconcile the parties consists of the "outsider's" depicting the negative aspects of State A's position to State A, so that its approach will become more reasonable. The disputing parties have often resorted to litigation when one of them is unwilling to listen to what the other has to say.

Conciliation places third-party dispute resolution assistance in a more formalized setting than negotiation or mediation. Like the commission of inquiry, a conciliation commission *may* engage in a fact-finding role. Yet, a conciliation commission normally attempts to promote a resolution. This is a step beyond fact-finding inquiries, although less formal than an arbitration or judicial proceeding.

In 1922, the League of Nations General Assembly resolved that States should conclude treaties requiring the submission of disputes to conciliation commissions—unless the parties were already willing to resolve the dispute via arbitration or by litigation in the Permanent Court of International Justice. Some twenty treaties thus contained a conciliation requirement—including the famous Locarno agreements between Germany, on the one hand, and on the other Belgium, France, Czechoslovakia, and Poland. The so-called Locarno Treaty was then incorporated into the League's 1928 General Act for the Pacific Settlement of Disputes. League members thus established either *ad hoc* or permanent conciliation commissions to act, unless they submitted their disputes to the PCIJ or to binding arbitration. Nearly 200 such treaties were concluded between the two World Wars.

Conciliation is no longer a creature of bilateral treaties. Certain multilateral treaties thus provide for conciliation as an alternative for the adopting States and international organizations in various regions. These include the following: 1957 European Convention for the Peaceful Settlement of Disputes; 1965 Washington Convention for the Settlement of Disputes Concerning Investments Between States and Nationals of Other States; 1963 Charter of the Organization of African Unity; 1975 Convention on the Representation of States in Their Relations with International Organizations of a Universal Character; 1978 Vienna Convention on Succession of States in Respect of Treaties; 1981 treaty establishing the Organization of Caribbean States; and 1982 UN Convention on the Law of the Sea.[11]

Although these treaties provide for conciliation, not all are effective. The 1957 European Convention for the Peaceful Settlement of Disputes has not come into force, because too few States have decided to ratify it. The Arbitral Tribunal of the Organization of African Unity (OAU) is another tribunal that never materialized. Instead, OAU members continue to rely on traditional diplomatic negotiations to settle disputes.

Minitrial

While quite similar to conciliation, the so-called minitrial is the latest approach to international dispute resolution. It is not a real trial. The parties confront one another in a similar context, however, and must verify their positions before a neutral third party. The "judge" is typically an expert in the particular field, and not necessarily a sworn judicial officer or lawyer. These "trials" often take place before negotiators who are senior employees of the respective parties. Each negotiator, in turn, then proceeds to illustrate the weaknesses to his or her employer's position—long before a costly arbitration or judicial proceeding at some point in the future.

Italy's Mauro Rubino-Sammartano, who practices in French and Italian courts, illustrates the successes with this comparatively new device in his book on international arbitration:

> Xerox Corporation entered into a distribution agreement with a Latin American company. . . . [T]he distributor construed the contract as applying not to one line of computers only, but to all the computers sold by Rank Xerox throughout Latin America rather than in a more limited territory. One year after proceedings had been started before the California courts [in the US], an extremely quick mini-trial took place (Rank Xerox presenting its case in 1 hour and forty minutes), which produced a positive result ending in a promptly performed settlement.
>
> Another positive mini-trial is the Telecredit-TRW dispute concerning trademarks, conducted before the parties' negotiators and a neutral advisor; the dispute was settled 60 days after completion of the mini-trial.
>
> A third positive mini-trial is reported as having taken place between a German manufacturer and an American distributor. Settlement was reached after a presentation of [just] one hour by each party.[12]

One must, of course, recognize some inherent limitations with this new ADR device. Goodwill is an essential element in such a process. Its absence has frustrated ADR schemes in virtually every legal system to date. On the other hand, large corporate enterprises have little to lose by such devices as—opposed to the time and expense associated with the more formal resolution mechanisms addressed in the remaining sections of this chapter.

■ 9.3 ARBITRAL CLASSIFICATION/ TRIBUNALS

Arbitration is a comparatively formal mode of international dispute resolution, in contrast to the devices addressed in § 9.2. States and private parties rely on a third party to actually resolve the dispute via a binding arbitral award. This section of the book covers the basic categories of arbitration, selected arbitral tribunals, and their fundamental purposes.

Classification

Arbitration may be classified as follows: temporal nature of the tribunal (*ad hoc* versus permanent); nature of the parties (inter-State or otherwise); composition of the tribunal (who decides?); and category of dispute (some tribunals handle only certain issues, such as investment disputes).

Ad Hoc/Permanent Arbitrations have been historically *ad hoc*—the parties to an arbitration must negotiate to determine *what* will be decided and *who* will do the deciding. They must agree on the general terms and limitations that they will impose upon the arbitrators. Such *ad hoc* arbitration had often occurred after the dispute has arisen, with no foreseeable basis for objective procedures that are satisfactory to all concerned.

The terms of an international arbitration agreement may thus leave much to the discretion of the arbitrator and the participants. In 1988, for example, an international arbitration panel ruled in Egypt's favor in a border dispute with Israel, leaving the parties to work out the details of actually determining the precise boundary line. Such freedom of choice in fashioning the ultimate resolution is not available when a court, permanently established, decides such disputes. The parties have less flexibility when they submit their case to a standing court that typically resolves all issues presented in the pleadings.

A permanently operating *arbitral* tribunal has its own set of rules and procedures. They are established *before* the particular dispute arises. In contrast, mutually acceptable arbitration procedures may be tailored, after the fact, to match the circumstances of the particular case. This flexibility avoids the jurisdictional objections that have plagued courts such as the UN's International Court of Justice since its inception. On the other hand, the over-whelming percentage of parties fulfill their international obligations established by binding arbitration—which also requires consent for the tribunal to act.[13]

Permanently established "institutional" arbitration tribunals provide predictability and stability in resolving business disputes. As aptly depicted by Professor Stephen Troope of McGill University in Canada:

> Since the 1960s, the international business community has manifested an increasing interest in arbitration as a dispute resolution mechanism. Concurrent with this increased attraction to arbitration has been the emergence and growth of more and more arbitral institutions . . . providing facilities and organisational mechanisms for the arbitral resolution of commercial disputes . . . [and] with the increasing scale of international trade, arbitration has very much come into its own. . . .
>
> Because of the potential application of contemporary commercial arbitration in many economic contexts . . . one can understand the superficial attraction of institutional arbitration which provides a stable organisational base for an arbitration, a staff trained to administer arbitration and more importantly, a set of pre-established procedural rules which should prevent renegotiation during a heated dispute, thereby helping to ensure that the arbitration goes forward even in the face of a recalcitrant party. It is asserted, therefore, that institutional arbitration enhances the values of certainty and predictability.[14]

Nature of the Parties The historical form of arbitration involved primarily inter-State disputes. Arbitral models flourished near the turn of the twentieth century. A prime example is the Permanent Court of Arbitration (PCOA), a product of the 1899 Hague Peace Conference. Various nations met in Holland to explore ways to achieve peace and disarmament. They adopted the Convention on the Pacific Settlement of International Disputes. It dealt with a variety of settlement devices, including the PCOA. The treaty participants viewed the PCOA as a method for implementing their goal of peaceful dispute resolution. It commenced operations in 1913 and still functions today at its seat in The Hague.

The PCOA is not a court, however. Its "judges" are mostly lawyers who have expertise in international business matters and are willing to travel. They serve on small arbitration panels. Each of the seventy-five participating countries appoints four individuals to provide arbitration services for a fixed number of years. The national parties to a dispute choose several of these experts to serve on a panel that will consider their particular problem.

The PCOA's panels were busiest before World War I. The postwar creation of the Permanent Court of International Justice in The Hague diminished national attention to the PCOA. Prior to 1931, the PCOA heard twenty-four cases. Since then, it has heard three—two of them inconsequential, and the other being the Iran-US Claims Tribunal (which the PCOA's 1990 Annual Report claims as its third case). The current use of panels of several judges of the International Court of Justice has further limited the need for this arbitral tribunal (discussed in § 9.4 on ICJ chambers).

The limited use of the PCOA does not mean that it has no utility. Its continuous availability makes it a convenient forum for implementing the details of major treaty agreements. The sixty-five-year-old PCOA was immediately available to carry out the details of the US/Iran 1980 Hostage Treaty. *Ad hoc* types of arbitration were not viable alternatives, due to the very sensitive atmosphere surrounding the hostage crisis. The PCOA was a somewhat untapped resource that could immediately begin to consider the difficult compensation issues arising out of this dispute. This arbitration was no small undertaking since the crisis so deeply divided the rivals.

Another "States-only" arbitral tribunal was established by the Charter of the Organization of African Unity (OAU). It is the OAU's Commission of Mediation, Conciliation and Arbitration, seated in Addis Ababa, Ethiopia. Its twenty-one members have "jurisdiction" (noncompulsory) to resolve any inter-State dispute referred to it by the parties, or by certain governmental entities of the OAU or its State members. The essential role of the OAU Commission is to facilitate alternative dispute resolution mechanisms between the various African States.

The flexibility of modern dispute resolution procedures supports arbitration on bases other than just between States. International arbitration between States achieved its heyday in the first half of the twentieth century. The occurrence of inter-State arbitration has significantly declined since World War II, however.[15] The growing infrastructure of the increasingly diversified community of nations has not provided the type of stability necessary for States to arbitrate their disputes.[16]

Contemporary "international" arbitrations typically occur between a private individual or corporation and a State, *and between* private persons, corporations, and international organizations. This flexibility may thus encourage State treaty parties to provide for virtually all such categories of arbitration in the same international agreement. The 1987 France-United Kingdom Channel Tunnel Treaty expressly authorizes the reference of disputes to arbitral tribunals for disputes *between*: (a) the State parties; (b) States and concessionaires; or (c) just concessionaires. All public and private entities thus have access to a convenient dispute-resolution mechanism without regard to the status of any particular tunnel-service provider. There are no sovereign immunity problems for concessionaires, no potential sovereignty objections between the States involved in the tunnel's operation, and no need for a business entity to first enlist the assistance of its home State in order to present a claim against an international person (for example, France or the United Kingdom). A private (nongovernmental) corporation may then arbitrate a dispute with its own home State, without resorting to the traditional International Law requirement that it seek sovereign representation on the international level. This procedure thus avoids the awkward scenario when the contractor's dispute is with it own country. The major *multilateral* treaties that provide for this form of mixed State–private party arbitration are the New York Convention, the Inter-American Convention on International Commercial Arbitration, and the Washington Convention.[17]

Composition/Category A functional classification of modern arbitration involves the nature of the respective parties and who/where they choose for the resolution of their dispute. While some treaties still provide for inter-State arbitration, the most reassuring results are attributed to other categories of arbitration. The common ones include (a) mixed international arbitration, (b) private disputes involving a public interest, and (c) administrative arbitration.

In "mixed" international arbitration, one party is a State and the other is either a private party or business entity. A classic instance is the Algiers Accords—the agreement creating the Iran-United States Claims Tribunal in 1981. The US hostages being held in Iran were released, and Iran was able to regain control over some of its assets that were frozen at the inception of the hostage crisis. US individuals and corporations were thus provided with a means of redress against Iran. The Tribunal then began its task of resolving claims seeking Iranian funds, which were disbursable as a result of its decisions. Due to the animosity between the parties and the high claims at stake, the Tribunal's lasting value was rather evident. It was unlikely that a negotiated settlement between the Us and Iran could have been reached without this independent mechanism for "post-hostility" claims adjudication—typical of postwar tribunals formed to resolve private claims against State parties.[18]

In 1991, the UN Security Council established the UN Compensation Commission (UNCC), headquartered in Geneva. Its mandate is to process, determine, and pay any claims against Iraq arising from the Persian Gulf War. This tribunal was created under the Council's Chapter VII powers, whereby the UN Charter was designed to control threats to peace. The UNCC's function is to decide the amount and validity of claims arising on or after August 2, 1990—the date of Iraq's invasion of Kuwait. It has issued approximately twenty decisions, awarding settlements in claims involving serious personal injury or death that resulted from Iraq's annexation of Kuwait.

Another form of international arbitration is "commercial" arbitration between business enterprises. While there are a number of such tribunals, several bear special mention. The International Court of Arbitration of the International Chamber of Commerce (ICC Court) is a prominent arbitral organization based in Paris. It has resolved commercial disputes since 1923, and currently receives approximately 350 cases per year. Under Article 1.1 of the ICC's Rules of Conciliation and Arbitration, the "function of the Court is to *provide for* the arbitration of business disputes of an international character. . . ."[19] The parties submit their requests for dispute resolution assistance to the Secretariat of the ICC Court of Arbitration. The "court" then delegates the power to arbitrate matters referred to it. The Secretariat appoints either one or three indi-viduals to consider the dispute, depending on its complexity. These individuals sit on the ICC National Committee, located in each of the participating countries.[20]

Another active commercial arbitral body is the International Centre for Settlement of Investment Disputes (ICSID). The 1966 Convention on the Settlement of Investment Disputes between States and Nationals of Other States established the ICSID,[21] which is sponsored by the UN's International Bank for Reconstruction and Development located in Washington, D.C. This tribunal was designed to develop confidence in private foreign investment through arbitration. It differs from other international arbitral bodies, such as the Hague Permanent Court of Arbitration, because the use of ICSID facilities is not limited to governmental parties. An individual or corporation may arbitrate directly with a foreign State (that is, "mixed" arbitration). Thus, an individual does not need to seek and obtain governmental or diplomatic assistance from his or her own country to arbitrate a claim. Like the ICC International Court of Arbitration, the ICSID does not directly arbitrate disputes at its headquarters. It maintains panels of legal and business experts who are willing to arbitrate claims submitted to it. They arbitrate many contract disputes between private corporations and the foreign States with which they deal.[22]

There are also "special purpose" commercial arbitral bodies specializing in specific areas of law or trade. The World Intellectual Property Organization (WIPO) is a specialized agency of the UN with headquarters in Geneva. It maintains panels for resolving international problems involving alleged copyright, patent, and trademark infringement claims. This body (with revised ADR rules that became effective in 1994) may thus facilitate a particularly expeditious and suitable means for accommodating the special problems associated with intellectual property disputes. A patent or trademark holder may thus have instant access to a body of intellectual property experts. A claim that a foreign company is making or marketing the owner's product, without entering into a licensing arrangement with the patent/trademark owner, may be lodged with the WIPO. The owner does not have to pursue either diplomatic or judicial remedies, which would depend on the willingness of the owner's home State to one day pursue such claims.

"Administrative" arbitration typically involves the inner workings of international organizations. In the case of *Yakimetz v. The Secretary-General of the United Nations*, a UN staff member from the Russian delegation at the UN in New York applied for asylum in the US. He also requested a career appointment at the UN, based on his excellent service record. When his request was denied, he filed an administrative action in the United Nations Administrative Tribunal. The UN Tribunal decided that the

Secretary-General's decision was "flawed," although it would not reverse the UN's employment denial.[23]

Selected Arbitral Tribunals

Given the number and scope of contemporary arbitral tribunals, complete coverage is not possible in an introductory text on International Law. Exhibit 9.2 does provides a snapshot, however, regarding existing arbitral tribunals and the roles they serve in international dispute resolution.

EXHIBIT 9.2 Selected International Arbitral Tribunals

Tribunal	Location/HQ	Dispute Category/Function
UN Compensation Commission	Geneva, Switzerland	Mixed arbitration/UN Security Council organ resolves individual claims against Iraq due to invasion of Kuwait
Court of Arbitration of International Chamber of Commerce (ICC)	Paris, France	International business between private persons or corporations/ICC delegates requests for ICC arbitration to local experts on National Committees in participating States
International Centre for Investment Disputes	Washington, USA	Mixed arbitration/individual or corporation may deal directly with State/builds confidence in private foreign investment
Iran/US Claims Tribunal	The Hague, Netherlands	Mixed arbitration/resolves claims from 1979–80 Hostage Crisis/hears claims of US nationals v. Iran
UN Administrative Claims Tribunal	New York, USA	Administrative arbitration/resolves claims between UN and its employees
Law of the Sea Tribunal	Hamburg, Germany	Inter-State/after 11/94 effective date LOS treaty, will be established to resolve treaty disputes (*see generally* § 6.3) involving the treaty "Area"
Chambers of the International Court of Justice	The Hague, Netherlands	Inter-State/parties may request special 3-judge chamber to arbitrate disputes (*see* § 9.4)
International Labour Organization Administrative Tribunal	Geneva, Switzerland	Inter-State and administrative/resolves disputes regarding international labor standards/jurisdiction extended to various UN agency labor practices

EXHIBIT 9.2 *(continued)*

Tribunal	Location/HQ	Dispute Category/Function
World Trade Organization	Geneva, Switzerland	International business and inter-State/panels determine whether a State's businesses are complying with "GATT" requirements (*see* § 13.3)
London Court of International Arbitration	London, England	International business/between private persons or corporations/highly reputed center for commercial arbitration
Stockholm Chamber of Commerce Arbitration	Stockholm, Sweden	International business/between private persons or corporations/highly reputed center for commercial arbitration

■ 9.4 INTERNATIONAL COURT OF JUSTICE

Introduction

The dream of world peace linked to adjudication is not new. The medieval Florentine poet Dante proposed a world State under a central court of justice in his "*De Monarchia.*" The twentieth century was the first millennium to produce a world organization dedicated to peace. The premier "World Court"—ironically designated the *Permanent* Court of International Justice—was spawned by the first World War, but effectively uprooted by the second.

The dream of a global judicial body, which might substitute the courtroom for the battlefield, was not completely shattered by the abrupt reality of World War II. In 1943, the "Four Powers" (China, Soviet Union, United Kingdom, United States) determined that another global international organization should replace the League of Nations—also the descendant of a prior World War. The possibility of a second World Court to replace the earlier Permanent Court of International Justice began with the UK's invitation to a group of International Law experts to confer in London. They agreed that another global court should be created. This would be a completely new court, thereby diffusing the criticism of the previous World Court: that it was a European institution designed by European jurists to dominate the legal affairs of the larger community of nations.

In 1944, the Four Powers published their proposals about world peace. These were ultimately debated during the 1945 UN development conference in San Francisco. These meetings forged the principles now contained in the UN Charter and its annexed *Statute of the International Court of Justice.* Contrary to the approach taken by the League of Nations, UN participants decided that the powers of the new Court must be directly incorporated into the UN Charter. The status of the International Court of Justice would thus be on a par with the other major organs of the UN (*see* Exhibit 3.3 in § 3.3).

This section describes the contemporary operations of the International Court of Justice (ICJ)—what it is, and is not, designed to do.

Charter Provisions

The UN's founding members decided to express a "constitutional" basis for the ICJ directly within the text of the UN Charter. This dovetailed the international organization and its new World Court—rather than maintaining a loose "association" between the League of Nations and the *distinct* Permanent Court of International Justice (PCIJ).[24] Contrary to popular belief, the PCIJ was *not* a part of the League of Nations. The ICJ, on the other hand, is the judicial arm of the UN. It shares responsibility with the other major UN organs for monitoring national observance of the principles set forth in the UN Charter.

Charter Article 95's description of the ICJ as the UN's "principal" judicial organ did not mean that other judicial organs would be developed or incorporated into a worldwide hierarchy—with the ICJ at the apex. The Charter did not prevent States from

The International Court of Justice in the Peace Palace at The Hague, in the Netherlands.

"entrusting the solution of their differences to other tribunals." Unlike the ICJ, however, any regional international tribunals were not to be formally linked to UN operations.

The *UN Charter* sets forth the general functions of the Court in Articles 92 through 96. The *Statute of the International Court of Justice* contains the procedures for submitting and resolving national disputes. The following materials survey the UN Charter provisions on the Court, summarize the Court's functions under its statute, and analyze how the Court's functions have been affected by State practice that developed after the Charter materialized in 1945.

The UN Charter provides that: (1) all State members are automatically parties to the Statute of the International Court of Justice; (2) members promise to comply with the decisions of the Court; and (3) the Security Council may undertake enforcement measures if this promise is breached. To encourage national use of the ICJ, Article 93.1 of the Charter requires all State members to become "*ipso facto* [by joining the UN] parties to the Statute of the International Court of Justice." This statute is often referred to as being "annexed" to the Charter. The drafters wanted the Charter and the ICJ's Statute to be jointly adopted by all States that would join the UN. This Statute, discussed below, became

The judges of the International Court of Justice seated for proceedings in the Peace Palace.

operative in 1951. Several States that were *not* UN members (for several decades after it came into existence) initially became parties to the ICJ Statute but not to the UN Charter (Liechtenstein, San Marino, and Switzerland—only the latter is not a current UN member).

Under Article 94.1 of the Charter, each UN member "undertakes to comply with the decision of the International Court of Justice in any case to which it is a party." This is a fundamental requirement of any organized judicial system. While the judgments of the ICJ have been honored by most State parties to its litigation, some States have ignored its judgments. And, as usual, journalists and certain commentators who concentrate on these negative aspects of the UN's judicial process may have misinterpreted the conduct of several scofflaws as a fatal blow to the continuing willingness of most States to abide by ICJ judgments—where they have consented to the jurisdiction of the Court. Of course, the majority of States have not consented to this form of the Court's jurisdiction, discussed below in this section. That limitation on the use of the

Court is *not* evidence that consenting parties have failed to abide by its judgments.

There are, of course, some conspicuous examples of State defiance of ICJ decisions: Libya disobeyed the Court's order to turn over the two Libyan terrorists allegedly responsible for blowing up Pan Am flight 103 over Lockerbie, Scotland in 1988 (*see* § 6.4). South Africa refused to honor the Court's "advisory" order in the 1971 *Namibia Presence* case to terminate control of the area, South West Africa, that is now the independent State of Namibia. (The Court's "advisory" jurisdiction is discussed below.) In the 1973 *Fisheries Jurisdiction* cases, the ICJ ordered Iceland and the United Kingdom to negotiate an equitable solution to foreign fishing rights in the international waters near Iceland's coast (*see* § 8.2). This matter was not seriously negotiated and has not been resolved. In the 1980 *Hostage Case*, Iran refused to release the US and Canadian diplomats held hostage in Tehran. And from 1984 to 1988, the US refused to participate in, or to honor, the ICJ's judgments in the *Nicaragua* case (discussed below).

Defiance does not go unnoticed under the UN Charter. Charter Article 94.2 provides that if "any party to a case fails to perform the obligations incumbent upon it under a judgment rendered by the Court the other party may have recourse to the Security Council, which may, if it deems necessary, make recommendations or decide upon measures to be taken to give effect to the judgment." Thus, a State may notify the Security Council when another State has failed to comply with any Charter obligations.

The Council has occasionally referred cases to the ICJ. But the Council has never undertaken *effective* enforcement action after an ICJ judgment. By the early 1950s, a handful of States had failed to perform their obligations as determined by the Court. Although the Charter does not specify *what* measures may be taken in this instance, the Security Council could have devised and announced post-judgment compliance measures.

The Security Council formulated what was probably its most significant (although unsuccessful) ICJ enforcement measure after the Court rendered its opinion in the 1971 *Namibia Presence* case (*see* § 2.3). The Court ordered South Africa to terminate its control of South-West Africa (Namibia). The Council then ordered South Africa to comply with

the ICJ's judgment. It also ordered other States to abstain from dealing with South Africa in any way that was inconsistent with the ICJ's divestment opinion. South Africa ultimately agreed to cooperate with the UN. Two decades later, South West Africa (Namibia) finally achieved its independence from South Africa.

The Security Council has had very limited experience with enforcing judgments—and little incentive to develop enforcement measures. Under UN Charter Article 36.3, "legal disputes should as a general rule be referred by the parties to the International Court of Justice in accordance with the provisions of the Statute of the Court." States do not, as a general rule, refer *significant* legal disputes to the ICJ. Most States litigating disputes in the ICJ have thus complied with its judgments. The result has not been particularly adverse to the critical political or economic interests of the litigants.

UN Trust Fund Access

One reason for limited utilization of the ICJ is the financial condition of the UN's smaller States. As noted in § 7.2, many of them do not have the resources to maintain a diplomatic presence in many other States. Many cannot operate any embassy *anywhere*, due to quite limited financial resources. The same problem has historically limited their access to the ICJ as a dispute resolution center. It is costly to maintain a local presence at The Hague (Netherlands), where the ICJ is located, even for the limited purpose of filing pleadings, conducting the research necessary to adequately participate in judicial proceedings on a distant continent, and paying the cost of scientific studies and expert testimony in the Court's proceedings. A partial remedy has been proposed at the UN.

In UN Secretary-General Boutros Boutros-Ghali's 1992 report on preventive diplomacy, he recognized that while the Court's docket has grown it is an underutilized resource. He thus urged UN members to "support the Trust Fund established to assist countries unable to afford the cost involved in bringing a dispute to the Court. . . ."[25] This is an inducement to States to submit their disputes to the UN's judicial organ.

This fund constitutes a form of international legal aid, established by Secretary-General Javier Perez de Cuellar in 1989. The UN's Secretary-General has an institutional obligation to promote the peaceful settlement of disputes. This fund is financed by voluntary contributions from the comparatively prosperous States, international organizations, and nongovernmental organizations. Thirty-four States had contributed over a half million dollars to the fund as of the Secretary-General's 1992 annual report. Chad is one State that disclosed its ability to participate in ICJ proceedings due to the availability of this fund (during a public hearing at the ICJ on July 14, 1993, in the ICJ *Territorial Dispute Case* between Libya and Chad).

While some commentators have focused on this fund as a device for creating more work for the Court, the ICJ itself is not an intended beneficiary. A permanent fund is preferable to the common scenario whereby needy States must seek financial assistance from other States. The latter may, of course, exact a future concession for such grants or loans.

As reported by a staff member of the ICJ, the fund's resources were essentially depleted (after only two successful applications). Thus, "new incentives are needed to raise the level of contribution by wealthier states and enable a larger number of less fortunate states to settle their disputes peacefully in the World Court."[26] It is unfortunately evident that smaller State access to the ICJ is not a priority of the larger States. The penchant for redistributing the world's wealth was discussed in Chapter 6 on the UN's two-decade drive to effectuate the Convention on the Law of the Sea in 1994. The UN still has a long way to go in terms of currying support in favor of funding the UN Secretary-General's Trust Fund.

ICJ Statute

Earlier materials in this section of the book summarized the application of the basic UN *Charter* provisions on the ICJ, as well as the novel Trust Fund approach to increasing State access to the ICJ for economically deprived States. The various provisions of the companion "Statute of the International Court of Justice" are examined in the following materials—regarding judges, functions of the Court, the "optional" clause, and the ICJ's "advisory" jurisdiction.[27]

Judges

The International Court of Justice is composed of fifteen judges, each from a different UN member-State. This number is obviously much smaller than the total membership of the UN. Recurring suggestions that there be more judges have not been

adopted, primarily because it would not be practical to conduct the Court's business with a larger number of jurists. Also, the cost of additional judges would not be supported by the Court's limited case load to date.

The UN Secretary-General invites State members who are parties to the Permanent Court of Arbitration to submit names of judicial candidates (*see generally* § 9.3 on PCOA). There are triennial elections of five judges to the Court, each of whom serves a nine-year term. They are then elected by the UN General Assembly and Security Council.

Article 2 of the Statute of the International Court of Justice establishes the eligibility requirements for its judges. They must be "independent judges, elected . . . from among persons of high moral character, who possess the qualifications required in their respective countries for appointment to the highest judicial offices, or are jurisconsults [learned in International Law] of recognized competence. . . ." About one-third of the judges actually have been judicial officers in their countries. Most have been law professors and practicing lawyers. Some of the judges have been senior government administrators, and two were heads of State.[28]

Unlike other branches of the UN and some regional tribunals, the ICJ does not consist of judges who represent their governments. They must act independently. Thus, under Articles 16 and 17 of the statute, judges cannot "exercise any political or administrative function, or engage in any other occupation of a professional nature." They cannot "act as agent, counsel, or advocate in any case." Since the judges are *not* national delegates, their respective governments cannot dismiss them from the ICJ for their judicial opinions. Only the Court itself can vote to dismiss a judge. It has never done so.

Function

The Court's basic function is to hear and determine all cases involving interpretations and applications of the principles set forth in the UN Charter. Under the ICJ Statute's Article 36.1, its jurisdiction consists of "all cases which the parties refer to it and all matters specially provided for in the Charter of the United Nations or in treaties. . . ."

Under Article 38 of the ICJ Statute, the Court executes its judicial function by applying the following sources of International Law to disputes submitted for its consideration: (1) treaty interpretation; (2) ascertaining the content of international customs practiced by the various members of the international community; (3) general principles of law used in civilized nations; (4) national and regional court decisions; (5) scholarly writings of experts in International Law; and (6) other sources, including the resolutions of international organizations (*see* Article 38 analysis in § 1.4 of this book).

The original UN members designed the ICJ to promote the peaceful settlement of international disputes—a function that the Court's early case law executed in a fitting manner. In the Court's first contentious case involving the 1948 *Corfu Channel* litigation, the United Kingdom sued Albania when UK warships hit mines laid in Albania's territorial waters. The Court decided that the UK had a right to navigate through these waters, thus holding Albania responsible for the damage to the UK war vessels. Hostilities then ceased. In the 1950 *Protection of French Nationals and Protected Persons in Egypt* case, France sued Egypt for harming French citizens residing in Egypt. After the suit was filed, Egypt rescinded its objectionable measures. The ICJ discontinued the proceedings because Egypt's remedy had satisfied France's claim. The Court was apparently headed for a significant future.

The manner in which the Court was constituted by the UN Charter and its companion ICJ Statute created special jurisprudential problems. As stated by Nigeria's former Judge and President of the ICJ, T.O. Elias: "The ICJ or World Court is unique in a number of ways and, as such, generates no international legal system of its own." Unlike national tribunals, the ICJ has no bailiffs or prison system to ensure compliance with its interim orders and judgments.[29] There was no one to go to Libya, for example, when the Court ordered Libya to turn over the two Libyan citizens who allegedly bombed Pan Am flight 103 over Lockerbie, Scotland, in 1988. Even if Libya had turned over those individuals, there would be no UN jail at the disposal of the ICJ—necessitating reliance, instead, on the aid of some State member to carry out such an order.

Another significant jurisprudential problem is that the ICJ is a trial court. It is *not* an appellate tribunal that can rely on an extensive judicial record from a lower court to refine the issues in the case. As aptly noted by Professor Thomas Franck of New York University on this inherent limitation:

the Court, as both trial court and court of ultimate jurisprudential recourse, is in a far

more difficult position than domestic [national] courts, where it is customary to make fact-determination the principal concern of the lower court while leaving it to a higher tribunal to devote itself almost exclusively to the jurisprudential issues applicable to predetermined facts. Moreover, to this burden of [the ICJ's resulting] duality should be added the disadvantage of distance. That The Hague is very far . . . [from] the forests of El Salvador or the jungles of Thailand and the desert of Western Sahara, is self-evident. Less immediately apparent is the . . . Court's cultural diversity, [because] few members can draw upon personal experience to imagine the substantive realities as to which the pleadings establish contradictory assertions. . . . In the [ICJ's] Peace Palace, the judges . . . cannot . . . reach into their life experiences to weigh the comparative probabilities. Even where contradictory witnesses are concerned, how can they rely on socio-culturally conditioned instinct to feel who is likely to be lying . . . when the witnesses are from a culture that is wholly unfamiliar to most members of the Court?[30]

While the ICJ has always functioned as a trial court, it could arguably undertake a form of judicial review of UN agency actions. In the so-called *Libya* (*see* § 10.7) and *Bosnia* (*see* § 11.1) cases, these countries claimed that the ICJ must review and overrule Security Council sanction decisions allegedly beyond the Council's powers under the UN Charter. In national courts, such as those of the US, balance-of-power principles unquestionably authorize judicial review of the constitutionality of executive action. The ICJ has never reviewed a sanction decision by the Security Council, however, for the similar purpose of determining its "constitutionality" under the UN Charter.

"Optional" Clause

Compulsory Jurisdiction Member States do *not have to* submit their disputes to the ICJ. All State members of the UN are automatically parties to the ICJ Statute, per Article 93.1 of the UN Charter. Its terms "dictate" as follows: "All Members of the United Nations are *ipso facto* parties to the Statute of the International Court of Justice." That rather commanding language does *not* mandate that all disputes be resolved by the ICJ, however. This "requirement" is one of form rather than substance. Those who created the ICJ anticipated that sovereign States would not be willing to vest the ICJ with the full judicial power needed to require them to appear when sued by another State. The prospect of a distant tribunal rendering judgments against the more powerful nations of the world was too myopic to *require* the members to submit to the compulsory jurisdiction of the Court in all cases. If such a mandate had been placed in the Charter or ICJ Statute, the UN would be a much smaller organization than it is today.

There are several ways in which States may expressly accept the compulsory (mandatory) jurisdiction of the ICJ. Article 36 of the ICJ Statute provides that the Court will have jurisdiction to hear and decide cases against a defendant State in the following circumstances:

- In "cases which the parties refer to it" [for example, by inserting a clause in a treaty specifically referring disputes to the ICJ; *or*]

- "States parties to the present Statute may . . . declare [*unilaterally*, by an appropriate filing with the UN Secretary-General that the filing State] recognizes as compulsory . . . and without special agreement [that is, a mutually agreeable treaty] the jurisdiction of the Court in all legal disputes concerning:

(a) the interpretation of a treaty;
(b) any question of international law;
(c) the existence of any fact which, if established, would constitute a breach of an international obligation;
(d) the nature or extent of the reparation [such as damages] to be made for the breach of an international obligation."

The ICJ Statute's provisions for "compulsory jurisdiction" depends completely on the will of States to accept the Court's power over them—in the specific circumstances expressed in their various Declarations of Acceptance. The methods for exercising these alternatives are conveniently summarized by Renata Szafarz, Professor of International Law at the Polish Academy of Sciences, in his book on the Court's compulsory jurisdiction:

The consent may be expressed *ad hoc* once a dispute has arisen. It may also be expressed *post hoc* by a party to the dispute when the case has been brought before the court by another party. Finally, consent may be expressed *ante hoc*, in advance, with reference to all legal disputes to be submitted in the future or to certain categories of dispute. The latter form of jurisdiction is usually, though not very precisely, termed compulsory or obligatory jurisdiction. Since the compulsory jurisdiction of the ICJ results either from the acceptance by states of the so-called optional clause . . . or from the acceptance of judicial clauses contained in treaties a considerable majority of states have accepted the compulsory jurisdiction of the ICJ, at least to some extent . . . even though . . . there should be more than the present 54 declarations accepting the optional clause and that there should be fewer reservations to [such] judicial clauses.[31]

Statute's Optional Clause This new UN blueprint for a judicial dispute resolution mechanism was a realistic compromise. The organization's judicial process could not mandate *compulsory* jurisdiction for all of the UN's sovereign members all of the time. They could not realistically be forced to agree to submit all future disputes to resolution by this new and untested tribunal. But the potential UN members could be given the *option* to do so, by giving them the prerogative of accepting the ICJ's jurisdiction. The compromise was thus a peculiar and unique application of the "compulsory" jurisdiction commonly exercised by *national* courts. States joining the UN would automatically "accept" the ICJ Statute, although it contained a "compulsory jurisdiction" clause. That clause would be triggered, however, only by the joining State's subsequent decision to actually subject itself to the jurisdiction and judgments of the UN's Court.

The unique limitation was that compulsory jurisdiction would materialize *only* when a UN member expressly consented to the Court's power to act. This so-called "optional clause" of the ICJ Statute, contained in Article 36.2, was thus drafted to provide that the "state parties to the present Statute *may at any time* declare that they recognize as compulsory . . . the jurisdiction of the Court in all legal disputes. . ." [emphasis supplied]. This limitation on the Court's jurisdiction to hear a case is another application of the treaty reservation theme examined in § 8.2 of this book. Limiting reservations would thus be compatible with the underlying compromise, designed to avoid an "all or nothing" decision about joining the UN. Lacking this option, the more powerful nations of the world would not be likely to swell the membership ranks of the new world organization—which otherwise provided a number of other devices for the peaceful settlement of international disputes.

The "compulsory" jurisdiction to hear cases is the most controversial and misunderstood feature of the ICJ's jurisdiction. States have unilaterally tendered a variety of acceptances—very *narrow* acceptances of the ICJ's compulsory jurisdiction, very *broad* ones, and others that linger between these two poles. Egypt's declaration of 1957 was probably the narrowest—accepting ICJ jurisdiction *only* in the event of an international dispute directly involving its operation of the Suez Canal. The broadest acceptance comes from countries like Nicaragua, which have submitted unconditional unilateral acceptances of the ICJ's jurisdiction to hear *any* case involving Nicaragua as a party. That country has little to lose in a forum where it can theoretically "square off" with the major powers of the world. Somewhere in between lies the declaration accepting ICJ jurisdiction on specified terms, such as those that function for a limited period of years (subject to renewal). Under Article 36.3, national declarations thus opting to accept the compulsory jurisdiction of the ICJ may be made (1) unconditionally, (2) for a limited time, or (3) on the condition of reciprocity.

Jurisdiction to Determine Jurisdiction A common, but *non*statutory, limitation on the ICJ's power to act arguably conflicts with the express terms of the ICJ Statute. State practice since the promulgation of the Statute's final draft in 1951 has created yet another obstacle to realization of the dream of substituting the courtroom for the battlefield. Article 36.6 states that in "the event of a dispute as to whether the Court has jurisdiction, the matter shall be settled by the decision of the Court." This provision was interpreted by the ICJ in the Court's 1955 *Nottebohm* case (set forth in the text of § 4.2). The relevant passage addresses the virtually global practice that a court has the jurisdiction to determine its own jurisdiction, when one of the parties questions the existence of judicial jurisdiction. Pursuant to the ICJ articulation of this seminal legal doctrine:

Paragraph 6 of Article 36 merely adopted . . . a rule consistently accepted by general inter-

national law . . . [whereby] an international tribunal has the right to decide to [resolve questions about] its own jurisdiction and has the power to interpret for this purpose the instruments which govern jurisdiction. This principle, which is accepted by general international law in the matter of arbitration, assumes particular force when the international tribunal . . . is an institution which has been pre-established by an international instrument defining its jurisdiction and regulating its operation, and is in the present case the principle judicial organ of the United Nations. . . . The judicial character of the Court and the rule of general international law referred to above are sufficient to establish that the Court is competent to adjudicate on its own jurisdiction in the present case.[32]

Notwithstanding the above ICJ passage, the ICJ does *not* possess the sole power to decide its own jurisdiction. The major powers tended to limit their declarations, when they filed acceptances of the Court's "compulsory" jurisdiction over them. They specified that *they*—and not the ICJ—would decide whether the Court could hear and decide international disputes naming them as a defendant.

Try to imagine a national judge's reaction if a defendant told the judge that the court did not have the power to act, that the *defendant* had decided this question, and that the judge could do nothing about it. This is exactly what many States have done when invoking the optional clause by so limiting their "acceptances." The ICJ Statute does not *require* a State to accept the Court's jurisdiction. The optional clause has been used by States to limit the Court's power to proceed with cases filed against them. This is the reason why the Court has been powerless to act in so many widely publicized instances.

France's acceptance (which was withdrawn in 1974) is a good example. The French acceptance "does not apply to differences relating to matters which are essentially within the national jurisdiction *as understood by the Government of France* [emphasis supplied]." In this instance, France extracted the language from Article 2.7 of the UN Charter—that nothing "contained in the present Charter shall authorize the United Nations to intervene in matters which are essentially within the domestic jurisdiction of any state. . . ." France (and a number of other nations) have thus used Article 2.7 to avoid ICJ disputes by invoking this "right" to classify a particular case against the defendant State as one that is "domestic" rather than "international" in scope.

Reciprocity The "reciprocity" basis for limiting national acceptances of the ICJ's compulsory jurisdiction recognizes that not all States are going to tender their recognition of the Court's jurisdiction on the identical basis. Thus, a potential defendant State might consider it unfair for a plaintiff State—which has previously tendered a *narrower* acceptance of the Court's jurisdiction—to sue in circumstances whereby the plaintiff State would not be similarly amenable to the Court's jurisdiction.

Assume that France and Norway independently tendered their separate Declarations of Acceptance of ICJ jurisdiction some years ago. Each thereby agreed, prior to any dispute arising between them, to accept the ICJ's power over them and to be bound by its judgments. Neither country did so, however, on an *un*conditional basis. Each accepted the so-called "compulsory" jurisdiction of the ICJ with a limitation. France's hypothetical declaration consents to jurisdiction in all matters, with one exception not included in Norway's acceptance: France's reservation was that "France will *not* appear as a defendant in cases involving armed conflicts between France and any another country." Assume that Norway's prior declaration also accepted the court's jurisdiction, but with a different reservation: "Norway accepts the Court's compulsory jurisdiction on the condition of reciprocity."

In this hypothetical situation, Norway attacks France. France then sues Norway in the ICJ, possibly for the psychological value of media reports depicting France as the victim in this armed conflict. The more limited nature of France's acceptance of the Court's compulsory jurisdiction would be borrowed by Norway to avoid litigating this dispute. Norway's previous acceptance was limited by its conditional acceptance of jurisdiction "on the condition of reciprocity." France previously limited its submission to the ICJ's jurisdiction by not consenting to (and effectively repressing) the Court's power to hear cases involving France as a party to an armed conflict. Norway may invoke the narrower acceptance of a State that is suing Norway. Norway can therefore substitute France's comparatively limited acceptance of the Court's jurisdiction. France could

avoid the same suit, if it had been filed by Norway. The Court would have to dismiss France's case against Norway. Norway's "reciprocity"-based acceptance of the Court's jurisdiction would permit Norway to invoke France's "armed conflict" reservation to the Court's jurisdiction.

The following ICJ case illustrates the problems spawned by national declarations containing individual reservations arguably not contemplated by the drafters of the ICJ Statute. This case demonstrates how both the "reciprocity" and the "domestic jurisdiction" limitations may deprive the ICJ of its fundamental judicial power to decide whether it can hear a case that arises under International Law.

From 1885 to 1909, the Norwegian Government borrowed money from French sources. Norway's loans were secured by bank notes, wherein the government promised to repay the loans in gold. In 1914 (when World War I began in Europe), Norway wanted to retain its gold reserves. It therefore suspended the convertibility of its banknotes into gold for an indefinite period. Norwegian law provided that when creditors refused to accept payment in Bank of Norway notes (rather than the promised gold), Norwegian debtors could postpone payment of their loans in gold. French citizens were unable to obtain their repayment in gold, as promised under the express terms of the loans to Norway.

The French government suggested that this dispute be submitted to either an international commission of financial experts or any mutually acceptable arbitral body; and, alternatively, to the International Court of Justice. Norway consistently refused all of these alternatives on the basis that this matter should be heard only in Norwegian courts. Norway considered this problem to be a local matter involving no more than an alleged breach of contract that was governed by the local laws of Norway. France ultimately filed this case in the ICJ. In its application for relief, the French government sought a judgment that Norway's loans should be discharged only by payment in gold as promised.

The ICJ did not reach the merits of France's case. The Court did not have the jurisdiction to hear this particular case. Its inherent power to proceed was vitiated by the combined effect of France's "domestic jurisdiction" reservation and Norway's "reciprocity" reservation. The opinion of the *majority* of the judges discusses why the ICJ did not have the power to act. Judge Lauterpacht's *concurring* opinion agreed with the result reached by the majority of the judges (that the court lacked jurisdiction). He based his conclusion on different footing—that France's purported submission to the compulsory jurisdiction of the court was illusory (a rather daunting theme that continues to plague the Court to this day).

Reading both opinions in this case will reveal how national limitations on the power of the ICJ to hear international disputes have frustrated the goals of the Statute of the International Court of Justice, as well as the full utilization of the Court's resources:

CASE OF CERTAIN NORWEGIAN LOANS

France v. Norway
International Court of Justice, 1957
1957 International Court of Justice Reports 9

[Author's Note: The emphasis in certain paragraphs is supplied by the author.]

[*Opinion.*] MAJORITY OPINION OF THE COURT

The Application [by France for a judgment against Norway] expressly refers to Article 36, paragraph 2, of the Statute of the Court and to the acceptance of the compulsory jurisdiction of the Court by Norway on November 16th, 1946, and by France on March 1st, 1949. The Norwegian Declaration reads:

I declare on behalf of the Norwegian Government that Norway recognizes as compulsory ipso facto and without special agreement . . . *on condition of reciprocity*, the jurisdiction of the International Court of Justice in conformity with Article 36, paragraph 2, of the Statute of the Court, for a period of ten years as from 3rd October 1946.

The French Declaration reads:

On behalf of the Government of the French Republic, and subject to ratification [which was later given], I declare that I recognize as compulsory ipso facto and without special agreement . . . *on condition of reciprocity*, the jurisdiction of the International Court of Justice . . . for all disputes which may arise [unless] the parties may have agreed or may agree to have recourse to another method of peaceful settlement. This declaration does *not apply* to differences relating to *matters which are essentially within the national jurisdiction* [of France] *as understood by the Government of the French Republic.*

. . .

The Norwegian Government maintained that the subject of the dispute was within the exclusive domain of the municipal [internal] law of Norway, and that the Norwegian Government relied upon the reservation in the French Declaration [excluding] matters which are essentially within the national jurisdiction [of France] as understood by the French Government.

. . .

[Norway explained that]

There can be no possible doubt on this point. If, however, there should still be some doubt, the *Norwegian Government would rely upon the reservations made by the French Government* in its Declaration of March 1st, 1949. By virtue of the principle of reciprocity, which is embodied in Article 36, paragraph 2, of the Statute of the Court and which has been clearly expressed in the Norwegian Declaration of November 16th, 1946, the Norwegian Government cannot be bound, vis-a-vis the French Government, by undertakings which are either broader or stricter than those given by the latter Government [of France].

. . .

[In a subsequent portion of the opinion, the Court responded as follows]:

In the Preliminary Objections filed by the Norwegian Government it is stated:

The Norwegian Government did not insert any such reservation in its own Declaration. But it has the right to rely upon the [narrower] restrictions placed by France upon her own undertakings.

Convinced that the dispute which has been brought before the Court by the Application of July 6th, 1955, is within the domestic jurisdiction the Norwegian Government considers itself fully entitled to rely on this right [as France would do if a defendant in this Court]. Accordingly, it requests the Court to decline, on grounds that it lacks jurisdiction, the function which the French Government would have it assume.

In considering this ground of the Objection the Court notes in the first place that the present case has been brought before it on the basis of Article 36, paragraph 2, of the Statute and of the corresponding Declarations of acceptance of compulsory jurisdiction; that in the present case the jurisdiction of the Court depends upon the Declarations made by the Parties in accordance with Article 36, paragraph 2, of the Statute on condition of reciprocity; and that, since two unilateral declarations are involved, such *jurisdiction is conferred upon the Court only to the extent to which the Declarations coincide* in conferring it. A comparison between the two Declarations shows that the French Declaration accepts the Court's jurisdiction within narrower limits than the Norwegian Declaration; consequently, the common will of the Parties, which is the basis of the Court's jurisdiction, exists within these narrower limits indicated by the French reservation.

. . .

France has limited her acceptance of the compulsory jurisdiction of the Court by excluding beforehand disputes relating to matters which are essentially within the national jurisdiction as understood by the Government of the French Republic. In accordance with the condition of reciprocity to which acceptance of the compulsory jurisdiction is made subject in both Declarations and which is provided for in Article 36, paragraph 3, of the Statute, Norway, equally with France, is entitled to except from the compulsory jurisdiction of the Court disputes understood by Norway to be essentially within its national jurisdiction.

. . .

The Court does not consider that it should examine whether the French reservation is consistent with the undertaking of a legal obligation and is compatible with Article 36, paragraph 6, of the Statute [the core of Justice Lauterpacht's concurring opinion] which provides:

> *In the event of a dispute as to whether the Court has jurisdiction, the matter shall be settled by the decision of the Court.*

The validity of the [French] reservation has not been questioned by the Parties.

. . .

The Court considers that the *Norwegian Government is entitled, by virtue of the condition of reciprocity, to invoke the reservation contained in the French Declaration* of March 1st, 1949; that this reservation excludes from the jurisdiction of the Court the dispute which has been referred to it by the Application of the French Government; that consequently by the Court is without jurisdiction to entertain the [French] Application.

. . .

[The ICJ then voted, twelve to three, that it lacked the necessary jurisdiction to hear and determine France's claim.]

SEPARATE OPINION OF JUDGE SIR HERSCH LAUTERPACHT

While I concur in the operative part of the Judgment inasmuch as the Court has declared itself incompetent to decide on the merits of the case submitted to it, I much regret that I do not find myself in agreement with the *grounds* of the Judgment.

. . .

I consider it *legally impossible for the Court to act in disregard of its Statute* which imposes upon it the duty and confers upon it the right to determine its jurisdiction. That right cannot be exercised by a party to the dispute. The Court cannot, in any circumstances, treat as admissible the claim that the parties have accepted its jurisdiction subject to the condition that they, and not the Court, will decide on its jurisdiction. To do so is in my view contrary to Article 36 (6) of the Statute which, without any qualification, confers upon the Court the right and imposes upon it the duty to determine its jurisdiction. Moreover, it is also contrary to Article 1 of the Statute of the Court and *Article 92 of the Charter of the United Nations which lay down that the Court shall function in accordance with the provisions of its*

Statute. It is that question which I now propose to consider in connection with the examination of the validity of the French Acceptance [whereunder it decides jurisdiction rather than the ICJ].

. . .

Moreover, the particular [French] *reservation now at issue is not one that is contrary to some merely procedural aspect of the Statute. It is contrary to one of its basic features.* It is at variance with the principal safeguard of the system of the compulsory jurisdiction of the Court. Without it, the compulsory jurisdiction of the Court being dependent upon the will of the defendant party, expressed subsequent to the dispute having been brought before the Court, has no meaning. *Article 36 (6) is thus an essential condition of the system of obligatory judicial settlement as established in the Statute.* That provision was inserted in the Statute with the deliberate intention of providing an indispensable safeguard of the operation of the system. Article 36 (2) speaks of the recognition by the parties to the Statute of the 'compulsory' jurisdiction of the Court. But there is no question of compulsory jurisdiction if, after the dispute has arisen and after it has been brought before the Court, the defendant State is entitled to decide whether the Court has jurisdiction.

. . .

Accordingly, in my view the entire *French Declaration* of Acceptance must be treated as *devoid of legal effect* and as incapable of providing a basis for the jurisdiction of the Court. It is for that reason that, in my view, the Court has no jurisdiction over the dispute.

■ NOTES & QUESTIONS

The *Norwegian Loans* case illustrates that there are fundamental problems with the so-called "compulsory" jurisdiction of the ICJ. While the legal relationship existed between the parties before the Court came into existence, both litigants had expressly agreed to use the Court to decide such international disputes. Yet both litigants were able to reserve the "right" to avoid the Court's compulsory jurisdiction. France's narrow acceptance retained the ability to characterize a claim as one arising under France's internal law—rather than International Law. Norway merely piggybacked onto France's narrower Declaration of Acceptance because Norway had accepted the ICJ's compulsory jurisdiction via its own "reciprocity" Declaration of Acceptance. Consider the following questions:

1. Under the Statute of the International Court of Justice, who decides whether the ICJ has jurisdiction?

2. What is the "optional clause," and which State or States invoked it in *Norwegian Loans*?

3. When a State invokes the optional clause, what obligation does it thereby accept?

4. The text of the optional clause includes the word *compulsory*. What does this term mean? What limitations does the ICJ Statute contain?

5. States do not have to unconditionally accept the jurisdiction of the ICJ in *all* matters. How did Norway further limit the declaration in which it previously submitted itself to the compulsory jurisdiction of the ICJ?

6. Why was Norway able to avoid litigating the *Norwegian Loans* case?

7. Why did Judge Lauterpacht characterize France's submission to the compulsory jurisdiction of the ICJ as invalid?

Advisory Jurisdiction

During the first forty years of its existence (1946–1986), the International Court of Justice had fifty-three "contentious" cases—wherein the State litigants argued either jurisdictional objections or the merits of their cases. During the same period, the ICJ also rendered eighteen "advisory" opinions in cases where States were *not* parties to the proceedings. The Court therein invites States or international organizations to provide information to assist in its advisory deliberations. Unlike the ICJ's contentious litigation, there is no plaintiff or defendant in advisory proceedings.

The ICJ has succinctly summarized the fundamental difference between its contentious and advisory jurisdiction as follows:

The participation of interested States had conferred on the present proceedings a wholly unusual character tending to obscure the difference in principle between contentious and advisory proceedings. Whereas in contentious proceedings the Court has before it parties who plead their cause and must, where necessary, produce evidence in support of their contentions, in advisory proceedings it is assumed that the Court will itself obtain the information it needs, should the States not have supplied it. In contentious proceedings, if a party does not succeed in producing good grounds for a claim, the Court has only to dismiss it, whereas in advisory proceedings the Court's task is not confined to assessing the probative force of the information supplied by States, but consists in trying to arrive at an opinion with the help of all the elements of information available to it.[33]

The ICJ's advisory jurisdiction has been useful for resolving general questions of International Law in a nonadversarial context. An advisory resolution fills the gap created by the general lack of State commitment to resolving sensitive international disputes in contentious (adversarial) litigation. States are normally unwilling to submit their major disputes to the Court. Some States have even registered objections, when a UN agency has sought an advisory opinion. But State consent is *not* required for an advisory opinion. As articulated in an early ICJ opinion on point (in 1950):

> It follows that no State, whether a Member of the United Nations or not, can prevent the giving of an Advisory Opinion which the United Nations considers to be desirable in order to obtain enlightenment as to the course of action it should take. The Court's [advisory] Opinion is given not to the States, but to the organ which is entitled to request it; the reply of the Court, itself an 'organ of the United Nations', represents its participation in the activities of the Organization, and, in principle, should not be refused.[34]

Who initiates advisory proceedings and why? Under Article 65 of the Statute of the International Court of Justice, the "Court may give an advisory opinion on any [international] legal question at the request of whatever body may be authorized by or in accordance with the Charter of the United Nations to make such a request." An individual State may thus bring a problem to the attention of one of these bodies. Under UN Charter Article 96, however, only the General Assembly, the Security Council, and specialized agencies authorized by the General Assembly may "request advisory opinions of the Court on legal questions arising within the scope of their activities." The Court then interprets and applies International Law in the absence of State litigants. In 1993, for example, the General Assembly's World Health Organization sought an advisory opinion from the ICJ—requesting guidance on the question of whether the threat or use of nuclear weapons is permitted in *any* circumstances (*see* §12.1).

National decisions during the earlier PCIJ era, not to invoke the "contentious" jurisdiction of the World Court, contributed to the need for "advisory" opinions to prod the progressive development of International Law. The drafters of the UN Charter thus recognized that the judicial arm of the organization might function to resolve conflicting interpretations of the Charter by different organs within the UN itself. In the 1945 Statement on Charter Interpretation contained in UN Conference Document No. 933, the drafting committee thus provided as follows:

> Difficulties may conceivably arise in the event that there should be a difference of opinion among organs of the Organization concerning the correct interpretation of the Charter. Thus, two organs may conceivably hold and may express or even act upon different views. . . . [I]t would always be open to the General Assembly or to the Security Council . . . to ask the International Court of Justice for an advisory opinion concerning the meaning of a provision of the Charter.

Another reason for the ICJ's advisory jurisdiction is that only *States* may be parties in the Court's contentious litigation. Unlike certain regional international courts (discussed in § 9.6), international organizations, their agencies, and individuals cannot be parties in ICJ litigation. They lack the international personality to directly participate in contentious litigation. Supplementing the ICJ's contentious jurisdiction with the power to hear cases by or against international organizations had been suggested but not implemented—mostly due to the uncertain contours of the relationship between States and international organizations when the UN Charter and ICJ Statute were created. Advisory opinions were thus designed to provide guidance about matters involving the UN's organs and specialized agencies. The Court thus settles disputes among the various organs of the UN.

Among the Court's more prominent advisory opinions are the 1950 *Competence of the Assembly* case, the 1951 *Genocide Reservations* case, and the 1988 *PLO UN Mission* case. In the first of these opinions, the ICJ resolved a dispute involving the respective powers of the UN's General Assembly and Security Council. The Court decided that the UN Charter could not be interpreted to permit the General Assembly to unilaterally admit members to the UN. It was *un*willing to condone the suggestion—contrary to the Charter's language—that a recommendation of the Security Council was not required. In a second advisory opinion, the General Assembly sought guidance about the permissibility of potential reservations to the Genocide Treaty. While the court did not clearly answer this question (*see* case set forth in text of § 8.2), it did decide that State treaty reservations must be generally compatible with the underlying purpose of a treaty. In the 1988 *PLO UN Mission* case, the Court decided that the US could not close the mission of the Palestine Liberation Organization in New York. The US obligations to the UN precluded closure of the PLO's UN Mission on the basis of antiterrorism.[35]

Given the political interest that States sometimes exhibit in proceedings related to an advisory opinion, the difference between advisory and contentious litigation can become obscured. Normally, the Court obtains what information it desires when exercising its advisory jurisdiction—particularly when one or more interested States are not forthcoming in providing factual details for the Court's legal analysis. But in some advisory cases, State interest generates a degree of participation virtually on a par with that manifested by the ICJ's contentious cases. In the 1975 *Western Sahara* advisory opinion set forth in the text of § 2.3, for example, the UN General Assembly requested an ICJ advisory opinion regarding the status of the referenced territory. The Court called upon Spain, Morocco, and Mauritania to submit information regarding their respective claims in this area. The proceedings thus resembled contentious litigation, due to the presentation of conflicting adversarial views to the Court—although the case technically involved only the advisory jurisdiction of the Court.

Chambers of the Court

Nations have been experimenting with the use of "chambers," or panels composed of less than all of the ICJ's judges. Under Article 26 of the ICJ Statute, the "Court may form from time to time one or more chambers, composed of three or more judges . . . for dealing with particular categories of cases." Upon the request of a party to a dispute, the president of the ICJ determines whether the other party is agreeable to the formation of a chamber to hear the dispute.

The original intent—to provide chambers to hear labor, transit, and communications cases—expanded as of 1982. Various ICJ chambers began to consider border disputes between the US and Canada, Mali and Upper Volta, El Salvador and Honduras.[36]

The chamber mode of dispute resolution offers two advantages. One is that the judges may decide matters on a summary basis. Article 29 of the ICJ Statute provides that with "a view to the speedy dispatch of business, the Court shall form annually a chamber composed of five judges which, at the request of the parties, may hear and determine cases by summary procedure." They can dispense with certain court rules and procedures when deemed appropriate. The other advantage is that States do not have to submit their cases for consideration by the *full* court. The entire tribunal of fifteen jurists may include judges from States having poor relations with a party to a particular dispute.

In 1972, the ICJ amended its court rules to permit its president to ascertain the litigants' views on the judicial composition of their particular chamber. The legality and desirability of those consultations is still being debated. Article 26 of the Statute of the International Court of Justice provides only for party approval of the *number* of judges. It does not defer to party approval regarding *which* judges will sit on a panel. The 1972 compromise is designed to encourage greater use of the Court. When this issue was being considered, the ICJ president stated that parties' input about which judges sat on their panel would breathe new life into the use of the Court. The receipt of their input does not change the fact that the Court itself still elects the members of its chambers. The president of the Court acknowledged that from "a practical point of view, it is difficult to conceive that in normal circumstances those [judicial] Members who have been suggested by the parties would not be elected."[37]

Others view this development as an indicator of the increased politicalization of the ICJ. As reported in a 1987 study by the American Society of International Law on the ICJ, the parties have a decisive impact on the composition of the chambers. They are able to comment on the makeup of the particular chamber, which relieves national apprehension about submitting cases to judges from unfriendly governments. Some States have recommended that the ICJ chambers device be supplemented by creating *regional* chambers. These devices for increasing the use of the ICJ would, in the view of some commentators, support the perspective that the Court has become a political institution.[38]

ICJ Assessment

Is the concept of global adjudication, as an alternative to war, too idealistic to be workable? In the UN Secretary-General's 1992 special report to the UN Security Council, Boutros Boutros-Ghali recommended the following steps to reinforce the role of the ICJ:

(a) All member States should accept the general jurisdiction [rather than the usual reliance on special treaty clauses] of the International Court, . . . without *any* reservation, before the end of the United Nations Decade of International Law in the year 2000.
(b) When submission of a dispute to the full Court is not practical, the Chambers jurisdiction should be used;
(c) States should support the Trust Fund established to assist countries unable to afford the cost involved in bringing a dispute to the Court. . . .[39]

It is unlikely that States will rekindle the interest in international adjudication that blossomed from 1944 through 1946. In 1944, even before World War II ended, some of the world's most powerful nations planned a global organization of states that would avert further wars. In 1945, they drafted unassailable principles calling for the peaceful settlement of disputes. These norms were then incorporated into both the UN Charter and the ICJ Statute. The language in these constituting documents expressed the hope that the Court would play a role in managing subsequent hostilities. UN Charter Article 36.3 thus states "that legal disputes should as a general rule be referred by the parties to the International Court of Justice in accordance with the provisions of the Statute of the Court." The Court was designed to serve as a buffer for adversaries who might thereby avoid the use of force to settle their disputes. If an offending State failed to comply with the Court's interim orders or final judgments, the Security Council was to devise measures to ensure compliance.

This paradigm did not, in practice, close the gap between hope and reality. Many of the original UN members refused to yield sovereign control over their own disputes to an international organization headquartered in a distant land—or its judicial organ in Europe. Charter Article 33, for example, provides that adversaries are expected to resort first to local or regional mechanisms before invoking the aid of the UN. This rather amorphous prescription provided a convenient basis for avoiding direct resort to the ICJ.

A fundamental problem of mistrust remains. Many UN delegates at the 1945 UN drafting conference mistrusted the first World Court (PCIJ), which had been conceived by the French and staffed with mostly European judges. To these delegates, it would be more palatable to entrust sensitive disputes to a local or regional judicial body, than to a global body hundreds or thousands of miles away in the Netherlands. Socialist States have generally avoided the submission of State disputes to a distant international tribunal, perceiving such pressures as a bourgeois threat to their sovereign decision-making prerogatives. Many lesser developed States lack familiarity with formal adjudication—and are thus rather cautious about formal mechanisms like "compulsory jurisdiction."[40]

On the other hand, the US and Russia tendered a joint proposal in 1993 at the UN, encouraging greater use of the ICJ—via its "chambers" process described above. The objective is to encourage resort to a convenient dispute resolution mechanism, at least in cases involving the terrorism and narcotics treaties signed by both States in the aftermath of the Cold War. The other UN Security Council members—France, Great Britain, and China—were asked to support, and ultimately join in, the US/Russia chambers proposal. Disputes would be resolved by "panels" of less than all fifteen judges.

But Great Britain and a number of commentators have characterized this proposal as a step backwards. It supposedly *dis*courages use of full-court powers. France and China remain so suspicious of the ICJ that their endorsement of this plan is unlikely.

A manifestation of the general sovereign mistrust of "outside" judicial resolutions is found in Article 59 of the ICJ Statute. The court's decisions "have no binding force except as between the parties and in respect of that particular case." Although the Court is expected to provide some direction in the development of International Law, its Statute expressly limits the binding effect of the ICJ's judgments for use in subsequent cases. Decisions legally bind *only* the immediate parties in the immediate suit. The parties are not necessarily bound in the event of a similar issue arising between them in the future.

The Court has nevertheless relied on its prior decisions as evidence of the content of International Law. It would be a waste of judicial resources, however, not to consider earlier decisions when the same point of law is later presented in another case.

Although numerous criticisms persist, the ICJ has in reality been useful. It has decided a number of significant disputes, and most of its decisions have been implemented by the participating States. In 1992, for example, El Salvador and Honduras accepted an ICJ border dispute judgment that ended a two-century dilemma in their international relations. As stated by Honduras's President Raphael Callejas, two Central American States thus illustrated "that any dispute, however complex, can be resolved in a civilized and conciliatory way." The Court has also been able to proceed to an important judgment, even in the absence of the defendant State. Such cases have significantly aided in the progressive development of International Law (as in the *Nicaragua* judgment against the US after its withdrawal—described earlier in this section, and in § 10.2).

The utility of the ICJ includes the plaintiff State's ability to file a case, with a view toward encouraging settlement when diplomatic negotiations are deadlocked. Nicaragua filed a transborder armed conflict claim against Honduras in 1988. Honduras responded by attacking the jurisdiction of the Court. The Court determined that it did have jurisdiction over this dispute. The parties then reached an out-of-court agreement, likely facilitated by Honduras's recognition that it could obtain more via settlement than by a possibly "all-or-nothing" court judgment. Nicaragua then requested that this case be discontinued after the two nations fully resolved their dispute diplomatically.

Success is, of course, tempered by the realization that States tend *not* to submit their most sensitive disputes to the Court. The Court has nevertheless played a tangible role in facilitating the continuous development of International Law, as it ebbs and flows with the complex developments of State practice. The Court is a good forum for distilling the contemporary practice of the nearly 190 members of the international community.

The ICJ, through no fault of its own, has *not* contributed significantly to the preservation of world peace. It cannot realistically control disputes arising under International Law, when those States that would be governed by its jurisprudence have failed to employ its resources. The ICJ cannot be fairly accused of "failing." It was never vested with the independent power to require the participation of potential defendant States or to render enforceable legal solutions. The so-called "compulsory" jurisdiction of the Court is, in the last analysis, solely dependent on State consent for its very existence. Some States have even deprived the Court of the otherwise universally exercised judicial power to determine its own jurisdiction to proceed. As stated by one of the most prominent members of the Court, Sir Hersch Lauterpacht of England:

> [I]t would be an exaggeration to assert that the Court has proved to be a significant instrument for maintaining peace. The degree of achievement of this end by an international court, as indeed by any other court, is dependent upon the state of political integration of the society whose law it administers. But international society has in this respect, in the years following the two World Wars, fallen short of the expectation of those who in the Covenant of the League of Nations and in the Charter of the United Nations intended to create, through them, the basis of the future orderly development of the international community.[41]

Some individuals claim that the International Court of Justice is the classic ivory tower—occupied by a group of theoreticians. Its jurists supposedly generate pointless discourses that are unrelated to how States actually behave in the real world. These criticisms are misdirected, however. The UN was not intended to be a world government, in the sense that its decisions would replace the primacy of national sovereignty. The UN's judicial arm was not intended to be a world court, in the sense that it might become a principal tool for dispute resolution. The *optional* nature of sovereign submission to the ICJ's power to hear and determine cases arising under International Law is the built-in Achilles heel of the UN's judicial process.

A more useful perspective is that the UN has not replaced States as the core element in the structure of the international system. Its members never transferred the necessary jurisdictional powers to the ICJ, nor the necessary enforcement powers to the UN. States did not want to vest such organizational entities with the power to resolve international disputes, absent the full consent of the participating States on virtually a case-by-case basis.

The original fifty-one members of the UN had various reasons for limiting the power of this judicial body. The older and more developed powers perceived the potential change in the postwar composition of the community of nations as an unwelcome shift in the balance of power. Nearly three-fourths of the UN's current members did not exist in 1945 when the other quarter created the organization. (*See* Exhibit 2.1 in § 2.2, illustrating this development.)

These new States do not share the same political and economic perspectives of certain of the older, powerful, and more economically established members. In the 1970s, these so-called "Third World" States expressed the common view that they should become members of the international community on equal terms with the original UN members. From the perspective of new States, many aspects of modern International Law (developed by Europeans incident to the 1648 Peace of Westphalia described in § 1.3) discourage the Third World's military and economic development. The ICJ, and the ability of the more powerful UN members to manipulate it, is just another facade for perpetuating the dominance of the older members of the community of nations.

The above perspective of the majority of UN members suggests that until international tribunals command a wider constituency, the national courts provide the most realistic medium for the *judicial* recognition and development of International Law.

The ICJ cannot be a talismanic cure for international disputes, absent greater political integration in the community of nations.

Many observers of the International Court of Justice exude a religious reverence for the Court and a demonic disdain for States that have not used it. This perspective is misleading. The ICJ is not like a national supreme court—typically exercising the powers to command the presence of adversaries and to enforce national court judgments. The States that produced the ICJ cast it onto a stage directed by world politics. In the absence of world government, they did not want the ICJ to function like their own national courts. As classically depicted by the improper US withdrawal from ICJ jurisdiction in the *Nicaragua Case* (without the minimum notice of withdrawal as promised in its acceptance of the Court's jurisdiction), the so-called compulsory jurisdiction of the Court is not serving the role envisioned by the UN drafters.

One response to the impotence created by national practices limiting ICJ jurisdiction has been the creation of a *private* alternative to the ICJ—the Provisional District World Court, which rendered its first decision in 1988. There, a three-judge court, composed of prominent American law professors, banned the stockpiling of nuclear weapons by any State.[42] In its second case, decided in 1994, a panel consisting of three law professors from Moscow, Warsaw, and San Diego held that there was no international rule requiring States to cast off their war potential—as accomplished by Japan after its surrender ending World War II. This court, based in Los Angeles, California, consists of panels of scholarly "judges," whose opinions do not bind the defendant States because the latter have not recognized this court. The operation of this private tribunal suggests that there is a growing dissatisfaction with the inability of existing international tribunals that cannot resolve the crucial issues of the day—which will never be heard in the ICJ, due to its lack of true compulsory jurisdiction over States.

US Position on the ICJ

The US has been rather reserved about the ICJ from the outset. In 1946, the US Senate debated whether the US should accept the jurisdiction of the UN's new court. Senator Connally, Chairman of the Senate Foreign Relations Committee, expressed his concern that the US would be effectively surrendering the fate of important national interests to the UN, by generally accepting the Court's compulsory jurisdiction. In his words: "I am in favor of the United Nations, but I am also for the United States of America. I do not want to surrender the sovereignty or the prestige of the United States with respect to any question which may be merely domestic in character . . . [when the] best hope of the world lies in the survival of the United States with its concepts of democracy, liberty, freedom, and advancement under its [own] institutions."[43]

The US "accepted" the ICJ's jurisdiction in 1946, but not without reservations. The key US limitations that would preclude the Court from acting involved disputes that were (a) entrusted to *other* tribunals by a special treaty provision; or (b) essentially within the domestic jurisdiction of the US, *as determined by the US*; or (c) cases arising under a multilateral treaty—unless all parties to the dispute were also parties to the particular treaty or otherwise agreed to by the US.

After accepting the Court's jurisdiction, subject to the above limitations, the US became a major proponent of increased use of the ICJ. In 1974, the US Senate asked the US president to consider the feasibility of increasing the nation's participation in the ICJ. In 1977, the resulting US Department of State study concluded that the "underlying presumption of this Senate Resolution is that it is desirable to widen access to the International Court of Justice in order to increase its activity, use and contributions to the development of international law. As a general proposition, the Department of State strongly endorses that presumption."[44]

In the 1980s, the US "rollercoaster" approach to ICJ adjudication began another descent. The US had begun to withdraw from various organs of the UN, refusing to pay its assessed share of UN dues (*see* § 3.3). In 1984, the US refused to participate in Nicaragua's suit, which claimed that the US Central Intelligence Agency had arranged the mining of key Nicaraguan harbors. The US withdrew its acceptance of the Court's jurisdiction, virtually on the eve of the filing of the case by the plaintiff Nicaragua. In its 1946 declaration accepting the jurisdiction of the ICJ, the US had promised a minimum of six months notice for any withdrawal. US Secretary of State George Schultz nevertheless stated that the immediate withdrawal from any case involving any Central American State was necessary "to foster the continuing regional dispute settlement process

which seeks a negotiated solution to the interrelated political, economic, and security problems of Central America." As the US could not legally withdraw without giving six months' notice, the Court proceeded with the case and entered a judgment against the US.[45]

A sharp debate nevertheless continues about the legality and political propriety of the US withdrawal. Professor Stuart Malawer of George Mason University in Arlington, Virginia makes the following observation in opposition to the US position:

The World Court [judges] in absolutely astonishing majorities rejected the American arguments concerning the lack of jurisdiction and inadmissibility of Nicaragua's claim against it. Reading the recent court decision, one must wonder how anyone ever believed the [Court's] decision could have been otherwise.

Why is it that the United States, the country which has championed international law in foreign affairs and the development of the World Court, has gotten itself into such an embarrassing position, and is now on the verge of being branded an outlaw state, when the transgressions of so many others are so great?

My answer is simple. The legal advice given by the lawyers in the State Department must have been terrible.[46]

Although scholars may debate the legality of the US withdrawal, one conclusion is inescapable. The US did not comply with its reservation promising to give six months' notice of its intent to withdraw its acceptance of the Court's compulsory jurisdiction.

Then in 1985, the US terminated its general acceptance (in 1946) of ICJ compulsory jurisdiction. The US position was that, of the five permanent members of the UN Security Council, only the US and the UK had accepted the Court's compulsory jurisdiction (in a rather limited form). Given the lack of universality hoped for by the US when it originally accepted the Court's jurisdiction, the US had never been able to bring a case against another State—while itself being sued three times. Therefore, the US presidential administration publicly blamed Nicaragua, Cuba, and the former Soviet

Union for using the Court's processes as a political weapon in the Cold War.

The US *unilateral* withdrawal from the ICJ's compulsory jurisdiction does not affect its obligation to appear as a defendant under a treaty clause that, as a matter of *mutual agreement*, requires the treaty parties to litigate their disputes in the ICJ. This is a *special* form of submission that is distinct from the former *general* submission to the Court's compulsory jurisdiction. Since the "general" withdrawal by the US when the *Nicaragua Case* was filed, the US has been a defendant in several such cases. In one, Libya accused the US and the UK of complicity in a conspiracy to avoid certain treaty obligations in relation to Libya's bombing of Pan Am flight 103 over Lockerbie, Scotland in 1988. In another case, filed in 1993, Serbia similarly accused the US of politicizing the Bosnia debate—by supposedly claiming that the Serbian military forces were perpetrating another genocide in the former Yugoslavia.

While a serious question remains about the merits of such cases, the US was nevertheless required to participate. It expressly consented to conferring jurisdiction on the Court to hear disputes arising under the relevant treaties. In a third such instance, the US agreed in a prior treaty to litigate the type of case filed by Iran in 1989. A US naval vessel mistakenly downed a commercial Iranian airbus over the Persian Gulf. The on-site commander misidentified the commercial passenger plane as a hostile military warplane. The US had refused to give its proposed compensation to the Iranian government, as opposed to the individual families who directly suffered the loss. Iran then brought this suit in the ICJ. In each of the above three cases naming the US as a defendant in ICJ proceedings, the prior US *treaty*-based consent to the Court's jurisdiction was unaffected by the US *unilateral* withdrawal from the Court's general compulsory jurisdiction (under the previously addressed optional clause).

The last indication of the ultimate US position on the Court can be gleaned from the 1993 *Final Report of the United States Commission on Improving the Effectiveness of the United Nations*. This special government commission, established by the US Congress under the Foreign Relations Authorization Act of 1988, studied the role of the UN and its place in US foreign policy. In the *Findings and Recommendations*, this Commission (consisting of House members and other special appointees) deter-

mined that the US should take the lead in advocating wider acceptance of the compulsory jurisdiction of the Court. The Commission recommended as follows: "that, to set a standard of leadership, the U.S. consider reaccepting the compulsory jurisdiction of the Court. ..."[47]

As to the Court's *advisory* jurisdiction, the Commission also recommended a gradual expansion of this facet of the ICJ's competence. Specifically, States are thus encouraged to refer questions of International Law from their national courts to the ICJ.

■ 9.5   INTERNATIONAL CRIMINAL COURT

Introduction

Victorious States have often punished the losing State or States. In earlier eras, the motivation was revenge. Today, the *disclosed* motivation is to obtain reparations for alleged violations of International Law. This section addresses an almost mythological entity often referred to as the "International Criminal Court" (ICC). These materials thus begin with the most famous and successful international tribunal—the World War II Nuremberg Trial of Nazi Germany's notorious war criminals—and the companion Tokyo Trial of the Japanese defendants. This section of the book then focuses on the Yugoslavian war crimes tribunal, which was not established by a treaty among victorious powers. The latter ICC was established, instead, by a UN resolution in 1993. Its task is to prosecute certain events associated with the so-called Bosnian War in the former Yugoslavia. Another UN ICC was created for Rwanda in 1994.

The concept of a war crimes trial is not unique to the Nuremberg trial in post–World War II Germany. There are accounts of a war crimes trial in 405 B.C., near what is now Turkey; a trial of a European governor for his actions in 1427, when his troops raped and killed innocent individuals; and a post–World War I trial of a submarine commander who torpedoed a British hospital ship and then sank its lifeboats. The League of Nations produced an international penal code and related Convention on the Establishment of the International Criminal Court (within the PCIJ)—signed by Belgium, Bulgaria, Cuba, Czechoslovakia, France, Greece, Spain, Monaco, the Netherlands, Romania, Turkey, the USSR, and Yugoslavia. This treaty never entered into force, however, due to the lack of sufficient ratifications.[48] In 1994, Ethiopia commenced war crimes trials against the leaders of its former Marxist dictatorship. After it seized power in 1974, some 250,000 people were killed or died in forced relocation programs. In one six-hour period during 1988, 2,500 civilians were killed by helicopter gun ships and fighter planes.

Between 1946 and 1993 (the dates of establishment of the respective ICCs), there were many calls for the creation of the second exclusively criminal international tribunal to try various types of "international" crimes. These would be the crimes that may serve as a basis for universal jurisdiction, such as war crimes, terrorism, and highjacking (*see* § 5.2). Building on the 1934 League of Nations draft Convention for the Creation of an International Criminal Court, an unofficial nongovernmental organization attempted to assert pressure on the community of nations to bring such a tribunal into existence. The Foundation for the Establishment of an International Criminal Court thus conducted two drafting conferences in 1972, attended by experts from all over the world. And in 1986, the US Congress asked US President Reagan to explore the possibility of international pressure to establish an ICC to deal with international terrorists. This theme was ignited by problems with securing the extradition of terrorists from reluctant nations. An asylum State would be in a very awkward position if it refused to yield an offender to such a tribunal—thus improving the prospects for a truly *international* response to terrorism and the convenient "political offense" exception to extradition treaties (discussed in § 5.3). And in 1992, the UN Secretary-General appointed a Commission of Experts to document violations of humanitarian law in the former Yugoslavia.[49]

In theory, the trial of "international" criminals would be best accomplished by an *international* court—as opposed to a *national* court. The 1921 Leipzig trials of German nationals, in Germany, for war crimes against the Allies, plus the 1961 Israeli trial of Hitler's chief exterminator, Adolf Eichmann, in Israel, are classic examples of the judicial dilemma associated with such *national* tribunals. It was obviously rather difficult for both sets of judges to exercise the impartiality that is the primary attribute of the judicial role. One could also claim that the impartiality of the 1990 US prosecution of Panama's former dictator was tainted by the prior relationship between Noriega and the US Central Intelligence Agency. As stated in a 1992 study of the future of international courts:

> The existence of international crimes and the recognition of individual responsibility for such crimes logically suggests that there should be an *international* tribunal with power to try individuals for the commission of international crimes. It is just as important to have an international criminal court to administer international criminal law as it is to have national criminal courts to administer national criminal law. For however objective and impartial national courts in fact may be, because they are courts of particular states there will inevitably be a suspicion of bias when a national court tries an international criminal. . . .
>
> [T]rying international criminals before municipal courts is haphazard, unjust and militates against the development of a *universal* criminal law. The administration of international criminal law will only become systematic, just and universal when the organ of its administration is a *permanent* international criminal court.[50]

On the other hand, some commentators argue that altering the Statute of the *existing* International Court of Justice would be preferable to creating new judicial machinery to deal with matters easily placed within the province of the UN's international court—already in place since 1946. This sentiment was proficiently summarized by Professor Barbara Yarnold of Florida International University in 1991:

> One issue that requires attention is whether it might be advisable to create a new international criminal tribunal, rather than utilizing the International Court of Justice. . . .
>
> [T]he International Court of Justice is the best forum for the adjudication of state and international crimes, for several reasons. . . . Although the ICJ has fallen into disuse recently, its performance has commanded the respect of many states in the world community over the years, due to its presumed expertise and impartiality. Hence, the International Court of Justice *already* has a certain level of

legitimacy and support among states [as opposed to any tribunal yet to be established].

Second, the concept of establishing a new international tribunal may be more difficult to sell than that of transferring new responsibilities to a preexisting international tribunal.

Third, much work has already been put into developing the International Court of Justice. . . . The Statute of the International Court of Justice would not have to be discarded. Instead, the [ICJ] *Statute could be amended* where necessary [to provide the requisite criminal jurisdiction].

Certainly, this recommendation that the International Court of Justice be given jurisdiction over international crimes [rather than leaving it to State jurisdiction] . . . *will be opposed by those superpowers* in the world community that historically have favored the use of force over the rule of law.[51]

Nuremberg/Tokyo Tribunals

The desire to establish the first modern and truly International Criminal Court surfaced in 1945 as a device for deterring future misuses of force. The victorious Allied powers established two major international tribunals to try war crimes. One, the eleven-nation International Military Tribunal of the Far East, tried twenty-five Japanese defendants for war crimes. All were found guilty and seven were sentenced to death. The most famous tribunal, however, was the four-nation body established by the Nuremberg Charter. The United States, Great Britain, France, and the former Soviet Union created the Nuremberg Tribunal by international agreement. The fundamental objective was to try Nazi "war criminals whose offenses have no particular geographical location whether they be accused individually or in their capacity as members of [military] organizations" of the German government.[52]

The treaty, known as the Nuremberg Charter, contained what the Allied powers perceived as a novel method for deterring the national misuse of force. Germany's key planners were tried and imprisoned or executed for their war crimes. The essential basis for their liability was the violation of prewar international agreements that outlawed war. The following excerpt from the resulting Nuremberg Judgment analyzes the role of international law in outlawing the tactics planned and executed by German leaders during World War II:

JUDGMENT OF THE INTERNATIONAL MILITARY TRIBUNAL (1946)

22 International Military Tribunal, Trial of the Major War Criminals 411 (1948)

[*Opinion:*] The charges in the indictment that the defendants planned and waged aggressive wars are charges of the utmost gravity. War is essentially an evil thing. Its consequences are not confined to the belligerent states alone, but affect the whole world.

To initiate a war of aggression, therefore, is not only an international crime; it is the supreme international crime differing only from other war crimes in that it contains within itself the accumulated evil of the whole.

The first acts of aggression referred to in the indictment are the seizure of Austria and Czechoslovakia; and the first war of aggression charged in the indictment is the war against Poland begun on the 1st September 1939. Before examining that charge it is necessary to look more closely at some of the events which preceded these acts of aggression. The war against Poland did not come suddenly out of an otherwise clear sky; the evidence has made it plain that this war of aggression, as well as the seizure of Austria and Czechoslovakia, was premeditated and carefully prepared, and was not undertaken until the moment was thought opportune for it to be carried through as a definite part of the preordained scheme and plan.

For the aggressive designs of the Nazi Government were not accidents arising out of the immediate political situation in Europe and the world; they were a deliberate and essential part of Nazi foreign policy.

From the beginning, the National Socialist movement claimed that its object was to unite the German people in the consciousness of their mission and destiny, based on inherent qualities of [an allegedly superior] race, and under the guidance of the Fuhrer.

The leading Nazi defendants are pictured during these proceedings in 1945 at Nuremberg, Germany. Hermann Goering, Rudolph Hess, and Joachim von Ribbentrop are seated in the dock's first row (left to right). All three were found guilty of war crimes, crimes against peace, and crimes against humanity. Goering and von Ribbentrop were sentenced to death. Hess was sentenced to life imprisonment.

For its achievement, two things were deemed to be essential: The disruption of the European order as it had existed since the Treaty of Versailles, and the creation of a Greater Germany beyond the frontiers of 1914. This necessarily involved the seizure of foreign territories.

War was seen to be inevitable, or at the very least, highly probable, if these purposes were to be accomplished. The German people, therefore, with all their resources, were to be organized as a great political-military army, schooled to obey without question any policy decreed by the State.

The Charter defines as a crime the planning or waging of war that is a war of aggression or a war in violation of international treaties. The Tribunal has decided that certain of the defendants planned and waged aggressive wars against 10 nations, and were therefore guilty of this series of crimes. This makes it unnecessary to discuss the subject in further detail, or even to consider at any length the extent to which these aggressive wars were also "wars in violation of international treaties, agreements, or assurances."

These treaties are set out in . . . the indictment. Those of principal importance are the following [which are herein summarized by the Tribunal]:

(A) HAGUE CONVENTIONS

In the 1899 Convention the signatory powers agreed: "before an appeal to arms . . . to have recourse, as far as circumstances allow, to the good offices or mediation of one or more friendly powers." A similar clause was inserted in the Convention for Pacific Settlement of International Disputes of 1907. In the accompanying Convention Relative to Opening of Hostilities, article I contains this far more specific language:

The Contracting Powers recognize that hostilities between them must not commence without a previous and explicit warning, in the form of either a declaration of war, giving reasons, or an ultimatum with a conditional declaration of war.

Germany was a party to [and thus bound by] these conventions.

(B) VERSAILLES TREATY

Breaches of certain provisions of the Versailles Treaty are also relied on by the prosecution . . . to "respect strictly the independence of Austria" (art. 80); renunciation of any rights in Memel (art. 99) and the Free City of Danzig (art. 100); the recognition of the independence of the Czecho-Slovak State; and the Military, Naval, and Air Clauses against German rearmament found in part V. There is no doubt that action was taken by the German Government contrary to all these provisions.

. . .

The question is, what was the legal effect of this [Kellogg-Briand] pact? The nations who signed the pact or adhered to it *unconditionally condemned recourse to war for the future as an instrument of policy, and expressly renounced it* [emphasis supplied]. After the signing of the pact, any nation resorting to war as an instrument of national policy breaks the pact. In the opinion of the Tribunal, the solemn renunciation of war as an instrument of national policy necessarily involves the proposition that such a war is illegal in international law; and that those who plan and wage such a war, with its inevitable and terrible consequences, are committing a crime in so doing. War for the solution of international controversies undertaken as an instrument of national policy certainly includes a war of aggression, and such a war is therefore outlawed by the pact.

■ NOTES

1. The Nuremberg result was not well-received in all sectors of the political spectrum. US Senator Robert Taft, Republican Majority Leader after the war, referred to this case as a "miscarriage of justice which the American people would long regret." In his opinion, "the trial of the vanquished leaders could not be impartial now matter how it was hedged about with the forms [appearance] of justice." This perspective, and others, are analyzed in Migone, *After Nuremberg, Tokyo*, 25 Texas L. Rev. 475 (1947).

2. Criticisms were not limited to just the Nuremberg proceedings. India's dissenting judge in the Tokyo trials complained that there was no body of law prior to World War II for the majority's decision that war was unlawful under International Law. In Justice Pal's words, national resort to war was a "recognized rule of international life." Although there were a number of noble statements made in treaties—most of which were honored in the breach—customary State practice necessitated the legal conclusion that "war was a legitimate instrument of self-help" when peaceful solutions failed. His views on this subject were published in R. Pal, *International Military Tribunal for the Far East: Dissident Judgment* 103 (Calcutta: Sanyal, 1953).

The principles enshrined in this Nuremberg Judgment were later approved by the UN General Assembly. In 1946, shortly after the Judgment was published, the Assembly adopted Resolution 95(1)—thus expressing its sentiment that the "Nuremberg principle" had been incorporated into International Law. Under this principle, a State and its agents who wage an aggressive war commit the supreme international crime, punishable by any nation able to bring the planners to justice. The responsible leaders thereby incur criminal responsibility—arising directly under *International* Law—for their conduct that causes them to be liable for this supreme crime. The validity under the internal laws of Germany did not provide them with a defense. They were thus tried and punished for their participation as agents of the State in its unlawful use of force against other States. As articulated by the judges at Nuremberg: "crimes against international law are committed by men, not by abstract entities, and only by punishing individuals who commit such crimes can the provisions of international law be enforced."

Neither the Nuremberg principles nor the ensuing UN resolution had a significant impact upon subsequent decisions to use or not use force. This was the last time that "victorious" nations ever established a tribunal to try agents of a defeated nation for waging war. (The 1993 UN "Yugoslavian" tribunal, discussed below, does not involve an entity that one could clearly characterize as "victorious." The closest entity would be the Bosnian Serbs—whereby the victors would be prosecuted as the perpetrators.) In 1974, Professor William Bishop of the University of Michigan thus expressed his frustration with this predicament by posing the following question:

> What then, has . . . international law done for the welfare of humanity since its promulgation? The answer is clear and simple: nothing. Since Nuremberg, there have been at least eighty or ninety wars (some calculators exclude armed invasions of neighbors too weak to attempt resistance), some of them on a very large scale. The list includes the Korean War, the Suez invasion [by France and Great Britain] of 1956, . . . the four Arab-Israeli wars, the Vietnam wars (including the accompanying fighting in Laos and Cambodia), and the invasion of Czechoslovakia by the Soviet Union and its myrmidons. In none of these cases, nor in any other, was an aggressor arrested and brought to the bar of international justice, and none is likely to be. For all the good it has done, the doctrine that aggressive war is a crime might as well be relegated to the divinity schools.[53]

A number of academic studies have been undertaken with a view toward identifying the steps that might be taken to establish a *standing* ICC. In 1970, the World Peace Through Law Center published its study, which included the lament that neither the UN nor the major States appeared willing to create a permanent war crimes tribunal. As stated in its Introduction, the last attempts to induce UN adoption of an ICC ended in the 1950s, and "it is to the States which then failed to establish such an international criminal court that the reproach should be addressed that Eichmann should have been tried by

an international rather than a national criminal court."[54]

Adolf Eichmann, perhaps the most infamous of the Nazi criminals, escaped to Argentina after the war. The Allied ICC had been disbanded due to its temporary nature. After the State of Israel was formed, it enacted a *national* law incorporating the Nuremberg Principles into its internal law as the mechanism for enforcing International Law. Israeli commandos learned of Eichmann's whereabouts, undertook a secret mission into Argentina, and extracted him for trial under Israel's Nazi Collaborator Punishment Law (*see* § 5.2). While this incursion violated Argentina's territorial sovereignty, there was no State or international organization to hinder Israel's application of the universal principle of criminal jurisdiction—thus completing this facet of the work of the Nuremberg tribunal.

The work of Professors M.C. Bassiouni of Chicago's DePaul University, and Benjamin Ferencz of New York, have done much to keep the vision of a permanent ICC from fading into complete obscurity. Their exhaustive studies have served as a model for the UN's creation of the current tribunal "established" in 1993.[55]

"Yugoslavian" Tribunal

The Institution UN Security Council Resolution 827 of 1993 set the foundation for the UN's International Tribunal for the Prosecution of Persons Responsible for Serious Violations of International Humanitarian Law Committed in the Territory of the Former Yugoslavia. (The acronym UNITY will be used to hereinafter describe this tribunal.) This modern version of an International Criminal Court is designed to bring to justice those who have committed crimes in the Bosnia arena since 1991—and ending at a "date to be determined by the Security Council upon restoration of peace," as stated in the Statute of the new International Tribunal. The events complained of occurred in the aftermath of the breakup of the former Yugoslavia (*see* § 2.3 and § 2.4). Security Council Resolution 877 of 1993 unanimously concluded the process of actually forming this contemporary "Nuremberg" tribunal, with its seat in The Hague in the Netherlands—also the seat of the International Court of Justice.

The International Tribunal consists of two trial chambers and an appellate chamber. The executive organs include a registry for the court and a prosecutor's office. In September 1993, the UN General Assembly elected eleven judges, to serve four-year terms, from a slate of candidates nominated by the UN Security Council. The judges are professors and lawyers from all over the world. The first president of the International Tribunal (and its appellate chamber) is from Italy. The vice-president is from Costa Rica. A female judge from the US is president of one of the two trial chambers—of particular importance, due to the alleged mass rapes of Muslim women perpetrated by Serbian soldiers as part of an ethnic cleansing plan (somewhat analogous to Nazi Germany's "Final Solution"). A Nigerian is the President of the other trial chamber.

The International Tribunal will apply the rules of international humanitarian law applicable to armed conflict. These are the 1949 Geneva Convention for the Protection of War Victims, the 1948 Genocide Convention, the crimes against humanity formulation contained in the 1946 Nuremberg Judgment, and the 1907 Hague Convention on the Laws and Customs of War on Land (further addressed in Chapter 10 on the use of force). The prosecution (assuming there is one) will be aimed at the following crimes: murder, rape, torture, ethnic cleansing, and other similar human rights violations (generally addressed in Chapter 11 on Human Rights) occurring in the former Yugoslavia.

The Problems The establishment of the International Tribunal regarding crimes in the former Yugoslavia (UNITY) is a noble step toward realizing the age-old dream of the supremacy of the rule of law rather than rule by men. There are a variety of problems, however. They involve the *focus* of the criminal investigation, *jurisdiction, evidence, finances,* and *inertia.*

Focus: A preliminary problem is the apparent focus on the Serbs, as opposed to Muslims and Croats. The latter are allegedly responsible for some of the same crimes that are typically attributed to the Serbs by the Western press. It is also unlikely that Bosnia's Serbs will formally arrive at a negotiated settlement without assurances of protection from war crimes prosecution. In the 1994 Haiti settlement, for example, the deplorable disregard of human rights by Haiti's military leader was one basis for the US intervention. Suddenly, he was protected from prosecution—as a cost of peace and the expeditious return of democratic rule in Haiti. In El Salvador, the two army officers who shot six Jesuit

priests were released under a government-sponsored amnesty program. One can only hope that *all* relevant crimes will be the focus of the prosecution, not just those for which the Bosnian Serbs could be prosecuted.

Jurisdiction: What is the UNITY's jurisdictional competence to act? The Security Council premised the tribunal's jurisdiction on its "Chapter VII" powers contained in the UN Charter. Article 39 contains the central theme of the Charter-vested powers: the "Security Council shall determine the existence of any threat to the peace, breach of the peace, or act of aggression and shall make recommendations, or decide what measures shall be taken . . . to maintain or restore international peace and security." Of course, no UN entity has the power to create a subsidiary organ to carry out functions not conferred upon the endowing UN entity by the Charter. As stated by Judge Onyeama in a 1973 ICJ opinion:

> [T]he General Assembly cannot legally establish a subsidiary body to perform functions which were not specifically assigned to the Assembly itself, or [are not] within the range of its functions. Thus the Committee on International Criminal Jurisdiction established by the Assembly by resolution 489 (V) to prepare preliminary draft conventions and proposals relating to the establishment and the statute of an international criminal court, stated in its report: 'Under the Charter, the [ICC] Court could only be established as a subsidiary organ. The principal organ would presumably be the General Assembly, but a *subsidiary organ could not have a competence falling outside the competence of its principal,* and it was questionable whether the General Assembly [rather than the ICJ] was competent to administer justice.'[56]

The typical legal foundation for an ICC would be a multilateral treaty. This premise presents the dual disadvantages, however, of taking too much time and risking another unratified treaty—due to the possible lack of sufficient ratifications. The UN Secretary-General's Report regarding implementation of the UNITY thus acknowledges that its creation, in "the normal course of events . . . would be . . . a treaty . . . drawn up and adopted by an appropriate international body (e.g., the General Assembly or a specially convened conference), following which it would be opened for signature and ratification. [But] . . . the treaty approach incurs the disadvantage of requiring considerable time to establish an instrument . . . [and] there would be no guarantee that ratifications will be received. . . ."[57]

The assumption that the Security Council is thus able to delegate the power to act to a tribunal separate from the existing UN judicial organ is not without controversy. China, for example, characterized its establishment as an unwarranted intrusion on State sovereignty to try international crimes and criminals. Brazil pointed out that the various UN resolutions, and even the UNITY's Statute, are not meant to establish new international norms. Other States have expressed the sentiment that establishing the UNITY via a Security Council Resolution, rather than treaty, is an infringement on their territorial sovereignty. This issue may well be raised should the Tribunal summon indicted defendants from one of these reluctant States for prosecution at its seat in the Netherlands.

UNITY jurisdiction, if ever actually exercised, will focus on breaches of the 1949 Geneva Conventions and the customary laws of war, crimes against humanity as set forth in the 1946 Nuremberg Charter, and genocide as defined by the 1948 UN Convention on Genocide.

Evidence: The most practical of all problems with the UNITY will be the securing of evidence for use by the prosecution. The Tribunal technically began to function in 1993. Its preliminary mandate is to develop appropriate rules of evidence and procedure. The relevant difference between the Nuremberg and Yugoslavian ICCs is that the Nazis left a paper trail that was a virtual prosecutor's dream. An *official* State policy promoted genocide, murder, torture, and other mistreatment directed at certain ethnic groups. There is no such *official* policy in the former Yugoslavia—and thus no paper trail to conveniently document what has occurred. It is also difficult to obtain evidence while a war is in progress.

Another important evidentiary distinction is the unofficial policy whereby Bosnian Serbs allegedly engaged in a policy of mass rape of Muslim women to defile the population as a whole, as well as to convince Muslims to leave Bosnia. The natural tendency not to recount such crimes (for distant court proceedings) is compounded by religious limitations that severely limit the likelihood that Muslim victims will come forth to testify. There is the related

problem of reported retaliatory threats by the perpetrators if the victims testify. The establishment of six UN-created "safe havens" would theoretically provide an opportunity for victims to appear for depositions. Yet, the UN peacekeeping forces in Bosnia have not been able to ensure the safety of those areas. Further, the UN has not established any "safe houses" for victims who might be willing to go to the Bosnian "safe havens" (or the ICC's Netherlands seat) to testify.

Assuming that the UNITY issues subpoenas, States sheltering the individual defendants will likely ignore the Tribunal's "command" to produce them for trial—not to mention that there is no current arrangement to house such defendants pending trial. The most severe reaction would be UN Security Council sanctions, a threat that has not been particularly effective in other UN proceedings.

Finances: The prospects for UNITY's success are also thwarted by the same financial problems that have plagued the UN for some time (*see* § 3.3). The estimate for the *first year* of UNITY's operation—after fighting has ceased—is 373 staff members and $30 million. Also, there are no specially earmarked funds available, on the cessation of hostilities. Given the severe budgetary constraints of current UN operations generally, even the most well-thought-out judicial operation would suffer from a lack of the requisite funding. There would be painstaking work necessary to obtain evidence, procure witnesses, pay for a witness protection program, and actually underwrite the prosecution of the perpetrators, who obviously could not be produced without substantial costs.

Inertia: The final problem with this ICC is that all of the above problems with the UNITY could combine to make it no more effective than the abandoned threats to prosecute Saddam Hussein for war crimes after hostilities ceased in the Persian Gulf War. A previous order of the International Court of Justice (April 1993) warned Serbia's leaders that their forces could not engage in genocide. There is no standing UN Army. The UN has been *un*able to control the various factions in the Bosnian theater. The existing international tribunal can thus be safely ignored by potential defendants, who are likely to cease hostilities only on condition of immunity from prosecution for their crimes.

Another basis for inertia is the concern that today's prosecutors may be tomorrow's defendants.

When US President Bush was considering a US-backed plan to prosecute Iraqi leader Hussein for war crimes in 1991, he was advised that this would not be a risk-free venture for the US. Such war crimes trials might also require the trial of members of the US-led Persian Gulf War coalition for war crimes incident to their driving the Iraqi army out of Kuwait. There were civilian deaths, for example, that were a by-product of bombing by coalition warplanes. A US warplane's bomb killed hundreds of civilians in a bunker in Baghdad. There is the daunting question of whether British soldiers slaughtered Argentinean soldiers in the Falkland Islands War in 1982, in violation of the same 1949 Geneva Conventions relied on by the UNITY. And of the five permanent members of the UN Security Council, only the former Soviet Union ratified the 1968 Convention on the Non-Applicability of Statutory Limitations to War Crimes and Crimes Against Humanity.[58]

It is ironic that the *UN* itself sought amnesty for two Serbs convicted in 1993 by a Bosnian military court for war crimes in Bosnia. Many of their forty victims were young women who were first raped as part of the Serb ethnic cleansing campaign of Bosnia's Muslim population. UN military commander Lt. General Philippe Morillon appealed these convictions on the basis that the UN was trying to shore up a three-day ceasefire—which was in effect at the time of the judgment in this case. This UN agent criticized the Bosnians for trying these Serbs, rather than holding them for prosecution by the (yet to actually function) UNITY. In Morillon's widely-reported words: "Let this [UN ICC] court prosecute the criminals. *This is not the time for them* [referring to the Bosnian Muslim government] *to take justice into their own hands*." He thus sought a general amnesty for accused war criminals as "the only way to calm the anguish and mistrust" between Muslims and Serbs. The justices of the local court responded that, after a fair trial, the only way to deter similar crimes would be a widely-reported execution.[59]

The hiatus in the work of the UNITY, occasioned partially by a long period of war in the former Yugoslavia, has meant that much of the evidence dissipated with the flight of refugees from Bosnia. In the meantime, the moral outrage associated with the Bosnian war crimes has deteriorated in proportion to the length of the Bosnian conflict. The horrors of rape camps, forced sodomy and castration, and systematic ethnic extermination have

effectively slipped into a somewhat resigned acquiescence. If the community of nations did not militarily intervene, then the establishment of UNITY is the moral equivalent of the position that "everyone is guilty, and there is nothing that the outside world can do except establish *another* international tribunal." The community of nations was, in fact, aware of the Nazi extermination camps as early as 1942, but disclaimed their existence until approximately 1944.[60] Taking a passive stance in the Yugoslavian theater, by establishing a new ICC, should thus be no surprise.

■ 9.6 REGIONAL COURT ADJUDICATION

International Law in Regional Courts

Article 33 of the UN Charter provides that the "parties to any dispute . . . shall, first of all, seek a solution by negotiation, . . . arbitration, . . . resort to regional agencies or arrangements, or other peaceful means of their own choice." This section of the book thus surveys *regional* litigation of international disputes, theoretical advantages, and practical problems with this form of dispute settlement.

For many centuries, international disputes were not resolved by international courts. Diplomatic negotiations and occasional *ad hoc* arbitrations served this purpose. For example, successful postwar diplomacy might result in the creation of international "Claims Commissions." These temporary bodies heard evidence from representatives of the States involved in the particular dispute. The resolution of claims would effectively dissolve the commission.

The trend has been away from the use of temporary regional tribunals in favor of more permanent institutions for resolving disputes. During the twentieth century, for example, a number of regional courts (and two global courts) have been created by international agreement. Full-time judges and permanent staffs are available to the parties thereby submitting disputes to these tribunals. This method of dispute resolution differs from the historical mode of *ad hoc* arbitration, because the parties to the dispute have immediate access to an *existing* court. They are unrestrained by the need for a fresh arbitration agreement—creating the tribunal and selecting the arbitrators—each time that they decide to settle a dispute with the assistance of an objective "outsider."

In theory, regional courts *should* be more viable dispute resolution mechanisms than global courts. But, like the International Court of Justice, they are generally underutilized. Mistrust of the institution should be, of course, less of a problem in a *regional* court. The local judges can thereby resolve international problems originating within their own region, and are more likely to be familiar with regional norms of conduct. The two so-called "World Courts," both seated in the heart of Europe, have been criticized for not fully comprehending the impact of regional practices.

The comparative enforceability of the judgments is a related benefit of the regional court process. Unlike judgments from the UN's International Court of Justice, which have sometimes been ignored, judgments from the regional tribunals in Europe are unquestionably incorporated into the fabric of the European Union's member States. With the exception of this particular region, however, it is not clear that regional courts have been more effective than global courts. A number of regional courts have not survived. Those that have, do not hear many cases. A Central American Court, the first regional international court, was established by treaty in 1907. The State participants soon decided that any need for regional courts would be supplanted by the Permanent Court of International Justice. The Central American Court was therefore disbanded in 1918.

The belief that regional courts would be viable dispute-resolution mechanisms resurfaced after the demise of the first "World Court." In 1945, the States that created the UN inserted Article 33 into the UN Charter—indicating that disputes might be considered first by "regional arrangements." This language therein incorporated the theme that regional courts could play an effective role in shifting international disputes from the battlefield to the courtroom.

The absence, or presence, of a major regional power has affected the viability of regional adjudication. The regional European legal process described below accommodates the major powers of France and Great Britain. Their influence has significantly advanced adjudication at the regional level. The comparative frailty of the Latin American regional court process could be attributed to the lack of resolve of the US to engage in regional adjudication with its OAS neighbors. The *lack* of a major regional power has limited the effectiveness of regional tribunals. International courts in other regions of the world are unlikely to achieve the European success, without a significant economic or military power to motivate this mode of dispute resolution.

A related limitation of the regional court system is that its success depends on the *solidarity* of the member States. In most cases, the political and economic unity of the region has been minimal. This discourages national resort to these courts for the resolution of disputes. In the European Union, on the other hand, members have demonstrated the necessary cohesiveness to support a regional court system for an entire generation. The participating States possess similar economic and political interests—a fact that has contributed significantly to the success of the region's political organization and judicial dispute-resolution processes. In most regions, the lack of political solidarity limits the potential for a more effective regional court process.

In a more perfect world, the resolution of international disputes would not be affected by political considerations. The decision about whether to go to court, however, is itself a major political consideration. Many States avoid regional (and global) courts for reasons unrelated to the legal issues or merits of their disputes. National leaders may decide that the filing of a lawsuit in a public forum will only exacerbate national differences—which can be otherwise managed more effectively through less sensitive avenues of diplomacy. A State may oppose *judicial* resolutions of international disputes because a public airing of the problem may escalate (or create) a rift in international relations. In a different political environment, the same State may seek a judicial resolution. Amicable relations may be preserved by submission of the case to an impartial international tribunal.

Another problem limits the viability of regional adjudication. States have not given regional courts the compulsory jurisdiction to litigate. When States have created regional courts, they theoretically agree that the availability of a standing tribunal is a good idea. In practice, however, they do not *require* themselves to submit to the judicial processes of the regional courts that they create. They fear the loss of sovereignty they typically associate with submitting sensitive cases to a public forum that they do not control.

The *lack of a defined relationship* between the global and regional court systems further limits the potential for the judicial resolution of international disputes. Issues arising under International Law have been adjudicated *both* in the various regional courts, *and* in the International Court of Justice. UN Charter Article 95 grants the ICJ the power to hear cases arising under International Law. No Charter provision, however, creates or even suggests that there is a relationship between the ICJ and the various regional courts. Charter Article 33 merely provides for prior resort to "regional agencies or arrangements" for the resolution of international disputes. The same case could be lodged in *both* a regional court and the ICJ. Certain State violations of an individual's human rights, for example, could be heard in the European Court of Human Rights, the International Court of Justice, or the UN's International Criminal Court for the trial of war crimes in the former Yugoslavia.

The *lack of a hierarchy* among regional and global courts is a related limitation on the viability of regional adjudication. While the litigants are expected to exhaust local remedies in *national* courts, before coming to the ICJ (*see* § 2.5 on State responsibility), the ICJ has never required its litigants to resort first to available *regional* courts. Neither the UN Charter nor the Statute of the ICJ give the ICJ power to suspend regional court proceedings, so that the ICJ might provide a global response to the problem at hand.

A *lack of uniformity* also limits the international system of adjudication. Regional courts operate independently of national courts, the ICJ, and each other. Regional international courts function as *trial* courts, from which there is no right of appeal—nor any forum to which an appeal could be taken. States have never ceded appellate powers to regional (or global) courts. When creating the international courts discussed later in this section of the book, States avoided the typical model existing within their own court systems. In many national court systems, cases normally proceed through a hierarchy of judicial levels. This progression creates a trial-court record resolving factual issues, so that an appellate tribunal may then concentrate on the legal issues involved in the dispute. This promotes uniformity of decision within national legal systems. A higher appellate court may then provide guidance to the various national trial courts, thus promoting uniform application of the law within that national system.

The general lack of a legal relationship among regional courts—and between regional courts and the ICJ—has generated other problems. The predicament of having entirely independent regional court systems was forecast by Professor Jenks of England. In 1943, prior to creation of the regional courts that exist today, he cautioned against such a system as follows: "[t]he coexistence of the Permanent Court of International Justice and of entirely independent regional international courts would involve at least two dangers. There would be a danger of conflicts regarding jurisdiction, and a danger that regional courts might be inspired by regional legal conceptions to such an extent that their decisions might prejudice the future unity of the law of nations in respect of matters regarding which uniform rules of worldwide validity are desirable."[61]

Jenk's concern about parochial definitions of International Law was well founded. The interpretation of what constitutes a local custom has jeopardized prospects for a smooth relationship between national, regional, and global courts. What one type of court perceives as falling within the general parameters of International Law may be a rather parochial perspective. The ICJ's 1950 *Asylum* case (set forth in the text of § 7.3) illustrates this problem. Colombia relied on a regional practice to establish its claim that Peru had failed to honor the right of asylum existing in the Latin American region of the world. This was in fact a regional practice. The ICJ did not affirm this regional right of asylum because it was not practiced on a global level. The ICJ thus ruled that Colombia "failed to meet its burden" of proving the existence of such a right under International Law. The ICJ was harshly criticized for its failure to recognize and apply this regional practice.

Who may be a party in regional proceedings? This question reveals a significant difference between the regional and global adjudication of international disputes. As analyzed in Chapter 4 on the status of the individual, International Law does not recognize the right of an *individual* to appear as a plaintiff or defendant in an international proceeding. As analyzed in § 9.4, *States* (contentious cases) and *international organizations* (advisory cases) may be parties to proceedings in the International Court of Justice. In the case of an individual or corporation, harmed by the act of a foreign sovereign, the State of citizenship must be willing to present the claims of such aggrieved citizens in the ICJ's proceedings. In certain regional courts, however, member States have permitted individuals and business entities to present their claims directly to an international tribunal. The States that created the European court system determined that individual access to international executive and judicial institutions would foster the economic and political goals of their union. A corporation harmed by a breach of European Union law, for example, may proceed with its claim in the European Court of Justice, rather than suing the responsible State in its own courts. A Belgian corporation, for example, would not have to sue Belgium in Belgium's national court system.[62]

The next subsection surveys the operations and aspirations of the various regional courts.

Operational Regional Courts

Several regional courts currently hear issues arising under International Law. They include the following courts, which are discussed below: (1) the European Court of Justice, (2) the European Court of Human Rights, (3) the Inter-American Court of Human Rights, and (4) the Andean Court of Justice. These courts essentially interpret the treaties that created the political or economic organizations they serve.

There have been other dormant or defunct regional courts. The former Central American Court of Justice ceased to function in 1918. While it was supposedly reestablished in 1965, it has not yet issued a case. The Court of Justice of the European Coal and Steel Community was replaced by the current European Court of Justice in 1973. The League of Arab States has contemplated establishing an Arab Court of Justice since 1950. The proposed court is described in a draft statute. However, insufficient political solidarity in the region has prevented its activation.[63]

Various regional courts are profiled in Exhibit 9.3.

EXHIBIT 9.3 Regional International Courts

Court	Location (date)[a]	Bench	Affiliations	Cases Heard
Court of Justice of the European Communities[b]	Luxembourg (1973)	13 judges—1 from each European Union member State and president	Council of Europe/ European Union	Commission v. State/private v. EU institution/cases referred from national court
European Court of Human Rights[b]	Strasbourg, France (1958)	23 judges—from member States of the Council of Europe	Council of Europe/ European Union	Determines State violations of European Convention on Human Rights
European Court of First Instance[b]	Luxembourg (1989)	12 judges—1 from each European Union member State	Council of Europe/ European Union	Actions brought by individual/appeals to Court of Justice
Inter-American Court of Human Rights	San Jose, Costa Rica (1979)	6 part-time judges and 1 full-time president /all from OAS member States	Organization of American States	Determines State violations of American Convention on Human Rights
Andean Court of Justice	Quito, Ecuador (1979)	5 judges—1 from each member State	Andean Pact/ Latin American Free Trade Association	Reviews State compliance with Pact economics

EXHIBIT 9.3 *(continued)*

Court	Location (date)[a]	Bench	Affiliations	Cases Heard
Central American Court of Justice	[c] (1907/1965)	Presidents of member States' judiciaries	Organization of Central American States	Disputes between States and between individual and State[d]
Arab Court of Justice	Cairo, Egypt (1965)	[d]	League of Arab States	[d]

[a] = Date established/reestablished

[b] = Compulsory jurisdiction over member States

[c] = Hiatus, from 1918 until reconstituted in 1965; *see* D. Bowett, *The Law of International Institutions* 287 (4th ed. London: Stevens & Sons, 1982)

[d] = Proposed but not yet operational

European Court of Justice The 1957 Treaty of Rome established the first European regional court—the Court of Justice of the European Coal and Steel Community. Article 3 of the 1973 Convention on Certain Institutions Common to the European Communities then transferred the powers of this court to the current ECJ located in Luxembourg. The ECJ's judges, who come from twelve countries, decide about two hundred cases per year.

The ECJ, sometimes called the "Supreme Court" of Europe, resolves disputes between the national laws of member States and European Community law (now called the European Union, or "EU"). For example, EU nations are not supposed to create import duties or nontariff barriers on most products imported from other EU members. This Court decided that Italy violated community transportation rules by prohibiting an Irish airline from picking up passengers in England and flying them to Milan.

The judicial power of this remarkably successful tribunal is succinctly described by Professor John Bridge of the University of Exeter in England as follows:

> The ECJ is an "international court in more than one sense of that term. It is international in the fundamental sense that it is a creation of international law through the joint exercise of the treaty-making powers of the Member States. In organizational terms it is international in that it is composed of judges of the different nationalities of the [EU] Member States. In jurisdictional terms it is international in the classic sense that it is competent to hear and determine cases alleging the failure of Member States to fulfil treaty obligations. Another aspect of its international character lies in its authority to review, with reference to the Treaties, the legality of acts and omissions by the institutions set up by the Treaties to serve the purposes of the Communities. The ECJ also has jurisdiction to rule on the compatibility with the EEC Treaty of proposed agreements between Community and either third states or an international organization. It also serves as an international administrative tribunal through its jurisdiction in disputes between the Communities and its servants.[64]

The ECJ differs from the traditional international tribunals. Unlike the practice of the global International Court of Justice, where only *States* may be parties, individuals and corporations may participate in certain proceedings before the ECJ (especially through its Court of First Instance). The first two cases heard by the European Court were filed by private (nongovernment) corporations. Individuals who have been fined by an administrative body of the European Union may appeal to the ECJ. Individuals and corporations may also ask the ECJ to annul administrative decisions and regulations of EU agencies that allegedly violate EU norms. In one case, a British citizen filed suit in the ECJ to recover damages incurred during an assault in Paris. The administrator of a French fund for French citizens had denied the British citizen's claim, on the basis of his foreign nationality. In another case of great constitutional significance, a

French political group was able to successfully attack the European Parliament's allocation of funds from its budget to certain political parties. This clarified the Court's position that the decisions of all EU institutions, including the European Parliament, were open to judicial review via suits brought by private individuals or nongovernmental entities.[65]

National tribunals may also invoke the aid of the ECJ. Under Article 177 of the EEC treaty and Article 150 of the Euratom treaty, courts and other tribunals from within the EU's member States have requested the ECJ to rule on a treaty matter arising within their particular national systems.

This Court's practice further differs from routine international litigation in the UN's International Court of Justice. The UN, unlike the EU, is composed of approximately 184 member States. The objectives of the UN members are quite diverse, in comparison to the much smaller EU—whose member States are comparatively homogenous. Also, the respective constitutional charters are quite different. The UN Charter is *not* a legally enforceable document. It did not create immediately enforceable obligations applicable to all of its member States. These were, instead, standards of achievement—or, a form of global political aspiration (*see* § 8.1). On the other hand, the various treaties applicable to the comparatively integrated European Union were intended to create legal obligations from the outset. Thus, EU member States are subject to the economic directives contained in its various self-executing treaties. The EU may thus enforce their provisions in the same manner that a national court may require compliance with its internal law. This difference accounts for the comparative volume of cases heard by the ECJ.

The range of the ECJ's jurisdiction has had an impact on States outside of the EU—including the US. Ironically, there is virtually a global obsession with the so-called "extraterritorial application" of the laws of the US.[66] The ECJ exercises similar power, under International Law and its own case law, to enforce Community legislation against nonmembers. The ECJ even relies on US antitrust caselaw in support of its power to control anticompetitive conduct abroad.

The following case depicts the novel ability of an international organization to enforce its economic solidarity through its integrated legislative, executive, and judicial policy. The ECJ acts in furtherance of the interest of the entire community of member States, so as to govern the conduct of citizens in nonmember States. This case illustrates how the ECJ effectively speaks for the region, when dealing with anticompetitive policies from abroad.

A cartel of US, Canadian, and other private wood pulp companies agreed to align their prices. This plan eliminated price competition, among these companies, for sales to various customers within the European Union (EU). This conduct did not violate US law. US companies may conspire to fix prices, as long as their arrangement involves only exports. The EU's executive authority (the "Commission") fined these foreign wood pulp companies for their anticompetitive conduct, based on their *activity outside* of the EU having an *effect within* the EU.

The defendants basically claimed that an international organization did not have the power to sanction the conduct of foreign companies that were not citizens of States within the European Economic Community. The ECJ herein resolved the related issues of whether the "EEC" (now European Union) could apply its laws to foreign individuals—on a par with *State* exercises of this so-called "extraterritorial" jurisdiction.

AHLSTROM OY AND OTHERS v. EC COMMISSION

Court of Justice of the European Communities, 1988
Case No. 89/85, Euro. Court Rep. 5193, 4 Common Mkt. L. Rep. 901*

[Author's Note: After the preliminary statement of the facts, the bulk of the reported ECJ case opinion contains the analysis by the Advocate-General assigned to this case. Six individuals, who are ECJ employees, serve in this special capacity and do not represent any party. Unlike the US system, where there is no similar judicial officer, the ECJ judges rely heavily on the analysis prepared by the Advocate-General assigned to this case. The "Commission" is the administrative body that developed the record in this case, and that fined the foreign companies before they appealed to the ECJ.

Emphasis and bolding have been supplied by the author at several points within this opinion. Citations to authority have been omitted.]

[*Opinion.*] These applications [for relief] are directed against the Commission Decision of 19 December 1984 establishing that 41 wood pulp producers, and two of their trade associations, all having their registered offices outside the Community, [illegally] engaged in concerted practices on prices. . . .

[I.] *A. The product and the producers*

Wood pulp is used in the manufacture of paper and paperboard.

. . . The product in question in these cases is a chemical pulp known as 'bleached sulphate pulp.' Of all wood pulps it is the best in quality and its characteristics are such that it can be used in the manufacture of quality paper (writing paper or printing paper) and quality paperboard (milk cartons).

. . .

The more than 800 paper manufacturers established in the Community are supplied by some fifty pulp producers from at least eighteen countries. The Community is the most important market for bleached sulphate pulp, relatively little of which is produced in the Community.

. . .

B. The contested decision

1. The operative part of the decision

In its decision, the Commission has established a number of infringements [of Community legislation and policies].

. . .

In respect of all those practices, the Commission imposed fines on 36 of the 43 addressees of the decision.

. . .

However, the Commission states that it also took into account the submission of the United States addressees that they were unaware that their behaviour infringed Community law.

. . .

2. **Whether the Community has jurisdiction to apply its competition rules in this case**

In its decision the Commission states:

Article 85 of the EEC Treaty applies to restrictive practices which may affect trade between member-States even if the undertakings and associations which are parties to the restrictive practices are established or have their headquarters *outside* the Community, and even if the restrictive practices in question also affect markets outside the EEC.

In this case all the [defendant] addressees of this decision were during the period of the infringement exporting directly to or doing business within the Community. Some of them had branches, subsidiaries, agencies or other establishments within the Community. The concertation [illegal agreement] on [fixing] prices, the exchange of sensitive information relative to prices, and the clauses prohibiting export or resale all concerned shipments made directly to buyers in the EEC or sales made in the EEC to buyers there. The shipments affected by these agreements and practices amounted to about two-thirds of total shipments of bleached sulphate wood pulp to the EEC and some 60 per cent of EEC consumption. . . . The effect of the agreements and practices on prices announced and/or charged to customers and on resale of pulp within the EEC was therefore not only substantial but intended, and was the primary and direct result of the agreements and practices.

. . .

D. Procedure before the Court

. . .

On 8 July 1987, the Court decided that the parties should first of all be heard on the question *whether the Community has jurisdiction to apply its competition rules* to undertakings whose registered office is situated *outside* the Community.

. . .

Questions asked by the Court

The Court asked the Commission the following question:

Does the Commission maintain that it has jurisdiction in these cases by reason of *conduct* which has taken place *within* the Community and, if so, what is that conduct? *Or* does it [the Commission] base its jurisdiction on the *effects within* the Community of conduct which took place outside the Community and, if so, what is that conduct and what are its effects?

The Commission answered that question as follows:

On the basis of Article 3(f) of the Treaty, the Commission considers that the primary objective of the rules on competition in the EEC Treaty is to ensure that the conduct of economic activity in the Community should not be distorted [by anti-competitive price-fixing]. Therefore, in considering what constitutes the relevant conduct for the purposes of Article 85, the Commission must determine how the agreement, decision or concerted practice has been implemented. In the case of a concerted practice, this means identifying the practices that have been concerted.

. . .

The Commission acknowledges that *it is not always easy to distinguish 'the effects' of 'conduct' from the conduct itself.*

. . .

Thus the communication of announced prices was made *in* the Community. The transaction prices themselves were charged in the Community by the producers themselves, by their subsidiaries, branches or other establishments, or by their agents or employees.

. . .

Finally, as regards . . . price recommendations, . . . that *conduct admittedly took place outside the Community. However, the substantial, foreseeable and direct effect of that conduct is a restriction of competition within the Common Market*, that is to say an effect which clearly took place within the Community.

Next, the Commission considers whether that kind of jurisdiction may be claimed under international law. . . .

In this case, the Commission considers that if the Community's jurisdiction in this case is considered to be based on conduct which occurred *within* the Community, it is not in breach of any prohibitive rule of international law. The same holds true in so far as its jurisdiction is based on the effects within the Community of conduct which occurred elsewhere. The Community has not acted in a manner which is contrary to the laws or national interests of non-member countries, nor has it substantially interfered with the economic policy of the countries concerned, as is clear from the lack of any reaction from those countries [that is, no diplomatic or other protest by non-Community countries to the Community's imposition of fines].

There is nothing in international law which obliges the Commission to interpret away the word 'effect' in Article 85 of the Treaty as soon as that effect is produced [from some other location] across international boundaries. Although the 'effects doctrine' is still contested under international law, the Commission considers that the objections come primarily from the United Kingdom and not from . . . other countries. The Commission maintains that, in that respect, the Community should not be subject to a more restrictive jurisdictional criterion than that accepted for *States* [merely because the Community is an international organization].

. . .

[I]t is said that there is nothing in the wording of Article 85 of the Treaty to *allow* it to be extended to cover undertakings outside the Community solely by reason of anti-competitive effects produced within the territory of the Community. Secondly, it is suggested that the case law of the Court can be construed as rejecting the effects doctrine. Let me state at once that I will advise the Court to uphold neither of those objections.

. . .

Principles laid down by the Court in its case law
Although the Court has not, in its decision to date, formally upheld the effects doctrine with regard to the application of competition law to undertakings outside the Community, that does not imply that it rejects the doctrine.

. . .

II. The effects doctrine in the light of international law

. . .

Is the location of effects doctrine, as a basis for jurisdiction, consistent with the rules of international law? In order to answer that question, it is necessary first of all to consider the very nature of international law. . . .

Academic writers are divided on that point. The discussion has revolved essentially around the significance and scope of the LOTUS judgment, delivered on 7 September 1927 by the Permanent Court of International Justice ((1927) PCIJ ser A, no 10). That judgment, adopted by the President's casting vote, states in particular that international law does not prohibit a *State* from exercising jurisdiction in its own territory, in respect of any case which relates to acts which have taken place abroad.

. . .

And what is thus permissible for *States* must necessarily also be permissible for the *Community*, as a ["person" who is a] subject of international law, where the jurisdiction of the Community has been substituted for that of the member-States.

. . .

That having been said, it is undoubtedly in United States law that are to be found the most far-reaching deliberations and efforts to determine the circumstances permitting a State to exercise its prescriptive jurisdiction in situations involving extraneous elements. That is not surprising. The [US]

Sherman [Antitrust] Act dates back to 1890. It has given rise to a very considerable body of case law and academic writing, evidencing the concern to reconcile legitimate national interests with the imperative requirements of international law and international relations. That is why I propose to refer to the most noteworthy decisions of the United States courts [in the following passages of this opinion].

III. The principles of United States law

. . .

In the context of this attempt to circumscribe the effects doctrine, reference should be made to the judgment of Judge Choy in the TIMBERLANE LUMBER case ((9th Cir 1977) 549 F 2d 597). . . .

Judge Choy came to the conclusion that, in certain circumstances, the interests of the United States were too weak and the incentive for restraint in order to preserve harmony in its international relations too strong to justify an assertion of extraterritorial jurisdiction.

. . .

In that regard, United States law, as it now stands, rests [firmly] on two principles. The first is that the United States will assert jurisdiction [over conduct outside the US] where the effects on its trade are direct, substantial and foreseeable. According to the second [principle], the courts should assess the 'balance of interests' in order to ensure that the exercise of such jurisdiction is reasonable [given the respective national interests involved].

. . .

DECISION [of the ECJ]:

. . .

The [wood pulp] producers in this case *implemented* their pricing agreement *within* the Common Market. . . .

Accordingly the Community's jurisdiction to apply its competition rules to such conduct is covered by the territoriality principle as universally recognised in public international law.

. . .

It should further be pointed out that the United States authorities raised no objections regarding any conflict of jurisdiction when consulted by the Commission pursuant to the OECD [regional Organization for Economic Co-operation and Development]

Council Recommendation of 25 October 1979 concerning Co-operation between member Countries on Restrictive Business Practices affecting International Trade (Acts of the Organisation, Vol 19, p 377).

. . .

Accordingly it must be concluded that the Commission's decision is not contrary to Article 85 of the Treaty or to the rules of public international law relied on by the applicants.

■ NOTES & QUESTIONS

1. The case of the *SS Lotus*, referred to in the ECJ's opinion, is set forth in the text of § 5.2 of this book on general jurisdictional principles under International Law. That case, from the Permanent Court of International Justice, differed in certain respects from the issues before the ECJ in *Ahlstrom*—how so?

2. The ECJ refers to the absence of a US protest to the Commission fine and the ECJ exercise of jurisdiction over the US wood pulp companies. Had there been such a protest, would it be likely to change the Court's decision—in a case where the US had militarily invaded Panama to get Noriega?

European Court of Human Rights The European Court of Human Rights (ECHR) is the other regional court in Europe. Established by the 1950 European Convention for the Protection of Human Rights and Fundamental Freedoms, the ECHR became operational in 1958 when the eighth European Community member State accepted its jurisdiction to hear cases arising under the regional Human Rights treaty. It began hearing cases in Strasbourg, France, in 1959. There are twenty-three European State signatories to this treaty. Its jurisdiction, while limited to human rights matters, is more extensive than that of the European Court of Justice—in terms of the number of State parties to the human rights treaty that provides the basis for this court's existence.

Article 45 of the Human Rights treaty provides that the ECHR may hear "all cases concerning the interpretation and application of the present Convention." The Court's basic role is to provide judicial protection for the fundamental rights of the individual. The ECHR thus hears cases that might not be heard under the laws of the aggrieved individual's home State. In Great Britain, for example, there is no written constitution that enumerates a list of individual rights. Neither the medieval Magna Charta nor any other document guarantees the right of British citizens against any capricious act of government agents. Great Britain's commitment to the preservation of human rights under the European treaty, however, does provide certain written guarantees to British citizens. They may file claims against their government in the ECHR, at its seat in Strasbourg, France.[67]

Member States, and the European Commission on Human Rights may litigate suits in the ECHR. Individuals do not have the legal capacity to be parties, although they may petition the European Commission on Human Rights to correct State action that fails to comply with the Human Rights treaty. The Commission is the major administrative organ for ensuring State compliance with the human rights treaty. If the Commission cannot reach a satisfactory settlement with the offending member State, it presents the aggrieved individual's claim to the ECHR (*see, e.g., Open Door Case*, set forth in text of § 3.4).

In one of the Court's more famous cases, it effectively deviated from the usual international practice of denying *individual* access to an international tribunal. In the *Lawless* case, an Irish citizen accused of terrorism was jailed under an Irish statute that could be used only during a state of emergency. Lawless claimed that Ireland improperly deprived him of his right to liberty because there was no "emergency." The Irish Supreme Court refused to release him, although he claimed that there was no legitimate basis for his incarceration. The European Court of Human Rights initially determined that "it is in the interests of the proper administration of justice that the [Human Rights] Court should have knowledge of and, if need be, take into consideration, the applicant's [Lawless's] point of view." In a related proceeding, the ECHR reconfirmed the validity of the treaty provision barring individuals from being litigants in the court but implicitly modified this limitation. It ruled that when the Commission presented Lawless's claim to the court, it could "place some person at its [the court's] disposal in order to fully present the point of view of the individual harmed by State action."[68] This meant that an individual (Lawless) could be present in the court to argue his own case directly, although he was supposedly not a party to the international proceedings. As a result of this case, the representatives of the European Commission rely on the "assistance" of individuals or their lawyers in ECHR proceedings.

Members of the European Community (and some nonmember states) have submitted disputes to the compulsory jurisdiction of the European Court of Human Rights. They have thus promised to participate in all cases alleging breaches of their treaty obligation to preserve fundamental human rights. State participation in this regional judicial process demonstrates a greater commitment than many of those same nations have shown to any global judicial process. They have thus relinquished some of the sovereign immunity that would otherwise shield them from being sued without their express consent. The resistance of the same States to the compulsory jurisdiction of the International Court of Justice illustrates their preference for *regional* enforcement of human rights under their regional treaty.

Another comparative advantage of the ECHR (versus the ICJ) is that ECHR judgments are directly enforceable in the national courts of the parties to the European Convention on Human Rights. This eliminates a major enforcement problem plaguing the ICJ. Even when States appear and litigate in the ICJ's proceedings, there is no supranational executive body to oversee national compliance with the ICJ judgments. Nor is there a comparable treaty provision making ICJ judgments directly enforceable by treating them as if they were made by a national court of the State parties to the dispute.

There are, of course, questions about the proper scope of the ECHR's decisional law, and how its exercise has affected the willingness of member States to submit to its compulsory jurisdiction. The classic example of this conflict was spawned by the Court's decision in the 1979 *Sunday Times* case—wherein the ECHR overturned a major decision by the British House of Lords. A summary of the events in this ECHR case follows:

British proceedings: The drug Thalidomide was made in (former West) Germany and marketed in Great Britain. In 1961, large numbers of pregnant women, who used this sedative, began to give birth to children with severe deformities. The manufacturer withdrew the drug from the British market that year. During the 1971 settlement negotiations regarding the funding of a charitable trust established in 1968 for the children, the British newspaper *Sunday Times* criticized the small amounts to be placed in this trust, considering the severity of its effect on the children involved. The *Times* announced that a future article would detail how this tragedy occurred arising from lack of proper testing of the drug. The British Attorney-General (AG) obtained a court injunction barring the publication of this story—subjecting the *Times* to contempt of court if it published the article. Unlike the US, British law prohibits "trial by newspaper" so as to avoid pretrial publicity that will adversely affect pending litigation. In this case, however, the trial judge decided that the public's need to know outweighed the rationale for banning the intended newspaper story on pending litigation. The British AG appealed. The appellate court refused the AG the relief sought. The AG then further appealed to the House of Lords—effectively the "court of last resort" in Great Britain. The House directed that the trial court issue an injunction against publication—which again subjected the newspaper to contempt of court sanctions if it published the subject article.

ECHR proceedings: The newspaper then sought relief from the European Commission on Human Rights—an administrative step prior to the court proceedings. The Commission found that the injunction violated Article 10 of the European Human Rights Convention. That article protects the right to freedom of expression, including the right "to hold opinions and to receive and impart information and ideas without interference by public authority and regardless of frontiers." The European Court Human Rights in Strasbourg, France then affirmed this administrative decision, thereby relieving the paper of liability for contempt of the court in London. The ECHR thus held that the House of Lord's injunction against publication was not necessary for the maintenance of public confidence in the British judicial system. (Other nations, including Canada, also generally prohibit pretrial publicity like that which hindered the objective conduct of the famous 1995 O.J. Simpson case in Los Angeles, California).

Criticism: A prominent British lawyer, F.A. Mann, wrote that the ECHR, sitting in France, effectively undermined confidence in its regional judging by this ruling, which uprooted the staunchly ingrained British legal tradition. In his incisive analysis:

> contempt of court is undoubtedly one of the great contributions the common law [of England] has made to the civilised behaviour of a large part of the world beyond the continent of Europe where [the ECHR sits but] the institution [of restraining pretrial newspaper publicity to preserve confidence in the courts] is unknown. . . . Yet it is that very branch of the law which the European Court of Human Rights has seriously undermined by, in effect, overturning the unanimous decision of the House of Lords . . . a unique event in the [extensive] history of English law. In fact, it is probably no exaggeration to say that the gravest blow to the fabric of English law has been dealt by the *majority of eleven judges* coming *from* Cyprus, Denmark, Eire, France, Germany, Italy, Portugal, Spain, Sweden and Turkey, who over the *dissent of nine judges from* Austria, Belgium, Holland, Iceland, Luxembourg, Malta, Norway, Switzerland and the United Kingdom, decided in favour of the *Sunday Times*. . . . The [real issue is] whether the Strasbourg Court arrogated unto itself powers . . . which it cannot possibly exercise convincingly . . . and whether the level of [sound] judicial reasoning is higher in London or Strasbourg?[69]

Inter-American Court of Human Rights The Organization of American States (OAS) is the regional political association of States in the Western hemisphere (*see* § 3.5). OAS member State representatives drafted the American Convention on Human Rights, which became effective in 1978.[70] Approximately two-thirds of the OAS's more than thirty member States have adopted this treaty. (It has not been adopted by the US.)

In 1979, the OAS established the Inter-American Court of Human Rights (IAC) in San Jose, Costa Rica. Its first case was heard in 1981. It has heard only several contentious cases, and has rendered about a dozen advisory opinions. The primary function of this court is to interpret the referenced OAS Human Rights Convention. The IAC thus has the power to hear claims that an individual's civil and political rights have been infringed by State action. Unlike the practice that developed in Europe's regional courts, individuals can never appear either directly or indirectly in the IAC. Under Article 61(1) of the Convention, "only States Parties and the [Human Rights] Commission shall have the right to submit a case to the Court." The Human Rights Commission is the other organ that oversees national performance of obligations arising under the OAS Human Rights Convention.

The IAC hears disputes between States, when one accuses the other of violating the individual freedoms guaranteed under the American Convention. The participating States must consent, however, to the jurisdiction of this court to resolve such disputes. Unlike the practice in the region served by the two European courts, only a few OAS member States have accepted the compulsory jurisdiction of the IAC.

The IAC may also issue "advisory" opinions that do not require the presence of the offending nation. The purpose of this power, similar to that of the UN International Court of Justice advisory jurisdiction, is to provide judicial guidance to member States about certain practices that may violate the Human Rights Convention.[71] Thus, the absence of the consent of an offending State does not prevent the IAC from evaluating the particular practice in question. The Court is thus able to develop the regional Latin American law on State compliance with the provisions of the American Convention.

The Convention prohibits a State from harming its citizens for political purposes. In a landmark trial in 1988, the IAC heard the first contentious trial against a Latin American State for murdering its own citizens for political purposes. Honduras was tried for the disappearance and murders of 90,000 people since the 1950s.[72] Thus, the IAC is only the second regional court (after the European Court of Human Rights) to judge States for violations of internationally recognized human rights. Given the tragic history of this region, associated with dictatorships since World War II, the IAC has thus functioned essentially as an International Criminal Court.

The IAC is something more than a temporary arbitral body and something less than a permanent judicial institution. Its seven jurists from different OAS nations do not conduct proceedings on a full-time basis. Funding has been withheld, pending development of the Court's jurisprudence to a point where full-time judges are necessary. This part-time status is, unfortunately, unique among the regional courts of the world. As stated in 1982 by its Chief Justice, Professor Thomas Burgenthal (now) at George Washington University in Washington, D.C.: "a part-time tribunal might give that body an ad hoc image, likely to diminish the prestige and legitimacy it might need to obtain compliance with and respect for its decisions in the Americas. But the [OAS] General Assembly opted instead for a tribunal composed of part-time judges . . . [who are] free to practice law, to teach, and to engage in whatever other occupations they may have in their native countries."[73]

This tribunal judicially oversees a rather ambitious set of goals set forth in the various regional human rights documents discussed in Chapter 11 of this book on regional human rights programs. Its theoretical utility has not been matched, however, by State usage. The region does not enjoy the comparatively lengthy period of development, and degree of solidarity that exists in the European Union's two regional tribunals. Absent the sense of liberal democracy enjoyed in other regions of the world, the work of this court will likely remain rather limited in terms of actual accomplishments. As aptly described by Professor Scott Davidson, of the University of Canterbury in New Zealand:

> The malaise which the nonuse of the contentious procedure signifies lies deeper than the pure mechanics of making an instrument and its institutions work more efficiently: it lies more likely in the political and economic structures of the states of the region and in the perceptions which these structures engender. If certain states continue to see the inter-American human rights system as a threat to entrenched positions rather than an aid to furthering support for the forms of liberal democracy which the Court and the instruments upon which it relies clearly support, then such states are unlikely to encourage its [expanded] use.[74]

Andean Court of Justice The 1969 Treaty of Bogota, often referred to as the "Andean Pact," was adopted by five South American nations. They hope to develop an economic union similar to that of the European Union. The national members are Bolivia, Colombia, Ecuador, Peru, and Venezuela. (Chile previously withdrew.)

In 1983, the Andean Pact countries created the Andean Court of Justice (ACJ), which sits in Quito, Ecuador. It has five judges—one from each member State. Contrary to the more flexible practice in the Inter-American Court of Justice, the judges of the ACJ must live near Quito and may not undertake any other professional activities.[75]

Under Article 32 of the 1983 treaty, judgments are directly enforceable in the national courts of member States. There is no need for any national incorporation of the regional court's judgments into internal law. Similar to the practice in the European Court of Justice, Article 33 provides that States cannot submit any controversy arising under the Andean Pact "to any [other] court, arbitration system or any other procedure not contemplated by this Treaty." This limitation is designed to promote uniformity of decision and application of the same judicial standards to economic disputes arising throughout the region. Judges of national courts within Andean Pact states may also request that the regional court interpret the Andean Pact's economic provisions, when such issues are litigated in their national courts. This power encourages regional solidarity in matters of Latin American economic integration.

The court is able to overrule decisions by the Andean Pact's other major organs. A member State's alleged noncompliance with the Pact's economic integration plan is first considered by either the Commission—the Pact's major administrative organ—or the Junta—its chief executive organ. These bodies may submit their disputes with a member nation to the Court. The Court may then nullify decisions of the Commission or the Junta, and require the offending State to comply. In the ACJ's first case, decided in 1987, Colombia questioned a resolution of the Junta. The Court ruled that the Junta improperly limited Colombia's introduction of protective measures against imports from Venezuela.[76]

Under Article 25 of the treaty creating the ACJ, the offending nation's noncompliance permits the court to "restrict or suspend, totally or partially, the advantages deriving from the Cartagena [Andean

Pact] Agreement which benefit the noncomplying member country." Suppose that, for example, a member State does not reduce its tariffs on exports of another member State—as required by the terms of the Andean Pact regulations. The ACJ Court has the power to render a judgment requiring the offending State to comply with the treaty or its related regulatory rules. The Court has never issued such an opinion, however.

Like other international courts, the ACJ may render advisory opinions. It may thus interpret the norms contained in the Andean Pact, when the offending State does not voluntarily participate in the regional processes.

The ACJ has not been utilized extensively, for a variety of economic and political reasons. The underlying Cartagena Agreement (Andean Pact) was modified in 1989 by the Quito Protocol, however, with a view toward bringing the Andean regional process in line with that of the European Union. In that year, the member States also issued a manifesto whereby they committed themselves to fully implementing the Andean Common Market.[77]

■ 9.7 NATIONAL COURT ADJUDICATION

National/International Nexus Revisited

Chapter 1 of this book depicted the contemporary "realist" perspective that International Law is primitive, in comparison to national law. Given the general movement in the direction of democracy, many State systems have more clearly established governmental institutions. A legislative body *makes* the law that governs the inhabitants; a chief executive *enforces* the law; and a judicial branch applies and *interprets* the law. Under International Law, there is no legislative body, no "supranational" mode of executive enforcement, and no court with compulsory jurisdiction—unless a State defendant expressly consents to its jurisdiction.

The *judicial* enforcement of International Law has thus been primarily the province of national courts. This section of the book therefore underscores the historical reliance of International Law on State court modes of enforcement. The European Court of Justice and the European Court of Human Rights are experiencing comparatively striking success in the true internationalization of the Rule of Law. It must stressed, however, that State enforcement has been the most traditional forum for the judicial role in developing International Law.

Chapter 1 addressed the relationship between the internal law of various nations and the International Law applicable to the conduct of nations. Two frequently quoted cases from Great Britain and the US contrast the potential impact of International Law on the internal law of an individual State. In the *British* courts, "whatever has received the common consent of civilized nations must have received the assent of our country, and that to which we have assented along with other nations in general may properly be called international law, and as such will be acknowledged and applied by our municipal tribunals when legitimate occasion arises for those tribunals to decide questions to which international law may be relevant." This language does not contain any reservations about the applicability of international law to issues rising in the English courts. In a representative judicial opinion from the *United States*, on the other hand, international "practice is law only in so far as we adopt it, and like all other common [judicial decisions by judges] and statute law it bends to the will of the Congress. It is not the function of the courts to annul legislation; it is their duty to interpret and by judicial decrees to enforce it." US courts will not uniformly employ International Law, at the expense of the internal law of the US.[78]

In practice, the apparently diverse approaches of British and US courts are in fact rather similar. British courts have never abandoned that country's critical interests in the name of International Law, while US courts often refer to International Law as a part of US law (*see* § 9.8).

The caselaw from various national courts within the European Union countries vividly depicts International Law as *necessarily* controlling when it conflicts with national law. In a case from the Belgian Supreme Court, for example, its judges remedied that country's executive and legislative attempts to enact laws contrary to Belgium's treaty commitments (not to impose import taxes on milk from within the European Community). As thus stated by the Court:

> States have the duty of ensuring that a rule of domestic law which is incompatible with a

rule of international treaty law may not validly be set up against the latter rule. This duty, sanctioned by [State] liability [for a breach] under international law, binds the legislator. It also binds the judge. . . .

The obligation of States . . . must have as a corollary the superiority of a norm of international treaty law over one of domestic law. If a rule of international law did not prevail, international law would be doomed, as it would constantly be threatened with obstacles preventing it from attaining or maintaining its general character.[79]

Certain countries have enacted legislation containing this principle—which *directs* national courts to apply International Law in the event of any treaty conflict. Article 133 of the Mexican Constitution expressly provides that treaty law always governs in the event of a conflict with a Mexican statute that is incompatible with a treaty commitment of Mexico.

Exhaustion of Local Remedies Requirement

Certain prerequisites govern the pursuit of claims in *international* tribunals. One is the requirement that, when seeking a remedy for a breach of International Law, an individual or corporation must first exhaust "local" remedies in the courts of the State that allegedly violated International Law. International diplomacy is often the first resort. If unsuccessful, the person or entity harmed by a State violation of International Law might then take the matter to a national or regional tribunal—to either arbitrate or adjudicate the matter.

The exhaustion of local remedies requirement was described by a member of the International Court of Justice in the Court's 1959 *Interhandel* case as follows: "When a State adopts the cause of its nationals as against a respondent State in a dispute which originally was one of national law, it is important to obtain the ruling of the local courts with regard to the issues of fact and law involved, before international aspects are dealt with by an international tribunal. It . . . [the defendant State] should have a fair opportunity to rectify the position [asserted by the plaintiff] through its own tribunals."[80]

Similarly, the UN General Assembly and Security Council normally decline to review alleged breaches of International Law, until local remedies have been exhausted. The affected States are expected to engage in diplomacy, mediation, or other peaceful means of their own choice—under Article 33 of the UN Charter—before seeking redress from the UN. They are not *required* to do so, however, if attempting to comply would be futile under the circumstances. A State that is functioning under martial law, or is at war, would be unlikely to provide timely redress to either local or foreign citizens.

■ 9.8   INTERNATIONAL LAW IN UNITED STATES COURTS

This section addresses the following themes:

■ *Is* International Law a part of the "laws" of the US?

■ *When* does national law take precedence over International Law?

■ In *what courts* can suits involving International Law be brought?

■ *How* may US courts *avoid* the resolution of such issues?

Incorporation of International Law

Is international law a part of the laws of the US? This question is answered by the US Constitution and various judicial decisions interpreting it. While the Constitution does not provide an explicit answer, its principal legislative article proclaims that Congress has the power "To define and punish . . . Offenses against the Law of Nations." Another constitutional article provides that treaties "shall be the supreme Law of the Land." Yet neither of these constitutional provisions expressly incorporated *International Law* (which includes more than just treaties) into the "laws" of the United States. The US Supreme Court appeared to do so in 1900 in the *Paquette Habana* case, when one of its major decisions announced that "International law is part of our law, and must be ascertained and administered by the courts . . . as often as questions of right depending upon it are duly presented for their determination."[81]

Resolution of Conflict with National Laws

May a national law take precedence over International Law? In practice, the above Supreme Court statement—and the constitutional language that treaties are part of the "supreme Law of the Land"—are subject to a number of qualifications. Nothing in the language of the US Constitution suggests any conflict with International Law. The constitution's drafters hoped that the new nation's law would progressively develop, so as to respond to the felt necessities of the particular era. On the other hand, making treaties with other nations the "Law of the Land" would give the least offense to the established European powers that might threaten the existence of the new republic. Nevertheless, a conflict may exist due to the hierarchy among the constitution, federal statutes, and treaties. The very existence of a hierarchy exposes the gap between national and International Law in US courts. The hierarchical relationship among these sources of US law means that the US Constitution, and occasionally a federal statute, are the "supreme Law of the Land" as follows.

Constitutional Supremacy The US Constitution *always* takes precedence over treaties, US statutes, and customary (nontreaty) rules of International Law.

The following case conveniently illustrates how an international treaty (presidential executive agreement), a federal statute (Uniform Code of Military Justice), and the US Constitution (Bill of Rights) might clash. In two cases being considered simultaneously by the Court, civilian wives killed their husbands who were members of the US armed forces assigned to bases overseas. Mrs. Covert killed her husband (a sergeant in the US Air Force) at a US base in Great Britain. Mrs. Smith killed her husband (an army officer) at a US military base in Japan. Mr. Reid was the nominal defendant because he was the Superintendent of the Jails that housed certain civilian dependents who were serving sentences imposed by military courts-martial overseas.

Some years before the homicides in this case, the president had entered into executive agreements, called "Status of Forces" (SOF) agreements, between the US and the countries where these homicides occurred. As a result of these prior agreements, civilian dependents accompanying their spouses were tried on US military bases in those countries under the UCMJ, which is the US statute governing

criminal trials of *military* personnel. The UCMJ and the SOF treaties with Great Britain and Japan assured these countries that crimes occurring at US military posts on their soil would be prosecuted; and, that those responsible would be punished by American military authorities.

A year before this opinion was rendered, the US Supreme Court had decided that the military trials of Mrs. Covert and Mrs. Smith did *not* violate their rights under the US Constitution. The Court had determined that their constitutional rights—including the right to a jury of one's peers (that is, a civilian jury rather than a military jury)—did *not* apply to American citizens for their conduct in foreign lands. The Supreme Court nevertheless granted a subsequent petition, resulting in the rehearing of the cases against Mrs. Covert and Mrs. Smith. On rehearing, the Court reversed its earlier decision that had approved the courts-martial of Covert and Smith. This time, the Supreme Court held that trial by courts-martial improperly deprived the civilian wives of their constitutional rights. The Uniform Code of Military Justice (UCMJ) permissibly altered the constitutional right to a jury trial, as applied to *military* personnel. The UCMJ could not be applied to authorize a military courts-martial of their civilian dependents.

Unlike the UCMJ, the US Constitution provides for civilian juries and related safeguards expressed in the constitutional Bill of Rights. The wives' lawyers argued that the presidential SOF agreements, which incorporated the UCMJ, could not override safeguards expressly guaranteed to civilians in the US Constitution.

As you read this case, bear in mind that the importance and applicability of International Law was *presumed* by the drafters of the US Constitution during the formative years of the new republic. That is one reason why they did not address the possibility of an express hierarchy between International Law and national law within the US Constitution of 1787:

REID v. COVERT

Supreme Court of the United States, 1957
354 U.S. 1, 77 S.Ct. 1222, 1 L.Ed.2d 1148

[Author's Note: The relevant portions of Justice Black's majority opinion follow, representing only four of the seven justices who participated in the case. Emphasis in certain passages of the Supreme Court's opinion has been supplied by the author.]

[*Opinion.*] These cases raise basic constitutional issues of the utmost concern. They call into question the role of the militia under our system of government. They involve the power of Congress to expose civilians to trial by military tribunals, under military regulations and procedures, for offenses against the United States thereby depriving them of trial in civilian courts, under civilian laws and procedures and with all the safeguards of the Bill of Rights. These cases are particularly significant because for the first time since the adoption of the Constitution wives of soldiers have been denied trial by jury in a court of law and forced to trial before courts-martial.

In No. 701 Mrs. Clarice Covert . . . was tried by a court-martial for murder under Article 118 of the Uniform Code of Military Justice (UCMJ). The trial was on charges preferred by Air Force personnel and the court-martial was composed of Air Force officers. The court-martial asserted jurisdiction over Mrs. Covert under Article 2 (11) of the UCMJ, which provides:

"The following persons are subject to this code:

. . .

"(11) Subject to the provisions of any treaty or agreement to which the United States is or may be a party or to any accepted rule of international law, all persons serving with, employed by, or accompanying the armed forces without the continental limits of the United States. . . ."

Counsel for Mrs. Covert . . . petitioned the District Court for a writ of habeas corpus to set her free on the ground that the Constitution forbade her trial by military authorities.

. . .

In No. 713 Mrs. Dorothy Smith . . . charged that the court-martial was without jurisdiction because Article 2 (11) of the UCMJ was unconstitutional insofar as it authorized the trial of civilian dependents accompanying servicemen overseas.

. . .

At the beginning *we reject* the idea that *when the United States acts against citizens abroad it can do so free of the [constitution's] Bill of Rights.* The United States is entirely a creature of the Constitution. Its power and authority have no other source. It can only act in accordance with all the limitations imposed by the Constitution. When the Government reaches out to punish a citizen who is abroad, the shield which the Bill of Rights and other parts of the Constitution provide to protect his life and liberty should not be stripped away just because he happens to be in another land. This is not a novel concept. To the contrary, it is as old as government. It was recognized long before Paul successfully invoked his right as a Roman citizen to be tried in strict accordance with Roman law.

. . .

The rights and liberties which citizens of our country enjoy are not protected by custom and tradition alone, they have been jealously preserved from the encroachments of Government by express provisions of our written Constitution.

Among those provisions, Art. III, § 2 and the Fifth and Sixth Amendments are directly relevant to these cases. Article III, § 2 lays down the rule that:

"The Trial of all Crimes, except in Cases of Impeachment, shall be by Jury; and such Trial shall be held in the State where the said Crimes shall have been committed; but when not committed within any State, the Trial shall be at such Place or Places as the Congress may by Law have directed."

The Fifth Amendment declares:

No person shall be held to answer for a capital, or otherwise infamous crime, unless on a presentment or indictment of a Grand Jury, except in cases arising in the land or naval forces, or in the Militia, when in actual service in time of War or public danger;"

And the Sixth Amendment provides:

"In all criminal prosecutions, the accused shall enjoy the right to a speedy and public trial, by an impartial jury of the State and district wherein the crime shall have been committed."

The [above] language of Art. III, § 2 manifests that constitutional protections for the individual were designed to restrict the United States Government when it acts outside of this country, as well as here at home. After declaring that *all* criminal trials must be by jury, the section states that when a *crime* is "*not committed within any State, the Trial shall be at such Place or Places as the Congress may by Law have directed.*" If this language is permitted to have its obvious meaning, § 2 is applicable to criminal trials outside of the States as a group without regard to where the offense is committed or the trial held. From the very first Congress, *federal statutes* have implemented the provisions of § 2 by providing for trial of murder and other crimes committed outside the jurisdiction of any State "*in the district where the offender is apprehended, or into which he may first be brought.*" The Fifth and Sixth Amendments, like Art. III, § 2, are also all inclusive with their sweeping references to "no person" and to "all criminal prosecutions."

This Court and other federal courts have held or asserted that various constitutional limitations apply to the Government when it acts outside the continental United States. While it has been suggested that only those constitutional rights which are "fundamental" protect Americans abroad, *we can find no warrant*, in logic or otherwise, *for picking and choosing among the remarkable collection of "Thou shalt nots" which were explicitly fastened on all departments and agencies of the Federal Government by the Constitution and its Amendments.* Moreover, in view of our heritage and the history of the adoption of the Constitution and the Bill of Rights, it seems peculiarly anomalous to say that trial before a civilian judge and by an independent jury picked from the common citizenry is not a fundamental right.

At the time of Mrs. Covert's alleged offense, an executive agreement was in effect between the United States and Great Britain which permitted United States' military courts to exercise exclusive jurisdiction over offenses committed in Great Britain by American servicemen or their dependents. For its part, the United States agreed that these military courts would be willing and able to try and to punish all offenses against the laws of Great Britain by such persons. In all material respects, the same situation existed in Japan when Mrs. Smith killed her husband. Even though a court-martial does not give an accused trial by jury and other Bill of Rights protections, the Government contends that Art. 2 (11) of the UCMJ, insofar as it provides for the military trial of dependents accompanying the armed forces in Great Britain and Japan, can be sustained as legislation which is necessary and proper to carry out the United States' obligations under the international agreements made with those countries. The obvious and decisive answer to this, of course, is that *no agreement with a foreign nation can confer power on the Congress, or on any other branch of Government, which is free from the restraints of the Constitution.*

Article VI, the Supremacy Clause of the Constitution, declares:

"This Constitution, and the Laws of the United States which shall be made in Pursuance thereof; and all Treaties made, or which shall be made, under the Authority of the United States, shall be the supreme Law of the Land; . . . ."

There is nothing in this language which intimates that treaties and laws enacted pursuant to them do not have to comply with the provisions of the Constitution. Nor is there anything in the debates which accompanied the drafting and ratification of the Constitution which even suggests such a result. These debates as well as the history that surrounds the adoption of the treaty provision in Article VI make it clear that the reason treaties were not limited to those made in "pursuance" of the Constitution was so that agreements made by the United States under the Articles of Confederation, including the important peace treaties which concluded the Revolutionary War, would remain in effect. It would be *manifestly contrary to the objectives of those who created the Constitution*, as well as those who were responsible for the Bill of Rights—let alone alien to our entire constitutional history and tradition—*to construe Article VI as permitting the United States to exercise power under an international agreement without observing constitutional prohibitions.* In effect, such construction would permit amendment of that document in a manner not sanctioned by Article V. The prohibitions of the Constitution were designed to apply to all branches of the National Government and they cannot be nullified by the Executive or by the Executive and the Senate combined.

. . .

This Court has also repeatedly taken the position that *an Act of Congress,* which must comply with the Constitution, *is on a full parity with a treaty, and* that *when a statute which is subsequent in time is inconsistent with a treaty, the statute* to the extent of conflict *renders the treaty null.* It would be completely anomalous to say that a treaty need not comply with the Constitution when such an agreement can be overridden by a statute that must conform to that instrument.

In summary, we conclude that the Constitution in its entirety applied to the trials of Mrs. Smith and Mrs. Covert. [The Court then ordered the release of Mrs. Covert and Mrs. Reid from custody, freeing them from any further prosecution.]

■ NOTES

1. The US President's SOF agreements, incorporating the federal statute (UCMJ), provided for trial and punishment of civilian dependents by military courts-martial. Those agreements accommodated Japanese and British sovereign concerns. When military personnel were killed on US bases on their soil, those countries were willing to cede their sovereign power or control over the civilian perpetrators to the US—so that they could be courts-martialed, rather than be tried in the local courts where the US Constitution would not apply. The SOF agreements were based on the expectation that such crimes would be punished. The *Reid* case illustrates that when the US takes action affecting its citizens abroad, it can do so only within the parameters imposed by the US Constitution. Under *US* law, the Constitution thus had to prevail, although it conflicted with the international obligations spawned by crimes on US military bases in other countries. As a result of *Reid,* however, these two murders went unpunished.

2. The US released the defendant wives from custody. They were not extradited to Great Britain or Japan. These defendants could not be prosecuted (at that time) because it had been presumed that such matters were exclusively governed by the UCMJ. By entering into the SOF agreements, there was no other law under which to prosecute them. The president had effectively ceded exclusive jurisdiction to hear such cases to US military courts.

3. In the dissenting opinion in *Reid,* certain members of the Court expressed their concern that the peacetime failure to apply the UCMJ to civilian dependents created a gap that would allow US citizens to be prosecuted by foreign authorities for crimes committed on US military bases overseas. The dissenters believed that it would be preferable to try Mrs. Smith by court-martial, rather than in the Japanese system, where there are *no juries.*

4. Under International Law, the US Constitution cannot be applied to events occurring in other countries. Only a foreign nation has the sovereign power to prosecute criminals for conduct occurring within its borders. Like the prior SOF agreements, a treaty may still provide the US and another country with the *concurrent* jurisdiction or mutual opportunity to try and punish such defendants. The US usually obtains "primary jurisdiction" to try its own military and civilian defendants. If it declines to prosecute, then the foreign country may do so. One such agreement is the subsequent US/Japanese Protocol Agreement. That agreement deals with *on-base* offenses against members of the American armed forces and their dependents. Under its terms, the US has the *primary* or first right to try the perpetrators of such offenses (courts-martial for military personnel, and civilian jury trial in the US for dependents). Civilians may be turned over to Japanese authorities, however, if the US declines its option to try them in civilian courts of the US under federal law enacted after the *Reid* decision. This Protocol was then approved by the US Supreme Court (after the *Reid* decision).[82]

Statutory Supremacy US legislators do not normally propose laws that purport to violate International Law. For example, the object of the Anti-Terrorism Act of 1987, which required the closure of the Palestine Liberation Organization's New York (UN) and Washington, D.C., offices, was to suppress terrorism. A US court nevertheless held that this law violated US obligations to the UN. A clearer example of the US breach of an international obligation would be a statute that, under US law, withholds or extinguishes the US obligation to pay assessed UN dues.[83]

What happens when a statute does conflict, either expressly or implicitly, with a treaty? The US rule is that the *later in time* prevails. This rule is derived from a judicial interpretation of Article VI of the Constitution providing that "the laws of the United States [including federal statutes] . . . and all Treaties . . . shall be the supreme Law of the Land." This equality means, however, that an obligation arising under an international treaty may be negated by a *subsequent* statute. Under the US Supreme Court's time-honored "parity" rule, which merely treats the last in time as controlling, "an Act of Congress . . . is on full parity with a treaty, and . . . when a statute which is subsequent in time is inconsistent with a treaty, the statute to the extent of the conflict renders the treaty null."[84]

What happens when a federal statute conflicts with a norm of International Law *not* contained in a treaty? This problem is presented when a criminal defendant claims that the application of a US statute to his or her crime cannot survive scrutiny, under International Law, due to its "extraterritorial" effect. Under US law, a statute that *expressly* proscribes criminal conduct abroad must be applied by a US judge, regardless of whether there may be a breach of International Law. A statute that is *silent*, however, is *presumed* not to apply to extraterritorial conduct. Yet this presumption may be overcome when the circumstances unmistakably lead to the *implication* that Congress intended to apply US law on an extraterritorial basis.

The judicial opinion in the *Noriega* case summarizes the basic paradigm for this potential conflict between a federal criminal statute and some norm of International Law. Panama's former military leader had been indicted in the US for drug trafficking—for misusing his position to direct the importation of thousands of pounds of cocaine into the US via Miami. After the US invasion of Panama, and Noriega's extraction for prosecution in the US, Noriega claimed that the relevant drug trafficking statutes (such as the US criminal code's § 959 below) could not be properly applied to him. The court disagreed as follows (quoting various authorities including the US Supreme Court):

> Section 959, prohibiting the distribution of narcotics intending that they be imported into the United States, is *clearly meant to* apply extraterritorially. The statute expressly states that it is 'intended to reach acts of manufacture or distribution committed outside the territorial jurisdiction of the United States.' 21 U.S.C. § 959(c). The remaining statutes, by contrast, do *not on their face* indicate an express intention that they be given extraterritorial effect. Where a statute is silent as to its extraterritorial reach, a *presumption* against such application normally applies. However, 'such statutes *may* be given extraterritorial effect if the nature of the law permits it and Congress intends it. Absent an express intention on the face of the statutes to do so, the exercise of that power *may be inferred* from the nature of the offenses and Congress' other legislative efforts to eliminate the type of crime involved.'[85]

Who Can Sue/Be Sued/Where?

When a claim arising under International Law is adjudicated in the US, who can sue—or be sued—and where? In US federal courts, all lawsuits must be based on a specific constitutional grant of power to hear and determine the particular type of case. Under Article III of the Constitution, for example, federal courts—but not state courts—resolve cases involving ambassadors and consuls.[86] This congressional grant of *exclusive* jurisdiction to hear such cases, to the federal courts only, preserves harmony in the judicial application of International Law when foreign diplomats and consular officers are sued in a court of the US.

Federal courts share certain *concurrent* powers with the states of the US. The respective court systems routinely resolve controversies *between* a state or its citizens *and* foreign countries or their citizens (*see* § 2.6 on "Sovereign Immunity"). Disputes involving issues of International Law, other than cases that are statutorily within the *exclusive* province of the federal courts, may be adjudicated in the courts of all fifty states—as well as in the ninety-five federal districts of the US.

The Supremacy Clause of the Constitution requires states of the US to apply *federal* law when dealing with issues of International Law. Decisions by federal courts thus take precedence over any conflicting decisions by state courts, when a question of International Law is presented in either system (state or federal). Put another way, state court judges cannot decide an issue concerning International Law in a manner that conflicts with a federal decision on that point of law. One reason is that, once the US was formed, the individual states of the US no longer exercised any *international* powers. The 1787 US Constitution thus established the US as a federal entity distinguishable from the thirteen colonies.

The sovereignty of the *federal* government in international affairs is thus complete. The US Supreme Court established this federal-state hierarchy when it reasoned that as "a member of the family of nations, the right and power of the United States in that field [international law] are equal to the right and power of the other members of the international family. Otherwise, the United States is not completely sovereign." When the federal government decides not to recognize a foreign government, for example, state court judges cannot allow that government to appear in its courts as either a plaintiff or a defendant.[87]

Avoiding International Law Issues

Can a US court completely avoid the resolution of an issue arising under International Law—without abdicating its judicial responsibility to resolve cases and controversies? US courts have devised a number of judicially-created doctrines to *avoid* the resolution of issues arising under International Law. The prominent ones are the Political Question Doctrine, the Act of State Doctrine, and the lack of Standing.

Political Questions The judicial branch of government was not designed to exercise political functions. Under the Political Question Doctrine, judges will not resolve controversies that should be resolved by the *political* branches of government—the executive and the legislative branches. The conduct of foreign affairs is constitutionally committed to the president, who is the chief of the executive branch of government. When it is claimed that the *US* has violated International Law, a "political question" is presented that may fall within the province of the president's foreign relations powers.

A number of these so-called political questions were presented in various state and federal courts during the Vietnam War. President Nixon's decisions to mine North Vietnamese harbors and to bomb Cambodia, for example, were challenged by individuals in the US Army and in the House of Representatives. Their lawsuits claimed that these US military actions violated the United Nations prohibition against the aggressive use of force in international relations. The courts dismissed such cases, however, on the grounds that they attacked military decisions that were insulated from judicial review and were thus *political* (rather than judicial) questions. The validity of these executive decisions under International Law could not be properly decided by the judicial branch of the US government. The courts did not wish to second-guess the President's military strategy in foreign conflicts.[88]

Acts of State The Act of State Doctrine (AOS) is another convenient device for avoiding the litigation of issues arising under International Law. This doctrine is used to avoid a judicial resolution of challenges to the conduct of *foreign* leaders or governments, performed within their own territories. For example, the Cuban government nationalized property belonging to US citizens in 1959. In the ensuing suits in various US courts, those citizens alleged violations of International Law spawned by Cuba's inadequate compensation for these nationalizations. The US courts dismissed these claims under the AOS Doctrine. Cuba's conduct in Cuba could not be challenged in US courts—even *assuming* that Cuba had violated International Law through its nationalization of alien property without the requisite compensation. In the famous *Sabbatino* case, the US Supreme Court authoritatively echoed the traditional position that every national government is "bound to respect the independence of every other sovereign State, and the *courts of one country will not sit in judgment on the acts of the government of another [country] done within its own territory.* Redress of grievances by reason of such acts must be obtained through the means open to be availed of by sovereign powers as between themselves [through diplomatic negotiations or litigation in *international* tribunals]."[89]

The dismissal of such suits under the AOS doctrine does not mean that there is no redress for the underlying grievances. It does mean that aggrieved individuals should pursue *legislative* or *executive* remedies. An example of the latter would be individual pressure on the US Department of State to negotiate for monetary compensation with Cuba, on behalf of the US sugar corporations adversely affected by the Cuban nationalizations.

The courts are reluctant to resolve issues that touch upon the constitutional powers of the executive branch of government. The president is constitutionally required to conduct foreign affairs—not the courts. Judges do not want to hinder the international diplomacy of the Department of State by making pronouncements on sensitive points of International Law. The State Department, acting on behalf of the president, may be engaged in negotiations with another government on behalf of *all* US citizens harmed by that foreign government's actions. A US court judgment for *one* US citizen in a particular case—heralding the foreign State's violation of International Law—could easily jeopardize those negotiations.

Congress disliked the US Supreme Court's well-intentioned AOS Doctrine, because judges were thereby encouraged to dismiss suits involving the acts of foreign governmental against US citizens that violated International Law. Congress responded to the Court's *Sabbatino* case by amending a federal statute to *encourage* courts to resolve such issues, *unless* the president deems it appropriate to seek a dismissal. Title 22 of the United States Code, Section 2370(e)(2), was thus amended by the so-called "Hickenlooper Amendment" to the US Foreign Assistance Act. The alteration of this legislation provides that the judge should proceed to decide cases—alleging foreign government violations of International Law harming US citizens. The exception is that the court should dismiss, however, if there is an executive suggestion that hearing and determining the case would adversely affect some sensitive diplomatic negotiations (or for any other political reason for not proceeding to judgment). The Hickenlooper Amendment thus provides as follows:

> Notwithstanding any other provision of law [that is, US Supreme Court authority], no court in the United States shall decline on the ground of the federal act of state doctrine to make a determination of the merits giving effect to the principles of international law in a case in which . . . [a] right to property is as-serted by any party . . . based on the confiscation . . . by an act of that state in violation of the principles of international law including the principles of compensation . . .: *Provided,* That this subparagraph shall not be applicable (1) in any case [where a bank letter of credit secures the claimant's right to the value of the nationalized property] . . . , or (2) . . . the President determines that application of the act of state doctrine [i.e., dismissing the case] is required in that particular case by the foreign policy interests of the United States and a suggestion to this effect is filed on his behalf in that case with the court.

If the president (through the Department of State) does *not* file a suggestion with the court requesting a dismissal, then the judge normally proceeds to decide the case—even if the court effectively passes judgment on the question of whether a foreign government or its agency has violated International Law.

Congress thus reversed the impact of the US Supreme Court's AOS Doctrine, which had directed trial courts to *automatically* decline to hear and determine such issues. This congressional directive thus dovetails the interests of the executive branch with those of the judicial branch, in a way that accomplishes the same result.[90] The courts need not be concerned about embarrassing the president in the conduct of foreign relations. The State Department receives notice from the courts, anytime such an issue is pending. The president thus has an opportunity to effectively intervene for the purpose of seeking a dismissal.

Lack of Standing This doctrine precludes a criminal defendant from asserting the rights of a third party, who is not present in the litigation. A related form of the "standing" motif was previously presented in § 5.3 of the text. The *Alvarez-Machin* case involved a claim by a kidnapped Mexican doctor who was a defendant in a US court after his abduction from Guadalajara. *He* could not assert *Mexico's* potential claim that the US had violated its territorial sovereignty by arranging the abduction of a Mexican citizen for trial in the US.

General Manuel Noriega presented a similar claim, after the US invasion of Panama. He was taken by US military forces to the US, for prosecution under US drug trafficking laws. The US judge relied on the standing doctrine to avoid resolving the issue of whether the US invasion violated International Law. The relevant passages of the court's standing analysis are set forth immediately below:

UNITED STATES OF AMERICA v. MANUEL ANTONIO NORIEGA

United States District Court of Southern Florida, 1990
746 Fed.Supp. 1506

[Author's Note: The Court's original footnotes 29–32 have been replaced by author's footnotes a–d in the text of this version of the opinion. Emphasis in certain passages has been supplied by the author.]

[Opinion.] B. Violations of International Law

In addition to his due process claim, Noriega asserts that the *invasion of Panama violated international treaties and principles of customary international law*—specifically, Article 2(4) of the United Nations Charter,[a] Article 20[17] of the Organization of American States Charter,[b] Articles 23(b) and 25 of the Hague Convention,[c] Article 3 of Geneva Convention I, and Article 6 of the Nuremberg Charter.[d]

Initially, it is important to note that individuals lack standing to assert violations of international treaties in the absence of a protest from the offended government. Moreover, the *Ker-Frisbie* doctrine establishes that violations of international law alone do not deprive a court of jurisdiction over a defendant in the absence of specific treaty language to that effect. To defeat the Court's personal jurisdiction [over the defendant], Noriega must therefore establish that the treaty in question is self-executing in the sense that it confers *individual* rights upon citizens of the signatory nations, and that it by its terms expresses "a self-imposed limitation on the jurisdiction of the United States and hence on its courts."

As a general principle of international law, *individuals have no standing to challenge violations of international treaties* in the absence of a protest by the sovereign involved. [Citing US case authorities:] "[R]ights under international common law must belong to the sovereigns, not to individuals"; "Under international law, it is [only] the contracting foreign government that has the right to complain about a violation." The rationale behind this rule is that treaties are "designed to protect the sovereign interests of nations, and it is up to the offended nations to determine whether a violation of sovereign interests occurred and requires redress." . . . Consistent with that principle, a treaty will be construed as creating enforceable *private rights* [assertable by criminal defendants in US courts] only if it expressly or impliedly provides a *private* right of action [assertable by nationals of the contracting States].

No such rights are created in the sections of the U.N. Charter, O.A.S. Charter, and Hague Convention cited by Noriega. Rather, those provisions set forth broad general principles *governing the conduct of nations toward each other and do not by their terms speak to individual or private rights*. [Citing US case

---

[a] Article 2(4) of the United Nations Charter provides, in relevant part, that 'All Members shall refrain in their international relations from the threat or use of force against the territorial integrity or political independence of any state, or in any other manner inconsistent with the Purposes of the United Nations.' [1946]

[b] Article 20[17] of the O.A.S. Charter provides that '[t]he territory of a State is inviolable; it may not be the object, even temporarily, of military occupation or of other measures of force taken by another State, directly or indirectly, on any grounds whatever. No territorial acquisitions or special advantages obtained either by force or by other means of coercion shall be recognized.' [1948]

[c] Article 23(b) states that 'it is especially forbidden . . . [t]o kill or wound treacherously individuals belonging to the hostile nation or army;' Article 25 provides that '[t]he attack or bombardment, by whatever means, of towns, villages, dwellings, or buildings which are undefended is prohibited.' [1907]

[d] Noriega also asserts that the United States military action in Panama violated the Protocol Additional to the Geneva Conventions of 12 August 1949, and Relating to the Protection of Victims of International Armed Conflicts (Protocol I) [1977]. The United States Congress, however, has expressly declined [1987] to ratify that Protocol on the grounds that it is 'fundamentally unfair and irreconcilably flawed' and 'would undermine humanitarian law and endanger civilians in war.'

authorities:] (articles phrased in "broad generalities" constitute "declarations of principles, not a code of legal rights"); (Articles 1 and 2 of the United Nations Charter "contain general 'purposes and principles,' some of which state mere aspirations and none of which can be sensibly thought to have been intended to be judicially enforceable at the behest of individuals." ([I]ndividual may not invoke Article 2(4) of the U.N. Charter or Article 20[17] of the O.A.S. Charter if the sovereign state involved does not protest); (Hague Convention confers no private right of action on individuals). . . . Thus, under the applicable international law, Noriega lacks standing to challenge violations of these treaties in the absence of a protest by the Panamanian government that the invasion of Panama and subsequent arrest of Noriega violated that country's territorial sovereignty.

It can perhaps be argued that reliance on the above body of law, under the unusual circumstances of this case, is a form of legal bootstrapping. Noriega, it can be asserted, is the government of Panama or at least its de facto head of state, and as such he is the appropriate person to protest alleged treaty violations; to permit removal of him and his associates from power and reject his complaint because a new and friendly government is installed, he can further urge, turns the doctrine of sovereign standing on its head. This argument is not without force, yet there are more persuasive answers in response. First, as stated earlier, the *United States has consistently refused to recognize* the Noriega regime as Panama's legitimate government, a fact which considerably undermines Noriega's position. Second, Noriega *nullified the results of the Panamanian presidential election held* shortly before the alleged treaty violations occurred. The suggestion that his removal from power somehow robs the true government of the opportunity to object under the applicable treaties is therefore weak indeed. Finally, there is no provision or suggestion in the treaties cited which would permit the Court to ignore the absence of complaint or demand from the present duly constituted government of Panama. The current government of the Republic of Panama led by Guillermo Endara is therefore the appropriate entity to object to treaty violations. *In light of Noriega's lack of standing to object, this Court therefore does not reach the question of whether these treaties were violated by the United States military action in Panama.*

Article 3 of Geneva Convention I, which provides for the humane treatment of civilians and other non-participants of war, applies to armed conflicts "not of an international character," i.e., internal or civil wars of a purely domestic nature. Accordingly, Article 3 does not apply to the United States' military invasion of Panama.

Finally, Defendant cites Article 6 of the Nuremberg Charter, which proscribes war crimes, crimes against peace, and crimes against humanity. The Nuremberg Charter sets forth the procedures by which the Nuremberg Tribunal, established by the Allied powers after the Second World War, conducted the trials and punishment of major war criminals of the European Axis. The Government maintains that the principles laid down at Nuremberg were developed solely for the prosecution of World War II war criminals, and have no application to the conduct of U.S. military forces in Panama. The Court cannot agree. As Justice Robert H. Jackson, the United States Chief of Counsel at Nuremberg, stated: "If certain acts in violation of treaties are crimes, they are crimes whether the United States does them or whether Germany does them, and we are not prepared to lay down a rule of criminal conduct against others which we would not be willing to have invoked against us." Nonetheless, Defendant fails to establish how the Nuremberg Charter or its possible violation, assuming any, has any application to the instant prosecution. As stated above, the *Ker-Frisbie* doctrine makes clear that *violations of treaties or customary international law alone do not deprive the court of jurisdiction over the defendant in the absence of limiting language to that effect.* Defendant has not cited any language in the Nuremberg Charter, nor in any of the above treaties, which limits the authority of the United States to arrest foreign nationals or to assume jurisdiction over their crimes. The reason is apparent; the Nuremberg Charter, as is the case with the other treaties, is addressed to the conduct of war and international aggression. It has no effect on the ability of sovereign states to enforce their laws, and thus has no application to the prosecution of Defendant for alleged narcotics violations. "The violation of international law, if any, may be redressed by other remedies, and does not depend upon the granting of what amounts to an effective immunity from criminal prosecution to safeguard individuals against police or armed forces misconduct." United States v.

Cadena, 585 F.2d at 1261. *The Court therefore refrains from reaching the merits of Defendant's claim under the Nuremberg Charter.*

■ NOTES & QUESTIONS

1. What is the court's rationale for saying that the cited treaties do not yield any protection to Noriega (or other criminal defendants)?

2. The court makes two interesting statements about Noriega's claims: First, "the United States has consistently refused to recognize the Noriega regime as Panama's legitimate government, a fact which considerably undermines Noriega's position." Second, "Noriega nullified the results of the Panamanian presidential election held shortly before the alleged treaty violations occurred." Do these judicial counters mean that lack of recognition and undermining an election are legal bases for the US invasion and the ensuing prosecution of Noriega?

3. Could Noriega have properly raised an Act of State defense to his prosecution?

■ SUMMARY

1. Arbitration differs from diplomatic and judicial methods of international dispute resolution. In diplomacy, the national participants do not submit their disputes for resolution by a third party or "outside" entity. In litigation, the court's composition and power to act are established *before* the dispute arises. In arbitration, the parties often determine who will decide and what will be decided—after the dispute arises.

2. The various *ad hoc* arbitration alternatives share a common problem: States must freshly design each arbitral body for every arbitration. Unlike a *permanent* arbitral entity, such as the Permanent "Court" of Arbitration, there are no preestablished rules and procedures predating the agreement to arbitrate. Permanent arbitral bodies are immediately available, with objective rules and procedures for resolving international disputes.

3. Three permanent arbitral entities are: (1) the Permanent Court of Arbitration, (2) the International Chamber of Commerce Court of Arbitration, and (3) the International Centre for Settlement of Investment Disputes. The Permanent Court of Arbitration (Netherlands) is not a court. Its "judges" serve on small arbitration panels available for the arbitration of *inter-State* disputes. The Court of Arbitration of the International Chamber of Commerce (France) facilitates the arbitration of *private* business disputes. The International Centre for Settlement of Investment Disputes (US) refers mixed arbitration disputes (between a State and a private individual or corporation) to panels of legal and business experts who arbitrate claims submitted to it.

4. A global court for judicially resolving international disputes between States materialized after World War I (Permanent Court of International Justice). The leaders of many nations believed that a universal judicial tribunal might one day supplant the use of military force to resolve conflicts. The 1939 outbreak of World War II signaled the demise of the first so-called World Court.

5. In 1945, the UN created a new World Court—the International Court of Justice—via UN Charter provisions and a new Statute of the International Court of Justice. All States that join the UN become parties to the relevant treaty provisions that establish the powers of the ICJ. The Court may hear cases referred to it as specifically provided in the UN Charter, in the ICJ Statute, or under international agreements between nations.

6. Under the "Optional Clause" of the ICJ Statute, States have the *option* of consenting to the jurisdiction of the ICJ. States may thus choose to submit themselves to the Court's jurisdiction, without imposing any conditions or limitations on their consent. Most States, however, have incorporated reciprocity or some other limitation into their acceptance of the ICJ's jurisdiction. This compromise facilitated the number of acceptances, although the actual acceptances have often been rather limited.

7. The ICJ possesses both "contentious" and "advisory" jurisdiction. In a contentious case, the plaintiff State and the defendant State take part in the proceedings as adversaries. The Court may also issue advisory opinions in *non*contentious cases. In such a case, there is no plaintiff and no defendant participating in the Court's proceedings. UN agencies, such as the General Assembly or the Security

Council, may request that the ICJ apply International Law to a given set of facts. The ICJ may then issue an advisory opinion to aid in the progressive development and interpretation of International Law.

8. The ICJ has been criticized for its ineffectiveness. The ICJ was formed within a political arena, however. The State participants did not really want it to decide all international disputes. In the absence of a true world government, they did not want this World Court to function like their national courts.

9. The first contemporary International *Criminal* Court (ICC) was the Nuremberg Tribunal—constituted by the victorious Allies after their defeat of the Axis Powers in 1945. German and Japanese defendants were thus prosecuted in an international forum for various crimes, including crimes against peace and humanity.

10. The UN established a contemporary ICC in 1993, to prosecute war crimes in the former Yugoslavia. It will be comparatively difficult to successfully prosecute those responsible for war crimes in Bosnia for several reasons: the absence of a paper trail (conveniently generated by the German defendants); the existing state of war, which has delayed access to proof; and the concerns of some powerful States that they, too, could become defendants in future ICC proceedings.

11. A number of regional courts have been created by an international treaty. Their judges hear disputes arising under International Law within their regions, as structured by the treaty creating the particular courts. There are several functioning regional courts. They are the European Court of Justice, the European Court of Human Rights, the Inter-American Court of Human Rights, and the Andean Court of Justice.

12. The future of regional courts will depend on the solidarity of the political organizations of the member States with which they are associated. In most instances, the limited political and economic integration of the member States discourages the use of regional courts for resolving international disputes. Some States avoid regional litigation for reasons that are unrelated to the legal issues or merits of a potential court case. They refuse to participate, due to fear of losing cases in a public forum consisting of third parties or judges that the defendant State does not control.

13. There is no defined relationship between the global and regional court systems. The UN Charter does not address the relationship between the International Court of Justice and regional courts. The Charter merely provides for the option of prior resort to "regional agencies or arrangements" for resolving international disputes. Appeal from a regional court decision to the global court is not possible. Regional judges do not defer cases for resolution by the ICJ, and the ICJ cannot order regional courts to delay their proceedings for a decision by the ICJ.

14. The European Court of Justice interprets the trade obligations contained in the treaties and regulations of the various segments of the European Union. The European Court of Human Rights, the other regional court in Europe, is one of the several organs within the European Union that enforces human rights. This court provides judicial protection of the fundamental rights of the individual under the European Convention on Human Rights.

15. The Organization of American States established the Inter-American Court of Human Rights. The primary function of that court is to hear disputes between States, when one accuses another of violating the fundamental freedoms guaranteed under the American Convention on Human Rights.

16. The Andean Pact is composed of five South American nations that created the Andean Court of Justice. Judges of *national courts* within Andean Pact states may request that the regional court interpret the Andean treaty's provisions, when such issues are litigated in their national courts. This promotes uniformity of judicial decision making on matters of regional economic integration. Several members of the Organization of American States created a separate organization of states known as the Central American Organization of States. Its judicial organ, the Central American Court of Justice, has not been as effective as other regional courts.

17. Conduct that harms an individual or a corporation may simultaneously violate both national and International Law. Individuals and corporations do not have the general capacity ("international personality"), however, to pursue remedies in international forums. Their home State must present their claims to an international tribunal.

18. Under the exhaustion of local remedies requirement, international claims should be presented in *national* tribunals before they are lodged with

international tribunals. The State that is allegedly responsible for a breach of International Law thus has the opportunity to rectify the alleged misconduct.

19. In the US, the Constitution provides that treaties are the "supreme Law of the Land." The US Supreme Court has added that "International law is part of our law." These provisions are subject to a number of qualifications, however. The US Constitution always takes precedence over treaties, statutes of the US, and customary (nontreaty) rules of International Law. When a treaty and a statute conflict, the later in time prevails. When the intent of Congress is clear, legislative violations of International Law do not excuse the courts from following the will of Congress. US courts do presume, however, that US legislation is intended to be in harmony with the rules of International Law.

20. US federal courts *exclusively* resolve cases involving ambassadors and consuls. State and federal courts in the US exercise *concurrent* jurisdiction over cases containing issues arising under international law. The Supremacy Clause of the US Constitution requires that states of the US apply federal law to issues arising under International Law.

21. A number of doctrines are used by US courts to avoid a judicial resolution of issues arising under International Law. Under the Political Question Doctrine, a judge will not resolve a controversy that should be resolved by the political branches of the government.

22. The Act of State Doctrine is used to avoid challenges to the conduct of foreign leaders occurring within their own territories. Judges do not want to hinder any diplomatic efforts by judicial pronouncements on sensitive questions of International Law. In 1964, the US Supreme Court directed judges to dismiss cases alleging a foreign sovereign's violation of International Law. The US Congress responded to that decision by its amendment to the US Foreign Assistance Act (Hickenlooper Amendment). Judges now proceed with such cases, and give notice to the Department of State that a relevant issue alleging a breach of International Law by a foreign sovereign is pending before the court. This notice provides the president with an opportunity to file a suggestion with the court that it would be in the best interests of the US for the judge to dismiss the case (due to ongoing political negotiations).

23. The lack of "standing" prevents a criminal defendant from asserting the rights of his or her home State, when brought before US courts via a violation of the territorial sovereignty of that foreign State. Absent a protest by the defendant's home State, US courts routinely proceed to resolve such cases.

■ PROBLEMS

Problem 9.1 (*§ 9.4 after* Norwegian Loans *case*): The ICJ opinion in *Reservations to the Convention on Genocide* is set forth in the text of this book in § 8.2. The Court held that to be an acceptable reservation to a multilateral treaty, a reservation must be "compatible" with the underlying purposes of the treaty. Under France's reservation, *France* decides if the ICJ has jurisdiction in certain cases. Under the ICJ Statute, the *ICJ* decides whether it has the power to act. Is France's reservation therefore *in*compatible with the underlying purpose of the ICJ Statute (which is a treaty)?

Problem 9.2 (*end of § 9.4*): Two groups of students will meet separately to draft their versions of a new "World Court Statute." Each group must draft clauses defining the court's power to act. These clauses will address whether the UN membership should do the following:

1. Automatically be parties to this new World Court Statute;

2. Have the option to accept the court's compulsory jurisdiction—

   a. without any possible reservation, or

   b. with reservations;

3. If 2(b) is permitted, make any reservations (conditional acceptances) necessary to ensure wide participation in the new "World Court Statute."

Problem 9.3 (*§ 9.6 after European Court of Human Rights* Sunday Times *case materials*): Unlike English law, the laws of many countries of continental Europe do *not* generally prevent pretrial publicity (via routine court injunctions against publishers of pretrial information). Similar to the famous O.J. Simpson murder case of 1994 in Los Angeles, California, there may be the same "publishers' feeding frenzy" prior to criminal trials—complete with interviews and opinion-editorials appearing in newspapers, tabloids, books, and on television and radio. One advantage of the public dissemination of such information is that the public can thereby learn about dangers to their safety and what is being done to protect them. On the other hand, it is also difficult (as in the US O.J. Simpson trial) to obtain an impartial finding of fact at trial due to the widespread effects of such publicity.

Assume that a contemporary "Jack the Ripper" has been arrested in London, after an extraordinary murder investigation. A number of individuals have been murdered in the same way that Jack allegedly killed a famous London socialite, who was well known for her exhaustive charity work in the slums of London. Jack's sensational murder trial will soon begin in London. There have been no similar murders since Jack's capture. A German-owned broadcasting company beams satellite-based information about Jack's pending trial throughout the continent of Europe, and into the British airwaves.

After obtaining the usual London trial-court injunction banning this form of pretrial publicity, British authorities prosecute this German company for its continued dissemination of the satellite-based information (from Germany) about the pending trial in London. After exhausting all appeals under the British system, the German company seeks relief from the European Court of Human Rights—based on the London court's violation of the Convention Article 10 right to free expression.

Great Britain's judiciary has had a long and unbroken history of banning pretrial publicity. German courts have rarely ever made such "gag orders." Great Britain did not express its concern in a reservation to Article 10 of the ECHR treaty regarding "free expression." Both countries are parties to the European Human Rights Convention, which does not contain any specific guidance as to the application of the treaty's "free expression" clause.

Two students (or groups) will debate whether the ECHR should rule as it did in the ECHR "Thalidomide" case set forth in § 9.6. Specifically, should this *regional* court once again overrule the British *national* court's injunction—designed to control the adverse effects of pretrial publicity on the English judicial system?

Problem 9.4 (*§ 9.8 after* Reid v. Covert *case*): Three students (or groups) will conduct this exercise. The first two students (or groups) are diplomats in the US and Japanese departments of state. The third student (or group) will sit as the US Supreme Court.

The first two groups will negotiate and draft a brief international agreement between Japan and the US, governing the prosecution of US citizens who commit crimes against Japanese citizens on US military bases. The diplomatic representatives will negotiate and produce treaty provisions that answer the following questions:

- Which country will prosecute US *soldiers* who murder Japanese citizens on base?

- Which country will prosecute *civilian dependents* (of US soldiers) who murder Japanese citizens on base?

The student who represents Japan does not want murder cases to remain unpunished, as occurred in *Reid.* The Japanese negotiator knows that civilian courts in the US now have the capacity—based on federal legislation enacted in response to *Reid*—to try such offenses, when the responsible person returns or is returned to the US. However, Japan does not want to completely yield its sovereign power over those individuals (committing murder in Japan) whom it would like to prosecute.

The US negotiator is concerned about the constitutional right to a jury of one's peers. None of the jury-related constitutional guarantees mentioned in *Reid* are provided in the Japanese court system—where there are no juries. The US representative must avoid a conflict between the proposed treaty and the constitutional requirements addressed in the *Reid* case.

The third student (or group) will act as the US Supreme Court. The issue for decision is whether the agreement drafted by the other students (or groups) complies with the US constitutional right to jury trial (as defined in *Reid*) and the treaty obligations just entered into by the US representative(s) with Japan.

Problem 9.5 (*§ 9.8 after* Noriega *case*): A US citizen is traveling in the Middle East. He is riding on the public bus that was the target of a terrorist "suicide bomb" in October 1994. He is killed when the bomb carrier leaves it on board the crowded bus—thus killing twenty-one people, and injuring many others, during rush hour in Tel Aviv.

"Hamas" claims responsibility. Hamas consists of people of Palestinian origin, who hope to use such terrorist events as political bargaining chips to defeat the Middle East peace process being negotiated by the PLO and various governments in the region. Hamas is seeking a greater Palestine than agreed to by the PLO's representative, Yasir Arafat.

The US Department of State is considering an Israeli plan that the US and Israel jointly undertake a secret mission to go into whatever State in which the Hamas perpetrators are ultimately found—to extract the perpetrator who left the bomb on the Israeli bus. Any other captured Hamas members will be tried in Israel for their participation in the 1994 bombing.

You are the judge in a trial court in your state of the United States, where the deceased US citizen lived. The spouse of the murdered citizen has recently filed a suit against Hamas in your court. Needless to say, Hamas does not respond to this suit. The US Department of State (acting on behalf of the US president) files papers in this suit asking you to dismiss this case—due to sensitive Department of State negotiations with Israel. The essential Department of State requests are as follows:

a. The Department of State lawyer says that the Political Question Doctrine requires dismissal of this case. How will you rule?

b. The Department of State lawyer says that the Act of State Doctrine is applicable and requires dismissal of this case. How will you rule?

c. The Department of State lawyer says that if you deny the US Government's request to dismiss this case, and the Hamas bomber is captured and returned to the US for trial, the perpetrator will have the standing to claim that your court cannot prosecute him. In other words, it is argued that you will have to dismiss this case anyway. How will you rule?

■ BIBLIOGRAPHY

§ 9.1 Arbitration/Adjudication Blueprint:
S. Muller & W. Mijs (ed.), *The Flame Rekindled: New Hopes for International Arbitration* (Dordrecht, Neth.; Boston: Martinus Nijhoff, 1994)

J. Ralston, *International Arbitration from Athens to Locarno* (Stanford, CA: Stanford Univ. Press, 1929)

§ 9.2 Alternative Dispute Resolution:
Ostrihansky, *The Future of Dispute Settlement within GATT: Conciliation v. Adjudication*, in M. Brus, S. Muller & S. Weimers (ed.), *The United Nations Decade of International Law: Reflections on International Dispute Resolution* (Dordrecht, Neth.; Boston: Martinus Nijhoff, 1991)

Panel, *New Trends in International Dispute Settlement*, in *Proceedings of the 87th Annual Meeting of the American Society of International Law* 2 (1993)

§ 9.3 Arbitral Classification/Tribunals:
S. Cromie & W. Park, *International Commercial Arbitration* (London; Boston: Butterworths, 1990)

A. Lowenfeld, *International Litigation and Arbitration* (St. Paul: West, 1993)

§ 9.4 International Court of Justice:
Coplin & Rochester, *The Permanent Court of International Justice, the International Court of Justice, the League of Nations and the United Nations: A Comparative Empirical Survey*, 66 Amer. Pol. Sci. Rev. 529 (1972)

R. Falk, *Reviving the World Court* (Charlottesville, Va.: Univ. Press of Va., 1986)

T. Franck, *Judging the World Court* (London: Allen & Unwin, 1986)

Gorove, *Formation of Internal Subdivisions of International Tribunals—Some Comparative Highlights and Assessment*, 38 American Journal of International Law 353 (1990)

B. MacPherson, *World Court Enhancements to Advance the Rule of Law* (Livingston, NJ: Center for UN Reform Education, 1994)

S. Rosenne, *The World Court and How it Works* (5th rev. ed. (Dordrecht, Neth.; Boston: Martinus Nijhoff, 1994)

Thirlway, *The Law and Procedure of the International Court of Justice 1960–1989*, 63 British Yearbook International Law 1 (1992)

§ 9.5 International Criminal Court:
Bres, *Toward Prosecution of Iraqi Crimes Under International Law: Jurisprudential Foundations and Jurisdictional Choices*, 22 California Western International Law Journal 127 (1991)

F. Buscher, *The U.S. War Crimes Trial Program in Germany, 1946–1955* (New York: Greenwood Press, 1989)

Harris, *A Call for an International War Crimes Court: Learning from Nuremberg*, 23 University of Toledo Law Review 229 (1992)

V. Morris & M. Scharf, *An Insider's Guide to the International Criminal Tribunal for the Former Yugoslavia: A Documentary History and Analysis* (Irvington, NY: Transnat'l Pub., 1994)

P. Piccigallo, *The Japanese on Trial: Allied War Crimes Operations in the East, 1945–1951* (Austin: Univ. of Texas Press, 1979)

§ 9.6 Regional Court Adjudication:
J. Bengoextea, *The Legal Reasoning of the European Court of Justice: Toward a European Jurisprudence* (Oxford, Eng.: Clarendon Press, 1993)

V. Berger, *Case Law of the European Court of Human Rights* (Dublin: Round Hall Press, 1991)

S. Davidson, *The Inter-American Court of Human Rights* (Aldershot, Eng.; Brookfield, VT, USA: Dartmouth Press, 1992)

M. Janis, *International Courts for the Twenty-First Century* 235 (Dordrecht, Neth.; Boston: Martinus Nijhoff, 1992)

C. Medina, *Project: The Inter-American Commission on Human Rights and the Inter-American Court of Human Rights,* 12 *Human Rights Quarterly* 439 (1990)

§ 9.7 National Court Adjudication:

The Impact of International Law Upon National Law, in B. Weston, R. Falk & A. D'Amato, *International Law and World Order* 171 (2nd ed. St. Paul: West, 1990)

International Law Before Municipal Courts, in R. Wallace, *International Law* 38 (2nd ed. London: Street & Maxwell, 1992)

International Law in Municipal Law, in L. Henkin, et al., *International Law* 158 (3rd ed. St. Paul: West, 1993)

§ 9.8 International Law in United States Courts:

Charney, *Judicial Deference in Foreign Relations,* in L. Henkin, M. Glennon & W. Rogers (ed.), *Foreign Affairs and the U.S. Constitution* 98 (Ardsley-on-Hudson, NY: Transnat'l Pub., 1990)

Foreign Relations Law in the United States, ch. 8 in T. Buergenthal & H. Maier, *Public International Law in a Nutshell* 186 (2nd ed. St. Paul: West, 1990)

M. Glennon, *Foreign Affairs and the Political Question Doctrine* in L. Henkin, M. Glennon & W. Rogers (ed.), *Foreign Affairs and the U.S. Constitution* 107 (Ardsley-on-Hudson, NY: Transnat'l Pub., 1990)

Henkin, *International Law as Law in the United States,* 84 *Michigan Law Review* 1555 (1984)

The Law of Nations as Incorporated into United States Law, ch. 2 in T. Franck & M. Glennon, *Foreign Relations and National Security Law* 108 (2nd ed. St. Paul: West, 1993)

■ ENDNOTES

1. *See* Sohn, *International Arbitration in Historical Perspective: Past and Present,* in A. Soons (ed.), *International Arbitration: Past and Prospects* 9 (Dordrecht, Neth.; Boston: Martinus Nijhoff, 1990).

2. 8 US Statutes at Large 196 (1802), US Treaty Series No. 108.

3. *See Introduction,* in A. Stuyt, *Survey of International Arbitrations: 1794–1989,* p.3 (3rd ed. Dordrecht, Neth.; Boston: Martinus Nijhoff, 1990) [hereinafter *Survey of International Arbitrations*].

4. *See generally, Survey of International Arbitrations* (cited in note 3 above).

5. *See generally, Survey of International Arbitrations* (cited in note 3 above).

6. A succinct history of the PCIJ is available in *The International Court of Justice* 14–16 (3rd ed. The Hague: Registrar of the ICJ, 1986) [hereinafter *The International Court*].

7. Reprinted in Appendix A to J. Merrills, *International Dispute Settlement* 255 (2nd ed. Cambridge, Eng.: Grotius, 1991) [hereinafter *International Dispute Settlement*].

8. An excellent discussion of this distinction, and ADR modes in general, is available in *International Dispute Settlement,* p.43 (cited in note 7 above).

9. The facts are available in *International Dispute Settlement,* pp.44–46 (cited in note 7 above).

10. C. Parry, et al., *Parry and Grant Encyclopaedic Dictionary of International Law* 71 (New York: Oceana, 1988) (citing authority).

11. *See International Dispute Settlement,* pp.59–75 (cited in note 7 above).

12. *Arbitration and Alternative Disputes Resolution,* ch. 1, in M. Rubino-Sammartano, *International Arbitration Law* 1, 8–9 (Deventer, Neth.; Boston: Kluwer Law and Taxation Pub., 1990).

13. *See generally, Survey of International Arbitrations* (cited in note 3 above). In the prior edition of this work, the author reported that a party failed to comply with only 3 of 443 reported decisions.

14. S. Troope, *Mixed International Arbitration* 200–201 (Cambridge, Eng.: Grotius, 1990).

15. For statistics, *see* text accompanying note 5 above.

16. *See* Exhibit 2.1, § 2.2, on the vast change in the makeup of the community of nations—especially since the 1960s.

17. **New York Convention:** United Nations Convention on Recognition and Enforcement of Arbitral Awards, 330 UN Treaty Series, No. 4739 (1958) (over 90 State parties). **Inter-American Convention:** *see* US implementing statutes in 9 US Code §§ 301–307 (1990) (approximately thirteen State parties and likely to increase with US ratification). **Washington Convention:** Convention on the Settlement of Investment Disputes between States and Nationals of Other States, 575 UN Treaty Series 159 (1965) (over 100 State parties) [hereinafter Washington Convention].

18. *See* Von Mehron, *The Iran-US Arbitral Tribunal,* 31 *Amer. J. Comp. L.* 713.

19. The ICC's arbitration rules are reprinted in 15 *Int'l Legal Mat'ls* 395 (1976) (emphasis supplied).

20. Further details about the work of the ICC are available in S. Jarvin, Y. Derains & J. Arnaldez, *Collection of ICC Arbitral Awards: 1986–1990* (Deventer, Neth.; Boston: Kluwer Law and Taxation Pub., 1994).

21. *See* Washington Convention (cited in note 17 above).

22. Further details about the work of the ICSID are available in R. Rayfuse (ed.), *ICSID Reports* (Cambridge, Eng.: Grotius, 1993).

23. Case No. 332, Judgment No. 333, reported in Judgments of the United Nations Administrative Tribunal, Nos. 301–370, p.239 (1992). *See also Broadbent v. OAS*, featured in the text of § 3.6 of this book (employee's termination of employment action against OAS dismissed as a matter internal to OAS).

24. *See* M. Hudson, *International Tribunals* 145 (Wash., DC: Carnegie Endowment for Int'l Peace, 1944).

25. B. Boutros-Ghali, *An Agenda for Peace* 23 (New York: UN, 1992), reprinted in 28 *Int'l Legal Mat'ls* 1589 (1989).

26. **Commentator:** *see* O'Connell, *International Legal Aid: The Secretary General's Trust Fund to Assist States in the Settlement of Disputes through the International Court of Justice*, ch. 12, in M. Janis, *International Courts for the Twenty-First Century* 235 (Dordrecht, Neth.; Boston: Martinus Nijhoff, 1992) [hereinafter *International Courts*]. **Resources quote:** Bekker, *International Legal Aid in Practice: The ICJ Trust Fund*, 87 *Amer. J. Int'l L.* 659, 668 (1993).

27. The ICJ Statute is reprinted in full in E. Osmanczyk, *Encyclopedia of the United Nations and International Agreements* 454 (2nd ed. New York: Taylor & Francis, 1990) [hereinafter *UN Encyclopedia*] and in L. Henkin, et al. *Basic Documents Supplement to International Law Cases and Materials* 123 (3rd ed. St. Paul: West, 1993).

28. A more detailed description is available in *The International Court* 23 (cited in note 6 above).

29. *The World Court and the International Legal System*, ch. 8, in T.O. Elias, *The United Nations Charter and the World Court* 111 (Lagos, Nigeria: Nigerian Inst. Advanced Legal Studies, 1989).

30. Franck, *Fact-Finding in the ICJ*, in R. Lillich, *Fact-Finding Before International Tribunals* 21–22 (Ardsley-on-Hudson, NY: Transnat'l Pub., 1992).

31. *The Compulsory Jurisdiction of the International Court of Justice* x (Dordrecht, Neth.; Boston: Martinus Nijhoff, 1993) (explanatory clauses deleted).

32. Nottebohm Case, 1953 I.C.J. Rep. 119–20 (preliminary order). The judgment in this case is set forth in this text § 4.2.

33. Western Sahara Case (Advisory Opinion), 1975 I.C.J. Rep. 3, 104 (Judge Petren's separate opinion).

34. Interpretation of Peace Treaties with Bulgaria, Hungary and Romania (Advisory Opinion) 1950 I.C.J. Rep. 71, para.71.

35. **Competence case:** Competence of the General Assembly for the Admission of a State to the United Nations, 1950 I.C.J. Rep. 4. **Reservations case:** Reservations to the Convention on Genocide, 1951 I.C.J. Rep. 15. **PLO case:** Applicability of the Obligation to Arbitrate Under Section 21 of the United Nations Headquarters Agreement of 26 June 1947, 1988 I.C.J. Rep. 12.

36. Accounts of these cases are available in Schwebel, *Ad Hoc Chambers of the International Court of Justice*, 81 *Amer. J. Int'l L.* 831, at 843 (1987).

37. De Archaga, *The Amendments to the Rules of Procedure of the International Court of Justice*, 67 *Amer. J. Int'l L.* 1, 3 (1973).

38. Leigh & Ramsey, *Confidence in the Court: It Need Not Be a "Hollow Chamber,"* in L. Damrosch, *The International Court of Justice at a Crossroads* 106, 112–17 (Dobbs Ferry, NY: Transnat'l Pub., 1987) [hereinafter *ICJ at a Crossroads*].

39. B. Boutros-Ghali, *An Agenda for Peace: Preventative Diplomacy, Peacemaking and Peace-keeping* 22–23 (New York: UN, 1992).

40. Analyses of this form of mistrust/caution are available in Anand, *Attitude of the "New" Asian-African Countries Toward the International Court of Justice*, in F. Snyder & S. Sathirathai, *Third World Attitudes Towards International Law* 163 (Dordrecht, Neth.; Boston: Martinus Nijhoff, 1987); E. Whinney, *The World Court and the Contemporary International Law-making Process* (Alphen aan den Rijn, Neth.: Sijthoff & Noordhoff, 1979).

41. H. Lauterpacht, *The Development of International Law by the International Court* 4 (Cambridge, Eng.: Grotius Publications, 1982).

42. *See Los Angeles Daily Journal*, August 29, 1988, at p.1.

43. 92 Congressional Record 10,696 (1946).

44. The Senate study is reprinted in 16 *Int'l Legal Mat'ls* 187 [quote p.188] (1977).

45. Case Concerning the Military and Paramilitary Activities in and Against Nicaragua (Nicaragua v. USA), 1986 I.C.J. Rep. 98.

46. S. Malawer, *World Court and the U.S.*, in *Essays on International Law* 95 (Buffalo, NY: Hein, 1986). The Department of State's counter is summarized in Stevenson, *Conclusion* to *ICJ at a Crossroads* 459–61 (cited in note 38 above).

47. Copies are obtainable from the UN Sales Office in New York City. Quote drawn from *Final Report*, p.28.

48. **Early trials:** *see* R. Hingorini, *Modern International Law* 353 (2nd ed. New York: Oceana, 1984). **League of Nations ICC:** this account is available in *UN Encyclopedia* p.202 (cited in note 27 above).

49. **NGO:** *see* Gross, *International Terrorism and International Criminal Jurisdiction*, 67 *Amer. J. Int'l L.* 508 (1973). **US Congress/political offense concern:** discussed in *The Political Offense Exemption*, ch. 6, in G. Gilbert, *Aspects of Extradition Law* 113, 156–62 (Dordrecht, Neth.; Boston: Martinus Nijhoff, 1991).

50. Bridge, *The Case for an International Court of Criminal Justice and the Formulation of International*

Criminal Law, ch. 11, in *International Courts* 213, 223 (cited in note 26 above) (emphasis supplied).

51. *The International Court of Justice as an Adjudicator of State Transnational and International Crimes*, ch. 7, in B. Yarnold, *International Fugitives: A New Role for the International Court of Justice* 104–105 (New York: Praeger, 1991) (emphasis supplied).

52. **Tokyo Trial:** *see* J. Ginn, *Sugamo Prison, Tokyo: An Account of the Trial and Sentencing of Japanese War Criminals in 1948* (Jefferson, NC: McFarland & Co., 1992); J. Keenan & B. Brown, *Crimes Against International Law* (Wash., DC: Public Affairs Press, 1950). **Nuremberg Trial:** G. Ginsburgs & V. Kudriavtsev, *The Nuremberg Trial and International Law* (Dordrecht, Neth.; Boston: Martinus Nijhoff, 1990); Fried, *The Great Nuremberg Trial* 70 *Amer. Pol. Sci. Rev.* 192 (1976).

53. W. Bishop, *Justice Under Fire* 284 (New York: Prentice-Hall, 1974).

54. J. Stone & R. Woetzel, *Toward a Feasible International Criminal Court* xi (Geneva: World Peace Through Law Center, 1970).

55. *See* Bassiouni, *The Time Has Come for an International Criminal Court*, 1 *Indiana Int'l & Comp. L. Rev.* 1 (1991) (one of the author's many publications in this field) & B. Ferencz, *An International Criminal Court: A Step Toward World Peace—A Documentary History and Analysis* (New York: Oceana, 1980) (two volumes).

56. Application for Review of Judgment No. 158 of the United Nations Administrative Tribunal (Advisory Opinion), 1973 I.C.J. Rep. 166, General List No. 57 (emphasis supplied).

57. *Report of the Secretary-General Pursuant to Paragraph 2 of Security Council Resolution 808 (1993), UN Doc. S/25704*, reprinted in 32 *Int'l Legal Mat'ls* 1163, 1168 (1993).

58. *See Recent Actions to Which the United States is Not a Party*, 31 *Int'l Legal Mat'ls* 1259 (1992).

59. This incident was reported in a number of US newspapers immediately after the March 30, 1993 Bosnian judgment.

60. *See* M. Gilbert, *Auschwitz and the Allies* (New York: Holt, Rinehart & Winston, 1981).

61. Jenks, *Regionalism in International Judicial Organization*, 37 *Amer. J. Int'l L.* 314 (1943).

62. *See, e.g.,* Minister for Economic Affairs v. S.A. Fromagerie Franco-Suisse "Le Ski," Supreme Court of Belgium (1971), 1972 *Common Market Law Rep.* 330 (1972).

63. **Central American Court:** *see* D. Bowett, *The Law of International Institutions* 287 (4th ed. London: Stevens & Sons, 1982). **Arab Court:** *see* E. Foda, *The Projected Arab Court of Justice: A Study in Regional Adjudication with Specific Reference to the Muslim Law of Nations* (Westport, CT: Hyperion Press, 1981).

64. *International Courts* 87–88 (cited in note 26 above).

65. Case 294/83, *Partie Ecologiste 'Les Verts' v. European Parliament*, 1986 Euro. Ct. Rep. 1339, analyzed in *Judicial Review of Community Acts*, ch. 7, in L. Brown & T. Kennedy, *The Court of Justice of the European Communities* 123, 128 et seq. (4th ed. London: Street & Maxwell, 1994).

66. *See, e.g.,* the US Supreme Court's validation of the US Drug Enforcement Administration's role in kidnapping a Mexican national from Mexico for trial in the US, as set forth in the text of § 5.3 on Extradition (*Alvarez-Machain* case).

67. *See* Newman, *Legal Anomaly: Lacking Bill of Rights, Britons Seek Redress at a Court in France, Wall Street Journal,* Oct. 21, 1985, at p.1.

68. Lawless v. Ireland (European Court of Human Rights) 31 Int'l L. Rep. 290 (Judgment of Nov. 14, 1960).

69. Mann, *Contempt of Court in the House of Lords and the European Court of Human Rights*, 95 *Law Quarterly Rev.* 348, 348–349 (1979) (emphasis supplied).

70. The text of this convention is reprinted in 9 *Int'l Legal Mat'ls* 673 (1970).

71. *See* Burgenthal, *The Advisory Practice of the Inter-American Human Rights Court*, 79 *Amer. J. Int'l L.* 1 (1985).

72. A detailed account of this and two related cases is available in Cerna, *The Inter-American Court of Human Rights*, in *International Courts*, 117, p.131 (cited in note 27 above).

73. Burgenthal, *The Inter-American Court of Human Rights*, 76 *Amer. J. Int'l L.* 231, 233 (1982).

74. S. Davidson, *The Inter-American Court of Human Rights* 207 (Aldershot, Eng.: Dartmouth Press, 1992).

75. The Andean Pact is reprinted in 8 *Int'l Legal Mat'ls* 910 (1969). The Andean Court agreement is reprinted in 18 *Int'l Legal Mat'ls* 1203 (1979).

76. Pierola, *The Andean Court of Justice*, 2 *J. Int'l Dispute Reso.* 11, 35–36 (1987).

77. **Alignment with European process:** *see* Quito Protocol, 28 *Int'l Legal Mat'ls* 1165 (1989). **Implementation goal:** *see* Manifest of Cartagena de Indias, 28 *Int'l Legal Mat'ls* 1282 (1989).

78. **British case:** West Rand Central Gold Mining Co. v. The King, 2 King's Bench 391 (1905). **US case:** Schroeder v. Bissell (The Over the Top), 5 Fed.Rptr.2d 838 (Dist. Ct. Conn., 1925).

79. Minister for Economic Affairs v. S.A. Fromagerie Franco-Suisse "Le Ski," Supreme Court of Belgium, 1972 Common Market Law Rep. 330, p.347 (1971).

80. Interhandel (Switzerland v. United States), 1959 I.C.J. Rep. 6 (Judgment of March 21, 1959) (Judge Winiarski dissenting on unrelated grounds).

81. **Punish Offenses Article:** Art. I, Section 8, Clause 10. **Law of the Land Article:** Article VI, clause 2. **Supreme Court confirmation:** the quoted case is reported in 175 U.S. 677 (1900), and is set forth in § 1.4 of this text.

82. The US/Japanese Protocol Agreement is discussed in Wilson v. Girard, 354 U.S. 524, 77 S.Ct. 1409, 1 L.Ed. 1544 (1957).

83. **PLO case:** US v. PLO, 695 Fed.Supp. 1456 (So.Dist. N.Y., 1988). The Reagan administration decided not to appeal the court's decision. **UN dues:** *see* § 3.3 of this text, regarding the *president's* potential breach (as opposed to the hypothetical statute—which has never been enacted).

84. Reid v. Covert, 354 U.S. 1, 77 S.Ct. 1222, 1 L.Ed. 2d 1148 (1957)—set forth earlier in the text of this section of the book.

85. US v. Noriega, 746 Fed.Supp. 1506, 1515 (So. Dist. Fla., 1990).

86. *See* 28 U.S.C.A. § 1351.

87. **Federal sovereignty over individual states:** United States v. Curtiss-Wright Export Corp., 299 U.S. Rep. 304, 57 S.Ct. 216, 220, 81 L.Ed. 255 (1936). **Effect of federal nonrecognition:** *see* Russian Socialist Federated Soviet Republic v. Cibrario, 235 N.Y. 255, 139 N.C. 259 (1923) [dismissing suit *against* Russia's unrecognized Bolshevik government]; Wulfsohn v. Russian Socialist Federated Soviet Republic, 234 N.Y. 372, 138 N.C. 24 (1923) [dismissing suit *by* that unrecognized government].

88. *See* DaCosta v. Laird, 471 F.2d 1146 (2d Cir. 1973) (Vietnam harbor mining); Holtzman v. Schlesinger, 484 F.2d 1307 (2d Cir. 1973) (Cambodian bombing).

89. Banco Nacional de Cuba v. Sabbatino, 376 U.S. Rep. 398, 416, 84 S.Ct. 923, 934, 11 L.Ed.2d 804 (1964) (emphasis supplied).

90. *See* Sen. For. Rel. Comm. Rpt on (the second) Hickenlooper Amendment, S. Rep. No. 1188, pt. I, 88th Cong., 2d Sess. 24 (1964).

CHAPTER TEN

Use of Force by States and Organizations

■ INTRODUCTION

Earlier chapters portray the sometimes hostile environment associated with the development of International Law, States, and international organizations. Later chapters on diplomacy, treaty relations, and dispute resolution mechanisms likewise illustrate the historical role of International Law in seeking ways to control the ultimate instrument of diplomacy—which is the use of force.

This chapter focuses on the legitimacy of using force, its many facades, and its capacity to adversely affect International Relations. The chapter begins by defining and classifying the contours of the term "force." The ensuing sections will make little sense without a good comprehension of its many forms. These materials next address the *control* of force—an essential UN Charter theme that is reinforced through multilateral agreements and UN peacekeeping operations.

The remaining sections depict concerns of the international community with some special uses of force: humanitarian intervention, rescue missions, the Laws of War, State terrorism, and arms sales. The chapter closes with a brief analysis of *US* attempts to control its use of military force via the War Powers Resolution. This theme is of special interest, now that the US is "the" remaining post–Cold War superpower—and often called on to intervene in foreign conflicts.

■ 10.1 DEFINING "FORCE" AND ITS ROLE

The topic of force significantly affected the overall development of International Law. Evidence of its impact is discernible from the direct, or indirect, impact on other facets of this course. Chapter 1 examines the development of International Law and the norms that States consider binding in their mutual relations. The most fundamental norm in International Law is the *contemporary* prohibition on the use of force (*see* § 10.2). Chapters 2 and 3 analyze the creation and extinction of States, and how certain international organizations were established for the explicit purpose of controlling the State misuses of force. Other chapters disclose how diplomats, treaty negotiators, and international tribunals promote alternatives to war.

Later chapters will address some other parameters of the use of force—its impact on human rights, the environment, and international trade.

Historical/Modern Roles

War was not condemned in either ancient Greece or Rome. On the other hand, wrote Aristotle, it was regarded as the antithesis of happiness and leisure: "We make war in order that we may live at peace. . . . Nobody chooses to make war or provokes it for the sake of making war; a man would be regarded as a bloodthirsty monster if he made . . . [friendly nations] into enemies in order to bring about battles and slaughter.[1]

Controlling the capacity for war is probably the most basic and most unsatisfied obsession of the nation-State system developed in the aftermath of the 1648 Peace of Westphalia—the dawn of the modern State system (*see* § 1.3). Much of international relations can be better understood by viewing war as a systemic essential. A valuable perspective is provided by Professor Michael Reisman of Yale, in his provocative essay on the global system that promotes war:

> The rhetoric of peace is more than neutralized by the symmetrical prominence of the military in competing governments. The manifest drive is for security, in a system which is structured for insecurity. . . . The allocation of power is, of course, an inescapable concern, but one of the functions of a system of nation-states . . . is to perpetuate insecurity through artifacts such as the "balance" or imbalance of power. . . . While a war system requires a culture of parochialism, self-sacrifice, and the paraphernalia of wars, it does not require wars. Rather it requires a pervasive *expectation* of impending violence in order to sustain and magnify personal insecurity. Small wars can be nourished as a neat means of keeping this expectation alive. . . .
>
> The viciousness of a war system is circular as well, for even those who concede its horror and absurdity [can readily] perceive . . . a situation in which the sense of insecurity can be quite accurate and rational. . . . In international politics there is, indeed, a very real enemy with very real operations-plans [prepared in anticipation of war].[2]

During the formation of modern international law in the eighteenth and nineteenth centuries, the use of force was often characterized as a necessity. The more powerful European States developed convenient justifications for their aggressive use of force. One such convenience was the common claim that force was the only effective device for *enforcing* International Law. An aggrieved State could not allow the violation of International Law to go unpunished, for fear of anarchy. Force was characterized as an inherent right—beyond question—when a State, in its discretion, deemed it necessary to employ force in the name of God and country.

One of the most prolific legal historians, teachers, writers, and judges of the International Court of Justice was Great Britain's Sir Hersch Lauterpaucht. His ubiquitous writings on war aptly described it as the ultimate instrument for enforcing national policy. It was also the self-acclaimed enforcement mechanism of International Law, needed in the absence of an international organization (prior to the twentieth century). Lauterpacht traced the development of the legal justification for the unilateral use of force as follows:

> [T]he institution of war fulfilled in International Law two contradictory functions. In the absence of an international organ for enforcing the law, war was a means of self-help for giving effect to claims based or alleged to be based on International Law. Such was the legal and moral authority of this notion of war as an arm of the law that in most cases in which war was in fact resorted to in order to increase the power and the possessions of a State at the expense of others, it was described . . . as undertaken for the defence of a legal right. This conception of war was intimately connected with the distinction, which was established in the formative period of International Law and which never became entirely extinct, between just and unjust wars.
>
> . . .
>
> In the absence of an international legislature it was a crude substitute for a deficiency in international organization. As [the English legal analyst] Hyde, writing in 1922, said 'It always lies within the power of a State to gain political or other advantages over another . . . by direct recourse to war." International Law

did not consider as illegal a war admittedly waged for such purposes.

. . .

War was in law a natural function of the State and a prerogative of its uncontrolled sovereignty.[3]

In the nineteenth century, the unbridled use of force became the centerpiece of national policy for certain leaders. They employed it to preserve the "national security."[4] The defensive tone of this term could not emasculate the very aggressive nature of their realpolitik. Napoleon used force to dominate Europe in the late eighteenth and early nineteenth centuries. Hitler's twentieth century use of force expanded Germany's national frontiers and influence throughout Europe. His aggressive policies sparked World War II.

The use of force has also been perceived as a useful dimension of the political struggle for achieving national objectives. Under this view, the use of force is necessary to achieve political power, both internally and in International Relations. China's revolutionary leader from another era in Chinese political thought, Mao Tse-tung, viewed "politics as war without bloodshed and war as politics with bloodshed." During and after his rise to power in 1949, Mao asserted that war would no longer be necessary after international communism eliminated the world's social and economic classes. Aggressive military force was thus justified by the end.

The former Soviet Union championed a distinct communist perspective designed to avoid the use of force. Prior to its demise in the 1990s, the use of force was characterized as becoming obsolete, once other nations fully comprehended the principle of "peaceful coexistence" enshrined in the Soviet Constitution. Its basic premise was that two nations with opposed political and economic ideologies can nevertheless coexist in peace—if each is able to pursue distinct social, political, and economic goals during the global transition from capitalism to communism. Thus, the Soviet Union's official foreign policy with the West was one of "detente." This policy necessitated tolerance of the western capitalist system until it could be overcome. As explained by Professor Grigori Tunkin of Moscow State University:

The principle of peaceful coexistence of states with different social systems presupposes the existence of other major principles of international law, such as non-use of force or threat of force, respect for sovereignty and non-intervention in internal affairs. It reflects their substance in a general form even though it goes beyond these principles. The principle of peaceful coexistence prohibits policies that are directed at confrontation between states belonging to different social systems and requires that policies be directed at developing co-operation between them, in short, be policies of detente.

. . .

It follows that the principle of peaceful coexistence is directed against anti-communism in interstate relations. That is why it is so strongly disliked by reactionary circles of capitalist countries who assert that this principle does not exist in international law.[5]

Contemporary "realists" discount the accuracy of claims that history has ever produced binding limitations on the use of force. Their perspective is that international rules about force are meaningless in a crisis. There is no practical utility in the legal formulations purporting to legally justify or control the State use of force. Analyzing the legitimacy of aggressive conduct is, in reality, theoretical and unproductive. The role of law in International Relations is thereby overstated. States have retained the inherent right to use force, notwithstanding the contemporary prohibition in the UN Charter. Under this perspective, it is unrealistic to expect States to justify their conduct to anyone. Professor D.W. Greig of the Australian National University explains this view as follows:

The extent to which a state is entitled to use force in the conduct of its international relations raises a profusion and a confusion of politico-legal problems which are scarcely capable of analysis, let alone solution.

. . .

In no area is international law more vulnerable to the taunt that "it really doesn't work" than in the context of the rules which are claimed to exist [about] prohibiting or restricting the use of force. The reason why this type of assertion is made is partly due to the fact that widespread publicity is given to instances of the use of force by states, while peaceful inaction or co-operation, that is, the normal situation in the relations of states, merits scarcely a mention in the news media. However, *the making of such an assertion discloses a fundamental misunderstanding of the role of international law.* It has already been demonstrated that legal principles are only allowed to be the sole determinants within a limited area (i.e. mainly within the jurisdictional competence of the International Court). The more important the issue, the less traceable it is to anything other than political compromise in which the part played by the legal rules is correspondingly limited. And if one assumes that states will only have recourse to force as a last resort when they consider their vital interests most gravely threatened or affected, the role of legal principle may well vanish altogether, even though the states concerned will often advance reasons which purport to establish the legality of their actions within the existing or supposed legal order.[6]

The contemporary norm is a bright-line rule that legally tolerates *no* use of aggressive force—including threats. This is the UN Charter perspective, proclaimed in the 1945 constitutive document of *the* international organization that has the "official" monopoly on the use of force. The contours of this unwavering approach, and the realities of its operation, are addressed in the next section of this book.

In practice, a number of States do not consider force, or certain of its applications, as necessarily "bad." Certain nations have employed various combinations of military action, threats, and economic coercion to achieve political objectives. Most nations ostensibly characterize force as being "bad" in the abstract. It often becomes a "necessary evil," however, when a critical national interest is at stake.

The above summary of just some of the perspectives on force suggests that there are probably more views on this subject than on any other within the field of International Law. Reaching the correct answer is not as important as recognizing the underlying question: Will the international community effectively control national uses of aggressive force, on a planet where sophisticated weaponry may trigger a nonbiblical Armageddon.

What Is "Force?"

Force is a broad term that applies to a variety of contexts. The legality of its use cannot be assessed until it is first defined and classified. Force has been applied when States are at war, on the brink of war, or exchanging political and economic potshots, and even when one State is unaware of the clandestine acts of another hostile State. States have thus invoked measures, short of war, that have had rather devastating effects on the target nation.

War Approximately 150 major "wars" have erupted since the end of World War II—mostly in the so-called Third World. From the time of fall of the Berlin Wall in 1989, through the end of 1994, there were 83 "medium-sized" conflicts—resulting in approximately 1,000 casualties. Various legal regimes apply, depending on the type of war. One may differentiate, for example, between declared and undeclared war; large-scale military combat and low-intensity conflict; civil and international war.

Declared wars, of course, refer to that point in international relations where one nation or group (such as the Allies and the Axis powers of World War II) advises another that a state of war exists between them. As discussed in prior chapters, this state of affairs normally vitiates diplomatic relations and may suspend treaty performance obligations. Early twentieth century agreements required formal advance notice, in the event of one State's plans to declare war on another.

Important legal distinctions must be drawn between a "declared" and an "undeclared" war. An undeclared war involves the participation of two or more States in hostilities that have not been formally declared a "war." During the Vietnam War, for example, successive US presidents were able to commit US military forces to this unpopular military conflict. These decisions created a significant conflict between Congress and those presidents. Congress never exercised its constitutional power to declare war on North Vietnam (*see* § 10.8). The North Vietnamese viewed the nondeclaration of war by any party, in what it perceived as a *civil* war, as not triggering the protections of the Geneva Conventions for military prisoners of war. Thus, US POWs did not have to be visited by the Red Cross, and conditions of incarceration were matters of local rather than International Law (*see* § 10.6).

The term *war* includes another point on the force spectrum, somewhere between an all-out war of nations and mere political hostility. It is the so-called "low-intensity conflict." The word *war* generates visions of the two World Wars of the twentieth century; or the more contemporary Persian Gulf War, where two dozen States joined in the fight to liberate the oil-rich sheikhdom of Kuwait from Iraq. In the shadow of such major conflicts, there have been hundreds—if not thousands—of smaller conflicts wherein death and destruction were just as brutal for those affected by its existence. The residents of the new State of Bosnia-Herzegovina are experiencing a so-called low-intensity conflict. These inhabitants would hardly consider their conflict as being anything less intense than a world war. Yet the conflict is designated by outsiders as a "low-intensity" conflict—in the sense that it is limited to one location, and often ignited or fueled by external military or political sparks keeping the fires of war burning.

The US military definition of this phenomenon provides some useful insight about this method of conducting foreign affairs:

> Low-intensity conflict is a politico-military confrontation between competing states or groups *below* conventional war and *above* the routine, peaceful competition among states. It frequently involves protracted struggles of competing principles and ideologies. Low-intensity conflict ranges from subversion to the use of armed force. It is waged by a combination of means, employing political, economic, informational, and military instruments. Low-intensity conflicts are often localized, generally in the Third World, but contain regional and global security implications.[7]

This category of "war" thus includes but is not limited to the following: large-nation interventions such as the 1994 US military operation in Haiti to restore democracy; border wars between Third World countries; the conflict between Israel and its Middle East neighbors; wars involving national liberation fronts, such as US support of the Contras, which was designed to topple Nicaragua's Sandinista government (*see Nicaragua* case in § 10.2). Such conflicts will continue to surface in the aftermath of

the Cold War. The post-1945 Soviet objective of worldwide communism, and any US exaggeration of the Soviet threat to control US allies in the North and its clients in the South, are no longer factors in the suppression of such conflicts.[8]

An analysis of this form of conflict is contained in a 1988 US Government Printing Office publication reporting the findings of the Commission on Integrated Long-Term Strategy. This publication was prepared before the demise of the Soviet Union. It still suggests the continuing interest in low-intensity conflicts with implications for US national security:

> To help protect U.S. interests and allies in the Third World we still need more of a national consensus on both means and ends. Our means should include:
>
> ▪ Security assistance at a higher level and with fewer legislative restrictions. . . .
>
> ▪ Versatile mobile forces, minimally dependent on overseas bases, that can deliver precisely controlled strikes against military targets.
>
> ▪ In special cases, U.S. assistance to . . . insurgents who are resisting a hostile regime that threatens its neighbors. The free world will not remain free if its options are only to stand still and retreat.[9]

"Civil" war is another category of war invoking special rules of International Law on the use of force. States not themselves involved in such a conflict may not participate, absent a declaration of war. Nor may they clandestinely support one of the belligerent parties. Great Britain violated this principle during the US Civil War, when it outfitted a number of the South's Confederate ships for use against the North. In the 1872 *Alabama Claims* arbitration, the British government was thus ordered to pay compensation to the US for this violation of the duty of neutrality (*see* § 2.4). The International Court of Justice rebuked the US on similar grounds in its 1986 *Nicaragua* case, holding that the US had not properly invoked a collective right of self-defense by aiding the Contras in their fight against the government of Nicaragua (discussed in § 10.2).

Brink of War Force has been used in a variety of contexts that one might characterize as brinkmanship—effectively lighting the fuse without actually firing. Examples include reprisals, countermeasures, and "gunboat diplomacy."

A *reprisal* is a coercive measure, typically involving the State-authorized seizure of property or persons. It retaliates for a prior wrong to the State, or its citizens, seeking reparation. While not uncommon during war, it is not authorized during times of peace. States should not undertake, or otherwise authorize others, to engage in self-help. The 1970 UN Declaration on Principles of International Law Concerning Friendly Relations and Cooperation Among States in Accordance with the Charter of the United Nations explicitly prohibits acts of reprisal involving the use of force.[10]

Reprisal was a more common strategy prior to the twentieth century. It took the forms of public and private reprisals. Public reprisals were once confined to injuries sustained by the State itself. In the eighteenth century, however, governments began to authorize reprisals for injuries to their citizens caused by foreign governments. When the ship of an English Quaker was seized in French waters, for example, England's Lord Cromwell demanded redress from the French government. When he was ignored, he sent orders to English warships to seize the French vessels and goods. Private reprisals were executed by individuals, as opposed to States, who were harmed by the acts of a foreign government. The individual would petition his or her State for the issuance of "letters of marque and reprisal." In times of peace, the carrier of such a letter would be authorized, in his or her home State, to seize property or citizens of the offending State under authority of the issuing State's letter.[11]

Countermeasures are a form of sanctions not employing military force. Examples include a State's decision not to apply a treaty in force in its relations with the targeted State; the confiscation of goods or freezing of assets, as when US President Carter froze Iranian bank accounts during the hostage crisis of 1979–1980 (*see* § 9.3); a boycott, such as the Arab boycott of Israel (*see* § 8.4); or an embargo or a military blockade. A reprisal is a countermeasure, although the peacetime use of this individualized remedy is rare.

Countermeasures often involve self-defense, a theme addressed in § 10.2. While there is some overlap, not all countermeasures are undertaken with a view toward self-defense. While legitimate self-defense is a justification for the use of force, certain countermeasures undertaken for other purposes may not be justifiable uses of "force." A State that clandestinely finances a terrorist group is, in effect, undertaking a countermeasure against the State where the terrorists strike (*see* § 10.7).

On the other hand, certain countermeasures may be undertaken to *avoid* what would otherwise trigger State responsibility for a breach of International Law. The International Law Commission, an organ of the General Assembly (discussed in § 8.1), addresses such countermeasures in its draft article on the law of State Responsibility (discussed in § 2.5). Article 30 thus provides that the wrongfulness of State A's act toward State B *may* be vitiated if A's countermeasure, that is, a sanction or other use of force, is "legitimate under international law against that other State [B], in consequence of an internationally wrongful act of that other State [B]." While the International Law Commission does not proceed to define what are acceptable countermeasures in this description, its commentary to Article 30 poses the example of State A's applying sanctions—or *armed* force—at the direction of a UN organ that is responding to B's international offense in violation of Charter principles.[12]

"*Gunboat diplomacy*" is a form of force. It is one State's somewhat hostile or threatening act designed to intimidate another State. In the International Court of Justice's 1949 *Corfu Channel* judgment, Great Britain successfully established that Albania was responsible for safe passage of international shipping through the channel between Albania and the Greek Island of Corfu. One of the British warships hit a mine while navigating within those waters. Albania had previously contested the presence of such vessels in these waters. One could argue that the presence of the warships in that strait was itself a hostile act provoking Albania to take countermeasures.

In the famous "Tonkin Gulf" incident of 1964, US warships were continuously present off the coast of North Vietnam while US military advisors were being introduced into South Vietnam. A Navy warship was supposedly attacked by North Vietnamese patrol boats, which provided the fodder for escalating the American involvement in the undeclared Vietnam war. US naval vessels then began to patrol the Gulf's international waters off North Vietnam in growing numbers. The message to North

Vietnam, sent by the mere presence of these vessels, was that the US was always on the horizon.

A more recent example of this form of force was the 1994 military buildup in southern Iraq. Its forces began to concentrate near the northern Kuwait border. The US responded to this show of force by conducting military exercises in the immediate area. US warplanes then dropped bombs on Iraqi tanks abandoned in the Kuwait desert during the Persian Gulf War. Then in March 1995, Iraq deployed 6,000 troops and chemical weapons at the mouth of the Persian Gulf. This buildup was apparently well beyond Iraq's reasonable defense requirements—and intended as a regional show of force. These events illustrate "gunboat diplomacy" in operation.

Other Variables Affecting Legitimacy

Economic/Political Force A number of contemporary political factors militate against the use of large-scale military force. Given the post–World War II development of weapons technology, plus the ability to move military forces over greater distances in less time, the majority of States do not consider the current potential use of military force to be as prominent a factor in International Relations as in recent eras. With the demise of the Cold War, the worldwide concern about nuclear war has diminished. Saddam Hussein gambled that Iraq's 1990 takeover of Kuwait would not trigger any responsive use of force. His strategy likely included an erroneous assessment that the end of the Cold War also meant the beginning of a new era of international isolation rather than military engagement.

States remain engaged in a significant degree of competition, often taking the form of economic and political uses of nonmilitary "force." Such force has always been employed, but there are no longer two superpowers that skew the day-to-day planning and acting out of international relations theory. There can be a fine line between devices that consist of mere competition versus "aggression."

The negative role of this form of force is classically illustrated by the four-decade-old Arab boycott of Israel. Just after the post–World War II establishment of the State of Israel, members of the Arab League unanimously planned the economic collapse of Israel as follows: a primary boycott of Israeli goods sold in the international marketplace; a secondary boycott, whereby Arab States encouraged other States not to trade with Israel; a tertiary boycott, whereby other States that did trade with Israel were "blacklisted" from obtaining international contracts of any kind with this boycott's overseers. (*See* § 8.4.)

Other, somewhat hostile, forms of economic coercion have been invoked in International Relations. In 1979, US President Carter ordered a freeze on the transferability of billions of dollars worth of Iranian assets found in the US, or controlled by US entities. This form of force was calculated to pressure Iran into releasing US diplomatic staff taken hostage after the storming of the US embassy and two consulates in Iran. Some may remember that episode for the unsuccessful US use of military force—the failed rescue mission in Iran. It should be recalled, however, that the freezing of Iran's vast financial assets ultimately played a quite more significant role in obtaining their release. Those funds helped to establish a tribunal for posthostility claims to settle Iran's State responsibility for the uncompensated taking of US property during this crisis.

Multilaterally imposed sanctions are another form of force. The breakdown of South African apartheid was, to a significant degree, facilitated by international sanctions assessed on the basis of that country's official policy of separating the races. The UN thus directed its member States to boycott South African goods and investments. The long-term effects of this economic deprivation was partially responsible for that government's decision to abandon its apartheid policy, in order to avoid the adverse long-term effects of the external economic pressures.

Aggressive/Defensive Force Another significant feature of any analysis or classification of "force" is the actor's posture as the aggressor, or the victim who has no choice but to defend its sovereign existence. As will be analyzed in § 10.2, on the actual application of this distinction under UN Charter principles, the term *force* can be rather ambiguous. The underlying question is whether the particular force is being used as a sword or a shield.

State/Organizational Actor Prior to commencing one's study of the complexities of whether the force used violates International Law, it is also important to consider whether the State actor is undertaking unilateral action, or merely acting at the directive of an international organization attempting to restore peace. A State member of the UN, or of NATO, could unilaterally decide to end the Bosnian War by bombing all known Serbian military positions in Bosnia outside of the UN-declared "safe havens." The same action, by the same State acting under direction of the UN or NATO, would not necessarily be an illegal use of force.

■ 10.2 UNITED NATIONS CHARTER PRINCIPLES

The UN Charter contains some deceptively simple rules on the use of force: (1) States may not use force aggressively, although the Charter does not define the term *force*; (2) States may use force defensively, when there is an "armed" attack; and, (3) the UN Security Council possesses the legal monopoly on the use of force. The UN's drafters thus hoped to control the aggressive behavior that led to World War II and the demise of the post–World War I League of Nations. The foundation for the Charter's provisions on the use of force was set in the following language:

Article 2.4 All Members shall refrain in their international relations from the threat or use of force against the territorial integrity or political independence of any state, or [behave] in any other manner inconsistent with the Purposes of the United Nations.

Article 51 Nothing in the present Charter shall impair the inherent right of individual or collective self-defence if an armed attack occurs against a Member of the United Nations, until the Security Council has taken measures necessary to maintain international peace and security. . . .

Article 39 The Security Council shall determine the existence of any threat to the peace, breach of the peace, or act of aggression and shall . . . decide what measures shall be taken in accordance with Articles 41 [countermeasures not involving armed force] and 42 [countermeasures involving armed force], to maintain or restore the peace.

How Is Article 2.4 Applied?

Scope of Article 2.4 This article is, without question, the most fundamental principle in International Law. Yet its proscription on force almost immediately generated a debate about whether this Charter prohibition is a *meaningful* norm. Unlike earlier multilateral treaties on the use of force—such as the 1928 Paris Peace Pact that expressly condemned war—the UN Charter does not mention the terms *war* or *aggression*. Nor does the Charter define a number of key terms that became subject to varied interpretations. Some commentators have therefore argued that Article 2.4 is deficient as a legal norm—because it is too broad to have any specific meaning. Others have argued that the drafters' use of such broad terms was intended to avoid any narrow interpretation of Article 2.4. Professor Oscar Schachter of Columbia University, and former Director of the UN Legal Division, provides a useful perspective on the position that Article 2.4 is entitled to an all-inclusive interpretation:

> Admittedly, the article does not provide clear and precise answers to all the questions raised. Concepts such as "force," "threat of force" or "political independence" embrace a wide range of possible meanings. Their application to diverse circumstances involves choices as to these meanings and assessments of the behavior and intentions of various actors. Differences of opinion are often likely even among "disinterested" observers; they are even more likely among those involved or interested. But such divergences are not significantly different from those that arise with respect to almost all general legal principles.
>
> . . . [A]rticle 2.4 has a reasonably clear core meaning. That core meaning has been spelled out in [subsequent] interpretive documents . . . adopted unanimously by the General Assembly. . . . The International Court and the writings of scholars reflect the wide area of agreement on its [intended] meaning. It is therefore unwarranted to suggest that article 2.4 lacks the determinate consent necessary to enable it to function as a legal rule of restraint.[13]

Some States and commentators nevertheless interpret Article 2.4 more narrowly. They do not view economic coercion, for example, as falling within the meaning of the Charter's prohibition against force. Under this delimiting view, a trade embargo against a particular State's products is not "force" within the meaning of the Charter.

In 1952, the General Assembly established the Special Committee on the Definition of Aggression. Many States, particularly those of "Western" origin, urged that since International Law had already banned the use of force, further definitions of "aggression" were unnecessary. The Committee and the General Assembly ought to concentrate, instead, on defining the Charter terms "armed attack" and "self-defence." A more detailed definition of aggression would only serve to hamper the UN's own organs when the Security Council was exercising its broad discretion to control breaches of the peace under its "Chapter VII" powers (that is, Articles 39, 41, and 42). This blocking move was countered with the argument that larger Western nations, in reality, wanted only to retain their own discretion to act in ways that were not *expressly* prohibited in UN-related terms.

While the US was objecting to UN attempts to define aggression, it had agreed to such definitions in its own hemisphere. In its 1956 Report to the United Nations Special Committee on the Definition of Aggression, the US representative asserted the futility of attempting to derive *global* definitions. Yet, it had signed a number of more specific *regional* definitions (including the OAS 1947 Inter-American Treaty of Reciprocal Assistance). Such "instruments belonged to the same geographical area and were united by many bonds, including a feeling of solidarity, which were not present to the same degree among the Members of the United Nations."[14] Further refinements of the term *force* were more readily controlled by a *regional* process, where the US was the major regional force.

Given the evolution of this definitional debate, something needed to be done to clarify the scope of the Charter's terse statement prohibiting the use of force or threats. Under Article 13.1(a) of the UN Charter, the General Assembly is tasked with the responsibilities of "promoting international co-operation in the political field and encouraging the progressive development of international law. . . ." The Assembly thus resolved to fill the Charter's use of force gap by proclaiming two major definitional resolutions—one in 1970, and the other in 1987.

Subsequent Declarations In 1970, the UN General Assembly further defined the term *force* in its Declaration on Principles of International Law concerning Friendly Relations and Co-operation among States in Accordance with the Charter of the United Nations.[15] This comparatively lengthy Declaration contains provisions drawn from a variety of interim UN documents regarding the use of force. The basic purposes of the 1970 Declaration were to interpret these documents, and to confirm that States should *broadly* construe the Charter principle concerning the prohibition against the use of force in International Law.

The 1970 Declaration "recalls" the duty of States to refrain from military, political, economic, or any other form of coercion directed at the political independence or territorial integrity of another State. It specifies that such "a threat or use of force constitutes a violation of international law and the Charter of the United Nations and shall never be employed as a means of settling international issues." This Declaration thus provides that a State may not use "propaganda," "terror," or "finance" to coerce another State into acting in a particular way.

The 1970 Declaration was a UN General Assembly resolution that was not debated, and was adopted without a vote. Thus, it was not the product of a negotiated process in which the national members of the UN exchanged concessions to achieve a workable agreement. It is another statement of laudatory principles containing common-sense provisions that belabor the obvious. In its final paragraph, for example, the Declaration provides that the "principles of the Charter which are embodied in this Declaration constitute basic principles of international law, and consequently [it] appeals to all States to be guided by these principles in their international conduct and to develop their mutual relations on the basis of the strict observance of these principles."

In 1987, the General Assembly approved another declaration, which even further refined the Charter prohibition on "force." This was the Declaration on the Enhancement of the Effectiveness of the Principle of Refraining from the Threat or Use of Force in International Relations. This second Declaration, which attempts to define aggression, was the product of ten years of committee work. It is the most recent statement of UN guidelines on the use of force. Like the UN's 1970 Declaration on Friendly Principles, the General Assembly ultimately adopted the 1987 UN Declaration without a vote.[16]

The 1988 Declaration contains significant clarifications. States must:

- Refrain from "organizing, instigating, or assisting or participating in paramilitary, terrorist or subversive acts, including acts of mercenaries, in other States";
- Abstain from threats against the economic elements of another State; and
- Avoid "economic, political *or any other type of measures* to coerce another State" for the purpose of securing advantages of *any* kind.

There are two significant similarities in the 1970 and 1988 Declarations. First, they broadened the Charter rule prohibiting "force," by expressly prohibiting particular uses of force not specifically mentioned in the 1945 Charter. Second, these Declarations share the same infirmity. In each of them, the national members of the General Assembly did not include concrete measures to *enforce* the principles they purported to add to the UN's trilogy of basic articles on force (2.4, 51, and 39). Thus, these

declarations are arguably thus just that—declarations. On the other hand, they do serve as clarifications or expanded definitions of what is intended by the Charter's prohibition on the use of force.

ICJ Position The 1986 opinion of the International Court of Justice, in the so-called *Nicaragua* case, takes the position that the Article 2.4 "armed attack" provision of the UN Charter is no longer the exclusive blueprint for employing force in International Law. While Nicaragua and the US agreed that Article 2.4 is the fundamental norm, this treaty language is only one module of the legal foundation for the use of force. Nicaragua alleged that the US had mined its harbors, trained counterinsurgents, and promoted civil dissent against a government that was unpopular with the US. The excerpted paragraphs address the interplay of Article 2.4 and customary State practice:

MILITARY AND PARAMILITARY ACTIVITIES IN AND AGAINST NICARAGUA

Nicaragua v. United States
International Court of Justice, 1986
1986 International Court of Justice Reports 14

. . .

183. . . . [T]he Court has next to consider what are the rules of customary international law applicable to the present dispute. For . . . the Court recently observed,

It is of course axiomatic that the material of customary international law is to be looked for primarily in the actual practice and *opinio juris* [commonly accepted practice] of States, even though multilateral conventions [such as the UN Charter] may have an important role to play in recording and defining rules deriving from custom, or indeed in developing them.

. . .

188. The Court thus finds that the Parties thus both take the view that the fundamental principle in this area is expressed in the terms employed in Article 2, paragraph 4, of the United Nations Charter. . . . The Court has however to be satisfied that there exists in customary international law an *opinio juris*

[commonly accepted State practice] as to the binding character of such abstention. This *opinio juris* may . . . be deduced from . . . the attitude of the Parties and the attitude of States towards certain General Assembly resolutions, and particularly . . . [the 1970 Declaration concerning Friendly Relations]. The effect of [unanimous] consent to the text . . . may be understood as an acceptance of the validity of the rule or set of rules declared by the resolution themselves. The principle of non-use of force, for example, may thus be regarded as a principle of customary international law.

. . .

191. As regards . . . the principle in question, it will be necessary to distinguish the most grave forms of the use of force (those constituting armed attack) from other less grave forms. In determining the legal rule which applies to these latter forms, the Court can again draw on the formulations contained in the Declaration [concerning Friendly Relations]. . . . Alongside certain descriptions which may refer to aggression, this text includes other . . . less grave

forms of the use of force. In particular, according to this resolution:

. . .

Every State has the duty to refrain from organizing or encouraging the organization of irregular forces or armed bands . . . for incursion into the territory of another State.

Every State [also] has the duty to refrain from . . . assisting or participating in acts of civil strife or terrorist acts in another State or acquiescing in organized activities within its territory directed towards the commission of such acts, when the acts . . . involve a threat or use of force.

192. Moreover, in the part of this same resolution devoted to the principle of non-intervention in matters within the national jurisdiction of States, a very similar rule is found:

Also, no State shall organize, assist, foment, finance, incite or tolerate subversive, terrorist or armed activities directed towards the violent overthrow of the regime of another State, or interfere in civil strife in another State.

In the context of the inter-American system, this approach can be traced back at least to 1928 (Convention on the Rights and Duties of States in the Event of Civil Strife, Art. 1 (1)); it was confirmed by resolution 78 adopted by the General Assembly of the Organization of American States on 21 April 1972. The operative part of this resolution reads as follows:

The [OAS] General Assembly Resolves:

1. To reiterate solemnly the need for the member states of the Organization to observe strictly the principles of nonintervention and self-determination of peoples as a means of ensuring peaceful coexistence among them and to refrain from committing any direct or indirect act that might constitute a violation of those principles.

2. To reaffirm the obligation of those states to refrain from applying economic, political, or any other type of measures to coerce another state and obtain from it advantages of any kind.

3. Similarly, to reaffirm the obligation of these states to refrain from organizing, supporting, promoting, financing, instigation, or tolerating subversive, terrorist, or armed activities against another state and from intervening in a civil war in another state or in its internal struggles.

. . .

■ NOTES

The ICJ ruled against the US in the above case in 1986. Nicaragua's claim for reparations was thus pending before the ICJ for the next five years. In 1991, the Nicaraguan government notified the Court that it had decided to "renounce all further right of action based on the case and did not wish to go on with the proceedings. . . ." As is typical in such cases, where a party has requested a discontinuance of the case, the US was given an opportunity to object to the "discontinuance." Two weeks later, the Legal Adviser to the US Department of State responded with a letter to the Court, "welcoming the discontinuance." The case was thus removed from the ICJ's list of active cases.

How Is Article 51 Applied?

"Armed" Attack Provision In 1945, self-defense could be justified only in the case of "armed attack" under the UN Charter. That year was also the dawn of the nuclear age, when the US bombed Hiroshima and Nagasaki—effectively persuading Germany and Japan to end World War II. The development of weapons technology mushroomed in the ensuing decades.

Other Sources The are divergent perspectives about whether the UN Charter is the *exclusive* source for defining the parameters of the Article 51 "self-defense" provision. The reason for this debate is that this article refers to self-defense only in the context of an "armed attack." Prior to World War II, an armed attack—such as Pearl Harbor—was not synonymous with annihilation of an entire country or region of the world. In 1945, however, only one nation had the monopoly on nuclear weapons. The sophistication of international weapon systems, which would heavily influence international relations during the Cold War, was unforeseeable.

The ensuing growth of the community of nuclear nations, and the general development of weapons technology, supported the view that the Charter-based definition of self-defense quickly became obsolete. The drafters could not have intended to prohibit self-defense until missiles were actually launched. Some nations and commentators still claim that this UN Charter provision has only one clear meaning, however. Self-defense is thus characterized as being limited to cases where an "armed attack" is underway. Professor D.W. Greig of the Australian National University criticizes the circuity of this narrow "plain meaning" argument, viewing it as an unrealistic interpretation of the UN Charter. The Charter did not, by using this term, become the *sole* source for defining the contours of self-defense. Customary State practice is thus a viable alternative for defining the contours of the justifications for self-defense. In his aptly worded account:

> Because Article 51 refers solely to situations where *armed* attack has actually occurred, it has been argued that the Charter only reserves the right of self-defense to this limited extent. Supporters of this view have inevitably been led into tortuous distinctions between different situations to decide whether each situation qualifies as an "armed attack." Once a missile is launched, it may be said that the attack has commenced; but does it also apply to the sailing of an offensive naval force? Does the training of guerrillas and other irregular forces for use against another state constitute an armed attack? . . .
>
> However, there would appear to be no need to adopt such an unrealistic approach to Article 51, because it is possible to reconcile its wording with the reasonable interests of states. It has already been pointed out that [under]

Article 51 [a State] retains the "inherent right of self-defence" independently of other provisions of the Charter in cases of an armed attack. In cases where there is no armed attack but where, under traditional [customary] rules of international law, there existed a wider right of action in self-defence . . . [it] still continues to exist, though made subject to the restrictions contained in the Charter [prohibiting the *aggressive* use of force].[17]

Anticipatory Self-Defense The Cuban Missile Crisis of 1962 presented another round in this debate. In 1959, communist-inspired revolutionaries seized power in Cuba. Their leader, Fidel Castro, pledged to spread that revolution to the other republics of Central America. The former Soviet Union was sending missiles to Castro.

In a unique incident in the history of the Organization of American States, Cuba was expelled in 1962. The OAS rationale was that the introduction of foreign armaments was "incompatible with the principles and objectives of the inter-American system." In September, US President Kennedy advised the American people that the "Soviets have provided the Cuban Government with a number of anti-aircraft missiles." In October, he ordered a US naval "quarantine" of Cuba (thus avoiding the more aggressive term *blockade*). Kennedy thus described the US action as "defensive" measure, taken in anticipation of an armed attack from Cuba. He also announced his willingness to go to war with the Soviet Union if it did not halt its missile shipments to Cuba. The following materials describe the definitional context of the era, as well as the relevant OAS legal documents serving as the basis for developments in the law of force:

THE SOVIET THREAT TO THE AMERICAS

Address by President John F. Kennedy
47 US Department of State Bulletin 715 (1962)

Neither the United States of America nor the world community of nations can tolerate deliberate deception and offensive threats on the part of any nation, large or small. We no longer live in a world where only the actual firing of weapons represents a sufficient challenge to a nation's security to constitute maximum peril. Nuclear weapons are so destructive and ballistic missiles are so swift that any substantially increased possibility of their use or any sudden change in their deployment may well be regarded as a definite threat to peace.

For many years both the Soviet Union and the United States, recognizing this fact, have deployed strategic nuclear weapons with great care, never upsetting the precarious status quo which insured that these weapons would not be used in the absence of some vital challenge. Our own strategic missiles have never been transferred to the territory of any other nation under a cloak of secrecy and deception; and our history, unlike that of the Soviets since the end of World War II, demonstrates that we have no desire to dominate or conquer any other nation or impose our system upon its people. Nevertheless, American citizens have become adjusted to living daily on the bull's eye of Soviet missiles located inside the U.S.S.R. or in [its] submarines.

In that sense missiles in Cuba add to an already clear and present danger—although it should be noted the nations of Latin America have never previously been subjected to a potential nuclear threat.

. . .

Acting, therefore, in the defense of our own security and of the entire Western Hemisphere, and under the authority entrusted to me by the Constitution as endorsed by the resolution of the Congress, I have directed that the following initial steps be taken immediately:

First: To halt this offensive buildup, a strict quarantine on all offensive military equipment under shipment to Cuba is being initiated. All ships of any kind bound for Cuba from whatever nation or port will, if found to contain cargoes of offensive weapons, be turned back. This quarantine will be extended, if needed, to other types of cargo and carriers. . . .

Second: I have directed the continued and increased close surveillance of Cuba and its military buildup. The Foreign Ministers of the OAS in their communiqué of October 3 rejected secrecy on such matters in this hemisphere. Should these offensive military preparations continue, thus increasing the threat to the hemisphere, further action will be justified. I have directed the Armed Forces to prepare for any eventualities; and I trust that, in the interest of both the Cuban people and the Soviet technicians at the sites, the hazards to all concerned of continuing this threat will be recognized.

Third: It shall be the policy of this nation to regard any nuclear missile launched from Cuba against any nation in the Western Hemisphere as an attack by the Soviet Union on the United States, requiring a full retaliatory response upon the Soviet Union.

. . .

Fifth: We are calling tonight for an immediate meeting of the Organ of Consultation, under the Organization of American States, to consider this threat to hemisphere security and to invoke articles 6 and 8 of the Rio Treaty in support of all necessary action. . . .

Sixth: Under the Charter of the United Nations, we are asking tonight that an emergency meeting of the Security Council be convoked without delay to take action against this latest Soviet threat to world peace. Our resolution will call for the prompt dismantling and withdrawal of all offensive weapons in Cuba, under the supervision of U.N. observers, before the quarantine can be lifted.

Seventh and finally: I call upon Chairman Khrushchev to halt and eliminate this clandestine, reckless, and provocative threat to world peace and to stable relations between our two nations. . . .

This nation is prepared to present its case against the Soviet threat to peace, and our own proposals for a peaceful world, at any time and in any forum—in the OAS, in the United Nations, or in any other meeting that could be useful—without limiting our freedom of action.

The following provisions were the bases for the OAS and US security measures taken in the name of "self defense":

INTER-AMERICAN (RIO) TREATY OF RECIPROCAL ASSISTANCE OF SEPTEMBER 2, 1947

43 American Journal of International Law 53 (1949 Supp.)

Article 6. If the inviolability or the integrity of the territory or the sovereignty or political independence of any American State should be affected by an aggression which is not an armed attack or by an extra-continental or intra-continental conflict, or by any other fact or situation that might endanger the peace of America, the Organ of Consultation shall meet immediately in order to agree on the measures which must be taken in case of aggression to assist the victim of the aggression or, in any case, the measures which should be taken for the common defense and for the maintenance of the peace and security of the Continent.

. . .

Article 8. For the purposes of this Treaty, the measures on which the Organ of Consultation may agree will comprise one or more of the following: recall of chiefs of diplomatic missions; breaking of diplomatic relations; breaking of consular relations; partial or complete interruption of economic relations or of rail, sea, air, postal, telegraphic, telephonic, and radiotelephonic or radiotelegraphic communications; and use of armed force.

CHARTER OF THE ORGANIZATION OF AMERICAN STATES

119 UN Treaty Series 3 (1948)

Article 15. No State or group of States has the right to intervene, directly or indirectly, for any reason whatever, in the internal or external affairs of any other State. The foregoing principle prohibits not only armed force but also any other form of interference or attempted threat against the personality of the State or against its political, economic and cultural elements.

RESOLUTION OF COUNCIL OF THE ORGANIZATION OF AMERICAN STATES MEETING AS THE PROVISIONAL ORGAN OF CONSULTATION

October 23, 1962
47 US Department of State Bulletin 722 (1962)

Whereas,

The Inter-American Treaty of Reciprocal Assistance of 1947 (Rio Treaty) recognizes the obligation of the American Republics to "provide for effective reciprocal assistance to meet armed attacks against any American state and in order to deal with threats of aggression against any of them"

. . .

The Council of the Organization of American States, Meeting as the Provisional Organ of Consultation, Resolves:

1. To call for the immediate dismantling and withdrawal from Cuba of all missiles and other weapons with any offensive capability;
2. To recommend that the member states, in accordance with Articles 6 and 8 of the Inter-American Treaty of Reciprocal Assistance, *take all measures, individually and collectively,*

including the use of armed force, which they may deem necessary to ensure that the Government of Cuba cannot continue to receive from the Sino-Soviet powers military material and related supplies which may threaten the peace and security of the Continent and to prevent the missiles in Cuba with offensive capability from ever becoming an active threat to the peace and security of the Continent. . . .

President Kennedy's subsequent proclamation, warning Cuba and the Soviet Union of the intended quarantine of Cuba, thus declared as follows:

UNITED STATES PROCLAMATION
INTERDICTION OF THE DELIVERY OF OFFENSIVE WEAPONS TO CUBA
47 US Department of State Bulletin 717 (1962)

[T]he United States is determined to prevent by whatever means may be necessary, including the use of arms, the Marxist-Leninist regime in Cuba from extending, by force or the threat of force, its aggressive or subversive activities to any part of this hemisphere, and to prevent in Cuba the creation or use of an externally supported military capability endangering the security of the United States; and

Whereas the Organ of Consultation of the American Republics meeting in Washington on October 23, 1962, recommended that the Member States, in accordance with Articles 6 and 8 of the Inter-American Treaty of Reciprocal Assistance, *take all measures, individually and collectively, including the use of armed force*, which they may deem necessary to ensure that the Government of Cuba cannot continue to receive from the Sino-Soviet powers military material and related supplies which may threaten the peace and security of the Continent and to prevent the missiles in Cuba with offensive capability from ever becoming an active threat to the peace and security of the Continent:

Now, Therefore, I, John F. Kennedy, President of the United States of America, acting under and by virtue of the authority conferred upon me by the Constitution and statutes of the United States, in accordance with the aforementioned resolutions of the United States Congress and of the Organ of Consultation of the American Republics, and to defend the security of the United States, do hereby proclaim that the forces under my command are ordered, beginning at 2:00 p.m. Greenwich time October 24, 1962, to interdict, subject to the instructions herein contained, the delivery of offensive weapons and associated matériel to Cuba.

For the purposes of this Proclamation, the following are declared to be prohibited matériel:

Surface-to-surface missiles; bomber aircraft; bombs, air-to-surface rockets and guided missiles; warheads for any of the above weapons; mechanical or electronic equipment to support or operate the above items; and any other classes of matériel hereafter designated by the Secretary of Defense for the purpose of effectuating this Proclamation.

To enforce this order, the Secretary of Defense shall take appropriate measures to prevent the delivery of prohibited matériel to Cuba, employing the land, sea and air forces of the United States in cooperation with any forces that may be made available by other American States.

. . .

The US premised its Article 51 self-defense posture on the progressive development of International Law, which arguably now recognized "anticipatory" self-defense. A State could not stand by, without taking decisive action, when an arch-rival's missiles were being introduced into another nation only ninety miles from its shores. But the UN Security Council was not given an opportunity to take control of this crisis, as envisioned by Article 51. It provides that a State may take unilateral action "*until* Security Council has taken measures necessary to maintain international peace and security." Under the US view, however, the Charter made the Security Council the *primary* entity for monitoring the defensive use of force. It was not the *exclusive* one. Kennedy was fully aware that the Soviet Union would undoubtedly block any Security Council action by exercising its veto power. Kennedy's Legal Advisor, Leonard Meeker, later wrote that "The quarantine was based on a collective judgment and recommendation of the American Republics made under the Rio Treaty. It was considered not to contravene Article 2, paragraph 4, because it was a measure adopted by a regional organization in conformity with the provisions of the [UN] Charter. Finally, in relation to the Charter limitation on threat or use of force, it should be noted that the quarantine itself was a carefully limited measure proportionate to the threat and designed solely to prevent any further build-up of strategic missile bases in Cuba."[18]

The former Soviet Union and the People's Republic of China opposed the legality of the US-imposed "quarantine" of Cuba. They did not perceive it as a measure that fairly anticipated imminent danger. The Soviet Union introduced a resolution in the Security Council condemning the US "blockade" of Cuba. It characterized this US action as a hostile act of aggression—not defensive in nature—because the US did not first seek the Security Council's approval. While the Council did not act on the Soviet resolution to condemn the US action in Cuba, there was a general consensus that the UN Secretary-General should have been given the opportunity to negotiate a settlement. And in November 1962, an article in the Chinese Government's *Chinese People's Daily* newspaper summarized the Sino-Soviet perspective on why this was an illegal blockade under International Law:

> Disregarding the severe condemnation and strong protest of the world's people, United States President Kennedy ruthlessly declared that a military blockade of Cuba was being put into effect. . . .
>
> It is extremely clear that American imperialism frivolously hopes to use the military blockade to exterminate the revolutionary regime of Cuba, to wipe out the Cuban people's right of self-determination. It is a serious act of criminal intervention in the internal affairs

of Cuba and infringement of the sovereignty and independence of Cuba. This naked aggression is also a thorough undermining of the Charter of the United Nations [Article 2.4] . . . and even [Article 15] of the "Charter of the Organization of American States". . . .

> This further proves that any rules or any rights confirmed by the Charter . . . can be torn to pieces by the United States in accordance with its own needs of aggression and war.[19]

Collective Self-Defense The next major development in the law of Charter Article 51 self-defense arose when the International Court of Justice heard and decided Nicaragua's suit against the US. (The US purported to withdraw from the ICJ's jurisdiction, as discussed in § 9.4.) The US had worked with counterinsurgents for the purpose of undermining the mid-1980s Sandinista government of Nicaragua. This case presented an opportunity for the ICJ to address the applicability of *collective* self-defense arguments, not determined during the Cuban Missile Crisis—and now ripe for decision. The issue was whether the US could assert *collective* self-defense as a legal justification for its political actions—which included the work of US CIA operatives who mined strategic harbors in various ports in Nicaragua.

The ICJ disagreed with the US position that its activities in Nicaragua constituted a proper case for an intervention that could be properly characterized as "collective self-defense." The US asserted that its intervention was justified as a form of self-defense against some *future* armed attack by Nicaragua on other OAS members. Premised on the UN Charter, as well as the above OAS provisions providing for collective defense against an attack, the US claimed that it had the right to intervene *before* Nicaragua aided opposition forces in other Latin American States. Nicaragua was allegedly helping antigovernment forces, in countries such as El Salvador, to overthrow democratically elected governments in the region.

The ICJ reaction to the US claim of collective self-defense was critically unaccepting. The Court nevertheless examined whether there might be indications of a recognized practice to legitimize US intervention, directly or indirectly, with or without armed force, in support of antigovernment forces in Nicaragua. The question posed by the US, then, was whether the "cause" of the opposition "Contras," which the US characterized as particularly worthy for political and moral reasons, could ripen into a right of intervention in the name of collective self-defense. US authorities supported intervention into the affairs of a foreign State based on factors including ideology, the level of its armaments, or the direction of its foreign policy—which the US would characterize as adverse not only to its own interests, but also to those of other countries in the region. The Court responded that this US policy was not supported by any existing rule of International Law. For such a general right to legally materialize, the US would have to prove a fundamental *modification* of the customary International Law principle of non-intervention. The ICJ thus disapproved the US basis for intervention in Nicaraguan affairs, as not being supported by the doctrine of self-defense. In the Court's words:

the United States has not claimed that its intervention, which it justified in this way on the *political* level, was also justified on the *legal* level, alleging the exercise of a new right of intervention regarded by the United States as existing in such circumstances. As mentioned above, the United States has, on the legal plane, justified its intervention expressly and solely by reference to the 'classic' rules involved, namely, collective self-defence against an armed attack. Nicaragua, for its part, has often expressed its solidarity and sympathy with the opposition [anti-government forces] in various States, especially in El Salvador. . . .

The Court therefore finds that no such general right of [US] intervention, in support of an opposition within another State [Nicaragua], exists in contemporary international law. The Court concludes that acts constituting a breach of the customary principle of non-intervention will also, if they directly or indirectly involve the use of force, constitute a breach of the principle of non-use of force in international relations.[20]

The next major opportunity to analyze Article 51 occurred during the Persian Gulf War. Four days after Iraq invaded Kuwait, the UN Security Council issued Resolution 661. That statement identified the application of self-defense by "*Affirming* the inherent right of individual and collective self-defence,

in accordance with Article 51 of the Charter. . . ."[21] The dozen resolutions during that war reflected a consensus about the existence of the inherent right of *collective* self-defense.

The novel question was whether either individual or collective self-defense could be undertaken, at any time, *without* the direct participation of the UN Security Council. Article 51 authorizes self-defense "until the Security Council has taken measures necessary to maintain international peace and security." Although time was allegedly of the essence, Article 51 does not condone a wholly *unilateral* exercise—whether by the US or other States. That would be inconsistent with the Security Council's traditional concerns about State responses to aggression in the name of self-defense. The Council was thus motivated to quickly, and incessantly, issue resolutions so as to remain openly involved with the US-directed process of extracting Iraq from Kuwait. It is at this point that one may integrate the Security Council's Chapter VII powers with self-defense.

How Is Article 39 Applied?

Charter Language This provision of the Charter provides that the "Security Council shall . . . decide what measures shall be taken in accordance with Articles 41 and 42, to maintain or restore the peace." The latter articles provide that the Council may initiate appropriate countermeasures. Those not involving force include the interruption of economic relations with the offending States. Those countermeasures involving force, when *non*forcible measures would be inadequate, include "action by air, sea, or land forces . . . includ[ing] demonstrations, blockade, and other operations by air, sea, or land forces of Members of the United Nations."

Sanctions The word *sanctions* is used by journalists and other commentators. It is normally avoided in international documents. It suggests the imposition of punishment—rather than mere deterrence. The UN Charter is most discreet in its Article 39 reference to "measures . . . to maintain or restore international peace and security."

The UN Charter envisions regional organizational measures (sanctions) undertaken as a means of regional dispute resolution that is not unilaterally imposed. The European Community's antiinvestment measures against South Africa were imposed as a means of participating in the broader UN policy of encouraging member States to dismantle apartheid. The Organization of American States imposed economic sanctions on Haiti, after military leaders deposed its first democratically elected leader in 1991. The 1992 OAS sanctions thus barred oil deliveries to Haiti as a measure for securing Haiti's observation of the democratic principles contained in the OAS Charter. The OAS also considered sanctions against Peru in 1992, when its leader closed Congress and suspended the Peruvian Constitution. In both instances, the US is *the* "strongman" in terms of a regional military and economic power. However, the application of sanctions on an international level, rather than unilaterally, increases the likelihood of consensus appropriate for the *organizational* imposition of sanctions via a regional process. Regionally imposed sanctions thus encourage the elimination of threats to peace. Unilaterally imposed sanctions encourage the escalation of threats to peace. The sanctioning State will not as readily be perceived as an aggressor, who is merely taking advantage of the situation to achieve some less-than-altruistic objective.

One should not construe unilateral *State*-imposed sanctions, employed for the asserted purpose of furthering UN Charter principles, as tantamount to compliance with the Charter. The UN, and not its individual member States, has the monopoly on the use of force. US President Carter applied a series of sanctions against Iran during the 1979 Hostage Crisis. Various UN organs—and virtually every nation of the world—condemned Iran's actions of seizing and then holding diplomatic hostages. This multilateral form of approval did not authorize President Carter's use of unilateral sanctions, however, in the absence of Security Council involvement.

US dealings with Cuba present a more blatant breach of UN Charter principles. In 1994, the UN General Assembly passed a resolution—for the third consecutive year—calling on the US to end its embargo against Cuba. Only Israel, of the 184 UN member States, has supported the US-imposed economic sanctions against Cuba. Cuba has always characterized US sanctions policy as a direct threat to its existence. A 1960 Cuban law thus characterized US economic countermeasures as follows: "the attitude assumed by the [US] government . . . constitutes an aggression, for political purposes, against the basic interests of the Cuban economy . . . [which] forces the Revolutionary government to

adopt, without hesitation, all and whatever means it may deem appropriate or desirable for the due defense of the national sovereignty and protection of our economic development process."[22]

It is this type of economic hostility that may ripen into more serious forms of conflict. The US, for example, launched the infamous 1961 Bay of Pigs assault—which Cuba used to justify Cuba's introduction of Soviet missiles during the following year's Cuban Missile Crisis. Cuba has since had reason to harbor lingering mistrust. The Castro government feared the almost insatiable US desire to economically crush Cuba. The Cuban defections to US shores of the 1980s and 1990s were caused, in part, by the resulting economic hardship of US sanctions policy. This is not a situation where the US has acted, under Security Council principles, to economically force compliance of some State to come to terms with UN-imposed sanctions. State sanctions against South African apartheid, or the aggression of the Bosnian Serbs, are a different matter. The Cuba sanctions are a matter of unilateral obsession, with the objective of the economic destruction of a State. One could thus draw a parallel with the Arab boycott of Israel. Both were designed to crush a particular government, or State in the case of the Arab boycott against Israel.

The Cuban impasse does not align with the Charter's Security Council monopoly on force. Nor is there likely to be an opinion from the International Court of Justice, which would at least create further pressure on the US to withdraw its unilateral sanctions against Cuba. Advisory opinions do not address *bilateral* disputes, notwithstanding the all-out economic warfare involved in this particular scenario. As thus lamented by Professor Richard Falk of Princeton University:

> In an era when economic relations with China are being actively promoted and relations with Vietnam are being gradually normalized, it would seem more anachronistic than ever for the United States to continue to regard its close neighbor Cuba as posing some sort of lethal threat to U.S. interests and values.

> . . .

> In the end it will probably require pressure from U.S. citizens to induce the White House to change U.S. policy toward Cuba . . . [to expose] the extent to which economic warfare

collides with international law and with the opportunities for peaceful and equitable international relations among sovereign states in the post-cold war world.[23]

Organizational Force The collective response during the 1991 Persian Gulf War expanded the concept of self-defense beyond merely repelling an aggressor. The objective was to defeat Iraq with sufficient force, so as to eliminate its potential for further threats to international peace. Security Council Resolution 678, for example, thus authorized "all necessary means" to force Iraq's withdrawal from Kuwait—in addition to restoring peace. The Council's Chapter VII powers indicate that the organization should authorize less forceful measures, before escalating the use of force as happened in Kuwait. The Security Council normally should authorize forcible sanctions *only* after less severe ones fail to work. But the Charter should also be a flexible document, and so interpreted as to ensure enforcement of its mandate to restore peace and *maintain* security. As articulately portrayed by David Scheffer of the Carnegie Endowment for International Peace:

> The Iraq-Kuwait crisis served to remind us that the Charter is a flexible document that can be interpreted as such. Narrow, rigid interpretation of the Charter by U.N. enthusiasts may have the unintended result of creating unnecessary obstacles to the effective implementation of critical Charter provisions. For example, there was some discussion during the early months of the Iraq-Kuwait crisis that trade sanctions must be proven to have failed before the Security Council could authorize use of force under Article 42 of the Charter. However, the text of Article 42 offers more latitude. . . . The Security Council could make a determination at any time that trade sanctions "would be inadequate" [under Article 41] and move on to Article 42 and the use of force.[24]

Scheffer's argument favoring a liberal Charter interpretation was borne out by the facts that Iraq was *militarily* defeated in the Persian Gulf War; yet, it restationed a large military force near the Kuwait border in late 1994. Applying economic sanctions, for a long enough period to determine their deter-

rent effect, would have had about the same effect as US economic sanctions against Iran during the 1979–1980 hostage crisis (*see* § 7.4).

Problems have arisen, of course, with obtaining the necessary national consensus to impose UN sanctions; and alternatively, with maintaining sanctions against the targeted State. During the Cold War, the Council's ability to use sanctions, as a basis for forcing State compliance with Charter principles, was thwarted by the veto power. One permanent member's veto would block the ability of the Council to take decisive action. Since the demise of the Cold War, the UN has been able to enter into geographical arenas (like Bosnia), once beyond its reach due to the superpowers' respective spheres of influence. After the demise of the Cold War, the Security Council was able to impose an embargo on the former Yugoslavia for the purpose of avoiding escalation of the so-called Bosnian War.

Maintaining UN sanctions policy may be another matter. Some States are reportedly ignoring the embargo and providing arms to Serbia and Montenegro to assist the Bosnian Serbs. The 1994 US decision to no longer honor the embargo adversely affected the Security Council's new-found activism—as well as alarming US allies in Europe. The US is concerned about the embargo's impact on Muslim and Croatian forces, who do not enjoy the benefit of receiving illicit arms. A unilateral national decision to ignore Security Council–imposed sanctions will likely create a diplomatic rift between the US and its NATO allies. The latter are concerned because the US Congress eliminated funding for the US enforcement of the UN's embargo on Yugoslavia. Now that the US has officially withdrawn its support of the UN-imposed sanctions, other Security Council members may question the lasting value of future sanction orders.

The UN Secretary-General has proposed a more forceful method for applying Charter principles to future hostilities. In 1992, UN Secretary-General Boutros Boutros-Ghali proposed that UN forces be made available for the rapid deployment of force under the Charter's Chapter VII enforcement powers. There had never been a standing army, as envisioned by Article 43. Yet the time was ripe, in the aftermath of the Cold War, to establish some force capable of quickly responding to threats to peace. In his *Agenda for Peace*, prepared in response to a request from the heads of State of the Council members (*see* § 3.3), Boutros-Ghali proposed that the Persian Gulf War had taught the community of nations an important lesson. A permanent body would need to be on call, in order to serve as a deterrent to future threats to peace. He thus proposed "Peace Enforcement Units." Under this proposal, the "ready availability of armed forces could serve, in itself, as a means of deterring breaches of the peace since a potential aggressor [like Iraq] would know that the Council had at its disposal a[n immediate] means of response."

This proposal seeks the introduction of a UN rapid deployment force into any conflict deemed appropriate by the Security Council. Boutros-Ghali's perspective is that the Council should thus consider "the ultization of peace-enforcement units in clearly defined circumstances."[25] Adoption by the Council would thus bolster the UN's role as diplomat—but armed with the power to be a peace-*maker*, rather continuing to serve in its perennial role as the mere peace*keeper*.

In 1994, President Clinton responded with new guidelines for US participation that would do two things. First, they would greatly limit future US involvement in UN operations involving the use of force (*see* § 3.3, on UN Reform). The essential feature is that "the President will never relinquish command over US forces. However, the President will, on a case-by-case basis, consider placing appropriate U.S. forces under the operational control of a competent UN commander for specific UN operations authorized by the Security Council."[26] Ample room is left within this new US executive policy for the provision of rapid deployment forces. It remains to be seen, however, whether this policy will survive congressional War Powers Act scrutiny.

■ 10.3 PEACEKEEPING OPERATIONS

Peacekeeping operations are normally analyzed in international organizations courses. They should not be ignored in an International Law course, where one may consider the degree to which international peacekeeping affects the use of force by States. While several non-UN peacekeeping operations of some significance have materialized, this section focuses on the UN operations. UN peacekeeping has been the focus of worldwide concern since its inception in 1947. Since then, nearly a half-million UN troops have been deployed in vari-

ous regions of the globe. Over 900 have lost their lives in that service.

The scope of these operations has dramatically increased from their inception, and particularly since the end of the Cold War. The first UN peacekeeping operation in 1947 involved a handful of UN employees attempting to limit the degree to which the Balkans were a source of support for guerrillas fighting in the Greek civil war. In 1992, the number of UN forces quadrupled from 11,000 to 44,000. By year's end in 1993, there were 80,000 UN peacekeepers—a number that would have to grow to an estimated 100,000 troops to provide adequate protection for the Bosnian "safe havens." And for the first time in UN history, US combat troops were assigned as UN peacekeepers—sent to Macedonia to aid in containing the Bosnian conflict so that it would not spill over into bordering States.

Non-UN Peacekeeping

The UN is not the only international organization for dispatching international peacekeeping forces. NATO, OAS, European Union, and other peacekeeping forces have attempted to control State uses of force.

NATO authorized the use of air strikes beginning in 1993, for example, under extensive international pressure to react to the Bosnian Serb attacks on civilian targets. NATO awaited UN authorization, before it carried out its "threat" by bombing some Serbian positions when they failed to retreat and then attacked UN-designated safe havens in Bosnia. NATO's 1994 air strikes were the first attacks on ground troops in NATO's existence. They could be the last, as French and British peacekeepers are already on the ground and there is fear of harming UN troops in this process.

NATO's earlier decision to conduct airstrikes should be insulated from any responsibility in Serbia and Montenegro's 1994 suit against NATO in the International Court of Justice. The former Yugoslavia therein challenged NATO's February 1994 decision to use air strikes as an illegal use of international force in this civil war. This case is unlikely to proceed, however, due to jurisdictional defects. First, NATO States have not generally consented to the jurisdiction of the ICJ (choosing instead to do so via specific international treaties). Second, the present "Yugoslavia" no longer holds the former UN seat and must reapply for admission to the UN. The plaintiff State is no longer a UN member, and thus not a party to the UN's Statute of the International Court of Justice (*see* § 9.4 on ICJ jurisdiction).

Other less publicized operations have been conducted by several international organizations. Examples include the following:

■ OAS (1993)—a sixteen-nation OAS civilian observer force was present in Haiti to assess the effect of the coup of its first democratically elected leader in 1991.

■ WEU (1992)—the Western European Union assisted NATO with enforcing a UN-imposed blockade. The warships of certain European States thus kept all vessels from passing in or out of the Adriatic Sea near the former Yugoslavia.

■ WAC (1990)—the sixteen-member West African Community sent a five-nation peacekeeping force into Liberia during its civil war. Its purpose was to locate the leader of the rebel forces in Liberia.

■ BRITISH COMMONWEALTH (1979)—some one thousand troops from five nations of the British Commonwealth were sent into Southern Rhodesia. Their goal was to keep the peace achieved as a result of a cease-fire agreement between antigovernment guerrillas and the government of Southern Rhodesia. The presence of this force enabled Southern Rhodesia to transfer political power to the new Zimbabwe government in 1980.

■ ARAB LEAGUE (1976)—the six-nation Inter-Arab Deterrent Force was sent into Lebanon by the Arab League. On Lebanon's request, the League sent more than thirty thousand troops there, for the purpose of monitoring the peace "established" by an agreement between Muslim and Christian factions during Lebanon's civil war.

■ OAS (1965)—the Dominican Republic was on the verge of a civil war. The US sent more than twenty thousand US troops, in a unilateral action that violated standing OAS regional security agreements. The OAS later replaced those troops with its own much smaller Inter-American Peace Force.

UN Peacekeeping

Introduction   Since its inception in 1945, the UN has conducted a number of UN "peacekeeping" operations—although the term was not employed until the 1956 Suez Canal Crisis. There were problems from the outset. No standing army ever materialized, as envisioned under Article 43 of the UN Charter. The Cold War blocked effective peace*making*. Contemporary UN peacekeeping problems include inadequate funding, insufficient national resolve to continue participation, and severely limited US guidelines promulgated by President Clinton in 1994 (*see* § 10.2).

Exhibit 10.1 provides a snapshot of the various UN peacekeeping operations to date.

EXHIBIT 10.1   United Nations Peacekeeping Operations*

Name	Date	Location	Function
UNMIH	1995	Haiti	Mission in Haiti to ensure transition to democracy
UNAMIR	1994	Rwanda	Humanitarian assistance mission
OUNMOZ	1992	Mozambique	Operation for maintaining peace
UNOSOM	1992	Somalia	Humanitarian assistance/civil war

EXHIBIT 10.1 *(continued)*

Name	Date	Location	Function
UNTAC	1992	Cambodia	Transitional authority subsequent to Vietnamese departure
UNPROFOR	1992	Yugoslavia	Civilian protection/State breakup
UNAVEM II	1991	Angola	Verify withdrawal Cuban troops
UNUSAL	1991	El Salvador	Verify elections after US and Nicaraguan indirect involvement
MINURSO	1991	Western Sahara	Mission for Referendum on status
UNIKOM	1991	Iraq-Kuwait	Monitor post–Persian Gulf War Iraqi observance of UN resolution
UNTAG	1989	Namibia	Transition assistance group/implement independence from South Africa
UNUCA	1989	Central America	Observe Central American peace treaties
UNGOMAP	1988	Afghanistan/Pakistan	Good office mission/control force
UNGOMOG	1988	Iran/Iraq	Supervise postwar ceasefire
MFO & MFN	1982	Middle East	Enforce peace treaties between Egypt, Israel, and Lebanon
UNIFIL	1978	Lebanon	Interim force/restore sovereignty
UNDOF	1974	Israel-Syria	Disengagement observer force/1973 War between Israel and Syria
UNEF II	1973	Gaza	Supervise Egypt/Israeli ceasefire
UNFICYP	1964	Cyprus	Buffer between Turkish and Greek Cypriot forces post-Turk invasion
ONUC	1964	Congo	Maintain independence from Belgium
UNYOM	1963	Yemen	Observe DMZ between Yemen/Saudi Arabia
UNSF	1962	West New Guinea	Security force/transfer to Indonesia
UNEF I	1956	Gaza	Buffer Egyptian/Israeli forces

EXHIBIT 10.1 *(continued)*

Name	Date	Location	Function
UNMOGIP	1949	India/Pakistan	Military observer group/ceasefire
UNTSO	1948	Palestine	Truce supervision/monitor cease-fires along Israeli borders
UNSCOB	1947	Balkans	Identify Greek guerrilla source

*Date = commencement of operation

Original Limitations State sovereignty problems limited the potential for successful UN peacekeeping from the outset. The Charter was drafted with a view toward ensuring that the UN would not become a form of world government with the requisite ability to override national sovereignty. Therefore, Article 2.7 of the Charter provides as follows: "Nothing contained in the present Charter shall authorize the United Nations to intervene in matters which are essentially within the domestic jurisdiction of any state. . . ." This constitutional limitation was ultimately interpreted to precluded the organization from operating in any theater without the consent of the States involved—giving rise to the perennial UN role as "peace*keeper*" rather than "peace*maker*."

This limitation supported the opposing perspective that expansion of the UN Somalia "Operation Restore Hope" was beyond the intended scope of UN involvement. Charter Article 2.7 provides that the UN may not intervene into the internal affairs of its member States. A peacekeeping invitation, in practice, had always been understood to mean that the UN troops would take on a somewhat passive role—not actively participating in local military conflicts, because they were only a buffer force. UN troops in Somalia seized arms and conducted raids in order to find a particular Somalian warlord. This organizational activity arguably violated the principle that the organization cannot use its presence to act in ways not authorized under its Charter-based peacekeeping role.

Another preliminary handicap limited the UN's peacekeeping potential. States did not stock the Article 43 "standing army." The UN Charter did not specify the intended composition of its peacekeeping forces. Under Article 43, members would "undertake to make available to the Security Council, on its call and in accordance with a special agreement or agreements, armed forces, [and] assistance . . . necessary for the purpose of maintaining international peace and security." Because the framers of this article did not have enough support to actually establish an international military force in 1945, they inserted this open-ended provision. The details would be resolved sometime after completion of the initial Charter-drafting process in 1945. Article 43 did not specify the size, makeup, and utilization of the international armed forces that were supposed to be placed at the Security Council's disposal. This lack of specificity allowed the national representatives to quickly conclude the drafting of the UN Charter in 1945. Unfortunately, it also vitiated the Security Council's power to effectively maintain peace, since it had no standing army available for potential police actions to deal with threats to international peace.

The other early UN peacekeeping problem was the Cold War. For four decades, the UN peacekeeping operations would not be established within the US and Soviet spheres of direct influence (*see* Exhibit 10.1). Their respective interests in the Third World was to keep one another's influence to a minimum. As noted by William Durch, a prominent policy analyst at the Henry Stimson Center in Virginia, "the UN offered a nominally impartial alternative that could meet this objective. . . . Peacekeeping missions more often served the West's interests in regional *stability*. Since Moscow's interest . . . was to foster regional *instability* . . . lead[ing] to radical political change and greater Soviet regional influence, Soviet support for UN peacekeeping was intermittent at best throughout this period."[27]

Uniting for Peace Frustration with the Security Council's potential for inaction led the General Assembly to adopt the 1950 Uniting for Peace Resolution (UFP). With the Security Council effectively precluded from controlling hostilities—due to the veto power of the five permanent members—the UN General Assembly decided to fashion its own method for taking action independently of the Council. The Assembly's UFP Resolution was designed to remedy the potential failure of the Security Council to discharge its responsibilities on behalf of all the member States, if continually rendered impotent by the veto of one permanent member. The resolution's supporters devised a strategy, not contemplated by the terms of the Charter, that purported to authorize the *General Assembly* to initiate measures to restore peace, including the use of armed force. This novel resolution is set forth below:

UNITING FOR PEACE, RESOLUTION 377(V)

UN General Assembly Official Record
5th Session (1950), Supp. No. 20 (A/1775), p.10

. . .

Conscious that failure of the Security Council to discharge its responsibilities on behalf of all the Member States . . . does not relieve Member States of their obligations or the United Nations of its responsibility under the Charter to maintain international peace and security,

Recognizing in particular that such failure does not deprive the General Assembly of its rights or relieve it of its responsibilities under the Charter in regard to the maintenance of international peace and security,

Recognizing that discharge by the General Assembly of its responsibilities in these respects calls for possibilities of observation which would ascertain the facts and expose aggressors; for the existence of armed forces which could be used collectively; and for the possibility of timely recommendation by the General Assembly to Members of the United Nations for collective action which, to be effective, should be prompt . . .

Resolves that if the Security Council, because of lack of unanimity of the permanent members, fails to exercise its primary responsibility for the maintenance of international peace and security in any case where there appears to be a threat to the peace, breach of the peace, or act of aggression, the General Assembly shall consider the matter immediately with a view to making appropriate recommendations to Members for collective measures, including in the case of a breach of the peace or act of aggression the use of armed force when necessary, to maintain or restore international peace and security. If not in session at the time, the General Assembly may meet in emergency special session within twenty-four hours of the request therefor. Such emergency special session shall be called if requested by the Security Council on the vote of any seven Members, or by a majority of the Members of the United Nations [General Assembly]. . . .

This resolution was important to the future of UN peacekeeping operations. The League of Nations had failed to prevent the outbreak of World War II. The promoters of this resolution did not want history to repeat itself. If the Security Council were unsuccessful in exercising its "primary" responsibility to maintain peace because of the vetoes of permanent members, the General Assembly must assist in the achievement of the fundamental objectives of the organization. This resolution effectively rewrote the UN Charter's Security Council provisions. The General Assembly, rather than the Security Council, now had an arguably valid basis for carrying out the UN peacekeeping function. The Uniting for Peace Resolution was the basis for the next UN peacekeeping operation, which, unlike the US-driven Korean operation, was *actually* under UN control. This was the 1956 Suez Canal Crisis.

The Middle East has been the site of a number of UN peacekeeping operations. The events leading to the Suez Canal Crisis provided an initial flashpoint. In 1956, the president of Egypt nationalized the Suez Canal, one of the major transshipping points of the world. Its closure would require the time and expense of circumnavigating continents to deliver goods or troops. Control of the canal would also affect the price of transporting Middle Eastern oil to the rest of the world.

The significant economic and military threats posed by Egypt's control of the Suez Canal concerned the entire world. Great Britain, France, and Israel secretly decided that Israel would attack Egypt. Great Britain and France would rely on that attack as the basis for their own police action. After the Israeli attack, England and France then vetoed a Security Council resolution calling on Israel and Egypt to cease their hostilities. These vetoes by permanent members of the Council temporarily precluded the establishment of a UN peacekeeping force. England, France, and Israel thus presumed that they could protect their own interests in the canal without any UN interference.[28]

The United Nations Emergency Force (UNEF) was established in 1956. The General Assembly invoked the Uniting for Peace Resolution, to enable it to act after the Security Council was stalemated by the British and French vetoes. A five-thousand-troop force was drawn from States that were *not* members of the Security Council. They were deployed to Egypt, to serve as a buffer between Egypt and its British, French, and Israeli adversaries. In 1967, at the request of Egypt, the UN Secretary-General took the controversial step of withdrawing this force at the time of the so-called Six Day War between Israel and its Arab neighbors. This suspended the UNEF operation until 1973, when it was revived to keep peace and order in the Sinai Desert and the Gaza Strip. This time, the Security Council exercised its Charter powers to establish the next of many Council operations to follow in that theater.

Contemporary Limitations In 1991, Secretary-General Javier Perez de Cuellar analyzed the impact of the UN's financial crisis on peacekeeping. The waning national commitment to paying dues assessments to the UN had begun to materialize (*see* § 3.3). The Secretary-General thus proposed a $1 billion Peace Endowment Fund to help defray costs of future peacekeeping operations. The UN was on the

brink of insolvency. Members, principally the US, were falling behind in their dues payments because of national concern about the soaring costs of membership in this organization. Only sixty-seven of 159 countries had paid in full. By the end of 1992, the UN would learn that it had undertaken the most expensive operation in its history in Cambodia—with its $2 billion price tag.

In 1992, UN Secretary-General Boutros Boutros-Ghali responded to a Security Council request for recommendations about the future of UN peacekeeping. In his report, he noted that demands are being placed on the UN for more peacekeeping operations than ever before. The demise of the Cold War had thrust open new geographical peacekeeping possibilities formerly controlled by superpower politics. These demands also were coming at a time when the UN's financial capacity was already overextended. He welcomed a broadening of the task of UN peacekeeping, but was unable to present a suggestion that would provide any long-term answer to the perennial lack of national resolve.

The Secretary-General's most concrete suggestion was that the members' national budgets use local infrastructure to carry out tasks previously undertaken by UN peacekeeping forces. National expenditures might, in this manner, include the use of facilities and development of budgets with some form of UN component in mind. From his perspective, one must recognize that UN peacekeeping is headed for oblivion unless UN members decide that they wish to cooperate in unprecedented ways to avoid the flashpoints resulting in even more costly wars in a global era of declining governmental resources.

Regardless of contemporary or anticipated limitations, one may refer to the judicial precedent of a past generation for an explicit articulation of the *legal* obligation of the UN members to pay for peacekeeping. A 1962 opinion of the International Court of Justice addressed the obligation of UN members to pay for extraordinary expenses incurred by the UN General Assembly for peacekeeping in the Congo and the Middle East. Article 17.2 of the Charter provides that the "expenses of the Organization shall be borne by the Members as apportioned by the General Assembly." France then proposed that future "extraordinary" expenditures, specifically those associated with peacekeeping, would necessitate the Court's review of whether they were decided in conformity with the Charter. The Court effectively rejected this approach in the following passage:

> Turning to paragraph 2 of Article 17 . . . the term "expenses of the Organization" means *all* the expenses and not just certain types of expenses which might be referred to as "regular expenses." An examination of other parts of the Charter shows the variety of expenses which must inevitably be included within the "expenses of the Organization" just as much as the salaries of the staff or maintenance of the buildings.

> . . .

> For the reasons stated, financial obligations which . . . the Secretary-General incurred on behalf of the United Nations, constitute obligations of the Organization for which the General Assembly was entitled to make provision under the authority of Article 17.[29]

The most serious threat to UN peacekeeping came in February 1995, when the US Congress began to consider legislation which would:

- Limit the president's authority to act in concert with the UN, without prior consultation with the Congress;

- Reduce the US share of UN peacekeeping from 31 to 20 percent; and

- Further reduce the US share by deducting costs incurred by the Pentagon when conducting unilateral "peacekeeping" missions.

If passed, this legislation would significantly alter the US's long-standing commitment to the UN. Other States would arguably withhold *their* assessed shares of the UN peacekeeping budget. The overall impact would jeopardize the ability of the UN to engage in future peacekeeping missions.

■ 10.4 MULTILATERAL AGREEMENTS ON FORCE

Attempts to control the use of force by States are briefly examined in this section. States and international organizations have used a variety of approaches, in the quest to limit the use of military force.

Attempts to control the State use of force are not just a twentieth century phenomenon. In 1789, English writer Jeremey Bentham published arms-control proposals, emphasizing disarmament as the prerequisite to achieving peace. He hoped to pacify Europe through treaties that would limit the number of troops that each State could maintain. He envisioned an international court that would resolve any differences regarding implementation. He did caution, with a relevance that has not faded with the passage of time: "such a court was not to be armed with any coercive powers."[30]

Modern Historical Setting

In the nineteenth century, a number of States met in Europe to consider the efficacy of drafting rules on the laws of war. They produced the Paris Declaration of 1856, a collection of principles on the methods for employing and conserving the use of force in armed conflicts.

In 1899, Russia's Czar Nicholas invited a number of national representatives to The Hague in the Netherlands for the first of two turn-of-the-century international peace conferences. The second occurred in 1907. The objective was to limit the national use of armaments. Once the conference participants realized that there would be no international agreement *eliminating* war, the central theme was how to *conduct* war—rather than how to stop it. The representatives agreed, for example, to provide advance warning when they intended to use a forceful means for settling a dispute.

The conference delegates prepared numerous declarations in the form of draft treaties. The titles depicted the prevailing concerns of the period. A representative list is provided below:

1899 Hague Conference:

- Convention for the Adaption to Maritime Warfare of the Principles of the Geneva Convention of 1864 on the Laws of War

- Declaration on Prohibiting Launching of Projectiles and Explosives from Balloons

- Declaration on Prohibiting the Use of Projectiles Diffusing Suffocating Gas

- Declaration on Prohibiting the Use of Expanding Bullets

- Hague Convention with Respect to the Laws and Customs of War on Land

1907 Hague Conference:

- Convention for the Pacific Settlement of International Disputes

- Convention Respecting the Limitation of the Employment of Force for the Recovery of Contract Debts

- Convention Relative to the Opening of Hostilities

- Convention Respecting the Rights and Duties of Neutral Powers and Persons in War on Land

- Convention Respecting Bombardment by Naval Forces in Time of War

The Hague Conference representatives did not establish a system to *remedy* violations of the principles contained in the above agreements. There would be no international military force to act as a peacekeeper at the scene of hostilities. Instead, they announced an arbitration system to settle international disputes (*see* § 9.1, on the Permanent Court of Arbitration). But they were not *required* to resort to arbitration before using force. All of their draft treaties thus contained rights, without effective remedies. Obligations were unenforceable.

Many of the Hague Conference principles nevertheless served as bases for later treaties and international conferences. The Hague draft agreement on suffocating gas was reconsidered during the 1925 Geneva Protocols on the manufacturing of chemical weapons for future use. These post–World War I agreements prohibited the use of poisonous gases in warfare, although nations could continue to stockpile such weapons. In 1971, UN delegates considered both of these earlier documents when they resolved to prohibit the development, production, and stockpiling of biological and toxic weapons. The Hague Conference chemical-weapons principles resurfaced in 1989. Discovery of a chemical-weapons plant in Libya focused new attention on the need for international control of chemical weapons to avoid their use by terrorists. There was a renewed fear about the effects described in the preparatory work for the early twentieth century chemical-weapons conferences. The former Soviet Union and the US then pledged that they would reduce their arsenals of chemical weapons.

League of Nations The 1919 Treaty of Versailles established global peace expectations following World War I—then referred to as "the war to end all wars." That treaty was the first to *outlaw* war. It was thus the direct ancestor of the League of Nations Covenant, which outlawed war in its Article 12.

Article 16 of the League's Covenant contained a significant innovation. It established the first collective security measure adopted by an international organization: War against one member of the League was tantamount to war against *all*. The League's representatives believed that they could deter hostile actions by agreeing to an interrelated mutual defense system. They opted for economic, rather than military, enforcement measures. Article 16 thus provided as follows:

> Should any of the . . . Parties break or disregard its covenants under Article XII, it shall thereby *ipso facto* [by that act automatically] be deemed to have committed an act of war against all the other members of the League, which hereby undertake immediately to subject it [the offending nation] to the severance of all trade or financial relations, the prohibition of all intercourse between their nationals and the nationals of the covenant breaking State, and the prevention of all financial, commercial, or personal intercourse between nationals of the covenant breaking State and the nationals of any other State, whether a member of the League or not. . . . The . . . Parties agree, further, that they will mutually support one another in the financial and economic measures which are taken under this Article [against any state that wages war]. . . .

Article 16 was first tested in the mid-1930s, during Italy's war against Abyssinia (now Ethiopia). The League did not intervene, even when Abyssinia sought its assistance to control Italy's aggression. The League instead responded by directing several nations to draft a report on Italy's hostile acts. Great Britain and France, with League approval, established an embargo against certain Italian exports. The products that were the object of this embargo, however, were insignificant because Great Britain and France did not want to risk war with their Italian trading partners. Japan then attacked Manchuria in 1939, with League action to implement the above collective security provisions of the multilateral agreement that legally prevented the use of force. The League's inability to take decisive action destroyed its credibility, and exposed its ineffectiveness as a device for controlling the State use of force.[31]

Kellogg-Briand Pact The 1928 Treaty for the Renunciation of War, or Kellogg-Briand Pact, was advocated by France and the United States. It was not designed to be merely a regional peace process. The participants focused on Europe, however, because it was the region most affected by World War I—not to mention the region most engaged in wars throughout the development of modern International Law since the 1648 Peace of Westphalia (described in § 1.3).

This pact *condemned* war and contained the agreement that States "shall" use only peaceful means to settle their differences. Under Articles 1 and 2, the "Parties solemnly declare in the names of their respective peoples that they condemn recourse to war for the solution of international controversies, and renounce it as an instrument of national policy in their relations with one another. The . . . Parties agree that the settlement or solution of all disputes or conflicts of whatever nature or of whatever origin they may be . . . shall never be sought except by pacific means."

This pact still exists, but it shares an important flaw with the defunct League of Nations Covenant. While both outlawed war, neither prevented the outbreak of a world war. They contained unassailable principles, yet lacked any effective enforcement provisions to control the State (mis)use of force.

Latin American Initiatives Some significant peace initiatives, like the 1928 Kellogg-Briand Pact, condemn war. The 1933 Montevideo Treaty provided that "settlement of disputes or controversies shall be effected only by the pacific means which shall have the sanction of international law." The 1948 Charter of the Organization of American States also prohibits the aggressive use of force. Its Article 21 provides that the "American States bind themselves in their international relations not to have recourse to the use of force." This treaty does not contain a specific arms control regime, however.

The "Cold War" between the former Soviet Union and the US began in the mid-twentieth century, dominating international affairs for the next forty years. During this period, States and international organizations concluded a number of agreements to prevent the escalation of that "conflict." The US and former Soviet Union agreed to a series of bilateral arms limitation agreements, beginning in 1972, to control the potential use of their respective nuclear weapons arsenals. Since the end of the Cold War, there have been fresh attempts to control the use of force—on both the regional and multilateral levels. Exhibit 10.2 provides a snapshot of selected agreements or resolutions designed to control today's uses of *military* force.

EXHIBIT 10.2 Selected Multilateral Arms Control Regimes

Date*	Title	Scope
1925 1928	Geneva Protocol	Prohibits use of asphyxiating, poisonous, and bacteriological warfare
1957	International Atomic Energy Agency created	Intergovernmental organization to promote peaceful uses of nuclear energy
1959 1961	Antarctic Treaty	Prohibits establishment of military bases, maneuvers, and testing

EXHIBIT 10.2 *(continued)*

Date*	Title	Scope
1961	Belgrade Declaration	29 nonaligned States from various regions of the globe, fearing escalation of Cold War, demand an immediate stop to armed action directed at any dependent peoples
1963 1963	Partial Test Ban Treaty	Prohibits use of nuclear weapons in atmosphere, outer space, under water—authorizes underground testing only 1967
1967	Outer Space Treaty	Prohibits orbit of weapons of mass destruction and any military presence in space or on any celestial body
1967 1968	Treaty of Tlatelolco	*Latin America:* regional nuclear-free zone prohibiting acquisition, manufacture, or any use of nuclear weapons
1968 1970	Non-Proliferation Treaty	Nuclear States may not transfer, and others may not receive, manufacture, or develop nuclear weapons/effect limited due to lack of ratification by key parties (China, France, India, Pakistan, South Africa)
1971 1972	Seabed Treaty	Prohibits nuclear weapons and other weapons of mass destruction on the seabed and ocean floor, and in subsoil
1972 1975	Biological Weapons Convention	Prohibits the production and stockpiling of bacteriological and toxin weapons/seeks destruction or diversion to peaceful purposes/national sovereignty withdrawal clause has rendered it ineffective
1977 1978	Enmod Convention	Prohibits military or other hostile use of environmental modification in, over, and above the Earth
1977	Mercenarism Convention	*Africa:* Organization of African Unity prohibition on placing or training mercenaries in Africa/created crime of mercenarism/guilty person denied POW status
1981 1983	Inhumane Weapons Convention	Prohibits/restricts certain conventional weapons deemed too injurious—mines, booby-traps, incendiary devices
1985 1986	Treaty of Rarotonga	*South Pacific:* declares nuclear-free zone/prohibits acquisition, testing of nuclear weapons, and dumping of waste

EXHIBIT 10.2 *(continued)*

Date*	Title	Scope
1986	CSCE Confidence and Security Building Measures and Disarmaments	*Europe:* facilitates abstention from threat or use of force, including advance notification of certain military activities such as major troop and battle tank movements 1990
1992	Conventional Armed Forces in Europe (CFE) Treaty	*Europe:* former Warsaw Pact nations to destroy 50,000 major weapons; NATO nations to destroy few weapons; all to reduce ground and air weapons; ceilings on certain combat equipment 1992
1992	CFE-1A Agreement	*Europe:* CFE-related treaty limiting conventional personnel strength
1991	START I & II Treaties	Would cut nuclear stockpiles by two-thirds: initially signed by US/USSR; now = US, Russia, and three former USSR republics
1991	Missile Technology Control Regime	UN Security Council permanent member sponsored arms export limitations and shared information regarding sales of all military weapons and control of missiles capable of delivering biological/chemical/nuclear weapons
1992	Chemical Weapons Convention	UN General Assembly Resolution 47/39 prohibiting use, development, stockpiling, of chemical weapons/seeks destruction 10 years after entry into force
1992	Nuclear Power in Outer Space	UN General Assembly Resolution 47/68: would control use of nuclear power in outer space
1992	General and Complete Disarmament	UN General Assembly Resolution 46/36: 12 resolutions calling for complete disarmament, rather than mere controls /Annex establishes UN Register of Conventional Arms, to track import or export of specified types of military systems

* Second date = year of entry into force, by minimum number of ratifications or by other special agreement

Contemporary Perspectives

Any study of the use of force must include the recognition that there remain diverse perspectives about the use of force after the Cold War. Some commentators, for example, believe that the use of force is still an important tool in the arsenal of contemporary alternatives. Ardent supporters of its use in Operation Desert Storm, during the 1991 Persian Gulf War with Iraq, argued that "force is a legitimate tool of [foreign] policy."[32] Yet the ramifications of even this UN-sponsored use of force should only emphasize that prevention must precede its use—which must be the *last* resort even when supreme national interests are at stake.

War is an expensive means of dispute resolution. Its use does not really "settle" an underlying dispute. The victor merely suppresses the effects of the dispute, and not its root causes. There is a need for a legal process that is, in the long run, satisfactory to all the disputing parties. An indigenous population can overcome the mightest show of force, when they believe that their losses are only temporary and unjustly inflicted. The Vietnamese were able to secure freedom from colonial control after France's decisive defeat in Indochina in 1954—and reunification of the North and South, despite the long-term commitment of far superior US military forces until 1973. The Iraq/Kuwait border dispute was not over, even after the thorough defeat of the Iraqi forces who were driven out of Kuwait in 1991. Iraq's 1994 renunciation of all claims to Kuwait is, presumably, the end of that ancient territorial dispute—initiated by Britain's rewriting of regional frontiers in the 1800s.[33]

Some nations have a different perspective. They have either renounced the use of *aggressive* military force, or have decided not to have *any* military force. Article 9 of Japan's Constitution provides that "the Japanese people forever renounce war as a sovereign right of the nation and [reject] the threat or use of force as a means of settling international disputes." Japan's army and navy are "self-defense" forces and greatly limited in the scope of their external operations. The nation has seen a number of constitutional problems, as the size of Japan's self-defense forces have gradually increased. In 1993, Japan issued special peacekeeping guidelines in response to international pressures for it to contribute forces for this UN role. This sensitive constitutional issue involves the extent to which Japanese forces can participate in a foreign conflict, although limited to a UN peacekeeping role.[34]

In 1992, the former Soviet nation of Kirgizstan decided not to maintain *any* military forces. The agrarian economy was the basis for its leaders deciding against maintaining a military force capable of defending it against attack. This new State is a would-be Switzerland—located in the midst of China's western border and neighboring former Soviet States that are arming and, in some cases, alarming the West.

Russia's President Boris Yeltsin has expressed another contemporary perspective on how to limit force on a multilateral basis. Russia, in his words,

should be the "guarantor of peace and stability in regions of the former U.S.S.R." In this March 1993 plea at the UN, Yeltsin sought to establish his own form of the US Monroe Doctrine. In 1823, US President James Monroe asserted the role of the US as protector of the Western Hemisphere from external threats. European States were thus warned not to intervene in hemispheric matters. On a similar note, Russia obtained the UN seat once occupied by the "Soviet Union." Thus, it could be the regional power responsible for maintaining peace, with UN approval. But Yeltsin's claim to this "right" was not welcomed by historic rivals such as Ukraine, a nation that has been effectively dominated by Russia for 600 years.

In the aftermath of the Cold War, traditional notions of sovereignty are changing (*see* Chapter 2 on States). Sovereignty is changing in terms of an increasing number of States. A number of regional and local conflicts are flaring up, now that the two superpowers no longer consider Third World powers as pawns in a global chess match for survival. There are no longer East-West zones of influence wherein armed conflict might be dealt with swiftly by one of the former superpowers. The war in the former Yugoslavia, where the West would not have ventured during the Cold War, is unfortunate evidence of this principle. The scourge of war that has besieged the globe since the inception of the modern system of nation-States 350 years ago, and of course long before, may ultimately engulf the planet in a series of flames that gradually burn out of control.

One of the most serious problems with implementing multilateral agreements on the control of force surfaced in 1991. The Cold War had ended. North Korea had been admitted to the UN in 1991 as a "peace-loving state," under Article 4.1 of the UN Charter. It signed a Treaty of Reconciliation with South Korea. The US had announced a major withdrawal of US troops, stationed in South Korea since the Korean War. North Korea had announced its agreement, in principle, with a US plan to purge the Korean peninsula of nuclear weapons. Under the Bush administration, the US had already removed its nuclear weapons from South Korea.

Suddenly, it appeared that one East-West remnant of the Cold War was about to resurface—another major threat to regional and global stability centered on the possession of nuclear weapons of mass destruction. North Korea announced that it would no longer permit inspections by the UN International Atomic Energy Agency, under the 1968 Nuclear Non-Proliferation Treaty. All foreigners except accredited diplomats were asked to leave North Korea in 1993, as this disruptive scenario continued to unfold. North Korea then announced its withdrawal from the 1968 nuclear control treaty, later scaled back to a "suspension," after extensive UN-sponsored negotiations. Japan and South Korea pleaded with the US not to impose sanctions on North Korea. The world was, once again, perceived by many commentators as being near the brink of nuclear confrontation. In 1994, the US sent in scores of Patriot antimissile batteries—to block North Korean Scud missiles in the event of the North's attack of the South. Later in 1994, North Korea finally agreed to permit inspectors to reenter to determine its nuclear weapons capability.

While tension was thus diminished, the related compromise has arguably set a risky precedent. The US agreed to North Korea's demand that inspections of its suspected nuclear sites be postponed for several years. The US will provide $4 billion in aid to help North Korea for energy assistance. North Korea will freeze any nuclear programs for several years. This incident may have sent an unintended message to rogue States, that violating the 1968 treaty has its rewards. North Korea is, effectively, free to proceed as it wishes. The international community was "put off" for several years, and (once again) North Korea remains free to disregard the nuclear control treaty when that time frame elapses. One member of the community of nations may have thus risked nuclear holocaust, with the result that this brinkmanship will resurface for those States that are able to develop nuclear weapons capabilities in the interim.

One might thus consider the following question: Just how well can multilateral agreements effectively control the use of force, as long as the international community tolerates such risks in the name of the preservation of sovereignty? Put another way, multilateral agreements on force, thus far, have failed to vitiate the nationalist penchant for agreements *in principle* without yielding the sovereign power to create enforcement machinery.

■ 10.5 HUMANITARIAN INTERVENTION

Various modes of intervention are used to assist people with some struggle in their homeland. *Unilateral* humanitarian interventions conflict, however, with a number of norms involving the use of force and territorial sovereignty. Intervention may also be *collective*. It may be authorized by an international organization pursuing the common objective of maintaining peace. The extent to which a State may unilaterally intervene, for the purpose of rescuing political figures or hostages, is also fraught with complex issues of legitimacy. This section thus deals with what are often *mis*characterized as "humanitarian" interventions.

Humanitarian Intervention

Definitional Contours Multilateral intervention is often undertaken by a regional or global organization for the purpose of aiding people who are suffering in a variety of circumstances. The underlying problem may be a civil war, or degradation at the hands of a despotic political regime. The intervention may be undertaken via military or economic actions designed to bring about a change in the targeted State. Too often, intervention in the name of humanitarian motives has been little more than another State justification for political domination via this form of force.

The application of this form of force is typically justified on the basis that the inhabitants of another State are not receiving the protection they deserve under the International Law of Human Rights (Chapter 11). In other words, their government is arbitrarily and persistently abusing all inhabitants, or a particular ethnic group. The US unilaterally intervened in Cuba in 1898, for example, to "put an end to barbarities, bloodshed, starvation, and horrible miseries. . . ."[35]

Further definition is difficult. The permissible contours of humanitarian intervention have not been defined in a way that represents any State consensus. The legitimacy of unilateral humanitarian intervention has thus been analyzed and debated for some six hundred years. States have long recognized the practical utility of characterizing their actions as legal because they are undertaken for "humanitarian" purposes.[36]

Public and private commentaries have thus focused on the following factors for assessing the criteria for *proper* humanitarian intervention—not always distinguishing between armed and unarmed intervention:

- What is the *nature of the right* that has been violated? Genocide may arguably support unilateral intervention undertaken to restore the regime to acceptable governmental control.

- What is the *purpose of the intervention*? Was the 1898 US unilateral intervention in Cuba really undertaken to avoid "barbarities, bloodshed, starvation, and horrible miseries" as noted above?

- What is the *nature of the intervention*? Was the intervention unilateral, collective, or universal? If the US and its allies had undertaken the Persian Gulf War to save Kuwait, without UN Security Council approval, such action would be more likely to be characterized a UN Charter violation. Was it really necessary and proportional to the conduct of the target State? Early US airdrops of humanitarian relief packages over Bosnia (as done with the Kurdish region of Iraq in 1991) were far less intrusive, for example, than NATO's air strikes to force Serbs away from "safe havens" such as Sarajevo and Bihac. This may necessitate a balancing of the choice among various alternatives to inaction, versus the results obtainable by a unilateral intervention to ameliorate suffering.

- Do the circumstances warrant a *balancing standard* favoring human rights protection, versus unbending adherence to preservation of national sovereignty? Just what type of community of nations is envisioned for the future?

- Should there be a brightline rule, either prohibiting all unilateral intervention—or alternatively, authorizing this conduct in appropriate treaty-based circumstances?

Collective Intervention Intervention that is collective in nature is more readily justifiable than unilateral intervention. A UN-based humanitarian mission, like the effort to rescue the failing State of Somalia in 1993, is the preferable form of humanitarian intervention. Chapter VII of the Charter gives the Security Council broad powers to intervene when there are threats to peace justifying intervention to carry out Security Council mandates. The inherent problem is that the Charter contains potentially conflicting norms. Members are expected to avoid the use of force that threatens peace, while at the same time encouraging respect for human rights. The Charter expectation is that members pledge "to take joint *and separate* action" in cooperation with the UN for the achievement of its humanitarian purposes. They must therefore promote "universal respect for, and observance of, human rights and fundamental freedoms for all without distinction as to race, sex, language, or religion." Yet, the UN may *not* interfere in matters within the national jurisdiction of another member.[37]

The UN Charter authorizes *regional* arrangements in Chapter VIII. It does not specify the interplay between that Chapter of the Charter and the Security Council's Chapter VII enforcement powers. Thus, a collective regional action, undertaken in the name of humanitarian intervention, would not be necessarily authorized by Security Council inaction or silence. Under Article 53, no enforcement actions are to be undertaken via regional arrangements without the authorization of the Security Council.[38]

On the other hand, there is room for the argument that customary State practice may augment or clarify the meaning of the term "humanitarian intervention." As articulated by the International Court of Justice's 1986 *Nicaragua* case: "There can be no doubt, that the provision of *strictly* humanitarian aid to persons or forces in another country, whatever their political affiliation or objectives, cannot be regarded as unlawful intervention, or as in any other way contrary to international law."[39] While this right supports another State's providing supplies in civil wars, or other emergencies, it does not include the right of armed penetration.

This humanitarian intervention facet of customary (nontreaty) International Law had contemporary application in Rwanda in 1994, and in Bosnia since 1991. Over 1 million people fled from Rwanda during a civil war, wherein belligerent tribes used machetes indiscriminately to kill or maim the people of Rwanda. France sought to intervene on the basis of humanitarian intervention. It was accused of employing this convenient basis for intervening into the affairs of its former French colony, rather than altruistically seeking an end to the massacres. France insisted that it was neutral with no such ulterior motives.

France and Belgium had previously sent "humanitarian aid" to Africa in the form of military troops to protect their respective citizens living in Zaire in 1991. That intervention provoked a number of protests, alleging that they had done no more than to intervene into the internal affairs of a weaker sovereign nation once controlled by French during the colonial era. In Rwanda, the UN established a peacekeeping operation after the loss of hundreds of thousands of lives. This force consists of American, British, and Canadian troops.

A case for international humanitarian intervention exists today in Bosnia. Claims of ethnic cleansing by Serbian military forces, mass rapes of Muslim women as a military tactic to drive them out of Bosnia, and other atrocities gave rise to the first International Criminal Court since Nuremberg (*see* § 9.5). While some food has been sent, even NATO air strikes on Serb positions did little to relieve the suffering of the civilian populace. In a January 1993 speech given by the Catholic Church's pope, he claimed that the international community had a "duty to disarm the aggressor" if other means failed. This sentiment was premised, in part, on the appeals of non-Serbian leaders for *any* form of intervention that would balance the playing field in the Bosnian War—where the Serbs stood accused of genocidal acts and being in defiance of UN mandates regarding their conduct of the war in violation of human rights. More humanitarian intervention could be authorized. The themes of sovereignty and nonintervention constitute barriers, however, that have precluded *effective* international action to control the murder and torture of civilians in Bosnia.

Private Intervention Humanitarian intervention is greatly limited by concerns about State sovereignty. There has been an interim development, however, that may one day bridge this gap between human rights and sovereignty. Given the difficulties of establishing criteria for legitimate humanitarian intervention, certain *non*governmental actors have sought the right to *private* intervention into appropriate conflicts. At France's insistence, the General Assembly supported this development in its three resolutions between 1988 and 1991 on "Humanitarian assistance to victims of natural disasters and similar emergency situations."[40] France sought to establish the right of private French groups to cross international borders, unhindered by sovereign limitations that would otherwise prevent them from treating the victims of armed hostilities or other disasters.

These General Assembly resolutions paved the way for Security Council Resolution 688 of 1991, which insisted that Iraq provide immediate access to those in need of humanitarian assistance—especially its Kurdish population that had been the subject of the government's poisoned gas attacks several years before. Resolution 688 did not, however, authorize *armed* intervention. Council members were reluctant to set any precedent, regardless of Iraq's extremely provocative conduct reminiscent of the Nazi Holocaust. International humanitarian organizations, such as the International Red Cross, were thus endowed with a new justification for humanitarian relief—so often blocked by competing notions of national sovereignty.

It is now arguable that States have a duty, under International Law, to provide humanitarian assistance to their *own* populations; and, alternatively, to accept external humanitarian assistance. If so, then this duty would also give rise to the duty of all States to facilitate humanitarian assistance. A breach would permit other States to provide such assistance without the sovereign consent of the State in need of such "intervention." As the basis for humanitarian intervention has always been to limit or eliminate suffering, then the freer accessibility of nongovernmental organizations to afflicted peoples would be a reasonable compromise that balances sovereign concerns with the developing human rights regime discussed in the next chapter of this book. As stated by Professor Dietrich Schindler of the University of Zurich:

> Access by private humanitarian organisations to victims without the consent of the government of the State concerned must be considered lawful in the following two cases. First, in a non-international armed conflict [civil war], an impartial humanitarian body, such as the International Committee of the Red Cross, may bring humane assistance to victims of the insurgent party without the consent of the legal government. . . .
>
> Second, if a State refuses a humanitarian organization [to have such] access to its territory in contradiction to its duties, such organizations can assert the same rights as a State. They may bring assistance to the victims in spite of the refusal of the government.[41]

Rescue

Certain States, and terrorists clandestinely supported by them, use various forms of force and coercion in their international relations. One form of coercion is the taking of hostages to place political pressure on another nation. The aggressor nation takes hostages, or financially supports a group of individuals, to force another nation to act pursuant to the captor's demands.

Hostage taking began to occur with alarming frequency in the 1970s, when it became a useful tool for accomplishing the national political objectives of certain countries. The UN responded to this phenomenon with the 1979 International Convention against the Taking of Hostages. The primary impetus for this convention was the Iranian hostage crisis, triggered by Iran's 1979 seizure of American diplomats and military personnel at the US embassy in Tehran. Article 1 of the Hostage Convention provides that any *person* who detains and threatens to kill another person in order to compel a State "to do or abstain from doing any act as an explicit or implicit condition for the release of the hostage commits the offense of taking hostages." Under International Law, a person acting on behalf of a State may not take a hostage to coerce another State to act in a certain way. When this occurs, the responsible State breaches this prohibition.

Some States have obviously disregarded this principle, giving rise to a related issue in International Law. When foreign hostages are kidnapped, there is intense national pressure to free them. It is difficult to yield to that pressure, since giving in to the captors' demands encourages further hostage taking. This dilemma has triggered the occasional but widely publicized use of an innovative form of countermeasure. Rescue missions have been carried out in other States, to save hostages facing certain death.

Military rescue missions present practical and legal problems. The nation that launches the rescue mission clearly breaches the territorial sovereignty of the nation where the hostages are located. The rescuing nation claims, however, that necessity dictates its action. One reason for the necessity is that International Law cannot enforce the Hostage Convention's principles when a nation takes or effectively condones hostage taking. Where no action has been taken, other than the usual diplomatic efforts to free the hostages, hostages have been harmed or

killed. It is therefore argued that the rescuing nation's right of self-defense supports the existence of a *limited* right to breach the sovereignty of the captor nation for this humanitarian purpose.

States and international organizations have undertaken occasional rescue missions to extract their citizens or agents who are likely to die at the hands of some terrorist or government. While not the completely altruistic form of humanitarian intervention, there are similar concerns regarding the violations of sovereignty that may accompany such forms of self-help.

There is, of course, a legal basis for UN activity that works to extract its agents who are involved in an enforcement action already authorized by the Security Council. In 1992, a UN antimine team rescued a convoy that had braved two days of crossfire in order to deliver food to the besieged Bosnian town of Gordaze. While returning to the Bosnian capital of Sarajevo, this convoy was trapped by land mines. Neither of the warring factions would come to the aid of these UN workers to ensure their safe return.

The major problem is the unilateral use of force, when danger invites rescue. The US has been involved in a number of such rescue attempts. In 1980, a US military operation in Iran failed to retrieve US diplomats held captive for over one year during the US-Iran Hostage Crisis (*see* § 7.4). In 1992, a US Navy SEAL team conducted a secret rescue mission in Haiti. It extracted a handful of former Haitian officials aligned with the then-ousted President Aristide. Their lives were in danger—according to Pentagon officials. US Congressman Charles Rangel condemned this rescue, promising that Congress would conduct an inquiry into this matter. US President Bush did not comment on the raid, although a White House spokesman said that the President was unaware of the rescue—a highly unlikely representation.

The classic illustration of a hostage rescue mission occurred in 1976. A French passenger plane, containing mostly Israeli citizens, was hijacked in Athens by a Middle East terrorist organization. They flew to Entebbe, Uganda. Some newspaper accounts of this event reported that a Middle Eastern nation clandestinely promoted this hijacking. The hijackers threatened to systematically kill the hostages unless other Middle Eastern citizens were freed from Israeli prisons. Uganda's President Amin refused to help the hostages, arguably out of a desire to avoid harming his political position with any Arab nation that may have sponsored the hijacking. A group of Israeli commandos then flew into Uganda without permission and rescued the hostages. They killed a number of Ugandan soldiers at the airport where the hostages were being held.

The chairman of the Organization of African Unity initiated a complaint in the UN, based on Israel's "act of aggression" against Uganda. Two draft resolutions condemning Israel's conduct were intro-duced in the Security Council—one by Great Britain and the United States—and the other by Tanzania, Libya, and Benin. The draft resolutions condemned Israel's rescue mission as a violation of the principle prohibiting the use of force in international relations. The following summary from the UN debate suggests the delicate nature of this problem—how to simultaneously condemn both Israel's violation of Uganda's territory *and* the future taking of hostages:

EXCERPTS FROM UNITED NATIONS SECURITY COUNCIL DEBATE ON THE ENTEBBE INCIDENT

13 UN Monthly Chronicle (August-September 1976)*

In the debate, Kurt WALDHEIM, Secretary-General of the United Nations, said he had issued a statement on 8 July immediately after his return from Africa in which he had given a detailed account of the role he had played in efforts to secure the release of the hostages at Entebbe.

The case before the Council raised a number of complex issues because, in this instance, the response of one State to the results of an act of hijacking involved an action affecting another sovereign State. In reply to a specific question, he had said: "I have not got all the details, but it seems to be clear that Israeli aircraft have landed in Entebbe and this constitutes a serious violation of the sovereignty of a State Member of the United Nations." The Secretary-General said he felt it was his obligation to uphold the principle of the territorial integrity and sovereignty of every State.

However, that was not the only element involved in considering cases of the kind which the Council was discussing. That was particularly true when the world community was required to deal with unprecedented problems arising from acts of international terrorism, which Mr. Waldheim said he had consistently condemned and which raised many issues of a humanitarian, moral, legal and political character for which, at the present time, no commonly agreed rules or solutions existed.

. . .

Percy HAYNES (Guyana) said the action taken by Israel against Uganda was nothing but naked and brutal aggression. Guyana strongly condemned Israel for its aggression against the black African country of Uganda.

It was being argued that the principle of sovereignty was subordinate to the principle of human freedom and that Israel had the right, whenever it chose, to violate the sovereignty of other States in order to secure the freedom of its own citizens. That was nothing but a modern-day version of gun-boat diplomacy.

Those who, like Israel, sought to give legitimacy to the violation of the sovereignty of other States were making many small States, whose faith in and commitment to international law were unshakable, hostage to the dictates of naked power.

. . .

Kaj SUNDBERG (Sweden) said the drama was started by an abhorrent act of terrorism perpetrated by a group of extremist Palestinian Arabs and Europeans. There was no excuse for that criminal act.

The world must react vigorously against terrorist acts and take all possible protective measures. New efforts must be undertaken to achieve broad international agreement to combat terrorism, in the form of generally recognized standards of international conduct. The international community must work towards general recognition of the clear obligation resting on every State to do everything in its power,

---

*Reprinted with permission of the United Nations.

where necessary in collaboration with other States, to prevent acts of terrorism and, even more, to refrain from any action which might facilitate the perpetration of such acts.

Any State where hijackers landed with hostages must be prepared to shoulder the heavy responsibility of protecting all victims under circumstances which were bound to be difficult and delicate.

. . .

Sweden, although unable to reconcile the Israeli action with the strict rules of the Charter, did not find it possible to join in a condemnation in such a case.

. . .

Mr. SCRANTON (United States) said the United States reaffirmed the principle of territorial sovereignty in Africa. In addition to that principle, the United States was deeply concerned over the problem of air piracy and the callous and pernicious use of innocent people as hostages to promote political ends. The Council could not forget that the Israeli operation in Uganda would never have come about had the hijacking of the Air France flight from Athens not taken place.

Israel's action in rescuing the hostages necessarily involved a temporary breach of the territorial integrity of Uganda. Normally, such a breach would be impermissible under the Charter. However, there was a well established right to use limited force for the protection of one's own nationals from an imminent threat of injury or death in a situation where the State in whose territory they were located was either unwilling or unable to protect them. The right, flowing from the right of self-defence, was limited to such use of force as was necessary and appropriate to protect threatened nationals from injury.

The requirements of that right to protect nationals were clearly met in the Entebbe case. Israel had good reason to believe that at the time it acted Israeli nationals were in imminent danger of execution by the hijackers. In addition, there was substantial evidence that the Government of Uganda cooperated with and aided the hijackers. The ease and success of the Israeli effort to free the hostages suggested that the Ugandan authorities could have overpowered the hijackers and released the hostages if they had really had the desire to do so.

. . .

Mikhail KHARLAMOV (USSR) said that the flight carried out, the material destruction wrought, the substantial number of Ugandans killed were all regarded by Israel as a measure which was just or at least justified. But there existed no laws in the world, no moral or international laws, which could justify such action.

However much the representative of Israel might have tried to refute the irrefutable, the armed action against Uganda was an act of direct, flagrant aggression and an outright violation of the Charter, especially of Article 2, paragraph 4, which stated: "All Members shall refrain in their international relations from the threat of use of force against the territorial integrity or political independence of any State, or in any other manner inconsistent with the purposes of the United Nations."

The Soviet Union consistently opposed acts of terrorism, and was prepared to do its part in order to end that phenomenon. But one could not replace one matter with another. The Council was considering not the matter of international terrorism but an attack on Uganda, the killing of Ugandans, the destruction of Entebbe Airport, and other material destruction inflicted by the Israeli action against that State.

. . .

The Council must condemn in the most vigorous manner the Israeli aggression against the sovereignty and territorial integrity of Uganda and compel Israel to recompense Uganda for the material damage done in connection with the attack. In addition, the Council must extend a serious warning to Israel that such acts of aggression would not go unpunished in future.

. . .

Isao ABE (Japan) said international terrorism, whatever form it might take, constituted an abhorrent crime against mankind and must be denounced in the strongest terms by the world community. The countries in the world must take effective measures to prevent and eliminate such a crime against humanity, and they were required to co-operate fully with each other in attaining that goal.

The Air France hijacking was terminated in an extraordinary circumstance—military action by a

State within the territory of another State. Although the motives as well as the circumstances which led Israel to take such action were presented in detail, nevertheless there was an act of violation by Israel of the sovereignty of Uganda.

Japan reserved its opinion as to whether the Israeli military action had or had not met the conditions required for the exercise of the right of self-defence recognized under international law, as the Israeli representative contended.

The Security Council did not adopt either of the previously mentioned draft resolutions condemning Israel's violation of Uganda's territorial sovereignty. Most nations were reluctant to officially condone Israel's acts, although their newspapers reported popular approval. One reason for this approval was that Israel did not initiate the crisis. Another was that Uganda's inaction acquiesced in terrorist hostage taking. Without some action by the Israeli government, the hostages faced certain death in Uganda at the hands of the hijackers.

Whether State practice prohibits this limited use of reactionary force remains unclear. Rescue missions *may* be an acceptable way of responding to hostage crises. Although the US coauthored a resolution that would have condemned Israel for its rescue mission in Uganda, it later argued in favor of a limited right to rescue hostages from certain death when there was a diplomatic impasse. Three years later, the US would undertake its own hostage rescue mission in Iran. That mission did *not* generate an international reaction like the one that was thrust upon Israel.

■ 10.6 LAWS OF WAR

SARAJEVO, Bosnia-Herzegovina, June 2, 1993—Serb mortar shells blasted a soccer game on a Muslim holy day yesterday, killing at least 15 people and wounding about 80 in one of the war's worst attacks on Sarajevo civilians.

An hour after two shells slammed into the crowd of spectators, the soccer ball remained on the parking lot where the game was played, surrounded by pools of blood. *Associated Press*

Definitional Introduction

The "Laws of War" consist of customary State practices and the treaties that limit or prohibit the *way* in which belligerents conduct war. *National* laws prohibit war-related crimes including espionage and treason. It is *International* Law, however, that provides the impetus for laws protecting the innocent and defenseless against the excesses of State actors who believe that the ends justifies the means. Democratic States tend to include these global expectations in appropriate battle manuals of military commanders in the field. The underlying concern is that expediency during hostilities must, in applicable cases, give way to legal and moral concerns about humane treatment. A less poignant concern influences the Laws of War. Certain norms relate to the expeditious conduct of war in ways that do not unnecessarily disrupt international commerce.

Areas of concern include the following: summary executions of civilians and military personnel; ethnic cleansing and forcible displacement; mistreatment in detention; indiscriminate use of force against *non*-military targets; attacks on medical and related relief personnel; looting and other destruction of civilian property with no military purpose; terrorizing and starving a civilian population; use of military or civilian human shields against further attack; and the use of particular types of warfare condemned under various international agreements mentioned in this section of the book.

Four general categories of the Laws of War impact what nations may or may not do when engaged in hostilities: These include the Laws of War on the ground, at sea, and in the air. Given the environmental terrorism perpetrated by Iraqi forces retreating from Kuwait during the Persian Gulf War, one must also emphasize environmental Laws of War as a special category—due to the pervasive impact of this mode of conduct on all three territorial dimensions.

There have been numerous attempts to control or outlaw the *ways* in which nations conduct war. A few of these regulatory regimes were addressed in §10.4. Exhibit 10.2 contains major multilateral agreements regarding the use of force. Earlier expressions, such as the 1928 "Kellogg-Briand" Pact's outright prohibition of war, may be disregarded when studying the Laws of War, as well-intentioned but myopic attempts to deal with the reality of State sovereignty. The materials in this section of the book thus overlook the presumption that International Law has outlawed aggressive uses of force. No nation openly defies that principle—many, however, disagree with its application.

Historical Setting

History is fraught with accounts of "man's inhumanity to man" in time of war. The Bible's Old Testament contains admonitions prohibiting the following: the slaughter of captured men; the transplanting of innocent women and children; the plunder of animals and other property; and the pillaging and wanton destruction of cities. In the Battle of Teutoburg Forest of 9, a Germanic tribal chieftain defeated several Roman legions. He declared at the point of victory that "those prisoners who were not hewn to pieces on the spot were only preserved to perish by a more cruel death in cold blood."

During the medieval Crusades, combatant forces routinely slaughtered enemy prisoners. Women were raped, and inhabitants' goods were forfeited. These prizes of war were available as an incentive for soldiers facing periods of protracted siege.[42]

Sporadic efforts limited the cruelty of warfare. A few military leaders and heads of State required their soldiers to observe certain minimum standards of humane conduct in warfare. In 559 B.C. and 333 B.C. respectively, the King of Persia and Alexander the Great ordered their troops to spare the civilian population of conquered areas and to avoid the intentional desecration of religious sites. In 70 B.C.,

the Roman commander Titus arranged for the safe departure of women and children from Jerusalem when it was under his siege. In 410, the Visigoth leader Alaric—known for his cruelty to foreign soldiers—forbade his soldiers to violate the women of Rome when he captured the city. In the Middle Ages, certain Christian and Muslim leaders humanized the conduct of war, partially out of a strategy of avoiding an overly desperate enemy.

"Just wars" were a part of the new international legal system established by the seventeenth century Peace of Westphalia (see § 1.3). The European perspective was that if the war was "just" then the enemy was by definition "unjust." Adversaries therefore were not entitled to humane treatment, other than that within the discretion of the on-scene military commander.

The beginnings of more "civilized" modes for killing other humans began to emerge in the Middle Ages. In Latin America, for example, Spanish conquistadors—representing the crown and the Catholic Church—were required to read the *El Requerimiento* to the Indians before hostilities could be legally commenced. Note the religious implications of the following declaration, which one could imagine as being read during contemporary Middle Eastern hostilities near Jerusalem. The South American Indian of the 1500s would thus be advised as follows, in the presence of a notary public who would record the fact of the required prewar declaration:

EL REQUERIMIENTO
THE DEVELOPMENT OF REGULATIONS FOR CONQUISTADORS
CONTRABUCIONES PARA EL ESTUDIO DE LA HISTORIA DE AMERICA

Lewis Hanke, Buenos Aires, Argentina (1941)

On the part of the King [and Queen] . . . subduers of the barbarous nations, we their servants notify and make known to you . . . [that the Lord made known to] St. Peter, that he would be would be Lord and Superior of all men in the world, that all should obey him, and that he should head the whole human race, wherever men should live. . . .

And he commanded him to place his seat in Rome, as the spot most fitting to rule the world from; but also he permitted him to have his seat in any other part of the world and to judge and govern all Christians, Jews, Gentiles, and all other sects.

This man was called Pope, as if to say, Admirable Great Father and Governor of men. . . .

One of these Pontiffs, who succeeded St. Peter as Lord of the world . . . made donation of these isles and Terra-firme [land territories] to the aforesaid King and Queen and to their successors. . . .

So their Highnesses are kings and lords of these islands and land. . . . Wherefore as best we can, we ask and require you that you consider what we have said to you, and that you take the time that shall be necessary to understand and deliberate upon it, and that you acknowledge the Church as the Ruler and

Superior of the whole world . . . and that you consent and give place that these religious fathers should declare and preach to you the aforesaid.

If you do so, you will do well. . . . And besides this, their Highnesses will award you many privileges and exceptions and will grant you many benefits.

But if you do not do this, and wickedly and intentionally delay to do so, I certify to you that, with the help of God, we shall forcibly enter into your country and shall make war against you in all ways and manners that we can and we shall subject you and your wives and your children, and shall make slaves of them . . . and we shall take away your goods, and shall do all harm and damage that we can. . . . And that we have said this to you and made this Requisition, we request the notary here present to give us his testimony in writing, and we ask the rest who are present that they should be witnesses of this Requisition.

By the mid-nineteenth century, the various modes for conducting, declaring, and waging war were no more than pretenses for justifying aggressive tendencies. Both States and private organizations such as the Red Cross understood that increasingly sophisticated weapon systems were capable of inflicting alarming consequences, if uncontrolled. Military theorists, theologians, and moralists believed that certain State practices were too inhumane to be condoned by a civilized society. The desire for control began to materialize in national and treaty-based Laws of War. Although there were several predecessors, the 1864 Geneva Convention for the Amelioration of the Condition of the Wounded in Armies in the Field was the first such treaty to be drafted and widely ratified. The International Law of the Laws of War would soon find its way into the national laws of many countries, as well as major international treaties.

The year 1847 was an important turning point. Swiss General Dufour ordered his officers to protect wounded enemy soldiers who were prisoners of war. He was one of the original members of the "Committee of Five," which later became the International Committee of the Red Cross in 1876.[43] The International Red Cross ultimately worked with the Swiss government, which would one day yield four treaties collectively known as the 1949 "Geneva Convention." Thus, it was actually a *non*governmental actor that ignited the international movement for regulating the treatment of civilians and prisoners in time of war.

Essence of Laws of War

The content of this body of law developed in terms of the environment wherein the particular military platform was operational—on land, in the air, or at sea.[44] Given the range of modern weapons systems, even this simple categorization is not sufficiently encompassing—especially now that environmental warfare has become so devastating. This section surveys some illustrative problems, including the need for observance of the Laws of War by national contingents of international peacekeeping forces. Exhibit 10.3 then depicts the currently applicable treaties and their scope.

Land Warfare on land is limited by norms regarding the use of bacteriological and gaseous substances. Hilter considered the use of such weapons in World War II. His field marshals convinced him, however, that Germans would likely suffer more than the enemy. Nevertheless, Germany used Soviet prisoners, and its own citizens, to conduct experiments in anticipation of its potential use.

Concentration camps have been used by captors for purposes regulated by the famous Geneva Conventions. One of the best—or worst—illustrations was the treatment of military prisoners and civilians by the infamous Nazi regime of World War II. The Nuremberg Military Tribunal's judgment describes the all-too-familiar scenario, where inhumane brutalization was relentlessly administered. The following passage succinctly describes a number of circumstances governed by the Laws of War. Each sentence, if not every phrase of the Court's description, is the subject of a Geneva Convention provision, designed after the war to prevent the repetition of the following violations:

the concentration camps were used to destroy all opposition groups. The persons arrested by the Gestapo . . . were conveyed to the camps in many cases without any care whatever being taken for them, and great numbers died on the way. Those who arrived at the camp were subjected to systematic cruelty. They were given hard physical labor, inadequate food, clothes and shelter, and were subject at all times to . . . the private whims of individual guards.

. . .

A certain number of concentration camps were equipped with gas chambers for the wholesale destruction of the inmates, and with furnaces for the burning of the bodies. Some of them were in fact used for the extermination of Jews. . . . Most of the non-Jewish inmates were used for labor although the conditions under which they worked made labor and death almost synonymous terms. Those inmates who became ill and were unable to work were either destroyed in the gas chambers or sent to special infirmaries, where they were given entirely inadequate medical treatment, worse food if possible than the working inmates, and left to die.[45]

Probably the most notorious breach, between World War II and the Bosnia of the 1990s, took place in the village of My Lai, Vietnam in 1973. The superior orders defense, previously unsuccessful at the Nuremberg and Tokyo Trials of 1945, also failed in this more recent application. The resulting court-martial provides a realistic "in the field" perspective about the soldier who must choose between punishment for disobeying the order of a superior, or alternatively, punishment for violating the Laws of War.

All three of the military judges in this appellate review of the defendant US Army Lieutenant Calley's conviction agreed that his conduct breached the Laws of War. Both what Calley did, and the citations of authority within this opinion, depict the content of this body of law in a combat scenario. The Army Manual's standard for measuring such liability is whether a soldier of "common" understanding would know that an order to summarily execute unarmed civilians is illegal and must be disobeyed. This standard makes it easier to convict a soldier of "low-grade" intelligence, who may not have the capacity to recognize that a superior officer's order should not be followed because it violates the Laws of War (as expressed in the US Army Field Manual). He, too, is subject to hindsight assessments of his conduct from the perspective of how any "common" soldier would react when so ordered.

The dissenter, who did not question the audacity of *Calley's* conduct, wrote a separate opinion about the application of this "common man" standard to other soldiers in combat situations. Appellate defense counsel, and the dissenting appellate judge, thus sought a change in the applicable legal standard that would make it more difficult to convict the "low-grade" or commonest soldier. They argued that continued application of the "common" soldier standard was unfair to soldiers of below-average or low-grade intelligence.

But the suggested change would have diminished the overall scope of liability for breaches of the Laws of War. If the legal yardstick was the soldier of lowest intelligence, rather than the soldier of common or average intelligence, then Calley (who was likely to be convicted under any standard) was convicted under the wrong standard.

UNITED STATES v. CALLEY

U.S. Court of Military Appeals, 1973
22 USCMA 534, 48 CMR 19

[Author's Note: Emphasis has been supplied by the author in certain passages. Most citations have been omitted.]

[Opinion.] QUINN, Judge:

. . .

Lieutenant Calley was a platoon leader in C Company, a unit that was part of an organization known as Task Force Barker, whose mission was to subdue and drive out the enemy in an area in the Republic of Vietnam known popularly as Pinkville. Before March 16, 1968, this area, which included the village of My Lai 4, was a Viet Cong stronghold. C Company had operated in the area several times. Each time the unit had entered the area it suffered casualties by sniper fire, machine gun fire, mines, and other forms of attack. Lieutenant Calley had accompanied his platoon on some of the incursions.

On March 15, 1968, a memorial service for members of the company killed in the area during the preceding weeks was held. After the service Captain Ernest L. Medina, the commanding officer of C Company, briefed the company on a mission in the Pinkville area set for the next day. . . .

Captain Medina testified that he instructed his troops that they were to destroy My Lai 4 by "burning the hootches, to kill the livestock, to close the wells and to destroy the food crops." Asked if women and children were to be killed, Medina said he replied in the negative, adding that, "You must use common sense. If they have a weapon and are trying to engage you, then you can shoot back, but you must use common sense." However, Lieutenant Calley testified that Captain Medina informed the troops they were to kill every living thing—men, women, children, and animals—and under no circumstances were they to leave any Vietnamese behind them as they passed through the villages enroute to their final objective. Other witnesses gave more or less support to both versions of the briefing.

. . .

Calley's platoon passed the approaches to the village with his men firing heavily. Entering the village, the platoon encountered only unarmed, unresisting men, women, and children. The villagers, including infants held in their mothers' arms, were assembled and moved in separate groups to collection points. Calley testified that during this time he was radioed twice by Captain Medina, who demanded to know what was delaying the platoon. On being told that a large number of villagers had been detained, Calley said Medina ordered him to "waste them." Calley further testified that he obeyed the orders because he had been taught the doctrine of obedience throughout his military career. Medina denied that he gave any such order.

One of the collection points for the villagers was in the southern part of the village. There, Private First Class Paul D. Meadlo guarded a group of between 30 to 40 old men, women, and children. Lieutenant Calley approached Meadlo and told him, "'You know what to do,'" and left, He returned shortly and asked Meadlo why the people were not yet dead. Meadlo replied he did not know that Calley had meant that they should be killed. Calley declared that he wanted them dead. He and Meadlo then opened fire on the group, until all but a few children fell. Calley then personally shot these

children. He expended 4 or 5 magazines from his M-16 rifle in the incident.

Lieutenant Calley and Meadlo moved from this point to an irrigation ditch on the east side of My Lai 4. There, they encountered another group of civilians being held by several soldiers. Meadlo estimated that this group contained from 75 to 100 persons. Calley stated, "'We got another job to do, Meadlo,'" and he ordered the group into the ditch. When all were in the ditch, Calley and Meadlo opened fire on them. Although ordered by Calley to shoot, Private First Class James J. Dursi refused to join in the killings, and Specialist Four Robert E. Maples refused to give his machine gun to Calley for use in the killings. Lieutenant Calley admitted that he fired into the ditch, with the muzzle of his weapon within 5 feet of people in it. He expended between 10 to 15 magazines of ammunition on this occasion.

With his radio operator, Private Charles Sledge, Calley moved to the north end of the ditch. There, he found an elderly Vietnamese monk, whom he interrogated. Calley struck the man with his rifle butt and then shot him in the head. Other testimony indicates that immediately afterwards a young child was observed running toward the village. Calley seized him by the arm, threw him into the ditch, and fired at him. Calley admitted interrogating and striking the monk, but denied shooting him. He also denied the incident involving the child.

Appellate defense counsel contend that the evidence is insufficient to establish the accused's guilt. They do not dispute Calley's participation in the homicides, but they argue that he did not act with the malice or mens rea [evil intent] essential to a conviction of murder; that the orders he received to kill everyone in the village were *not* palpably illegal; that *he was acting in ignorance of the laws of war*; that since he was told that only "the enemy" would be in the village, his honest belief that there were no innocent civilians in the village exonerates him of criminal responsibility for their deaths; and, finally, that his actions were in the heat of passion caused by reasonable provocation.

. . .

Enemy prisoners are not subject to summary execution by their captors. Military law has long held that the killing of an unresisting prisoner is murder. While it is lawful to kill an enemy "in the heat and exercise of war," yet "to kill such an enemy after he has laid down his arms . . . is murder." Digest of Opinions of the Judge Advocates General of the Army, 1912.

Conceding . . . that Calley believed the villagers were part of "the enemy," the uncontradicted evidence is that they were under the control of armed soldiers and were offering no resistance. In his testimony, Calley admitted he was aware of the requirement that prisoners be treated with respect. He also admitted he knew that the normal practice was to interrogate villagers, release those who could satisfactorily account for themselves, and evacuate the suspect among them for further examination. Instead of proceeding in the usual way, Calley executed all, without regard to age, condition, or possibility of suspicion. On the evidence, the court-martial could reasonably find Calley guilty of the offenses before us.

. . .

[A]ppellate defense counsel [also] assert gross deficiencies in the military judge's instructions to the court members [serving as the jury in Calley's trial].

. . .

After fairly summarizing the evidence, the *judge gave the following instructions [on the law] pertinent to the issue:*

The killing of resisting or fleeing enemy forces is generally recognized as a justifiable act of war, and you *may* consider any such killings justifiable in this case. The law attempts to protect those persons not actually engaged in warfare, however; and limits the circumstances under which their lives may be taken.

Both combatants captured by and noncombatants detained by the opposing force, regardless of their loyalties, political views, or prior acts, have the right to be treated as prisoners until released, confined, or executed, in accordance with law and established procedures, by competent authority sitting in judgment of such detained or captured individuals. Summary execution of detainees or prisoners is forbidden by law. Further, it's clear under the evidence presented in this case, that hostile acts or support of the enemy North Vietnamese or Viet Cong forces by inhabitants of My Lai (4) at some time prior to

16 March 1968, would not justify the summary execution of all or a part of the occupants . . . nor would hostile acts committed [even on] that day, if, following the hostility, the belligerents surrendered or were captured by our forces. *I therefore instruct you* [the military jury], as a matter of law, that if unresisting human beings were killed at My Lai (4) while within the effective custody and control of our military forces, their deaths cannot be considered justified, and any order to kill such people would be, as a matter of law, an illegal order. Thus, if you find that Lieutenant Calley received an order directing him to kill unresisting Vietnamese within his control or within the control of his troops, that order would be an illegal order.

A determination that an order is illegal does not, of itself, assign criminal responsibility to the person following the order for acts done in compliance with it [as a general rule]. Soldiers are taught to follow orders, and special attention is given to obedience of orders on the battlefield. *Military effectiveness depends upon obedience to orders. On the other hand, the obedience of a soldier is not the obedience of an automaton.* A soldier is a reasoning agent, obliged to respond, not as a machine, but as a person. The law takes these factors into account in assessing criminal responsibility for acts done in compliance with illegal orders.

The *acts of a subordinate done in compliance with an unlawful order given him by his superior are excused* and impose no criminal liability upon him *unless* the superior's order is one which a *man of ordinary sense and understanding would, under the circumstances, know to be unlawful,* or if the order in question is actually known to the accused to be unlawful.

. . .

Appellate defense counsel contend that . . . the standard stated by the [trial] judge is too strict and unjust; that it confronts members of the armed forces who are not persons of ordinary sense and understanding with *the dilemma of choosing between the penalty of death for disobedience* of an order in time of war on the one hand *and* the *equally serious punishment for obedience* on the other. Some thoughtful commentators on military law have presented much the same argument.

The "ordinary sense and understanding" standard is set forth in the present Manual for Courts-Martial, United States, 1969 and was the standard accepted by this Court. It appeared as early as 1917. Manual for Courts-Martial, U.S. Army, 1917. . . .

Colonel William Winthrop, the leading American commentator on military law, notes: . . . *Where the order is apparently regular and lawful on its face, he [the subordinate] is not to go behind it to satisfy himself that his superior has proceeded with authority,* but is to obey it according to its terms, *the only exceptions* recognized to the rule of obedience being cases of *orders so manifestly beyond the legal power or discretion of the commander as to admit of no rational doubt of their unlawfulness.* . . . Except in such instances of palpable illegality, which must be of rare occurrence, the inferior should presume that the order was lawful and authorized and obey it accordingly. . . . Winthrop's Military Law and Precedents, 2d ed., 1920 Reprint, at 296–297.

In the stress of combat, a member of the armed forces cannot reasonably be expected to make a refined legal judgment and be held criminally responsible if he guesses wrong on a question as to which there may be considerable disagreement. But *there is no disagreement as to the illegality of the order to kill in this case.* For 100 years, it has been a settled rule of American law that even in war the summary killing of an enemy, who has submitted to, and is under, effective physical control, is murder. Appellate defense counsel acknowledge that rule of law and its continued viability, but they say that Lieutenant Calley should not be held accountable for the men, women and children he killed because the court-martial could have found that he was a person of "commonest understanding" and such a person might not know what our law provides; that his captain had ordered him to kill these unarmed and submissive people and he only carried out that order as a good disciplined soldier should.

Whether Lieutenant Calley was the most ignorant person in the United States Army in Vietnam, or the most intelligent, he must be presumed to know that he could not kill the people involved here. . . . An order to kill infants and unarmed civilians who were so demonstrably incapable of resistance to the armed might of a military force as were those killed by Lieutenant Calley is, in my opinion, so palpably illegal that whatever conceptional differ-

ence there may be between a person of "*commonest* understanding" [the proposed standard that would lower the threshold of liability] and a person of "*common* understanding" [the established standard that extends criminal responsibility to virtually all soldiers], that difference could not have had any "impact on a court of lay members receiving the respective wordings in instructions," as appellate defense counsel contend. In my judgment, there is no possibility of prejudice to Lieutenant Calley in the trial judge's reliance upon the established standard of excuse of criminal conduct, rather than [applying] the standard of "*commonest* understanding" presented by the defense, or by [applying] the new variable test postulated in the dissent, which, with the inclusion of such factors for consideration as grade and experience, would appear to exact a higher standard of understanding from Lieutenant Calley than that of the person of ordinary understanding.

. . .

[The opinion of another judge, who concurred in the conviction of Lieutenant Calley, is omitted. In his opinion: "Contrary to Judge Quinn, I do not consider that a *presumption* arose that the appellant knew he could not kill the people involved. The Government . . . is not entitled to a presumption of what the appellant knew of the illegality of an order."]

DARDEN, Chief Judge (dissenting):

Although the charge [instructions to the jury] the military judge gave on the defense of superior orders was not inconsistent with the [US Army Field] Manual treatment of this subject, *I believe the Manual provision is too strict* in a combat environment. Among other things, this standard permits serious punishment of persons whose training and attitude incline them either to be enthusiastic about compliance with orders or not to challenge the authority of their superiors. The [current] standard also permits conviction of members who are not persons of ordinary sense and understanding.

. . .

My impression is that the weight of authority, including the commentators whose articles are mentioned in the principal opinion, supports a *more liberal* approach to the defense of superior orders. Under this approach, superior orders should constitute a defense except "in a plain case of excess of authority, where at first blush it is apparent and palpable to the commonest understanding that the order is illegal."

While this test is phrased in language that now seems "somewhat archaic and ungrammatical," the test recognizes that the essential ingredient of discipline in any armed force is obedience to orders and that this obedience is so important it should not be penalized unless the order would be recognized as illegal, *not by what some hypothetical reasonable soldier would have known*, but also by "those persons at the lowest end of the scale of intelligence and experience in the services." This is the real purpose in permitting superior orders to be *a defense*, and it *ought not to be restricted by the concept of a fictional reasonable man* so that, regardless of his personal characteristics, an accused judged after the fact may find himself punished for either obedience or disobedience.

. . .

But while humanitarian considerations compel us to consider the impact of actions by members of our armed forces on citizens of other nations, I am also convinced that the phrasing of the defense of superior orders should have as its principal objective fairness to the unsophisticated soldier and those of somewhat limited intellect who nonetheless are doing their best to perform their duty.

. . .

In the instant case, Lieutenant Calley's testimony placed the defense of superior orders in issue, even though he conceded that he knew prisoners were normally to be treated with respect and that the unit's normal practice was to interrogate Vietnamese villagers, release those who could account for themselves, and evacuate those suspected of being a part of the enemy forces. Although crucial parts of his testimony were sharply contested, according to Lieutenant Calley, (1) he had received a briefing before the assault in which he was *instructed that every living thing in the village was to be killed, including women and children;* (2) he was informed that *speed was important* in securing the village and moving forward; (3) he was ordered that *under no circumstances were any Vietnamese to be allowed to stay behind* the lines of his forces; (4) the *residents* of the village who were *taken into custody were hindering the progress* of his platoon in taking up the position it was to occupy; and (5) when he informed Captain Medina of this hindrance, he was [*again*] ordered to kill the villagers and to move his platoon to a proper position.

In addition to the briefing, Lieutenant Calley's experience in the Pinkville area caused him to know that, *in the past*, when villagers had been left behind his unit, the unit had immediately received *sniper fire from the rear* as it pressed forward. Faulty *intelligence* [information] apparently led him also to believe that those persons in the village were *not innocent civilians* but were either enemies or enemy sympathizers. For a participant in the My Lai operation, the *circumstances* that could have obtained there *may have caused the illegality of alleged orders to kill* civilians to be *much less clear than* they are in a *hindsight review.*

Since the defense of superior orders was not submitted to the military jury under what I consider to be the proper standard, I would grant Lieutenant Calley a rehearing [so that his culpability would be determined under the dissenting judge's proposed "commonest" or simplest soldier standard].

■ NOTES & QUESTIONS

1. In subsequent proceedings, Calley was ordered released, due to the extent of pretrial publicity with this sensational case. That order was reversed. While various appeals were in progress, the US Army released him from custody in 1974. In 1976, the Army decided not to return him to custody. Thus, he did not serve the remainder of his twenty-year sentence. *See New York Times*, April 6, 1976, p.1.

2. Regardless of what standard is applied, the combat soldier may have to choose between punishment for obeying a superior's order, and that for disobeying the order. Is it fair to expect the "simplest" soldier to break ranks with military discipline and disobey a superior's order in a combat environment?

3. What can a State do to limit the possibility of such dilemmas for its combat soldiers? The April 1992 US Department of Defense Report to Congress suggests one means of using national laws to ensure the observance of international limitations on State uses of force. This report was provided under the Persian Gulf Conflict Supplemental

Authorization and Personnel Benefits Act of 1991. Section 501(b)(12) requires a report that must discuss the following matters:

> the role of the law of armed conflict in the planning and execution of military operations by United States forces and the other coalition forces and the effects on operations of Iraqi compliance or noncompliance with the law of armed conflict, including a discussion of each of the following matters: (A) Taking of hostages. (B) Treatment of civilians in occupied territory. (C) Collateral damage and civilian casualties. (D) Treatment of prisoners of war. (E) Repatriation of prisoners of war. (F) Use of ruses and acts of perfidy. (G) War crimes. (H) Environmental terrorism. (I) Conduct of neutral nations.

The Role of the Law of War Report to Congress requirements are reprinted in 31 *International Legal Materials* 612 (1992).

4. In 1985, a federal court in Ohio decided that it had the responsibility to honor Israel's request for the extradition of "Ivan the Terrible" Demjanjuk. Prior to his naturalization as a US citizen after World War II, he allegedly murdered tens of thousands of defenseless people while operating the gas chambers at the infamous Treblinka concentration camp in Poland in 1942. An Israeli court later found that there was insufficient evidence to establish his identity. The US portion of this case is important for this reason: This decision is an expression of American caselaw addressing the Laws of War. A national *civilian* court thus has the power to consider extradition for wartime crimes, as well as military tribunals in appropriate circumstances. In other words, US law recognizes the power of both civilian and military tribunals to hear cases involving war crimes. Matter of Demjanjuk, 603 Fed.Supp. 1468 (No.Dist. Ohio, 1985), appeal dismissed 762 Fed.Rptr. 1012 (6th Cir. 1985). There were several appeals on a variety of grounds.

A number of atrocities were allegedly committed by the Bosnian Serbs against the indigenous Muslim and Croatian civilian and military forces in Bosnia-Herzegovina. These breaches of the Laws of War were the impetus for the UN establishment of a new war crimes tribunal in the Netherlands in 1993 (*see* § 9.5). In a 1994 war crimes trial in Bosnia, a Serbian defendant was convicted of torturing numerous prisoners in ways that defy description in this book.[46] In late 1994, Serbian forces immobilized 200 UN troops and observers near Sarajevo, and fifty Canadian peacekeepers at another location. After several NATO air strikes, this tactic rendered those UN troops virtual hostages and potential human shields against further NATO strikes. It was at this point that NATO and the UN announced their intent to withdraw from Bosnia.

The purpose of the new UN tribunal is to send a message that responsible parties in any quarter of the Bosnian struggle will be subject to prosecution at war's end. Thus far, this message has been ignored by many perpetrators who apparently believe that they can seek immunity from prosecution—in what they perceive as the remote event of a military loss after ineffective UN and NATO actions to date. Further, it is most likely that a negotiated end to this conflict will incorporate immunity from subsequent international war crimes trials.

There are other serious breaches of the Laws of War imputable to States. Victorious armies may not intentionally destroy cultural objects. These include certain buildings, works of art, libraries, and the like. Although Hitler ordered the bombing of Paris, which would have destroyed the Cathedral of Notre Dame, his own military leader in the field chose to stable German horses in the cathedral to avoid any destruction of this special landmark in French history. Under the early Lieber Code of 1856 and the ensuing 1907 Hague Regulations on the Laws of War, there would have been responsibility for violating this regulation prohibiting destruction of cultural property unless a case of military necessity.

The 1949 Geneva Convention also prohibits the desecration of dead bodies. This provision was inspired by the Nazi policy of extracting gold teeth and fillings from the heads of corpses. After cremation, ashes were used as fertilizer. There were also attempts to use fat from deceased bodies for making soap.[47]

The Japanese undertook some rather infamous measures against prisoners of war in World War II. The 1942 Bataan Death March drew the ire of the international tribunal prosecuting the Japanese defendants. After the American surrender in the Philippines, the US general was assured that his soldiers would be treated humanely. This seventy-five-mile march in intense heat was the last for the sick and wounded. The American and Filipino prisoners were shot if they fell behind. Others were taken from the ranks, and beaten or killed. Approximately 8,000 died as a result of this forced march.[48] In 1994, a South Korean escaped from North Korea after forty-three years. He spent twenty-six of those years as a coal miner. This was an egregious violation of the State duty to repatriate prisoners of war, after the war has ended.

Civilians may not be deported from occupied territory. The Nazis deported millions of civilians from every occupied territory, to meet the labor needs of the Third Reich. In 1994, Japan apologized to surviving "comfort girls" (mostly Korean) who were forced to become sex slaves for occupying Japanese troops. These examples of slave labor are prohibited by the Geneva Conventions and resulting national laws.

Prisoners of war may not be tortured to compel them to divulge information. Nor can they be legally punished for giving false information during an interrogation. Article 17 of the 1949 Geneva (Third) Convention thus provides as follows: "No physical or mental torture, nor any other form of coercion may be inflicted on prisoners of war to secure from them information of any kind whatsoever. Prisoners of war who refuse to answer may not be threatened, insulted, or exposed to any unpleasant or disadvantageous treatment of any kind." During the Vietnam War, there were widespread reports that captured North Vietnamese soldiers and South Vietnamese Viet Cong were pushed from helicopters for failing to answer questions during US military interrogations. If true, this form of questioning clearly violated the Geneva Conventions.

Sea There have been fewer reported incidents of violations of the naval Laws of War. This does not mean that they have not occurred or are less heinous in their potential effect. During the Nazi war crimes trials at Nuremberg, two U-boat captains were accused of ordering totally unrestricted submarine warfare. One was found guilty of sinking all vessels within a particular zone, including neutral shipping. The other was charged (although there was insufficient evidence for conviction) with the crime of killing survivors of sunken ships. Naval captors may not deny quarters to, or kill, a defenseless enemy.

They were not found guilty of this particular charge, however, as the tribunal found that this was also the US practice in the Pacific.[49]

The 1980–1988 Iran–Iraq war was the first opportunity since the 1945 UN Charter to more fully examine the relevant principles that States consider binding in their international relations. The 1991 Persian Gulf War (PGW) provided further insights to its content. The following practices amount to what may be the modern naval Laws of War.

First, belligerents have a right to visit and search neutral-flagged merchant vessels. While this was done routinely in the Vietnamese conflict, it was basically just one State (the US) that exercised this "right." Visit and search occurred with much greater frequency during the PGW, thus giving rise to the rather clear expectation that States at war may undertake this form of intrusion. It is a necessary incident to maintaining security from various forms of infiltration by belligerents and violations of neutrality by third parties (*see* § 2.4, on recognition of belligerency).

Mine-laying is permitted, but not without limitation. The 1907 Hague Convention Relative to the Laying of Automatic Submarine Contact Mines precludes indiscriminate mine-laying, without proper monitoring by the responsible State. Notification is an essential requirement. The International Court of Justice commented on this expectation in both its 1949 *Corfu Channel* case and the 1986 *Nicaragua* case. In the first case, Albania was at fault for not removing surface mines hit by British ships passing through an international strait. In the second case, the US was responsible for its role in assisting indigenous forces to lay mines in key harbors to interrupt Nicaraguan shipping.[50]

Another mine-laying limitation is that States may not lay mines in the high seas, if doing so endangers shipping of nonbelligerent States. UN Security Council Resolution 540 of 1983 thus provides that States may not thereby threaten "the right of free navigation and commerce in international waters."

The right of passage by neutral ships through international straits cannot be suspended. The ICJ so ruled in the above 1949 *Corfu Channel* case. This norm was tested during the PGW, when Iran threatened to close the Straits of Hormuz—the only entry to the oil-exporting Persian Gulf. Professors Guttry and Ronzitti of the University of Pisa in Italy comment on the scope of this right of passage as follows:

> neutral warships are granted the right of passage through international straits even if the littoral [coastal] State is at war. If such right is accorded to warships, so much the more will it be binding for merchant vessels flying a neutral flag. Not all scholars agree on this, but it seems to us that practice in the Gulf is perfectly in tune with what appears to be the dominant trend, a trend which probably now corresponds to precise customary rules.
>
> Faced with Iran's repeated threat to close the Strait, the USA, the United Kingdom, France and Italy . . . firmly emphasized that the right of passage through international straits can never be suspended, even when the littoral State is one of the belligerents.[51]

Air The comparatively recent appearance of the airplane in military warfare may account for the fact that there were no relevant charges made at either the Nuremberg or Tokyo trials. The only reference therein was a statement addressing the bombing of a city that kills innocent civilians (without mention of the 1945 US atomic bombings of Hiroshima and Nagasaki). In the words of the Nuremberg tribunal:

> This is . . . an unavoidable corollary of battle action. The civilians are not individualized. The bomb falls, it is aimed at railroad yards, houses along the tracks are hit and many of their occupants killed. But that is entirely different, both in facts and in law, from an armed force marching up to these same railroad tracks, entering those houses abutting thereon, dragging out the men, women, and children and shooting them.[52]

Post-Nuremberg air tactics are also regulated by the 1977 Geneva Protocol and the 1980 Convention on Prohibition or Restrictions on the Use of Certain Conventional Weapons. The relevant portions of these documents contain prohibitions on air warfare. Article 42 of the Geneva Protocol, for example, prohibits ground or air attacks on persons parachuting from aircraft in distress. Such individuals must also be given an opportunity to surrender, before engaging them as enemy soldiers. *Airborne* troops are excepted from this protection. One reason for the Protocol was the North Vietnamese position that the 1949 Geneva Conventions did not apply to an undeclared conflict.

Environmental Warfare The 1976 Environmental Modification Convention prohibits military and other hostile uses of the environment to destroy the enemy. Ensuing protocols exhibited the international concerns regarding acts that affected lives far beyond the immediate military theater. The 1977 Protocol precludes any use that would cause "widespread, severe damage to the environment." Reprisals via the environment are also prohibited.

These conventions were not in effect when the most disastrous environmental act of war occurred. During its retreat from Kuwait during the 1991 Persian Gulf War, Iraq's military forces set fire to 700 oil wells, sending flames and smoke into the upper atmosphere for a period of nine months (until all wells could be capped). This event also generated the call for a new "Fifth" Geneva Convention, dedicated solely to the protection of the environment in time of armed conflict.[53]

International Organizations No treaties specifically address the responsibility of an *international organization* to observe the Laws of War. The UN is not a member to the Geneva Conventions dealing with the Laws of War. Those Conventions form the heart of the norms that address *State* practice. By analogy, however, national contingents operating within the service of the UN, NATO, or other organizations should be bound by the same requirements as if they were operating on behalf of their own States.

The International Committee of the Red Cross has thus requested that the UN promote the practice of having its State members provide renewed instructions to their national contingents, prior to departure for UN service. In 1956, there were reports that UN emergency forces were violating the Laws of War during the UN operation in the Congo. Now that the UN peacekeeping operations have exercised the option of firing first in situations carefully prescribed in the Somalian conflict, this concern has taken on a new significance. Geneva Convention Articles 47, 48, 127, and 144 incorporate the State responsibility of instructing State military forces about the Laws of War. Thus, the Red Cross document addressed to UN member States requests "that such contingents receive, before leaving their own countries, appropriate instruction so that they may acquire a sufficient knowledge of these Conventions."[54]

Modern treaties contain various provisions that one might describe as the sources of the Laws of War. Exhibit 10.3 provides a capsule overview of selected treaties.

EXHIBIT 10.3 Selected Treaties Illustrating the Laws of War

Date	Treaty	Scope
1899	Hague Conventions on the Laws and Customs of War	Series of draft controls on customs of war on land/at sea limiting poisonous gas, expanding bullets/required recourse to third-party mediation before resorting to war
1906	Geneva Convention	Updated 1864 Geneva Convention/although not extensively followed, it contains provision requiring parties to pass or encourage legislation punishing violations of Laws of War
1906 1907	Geneva Convention and Hague Convention	Parties must enact criminal laws punishing misuses of protective markings such as Red Cross insignia to trick enemy
1907	Hague Second Conference on Laws and Customs of War (12 treaties, some updating 1899 Hague Conference draft)	Prohibits acts including uncontrolled unanchored contact mines, naval bombardment of undefended towns, capturing hospital ships/ requires humane treatment of POWs who cannot be summarily killed or wounded
1925	Geneva Convention	Prohibits use of asphyxiating, poisonous, and bacteriological warfare
1945	London Charter (the Nuremberg Tribunal)	Prohibits conduct including: murder, ill-treatment, deportation to slave labor, plunder of public or private property, destruction of cities in absence of military necessity
1946	UN General Assembly Resolution 95(1)	Prohibits the Crime of Genocide—includes annihilation of particular ethnic or national group
1949	Geneva Convention I (Wounded and sick in the field)	Updated original 1864 Convention to adapt to modern warfare/requires respect and care for defenseless combatants
1949	Geneva Convention II (Wounded, sick, and shipwrecked at sea)	Updated 1868 principles and 1907 Hague Convention laws in conduct of maritime warfare

EXHIBIT 10.3 *(continued)*

Date	Treaty	Scope
1949	Geneva Convention III (Prisoners of War)	Most extensive of four 1949 Conventions/updates 1929 Geneva Convention/regulates conditions of captivity to safeguard human dignity
1949	Geneva Convention IV (Civilian protection in time of war)	Second most extensive Geneva Convention/prohibits torture, mutilation, violence, outrages on personal dignity/designed to protect innocent civilians, not involved in hostilities, from being terrorized by enemy military forces
1972	Bacteriological Warfare Convention	Prohibits the production and stockpiling of bacteriological and toxic weapons/seeks destruction or diversion to peaceful purposes/national sovereignty withdrawal clause has limited effectiveness
1977	Geneva Protocols	Refinements: most significant one protects POWs in conflict described as *non*international or undeclared (North Vietnamese bases for nonapplication of Geneva POW Convention in Vietnam)
1977	Environmental Modification Convention	Prohibits military or other hostile use of environmental modifications in, over, and above the Earth
1981	Inhumane Weapons Convention	Prohibits and restricts certain conventional weapons deemed too injurious/e.g., land mines, boobytraps, incendiary devices, weapons escaping even X-ray detection in human body
1992	Chemical Weapons Convention	Priority is post–Cold War destruction of chemical and bacteriological weapons stock

■ 10.7 STATE TERRORISM/ARMS SALES

The "Terrorism" Problem

Another weapon in the State arsenal of force is international terrorism. What was once the high-water mark of such terrorism was the rash of commercial aircraft hijackings in the 1970s. On December 18, 1973, for example, Arab terrorists killed thirty-two people in Rome's Leonardi Da Vinci Airport during an attack on a US *commercial* passenger jet. Hostages were taken to Athens in support of their demand for the release of two Palestinian terrorists imprisoned in Greece. The aircraft was granted free passage to Kuwait (defended by the US in the 1991 Persian Gulf War), where local authorities indicated that they had no plans to try the hijackers.[55]

Another event drew international attention to terrorism: the 1985 hijacking of the Achille Lauro passenger cruiseliner by members of the Palestine

Liberation Organization (supported by the US during the 1993 Washington Peace Accords). The perpetrators succeeded in drawing attention to their cause by throwing a wheelchair-bound elderly Jewish man to his watery grave. This act was, in part, responsible for the 1987 US Anti-Terrorism Act. The legislative history for this congressional response includes the following findings:

The Congress finds that—

(1) Middle East terrorism accounted for 60 percent of total terrorism in 1985;

(2) the Palestine Liberation Organization . . . was directly responsible for the murder of an American citizen on the Achille Lauro cruise liner in 1985, and a member of the PLO's Executive Committee is under indictment in the United States for the murder of that American citizen;

(3) the head of the PLO has been implicated in the murder of a United States Ambassador overseas;

(4) the PLO and its constituent groups have taken credit for, and been implicated in, the murders of dozens of American citizens abroad. . . .

Therefore, the Congress determines that the PLO and its affiliates are a terrorist organization and a threat to the interest of the United States, its allies, and to international law. . . .[56]

The 1990s spawned a new wave of what has been described as either "terrorism" or "necessity" by the respective victims and perpetrators. One person's "terrorist" is often another's "hero." This particular difference of opinion exists largely due to clandestine State-sponsored terrorism. Selected examples follow, with datelines from around the globe:

- BONN (Feb. 1995)—German intelligence services report a "quantum leap" in the black market smuggling of nuclear weapons from the former Soviet Union during 1994. Worldwide, there were 124 attempts to obtain radioactive weapons-grade materials—compared to only 53 such attempts in 1992.

- TEL AVIV (Oct. 1994)—twenty killed and forty-six commuters are wounded during rush hour by a powerful bomb that blew apart their passenger bus. The radical PLO wing, Hamas, claims responsibility for the purpose of disrupting the Middle East peace process.

- LONDON (Apr. 1993)—one killed and forty wounded in financial district blast. A previous Irish Republican Army code word was telephoned, just prior to the incident, to establish the IRA's complicity.

- BUENOS AIRES (Jul. 1994)—a bomb rips the heart of largest Jewish community in Latin America, killing over 100 and wounding another 200 people. Many attribute to Islamic extremists, although they had not claimed responsibility for such an attack during the two previous years.

- SARAJEVO (Feb. 1994)—a Serbian mortar shell exploded in the middle of a busy downtown marketplace at noon, killing sixty-six and wounding over 200 people.

- CALCUTTA & BOMBAY (Mar. 1993)—within the same week, a bomb reducing a tenement dwelling to rubble kills sixty people in Calcutta, and other bombs kill 317 in Bombay. These are assumed to be work of Muslims in aftermath of Hindu-Muslim riots.

- NEW YORK (Feb. 1993)—six are killed and more than 1,000 hurt in bomb attack on World Trade Center during business hours. (Foreign Muslim extremists would later be arrested and convicted.)

- CAIRO (Dec. 1993)—attackers hurl bombs at a tour bus, wounding sixteen people inside, including eight Austrians. Muslim militants claim responsibility as part of renewed campaign of violence against Western tourists in Egypt.

- BAGHDAD (Feb. 1991)—a US stealth aircraft releases two bombs that kill nearly 300 Iraqi woman and children civilians in a Baghdad air raid shelter during the Persian Gulf War. (The US claimed that this center-city building was a military center, while Iraq claimed it was an air raid shelter.)

Even for those events considered to be the work of *individual* extremists, where do they get the money to finance their operations? How do they manage to become so well armed, when they must pass border check points in order to gain access to the target population? Is there clandestine support for international terrorism by some State or States that privately support the effects caused by such force?

Causes Terrorism cannot be eradicated without recognizing and solving its cause: clandestine support from States that have something to gain from the resulting disruption. Many have blamed Syria, for example, for its alleged role in promoting terrorism in the Middle East. Whether these accusations are true, or not, the study of this form of force would be incomplete without recognizing two essential points: (1) the perpetrators do not consider their victims innocent; and (2) the ends justify the means.

A State that perpetrates or tolerates international terrorism uses it as a device for furthering national objectives. The rich history of State terrorism may now be augmented by massive improvements in technology, communications, and technology. Today's terrorists can strike at targets of opportunity— virtually anywhere in the world—within hours from start, to finish, and to escape. In many cases, national boundaries are virtually irrelevant.

The more democratic societies provide atmospheres that may conveniently serve the needs of a terrorist operation, comparatively free from the constraints of less democratic societies. Freedom of travel, communications, and weaponry are relatively unrestricted. Private industry in these advanced societies is also a potential contributor to future problems. One perspective is that corporate activity is guided by a profit motive in producing counterterror devices to protect against terrorism. There is a vicious cycle, then, that feeds on the continued vitality of promoting the same products on "both sides of the fence."

The balance between human rights and antiterrorism legislation also presents a problem for such societies. Under recent British law, for example, a suspected terrorist could be arrested and detained for seven days. But if there are no limits on the State's pursuit of terrorists, then the State may be in violation of human rights treaty obligations. In 1988, the European Court of Human Rights thus decided that Britain's seven-day power of extra-judicial arrest and detention, *without a hearing*, violated the provision of the European Human Rights Convention that mandates a "prompt appearance" before a neutral judicial officer to determine the validity of the detention.[57]

Another distinction must be made between traditional modes of terrorism and contemporary "improvements." The 1988 bombing of Pan Am flight 103 over Lockerbie, Scotland is a useful event for illustrating this new focus. Two Libyan nationals appear to have blown up that flight, killing hundreds of British and American citizens on the basis of their nationality—rather than targeting a *specific* individual. Libya and Iran allegedly planned this event. Iran supposedly participated, as its revenge for the midair destruction of an Iranian commercial airliner by a US warship in 1988. Iran allegedly commissioned the Popular Front for the Liberation of Palestine General Command to carry out this bombing.[58] Notwithstanding UN Security Council and International Court of Justice efforts to extract the two Libyans from Libya for trial, its leader has refused to comply. As discussed in § 6.4, there are multilateral treaties that prohibit such conduct and require all States to try and punish the perpetrators. The apparent perpetrators were undoubtedly aided by Libya's leader. Col. Ghaddafi shielded them from prosecution for this act by British and US authorities seeking their extradition for trial.

This terrorist event foreshadows the emergence of a varied terrorist approach for the future. In the past, individuals including Prime Minister Gandhi of India, President Sadat of Egypt, and the prime ministers of Argentina and Italy, were allegedly killed by terrorist acts financed from external sources to these assassinations. These leaders were thus punished, with the aid of other State force, for political conduct while in office. This brand of terrorism was then directed at *specific* individuals. But the Pan Am flight 103 scenario suggests the emergence of international terrorism now directed at groups—rather than targeting a particular individual. The Muslim extremists who bombed New York's World Trade Center in 1993 had no particular person within their sights.

Contemporary terrorism is being fueled by religious zealotry, as is now evident in Bosnia. There, State-sponsored terrorism is designed to accomplish the political goal of ethnic cleansing. The participation of groups with religious motivations is the principal reason for the deadliness of contemporary terrorism. In a study done by Bruce Hoffman, a Rand Corporation analyst, it was obvious that secular terrorists understand that indiscriminate killing is antithetical to the goals of the well-trained and well-financed terrorist. Religious terrorists in the Middle

East and South Asia, on the other hand, act in the name of religious values. Their logic is not restrained by such ethical restraint: "For the religious political terrorist violence is viewed as a sacramental act or divine duty. Terrorism thus assumes a transcendental dimension, and its perpetrators have none of the political, moral or practical constraints that affect other terrorists."[59] Thus, one person's terrorist is another's hero.

This form of international terrorism has had its impact on international organizations, in addition to targeted States. Ironically, some of the great powers of the world view the UN as being controlled by the so-called Third World. Yet, many religious terrorists view the UN as being antithetical to their struggles—thus necessitating the employment of terrorism. This is one reason why the UN itself was the target of terrorist threats, just after the 1993 World Trade Center bombing described earlier in this section. The UN, in their view, is no longer capable of accomplishing their objectives. In a letter sent to the Secretary-General from the Islamic Jihad (or Holy War), this organization described the conditions that it relies on as the basis for its use of terrorism:

CONDITIONS FOR ENDING HOSTAGE-TAKING: A LETTER FROM THE ISLAMIC JIHAD

Letter to the United Nations Secretary-General
Received and translated from Arabic on August 11, 1991
Reprinted in *Washington Post*, August 13, 1991

. . .

The role that the United Nations has played in our contemporary history . . . particularly the cause of the Muslim people of Palestine . . . the question of the occupied territories in Jordan, Syria and Lebanon and, subsequently, the [Persian] gulf crisis, gives us an extremely unfavorable impression of the situation of the United Nations, which has become a plaything in the hands of the superpowers.

Why has the United Nations been given an effective and important role . . . in solving the crisis that arose in the [Persian] gulf while it has been prevented from playing a role in helping to find a just solution to the question of the Muslim people in Palestine in spite of the fact that more than 50 years have passed since [the UN partition of Palestine creating Israel, whereby] the Israeli enemy usurped the land of Palestine?

Whenever an American, a Westerner or an Israeli is involved in [a] simple incident, there is an international hue and cry, all the United Nations organizations spring into action and governments throughout the world rise up in his defense under the slogan of protection of human rights, in contrast to their attitudes toward the massacres . . . [in vari-

ous parts of the Muslim world including] the [US] shooting down of a civil aircraft over the gulf, which led to the death of its 300 passengers . . . and the other equally odious massacres that have been committed against our people engaged in the intifada in occupied Palestine. . . . [T]he conventions that have been adopted to protect human rights have been formulated in such a way as to protect the nationals of superpowers, which, in their customary statements, attach no value to persons who do not hold their citizenship.

. . .

If the slogan of the need to combat international terrorism is an attempt to divert us from our course of holy struggle in the face of international arrogance, we will continue along the difficult path that we have chosen for ourselves without giving an inch.

. . .

Consequently, the question of the detainees [hostages] was a reaction on the part of the Muslim freedom fighters to all those [above] practices and an endeavor to secure the release of our incarcerated fighters. This action will continue as long as they remain incarcerated.

The sorrow associated with such detentions was, of course, personified in the grief of the parents of the young Israeli soldier captured and held hostage by Hamas, prior to his death in October 1994. The "terrorists," on the other hand, are seeking self-determination so as to secure their geographical version of the true State of Palestine. They are dissatisfied with the geographical version of Palestine accepted by PLO Chairman Yasir Arafat, during the 1993 Washington Peace Accords with Israel that brought some degree of autonomy to the Palestinians in Gaza and the city of Jericho. It is the perspective that, without possessing the military power of the "occupying powers," terrorism is their only weapon. Funding and training necessarily involve the aid of one or more States that clandestinely support the objectives of the Islamic Jihad, Hamas, and other "terrorist" organizations.

Solutions? States themselves must decide whether they are willing to accept the long-term consequences of allowing their territories to be used as launching pads for operations against other States. Further, they must determine what is to be gained from allowing groups or individuals to use their territories for the such purposes. Put more bluntly, the reason that State-sponsored terrorism is *clandestinely* supported is that it is an act of war and an unjustified use of force in violation of all UN Charter principles. The perpetrators would violently disagree. But *why* is the obvious financial backing by one or more States *secretly* given to the perpetrators?

One answer may be the unfortunate difference between word and deed. There have been several multilateral attempts at the UN to legislate solutions to international terrorism. One is the 1973 General Assembly Resolution on Measures to Prevent International Terrorism. There was a lack of precision, however, in articulating a definition of "terrorism." That consequence narrowed the Resolution's potential effectiveness as an agreed-upon strategy for ending the exportation of terrorism on a global scale.

The companion UN General Assembly's 1973 *Report of the Ad Hoc Committee on International Terrorism* (after seventeen meetings) did not arrive at any conclusions, except that this was a complex problem requiring further study. Only one of the delegations submitted a draft proposal dealing with State terrorism, and the eradication of its underlying causes as a solution. This nonaligned delegation, led by Algeria, thus proposed that the following had to

occur: the elimination of colonial domination and racial discrimination; taking measures at the *national* level; and strict implementation of the Declaration on Principles of International Law Concerning Friendly Relations and Co-operation Among States in accordance with the Charter of the United Nations (*see* § 10.2).[60]

The UN's 1979 Hostage Convention was spawned by events such as the Iranian Hostage Crisis. It violated the international norms regarding diplomatic protection and the immunities associated with consular and embassy premises (*see* § 7.4). Hostage taking has also violated the various air hijacking conventions of the 1970s (*see* § 6.4). The 1976 Entebbe incident was fresh on the minds of those who wanted to limit the problem of danger inviting rescue, thus spawning State rescue missions in response to international terrorism (*see* § 10.5). Since its drafting, there have been a number of hostage taking incidents in the Middle East with support allegedly provided by a State or States in the region. There has been a piecemeal approach to the various facets of terrorism. This treaty presents a comprehensive approach to the narrow problem of hostage taking. The reality, of course, is that significant steps will only come by steps taken at the *national* level within each State. There must be a willingness to directly address this problem, through legislation to implement the principles of treaties like the 1979 Hostage Convention.

In the same month in 1985, the UN Security Council and General Assembly adopted similar terrorism declarations: the Resolution Condemning Hostage Taking (Council) and Measures to Prevent International Terrorism (Assembly).[61] The Security Council Resolution was adopted unanimously. The General Assembly Resolution was adopted without a vote. Neither document mentioned specific instances of *State* terrorism. Both articulations were geared toward *individual* acts of terrorism, rather than directly confronting the questions of what *States* were acting in ways condemned in these unassailable resolutions. Thus, any State clandestinely pursuing international terrorism would not be likely to disagree in principle.

Thus, UN attempts to control international terrorism are at best dismal. The UN definition of aggression effectively works at cross purposes with controlling State-sponsored terrorism. As articulately analyzed by Robert Friedlander, Chief Counsel to the US Senate Foreign Relations Committee in 1993:

The Definition of Aggression, adopted by the General Assembly resolution of December 14, 1974, after a quarter-century of debate and disagreement, clearly indicates that forcible attacks against a victim state by "armed bands, groups, irregulars or mercenaries," sponsored by another state, are in direct violation of the U.N. Charter. However, there is an exception . . . for violent national liberation movements, thus legitimating a legal cloak which many terrorist organizations (such as the PLO) have since wrapped around themselves. Therefore, armed attacks—presumptively by terrorist groups—under the banner of self-determination become . . . [they are] not only permissible, but also legally justified. The implications for a global rule of law are distressingly self-evident.[62]

Some *regional* approaches directly address State terrorism. Certain European pronouncements prohibit State-sponsored terrorism, although they are not treaties and do not yet have any legally binding force. But they do represent the most concrete consensus of a large bloc of States on the following general principles. The 1975 Helsinki Accords, or Final Act of the Conference on Security and Co-operation in Europe (CSCE), *recommends* that CSCE members (*see* § 3.5) refrain from direct or indirect assistance to terrorist activities, or to subversive or other activities directed toward the violent overthrow of the regime of another participating state. Subsequent confidence-building measures add that no State member is to allow the use of its territory by terrorist groups.[63]

The other multilateral denunciation of State-terrorism is the Bonn Anti-Hijacking Declaration pronounced by the Group of Seven Economic Summit Industrial Powers in 1978 (US, UK, France, Canada, Italy, West Germany, and Japan). It was designed to admonish those State regimes that harbor air hijackers and hostage takers. They threatened to terminate air travel to any State providing a safe haven to such individuals. In 1981, their Ottawa Economic Summit produced a sanction against Afghanistan.

Arms Sales

A dimension of the State exportation of terrorism is the unrestricted sales of weapons to States or private organizations. This is a high-profit, high-demand international business. The lull in the nuclear arms race, occasioned by the demise of the Cold War, does not mean that other forms of arms races are not still underway. The question is whether an arms race can merely go on without "going off."

The notion of limiting arms sales is not new. In 1789, the English philosopher and writer Jeremy Bentham (who coined the term *International Law*) proposed an arms control regime. This was the only realistic way for curbing the widespread use of armaments. Otherwise, peace would not be attainable because Europe would fail to limit the number of troops, to implement treaty controls on the quantity of armaments, and to establish a court for settling international differences. As one commentator aptly characterizes the historical penchant for arms races: "The threat of war and the need to prepare for it are as old as civilization itself. . . . The reason is simple and stated in the [biblical] quotation from Joel: 'Let the weak say I am strong.' The status quo is not universally accepted and is challenged by a variety of groups with some frequency. War, the preparation for war, and strategies to change the status quo with the least cost to the challenger are an integral part of human history."[64]

The establishment of the UN did not exactly beat swords into plowshares. The five permanent members of the UN Security Council account for 85 percent of the world's international trade in armaments. During Iraq's 1980–1988 war with Iran, for example, the US exported huge amounts of weapons to Iraq. During the fourteen-year period prior to the Persian Gulf War arms embargo on Iraq, the five permanent members sold arms in the Middle East worth $163 billion. Then in 1991, the five Council members agreed, in principle, on arms export rules to limit the ability of States like Iraq to amass huge weapons arsenals. The 1991 "rules" contained no sanctions, however. Thus, only peer pressure could limit their engagement in international arms sales on a smaller scale than in previous decades. By 1992, it appeared that these rules would not be considered in future negotiations. One source for this conclusion is the UN Conventional Arms Register established in 1992. Its purpose is to obtain disclosure of *all* international arms sales. Of course, not all are reported. Of those that have been disclosed, it is clear that arms sales are decreasing. But the decrease is not at the levels hoped for, as a result of the 1991 "agreement" between the major arms exporters—the five permanent members of the UN Security Council.

Since the 1991 Security Council Permanent Five agreement, sales have both increased and decreased—depending on the affected region. There has been a reduction in the *world* aggregate military expenditure. On the other hand, procurement in two regions greatly *increased.* A Turkish economist, Dr. Saadet Deger, who is senior researcher for the Stockholm World Military Expenditure Project (1989–1992), traces the essential changes in such expenditures in the 1990s: "The central reason for the fall in world military expenditure in [the] aggregate is the halving of defence spending in one year by the Commonwealth of Independent States (CIS) countries [after the Cold War]. This aspect of 'shock therapy' in those countries has made the major contribution to international demilitarization. In the developing world [however], military spending rose in the Middle East and the Far East but fell in all other regions."[65]

The Middle East is not the only region adversely affected by the lucrative arms sales business. In 1994, Africa's Catholic bishops pleaded with Western nations to halt their arms sales on that continent. Weapons exports were kindling ethnic bloodshed in Rwanda, for example. They complained that the West was contributing to tribal warfare via the introduction of arms into African nations.

The ultimate control of arms exports will depend, of course, on the degree to which the international community determines that there is a State obligation to regulate arms exports. If so, then there would be State responsibility for its breach. For example, Iraq's decade-long weapons buildup during its war with Iran was facilitated by Western arms sales for a variety of purposes: to defeat Iran; to spar with Cold War adversaries; to control *which* Middle East power would have superior weaponry; and to obtain the profits that another major weapons-exporting power would obtain in the event of any unilateral cutback.

The arms race is currently limited to the Planet Earth. Will today's arms exporting States comply with the international treaties (addressed in § 6.4) requiring that outer space remain a weapons-free environment?

■ 10.8 UNITED STATES WAR POWERS RESOLUTION

This chapter on the use of force ends with an appropriate discussion of *US* control of its own force. As the growing trend toward democracy continues to sweep the globe, in the aftermath of the Cold War, the pressures on the remaining superpower to use its military force have also grown. Other States, international organizations such as the UN and the European Union, nongovernmental actors, and private entities often look to the US for various forms of support in this facet of their international relations. While many Americans do not want the US to act as the world's international policeman, many others would like to see *more* American involvement in foreign conflicts.

Balance of Powers

The extent to which US law tends to concentrate the national war power in either the congressional or the executive branch of government is a major question of constitutional significance. What remains unclear is the degree to which the so-called balance of powers between the various branches of the federal government directs the injection of American military forces into foreign hostilities.

The constitutional separation-of-powers analysis actually hinges on the allocation of power between the legislative and executive branches of government. Article I § 8 of the US Constitution gives the *Congress* the following relevant powers: to declare war; to raise and support armies; to provide and maintain a navy; and to make rules governing their operations. Article II § 2 makes the *president* the Commander in Chief of the army and navy, as well as the militia of the states (reserve units) when called on for active duty. The basic problem arises when Congress does *not* declare war, yet the president sends military units to foreign conflicts.

The *judicial* branch of the federal government now plays a comparatively minor role in foreign affairs, interpreting the Constitution or federal legislation regarding the use of power in ways that allegedly violate the Constitution. The courts usually dismiss cases involving "political" questions about the president's decision to engage US military forces in a particular foreign conflict (*see* § 9.8).

Prior to the 1973 Watergate incident, it was the US Supreme Court (rather than Congress) that controlled claimed executive excesses in the president's use of the national war power. For example, the US Supreme Court invalidated President Truman's seizure of the US steel mills when he sought to thereby avert a strike during the Korean War.[66] Since the Korean conflict, US presidents undertook numerous foreign engagements that frustrated the Congress. That body reacted to what its members perceived as relative powerlessness to control the presidential conduct of foreign military affairs. After the Watergate incident, resulting in the first US president having to resign from office, the Congress seized on the opportunity to legislate a greater role for itself in military matters. As stated by Elliot Richardson, former US cabinet member and ambassador:

> Congress became ever more frustrated as Presidents unilaterally committed this country to a series of controversial policies, including the Berlin airlift, the Bay of Pigs invasion, intervention in the Dominican Republic, and engagement in the Cuban Missile Crisis—seeking legislative approval after the fact, if at all. It was not until the Nixon Presidency was weakened by the dual political crises of Vietnam and Watergate that Congress was able to reassert itself. Thus, the stage was set, with a restless and increasingly active Congress seeking to assert its powers by confronting a President whose personal and political powers were waning.[67]

War Powers Resolution

Congress then passed the War Powers Resolution (WPR) in 1973. The stated purpose of this legislation is to "insure that the *collective* judgment of both the Congress and the President will apply to the *introduction* of United States Armed Forces into hostilities . . . and to the *continued use* of such forces in hostilities. . . ."[68] The objective was to limit the presidential exercise of the Commander in Chief's power to introduce military forces into foreign conflicts, or potential conflicts, *only* in the following circumstances: when Congress has already declared war; when Congress has specifically provided statutory authorization to do so; or in cases of national emergency created by an attack on the US.

This legislation thus requires the president, "in every possible instance," to consult with Congress *prior* to introducing armed forces into hostilities *and after* they are sent abroad. This legislation requires the president, absent a declaration of war (as in the Vietnam impasse), to submit a written report to the House and the Senate within two days of sending forces abroad for combat purposes. The president must report on the need for such action, the constitutional or legislative authority for such action, and the "estimated scope and duration of the hostilities or [other] involvement." Within sixty days of the report, the president must terminate the foreign involvement. Exceptions occur when Congress has declared war in the interim, has extended the involvement, or is unable to meet due to an armed attack on the US. And under *any* circumstances, the Congress may cause the president to withdraw US armed forces from a foreign involvement "if the Congress so directs by concurrent resolution."

This congressional augmentation of its role in foreign conflicts has by no means put to rest the question of its legitimacy. The WPR invades the separation of powers doctrine, if it too fully restricts the ability of the Commander in Chief to carry out his or her function of leading the nation's military in appropriate conflicts. Presidents always assert that they know best. Alternatively, it gives the Congress at least some power to exercise its intended role in foreign affairs that would otherwise lie dormant when it has chosen not to declare war. In the final analysis, it is the Congress that can control the purse-strings, in terms of financing US military operations abroad.

While there have been some two dozen general presidential reports to Congress, one could argue that the WPR is not working as Congress intended. The reporting clause has not stopped US presidents, since passage in 1973, from introducing military forces into combat or near-combat situations—Haiti, Iraq, Panama, and Grenada, for example. Only President Ford thought it necessary to make the specific type of report that triggers the sixty-day reporting period and the ability of Congress to force termination of the action.

Poor drafting of the WPR has also yielded a number of circumventions by US presidents, to avoid making the type of report giving Congress the ability to terminate the particular action. As aptly characterized by Professor Thomas Franck of New York University: "The War Powers Resolution was a good idea, but its drafting and execution were faulty. Instead of authorizing the President to use the armed forces in limited circumstances—such as armed attack on U.S. forces, possessions or, perhaps, citizens—for as long as necessary, it authorized their use in unlimited circumstances for a fixed period. This stands the Constitution on its head."[69]

The August 1994 100–0 unanimous vote of the Senate determined that UN Security Council measures regarding Haiti would *not* relieve President Clinton of the obligation to comply with the WPR. This was reminiscent of the prior 177–37 House vote that "required" President Bush to obtain congressional approval for the deployment of troops for the Persian Gulf War. President Clinton nevertheless responded that "like my predecessors of both parties, I have not agreed that I was constitutionally mandated to get prior congressional authorization" [for US intervention in Haiti].

The daunting question about the US War Powers Resolution is whether it makes sense in an International Law context. The UN supposedly has the monopoly to use force to deal with threats to peace. President Bush did not go to the Congress for approval when the US participated in the Persian Gulf War. There had been numerous UN Security Council resolutions that condemned Iraq's various threats to peace. Legislation introduced in 1995, if enacted into law, would significantly alter the existing war powers statute. It would limit US involvement in future UN peacekeeping operations, and the ability of the US President to delegate control of US military forces to a foreign commander.

Arguments can be made that the WPR violates the no-concentration of power theme associated with the legislative-executive balance of powers in the US Constitution. Does the WPR *also* violate the spirit of the UN Charter? Is US membership in the UN consistent with the notion that each State member may thus delay compliance with Security Council mandates until it has consulted its own legislature?

■ SUMMARY

1. In prior eras, war was not condemned. It was often waged as a "just" war, based on the alleged unjustness of another nation's conduct. At the beginning of the twentieth century, Russia thus promoted the Hague Conferences designed to *control* the ways in which war would be conducted. While war was condemned in the 1928 Kellogg-Brian Peace Pact, this paradigm was ignored by many members of the international community. Now, the most funda-

mental norm in International Law is the contemporary prohibition on the use of force, embodied in Article 2.4 of the UN Charter.

2. The contemporary "realist" perspective is that requiring an explanation for aggressive conduct is both theoretical and unproductive. The role of law in International Relations is overstated. States have retained the inherent right to use force, notwithstanding the contemporary prohibition in the UN Charter. Under this perspective, it is unrealistic to expect States to justify their conduct to anyone when their supreme interests are at stake.

3. *Force* is a broad term that encompasses many variables. Some relevant factors in assessing its legality include whether the particular mode is: aggressive or defensive; military, economic, or some other form of coercion; used unilaterally by a State, or multilaterally by an international organization whose function is to control threats to peace.

4. The various forms of force include coercive measures such as reprisals; low-intensity conflicts, as where one State supports a rebel force within another State; economic countermeasures, such as freezing assets or boycotting goods from a certain country; embargoes to keep goods from entering the target nation; and "gun-boat" diplomacy, where one State stations its forces near another's borders in a threatening show of military strength.

5. The key UN Charter provisions regarding the use of force are Articles 2.4 and 51. The first prohibits force or threatening to use it in International Relations. The latter article authorizes the use of force as a legitimate response to an "armed" attack. The phenomenal "improvements" in weapons technology have prompted reliance on "anticipatory" self-defense in State practice. Attempting to respond *after* an armed attack would be suicidal.

6. Chapter VII of the UN Charter otherwise vests the Security Council with the legal monopoly on the use of force. The standing army provision of Article 43 never materialized. The Council may thus authorize multilateral action via its resolutions, which other powerful States may then employ as bases for their use of force to alleviate the particular threat to peace.

7. Given the breadth of the Charter norms, and their lack of definitional precision, the UN General Assembly promulgated two subsequent declarations. The 1970 Declaration prohibits "propaganda, terror, and finance" as means of coercing another State into acting in a particular way. The 1987 Declaration

prohibits organizing or assisting in the execution of paramilitary, terrorist, or subversive acts. States must also avoid "economic, political, or any other type of measure to coerce another State" for the purpose of securing advantages of *any* kind.

8. There is a contemporary problem with ascertaining the precise nature of the "right" of *collective* self-defense. In the 1986 *Nicaragua* case, the International Court of Justice denied the US reliance on this principle as a basis for justifying its intervention in Nicaragua. This *was* a legal basis, however, for multilateral action in the UN-authorized Persian Gulf War against Iraq after its 1990 invasion of Kuwait.

9. UN operations have traditionally been undertaken as peace*keeping*, rather than peace*making*. State consent of the involved territories has thus been a condition precedent to UN involvement. UN efforts to incorporate an offensive, or first-strike, posture (Somalia) resulted in numerous problems and added dangers. There was a lack of clarity about the UN's role as a military force that is only supposed to maintain the status quo rather than changing it.

10. The Security Council's impotence is caused by insufficient State resolve to endow the UN with the requisite degree of power to act independently of the wishes of its member States. The veto power of any one of the five permanent members is a contributing factor. The members' frustration materialized in the Uniting for Peace Resolution of 1950. The General Assembly therein proclaimed its right to act, in lieu of the Security Council, where the Council would not exercise its "primary" obligation to control threats to peace. This resolution served as the basis for certain peacekeeping operations.

11. There have been a number of multilateral attempts to control State uses of force via international treaties. Key regional and global initiatives are summarized in Exhibit 10.2.

12. Humanitarian intervention is often claimed as the legitimizing basis for State uses of force. The objective is to come to the aid of people in other nations who are unable to fend for themselves in times of need. What constitutes this "need" is, of course, subject to much disagreement. The UN Charter does not answer the question of the degree to which States may undertake collective humanitarian intervention without UN approval.

13. It is often said that danger invites rescue. There may thus be a limited basis for justifying unilateral rescue missions, when a State's citizens face certain death at the hands of terrorists or a State that is unwilling to come to the aid of those in danger.

14. The Laws of War are designed to govern the treatment of various classes of individuals during military hostilities. The famous 1949 Geneva Conventions are the primary source of this use of force. Defenseless civilians and prisoners of war are thus entitled to a minimum level of treatment, so as to avoid the degradation that occurs in the absence of control.

15. Terrorism is a form of force that is theoretically subject to multilateral control via various treaties. Unfortunately, one person's terrorist is often another's hero. For the perpetrators, the end justifies the means. Methods include the sabotaging of commercial aircraft to indiscriminately kill civilian passengers. Such acts bring attention to the plights of the terrorist. But dealing with the effects, rather than the causes, will not eradicate this form of force.

16. The powerful States of the world are responsible for some of the contemporary problems with the many conflicts that arose before and after Cold War. The five permanent members of the Security Council—the US, Great Britain, France, Russia, and China—are responsible for approximately 85 percent of global arms sales. In 1991, they promulgated guidelines to limit such sales. These "rules" have not been followed, however.

■ PROBLEMS

Problem 10.1 (*§ 10.2 after 1970/1987 UN Declarations*): Refer to the *Alvarez-Machain* case, contained in the text of § 5.3 of this book. Assume that the same incident occurred in Panama, *prior to* General Noriega's extraction by US military forces during the US invasion of Panama in 1990 (discussed in § 9.8). In this hypothetical scenario in Panama, a Panamanian doctor is extracted by US Drug Enforcement agents from Panama during a clandestine mission, resulting in Doctor X having to stand trial in the US on international drug-trafficking charges.

Noriega decides that he must take decisive action, in order to strengthen his position in relation to the US abduction of the Panamanian doctor. In a speech to the people of Panama, General Noriega thus declares as follows:

> The atrocity perpetrated this week by US authorities demonstrates the imperialistic attitude of the US toward Panama's political independence, territorial sovereignty, and its indisputable right to self-determination. I am thus forced to take measures to counter the continued unlawful operations of US forces in our beloved nation. Because humanitarian concerns do not guide the actions of the US, I must focus US attention upon our sovereign rights by using economic countermeasures. This morning, I ordered Panama's Minister of Banking and Commerce to seize all bank accounts and assets belonging to US citizens.

The US president responds to this expropriation by imposing an embargo on all goods from Panama. The US Customs Service thus refuses to allow any products from Panama to enter into the US.

Do Panama's bank account seizures and the US embargo violate the principle of International Law that prohibits the State use of force? If so, *how*?

Problem 10.2 (*§ 10.2 after 1970/1987 UN Declarations*): In the 1970s, Ecuador and the US were embroiled in a fishing dispute over the breadth of Ecuador's territorial water zone. Ecuador claimed a territorial sea of two hundred nautical miles. The US claimed that customary State practice permitted only a twelve-mile claim.

Ecuador seized fourteen US tuna fishing boats in its "territorial sea"—well beyond twelve miles from its coast—and did not return them unless the owners paid significant licensing fees. At the same time, the US encouraged its commercial fishing fleet to fish in Ecuador's two-hundred-mile zone. Congress passed legislation under which the owners of the captured tuna boats were reimbursed when their boats were seized or they had to pay Ecuador's license fees. The US responded to these boat seizures by suspending its sales of military supplies to Ecuador. Ecuador then claimed that the US had used illegal economic and political force by withholding these vital exports needed for its defense.

Assume that representatives of the US and Ecuador are debating this incident in the UN General Assembly. Two students (or groups) will present the positions of Ecuador and the US on the following

question: Did either the US or Ecuador violate the UN Charter's prohibition against the use of force?

Problem 10.3 (*§ 10.2 after Cuban Missile Crisis materials*): Did the US violate UN Charter Article 51's provision regarding the use of self-defense in the case of an "armed attack?"

Problem 10.4 (*§ 10.2 after Article 51 materials*): In April 1993, after US President Bush left office, he traveled to Kuwait. After returning, the US discovered that Saddam Hussein had planned the assassination of President Bush during this visit. The US responded, in June 1993, by launching several missiles into Baghdad. The US claimed that an unsuccessful armed attack on a former head of State justified this responsive use of force as Article 51 self-defense.

The UN Security Council had authorized States to take "all necessary measures" to subdue Iraq's behavior related to the Persian Gulf War over its aggression in Kuwait. Not responding might suggest to Saddam Hussein that Iraq might continue to operate as a rogue State, with no countermeasures to control his excesses.

Two students—one representing Iraq, and one representing the US—will debate whether a State's use of force in these circumstances is justifiable self-defense, as opposed to a mere reprisal.

Problem 10.5 (*end of § 10.4*): In 1981 and 1982, fourteen petitions on behalf of approximately 5,000 inhabitants of the Marshall Islands were filed in the US Court of Claims (Washington, D.C.) to claim damages said to result from the US program to test nuclear weapons during the period June 30, 1946, to August 18, 1958. The US program included detonation of 23 atomic and hydrogen bombs at Bikini Atoll and 43 nuclear bombs at Enewetak Atoll, and required the removal of the inhabitants and their relocation. There was severe physical destruction at Bikini Atoll and Enewetak Atoll, and radioactive contamination of parts of the Marshall Islands chain. Claimed damages ranged from $450 million to $600 million. This case and similar ones have been dismissed on a variety grounds including the statute of limitations, US sovereign immunity from suit, and lack of the court's power to hear this type of case because it poses a "political question." *See, e.g.,* Juda v. U.S., 13 Claims Ct. 667 (1987), appeal dismissed by People of Bikini v. U.S., 859 Fed.Rptr.2d 1482 (Fed. Cir. 1988).

In 1994, US newspapers ran stories regarding the US disclosure of more than 200 previously undisclosed underground nuclear tests in the US since World War II. Assume that some of these 200 nuclear tests occurred in 1994. Would the US thereby have violated any of the multilateral agreements mentioned in this chapter? Would it matter if the 1994 tests were conducted within or outside of the US?

Problem 10.6 (*end of § 10.5*): The border separating the hypothetical nations of North Alpha and South Bravo is lined with military installations on both sides. Both nations are members of the United Nations. Alpha and Bravo recently signed a bilateral treaty in which they agreed that neither State may use or encourage the use of coercive measures, of an economic or political character. They further agreed that neither could force its objectives on the sovereign will of the other State, or attempt to use force so as to obtain advantages of any kind.

Their international relations are now very poor. A small band of Alpha's military troops covertly crossed the border into Bravo and disappeared into Bravo's heartland. Bravo's leader learns about this clandestine military operation and decides that he must respond to this threat. He takes some prominent Alpha citizens, who are visiting Bravo, as hostages. He then announces that they will remain under house arrest in an unknown location in Bravo. The Alpha troops in Bravo are given an ultimatum by Bravo's leader in a widely broadcasted radio and television message: The Alpha soldiers must surrender to Bravo authorities, or the Alpha civilian hostages will be executed, one each day, until Alpha's troops surrender.

Alpha's military forces in Bravo decide not to surrender. Instead, they plan a hostage rescue mission. An Alpha military plane, loaded with specially trained Alpha soldiers, flies into Bravo to assist them. All of the Alpha soldiers in Bravo then join forces at a predetermined rendezvous point near the city where the Alpha citizens are being held. Bravo is not surprised. Bravo's military troops ambush and kill all of the Alpha soldiers. Bravo's leader then orders the mass execution of all Alpha hostages.

Did Alpha's rescue mission violate any of the international norms presented thus far in this chapter of the book? Was there any justification?

Problem 10.7 (*end of § 10.6*): The US conducted "carpet" bombings of Hanoi in 1972. During the negotiations to end the Vietnam War, President Nixon decided to bomb Hanoi, in order to bring an end to the Vietnam War. The city contained many military targets. Being the seat of government for North Vietnam, the city was also home to a large number of civilians who were killed by the thousands.

The following news report explains carpet bombing, its impact upon the civilian populace, and the basis for a claim arising under the Geneva Conventions:

Air raid sirens scream day and night. The earth trembles with the violence of an earthquake, and whole sections of the city crumble in a roar of flames and jagged steel. For the first time in the war the people seem afraid.

This is Hanoi under attack by American B-52's, as described by Westerners who have been there. The big bombers, flying in wedges of three, lay down more than 65 tons of bombs at a time in a carpet pattern a mile and a half long and a half mile wide.

For nearly two weeks now the city has been the focal point of a siege by American bombers that has extended across the densely populated heart of North Vietnam. Hundreds, if not thousands, of civilians are believed to have been killed. (*New York Times*, Dec. 31, 1972.)

This incident focused attention on the 1949 Geneva Convention on the Protection of Civilian Persons in Time of War. A belligerent may not intentionally direct military force at civilian targets. While some civilian casualties cannot be avoided, a State cannot annihilate the civilian populace of the enemy, in order to gain tactical or psychological advantages in time of war. North Vietnam's claimed violation of the Geneva Convention was never tested in an international tribunal. (Nor was its mistreatment of American POWs, particularly downed pilots captured in North Vietnam.)

The following account was written by a seven-year inmate of the infamous "Hanoi Hilton" (the subject of several American movies). This was a North Vietnamese prison complex—where the interrogations brutalized mostly American pilots shot down over North Vietnam. One American inmate, Render Crayton, wrote that the Christmas bombings were responsible for bringing an end to the war (not unlike President Truman's 1945 decision to drop atomic bombs on the cities of Hiroshima and

Nagasaki to end the war with Japan). In support of the US bombings, Crayton wrote as follows:

> Maybe North Vietnam was willing to *talk* about peace, but during the bombing pause that began in October 1972, Hanoi was re-supplying its troops and rebuilding its air defense system. . . . The B-52 strikes during Christmas conveyed the required notice that it was time to talk seriously or else.
>
> From a cell in the Hanoi Hilton, I and many other Americans had close encounters during those 11 days of bombings. After seven years of sitting out an on-again, off-again war . . . it was clear to me that the B-52s carried a . . . message: this time we meant business. It was a long-awaited Christmas present. . . .
>
> The same fear that overcame the guards and the people in the streets undoubtedly was reflected in the willingness of their leaders to hustle back to the [negotiating] table [in Paris], this time ready for serious talks.
>
> [I]t was Congress . . . that helped drag out the Vietnam War. It was President Nixon, with the Christmas bombings, who put an end to it. (*San Diego Union-Tribune*, Jan. 7, 1993.)

Were any Laws of War violated? Was there any justification?

■ BIBLIOGRAPHY

§ 10.1 Defining "Force" and Its Role:

I. Brownlie, *International Law and the Use of Force by States* (Oxford, Eng.: Oxford Univ. Press, 1963) (classic study)

W. Butler, *The Non-Use of Force in International Law* (Dordrecht, Neth.; Boston: Martinus Nijhoff, 1989)

E. Corr & S. Sloan (ed.), *Low-Intensity Conflict: Old Threats in a New World* (Boulder, CO: Westview Press, 1992)

Dixon, *Democracy and the Peaceful Settlement of International Conflict*, 88 *American Political Science Review* 14 (1994)

T. Ehrlich & M. O'Connell, *International Law and the Use of Force* (Boston: Little, Brown & Co., 1993)

International Conflicts, ch. 4, in B. Jankovic, *Public International Law* 347 (Dobbs Ferry, NY: Transnat'l Pub., 1984) (Yugoslavian author)

Reisman, *Coercion and Self-Determination: Construing Charter Article 2(4)*, 78 *American Journal of International Law* 642 (1984)

A. Rifat, *International Aggression—A Study of the Legal Concept: Its Development and Definition in International Law* (Stockholm: Almqvist & Wiksell Int'l, 1979)

Schachter, *In Defense of International Rules on the Use of Force*, 53 *University of Chicago Law Review* 113 (1986)

§ 10.2 United Nations Charter Principles:

R. Amer, *The United Nations and Foreign Military Interventions: A Comparative Study of the Application of the Charter* (Uppsala, Sweden: Uppsala Univ., 1992)

Chayes, *Law and the Quarantine of Cuba*, 41 *Foreign Affairs* 550 (1963)

Y. Dinstein, *War, Aggression and Self-Defence* (2nd ed. Cambridge, Eng.: Grotius, 1994)

Henkin, *Law and War after the Cold War*, 15 *Maryland J. Int'l L. & Trade* 147 (1991) (published speech)

International Organizations, Peace and Defense, § 3-24 to § 3-27 in T. Buergenthal & H. Maier, *Public International Law in a Nutshell* 57 (2nd ed. St. Paul: West, 1990)

I. Johnstone, *Aftermath of the Gulf War: An Assessment of UN Action* (Boulder, CO: Lynne Reinner, 1994)

§ 10.3 Peacekeeping Operations:

L. Davis, *Peacekeeping and Peacemaking After the Cold War* (Santa Monica, CA: Rand Inst., 1993)

P. Diehl, *International Peacekeeping* (Baltimore: Johns Hopkins Press, 1993)

R. Diekmann, *Basic Documents on United Nations and Related Peace-keeping Forces* (2nd ed. Dordrecht, Neth.; Boston: Martinus Nijhoff, 1989)

Garvey, *United Nations Peacekeeping and Host State Consent*, 64 *American Journal of International Law* 642 (1984)

UN, *The Blue Helmets: A Review of United Nations Peacekeeping* (2nd ed. New York: UN, 1990)

§ 10.4 Multilateral Agreements on Force:

D. Bourantonis, *The United Nations and the Quest for Nuclear Disarmament* (Brookfield, VT: Dartmouth, 1993)

S. Croft (ed.), *The Conventional Armed Forces in Europe Treaty: The Cold War Endgame* (Brookfield, VT: Dartmouth, 1994)

D. Paul (ed.), *Disarmaments Mission Dimension: A UN Agency to Administer Multilateral Treaties* (Toronto: S. Stevens, 1990)

R. Powell, *Crisis Bargaining, Escalation and Mad*, 81 *American Political Science Review* 717 (1987)

D. Schindler & J. Toman (ed.), *The Law of Armed Conflict: A Collection of Conventions, Resolutions and Other Documents* (3rd rev. ed. Geneva: Henry Durant Inst., 1988)

§ 10.5 Humanitarian Intervention:

R. Lillich (ed.), *Humanitarian Intervention and Developing Public International Law*, 1983 *Duke Law Journal* 748 (1983)

P. Schraeder, *Intervention in the 1990s: U.S. Foreign Policy in the Third World* (Boulder, CO: Lynne Reinner Pub., 1992)

F. Teson, *Humanitarian Intervention: An Inquiry into Law and Morality* (2nd ed. Irvington, NY: Transnat'l, 1994)

Unilateral Intervention, in B. Weston, R. Falk & A. D'Amato, *International Law and World Order* 867 (2nd ed. St. Paul: West, 1990)

§ 10.6 Laws of War:

Gasser, *Agora: The U.S. Decision Not to Ratify Protocol I to the Geneva Conventions on the Protection of War Victims*, 81 *American Journal of International Law* 910 (1987)

W. Krutzsch & R. Trapp, *A Commentary on the Chemical Weapons Convention* (Dordrecht, Neth.; Boston: Martinus Nijhoff, 1994)

The Law of War and the Control of Weapons, in L. Henkin, et al., *International Law* 1019 (3rd ed. St. Paul: West, 1993)

M. McDougal & F. Feliciano, *The International Law of War: Transnational Coercion and World Public Order* (Dordrecht, Neth.; Boston: Martinus Nijhoff, 1994)

Mushkat, *When War May Justifiably Be Waged: An Analysis of Historical and Contemporary Legal Perspectives*, 15 *Brooklyn J. Int'l L.* 223 (1989)

Symposium, *The International Humanitarian Law Applicable to Armed Conflict at Sea: Round Table of Experts*, 14 *Syracuse Journal of International Law & Commerce* 571 (1988)

D. Wells, *War Crimes and the Laws of War* (Lanham, NY: Univ. Press of Amer., 1984)

§ 10.7 State Terrorism/Arms Sales:

M.C. Bassiouni (ed.), *Legal Responses to International Terrorism: U.S. Procedural Aspects* (Dordrecht, Neth.; Boston: Martinus Nijhoff, 1988)

D. Dahlitz & D. Dicke (ed.), *The International Law of Arms Control and Disarmament* (New York: UN, 1991) (symposium)

Greene, *Terrorism as Impermissible Political Violence: An International Law Framework*, 16 *Vermont Law Review* 461 (1992)

J. Lambert, *Terrorism and Hostages in International Law: A Commentary on the Hostages Convention 1979* (Cambridge, Eng.: Grotius, 1990)

McCredie, *Contemporary Uses of Force Against Terrorism: The United States Response to Achille Lauro—Questions of Jurisdiction and Its Exercise*, 16 *Georgia J. Int'l & Comp. L.* 435 (1986)

SIPRI Yearbook 1993: World Armaments and Disarmament (New York: Oxford Univ. Press, 1993)

§ 10.8 United States War Powers Resolution:

Franck, *After the Fall: The New Procedural Framework for Congressional Control over the War Power*, 71 *Amer. J. Int'l L.* 605 (1977)

Keynes, *The War Powers Resolution: A Bad Idea Whose Time Has Come and Gone*, 23 *Univ. Toledo L. Rev.* 343 (1992)

■ ENDNOTES

1. Aristotle, *Nichomachaean Ethics* 329 (New York: Penguin, 1976) (H. Tredennick revision, J. Thompson translation).

2. W. Reisman, *Private Armies in a Global War System: Prologue to Decision*, in M. McDougal & W. Reisman, *International Law Essays* 142, 154–55 (Mineola, NY: Foundation Press, 1981).

3. *War as a Lawful Instrument of National Policy*, 2 *Oppenheim's International Law* 177–78 (Essex, Eng.: Longman, 7th ed. 1952) (H. Lauterpacht edition).

4. *See* M. Mandelbaum, *The Fate of Nations: The Search for National Security in the Nineteenth and Twentieth Centuries* (New York: Cambridge Univ. Press, 1988).

5. *See Law Functioning in the International System*, ch. 2 in *Law and Force in the International System* 43, 80 (Moscow: Progress Publishers, 1983) (1985 English translation).

6. *The Use of Force by States*, ch. 16, in D. Greig, *International Law* 867 (2nd ed. London: Butterworths, 1976) (emphasis supplied).

7. Dep't of the Army and the Air Force, *Military Operations in Low Intensity Conflict, Army Field Manual 100-20, Air Force Pamphlet 3-20*, p.1 (Dec. 1990).

8. *See, e.g.,* the comment of one commentator that "American administrations have exaggerated the Soviet threat so as to keep in line their allies in the North and their clients in the South." *Introduction*, G. Arnold, *Wars in the Third World Since 1945* xii (London: Casell, 1991).

9. Commission on Integrated Long-Term Strategy, *Discriminate Deterrence* 2–3 (Wash., DC: US Gov't Print. Off., 1988).

10. Gen. Ass. Res. 2625(XXXV), Part 1 Principles (1970).

11. *See The Development of the Doctrine of Reprisals in the Seventeenth and Eighteenth Centuries*, ch. 1, in O. Elagab, *The Legality of Non-Forcible Counter-measures in International Law* (Oxford, Eng.: Clarendon Press, 1988).

12. The draft articles are reproduced in S. Rosenne, *The International Law Commission's Draft Articles on State Responsibility: Part I, Articles 1–35* 319 (Dordrecht, Neth.; Boston: Martinus Nijhoff, 1991).

13. Schachter, *The Right of States to Use Armed Force*, 82 *Mich. L. Rev.* 1620, 1633 (1984).

14. *Report of the Special Committee on the Definition of Aggression* 12 UN Gen. Ass. Off. Rec. (Supp. No. 16) 13 (1956). Further details are available in *Aggression and Armed Attack*, ch. 3, in H. McCoubrey & N. White, *International Law and Armed Conflict* 39 (Brookfield, VT: Dartmouth Pub., 1992).

15. Gen. Ass. Res. 2625(XXXV 1970), reprinted in 9 *Int'l Legal Mat'ls* 1292 (1970).

16. Gen. Ass. Res. 42/22 (1987), reprinted in 27 *Int'l Legal Mat'ls* 1672 (1988). The approving resolution in 1988 adopted an earlier draft resolution from 1986.

17. D. Greig, *International Law* 892–93 (2nd ed. London: Butterworths, 1976) (emphasis supplied).

18. Meeker, *Defensive Quarantine and the Law*, 57 *Amer. J. Int'l L.* 515, 523 (1963).

19. Chao Li-hai, *American Imperialism Tramples on International Law*, Chinese People's Daily, Nov. 14, 1962, at 4, reprinted in Vol. 2 J. Cohen & H. Chiu, *People's China and International Law: A Documentary Study* 1461–1464 (Princeton: Princeton Univ. Press, 1974).

20. Military and Paramilitary Activities in and Against Nicaragua, (Nicaragua v. United States), 1986 I.C.J. Rep. 14, para. 208–9 (emphasis supplied) [hereinafter *Nicaragua* case].

21. The various Gulf War resolutions, and numerous related documents, are collected in W. Weller (ed.), *Iraq and Kuwait: The Hostilities and Their Aftermath* (Cambridge, Eng.: Grotius Pub., 1993).

22. **Cuban law:** No. 851, July 6, 1960. **Bay of Pigs:** *see* P. Wyden, *Bay of Pigs: The Untold Story* (New York: Simon & Schuster, 1981) (detailing author's six-hour interview with Fidel Castro). **Cuban missile crisis:** *see* self-defense analysis earlier in this section.

23. R. Falk, *Introduction* to M. Krinsky & D. Golove, *United States Economic Measures Against Cuba: Proceedings in the United Nations and International Law Issues* 1, 10–11 (Northhampton, MA: Aletheia Press, 1993).

24. D. Sheffer, *Commentary on Collective Security*, ch. 8 in L. Damrosch & D. Scheffer (ed.), *Law and Force in the New International Order* 101, 103–4 (Boulder, CO: Westview Press, 1991) [hereinafter *Law and Force*].

25. B. Boutros-Ghali, *Agenda for Peace* 25–26 (New York: UN, 1992).

26. *Opening Statement of Dr. Edward Warner before the Senate Armed Services Subcommittee on Coalition Defense and Reinforcing Forces*, in *U.S. Department of Defense Statement on Peacekeeping*, 33 *Int'l Legal Mat'ls* 814 (1994). *See also* Scheffer, *U.S. Administration Policy on Reforming Multilateral Peace Operations*, 33 *Int'l Legal Mat'ls* 795 (1994) and *U.S. Department of State Statement on the Legal Authority for UN Peace Operations*, 33 *Int'l Legal Mat'ls* 821 (1994).

27. W. Durch (ed.), *The Evolution of UN Peacekeeping* 7 (New York: St. Martin's Press, 1993) (emphasis supplied).

28. A detailed account is provided in D. Neff, *Warriors at Suez*, (New York: Simon & Schuster, 1981).

29. Certain Expenses of the United Nations (Advisory Opinion), 1962 I.C.J. Rep. 151, para. 161 & 177.

30. This account is provided in McNeill, *Commentary on Dispute Resolution Mechanisms in Arms Control Agreements*, ch. 26, in *Law and Force* 258, 259 (cited in note 24 above).

31. An account of this incident is provided in Spencer, *The Italian-Ethiopian Dispute and the League of Nations*, 31 *Amer. J. Int'l L.* 614 (1937).

32. Editorial, *Wall Street Journal*, Feb. 25, 1991.

33. *See* J. Wilkinson, *Arabia's Frontiers: The Story of Britain's Boundary Drawing in the Desert* (London: I.B. Tauris & Co., 1991).

34. **Constitutional dilemma:** Slomanson, *Judicial Review of War Renunciation in the Naganuma Nike Case: Juggling the Constitutional Crisis in Japan*, 9 *Cornell Int'l L.J.* 24 (1975). **Peacekeeping guidelines:** *Law Concerning Cooperation for United Nations Peace-keeping Operations and Other Operations*, 32 *Int'l Legal Mat'ls* 215 (1993).

35. *See* Franck & Rodley, *After Bangladesh: The Law of Humanitarian Intervention by Military Force*, 67 *Amer. J. Int'l L.* 275, 285 (1973).

36. **Historical background:** J. Fonteyne, *The Customary International Law Doctrine of Humanitarian Intervention*, 4 *Calif. West. Int'l L.J.* 203 (1974). **Varied definitions:** Bazyler, *Reexamining the Doctrine of Humanitarian Intervention in Light of the Atrocities in Kampuchea and Ethiopia*, 23 *Stanford J. Int'l L.* 547 (1987).

37. **Humanitarian purposes:** Article 55(c). **Action pledge:** Article 56. **No UN interference:** Article 2.7.

38. *See* R. Lillich (ed.), *Humanitarian Intervention and the United Nations* (Charlottesville, Va.: Univ. Press of Va., 1973).

39. *Nicaragua* case, para. 242 (cited in note 20 above) (emphasis supplied).

40. UN Gen. Ass. Resolutions: 43/131, Dec. 8, 1988; 45/100, July 29, 1991; 46/182, Dec. 19, 1991.

41. Schindler, *Humanitarian Assistance, Humanitarian Interference and International Law*, ch. 46, in R. Macdonald (ed.), *Essays in Honour of Wang Tieya* 689, 700 (Dordrecht, Neth.; Boston: Martinus Nijhoff, 1994).

42. These accounts are provided in *Historical Background*, ch. 1, in H. Levie, *Terrorism in War—The Law of War Crimes* 9–10 (Dobbs Ferry, NY: Oceana, 1992) [hereinafter *Law of War Crimes*].

43. Kuhn, *Responsibility for Military Conduct and Respect for International Humanitarian Law*, in *Dissemination* p.1 (Aug. 1987) (magazine of the International Committee of the Red Cross).

44. The organization for any useful analysis of this field of law is conveniently structured by reference to Levie's *Law of War Crimes* (cited in note 42 above).

45. 1 *Trial of Military War Crimes* 234–35 [German defendants](this is a multivolume set containing an exhaustively complete record of the lengthy case set forth in the text of § 9.5) [hereinafter referred to as the *Nuremberg Trial*]. It also contains the record of the similar proceedings of the Tokyo defendants also tried by the Allies [hereinafter *Tokyo Trial*].

46. *See Violations of the Rules of War*, Helsinki Watch, *War Crimes in Bosnia-Hercegovina* 50 (New York: Human Rights Watch, 1992).

47. 1 Nuremberg Trial, 252 (cited in note 45).

48. 1 Tokyo Trial, 231 (cited in note 45).

49. 1 Nuremberg Trial, 313 (cited in note 45).

50. **Corfu:** 1949 I.C.J. Rep. 4, p.22. **Nicaragua:** 1986 I.C.J. Rep. 14, p.112.

51. A. Guttry & N. Ronzitti (ed.), *The Iran-Iraq War (1980–1988) and the Law of Naval Warfare* 7 (Cambridge, Eng.: Grotius, 1993).

52. 4 Nuremberg Trial, 466–67 (cited in note 45).

53. The so-called "London Conference" of 1991 is discussed in G. Plant, *Environmental Protection and the Law of War: A 'Fifth Geneva' Convention on the Protection of the Environment in Time of Armed Conflict* (London: Belhaven Press, 1992).

54. Memorandum of the ICRC to the Governments of States Party to the Geneva Conventions and Members of the United Nations on the Application of the Geneva Conventions by the Armed Forces Placed at the Disposal of United Nations, 10 November 1961 reprinted in *International Review of the Red Cross* (Geneva: 1961).

55. This widely reported event, and others of that era, are discussed in Slomanson, *I.C.J. Damages: Tort Remedy for Failure to Punish or Extradite International Terrorists*, 5 *Calif. West. Int'l L.J.* 121 (1973), reprinted in 14 *Comp. Juridical Rev.* 139 (1977).

56. Anti-Terrorism Act, Pub. Law No. 100–204, Title X, § 1002, Dec. 22, 1987, 101 Statutes at Large 1406, Legislative Findings and Determinations, set forth in 22 US Code § 5201.

57. Case of Brogan and Others, 145-B Euro. Ct. Hum. Rts. (series A) (1988). Analyzed in Note, *The United Kingdom's Obligation to Balance Human Rights and its Anti-Terrorism Legislation: The Case of Brogan and Others*, 13 *Fordham Int'l L.J.* 328 (1990).

58. *See* Hearings of March 21, 1988, and April 25, 1989, Sub-Comm. on Aviation of the Comm. on Public Works and Transportation, U.S. House of Representatives (Wash., DC: US Gov't Print. Off., 1989).

59. B. Hoffman, *The Contrasting Ethical Foundations of Terrorism in the 1980s*, in *Terrorism and Political Violence* 360, 369 (July, 1989).

60. **Report:** UN Gen. Ass. Off. Records: 28th Sess., Supp. No. 28 (A/9028). **Resolution:** UN Gen. Ass. Reso. 3034(XXVII), UN Doc. A/RES/3068 (1973), reprinted in 13 *Int'l Legal Mat'ls* 218 (1973).

61. **Council:** Resolution 579, Dec. 9, 1985. **Assembly:** Resolution 40/61, Dec. 18, 1985. Both are reprinted in 25 *Int'l Legal Mat'ls* 239 & 243 (1986).

62. Friedlander, *Terrorism and the World Community*, Epilogue to H. Han (ed.), *Terrorism & Political Violence: Limits and Possibilities of Legal Control* 447, 449–50 (New York: Oceana, 1993).

63. *See* 1983 Concluding Document of Madrid, 1986 Document of the Stockholm Conference, and the 1989 Concluding Document of Vienna, reproduced in A. Bloed, *The Conference on Security and Co-operation in Europe: Analysis and Basic Documents, 1972–1993* (Dordrecht, Neth.; Boston: Martinus Nijhoff, 1993).

64. **1789 proposal:** This historical account of early attempts at arms control is available in McNeil, *Commentary on Dispute Resolution Mechanisms in Arms Control Agreements*, ch. 26 in L. Damrosch & D. Scheffer (ed.), *Law and Force in the New International Order* 258 (Boulder, CO: Westview Press, 1991). **Quote:** *Why Study Arms Races?*, ch. 1 in G. Hammond, *Plowshares into Swords: Arms Races in International Politics, 1840–1991* 3–4 (Columbia, SC: Univ. of So. Caro. Press, 1993).

65. Deger, *World Military Expenditure*, ch. 9, in *SIPRI Yearbook 1993: World Disarmaments and Disarmament* 337 (Oxford, Eng.: Oxford Univ. Press, 1993). Earlier statistics are available in D. Galik (ed.), *World Military and Arms Transfers 1987* (Wash., DC: US Arms Control and Disarmament Agency, 1988).

66. Youngstown Sheet & Tube v. Sawyer, 343 U.S. 579, 72 S.Ct. 863, 96 L.Ed. 1153 (1952).

67. E. Richardson, *Checks and Balances in Foreign Relations* in L. Henkin, M. Glennon & W. Rogers (ed.), *Foreign Affairs and the U.S. Constitution* 27 (Ardsley-on-Hudson, NY: Transnat'l, 1990) [hereinafter *Foreign Affairs and the Constitution*].

68. Pub. Law No. 93-148, 87 Statutes at Large 555, 50 US Code § 1541 (emphasis supplied). The following quotes are taken from the remainder of this legislation contained in 50 US Code §§ 1541–48.

69. Franck, *Rethinking War Powers: By Law or by "Thaumaturgic Invocation?"* in *Foreign Affairs and the Constitution* 56, 58–59 (cited in note 67 above).

Human Rights

■ INTRODUCTION

The first ten chapters of this book address the fundamentals of International Law. The remaining chapters contain cross-cutting themes offered as separate courses in both undergraduate and law school curriculums—human rights, environment, and international economic relations. This survey course in Public International Law would be incomplete, however, without coverage of the basic principles in each of these subject areas.

This chapter addresses the first of these themes—human rights. After a preliminary exploration of this topic in the field of International Law, these materials then summarize the International Bill of Human Rights. To enable the student to appreciate the overall successes and dilemmas, the remaining sections proceed through the prominent global and regional approaches to human rights—including the role of private nongovernmental organizations in the evolution of human rights.

The final substantive section addresses *US* treaty ratification obstacles, together with legislative/judicial enforcement policy affecting those whose human rights have been violated abroad.

■ 11.1 HUMAN RIGHTS IN CONTEXT

Course Affiliation

Some component of what is now referred to as "human rights" impacted virtually all facets of the development of International Law. The first chapter of this book defined International Law as the body of norms that States consider binding in their international relations. UN Charter norms, current State practice, international treaties or declarations, and national legislation are the sources of International Law that echo the aging human rights adage "Never again!"

Chapters 2, 3, and 4 present the essential "players" in International Law—States, international organizations, and the individual. Human rights have been a critical catalyst in their interaction.

Other chapters in this book (5 and 6) analyzed "international" jurisdiction to act and the range of sovereignty. The relevant facet of that particular survey was the "universal" basis for jurisdiction to seek extradition or to punish offenders of human rights law who commit genocide, war crimes, and like offenses against the law of nations.

The diplomatic relations and treaty chapters of this book (7 and 8) explored international relations aspiring to eliminate or ameliorate State conduct violating human rights. Political and diplomatic asylum are often sought due to intolerable conditions in the applicant's home State. Many treaties focus on the varied forms of human rights abuses that underlie the International Bill of Human Rights discussed later in this chapter.

Chapter 9 addresses international adjudication and the Nuremberg/Tokyo Trials of World War II. The military agents of the Axis powers were therein brought to justice for human rights violations that rose to the level of "Crimes Against [all] Humanity"—as charged in the indictments.

Chapter 10 addresses the use of force by States and their agents, as well as limitations imposed by the Laws of War. The Vietnam-era *Calley* trial of a soldier who unmercifully murdered a village-full of nonresisting men, women, and children is but one contemporary example of the ubiquitous inhumanity sought to be regulated by human rights advocates. That "Use of Force" chapter is also relevant to the law of human rights for another reason. The seventeenth century Grotian formulation of the law of humanitarian intervention was that one nation could enter another nation to enforce international human rights recognized by the community of nations. Some nations, however, boldly invaded other nations in the name of humanitarian intervention without just cause. This historical abuse thus fostered future generations of national distrust for human rights initiatives. It later retarded international attempts to secure those rights for oppressed individuals, due to sovereign claims that no international organization of States had the power to interfere with "internal" affairs involving how a State treated its *own* citizens.[1]

Doctrinal Evolution

What does the term *human rights* mean? There are, of course, differences in State practice, and differences in definitional perspectives. Certain universal norms, however, are purportedly recognized by all States. A very general starting point is that human rights are those rights possessed by an individual that cannot be withheld by the State. Some specificity is provided by scholars who would refer to this body of law as involving the "protection of individuals and groups against governmental violations of their internationally guaranteed rights."[2]

The English Magna Charta (1215), the French Declaration of the Rights of Man (1789), and the US Constitution's Bill of Rights (1791) are documents that specifically listed inherent rights of the individual, considered to be irrevocable by government action. Contemporary human rights norms originated in documents such as these, because the legacy of the Middle Ages was that life was seen to be anchored in rigid religious and social structures. Any human rights guarantees addressed entitlements of classes rather than individuals.

The coincidental French Declaration and the US Constitution first expressed one of the most fundamental of all modern human rights: that no person shall "be deprived of life, liberty, or property, without due process of law." The US Bill of Rights was added to the US Constitution in the form of constitutional amendments guaranteeing freedom of religion, speech, press, and assembly.

In democratic societies, the rights of the individual have historically focused on *political* liberty. In lesser-developed societies, social and economic benefits are the individual's primary concern. Food, shelter, health care, some form of social security, and a minimal education—these are the "human rights" of primary importance. In these troubled societies, many individuals must struggle for their daily existence in terms of obtaining food and shelter. Such "rights" are, of course, subject to budgetary constraints (further discussed below).

Contemporary Influences

One could view World War II as a war fought to promote human rights. Certain States had deprived their inhabitants of life, liberty, and property by instituting sweeping social reforms to eliminate particular racial or ethnic groups. Germany's Nazi government, for example, deported a large portion of the German population to concentration camps in Poland. The government's goal was to eliminate what it branded as "inferior" segments of its society. Some nations entered the war, professing that the international community must fight to avoid the proliferation of such atrocities. After the war, these States thus formed an international organization of States (the United Nations) that would develop the various human rights initiatives discussed later in this chapter. Ironically, many supportive States continued to *violate* human rights within their own territories, while professing the importance of developing global and regional regimes to *protect* human rights.

The development of human rights law thus is fraught with a number of ironies. The UN Charter's human rights provisions, for example, were influenced by Hitler's "Final Solution." That State policy was designed to eradicate certain individuals and groups from German society and all of Europe. This key event in the evolution of "the Holocaust" was probably the ultimate discrimination based on "race, language, and religion"—a familiar trilogy in contemporary human rights instruments. Yet in 1975, a UN resolution equated "Zionism" with racism. This General Assembly position was not repealed until 1991. And it was not until 1994 that the UN—via its Human Rights Commission, rather than the General Assembly—condemned anti-Semitism as a form of human rights abuse.

Unfortunately, the Nazi Holocaust was neither the first nor the last example of such widespread practice within a State. There was no international human rights program, for example, to limit the twentieth century's first major genocide—in 1915, when Turkey deported 1.75 million Armenians to arid deserts where few survived. Nor did anyone stand in the way of Stalin's "Terror Famine" during the winter of 1932–1933 in the Ukraine. Russia thus starved between 8 and 10 million rural farmers of the Ukraine, pursuant to Stalin's State policy to break the populace of the Ukraine based on class ha-

tred. The subsequent holocaust in Bosnia was premised on ethnic cleansing in the former Yugoslavia, beginning in 1991 after the close of the Cold War. The nature of the atrocities led the UN to reestablish the first International Criminal Court since Nuremberg. The scale of human rights violations has yet to be fully reported.

The mid-twentieth century was, practically speaking, the period for dating the development of the contemporary International Law of Human Rights. A brief history of the endeavors of States, and associations of States, is provided below by a British author. It provides a useful perspective for understanding how contemporary human rights developed, why certain States began to appreciate the importance of protecting individuals, and in what way the renewed fervor would form the basis for the contemporary UN human rights model. This passage further illustrates the early proposals that would have provided much greater definitional specificity—and offers reasons why these proposals were rejected (in the name of State sovereignty):

THE INTERNATIONAL LAW OF HUMAN RIGHTS IN THE MIDDLE TWENTIETH CENTURY

in The Present State of International Law and Other Essays 75 (1973)*
John Humphrey, United Nation's Director of Division of Human Rights
from 1946 to 1966

I. TRADITIONAL DOCTRINE AND PRACTICE

[L]egal historians will surely be saying that one of the chief characteristics of mid-twentieth century international law was its sudden interest in and concern with human rights. The human rights were—and indeed still are—essentially a relationship between the State and individuals—usually its own citizens—residing in its territory, th[at] were, in *traditional theory* and practice, considered to fall *within domestic jurisdiction and hence beyond the reach of international law*, the norms of which governed the relations of States only [as opposed to relations between the State and its own citizens].

. . .

[I]n the nineteenth and early twentieth centuries an increasing number of treaties were entered into

the purpose of which was to protect, if only indirectly, the rights of certain classes of people. The most important of these [treaties] were the treaties aimed at slavery and the slave trade. By 1885, it was possible to affirm, in the General Act of the Berlin Conference on Central Africa, that "trading in slaves is forbidden in conformity with the principles of international law." [This European "revelation" appeared after the success of the North in the American Civil War.] And in 1889, the Brussels Conference not only condemned slavery and the slave trade but agreed on measures for their suppression, including the granting of reciprocal rights of search, and the capture and trial of slave ships [on the high seas]. This work was continued by both the League of Nations and the United Nations. Steps were also taken in the nineteenth century for the relief of sick and wounded soldiers and prisoners of

---

*Reprinted with permission of the International Law Association of London. Italics has been supplied in certain passages.

war. By the Geneva Convention of 22 August, 1864, twelve States undertook to respect the immunity of military hospitals and their staffs, to care for wounded and sick soldiers and to respect the emblem of the Red Cross. The Convention was revised in 1929 and has been widely ratified [by States as a binding obligation rather than being a mere statement of moral principles].

In 1906, the second Berne Conference opened two conventions for signature [so that States could later ratify them] which were forerunners of the many labor conventions which, after the First World War, would be adopted by the International Labor Organization: the International Convention respecting the Prohibition of Night Work for Women in Industrial Employment and the International Convention respecting the Prohibition of the Use of White (Yellow) Phosphorus in the Manufacture of Matches.

II. THE LEAGUE OF NATIONS

The peace settlement at the end of the First World War brought still more important developments. Attempts were made to enshrine human rights in the Covenant of the League of Nations. [US] President Wilson sponsored an article on religious freedom, but when the Japanese suggested that mention *also* be made of the equality of nations and the just treatment of their nationals (which frightened some countries the laws of which restricted Asiatic immigration) both suggestions were *withdrawn*. Wilson put into his second draft an article under which the League would have required all new States to bind themselves, as a condition precedent to their recognition, to accord all racial and national minorities "exactly the same treatment and security, both in law and in fact, that is accorded the racial and national majority of their [*own*] people." But the Peace Conference decided that the protection of minorities—though only in certain countries—would be dealt with *not in the Covenant* but by other treaty provisions and by declarations which certain States were required to make on their [subsequent] admission to the League.

. . .

Human rights were expressly dealt with in Article 23 of the Covenant. Members of the League, it said, would "endeavour to secure and maintain" fair and humane labor conditions, undertake to secure just treatment for the native inhabitants of territories under their control, and entrust the League with the supervision of agreements relating to the [slave] traffic in women and children. [The US never joined the League.]

Although President Wilson's suggestion that the Covenant contain a provision protecting minorities was not pursued, the Allied and Associated Powers did require certain *newly created* States and [other] States, the territory of which had been increased by reason of the war, to grant the enjoyment of certain human rights to all inhabitants of their territories and to protect the rights of their racial, religious and linguistic minorities. These obligations were imposed by treaty and by the declarations which certain States were required to make on their admission to the League—the provisions relating to minorities being put under the guarantee of the League Council.

. . .

The League of Nations also did important work on slavery. It created a special committee to *study* the question, was responsible for the drafting of the Slavery Convention of 1926, and, when Ethiopia applied for readmission to the League, it required from her an undertaking to make special efforts to abolish slavery and the slave trade, Ethiopia recognizing that this was not a purely internal matter but one on which the League had a right to intervene.

. . .

To sum up, international law recognized, by the beginning of the Second World War, a whole series of rules and institutions . . . the effect of which was to protect the rights of individuals and groups, even though, in the dominant theory, *the individual was neither a subject of international law nor directly protected by it.* International law protected the rights of aliens through their States.

. . .

III. THE IMPACT OF THE SECOND WORLD WAR AND THE UNITED NATIONS

The Second World War and the events leading up to it was the catalyst that produced the revolutionary developments in the international law of human rights that characterize the middle twentieth century. So potent was this catalyst that it produced not only an unprecedented growth in human rights law, but the very theory of international law had to be adapted to the new circumstances. *The individual now becomes a subject of international law.* . . . He is directly protected by this law and can even in some cases seek his own remedy. And States can no longer rely on the plea of domestic jurisdiction [over its own citizens to avoid human rights obligations under International Law]. It was not only a matter of new norms being added within the confines of an existing order, but the very nature of that order had changed. What had happened was revolutionary.

The Second World War was, as no other war has ever been, a war to vindicate human rights. This was recognized by the leaders of the Grand Alliance and perhaps best expressed by President Roosevelt when, in January 1941, before the United States entered the war, he defined four freedoms: freedom of speech, freedom of worship, freedom from want, freedom from fear—"everywhere in the world." These he said, were "the necessary conditions of peace. . . ." Yet, when the *Dumbarton Oaks Proposals* [creating the blueprint for the UN] were published in the fall of 1944 they contained only the [most] general reference to human rights. The United Nations would . . . "promote respect for human rights and fundamental freedoms"—something which considering its context and the generality of the language used *hardly met the expectations of a public opinion shocked by the atrocities of the war.*

The *relatively strong human rights provisions in the Charter* . . . were largely, and appropriately, the *result of determined lobbying by non-governmental organizations* at the San Francisco Conference. Some of the countries represented at San Francisco would have accepted even stronger human rights provisions than found their way into the Charter. There was even an attempt, which failed, to incorporate in the Charter an International Bill of Rights. But the Charter did provide for the creation of a Commission on Human Rights which, as [US] President Truman said in the speech by which he closed the Conference, would, it was generally understood, draft the bill [of rights. The UN Economic and Social Council later established the Commission that drafted the ensuing UN human rights instruments].

. . .

Implementation systems created by *treaty* have the *inherent weakness* that they are *unlikely to reach those countries where human rights are the least respected* and where, therefore, they are the most needed. There is no way by which the governments of such countries can be forced to ratify the treaties. Even those governments which are the most com-

mitted to respecting human rights are cautious about committing themselves in advance to limitations on their discretionary powers; and, in the experience of the United Nations in any event, treaty provisions for implementation have been extremely limited in their scope and operation.

. . .

The principal characteristic of the twentieth century approach to human rights has been its unambiguous recognition of the fact that all human beings are entitled to the enjoyment not only of the traditional civil and political rights but also the economic, social and cultural rights without which, for most people, the traditional rights have little meaning.

. . .

The United Nations, however, has always recognized that there is a *difference between* what can be expected from States in the implementation of *economic and social rights* and in the enforcement of *civil and political rights.* The former are looked upon as programme rights, [that is, mutually agreeable principles] the implementation of which is to be progressive. This is particularly true of economically underdeveloped countries with large populations to feed, which can hardly be expected to guarantee the immediate implementation of all economic and social rights. Even highly industrialized States will hesitate before guaranteeing the right, for example, to work—on any literal interpretation of the meaning of that right.

. . .

[There is] the question of the increasing politicalization of human rights in the United Nations. Human Rights cannot, nor is it desirable that they should, be divorced from politics. To do so would be to divorce them from reality. And as a matter of fact there has always been a good deal of political controversy in the debates on human rights. . . . In recent years, however, the debates have become political to the exclusion of almost all constructive work, and one has the impression that governments are chiefly motivated by their [unrelated] conflicts with other countries. This, and *the absence of any effective public opinion capable of putting pressure on governments, has resulted in a slowing down*, in the United Nations at least, of effective work for the international promotion of respect for human rights.

The above perspective of the UN's first Human Rights Director depicts the political reasons for disparate applications of the Charter and ensuing Charter-based "fundamental" human rights. Today's so-called International Law of Human Rights —initiated by the UN—has not been adopted by all social and political systems. Thus, many States continue to assert that the scope of human rights is an internal matter, reserved exclusively for national implementation on a discretionary basis that must reflect local rather than internationally defined conditions. But as stated by the Permanent Court of International Justice, as early as 1923, and long before the post–World War II "internationalization" of human rights:

> The question whether a certain matter is or is not solely within the jurisdiction of a State is an essentially relative question; it depends on the development of international relations . . . [and] it may well happen that, in a matter which . . . is not, in principle, regulated by international law, the right of a State to use its discretion is nevertheless restricted by obligations which it may have undertaken towards

other States. In such a case, jurisdiction which, in principle, [allegedly] belongs solely to the State, is limited by the rules of international law.[3]

The study of human rights would be incomplete, if the student merely viewed the UN's global regime as the only reasonable perspective. The following analysis of human rights in distinct political regimes explains the problem with the prevailing attitude in many Western countries—that the UN's globally defined human rights regime is adaptable to *all* legal systems. The Canadian and American professors who conducted this study disagree with that premise. They contend that human rights *cannot* flourish in certain political systems, such as communist regimes (like the People's Republic of China, North Korea, and Cuba). The human rights of the individual cannot prevail in a society where the rights of the State necessarily take priority over the rights of the individual when they conflict. Internationally defined human rights are *not* common to all cultures and cannot be readily incorporated into all of the world's social and political systems:

HUMAN DIGNITY, HUMAN RIGHTS, AND POLITICAL REGIMES

80 American Political Science Review 801 (1986)*
Rhoda Howard & Jack Donnelly

We argue, however, that international human rights standards are based upon a distinctive substantive conception of human dignity. They therefore require a particular type of "liberal" regime, which may be institutionalized in various forms, but only within a narrow range of variation.

. . .

Human rights are viewed as (morally) prior to and above society and the state, and under the control of individuals, who hold them and may exercise them against the state in extreme cases.

In the areas and endeavors protected by human rights, the individual is the "king. . . ."

. . .

Communitarian societies are antithetical to the implementation and maintenance of human rights, because they deny the autonomy of the individual, the irreducible moral equality of individuals, and the possibility of conflict between the community's interests and the legitimate interests of any individual.

. . .

Communist societies obviously must violate a wide range of civil and political rights during the revolutionary transition, and necessarily, not merely as a matter of unfortunate excesses in practice. Even after communism is achieved, the denial of civil

and political rights remains necessary to preserve the achievements of the revolution. The permanent denial of civil and political rights is required by the

---

*Reprinted with permission of the *American Political Science Review*.

commitment to build society according to a particular substantive vision, for the exercise of personal autonomy and civil and political rights is almost certain to undermine that vision.

One must also acknowledge the implicit impact of a generally declining economic commitment to UN processes, discussed earlier in this book (*see* § 3.3). This diminished State commitment will likely have an adverse impact on the ability to consummate UN human rights objectives. The UN's annual human rights budget is approximately $11 million, or less than 1 percent of its regular (nonpeacekeeping) budget. But the work of the UN Commission on Human Rights *tripled* during the ten years between the early 1980s and the early 1990s. Thus, the Human Rights Commission's increased caseload has not been offset by an increased economic commitment to the UN's role in monitoring State human rights observance.

■ 11.2 UNITED NATIONS PROMOTIONAL ROLE

Historical Perspective

Prior to the creation of the UN Charter, there were a variety of impediments to the fulfillment of human rights. There was no International Bill of Human Rights. An individual had to rely on the internal law of his or her own State to remedy abuses by State actors affiliated with the

The concentration camps in Poland were the sites for implementing the Nazi government's "Final Solution." Hitler thus planned to destroy entire classes of people, including Europe's Jewish and Gypsy populations.

government. States were (and still are) reluctant to admit responsibility for human rights problems within their borders. Lack of consensus regarding the definition of the term *human rights* rendered discussion even more difficult.

During the early twentieth century, occasional bilateral treaty agreements specified what two contracting nations considered the fundamental rights of their citizens. League of Nations members occasionally expressed concern about this problem. None of its efforts, however, prevented war crimes, genocide, and the other atrocities addressed in the contemporary myriad of UN human rights treaties and declarations.

The United Nations thus inaugurated a human rights program. Members drafted a number of human rights documents, beginning with the UN Charter itself. These documents constitute what is sometimes referred to as the International Bill of Human Rights. It consists of the documents described in Exhibit 11.1. The Charter is considered the basic constitutive instrument. The 1948 Universal Declaration and the two 1966 Covenants constitute the nucleus of the International Law of Human Rights. Compared to the myriad of special-interest human rights instruments, they receive the most attention and enjoy the widest acclamation of States. Each is profiled below, as the centerpieces of modern human rights law.

International Bill of Human Rights

During World War II, the Nazi political regime totally disregarded the inherent dignity of the individual. If anything positive can be drawn from that experience, it is that this form of fascism spawned an international consensus that the dignity of the individual is *not* solely a matter of State consent. Postwar treaties, declarations, and commentaries stand as evidence of an international moral order that limits the State's discretion in the treatment of its own citizens. States have thus been restrained, although

only theoretically in the case of certain rogue regimes, in their historical discretion to exercise State power over human rights.

It has thus become increasingly difficult for modern States to successfully claim that human rights are measured only by the degree of State willingness to protect the individual. The international instruments in this section thus strengthen the position of the individual vis-à-vis the State. The 1989 Chinese massacre of pro-democratic students in Tiananmen Square, for example, still haunts the PRC in its trade relations with the US.

Any analysis of international human rights will be aided by a streamlined synopsis of the components of the "International Bill of Human Rights." The four *principal* documents in this collection are the UN Charter, the clarifying Universal Declaration of Human Rights of 1948, and the two 1966 treaty expansions—the International Covenant on Civil and Political Rights (CPR) and the International Covenant on Economic, Social and Cultural Rights (ESCR).

Some commentators view only these four documents (some even excluding the Charter) as falling within the so-called "Bill of Rights." One may also add a number of ancillary UN conventions to this cache of human rights instruments. Many of them have been "declared" by the General Assembly, and thus opened for signature as treaties. They typically address a very specific agenda that builds on the broad principles contained in the four principal UN documents.

Exhibit 11.1 illustrates the core of these UN-generated treaties and declarations forming the core of International Human Rights Law. Subsequent protocols have not been included, so as to provide an illustrative snapshot. After the following Exhibit, the materials in this section of the book highlight the essentials of the four principal documents in this series.

EXHIBIT 11.1 Selected Human Rights Agreements in Force*

Year	Title	Objective
1926 1927	Slavery, Servitude, Forced Labour and Similar Institutions and Practices[a]	Amended 1956 to avow League Nations principles
1945	United Nations Charter calls for respect and observance of "human rights . . . without distinction as to race, sex, language, or religion" (Articles 1.3 and 55c)	The basic constitution for human rights interpretation
1948	Universal Declaration of Human Rights— every organ of society to promote progressive measures for universal recognition and observance of UN Charter's human rights objectives	Clarifying declaration of essential principles of the global human rights program
1948 1951	1948 Convention on the Prevention and Punishment of the Crime of Genocide[b]	Affirm Nuremberg Principle (US became a party in *1988*)
1949 1951	Convention for the Suppression of the Traffic in Persons and of the Exploitation of the Prostitution of Others[c]	(US *not* party)
1951 1954	Convention Relating to the Status of Refugees	*See* text § 4.2 (US *not* party)
1952 1954	Convention on the Political Rights of Women[d]	
1954 1960	Convention Relating to the Status of Stateless Persons	*See* text § 4.2 (US *not* party)
1957 1958	Convention on the Nationality of Married Women[e]	(US *not* party)
1960 1962	Convention against Discrimination in Education[f]—"discrimination" includes distinctions based on race, sex, language, religion, political opinion, and economic condition	Eliminates distinctions not expressed in Charter Articles 1.3/55c (US *not* party)
1962 1964	Convention on Consent to Marriage, Minimum Age for Marriage and Registration of Marriages[g]	(US *not* party)
1965 1969	International Convention on the Elimination of All Forms of Racial Discrimination[h]	(US *not* party)

EXHIBIT 11.1 *(continued)*

Year	Title	Objective
1966 1976	International Covenant on Civil and Political Rights—treaty opened for signature, as opposed to mere declaration	(US became a party in 1992)
1966 1976	International Covenant on Economic, Social and Cultural Rights—treaty opened for signature, as opposed to mere declaration	(US *not* party)
1968 1970	Convention on the Non-Applicability of Statutory Limitations to War Crimes and Crimes Against Humanity	*See* § 10.6 (US *not* party)
1973 1976	International Convention on the Suppression and the Punishment of the Crime of Apartheid[i]	(US *not* party)
1979 1981	Convention on the Elimination of All Forms of Discrimination against Women[j]	(US *not* party)
1984 1987	Convention against Torture and Other Cruel, Inhuman or Degrading Treatment[k]	(US has signed but not ratified)
1989 1990	Convention on the Rights of the Child[l]	Protects from discrimination (US has signed but not ratified)
1989 1991	Convention Concerning Indigenous and Tribal Peoples in Independent Countries[m]	*Maintain* distinctions (US *not* party)

Exhibit Descriptive Information:
*Second date = year of entry into force
See § ___.___ in third column refers to a section of this text
IBHR = International Bill of Human Rights discussed in text in relation to UN Charter principles
US *not* party = some treaties *signed*, but not *ratified* by the United States/many States have signed, but not ratified, a number of human rights treaties
US not party to 1951 Convention; US is a party to the 1967 Protocol (*see Sale v. Haitian Centers Council* case in § 4.2)
Citations:
[a] Amendment entered into force 1957/ECOSOC Resolution 608 of 4/30/56
[b] 78 United Nations Treaty Series 277 (1951)
[c] General Assembly Resolution 260 A(III) of 12/9/48
[d] General Assembly Resolution 640(VII) of 12/20/52
[e] General Assembly Resolution 1040(XI) of 1/29/57
[f] General Conference, ECOSOC, adopted 12/14/60
[g] General Assembly Resolution 1763 A(XVII) of 11/7/62
[h] General Assembly Resolution 2106 A(XX) of 12/21/65
[i] General Assembly Resolution 3068(XXVIII) of 11/30/73
[j] General Assembly Resolution 34/180 of 12/18/79
[k] General Assembly Resolution 39/46 of 12/10/84
[l] General Assembly Resolution 44/25 of 11/20/89
[m] General Conference, International Labour Organization, adopted 6/27/89

Four Basic Instruments

UN Charter The UN Charter contains aspirational provisions designed to internationalize human rights norms. UN members incorporated a rather brief human rights statement into the Charter. It nevertheless altered the historical perception that individual rights were protected *only* under State law and not by International Law. Under Article 1.3, a basic purpose of the Charter is to "achieve international co-operation in solving international problems of an economic, social, cultural, or humanitarian character, and in promoting and encouraging respect for human rights. . . ." Article 55 of the Charter further provides that "the United Nations shall promote. . . universal respect for, and observance of, human rights and fundamental freedoms for all without distinction as to race, sex, language, or religion." Article 56 continues with the objective that all UN members therein "pledge themselves to take joint and separate action in co-operation with the Organization for the achievement of the purposes set forth in Article 55."

Contemporary instances of improper discrimination based on race, sex, and religion are all too familiar, however. For more than four decades, the white South African government would refuse to cease its State policy of discrimination against the black racial majority—contrary to the above Charter principle (as well as the Apartheid and Racial Discrimination Conventions listed in Exhibit 11.1). Even today, women in many States are not given equal pay for equal work—contrary to the Charter's principles and the Discrimination against Women Convention.

States may also bear responsibility for violating human rights on the basis of linguistic discrimination. In the mid-1960s, for example, five French-speaking towns in Belgium lodged a claim against the Belgian government, asserting that it failed to provide an education for their children in the French language. This inaction allegedly violated the UN Charter and the European Human Rights Convention prohibitions against discrimination based on language.[4]

In 1959 and 1960, an epidemic of anti-Semitism took the form of swastika-painting in Europe and Latin America. The UN's Sub-Commission on Prevention of Discrimination and Protection of Minorities condemned these manifestations of racial hatred as violations of the UN Charter. The sub-committee's work ultimately resulted in the drafting of the 1981 Declaration on the Elimination of All Forms of Intolerance and of Discrimination Based on Religion or Belief.[5]

In 1970, the General Assembly announced the Declaration on the Occasion of the Twenty-Fifth Anniversary of the United Nations (Charter entering into force). State representatives therein lauded the UN's work, while recognizing that there remained much to be done. In the words of the Assembly, "serious violations of human rights are still being committed against individuals and groups in several regions of the world."[6]

Do the human rights provisions of the UN Charter impose legally binding obligations, or are they merely a statement of goals? This question has been asked throughout the fifty-year existence of the United Nations. The answer is the same as the answer to the question whether the Charter itself imposes binding obligations. In both instances, the answer is no. The Charter, together with its human rights provisions, contains a statement of aspirational standards for all member States. Article 56, for example, contains the oath that members "pledge themselves to take joint and separate action in co-operation with the Organization" to achieve the human rights goals specified in the Charter. If this language were designed to require *immediate* steps to implement the Article 56 pledge, joining the UN would have required immediate compliance with the Charter's human rights provisions. But the Charter's provisions are broad statements of principle, requiring a State's *moral commitment* to provide these rights to its inhabitants. In 1945, many States were in shambles as a result of World War II. It was readily foreseeable that providing all such rights would be prohibitively expensive. The precise date of compliance was thus expected to vary with the respective UN members' economic, social, and political ability to fully implement the Charter's expectations. Professor Louis Henkin of Columbia University offers this explanation for including the human rights "pledge" in the Charter:

> Because, in general, the condition of human rights seemed to have little relation to the foreign policy interests of states, traditional policy-makers and diplomats tended to have little concern for the human rights movement, but neither did they see any need to court the public embarrassment of opposing it. In the

United Nations General Assembly . . . governments could take part in the . . . [human rights] process without any commitment to adhere to the final product, trying nevertheless to shape emerging international norms so that their country's behaviour would not be found wanting . . . and it might even be possible to adhere to them [human rights norms] without undue burden if that later appeared desirable.[7]

The transformation, from a moral imperative to a legal duty, may be accomplished by (a) ratifying the *global* treaties in the International Bill of Human Rights (*see* Exhibit 11.1); (b) enacting *national legislation* to implement the various UN Charter pledges regarding human rights (*see* § 11.5 of this book); and/or (c) ratifying *regional* treaties containing human rights provisions acceptable to certain UN members in a more localized context.

Thus, one could characterize the initial drafting process producing the UN Charter's human right provisions as apparently saying one thing but actually meaning another. No State would openly object to the Charter (or other components of the International Bill of Human Rights). However, no State need consider itself obliged to *act* on the above "Article 56 pledge." Each State was thus implicitly authorized to defer the decision on the "how," "what," and "when" of implementation. The UN Charter was therefore devoid of any self-executing language (*see* § 3.3 on the UN, and § 8.2 on treaty formation). No State had the legal obligation to implement the Charter's provisions by immediately guaranteeing all possible "human rights" to its citizens. In the most prominent judicial opinion in US case law, the 1952 California Supreme Court candidly analyzed the nonobligatory nature of UN Charter's human rights provisions:

It is clear that the provisions . . . are not self-executing [binding by their own terms]. They state general purposes and objectives of the United Nations Organization and do not purport to impose legal obligations on the individual member nations or to create rights in private persons. . . . Although the member nations have obligated themselves to cooperate with the international organization in promoting respect for, and observance of, human rights, it is plain that it was contemplated that future legislative action by the several nations would be required to accomplish the declared

objectives, and there is nothing to indicate that these provisions were intended to become [immediately binding] rules of law for the courts of this country upon the ratification [by the United States] of the charter.[8]

The States creating the UN had very practical reasons for characterizing the human rights provisions of the UN Charter as nonobligatory—in the *legal*, as opposed to the *moral*, sense. They did not want to accept an obligation that had not been precisely defined. Further, they did not wish to risk the embarrassment of a UN inquiry into matters that they might prefer to characterize as *national*, rather than *international*, in scope. In 1945, for example, the internal laws of the US permitted racial segregation and, in some cases, even prohibited interracial marriages. The former Soviet Union had its gulags—the forced-labor camps where individuals who resisted State policy in peaceful ways were incarcerated.[9]

Universal Declaration The other cornerstone of the UN's role in promoting human rights is the Universal Declaration of Human Rights (UDHR). This 1948 UN General Assembly Resolution was adopted without dissent, although five members of the Soviet bloc, plus Saudi Arabia and South Africa, abstained from voting either for or against it. This Declaration was the first *comprehensive* human rights document to be adopted on a global scale. The Charter's provisions were not as narrowly drawn.

The UDHR promotes two general categories of rights. The first is "civil and political rights" including the following: the right to life, liberty, and security of the person; the right to leave and enter one's own country; the prohibition of slavery and torture; freedom from discrimination, arbitrary arrest, and interferences with privacy; the right to vote; and freedom of thought, peaceable assembly, religion, and marriage. The second category of rights consists of "economic, social, and cultural rights" such as the rights to own property, to work, to maintain an adequate standard of living and health, and the right to an education.

The Declaration is also a statement of principles. Like the 1945 UN Charter's human rights provisions, the 1948 Universal Declaration does not *require* a State to provide the listed rights to its populace immediately. One reason for this limitation is that the various UN members have diverse economic bases. A poor country will not be able to give its citizens what a more developed country considers an adequate standard of living or education. UN member States were expected to accomplish the laudatory goals of the Universal Declaration at their own pace, and according to their financial ability to comply with the laudatory principles now specified in this fundamental global human rights instrument. Eleanor Roosevelt, the Chair of the United States Commission on Human Rights, and the US Representative to the UN General Assembly, expressed the sentiment of the nations proclaiming this "universal" statement of principles in 1948:

> In giving our approval to the declaration today, it is of primary importance that we keep clearly in mind the basic character of the document [the Universal Declaration of Human Rights]. It is not and does not purport to be a statement of law or of legal obligation. It is a declaration of basic principles of human rights and freedoms, to be stamped with the approval of the General Assembly by formal vote of its members, and to serve as a common standard of achievement for all peoples of all nations.[10]

While the UDHR contained only goals when adopted in 1948, a number of commentators have since characterized it as being something more. Certain jurists, including the Vice President of the International Court of Justice in 1971, commented that the human rights provisions of the Declaration have ripened into general practices that became "accepted as law." In his separate opinion in the *Namibia* case, Judge Ammoun (Lebanon) made this statement while condemning racial discrimination as a violation of the Declaration and the Charter. In his view, the degree of State observance of human rights provisions in the Charter, and especially the UDHR, ripened what were initially only moral commitments into binding obligations under *customary* International Law. In the following passage from that case, Lebanon's Judge Ammoun explained this view as follows:

> [The] Universal Declaration of Human Rights . . . stresses in its preamble that "it is essential, if man is not to be compelled to have recourse, as a last resort, to rebellion against tyranny and oppression, that human rights

should be protected by the rule of law. . . . The Court could not remain an unmoved witness in face of the evolution of modern international law which is taking place in the United Nations through the implementation and the extension to the whole world of the principles of equality, liberty and peace in justice which are embodied in the Charter and the Universal Declaration of Human Rights. By referring . . . to the Charter of the United Nations and the Universal Declaration of Human Rights, the Court [in the main opinion of the *Namibia* case] has asserted the imperative character of the right of peoples to self-determination and also of the human rights whose violation by the South African authorities it [the Court] has denounced. . . .

> The violation of human rights has not yet come to an end in any part of the world. . . . Violations of personal freedom and human dignity, the racial, social or religious discrimination which constitutes the most serious of violations of human rights . . . all still resist the currents of liberation on the five continents. That is certainly no reason why we should close our eyes to the conduct of the South African authorities. . . . Although the affirmations of the Declaration are not binding *qua* international convention [that is, not possessing legal capacity as an immediately binding treaty obligation] . . . they can bind states on the basis of custom . . . because they have acquired the force of custom through a general practice accepted as law. . . .

> The equality demanded by the Namibians and by other peoples of every colour . . . is something of vital interest here . . . because it naturally rules out racial discrimination and *apartheid*, which are the gravest of the facts with which South Africa, as also other States, stands charged. . . .

> It is not by mere chance that in Article 1 of the Universal Declaration of the Rights of Man there stands, so worded, this primordial principle or axiom: All human beings are born free and equal in dignity and rights. . . . The condemnation of *apartheid* has passed the stage of declarations and entered the phase of binding conventions.[11]

Some US commentators share Judge Ammoun's belief that certain human rights provisions of the UN Declaration are now binding under customary State practice. In 1987, a nationwide group of US judges, academicians, and government lawyers published their assessment of International Human Rights Law after years of study. Like Judge Ammoun of the International Court of Justice, they asserted that:

Almost all States are parties to the United Nations Charter, which contains human rights obligations. There has been no authoritative determination of the full content of those obligations, but it is increasingly accepted that states parties to the [UN] Charter are legally obligated to respect some of the rights recognized in the [UN] Universal Declaration. . . . It has been argued that the general pledge of the members in the Charter [to promote human rights] . . . has been made definite by the Universal Declaration, and that failure by any member to respect the rights recognized in the declaration is a violation of the Charter. Alternatively, it has been urged, the Charter, the Universal Declaration . . . and other practice of states have combined to create a customary international law of human rights requiring every state to respect the rights set forth in the Declaration [of Human Rights].[12]

One persistent criticism of the 1948 UDHR has been its "western" or "northern" derivation. It lacked input from either lesser-developed nations, or those nations with more diverse political and social viewpoints. As argued by Norway's Ashborn Eide and Iceland's Gudmundur Alfredsson (of the UN Secretariat) in 1992, however, this perspective is greatly exaggerated. In their comprehensive study of the UDHR, they depict the evolution of the UDHR as follows: "participants came from all over the world. Admittedly, there was only one participant from the African continent (Egypt). Indigenous peoples and minorities had no representation during the drafting and adoption stages. While this may be true, today the broad wording of the Declaration and its general principles together with subsequent standard-setting and implementation activities [see Exhibit 11.1] reduce the value of this statement to history.[13]

Ironically, the June 1993 Vienna World Conference on Human Rights appeared to take a step backwards in terms of *globally* defining human rights entitlements. China and Indonesia were the frontrunners in the final conference statement. It contends that western-derived human rights standards should now be tempered by "regional peculiarities and various historical, cultural and religious backgrounds." This statement, contained in the Vienna Declaration and Programme of Action,[14] may arguably diminish the efforts to eliminate barriers to the internationalization of human rights enforcement.

Philosophical debates about the scope of national human rights commitments must be juxtaposed with what nations are actually doing. The annual reports of Amnesty International (AI) furnish some insight into the actual content of State practice. AI is the most active of the private "watchdog" organizations keeping track of claimed human rights abuses throughout the world. In its 1988 report, AI observed that many UN member nations consider the 1948 Declaration of Human Rights *"subversive."* It was the first UN document to assert that individuals have a right to direct protection by the international community. That clashes with the perceived national right to freedom from international interference with matters essentially within the local jurisdiction of each sovereign State. As reported by AI:

In at least half the countries of the world, people are locked away for speaking their minds, often after trials that are no more than a sham. In at least a third of the world's nations, men, women and even children are tortured. In scores of countries, governments pursue their goals by kidnapping and murdering their own citizens. More than 120 states have written into their laws the right to execute people convicted of certain crimes, and more than a third carry out such premeditated killings every year.[15]

The UN Commission on Human Rights documented alleged cases of torture in *seventy-seven* countries during 1994. India (twenty-three deaths) and Pakistan were singled out for some of the sharpest criticism.

International Covenants In 1966, the UN General Assembly added two other core documents to the International Bill of Human Rights in the form of multilateral *treaties*: the International Covenant on Civil and Political Rights (CPR), and the International Covenant on Economic, Social and Cultural Rights (ESCR). By 1976, the minimum number of States ratified both of these treaties—meaning that they became *binding* obligations for those States. This is how they differ from the UN Charter and the Universal Declaration of Human Rights, because they are *not* mere declarations of principle.[16]

The two covenants share a number of common substantive provisions. Both restate the human rights provisions contained in the Universal Declaration. The distinguishing feature of the Covenants is that they obligate States to establish conspicuous and effective machinery for filing charges of, and dealing with, alleged violations of human rights. Article 2 of the CPR Covenant requires parties "to adopt such legislative or other measures as may be necessary to give effect to the rights recognized in the present Covenant." States must also "ensure that any persons whose rights or freedoms as herein recognized are violated shall have an effective remedy . . . determined by competent judicial, administrative or legislative authorities, or by any other competent authority provided for by the legal system of the State. . . ."

The ESCR Covenant requires the State to provide for improved living conditions for its inhabitants and to facilitate international cooperation in achieving this objective. Article 11 (and Article 28 of the Universal Declaration of Human Rights) thus provides as follows: "The States Parties to this Covenant recognize the right of everyone to an adequate standard of living for himself and his family including adequate food, clothing and housing, and to the continuous improvement of living conditions. The States Parties will take appropriate steps to ensure the realization of the right. . . ."

To monitor compliance with the CPR Covenant, and other UN guidelines, a Human Rights Committee composed of eighteen State representatives examines the periodic compliance reports that the treaty parties must submit to the UN. That Committee cannot, however, conduct its own investigations to ensure the accuracy of the reports. A separate protocol to these covenants permits *individuals* to submit their complaints directly to the Human Rights Committee. This was made possible under UN Resolution 1503 of 1970, providing the individual right to petition the UN as a basic human right. This right of petition has not been particularly successful, partially due to the difficulty of individual access that is effectively controlled by the State.

An example of an individual petition submitted to this Committee is the first that it received and "acted" on. It is also a classic example of the types of human rights entitled to protection under the International Covenant. As you read this passage, note the subjectivity of the government's basis for the arrests in this case:

REPORT OF THE HUMAN RIGHTS COMMITTEE
24 UN Monthly Chronicle 66 (June 1979)

. . .

The Committee also concluded, for the first time, consideration of a communication submitted to it by a Uruguayan national in accordance with the Optional Protocol to the International Covenant on Civil and Political Rights. Under the terms of the Protocol, individuals who claimed that any of their rights enumerated in the Covenant had been violated and who had exhausted all available remedies, might submit written communications to the Committee for consideration. The Committee, after examining the communication in question, took the view that it revealed a number of violations by Uruguay, the State Party concerned, of the Covenant provisions.

It held that the State Party was under an obligation to take immediate steps to ensure strict observance of the Covenant provisions and to provide effective remedies to the victims.

The communication was written by a Uruguayan national residing in Mexico, who submitted it on her own behalf, as well as on behalf of her husband, Luis Maria Bazzano Ambrosini, her stepfather, Jose Luis Massera, and her mother, Martha Valentini de Massera.

The author alleged, with regard to herself, that she was detained in Uruguay from 25 April to 3

May 1975 and subjected to psychological torture. She stated that she was released on 3 May 1975 without having been brought before a judge.

The author claimed that her husband, Luis Maria Bazzano Ambrosini, was detained on 3 April 1975 and immediately thereafter subjected to torture.

She also claimed that her stepfather, Jose Luis Massera, professor of mathematics and former Deputy to the National Assembly, had been arrested on 22 October 1975 and held incommunicado until his detention was made known in January 1976, and that her mother, Martha Valentini de Massera, had been arrested on 28 January 1976 without any formal charges and that in September 1976 she was accused of "assistance to subversive association," an offence which carried a penalty of two to eight years imprisonment.

. . .

The Committee decided to base its views on the following facts which had not been contradicted by the State Party. Luis Maria Bazzano Ambrosini was arrested on 3 April 1975 on the charge of complicity in "assistance to subversive association." Although his arrest had taken place before the coming into force of the International Covenant on Civil and Political Rights and of the Optional Protocol thereto, on 23 March 1976, his detention without trial continued after that date. After being detained for one year, he was granted conditional release, but that judicial decision was not respected and the prisoner was taken to an unidentified place, where he was confined and held incommunicado until 7 February 1977. On that date he was tried on the charge of "subversive association" and remained imprisoned in conditions seriously detrimental to his health.

Jose Luis Massera, a professor of mathematics and former Deputy to the National Assembly, was arrested in October 1975 and has remained imprisoned since that date. He was denied the remedy of habeas corpus [whereby a neutral judge would assess the basis for his incarceration] and another application for remedy made to the Commission on Respect for Human Rights of the Council of State went unanswered. On 15 August 1976 he was tried on charges of "subversive association" and remained in prison.

Martha Valentini de Massera was arrested on 28 January 1976. In September 1976 she was charged with "assistance to subversive association." She was kept in detention and was initially held incommunicado. In November 1976 for the first time a visit was permitted, but thereafter she was again taken to an unknown place of detention. She was tried by a military court and sentenced to three-and-a-half years imprisonment.

The Committee, acting under article 5(4) of the Optional Protocol to the International Covenant on Civil and Political Rights, took the view that those facts, in so far as they had occurred after 23 March 1976, disclosed violations of the International Covenant on Civil and Political Rights [by Uruguay].

■ NOTES

Subsequent developments suggest that the shift to civilian control of the Uruguay government had a positive impact on its observance of international human rights norms. Ten years after the Commission's consideration of this claim of human rights abuses in Uruguay (June 1989), a court in Montevideo, Uruguay, ordered Uruguay's Defense Ministry to pay the equivalent of $47 million to an electrician tortured with his own equipment for eighteen months during 1976 and 1977. This was the first time that such a judgment was rendered in Uruguay—where such incidents were commonplace during the military dictatorship of the 1970s to the mid-1980s. In 1994, UN Secretary-General Boutros-Ghali appointed a citizen of Uruguay, who was then Uruguay's Education Ambassador to the UN, to be the first UN High Commissioner for Human Rights.

Systemic Problems/Solutions

Individual Access The UN Human Rights Committee has dealt with a number of such complaints—which somehow arrived in New York from unknown locations. This is another example of the significant role played by NGOs (nongovernmental organizations) in monitoring State observance of human rights. Many of them have been denied, however, on the basis that the complaining individual did not exhaust domestic remedies, or that the same complaint was being examined by some other investigative process of either the UN or another international agency. As suggested by the above process, especially in the absence of a response from Uruguay, many States remain unwilling to submit themselves to external scrutiny in the field of human rights.[17]

The UN human rights program is apparently comprehensive and has received much publicity. Commentators argue, however, that many State participants merely "pay lip service" to these programs while their inhabitants suffer. Professor Theodore Meron of New York University presents the view that, rather than editing or somehow beefing up existing treaties, a completely *new* instrument there is needed. His perspective is as follows:

> In recent years there has been a proliferation of human rights instruments, not all of them necessary and carefully thought out. It would nevertheless appear that the international community needs a short, simple, and modest instrument to state an irreducible and non-derogable core of human rights. . . .
>
> Some might argue that a solution could be found in better implementation of the existing law, rather than in the adoption of new instruments. But attainment of an effective system to implement the existing law, rather than in the adoption of new instruments. But attainment of an effective system to implement the existing law is not probable in the near future. Neither would it help to remedy the weakness inherent in the quantity and quality of the applicable norms.[18]

There is another view. Insufficient emphasis has been placed on *individual* responsibility under International Law for serious human rights violations. The majority of human rights instruments focus on the *State* as the primary actor in need of external controls. Of course, the State is the primary actor in International Law. The State is vested with the power to control the lives of its inhabitants, and to decide which international agreements it will ratify (*see* § 8.2). Therefore, international human rights instruments obligate the State, as opposed to its citizens, not to act in ways that will deprive other individuals of their human rights. Some States are oblivious to their human rights obligations, as demonstrated by their failing to honor treaty commit-

ments or their failure to follow customary State expectations.

Rather than "starting over," as suggested above by Professor Meron, Professor Lyal Sunga's study from the Graduate Institute of International Studies at Geneva proposes supplementation of the existing regime. There should be an increased emphasis on *individual* responsibility for human rights violations. His starting point would be to establish the legal liability of individuals for serious violations in the context of the Laws of War. The Nuremberg Judgment, followed by the 1949 Geneva Conventions, appeared to do this. Dr. Sunga argues that there should be a general rule of *individual* responsibility under International Law for serious human rights violations, to supplement existing rules of *State* responsibility for such violations.[19] How to accomplish this objective remains an open question.

UN High Commissioner In December 1993, the UN General Assembly decided on a "new" solution to this aging problem of matching word and deed. It resolved to establish the post of "UN High Commissioner for the Promotion and Protection of All Human Rights," a proposal first made by Uruguay in 1951. The Commissioner is appointed by the Secretary-General, subject to approval by the General Assembly. The first Commissioner is Jose Ayala Lasso, Ecuador's Education Ambassador to the UN (appointed in 1994).[20]

The UN has a good track record, in terms of setting human rights standards through its International Bill of Human Rights. But according to the UN itself, over half the people of the world suffer some form of violation of those rights. The lack of adequate enforcement resources has made it difficult for the UN to more fully implement its stated human rights programs.

The Commissioner is expected to be the focal point for coordinating the UN's fragmented efforts to implement the rights enshrined in its numerous problem-specific treaties (*see* Exhibit 11.1). This UN official will focus on managing the UN's Center for Human Rights, at a time when economic efficiency is of utmost importance. This individual might act more swiftly and convincingly than just the overburdened Human Rights Commission, whose work tripled between the early 1980s and the early 1990s.

The task of the first UN Commissioner (from Ecuador) began with a compromise. Western States agreed to modify language that would have given the Commissioner responsibility for "elimination and prevention" of human rights violations. His task is now worded to make him play "an active role in removing the current obstacles" to the global enjoyment of human rights. This attenuated version of the Commissioner's role may ultimately relegate this office to bureaucratic obscurity.

Human Rights Police Force In 1992, Russia proposed a UN global police force for protecting human rights throughout the world. Russia's Foreign Minister to the UN, Andrei Kozyrev, made this proposal in February 1992, before the UN Human Rights Commission. In his speech, he recognized the "effectiveness of the international monitoring mechanism in the field of human rights and if need be to create new ones." The Russian minister thus proposed an independent body of moral leaders who could study a particular situation and render advisory judgments on the particular State's conduct toward its citizens.

This proposal suggested a radical change from prior Soviet doctrine. Human rights enforcement was uniformly characterized as an issue that fell within the internal affairs of the former Soviet Union—as opposed to activating the international jurisdiction of the UN. The problem with such a proposal is that the UN could thus be fairly accused of intervening in the internal affairs of the target State. It is one thing to complain in a General Assembly context. It is quite another to dispatch a UN police force, against the wishes of a member of the international community.

It is evident from the Bosnian crisis of the 1990s, where UN peacekeepers were virtual hostages, that powerful States will not risk either humanitarian intervention or any military form of commitment to human rights objectives. For example, to what degree is the most powerful State, the US, willing to risk losing trade with a State such as the People's Republic of China over human rights issues? Notwithstanding US claims about what it regards as slave labor, forced sterilization, and other human rights abuses in China, the US approach is one of first seeking economic accords rather than risking adverse international relations via public confrontations over human rights.

■ 11.3 REGIONAL HUMAN RIGHTS APPROACHES

Several *regional* human rights programs coexist with the UN program. The degree to which they have been successful, in comparison to the UN's global program, depends on the political solidarity of the particular region. This section addresses human rights initiatives in Europe, Latin America, Africa, and Asia.

European Programs

Historical Evolution The Council of Europe is an international organization composed of twenty-one Western European nations. The Council's essential goals are the maintenance of political and economic stability in Europe. Member States have characterized the preservation of individual rights as being an important method for achieving those goals. The constitution of the Council of Europe provides that each member must ensure "the enjoyment by all persons within its jurisdiction of human rights and fundamental freedoms." This provision was implemented by the creation of two human rights treaties, the European Human Rights Convention (EHR) and the European Social Charter. On ratification, the participants bound themselves to grant the rights contained in the treaties to their inhabitants.[21]

The EHR treaty contains civil rights that are virtually identical to those set forth in the United Nations Covenant on Civil and Political Rights (*see* § 11.3). The EHR treaty thus protects the rights to life, public and fair hearings, peaceful enjoyment of possessions, an education, freedom from torture or other degrading treatment, and the freedoms of thought, conscience, religion, expression, and peaceful assembly.

The European Social Charter provides for economic and social rights that are similar to those set forth in the United Nations Covenant on Economic, Social and Cultural Rights (*see* §11.3). The European Social Charter guarantees the rights to work, safe working conditions, employment protection for women and children, vocational training, and to engage in gainful occupations in the territories of other member states.

Enforcement Europe's human rights enforcement machinery consists of specialized executive and judicial institutions. The executive body is the European Commission on Human Rights, composed of one or more representatives from each member of the Council of Europe. The Commission conducts periodic conferences to monitor member State compliance. This Commission remedies human rights violations through an administrative process. If that does not succeed, the other avenue for prosecuting such claims is the European Court of Human Rights, the judicial arm of the EHR treaty. The Court hears cases arising under the EHR treaty (*see* § 9.6). The Commission and the Court are both seated with the Council of Europe in Strasbourg, France. It was this court that directed Ireland to permit a pregnant minor to leave the country for the purpose of obtaining an abortion in Great Britain, although the Irish Constitution forbade abortions under the circumstances.[22]

The existence of this comprehensive human rights machinery does not mean that the interests of the national participants always yield to the rights of the individual. For example, England's 1988 Prevention of Terrorism Act extended prearraignment detention, for those suspected of terrorism, from two to seven days. In the major national case to be prosecuted under that act, four men from Northern Ireland were held for periods of from five to *seventeen* days. They were never charged with a crime. They were unable to seek redress in the English courts and thus filed a claim in the European Court of Human Rights. The Court held that England's law permitting police to detain suspected terrorists for even seven days, without a hearing, violated the European Convention on Human Rights. The ECHR requires "prompt" access to a judicial officer after an arrest. The ECHR also provides for "an enforceable right to compensation." Rather than comply with the court's ruling, the British government announced that it would withdraw from the applicable sections of the ECHR treaty.

One difference between the UN and European human rights programs is the ability of individuals and State members of these international organizations to directly enforce human rights violations.[23] In the UN's International Court of Justice, for example, only the victim's home State may litigate claims on behalf of an individual whose rights have been violated by State action (*see* § 9.4). Under customary International Law, an individual has no capacity to institute a claim against his or her State before an international body. Under the European procedure, aggrieved individuals do *not* have to be represented by the State of their nationality in European Human Rights Commission or Court of Human Rights proceedings.

An individual may petition both of these UN and European human rights commissions with grievances against his or her home State. Unlike the more liberal UN process, however, petitions to the European Human Rights Commission can be presented *only* with the consent of the accused nation. Under Article 25 of the EHR treaty:

> The Commission may receive petitions . . . from any person, non-governmental organization or group of individuals claiming to be the victim of a violation by one of the High Contracting Parties [states that ratified the treaty] of the rights set forth in this Convention, provided that the High Contracting Party against which the complaint has been lodged has declared that it recognizes the competence of the Commission to receive such petitions. Those of the High Contracting Parties who have made such a declaration undertake not to hinder in any way the effective exercise of this right.

This article thus permits the EHR treaty signatories to defeat the right of individual petition by withholding recognition of the Commission's competence to hear individual petitions. Most States have nevertheless filed Article 25 declarations triggering the European Commission's competence to consider individual complaints against them. The few that have not vested the Commission with this power are not thereby insulated from an examination of their human rights records. Article 24 of the ECHR permits State members of the European Council to file complaints alleging a human rights violation occurring in another State.

In a case against Sweden, one of its citizens was paid a $50,000 tax settlement in 1987. Actor Max von Sydow, a US Oscar nominee, thus ended a sixteen-year dispute with Swedish tax authorities over a fine collected for alleged underpayment of his 1973 tax bill. Since von Sydow had no way to appeal the fine under Swedish law, he sued in the European Court of Human Rights. Sweden resolved this claim by returning his fine.

Under the ECHR, *any* State may pursue a remedy for another State's violation of an individual's human rights. The individual's citizenship is unimportant. This differs from the customary requirement in International Law that an individual's claim be espoused at the international level by his or her home State.

One of the most significant cases considered by the European Human Rights Commission consisted of the 1967 Scandinavian claims against Greece, filed on behalf of Greek nationals who were denied their constitutional rights by the new military government of Greece. The Greek military government had renounced the ECHR in the 1960s. The Commission responded by publishing its findings that Greece had thus violated the ECHR. Greece freed these political prisoners in 1973 and restored their individual civil rights arising under the ECHR.[24]

Oxford University Professor Mark Janis, and University of Connecticut Professor Richard Kay, have summed up the very positive impact of the European human rights approach as the paradigm for other regions of the world to consider. The region's ability to overcome national sovereignty barriers illustrates effective enforcement of International Human Rights Law:

> Nowadays, the European Court of Human Rights *regularly* finds nations in breach of their obligations under the international human rights law. . . . Remarkably, sovereign states have respected the adverse judgments of the Court . . . [and] have reformed or abandoned police procedures, penal institutions, child welfare practices, administrative agencies, court rules, labor relations, moral legislation, and many other important public matters. The willingness with which the decisions of the European Court have been accepted demonstrates the *emergence of a crucial new fact in the Western legal tradition*: an effective system of international law regulating some of the most sensitive areas of what previously had been thought to be fields within the exclusive domain of national sovereignty.[25]

CSCE Process The "Helsinki Final Act" of 1975, and its subsequent addendums, forms the latest regional human rights agreements undertaken by predominantly European nations. Thirty-five nations (now fifty-two) convened the Conference on Security and Co-operation in Europe (CSCE), meeting in Finland from 1973 through 1975 (with follow-up conferences). Driving forces for this develop-

ment were the former Soviet Union and other Warsaw Pact nations. They had pursued the concept of a regional political and security arrangement for several decades. Canada and the US were invited to participate, due to their prominent positions in NATO.[26]

The so-called *Final Act* is not a treaty in the traditional sense. It is a declaration of "Principles Guiding Relations between Participating States." Like the UN Charter and the Universal Declaration of Human Rights, it is a political statement of principles that is not independently binding. It thus provided a regional standard of achievement. The State participants decided not to commit themselves to anything other than general principles, due to a lack of consensus on the question of how to achieve regional security. The CSCE process does not consist of the small number of comparatively homogenous States that formed the European Union.

Regional security was not the only CSCE goal. The participants also intended to overcome national inertia in the region's observance of human rights. They wanted to further *implement* the stockpile of principles contained in numerous contemporary human rights documents. The fundamental human rights provision of the Helsinki Final Act is Principle VII of its Declaration of Principles. It provides that in "the field of human rights and fundamental freedoms, the participating States will act in conformity with the purposes and principles of the Charter of the United Nations and the Universal Declaration of Human Rights. They will also fulfill their obligations as set forth in the international declarations and agreements in this field, including inter alia the [1966] International Covenants on Human Rights. . . ."

International disagreement about the right to travel was one reason for the early inability of conference participants to achieve a concrete agreement on security and human rights. Certain nations, particularly the US, actively pursued implementation of the right of international travel. The US State Department issued annual reports for ten years *after* the initial 1975 CSCE conference, focusing on travel restrictions between East and West. The US vetoed the Helsinki Final Act in 1986. It denounced Eastern European travel restrictions, typified by the former "Berlin Wall," as being contrary to the human rights principles stated in the Helsinki Declaration.

The CSCE played a prominent role in monitoring the Russian assault on Chechnya, which began in 1994. In 1995, Russian President Boris Yeltsin agreed to allow a CSCE human rights mission to maintain a permanent presence in this secessionist region. Yeltsin thus assured the foreign ministers of Germany, France, and Spain—while on a mission from the European Union—that Russia was committed to a political settlement of the Chechnya crisis, to be undertaken in conformity with CSCE human rights objectives.

Latin American Programs

Human rights norms in Latin American are expressed in the Charter of the Organization of American States (OAS),[27] the American Declaration of the Rights and Duties of Man, and the American Convention on Human Rights. These norms are monitored by the Inter-American Commission on Human Rights.

The human rights provisions of the OAS Charter are contained in Articles 5 and 16. Article 5 provides that the "American States proclaim the fundamental rights of the individual without distinction as to race, nationality, creed or sex." This language is obviously drawn from Article 55c of the UN Charter (*see* § 11.2 of this text). Article 16 provides that each "State has the right to develop its cultural, political and economic life freely and naturally. In this free development, the State shall respect the rights of the individual and the principles of universal morality." The human rights provisions of the OAS Charter, like its UN counterpart, are aspirational statements of moral principles. They were designed to guide Latin American nations in their treatment of individuals, although neither charter imposes specific legal obligations.

State rights thus have priority over individual rights. The first sentence of Article 16 expresses the rights of the State. The State is thus guaranteed the right to develop "freely and naturally." The delegates to the drafting conference thereby ensured that each OAS member retained its complete sovereignty on affiliation with the OAS. The second sentence of the article says that States must also "respect the rights of the individual." This language ostensibly limits that sovereignty. The Charter is not specific, however, about the content of the rights to be respected. Nor does it express any obligation to treat the individual in a particular way.

Certain events have favorably affected the course of international human rights observance in Latin America. One was the OAS reaction to the harsh measures imposed by Cuba's revolutionary government beginning in 1959, when the Castro regime imprisoned anyone suspected of disloyalty. The OAS Inter-American Commission on Human Rights quickly conducted an international human rights investigation. Since Cuba did not allow the commission to inspect, the Commission conducted its hearings in Florida, where it interviewed Cuban refugees. The Commission found that there was a widespread suspension of the human rights implicit in the OAS Charter and the other Latin American human rights declarations discussed below. Cuba was ultimately expelled from the OAS. Yet many commentators—recognizing that similar problems occurred during the same period elsewhere in Latin America—espouse the conviction that superpower politics (related to the former Cold War) played a larger role in this expulsion than any claimed human rights abuses. Numerous military dictatorships in Latin America used similar tactics to control their people, but were not the object of such human rights scrutiny.

Another regional development suggests the potential for greater adherence to the OAS Charter promise that the "State shall respect the rights of the individual." That development has been the shift away from military to democratic governments in all Latin American countries (except Cuba). In the 1960s and the 1970s, the military dictators in this region were known for their *desaparecidos*—the "disappeared" individuals who were political or personal enemies of government officials. Many of these dictatorships exhibited little concern for human rights, and subsequently became democracies in the next decade.

This change should have had a favorable impact on human rights in a number of Latin American nations. The evidence of improvement, however, is far from conclusive. Some commentators are reservedly positive. Others believe that little has changed in Latin America after the shift from military to civilian rule. The collapse of military dictatorships during the 1980s did *not* minimize the degree of human rights violations. The following excerpt from the US-based Pacific News Service suggests why:

HUMAN RIGHTS CHALLENGE: WHY TERROR STILL PERSISTS IN LATIN AMERICAN DEMOCRACIES

Robin Kirk, Reporter
Los Angeles Daily Journal, July 14, 1987 at 4*

In Latin America today, where democracy is flourishing, terror still persists, in the form of mass arrests, disappearances, executions, and torture. No longer associated with just dictatorships like those in Chile or Paraguay, today terror exists—and is even on the rise—within democracies whose newly elected civilian governments are unable to prevent it.

The most telling clue to what sustains terror in democracies lies in Argentina where last April [1987], President Raul Alfonsin reached an accord with military officers. The accord followed protests in which some military [personnel] occupied bases to block the prosecution of fellow officers for human rights abuses committed during the 1970s.

The Argentine military functions almost like an American political party—with its own leaders, hierarchy, and civilian constituents who support it either out of blood ties or . . . the conviction that any drastic action to preserve law and order is justified. But it is a party with a difference—it has a monopoly on modern weapons and a fiercely loyal membership. Government officials have little weight with military officers, who have risen in rank because of their allegiance to generals, not to democracy.

Threatened with a coup, President Alfonsin agreed not to prosecute lower ranking officers—and to preserve democratic rule. He made a "convivencia," or "living together" [arrangement of convenience].

. . .

Nor is the convivencia unique to Argentina. Similar agreements exist in Guatemala, Peru, Columbia, Ecuador, Bolivia, El Salvador, and Uruguay, where civilian governments no longer [bother to] determine the level of human rights abuse.

In democratically ruled Guatemala, infamous secret police still "disappear" government critics—425 political assassinations were recorded by the local press in the first two months of 1987 alone, according to U.S. Embassy sources.

. . .

And death squads continue to haunt such democratically run countries as Brazil, El Salvador, and Ecuador.

. . .

For the international human rights movement, convivencias pose a formidable challenge. Even as the [human rights] movement gains new converts and worldwide prestige, it is having to rethink its traditional tactic of pressuring government bureaucracies to get abuses halted and prisoners released. Under convivencias, government officialdom no longer calls the shots on human rights.

The OAS Charter was not the only regional human rights document promulgated in 1948. That year, an international conference of Latin American States proclaimed the American Declaration of the Rights and Duties of Man. This declaration of principles contains various political and civil rights—basically the same rights as those contained in the UN's 1948 Universal Declaration of Human Rights (*see* § 11.2). The *duties* include the specific duty of the *individual* to obey the law, and a general duty to

conduct oneself in a way that serves the immediate community and the nation.

Like the UN Declaration, the rights contained in the American Declaration were not intended to immediately bind the participating Latin American States. It would have been a national embarrassment *not* to agree to such lofty human rights principles. This Declaration is yet another example of the treaty process whereby the signatories only agree to a general statement of principles. Until subsequent

---

*Reprinted with permission of the Pacific News Service, San Francisco.

ratification by the signatories, States are free to delay actual implementation of the American Declaration's human rights goals.

The most recent Latin American human rights document is the American Convention on Human Rights. In the mid-1970s, OAS members met to decide whether they should expand on the minimal human rights provisions contained in the 1948 OAS Charter (as amended in 1970) and the 1948 American Declaration of the Rights and Duties of Man. They were concerned because the latter document emphasized the duties of the individual rather than those of the State. The product of their work was the American Convention on Human Rights, which became effective in 1978. It contains many of the human rights mentioned in the UN Charter and Universal Declaration of Human Rights.

The American Convention became effective after a number of Latin American countries altered their form of government from military dictatorships to democracies. It was a written response to the excesses of the military governments of the 1960s and 1970s. Prior to 1978, the Inter-American Commission on Human Rights did not have a foundation that was traceable to any document drawn up by OAS member nations. The American Convention thus provided an express source for the Commission's power to hear and determine human rights violations. This would, in theory, confirm the Commission's power to prevent several more decades of human rights violations in Latin America. State parties should not only respect human rights. They are required "to ensure" the free and full exercise of these rights.

Certain countries (including the US) have not ratified the American Convention on Human Rights. Their rationale is that they cannot determine the extent of their commitments under the "full and free exercise of human rights" provision of the Convention. Without specific obligations being set forth in that agreement, they are unwilling to commit themselves to a process that does not more fully identify the outer parameters of the State's obligation to the individual.

Some OAS nations are reluctant to ratify the 1978 American Convention for yet another reason. A unique human rights provision was inserted into the 1978 American Convention stating that judicial remedies for certain rights cannot be suspended. The treaty right of *habeas corpus* means that prison officials can be forced to produce a prisoner for a prompt judicial examination of the legality of his or her incarceration. That right *cannot* be suspended, *even in time of emergency*.[28]

Another stumbling block to ratification of the 1978 Convention lies in the regional enforcement mechanisms. The Inter-American Commission on Human Rights and the Inter-American Court on Human Rights both predate the 1978 Convention. Neither the OAS Charter nor the American Declaration on the Rights and Duties of Man even mentions these human rights institutions, however. Under the American Convention, the Commission and the Court would be expressly vested with the power to monitor state compliance with the human rights goals of the earlier OAS agreements. Signatories would be required to respond to human rights inquiries by these institutions.

The Inter-American Commission on Human Rights encourages members to implement the human rights norms in the OAS Charter and the American Declaration of the Rights and Duties of Man. It conducts country studies and makes recommendations to member states. Latin American States are encouraged to use their national legislative processes to implement the recommendations of the Commission.

Under the American Convention on Human Rights, cases must be first considered by the Commission before they can be heard by the Court. The Commission will not normally consider a case unless the aggrieved person has sought his or her remedies in the courts of the State accused of the human rights violation. Another limitation is that individuals may present claims to the Commission, but not to the Court. After all remedies have been exhausted before the Human Rights Commission, a State party to a dispute may then lodge the matter—on behalf of the aggrieved individual—in the Inter-American Court on Human Rights (established under the 1978 Convention).

§ 9.4 of this book addressed the extent to which the UN's International Court of Justice (ICJ) could advance International Law via its advisory opinions. This facet of the Court's judicial power is typically initiated by a UN organ, when it is unlikely that the sensitivity of a particular situation will result in one or both of the disputing States agreeing to an adversarial resolution through their respective presentations of the evidence for resolution by the ICJ. In

Latin America, the ability of the Inter-American Court of Human Rights to enhance the development of human rights is not as clear. The various treaties and declarations containing human rights provisions do not expressly provide that the Court can address regional human rights problems without the express consent of member States of the Organization of American States. In 1988, this question was squarely presented by a petition to the Court, and member States of the OAS. The Court's ensuing 1989 decision, dealing with its ability to aid in the regional protection of human rights, appears immediately below.

Colombia requested an advisory opinion regarding, first, whether the Court has the jurisdiction to interpret the American Declaration; and, second,

the scope of its ability to interpret the Declaration in future human rights cases. Written comments were requested from all OAS member States. The Court, sitting in San Jose, Costa Rica, received responses from Costa Rica, Peru, Uruguay, the US, and Venezuela.

Costa Rica, the US, and Venezuela responded with their views that the Court did *not* have the authority to interpret this expression of human rights in the Americas—because it is not a treaty. Peru and Uruguay disagreed. Their view was that the *juridical* nature of the American Declaration is such that the Court has authority to render advisory opinions on its proper interpretation. Otherwise, the region's human rights provisions would be meaningless.

INTERPRETATION OF THE AMERICAN DECLARATION OF RIGHTS AND DUTIES OF MAN WITHIN THE FRAMEWORK OF ARTICLE 64 OF THE AMERICAN CONVENTION ON HUMAN RIGHTS

Advisory Opinion OC-10/89
Inter-American Court of Human Rights, 1989
29 International Legal Materials 379*

[*Author's Note: The first issue for the Court was whether it possessed the jurisdiction to interpret a 1948 Organization of American States Declaration concerning human rights. Unlike the 1978 OAS treaty concerning human rights, the earlier Declaration at issue in this case was not a treaty. The Court nevertheless determined that the Declaration's "juridical" or legal nature, in relation to the later treaty (American Convention), did establish legal norms—thus vesting this international human rights court with the requisite authority (a) to interpret the Declaration, and (b) to define how it applies to OAS member States.*

As you read the following opinion, consider the varied characterizations of the Declaration by the OAS member governments that responded to the OAS request for State interpretations to aid the Court in its opinion.

The numbered paragraphs are those of the Court. Citations have been omitted, and emphasis has been supplied, in certain passages of this edited opinion.]

[*Opinion.*] 1. . . . [T]he Government of the Republic of Colombia (hereinafter "the Government") submitted to the Inter-American Court of Human

Rights (hereinafter "the Court") a request for an advisory opinion on the interpretation of Article 64 of the [1978] American Convention on Human Rights (hereinafter "the Convention" or "the American Convention") in relation to the [1948] American Declaration of the Rights and Duties of Man (hereinafter "the Declaration" or "the American Declaration").

2. The Government requests a reply to the following questions:

Does Article 64 [*see* paragraph 20 below] authorize the Inter-American Court of Human Rights to render advisory opinions at the request of a member state or of one the organs of the OAS, regarding the interpretation of the American Declaration of the Rights and Duties of Man, adopted by the Ninth International Conference of American States in Bogota in 1948?

The Government adds:

The Government of Colombia understands, of course, that the [1948] Declaration is not a treaty. But this conclusion does not automatically answer the question. It is perfectly

---

reasonable to assume that the interpretation of the human rights provisions contained in the [1948] Charter of the OAS . . . involves, in principle, an analysis of the rights and duties of man proclaimed by the [1948] Declaration, and thus requires the determination of the normative status of the Declaration within the legal framework of the inter-American system for the protection of human rights.

The applicant government points out that

(1) for the appropriate functioning of the inter-American system for the protection of human rights, it is of great importance to know what the juridical status of the Declaration is, whether the Court has jurisdiction to interpret the Declaration, and if so, what the scope of its jurisdiction is within the framework of Article 64 of the Convention.

. . .

I

11. In its written observations, the Government of *Costa Rica* believes that notwithstanding its great success and nobility, the American Declaration of the Rights and Duties of Man is not a treaty as defined by international law, so Article 64 of the American Convention does not authorize the Inter-American Court to interpret the Declaration. Nevertheless, that could not in any way limit the Court's possible use of the Declaration and its precepts to interpret other, related juridical instruments or a finding that many of the rights recognized therein have become international customary law.

12. The Government of the *United States* of America believes The American Declaration of the Rights and Duties of Man represents a noble statement of the human rights aspirations of the American States.

Unlike the American Convention, however, it was not drafted as a legal instrument and lacks the precision necessary to resolve complex legal questions. Its normative value lies as a declaration of basic moral principals and broad political commitments and as a basis to review the general human rights performance of member states, not as a binding set of obligations.

The United States recognizes the good intentions of those who would transform the American Declaration from a statement of principals into a binding legal instrument. *But good intentions do not make law.* It would seriously undermine the process of international lawmaking—by which sovereign states voluntarily undertake specified legal obligations—to impose legal obligations on states through a process of "reinterpretation" or "inference" from a nonbinding statement of principles.

13. For its part, the Government of *Peru* said that although the Declaration could have been considered an instrument without legal effect before the American Convention on Human Rights entered into force, the *Convention* has recognized its special nature by virtue of *Article 29*, which prohibits any interpretation "excluding or limiting the effect that the American Declaration of the Rights and Duties of Man and other international acts of the same nature may have" and *has thus given the Declaration a hierarchy [as a source of law] similar to that of the Convention* with regard to the States Parties, thereby contributing to the promotion of human rights in our Continent.

14. The Government of *Uruguay* affirmed that

i) The Inter-American Court of Human Rights is competent to render advisory opinions on any aspect of the American Declaration of the Rights and Duties of Man in relation to the revised Charter of the Organization of American States and the American Convention on Human Rights, within the scope of Article 64 of the latter.

ii) The juridical nature of the Declaration is that of *binding, multilateral instrument* that enunciates, defines and specifies fundamental principles recognized by the American States and which *crystallizes norms of customary law generally accepted by those States.*

15. The Government of *Venezuela* asserted that

as a general principle recognized by international law, a declaration is not a treaty in the true sense because it does not create juridical norms, and it is limited to a statement of desires or exhortations. A *declaration creates political or moral obligations for the subjects of international law*, and its *enforceability* is *thus limited in contrast to a treaty*, whose legal obligations are enforceable before a jurisdictional body.

. . .

III

19. The Court will first examine the admissibility of the instant advisory opinion request [that is, whether the Court has the jurisdiction to hear and determine Colombia's application for an advisory opinion].

20. Article 64(1) provides:

The member states of the Organization may consult the Court regarding the interpretation of this Convention or of other treaties concerning the protection of human rights in the American states. Within their spheres of competence, the organs listed in Chapter X of the Charter of the Organization of American States . . . may in like manner consult the Court.

. . .

28. The Court holds that it has the requisite competence to render the present request advisory opinion and therefore rules it to be admissible. [This was the *procedural* hurdle.]

IV

29. The Court will now address the merits [of the *substantive* legal] question before it [having ruled that it has the jurisdiction to determine such matters].

30. Article 64(1) of the Convention authorizes the Court to render advisory opinions "regarding the interpretation of this Convention or of other *treaties* concerning the protection of human rights in the American states."

. . .

33. In attempting to define the word "treaty" as the term is employed in Article 64(1), it is sufficient for now to say that a "treaty" is, at least, an international instrument of the type that is governed by the two Vienna Conventions [*see* § 8.1]. . . . What is clear . . . is that the *Declaration is not a treaty* as defined by the Vienna Conventions because it was not approved as such, and that, consequently, it is also not a treaty within the meaning of Article 64(1) [of the 1978 American Human Rights Convention].

34. . . . *In order to obtain a consensus, the Declaration was conceived as the initial system of protection* considered by the American States as being suited to the present social and juridical conditions, not without a recognition on their part that they should increasingly strengthen that system in the international field as [political and economic] conditions become more favorable. ([1948] American Declaration, Considerandum 4).

This same principle was confirmed on September 25, 1949, by the Inter-American Committee of Jurisconsults, when it said:

It is evident that the [American] Declaration of Bogota does not create a contractual juridical obligation, *but it is also clear that it demonstrates a well defined orientation toward the international protection of the fundamental rights of the human person.*

35. The mere fact that the Declaration is not a treaty does not necessarily compel the conclusion that the Court lacks the power to render an advisory opinion containing an *interpretation* of the American Declaration.

36. In fact, the [1978] American Convention refers to the [1948 American] Declaration in paragraph three of its [Convention] Preamble which reads as follows:

Considering that these principles have been set forth in the *Charter* of the Organization of the American States, in the *American Declaration* of the Rights and Duties of Man, *and in the [UN's 1948] Universal Declaration* of Human Rights, and that they have been reaffirmed and defined in other international instruments, worldwide as well as regional in scope.

And in [treaty] Article 29(d) which indicates:

No provision of this convention shall be interpreted as:

. . .

d. *excluding or limiting the effect that the American Declaration* of the Rights and Duties of Man and other international acts of the same nature *may have.*

From the foregoing, it follows that, in interpreting the Convention in the exercise of its advisory jurisdiction, the Court may have to [thus] interpret the Declaration.

37. The American Declaration has its basis in the idea that "the international protection of the rights of man should be the principal guide of an evolving American law" (Third Considerandum). This American law has evolved from 1948 to the present; international protective measures, subsidiary and complementary to national ones, have been shaped by new instruments. As the International Court of Justice said: "an international instrument must be interpreted and applied within the overall framework of the juridical system in force at the time of the interpretation." That is why the [Inter-American] Court finds it necessary to point out that to determine the legal status of the American Declaration it is appropriate to look to the inter-American system of *today* in the light of the evolution it has undergone since the adoption of the Declaration, rather than to examine the normative value and significance which that instrument was believed to have had in 1948.

38. The evolution of the here relevant "inter-American law" mirrors on the regional level the developments in contemporary international law and especially in human rights law, which distinguished that law from classical international law to a significant extent. That is the case, for example, with the duty to respect certain essential human rights, which is *today* [a duty that also empowers international courts to use pretreaty declarations of intent to interpret current human rights obligations]. . . .

39. The Charter of the Organization refers to the fundamental rights of man in its Preamble and in [various] Articles, but it does not list or define them. The member states of the Organization have, through its diverse organs, given specifically [specificity] to the human rights mentioned in the Charter and to which the Declaration refers.

. . .

41. These norms authorize the Inter-American Commission to protect human rights. *These rights are none other than those enunciated and defined in the American Declaration.* That conclusion results form Article 1 of the Commission's Statute, which was approved by Resolution No. 447, adopted by the General Assembly of the OAS at its Ninth Regular Period of Sessions, held in La Paz, Bolivia, in October, 1979. That Article reads as follows:

1. The Inter-American Commission on Human Rights is an organ of the Organization of American States, created to promote the observance and defense of human rights and to serve as consultive organ of the Organization in this matter.

2. For the purpose of the present Statute, *human rights are understood to be*:

a. The rights set forth in the American Convention on Human Rights, in relation to the States Parties thereto;

b. The *rights set forth in the American Declaration* of the Rights and Duties of Man, in relation to the other member states.

. . .

42. The *General Assembly* of the Organization has also *repeatedly recognized* that the *American Declaration is a source of international obligations for the member states of the OAS*. For example, in resolution 314 (VII-0/77) of June 22, 1977, it charged the Inter-American Commission on Human Rights with the preparation of a study to "set forth their obligation to carry out the *commitments assumed in the American Declaration* of the Rights and Duties of Man." In Resolution 371 (VIII-0/78) of July 1, 1978, the General Assembly reaffirmed "its commitment to promote the observance of the American Declaration of the Rights and Duties of man," and in Resolution 370 (VIII-0/78) of July 1, 1978, it referred to the "*international commitments*" of a member state of the Organization to respect the rights of man "*recognized in the American Declaration* of the Rights and Duties of Man." The Preamble of the American Convention to Prevent and Punish Torture, adopted and signed at the Fifteenth Regular Session of the General Assembly in Cartagena de Indias (December, 1985), reads as follows:

Reaffirming that all acts of torture or any other cruel, inhuman, or degrading treatment or punishment constitute an offense against human dignity and a denial of the principles set forth in the Charter of the Organization of American States and in the Charter of the United Nations and are violations of the fundamental human rights and freedoms proclaimed in the American Declaration of the Rights and Duties of Man and the Universal Declaration of Human Rights.

43. Hence it may be said that by means of an authoritative interpretation, the member states of the Organization have signaled their agreement that the Declaration contains and defines the fundamental human rights referred to in the Charter. Thus *the Charter of the Organization cannot be interpreted and applied as far as human rights are concerned without relating* its norms, consistent with the practice of the organs of the OAS, *to the corresponding provisions of the Declaration.*

44. In view of the fact that the *Charter* of the Organization *and* the American *Convention are treaties* with respect to which the Court has advisory jurisdiction by virtue of Article 64(1), it follows that the Court is authorized . . . to interpret the American Declaration and to render an advisory opinion relating to it whenever it is necessary to do so in interpreting those instruments.

. . .

■ NOTES & QUESTIONS

1. The Court decided that it was competent to render this advisory opinion. Having done so, what did the Court actually decide?

2. During 1994, the OAS promulgated two new human rights instruments: (1) the Inter-American Convention on Forced Disappearance of Persons; and (2) the Inter-American Convention on the Prevention, Punishment and Eradication of Violence Against Women. *See 23 Int'l Legal Mat'ls* 1529 and 1534 (1994). The OAS is taking important steps toward eliminating the historical characterization of Latin America as a region of the world where States are committed—*only* in principle—to the international rule of law in human rights matters.

African Programs

The Organization of African Unity (OAU) is Africa's political organization of States (*see* § 3.5). The 1963 OAU Charter reaffirms the human rights principles of the UN Charter and the UN's Universal Declaration of Human Rights. It adds certain rights not contained in those documents, such as the rights to the "eradication of colonialism" and to the well-being of the African people.

Like other regional human rights documents, the OAU Charter provisions are moral rights that exist on paper awaiting implementation. As stated by Professor U.O. Umozurike of Nigeria's University of Calabar in 1983:

During the 1970s human rights appeared to enjoy low esteem in Africa. . . . The O.A.U. maintained an indifferent attitude to the suppression of human rights in a number of independent African states by *unduly emphasizing the principle of noninterference in the internal affairs of member states* at the expense of certain other principles, particularly the customary law principle of respect for human rights. . . . For instance, the massacres of thousands of Hutu [tribes people] in Burundi in 1972 and 1973 were neither discussed nor condemned by the O.A.U., which regarded them as matters of [Burundi's] internal affairs. The notorious regimes of Idi Amin of Uganda

(1971–1979) [and other African leaders] escaped the criticism of the O.A.U. and most of its members. . . .[29]

In his 1993 treatise on International Law, Professor Umozurike characterized the positive potential of the Banjul (African) Charter on Human and Peoples' Rights—which entered into force in 1986. It contains rights like those in the above UN's 1966 Covenants (*see* § 11.2). A number of those rights can be derogated by law, however, without any significant limitations on the State parties. While the African Charter thus internationalizes human rights on the African Continent, "there are practically no effective measures for enforcement."[30]

The analysis of African perspectives would be incomplete without acknowledging the distrust of *internationally* derived human rights values. Some African scholars perceive these "global" rights as yet another attempt to impose western cultural values on the African Continent. Professor T.W. Bennett of the University of Cape Town summarizes this position in his 1991 study of human rights in southern Africa (just prior to South Africa's cessation of minority white political governance):

The talk about human rights that currently permeates discussions about South African law has its origins in the [external] international and constitutional human rights movement.

The universality claimed for this movement should not obscure its actual cultural provenance. Although the accession of many developing countries to United Nations' declarations and international [human rights] conventions gives a superficial impression of universalism, human rights are the product of bourgeois western values. In many parts of Africa this has given cause for suspicion about a renewed attempt to impose western cultural hegemony.

[The author then refutes the argument that human rights are irrelevant to the situation in Africa, with counterarguments including the following:] . . . Feminist studies, for instance, have revealed that women used to be assured of material protection and support within the framework of the extended family; after the introduction of capitalism, however, the system of labour migration caused the breakdown of this family structure to the detriment of women (amongst others). They have now been rendered vulnerable, and at the same time forced to undertake roles (for which they have no formal legal powers) that were previously prescribed for all men.[31]

Like Latin America's 1948 American Declaration on the Rights and Duties of Man, the 1986 African Charter focuses on a number of *duties*. The individual thus has duties to preserve family, society, the State, and even the OAU. For example, individuals must care for their parents and always conduct themselves in a way that "preserves social and national solidarity."

The expression of these duties in Africa's human rights charter may be misused by a national leader. Idi Amin suppressed individual rights in Uganda, leading to thousands of citizens' being killed or jailed without just cause in the 1970s. While no human rights document would mean anything to a leader like Amin, the 1986 African Charter conveniently emphasized *duties*, rather than the minimal rights denied to Ugandans under Amin. As stated by Professor Umozurike, the "concept of duties stressed in the Charter is quite likely to be abused by a few regimes on the continent, if the recent past can be any guide to future developments. Such governments will emphasize the duties of individuals to

their states but will play down their rights and legitimate expectations."[32]

The 1986 African Charter also established the African Commission on Human Rights. This Commission is an eleven-member body composed of representatives from the fifty-two member nations of the OAU. The Commission, seated in Bangul, Gambia, is supposed to promote national observance of human rights on the African Continent. Like the Inter-American Commission on Human Rights, the African commission may only study, report, and recommend. It has no enforcement powers. It conducts country studies and makes recommendations to member governments. The Commission has the power to publish its reports when it concludes that an OAU State has violated the human rights provisions of the African Charter. This Commission's very existence represents a significant aspirational improvement after centuries of slave trade, colonialism, and despotic regimes. But no regional mechanism has been able to halt egregious human rights violations exemplified by the Rwandan slaughter of 1994.

If one were to characterize the Commission's power of publication of negative reports as a voice for enforcing human rights in Africa, that voice may be easily silenced. Individuals and States may report violations of the African Charter to the commission. The Commission then explores the basis for such claims, drafts confirming reports, and may publish them in all OAU countries. The allegedly offending nation's leader, however, may avoid that negative publicity by requesting a vote from the OAU Assembly (Africa's heads of State) to block publication. Since its creation, the Commission has not published one adverse report of mistreatment of individuals by an OAU member State.

Asian Perspectives

A number of Chinese scholars have expressed the perception that the existing International Law of Human Rights is a pretext for intervention in the internal affairs of socialist nations. They believe that the field of human rights is primarily a matter governed by the internal law of a State, rather than one falling within the competence of International Law. Any pressure to make China use Western standards in the treatment of its citizens would be considered an interference with the internal affairs of China. The Chinese were quite offended, for example, when the 1989 government restraints on the democratic student uprisings in Beijing were characterized in the Western press as a return to Maoist-era restrictions on internationally recognized human rights.

As verbalized by one Chinese scholar from the earlier "Maoist" era, human rights are intact in China—without any need of the global approach expressed in the UN's International Bill of Human Rights. The elimination of private ownership of property, for example, is perceived as a guarantee of the genuine realization of human rights of the Chinese people. As stated by Professor Ch'ien Szu, the "rights of landlords and bourgeoisie arbitrarily to oppress and enslave laboring people are eliminated; the privilege of imperialism and its agents to do mischief . . . is also eliminated. To the vast masses of people, this is a wonderfully good thing; this is genuine protection of the human rights of the people. The bourgeois . . . international law scholars, however, consider this to be a bad thing, since it encroaches upon the 'human rights' of the oppressors and exploiters."[33]

Contemporary human rights perspectives are not solely State-oriented as in previous eras. Hong Kong, for example, incorporated the UN Covenant on Civil and Political Rights into its domestic law after the close of the Cold War (at least through 1997). The 1991 Bill of Rights Ordinance thus made the UN Covenant the essential source of human rights law in Hong Kong. Also, in the aftermath of the Cultural Revolution of 1966–1976, Professor Szu's perspective would no longer be representative of more recent Chinese scholarship on human rights. Contemporary thought is that the way in which one country or group establishes a human rights model is not necessarily the sole criterion for judging the performance of other countries. Chinese citizens enjoy far greater human rights protection now than in the Mao era.[34]

Scholars in Asia's *democratic* States have a different criticism of what they characterize as arrogant Western human rights standards. Indian scholars, for example, believe that the Western-derived concepts of human rights—stated in the UN Charter and the various regional programs modeled after the Charter—benefit only developed States. Thus, the UN's international human rights program has little meaning for a State whose people do not all have the basic necessities of life. As articulated by Dean Hingorini of India's Patna University, traditional

"human rights have no meaning for these States and their peoples. Their first priority is [obtaining] basic necessities of life. These are bread, clothing and shelter. These necessities of life could be termed as basic human rights for them."[35]

Dean Hingorini's perspective does not mean that Indian scholars *oppose* the human rights principles set forth in the various UN and regional charters. Rather, his perspective is that many of those political and economic rights are—for the time—irrelevant, and thus of little practical value to the people of India today. Attaining the rights expressed in the UN model cannot take precedence over India's need to first provide more basic rights to its populace. The more-developed nations can afford to be the champions of political and economic human rights, such as the rights to work and an education. Developed nations proclaim the importance of such rights for the convenient purpose of ensuring that their multinational corporations can exploit the Indian masses. As articulated by Professor S.B.O. Gutto of India:

> Historical developments in the Third World countries in the last few decades have firmly fashioned the Third World as theaters for the violation of human rights. . . . Classical international law, under the umbrella of 'law of nations' developed as a major super-structural tool for facilitating and justifying the actions of some states and their agents, in ensuring the dominant economic classes and institutions, and in dividing the world into spheres where . . . enslavement, dehumanization, super-exploitation of peoples labour and resources takes place. The unsatisfactory condition of human rights in the Third World today is therefore not solely a reflection of inherent social factors in the Third World but rather products of the historical relations in the world system corresponding to the international division of labor.[36]

The degree of national economic development may thus be correlated to the degree of affordable human rights enjoyed by a nation's populace. A high percentage of unemployment may be characterized as the State's failure to afford the right to work, for example. An underdeveloped country like India is not economically equipped to create and implement such human rights, or to establish commissions to monitor human rights observance. Such countries must first achieve a comparatively minimal degree of economic development. Professor T.O. Elias of India, formerly a judge of the International Court of Justice, published the following assessment of this correlation when he described the 1964 Seminars on Human Rights in Developing Countries conducted in Kabul, Afghanistan: "the existence of adequate material means and a high standard of economic development were essential prerequisites of the full and effective enjoyment of economic, social and cultural rights, and contributed to the promotion of civil and political rights. . . . [T]he right to work was meaningless in countries where employment opportunities were grossly inadequate owing to overpopulation combined with economic underdevelopment."[37]

Under this view, a poor and undeveloped economy simply cannot afford the package of human rights espoused by the more-developed nations. Any attempt to implement Western political and economic rights would detract less-developed nations from other national priorities. They must necessarily delay realization of these "advanced" rights contained in the Western human rights documents until the far more "basic" human rights to food and adequate living conditions are first realized.

The apparent drawback of this "Third World" human rights perspective is that the State can continue to rely on economic grounds to indefinitely postpone implementation of globally recognized human rights. The State could thus characterize the right to food as too important to justify national attention to rights to vote or to be free from imprisonment without due process of law.

■ 11.4 OTHER HUMAN RIGHTS ACTORS

The previous sections of this chapter addressed the global and regional efforts of international organizations to secure the human rights of the individual. Other human rights organizations and entities also act as advocates. The most common are the privately constituted nongovernmental organizations (or NGOs). They have undertaken the rather daunting task of setting the tone for the national observance of international human rights norms—when many State actors pay only lip service. The State-centric system of International Law thus brands them as "*non*governmental" institutions, notwithstanding their function of ascertaining and disseminating grass roots human rights concerns to governments and international organizations such as the UN.

A State may, of course, incorporate human rights norms into its local laws. The Hong Kong Bill of Rights is one example (*see* § 11.3). Israel's State Ministry of Justice has a Human Rights Department that is responsible for responding to concerns (usually raised by NGOs) regarding the status of human rights enforcement in Israel. US legislation addressed in the next section of this book is an example of national programs addressing human rights abuses in *other* States—in circumstances where the US is willing to take appropriate enforcement action or provide a forum for dispute resolution.

States sometimes attempt to collaborate with one another, in order to achieve the human rights objectives of the International Bill of Human Rights. In mid-1993, for example, 167 State representatives convened the Second UN World Human Rights Conference in Vienna. Their work product was the "Vienna Declaration and Programme of Action."[38] Two key objectives were the creation of both an International Criminal Court and the Office of the UN High Commissioner for Human Rights (*see* § 9.5 & § 11.2). While the primary credit for these developments in the Law of Human Rights goes to other institutions—the UN's International Law Commission for the Court, which initiated its operation in 1993, and the UN General Assembly for the High Commissioner, who commenced service in 1994—this 1993 human rights conference provided a spark that helped kindle the fervor for enforcement apparatus.

Unfortunately, there were evident limitations on what States were willing to accomplish. It initially appeared that the 1993 World Human Rights Conference would serve as a catalyst for the nongovernmental organization movement. One-thousand five-hundred NGOs sent representatives. The UN ousted them, however, from the drafting of the Conference's resulting Vienna Declaration and Programme for Action. The more powerful NGOs such as Amnesty International bitterly protested. But China's threatened boycott succeeded in convincing the UN to bar NGOs from participation. China's perspective is that the UN does not need NGOs. The PRC's position reflects that of a number of Asian States. They perceive Western States as attempting to impose their religious and cultural values, under UN authority, when they denounce human rights abuses in politically targeted regions or countries. The NGOs responded by accusing the UN of bowing to such pressures, thus retarding the achievable degree of accountability for human rights violations.

These private organizations have nevertheless played a very critical role in human rights monitoring. The International Red Cross is one of the most prominent. Its efforts included relentless pressure for internationalizing the Laws of War (*see* § 10.6). The most important result has been the 1949 Geneva Conventions, and their Protocols, dealing with the treatment of civilians and prisoners during time of war (*see* Exhibit 10.3). The Red Cross is the NGO that routinely inspects various national detention centers holding political prisoners, so that inmates might receive medical and other basic necessities.

Amnesty International (AI) is probably the most prominent "watchdog" group. This NGO has offices and individual members throughout the world. AI produces annual reports on national compliance with the various human rights treaties and declarations on human rights. It is one of the many private monitors that publicize the human rights problems discussed in this chapter.

The major human rights NGOs enjoy consultative status in various international organizations including the Council of Europe, the OAS, and UNESCO (UN). Their representatives may thus present reports to these organizations as a means of maintaining public scrutiny of offending State practices. The Civil Liberties Organization of Nigeria, for example, reported that fifty-four detainees in a single prison in Lagos died during the first six months of 1988 while awaiting trial. This group filed a class-action lawsuit in Nigeria in 1989, challenging the incarceration of seventy other prisoners who had been detained without a trial for periods from three to ten years.

The major human rights NGOs include the following:

- Amnesty International (London)

- Canadian Human Rights Foundation (Montreal)

- Civil Liberties Organization (Nigeria)

- Committee for the Defense of Democratic Freedoms and Human Rights in Syria (Damascus)

- Human Rights Watch (New York)

- International Association of Democratic Lawyers (Brussels)

- International Commission of Jurists (Geneva)

- International Committee of the Red Cross (Geneva)

- International Federation for the Rights of Man (Paris)

- International Helsinki Federation for Human Rights (Vienna)

- International League for Human Rights (New York)

- Lawyers Committee for Human Rights (New York)

- Punjab Human Rights Organization (Chandigarh)[39]

■ 11.5 UNITED STATES RATIFICATION/ LEGISLATION

This section of the book focuses on several centerpieces of US human rights policy: first, the US Senate's dilemma with ratifying the relevant regional and global human rights treaties identified earlier in this chapter; second, US military and economic incentives for improving human rights via its foreign assistance policy; and third, US judicial perspectives on the availability of a forum for resolving human rights disputes arising in other countries.

Treaty Participation Dilemma

The US is not a party to a number of international human rights instruments (*see* Exhibit 11.1 in § 11.3). Ratification has typically taken decades. The Senate did not ratify the 1948 Genocide Convention until 1986. It did not ratify the 1966 International Covenant on Civil and Political Rights until 1992. The US is not a party to the International Convention to Eliminate All Forms of Racial Discrimination, nor the American Convention on Human Rights, nor a number of such treaties (*see* Exhibit 11.1 in § 11.3). While a number of *bilateral* treaties with other countries contain human rights provisions, the US has not been willing to generally ratify *multilateral* agreements. Why?

One perspective is that—at the time of the 1945 UN Charter, the 1948 Universal Declaration of Human Rights (global), and the 1948 American Convention on Human Rights (regional)—racial discrimination was permitted or mandated in the US. Thus, many southern Senators were not willing to embrace the postwar wave of UN human rights instruments. They feared that they would subject the US to embarrassing international inquiries based on noncompliance with certain human rights instruments. This form of discrimination was not limited to the South. As asserted by US Supreme Court Justice Black in 1948, the majority opinion in that particular case ignored the UN Charter's human rights provisions. The US Supreme Court's other judges allowed a state of the US to legally discriminate against Japanese citizens residing in the US. Aliens were thereby prohibited from owning land under California law. In Justice Black's words:

> California should not be permitted to erect obstacles designed to prevent the immigration of people whom Congress has authorized to come into and remain in the country. . . . [I]ts law stands as an obstacle to the free accomplishment of our policy in the international field. One of these reasons is that we have recently pledged ourselves to cooperate with the United Nations to 'promote . . . universal respect for, and observance of, human rights and fundamental freedoms for all without distinction as to race, sex, language, or religion.' How can this nation be faithful to this international pledge if state laws which bar land ownership and occupancy by aliens on account of race are permitted to be enforced?[40]

It was not until 1954 that the US Supreme Court decided *Brown v. Board of Education*—whereby "separate but equal facilities" were, for the first time, characterized as unconstitutional under US law. *De facto* racial discrimination did not end with *Brown*. Governmental agencies continued to struggle with the full implementation of *Brown* and its progeny.

At the same time, Ohio's Senator John Bricker sought an amendment of the US Constitution's treaty power that would have eliminated the president's executive agreement power (*see* § 8.3 of this book). If successful, that measure would have required the president to obtain the "Advice and Consent of the Senate" for *all* treaties—not just the ones that the executive branch perceived as falling within the meaning of this constitutional phrase. The senator's underlying fear was the California *Sei Fujii* case (*see* text of this case in § 8.1). The trial court had just ruled against discriminatory land laws barring alien ownership, which could be upheld by the US Supreme Court or impacted by a presidential executive agreement without input from Congress (neither of which occurred). In the meantime, Senator Bricker relentlessly expressed his concern that numerous state and federal laws might fall, in the wake of presidential agreements that the Senate would not be able to bar or control.[41]

In the 1960s and 1970s, Presidents Kennedy and Carter submitted various human rights treaties to the US Senate for its Advice and Consent. Few, however, were ratified. The Genocide Convention was ratified during the Reagan years, but not without significant concern about how it might later haunt the US. Like most multilateral instruments, it is broadly worded with rather general principled statements.

A new constitutional concern supplanted the internal balance of power concerns of Senator Bricker. Threats to the constitutionally protected right to freedom of speech emerged as the contemporary argument for opposing US ratification of human rights treaties. Under US law, treaties cannot override the Constitution (*see* § 9.8). Thus, a variety of international provisions might require the US to abandon its staunchly ingrained judicial posture—that the US Constitution cannot be overcome by a treaty. When the US Senate finally ratified the 1948 Genocide Convention forty years after the UN General Assembly's unanimous adoption, it did so on the basis of its reservation providing that "nothing in the [Genocide] Convention requires or authorizes legislation or other action by the United States of America as interpreted by the United States."

This Convention, like a number of other human rights instruments, contains wording that essentially prohibits racial or religious hatred constituting an incitement to discrimination of any kind. In 1978, for example, the American Civil Liberties Union successfully litigated the First Amendment right of Neo-Nazis to parade in Skokie, Illinois—complete with swastikas.[42] Assuming that the US had ratified the Genocide Convention at the time of that march (absent an appropriate reservation), the judicial approval and city-issued permit for this march might have subjected the US to international responsibility for government-approved activity inciting religious hatred.

The question of whether ratification of human rights treaties would yield unintended State responsibility for violations is not limited to free speech concerns. Rationales include the following. (1) Many States of the world advocate abolition of the death penalty.[43] Many states of the US, however, punish certain crimes by imposing a death penalty. This would arguably subject the US to criticism, based on the developing State practice condemning the death penalty. (2) US President Clinton discouraged the 1994 flogging of Michael Fay, an eighteen-year-old US citizen convicted of vandalism in Singapore. Yet the US has had a long history of public flogging. Until the 1960s, public flogging was authorized in several states for crimes such as robbery and certain assaults. The most recently publicized event was the 1952 flogging of a young bricklayer in Delaware for beating an elderly woman. (3) The US invasion of Panama may have violated the 1977 Geneva Convention Protocol relating to the protection of civilian victims in armed conflict. The US Senate had previously declined ratification, however, on grounds that the Protocol is "fundamentally unfair and irreconcilably flawed" because it "would undermine humanitarian law and endanger civilians in war."

Foreign Assistance Act

Specific US statutory human rights provisions target conduct abroad (rather than within the US). Title 22 of the US Code contains the Foreign Assistance Act. Section 2304 thus provides as follows:

(a)(1) The United States shall, in accordance with its international obligations as set forth in the Charter of the United Nations and in keeping with the constitutional heritage and traditions of the United States, promote and encourage increased respect for human rights and fundamental freedoms throughout the world without distinction as to race, sex, language, or religion. Accordingly, a principal goal of the foreign policy of the United States shall be to promote the increased observance of internationally recognized human rights by all countries.

(a)(2) Except under circumstances specified in this section, no security assistance may be provided to any country the government of which engages in a consistent pattern of gross violations of internationally recognized human rights.

This legislation thus prohibits the provision of security or police assistance to any foreign government that "engages in a consistent pattern of gross violations of internationally recognized human rights unless the President certifies in writing [to Congress] . . . that extraordinary circumstances exist warranting provision of such assistance . . . ." No military or law enforcement training may be provided to offending regimes. The term *gross violations* is statutorily defined as "torture or cruel, inhuman, or degrading treatment or punishment, prolonged detention without charges and trial, causing the disappearance of persons by the abduction and clandestine detention of those persons, and [any] other flagrant denial of the right to life, liberty, or the security of person. . . ."

Section 2151(n) of the Foreign Assistance Act is designed to protect abused children. No assistance may be provided to any government that fails to take appropriate measures, *within its means*, to protect children from exploitation, abuse, or forced conscription into military or paramilitary services. The "within its means" provision thus recognizes that certain governments may not have the economic competence to provide the degree of protection expected under US standards.

Under the Foreign Assistance Act, the US Secretary of State must transmit an annual report to the Speaker of the House of Representatives and the Senate Committee on Foreign Relations on foreign practices of assisted nations involving "coercion in population control, including coerced abortion and involuntary sterilization. . . ." This latter provision places the relationship between the US and the People's Republic of China at odds, due to the PRC's official policy of depriving State benefits of those parents who have more than one child (which is generally enforced in urban areas).[44]

The Foreign Assistance Act formerly provided for an "Assistant US Secretary of State for Human Rights and Humanitarian Affairs." This position was statutorily repealed in 1994 under Vice President Gore's "restructuring" program to reduce the size of the US Government. The new title for the officer in charge of this monitoring function is the "Assistant Secretary of State for the Bureau of Democracy, Human Rights, and Labor."[45] That arguably minor title change raises the issue of whether this "restructuring" contracts this officer's human rights monitoring duties—because it expands the job description.

Judicial Perspectives

One could assert that the most significant human rights treaty of all times is the UN Charter. But it is also important to recall that the Charter has been consistently characterized by US courts as being an aspirational standard of achievement. It is not "self-executing." It does not impose immediately binding legal obligations to honor the Charter's human rights provisions (see § 8.3).

Yet much of international human rights law consists of customary practice, as evidenced by what States do and their related judicial decisions (see § 1.4). As of 1980, a flourishing body of US human rights law has developed in the US. The following case was the judicial springboard:

FILARTIGA v. PENA-IRALA

United States Court of Appeals, Second Circuit
630 F.2d 876 (1980)

[Author's Note: Citations have been omitted and emphasis supplied in certain passages.]

[Opinion.] IRVING R. KAUFMAN, Circuit Judge:

. . .

Implementing the constitutional mandate for national control over foreign relations, the First Congress established original district court jurisdiction over "all causes where an alien sues for a tort only (committed) in violation of the law of nations." Judiciary Act of 1789, codified at 28 U.S.C. § 1350. Construing this rarely-invoked provision, we hold that deliberate torture perpetrated under color of official authority violates universally accepted norms of the international law of human rights, regardless of the nationality of the parties. Thus, whenever an alleged torturer is found and served with process by an alien within our borders, § 1350 provides federal jurisdiction. Accordingly, we reverse the judgment of the district court dismissing the complaint for want of federal jurisdiction [to hear and decide this type of case].

I

The appellants, plaintiffs below, are citizens of the Republic of Paraguay. Dr. Joel Filartiga, a physician, describes himself as a longstanding opponent of the government of President Alfredo Stroessner, which has held power in Paraguay since 1954. His daughter, Dolly Filartiga, arrived in the United States in 1978 under a visitor's visa, and has since applied for permanent political asylum. The Filartigas brought this action in the Eastern District of New York against Americo Norberto Pena-Irala (Pena), also a citizen of Paraguay, for wrongfully causing the death of Dr. Filartiga's seventeen-year old son, Joelito. . . .

The appellants contend that on March 29, 1976, Joelito Filartiga was kidnapped and tortured to death by Pena, who was then Inspector General of Police in Asuncion, Paraguay. Later that day, the police brought Dolly Filartiga to Pena's home where she was confronted with the body of her brother, which evidenced marks of severe torture. As she fled, horrified, from the house, Pena followed after her shouting, "Here you have what you have been looking for so long and what you deserve. Now shut up." The Filartigas claim that Joelito was tortured and killed in retaliation for his father's political activities and beliefs.

Shortly thereafter, Dr. Filartiga commenced a criminal action in the Paraguayan courts against Pena and the police for the murder of his son. As a result, Dr. Filartiga's attorney was arrested and brought to police headquarters where, shackled to a wall, Pena threatened him with death. This attorney, it is alleged, has since been disbarred without just cause.

. . .

In July of 1978, Pena sold his house in Paraguay and entered the United States under a visitor's visa. He was accompanied by Juana Bautista Fernandez

Villalba, who had lived with him in Paraguay. The couple remained in the United States beyond the term of their visas, and were living in Brooklyn, New York, when Dolly Filartiga, who was then living in Washington, D. C., learned of their presence. Acting on information provided by Dolly the Immigration and Naturalization Service arrested Pena and his companion, both of whom were subsequently ordered deported on April 5, 1979 following a hearing. They had then resided in the United States for more than nine months.

Almost immediately, Dolly caused Pena to be served with a summons and civil complaint at the Brooklyn Navy Yard, where he was being held pending deportation. The complaint alleged that Pena had wrongfully caused Joelito's death by torture and sought compensatory and punitive damages of $10,000,000. The Filartigas also sought to enjoin Pena's deportation to ensure his availability for testimony at trial. The cause of action is stated as arising under "wrongful death statutes; the U.N. Charter; the Universal Declaration on Human Rights; the U.N. Declaration Against Torture; the American Declaration of the Rights and Duties of Man; and other pertinent declarations, documents and practices constituting the customary international law of human rights and the law of nations" . . . Jurisdiction is claimed . . . principally on this appeal, under the Alien Tort Statute, 28 U.S.C. § 1350.

[Trial] Judge Nickerson stayed the order of deportation, and Pena immediately moved to dismiss the complaint on the grounds that subject matter jurisdiction was absent [in a case between citizens of Paraguay, regarding conduct occurring there] and for forum non conveniens [better forum elsewhere]. On the jurisdictional issue, there has been no suggestion that Pena claims diplomatic immunity from suit. The Filartigas submitted the affidavits of a number of distinguished international legal scholars, who stated unanimously that the law of nations prohibits absolutely the use of torture as alleged in the complaint. Pena, in support of his motion to dismiss on the ground of forum non conveniens, submitted the affidavit of his Paraguayan counsel, Jose Emilio Gorostiaga, who averred that Paraguayan law provides a full and adequate civil remedy for the wrong alleged. Dr. Filartiga has not commenced such an action, however, believing that further resort to the courts of his own country would be futile [where a criminal investigation had been pending against

Pena for four years, Filartega's lawyer was thus disbarred without cause, and Pena had left Paraguay to live in the US].

Judge Nickerson . . . dismissed the complaint on jurisdictional grounds. The district judge recognized the strength of appellants' argument that official torture violates an emerging norm of customary international law. Nonetheless, he felt constrained . . . to construe narrowly "the law of nations," as employed in § 1350, as excluding . . . [the] law which governs a state's treatment of its *own* citizens i.e., precluding US jurisdiction over cases arising abroad.

The district court continued the stay of deportation for forty-eight hours while appellants applied for further stays. These applications were denied by a panel of this Court on May 22, 1979, and by the Supreme Court two days later. Shortly thereafter, Pena and his companion returned to Paraguay.

II

Appellants rest their principal argument in support of federal jurisdiction upon the Alien Tort Statute, 28 U.S.C. § 1350, which provides: "The district courts shall have original jurisdiction of any civil action by an alien for a tort only, committed in violation of the law of nations or a treaty of the United States." Since appellants do not contend that their action arises directly under a treaty of the United States, a threshold question on the *jurisdictional issue is whether the conduct alleged violates the law of nations.* In light of the universal condemnation of torture in numerous international agreements, and the renunciation of torture as an instrument of official policy by virtually all of the nations of the world (in principle if not in practice), we find that an act of torture committed by a state official against one held in detention violates established norms of the international law of human rights, and hence the law of nations.

. . .

The United Nations Charter (a treaty of the United States, see 59 Stat. 1033 (1945)) makes it clear that in this modern age a state's treatment of its own citizens is a matter of international concern. It provides: With a view to the creation of conditions of stability and well-being which are necessary for peaceful and friendly relations among nations . . . the United Nations shall promote . . . universal respect for, and observance of, human rights and fundamental freedoms for all without distinctions as to race, sex, language or religion. And further: All members pledge themselves to take joint and separate action in cooperation with the Organization for the achievement of the purposes set forth in Article 55. Id. Art. 56.

While this broad mandate has been held not to be wholly self-executing, . . . this observation alone does not end our inquiry. For although there is no universal agreement as to the precise extent of the "human rights and fundamental freedoms" guaranteed to all by the Charter, there is at present no dissent from the view that the guaranties include, at a bare minimum, the right to be free from torture. This prohibition has become part of customary international law, as evidenced and defined by the Universal Declaration of Human Rights, General Assembly Resolution 217 (III)(A) (Dec. 10, 1948) which states, in the plainest of terms, "no one shall be subjected to torture." The General Assembly has declared that the Charter precepts embodied in this Universal Declaration "constitute basic principles of international law." Gen. Ass. Reso. 2625 (XXV) (Oct. 24, 1970). [Here, the opinion notes that eighteen nations had—by 1978— incorporated the Universal Declaration into their own national constitutions.]

Particularly relevant is the Declaration on the Protection of All Persons from Being Subjected to Torture, General Assembly Resolution 3452 (1975). . . . The Declaration expressly prohibits any state from permitting the dastardly and totally inhuman act of torture. Torture, in turn, is defined as "any act by which severe pain and suffering, whether physical or mental, is intentionally inflicted by or at the instigation of a public official on a person for such purposes as . . . intimidating him or other persons." The Declaration goes on to provide that "(w)here it is proved that an act of torture or other cruel, inhuman or degrading treatment or punishment has been committed by or at the instigation of a public official, the victim shall be afforded redress and compensation, in accordance with national law."

. . .

These U.N. declarations are significant because they specify with great precision the obligations of member nations under the Charter. Since their adoption, "(m)embers can no longer contend that they do not know what human rights they promised in the Charter to promote." Sohn, "A Short History of United Nations Documents on Human Rights," in The United Nations and Human Rights, 18th Report of the Commission (Commission to Study the Organization of Peace ed. 1968). . . .

Turning to the act of torture, we have little difficulty discerning its universal renunciation in the modern usage and practice of nations. The international consensus surrounding torture has found expression in numerous international treaties and accords. . . . *Although torture was once a routine concomitant of criminal interrogations in many nations*, during the modern and hopefully more enlightened era it has been universally renounced. According to one survey, torture is prohibited, expressly or implicitly, by the *constitutions* of over fifty-five nations, including both the United States and Paraguay. . . .

Having examined the sources from which customary international law is derived [including] the usage of nations, judicial opinions and the works of jurists we conclude that official torture is now prohibited by the law of nations. The prohibition is clear and unambiguous, and admits of *no distinction between treatment of aliens and citizens*. Accordingly, we must conclude that the dictum [nonessential language] in *Dreyfus v. von Finck, supra*, 534 F.2d at 31, to the effect that "violations of *international* law do not occur when the aggrieved parties are nationals of the *acting* state," is clearly out of tune with the current usage and practice of international law. . . . We therefore turn to the question whether the other requirements for jurisdiction are met.

III

Appellee submits that even if the tort alleged is a violation of modern international law, federal jurisdiction may not be exercised consistent with the dictates of Article III of the Constitution [under US law]. The claim is without merit. . . .

It is not extraordinary for a court to adjudicate a tort claim arising outside of its territorial jurisdiction. A state or nation has a legitimate interest in the orderly resolution of disputes among those [who happen to later live] within its borders.

. . .

[W]e proceed to consider whether the First Congress acted constitutionally in vesting jurisdiction over "foreign suits," alleging torts committed in violation of the law of nations. A case properly "aris(es) under the . . . laws of the United States" for Article III purposes if grounded upon statutes enacted by Congress or upon the common law of the United States. The law of nations forms an integral part of the common law, and a review of the history surrounding the adoption of the Constitution demonstrates that it became a part of the common law of the United States upon the adoption of the Constitution. Therefore, the enactment of the Alien Tort Statute was authorized by Article III.

During the eighteenth century, it was taken for granted on both sides of the Atlantic that the law of nations forms a part of the common law [of the courts of the US].

. . .

As ratified, the [US Constitution's] judiciary article contained no express reference to cases arising under the law of nations. Indeed, the only express reference to that body of law is contained in *Article I, sec. 8, cl. 10*, which grants to the Congress the power to *"define and punish . . . offenses against the law of nations."* Appellees seize upon this circumstance and advance the proposition that the law of nations forms a part of the laws of the United States *only to the extent that Congress has acted to define it.* This extravagant claim is amply refuted by the numerous decisions applying rules of international law uncodified in any act of Congress.

. . .

The Filartigas urge that 28 U.S.C. § 1350 be treated as an exercise of Congress's power to define offenses against the law of nations. While such a reading is possible, . . . we believe it is sufficient here to construe the Alien Tort Statute, not as granting new rights to aliens, but simply as opening the federal courts for adjudication of the rights already recognized by international law. The statute nonetheless does inform our analysis of Article III, for we recognize that questions of jurisdiction "must be considered part of an organic growth part of an evolutionary process," and that the history of the judiciary article gives meaning to its pithy phrases.

The Framers' overarching concern that control over international affairs be vested in the new national government to safeguard the standing of the United States among the nations of the world therefore reinforces the result we reach today.

Although the Alien Tort Statute has rarely been the basis for [successfully asserting § 1350] jurisdiction during its long history, in light of the foregoing discussion, there can be little doubt that [*now*] this action is properly brought in federal court. . . . Thus, the narrowing construction that the Alien Tort Statute has previously received reflects the fact that earlier cases did not involve such well-established, universally recognized norms of international law that are here at issue.

. . .

In the twentieth century the international community has come to recognize the common danger posed by the flagrant disregard of basic human rights and particularly the right to be free of torture. Spurred first by the Great War, and then the Second, civilized nations have banded together to prescribe acceptable norms of international behavior. From the ashes of the Second World War arose the United Nations Organization, amid hopes that an era of peace and cooperation had at last begun. Though many of these aspirations have remained elusive goals, that circumstance cannot diminish the true progress that has been made. In the modern age, humanitarian and practical considerations have combined to lead the nations of the world to recognize that respect for fundamental human rights is in their individual and collective interest. Among the rights universally proclaimed by all nations, as we have noted, is the right to be free of physical torture. Indeed, for purposes of civil liability, the torturer has become like the pirate and slave trader before him *hostis humani generis*, an enemy of all mankind. Our holding today, giving effect to a jurisdictional provision enacted by our First Congress, is a small but important step in the fulfillment of the ageless dream to free all people from brutal violence.

■ NOTES & QUESTIONS

1. Several other issues were addressed by the various courts involved in the *Filartega* litigation:

First: Pena's US lawyer argued that the relevant human rights treaties were not "self-executing." As described in § 8.1 of this book, a self-executing treaty either expressly or impliedly creates immediately binding obligations. The referenced multilateral human rights treaties are *not* "self-executing." Instead, they set aspirational standards of achievement—which all nations are at least morally obliged to achieve, but only when ready to *ratify* the relevant human rights treaties. This treaty-based defense was correct, but not the end of the case. Customary State practice—and US national law—had already recognized the pervasive nature of the prohibition against torture.

Second: Defendant Pena claimed that the Act of State (AOS) doctrine barred US courts from hearing this case, because Pena was a police official when the "alleged" torture occurred in Paraguay. As discussed in § 9.8 of this book, the AOS doctrine would not apply. An action by a State official—in violation of the antitorture provision of the Constitution of the Republic of Paraguay, and not ratified by Paraguay—could hardly be characterized as an AOS.

Third: Pena's *forum non conveniens* argument—essentially that Paraguay was a better forum for resolving this case—underscores the wisdom of the First US Congress in vesting jurisdiction over such claims in the federal district courts through the Alien Tort Statute (Judicial Code § 1350). Put another way, if the US were to dismiss this suit on the basis that Paraguay was a better forum, would the US be further discouraging an already ineffective International Law of Human Rights? *Filartega* thus sent a message abroad that US courts would apply international human rights doctrine, even when foreign citizens torture others in foreign countries. The practical limitation is that the tortured plaintiff (or relative, in the case of wrongful death) must find a defendant in the US, who is not subject to some immunity while present, in order to serve the defendant with a "*Filartega*" suit.

2. Four years after the appellate court's finding that the *Filartega* plaintiffs had stated a valid claim under US human rights laws, and remanded the case back to the trial court for further proceedings, they were awarded judgments totaling $10,385,364. The Pena defendants made no appearance in these subsequent proceedings. They had previously been deported from the US to Paraguay. The plaintiffs would then have to seek to enforce their judgments in Paraguay, on the assumption that the defendants were not effectively judgment-proof due to lack of money to pay that judgment. The final *Filartega* judgment nevertheless makes the US position clear for those perpetrators who are subject to US juris-

diction after committing such egregious conduct. That US judicial opinion thus provides as follows:

> The record in this case shows that torture and death are bound to recur unless deterred. This court concludes that an award of punitive damages of no less than $5,000,000 to each plaintiff is appropriate to reflect adherence to the world community's proscription of torture and to attempt to deter its practice.

Filartega v. Pena, 577 F.Supp. 860, 867 (E.D.N.Y. 1984).

3. In 1991, Congress enacted a refinement to the Alien Tort Statute (28 U.S. Code § 1350) which thus codified the *Filartega* decision. This legislation is called the Torture Victim Protection Act. It prohibits torture and "extrajudicial killings." Congress defined the latter term to create liability for an "individual who, under actual or apparent authority, or color of law, of any foreign nation . . ." tortures another human being or perpetrates "a deliberated killing not authorized by a previous judgment pronounced by a regularly constituted court affording all the judicial guarantees which are recognized as indispensable by civilized peoples." This term excludes "killing that, under international law, is lawfully carried out under the authority of a foreign nation." Congressional objectives for enacting this 1991 legislation included the availability of a US judicial forum for resolving the civil liability when foreign officials or State agents perform torture, and then seek to defend their actions on the procedural grounds of sovereign immunity (*see* § 2.6 of this book) or Act of State (*see* § 9.8).

4. The 1991 Torture Prevention Act did *not* thereby adopt the 1984 *UN Convention* Against Torture. Principle 6 of the 1984 UN Convention on Torture provides that "No circumstances *whatever* may be invoked as a justification for torture. . . ." Although the Senate gave its Advice and Consent for ratification in 1990, the US cannot become a party until further legislation, implementing the Convention's applicability under US law, has been enacted. International Law is nevertheless quite specific in terms of the content of treaty-based prohibitions of torture. It is also prohibited by the fundamental 1966 International Covenant on Civil and Political Rights: "No one shall be subjected to torture *or* to cruel, inhuman or degrading punishment." (The US *is* a party.)

5. The internationally recognized jurisdictional principles were discussed in § 5.2 of this book. None of these was expressly mentioned in Judge Kaufman's opinion. Which of these effectively served as a viable *international* basis for jurisdiction under Judge Kaufman's analysis in *Filartega*? Did the US violate any obligation by thus deporting Pena back to Paraguay?

■ SUMMARY

1. Early "humanitarian interventions" were undertaken to enforce international human rights supposedly recognized by the international community of nations. Some nations, however, abused this notion by invading other nations for other political and military purposes. They thereby fostered national distrust of human rights initiatives and retarded international attempts to secure those rights for oppressed individuals.

2. The UN inaugurated a human rights program, often referred to as the International Bill of Human Rights. The essential rights are contained in various UN documents, especially in the 1948 Universal Declaration of Human Rights (UDHR), the 1966 International Covenant on Civil and Political Rights, and the 1966 International Covenant on Economic, Social and Cultural Rights.

3. All States profess their support for the human rights of their citizens. Many States disagree, however, about the precise content of this body of rights. Some deny that these rights are governed by International Law. Others "pay lip service" to the International Bill of Human Rights, without actually observing them.

4. Human rights declarations, such as the Universal Declaration of Human Rights, are aspirational standards of achievement—as opposed to treaties necessitating immediately binding obligations. Treaties, such as the 1966 International Covenants, are binding—which is why many States have either not ratified them or have done so with reservations.

5. The 1948 UDHR was the first comprehensive human rights document to be announced on a global scale. It is a General Assembly Resolution that was unanimously adopted by all UN members in 1948. It contains two categories of rights. The first is civil and political rights. The second is economic, social, and cultural rights. Like the UN Charter, the Universal Declaration does not require a State to immediately provide these rights to its populace. Universal acceptance of this resolution arguably made it binding as a matter of *customary* international law, however.

6. In 1966, the UN General Assembly produced two key human rights instruments: the International Covenant on Civil and Political Rights and the International Covenant on Economic, Social and Cultural Rights. They differ from earlier human rights instruments in that they were drafted in the form of a multilateral treaty. Those countries that specifically accept their obligations, by ratifying these Covenants, must establish conspicuous and effective machinery for dealing with alleged violations of human rights.

7. The UN's eighteen-nation Human Rights Committee examines periodic compliance reports submitted by the treaty parties. In 1993, the UN established the post of the UN High Commissioner on Human Rights for the purpose of monitoring and enhancing the various UN human rights programs.

8. There are several *regional* human rights programs. Most reiterate the same rights contained in the UN-based human rights documents. Europe has two basic human rights treaties: the European Human Rights Convention (EHR treaty) and the European Social Charter. The EHR treaty contains civil and political rights that are virtually identical to those set forth in the United Nation's Covenant on Civil and Political Rights. The European Social Charter contains the same economic and social rights set forth in the United Nation's Covenant on Economic, Social and Cultural Rights. Europe's enforcement machinery consists of specialized executive and judicial bodies. The executive body is the European Commission on Human Rights. The judicial body is the European Court of Human Rights.

9. Latin America's human rights norms are expressed in the 1948 Charter of the Organization of American States (OAS), the 1948 American Declaration of the Rights and Duties of Man, and the 1978 American Convention on Human Rights. These norms are monitored by the Inter-American Commission on Human Rights. The OAS Charter and the American Declaration are—in comparison to other regional instruments—not as specific about the content of human rights in Latin America.

Thus, the State's sovereignty to act is not as effectively limited as is European practice.

10. Africa's human rights program is premised on the 1986 African Charter on Human and Peoples' Rights. The African Charter contains many of the human rights principles mentioned in the UN Charter and the UN Universal Declaration of Human Rights. Like many other regional human rights documents, the African Charter contains only "rights" in principle that have not been implemented by a binding multilateral treaty. Further, the African Charter establishes that individuals have a number of *duties* to society, the State, and the Organization of African Unity. The 1986 African Charter established the African Commission on Human Rights, which is tasked with the responsibility to monitor human rights enforcement on the African Continent. Like its Latin American counterpart, the African Commission may only study, report, and recommend. It has no enforcement powers.

11. Some Asian scholars have traditionally characterized the so-called International Law of Human Rights as an "imperialist" tool for intervening in the internal affairs of socialist nations. Their view is that the field of human rights is a matter governed *solely* by internal law. Human rights are considered intact in China. State ownership of all resources is characterized as an effective guarantee of the genuine realization of human rights of the Chinese people. Contemporary, post–Cultural Revolution scholars claim that human rights in China are now more protected than in any prior generation.

12. Asian scholars in *democratic* nations criticize the UN's "global" human rights standards for a different reason. Indian scholars believe that this Western-derived conception of human rights has little meaning for people lacking the basic necessities of life. The human rights contained in the UN Charter, and the cloned regional instruments, address mostly political rights that have no practical value for the people of today's India.

13. The advocation of human rights is not limited to international organizations. Some States have expressly incorporated various human rights instruments directly into their constitutions or national laws. A number of nongovernmental organizations—including the Red Cross and Amnesty International—also expose State violations of international human rights principles to public scrutiny.

14. The US Senate has historically evaded US ratification of global human rights instruments. The reasons include a lack of clarity in the precise content of the typically broadly-worded human rights instrument. They tend to speak in terms of morally unobjectionable, but undefined moral principles. Treaty commitments could thus subject the US to unintended obligations. Precise definitions are not a common characteristic of multilateral treaties, which depend on broad consensus for the incremental development of International Law.

15. US human rights policy nevertheless includes legislation specifically designed to address human rights violations abroad. The Foreign Assistance Act prohibits the provision of aid or technical assistance to States that perpetrate gross violations of legislatively defined human rights. The Alien Tort Statute implements the Constitutional provision authorizing Congress to "define and punish . . . offenses against the law of nations."

■ PROBLEMS

Problem 11.1 (*end of § 11.3*): Assume that Nicaragua's Sandinista government of the mid-1980s has just learned about a US Central Intelligence Agency plot to disrupt the daily affairs of Nicaragua. Key harbors have thus been mined, and US financial aid is being provided to a rebel group known as the "Contras." (Additional details are available from the *Nicaragua* case, set forth in the text of § 10.2 of this book.) The US President has just said, in a widely reported announcement: "I, too, am a Contra."

You are the national leader in Nicaragua. To defend your borders against this form of aggression, you declare martial law. Military forces now control all of Nicaragua. Civil rights, including access to the courts, is suspended. Martial law has further limited opposition from the Roman Catholic Church, from Nicaragua's human rights groups, and from individuals who may incur criminal liability for the crime of "civil disobedience." Nicaragua is a party to, and has publically embraced, the UN's International Bill of Human Rights.

You now decide to dispatch a series of warnings to local groups that you suspect of being supporters of the antigovernment Contras. First, you warn the Catholic Bishop of Nicaragua that "the Church must stay out of political affairs and cannot be used as a vehicle for influencing governmental decision making." Amnesty International (AI) is part of a worldwide organization designed to monitor progress toward the accomplishment of UN human rights goals. AI has more offices in the US than in any other country. After opposition to martial law from the local office of AI, you close the AI office in Nicaragua because it was publishing unapproved literature.

Martial law has also resulted in the arrest of Nicaraguan citizens charged with "civil disobedience." You believe that their detention is necessary because they may be aiding the rebel "Contra" forces. On the basis of national emergency, you have established "People's Tribunals" to accelerate the prosecution of subversion cases. The People's Tribunals have the power to summarily imprison anyone in Nicaragua. They have exercised this power to jail Nicaraguan citizens who are Catholic, or members of Amnesty International, or suspected of "civil disobedience." This term is not defined, so that arresting authorities and the prosecuting Tribunals will have the necessary discretion to operate on a case-by-case basis.

The national emergency has therefore temporarily suspended "due process of law," one of the fundamental features of various human rights treaties. The inhabitants of Nicaragua, in other words, are not necessarily charged with crimes when they are arrested. There is no independent judicial officer available to verify the propriety of incarcerations by the agents of the People's Tribunals. Each Tribunal has the complete discretion to orchestrate what Amnesty characterizes as the "disappearance" of many Nicaraguan citizens. No one jailed under your proclamation can question the legal basis for his or her incarceration.

While in jail, prisoners are routinely tortured. Although this is not State policy, it is difficult to control because your police force is your first line of defense in finding information about the US-supported "Contras." Given this emergency, torture is an unpleasant necessity for extracting vital information necessary for identifying all citizens who seek the imminent overthrow of your government. You thus impose curfews on travel at night, and on any travel between all rural and urban areas of Nicaragua (without a permit).

You have undertaken all of the above steps to maintain public order in Nicaragua. It is clear that a major foreign power has effectively launched a war on your nation—including the bombing of your harbors, the financing of the Contras, and the potential use of the Church and other private organizations to disseminate information to incite the populace to rise against your government. Have you violated the UN's International Bill of Human Rights? If so, were you justified in doing so?

Problem 11.2 (*end of § 11.5*): In a December 1993 report, the World Health Organization (WHO) estimated that "over 80 million [living] female infants, adolescents, and women in over 30 countries . . . have been subject to female genital mutilation." This procedure is commonly referred to as "female circumcision." This practice is a "tradition" that dates from ancient Egypt. Now, in Somalia for example, all females undergo this process. Young women, mostly in Africa and the Middle East, are social outcasts if they do not undergo this process—associated with the retention of virginity due to the resulting lack of any sensation. In countries where this technique is practiced, most men will not marry women who have not undergone this procedure.

While it appears that no religion specifically endorses it, leading Muslim scholars have endorsed female circumcision as a *duty* recommended by the ancient Prophet Mohammed himself and currently "a noble practice which does honor to women." *Washington Post*, Apr. 11, 1995, p.A14. While it is not officially endorsed as a State policy in any country, female circumcision is effectively condoned in those countries in Africa and the Middle East that have never taken any steps to curtail its known practice.

At approximately age ten, the young girl is held down by several women, while a "practitioner" with no training uses a razor or paring knife to do this procedure in the home. It is extremely painful and performed without anesthesia. The WHO is concerned about the resulting hemorrhaging, tetanus, infections, infertility, and death. In the West, women's rights groups seek the global abolition of female circumcision (such as the National Organization for Women, Global Campaign for Women's Human Rights, Population International, and Women's International Network).

This procedure has been outlawed *only* in France and Great Britain. In 1993, US House of Representatives Resolution 3247 was the first congressional bill to deal with what western newspapers have described as "the most widespread existing violation of human rights in the world."

In 1994, a US immigration judge in Boston had to decide whether two US-born Nigerian girls—aged five and six—would be returned to their father in Nigeria or remain in the US after their parents divorced. The judge decided to overturn the mother's deportation order on humanitarian grounds: genital mutilation would be performed, like that undergone by the mother when she was a child in Nigeria. There are an estimated two million living women in Nigeria who have experienced this "tradition." The judge thus permitted the daughters to remain in the US with their mother. Had the girls returned home with their father, they would have been required to undergo this traditional procedure. In the judge's words: "This court attempts to respect traditional cultures, but this is cruel and serves no medical purpose." Ins v. Oluloro (unreported case reviewed in *Maui News*, March 29, 1994).

Also in 1994, the US Department of State first focused on this treatment of women in its annual human rights report (pursuant to a legislative enactment discussed in § 11.5). This report referred to this practice as "ritual mutilation." An analysis of this phenomenon is available in Gifford, *The Courage to Blaspheme*, 4 *UCLA Women's L.J.* 329 (1994).

Assume that a wealthy African family vacations in the US each year, during the period that the heat is most intense in their home State—herein referred to as State X. Mrs. X is a citizen of State X. Her husband is a ranking government official in State X. While it would be inappropriate for him to ever attend one of his wife's "procedures," he nevertheless agrees with the purpose of her work—as do most of the officials in the State X government who are fully aware of this practice.

Mrs. X is a devout religious woman, who has herself undergone the "procedure"—and has performed it on her daughters, as well as hundreds of ten- to twelve-year-old girls in State X. This practice has been passed on, from generation to generation in her family, for hundreds of years. Religious teachings in her faith convince her that it is her "God-given" duty to perpetuate her faith by performing this ritualistic circumcision procedure. She believes that this work is especially important, in contemporary times when adolescent behavior in other regions of the world subject young women in State X to many adverse influences, which will certainly debase the family's cultural and religious beliefs.

During her annual vacation in New York City, she is served with process accusing her of torture in violation of International Law. The plaintiff is the mother of a Middle Eastern woman who underwent this procedure, only after Mrs. X convinced the mother that this tradition cannot be changed and that "The Divine Order" requires that only faithful women be thus made available for marrying State X males. "Otherwise," Mrs. X explained to the plaintiff mother, "the social, cultural, and religious traditions of State X will be vitiated by western influences." Although unusual, this particular child died of complications several very painful weeks after Mrs. X performed the "procedure."

The plaintiffs' lawyer decides not to sue on the basis of the gender discrimination provisions in International Human Rights Law. The relevant instruments address *State* responsibility for such discrimination—rather than individual responsibility under International Law. Also, the plaintiff's lawyer decides not to name the father as a defendant in this matter because he will likely be entitled to immunity.

This case is filed in a New York court against Mrs. X, alleging torture resulting in violation of her daughter's death. The plaintiff's lawyer also decides to bring this matter to the attention of the UN by filing a § 1503 petition with the UN High Commissioner for Human Rights. In it, the plaintiff mother claims that her daughter's rights have been also violated by State X because it has failed to provide sufficient information or any medical licensing regime for this procedure.

Two students will play roles in this hypothetical case: *Student #1—the New York trial judge.* The defense lawyer for Mrs. X claims that the judge cannot proceed with this case, because US courts cannot exercise *Filartega* "§ 1350 jurisdiction" over this type of case. *Student #2—the UN High Commissioner for Human Rights.* The same lawyer presents a defense to the "UN" petition, on the grounds that State X is not liable for torture under International Law. How should the US judge and the UN Commissioner rule?

■ BIBLIOGRAPHY

§ 11.1 Human Rights in Context:
T. Buergenthal, *International Human Rights in a Nutshell* (St. Paul: West, 1988)

J. Friedman & M. Sherman, *Human Rights: An International and Comparative Law Bibliography* (Westport, CT: Greenwood Press, 1985)

Gunter Hoog & A. Steinmetz (ed.), *International Conventions on Protection of Humanity and Environment* (Berlin: Walter de Gruyter & Co., 1993) (full text of forty-eight treaties)

E. Lawson, *Encyclopedia of Human Rights* (New York: Taylor & Francis, 1991)

R. Lillich, *International Human Rights: Problem of Law, Policy, and Practice* (2nd ed. Boston: Little, Brown & Co., 1991

T. Meron, *Human Rights in International Law: Legal and Policy Issues* (New York: Oxford Univ. Press, 1984) (two volumes)

UN, *Status of International Instruments* (New York: Geneva Centre for Human Rights, 1987)

§ 11.2 United Nations Promotional Role:

P. Alston (ed.), *The United Nations and Human Rights: A Critical Appraisal* (Oxford, Eng.: Clarendon Press, 1992)

A. Eide & G. Alfredsson (ed.), *The Universal Declaration of Human Rights: A Commentary (Oslo, Norway: Scandinavian Univ. Press, 1992)*

L. Henkin (ed.), *The International Bill of Rights: The Covenant on Civil and Political Rights* (New York: Columbia Univ. Press, 1981)

UN, *A Compilation of International Instruments: Universal Instruments* (Vol. 1) (New York: Geneva Centre for Human Rights, 1994)

§ 11.3 Regional Human Rights Approaches:

Gittleman, *The African Commission on Human Rights and Peoples' Rights: Prospects and Procedures*, in H. Hannum, *Guide to International Human Rights Practice* 153 (Deventer, Neth.: Kluwer, 1987)

Human Rights and Peace in the Middle East: A Conference, 13 *Syracuse J. Int'l L. & Comm.* 391 (1987)

A. Mower, *Regional Human Rights: A Comparative Study of the West European and Inter-American Systems* (New York: Greenwood Press, 1991)

Nagan, *African Human Rights Process: A Contextual Policy-Oriented Approach*, 21 *Southwestern L. Rev.* 157 (1992)

A. Rosas (ed.), *International Human Rights Norms in Domestic Law: Finnish and Polish Perspectives* (Helsinki: Finnish Lawyers' Pub., 1990)

UN, *A Compilation of International Instruments: Regional Instruments* (Vol. 1) (New York: Geneva Centre for Human Rights, 1994)

Weiler, *Eurocracy and Distrust: Some Questions concerning the Role of the European Court of Justice in the Protection of Fundamental Human Rights within the Legal Order of the European Communities*, 61 *Wash. L. Rev.* 1103 (1986)

§ 11.4 Other Human Rights Actors:

M. Bronson, *Amnesty International* (New York: Macmillan Children's Book Group, 1994)

Posner & Whittome, *The Status of Human Rights NGOs*, 25 *Colum. Hum. Rts. L. Rev.* 269 (1994)

When Do Individuals and Non-Governmental Organizations Have the Right to Petition the UN and What Happens? in R. Lillich, *International Human Rights: Problems of Law, Policy, and Practice* (2nd ed. Boston: Little, Brown & Co., 1991)

§ 11.5 United States Ratification and Legislation:

M. Gibney (ed.), *World Justice? U.S. Courts and International Human Rights* (Boulder, CO: Westview Press, 1991)

Human Rights Violations in the U.S.: A Report on U.S. Compliance with the International Covenant on Civil and Political Rights (New York: Human Rights Watch, 1994)

K. Randall, *Federal Courts and the International Human Rights Paradigm* (Durham, NC: Duke Univ. Press, 1991)

Stark, *Economic Rights in the United States and International Human Rights Law: Toward an "Entirely New Strategy,"* 44 *Hastings L.J.* 79 (1992)

Special Human Rights Issues:

S. Chandra (ed.), *International Protection of Minorities* (Delhi, India: Mittal, 1986)

S. Chowdhury, *The Rule of Law in a State of Emergency: The Paris Minimum Standards of Human Rights Norms in a State of Emergency* (New York: St. Martin's Press, 1989)

S. Chowdhury, E. Denters & P. Waart, *The Right to Development in International Law* (Dordrecht, Neth.; Boston: Martinus Nijhoff, 1992)

Engle, *International Human Rights and Feminism: When Discourses Meet*, 13 *Mich. J. Int'l L.* 517 (1992)

M. Halberstam & E. Defels, *Women's Legal Rights: International Covenants an Alternative to ERA?* (Ardsley-on-Hudson, NY: Transnat'l Pub., 1987)

Human Rights in Developing Countries 1986–1994 (Oslo, Norway: Norwegian Inst. Human Rts, 1994) (seven volumes)

M. Jakobson, *Origins of the Gulag: The Soviet Prison-Camp System, 1917–1934* (Lexington, KY: Univ. Press of Kentucky, 1992)

G. van Bueren, *International Law on the Rights of the Child* (Dordrecht, Neth.; Boston: Martinus Nijhoff, 1994)

■ ENDNOTES

1. *See* E. Stowell, *International Law* 126 (London: Pitman, 1921) & H. Wheaton, *Elements of International*

Law (Boston: Little Brown, 1863), reprinted in *The Classics of International Law* 79 (Scott ed., New York: Oceana, 1936).

2. *See Historical Antecedents of International Human Rights Law*, ch. 1, in T. Buergenthal, *International Human Rights in a Nutshell* 1 (St. Paul: West, 1988) [hereinafter *Nutshell*].

3. Advisory Opinion on Nationality Decrees Issued in Tunis and Morocco, P.C.I.J., ser. B, No. 4 (1923).

4. Belgian Linguistics Case (Merits), European Court of Human Rights, 45 Int'l Law Rep. 114 (1968).

5. Gen. Ass. Reso. 36/55, reprinted in 21 *Int'l Legal Mat'ls* 205 (1982).

6. Gen. Ass. Reso. 2627(XXV), of Oct. 24, 1970, reprinted in E. Lawson, *Encyclopedia of Human Rights* 375, 376 (New York: Taylor & Francis, 1991).

7. *Idealism and Ideology: The Law of Human Rights*, ch. 12, in L. Henkin, *How Nations Behave: Law and Foreign Policy* 231 (2nd ed. New York: Columbia Univ. Press, 1979).

8. Sei Fujii v. State of California, 38 Cal. 2d 718, at 722, 242 P.2d 617, at 620 (1952). This case is set forth in § 8.1, on the distinction between "self-executing" treaties and "standards of achievement."

9. **US segregation:** Plessy v. Ferguson, 163 U.S. 537, 16 S.Ct. 1138, 41 L.Ed. 256 (1898). *Plessy* was not overruled until 1954. **US interracial marriages:** the applicable state prohibitions were not ruled unconstitutional until 1967. *See* Loving v. Virginia, 388 U.S. 1, 87 S.Ct. 1817, 18 L.Ed.2d 1010 (1967). **Soviet gulags:** A. Solzhenitsyn, *The Gulag Archipelago* (New York: Harper & Row, 1974).

10. 5 M. Whiteman, *Digest of International Law* 243 (Wash., DC: US Gov't Print. Off., 1965).

11. Namibia (South West Africa) Advisory Opinion, 1971 I.C.J. Rep. 16, 55 (concurring opinion of Judge Ammoun).

12. American Law Institute, 2 *Restatement of the Foreign Relations Law of the United States* § 701, at 153 & 155 (3rd ed. Wash., DC: Amer. Law Inst., 1987).

13. *A Western Approach?*, in A. Eide & G. Alfredsson (ed.), *The Universal Declaration of Human Rights: A Commentary* 11 (Oslo, Norway: Scandinavian Univ. Press, 1992).

14. Reprinted in 32 *Int'l Legal Mat'ls* 1661 (1993).

15. *Rights Report Finds Continuing Abuses around the Globe, Los Angeles Daily Journal*, October 5, 1988, p.1.

16. **ICCPR:** 999 United Nations Treaty Series 171 (1976). **ICESCR:** 993 United Nations Treaty Series 3 (1976).

17. **Lack of State commitment:** *Nutshell*, p.42 (cited in note 2 above). **Contrary view:** *see* De Zayas, Moller & Opsahl, *Application of the International Covenant on Civil and Political Rights under the Optional Protocol by the Human Rights Committee*, 2 *German Yearbk. Int'l L.* 9 (1985).

18. Meron, *On the Inadequate Reach of Humanitarian and Human Rights Law and the Need for a New Instrument*, 77 *Amer. J. Int'l L.* 589, 604–605 (1983).

19. *See* L. Sunga, *Individual Responsibility in International Law for Serious Human Rights Violations* (Dordrecht, Neth.; Boston: Martinus Nijhoff, 1992).

20. Gen. Ass. Reso. 48/141, of Dec. 20, 1993, reprinted in 33 *Int'l Legal Mat'ls* 303 (1994).

21. **Convention:** European Convention for the Protection of Human Rights and Fundamental Freedoms, 213 UN Treaty Series 221 (1955). **Charter:** *see* D. Harris, *The European Social Charter* (Charlottesville, VA: Univ. Press of Va., 1984).

22. *See* Case of Open Door and Dublin Well Woman v. Ireland, set forth in § 3.4 of this book.

23. *See* European Convention for the Protection of Human Rights and Fundamental Freedoms: Report regarding Its Differences from the UN Covenants, 9 *Int'l Legal Mat'ls* 1310 (1970).

24. The case is analyzed in 12 *Yearbook of the European Convention on Human Rights* (1969) ("Greek Case").

25. M. Janis & R. Kay, *European Human Rights Law*, vii (Hartford, CT: Univ. of Conn. Law School Foundation Press, 1990).

26. **Final Act:** reprinted in *Declaration of Principles Guiding Relations between Participating States*, 70 *Amer. J. Int'l L.* 417 (1976). **Conference documents:** A. Bloed (ed.), *The Conference on Security and Co-operation in Europe: Analysis and Basic Documents*, 1972–1993 (Dordrecht, Neth.; Boston: Martinus Nijhoff, 1993).

27. 119 UN Treaty Series 3 (1952) (as amended).

28. *See generally*, Hartman, *Derogation from Human Rights Treaties in Public Emergencies*, 22 *Harv. Int'l L.J.* 1 (1981).

29. U. Umozurike, *The African Charter on Human and Peoples' Rights*, 77 *Amer. J. Int'l L.* 902–903 (1983) (emphasis supplied) [hereinafter *African Charter*].

30. *Human Rights*, ch. 12, in U. Umozurike, *Introduction to International Law* 153 (Ibadan, Nigeria: Spectrum Law Publishing, 1993).

31. T. Bennett, *A Sourcebook of African Customary Law for Southern Africa* viii (Wetton, So. Africa: Juta & Co., 1991).

32. *African Charter*, at 911 (cited in note 29 above).

33. Ch'ien Szu, *A Criticism of the Views of Bourgeois International Law on the Question of Population*, reprinted in 1 J. Cohen & H. Chiu, *People's China and International Law* 607 (Princeton: Princeton Univ. Press, 1974).

34. **Hong Kong Bill:** Lillich, *Sources of Human Rights Law and the Hong Kong Bill of Rights*, in H. Chiu (ed.), 10 *Chinese Yearbook Int'l L. & Affairs* 27 (Baltimore: Chinese Soc. Int'l Law, 1992). **Contemporary rights of Chinese citizens:** H. Chiu, *Chinese Attitudes Toward*

International Law of Human Rights in the Post-Mao Era, in *Occasional Papers/Reprints Series in Contemporary Asian Studies*, Paper No. 5 (Baltimore: Univ. of Maryland, 1989).

35. R. Hingorini, *Modern International Law* 258 (New York: Oceana, 1984).

36. Gutto, *Violation of Human Rights in the Third World: Responsibility of States and TNCs*, reprinted in F. Snyder & S. Sathirathai (ed.), *Third World Attitudes Toward International Law* 275 (Dordrecht, Neth.; Boston: Martinus Nijhoff, 1987).

37. T. Elias, *New Horizons in International Law* 167 (Alphen an den Rijn, Neth.: Sitjhoff & Noordhoff, 1979).

38. Reprinted in 32 *Int'l Legal Mat'ls* 1661 (1993).

39. **Amnesty:** *Amnesty International: The 1994 Report on Human Rights Around the World* (London: Amnesty Int'l Pub., 1994). **Commission of Jurists:** H. Tolley, *The International Commission of Jurists: Global Advocates for Human Rights* (Baltimore: Univ. of Pa. Press, 1994). **NGOs:** Posner & Whittome, *The Status of Human Rights NGOs*, 25 *Colum. Hum. Rts. L. Rev.* 269 (1994).

40. Oyama v. California, 332 U.S. 633, 649–50, 68 S.Ct. 269, 277, 92 L.Ed. 249 (1948) (Justice Black, Concurring Opinion).

41. **Brown case:** 347 U.S. 483, 74 S.Ct. 686, 98 L.Ed. 873 (1954). **Sei Fujii case:** 38 Cal.2d 718, 242 P.2d 617 (Cal. S.Ct., 1952). **Racial rationale:** *see The U.S. Senate and Human Rights Treaties*, § 7.3 in *Nutshell* (cited in note 2 above).

42. *See* Collin v. Smith, 578 F.2d 1197 (7th Cir. 1978), *cert. denied* 439 U.S. 916.

43. **Treaty:** Organization of American States Protocol on the American Convention on Human Rights to Abolish the Death Penalty, 29 *Int'l Legal Mat'ls* 1447 (1990). **Scholarship:** W. Schabas, *The Abolition of the Death Penalty in International Law* (Cambridge, Eng.: Grotius Pub., 1993).

44. For a discussion of this US statute and a related policy analysis, *see generally*, Cohen, *Conditioning U.S. Security Assistance on Human Rights Practices*, 76 *Amer. J. Int'l L.* 246 (1982).

45. **Repealed position:** 22 US Code § 2384(f). **New job description:** provided by telephone call to US Department of State on January 18, 1995.

CHAPTER TWELVE

International Environment

CHAPTER OUTLINE

■ INTRODUCTION

Wororld wars, the Cold War, and the possibility of a nuclear holocaust have all subsided as perceived threats to the inhabitants of the Planet Earth. It is environmental problems that may cause the breakdown of international society as we now know it.

This chapter opens with a contemporary incident involving one State's disruption of the environmental activities of a nongovernmental organization in another State. This scenario thus integrates environmental responsibility with a number of other previously studied matters of State responsibility in International Law. The materials then analyze the international liability standards for "transboundary environmental interference" and remedial expectations when one State degrades another's environment.

One section provides a representative snapshot of the numerous contemporary international treaties and declarations on the environment. The chapter closes with a final substantive section on legislation in the United States and related judicial interpretation of environmental issues having global implications.

■ 12.1 THE ENVIRONMENT'S DOMINION

Environmental Degradation

Earlier chapters depicted numerous examples of "man's inhumanity to man." This chapter illustrates that theme in a different context: the degradation of the environment of another State or "global common" areas—such as Antarctica, the oceans, and outer space.

Ancient Greek and Roman smelters emitted enough lead to contaminate the entire Northern Hemisphere, thus rivaling gasoline as a cause of modern pollution. Silver refining, 2,500 years ago, was thus the oldest large-scale hemispheric pollution ever reported prior to the Industrial Revolution of the nineteenth century.[1]

The mid-twentieth century initiated further attacks on the environment. Examples include the radioactive fallout from the US bombing of Nagasaki and Hiroshima, which either killed or harmed *another* 100,000 individuals for several years after the dawn of the nuclear era. The next generation would spawn extensive atmospheric and underground testing by the nuclear nations during the Cold War.

A parade of horribles, in the last decade of the twentieth century, dramatically illustrates that the

On December 2, 1984, there was a massive leak of toxic gas from a storage tank at the Union Carbide plant (the subsidiary of a US corporation) in Bhopal, India. A deadly fog blanketed the city, killed over 3,000 people, and injured approximately 200,000 others.

importance of environmental protection may be the ultimate international exigency. In 1984, toxic chemical gas leaked from a plant at a US corporation's subsidiary in Bhopal, India. Over 3,000 people were killed and some 200,000 more were injured in the worst industrial disaster in history. In 1986, an explosion at the Chernobyl nuclear reactor in the Ukraine caused the first *officially* reported radiation deaths in a nuclear power plant accident. This incident hurled radioactive material into the atmosphere that traveled as far away as the US. Also in that year, a fire in Switzerland resulted in thirty tons of chemicals being washed into the nearby Rhine River. This event was one of Europe's most serious environmental catastrophes. In 1991, retreating Iraqi forces set fire to 700 Kuwaiti oil wells near the close of the Persian Gulf War. That single military campaign sent millions of tons of contaminants into the biosphere for the nine-month period it took to extinguish all of these fires. In 1993, a Norwegian tanker lost 4,000 tons of sulfuric acid at sea off the Mexican coast.

The above are examples of *sudden* disasters. Equally severe are long-term *incremental* threats—ozone depletion, climate change, deforestation of entire regions, and many other potentially incalculable dangers to human survival. Many of these hazards have reportedly caused skin cancer, cataracts, suppression of the human immune system, and agricultural degradation. The circulation of industrial contaminants throughout the atmosphere may further lead to catastrophic rises in sea levels, and even the so-called "greenhouse effect" whereby unnatural warming of the biosphere would cause heat waves and the melting of polar icepacks.

Much remains to be done in terms of international cooperation in controlling the effects of transboundary responses to all of these sudden and incremental environmental disasters. Unfortunately, those in control are often those in denial. The Mexican government initially claimed that there was no major leak, when a tanker lost 4,000 tons of acid in 1993 (presumably not wishing to tarnish its "NAFTA" image). In the same year, the head environmental adviser to Russia's President Yeltsin revealed that the former Soviet Union clandestinely dumped vast amounts of highly radioactive waste at sea during the previous thirty years—twice the combined amount of all twelve of the other nuclear nations. That amount was 2.5 million curies of

radioactive waste, plus eighteen nuclear reactors dumped into the Arctic Sea and the Sea of Japan.

The impact of such disasters is not limited to the territorial borders of the State of occurrence. Environmental pollution knows no boundaries. Thus, States may no longer rely on territorial sovereignty to conveniently brush aside international programs to control the environmental effects and legal consequences of such incidents. Transboundary pollution is arguably the least logical of all modes of State conduct for invoking a familiar defense—that such matters fall exclusively within the *national* jurisdiction of the offending State, rather than being within the province of *International* Law.

The possibly defining crisis in the "incremental" category of environmental degradation may be world overpopulation. In 1994, the Worldwide Watch Institute, a Washington, D.C. research institute, issued its grimmest annual report ever. According to Worldwide Watch, this planet is nearing its capacity to produce food. If the earth's geometrically increasing population remains uncontrolled, and soil and water resources continue to be degraded, there will be no symmetry between food production and human consumption. The Institute projected that the world's population will *increase by* 3.6 billion people in the next forty years (*currently* 5.4 billion). But the world's per capita seafood catch fell 9 percent during the four-year period between 1989 and 1993. Grain production, which expanded 3 percent between 1950 and 1984, dropped to a 1 percent annual growth rate between 1984 and 1994. Just as ideological conflict dominated the *last* four decades of the Cold War, the Earth's physical capacity to satisfy the growing demand for food may thus dominate the *next* four decades.

It was these statistics that motivated 180 nations to develop a twenty-year plan for slowing population growth at the 1994 UN Population Conference in Cairo. This conference focused on birth control, economic development, and providing women in certain societies and religious backgrounds with more power over their lives. The Vatican, for example, had previously rejected the final documents of the earlier Bucharest (1974) and Mexico City (1974) world population conferences. At the 1994 conference, however, the pope partially supported the final result in principle—although still adverse to the abortion alternative. The Cairo Program of Action thus calls on States to provide better education for women in traditionally male-dominated societies, wider access to modern birth control methods, and the right to choose if and when to become pregnant. The consensus-oriented reservation is that these program objectives must not conflict with national laws, religious beliefs, and cultural norms.[2]

Concerns about environmental degradation are not limited to periodic conferences of States. An exhaustive academic study by the editors of an American law review succinctly summarized the related swell of environmental studies in the universities:

DEVELOPMENTS IN THE LAW—
INTERNATIONAL ENVIRONMENTAL LAW
104 Harvard Law Review 1484, 1489 (1991)

. . .

[I]nternational environmental law has emerged as a distinct academic discipline. A growing number of commentators, diplomats, and practitioners are concentrating on transboundary and global environmental issues, and in the last few years many of the . . . schools in the United States have begun to offer classes devoted to the study of legal responses to international environmental problems. This surge in scholarly attention heralds a period of intense development of international environmental law.

The international environmental regime is composed of customary law, treaties, institutions, and extraterritorial application of domestic environmental law. In an attempt to use customary international law [in support of a legal basis] to protect the environment, commentators have spent the last two decades elaborating rules of state responsibility and

liability specifically designed to address transboundary pollution. States have begun to build on this liability regime by developing international agreements designed to prevent harmful environmental activity. Furthermore, to develop explicit regulation to address special environmental problems, states continue to experiment with different modes of treaty creation such as the convention-protocol method, and to search for new methods of treaty enforcement. Meanwhile, a plethora of intergovernmental organizations now monitor pollution and regulate environmentally harmful behavior. Finally, frustrated by the slow pace of public international law, scholars and litigants have stepped up their calls for states with strong environmental laws to extend unilaterally their jurisdiction to environmentally harmful activities occurring in other states.

. . .

Definitional Perspective

What does the term *International Environmental Law* (IEL) mean? This is a relatively novel question, because the expression is a relatively new one. The term "International Law" was coined some three hundred years ago, near the dawn of the 1648 Westphalian concept of Statehood (*see* § 1.3). The term *Environmental Law*, until the last generation of the twentieth century, was essentially governed by national laws. National legislation was thus the predominant focus of private environmental organizations. International codification had been perceived as inconsequential. Transboundary control was almost exclusively the province of special interest groups within the industrial States, such as Greenpeace International (based in Amsterdam).

This distinct systemic attention to environmental problems was, for too long, entirely artificial. The environment respects no territorial sovereignty—nor the diversity of political or economic systems within the community of nations. The environment does not distinguish between industrialized and developing societies. Unlike the members of that community, the environment does not observe distinctions between treaty obligations and mere statements of principle. What is now referred to as IEL is thus the lineal descendant of the formerly distinct branches of the national and international legal systems.

The following scenario provides some insight into the link between IEL and the traditional subject matter of courses in International Law, as well as indicating the pervasiveness of the environment as a key to future international relations.

Rainbow Warrior Incident[3]

Greenpeace International is a nongovernmental organization (NGO), headquartered in Amsterdam. The task of this private international organization is to protect the environment, not just monitor State management. Supported through worldwide private donations, Greenpeace thus monitors threats to what it characterizes as an increasingly fragile environment. It has thus operated a small fleet, including the former British-registered flagship *Rainbow Warrior*, which began to make international port calls in 1971. French nuclear testing has been a popular target for Greenpeace activity.

In 1973, New Zealand and Australia sued France in the International Court of Justice, seeking a judgment that would require France to cease its nuclear testing in the South Pacific. The plaintiff States feared that radioactive fallout would adversely affect the atmosphere throughout the South Pacific. Rather than participating in this litigation, France withdrew. The ICJ dismissed the case in 1974, on the basis of France's unilateral declaration that it would cease such testing (which in fact was later resumed).[4]

The private multinational crews of Greenpeace vessels had recently begun to follow various ocean-going vessels engaged in activities constituting what Greenpeace determined to be threats to the environment. These threats included excessive whaling and other fishing enterprises in violation of international norms; transporting and dumping of nuclear fuels and waste materials; and the dumping of other toxic substances into the ocean. Given the mid-1970s case filed by two State opponents of France's nuclear testing, Greenpeace believed that it was in a far better position to bring worldwide attention to France's resumption of nuclear testing.

The most famous "collision" between Greenpeace and the French government occurred in 1980 at a harbor's entrance to a port in France. A Japanese merchant vessel was carrying nuclear reactors to France, which Greenpeace characterized as a major hazard due to the potential radiation hazard of transferring this material by sea. Put another way, this was a nuclear *Exxon Valdez* waiting to happen. As the *Rainbow Warrior* began to shadow the Japanese vessel, the Greenpeace vessel was rammed by a French police ship. After its seizure by the French port authorities, the Greenpeace vessel was released and ordered never to return to French waters.

The primary newsworthiness of the *Rainbow Warrior* was its subsequent "shadowing" of French, Russian, and Spanish naval vessels—in attempts to protest French nuclear testing in French Polynesia (not far from New Zealand). Greenpeace was the target of a plot by a French governmental intelligence agency—the Directurat-Générale de Sécurité Extérieure (DGSE). A DGSE agent, purporting to be a Greenpeace supporter, worked undercover in the Auckland, New Zealand office of Greenpeace International. She photographed Auckland's harbors as part of a plan to sink the *Rainbow Warrior* after a decade of its shadowing French military vessels. New Zealand, as part of its Nuclear Free Zone policy, had banned French nuclear vessels from its harbors. This agent's photographs were sent to Paris for intelligence gathering purposes, which would soon bring worldwide attention to the ongoing Greenpeace/French connection.

While in Auckland Harbor in 1985, the *Rainbow Warrior* was bombed and sunk by a group of at least eight DGSE agents. Two bombs, exploding near midnight, resulted in the death of a Dutch citizen who was the Greenpeace onboard photographer. The explosion injured several crew members of various nationalities (other than New Zealand) and sank this British-flagged ship. Most of the French agents escaped. It appears that the nearby French submarine sank the boat in which they escaped from Auckland Harbor, after bringing them aboard for their probable return to France via French Polynesia.

New Zealand captured two of the French DGSE agents, tried them, and sentenced them to ten-year sentences for manslaughter and arson (to name a few of the charges). The New Zealand public was outraged. The *Rainbow Warrior* incident was the first operation by a foreign government involving a bombing, death, and sinking of a vessel in a New Zealand harbor. New Zealand thus lodged a diplomatic protest with France, and demanded reparations based on France's alleged State responsibility for various violations of national and International Law. The UN Secretary-General then arbitrated an agreement between France and New Zealand, whereby: France was to pay damages to New Zealand—but no damages on account of the death or damage to the vessel caused by the bomb blast; New Zealand would transfer the two convicted agents to a prison in French Polynesia to serve out the remainder of their terms; and France would not impose the threatened trade barriers against New Zealand butter and meat imports, threatened by France during the *Rainbow Warrior* negotiations. New Zealand thus agreed to release the two captured French army officers to French custody so that they would serve the remainder of their jail terms in a French Polynesian prison.[5]

Within four years, the two transferred prisoners "escaped" from the French island prison. They were repatriated to France, but never taken into custody in France (for what would otherwise be their return to the prison in French Polynesia). France claimed that there was no basis for New Zealand's demanding their continued incarceration, because they were

acting on "superior orders." The other French agents were never arrested or tried. The French government conceded its role in their bombing of the *Rainbow Warrior,* but claimed that its agents had exceeded their authority. France nevertheless threatened to use further force if any other Greenpeace vessel ever attempted to disrupt future French nuclear testing.

In 1991, another French agent involved in the *Rainbow Warrior* bombing was arrested in Switzerland. Greenpeace immediately pressured the New Zealand government to seek his extradition from Switzerland. New Zealand decided not to pursue the harbor-bombing incident any further. Switzerland allegedly bowed to French pressure to release him from custody, complete with a diplomatic escort to the French border.

■ NOTES

1. This was not the last such incident involving Greenpeace and a foreign government over environmental issues. In October 1992, Russia's coast guard seized a Greenpeace vessel attempting to investigate nuclear waste sites in Arctic waters. In November 1992, a Japanese coast guard vessel accompanying a Japanese freighter rammed a protesting Greenpeace vessel. The Greenpeace vessel was shadowing the freighter—which was carrying nearly two tons of radioactive plutonium out of the French port of Cherbourg. This was the largest such shipment in history.

2. The above abbreviated version of the *Rainbow Warrior* affair suggests a number of breaches of International Law, some of which were related to environmental concerns. It thus serves as a useful tool for integrating various segments of this course in an environmental context.

ICJ Environment

Environmental Chamber The Secretary-General's 1987 arbitration of the *Rainbow Warrior* affair was not the only significant UN event in contemporary international environmental dispute resolution. There is now a specialized Environmental Chamber within the International Court of Justice (ICJ).

§ 9.4 of the arbitration/adjudication chapter addressed the "Chambers" process, whereby States may access the expertise of certain ICJ members to resolve their conflicts. Thus, Article 26.1 of the Statute of the ICJ provides for "chambers, composed of three or more judges . . . for dealing with particular categories of cases; for example labour cases and cases relating to transit and communications."

In 1993, the ICJ thus formed a "Chamber of the Court for Environmental Matters." That Chamber's Constitution proclaims that the ICJ *was* willing, until the 1990s, to deal with environmental matters on an *ad hoc* basis. But due to increased concern with environmental conflicts between State parties, the judges of the Court implemented this novel environmental dispute resolution procedure. The special "Constitution of a Chamber of the Court for Environmental Matters" thus provides as follows: "In view of the developments in the field of environmental law and protection which have taken place in the last few years [*see* Exhibit 12.1], and considering that it should be prepared to the fullest possible extent to deal with any environmental case falling within its jurisdiction, the Court has now deemed it appropriate to establish a *seven*-member Chamber for Environmental Matters. . . ."[6]

The Environmental Chamber has not yet decided any cases. Given the intense interest in major environmental disasters of the current generation (Kuwait and Bhopal, for instance), however, States will hopefully refer such matters to this specialized forum by treaty or other special agreement. The anticipated advantages include the development of a special body of expertise and a group of judges who are readily available for a quicker resolution than possible under the traditional full Court procedure. Judges can also be selected so as to seat judges of particular nationalities, rather than the full court—a preferred posture for some litigants.

Environmental Advisory Jurisdiction The demise of the Cold War threat of nuclear proliferation did not diminish concerns about environmental disasters caused by the potential use of nuclear weapons in other conflicts. Black marketeers, ethnic or religious zealots—like those who used poisonous gas in Tokyo's subways in March 1995—and terrorists all still present the danger of a *nuclear* environmental disaster. Thus, the UN's World Health Organization (WHO) requested an advisory opinion from the full bench of the ICJ in 1993. The WHO is therein questioning, as indicated by the name of this case, the *Legality of the Potential State Use of Nuclear Weapons in Armed Conflict.*[7] All States and international organizations with an interest in the resolution of this issue were required to submit their written input to the Court by June 1995. The global interest in preventing environmental degradation will likely be balanced against the national prerogative to use any means to successfully preserve the State's existence in an armed conflict, and to procure state-of-the-art technology in the name of national defense.

Environmental Contentious Jurisdiction The ICJ considered its first major environmental case in 1993. The small, formerly resource-rich State of Nauru alleged that Australia had incurred State responsibility for the environmental degradation of Nauru. The plaintiff State thus claimed that Australia breached its UN Charter Article 73 "sacred trust duties" via Australia's exploitation of the UN Trusteeship Council program. Australia (and others) mined the phosphate-rich soil of Nauru, to satisfy the needs of a large agricultural industry for fertilizer refined from Nauru's natural resources. Nauru received a woefully inadequate share of the profits from its natural resources, in addition to experiencing a depletion that degraded its economic, social, and cultural environment. This was the case against Australia for mismanaging this tiny island territory prior to its 1968 independence. Australia (and others) thus depleted Nauru's vast deposits of the richest phosphates in the world—as found by the independent Commission of Inquiry mentioned below—in violation of its UN-imposed trusteeship assignment.[8]

The parties settled this case, shortly after the ICJ announced its above-described Environmental Chambers Constitution in 1993. One might presume that the Court's willingness to hear Nauru's contentious case, coupled with its establishment of a specialized environmental chamber, may have pressured Australia into pursuing a settlement—rather than facing the consequences of an adverse ICJ judgment. One consequence was the possible court-mandated requirement that Australia restore Nauru to the position it would have enjoyed but for the breach of the sacred trust duty. A Commissioner's book-length account of the work of the Commission of Inquiry (undertaken prior to Nauru's post-independence ICJ litigation) depicts the resulting environmental degradation of Nauru by the partnership of Australia, New Zealand, and Great Britain. A scientific report used by the Commission of Inquiry illustrates the relevant findings:

> Land shortage resulting from mining has given Nauru one of the most important social problems which the country now faces.
>
> In relation to fauna and flora, [scientists who prepared this report] . . . have described how centuries will be needed for the forest to reestablish itself naturally even in modified form, and how numerous plant species are scattered and stunted as compared with their growth in the unmined forest. . . . These scientists have stressed 'the disastrous effects and almost total disruption of island ecosystems that resulted from inappropriate development projects and land use.' Natural forest microclimates have been transformed into new microclimates with increased sunlight and lower humidity, resulting in greatly altered patterns of vegetation. A number of indigenous plant species are endangered.
>
> With the changes in vegetation, Nauruan diet too has suffered a drastic change.[9]

UN Environmental Conferences

1972 Stockholm Conference In 1972, the UN convened its first Conference on the Human Environment.[10] The resulting proclamations essentially recognized that preservation of the environment is essential to the continued enjoyment of human rights, including life itself. The importance of preserving the environment was succinctly stated in that conference's aspirational proclamation providing (in part) as follows:

1. . . . In the long and tortuous evolution of the human race on this planet a stage has been reached when, through the rapid acceleration of science and technology, man has acquired the power to transform his environment in countless ways and on an unprecedented scale. . . . [M]an's environment . . . [is] essential to his well-being and to the enjoyment of basic human rights—even the right to life itself.

2. The protection and improvement of the human environment is a major issue which affects the well-being of peoples and economic development throughout the world; it is the urgent desire of peoples of the whole world and the duty of all Governments.

The bulk of the work product of the Stockholm Conference was a series of twenty-six principles, calling on States and international organizations to "play a co-ordinated, efficient and dynamic role for the protection and improvement of the environment" (Principle 25). In 1972, the UN thus responded by resolving the establishment of the Governing Council of the United Nations Environment Programme. The functions of this Council included the implementation of environmental programs and "To keep under review the world environmental situation in order to ensure that emerging environmental problems of wide international significance receive appropriate and adequate consideration by Governments. . . ."[11]

In 1972, States thus focused on the emerging debate about whether environmental protection and economic development helped or hindered one another. There were few international agreements concerning the environment. Since then, virtually all States have enacted *national* legislation providing for varying degrees of environmental protection. And there are nearly 900 *international* instruments, consisting of further UN declarations, plus regional or multilateral treaties (*see,* for example, Exhibit 12.1 in § 12.3).[12]

The new focus was on "sustainable development." This phrase represents a somewhat symbiotic relationship between economic development (the benefit) and environmental degradation (the cost). The improvement of underdeveloped economies is not supposed to occur through unacceptable costs to the environment. As recognized in Proclamation 4 of the 1972 Stockholm Resolution, "In the developing countries most of the environmental problems are caused by under-development. . . . Therefore, the developing countries must direct their efforts to development, bearing in mind their priorities and the need to safeguard the environment." One might characterize this aspiration as an attempt to impose the rough equivalent of an environmental impact statement requirement—cast in terms of an international declaration of States.

On the twentieth anniversary of the Stockholm Conference, nations assembled once again, this time to reassess the interplay between the potentially conflicting objectives of sustaining the quality of the Earth's environment and sustaining the development of its "Third World" nations.

1992 Rio Conference In 1992, nearly 180 States gathered in Rio de Janeiro for the second United Nations Conference on Environment and Development (UNCED). A central issue, again, was how to manage the connected but sometimes competing themes of environmental protection and economic development. This widely heralded gathering of diverse States produced five major documents, setting the international environmental agenda for the twenty-first century. The primary components of this "Agenda" for the environmental future include (1) Agenda 21; (2) Rio Declaration; (3) Climate Change Convention; (4) Biological Diversity Convention; and (5) the Forest Principles.[13]

Agenda 21 is the 800-page blueprint for managing the various sectors of the environment in the twenty-first century. Many of the action items are quite specific, yet they aspire to degrees of protection that are well beyond the existing capacity of many States. The most controversial of these was protection of the atmosphere. Rio Conference participants such as Saudi Arabia sought to avoid any mention of "renewable sources" (that is, other than oil) as environmentally preferable. Thus, this portion of Agenda 21 was totally rewritten during the Conference process.

Financing was also a critical issue. There was agreement that fresh funding sources were needed, if the dual objective of sustainable development were to be something more than just "lip service" to an unattainable ideal. However, the developed States did not succumb to pressure from proponents of the "Group of 77" (*see* § 13.4) to commit even a small fraction of their GNP to assisting developing States.

Agenda 21 has some drawbacks. It does not contain any mandatory rules, and depends largely on follow-up processes to attain the laudable goals within its 800-page Program of Action. Stanley Johnson, author of several environmental books, thus laments in his description of Agenda 21 that it

> may suffer from its own sheer bulkiness . . . as well as from the fact that it does not lay down any mandatory rules, nor on the whole does it require truly bankable commitments to be made by any of the [State] parties involved. Agenda 21 is in reality the softest of "soft law," exhortory in nature, a cafeteria where self-service is the order of the day.
>
> Much hope is placed in the "follow-up" process, i.e., how the implementation of Agenda 21 at [the] national and international level will be monitored, but this is an area where much confusion still has to be dissipated.
>
> UNCED [merely] agreed on new institutional arrangements, particularly an intergovernmental Commission on Sustainable Development reporting to the General Assembly through ECOSOC [the Economic and Social Council discussed in § 3.3], whose primary responsibility would be to investigate the extent to which states were fulfilling their duties under Agenda 21. . . . With so many uncertainties, it is hard to enthuse . . . over the creation of another new institution in the UN framework [referring to the UN Commission for Sustainable Development].[14]

The *Rio Declaration* on Environment and Development was the 1992 conference update of the first environmental conference held in Stockholm.[15] The Rio Declaration consists of twenty-one principles, including the right to development and Principle 24—which is certain to reappear in scholarly and judicial discussions of the relationship between novel environmental concerns and traditional international legal theory. That Principle provides as follows: "Warfare is inherently destructive of sustainable development. States shall therefore respect international law providing protection for the environment in times of armed conflict and cooperate in its further development, as necessary."

The drafters of this Principle likely had in mind the virtually incomprehensible devastation wrought by Iraq's armed forces during their retreat from Kuwait. They set fire to 700 Kuwati oil wells. It took nine months to bring these infernos fully under control. In the interim period, millions of tons of hazardous gases belched into the air over Kuwait during 1991. UN Security Council Resolution 687 affirmed that Iraq was "liable under International Law for any direct loss, [or] damage, including environmental damage and the depletion of natural resources . . . as a result of Iraq's unlawful invasion and occupation of Kuwait." Yet, it is unclear whether State *practice* (as opposed to nonbinding resolutions) characterizes this use of the environment as invoking criminal responsibility under customary International Law. No ratified *treaty* has yet to specifically designate this form of environmental degradation as a violation of International Law. One reason is that States may fear expansions of Resolution 687's principle, which could thus criminalize other less egregious forms of transborder pollution.

The 1992 Rio Conference spawned another major dispute. It involved the Convention on Biological Diversity.[16] This treaty was opened for signature at the Conference. The so-called "Biodiversity Treaty" mandates national development, monitoring, and preservation of biological diversity. It also requires the maintenance of "variability" among living organisms from all sources and ecosystems—a form of endangered species protection. The relevant dispute occurred when President Bush declared that the US would not endorse this treaty, even in principle. He objected to the required transfer of technology and intellectual property rights held by US corporations, the sharing of access to profitable biotechnologies with developing countries, and a required financial commitment to advancing the relative economic position of developing countries. The gist of the US objection was that the US did not want to donate its biotechnology, nor to provide financing for other countries to develop competitive capabilities.

The US then stood alone among the world's leaders against implementation of the Biodiversity Treaty. Some 120 States had signed this treaty at or shortly after the Rio Convention. In 1993, however, incoming President Clinton reversed the US position. He announced that the US would "sign" this treaty, meaning an agreement in principle—although the US would not ratify it as a binding instrument (*see* § 8.2). President Clinton announced that the US would subsequently work with the European Union to develop an interpretive agreement that would not debase the intellectual property rights of US and European companies using genetic resources in their research and development programs.

Article 3 of the Biodiversity Treaty contains an important principle that will be of lasting value in dovetailing environmental protection and sustainable development: "States have, in accordance with the Charter of the United Nations and the principles of international law, the sovereign right to exploit their own resources pursuant to their own environmental policies, and the [concomitant] responsibility to ensure that activities within their jurisdiction or control do not cause damage to the environment of other States or areas beyond the limits of national jurisdiction."

■ 12.2 INTERNATIONAL LIABILITY STANDARDS

Do international legal standards exist for determining a State's responsibility for *environmental* harm?

Arbitral/Judicial Decisions

The preliminary analysis of this complex question begins with the recognition that the presence of an international border cannot vest total discretion in the border States to alter natural conditions on the basis of State sovereignty. Several opinions of the Permanent Court of International Justice in the 1920s and 1930s thus limited State control of international waterways used for navigation or irrigation.[17]

The 1941 *Trail Smelters Arbitration* may be the classic case for articulating the fundamental norm in contemporary International Environmental Law. Some prior international cases dealt with water pol-

lution. This was the first to deal authoritatively with cross-border air pollution. A Canadian smelter, seven miles from the US state of Washington, emitted extraordinary sulfur dioxide fumes, harming the atmosphere and the agricultural industry in the state of Washington for over a decade. The US and Canada established an arbitral tribunal, consisting of individual Canadian, US, and Belgian arbitrators (the third being a neutral arbitrator selected by the other two). Their task was to resolve this controversy between the two governments. This tribunal determined that Canada had thus incurred State responsibility for environmental damage, although the smelter was a nongovernmental operation by private industry in Trail, Canada.

In one passage, the arbitrators effectively predicted the direction of future environmental analyses by referring to the competing interests of industrial development and agricultural degradation in the region encompassing both British Columbia and Washington. Drawing from commonly accepted sources, the arbitral decision thus provides that "[i]t would not be to the advantage of the two countries concerned that industrial effort should be prevented by exaggerating the [environmental] interests of the agricultural community. Equally, it would not be to the advantage of the two countries that the agricultural community should be oppressed to advance the interest of industry."[18]

While the State parties ineffectively juggled the final resolution of this decision for the next forty years, it authoritatively restated an emerging principle—subsequently cited in national and international litigation. A State must not knowingly permit the use of its territory to harm other States. State A has the obligation to protect State B from the injurious acts of individuals and corporations within State A. Sovereignty includes certain rights. It also includes the responsibility to respect the territory of other States.

The UN's International Court of Justice (ICJ) addressed the obligation of States not to allow the use of their territories to interfere with the rights of other States in two major cases since the *Trail Smelters Arbitration*. Albania was held liable for its failure to notify Great Britain about the presence of mines in Albanian waters within an international strait. The ICJ also ordered France to cease its nuclear atmospheric testing (discussed in relation to the *Rainbow Warrior* incident in § 12.1), because radioactive fallout would prejudice various health and agricultural interests of the citizens of Australia and New Zealand.[19]

International Codification Struggle

Various UN initiatives have attempted to codify the standard for establishing international environmental wrongs. The UN Conferences on Environment and Development (UNCED) contain draft standards (*see* § 12.1). Principle 21 of the 1972 Stockholm Declaration on the United Nations Conference on the Human Environment restated the above *Trail Smelters* formulation as follows:

Principle 21 States have, in accordance with the Charter of the United Nations and the principles of international law, . . . the responsibility to ensure that activities within their jurisdiction or control do not cause damage to the environment of other States or of areas beyond the limits of national jurisdiction.

Principle 22 States shall cooperate to develop further international law regarding liability and compensation for the victims of pollution and other environmental damage caused by activities within the jurisdiction or control of such States beyond their jurisdiction.

The next UN conference attempt to codify environmental responsibility appeared in the 1992 UNCED Rio Declaration. Principle 2 repeated *verbatim* the above-quoted Stockholm Principle 21 on the general duty not to permit any use that harms another State's interests. Principle 7 of the Rio Declaration expanded the Stockholm Principle 22 statement of environmental expectations. The 1992 articulation distinguished between the responsibilities of developed and other countries, specifically referring to the new goal of "sustainable development." Rio Principle 7 thus provides as follows:

States shall cooperate in a spirit of global partnership to conserve, protect and restore the health and integrity of the Earth's ecosystem. In view of the different contributions of global environmental degradation, States have common but differentiated responsibilities. The developed countries acknowledge the responsibility that they bear in the international pursuit of sustainable development in view of the pressures their societies place on the global environment and of the technologies and financial resources they command.

Several years prior to the Rio Conference, a UN group of experts drafted principles that may also serve as a yardstick for measuring the acceptable scope of the "sustainable development" for developing countries. They must be vigilant about their responsibility not to use their territory in ways that harm other States. In 1987, this Experts Group on Environmental Law of the World Commission on Environment and Development thereby promulgated their Legal Principles for Environmental Protection and Sustainable Development.[20] Article 11 provides for liability when transboundary environmental harm results from *permissible* activities. An activity that creates a risk of substantial harm, caused by "transboundary environmental interference," gives rise to State liability if "the overall technical and socio-economic cost . . . far exceeds the long run advantage." Article 21 provides for liability when the State act or omission is *not permissible* under International Law. A State may be thereby responsible when it uses its natural resources in a way that results in (or fails to prevent) an environmental interference with the rights of another State.

The UN Experts' list includes the following alternative remedies:

- The responsible State must thereby cease the wrongful act or omission resulting in the environmental interference;

- It may have to reestablish the circumstances—as they were prior to its wrongful act;

- The responsible State may, instead, have to pay compensation to the State(s) harmed by its transborder environmental interference.

Other UN Conventions contain articles addressing environmental responsibilities, within the more specific context of the sea and the airspace. The 1982 Conference on the Law of the Sea produced articles that would form the constitution of the seas that entered into force in 1994 (*see* § 6.3). Section 9 of that treaty addresses "Responsibility and Liability." It contains several articles involving that regime's particular legal standards. The relevant portion of Article 235 provides as follows:

1. States are responsible for the fulfillment of their international obligations concerning the

protection and preservation of the marine environment. They shall be liable in accordance with international law.

2. States shall ensure that recourse is available in accordance with their [national] legal systems for prompt and adequate compensation or other relief in respect of damage caused by pollution of the marine environment by natural or juridical [that is, corporate] persons within their jurisdiction.

Environmental concerns with the space above the earth are expressed in the various UN draft instruments such as the 1992 Rio Climate Change Convention.[21] This was the only treaty opened for signature at the Rio Conference. It addresses the so-called "greenhouse" emissions, including carbon dioxide. Signatories would thus submit inventories and periodic reports to an environmental agency concerning the gaseous emissions harming the atmosphere—such as those that are depleting the ozone layer above the earth. Some 6 percent of the world's industrialized population now produces 30 percent of the gases responsible for the "Greenhouse Effect." Signatories would thus be subject to international review of their compliance with the treaty goal of controlling these environmentally adverse emissions.

The Climate Convention also provides for financial assistance to the lesser-developed countries. Funding would become available through the "Global Environmental Facility of the World Bank"—an intergovernmental institution previously responsible for the rebuilding of postwar Europe and assisting with the establishment of national economic development programs. The Global Environmental Facility would thus be the world's environmental banker. Article 9 of the Climate Convention also calls for the State parties to continually assess scientific evidence, as it becomes available, for controlling climate change and incorporating the relevant technologies for achieving better national control of the environment.

The World Bank, in conjunction with the International Monetary Fund, is currently working to fund the cleanup and restoration of the Amazon forests in Brazil. These are "lungs" of the earth, in the sense that 50 to 80 percent of the Western Hemisphere's oxygen comes from these rain forests. Each year, approximately twenty-five million acres of forests are cleared from the rain forests of the world. In 1994, the US Agency for International Development estimated that Guatemala and Colombia will lose 33 percent of their remaining forests. Ecuador and Nicaragua will lose 50 percent of their rain forests. This form of environmental depletion is thus affecting all other nations throughout the hemisphere.

Several archetypal problems may be noted with the Climate Change Convention. Given existing concerns with the objectivity of the World Bank, it is not clear that the more developed nations will ratify this device for financing sustainable development.[22] Also, the Convention doe *not* require the signatories to actually control their harmful emissions. Nor does it contain any target date for doing so. The implicit agreement, however, was to strive for a return to the emission levels of 1990—by the year 2000. Finally, preventative measures are costly. The estimated cost would be $120 billion per year to control global warming. Not many States will have the economic capacity to provide the requisite funding. Future global warming conferences will have to focus on an acceptable framework for controlling nations like the US, with its highest rate of greenhouse gas emissions in the world—twenty tons per person in 1995.

Liability Summary

One may nevertheless conclude that States are liable for their conduct or omissions constituting "transboundary environmental interference," as defined in principle by the 1992 UN Rio Conference documents. This theme was similarly expressed in the only relevant treaty to enter into force (in 1994): the Convention on the Law of the Sea. Article 235 of that treaty thus provides that States are liable for "damage caused by pollution of the marine environment by natural or juridical persons within their jurisdiction." And as formulated by Article 21 of the UN World Commission on the Environment 1987 Principles, a State is responsible when it uses a natural resource, or fails to prevent an environmental interference, in a manner that results in an adverse environmental impact in another State. The offending State thus has several resulting duties under the UN environmental Experts Principles. It must cease the wrongful act; reestablish the circumstances as they were prior to the wrongful act; and otherwise provide compensation to the State harmed by the environmental interference.

Now that the varied articulations of international environmental legal standards have been presented and summarized, one must recognize that there are some familiar defenses to the ready resolution of international environmental claims. First, the very nature of environmental harm blurs the ability to determine exactly *how it happened.* One must sometimes search for a causal link between the activity and the actor supposedly responsible for the damage and the effect. The result may occur long after the incident (if there is one) allegedly causing the degradation ("transboundary environmental interference"). Further, *existing* environmental degradation may be a significant factor in causation and potential liability of other contributing actors. Carbon dioxide, or so-called acid rain, was sent into the atmosphere in the above *Trail Smelters Case*—across the border from Canada to the US state of Washington. Assuming that the Washington fog became thicker and more dense in subsequent years later, it would be difficult for the state of Washington to trace the fog problem directly or exclusively to the Canadian smelter. Events in the *US* may have contributed to that fog, including industrialization in the region near the border and the ensuing smoke contaminants created within the US. The local US pollution may thus originate from a variety of sources, including US automobiles, forest depletion machinery operations, and other industrial activities—in addition to a smelter operation just on the other side of the border.

Liability is not the only facet of this complex problem of establishing State responsibility for environmental degradations. Even assuming that the liability is clear, what remedy is the most appropriate? Should the responsible State pay *damages* for the "environmental interference"? If so, *how much* would appropriately compensate the harmed State? Would it be fairer to require the offending State to *restore* the status quo, as it existed prior to the environmental degradation? Further, the developments in International Environmental Law (EIL) signal a shift to the paradigm of "sustainable development." This model authorizes risk assessments when balancing the competing interests of protecting the environment while encouraging underdeveloped nations to improve the conditions of life for their inhabitants. This evolution in the contemporary UN treaty instruments will surely make both liability and remedy assessments even more complex, given the ambiguities associated with implementation of the ill-defined term *sustainable development.*

The 1991 joint research project of the Italian universities of Sienna and Parma analyzes the practical problems with international responsibility for environmental harm. The president of the European Council for Environmental Law therein cautions that environmental damage cases are comparable to a *legal steeplechase.* His analogy is as follows: "The procedure of compensation for environmental damage can be compared to a steeple-chase where different obstacles must be overcome before arriving to the final result. Some obstacles—and maybe the hardest ones to overcome—result from *facts* while others have a *legal* character. The first category characterizes all environmental compensation situations [that is, causation] while the second [the remedy] mainly consists in problems arising from the transnational nature of the damage."[23]

■ 12.3 ENVIRONMENTAL INSTRUMENTS

The 1972 and 1992 UN Conferences on the Environment spawned an unprecedented political and diplomatic awakening. The UN, together with regional environmental organizations and world leaders, has repositioned international environmental issues from the periphery to the center of their political and diplomatic agendas. Conferences of States, UN initiatives, and intergovernmental treaties permeated the public consciousness in the last portion of the twentieth century. As a result, environmental issues are finally sharing center stage with the other traditional concerns of International Law depicted in the first ten chapters of this book.

This section provides a *snapshot* of some of the major international environmental instruments. The overview contained Exhibit 12.1 will help to visualize the various campaigns designed to save the environment from further unplanned assault. Recent entries address the herculean task of discouraging environmental degradation while encouraging sustainable development in underdeveloped countries.

EXHIBIT 12.1 Major Global Environmental Instruments

1967	Treaty on Principles Governing Activities of States in the Exploration and Use of Outer Space, Including the Moon and Other Celestial Bodies—prohibits weapons testing (and military maneuvers) on celestial bodies[a]
1972	Stockholm Declaration of UN Conference on Human Environment—first global statement of environmental principles
1972	Resolution 2997 on Institutional and Financial Arrangement for International Environment Cooperation—established UN's environmental fund and Governing Council for policy guidance[b]
1973	Resolution 3129 on Co-operation in the Field of the Environment Concerning Natural Resources Shared by Two or More States—Governing Council to report on measures taken[c]
1974	Convention for the Prevention of Marine Pollution from Land-Based Sources—ecological protection[d]
1977	Environmental Modification Convention—prohibits military and other hostile uses of the environment[e]
1978	Protocol Relating to International Convention for the Prevention of Pollution from Ships—ecological protection[f]
1980	Resolution 35/48[g] on Historical Responsibility of States for Preservation of Nature for Present and Future Generations
1983	World Charter for Nature—nature's essential processes not to be impaired; genetic viability not compromised; all areas of earth subject to conservation; ecosystems managed for optimum sustainable productivity; no degradation by warfare or other hostile activities[h]
1985	Vienna Convention for the Protection of the Ozone Layer—protects layer of atmospheric zone above planetary layer[i]
1986	International Atomic Energy Agency Convention on Early Notification of a Nuclear Accident—designed to minimize consequences and protect life, property, and environment[j]
1987	Experts Group on Environmental Law of World Commission on Environment and Development—legal principles for maintaining "sustainable development" of developing countries
1988	Protocol to the 1979 Convention on Long-Range Transboundary Air Pollution Concerning the Control of Emissions of Nitrogen Oxides or Their Transboundary Fluxes—States to control or reduce emissions to 1987 levels[k]
1989	Hague Declaration on the Environment—cooperation in controlling ozone layer deterioration, caused by emissions from industrialized States adversely affecting the right to live[l]

EXHIBIT 12.1 *(continued)*

1991	Protocol on Environmental Protection to the Antarctic Treaty—updates 1959 treaty (prohibiting nuclear testing and hazardous waste disposal) to enhance protection of all ecosystems, prevent jeopardy of endangered species, and prohibit mineral resource activities except scientific[m]
1992	Rio Declaration on Environment and Development—second major conference of States; establishes current program for global partnership discouraging environmental degradation while *encouraging sustainable development*
1992	Agenda 21—most extensive statement of priorities including review/assessment of International Law, development of implementation and compliance measures, effective participation by all States in law-making process, study of range and effectiveness of dispute resolution procedures
1992	Framework Convention on Climate Change—measures to combat greenhouse effect of emissions of carbon dioxide and similar gases and to finance controls
1992	Convention on Biological Diversity—national monitoring and strategies for conserving biological diversity of all ecosystems (US opposition was a major barrier to Conference success)
1992	Non-Legally Binding Authoritative Statement of Principles for Global Consensus on the Management, Conservation and Sustainable Development for All Types of Forests—principles encouraging *sustainable* development, reforestation, reduction of pollutants, especially acid rain
1993	Resolution on Institutional Arrangement to Follow up the [1992] UN Conference on Environment and Development—UN General Assembly follow-up resolution welcoming adoption of Agenda 21, stressing integration of environmental protection and sustainable development[n]

Note: instruments *not* cited below are discussed in § 12.1 or § 12.2; (*19__) below = year treaty entered into force

[a] Reprinted in 6 Int'l Legal Mat'ls [hereinafter ILM] 386 (*1979)
(prohibits nuclear weapons in orbit) 18 ILM 1434 (*1984)
[b] UN Doc. A/8370, 13 ILM 234
[c] Subsequent principles, 17 ILM 1097
[d] 13 ILM 352 (*1978) (one of numerous treaty controls)
[e] 16 ILM 88 (*1978)
[f] 17 ILM 546 (*1983) (one of numerous treaty controls)
[g] UN Doc. A/35/48, General Assembly Official Records, 35th Session, Supp. No. 48
[h] General Assembly Resolution 37/7 (*see* Annex), 22 ILM 455
[i] 26 ILM 1529 (*1988); protocols—28 ILM 1335
[j] 25 ILM 1369 (*1986)
[k] 28 ILM 212 (*1991); 1979 treaty in 18 ILM 1442 (*1983)
[l] UN Doc. A/44/340-E/1989/120 (*see* Annex), 28 ILM 1308
[m] 30 ILM 1461; 1959 treaty—19 ILM 860 (*1961)
[n] UN Doc. A/47/191, 32 ILM 238

■ 12.4 UNITED STATES ENVIRON-MENTAL LEGISLATION

Principle 11 of the 1992 Rio Declaration of the UN Conference on the Environment and Development (*see* § 12.1) provides, in part, that "States shall enact effective environmental legislation." States are thus expected to develop national programs that will both implement and supplement International Environmental Law (IEL). Commentators have characterized this body of law as "soft law." It contains many declarative statements of principle but too few legally binding provisions.

The United States previously enacted environmental legislation originally intended to manage the environment *within* the US. "Transboundary environmental interferences," a subsequently established term of art contained in international instruments, is not limited to the boundaries of the responsible State, however. And the myriad of physical assaults on the environment illustrate that States cannot wait until IEL moves from "soft law" principles to "hard law" obligations. In 1969, the US Congress enacted legislation designed to control degradation of the environment. It has been interpreted, since the 1992 UN Rio Conference on the Environment and Development, as applying in a broader context than likely intended by the original congressional blueprint.

First, the basic legislation is provided immediately below—the National Environmental Policy Act, as amended to date (emphasis supplied):

TITLE 42. THE PUBLIC HEALTH AND WELFARE
CHAPTER 55—NATIONAL ENVIRONMENTAL POLICY
SUBCHAPTER I—POLICIES AND GOALS

§ 4332. Cooperation of agencies; reports;
availability of information; recommendations;
international and national coordination of efforts

The Congress authorizes and directs that, to the fullest extent possible: . . . *all agencies of the Federal Government shall—*

(A) utilize a systematic, interdisciplinary approach which will insure the integrated use of the natural and social sciences and the environmental design arts in planning and in decisionmaking which may have an impact on man's environment;

(B) identify and develop methods and procedures, in consultation with the Council on Environmental Quality established by subchapter II of this chapter, which will insure that presently unquantified environmental amenities and values may be given appropriate consideration in decisionmaking along with economic and technical considerations;

(C) *include* in every recommendation or report on proposals for legislation and other major Federal actions significantly affecting the quality of the human environment, *a detailed statement* by the responsible official *on—*

(i) *the environmental impact of the proposed action,*

(ii) any adverse environmental effects which cannot be avoided should the proposal be implemented,

(iii) alternatives to the proposed action,

(iv) the relationship between local short-term uses of man's environment and the maintenance and enhancement of long-term productivity, and

(v) any irreversible and irretrievable commitments of resources which would be involved in the proposed action should it be implemented.

. . .

(F) *recognize* the worldwide and long-range character of environmental problems and, where consistent with the foreign policy of the United States, lend appropriate support to initiatives, resolutions, and programs designed to maximize international cooperation in anticipating and preventing a decline in the quality of mankind's world environment. . . .

A variety of novel legal issues, regarding application of the National Environmental Protection Act (NEPA), surfaced since the 1972 Stockholm Declaration and the 1992 Rio Declaration. The following examples provide some insight into how these international issues have arisen in the *national* legal context involving the NEPA:

■ WASHINGTON, D.C. (Jul. 1993)—An environmental group sued the federal government, when the president was negotiating the North American Free Trade Agreement. The president, who is a federal officer, had not obtained an environmental impact statement as required in proposals "for legislation and other major Federal actions significantly affecting the quality of the human environment." A US trial judge thus declared the government to be in violation of the NEPA. The court of appeals reversed, however, on the basis that the plaintiff environmentalists did not have the legal capacity to sue—although the NEPA statutory mandate had been disregarded. The US Supreme Court decided not to review this case.[24]

■ WASHINGTON, D.C. (Oct. 1993)—The Clinton administration revealed a new plan to reduce the waste of carbon dioxide and other gaseous emissions that threaten to warm the global climate by trapping heat within the atmosphere. The US Environmental Protection Agency therein proposed an amendment to the federal Clean Air Act. It would call on landfill operators to voluntarily remove organic waste that releases methane, a greenhouse gas, when it decomposes. Another program goal would be the augmentation of household appliance standards, to further reduce harmful emissions into the atmosphere. The basic objective is to reduce this category of emissions, by the year 2000, to 1990 levels.[25]

■ COLUMBIA, S.C. (Sept. 1994)—A federal appeals court decided that European nuclear waste may enter the US. South Carolina had sued the US Energy Department, due to its failure to provide a "detailed" environmental impact statement as required under the NEPA. Two ships waiting in the Atlantic were thus able to proceed to port to offload 409 spent fuel elements from nuclear reactors in Austria, Denmark, Sweden, and the Netherlands. The court nevertheless criticized the US Energy Department for evading environmental rules, because this was not an isolated incident. The federal government had arranged the return of the highly enriched uranium to the US, where it was originally manufactured. The US plans to thus "return" another ten to fifteen thousand spent fuel rods over the next dozen years. Receipt is crucial to US nuclear nonproliferation policy.

■ SAN DIEGO, CA (Dec. 1994)—A federal trial court sentenced the nation's first defendant convicted of freon trafficking. An automotive air conditioning repair business had illegally imported 200 containers of chlorofluorocarbons (CFCs). CFCs are currently used in an estimated 140 million US automobiles and 160 million refrigerators. Although these units will need replenishing, the US stopped importing any freon in 1995, due to concerns with ozone depletion causing skin cancer. The US Customs Service anticipates that freon will become the second major illegal import, after cocaine. (Continued production in Mexico may facilitate added black market importation.) Under a 1987 treaty, CFC production has been terminated in the US—but not elsewhere.

Although International Environmental Law is commonly criticized as being "soft law" without binding obligations, it nevertheless sets standards for a broader application of national legislation to accommodate international environmental concerns. US judges are becoming more and more aware of the "larger picture" when they interpret conduct in one country that may impact others. As discussed in other chapters in this book, the perennial problem with expanded applications of national law is the degree to which US laws apply to conduct occurring *elsewhere*. The root question is typically whether or not an event occurring *outside* of the State attempting to exercise its jurisdiction has the requisite "effect" *within* that State for the purpose of applying its law to the event (*see,* for example, § 5.2).

Environmental litigation presents the converse question of the degree to which national law can be applied by a national court, based on effects *outside* of the particular jurisdiction. If the community of nations is ever to make significant strides, in the grand design of the UN's environmental instruments (*see* Exhibit 12.1), then the judges of other countries might well consider adopting the novel analysis of the following decision—construing the

US National Environmental Protection Act (NEPA). Note the dichotomy as you read the rationale for its result: The Court authorizes the application of US law to environmental concerns in Antarctica, while retaining the sovereign right to choose the "public benefit" over "environmental costs" in other cases.

ENVIRONMENTAL DEFENSE FUND, INC. v. MASSEY

United States Court of Appeals,
District of Columbia Circuit
986 F.2d 528 (1993)

[*Author's Note: Most citations have been omitted. Emphasis has been supplied in selected passages.*]

[*Opinion.*] Before: MIKVA, Chief Judge, WALD and EDWARDS, Circuit Judges.

The Environmental Defense Fund ("EDF") appeals the district court's order [by a federal trial judge] dismissing its action . . . under the National Environmental Policy Act ("NEPA"). EDF alleges that the National Science Foundation ("NSF") violated NEPA by failing to prepare an environmental impact statement ("EIS") in accordance with Section 102(2)(C) [*see* § 4332(C) above] before going forward with plans to incinerate food wastes in Antarctica. The district court dismissed EDF's action for lack of subject matter jurisdiction [to hear this type of claim]. The [trial] court explained that while Congress utilized broad language in NEPA, the statute nevertheless did not contain "a clear expression of legislative intent through a plain statement of [congressional intent that the NEPA should be interpreted to have] extraterritorial statutory effect". . . .

We reverse the district court's decision, and hold that the presumption *against* the extraterritorial application of statutes . . . does not apply where the conduct regulated by the statute occurs primarily, if not exclusively, in the United States, and the alleged extraterritorial effect of the statute will be felt in Antarctica—a continent without a sovereign, and an area over which the United States has a great measure of legislative control. . . .

I.

As both parties readily acknowledge, Antarctica is not only a unique continent, but somewhat of an international anomaly. Antarctica is the only continent on earth which has never been, and is not now, subject to the sovereign rule of any nation [*see* § 6.1 of this book on territory that is *res communis*]. Since entry into force of the Antarctic Treaty in 1961, the United States and 39 other nations have agreed not to assert any territorial claims to the continent or to establish rights of sovereignty there. Hence, Antarctica is generally considered to be a "global common" and frequently analogized to outer space.

Under the auspices of the United States Antarctica Program, NSF operates the McMurdo Station research facility in Antarctica. McMurdo Station is one of three year-round installations that the United States has established in Antarctica, and over which NSF exercises exclusive control. All of the installations serve as platforms or logistic centers for U.S. scientific research; McMurdo Station is the largest of the three, with more than 100 buildings and a summer population of approximately 1200.

Over the years, NSF has burned food wastes at McMurdo Station in an open landfill as a means of disposal. In early 1991, NSF decided to improve its environmental practices in Antarctica by *halting its practice* of burning food wastes in the open by October, 1991. After discovering asbestos in the landfill, . . . NSF decided to cease open burning . . . and to develop quickly an alternative plan for disposal of its food waste. NSF stored the waste at McMurdo Station from February, 1991 to July, 1991, but *subsequently decided to resume* incineration in an "interim incinerator" [not in an open landfill] until a state-of-the-art incinerator could be delivered to McMurdo Station. EDF contends that the planned incineration may produce highly toxic pollutants which could be hazardous to the environment, and that NSF failed to consider fully the consequences of its decision to *resume* incineration as required by the decisionmaking process established by NEPA.

Section 102(2)(C) of NEPA requires "all federal agencies" to prepare an EIS [Environmental Impact Statement] in connection with any proposal for a "major action significantly affecting the quality of the human environment." The EIS requirement, along with the many other provisions in the statute, is designed to "promote efforts which will prevent or eliminate damage to the environment and biosphere." Following the passage of NEPA, NSF promulgated regulations applying the EIS requirement to its decisions regarding proposed actions *in Antarctica*. Since the issuance of [Presidential] Executive Order 12114, however, NSF has contended that proposed action affecting the environment in Antarctica is governed by the Executive Order, not NEPA.

Executive Order 12114 declares that federal agencies are required to prepare environmental analyses for "major Federal actions significantly affecting the environment of the global commons *outside* the jurisdiction of any nation (e.g., the oceans or Antarctica)." According to the Executive Order, major federal actions significantly *affecting the environment of foreign countries* may also require environmental analyses under certain circumstances. Although the procedural requirements imposed by the Executive Order are analogous to those under NEPA, the Executive Order does not provide a cause of action to a [private] plaintiff [who might thus sue,] seeking agency compliance with the EIS requirement. The Executive Order explicitly states that the requirements contained therein are "solely for the purpose of establishing internal procedures for Federal agencies . . . and nothing in [the Order] shall be construed to create a cause of action." Thus, what is at stake in this litigation is *whether a federal agency may decide to take actions* significantly affecting the human environment in Antarctica *without complying with NEPA* and without being subject to judicial review.

II.

A. The Presumption Against Extraterritoriality

As the district court correctly noted, the Supreme Court recently reaffirmed the general presumption against the extraterritorial application of statutes. . . . [*See* § 5.1 of this book.]

. . .

[T]he district court below [completely] bypassed the threshold question of whether the application of NEPA to agency actions in Antarctica presents an extraterritoriality problem at all. In particular, the court failed to determine whether the statute seeks

to regulate conduct [*either*] in the United States or in another sovereign country. It also declined to consider whether NEPA would create a potential for "clashes between our laws and those of other nations" if it was applied to the decisionmaking of federal agencies regarding proposed actions in Antarctica. After a thorough review of these relevant factors, we conclude that this case does not present an issue of extraterritoriality.

B. Regulated Conduct Under NEPA

NEPA is designed to control the decisionmaking *process* of U.S. federal agencies, not the substance of agency decisions. By enacting NEPA, Congress exercised its statutory authority to determine the factors an agency must consider when exercising its discretion, and created a process whereby American officials, while acting *within* the United States, can reach enlightened policy decisions by taking into account environmental effects.

. . .

In many respects, NEPA is most closely akin to the myriad laws directing federal decisionmakers to consider particular factors before extending aid or engaging in certain types of trade. See Comment, *NEPA's Role in Protecting the World Environment*, 131 U. PA. L.REV. 353, 371 (1982). For example, the Foreign Assistance Act of 1961 requires the Agency for International Development, before approving developmental assistance, to consider the degree to which programs integrate women into the economy, as well as the possibility of using aid to "support democratic and social political trends in recipient countries." Similarly, the Nuclear Nonproliferation Act requires the Nuclear Regulatory Commission to consider a nation's willingness to cooperate with American nonproliferation objectives before approving a nuclear export license. Just as these statutes . . . [do not address agency] action in *foreign* jurisdictions, and are instead directed at the regulation of agency decisionmaking [in the US], NEPA . . . simply prescribes by statute the factors an agency must consider when exercising its discretionary authority [to undertake federal agency action].

. . .

C. The Unique Status of Antarctica

Antarctica's unique status in the international arena further supports our conclusion that this case does not implicate the presumption against extraterritoriality. . . . Thus, where the U.S. has some real measure of legislative control over the region at issue, the presumption against extraterritoriality is much weaker. *See, e.g., Sierra Club v. Adams*, 578 F.2d 389 (D.C. Cir. 1978) (NEPA assumed to be applicable to South American highway construction where the United States had two-thirds of the ongoing financial responsibility and control over the highway construction); *People of Enewetak v. Laird*, 353 F.Supp. 811 (D. Hawaii 1973) (concluding that NEPA applies to the United States trust territories in the Pacific). And where there is no potential for conflict "between our laws and those of other nations," the purpose behind the presumption is eviscerated, and the presumption against extraterritoriality applies with significantly less force.

. . .

D. Foreign Policy Considerations

. . . NSF argues that the EIS requirement *will interfere* with U.S. efforts to work cooperatively with other nations toward solutions to environmental problems in Antarctica. In NSF's view, joint research and cooperative environmental assessment would be "placed at risk of NEPA injunctions, making the U.S. a doubtful partner for future international cooperation in Antarctica" [that is, agency decisions/agreements are subject to judicial review under the NEPA].

NSF also argues that the Protocol on Environmental Protection to the Antarctic Treaty, which was adopted and opened for signature on October 4, 1991, *would, if adopted* by all the proposed signatories, *conflict with* the procedural requirements adopted by Congress for the decisionmaking of federal agencies under *NEPA*. See Protocol on Environmental Protection to the Antarctic Treaty, with Annexes, XI ATSCM, reprinted in 30 Int'l Legal Materials 1461 (1991). According to NSF, since NEPA requires the preparation of an EIS for actions with potentially "*significant*" impacts, while the Protocol requires an environmental analysis even for actions with "*minor or transitory*" impacts on the Antarctic environment, the two regulatory schemes are incompatible and will result in international discord.

We find these arguments unpersuasive. First, it should be noted that the Protocol is not in effect in any form and is years away from ratification by the

United States and all 26 signatories [none of which have *ratified* the Protocol]. . . .

More importantly, we are not convinced that NSF's ability to cooperate with other nations in Antarctica in accordance with U.S. foreign policy will be hampered by [the possibility of] NEPA injunctions. We made clear in [case citation omitted], that where the EIS requirement proves to be incompatible with Section 102(2)(F) [regarding worldwide assessment], federal agencies will *not* be subject to injunctions forcing compliance with Section 102(2)(C) [otherwise requiring an EIS]. Section 102(2)(F) specifically requires all federal agencies to recognize the worldwide and long-range character of environmental problems and, where consistent with the foreign policy of the United States, lend appropriate *support to initiatives, resolutions, and programs designed to maximize international cooperation.*

NRDC [omitted case] was not the first case to hold that NEPA's EIS requirement must yield where overriding [international] policy concerns are present. In *Committee for Nuclear Responsibility v. Seaborg*, 463 F.2d 796 (D.C.Cir.1971), for example, we refused to issue an injunction under NEPA, despite the real potential for significant harm to the environment, because the government made "assertions of harm to national security and foreign policy." In that case, conservation groups sought to enjoin an underground nuclear test on the grounds that the Atomic Energy Commission failed to comply fully with NEPA. Although there was reason to believe that the petitioners would succeed on the merits of their claim, we denied the requested injunction in light of the foreign policy concerns.

NRDC and *Seaborg* illustrate that the government may avoid the EIS requirement where U.S. foreign policy interests outweigh the benefits derived from preparing an EIS. . . . Thus, contrary to NSF's assertions, where U.S. foreign policy interests outweigh the benefits of the EIS requirement, NSF's efforts to cooperate with foreign governments regarding environmental practices in Antarctica will not be frustrated by forced compliance with NEPA.

. . .

We also note, that prior to the issuance of Executive Order 12114, the Council on Environment Quality ("CEQ") maintained that NEPA *applies* to the decisionmaking process of federal agencies regarding actions *in Antarctica*. CEQ is the agency created by Congress to oversee the implementation of NEPA, and its interpretation of that statute is generally entitled to "substantial deference." . . .

CONCLUSION

Applying the presumption against extraterritoriality here would result in a federal agency being allowed to undertake actions significantly affecting the human environment in Antarctica . . . without ever being held accountable for its failure to comply with the decisionmaking procedures instituted by Congress. . . . NSF has provided no support for its proposition that conduct occurring within the United States is rendered exempt from otherwise applicable statutes merely because the effects of its compliance would be felt in the global commons. We therefore reverse the district court's decision, and remand for a determination of whether the environmental analyses performed by NSF, prior to its decision to resume incineration, failed to [fully] comply with Section 102(2)(C) of NEPA [requiring an appropriately considered EIS].

■ SUMMARY

1. Environmental pollution is not an exclusively modern phenomenon. Sudden disasters and incremental degradations in the final decade of the twentieth have made it one of the most prominent of international concerns.

2. Numerous environmental instruments have been declared in the closing decades of the twentieth century. Two major conferences of States produced draft treaties, declarations, and principles designed to maintain the quality of the environment.

3. There are twin objectives in contemporary environmental instruments: discouraging environmental degradation and encouraging sustainable development. Whether these will ultimately be compatible depends on the degree to which underdeveloped States will be able to close the gap with developed States, without significant adverse effects on regional and global ecosystems.

4. The term *International Environmental Law* is a blend of national and international attempts to legally control the effect of development on the environment. The many draft treaties and declarations arguably consist of "soft law," in the sense that there are many principles but few binding obligations—due to the varying degrees of concern with the effects of development on the environment.

5. Alternative modes of dispute resolution are available in the International Court of Justice. The full Court has now considered several important environmental issues. In 1993, the Court announced the availability of a seven-judge "chamber" to hear only environmental disputes.

6. The 1992 UN Conference on the Environment and Development produced a series of draft treaties and declarations. The most prominent was Agenda 21—an extensive blueprint for environmental control and sustainable development in the twenty-first century. One potential drawback is the lack of mandatory obligations and Agenda 21's dependence on "follow-up processes."

7. There is legal liability for one State's "environmental interference" with another. The legal standards are emerging. States no longer have the *exclusive* discretion to manage and resolve environmental issues, because degradations often have transboundary effects. The clearest norm is that a State may not use, or allow the use of, its territory in a way that harms another.

8. Both the 1972 and 1992 UN environmental conferences affirmed the expectation that States must cooperate in developing programs to jointly manage the environment. The latter conference added that developing countries, in their pursuit of "sustainable development," must incorporate appropriate technologies and financial resources so that the *environmental* cost of development does not far exceed the economic benefit.

9. Determining the legal cause of an "incremental" category of transboundary environmental interference may be rather complex. Assuming that liability is established, the alternative remedies are relatively clear. The offending State must halt its role in perpetuating the environmental degradation. It may have to restore the harmed State to the position it would have enjoyed, but for the environmental interference. Money damages may also be an appropriate remedy, depending on the circumstances of the particular case and the theoretical ability to actually restore the harmed State to its prior position.

10. The 1992 Rio Declaration prompts States to develop environmental programs that will augment or implement international environmental efforts. The major US legislation, predating the conference, is the National Environmental Protection Act

(NEPA). It requires federal agencies to prepare an Environmental Impact Statement (EIS) for proposed activities that may "significantly" affect the environment. International instruments tend to require assessments of even a "minor" impact on the environment.

11. The NEPA has been judicially interpreted to apply to federal agency action in areas referred to as the "Global Commons." This term refers to Antarctica, the oceans, and outer space. US courts would not necessarily issue an injunction against agency action *not* based on an EIS, however, if national security interests were sufficiently clear.

■ PROBLEMS

Problem 12.1 (*§ 12.1 after* Rainbow Warrior *materials*):

1. Did New Zealand originally have the jurisdiction, under international legal principles, to prosecute the French agents? On what basis or bases?

2. Did France or its DGSE agents have any available defenses?

3. Why did France thereby incur State responsibility under International Law for its role in the *Rainbow Warrior* affair?

4. Why did the UN Secretary-General *not* award money damages to New Zealand for the death of the Greenpeace photographer or the sinking of the *Rainbow Warrior*?

Problem 12.2 (*end of § 12.3*):

Basic Facts

Refer to the *Rainbow Warrior* incident presented near the beginning of § 12.1. In addition to the given facts, assume the following *hypothetical* facts.

Additional "Facts"

First: The explosion and sinking of the *Rainbow Warrior* in Auckland Harbor contaminates it, due to the nature and large volume of the just on-loaded chemicals that were to be used for testing purposes. The New Zealand authorities were unaware of the presence of these chemicals aboard the Greenpeace vessel when it entered the harbor. While testing aboard the vessel did nothing to pollute the air, the combination of existing pollutants in Auckland Harbor and the chemicals aboard the sunken *Rainbow Warrior* further contaminates the fish within the harbor. One month after the explosion and sinking, the fish in Auckland Harbor are no longer fit for human consumption.

Second: France continues to conduct nuclear testing in French Polynesia. France actually conducted fifty such reported tests, both before and after the 1985 *Rainbow Warrior* incident. The people of New Zealand begin to experience a severe form of "cold," which makes the average healthy person sick for several months at a time. The common symptoms are flu, fever, and skin rash. This form of cold did not exist in New Zealand prior to the commencement of French and US nuclear testing in the South Pacific since the 1950s. Since the 1970s, a small percentage of the population exhibited these symptoms. It has become a fact of life for most New Zealanders in the last five years.

New Zealand (NZ) lodges a diplomatic claim with France in 1995. NZ accuses France of "transboundary environmental interference" within the meaning of the various UN instruments—especially the various 1992 Rio declarations—which NZ characterizes as the essence of International Environmental Law. NZ and France agree to arbitrate this matter. Both are parties to the UN Law of the Sea Treaty, the only agreement *in force* containing relevant environmental provisions. NZ thus seeks remedies for the flu that its citizens now suffer and the contamination of Auckland Harbor.

The Forum

Two students (or groups) will represent France and NZ, as the arbitrators chosen by the respective parties to today's "Flufish Arbitration." A third student will sit as the third and neutral arbitrator selected by the other arbitrators. This arbitral body will report on its resolution of whether France has thus incurred State responsibility under International Law for harm to NZ. In the event of a split decision, the dissenting arbitrator will report his or her decision for further class discussion.

Issues for Resolution

1. What rule or rules should the arbitrators use to determine France's liability?

2. Is France responsible for a "transboundary environmental interference" in New Zealand?

3. If France is found to be liable for New Zealand's claimed environmental degradation, what remedy would be appropriate?

■ BIBLIOGRAPHY

§ 12.1 The Environment's Dominion:

S. Chowdhury, E. Denters & P. de Waart, *The Right to Development in International Law* (Dordrecht, Neth.; Boston: Martinus Nijhoff, 1992)

L. Guruswamy, G. Palmer & B. Weston, *International Environmental Law and World Order: A Problem-Oriented Coursebook* (St. Paul: West, 1994)

S. Johnson, *World Population—Turning the Tide: Three Decades of Progress* (Dordrecht, Neth.; Boston: Kluwer, 1994)

M. Miller, *The Third World in Global Environmental Politics* (Boulder, CO: Lynne Reiner, 1995)

P. Muldoon & R. Lindgren, *The Environmental Bill of Rights* (Toronto: Edmond Montgomery, 1995)

H. Munoz, *Environmental Diplomacy in the Americas* (Boulder, CO: Lynne Reinner, 1992)

M. Quinn, *International Environmental Law*, in *Going International: International Trade for the Nonspecialist* 91 (Philadelphia: Amer. L. Inst., 1994)

G.C. Reijnen & W. de Graaf, *Pollution of Outer Space, in Particular the Geostationary Orbit: Scientific, Policy and Legal Aspects* (Dordrecht, Neth.; Boston: Martinus Nijhoff, 1989)

J. Salter, *European Environmental Law* (Dordrecht, Neth.; Boston, MA: Graham & Trotman/Martinus Nijhoff, 1994)

C. Stone, *Beyond Rio: "Insuring" Against Global Warming*, 86 *Amer. J. Int'l L.* 445 (1992)

§ 12.2 International Liability Standards:

J. Cassels, *The Uncertain Promise of Law: Lessons from Bhopal* (Toronto: Univ. of Toronto Press, 1993)

P. Dupuy, *Soft Law and the International Law of the Environment*, 12 *Mich. J. Int'l L.* 420 (1991)

G. Goldenman, *Environmental Liability and Privatization in Central and Eastern Europe* (Dordrecht, Neth.; Boston: Graham & Trotman/Martinus Nijhoff, 1994)

A. Libler, *Deliberate Wartime Environmental Damage: New Challenges for International Law*, 23 *Calif. West. Int'l L.J.* 67 (1992)

C. Tinker, *Strict Liability of States for Environmental Harm: An Emerging Principle of International Law*, 3 *Touro J. Int'l L.* 155 (1992)

E. Urbani & C. Rubin (ed.), *Transnational Environmental Law and Its Impact on Corporate Behavior* (Irvington-on-Hudson, NY: Transnat'l 1994) (Fletcher School symposium)

§ 12.3 Environmental Instruments:

The Environment Encyclopedia & Directory (New York: Taylor & Francis, 1993)

H. Hohmann (ed.), *Basic Documents of International Environmental Law* (Dordrecht, Neth.; Boston: Graham & Trotman/Martinus Nijhoff, 1992)

B. Kwiatkowsa & A. Soons (ed.), *Transboundary Movements & Disposal of Hazardous Wastes in International Law: Basic Documents* (Dordrecht, Neth.; Boston: Graham & Trotman/Martinus Nijhoff, 1992)

Multilateral Treaties in the Field of the Environment (Cambridge, Eng.: Grotius Pub., 1991) (two volumes)

§ 12.4 United States Environmental Legislation:

B. Bobertz, *The Tools of Prevention: Opportunities for Promoting Pollution Prevention Under Federal Environmental Legislation*, 12 *Va. Environmental L.J.* 1 (1992)

Note, *The Long Arm of the Law? Extraterritorial Application of U.S. Environmental Legislation to Human Activity in Outer Space*, 6 *Georgetown Int'l Environmental L. Rev.* 455 (1994)

■ ENDNOTES

1. Dr. Claude Boutron of France's Domaine University thus depicted Europe's extensive toxic fallout in the journal *Science*, reported in various US newspapers in mid-1994.

2. **Conference:** *see, generally*, N. Taub, *International Conference on Population and Development* (Wash., DC: Amer. Soc. Int'l L., 1994). **Statistics:** *World Population Statistics 1985–2025* (appendix) in E. Osmanczyk, *The Encyclopedia of the United Nations and International Relations* 1085 (New York: Taylor & Francis, 1990).

3. The author thanks Greenpeace International of Amsterdam, for providing detailed information regarding this incident.

4. *See* Nuclear Tests Case (New Zealand v. France), 1974 I.C.J. Rep. 253. Australia filed an identical case against France.

5. The Secretary-General's arbitral decision is reprinted in 26 *Int'l Legal Mat'ls* 1346 (1987).

6. International Court of Justice Communique No. 93/20, of 19 July 1993 (emphasis supplied). The usual chamber consists of three judges.

7. **WHO case:** 1993 I.C.J. Rep. 467. **1995 time limit:** 1994 I.C.J. Rep. 109.

8. **Trusteeship duties:** *see* § 3.3, regarding UN Charter articles 73–91. **ICJ case:** Certain Phosphate Lands in Nauru (Nauru v. Australia), 1989 I.C.J. Rep. 12. **Settlement:** 1993 I.C.J. Rep. 322.

9. *Social Impact of Phosphate Mining*, ch. 3, in C. Weeramantry, *Nauru: Environmental Damage under International Trusteeship* 28, 30–31 (Oxford, Eng.: Oxford Univ. Press, 1992).

10. *See Report on the UN Conference on the Human Environment*, UN Doc. A/CONF.48/14/Rev.1, reprinted in 11 *Int'l Legal Mat'ls* 1416 (1972).

11. Section I, 2(d), Resolution on the Institutional and Financial Arrangement for International Environment Cooperation, Gen. Ass. Reso. 2997, UN Doc. A/8370 (1973), reprinted in 13 *Int'l Legal Mat'ls* 234 (1974).

12. The most comprehensive, but conveniently assembled, collection is available in L. Guruswamy, G. Palmer & B. Weston, *Supplement of Basic Documents to International Environmental Law and World Order* (St. Paul: West, 1994).

13. These documents, with the exception of Agenda 21, are reprinted in 31 *Int'l Legal Mat'ls*, beginning with Georgetown Professor Edith Brown Weiss's summary at 814 (1992).

14. *Did We Really Save the Earth at Rio?*, in *Introduction*, S. Johnson, *The Earth Summit: The United Nations Conference on Environment and Development (UNCED)* 6 (Dordrecht, Neth.; Boston: Graham & Trotman/Martinus Nijhoff, 1993).

15. **Rio:** reprinted in 31 *Int'l Legal Mat'ls* 874 (1992). **Stockholm:** *see* note 10 above.

16. Reprinted in 31 *Int'l Legal Mat'ls* 818 (1992).

17. *See, e.g.*, Territorial Jurisdiction of the International Commission of the River Oder, 1929 P.C.I.J., ser. A, No. 23 (Versailles Treaty Commission jurisdiction over river running through former nations at war) & Diversion of Water from the Meuse Case (Netherlands v. Belgium), 1937 P.C.I.J., ser. A/B, No. 70 (Belgium's control of canal based on treaty).

18. Trail Smelter Arbitration (US v. Canada), 3 UN Rep. Int'l Arb. 1938 (1949).

19. **Mines case:** Corfu Channel Case (Great Britain v. Albania), 1949 I.C.C. Rep. 4. **Nuclear case:** Nuclear Tests Cases (New Zealand v. France), 1974 I.C.J. Rep. 253.

20. UN Doc. WCED/86/23/Add. 1 (1986).

21. **Treaty:** Framework Convention on Climate Change, reprinted in 31 *Int'l Legal Mat'ls* 849 (1992). **Environmental background:** Vandevelde, *International Regulation of Fluorocarbons*, 2 *Harv. Environmental L. Rev.* 474 (1977).

22. *See generally*, B. Brown, *The United States and the Politicalization of the World Bank: Issues of International Law and Policy* (London: Kegan Paul Int'l, 1992).

23. Kiss, *Present Limits to the Enforcement of State Responsibility for Environmental Damage*, ch. 1, in F. Francioni & T. Scovazzi, *International Responsibility for Environmental Harm* 3, 4–5 (Dordrecht, Neth.; Boston: Graham & Trotman/Martinus Nijhoff, 1991) (emphasis supplied).

24. Public Citizen v. US Trade Rep., 5 F.3d 549 (D.C. Cir. 1993), *cert. den'd* 114 S.Ct. 685 (1994). Reviewed in 88 *Amer. J. Int'l L.* 526 (1994).

25. *See* Lee, *O'Leary Says U.S. Is Cutting Gas Emissions*, *Wash. Post*, Apr. 20, 1994, p.A3.

CHAPTER THIRTEEN

International Economic Relations

■ INTRODUCTION

This final chapter deals with several components of a subject historically regarded as a distinct discipline: the *economic* relations of States. Its substantive content has been covered in various economics courses in both graduate and undergraduate curriculums. When taught as a separate course, the titles include International Business, International Business Transactions, International Commerce, International Economics, International Finance, International Trade, and Transnational Business Problems—to name a few. The common theme is that each covers some facet of the relationship between economics and international relations. The objective of this particular treatment is to provide the student of International Law with a more rounded perspective. One may thus leave this course with a general sense of the pervasive impact of international commercial transactions on the evolution of International Law.

The initial section of this chapter identifies some of the very practical problems that corporate management must contemplate when the enterprise is engaged in an international commercial venture. It also presents the tip of the economic iceberg that underlies the historical and contemporary evolution of International Law.

The materials next focus on contemporary international economic integration—the organizations, their objectives, and the major economic treaties. Economic integration has been a very positive development in international relations, due to its potential for achieving lasting peace.

The two remaining topics have shared a virtually symbiotic relationship—the World Trade Organization and the New International Economic Order. These coexisting features of international economic relations have different objectives. The WTO, and the related General Agreement on Tariffs and Trade, were created to improve the economic position of *all* member States. The NIEO, on the other hand, was designed to improve the economic position of *underdeveloped* States in relation to developed States.

■ 13.1 ECONOMICS AND INTERNATIONAL RELATIONS

Chapter Rationale

Books on Pubic International Law have traditionally avoided any detailed discussion of commercial transactions. The rationale was that a course on "Public" International Law should deal with State behavior or the work of international organizations of States with political and military objectives. "Private" International Law, by contrast, could be readily distinguished. That body of law deals with the impact of differing national legal systems on individuals—like merchants engaged in cross-border commercial transactions (see § 1.5).

In the late 1970s and 1980s, the academic environment began to change. A law school casebook in *International Economic Relations* materialized in 1977. The first casebook in *International Business Transactions* appeared in 1986. Business and undergraduate schools were similarly slow to respond to the internationalization of United States commercial life in the closing decades of the twentieth century. The American Assembly of Collegiate Schools of Business (AACSB), the major accrediting agency for US graduate and undergraduate business schools, thus took action in 1984. The AACSB announced the requirement that business curriculums be internationalized. Many graduate and undergraduate institutions began to stress the importance of distinguishing between national and international business models. Many teachers understandably remained reluctant to "cram" Private International Law themes into a course in Public International Law.

Terms like *GATT, NAFTA,* and *World Trade Organization* have become relatively commonplace terms in numerous publications and other forms of communication. Thus, this will hopefully be the last edition of this book containing a justification explanation for including an International Economic Relations chapter. While international business has become a separate academic offering in many universities, its role in the evolution of Public International Law should be at least briefly addressed. The student of International Law may thus leave this course with a better sense of another significant factor in its evolution.

Historical Evolution

Trade was a central theme for ancient and medieval nations. *Some* of the great powers, like Persia and Rome, could afford to be relatively indifferent to foreign trade. They maintained well-developed agricultural bases. For other nations, trade was a method for raising revenue and exercising a degree of political power. From ancient Athens through the medieval city-States, the role of trade was to create wealth—in turn, leading to social and cultural de-

velopment. Trade thus provided access to broader social and cultural perspectives, as merchants traveled in search of trading opportunities. Civilization developed, in part, from the concentration of people on or near trade routes and major ports. Trade led to diplomatic and other exchanges between these congregations of people.

Early medieval international agreements thus focused on economic matters. The treaty of A.D. 860 between Byzantium—the major trading empire of that era—and Russia formalized their initial diplomatic and commercial relations. Under Article 4 of their agreement, Russia removed its previous ban on Byzantine exports. Trade was thus the ideal vehicle for developing international relations with which to usher in an era of relative peace. That concession also launched Russia's development of international trade relations with other nations.[1]

Links between commerce and law were thus forged by trade and exploration. Many territories of the world were "discovered" by explorers seeking new trading opportunities. The ancient Phoenicians traveled the Mediterranean Sea and the north Atlantic Ocean in search of new trading partners. Portuguese and Spanish explorers discovered the New World during their trade development programs of the fifteenth and sixteenth centuries.

Modern international commercial law is rooted in trade practices that developed during the resulting interaction of national legal systems. Many standard contractual expectations were expressed in the medieval "Lex Mercatoria" (Law Merchant). This body of law was created and developed by specialized commercial tribunals, typically located in major port cities. Private merchants could thus resolve their local and international business disputes. The Lex Mercatoria flourished in the twelfth century Italian city-States, and later spread to other commercial centers. The customary practices of these tribunals were ultimately incorporated into the commercial laws of many nations.[2]

An old English case suggests how judges continued to apply the Lex Mercatoria when resolving subsequent maritime disputes. A shipment of goods was en route from San Francisco to London during a long sea voyage at the turn of this century. The contract did not include a clause regarding *when* payment was due—thus failing to express the buyer's and seller's intent. While the goods were en route, the seller's agent presented the bill of lading (document of title) to the buyer. The buyer refused payment, however. He wanted to inspect the goods on arrival in London. The seller sued the buyer for breach of contract, prior to the arrival of the goods. Under the medieval maritime practice, a buyer was required to pay for goods when the seller's agent provided a bill of lading for cargos still en route by sea—unless the parties expressly contracted for payment at another time. The London court incorporated this old commercial practice into the contract, which thus supplied the missing terms.[3] Arbitrators and judges thus merged certain commercial practices into the decisional law and legislative enactments of maritime nations. Those practices then became customary rules of international commercial practice. Some were then codified into modern legislation or treaties.

The global business climate changed dramatically after World War II. The postwar Marshall Plan, announced by the US in 1947, was the largest and most successful foreign assistance program ever devised. The US was unable to agree with the Soviet Union about the scope of German reparations for the latter's role in causing the economic devastation of Europe. Just like US President Clinton's assessment of the 1995 upgraded Russian assaults on Chechnya, each day of World War II could be characterized as a lost opportunity. The Marshall Plan was the US substitute for the dismal failure of the post–World War I Versailles Treaty process—which isolated Germany and rendered its economy stagnant. The resulting international isolation contributed significantly to the conditions allowing Hitler to lead Germany's resurgence as a military power in the 1930s.

After World War II, the US wanted Germany and Japan to rise from the ashes of defeat to become prosperous allies. Helping to rebuild their economies was an important factor in maintaining an enduring peace. A prosperous *West* Germany could ultimately "showcase" the advantages of market capitalism during the Cold War. Improved economic conditions in Germany and Japan would also create new long-term markets for US exports. A similar concern drives the West's promotion of democracy through economic strategies in the former Soviet Union republics. Aid is linked to reform, arms control, nonproliferation of nuclear weapons, and the development of new consumer markets.

What occurred in the US is a good example of the development of economic ties that can lead to lasting peace. US economic interaction with Germany and Japan strengthened the political and economic ties between these nations. The stage was set for a comparative frenzy of international business transactions, unlike the isolationist tendencies of earlier eras. The US government's postwar objectives impacted corporate life in the US, as well as other countries. Corporate managers historically concerned themselves only with local or nationwide business ventures. The country's vast internal markets did not encourage medium and small entrepreneurs to engage in foreign commerce. By the 1970s, however, foreign competitors began to enter into US markets in unprecedented numbers. The rebuilding programs of an earlier generation had virtually created economic Frankensteins. As the US demand for foreign products increased, a trade imbalance developed. US export growth lagged behind that of imports. Jobs in the affected US industries were at risk, for those enterprises unwilling to accommodate the surge of foreign competition.

A price would have to be paid for the unexpected degree of success of the US plans to develop foreign consumer markets. Some commentators began to regard countries like Germany and Japan as economic Frankenstein's monsters. In order to compete, many US companies had to develop an expertise in problems that they had not previously encountered in the local or even nationwide business context. Even those companies that did not engage in *international* business had to respond in their own markets to foreign competitors. There was a growing consumer demand for foreign-made goods, a major contributor to the commonly articulated problem of "the foreign trade deficit."

Multinational enterprises in regions like Europe had never been as isolated from international commercial transactions. There, natural proximity to foreign borders—coupled with some limitations in the local availability of natural resources—presented a business environment more intuitively driven toward foreign markets. The same aggregate space between the US borders—the Atlantic and Pacific Oceans—could be geographically occupied by virtually all of Europe, with its ubiquitous international frontiers. One reason for the success of the European Union's economic integration is that many national economies contained a significant degree of international business activity.

Contemporary managers contemplating international business opportunities had to become familiar with the intricacies of importing, exporting, and producing in or for foreign markets. Assume that the CEO of Widget, Inc., a large US manufacturer, is contemplating export sales of its generic product known as "widgets." Widget's product has been quite successful in the US. But there is no guarantee that foreign markets will similarly respond to the same product. A representative cafeteria of entrees for Widget, Inc.'s consumption might include the following:

■ Should our company export widgets to another country or region of the world? By what percentage should we increase our current production, in order to do this? Alternatively, should we merely *advertise* our product to foreign market wholesalers?

■ Should we, instead, commit our capital to a joint venture with a foreign producer? We might thus combibe our expertise in widget-making with the reduced-cost benefit of producing widgets in the foreign market? But *which* foreign market?

■ Would any export restrictions apply to our widgets—particularly if they contain high-technology components that could be copied or used for purposes contrary to US military interests? The technical components of our product may be subject to federal agency review. That decision may adversely impact our export plans after an inordinate amount of company resources have been committed to developing a foreign marketing plan.

■ Will a foreign environmental regulation bar our product from the preferred market?

■ If our widgets are defective, or inoperable due to conflicting technologies, will our company be able make the necessary modifications to sell our product overseas?

■ Would the laws of the country where we want to market our product preclude us from forming the *type* of enterprise that we prefer? Put up barri-

ers to profitability? Require us to share our technology as a condition of marketing our product?

■ What would be the tax consequences of our business transactions under US law? Under foreign tax law? Is there a tax treaty between the US and that country to insulate us from double taxation?

■ What will be the foreign investment risks if we establish a widget enterprise in another country? Will too much success result in our corporate assets being nationalized?

■ Will we be able to get insurance for our operations in a foreign country? Can we insure against losses such as nationalization? Suddenly limiting or prohibiting the repatriation of profits back to the US? Imposing currency-exchange limitations that would preclude the free transfer of capital out of the country?

■ Will the US intervene, in the event of a dispute between Widget, Inc. and the host country? Or, in the event of some other action that effectively takes control of our enterprise away from Widget, Inc. management?

■ Does that country have national laws that preclude us from seeking US help as a condition of doing business? If so, we might lose the diplomatic protection normally afforded to aliens subject to governmental expropriation.

Negotiation Procedures

Now assume that Widget, Inc. decides to enter into a business arrangement with a foreign company to market and sell widgets. It is critically important to acknowledge differences in business customs, language, culture, and attitude. Merely speaking the language, or having translators and lawyers present, does not ensure that the parties will achieve their objectives. This is a significant component of the bargaining process between or among business negotiators from different countries. The following excerpt succinctly summarizes some significant highlights in this process:

INTERNATIONAL BUSINESS TRANSACTIONS IN A NUTSHELL 4th edition

R. Folsom, M. Gordon, & J. Spanogle, Jr.

Negotiating International Business Transactions, 46–54*

TIMING

Understanding the . . . framework for a successful negotiation is sometimes difficult for . . . United States attorneys and business executives. . . . [I]t took the Vietnamese two years to agree about the shape of the negotiating table at the Paris Peace Talks. The Chinese people from many other countries negotiate with a recognition that what cannot be settled today perhaps can be settled tomorrow or next week. Japanese are reluctant to do business with someone in whom they do not have sufficient trust and with whom they do not sense reciprocal feelings of friendship. . . . It may take weeks spent together on a golf course before such trust is engendered. People in other countries do not prefer to negotiate during certain times of the years, e.g., Ramadan in Islamic nations. In some countries the "weekend" is on days other than Saturday and Sunday, those days being normal business days. Some hours which in the United States are considered the normal business day are not considered appropriate for doing business in other countries. In parts of Africa "noon" may be any time between 10 a.m. and 2 p.m. The hours between 2 p.m. and 5 p.m. are inappropriate for doing business in Saudi Arabia.

IMPORTANCE OF PROCEDURE

It may be, and often is, that the procedure employed in international business negotiations is the single most important cause of their success or failure. The careful lawyer or executive will make advance inquiry about whether contacts preliminary to the negotiation are advisable and about which locations may be preferable for conducting negotiations. Procedures calculated to facilitate the building of personal relationships increase prospects for a successful negotiation, especially in Asia. In tough moments during a negotiation, courtesy alone may keep a consensus momentum going. Enduring courtesy is the essential lubricant of international negotiations. A negotiating opposite may not want to admit that an apparent unwillingness to agree to a suggested point is caused by bureaucratic foot dragging, lack of coordination, lack of technical understanding or simple confusion on its side. Procedures that are flexible enough to allow time to work out such problems may cultivate ego, avoid a loss of "face" and continue [meaningful] participation in the negotiations. For example, a negotiating opposite may be unwilling to let you know that failure to reach quick agreement is due to the fact that he or she, despite having a lofty sounding title or other credentials, does not have authority to make a final agreement or will not assume personal responsibility for the consequences of an agreement. The latter case occurs frequently in Japan. Some nations find it prudent to advertise publicly that only certain government agencies are authorized to carry out sales or purchases.

Procedures which cause surprise are intimidating and can engender hostility and distrust. Obvious examples include emotional displays used as smokescreens, changing the agreed agenda for negotiation, unannounced or late arrivals and departures of negotiating personnel, and retreating from agreements already made. The surprise introduction of a written document . . . the contents of which a negotiating opposite is asked to consider or even to read on the spur of the moment, often causes similar reactions. Taking [written] minutes of a negotiation and preparing written summaries of points of agreement often speeds the consensus building process, but the surprise transmission of such documents to a negotiating opposite can work a greater and opposite effect. Of course, these procedures may be useful if negotiating by contest rather than consensus. Because the intimidating nature of a written document increases with its thickness, a one page summary of the contents stands a better chance of being read.

. . .

---

*Reprinted with permission of West Publishing Company. Emphasis has been supplied in certain passages.

Although giving gifts of modest value is appreciated in virtually all cultures, it is an *expected* occurrence between negotiating opposites in some countries. Certain gifts, such as books depicting the natural beauty of the investor's home area, are generally appreciated while more specialized gifts may be preferred in a particular country. For example, Johnny Walker Black Label Scotch is appreciated in Japan, but Red Label is valued in Thailand and Burma.

There is an almost universal cultural importance attached to sharing a meal with a negotiating opposite. Meal time affords a good opportunity for an investor to show an interest in and sensitivity about the host's culture. In many cultures [however,] talking about business matters during a meal is considered impolite and is counter-productive.

There is considerable cultural diversity about the meaning in international negotiations of *silence* and *delay*. The common law rule [in English-speaking countries] that, under appropriate circumstances, "silence is acceptance" is not shared widely in many countries. In some countries silence may mean "no," while in other countries periods of silence are an acceptable and common occasion during which thoughts are arranged and rearranged. For example, an investor in Indonesia brought the final draft of a completely negotiated agreement to a counterpart for signature and, following some pleasant conversation, placed the agreement on the desk. In complete silence, the counterpart simply returned the document, unsigned, to the investor. The investor later learned that this day was not considered propitious in Indonesia for signing one's name. Delays of days or even of months may not be signs that a negotiation is in difficulty, nor represent an attempt at increasing the costs of negotiating. Such delays may simply be the minimum time period in which a necessary consensus or authority is being achieved within a negotiating team.

THE LANGUAGE OF NEGOTIATIONS

Differences in language skills between negotiating opposites raise some peril in every international business transaction. Each negotiating party prefers quite naturally to use the language whose nuances are best known. Words that have a clear and culturally acceptable meaning in one language may be unclear or culturally offensive in another tongue. The converse may be true as well. . . . Because some hand gestures and body movements are acceptable in one culture yet deeply offensive in another culture, they are rarely an appropriate communications aid in international negotiations. For example, raising an open hand in the direction of another party can mean in North Africa that you hope that person will lose all five senses.

The use of interpreters substantially slows the pace of negotiations and may spawn further difficulties because the interpreter is one more fallible person taking part in the negotiations. Interpreting is exhausting work and rarely exact. During an international commercial arbitration in Los Angeles, a witness testified in German alongside a skilled interpreter whose job it was to translate the testimony into English. While the arbitrators waited, it required the interpreter's efforts, the efforts of a United States lawyer fluent in German, and the efforts of a German lawyer fluent in English to produce an oral translation which all agreed was sufficiently accurate. Even assuming the availability of an accurate literal translation, a Japanese person saying "yes" in answer to a question may not be signifying agreement but may only mean, "Yes, I understand the question."

The peril of language difficulty can be equally acute in negotiations between a lawyer from the United States and a negotiating opposite who speaks the English language. Each party may be [too] embarrassed to raise a language question. For example, in the middle of a telephone conversation between a lawyer from the United States and a negotiator in England, a London operator interrupted to ask if the lawyer was "through." Not wishing to terminate the conversation, the American answered, "No, I am not through". The operator disconnected the circuit, apologized, and once again dialed to get the call "through." A few minutes later the London operator came on the line again, interrupting the parties' conversation, to ask again if the United States caller was "through." Desiring to continue the conversation without further interruption, the American lawyer this time said "Yes, thank you," and the operator left the line connected.

Certain foreign MNEs require their negotiators to speak English when negotiating with Americans. The problem is that their English seldom tracks American English, and embarrassing moments occur when U.S. negotiators must delicately seek clarification of the opponent's words. Such clarifications must be undertaken with the utmost politeness and goodwill in order not to insult or intimidate the foreign party.

Even exceptionally able interpreters may have difficulty if a United States lawyer or executive uses American slang in communicating during an international negotiation. The American penchant for using "ball park" figures may not be shared or understood in countries where baseball is not a popular sport. Slow and distinct patterns of speech combined with simple declarative sentences will always facilitate international business negotiations.

LANGUAGE IN THE AGREEMENT

The careful language normally used by American lawyers in commercial contracts may prove controversial. While legally trained persons in some countries (e.g., the former Soviet Union) share an affinity for written contracts that set out the full extent of every right and duty of each party, the practice in many other countries tends toward more generally worded agreements that leave it to the parties (e.g., in Japan) or to the courts (e.g., in Germany) to supply any necessary details. A detailed, exhaustively worded, draft contract which is introduced during negotiations with Japanese or Chinese persons may arouse distrust. To them, a contract relationship is perceived as something that is shaped mutually as understanding develops. A German negotiating opposite may not be willing to sign an exhaustively worded contract because German courts dislike such agreements. The German courts take the position that they know the law and do not need a contract to state what is known already.

This attitude may trap unwary U.S. parties. Chinese negotiators, for example, will resist bargaining on the details of a contract or joint venture, saying "All that is of course understood" or "a part of our law." They may even show resentment at attempts to detail business agreements. However, during performance at a later date, other representatives of a Chinese entity may . . . say: "That is not written expressly in the contract and is not our duty." If a detail is important to the transaction, spell it out in the agreement. Many U.S. attorneys involved with Chinese business transactions have learned the hard way.

Permissible contract clauses in one country may be impermissible in another country and *vice versa*. For example, penalty clauses which are not legally enforceable in the United States are enforced routinely by French and, to a lesser extent, Italian courts. One-sided (adhesion) contracts may be fun for lawyers to draft, but they may serve only to raise suspicion by identifying the drafter as an adversary or to generate hostility and ill will. Draft adhesion contracts do not promote the consensus building style of international business negotiations. German courts will eviscerate an unfair adhesion contract without mercy.

One of the most frustrating features of international business agreements is the presence of texts in different languages, each of which is considered authoritative. Counsel to an American enterprise will always seek to make English the sole language of the agreement, and sometimes succeed since English has become the predominant language of international business. Especially when negotiations have been conducted exclusively in English, time, expense, clarity and mutual understanding favor such a result. Even parties who do not natively speak English may use it as the language of agreement for these reasons. Agreements between Japanese and Indonesian businesses, for example, are often in English. But cultural pride (especially with French speaking negotiators) or fear of unfair dealing (especially with Chinese negotiators) may leave multiple texts in different languages [as] the only acceptable solution once "agreement" is reached.

Another important linguistic feature of international transactions, particularly of concern to lawyers, is the existence of different language texts of relevant laws. In the EEC, for example, there are nine official, authoritative texts for every treaty, regulation, directive, parliamentary report, etc. The nuances of nine languages can significantly affect the legality of any business transaction subject to EEC law. Those same nuances can undermine any carefully constructed "consensus" international negotiators have worked hard to create.

Public International Law Connection

This portion of the chapter will now illustrate the connection between international economic relations and Public International Law—the body of norms covered in the first twelve chapters of this book. This subsection will address some subjects covered in prior chapters—this time, emphasizing the economic perspective. It will also depict the employment of some other commercial transactions to resolve prominent crises, or to facilitate routine inter-State relations.

International Legal Personality The preliminary chapters on the actors in International Law introduced the concept of international personality—the legal capacity to participate in certain matters on an international level. Given the leading role of the State, the nature of its international personality naturally induced its protection via sovereign immunity.

After World War II, States engaged in international transactions with individuals and corporations in other States on an unprecedented scale. Previously, when State A was asked to appear as a *defendant* in State B litigation, B's courts would automatically dismiss suits by individuals or corporations against State A—even if State A could appear as a *plaintiff* in B's courts. National and international tribunals thus reconsidered the traditional rule of Public International Law that the State's legal status necessarily precluded a lawsuit against it. The former State practice of *absolute* sovereign immunity from suit gave way to the *restrictive* application of sovereign immunity. The routine appearance of States in the international marketplace, where their profit motive resembled that of any other trader, accordingly altered State sovereign immunity practice (*see* § 2.6).

Even business transactions within a State became subject to external controls by *other* international actors possessing the necessary international legal personality. The post–World War II evolution of international organizations of States, such as the UN and the European Union, is depicted in Chapter 3. As these organizations began to function on an unprecedented scale, certain ones amassed powers that were previously exercisable on the international level only by States. Their international legal personality thus blossomed as they cultivated organizational objectives. Certain organizations, notably the European Economic Community (now European Union), possessed the legal capacity to require a State—once the *only* actor in Public International Law—to act in ways that would not otherwise occur.

This postwar expansion of organizational legal capacity is typically expressed in a commercial context. A classic example is the "German Beer" case of 1987. The Commission of the European Commu-

nities sued the Federal Republic of Germany, claiming that the State had breached its obligations under European Community Law. The relevant treaty ceded the capacity to the Council of Europe to enact directives limiting a member State's ability to use restrictive business practices against other members of the European Community. The relevant German law, dating from the year 1516, prohibited additives in the manufacturing of beer. Germany's nondiscriminatory national beer law thus barred the importation of beer from *any* country, when the beer contained *substitutes* for malted barley—the basic and unadulterated substance for making German beer. Other Community member States wanted to export a different kind of beer to the German market containing a substitute for malted barley. They claimed the right to do so, as long as they called their beer "bier." Germany defended its restrictive "beer" law, on the basis that consumers would be misled by the similarity of the term "bier." That name change, while reflecting the beer's origin as non-German, nevertheless violated German law that has been in existence for four centuries. The Court of Justice of the European Communities nevertheless ruled that Germany's vintage restrictions did not survive 1985 European Council Directives barring nontariff barriers. Germany's legislative protection thus impeded the free importation of member-State products throughout the Community.[4]

Sovereignty The legal personality of international organizations also affects commerce in far more sensitive ways. After the breakup of the former Yugoslavia, one of the new republics took the same name as the neighboring Greek province of Macedonia. Greece imposed a trade ban on the new State of Macedonia. As discussed in the Chapter 2 materials on statehood and recognition, Greece's objection was not limited to the resulting confusion of coexisting Macedonias. Greece questioned whether this fragment of the former Soviet Union would ultimately seek to expand its territorial boundaries to include the adjacent Macedonian portion of Greece (*see* Problem 2.5).

In April 1994, the European Union threatened legal action against Greece. This trade dispute involved significant sovereignty concerns for Greece. The EU nevertheless advised Greece of its intent to sue in the European Court of Justice—a somewhat awkward decision since the president of the EU was a Greek citizen. The EU concern was that Greece's trade blockade also affected the ability of fellow EU members to access the nearby Greek port of Salonika. This is the usual Greek port for the passage of goods going to and from the new Republic of Macedonia. Salonika is thus the exchange point for 80 percent of Macedonian trade, and all of its oil imports. EU member States Great Britain and Germany pressured the EU to take this action for political reasons. The continued trade blockage of Macedonia might trigger a new round of Balkan destabilization.

Jurisdiction Chapters 5 and 6 presented the interwoven themes of "jurisdiction" under International Law, and the permissible range of State "sovereignty" when exercised beyond territorial borders. The limitations on "extraterritorial" jurisdiction are not limited to States. An international organization must also be cautious about overreaching. The potential for such conduct typically arises in a commercial context.

A classic example was presented in the adjudication chapter (Chapter 9). An international cartel including US wood pulp producers conspired to fix prices in member States of the European Community during the 1980s. The organization's executive and judicial bodies fined them, under European Community Law, because their price-fixing conspiracy violated Community antitrust laws. These legal actions, although taken against businesses as far away as the US, did *not* constitute an improper "extraterritorial" regulation of commercial transactions.[5] The conduct of the foreign enterprises had the requisite effect within the territory of the European Community—thus triggering a civil application of the territorial principle of international criminal jurisdiction (*see* § 5.2).

A number of countries have legislatively reacted to what they construe as extraterritorial assertions of another State's law against their citizens. The greatest concern is with applications of US law to foreign corporate activity in the US. Other States have thus enacted "blocking statutes." These statutes are countermeasures whereby State X "blocks" the potential application of US law to the corporate activities of State X individuals or corporations, when they are subjected to US legal processes. Blocking statutes typically make it a crime for its citizens to reveal in-

formation, as with the famous Swiss bank secrecy laws.

The Chinese State Secrecy Law generally forbids the disclosure of financial data by Chinese corporations. This statute is designed to protect Chinese State agencies from disclosing information requested by authorities in other countries. But it creates a problem for the Chinese entity that is subject to conflicting demands. When Chinese companies do business in the US, for example, they have generally been required to disclose financial information when demanded by a US judge. Thus, these companies are held to the more liberal US disclosure standard. In 1992, a federal judge in San Francisco thus imposed a fine of $10,000 per day, for each day that a Chinese corporation refused to comply with an American company's right to obtain business information.

In other business litigation, the US Supreme Court similarly held that a French company could not rely on French blocking legislation. French law prohibited the defendant French company from giving evidence in foreign litigation. In this case, the corporate liability for an allegedly faulty aircraft involved an accident that arose within the US, however. The corporation had injected itself into business activities and could not avoid its litigation responsibilities arising in the country where it was operating.[6]

Diplomacy The diplomacy chapter (Chapter 7) covered the importance of diplomatic protection in time of crisis. Recalling those materials in this chapter will further unsheathe the *economic* aspects of diplomacy.

In 1991, the European Community withheld a one-billion-dollar food/aid package destined for what was then the Soviet Union. The Community also delayed execution of a half-billion-dollar technical assistance agreement with Moscow. The Community thus announced its intent to file a human rights complaint with the Conference on the Security and Co-operation in Europe regional organization (*see* § 3.5 on CSCE). The reason was that the Soviet president, Mikhail Gorbachev, had just imposed a military "crackdown" on proindependence groups in the Baltic republics within the former Soviet Union. The European Community action was a protest to the Soviet response after violence erupted in Latvia. France and Germany simultaneously announced that they would also work toward tempering the Soviet hardline attitude toward the independence movement in the Balkan States of Lithuania, Latvia, and Estonia—which had themselves always protested their incorporation into the Soviet Union under a treaty between Hitler and Stalin in 1940.

The US pursued a different trade-related posture. US President Bush negotiated with Gorbachev, offering that the US Congress might grant the Soviets special trading status. The objective was to normalize international economic relations between the two superpowers. Bush's announced "global partnership" was designed to prevent the US and the Soviet Union from rekindling the tensions that symbolized their former Cold War. This was another example of employing economic relations to reduce the risk of political and military hostilities, while exploring the possibility of new Eastern European markets for US exports.

Treaty Norms The treaty chapter (Chapter 8) presented another perspective on international economic relations. The nearly half-century Arab economic boycott of Israel was a centerpiece that illustrated various facets of the treaty process (*see* § 8.4). That particular economic agreement illustrated another crossover with Public International Law. The Arab boycott was also a show of force designed for the political purpose of bankrupting the State of Israel. The Arab League thus sought to drive Israel out of existence—effectively, a reaction to the UN's 1947 partition of Palestine to create the State of Israel. The boycott thus depicts a worst-case scenario, in the sense that it used international economic relations for the purpose of annihilating a State made possible by the larger community of nations through the UN.

"Private" International Law This concept was mentioned early in this book, so as to distinguish so-called "Private" International Law from "Public" International Law (*see* § 1.5). It is becoming increasingly difficult to justify this distinction.[7] Several differences in national legal culture follow, which will identify some reasons for the "private" law integration with Public International Law.

Different legal systems may yield different results for the same transaction. Also, traders in different countries may operate quite differently. Socialist countries, for example, have historically conducted

their trade via national trade agencies, rather than through private enterprise. Nonsocialist nations depend on a market economy to conduct trade—which is done by private enterprises and for their profit, rather than for the direct benefit of the State. The government agencies in socialist States are characteristically bureaucratic and desperately in need of predictability. This one reason why intersystem dealing is a much more cumbersome process than negotiating transactions between traders in private market economies.

Other important systemic differences should now be noted. For example, business contracts in *developing* countries emanate from a different legal culture than that of comparatively developed Western countries. And as suggested in the previous "Nutshell" excerpt in this section of the book, very different attitudes are associated with the conduct of international business transactions. A resource-rich country, anxious to obtain money for its socioeconomic development programs, is likely to send comparatively eager but less-experienced negotiators to the bargaining table. They may not be as experienced as the negotiators sent by a potential trading partner, especially a large multinational corporation. The local legal enforcement mechanisms of the lesser-developed States tend to be less equipped to handle sophisticated business litigation—in relation to the older systems in *both* socialist and Western legal cultures.[8]

To illustrate how these differences might affect a common commercial setting, assume that X Corporation agrees to sell a load of widgets to Y Corporation. X is a corporation that does business in its home country of State X. Y corporation does business in its home country of State Y. X Corporation then sends its first shipment of widgets to Y corporation. It has some defects. Their written contract does not include a seller's promise that the goods will arrive without defects. Under the national law of the importing State Y, an importer cannot ask a Y court to *imply* a contractual term not expressed by the parties in their contract. The courts of State Y do not want to thereby rewrite business contracts for the parties—to include terms that *might* have been included but were not. Under the national law of the exporting State X, the lack of contractual warranties does not preclude Y Corporation from seeking a judicial remedy in State X. Y Corporation could thus sue for breach of the contract in State X, based on an *implied* warranty (not mentioned in the contract) that the goods will arrive without substantial defects. In the absence of an international treaty that deals with this "private" international law problem, the result will depend on the country in which enforcement is sought.

Given this recurring type of problem, generated by differences in national legal systems, the UN opened the 1980 Convention for the International Sale of Goods (CISG) for signature and ratification by interested nations.[9] Under Public International Law, two States that ratify the CISG treaty thereby chose a uniform rule that will govern the contractual relationships of their respective traders. The CISG treaty does not deprive the parties of some advantage that both might prefer under the law of one of the countries involved in their transaction. The CISG authorizes them to agree that the national law of either State X or State Y will apply. Freedom of contract is thus preserved. One of the best articulations for any nation to adopt the CISG was provided by US President Ronald Reagan, in the following excerpt from his letter to the US Senate recommending that the US adopt this treaty:

> International trade law is subject to serious legal uncertainties. Questions often arise as to whether our law or foreign law governs the transaction, and our traders and their counsel find it difficult to evaluate and answer claims based on one or another of the many unfamiliar foreign legal systems [whose law might apply]. The Convention's uniform rules offer effective answers to these problems.
>
> Enhancing legal certainty for international sales contracts will serve the interests of all parties engaged in commerce by facilitating international trade.[10]

Letter of Credit The Letter of Credit (LOC) is probably the most useful mechanism for facilitating the conclusion of an international commercial transaction. The International Chamber of Commerce (ICC), located in Paris, provides the services of experts to private business enterprises for resolving various problems in international commerce (*see* § 9.3). It has also produced standardized commercial documents, contract terms, and rules of interpretation. One of the ICC's most prominent contributions is the Uniform Customs and Practices for Documentary Credits (UCP). The UCP contains a series of articles that standardize the use of the LOC in international banking. A letter of credit expedites completion of the transaction between a buyer and a seller in different countries. It is particularly useful when the parties do not have a history of dealing with each other. The LOC is not required merely because the contract is international in scope. But some governments require it for all transactions involving foreign trade.

The buyer (importer) makes credit arrangements with the buyer's local bank. The buyer thus obtains a letter of credit from the bank. Its LOC guarantees that the seller (exporter) will be paid for the goods. The buyer bank thus promises to pay. This promise is essentially substituted for that of the buyer. The buyer's bank is the "issuing bank," charging a fee to the buyer for issuing its LOC. The LOC is typically sent to the "confirming bank" located in the seller's country. Assuming that everything is in order with the issuing bank's LOC, the confirming bank then advises the seller that payment has been guaranteed. There may be some condition that must be satisfied before the confirming bank forwards the payment—such as the buyer's right to inspect the goods. The seller is then willing to ship or release its goods to the buyer, because payment has been guaranteed by an institution with which the seller is familiar.

An actual application for a letter of credit is reproduced below in Exhibits 13.1 and 13.2. Exhibit 13.1 is the buyer's application for a LOC. Exhibit 13.2 is the issuing bank's LOC, which is forwarded to the confirming bank.

The LOC has an important but little known connection with Public International Law. It has been used to settle conflicts between States at war or to mitigate problems spawned by poor international relations. One of the classic examples occurred during the 1961 Bay of Pigs invasion of Cuba by Cuban rebels who had previously migrated to the US. They were sent on this clandestine mission by US President Kennedy, as part of a US strategy to overthrow Fidel Castro. Shortly after landing, their presence was detected and they were captured. A US naval destroyer was shelled as it monitored these events. One reason that this mission failed was the President Kennedy was reluctant to provide air support, once the plot was discovered.

A New York law firm attempted to negotiate the release of the invading Cuban immigrants thus sent to Cuba by the Central Intelligence Agency. The ensuing 1962 Cuban Missile Crisis did not derail

EXHIBIT 13.1 Application for Letter of Credit

TO: **FIRST INTERSTATE BANK OF CALIFORNIA** LETTER OF CREDIT APPLICATION AND SECURITY AGREEMENT
Formerly United California Bank

Please issue your irrevocable Letter of Credit as follows: ☐ Airmail ☒ Cable L/C No. SAMPLE

IN FAVOR OF (name and address)
PHILIPPINE LAUAN, LTD., C.P.O. BOX 1776, MAKATI, RIZAL, PHILIPPINES

FOR ACCOUNT OF (person or firm requesting this credit)
RED LAUAN PLYWOOD CO., 108 W. 6th ST., LOS ANGELES, CA

TENOR OF DRAFTS
SIGHT

DRAWINGS FOR 100 % OF INVOICE VALUE ☒ NOT TO EXCEED ☐ APPROXIMATELY

AMOUNT
US$25,000.00

DRAFTS TO BE ACCOMPANIED BY THE FOLLOWING DOCUMENTS: (Which the negotiating bank is authorized to forward to you in one mailing.)

☒ COMMERCIAL INVOICE(S) (indicate number of copies) triplicate ☐ SPECIAL CUSTOMS INVOICE(S)

☐ INSURANCE POLICY(IES) COVERING THE FOLLOWING RISKS (such as marine and war risk, etc.)

INSURANCE EFFECTED BY OURSELVES (name of ins. co. and policy no.)
I/We agree to furnish you, upon request, such policy.

☒ OTHER DOCUMENTS PACKING LIST IN TRIPLICATE

☒ FULL SET OF CLEAN ON BOARD OCEAN BILLS OF LADING, TO ORDER OF SHIPPER, BLANK ENDORSED
PERSON OR FIRM TO BE NOTIFIED BY CARRIER UPON ARRIVAL OF SHIPMENT
NOTIFY: RED LAUAN PLYWOOD CO., 108 W. 6th ST., LOS ANGELES, CA

☐ AIRWAY BILL/AIR CONSIGNMENT NOTE CONSIGNED TO

☐ RAILROAD/TRUCK BILL OF LADING CONSIGNED TO

EVIDENCING SHIPMENT OF:
COMMODITY (omit details of price, quality, etc.) RED LAUAN PLYWOOD AS PER ACCOUNTEE'S PURCHASE ORDER

NUMBER 1776

FROM (country or port of shipment)
PHILIPPINE PORT

DESTINATION (port of arrival)
LOS ANGELES HARBOR, CA

SHIPPING TERMS (check one)
☐ FAS ☒ FOB ☐ C&F ☐ CIF

SHIPMENT TO BE MADE NO LATER THAN
June 15, 1989

DATE THIS CREDIT TO EXPIRE
June 30, 1989

TRANSHIPMENT
☒ ALLOWED ☐ NOT ALLOWED

PARTIAL SHIPMENTS (check one)
☒ ALLOWED ☐ NOT ALLOWED

SPECIAL INSTRUCTIONS

We, and each of us, agree that the terms and conditions set forth on this and the reverse page hereof are hereby made a part of this application and are hereby accepted and agreed to by us.

March 31, 1989
DATE

RED LAUAN PLYWOOD CO.
APPLICANT'S NAME

FOR BANK USE ONLY

CUSTOMER'S CURRENT LIABILITY

OFFICE NO SIGNATURE OF LOAN OFFICER AUTHORIZING CREDIT

AUTHORIZED SIGNATURE TITLE

IB-117 8-82

Source: First Interstate Bank (San Diego, California)

EXHIBIT 13.2 Letter of Credit

First Interstate Bank, Ltd.
401 'B' Street, Suite 303
San Diego, CA 92101
619 699-3026

TO: PHILIPPINE NATIONAL BANK   FROM: FIRST INTERSTATE BANK, LTD.
     MAKATI, RIZAL, PHILIPPINES   SAN DIEGO, CALIFORNIA

PLEASE ADVISE BENEFICIARY THAT WE HAVE ISSUED OUR IRREVOCABLE DOCUMENTARY
CREDIT AS FOLLOWS:

OUR NUMBER: SAMPLE 89-01
PLACE AND DATE OF ISSUE: SAN DIEGO, 31MAR89
DATE AND PLACE OF EXPIRY: 30JUN89, AT NEGOTIATING BANK

BENEFICIARY: PHILIPPINE LAUAN, LTD. APPLICANT: RED LAUAN PLYWOOD CO.
              C.P.O. BOX 1776   108 WEST SIXTH STREET
              MAKATI, RIZAL, PHILIPPINES   LOS ANGELES, CALIFORNIA

AMOUNT: USD25,000.00   TWENTY FIVE THOUSAND AND 00/100 USD

THIS LETTER OF CREDIT IS AVAILABLE WITH: NEGOTIATING BANK
BY: NEGOTIATION, AGAINST PRESENTATION OF THE DOCUMENTS DETAILED HEREIN
AND OF YOUR SIGHT DRAFT(S) AT SIGHT DRAWN ON FIRST INTERSTATE BANK, SAN
DIEGO, CALIFORNIA

PARTIAL SHIPMENTS PERMITTED   TRANSHIPMENT PERMITTED

SHIPMENT/DISPATCH TAKEN IN CHARGE
FROM/AT: PHILIPPINE PORT
NOT LATER THAN: 15JUN89
FOR TRANSPORTATION TO: LOS ANGELES HARBOR, CALIFORNIA

SIGNED COMMERCIAL INVOICE IN TRIPLICATE
PACKING LIST IN TRIPLICATE
FULL SET OF CLEAN ON BOARD OCEAN BILL OF LADING, TO ORDER OF SHIPPER,
BLANK ENDORSED, NOTIFY: RED LAUAN PLYWOOD CO., 108 WEST SIXTH STREET, LOS
ANGELES, CALIFORNIA

EVIDENCING SHIPMENT OF: RED LAUAN PLYWOOD AS PER ACCOUNTEE'S PURCHASE
ORDER NUMBER 1776; FOB VESSEL PHILIPPINE PORT TO LOS ANGELES HARBOR,
CALIFORNIA, NOT LATER THAN 15JUN89

WE UNDERSTAND THAT THE INSURANCE WILL BE EFFECTED BY RED LAUAN PLYWOOD CO.

DRAFTS DRAWN HEREUNDER MUST BE PRESENTED TO THE NEGOTIATING BANK WITHIN
FIFTEEN DAYS AFTER DATE OF SHIPMENT, BUT WITHIN THE VALIDITY OF THIS
LETTER OF CREDIT.

WE HEREBY ISSUE THIS DOCUMENTARY CREDIT IN YOUR FAVOR. IT IS SUBJECT TO
THE UNIFORM CUSTOMS AND PRACTICE FOR DOCUMENTARY CREDITS (1983 REVISION,
INTERNATIONAL CHAMBER OF COMMERCE, PARIS, FRANCE PUBLICATION NO.400) AND
ENGAGES US IN ACCORDANCE WITH THE TERMS THEREOF. THE NUMBER AND DATE OF
THE CREDIT AND THE NAME OF OUR BANK MUST BE QUOTED ON ALL DRAFTS
REQUIRED.   IF THE CREDIT IS AVAILABLE BY NEGOTIATION EACH PRESENTATION
MUST BE QUOTED ON THE REVERSE OF THIS ADVICE BY THE BANK WHERE THE CREDIT
IS AVAILABLE.

Source: First Interstate Bank (San Diego, California)

the negotiations for their release. A secret bargain was struck. Cuba was to receive $53 million worth of food and medical supplies in return for their release. But Cuba had no way of knowing whether the US would renege on its part of the bargain once Cuba released these prisoners. Even if the US did comply, there was no guarantee about the quality of supplies that the US might ultimately ship to Cuba. It would be quite difficult to provide assurances via diplomatic representations—which the Cuban government was understandably unlikely to trust. The absence of formal diplomatic ties between Cuba and the US was but one of the problems with making this exchange.

The US negotiator successfully requested the Red Cross to apply for a LOC from a Canadian bank, executed in favor of Cuba. Once the bank issued an irrevocable LOC, Cuba would collect $53 million if the US failed to provide the supplies, or if they were inferior. Cuba could thus be assured that the Canadian bank would make the payment. To subsequently dishonor its LOC, even if prodded to do so by the US government, would ruin that bank's credibility in all future banking matters. LOCs are governed by the marketplace. Diplomacy is governed by politics. Thus, the US government's use of a LOC resolved this most sensitive of matters, at a time when tensions were already peaked by the Cuban Missile Crisis (see § 10.2).[11]

Adjudication   The adjudication chapter (Chapter 9) dealt with the resolution of disputes by specialized tribunals, created for the finite purpose of winding down hostile relations in a commercial context. A classic example is the Iran/US Claims Tribunal, which still functions in a building near the International Court of Justice in the Netherlands. This commercial adjudication scenario effectively concluded an episode involving numerous principles of International Law.

During the 1979–1980 Iranian Hostage Crisis, both Iran and the US acted in ways that violated accepted norms of State practice. Iran incurred State responsibility for the public storming of the US Embassy and consulates in Iran (see § 7.4). The US undertook its ill-fated military hostage rescue mission, three years after supporting a UN Security Council resolution condemning Israel's clandestine hostage mission in Uganda (see § 10.5). Here, both Iran and the US ultimately resolved their hostage crisis via the "good offices" (see § 9.2) of the Algerian govern-

ment. Iran released the US and Canadian hostages to Algeria. But this arrangement arguably violated the State practice, later codified as the Vienna Convention on the Law of Treaties, prohibiting treaties made under duress (see § 8.2). The US thus released a portion of Iran's assets frozen by US President Carter at the outset of the crisis. This countermeasure was a use of economic force that arguably violated the UN Charter principle prohibiting such unilateral action (see § 10.1). Since then, the Iran/US Claims Tribunal has steadily worked to resolve the private claims of US businesses that would otherwise lack the international personality to pursue claims in an international tribunal (see § 4.1). Thus, this third-party dispute resolution mechanism (see § 9.1) peacefully resolved one of the most sensitive disputes ever to arise under Public International Law.

Human Rights   A significant connection is to be observed between human rights doctrine and international commerce. The US is the largest consumer nation in the world, and one of its strongest economies. The US is therefore in a comparatively affluent position to employ international economic strategies to further various global human rights objectives. Of many contemporary examples, several follow. In mid-1994, the US opposed Singapore as the initial host of the World Trade Organization's premier 1995 ministerial meeting. The US Trade Representative objected to a Singapore site due to its 1994 "caning" (severe corporeal punishment via a whip-like cane) of an eighteen-year-old US citizen. President Clinton was unable to dissuade Singapore from carrying out this punishment for the youth's spray-painting of several cars. Given global concerns with this form of State action, as constituting either torture or cruel and degrading punishment under International Human Rights Law, the US was able to sidetrack Singapore's bid for hosting this major event at the dawn of the new World Trade Organization's operations.[12]

Contemporary US presidential administrations have complained about human rights abuses in the People's Republic of China. They have reportedly threatened to revoke the PRC's "most favored nation" (MFN) trade status with the US. MFN status, to be discussed in § 13.3 in some detail, essentially means that one State agrees to trade with another State on the same basis as its most favorable trade partner of all. For example, State A may *generally* charge a 15 percent tariff on "widgets" imported from other nations of the world (States D, E, F, and so on). A's import tariff is *10* percent, however, for its most favored trading partner State B. Assume that A and C decide to initiate trade relations. C will seek, and probably be given, the lowest tariff that A charges on the commodity that is, the subject of the A/C transaction—that is, 10 percent on the widgets that A imports from B. A will then charge only a 10 percent tariff on State C's imports.

There has been a relatively long and tortuous political history associated with the decisions of various US presidents regarding China's "MFN" status. In 1951, US President Truman denied MFN status to all communist countries, in the early stages of the Cold War. President Nixon unsuccessfully attempted to extend MFN status to China in 1972, when he initiated US relations with China. In 1980, President Carter finally extended MFN status to the PRC. In 1990, President Bush decided that China would receive MFN status—but not the former Soviet Union, because of obstacles it erected to Jewish emigration from that country to Israel. This appeared to set a double standard for US MFN policy. *Candidate* Clinton thus campaigned in 1991 that, if elected, he would revoke China's MFN status due to continuing concerns with China's human rights performance (*see* §§ 11.2 and 11.3). In 1992, *President* Clinton scaled this pledge back to denying MFN status only to *State* entities. Full MFN status was revived in 1993, and continued thereafter.

The threatened revocation of China's MFN status has thus been a commercial wrinkle in diplomatic relations. It has continued to resurface since the PRC's massacre of prodemocratic Chinese students in Tiananmen Square in 1989. In 1994, the US Trade Representative thus announced a new tactic in the pursuit of Chinese human rights improvement—a cutback of 25 to 35 percent on the US importation of Chinese textiles and clothing. Of course, the US is experiencing a major trade deficit with the PRC. But the expressed rationale for this particular round of human rights diplomacy was that China continues to display a poor human rights record after a decade of prodding by various human rights organizations.

Economic Force Chapter 10 addressed State uses of force that violate international legal principles. In this commercial chapter, one may productively re-consider the materials on force, so as to cultivate the commercial roots in the genealogy of Public International Law. The International Law texts of prior decades were Cold War–driven. That unfortunate episode in superpower international relations skewed the operation of the UN Security Council from the outset. It also nourished a disproportionately skeptical view, in the latter part of the twentieth century, that there was really no "law" to control State behavior. The Cold War shrouded the reality that, in Columbia University Professor Louis Henkin's provocative articulation: *"almost all nations observe almost all principles of international law and almost all of their obligations almost all of the time."*[13] During the Cold War, the UN Security Council invoked its UN Charter powers to impose international economic sanctions—with varying degrees of success—on South Africa, to eliminate the State policy of apartheid; on parts of the former Yugoslavia, to reduce the flow of arms entering the Bosnian conflict; and on Iraq, to keep it from perpetrating additional affronts to Kuwait's sovereignty during and after the 1991 Persian Gulf War.

Terrorist Targets The exceptions to Professor Henkin's above articulation, on the quality of State observance of International Law, include State-sponsored terrorism. Terrorists have targeted international commercial ventures in their zeal to use force as the means for accomplishing political ends. Attacks on foreign economic interests are a common method for bringing worldwide attention to local and regional political issues. In 1995, religious fundamentalist groups in Algeria continued to target foreign businesses as one device for ridding Algeria of all foreign influence. The cost of doing business in a foreign country increases with such political risks. There is thus an inverse correlation between being profitable and being the target of local extremists whose goal is to make it impossible for businesses to operate. In mid-1994, for example, the terrorist Group "November 17" claimed responsibility for two antitank missiles that struck the Athens offices of International Business Machines.

Cold War Conversion The contemporary "scaling down" of national war potential is another positive development in the ongoing relationship between war and commerce. In 1994, the US began its post–Cold War diversion of intercontinental ballistic missiles and nuclear warheads to commercial uses. The Pentagon has thus drawn Minuteman, Poseidon, and Trident rockets from active service. These former outposts of US defense readiness are now being sold to private US satellite makers, thus recycling missiles so that they can be mechanisms for communication rather than death. A European company had been doing so for many years, before the close of the Cold War. Russia and China are also pursuing this form of weapons conversion. In March 1995, for example, Russia launched two commercial satellites which were mounted on former nuclear-warhead rockets.

Environmental Role The environmental chapter (Chapter 12) embraced a variety of links between business and law. The 1992 Rio Conference and related international environmental programs have strived to accomplish sustainable economic development for the underdeveloped countries of the world (*see* § 11.2). But there is continuing concern with the environmental cost of such development. The flourishing industrial-chemical plants of the 1970s and 1980s in Ireland, for example, helped to raise the economic standard of living in Ireland—one of the European Union's poorest members. But they also produced one of the most polluted atmospheres in the Northern Hemisphere.[14]

At least one disadvantage is associated with prospering international business ventures and the insatiable desire of underdeveloped countries to obtain a more equitable share of global resources under the New International Economic Order (*see* § 13.4). Many members of the community of nations are now free of *de jure* colonial rule, under the UN program described in the self-determination materials in this book (*see* § 2.3).

But they are now challenged by the sometimes mutually exclusive objectives of brisk economic development and the drain of long-term environmental degradation. The citizens of Bhopal, India certainly gained from the presence of a major US corporate operation in their territory, making chemicals for agricultural use. Thousands of jobs were created. India's economy was favorably impacted by the presence of the multinational corporate activity. More money was spent locally, in the form of the added spending power of corporate employees, steady jobs, and a decline in unemployment. There would be a significant environmental price to be paid in 1984, however, for hosting a for-

eign corporation's operations in Bhopal. Several thousand people were killed, and 200,000 people became ill, as a result of the toxic gas leak in one of the worst environmental disasters in history (*see* § 12.1).

■ 13.2 ECONOMIC ASSOCIATIONS OF STATES

Chapter 3 analyzed the various categories of international organizations of States. That material introduced the essential characteristics of international organization, many of which are shared by all such "international persons." It emphasized political and military associations of States, with the exception of the European Union, which has enjoyed the greatest degree of success of any regional organization.

This chapter includes materials on *economic* associations of States: first, the economic summit mechanism in international relations; second, a snapshot of *regional* economic organizations; and third, a summary of one major regional organization (NAFTA). The final section of this chapter then focuses on *global* economic integration.

Summits

"G-7" National leaders have used economic summits as a basis for developing special-purpose economic associations. Solidarity of approaches to a variety of problems is thus promoted through an emphasis on trade and financial issues. For twenty years, the leaders of the world's major industrialized democracies have thus met at various locations for the annual "G-7" summit.

The Group of Seven, the world's richest countries, traditionally consisted of Canada, France, Japan, Germany, Great Britain, Italy, and the United States. In mid-1994, the G-7 became the G-8 via Russia's admission. At the Naples meeting of the association, President Boris Yeltsin described this occasion as a "large step to[ward] full security of peace on Earth." During the Cold War, there could be no such association. The former Soviet Union was politically opposed to democracy and to the capitalist market system. Now, the two superpowers have joined in a *loose* economic association designed to help extinguish the mistrust associated with their forty-year political adversity.

The 1994 summit communiqué of this ostensibly economic grouping of States went much further than just economics. It contained joint positions on Bosnia, Haiti, the Middle East, and North Korea, as well as on nuclear proliferation. At the same time, the two most powerful members, Japan and the US are involved in a major economic confrontation over the US trade deficit and US access to Japanese markets. Nevertheless, this annual summit procedure provides the opportunity for the leaders to review their drive toward a coordinated economic policy.

Summit of the Americas In December 1994, the heads of the Western Hemisphere's thirty-four democracies met in Miami for the first Summit of the Americas. Their goal is to convert the hemisphere into a free trade zone by the year 2005—called the Free Trade Area of the Americas. Their first (and last) summit on this topic was in 1967. Although the General Agreement on Tariffs and Trade has prodded freer trade since 1947, it was the 1993 North American Free Trade Agreement (NAFTA) that provided the impetus for this hemispheric economic summit.

The anticipated benefit for the US is that it would enjoy more trade within Latin America, by the year 2010, than it would in its *combined* trade with Japan and the European Union. This economic goal also involves much more than what is expressed by its apparent economic emphasis. The Summit's final decree called for joint action to combat crime and poverty. The summit leaders further agreed, in principle, to promote environmental cooperation, democracy, and literacy. This regional effort may bear more fruit than the UN's *global* poverty summit of March 1995 in Copenhagen. There, world leaders produced few hard promises to attack the related problems of poverty, unemployment, and political instability—which effectively isolate approximately 1 billion people of the planet in absolute poverty.

Some impediments may limit potential implementation by their target date of 2005. Due to the summit's rather progressive environmental and worker's rights objectives, it will be more difficult for certain States in the hemisphere to adopt or implement every item contained in the final decree's statement of intent. Further, Latin American States do not support the US policy on Cuba (*see* § 10.2)—the only State not invited to this summit of the hemisphere's "democracies." The Bolivia

Summit of 1996 is scheduled to address the difficult balance between sustainable economic growth and environmental degradation.

APEC Summit In 1993, fifteen Pacific Rim nations met in Seattle, Washington. Members of this "rim" of nations all have borders on the Pacific Ocean. This Asia-Pacific Economic Cooperation (APEC) meeting was the largest of world leaders in the US, since the 1945 UN Conference in San Francisco. It also brought a great deal of attention to APEC, in the aftermath of President Clinton's success in negotiating NAFTA. This economic association of States contains just over 50 percent of the world's economic production capabilities, and approximately 40 percent of the world's population. For the US, trade across the Pacific surpassed trade across the Atlantic by 1983. By 1992, Pacific trade amounted to $315 billion—one-third more than the US trade across the Atlantic.

APEC has thus associated the world's three largest economies—China, Japan, and the US. The 1993 summit was the first opportunity for a US president to meet a Chinese leader since the 1989 Tiananmen Square massacre. That particular event widely impacted subsequent Sino-US trade and human rights discourses. Meeting under the auspices of APEC thus provides an opportunity to develop a personal dialogue that could ease tensions associated with the Beijing massacre (*see* § 11.2).

The APEC nations established an inter-summit *Group of Eminent Persons* at the 1993 summit. Its task is to follow up on the declarations made at the 1993 summit. In September 1994, this group's report thus pronounced the objective to "commit the region to achieve trade in all goods, services, capital and investment by the year 2020 with implementation to begin by 2000." The 1994 follow-up summit in Indonesia generated the declaration that the *developed* members of APEC would remove such barriers by the year 2010.

This group rejected both the European Union and the NAFTA trade bloc approach to economic integration. Instead, it encourages "open regionalism." APEC is thus willing to accept new member States if they internationalize their economies. Unlike the EU and NAFTA, APEC does not intend to sustain trade discrimination against outsiders. It encourages APEC members to extend trade liberalization to non-APEC members.

For the US, this economic association could be characterized as a shift from the Cold War "East-West" focus to a "West-East" orientation in economic integration. The US attention to international economic matters is shifting away from the sagging economies of post–Cold War Europe toward the comparatively vibrant markets on the Pacific Rim. Economic integration in the Pacific is one way that the nations of the Western Hemisphere can respond to the European Union's very successful European economic integration strategy.

APEC solidarity is limited by its being the most diverse economic organization of States. China has the least codified trade policies. Japan and South Korea have the most intricate nontariff barriers to international trade. China and Taiwan are the two largest economies that were not members of the General Agreement on Tariffs and Trade, to be discussed in § 13.3. (China immediately joined the WTO, while Taiwan did not). The 1993 APEC summit was boycotted by the Prime Minister of Malaysia, due to a concern that APEC will become a device for forcing Western-style democracy and market reforms on its smaller members.

Regional Organization

This section of Chapter 13 provides a glimpse of the diverse array of *economic* integrations. One could describe the contemporary thrust toward *regional* economic organization as virtually eclipsing the importance of global devices such as the General Agreement on Tariffs and Trade. Whether this characterization proves accurate in the twenty-first century depends on the continued success of the new World Trade Organization, discussed in the next section of this book.

First, one must distinguish the basic objectives of the particular economic association of States. There are five categories, in ascending order of degree of integration:

- *Preferential trade*—Trade preferences are granted in the form of freer access to the respective markets. This is the most basic form of trade association. The US negotiated this form of agreement with its Caribbean neighbors in the 1983 Caribbean Basin Initiative.

- *Free trade area*—Tariffs between the member States are initially reduced, and ultimately eliminated. Each member may keep its original tariffs as against countries outside of the free trade area. There is no organized policy among the members as to other countries. The North American Free Trade Agreement among Canada, Mexico, and the United States is an example.

- *Customs union*—The members liberalize trade among themselves, while erecting a common tariff barrier as against all nonmember States. The 1969 South African Customs Union is an example.

- *Common market*—A common market is the next higher degree of integration beyond a customs union. The members thus remove restrictions on the internal movement of the means of production and distribution of all commodities. The European Union is the most successful of all common markets (*see* § 3.4).

- *Economic union*—This is a true common market, but with a unified fiscal and monetary policy within the union. The result is similar to the linkage among the fifty states of the US. The difference is that an economic union consists of *international* States, rather than states within one federated State. The European Union, formerly the European Economic Community, made a significant step toward becoming a fully integrated economic union through the implementation of the Single European Act commonly referred to as "1992." The EU, however, has not yet implemented the use of a common currency for all citizens and agencies within the union.[15]

The contemporary regional trading blocs currently number over thirty. They function in a variety of ways. Blocs range from those that act like super-States to those that are more like political arrangements merely cast in the form of economic blocs. Many commentators characterize trade blocs as sharing a common bond—with each one being the product of protectionist fears. A Washington, D.C. legal practitioner offers the following assessment of economic integration:

THE NEW WORLD ORDER OF REGIONAL TRADE BLOCKS

8 American University Journal of
International Law & Policy 155, 155–57 (1992)
Joseph Brand, of the District of Columbia Bar

. . .

Our world today is dividing into trading blocs. Some have the superstructure of nation states. The European Communities (the official name of what we commonly call the European Community), with a parliament and courts and the supremacy of Community laws over those of its members, begins to look more and more like a state; others are multinational agreements that may be more political negotiating arrangements than cohesive trading blocs. ASEAN (Association of Southeast Asian Nations) is a relevant candidate. These blocs, however strong or weak, are growing all around the world. Like the empires [from Rome to the Soviet Union] that preceded them, the regional trading blocs of the new economic world order may divide into a handful of protectionist superstates. If by the new political world order we mean increased American hegemony disguised as international cooperation, we may come to know the new economic world order as regional hegemony disguised as free trade.

. . .

[A variety of reasons explain their formation.] First, they are born of political fear. The European Community was proposed . . . just five years after the end of the Second World War. European unity was perceived as the antidote to European war. Fear of war gave birth to the union. Another kind of fear seems relevant to the extension of the U.S.-Canada Free Trade Agreement into a wider hemispheric economic bloc. Critics of the North American Free Trade Agreement (Canada, Mexico, and the United States) believe fear of a successful EC 1992 and the economic eminence of Japan underlies the political imperative that moves these negotiations.

Second, blocs espouse trade liberalization internally, but achieve trade protection externally. For example, the Uruguay Round of trade liberalization is now held hostage to the Europeans' protective treatment of their farmers.

. . .

This rather bleak perspective regarding the motivation for regional trade groupings is not the only one. Professor Gilbert Wickham of the Political Science Department at Dalhousie University in Canada espouses a very different perspective—not as negative, but certainly more buoyant—in his 1992 book on the evolution of trade agreements:

What is the role of international trade agreement[s] in the modern nation-state system? The answer is to *reduce* protectionist national regulation, but even more important [it is] to reduce the uncertainty and unpredictability of the international trade regime, and to promote stability. The greatest cause of uncertainty in the contemporary trading system comes from the self-serving actions of self-interested nation states. Thus, it can be said that

one nation's sovereignty is another nation's uncertainty.[16]

This perspective explains why, for example, members of the Association of Southeast Asian Nations (ASEAN)—Brunei, Indonesia, Malaysia, Philippines, Singapore, Thailand, and potentially Vietnam—seek regional "economic" stability in the form of the ASEAN trade agreement. They may thereby seek protection by their economic integration with similarly situated powers, who also seek freedom from external influences over their sovereign affairs. China and Japan, for example, have exhibited territorial designs over the affairs of these nations over a long period. The ASEAN States have thus expressed their fear that history may repeat itself. From their perspective, there is no reason to believe that the contemporary epoch will necessarily differ. Domination by war or by trade may thus be perceived as only a matter of degree.

Regardless of what perspective accurately depicts the motivation for pursuing international trade relations, economic integration is clearly going to be a very prominent feature in international relations for the foreseeable future. To appreciate its current contours, Exhibit 13.3 lists the major economic associations of States.

EXHIBIT 13.3 Selected Regional Economic Associations of States

Name[a]	Members—Objectives[b]
ANCOM	Andean Common Market: Bolivia, Colombia, Ecuador, Peru, Venezuela/Chile withdrew (1969)—as moved toward integration; conflicting national interests have inhibited achieving common market
APEC	Asia-Pacific Economic Cooperation: Australia, Brunei, Canada, China, Hong Kong, Indonesia, Japan, Malaysia, Mexico, New Zealand, Papua New Guinea, Philippines, Singapore, South Korea, Taiwan, Thailand, United States (1990)/Chile has applied—Pacific Rim trade cooperation (*see* § 13.2 above)[c]
ASEAN	Association of Southeast Asian Nations: Brunei, Indonesia, Malaysia, Philippines, Singapore, Thailand (1976)/Vietnam potential member—promotes regional economic stability and protection from external influences (China/Japan); 1992 program to create common market responding to economic alliances in Europe/North America[d]
CARICOM	Caribbean Community and Common Market: Anguilla, Barbados, Belize, Dominica, Grenada, St. Kitts-Nevis, St. Lucia, St. Vincent, Trinidad, Tobago (1974)—elimination of internal trade barriers and common external tariff[e]
ECOWAS (Lagos,Nigeria)	Economic Community of West African States: 16 West African nations (1975)—promotes cooperation and development; seeks creation of a customs union[f]
EFTA	European Free Trade Association: Austria, Denmark, Iceland, Norway, Portugal, Sweden, Switzerland (1959)—Great Britain, initially refused membership in EU, then led this rival scheme before withdrawing (after becoming EU member)[g]
European Union (Brussels)	Austria, Belgium, Denmark, Finland, France, Germany, Great Britain, Greece, Ireland, Italy, Luxembourg, Netherlands, Portugal, Spain, Sweden (1957)—only free trade zone with *no* tariff barriers (*see* § 3.4)[h]
Group of Eight (G-8)	Canada, France, Germany, Great Britain, Italy, Japan, Russia, US (1974)—annual summits on economic policies of major industrial democracies[i]
Gulf Cooperation Council	Bahrain, Kuwait, Oman, Qatar, Saudi Arabia, United Arab Emirates (1981)—standardized subsidies; eliminating trade barriers; negotiating with European Union and other regional organizations to obtain favorable treatment[j]

EXHIBIT 13.3 *(continued)*

Name[a]	Members—Objectives[b]
IECO (Islambad, Pakistan)	Islamic Economic Cooperation Organization: Iran, Pakistan, Turkey (1964)—seven former Soviet republics joined in 1992 to promote trade among Islamic States
NAFTA	North American Free Trade Agreement: Canada, Mexico, US (1994)—free trade zone treaty promoting reduction/elimination of tariffs and other trade barriers (*see* § 13.2)
OECD (Paris)	Organization for Economic Cooperation and Development (1961): 24 mostly Western European industrialized States—promotes world trade on nondiscriminatory basis for economic advancement of lesser-developed countries
OPEC (Vienna)	Organization of Petroleum Exporting Countries: Algeria, Ecuador, Gabon, Indonesia, Iran, Iraq, Kuwait, Libya, Nigeria, Qatar, Saudi Arabia, United Arab Emirates, Venezuela (1960)—control production and international pricing of oil[k]
SELA	Acronym for 25-nation Latin American Economic System (1975)—goal to establish system for pooling resources, creating agencies to sell resources on world market similar to OPEC
Summit of the Americas	Summit of Western Hemisphere's 34 heads of State (1994)—Free Trade Area goal by 2005

[a] City = headquarters of organizations with a permanent site

[b] Date = date when the association was originally formed

[c] K. Okuizumi (ed.), *The U.S.-Japan Economic Relationship* in *East and Southeast Asia: A Policy Framework for Asia Pacific Economic Cooperation* (Wash., DC: CSI Studies, 1992)

[d] *See* Framework Agreement on Enhancing ASEAN Economic Cooperation, 31 *Int'l Legal Mat'ls* 506 (1992)

[e] *See* A. Payne, *The Politics of the Caribbean Community, 1961–1979: Regional Integration Among New States* (New York: St. Martin's Press, 1980)

[f] *See Economic Community of West African States: An Overview of the Economies of West African States* (Lagos, Nigeria: ECOWAS Secretariat, 19__) (date not given)

[g] *See* M. Sheridan, J. Cameron & J. Toulin, *EFTA Legal Systems: An Introductory Guide* (London: Butterworths, 1993)

[h] *See* R. Folsom, *European Community Law in a Nutshell* (St. Paul, MN: West, 1992)

[i] *See* A. Mep & H. Ulrich, *Partners for Prosperity: The Group of Seven and the European Community* (Upland, PA: Diane Pub., 1994)

[j] *See* G. Dietl, *Through Two Wars and Beyond: A Study of the Gulf Cooperation Council* (New York: Advent, 1991)

[k] *See OPEC Official Resolutions and Press Releases 1960–1990* (Vienna: OPEC Secretariat, 1990)

NAFTA

The North American Free Trade Agreement (NAFTA) is an economic association consisting of Canada, Mexico, and the United States. NAFTA is now summarized to provide a better appreciation of how a regional trade agreement operates. The next section of the book profiles the major *global* agreements.

NAFTA is essentially a free trade area. Its members thus decided to initially reduce tariffs, with the objective of eliminating them after fifteen years. Unlike a customs union, each member State remains free to retain the tariffs of its choosing for nonmember countries. Prior to NAFTA, Mexico had an *average* tariff (the combined rate on all tariff items) of about 10 percent. The US average tariff rate was then about 4 percent. The NAFTA agreement established a schedule to reduce tariffs between members, and to eliminate other barriers like Mexico's special agricultural licensing system. Upon total elimination of tariffs and nontariff barriers to importation, there will be free market access within the free trade area by exporters in all three member countries.

The projected benefits include a 6 percent "real" growth rate (factoring in the effect of inflation) and a doubling of US exports to Mexico. It is thus estimated that, in the first five years of NAFTA, the US will sell $17 billion more in goods and services—just in Mexico—than it would have sold without NAFTA. Mexico's exports are expected to amount to an added $8 billion in the same period, as a result of the NAFTA treaty.

The NAFTA was not adopted without its critics. US presidential candidate Ross Perot predicted that the US/Mexican wage differential would unwittingly result in the mass exportation of US jobs to Mexico. US corporations would opt to relocate there because of Mexico's cheaper labor costs. He expressed another concern—that US companies would thus be able to take undue advantage of the average Mexican worker, given Mexico's less stringent labor and occupational protection laws. Many opponents also criticized the NAFTA, because it would result in greater environmental degradation. For example, the average US-licensed truck on US highways weighs 80,000 pounds when loaded. The Mexican equivalent is 170,000 pounds per truck. The added weight on US border-state highways, and the less stringent pollution standards for vehicle licensing in Mexico, would combine to bring further environmental damage to the US atmosphere and its highways.

On the positive side, there is little doubt that NAFTA will spur production and create more US jobs in certain industries. The NAFTA benefits include new restrictions in various trades that will make it more costly to import foreign (as opposed to North American–made) commodities. The US television industry has battled greatly increased foreign completion from Asia. Asian corporations previously took advantage of contemporary customs laws on both sides of the US/Mexico border—specifically, the 1985 twin-plant "maquiladora" pro-

gram. Asian companies have been able to complete final assembly of their products in Tijuana—one of the largest television assembly areas in the world. They shipped 10,000 units per month (in the non-recessionary period prior to 1995). In Tiajuana alone, manufacturers including Sony, Hitachi, Matsushita, and Samsung employ thousands of Mexican workers in the maquiladoras. The final assembly of a completed television set in Tiajuana allows these Japanese corporations to avoid the higher US tariff required when the same television is assembled in Japan and shipped directly to the US. Under the relevant "rules of origin," Mexico becomes the origin of the finished product for customs purposes. The US generally charges Mexico a lower tariff on imported goods than Japan. Under NAFTA, all televisions imported into the US will ultimately have to contain North American–made picture tubes to qualify for duty-free treatment. Thus, some of these Asian producers may shift their production centers from the maquiladoras of Mexico to new production plants in the US—creating jobs and added governmental revenues.

The 2,000-page NAFTA agreement accords preferential treatment to 9,000 categories of goods exchanged between the three member nations. This has certain benefits for the US. For example, the 1988 US/Canada Free Trade Agreement provided that an automobile was entitled to preferential tariff treatment if 50 percent of its components were made in the US. It was considered to have its "origin" in North America and could thus be imported from Canada without the imposition of a US tariff. Under the NAFTA agreement, the same car will have to consist of 65 percent US-made components to qualify for duty-free import into the US.

One may make several functional contrasts between NAFTA and other trade agreements. NAFTA contains protectionist measures. The above automobile example is one of them. There are preferential tariffs between the NAFTA members. In the twenty-first century, no tariffs will be assessed on the imports of many industries. Each NAFTA member remains free to assess whatever tariff it wishes on products not imported from member nations. This is the type of regional protectionism that the global World Trade Organization will likely seek to change, under the "most favored nation" tariff treatment discussed in § 11.4 of this book. Another contrast is that the NAFTA does not yield sovereign powers to an international entity that will control the independent actions taken by member governments. The European Union, on the other hand, is an example of economic integration where member States have ceded substantial sovereignty to the EU's organizational institutions (*see,* for example, Exhibit 3.5 in § 3.4).

Whether the NAFTA will achieve what proponents claimed will depend on the continuing solidarity of its trading partners. One year after NAFTA went into effect, Mexico experienced some major financial problems. The peso was devaluated, largely as a countermeasure to the intense borrowing of the prior Mexican presidential administration. Mexico began to experience a reversal of its ability to control inflation, coupled with a very troubled 1995 in terms of the stability of its stock market and other investment opportunities. In mid-1994, Mexico imposed a new 9 percent tariff on US milk-exports to northern Mexico. That came at a time when the NAFTA was supposed to *reduce* tariffs. US milk was temporarily banned from the shelves of Calimax, Tiajuana's major supermarket chain store. If protectionist measures continue to emerge, the thrust that was necessary for NAFTA's implementation will likely dissipate, along with the national willingness to continue this experiment in regional economic integration.

■ 13.3 GATT/WORLD TRADE ORGANIZATION

The World Trade Organization (WTO) became effective in 1995—in the form of a 26,228-page document. Due to the complexity of this global agreement, it will take some time to fully interpret all of its provisions. A Preparatory Committee at its headquarters in Geneva, Switzerland, is tasked with the duty to consider issues as they arise. This Committee will also interpret the WTO document for application in future international trade matters. The new agreement includes a six-part program designed to reduce barriers in contemporary international commerce. Its key elements are as follows:

■ *Tariffs*—Import taxes and other tariff barriers would be reduced on 85 percent of the world's trade, with some tariff cuts taking effect immediately. These taxes are commonly referred to as customs duties, charges, tolls, assessments, or levies. The most common term is "tariff."

■ *Dumping*—This is the predatory practice of temporarily selling imports, at a price below cost, to eliminate competition. After market access is secured, the pricing structure increases significantly, so that profits recoup previous losses.

■ *Agriculture*—Farm subsidies, which artificially reduce the cost of production, would be reduced by an average of 36 percent.

■ *Textiles*—Import quotas on textiles from developing countries, currently helping the local market's competitors maintain a greater market share, would be phased out over a ten-year period.

■ *Service sectors*—Markets in "service" sectors, such as banking, shipping, and insurance, will be subject to international trade controls for the first time. Only "goods" were regulated under the 1947–1994 version of the WTO.

■ *Intellectual property*—This extends protection against unauthorized copying of "intellectual" property such as books, films, music, and computer programs.

The WTO basically is intended to be the successor of the General Agreement on Tariffs and Trade (GATT) institution. It will also be something much more. This global trade arrangement was first called GATT, when it was negotiated in 1947. This institution did not previously operate as an "international organization" as such. It has nevertheless been *the* global agreement in international trade. "GATT 1994," meaning GATT as amended due to interim negotiated changes, will continue to operate for those few nations that did not become charter members or ratify the WTO agreement. The shift from GATT to WTO will be something more than just a name change. The GATT thus shifts from a *de facto* arrangement to a truly international organization that is intended to become the treaty-based centerpiece of International Trade Law. The primary reason for this upgraded status is that the WTO has radically changed dispute settlement procedures in international commerce.

This section of Chapter 13 will summarize the WTO's operation; tell how it fits into the overall scheme of international trade; give its essential operation in day-to-day trade matters; and explain why there was significant congressional opposition to continued US participation GATT/WTO after

1994—which was overcome by President Clinton's administration only in the eleventh hour.

Evolution of GATT

One might first consider the likely scenario *if there were no GATT*. One would have to assume that no nation had ever erected a trade barrier. Managerial skill and economic efficiency would then be the essential market forces for determining the nature and quantity of international business transactions. Instead, governments have introduced a variety of impediments to the free flow of cross-border commerce. There have been definite costs and benefits. Professor Christopher Korth, of the University of South Carolina Business School, explains this development in terms of special interests that skew otherwise natural market processes:

INTERNATIONAL BUSINESS: ENVIRONMENT AND MANAGEMENT 2nd ed. 1985

Christopher Korth
Barriers to International Business, p.84

[W]hile the world, nations, and even most regions would enjoy higher living standards as a result of the freedom of trade . . . some individuals and groups [in certain industries] would be worse off. Thus these groups are often protected, for example, much of the U.S. textile industry or the auto industry in most developing countries. In addition, the losses suffered by such groups tend to be quite concentrated and noticeable. On the other hand, the gains from free trade . . . for the entire country, although much greater in total than the losses of those who are adversely affected, are spread over much or all [of] the economy and are less readily quantifiable. As a result, those who would be hurt by freedom of trade . . . tend to frequently speak much louder than those who benefit. Therefore, the will of the minority often overrides the welfare of the majority.

The economy will likely suffer if the government of a country accedes to [excessive] protective pressures, regardless of the specific nature of the argument and regardless of whether the interested group represents the private or governmental sector. *Protectionism* means that a higher price must be paid by the majority in order to benefit the few.

The list of arguments on behalf of controls is long. The list of "reasonable" arguments from the viewpoint of the public good (as opposed to that of special interest groups) is very short. Even in these cases, however, both national and world efficiency, income, and living standards will decline.

The tariff thus developed as the primary international trade barrier. When a government so taxes a foreign-made commodity, its tariff increases the cost of doing business in that particular market. The higher the tariff, the higher the cost—and the less likely the importation of foreign goods. One reason that governments impose tariffs is to raise revenue. But the intended or unintended economic effect is that tariffs help local manufacturers to compete with cheaper imports from more efficient and established competitors in another country. While the taxing nation's products are protected by such tariffs, that protection has a price. That nation can expect its trading partners to counter with their own tariffs. The cost of the import so taxed is that it is more expensive for that nation's consumers. The wholesaler will pass this cost along to the customer as a cost of doing business.

There has often been an inverse relationship between tariffs and the magnitude of a nation's international commerce. A general increase in local tariff rates will likely cause a decrease in imports. The tariff thus increases the cost of doing business in that country—necessitating continuing management assessments of whether to continue exporting to a country that has increased its tariff on the imported product.

This inverse relationship between the level of tariffs and trade is illustrated by the effect of the US tariff law of 1930. It imposed the highest tariffs ever levied on foreign-made products. The US Congress then believed that this trade restriction would *stimulate* local industry and agriculture, and that the US would not be harmed by this tariff legislation. The opposite occurred. The other major industrial countries retaliated by placing higher tariffs on US exports. The foreign demand for American products fell immediately, resulting in a loss of jobs in the US. These events contributed to the Great Depression of the 1930s—and the global recession of that era.

In 1934, President Roosevelt and the Congress reversed this high-tariff approach. There was a need to stimulate the domestic economy. Congress thus enacted the Reciprocal Trade Agreements Program to encourage international competition. It generally reduced US tariff rates, thus encouraging similar reductions by other countries. The legislative goal was to vitiate the adverse effect of the high tariffs that strangled the flow of international commerce—both in and out of the US. Congress then authorized the president to negotiate mutual tariff reductions with individual nations. The US Trade Representative thus began to negotiate an exhaustive series of *bilateral* agreements to reduce tariffs. This program increased the volume of US exports and stimulated worldwide trade benefits, as other countries responded by reducing their tariffs. The US tariffs gradually declined to the lowest levels in the nation's history.

During World War II, certain nations explored the possibility of a *multilateral* trade organization. They advocated a single, global trade agreement that would replace the hundreds of independent bilateral agreements. The US pursued this objective by lobbying for creation of the International Trade Organization (ITO) to develop and maintain a global trade agreement. Representatives from several nations met to draft an ITO Charter. They simultaneously created a comparatively informal document called the General Agreement on Tariffs and Trade (GATT) at Geneva in 1947. The GATT was originally supposed to be a statement of principles related to—but distinct from—the anticipated ITO Charter.[17]

The ITO never materialized. Since the US Congress resurrected its isolationist trade posture after World War II, it decided against US participation in the proposed ITO. The US had the most prosperous postwar economy. Many of today's major economic powers were in ruins, or economically depressed, after the war. Without US support, the ITO became impractical. Since then, GATT continued to be a *de facto* arrangement that was useful, even if not legally enforceable when its obligations (discussed below) were breached by a participating State.

GATT became the device for coordinating policies on international commerce, for accomplishing trade objectives, and for overcoming the inertia of the US Congress. In 1948, twenty-two nations thus executed an interim Protocol of Provisional Application—the original GATT agreement referred to as "GATT 1947." A GATT General Secretariat and administrative staff were established by 1955 in Geneva. Its task was to better implement the trade objectives of the participating countries—which could not be called "members" because the GATT did not achieve official status as an international organization of States. GATT did not possess its own power to act when a State decided to ignore its GATT "obligations" during the next forty years.

Some market economies historically resisted membership in GATT out of a desire to protect their local industries from foreign competition. Mexico, for example, was opposed to GATT membership because it was not ready to open its economy to imports. Mexico's private industrialists equated GATT membership with a flood of cheap imports that would destroy certain domestic industries and remove the protective barriers that fostered their growth. Mexico finally applied for GATT membership in 1985, however, to breathe life into its sagging export program. President Roberto de La Madrid convinced Mexico's private industrialists that Mexico could not expand its export sales if it maintained barriers to imports from other nations. Mexico's participation in GATT has now removed many of those barriers.

In 1994, the status of the GATT arrangement changed. Most nations of the world either joined, or sought accession to, the various agreements produced by the seven-year "Uruguay Round" of GATT negotiations. This was the last of five such periodic rounds conducted since GATT's inception, and referred to as "GATT 1994." During that session, the national representatives produced the "Final Act," referring to the World Trade Organization (WTO).[18] As of January 1995, sixty nations thus became charter members of the WTO. Some have signed but have not yet ratified the WTO agreement. Twenty-one others immediately began to negotiate for their admission. Some States have decided to remain in GATT, rather than accept the WTO provisions on mandatory dispute settlement.

The new title was more than just a name change. First, there is now a *de jure* international organization endowed with jurisdictional powers provided by its member States. Second, the WTO has a power denied to GATT by its participating States. The WTO can enforce compliance when a member breaches the obligations undertaken by joining this global trade organization. Third, there is also room in the WTO for economies that have not been historically free-market economies. The former Soviet Union and the People's Republic of China had expressed interest in participating in the earlier GATT agreement. The US opposed China's participation, however, due to its extensive piracy of patented and copyrighted US materials. These products include computer hardware and software, books, movies, and a host of other items protected by treaty. US estimates are that China's breach of international copyright and patent treaties has cost over $1 billion a year in lost revenues, because 94 percent of US-made products in China are pirated copies. Notwithstanding the US concern, China became a member of the WTO. Russia's relatively recent shift to a market economy—assuming that democracy and capitalism continue to flourish—renders it a likely candidate for ultimate inclusion.

One major difference between the WTO and GATT is that a GATT State could pick and choose among which provisions of the various agreements it deemed appropriate to apply. That produced a very complex web of varied obligations, which did little to promote the universal appeal of the GATT. This is one of the reasons why regional trade organization virtually eclipsed the GATT in importance (*see,* for example, Exhibit 13.1). The WTO agreement thus requires that participating States must agree to all of the *basic* provisions, with some temporary exceptions.

The WTO also differs from GATT because it expanded GATT's limited application to only commodities. WTO membership thus requires accession to the four fundamental parts of the 1994 Final Act:

(1) trade in goods—GATT's sole focus; and the three new components on (2) services, (3) intellectual property rights, and (4) investment rules. The *goods* portion of international commerce continues to be the primary area of concern. It will thus be summarized below as the central portion of this section of the book. First, however, one should digest the major difference between GATT and the WTO. It caused the greatest concern for the Clinton administration when Congress considered it in late 1994. Had it not survived that debate, the WTO would have been rendered as impotent as the 1947 ITO proposal (discussed above).

The primary legal difference between GATT and the WTO is the latter's *mandatory* dispute-resolution mechanism (summarized in Exhibit 13.4). The former GATT panels of experts often issued their determinations without the ability to force compliance with the basic GATT obligations described below. A more formal adjudicatory system now exists, designed to provide enforceable remedies. The significance is succinctly explained by Professor Andreas Lowenfeld of New York University Law School, also a prominent international arbitrator:

> Until now dispute settlement in the GATT has generally reflected a certain ambivalence. Some states and many "old GATT hands" within the secretariat and among the delegations in Geneva believed that GATT dispute settlement should aim at lowering tensions, defusing conflicts, and promoting compromise; others, notably American officials and writers, have looked to the dispute mechanism of GATT as an opportunity to build a system of rules and remedies. Over the forty years of GATT dispute settlement, there has been an ebb and flow between the diplomatic and the adjudicatory models. It seems clear that the adjudicatory model prevailed in the Uruguay Round.[19]

EXHIBIT 13.4 World Trade Organization Dispute Resolution

Action	Nature	Actor(s)	Objective
Creation of rules and procedures	Administrative	DSB[a]	Administer procedure; establish panels and appeal process; monitor implementation
Request for consultation	Initiate resolution process	Plaintiff State (P)	Offending State has ten days to respond
Response	Initiates consultation	Defendant State (D)	Must respond within thirty days and settle within sixty days
Establish panel	Administrative	DSB	Either no D response or unsettled by P and D
Decision	Adjudicatory —first level	3 judges[b]	Complete work within six months; issue decision called "Report"
Appellate body	Adjudicatory —second level	3 judges[c]	Complete work within three months; three more months possible in complex cases
Adoption of report	Accept or reject	DSB	Panel/appellate report may be rejected by consensus of DSB
Compliance	Cease offending practice	Defendant State	Defendant must inform DSB of intent to comply and date by which it will comply
Arbitration agreement on *date* for compliance	Mutual agreement	P and D	Submit case to *binding* arbitration from which there can be no appeal
Arbitration	Final resort	Parties or WTO Director	Limited to *time* within which D must comply; no substantive issue considered

Source: Agreement Establishing WTO, reprinted in 33 *Int'l Legal Mat'ls* 13 (1994)

[a] DSB = Dispute Settlement Body formed by the WTO General Council.

[b] These will normally be members of GATT delegation in Geneva; panel member with same citizenship as a party may not serve on panel, absent specific request—providing option for panelists knowledgeable on laws of countries of respective parties.

[c] Seven-person organ, three of whom serve during Appellate Body review of panel report.

Under GATT, the losing party could essentially ignore or "block" a GATT "panel report." States could disregard the findings of the GATT panel when told to cease an offending practice. A powerful trading partner like the US could even block the GATT Secretariat from organizing a panel that was supposed to decide a complaint.[20]

Another difference is that GATT formerly permitted States to make their own unilateral determination that there had been a violation of the GATT rules. The US, for example, had freely wielded its "§ 301" procedure of the 1974 Trade Act. The congressional statement of purpose was "to strengthen economic relations between the United States and foreign countries through open and nondiscriminatory world trade. . . ." But the US Trade Representative thereby made determinations that there had been an unfair trade practice emanating from another country. Such unilateral determinations often led to the opposite result. They preceded (or announced) threatened trade wars and exacerbated the instability that such unilateral action connotes.

The WTO discourages this form of unilateral fact-finding by an individual member of the organization. Article 23 of Annex 2 to the Agreement Establishing the World Trade Organization thus provides that should a member seek redress for a violation of GATT obligations, it "shall have recourse to, and abide by, the rules and procedures of this Understanding. . . ." Members may not make their own determinations, and must instead seek "recourse to dispute settlement in accordance with the . . . [WTO] Understanding."[21]

Under this Understanding on Rules and Procedures Governing the Settlement of Disputes, there is a still a panel process. State members of the WTO can no longer dodge a panel decision, for three reasons. First, there is an initial consultation process. The aggrieved party may institute a relatively informal consultation with the allegedly offending party. This informal process has a short fuse, so that the aggrieved party may then secure the establishment of a formal panel if the matter remains unresolved for sixty days. Second, one State may not unilaterally block the establishment of a panel, when another has lodged a complaint in the WTO's headquarters in Geneva. Third, the unlikely acceptance of an adverse panel decision, without any form of review, would place the WTO and the entire GATT process at risk. States have been traditionally reluctant to yield sovereign powers to an external decision-maker without any recourse. The panels can make mistakes. Thus, the losing party may *temporarily* block a panel decision, unlike the former panel "process," which might drag on for months with no resolution.

The losing party must now seek immediate appellate review by the WTO's "Appellate Body" in Geneva. This will be a standing organ consisting of seven persons, three of whom will review the lower panel decisions. The existence of an appellate process is an innovation not present under prior GATT practice. This novelty has been criticized, on the basis that the availability of appellate review reduces the prestige of the "trial" panel. It offers a clear advantage, however. The losing party has the opportunity to rectify a perceived mistake—a common attribute of democratic systems of governance that should ultimately *add* to the integrity of the WTO process.[22]

The congressional concern, supplemented by interest groups and those of outspoken citizens such as Ralph Nader, was that the US would thereby unwittingly cede its sovereignty to the WTO in Geneva. The US, for example, would be unable to avoid the impact of a WTO panel or appellate decision that it deemed erroneous or prejudicial to US interests. A three-person WTO Appellate Body in a distant land would thus be able to trump US international commercial policy. On the other hand, the Clinton administration was able to convince a sufficient number of congressional decision-makers that the US could withdraw—in the event that the new WTO operation proved hostile to long-term US interests.

It is still possible that any of the WTO's trade power brokers—including the European Union and Japan—may ultimately withdraw. Proponents of the traditional "diffusion-not-adversarial" philosophy, discussed above, may ultimately prove to be right. In other words, "better to have a flexible, imperfect system that protects major principles than a system *so disciplined* that it provokes violation and defiance."[23]

Predictions about the consequences of WTO participation are quite diverse. Contemporary figures have been used—both to support and to negate the anticipated impact of *US* adoption of the WTO. Proponents anticipate a $1 trillion benefit, over the first five-year period through the year 2000. Other estimates are quite dismal—based on the

$1.4 trillion that the US supposedly lost, as a result of the trade deficit incurred since the Tokyo Round ended in 1979.

The WTO's above mandatory dispute resolution mechanism was the major procedural hurdle. But what are its *substantive* obligations?

GATT/WTO Trade Obligations

What exactly does participation in GATT and its successor WTO mean? What obligations does a State thereby undertake when it opts to join this international organization of States? The fundamental GATT/WTO purpose is to combat trade barriers. National representatives thereby attempt to reduce or eliminate the varied forms of trade barriers: tariffs, nontariff barriers, and discriminatory trade practices.

The essential articles are the articles I, II, III, and VI. The relevant portion of each is set forth below, followed by a brief explanation. (Emphasis has been supplied in certain passages.)

Article I General Most-Favoured-Nation Treatment

(1) With respect to customs duties and charges of any kind imposed on or in connection with importation or exportation or imposed on the international transfer of payments for imports or exports, and with respect to the method of levying such duties and charges . . . any advantage, favour, privilege or immunity granted by any contracting country shall be accorded immediately and unconditionally to the *like* product originating in or destined for the territories of all other contracting parties.

Under International Law, States are free to discriminate in their commercial dealings. That is an attribute of the sovereign power to engage in international relations with other States. As explained by Professor Georg Schwarzenberger of the University of London, in "the absence of bilateral and multilateral treaty obligations to the contrary, international law does not ordain economic equality between States nor between their subjects. Economic sovereignty reigns supreme. It is for each subject of international law to decide for itself whether and, if so, in which form, it desires to grant equal treatment to other States and their subjects or give privileged treatment to some and discriminate against oth-

ers."[24] Tariffs may thus discriminate against the goods from one country and in favor of those from another. Groups of States may combine to charge discriminatory tariffs. If the fifteen members of the European Union want to *eliminate* tariffs on the exported commodities of only its members, they do not have to extend this favorable tariff treatment to *other* countries.

The Article I "Most Favoured Nation" (MFN) clause has been a centerpiece of GATT. Even prior to its creation, many bilateral trade treaties contained such a clause. Each nation thereby promised that the tariff rate on the imports of its trading partner would be the lowest rate imposed on like imports from any other nation. Under the GATT, member nations likewise agreed to grant MFN status to the imported products from other GATT members.

Assume that South Africa imposes a 10 percent tariff on imported Italian shoes. Both States are members of the GATT/WTO. The above MFN article requires South Africa to charge Italy the lowest shoe tariff that it levies on like shoes from any other country. South Africa may charge a *higher* 12 percent tariff on shoes from State X if it is not a GATT member. South Africa may also impose a *lower* 8 percent tariff on shoes imported from State X. But it must then also extend this lowest tariff to Italian shoes.

Article II Schedules of Concessions

(1.b) The products described in *Part I* of the Schedule relating to any contracting party, which are the products of territories of other contracting parties, shall, on their importation . . . be exempt from ordinary customs duties in excess of those set forth therein. . . .

(1.c) The products described in *Part II* of the Schedule relating to any contracting party which are the products of territories entitled under Article I to receive *preferential treatment* upon importation into the territory to which the Schedule relates shall, on their importation . . . be exempt from ordinary customs duties in excess of those set forth and provided for in Part II of that Schedule.

Each State's tariff commitments are listed in "concessions" referred to as "schedules." These schedules have been renegotiated during the five periodic GATT rounds since the original 1947 agreement. Members then update and publish their latest tariff schedules, giving their maximum tariff for each item on the list of items governed by the GATT.

There is a dual system of tariffs under the GATT. Article II(1.c) above authorizes a GATT member to place the imports of designated nations on that member's "Part II Schedule" of tariffs. This results in lower tariffs on the imports from that nation. Each GATT member may thus publish *different tariffs* for the same type of import on its *Part I* list of imports and its Part II list. The lower tariffs on a member's *Part II* Schedule of tariffs favor the products of certain *developing* countries, thus encouraging their development. The more that they develop, the larger their markets will be for the other developed GATT nations.

Article III   National Treatment on Internal Taxation and Regulation

> (2) The products of the territory of any contracting party imported into the territory of any other contracting party shall not be subject, directly or *indirectly*, to internal taxes or other internal charges of any kind *in excess of* those applied, directly or indirectly, to like *domestic* products.

A tariff is normally a *surmountable* barrier to the importation of a foreign product. It increases the cost of getting that product to the foreign market for sale. A local business that is already in that market does *not* have to pay any import tariff. It can compete without having to factor in the additional tariff as a cost of doing business. If a US company wants to sell steel to Germany, for example, the latter's tariff on that steel is an added cost to the American company of doing business in Germany. German steel producers do not have to pay this same cost in their own German markets. If competition in the international steel market is very high, price differences will normally be minimal. Thus, the German tariff—or a sudden increase in it—may present an *insurmountable* cost barrier, making it unprofitable for a US company to sell steel in the German steel market.

In addition to *direct* import tariffs, many States have enacted, or more subtly imposed, *indirect* barriers to trade. Such an indirect tariff is called a non-tariff barrier (NTB) to competition from goods imported from another country. NTBs protect local industries from foreign competition. They create an added cost assessed on imports—in addition to the import tax that has already been paid. Article III(2) prohibits such indirect barriers on imports.

Assume that a US steel company determines that, even with the German tariff, it is still profitable to export steel to German markets. But representatives of the German steel industry then convince the German legislature to enact a law to require new inspections for structural defects in steel. This new law applies *only* to foreign-made steel imported into Germany. The US steel company must now pay the added cost of this new inspection procedure. This law is a GATT-prohibited NTB because it discriminates against foreign steel producers.

NTBs have often been imposed to make it harder for foreign imports to compete with products made in the local market. The simplest NTB is a quota on the quantity of foreign imports from a particular country. Another example is the so-called "buy national" law. It provides economic incentives to a country's consumers to buy domestic-made, rather than foreign-made, products.

A law may also discriminate in a way that violates a nation's GATT obligations. The US Congress, for example, passed environmental protection legislation in 1986 that discriminated against foreign oil. Congress thereby created a new tax on oil, to establish the so-called "Superfund" for cleaning up US waste disposal sites. The tax was set at 11.7 cents per barrel of *imported* oil—but only 8.2 cents per barrel for *domestic* oil. Many oil-exporting States complained that this was an indirect tariff on their oil sold in the US. A GATT dispute panel found that this tax violated the GATT because it was a NTB to competition with foreign oil. The US accepted the findings of the GATT panel and changed the law to delete its discriminatory effect.[25]

NTBs can discriminate against foreign imports in more subtle ways. A good example, although arising in a non-GATT context, was a French tax struck down in 1985 by the European Court of Justice (an entity discussed in § 9.6). France had imposed a tax on automobiles based on their horsepower. The French tax applied only to those automobiles with a very high horsepower. It was five times the tax imposed on cars with the usual horsepower for cars in France. France's automobile makers could not, effectively, be subject to this tax. None of them made vehicles with this high rate of horsepower. Although the French tax law purportedly applied to *all* automobile makers, its actual impact was limited to *foreign* automobile makers. France was thus required to repeal this tax. It was an NTB to international trade, which effectively imposed higher costs on foreign enterprises doing business in the French market.[26]

Article VI Dumping

(1) The contracting parties recognize that . . . dumping, by which products of one country are introduced into the commerce of another country at less than the normal value of the products, is to be condemned if it causes or threatens material injury to an established industry in the territory of a contracting party or materially retards the establishment of a domestic industry. . . .

A nation may not "dump" its products into another nation, at a price that is *below the fair market value* of that product in the *exporting* nation. Although a company could theoretically sell below cost without an anticompetitive effect, such conduct inherently "causes or threatens material injury to an established industry." Dumping is the type of business conduct that most likely "retards the establishment of a domestic industry" if there is none already present when the import arrives in the target market. Cheaper imports are one of the intended benefits of participation in the GATT. This provision controls a temporary flood of cheap imports, sold initially at a price below their value in the country of their origin (after considering shipping and insurance costs).

Article VI Countervailing Duties

(2) In order to offset or prevent dumping, a contracting party may levy on any dumped product an anti-dumping duty not greater in amount than the margin of dumping in respect to such product.

A State may thus augment its scheduled (published) tariff concession on that product, when it suspects that imports are being dumped. This is the so-called antidumping or countervailing "duty"— meaning a special tax on imports in addition to the usual tariff for that commodity. The purpose is to offset the anticompetitive effect of dumped products. The importing State thus raises the cost of exporting them into the "dumped" market, to a level that approximates their normal cost.

A major change, from the former GATT to the "New GATT," is the introduction of the more specific "Agreements on Implementation of the General Agreement on Tariffs and Trade." These new features embody the results of the seven-year Uruguay Round of GATT negotiations. The following portion of one of those implementing agreements is an example of the much greater detail for defining mutual trading expectations of GATT/WTO member States. Article 3.5 of the Agreement on Implementation of Article VI thus provides as follows:

It must be demonstrated that the dumped imports are, through the effects of dumping . . . causing injury within the meaning of this Agreement. The demonstration of a causal relationship between the dumped imports and the injury to the domestic industry shall [include] . . . any known factors *other than the dumped imports* which . . . are injuring the domestic injury, and the injuries caused by these other factors [such as contraction of demand, developments in technology, or domestic productivity.]

The various implementing agreements thus flesh out the skeletal detail provided by prior versions of the GATT, so as to clarify what factors should— and should not—affect the determination of whether dumping is actually occurring; and if it is, whether the dumping is in fact *causing* the alleged harm to the importing market's domestic industry.

■ 13.4 NEW INTERNATIONAL ECONOMIC ORDER

Historical Evolution

The roots of the so-called "New International Economic Order" (NIEO) may be traced to the early years of the twentieth century. The major political and economic powers engaged in extensive overseas investment, and took protective measures to ensure their continued profitability. They did not conduct their business operations with a view toward improving conditions in the host countries. The decades of environmental degradation, associated with the mining of phosphates in the former colony of Nauru, is one of the classic instances of profit at any cost (*see* § 12.1).

The decolonization movement of the 1960s did not extinguish smoldering claims that Western hegemony survived independence. A vast change affected the infrastructure of International Law—with a deluge of underdeveloped States suddenly appearing on the international level, and thus having a world forum available in which to express their desire for equality (*see* Exhibit 2.1 in § 2.2).

An embryonic movement of these States, which would come to be known as the NIEO, erupted when these new UN General Assembly members united with some other lesser-developed States to articulate their perspective about the application of UN Charter phrases, including the following:

- "equal rights of . . . nations large and small" (Preamble)

- "international machinery for the promotion of the economic and social advancement of all peoples" (Preamble)

- "international co-operation in solving international problems of an economic . . . character" (Art. 1.3)

- "The Organization is based on the principle of the sovereign equality of all its Members" (Art. 2.1)

- "promoting international co-operation in the economic . . . field" (Art. 13b)

- "the United Nations shall promote: higher standards of living . . . and conditions of economic and social progress and development" (Art. 55a)

A group of lesser-developed States thus began to articulate their right to economic independence by challenging the international status quo—specifically, the international legal principles on foreign investment, nationalization, and host State compensation for nationalization. They characterized International Law as a Eurocentric web of control, spun by the more powerful members of the UN to entrap their former "colonial" partners.

A series of UN developments surfaced in the 1960s that forged the early statement of this "Third World" position during the concurrent decolonization movement. In 1962, the UN General Assembly proclaimed the Resolution on the Permanent Sovereignty over Natural Wealth and Resources. Developing States therein complained about their required abdication of sovereignty—the price tag for encouraging foreign investment. The follow-up Resolution (1973) expressed the essence of the NIEO movement, wherein the General Assembly expressed that it:

> 2. *Supports resolutely* the efforts of the developing countries and of the peoples of the territories under colonial and racial domination and foreign occupation in their struggle to regain effective control over their natural resources;
>
> 3. *Affirms* that the application of the principle of nationalization carried out by States, as an expression of their sovereignty in order to safeguard their natural resources, implies that each State is entitled to determine the amount of possible compensation and the mode of payment, and that any disputes which might rise should be settled in accordance with the national legislation of each State . . . .[27]

The next major development of the 1960s occurred when a group of "Third World" States, known as the Group of 77 ("G-77"), advocated the creation of a NIEO in order to address the objectives of equality expressed in the UN Charter (quoted above). They initiated a fresh debate on the question of whether the Western foundations of modern International Law could continue to be operative, given the inequitable distribution of global wealth. G-77 thus prompted creation of the United Nations Conference of Trade and Development (UNCTAD) in 1966—a form of collective bargaining with the States that they characterized as economic rivals who dominated their existence. An UNCTAD resolution purported to demolish the basic tenet that *International* Law, rather than *national* law, provided the yardstick for measuring the scope of compensation for nationalized property. UNCTAD then began to promulgate a series of codes that purported to govern the conduct of multinational corporations. These included a Restrictive Business Practices Code and a Transfer of Technology Code. These were essentially guidelines for an international antitrust law designed to equitably distribute the proceeds of multinational corporate activity in developing nations.[28] Their efforts would later surface in the 1974–1982 negotiations during the UN Conference on the Law of the Sea—

producing draft provisions designed to redistribute the natural wealth found in and under the high seas (*see § 6.3*).

In 1966, the G-77 established the United Nations Industrial Development Organization (UNIDO). UNIDO's primary objective, contained in Article 1 of its Constitution, was the "promotion and acceleration of industrial development in the developing countries with a view to assist in the establishment of a New International Economic Order."[29]

The UN's establishment of UNIDO and UNCTAD suggested that developing nations would have a more prominent role on the economic-political horizon. The creation of these institutions reflected the growing thirst of the newly independent States for a greater role in world economic and political affairs. The G-77 firmly believed that the GATT operated primarily to preserve the economic hegemony of the relatively powerful and developed States. G-77 was also displeased with the operation of the postwar Breton Woods Agreement, establishing the International Monetary Fund. It was not designed to effectively further the economic interests of the developing nations.

Prior to the embryonic period of the NIEO, multinational corporations experienced a commanding expansion since World War II—roughly coinciding with the decolonization movement of the 1960s (*see § 2.3* on self-determination). Parent companies thus established foreign subsidiaries, with the ability to shift capital in and out of the foreign theater of operations. The foreign subsidiary was incorporated under the national laws of the host State. But the corporate operation was not thereby subject to the effective control of the host State. The corporate parent in a developed State fostered this evolution, while the host States assisted because they sought the infusion of foreign investment. The people of the host State became more and more dependent on the multinational corporation for economic survival—especially in nations where the cost of labor was cheap due to high unemployment. The multinational corporation's arrival created and supported a job base. This presence conferred certain economic benefits on the underdeveloped State. It improved the quality of life for its citizens where there was high unemployment.

The member States of G-77 nevertheless decided to change the state of International Law, particularly its special protection for aliens. Multinational corporations facing uncompensated nationalizations of their enterprises could thus resort to the "State responsibility for injury to aliens" feature of International Law. Developing States, in turn, perceived this reliance as perpetuating their economic independence long after the successful decolonization movement at the UN.

The G-77 thus promulgated the 1974 UN Charter of Economic Rights and Duties of States.[30] Its essential purpose was to further regulate the multinational corporations and change the legal status quo. The NIEO's Economic Charter, supported by a majority of the UN's member States, thus demanded that International Law be modified to accommodate their economic development in relation to the UN's economically dominant members. G-77's goal was to effectuate a redistribution of global wealth. One of the primary methods would be to recapture some of the wealth derived by multinational corporations—which were otherwise free to operate without constraints in their own sovereign territories.

The 1974 UN Economic Charter thus became the centerpiece of the NIEO. The State, in its capacity as a sovereign entity, may set the standard of compensation. Whether, and how much, to compensate a multinational enterprise was thus characterized as a matter governed by the host State's own laws and policies—not International Law, as it was articulated by the economically developed States. Under Article 2.2 of the NIEO's Economic Charter, each State has the following "right:"

> To nationalize, expropriate or transfer ownership of foreign property, in which case appropriate compensation should be paid by the State adopting such measures, taking into account its relevant laws and regulations and all circumstances that the State considers pertinent. In any case where the question of compensation gives rise to a controversy, it shall be settled under the domestic law of the nationalizing State and by its tribunals, unless it is freely and mutually agreed by all States concerned that other peaceful means be sought [to resolve compensation issues] on the basis of the sovereign equality of States and in accordance with the principle of free choice of means.[31]

Article 2 is a variation on the "Calvo Doctrine." As a condition of doing business, the foreign enterprise must waive the protections of International Law prohibiting the discriminatory treatment of aliens. A Calvo clause, stated either in the contract or mandated by host State law, precludes a nationalized entity from seeking the diplomatic assistance of its home State. The enterprise is thereby considered to be a citizen of the nationalizing State—in which case, it must look to *national* law for a remedy. The nationalizing State's decision, *whether* and *how* to compensate, is thereby based on its national law, rather than International Law (*see* § 4.4 on confiscation of property).

The promoters of the NIEO hoped to alter the reliance of these past decisions, as well as to modify or create a legal principle that would deem all such compensation decisions to fall solely within the discretion of the host State. If, for example, a nationalizing State's court or other tribunal finds that the multinational enterprise had taken unfair advantage of its position over a period of time, then the host State would not *necessarily* have to pay any compensation for its taking of property. Compensation would not necessarily have to be "prompt, adequate, and effective"—the common articulation of the Western-derived principle. Latin American States had already objected to "international" authority via the Calvo Clause. Now was the time to build on that model via the NIEO perception that host State law should govern such matters.[32]

The NIEO's obstacle would be the commonly applied standard, requiring prompt, adequate, and effective compensation for a governmental taking of foreign corporate assets. The source for this principle is ascertainable from customary State practice and international arbitrations. No multilateral treaty exists to express the consensus of States. The decisions of various international tribunals typically reasoned that a nationalizing State must compensate the owner of foreign assets under the "prompt, adequate, and effective" rule. (*See* § 4.4—Iran/US Claims Tribunal). This meant the fair market value of the seized property in freely transferable currency—the preferred yardstick of the Western capital exporters.

The posture of the International Court of Justice is that there is no clear rule on this point. The Court explains why, in the following passage from a 1970 case involving Belgian stockholders, a Canadian corporation, and a Spanish nationalization:

Considering the important developments of the last half-century, the growth of foreign investments and the expansion of the international activities of corporations, in particular of holding companies, which are often multinational, and considering the way in which the economic interests of States have proliferated, it may at first sight appear surprising that the evolution of law has not gone further and that *no generally accepted rules* in the matter have crystallized on the international plane.[33]

Some Western commentators have relied on the 1928 *Chorzow Factory* case, decided by the Permanent Court of International Justice, for a clear statement of the compensation principle attacked by the NIEO. The Court therein stated that established international practice required compensation that would "wipe out all the consequences of the illegal act. . . . To this obligation, in virtue of the general principles of international law, must be added that of compensating loss sustained as the result of the seizure."[34] This reliance is misplaced, because that case involved an *illegal* taking of alien property. In that instance, a treaty-based obligation precluded the sovereign State from exercising its customary power of nationalization.

New, New International Economic Order

During the 1980s, the multinational corporations in developed nations—particularly in the US—reacted to the UN-based articulation of the NIEO in a way that was not anticipated by its proponents. Corporate management diverted the flow of foreign investment from "Third World" nations to other developed nations. What was thought to be a clear legal standard—permitting nationalization but *requiring* compensation of foreign investment—had blurred. Corporate management decided to avoid the potential impact of the NIEO, stimulating a capital flight into other developed nations. The instability wrought by the NIEO thus backfired on the G-77, although it had grown to 120 nations during the 1970s and 1980s.[35]

As a result, the lesser-developed countries began to negotiate bilateral investment treaties (BITs) with the capital-rich States in order to reattract foreign investment. These treaties are typified by clauses protecting the right of the multinational corporation to fair market value compensation, in readily transferrable currency, in the event of a nationalization.[36]

This has been the wave of the 1990s. The Uruguay Round of the GATT process presented a similar device. Under GATT, Trade Related Investment Measures (TRIM) have been employed to protect foreign investors and to reverse the capital flight of the 1980s.

This bilateral treaty approach has not been accepted by all original members of the G-77. The BITs are virtually treasonous competitors with the UN process that pioneered the NIEO. One might argue that a *New*, New International Economic Order thus surfaced, signaling a movement in the direction of the *old* international economic order that prevailed prior to the heyday of the G-77 movement. The *new* NIEO appears to be coming full circle to the *old* order. Foreign investment cannot be attracted without sufficient protection from uncompensated nationalizations.

One could thus characterize the 1974 UN Economic Charter "establishing" the NIEO as showing evidence of excessive wear. Just as the global GATT process is scrambling to subdue the State penchant for regional economic integration, the NIEO is falling by the wayside. In both instances, sufficient attention may not have been paid to the reality that inherent differences exist within the community of nations. Thus, attempts to develop bipolarized paradigms may be doomed to failure, if not merely great frustration. The diverse nature of the State infrastructure that drives the international legal system need not be pressed into a dominant model for worldwide application. The key feature of a successful international legal system is the recognition by its decision-makers that emphasizing differences may eclipse values common to all. Professor Helen Hartnell of the Central European University in Budapest, Hungary has aptly characterized this problem with the NIEO as follows:

> The failed Charter of Economic Rights and Duties of States, like the failed Soviet Union, was built by "levellers." Their failure is rooted in [not conceding] the inevitability of diversity. Today's scrambling toward political, economic and legal integration in the eastern and western hemispheres might be seen to stem from fear of the consequences of too much difference, or [alternatively] from a recognition that cooperation can erase destructive differences. In any case, integration always has its

limits . . . the point at which differences begin to overshadow common values and interests.[37]

■ SUMMARY

1. International economic relations have continuously influenced the creation and evolution of modern International Law. Early treaties, and the medieval "Lex Mercatoria," or merchant law that flourished on the Mediterranean Sea, contained the norms for resolving disputes with distant lands. National leaders and their diplomats soon recognized that a solid trade foundation with other areas of the world could lead to benefits, including peace.

2. Recent applications of International Economic Law include the treaties standardizing the consequences of an international business transaction when it has different legal effects in the respective trading nations. States have used letters of credit, in the absence of diplomatic negotiations, to conclude sensitive arrangements. Trade is now used as a political vehicle for improving the human rights and environmental performance of other nations.

3. States are currently engaged in a frenzy of *regional* economic integration. They have thus undertaken preferential trade agreements, establishing free trade areas, customs unions, common markets, and economic unions to facilitate international commerce.

4. The *global* trade organization established in 1994/1995 consists of "GATT 1994" and "WTO 1995." GATT is the General Agreement on Tariffs and Trade. WTO 1995, GATT's successor organization, is the World Trade Organization. GATT/WTO will concurrently operate for some time into the early twenty-first century.

5. The GATT is basically a series of agreements that are periodically renegotiated and revised during multilateral trade negotiation "rounds" among the nations of the world. Its essential objective is to combat trade barriers by limiting tariffs and discriminatory barriers to trade.

6. The original GATT was not an international organization, in the sense that it could not command its "Participating States" to comply with its various negotiated trade rounds from 1947 to 1994. The WTO differs, largely because the State members *must* confer the ultimate dispute resolution authority on its panels in Geneva. GATT/WTO

now covers additional trade matters including services, intellectual property, and investment rules.

7. The essential GATT/WTO articles are I, II, III, and VI. Article I requires that "most favoured nation treatment" be accorded to the traders of other member States. A nation must thereby charge the same tariffs on like goods imported from other members. That nation is free, however, to charge a higher tariff on imports from nonmember nations.

8. Article II prohibits member nations from charging greater tariffs than those published in their tariff schedules, referred to as "concessions." They may charge lower tariffs in the case of certain lesser-developed countries. These are called preferential tariffs.

9. Article III prohibits nontariff barriers (NTBs) to imports. NTBs are charges assessed on foreign commodities in addition to Article II import duties. NTBs discriminate against foreign goods because like goods made within the same market are not subject to these practices.

10. Article VI prohibits "dumping"—the exporter's sale of goods in a foreign market at prices below their fair market value in the exporting country. When this occurs, importing nations may assess an additional "countervailing duty" on the dumped product to offset the effect of this anticompetitive practice.

11. The essential premise of the New International Economic Order (NIEO) was proclaimed in the 1974 UN Economic Charter on the Rights and Duties of States. That was that the host State has the sovereign right to determine *whether* and *how much* compensation is payable for the taking of foreign property. The NIEO was conceived for the purpose of increasing host State control over multinational enterprises.

12. The NIEO's announcement encouraged the large multinational corporations to withdraw their capital, once the compensation standards were in question. The Western capital-exporting nations believe the norm to be "prompt, adequate, and effective compensation in readily transferrable currency." Thus, they invested in other developed nations during the 1980s.

13. In the 1990s, a number of the G-77 countries began to negotiate bilateral investment treaties (BITs) in order to reattract foreign investment. These treaties are evidence of a withdrawal from the NIEO's 1974 Economic Charter.

■ PROBLEM

Problem 13.1 (*end of § 13.3*): *Hypothetical Problem*

Brazil and the United States are parties to "GATT 1994" and "WTO 1995." In 1994, Brazil announced a major discovery. After years of research in its rain forests, Brazilian chemists developed a generic drug substitute for a popular but expensive drug made by a US company in the US. The brand-name of the US drug is "A-1." The Brazilian generic substitute is called "B-2." Both drugs are the best nonprescription treatments for the "common cold."

Brazen, Inc. is a Brazilian State-owned corporation. Brazil uses the profits to raise revenue for the social and economic advancement of the people of Brazil. Brazen's corporate management realizes the extraordinary potential for B-2 to become a substitute for A-1. The latter drug has been used by most US consumers to treat their cold symptoms. Brazen begins its marketing plan by selling B-2 to associated US companies wishing to compete with the US maker of A-1. Several US importers are thus licensed to market B-2 to US consumers. The price charged is slightly less than that what US consumers pay for a bottle of A-1. The US tariff rate is low enough to make the exportation and sales of B-2 sufficiently profitable to encourage Brazen's entry into the US market.

Brazen exports B-2 to the US for $2 per unit shipped. It costs Brazen the equivalent of $1, per unit shipped, to produce B-2 in Brazil and then market it in the US. In 1995, some parts of the US market slowly begin to accept B-2 as the cheaper generic substitute for A-1. Brazen and its US associates then decide to lower the price charged to US consumers to 95¢ per unit. This price reduction yields immediate benefits for US customers. They now pay *substantially* less for B-2 than the cost of A-1. More consumers can now afford this relatively expensive but very effective cold remedy. B-2's unusually low prices quickly generate a large US demand. A-1 sales plummet, because US consumers can obtain B-2 at a substantially lower cost than A-1. The maker of A-1 thus reduces its production capacity and begins to look for profits in some other line of pharmaceuticals.

In 1996, Brazen's Minister of Commerce increases B-2 prices in gradual steps. By the end of the year, the cost to US consumers increases beyond the initial cost of B-2. Brazen begins to profit again, from the large volume of B-2 sales in the US. It had lost money during the 1995 marketing campaign. Brazen's 1995 "below cost" pricing strategy had resulted in US consumers relying almost exclusively upon B-2. Brazen's cost remained constant, at $1 per unit shipped. The retail price of B-2 has now settled at $2.50 per unit shipped, and will remain the same for the foreseeable future. Charging more would likely result in other companies pursuing this particular market.

The maker of A-1 reconsiders its decision to completely withdraw from manufacturing A-1. It begins by having its lobbyist in Washington, D.C. convince the US Customs Service to issue a new series of special regulations governing the importation of foreign cold remedies. These tests are not used on A-1. The expressed purpose of these new requirements is to ensure the quality control and consumability of imported drugs. The new customs procedures thus reduce the risk of unauthorized or unsafe pharmaceuticals entering the US. First, the new regulations require special customs inspections for imported cold remedies. Second, the new regulations impose strenuous quality testing of foreign cold remedies arriving at US ports of entry. All of these new procedures—the special inspections and quality testing—are uniformly applied to all pharmaceuticals, regardless of the source of origin. The new regulations result in the rejection of most of the Brazilian B-2 shipped to the US, but very little of other similar imported drugs.

Brazil lodges a complaint with the US Department of State, claiming discriminatory treatment that has targeted foreign-made cold remedies from Brazil. Brazen, Inc. is thus unable to reap the benefits of the Brazilian discovery of B-2 for Brazil's economy. The US consumer is paying more for A-1 than the previous cost of B-2. Brazil therefore claims as follows: US consumers no longer have the ability to choose between B-2 and A-1; this predicament has resulted in the lack of any significant competition for the maker of A-1 in US markets; and there has been a lack of access to B-2, which can only hurt the US customer.

Questions

1. Did Brazil's state-owned company violate the GATT/WTO?

2. Did the US, through its new customs regulations, violate the GATT/WTO?

3. Would this matter likely be resolved through Department of State diplomacy between Brazil and the US?

4. What steps could the parties anticipate in the resolution of this dispute under WTO procedures?

■ BIBLIOGRAPHY

§ 13.1 Economics and International Relations:

R. Folsom, M. Gordon & J. Spanogle, *International Business Transactions: A Problem-Oriented Coursebook* (2nd ed. St. Paul: West, 1991)

R. Folsom, M. Gordon & J. Spanogle, *International Business Transactions in a Nutshell* (4th ed. St. Paul: West, 1992)

T. Howell (ed.), *Conflict Among Nations: Trade Policies in the 1990s* (New York: Westview Press, 1992)

J. Jackson, W. Davey & A. Sykes, *Legal Problems of International Economic Relations: Cases, Materials and Text* (3rd ed. St. Paul: West, 1995)

P. Kinig, N. Lau & W. Meng (ed.), *International Economic Law: Basic Documents* (2nd ed. Berlin: de Gruyter, 1993)

R. Shaffer, B. Earle & F. Agusti, *International Business Law and Its Environment* (St. Paul: West, 1990)

P. Stephan, D. Wallace & J. Roin, *International Business and Economics: Law and Policy* (Charlottesville, VA: Michie, 1993)

S. Zamora & R. Brand (ed.), *Basic Documents of International Economic Law* (Chicago: CCH, 1990) (two volumes)

§ 13.2 Economic Associations of States:

R. Bernal, *Regional Trade Agreements in the Western Hemisphere*, 8 *Amer. Univ. J. Int'l L. & Policy* 683 (1993)

V. Nanda, R. Lake & R. Folsom, *European Community Law after 1992: A Practical Guide for Lawyers Outside the Common Market* (Boston: Kluwer, 1993)

§ 13.3 GATT/World Trade Organization:

Abbott, *GATT and the European Community: A Formula for Peaceful Coexistence*, 12 *Mich. J. Int'l L.* 1 (1990)

J. Jackson, *The World Trading System: Law and Policy of International Economic Relations* (6th rev. ed. Cambridge, MA: MIT Press, 1994)

Patterson & Patterson, *The Road from GATT to MTO* [now WTO], 3 *Minn. J. Global Trade* 35 (1994)

R. Weaver & D. Abellard, *The Functioning of the GATT System*, in T. Stewart (ed.), *The GATT Uruguay Round: A Negotiating History (1986–1992)* (Boston: Kluwer, 1993) (separately published booklet)

§ 13.4 New International Economic Order:

P. Ghosh (ed.), *New International Economic Order: A Third World Perspective* (Westport, CT: Greenwood Press, 1984)

Panel, *The New International Economic Order*, in *Proceedings of the 87th Annual Meeting of the American Society of International Law* 459 (1993)

Rubin, *Economic and Social Human Rights and the New International Economic Order*, 1 *Amer. J. Int'l L. & Policy* 67 (1986)

Thessaloniki Institute of Public International Law and International Relations, *North-South Dialogue: The New International Economic Order* (Thessaloniki, Greece: Inst. Public Int'l Law, 1982)

■ ENDNOTES

1. Braychevskiy, *On the Legal Content of the First Treaty of Russia with the Greeks*, 1982 *Soviet Yearbk. Int'l L.* 296 (Moscow: Nauka Pub., 1983) (English translation).

2. *See* V. Nanda, U. Draetta & R. Lake, *Breach and Adaptation of International Contracts: An Introduction to Lex Mercatoria* (Salem, NH: Butterworths, 1992).

3. E. Clemens Horst Co. v. Biddell Bros., 1911–1913 All England Law Reports 93, at 101 (Loreburn, Judge) (London: Butterworths, 1962).

4. Comm. of European Communities v. Fed. Rep. Germany, Case No. 178/84 (1987).

5. *See Ahlstom Oy v. EC Comm.* case in the text of § 9.6.

6. **Chinese case:** Richmark Corp. v. Timber Falling Consultants, 959 F.2d 1468 (1992), *cert. den'd* 113 S.Ct. 454. **French case:** Societe Nationale Industrielle Aerospatiale v. US Dist. Ct., 482 U.S. 522, 107 S.Ct. 2542, 96 L.Ed.2d 461 (1987). *See* Slomanson, *The U.S. Supreme Court Position on the Hague Evidence Convention*, 37 *Int'l & Comp. L.Q.* 391 (1988).

7. *See generally,* Janis, *Academic Workshop: Should We Continue to Distinguish between Public and Private International Law?*, in *Proceedings of the 79th Annual Meeting of the American Society of International Law* 352 (Wash., DC: Amer. Soc. Int'l Law, 1985) (panel discussion).

8. Further details on problems and conflict resolution mechanisms in different legal systems are available in P. North & J. Fawcett, *Private International Law* (12th ed. London: Butterworths, 1992).

9. *See* D. Magraw & R. Kathrein (ed.), *The Convention for the International Sale of Goods: A Handbook of Basic Materials* (2nd ed. Chicago: Amer. Bar Ass'n, 1990) [hereinafter *Handbook*].

10. Message from the President of the United States, *Handbook*, 75 (cited in note 9 above).

11. **The invasion:** an account, including interviews with Fidel Castro, is available in P. Wyden, *Bay of Pigs:*

The Untold Story (New York: Simon & Schuster, 1979). **The LOC:** McLaughlin, *How the Marketplace Can Help in International Crises, Los Angeles Daily Journal*, Dec. 24, 1992, p.6.

12. For an insightful analysis of a 1989 Zimbabwe Supreme Court decision involving caning, *see* Hannum, *Juvenile v. State*, 84 *Amer. J. Int'l L.* 768 (1990).

13. L. Henkin, *How Nations Behave: Law and Foreign Policy*, in Preface (1st ed. New York: Columbia Univ. Press, 1968); *quote:* 2d ed. (1979), p.47. *See* analysis in § 1.6.

14. A fascinating account of this phenomenon is available in R. Allen & T. Jones, *Guests of the Nation: People of Ireland versus the Multinationals* (London: Earthscan Pub., 1990).

15. **Caribbean initiative:** Caribbean Basin Recovery Act of 1983, as amended, 97 Statutes at Large 369 (1990). **Free trade area:** *see* NAFTA textual discussion in this section. **Customs union:** 1969 Agreement Establishing the South African Customs Union, 2 *Yearbk. Int'l Org.* 975 (1990–1991). **Common market:** *see* R. Keohane & S. Hoffman (ed.), *The New European Community: Decisionmaking and Institutional Change* (Boulder, CO: Westview Press, 1991). **Economic union:** Single European Act, reprinted in 25 *Int'l Legal Mat'ls* 503 (1986). The Treaty of Maastricht anticipates formation of a monetary union—the original objective of the "1992" program. *See* Treaty on the European Union and Final Act, reprinted in 31 *Int'l Legal Mat'ls* 247 (1991). A valuable analysis is available in Brand, *The New World Order of Regional Trade Blocs*, 8 *Amer. Univ. J. Int'l L. & Policy* 155 (1992).

16. G. Winham, *Lessons from History*, ch. 1, in *The Evolution of International Trade Agreements* 3, 21 (Toronto: Univ. Toronto Press, 1992) (emphasis added).

17. **ITO:** U.N. ECOSOC Res. 13, UN Doc. E/22 (1946). **GATT:** 55 UN Treaty Series 194 (1950).

18. *Final Act*, 33 *Int'l Legal Mat'ls* 1143 (1994). Explanatory introductions to the actual agreements are available in Porges, *General Agreement on Tariffs and Trade: Multilateral Trade Negotiations & Final Act*, 33 *Int'l Legal Mat'ls* 1 (1994) (Negotiations) & 33 *Int'l Legal Mat'ls* 1125 (1994) (Final Act).

19. Lowenfeld, *Remedies Along with Rights: Institutional Reform in the New GATT*, 88 *Amer. J. Int'l L.* 477, 479 (1994) [hereinafter *New GATT*].

20. Blocking examples are available in *New GATT*, 478 n.7 & n.8 (cited in note 19 above).

21. **Statement of purpose:** 19 US Code § 2102(1). **"301" procedure:** Omnibus Trade and Competitiveness Act of 1988, 19 US Code §§ 2901–3111. *See Changing the Rules: The Rise of Administrative Trade Remedies*, ch. 6, in I. Destler, *American Trade Politics* 139 (2nd ed. Wash., DC: Inst. Int'l Econ., 1992). **GATT/WTO limitation:** Agreement Establishing the World Trade Organization,

Part II, Annex 2, Final Act Embodying Results of the Uruguay Round of Multilateral Trade Negotiations, GATT Doc. MTN/FA (Dec. 15, 1993), reprinted in 33 *Int'l Legal Mat'ls* 1, 13 (1994). **Note:** this agreement refers to a "Multilateral" Trade Organization. In a 1994 follow-up meeting, the State representatives substituted the word "World" in the organization's title.

22. **Rules:** reprinted in 33 *Int'l Legal Mat'ls* 112 (1994). **Consultations:** Rule 4. **Panels:** Rule 6. **Appeals:** Rule 17. **Criticism of appellate process:** Pescatore, *The GATT Dispute Settlement Mechanism: Its Present Situation and Its Prospects*, 10 *J. Int'l Arb.* 27 (1993).

23. *New GATT*, 481 (cited in note 19 above) (emphasis supplied).

24. Schwarzenberger, *Equality and Discrimination in International Economic Law*, 25 *Yearbk. World Affairs* 163 (London: Sweet & Maxwell, 1971).

25. *See* discussion in 4 *Bureau Nat'l Affairs Int'l Trade Rep.* 786 (Wash., DC: BNA, 1987).

26. Humblot v. Directeur (Case No. 112/84), 46 Common Mkt. L. *Rep.* 338 (London: European Law Centre, 1986).

27. **Permanent Sovereignty resolution:** Gen. Ass. Reso. 1803(XVII), reprinted in 2 *Int'l Legal Mat'ls* 223 (1963). **1973 resolution:** Gen. Ass. Reso. 3171(XXVIII), reprinted in 13 *Int'l Legal Mat'ls* 238 (1974).

28. **Business practices code:** *see* Report of the Intergovernmental Working Group on the Formulation of a Code of Conduct, 16 *Int'l Legal Mat'ls* 719 (1977). **Technology transfer code:** *see* Group of 77 Manila Declaration and Program of Action for Commodities, Trade Negotiations, Transfer of Resources and Technology, and Economic Co-operation, 15 *Int'l Legal Mat'ls* 426 (1976).

29. *See* Y. Lambert, *The United Nations Industrial Development Organization: UNIDO and Problems of International Economic Cooperation* 61 (Westport, CT: Praeger, 1993).

30. UN Declaration on the Establishment of a New International Economic Order, Gen. Ass. Reso. 3201(S-VI), UN Doc. A/Res/3201(S-VI), reprinted in 13 *Int'l Legal Mat'ls* 715 (1974).

31. Gen. Ass. Reso. 3281, UN Doc. No. A/9631 (1975), reprinted in 14 *Int'l Legal Mat'ls* 251 (1975).

32. **Classic Western articulation:** 2 *Restatement of the Law of Foreign Relations of the United States* § 712 (3rd ed. Wash., DC: 1987). **NIEO summary:** Sandrino, *The NAFTA Investment Chapter and Foreign Direct Investment in Mexico: A Third World Perspective*, 27 *Vand. J. Transnat'l L.* 259 (1994). **Classic Calvo Clause analyses:** Freeman, *Recent Aspects of the Calvo Doctrine and the Challenge to International Law*, 40 *Amer. J. Int'l L.* 121 (1940) & D. Shea, *The Calvo Clause: A Problem of Inter-American and International Law and Diplomacy* (Minneapolis: Univ. of Minn. Press, 1955).

33. Barcelona Light & Traction Company (Belgium v. Spain), 1970 I.C.J. Rep. 3, 46–47, para. 89 (emphasis supplied). An edited version of the full case is set forth in § 4.3.

34. 1 World Ct. Rep. 646 (1928).

35. *See, e.g.,* Rewat, *Multilateral Approaches to Improving the Investment Climate of Developing Countries: The Cases of ICSID and MIEA*, 33 *Harv. Int'l L.J.* 102 (1992)

36. An analysis of BIT development is available in UN Centre on Transnational Corporations, *Bilateral Investment Treaties* (New York: UN, 1988).

37. Hartnell, *The New New International Economic Order: Private International Law*, in *Proceedings of the 79th Annual Meeting of the American Society of International Law* 352 (Wash., DC: Amer. Soc. Int'l Law, 1985) (panel discussion).

GLOSSARY

ABSOLUTE THEORY OF SOVEREIGN IMMUNITY under this historical theory that prevailed prior to World War II, a foreign State may not be subjected to a local suit—even when engaged in a commercial enterprise.

ACCREDITATION general term describing the process of exchanging diplomats. Foreign diplomats thereby present their *credentials* to the appropriate representative of the host government.

ACCRETION a method for obtaining legal title to land via slow or imperceptible change. Avulsion, or a sudden change caused by natural events, does not affect the prior legal boundaries of the affected territory.

ACT OF STATE DOCTRINE US practice whereby the courts will not sit in judgment of another State that has allegedly violated International Law. Under the "Hickenlooper Amendment," US courts are expected to hear such cases, unless the president intervenes to request that the case be dismissed for political reasons.

ADVISORY JURISDICTION an alternative form of jurisdiction exercised by international tribunals, typically in response to an organization's request for guidance, on some general question of International Law when there are no contentious parties before the court.

ANTICIPATORY SELF-DEFENSE rather than awaiting an "armed" attack (per the 1945 UN Charter requirement), a State takes what it characterizes as "defensive" action designed to avoid the aggressive conduct of another State.

ARBITRATION a third-party dispute resolution mechanism whereby States appoint an experienced arbitrator or panel to decide their dispute.

"AREA" under the Law of the Sea Treaty, "The Area" is the ocean floor and its subsoil beyond the limits of national jurisdiction; that is, the deep seabed area *under* the oceans that does not otherwise fall within any of the other coastal zones. Its resources are the common heritage of all mankind.

"AUTHORITY" under the Law of the Sea Treaty, an organization called the International Sea-bed Authority will control deep seabed mining in "The Area" (*see* above).

BASELINE the low-water line along the coast, as marked on charts officially recognized by the coastal State. It marks the inner boundary of the various coastal sea zones.

BAY a well-marked indentation of internal water whose penetration constitutes more than a mere curvature of the coast. The indentation must be as large as, or larger than, that of a semicircle whose diameter is a line drawn across the mouth of that indentation. A *historic* bay may be larger, thus excluding any international waters, if State practice has honored the coastal State's territorial claim over the entire body of water.

CALVO CLAUSE foreign enterprises are treated as if they were citizens of the host State, thus depriving them of the special protection afforded aliens under International Law. Foreign nationals must thereby rely exclusively on local remedies for the resolution of disputes, usually over compensation for a nationalization, thereby waiving their right to diplomatic intervention on their behalf.

CESSION the deeding of territory by one nation to another via international treaty. The grantee nation's right to title is thus derived from an agreement of the nations involved in the transfer.

CHAMBERS a typically three-judge panel of the International Court of Justice, providing the option of proceeding without a decision by all fifteen members of the Court.

CHARGE D'AFFAIRES normally the second-ranking official in an embassy's delegation who takes charge of the mission and premises in the absence of the primary diplomat.

COLLECTIVE SELF-DEFENSE a treaty provision whereby an armed attack on one member of the particular organization of States constitutes an attack on all, thus resulting in a *collective* response.

COMPARATIVE LAW the study of the internal law of various legal systems. Rather than attempting standardization, it compares the variances in legal relationships in different legal systems.

COMPULSORY JURISDICTION the ability of an international tribunal to require a defendant State to litigate a dispute before the court.

CONCILIATION a commission of persons who clarify the facts in an attempt to facilitate a resolution, typically via a report containing proposals for settlement.

CONGRESSIONAL-EXECUTIVE AGREEMENT under US treaty practice, the president requests the consent of *both* houses in a joint resolution of Congress—rather than seeking the consent of just the Senate under the federal Constitution's Treaty Clause.

CONQUEST the forcible taking of another State's territory, which is no longer an acceptable basis for acquiring title to land under contemporary International Law.

CONSTITUTIVE THEORY OF RECOGNITION other States must recognize an entity's statehood before it is entitled to *de jure* status as an international legal person.

CONSUL official agents of the sending State who are not "accredited" like diplomats. Consular officers often conduct "diplomatic" negotiations in international trade matters.

CONTIGUOUS ZONE twenty-four-nautical-mile zone of water adjacent to coastal State wherein it may exercise certain limited authority, as when deterring contraband or illegal entry.

CONTINENTAL SHELF the coastal State's seabed and subsoil of the submarine areas extending beyond its territorial sea throughout the natural prolongation of its land territory. Its range varies from 200 nautical miles from the coastal baseline to 350 nautical miles, depending on the natural extension of the coastal State's underwater land mass.

CONTRACTUAL TREATY merely restates existing norms deemed to expressly apply between the contracting nations; does not create new norms of International Law.

CONVENTIONS typically a multilateral law-making treaty, although sometimes used to describe bilateral contractual (as opposed to law-making) treaties. The former category of convention is a primary source for ascertaining the content of International Law (*see* TREATY).

COUNTERMEASURES sanctions taken in response to another State's conduct, not necessarily undertaken as justifiable self-defense. Like other forms of force, the unilateral use of countermeasures is outside the scope of the UN Charter's objective of limiting the use of force to the UN Security Council.

COUNTERVAILING DUTY an offsetting tax on an imported product suspected of being "dumped" on the market, designed to eliminate the anticompetitive conduct of dumping (*see* DUMPING).

CUSTOM/CUSTOMARY INTERNATIONAL LAW the component of International Law that is a blend of State practice and related expectations. This category of International Law is based essentially on what States do and what they consider legally binding in their mutual relations. It is thus a general practice accepted as law.

DECLARATIVE THEORY OF RECOGNITION once the elements of statehood are achieved, formal recognition by other States merely acknowledges the previously existing *de facto* status of the territory as an international person.

DIPLOMATIC ASYLUM protection from arrest or extradition, typically given to a host-State political refugee by a foreign-State diplomat.

DIPLOMATIC/CONSULAR IMMUNITY general treaty-based protection from host State laws and lawsuits. The "diplomatic bag" is thus immune from search and seizure, as are the premises of the mission and key diplomatic personnel.

DUALISM under this view of the legal relationship between national and International Law, each is a distinct legal system representing two separate legal orders—one binding the individual and the other binding the State.

DUMPING a foreign good sold at a price below fair market value, as part of a market strategy first to capture the market and then to eliminate competition in that market.

ECONOMIC AND SOCIAL COUNCIL OF THE UNITED NATIONS promotes observance of human rights and the general welfare of the individual. ECOSOC thus conducts studies and issues reports on economic, social, cultural, educational, and health matters.

EFFECTS DOCTRINE application of territorial jurisdiction, whereby a State may regulate conduct occurring abroad when that conduct has the requisite effect within the State.

EMBASSY under the Vienna Convention on Diplomatic Relations, the function or position of the ambassador; used as a common reference to the building where diplomatic functions are carried out.

ENVIRONMENTAL DEGRADATION the contemporary concern of public and private environmental organizations, seeking to protect the planet from pollution that does not respect any international boundary.

ENVIRONMENTAL IMPACT STATEMENT under US law, a requirement that federal agencies prepare a report that considers the potential impact of proposed agency action on the local and global environments.

EUROPEAN COMMUNITY LAW the European Union's body of rules and regulations governing community legal relations on a regional basis. The sovereign members have given EU organs the power to require State compliance with Community Law.

EXCLUSIVE ECONOMIC ZONE the economic zone, overlapping the Territorial Sea and Contiguous Zones, but extending coastal State authority up to 200 nautical miles from the baseline. Other States are therein subject to coastal State regulation of their economic activities including fishing and deep seabed mining.

EXECUTIVE AGREEMENT under US treaty practice, an international treaty concluded by the president *without* the advice and consent of the Senate. US practice thus distinguishes such agreements from the US Constitution's treaty provision requiring the Senate's consent to (certain) treaties.

EXHAUSTION OF LOCAL REMEDIES requirement that an individual or corporate entity first seek redress in the courts of the State that allegedly violated International Law, prior to resorting to international remedies.

EXTRADITION the arrest and transfer of an individual from one State to another, typically based on a bilateral treaty containing a schedule of extraditable crimes.

EXTRATERRITORIAL JURISDICTION (1) the State's legal ability to act or regulate conduct beyond its territorial borders; alternatively, (2) a State's illegal exercise of sovereign power beyond internationally recognized limits.

FORCE a broad term encompassing an array of unacceptable State behavior prohibited by UN Charter principles—including military, economic, and political uses of force.

GENERAL AGREEMENT ON TARIFFS AND TRADE (GATT) originally the only global arrangement covering import tariffs, and now one of several such agreements on services and other matters. It contains thousands of tariff "concessions" or negotiated tariff schedules.

GENERAL ASSEMBLY OF THE UNITED NATIONS a deliberative body, with many associated agencies, consisting of all UN member States. The General Assembly issues studies, reports, and resolutions designed to implement the UN's overall objectives.

GENERAL PRINCIPLES a norm existing in the internal law of many nations that is commonly used in all major legal systems. When such a norm has the requisite degree of usage, it may thus be a source of the substantive content of International Law.

GOOD OFFICES a variation of the "mediation" technique (*see* below), in which the third party communicates statements of the disputing parties to each other—particularly helpful when the respective States do not have diplomatic ties.

GUNBOAT DIPLOMACY a prohibited form of force whereby one State instigates a hostile or threatening act, short of war or a violation of sovereignty, that is designed to intimidate another State.

HIGH SEAS that portion of the oceans not subject to the control of any State due to the applicable regime of *res communis* (*see* below).

HUMANITARIAN INTERVENTION a claimed basis for legitimizing territorial encroachment, often misused by States to unilaterally intervene in the affairs of another State. The expressed purposes include rescuing the populace at large, certain political figures, or hostages possessing the nationality of the intruding State.

HUMAN RIGHTS those rights possessed by an individual that cannot be withheld by the State. Most are the subject of the UN-driven International Bill of Human Rights, which consists of a multitude of special-purpose treaties.

INJURY TO ALIENS a form of State responsibility incurred when governmental action discriminates against a foreign citizen on the basis of nationality. A State is thus accountable for the acts of its agents harming aliens in a way that treats them differently from its own citizens.

INNOCENT PASSAGE passage through territorial waters that does not disturb the peace, good order, or security of the coastal State (*see* STRAIT PASSAGE).

INQUIRY a commission of individuals, not associated with the State parties to the dispute, who attempt to provide an objective assessment of the facts of the case.

INTERNAL WATERS waters on the landward side of the baseline marking the inner edge of the coastal State's territorial sea.

INTERNATIONAL COURT OF JUSTICE the judicial arm of the United Nations, consisting of fifteen rotating judges who are located at its seat in the Netherlands. Its resolves contentious disputes arising under International Law, and issues advisory opinions when requested from certain UN organs and agencies.

INTERNATIONAL CRIMINAL COURT a formal judicial body, also referred to as a war crimes tribunal, established by treaty (Nuremberg) or by UN resolution (former Yugoslavia). It tries individual defendants for their violations of International Law.

INTERNATIONAL LAW the body of rules that international persons, such as States, recognize as binding in their mutual relations. Its major components are custom and treaties (*see* CUSTOM, MODERN INTERNATIONAL LAW, OPINIO JURIS, and TREATY).

INTERNATIONAL MINIMUM STANDARD a State may treat both aliens and its own citizens alike; but such equal treatment may nevertheless fall below the minimum level of treatment required by International Law.

INTERNATIONAL ORGANIZATION OF STATES a governmental organization, created by States, to accomplish treaty-based objectives. Some organizations, including those of the European Union, have the juridical power to enforce State compliance with their decisions.

INTERNATIONAL PERSONALITY the legal capacity, historically possessed by only States, to act on the international level—by bringing or defending claims between States. This legal personality, now possessed by certain organizations and individuals, yields reciprocal rights and duties arising under International Law.

INTERNATIONAL RELATIONS a broad scope of activities involving inter-State relations not limited to just legal expectations.

JURISDICTION the State's right, under International Law, to regulate conduct not exclusively of national concern.

JUS COGENS compulsory law, or a peremptory norm, from which no State may derogate. Such a norm does not depend on State sovereignty for its existence, thus constituting a derogation from unequivocal sovereignty.

JUS SANGUINIS individual nationality based on the blood or parentage rule applied by some countries.

JUS SOLI individual nationality based on the soil or place-of-birth rule applied by some countries.

LAST IN TIME RULE US practice for resolving conflicts between federal statutes and treaties, since they are equal in rank under the US Constitution.

LAW-MAKING TREATY creates new norms designed to modify existing State practice.

LAWS OF WAR essentially, the Red Cross–generated Geneva Conventions protecting private citizens and foreign soldiers during time of war.

LETTER OF CREDIT a banking device that expedites completion of the transaction between a buyer and a seller in different countries. The financial transaction guarantees payment to the seller, after the buyer applies for and receives the issuing bank's LOC.

MEDIATION unlike a fact-finding "commission of inquiry" (*see* INQUIRY above), a mediator is expected to advance his/her own proposal for resolving the dispute.

MINITRIAL the parties confront each other in an abbreviated trial-like context, with a view toward illustrating the weaknesses of the respective positions—before undertaking a comparatively costly arbitration or judicial proceeding.

MISSION (1) per treaty, the actual process of maintaining permanent diplomatic offices in another country; (2) and popularly, the physical location of the embassy—the correct term being the "premises."

MODERN INTERNATIONAL LAW originated with the 1648 Peace of Westphalia. After a long period of war, European nations entered into a period of relative peace based on a broader notion of sovereignty. The "State" would effectively replace local sovereignty exercised by indigenous groups during the rather bellicose feudal period of the early Middle Ages.

MONISM under this view of the legal relationship between national law and International Law, each is part of a unified system that binds both the State and the individual.

MOST FAVORED NATION TREATMENT a nation promises to trade with a particular partner on the most favorable tariff terms available for like goods, thus taxing that MFN nation's imports at the lowest amount of any nation.

MUNICIPAL LAW the historic description of the internal law of a nation, as opposed to the International Law applied by the community of nations.

NATION although often used synonymously with "State," a nation may technically be limited to an entity that has not yet achieved statehood.

NATIONALITY a legal bond based on individual or corporate attachment with the State conferring nationality. It is a genuine connection associated with the existence of reciprocal rights and duties between a State and its nationals.

NATIONALITY PRINCIPLE OF JURISDICTION the State regulation of conduct based on the nationality of the *defendant*, regardless of the location of the conduct.

NEW INTERNATIONAL ECONOMIC ORDER a 1974 UN General Assembly resolution establishing a revised Charter of Economic Rights and Duties of States. Its objective is to alter the traditional requirement of effective compensation for nationalizations. The internal law of the nationalizing State would thus govern, rather than the traditional customary State practice establishing a right of compensation for the taking of alien property.

NONGOVERNMENTAL ORGANIZATION (NGO) an association, not necessarily created by States, that may pursue objectives similar to those pursued by States and governmental international organizations.

NONTARIFF BARRIER Special licensing or other restrictions posing barriers to competition by exported goods—in addition to the import tax on that commodity (or service).

OCCUPATION exclusive occupation for an extended period of time as a basis for claiming valid ownership of territory. This mode of acquisition is referred to as an "original" claim to territory.

OPEN FOR SIGNATURE a step in the multilateral treaty process, whereby States or international organizations may sign the draft of a treaty after it has been developed by a conference of States or declared by a General Assembly resolution.

OPINIO JURIS the short form of *opinio juris sive necessitatis*. It is not enough that States consistently engage in a particular practice. To qualify as a binding norm of customary International Law, States must also accept that practice as legally binding them to act or refrain from acting in a certain way. When this is established, the custom is referred to as being with the *opinio juris*.

OPTIONAL CLAUSE a provision in the Statute of the International Court of Justice, whereby States may give their advance consent to generally litigate their disputes before the Court—as opposed to doing so on a treaty-by-treaty basis.

PACTA SUNT SERVANDA good faith performance of treaty obligations; the expectation that treaty parties will do nothing to frustrate the purpose of a treaty.

PASSIVE PERSONALITY PRINCIPLE OF JURISDICTION the State regulation of conduct based on the *victim's* nationality; normally requires the presence of some other jurisdictional basis for the State to exercise jurisdiction under International Law.

PERSONA NON GRATA the host State declares a diplomat unwelcome. He or she must then leave the host State to return home.

POLITICAL QUESTION DOCTRINE US judicial practice whereby a court will not resolve matters committed by the Constitution to the political branches of government.

PORT a long entryway consisting of natural twists and turns, extending to the outermost permanent harbor facility forming an integral part of the harbor system.

PORT TRANQUILITY DOCTRINE while bilateral treaties normally cede primary jurisdiction over vessels to the State of the vessel's nationality, this common treaty exception authorizes the port State to exercise authority when activity aboard such vessels disturb the port's tranquility.

PRESCRIPTION title derived from foreign occupation of a territory, for some period of time, without objection by the former sovereign occupant.

PRIVATE INTERNATIONAL LAW the body of rules governing the resolution of disputes when individuals or corporations have significant contacts with two or more States. The relevant treaties standardize the applicable law, which would otherwise yield different results—depending on which State's law is applied.

PROTECTIVE PRINCIPLE OF JURISDICTION the State regulation of conduct when the State's interest is sufficiently strong that neither the conduct nor its demonstrable effect needs to occur within its territory.

PUBLICIST international legal scholar whose writings are a subsidiary source for determining the rules of International Law.

RATIFICATION the final step in the multilateral treaty process whereby an individual State or international organization expressly accepts all or a portion of the draft treaty.

REBUS SIC STANTIBUS a change in circumstances whereby a State or international organization seeks to avoid or renegotiate its treaty obligations because the objective of the treaty is rendered difficult or impossible.

RECIPROCITY a provision in the Statute of the International Court of Justice used by a State to limit its consent to the Court's "compulsory jurisdiction" (*see* above). This form of consent to suit imposes the condition that—in future litigation—that State may invoke a *plaintiff* State's narrower terms of general consent to an ICJ suit. Reciprocity thus enables the consenting State to avoid a suit on the same basis that would be available to the plaintiff State, if the latter were a defendant in similar ICJ litigation.

RECOGNITION one State's recognition of another State, government, or belligerency. It is a political act with legal consequences, such as the recognized entity's acquisition of international legal personality with its attendant rights and obligations.

REGISTRATION sent to the UN Secretariat or other appropriate international institution for dissemination to interested parties. Registration ensures that international agreements are public documents, as opposed to secret treaties (such as those that led to World Wars I and II).

RENUNCIATION one nation's relinquishment of title to territory, without the formality of a "cession" treaty (*see* above). This mode of acquisition has often been orchestrated by victorious nations as a form of war reparation.

REPRISAL a coercive measure, typically involving the State-authorized seizure of property or persons. It retaliates for a prior wrong to the State, or its citizens, and is now an unacceptable means of seeking reparations.

RES COMMUNIS territory that is not subject to legal ownership by any State, such as the oceans and outer space.

RESERVATION a unilateral variation, submitted at the time of acceptance of the treaty. It excludes or modifies the legal effect of certain provisions as applied to the reserving State.

RESTRICTIVE THEORY OF SOVEREIGN IMMUNITY under this modern theory, a foreign State *may* be subjected to a local suit when it is engaged in a commercial enterprise. If acting as a trader, the foreign State must defend itself in local suits arising out of its commercial conduct.

SCHOOLS OF THOUGHT Natural Law, Positivism, and Eclectics. Natural Law reflects harmony with the essential nature of all peoples. The Naturalist school of thought thus espouses the belief that the rules of International Law are drawn from the moral law of nature rooted in human reason. These fundamental rules are thus discernible without regard to positive law. Positive International Law refers to custom and treaty-based norms, in some cases and eras denying the existence of Natural Law. The Eclectic School covers a broad range of International Law theories incorporating various components of either or both of the Natural and Positive Law Schools.

SECESSION one territory secedes from its legal ties with another territory, as when a State divides into two or more sovereign States. Unlike *succession*, there is no mere transfer of sovereignty. The seceding portion of the former territory exercises independent sovereignty as a new international legal person.

SECRETARIAT OF THE UNITED NATIONS   administers all UN programs, and is headed by the UN Secretary-General—the chief administrative officer of the UN.

SECURITY COUNCIL OF THE UNITED NATIONS   the rotating fifteen-State body designed to manage threats to peace. It was formed as a smaller organ than the General Assembly of all members, so that the Security Council could quickly react to threats to peace.

SELF-DETERMINATION   the right of an indigenous population to choose self-governance or some related form of autonomy. The people within the effected territory acquire the right to govern themselves—free of another State's control.

SELF-EXECUTING TREATY   creates immediately binding obligations by the terms of the treaty, as opposed to stating a declaration of principled intent constituting a standard for future achievement.

SIGNATURE   an interim step in the multilateral treaty process whereby representatives of the States or organizations generally agree on draft articles with a view toward ultimate ratification by the parties. A signature is a *provisional* acceptance, as opposed to *final* acceptance of the treaty's obligations through ratification.

SOURCE OF INTERNATIONAL LAW   where a decision maker, such as a judge or diplomat, looks for evidence of the content of International Law—customary State practice, treaties, general principles of law found in civilized legal systems, judicial opinions, the teachings (writings) of highly-qualified publicists (and possibly certain UN General Assembly resolutions/documents).

SOVEREIGN IMMUNITY   the immunity from suit enjoyed by States (and certain international organizations) in the courts of other States. This status is an attribute of sovereignty, whereby one State does not allow its judicial processes to be exercised against another State.

SOVEREIGNTY   the various attributes of statehood. A territory, coexisting with other such entities in an international system of independent States, is characterized as being a sovereign entity entitled to equality and territorial control.

STATE   historically, the only entity possessing the capacity to act on the international level. It is a group of societies within a readily defined geographical area, united to ensure their mutual welfare and security (*see* NATION). It consists of a permanent territory, a defined populace, and a government that is capable of engaging in international relations.

STATELESSNESS   the absence of nationality, whereby an individual is generally a refugee lacking the international protection afforded by a legal connection with any particular State.

STATE RESPONSIBILITY   a body of evolving norms containing the obligations incurred as a consequence of a State's international legal personality. Failure to observe a norm of State practice, or a treaty obligation, thus renders the State responsible under International Law for its wrongful act or omission.

STRAIT PASSAGE   passage through territorial waters that is not subject to the restrictive rules of the coastal State, due to the strategic nature of the particular strait. These waters are, for the purpose of strait passage, permitted free passage as if in high seas (*see* INNOCENT PASSAGE).

SUCCESSION   one or more States takes the place of a former State. The new entity thus succeeds to the sovereign attributes of the predecessor State, which no longer exists due to this transfer of sovereignty.

TARIFF   a tax on imports.

TERRA NULLIUS   territory capable of ownership, although not yet under sovereign control. The land is characterized as belonging to no one and thus is capable of ownership through some act of occupation.

TERRITORIALITY   the State regulation of conduct based on acts or effects felt within its territory. Recognized extensions authorize the exercise of a State's jurisdiction over its aircraft and sea-going vessels regardless of location.

TERRITORIAL SEA   twelve-nautical-mile strip of water adjacent to the coast, wherein the coastal State exercises total sovereignty as if on land.

TREATY   an international agreement, concluded between States or international organizations, typically in written form. Oral agreements also qualify, although their use has receded in the twentieth century.

TRUSTEESHIP COUNCIL OF THE UNITED NATIONS consists of selected UN members responsible for the administration of territories until they are capable of self-government. The bulk of its work was completed with the decolonization movement of the 1960s.

UNITED NATIONS the global association of States formed in 1945 to maintain international peace, as well as other social and economic objectives for the embetterment of all individuals.

UNIVERSALITY PRINCIPLE OF JURISDICTION the State regulation of conduct in circumstances where the actor's conduct is so heinous that it constitutes a crime against all nations. Each State may thus prosecute or extradite the individual criminal for trial, regardless of the location of the conduct.

WAR POWERS RESOLUTION US legislation, initially enacted in 1973 but never closely followed, designed to limit the president's ability to commit US combat troops to foreign conflicts for more than sixty days without congressional approval.

WORLD TRADE ORGANIZATION the 1995 global trade entity based in Geneva. It will ultimately oversee all facets of GATT (*see* above) and the related 1994 Uruguay Round agreements covering services and intellectual property.

Charter of the United Nations

WE THE PEOPLES OF THE UNITED NATIONS DETERMINED
to save succeeding generations from the scourge of war, which twice in our lifetime has brought untold sorrow to mankind, and
to reaffirm faith in fundamental human rights, in the dignity and worth of the human person, in the equal rights of men and women and of nations large and small, and
to establish conditions under which justice and respect for the obligations arising from treaties and other sources of international law can be maintained, and
to promote social progress and better standards of life in larger freedom,
AND FOR THESE ENDS
to practice tolerance and live together in peace with one another as good neighbours, and
to unite our strength to maintain international peace and security, and to ensure, by the acceptance of principles and the institution of methods, that armed force shall not be used, save in the common interest, and
to employ international machinery for the promotion of the economic and social advancement of all peoples,
HAVE RESOLVED TO COMBINE OUR EFFORTS TO ACCOMPLISH THESE AIMS
Accordingly, our respective Governments, through representatives assembled in the city of San Francisco, who have exhibited their full powers found to be in good and due form, have agreed to the present Charter of the United Nations and do hereby establish an international organization to be known as the United Nations.

■ Chapter I
PURPOSES AND PRINCIPLES

Article 1

The Purposes of the United Nations are:

1. To maintain international peace and security, and to that end: to take effective collective measures for the prevention and removal of threats to the peace, and for the suppression of acts of aggression or other breaches of the peace, and to bring about by peaceful means, and in conformity with the principles of justice and international law, adjustment or settlement of international disputes or situations which might lead to a breach of the peace;

2. To develop friendly relations among nations based on respect for the principle of equal rights and self-determination of peoples, and to take other appropriate measures to strengthen universal peace;

3. To achieve international co-operation in solving international problems of an economic, social, cultural, or humanitarian character, and in promoting and encouraging respect for human rights and

for fundamental freedoms for all without distinction as to race, sex, language, or religion; and

4. To be a centre for harmonizing the actions of nations in the attainment of these common ends.

Article 2

The Organization and its Members, in pursuit of the Purposes stated in Article 1, shall act in accordance with the following Principles.

1. The Organization is based on the principle of the sovereign equality of all its Members.

2. All Members, in order to ensure to all of them the rights and benefits resulting from membership, shall fulfil in good faith the obligations assumed by them in accordance with the present Charter.

3. All Members shall settle their international disputes by peaceful means in such a manner that international peace and security, and justice, are not endangered.

4. All Members shall refrain in their international relations from the threat or use of force against the territorial integrity or political independence of any state, or in any other manner inconsistent with the Purposes of the United Nations.

5. All Members shall give the United Nations every assistance in any action it takes in accordance with the present Charter, and shall refrain from giving assistance to any state against which the United Nations is taking preventive or enforcement action.

6. The Organization shall ensure that states which are not Members of the United Nations act in accordance with these Principles so far as may be necessary for the maintenance of international peace and security.

7. Nothing contained in the present Charter shall authorize the United Nations to intervene in matters which are essentially within the domestic jurisdiction of any state or shall require the Members to submit such matters to settlement under the present Charter; but this principle shall not prejudice the application of enforcement measures under Chapter VII.

■ Chapter II
MEMBERSHIP

Article 3

The original Members of the United Nations shall be the states which, having participated in the United Nations Conference on International Or-

ganization at San Francisco, or having previously signed the Declaration by United Nations of 1 January 1942, sign the present Charter and ratify it in accordance with Article 110.

Article 4

1. Membership in the United Nations is open to all other peaceloving states which accept the obligations contained in the present Charter and, in the judgment of the Organization, are able and willing to carry out these obligations.

2. The admission of any such state to membership in the United Nations will be effected by a decision of the General Assembly upon the recommendation of the Security Council.

Article 5

A Member of the United Nations against which preventive or enforcement action has been taken by the Security Council may be suspended from the exercise of the rights and privileges of membership by the General Assembly upon the recommendation of the Security Council. The exercise of these rights and privileges may be restored by the Security Council.

Article 6

A Member of the United Nations which has persistently violated the Principles contained in the present Charter may be expelled from the Organization by the General Assembly upon the recommendation of the Security Council.

■ Chapter III
ORGANS

Article 7

1. There are established as the principal organs of the United Nations: a General Assembly, a Security Council, an Economic and Social Council, a Trusteeship Council, an International Court of Justice, and a Secretariat.

2. Such subsidiary organs as may be found necessary may be established in accordance with the present Charter.

Article 8

The United Nations shall place no restrictions on the eligibility of men and women to participate in any capacity and under conditions of equality in its principal and subsidiary organs.

■ Chapter IV
THE GENERAL ASSEMBLY

Article 9
Composition

1. The General Assembly shall consist of all the Members of the United Nations.

2. Each member shall have not more than five representatives in the General Assembly.

Article 10
Functions And Powers

The General Assembly may discuss any questions or any matters within the scope of the present Charter or relating to the powers and functions of any organs provided for in the present Charter, and, except as provided in Article 12, may make recommendations to the Members of the United Nations or to the Security Council or to both on any such questions or matters.

Article 11

1. The General Assembly may consider the general principles of cooperation in the maintenance of international peace and security, including the principles governing disarmament and the regulation of armaments, and may make recommendations with regard to such principles to the Members or to the Security Council or to both.

2. The General Assembly may discuss any questions relating to the maintenance of international peace and security brought before it by any Member of the United Nations, or by the Security Council, or by a state which is not a Member of the United Nations in accordance with Article 35, paragraph 2, and, except as provided in Article 12, may make recommendations with regard to any such questions to the state or states concerned or to the Security Council or to both. Any such question on which action is necessary shall be referred to the Security Council by the General Assembly either before or after discussion.

3. The General Assembly may call the attention of the Security Council to situations which are likely to endanger international peace and security.

4. The powers of the General Assembly set forth in this Article shall not limit the general scope of Article 10.

Article 12

1. While the Security Council is exercising in respect of any dispute or situation the functions assigned to it in the present Charter, the General Assembly shall not make any recommedation with regard to that dispute or situation unless the Security Council so requests.

2. The Secretary-General, with the consent of the Security Council, shall notify the General Assembly at each session of any matters relative to the maintenance of international peace and security which are being dealt with by the Security Council and shall similarly notify the General Assembly, or the Members of the United Nations if the General Assembly is not in session, immediately the Security Council ceases to deal with such matters.

Article 13

1. The General Assembly shall initiate studies and make recommendations for the purpose of:

(a) promoting international co-operation in the political field and encouraging the progressive development of international law and its codification;

(b) promoting international co-operation in the economic, social, cultural, educational, and health fields, and assisting in the realization of human rights and fundamental freedoms for all without distinction as to race, sex, language, or religion.

2. The further responsibilities, functions and powers of the General Assembly with respect to matters mentioned in paragraph 1(b) above are set forth in Chapters IX and X.

Article 14

Subject to the provisions of Article 12, the General Assembly may recommend measures for the peaceful adjustment of any situation, regardless of origin, which it deems likely to impair the general welfare or friendly relations among nations, including situations resulting from a violation of the provisions of the present Charter setting forth the Purposes and Principles of the United Nations.

Article 15

1. The General Assembly shall receive and consider annual and special reports from the Security

Council; these reports shall include an account of the measures that the Security Council has decided upon or taken to maintain international peace and security.

2. The General Assembly shall receive and consider reports from the other organs of the United Nations.

Article 16

The General Assembly shall perform such functions with respect to the international trusteeship system as are assigned to it under Chapters XII and XIII, including the approval of the trusteeship agreements for areas not designated as strategic.

Article 17

1. The General Assembly shall consider and approve the budget of the Organization.

2. The expenses of the Organization shall be borne by the Members as apportioned by the General Assembly.

3. The General Assembly shall consider and approve any financial and budgetary arrangements with specialized agencies referred to in Article 57 and shall examine the administrative budgets of such specialized agencies with a view to making recommendations to the agencies concerned.

Article 18

Voting

1. Each member of the General Assembly shall have one vote.

2. Decisions of the General Assembly on important questions shall be made by a two-thirds majority of the members present and voting. These questions shall include: recommendations with respect to the maintenance of international peace and security, the election of the non-permanent members of the Security Council, the election of the members of the Economic and Social Council, the election of members of the Trusteeship Council in accordance with paragraph 1(c) of Article 86, the admission of new Members to the United Nations, the suspension of the rights and privileges of membership, the expulsion of Members, questions relating to the operation of the trusteeship system, and budgetary questions.

3. Decisions on other questions, including the determination of additional categories of questions to be decided by a two-thirds majority, shall be made by a majority of the members present and voting.

Article 19

A Member of the United Nations which is in arrears in the payment of its financial contributions to the Organization shall have no vote in the General Assembly if the amount of its arrears equals or exceeds the amount of the contributions due from it for the preceding two full years. The General Assembly may, nevertheless, permit such a Member to vote if it is satisfied that the failure to pay is due to conditions beyond the control of the Member.

Article 20

Procedure

The General Assembly shall meet in regular annual sessions and in such special sessions as occasion may require. Special sessions shall be convoked by the Secretary-General at the request of the Security Council or of a majority of the Members of the United Nations.

Article 21

The General Assembly shall adopt its own rules of procedure. It shall elect its President for each session.

Article 22

The General Assembly may establish such subsidiary organs as it deems necessary for the performance of its functions.

■ Chapter V
THE SECURITY COUNCIL

Article 23

Composition

1. The Security Council shall consist of fifteen Members of the United Nations. The Republic of China, France, the Union of Soviet Socialist Republics, the United Kingdom of Great Britain and Northern Ireland, and the United States of America shall be permanent members of the Security Council. The General Assembly shall elect ten other Members of the United Nations to be non-permanent members of the Security Council, due regard being specially paid, in the first instance to the contribution of Members of the United Nations to the maintenance of international peace and security and

to the other pruposes of the Organization, and also to equitable geographical distribution.

2. The non-permanent members of the Security Council shall be elected for a term of two years. In the first election of the non-permanent members after the increase of the membership of the Security Council from eleven to fifteen, two of the four additional members shall be chosen for a term of one year. A retiring member shall not be eligible for immediate re-election.

3. Each member of the Security Council shall have one representative.

Article 24

Functions And Powers

1. In order to ensure prompt and effective action by the United Nations, its Members confer on the Security Council primary responsibility for the maintenance of international peace and security, and agree that in carrying out its duties under this responsibility the Security Council acts on their behalf.

2. In discharging these duties the Security Council shall act in accordance with the Purposes and Principles of the United Nations. The specific powers granted to the Security Council for the discharge of these duties are laid down in Chapters VI, VII, VIII, and XII.

3. The Security Council shall submit annual and, when necessary, special reports to the General Assembly for its consideration.

Article 25

The Members of the United Nations agree to accept and carry out the decisions of the Security Council in accordance with the present Charter.

Article 26

In order to promote the establishment and maintenance of international peace and security with the least diversion for armaments of the world's human and economic resources, the Security Council shall be responsible for formulating, with the assistance of the Military Staff Committee referred to in Article 47, plans to be submitted to the Members of the United Nations for the establishment of a system for the regulation of armaments.

Article 27

Voting

1. Each member of the Security Council shall have one vote.

2. Decisions of the Security Council on procedural matters shall be made by an affirmative vote of nine members.

3. Decisions of the Security Council on all other matters shall be made by an affirmative vote of nine members including the concurring votes of the permanent members; provided that, in decisions under Chapter VI, and under paragraph 3 of Article 52, a party to a dispute shall abstain from voting.

Article 28

Procedure

1. The Security Council shall be so organized as to be able to function continuously. Each member of the Security Council shall for this purpose be represented at all times at the seat of the Organization.

2. The Security Council shall hold periodic meetings at which each of its members may, if it so desires, be represented by a member of the government or by some other specially designated representative.

3. The Security Council may hold meetings at such places other than the seat of the Organization as in its judgment will best facilitate its work.

Article 29

The Security Council may establish such subsidiary organs as it deems necessary for the performance of its functions.

Article 30

The Security Council shall adopt its own rules of procedure, including the method of selecting its President.

Article 31

Any Member of the United Nations which is not a member of the Security Council may participate, without vote, in the discussion of any question brought before the Security Council whenever the latter considers that the interests of that Member are specially affected.

Article 32

Any Member of the United Nations which is not a member of the Security Council or any state which is not a Member of the United Nations, if it is a party to a dispute under consideration by the Security Council, shall be invited to participate, without vote, in the discussion relating to the dispute. The Security Council shall lay down such conditions as it deems just for the participation of a state which is not a Member of the United Nations.

■ Chapter VI
PACIFIC SETTLEMENT OF DISPUTES

Article 33

1. The parties to any dispute, the continuance of which is likely to endanger the maintenance of international peace and security, shall, first of all, seek a solution by negotiation, enquiry, mediation, conciliation, arbitration, judicial settlement, resort to regional agencies or arrangements, or other peaceful means of their own choice.

2. The Security Council shall, when it deems necessary, call upon the parties to settle their dispute by such means.

Article 34

The Security Council may investigate any dispute, or any situation which might lead to international friction or give rise to a dispute, in order to determine whether the continuance of the dispute or situation is likely to endanger the maintenance of international peace and security.

Article 35

1. Any Member of the United Nations may bring any dispute, or any situation of the nature referred to in Article 34, to the attention of the Security Council or of the General Assembly.

2. A state which is not a Member of the United Nations may bring to the attention of the Security Council or of the General Assembly any dispute to which it is a party if it accepts in advance, for the purposes of the dispute, the obligations of pacific settlement provided in the present Charter.

3. The proceedings of the General Assembly in respect of matters brought to its attention under this Article will be subject to the provisions of Articles 11 and 12.

Article 36

1. The Security Council may, at any stage of a dispute of the nature referred to in Article 33 or of a

situation of like nature, recommend appropriate procedures or methods of adjustment.

2. The Security Council should take into consideration any procedures for the settlement of the dispute which have already been adopted by the parties.

3. In making recommendations under this Article the Security Council should also take into consideration that legal disputes should as a general rule be referred by the parties to the International Court of Justice in accordance with the provisions of the Statute of the Court.

Article 37

1. Should the parties to a dispute of the nature referred to in Article 33 fail to settle it by the means indicated in that Article, they shall refer it to the Security Council.

2. If the Security Council deems that the continuance of the dispute is in fact likely to endanger the maintenance of international peace and security, it shall decide whether to take action under Article 36 or to recommend such terms of settlement as it may consider appropriate.

Article 38

Without prejudice to the provisions of Articles 33 to 37, the Security Council may, if all the parties to any dispute so request, make recommendations to the parties with a view to a pacific settlement of the dispute.

■ Chapter VII
ACTION WITH RESPECT TO THREATS TO THE PEACE, BREACHES OF THE PEACE, AND ACTS OF AGGRESSION

Article 39

The Security Council shall determine the existence of any threat to the peace, breach of the peace, or act of aggression and shall make recommendations, or decide what measures shall be taken in accordance with Articles 41 and 42, to maintain or restore international peace and security.

Article 40

In order to prevent an aggravation of the situation, the Security Council may, before making the recommendations or deciding upon the measures provided for in Article 39, call upon the parties concerned to comply with such provisional measures as it deems necessary or desirable. Such provisional measures shall be without prejudice to the rights, claims, or position of the parties concerned. The Security Council shall duly take account of failure to comply with such provisional measures.

Article 41

The Security Council may decide what measures not involving the use of armed force are to be employed to give effect to its decisions, and it may call upon the Members of the United Nations to apply such measures. These may include complete or partial interruption of economic relations and of rail, sea, air, postal, telegraphic, radio, and other means of communication, and the severance of diplomatic relations.

Article 42

Should the Security Council consider that measures provided for in Article 41 would be inadequate or have proved to be inadequate, it may take such action by air, sea, or land forces as may be necessary to maintain or restore international peace and security. Such action may include demonstrations, blockade, and other operations by air, sea, or land forces of Members of the United Nations.

Article 43

1. All Members of the United Nations, in order to contribute to the maintenance of international peace and security, undertake to make available to the Security Council, on its call and in accordance with a special agreement or agreements, armed forces, assistance, and facilities, including rights of passage, necessary for the purpose of maintaining international peace and security.

2. Such agreement or agreements shall govern the numbers and types of forces, their degree of readiness and general location, and the nature of the facilities and assistance to be provided.

3. The agreement or agreements shall be negotiated as soon as possible on the initiative of the Security Council. They shall be concluded between the Security Council and Members or between the Security Council and groups of Members and shall be subject to ratification by the signatory states in accordance with their respective constitutional processes.

Article 44

When the Security Council has decided to use force it shall, before calling upon a Member not represented on it to provide armed forces in fulfillment of the obligations assumed under Article 43, invite that Member, if the Member so desires, to participate in the decisions of the Security Council concerning the employment of contingents of that Member's armed forces.

Article 45

In order to enable the United Nations to take urgent military measures, Members shall hold immediately available national airforce contingents for combined international enforcement action. The strength and degree of readiness of these contingents and plans for their combined action shall be determined, within the limits laid down in the special agreement or agreements referred to in Article 43, by the Security Council with the assistance of the Military Staff Committee.

Article 46

Plans for the application of armed force shall be made by the Security Council with the assistance of the Military Staff Committee.

Article 47

1. There shall be established a Military Staff Committee to advise and assist the Security Council on all questions relating to the Security Council's military requirements for the maintenance of international peace and security, the employment and command of forces placed at its disposal, the regulation of armaments, and possible disarmament.

2. The Military Staff Committee shall consist of the Chiefs of Staff of the permanent members of the Security Council or their representatives. Any Member of the United Nations not permanently represented on the Committee shall be invited by the Committee to be associated with it when the efficient discharge of the Committee's responsibilities requires the participation of that Member in its work.

3. The Military Staff Committee shall be responsible under the Security Council for the strategic direction of any armed forces placed at the disposal of the Security Council. Questions relating to the command of such forces shall be worked out subsequently.

4. The Military Staff Committee, with the authorization of the Security Council and after consultation with appropriate regional agencies, may establish regional sub-committees.

Article 48

1. The action required to carry out the decisions of the Security Council for the maintenance of international peace and security shall be taken by all the Members of the United Nations or by some of them, as the Security Council may determine.

2. Such decisions shall be carried out by the Members of the United Nations directly and through their action in the appropriate international agencies of which they are members.

Article 49

The Members of the United Nations shall join in affording mutual assistance in carrying out the measures decided upon by the Security Council.

Article 50

If preventive or enforcement measures against any state are taken by the Security Council, any other state, whether a Member of the United Nations or not, which finds itself confronted with special economic problems arising from the carrying out of those measures shall have the right to consult the Security Council with regard to a solution of those problems.

Article 51

Nothing in the present Charter shall impair the inherent right of individual or collective self-defence if an armed attack occurs against a Member of the United Nations, until the Security Council has taken measures necessary to maintain international peace and security. Measures taken by Members in the exercise of this right of self-defence shall be immediately reported to the Security Council and shall not in any way affect the authority and responsibility of the Security Council under the present Charter to take at any time such action as it deems necessary in order to maintain or restore international peace and security.

■ Chapter VIII
REGIONAL ARRANGEMENTS

Article 52

1. Nothing in the present Charter precludes the existence of regional arrangements or agencies for dealing with such matters relating to the maintenance of international peace and security as are appropriate for regional action, provided that such arrangements or agencies and their activities are consistent with the Purposes and Principles of the United Nations.

2. The Members of the United Nations entering into such arrangements or constituting such agencies shall make every effort to achieve pacific settlement of local disputes through such regional arrangements or by such regional agencies before referring them to the Security Council.

3. The Security Council shall encourage the development of pacific settlement of local disputes through such regional arrangements or by such regional agencies either on the initiative of the states oncerned or by reference from the Security Council.

4. This Article in no way impairs the application of Articles 34 and 35.

Article 53

1. The Security Council shall, where appropriate, utilize such regional arrangements or agencies for enforcement action under its authority. But no enforcement action shall be taken under regional arrangements or by regional agencies without the authorization of the Security Council, with the exception of measures against any enemy state, as defined in paragraph 2 of this Article, provided for pursuant to Article 107 or in regional arrangements directed against renewal of aggressive policy on the part of any such state, until such time as the Organization may, on request of the Governments concerned, be charged with the responsibility for preventing further aggression by such a state.

2. The term enemy state as used in paragraph 1 of this Article applies to any state which during the Second World War has been an enemy of any signatory of the present Charter.

Article 54

The Security Council shall at all times be kept fully informed of activities undertaken or in contemplation under regional arrangements or by regional agencies for the maintenance of international peace and security.

■ Chapter IX
INTERNATIONAL ECONOMIC AND SOCIAL CO-OPERATION

Article 55

With a view to the creation of conditions of stability and well-being which are necessary for peaceful and friendly relations among nations based on respect for the principle of equal rights and self-determination of peoples, the United Nations shall promote:

(a) higher standards of living, full employment, and conditions of economic and social progress and development;

(b) solutions of international economic, social, health, and related problems; and international cultural and educational co-operation; and

(c) universal respect for, and observance of, human rights and fundamental freedoms for all without distinction as to race, sex, language, or religion.

Article 56

All Members pledge themselves to take joint and separate action in co-operation with the Organization for the achievement of the purposes set forth in Article 55.

Article 57

1. The various specialized agencies, established by intergovernmental agreement and having wide international responsibilities, as defined in their basic instruments, in economic, social, cultural, educational, health, and related fields, shall be brought into relationship with the United Nations in accordance with the provisions of Article 63.

2. Such agencies thus brought into relationship with the United Nations are hereinafter referred to as specialized agencies.

Article 58

The Organization shall make recommendations for the coordination of the policies and activities of the specialized agencies.

Article 59

The Organization shall, where appropriate, initiate negotiations among the states concerned for the creation of any new specialized agencies required for the accomplishment of the purposes set forth in Article 55.

Article 60

Responsibility for the discharge of the functions of the Organization set forth in this Chapter shall be vested in the General Assembly and, under the authority of the General Assembly, in the Economic and Social Council, which shall have for this purpose the powers set forth in Chapter X.

■ Chapter X
THE ECONOMIC AND SOCIAL COUNCIL

Article 61
Composition

1. The Economic and Social Council shall consist of twenty-seven Members of the United Nations elected by the General Assembly.

2. Subject to the provisions of paragraph 3, nine members of the Economic and Social Council shall be elected each year for a term of three years. A retiring member shall be eligible for immediate re-election.

3. At the first election after the increase in the membership of the Economic and Social Council from eighteen to twenty-seven members, in addition to the members elected in place of the six members whose term of office expires at the end of that year, nine additional members shall be elected. Of these nine additional members, the term of office of three members so elected shall expire at the end of one year, and of three other members at the end of two years, in accordance with arrangements made by the General Assembly.

4. Each member of the Economic and Social Council shall have one representative.

Article 62
Functions And Powers

1. The Economic and Social Council may make or initiate studies and reports with respect to international economic, social, cultural, educational, health, and related matters and may make

recommendations with respect to any such matters to the General Assembly, to the Members of the United Nations, and to the specialized agencies concerned.

2. It may make recommendations for the purpose of promoting respect for, and observance of, human rights and fundamental freedoms for all.

3. It may prepare draft conventions for submission to the General Assembly, with respect to matters falling within its competence.

4. It may call, in accordance with the rules prescribed by the United Nations, international conferences on matters falling within its competence.

Article 63

1. The Economic and Social Council may enter into agreements with any of the agencies referred to in Article 57, defining the terms on which the agency concerned shall be brought into relationship with the United Nations. Such agreements shall be subject to approval by the General Assembly.

2. It may co-ordinate the activities of the specialized agencies through consultation with and recommendations to such agencies and through recommendations to the General Assembly and to the Members of the United Nations.

Article 64

1. The Economic and Social Council may take appropriate steps to obtain regular reports from the specialized agencies. It may make arrangements with the Members of the United Nations and with the specialized agencies to obtain reports on the steps taken to give effect to its own recommendations and to recommendations on matters falling within its competence made by the General Assembly.

2. It may communicate its observations on these reports to the General Assembly.

Article 65

The Economic and Social Council may furnish information to the Security Council and shall assist the Security Council upon its request.

Article 66

1. The Economic and Social Council shall perform such functions as fall within its competence in connexion with the carrying out of the recommendations of the General Assembly.

2. It may, with the approval of the General Assembly, perform services at the request of Members of the United Nations and at the request of specialized agencies.

3. It shall perform such other functions as are specified elsewhere in the present Charter or as may be assigned to it by the General Assembly.

Article 67

Voting

1. Each member of the Economic and Social Council shall have one vote.

2. Decisions of the Economic and Social Council shall be made by a majority of the members present and voting.

Article 68

Procedure

The Economic and Social Council shall set up commissions in economic and social fields and for the promotion of human rights, and such other commissions as may be required for the performance of its functions.

Article 69

The Economic and Social Council shall invite any Member of the United Nations to participate, without vote, in its deliberations on any matter of particular concern to the Member.

Article 70

The Economic and Social Council may make arrangements for representatives of the specialized agencies to participate, without vote, in its deliberations and in those of the commissions established by it, and for its representatives to participate in the deliberations of the specialized agencies.

Article 71

The Economic and Social Council may make suitable arrangements for consultation with nongovernmental organizations which are concerned with matters within its competence. Such arrangements may be made with international organizations and, where appropriate, with national organizations after consultation with the Member of the United Nations concerned.

Article 72

1. The Economic and Social Council shall adopt its own rules of procedure, including the method of selecting its President.

2. The Economic and Social Council shall meet as required in accordance with its rules, which shall include provision for the convening of meetings on the request of a majority of its members.

Chapter XI
DECLARATION REGARDING NON-SELF-GOVERNING TERRITORIES

Article 73

Members of the United Nations which have or assume responsibilities for the administration of territories whose peoples have not yet attained a full measure of self-government recognize the principle that the interests of the inhabitants of these territories are paramount, and accept as a sacred trust the obligation to promote to the utmost, within the system of international peace and security established by the present Charter, the well-being of the inhabitants of these territories, and, to this end:

(a) to ensure, with due respect for the culture of the peoples concerned, their political, economic, social, and educational advancement, their just treatment, and their protection against abuses;

(b) to develop self-government, to take due account of the political aspirations of the peoples, and to assist them in the progressive development of their free political institutions, according to the particular circumstances of each territory and its peoples and their varying stages of advancement;

(c) to further international peace and security;

(d) to promote constructive measures of development, to encourage research, and to co-operate with one another and, when and where appropriate, with specialized international bodies with a view to the practical achievement of the social, economic, and scientific purposes set forth in this Article; and

(e) to transmit regularly to the Secretary-General for information purposes, subject to such limitation as security and constitutional considerations may require, statistical and other information of a technical nature relating to economic, social, and educational conditions in the territories for which they are respectively responsible other than those territories to which Chapters XII and XIII apply.

Article 74

Members of the United Nations also agree that their policy in respect of the territories to which this Chapter applies, no less than in respect of their metropolitan areas, must be based on the general principle of good neighbourliness, due account being taken of the interests and well-being of the rest of the world, in social, economic, and commercial matters.

Chapter XII
INTERNATIONAL TRUSTEESHIP SYSTEM

Article 75

The United Nations shall establish under its authority an international trusteeship system for the administration and supervision of such territories as may be placed thereunder by subsequent individual agreements. These territories are hereinafter referred to as trust territories.

Article 76

The basic objectives of the trusteeship system, in accordance with the Purposes of the United Nations laid down in Article 1 of the present Charter, shall be:

(a) to further international peace and security;

(b) to promote the political, economic, social, and educational advancement of the inhabitants of the trust territories, and their progressive development towards self-government or independence as may be appropriate to the particular circumstances of each territory and its peoples and the freely expressed wishes of the peoples concerned, and as may be provided by the terms of each trusteeship agreement;

(c) to encourage respect for human rights and for fundamental freedoms for all without distinction as to race, sex, language, or religion, and to encourage recognition of the interdependence of the peoples of the world; and

(d) to ensure equal treatment in social, economic, and commercial matters for all Members of the United Nations and their nationals, and also equal treatment for the latter in the administration of justice, without prejudice to the attainment of the foregoing objectives and subject to the provisions of Article 80.

Article 77

1. The trusteeship system shall apply to such territories in the following categories as may be placed thereunder by means of trusteeship agreements:

(a) territories now held under mandate;

(b) territories which may be detached from enemy states as a result of the Second World War; and

(c) territories voluntarily placed under the system by states responsible for their administration.

2. It will be a matter for subsequent agreement as to which territories in the foregoing categories will be brought under the trusteeship system and upon what terms.

Article 78

The trusteeship system shall not apply to territories which have become Members of the United Nations, relationship among which shall be based on respect for the principle of sovereign equality.

Article 79

The terms of trusteeship for each territory to be placed under the trusteeship system, including any alteration or amendment, shall be agreed upon by the states directly concerned, including the mandatory power in the case of territories held under mandate by a Member of the United Nations, and shall be approved as provided for in Articles 83 and 85.

Article 80

1. Except as may be agreed upon in individual trusteeship agreements, made under Articles 77, 79, and 81, placing each territory under the trusteeship system, and until such agreements have been concluded, nothing in this Chapter shall be construed in or of itself to alter in any manner the rights whatsoever of any states or any peoples or the terms of existing international instruments to which Members of the United Nations may respectively be parties.

2. Paragraph 1 of this Article shall not be interpreted as giving grounds for delay or postponement of the negotiations and conclusions of agreements for placing mandated and other territories under the trusteeship system as provided for in Article 77.

Article 81

The trusteeship agreement shall in each case include the terms under which the trust territory will be administered and designate the authority which will exercise the administration of the trust territory.

Such authority hereinafter called the administering authority, may be one or more states or the Organization itself.

Article 82

There may be designated, in any trusteeship agreement, a strategic area or areas which may include part or all of the trust territory to which the agreement applies, without prejudice to any special agreement or agreements made under Article 43.

Article 83

1. All functions of the United Nations relating to strategic areas, including the approval of the terms of the trusteeship agreements and of their alteration or amendment, shall be exercised by the Security Council.

2. The basic objectives set forth in Article 76 shall be applicable to the people of each strategic area.

3. The Security Council shall, subject to the provisions of the trusteeship agreements and without prejudice to security considerations, avail itself of the assistance of the Trusteeship Council to perform those functions of the United Nations under the trusteeship system relating to political, economic, social, and educational matters in the strategic areas.

Article 84

It shall be the duty of the administering authority to ensure that the trust territory shall play its part in the maintenance of international peace and security. To this end the administering authority may make use of volunteer forces, facilities, and assistance from the trust territory in carrying out the obligations towards the Security Council undertaken in this regard by the administering authority, as well as for local defence and the maintenance of law and order within the trust territory.

Article 85

1. The functions of the United Nations with regard to trusteeship agreements for all areas not designated as strategic, including the approval of the terms of the trusteeship agreements and of their alteration or amendment, shall be exercised by the General Assembly.

2. The Trusteeship Council, operating under the authority of the General Assembly, shall assist the General Assembly in carrying out these functions.

Chapter XIII
THE TRUSTEESHIP COUNCIL

Article 86

Composition

1. The Trusteeship Council shall consist of the following Members of the United Nations:

(a) those Members administering trust territories;

(b) such of those Members mentioned by name in Article 23 as are not administering trust territories; and

(c) as many other Members elected for three-year terms by the General Assembly as may be necessary to ensure that the total number of members of the Trusteeship Council is equally divided between those Members of the United Nations which administer trust territories and those which do not.

2. Each member of the Trusteeship Council shall designate one specially qualified person to represent it therein.

Article 87

Functions And Powers

The General Assembly and, under its authority, the Trusteeship Council, in carrying out their functions, may:

(a) consider reports submitted by the administering authority;

(b) accept petitions and examine them in consultation with the administering authority;

(c) provide for periodic visits to the respective trust territories at times agreed upon with the administering authority; and

(d) take these and other actions in conformity with the terms of the trusteeship agreements.

Article 88

The Trusteeship Council shall formulate a questionnaire on the political, economic, social, and educational advancement of the inhabitants of each trust territory, and the administering authority for each trust territory within the competence of the General Assembly shall make an annual report to the General Assembly upon the basis of such questionnaire.

Article 89

Voting

1. Each member of the Trusteeship Council shall have one vote.

2. Decisions of the Trusteeship Council shall be made by a majority of the members present and voting.

Article 90

Procedure

1. The Trusteeship Council shall adopt its own rules of procedure, including the method of selecting its President.

2. The Trusteeship Council shall meet as required in accordance with its rules, which shall include provision for the convening of meetings on the request of a majority of its members.

Article 91

The Trusteeship Council shall, when appropriate, avail itself of the assistance of the Economic and Social Council and of the specialized agencies in regard to matters with which they are respectively concerned.

Chapter XIV
THE INTERNATIONAL COURT OF JUSTICE

Article 92

The International Court of Justice shall be the principal judicial organ of the United Nations. It shall function in accordance with the annexed Statute, which is based upon the Statute of the Permanent Court of International Justice and forms an integral part of the present Charter.

Article 93

1. All Members of the United Nations are *ipsa facto* parties to the Statute of the International Court of Justice.

2. A state which is not a Member of the United Nations may become a party to the Statute of the International Court of Justice on conditions to be determined in each case by the General Assembly upon the recommendation of the Security Council.

Article 94

1. Each Member of the United Nations undertakes to comply with the decision of the International Court of Justice in any case to which it is a party.

2. If any party to a case fails to perform the obligations incumbent upon it under a judgment rendered by the Court, the other party may have recourse to the Security Council, which may, if it deems necessary, make recommendations or decide upon measures to be taken to give effect to the judgment.

Article 95

Nothing in the present Charter shall prevent Members of the United Nations from entrusting the solution of their differences to other tribunals by virtue of agreements already in existence or which may be concluded in the future.

Article 96

1. The General Assembly or the Security Council may request the International Court of Justice to give an advisory opinion on any legal question.

2. Other organs of the United Nations and specialized agencies, which may at any time be so authorized by the General Assembly, may also request advisory opinions of the Court on legal questions arising within the scope of their activities.

■ Chapter XV
THE SECRETARIAT

Article 97

The Secretariat shall comprise a Secretary-General and such staff as the Organization may require. The Secretary-General shall be appointed by the General Assembly upon the recommendation of the Security Council. He shall be the chief administrative officer of the Organization.

Article 98

The Secretary-General shall act in that capacity in all meetings of the General Assembly, of the Security Council, of the Economic and Social Council, and of the Trusteeship Council, and shall perform such other functions as are entrusted to him by these organs. The Secretary-General shall make an annual report to the General Assembly on the work of the Organization.

Article 99

The Secretary-General may bring to the attention of the Security Council any matter which in his opinion may threaten the maintenance of international peace and security.

Article 100

1. In the performance of their duties the Secretary-General and the staff shall not seek or receive instructions from any government or from any other authority external to the Organization. They shall refrain from any action which might reflect on their position as international officials responsible only to the Organization.

2. Each Member of the United Nations undertakes to respect the exclusively international character of the responsibilities of the Secretary-General and the staff and not to seek to influence them in the discharge of their responsiblities.

Article 101

1. The staff shall be appointed by the Secretary-General under regulations established by the General Assembly.

2. Appropriate staffs shall be permanently assigned to the Economic and Social Council, the Trusteeship Council, and, as required, to other organs of the United Nations. These staffs shall form a part of the Secretariat.

3. The paramount consideration in the employment of the staff and in the determination of the conditions of service shall be the necessity of securing the highest standards of efficiency, competence, and integrity. Due regard shall be paid to the importance of recruiting the staff on as wide a geographical basis as possible.

■ Chapter XVI
MISCELLANEOUS PROVISIONS

Article 102

1. Every treaty and every international agreement entered into by any Member of the United Nations after the present Charter comes into force shall as soon as possible be registered with the Secretariat and published by it.

2. No party to any such treaty or international agreement which has not been registered in accordance with the provisions of paragraph 1 of this Article may invoke that treaty or agreement before any organ of the United Nations.

Article 103

In the event of a conflict between the obligations of the Members of the United Nations under the present Charter and their obligations under any other international agreement, their obligations under the present Charter shall prevail.

Article 104

The Organization shall enjoy in the territory of each of its Members such legal capacity as may be necessary for the exercise of its functions and the fulfilment of its purposes.

Article 105

1. The Organization shall enjoy in the territory of each of its Members such privileges and immunities as are necessary for the fulfilment of its purposes.

2. Representatives of the Members of the United Nations and officials of the Organization shall similarly enjoy such privileges and immunities as are necessary for the independent exercise of their functions in connection with the Organization.

3. The General Assembly may make recommendations with a view to determining the details of the application of paragraphs 1 and 2 of this Article or may propose conventions to the Members of the United Nations for this purpose.

■ Chapter XVII
TRANSITIONAL SECURITY ARRANGEMENTS

Article 106

Pending the coming into force of such special agreements referred to in Article 43 as in the opinion of the Security Council enable it to begin the exercise of its responsibilities under Article 42, the parties to the Four-Nation Declaration, signed at Moscow, 30 October 1943, and France, shall, in accordance with the provisions of paragraph 5 of that Declaration, consult with one another and as occasion requires with other members of the United Nations with a view to such joint action on behalf of the Organization as may be necessary for the purpose of maintaining international peace and security.

Article 107

Nothing in the present Charter shall invalidate or preclude action, in relation to any state which during the Second World War has been an enemy of any signatory to the present Charter, taken or authorized as a result of that war by the Governments having responsibility for such action.

■ Chapter XVIII
AMENDMENTS

Article 108

Amendments to the present Charter shall come into force for all Members of the United Nations when they have been adopted by a vote of two thirds of the members of the General Assembly and ratified in accordance with their respective constitutional processes by two thirds of the Members of the United Nations, including all the permanent members of the Security Council.

Article 109

1. A General Conference of the Members of the United Nations for the purpose of reviewing the present Charter may be held at a date and place to be fixed by a two-thirds vote of the members of the General Assembly and by a vote of any nine members of the Security Council. Each Member of the United Nations shall have one vote in the conference.

2. Any alteration of the present Charter recommended by a two-thirds vote of the conference shall take effect when ratified in accordance with their respective constitutional processes by two thirds of the Members of the United Nations including all the permanent members of the Security Council.

3. If such a conference has not been held before the tenth annual session of the General Assembly following the coming into force of the present Charter, the proposal to call such a conference shall be placed on the agenda of that session of the General Assembly, and the conference shall be held if so decided by a majority vote of the members of the General Assembly and by a vote of any seven members of the Security Council.

■ Chapter XIX
RATIFICATION AND SIGNATURE

Article 110

1. The present Charter shall be ratified by the signatory states in accordance with their respective constitutional processes.

2. The ratifications shall be deposited with the Government of the United States of America, which shall notify all the signatory states of each deposit as well as the Secretary-General of the Organization when he has been appointed.

3. The present Charter shall come into force upon the deposit of ratifications by the Republic of China, France, the Union of Soviet Socialist Republics, the United Kingdom of Great Britain and Northern Ireland, and the United States of America, and by a majority of the other signatory states. A protocol of the ratifications deposited shall thereupon be drawn up by the Government of the United States of America which shall communicate copies thereof to all the signatory states.

4. The states signatory to the present Charter which ratify it after it has come into force will become original Members of the United Nations on the date of the deposit of their respective ratifications.

Article 111

The present Charter, of which the Chinese, French, Russian, English, and Spanish texts are equally authentic, shall remain deposited in the archives of the Government of the United States of America. Duly certified copies thereof shall be transmitted by that Government to the Governments of the other signatory states.

Research Guide

■ CATEGORIES COVERED

This Appendix is a guide to the following tools for ascertaining the content of International Law:

- Research guides
- Treatises
- Periodicals/indexes
- On-line computerized sources
- CD-ROM
- Treaties
- Judicial decisions
- Encyclopedias/yearbooks
- Coursebooks
- Bibliographies
- Document delivery services

Introduction

A multilateral treaty, ratified by most States, is the most precise evidence of International Law. It is a *primary* source, as opposed to a *secondary* source such as a judicial opinion or scholarly work. One normally achieves more immediate results, however, by initially examining the secondary sources. This is especially true for a student preparing a research project, as opposed to an experienced lawyer or diplomat seeking direct evidence of a particular agreement. After listing some research guides immediately below, this Appendix lists the standard publications for quickly gathering the essentials of International Law. Entries will be listed, normally in descending order, either by usefulness or date. This form of ranking is obviously influenced by one person's subjective assessments.

Research Guides

- *Guide to International Legal Research* (2nd ed. London/Austin, TX: Butterworth, 1993)
- E. Beyerly, *Public International Law: A Guide to Information Sources (London/New York: Mansell, 1991)*
- C. Germain, *Germain's Transnational Law Research: A Guide for Attorneys* (Ardsley-on-Hudson, NY: Transnational Juris, 1991)
- A. Sprudzs, *International Legal Research Perspectives* (Buffalo, NY: Hein, 1988)
- S. Rosenne, *Practice and Methods of International Law* (London/New York: Oceana, 1984)
- *International Law Symposium*, 76 *Law Library Journal* 421–570 (1983) (covering most phases of international legal research).

Treatises

Scholarly publications are a useful starting point for one who is unfamiliar with International Law or the general topic being researched. The treatise author has undertaken painstaking efforts to collate, digest, and present a large body of complex material so that the reader may readily grasp the essentials. Exhibit B.1 presents the major scholarly publications from various countries, written or translated into English. The foreign entries are usually available from US publishers or distributors.

EXHIBIT B.1 General Treatises on International Law

Country of Origin	Author/Title/Publisher/Date
Australia	D. Grieg, *International Law* (3rd ed. London: Butterworths, 1995); I.A. Shearer, *Starke's International Law* (11th ed. London: Butterworths, 1994)
Canada	H. Kindred (ed.), *International Law: Chiefly as Interpreted and Applied in Canada* (5th ed. Edmond Montgomery, 1993) and documentary supplement
China	J. Cohen & H. Chiu, *People's China's and International Law: A Documentary Study* (Princeton, NJ: Princeton Univ. Press, 1974) two volumes
European Community	J. Steiner, *Textbook on EEC Law* (3rd ed. London: Blackstone Press, 1992)
Finland	V. Heiskanen, *International Legal Topics* (Helsinki: Finnish Lawyers' Publishing, 1992) (emphasizing municipal law interface, sanctions, and force)
Hungary	H. Bokor-Szego, *Questions of International Law: Hungarian Perspectives* (Dordrecht, Neth./Boston: Martinus Nijhoff, 1986)
India	R. Hingorini, *Modern International Law* (2nd ed. New Delhi/Dobbs Ferry, NY: IBH Pub. & Oceana, 1984)
Italy	A. Cassese, *International Law in a Divided World* (Oxford, Eng./New York: Clarendon Press, 1986)
Latin America	C. Fenwick, *International Law* (4th ed. New York: Appleton-Century-Crofts, 1965) (Latin American perspectives provided by former Director of Department of Legal Affairs of Pan American Union)
Netherlands	H. Panhuys, et al. (ed.), *International Law in the Netherlands* (Alphen aan den Rijn, Neth./Dobbs Ferry, NY: Sijthoff & Oceana, 1978) three volumes
Nigeria	U. Umozurike, *Introduction to International Law* (Ibadan, Nig.: Spectrum Law Pub., 1993); C. Okeke, *The Theory and Practice of International Law in Nigeria* (Enugu, Nig.: Fourth Dimension, 1986)
Philippines	E. Paras, *International Law and World Organizations* (5th rev. ed. Manila: Rex Book Store, 1985)
Russia	G. Tunkin, *International Law: A Textbook* (Moscow: Progess, 1982) (1986 translation); G. Tunkin, *Theory of International Law* (Cambridge, MA: Harv. Univ. Press, 1974); V. Grabar, *The History of International Law in Russia, 1647–1917: A Bio-Bibliographical Study* (Oxford, Eng./New York: Clarendon Press, 1990)
Swaziland	P. Bischoff, *Swaziland's International Relations and Foreign Policy: A Study of a Small African State in International Relations* (Bern/New York: Peter Lang, 1990) (emphasizes international relations)

EXHIBIT B.1 *(continued)*

Country of Origin	Author/Title/Publisher/Date
Sweden	I. Detter, *International Law* (Stockholm: Stockholm Inst. Res. Int'l Law, 1991) Third World F. Snyder & S. Sathirathai (ed.),
Third World	Attitudes Toward International Law: An Introduction (Dordrecht, Neth./Boston: Martinus Nijhoff, 1987)
United Kingdom	R. Jennings & A. Watts (ed.), *Oppenheim's Interna- tional Law* (9th ed. Essex, Eng.: Longman, 1992) two volumes; I. Brownlie, *Principles of Public International Law* (4th ed. Oxford, Eng./New York: Clarendon Press, 1990); M. Shaw, *International Law* (3rd ed. Cambridge, Eng.: Grotius, 1991); M. Akehurst, *A Modern Introduction to International Law* (6th ed. London/Boston: Allen & Unwin, 1987); R. Wallace, *International Law* (2nd ed. London: Street & Maxwell, 1992); M. Dixon, *Textbook on International Law* (2nd ed. London: Blackstone Press, 1990)
United States	M. Janis, *An Introduction to International Law* (2nd ed. Boston: Little, Brown & Co., 1993); G. von Glahn, *Law Among Nations: An Introduction to International Law* (6th ed. New York: Macmillan, 1992); O. Schachter, *International Law in Theory and Practice* (Dordrecht, Neth./Boston: Martinus Nijhoff, 1991); W. Levi, *Contemporary International Law: A Concise Introduction* (2nd ed. Boulder, CO: Westview Press, 1991); L. Chen, *An Introduction to Contemporary International Law: A Policy-Oriented Perspective* (New Haven, CT: Yale Univ. Press, 1989); R. Falk, et al. (ed.), *International Law: A Contemporary Perspective* (Boulder, CO: Westview, 1985); G. Maris, *International Law: An Introduction* (Lanham, MD: Univ. Press of Amer., 1984)
Yugoslavia	B. Jankovic, *Public International Law* (Dobbs Ferry, NY: Transnat'l, 1984) (University of Belgrade)
Special Compilations*	M. Bedjaoui (ed.), *International Law: Achievements and Prospects* (Paris/Boston: UNESCO & Martinus Nijhoff, 1991); R. Macdonald (ed.), *Essays in Honour of Wang Tieya* (Dordrecht, Neth./Boston: Martinus Nijhoff, 1994)

*Each listed compilation is an approximately 1,000 volume containing numerous chapters and contributors from all regions of the world. The editors have arranged these books so as to cover the majority of contemporary topical issues in International Law.

One form of "treatise" requires special mention. Each year, students travel to famous learning centers where experts from all over the world give summer courses in International Law. These offerings are later published in bound volumes. The most prominent is offered at The Hague, in the Netherlands—established in 1923 by the Hague Academy of International Law. The resulting publication, published in both French and English, is the annual *Recueil des Cours*. Probably the next most well known is the annual summer program of lectures at the Institute of International Public Law and International Relations of Thessaloniki (Greece)—which began to publish its lectures in 1973. The resulting publication is the *Thesaurus Acroasium*. Unlike the above *Recueil*, the Greek counterpart delivers and publishes its lectures in English.

Periodicals/Indexes

Legal The Exhibit B.1 treatises are more comprehensive than the law-related articles found in periodicals. Those books provide a general approach to the *entire* field of International Law. Periodical literature, on the other hand, is more narrow. The author tends to analyze one finite issue or area of the law. When seeking more detailed information about a particular issue, the researcher should investigate this form of literature.

One should, of course, consult the various indexes to periodical literature. The *Index to Legal Periodicals* is available in all law schools—at or near the library reference desk. Most law schools also carry the *Index to Foreign Legal Periodicals.* Canadian materials may be accessed through the *Index to Canadian Legal Periodical Literature* (as of 1961).

Each of these works provides monthly lists of the many articles written both in the US and in other English-speaking countries.

Undergraduate The *Reader's Guide to Periodical Literature* is the standard reference work for most research—not limited to legal topics. It lists articles from journals incorporating international topics, such as the *American Political Science Review.*

Original Documents Several "periodicals" carry recent treaty documents, diplomatic exchanges, and full-text or excerpted foreign judicial opinions and international tribunals. Pertinent examples include the following sources carried by most midsized libraries:

- *International Legal Materials,* published by the American Society of International Law in Washington, DC (also available in on-line format in Westlaw and Lexis);

- *Inter-American Legal Materials,* published by the American Bar Association's Section of International Law and Practice in Chicago, IL, from 1984 to 1992 (further publication temporarily delayed).

Exhibit B.2 lists a representative sampling of foreign periodicals containing scholarly articles on comparatively finite themes in International Law.

EXHIBIT B.2 Foreign Periodical Literature on International Law

Country of Origin	Scope of Coverage
Canada	*Canada-United States Law Journal,* published by the Case Western Reserve Journal of International Law (Cleveland, OH). Coverage includes topics in international trade and maritime matters.
China	*China Law Reporter,* published by the American Bar Association's Section of International Law and Practice. Its primary contribution to the literature is timely articles and documents on legal problems and institutions in the PRC.
European Community	*Common Market Law Review,* published by Martinus Nijhoff (Netherlands), containing articles and court decisions by the Court of Justice of the European Communities.
India	*Eastern Journal of International Law,* published by the Eastern Centre of International Studies (Madras), concentrating on human rights.
Japan	*Law in Japan,* published by the Japanese American Society for Legal Studies (Tokyo), emphasizing Japanese-American relations.

EXHIBIT B.2 *(continued)*

Country of Origin	Scope of Coverage
Netherlands	*Encyclopedia of Public International Law,* published by Max Plank Institute of Heidelberg, Germany/Elsevier Science (Amsterdam/New York), consisting of five volumes and over 1,300 articles covering every facet of International Law; *Netherlands International Law Review,* published by Martinus Nijhoff (Netherlands), containing legal articles on various issues arising under International Law.
Socialist Nations	*Review of Socialist Law,* published by the University of Leiden (Netherlands), emphasizing the legal systems of socialist countries and how they relate to those of other countries.
South Africa	*Comparative and International Law Journal of South Africa,* published by University of South Africa (Pretoria), analyzing international issues affecting South Africa.
South Korea	*Korea and World Affairs,* published by the Research Center for Peace and Unification of Korea (Seoul).
United Kingdom	*Anglo-American Law Review,* published by Barry Rose Law Periodicals, (Chichester, Eng.), covering a variety of issues arising in the context of US and English international practice; *International Business Lawyer,* published by the International Bar Association of London, containing articles and summaries of English caselaw on international commercial matters; *International and Comparative Law Quarterly,* published in Oxford, analyzing all facets of International Law affecting the English Commonwealth and the European Community; *Oxford Journal of Legal Studies,* by Oxford University, addressing the interface of law with other disciplines.
United States	Approximately eight hundred law and law-related journals are published in the US. Many of these contain articles on International Law. About eighty of these journals are specialized journals, whose names include the terms "International," "Transnational," or "Comparative." The on-line and hardcopy versions of *Index to Legal Periodicals* provide monthly indexing to articles appearing in these journals. One may also consult the *Reader's Guide to Periodical Literature* in graduate and undergraduate libraries.

On-Line Computerized Sources

Introduction An unprecedented explosion has enormously expanded the research capacity of on-line resources on International Law during the late 1980s and 1990s. This portion of Appendix B highlights some of the more useful resources available in most libraries—or through personal computer links. Exhibit B.3 lists the prominent features of this popular and greatly beneficial medium for accessing research materials.

EXHIBIT B.3 On-Line Computerized Research in International Law

Access Tool or Database Name	Relevant Databases (DBs) on International Law
Westlaw	Legal DB containing US cases and statutes plus useful IL DBs (**IDEN**=description of all Westlaw DBs): **CELEX**=on-line DB of the European Community, containing documents of the Commission, member States, Court of Justice, and parliamentary decisions; **CELEX-TRTY**=EC treaties and other legal acts; **CELEX-NP** =national implementing provisions; **CHINALAW**=laws and regulations of the PRC; **IEL**=documents/ treaties of international economic law such as GATT; **ILM**=Int'l Legal Mat'ls, the source for the latest treaties, and other documentary developments; **INT-ICJ**=Int'l Court of Justice cases; **INT-IRAN**=decisions of US/Iran Claims Trib.; **INT-TP**=international law reviews, texts, bar journals; **NAFTA**=treaty text; **RPD**=translated summaries of 100 Russian newspapers, many on international developments; **TP-ALL**=law review periodicals, texts, bar journals; **USTREATIES**=full text of treaties where US a party (from 1979).
Dialog	Nonlaw DB accessible via Westlaw: **AP-NEWS**=Associated Press News; **BIP**=Books in Print; **BBIP**=British Books in Print; **EOA**=Encyclopedia of (10,000 worldwide) Associations; **KOMPASS-E**=business information on 210,000 European companies; **MAGINDEX**=index of magazine articles; **PAIS**=Public Affairs Information Service, a bibliographic index to public policy literature of business, economics, government, international relations, political science, law; **PAPERS** =combined US newspapers; **NEWSWIRES**=newswire news; **PD&W**=addresses for 21,000 publishers, 15,000 association, 7,000 software producers, 1,500 wholesalers; **REUTER NEWS**=worldwide news coverage; **ULRICHS**=index of all international periodicals; **UPI-OLD**=United Press Int'l News (1983 to present). Foreign language newswires are available in DBs such as **AFP-ENG** and **AFP-FRENCH**.
Lexis	Legal DB containing US cases and statutes, based on license from West Publishing Co., and useful IL DBs (**GUIDE**=description of all Lexis DBs): **BNAITD**=daily report of events in international trade; **ECLAW**=documents of the EC; a number of European Community DBs are available; **LAWREV**=law review articles; **UNCHRN**=UN Chronicle of various UN developments.
Nexis	Nonlaw DB accessible via Lexis: **MARHUB-IBIO**=international professional biography listing; **MARHUB-ILIST**=list international colleges, universities, and law schools (**MARHUB** contains many lists, including lawyers' addresses).
Internet	**The Legal List:** on-line book containing an organizational blueprint of all legal databases on Internet, including UN Security Council or General Assembly materials (see Appendix B text); UNDP Gopher=full text of most UN treaties; DIANA (World Wide Web site)=full text of most human rights treaties.
Index to Legal Periodicals	Monthly listing of legal periodicals published in the US—and major schools in Australia, Canada, Ireland, Great Britain, and New Zealand (1981–present)

EXHIBIT B.3 *(continued)*

Access Tool or Database Name	Relevant Databases (DBs) on International Law
"Information Highway Tools" (also Internet gateways)	Prodigy, Compuserve, etc.: encyclopedic coverage of countries, international organizations, historical/contemporary events, and other general inquiries.

BOLD CAPS=name of on-line database for accessing above-listed information. The listed DBs are only a representative sampling of information available in these on-line systems.

Italicized entries=names of books or services available in both hardcopy and on-line format.

Legal Databases Westlaw and Lexis terminals resembling a personal computer exist in most, if not all, law schools. The specialized console permits access to system contents by entering a word or phrase on the screen. Most law schools employ student research assistants who provide training to other students wishing to use these relatively user-friendly systems. If there is no available training assistant, the computer terminals have user guides (Westlaw—"Westmate Tutorial") for quickly learning enough detail to access the particular system and its respective databases.

Most law schools have both Westlaw and Lexis, although some may have only one of these two legal database systems. Each system publishes a pamphlet listing of all available databases and a general softbound guide for new users. There are also specialized *international* primers entitled *Guide to International Law Research for Law Review Students* (Westlaw) and *Sources of International Law on Lexis/Nexis: Law School Menu* (Lexis). Representative on-line international resources on Westlaw and Lexis are identified in Exhibit B.3.

Internet An indescribable volume of information about all disciplines, occupations, and professions now appears on the Internet. There is every indication that its 30 million-plus users will continue to generate the demand for virtually every type of resource that is thinkable. For example, one may obtain many full-text UN resolutions or decisions of the General Assembly and Security Council (*see* Exhibit B.3).

The Internet is available at many universities to both graduate and undergraduate users, usually at on-campus locations. Anyone having a personal computer and a modem can also access Internet.

There are books available in most bookstores on Internet usage. Some of the more popular guidebooks are:

- H. Hahn & R. Stout, *The Internet Complete Reference* (Berkeley, CA: Osborne McGraw Hill, 1993) (818 pages, $29.95)

- E. Krol, *The Whole Internet User's Guide & Catalog* (Cambridge, MA: O'Reilly & Associates, 1994) ($24.95)

- J. Blackman, *The Legal Researcher's Internet Directory* (New York: Legal Research, 1993/1994) (137 pages, $49.95)

The above publications provide the essential details regarding Internet access and navigation through its somewhat infinite resources. Some contain pocket-part diskettes explaining how to use the Internet. Probably the best resource for conveniently navigating the many *legal* resources available on the Internet is Erik Heels, *The Legal List: Law-Related Resources on the Internet and Elsewhere.* This is an electronic book that is on-line on the Internet. Users may download to disk, but must pay $29.95 if they print any part of this electronic book. Printed paperback copies are also available from the author—Erik Heels, 39 Main St., Eliot, ME 03903 USA. Updated on-line versions are available at periodic intervals.

ILP A number of law schools have an on-line version of the *Index to Legal Periodicals* (available in the Westlaw or Lexis on-line database systems). All will have hardcopy versions in the vicinity of the library's law review section or reference desk.

CD-ROM

The compact disk–read only memory technology has appeared in academic, business, and home-office settings throughout the world. This technology is available in many institutions and through commercial computer vendors, as a means of integrating the related objectives of keeping current and preserving library shelf space. For example, a large number of volumes was once required to maintain an on-campus legal library of all cases published—even in just one state. With the availability of CD-ROM technology, one disk can store the same amount of information as 100 hardbound volumes.

The *Public Affairs Information Service (PAIS)* is available in CD-ROM format. A visit to the reference librarian or card catalogue should determine if the various CD-ROM offerings, mentioned in this part of Appendix B, are available at the particular institution. Most medium (250,000 volumes) to large-sized libraries will have *PAIS* in either CD-ROM or print format.

Infotrac is one of the most complete, readily accessible, and user-friendly CD-ROM products (provided by Information Access Corporation of Foster City, CA). It contains materials on all academic disciplines. A special *Infotrac* console, resembling a personal computer, permits access to its contents by entering a word or phrase. In a law school library, the related *LegalTrac* database on the *Infotrac* console thereby retrieves citation information on all of the legal periodicals and newspapers containing the user-entered word in their title. (Neither is a full-text service.) Coverage in the *LegalTrac* portion of *Infotrac* began in 1980, and is updated monthly.

The *Index to Legal Periodicals* is available in CD-ROM format in the larger law school library collections (and from SilverPlatter Information of Norwood, MA). The *Index to* Foreign *Legal Periodicals* is also available in this format, usually at the same location within the library.

Oceana Publications in New York City publishes *United States Treaties & International Agreements on CD-ROM.* This format thus provides 50,000+ pages of US treaty documents, dating from 1783 to present.

There are many other law-related CD-ROM products available. Probably the best resource for ascertaining *what* is published in this particular format is the softbound book by Arlene Eis, *Directory of Law-Related CD-ROMS 1994* (Teaneck, NJ: Infosources Publishing, 1994). CD-ROMs are published by various companies on a variety of topics, including Eastern Europe, European Community, government documents, international trade, Latin America, legal bibliography, legal periodicals, maps, treaties, United Nations, and various countries (154 pages, $49 plus $5 shipping). Infosources also provides the convenient *Law-Related CD-ROM Update*—a periodic update of its CD-ROM *Directory.*

Treaties

Treaties series have been published by the League of Nations and the United Nations. The League of Nations published treaties from 1920 to 1946 in its *League of Nations Treaty Series: Treaties and International Engagements Registered with the Secretariat of the League* (*LNTS*)—found in some midrange library collections and in all larger collections. The UN publishes treaties in the *United Nations Treaty Series: Treaties and International Agreements Registered or Filed and Recorded with the Secretariat of the United Nations* (*UNTS*)—approximately 1,500 volumes. This latter series contains the full text of treaties since 1946. All treaties are supposed to be registered (*see* § 8.2). *UNTS* is indexed, although the indexing does not appear until approximately ten years after publication date.

Each treaty in *UNTS* is assigned a sequenced number when it is submitted for publication. Unfortunately, the treaties do not appear in chronological order of adoption. Treaty No. 19941, for example, is a 1966 treaty. Treaty No. 19942 is a 1978 treaty. The absence of convenient indexing makes *UNTS* hard to use for up-to-the-minute research projects. The researcher must invest the necessary time to review the table of contents in each recent volume of UNTS to obtain the list of treaties in that particular volume.

Several sources help to reduce the drudgery of treaty research. One is Peter Rohn's *World Treaty Index* (*WTI*), a five-volume work available in many libraries (and from ABC-Clio of Santa Barbara, CA). Unlike other sources, *WTI* includes treaties in force when the US is not a party. Igor Kavass's *A Guide to the United States Treaties in Force 1991–* is a source for obtaining recent US treaty information (published by William Hein Company of Buffalo, NY).

Another source for obtaining the full text of recently concluded treaties is *International Legal Materials* (*ILM*), published by the American Society of International Law of Washington, DC, since 1961.

The society has published three indexes, entitled *International Legal Materials: Cumulative Index* for the years 1962 to 1969, 1970 to 1979, and 1980 to 1989. There is also an *annual* index in the rear of the final bimonthly issue of each year. The contents of most major treaties are now listed on the outside front cover as "Documents Highlights." Since the *UNTS* is typically published *years* after a treaty is ratified, *ILM* is a more up-to-date source for locating treaties and other forms of international agreements, such as US presidential executive agreements. It also contains the major diplomatic exchanges between various nations.

Regional treaty series are useful for finding the content of International Law, particularly for those countries that do not comply with the UN Charter requirement to provide a copy of all treaties to the UN. While *ILM* contains the text of certain Latin American treaties, a special series is separately published for that region. *Inter-American Legal Materials* has been published by the American Bar Association's Section of International Law and Practice from 1984 to 1992 (publication temporarily suspended). In the Western Hemisphere, the Organization of American States (OAS) published the *Pan American Union Treaty Series* from 1934 to 1956. The OAS now publishes the *Organization of American States Treaty Series*. In Western Europe, the Council of Europe publishes the treaties of approximately twenty European nations in both the *European Treaty Series* (official reporter) and the *European Conventions and Agreements* (Strasbourg, France). The treaties contained in these series cover the years from 1949 to the present. The other regional treaty series is published in Africa in the French language. *Accords et Conventions de l'Union Africaine et Malgache*, first published in 1967, is comparatively limited in scope. It contains diplomatic exchanges and materials on technical assistance between developing African nations. More recent African materials are available in *Basic Documents of African Regional Organizations*, a multivolume work published by Oceana in Dobbs Ferry, NY. Oceana also publishes *Basic Documents of Asian Regional Organizations* and *Instruments of Economic Integration in Latin America and the Caribbean*. These series by Oceana contain subject indexes.

Other formats for treaty research are discussed elsewhere in this appendix (Westlaw, Lexis, Internet, CD-ROM).

Several countries publish *national* treaty series. US treaties, for example, are contained in three standard print format sources (as well as the DSTATE database on Lexis). One is *Treaties in Force: A List of Treaties and Other International Agreements of the United States in Force as of January 1, 19__*, published by the US Department of State. Each annual paperback volume is arranged in two parts. Part 1 contains *bilateral* agreements by country, with subject headings for each topic. Part 2 lists *multilateral* agreements to which the US is a party. A second source for US treaties is *United States Treaties and Other International Agreements* (*UST*), published by the US State Department since 1950. This is the official publication for each agreement to which the US is a party. The William S. Hein Company publishes the other print format service called *A Guide to the United States Treaties in Force*. This publication has a convenient "Subject Reference Index" for each topic appearing in the *Guide's* listings.

The State Department has another publication that carries the same treaties as those published in the *UST*. US treaties are published in numerical order of their publication—in an *unofficial* pamphlet form—in the *Treaties and Other International Acts Series* (*TIAS*). The numerical order of the treaties contained in this series does not correlate with their chronological dates, however. There is no relationship between the sequence of treaties in pamphlet form and the official bound volumes of *UST*.

An efficient method for locating a US treaty on a particular subject is to use the comprehensive indexes, called the *United States and Other International Agreements Cumulative Index, 1776–1949* and the *UST Cumulative Indexing Service, 1976–present*. These publications index materials contained in *UST* and *TIAS*. This indexing system consists of several volumes. The most useful is the final volume containing the "Subject Index."

Judicial Decisions

This source of International Law is drawn from the decisions of international courts, arbitral tribunals, and national courts. Judicial opinions are typically collected and published in a series called a "reporter." The most comprehensive collection of judicial opinions and arbitrations is published in the worldwide English-language publication called the *International Law Reports (ILR)*, by Grotius Publications in Cambridge, Eng. (1919–present). In addition to bound volumes, *ILR* also publishes its companion *Consolidated Indexes and Tables*. The title for early volumes in this series was the *Annual Digest of Reports of Public International Law Cases*.

The decisions of the Permanent Court of International Justice are published in the *Hague Permanent Court of International Justice Publications— Series A: Judgments* (The Hague, Netherlands) and in *Hudson's World Court Reports* published by Oceana Publications (New York). The decisions of the International Court of Justice appear in the *International Court of Justice Reports of Judgments, Advisory Opinions and Orders* (also in Westlaw on-line database system).

Arbitral decisions are reported in United Nations Reports of International Arbitrational Awards, published by the UN. It contains arbitrations decided under auspices of the UN. The decisions of a number of arbitral tribunals involving the US are reported in *International Arbitrations—History and Digest of the International Arbitrations to Which the United States Has Been a Party*. This collection contains many important arbitrations *prior to* the twentieth century.

Decisions of *national* courts on issues involving International Law are published in the various local reporters. In the US, such cases can quickly be found by using the West Publishing Company's "Key Numbers" in the West National Reporter system of case reporting. To find a case containing a particular issue, the researcher should first consult West's *General Digest* and West's *Decennial Digest*. Cases containing international issues during the period 1981 through 1986, for example, are located by turning to Volume 27 of the *Ninth Decennial Digest*, Part 2, at page 328. The subheadings within the topic "International Law" are listed with related key numbers. This system assigns a number to a specific issue that has appeared in all cases in the US from 1981 through 1986. The listed number for "Sources and Scope" of International Law is "2." The researcher can then turn to the case digests beginning on page 330 of Volume 27 under West Key Number 2 for all cases decided in US courts expressly referring to "sources" of International Law. This research methodology is explained in the front of Volume 27 at page III.

Alternative formats for researching judicial opinions are discussed in other portions of this Appendix—Westlaw, Lexis, and the Internet.

Specialized case reporters contain *only* international law cases. The US Government Printing Office produces the *United States Court of International Trade Reports* on issues involving international commerce. Oceana (New York) publishes a series called *American International Law Cases*, containing cases decided in various US courts since 1971. Oceana previously published the nine-volume set of *British International Law Cases*, containing international law issues decided in English courts from 1964 through 1970.

Encyclopedias/Yearbooks

Encyclopedias and yearbooks contain a variety of materials on International Law, including articles, documents, and recent developments. The prominent encyclopedias appear in several languages, including French and German. The major English-language encyclopedia is the *Encyclopedia of Public International Law*, compiled by the Max Planck Institute for Comparative Public Law and International Law in Germany (published by North Holland Publishers of Amsterdam). Since 1981, this institute has published the work of scholars on every aspect of International Law.

Yearbooks are often prepared and published by the major legal society within a particular country. That society's members therein comment on International Law, as interpreted by their local decision-makers. A listing of major yearbooks is available in Volume 10 of the *Fordham International Law Journal*, Summer 1987 Supplement, at page 965–67.

The annual *Yearbook of the United Nations* summarizes decisions made by the various organs of the UN, especially those characterized by the UN as being inadequately covered by the world press. The researcher should consult both the contents page at the front and the rear indexes at the back of each *UN Yearbook* for specific subject areas.

Coursebooks

Although "casebooks" or "coursebooks" for academic courses are not direct sources of International Law, they can be useful research tools. Each contains a collection of materials, information on customary State and organizational practice, key cases, and excerpts from other scholarly writings. Casebooks are also useful for the researcher who wants to consider the author's organizational approach to the field of International Law or some issue within this discipline. Unlike legal treatises or judicial decisions, academic coursebooks do not assume that the reader is a lawyer or an experienced researcher.

There are also specialized international texts covering particular topics—rather than the entire field of International Law. They contain cases, correspondence, and documents designed for use in the more advanced courses. Exhibit B.4 contains the major books in this category that are published in the English language.

EXHIBIT B.4   Major Contemporary International Coursebooks

Country* or Theme	Author/Title/Publisher/Date
Canada	L. Green, *International Law Through the Cases* (4th ed. Toronto: Carswell, 1978)
China	J. Cohen & H. Chiu, *People's China and International Law: A Documentary Study* (Princeton, NJ: Princeton Univ. Press, 1974) [two volumes]
European Community	G. Berman, et al., *Cases and Materials on European Community Law* (St. Paul, MN: West, 1992); S. Weatherhill, *Cases & Materials on EEC Law* (London: Blackstone Press, 1992)
Foreign Relations	T. Franck & M. Glennon, *Foreign Relations and National Security Law* (2nd ed. St. Paul: West, 1993)
Human Rights	R. Lillich, *International Human Rights: Problems of Law, Policy, and Practice* (2nd ed. Boston: Little, Brown & Co., 1991)
Immigration	T. Alexander & D. Martin, *Immigration: Process and Policy* (St. Paul: West, 1985)
International Business	R. Folsom, et. al, *International Business Transactions: A Problem-Oriented Coursebook* (2nd ed. St. Paul: West, 1991); D. Vagts, *Transnational Business Problems* (Mineola, NY: Foundation Press, 1986)
International Economic Relations	J. Jackson, et. al, *Legal Problems of International Economic Relations: Cases, Materials and Text* (3rd ed. St. Paul, West, 1995)
International Environment	L. Guruswamy, *International Environmental Law and World Order: A Problem-Oriented Coursebook* (St. Paul: West, 1994)
International Organizations	F. Kirgis, *International Organizations in Their Legal Setting* (2nd ed. St. Paul: West, 1993)
International Trade	J. Barton & B. Fisher, *International Trade and Investment: Regulating International Business* (Boston: Little, Brown & Co., 1986)
Russia	G. Tunkin, *International Law: A Textbook* (Moscow: Progress Publishers, 1982) [1986 English trans.]

EXHIBIT B.4 *(continued)*

Country* or Theme	Author/Title/Publisher/Date
United Kingdom	D. Harris, *Cases and Materials on International Law* (4th ed. London: Street & Maxwell, 1991); M. Dixon & R. McCorquodale, *Cases & Materials on International Law* (London: Blackstone Press, 1991)
United States	H. Steiner, et al., *Transnational Legal Problems: Materials and Text* (4th ed. Mineola, NY: Foundation Press, 1994); L. Henkin, et al., *International Law: Cases and Materials* (3rd ed. St. Paul: West, 1993); D. Partan, *The International Law Process: Cases and Materials*, 1992); G. von Glahn, *Law Among Nations* (6th ed. New York: Macmillan, 1992); B. Carter & P. Trimble, *International Law* (Boston: Little, Brown & Co., 1991); B. Weston, et al., *International Law and World Order: A Problem-Oriented Coursebook* (2nd ed. St. Paul: West, 1990); J. Sweeney, C. Oliver & N. Leech, *The International Legal System: Cases and Materials* (3rd ed. Westbury, NY: Foundation Press, 1988)

*Country signifies nationality of author/publisher.

Bibliographies

A number of periodicals occasionally publish bibliographies on specialized subjects. These are not readily accessible, without going on-line (Westlaw or Lexis) or searching individual print-format shelved periodicals. One source may improve access to international materials via a bibliographic format—Juergun Goedan's *International Legal Bibliographies: A Worldwide Guide and Critique* (Ardsley-on-Hudson, NY: Transnational, 1992) (John Pickron's English translation). This is the successor edition to the author's 1975 German-language publication *Die internationaln allgemein juristischen Fachbibliographien.*

The traditional comparative law bibliography is the former Charles Szladitz publication, *A Bibliography on Foreign and Comparative Law* (1972–1983). This work is supposed to be continued by Columbia University's Parker School of Foreign and Comparative Law.

Document Delivery Services

The Law School Library of Columbia University houses one of the largest academic law libraries in the US and the world. In 1994, it commenced the operation of its "Document Delivery Service." Researchers anywhere can call (800) 332-4529 for a print, facsimile, or telephonic version of cases, treaties, academic writings, etc.—subject to certain copyright requirements. There is a $25 minimum fee for this service, plus expenses, which may include the cost of expressing or mailing larger documents to the caller.

A similar service is provided for researchers desiring translations of foreign laws and related materials. GEOLEX [call (800) 446-0906] is also an on-demand publisher, specializing in the foreign regulation of business. There is a service charge for providing the translated materials to the user.

APPENDIX C

Career Opportunities in International Law

Handbooks

- E. Kocher, *International Jobs: Where They Are [and] How to Get Them* (4th ed. Reading, MA: Addison-Wesley Publishing, 1993) [394 pages]. This sourcebook contains information about US federal agencies, the UN, various international organizations, banks, lawfirms, and educational offerings. Part I is International Career Planning and Job Strategy, including a chapter on "Making Your Academic Studies Work for You." Part II is The International Job Market, with detailed information on the who and where of international job hunting. The names and addresses of the relevant staff members and job descriptions/qualifications are provided for the listed jobs.

- M. Territo (ed.), *Career Choices for the 90's: For Students of Political Science and Government* (New York: Walker and Company, 1990) [157]. This publication provides suggestions on pursuing careers in various fields: broadcasting, government, human services, law (p.58), publishing, politics, public relations, and sales. Brief introductory essays cover the particular field's Job Outlook, Geographic Job Index, Major Employers, and How to Break into the Field.

- J. Green, D. Hodge & R. Kemp (ed.), *Guide to Education and Career Development in International Law* (Wash., DC: Int'l Law Students Ass'n/Amer. Soc. Int'l Law, 1991) [246]. The Introduction covers four areas for career development: obtaining information, education, experience, and colleague/client development. Five essays follow, covering legal practice opportunities overseas. The next section surveys the major international law firms in ten countries. The several directories include summer and semester programs abroad and information about advanced degree programs.

- J. Muldoon (ed.), *Internships and Careers in International Affairs* (4th ed. New York: UN Ass'n, 1994) [74]. This pamphlet contains detailed information on internships and organizations available to students in the US and abroad. It provides suggestions on how to apply for positions with governmental and nongovernmental organizations (UN, US government agencies, etc.). Part I lists available internships. Part II provides information on placement services. The information is generally oriented toward the pursuit of *non*legal careers.

- M. Janis (ed.), *Careers in International Law* (Wash., DC: Amer. Bar Ass'n, 1993) [229]. This booklet consists of sixteen chapters by different essay writers. They review varied career opportunities in International Law. Part I covers the private sector. Chapter topics include practice in and outside of the US (Miami, Canada, Great Britain, etc.); corporate practice; and admiralty practice. Part II covers careers in the public sector (Department of State, environmental opportunities; alternative careers). The appendixes include address lists for international and nongovernmental organizations in Washington, DC.

- J. Williams (ed.), *Career Preparation and Opportunities in International Law* (2nd ed. Wash., DC: Amer. Bar Ass'n/Int'l Law Inst., 1984) [143]. The above *Careers in International*

Law publication (by Janis) is actually a new version of this earlier work. The Williams version contains more detailed information about the subject covered. Part I consists of several essays on international studies and career preparation/opportunities. Part II contains five entries on practice with the federal government. Part III contains seven essays on private and corporate practice. Part IV covers nonprofit practice.

Volunteer Work

■ M. Shapiro, et al., *Directory of Pro Bono Opportunities in International Law* (Wash., DC: Dist. Columbia Bar Ass'n, 1993) [71]. This pamphlet contains information about the fifty organizations and institutions in the Washington, D.C. area in need of volunteer legal services. This is the first directory of its kind. While designed to promote "legal" assistance to these international agencies, nothing in the program inhibits law students or undergraduates from volunteering their assistance. The booklet is arranged by subject area: arms control, business and trade, environment, human rights, immigration, rule of law, and miscellaneous.

■ United Nations, *General Information on United Nations Employment Opportunities and Internship Programme* (New York: UN, 1991) (periodic revisions) [4]. This is the UN handout that is available at the UN Plaza's employment office. It summarizes the many classes of employment opportunities and offers information regarding the appropriate UN contact personnel. It also describes the UN's Headquarters Internship Programme for graduate students. Given the state of the UN budget, interns must obtain funding from their host countries or institutions.

Scholarships/Internships

■ G. Mattox, *Fellowships in International Affairs: A Guide to Opportunities in the United States and Abroad* (Boulder, CO: Lynne Reinner, 1994) [193]. This book identifies available grants, which is one facet of career development in international affairs. The publication identifies minimum qualifications, and lists conditions of various offerings for both the traditional and lesser-known grant opportunities. The entries are derived from various directories, computerized databases, academic journals, newsletters,

and direct contacts with verified grant-making organizations.

■ D. Cassidy, *The International Scholarship Directory: The Complete Guide to Financial Aid for Study Abroad* (3rd ed. Old Tappan, NJ: Prentice-Hall, 1993) [333]. This is a funding sourcebook for students wishing to study abroad, containing the relevant detail for most countries of the world. It contains information about study stipends and internships, for candidates from high school to postdoctoral studies. Over 80 percent of the grant applications to the 23,000 foundations in the US are either misdirected or filled out improperly. This directory thus provides the details for expeditious access to private sector funding.

■ *Fellowships for Professionals and Scholars: Information and Applications* (Wash., DC: US Inst. for Peace, 1992) [18]. The US Institute for peace is a nonpartisan federal institution created by Congress. This pamphlet contains information for practitioners, scholars, and students to focus their learning on a variety of issues concerning conflict and peace. The job descriptions are for annual fellowships in Washington, D.C.

■ R. Whitman, *Internships in Congress* (3rd ed. West Hartford, CT: Graduate Group, 1994) [150]

■ R. Whitman, *Internships in Federal Government* (7th ed. West Hartford, CT: Graduate Group, 1995) [200]

■ R. Whitman, *Internships in State Government* (6th ed. West Hartford, CT: Graduate Group, 1995) [200]

Research and Training

■ UN Economic and Social Council, *World Directory of Peace Research and Training Institutions in International Law* (7th ed. Paris: UNESCO, 1991) [354]. This directory lists institutions conducting peace research and training in sixty countries. Section I indexes the names or acronyms of the responding institutions. Section II is the bulk of this directory. It lists details about each of the alphabetically listed institutions (previously listed in Section I). Section III is a subject index, alphabetically listing the countries where the institutions associated with that particular subject are found.

- UN Economic and Social Council, *World Directory of Teaching and Research Institutions in International Law* (2nd rev. ed. Paris: UNESCO, 1990) [387]. This directory contains information on diploma courses, entrance formalities, financial assistance, structure of teaching programs, and continuous educational training facilities. Section I indexes the names and acronyms of the institutions. Section II contains descriptive entries of degrees and courses, international and regional institutions, and national institutions with international components. Section III lists associations and societies of international law. Section IV provides a personal name index of faculty. Section V is an index of international law subject matter emphasized in the listed institutions.

Study Programs

- *American Institute for Foreign Study Catalogue—Academic Year 1995–1996* (Greenwich, CT: AIFS, 1995) [various pagings] (published annually)

- R. Whitman, *Global Directory of Schools of Law* (2nd ed. West Hartford, CT: Graduate Group, 1994/1995) [132]

- R. Whitman, *Directory of Law School Summer Programs in the United States and Abroad* (7th ed. West Hartford, CT: Graduate Group, 1995) [73]

- R Whitman, *4th Annual Directory of Graduate Law Programs in the United States* (West Hartford, CT: Graduate Group, 1994/1995) [115]

- R. Hermann, L. Sutherland & J. Cox (ed.), *Directory of Graduate Law Degree Programs* (3rd ed. Wash., DC: Federal Reports, Inc., 1992) [99] (US only)

- *Commonwealth Directory of Post-Graduate Legal Programmes* (London: Commonwealth Legal Education Ass'n, 1987) [various pagings]

- C. Green (ed.), *Directory of Graduate Programs for Foreign Lawyers* (Wash., DC: Ass'n Amer. Law Schools, 1992) [52]

Essays

- *Ambassadorial Backgrounds: Who Are They?*, ch. 2, in D. Mak & C. Kennedy, *American Ambassadors in a Troubled World* 7 (Westport, CT: Greenwood Press, 1992)

- *International Law as a Career*, Postscript to A. D'Amato, *International Law: Process and Prospect* 233 (Dobbs Ferry, NY: Transnat'l Pub., 1987)

- D. Kennedy, *International Legal Education*, 26 Harv. Int'l L.J. 361 (1985)

Political Map of the World

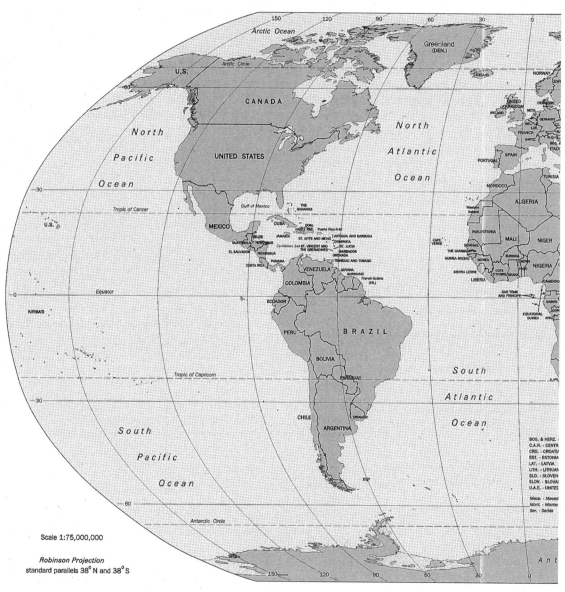

Source: The World Fact Book by the CIA

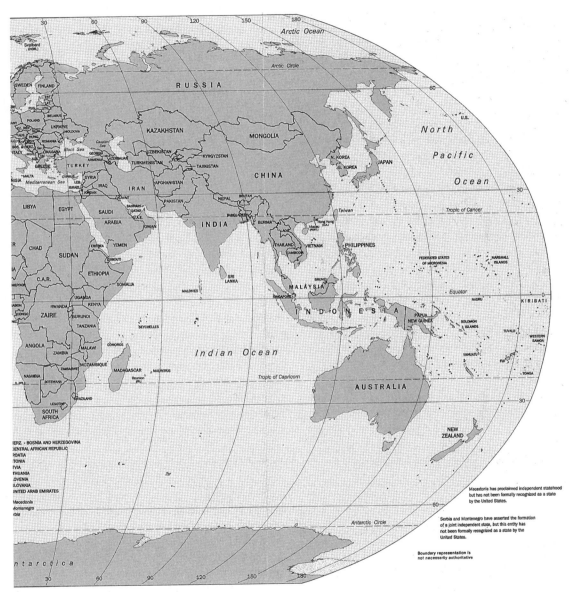

Arctic Ocean

Arctic Circle

SWEDEN FINLAND
Svalbard
(NOR.)

RUSSIA

60

EST
LAT
LITH
RUS
BELARUS
POLAND
UKRAINE
MOLDOVA
ROMANIA
HUNG
BULGARIA
ITALY
GREECE
MALTA
TURKEY
Mediterranean Sea
TUNISIA

KAZAKHSTAN

Caspian
Sea
Black Sea
GEORGIA
ARMENIA AZERBAIJAN
UZBEKISTAN
TURKMENISTAN
KYRGYZSTAN
TAJIKISTAN

MONGOLIA

N. KOREA
S. KOREA

JAPAN

North

Pacific

U.S.

Ocean

CYPRUS
LEB
ISRAEL
SYRIA
JORDAN
IRAQ
KUWAIT
IRAN
AFGHANISTAN
PAKISTAN

CHINA

30

LIBYA
EGYPT
SAUDI
ARABIA
BAHRAIN
QATAR
U.A.E.
OMAN
YEMEN

NEPAL
BHUTAN

BANGLADESH
BURMA

Taiwan

Tropic of Cancer

Hong Kong
(PORT)

INDIA

CHAD
SUDAN
ERITREA
DJIBOUTI
ETHIOPIA
SOMALIA

SRI
LANKA

MALDIVES

ACEH

THAILAND
CAMBODIA
VIETNAM

Macau
(PORT)

PHILIPPINES

C.A.R.
CAMEROON

MALAYSIA

FEDERATED STATES
OF MICRONESIA

MARSHALL
ISLANDS

BRUNEI

GABON
CONGO
RWANDA
BURUNDI
KENYA
UGANDA
ZAIRE
TANZANIA

SEYCHELLES

SINGAPORE

Equator

I N D O N E S I A

NAURU

KIRIBATI

PAPUA
NEW GUINEA

SOLOMON
ISLANDS

ANGOLA
ZAMBIA
MALAWI
COMOROS
ZIMBABWE
MOZAMBIQUE
MADAGASCAR
MAURITIUS

Indian Ocean

Reunion
(FR.)

Tropic of Capricorn

TUVALU

VANUATU

WESTERN
SAMOA

FIJI

NAMIBIA
BOTSWANA

SWAZILAND

AUSTRALIA

TONGA

LESOTHO
SOUTH
AFRICA

30

BIH. = BOSNIA AND HERZEGOVINA
C.A.R. = CENTRAL AFRICAN REPUBLIC
CROATIA
ESTONIA
LATVIA
LITHUANIA
SLOVENIA
U.A.E. = UNITED ARAB EMIRATES

Macedonia
Montenegro
Serbia

NEW
ZEALAND

Macedonia has proclaimed independent statehood
but has not been formally recognized as a state
by the United States.

60

Serbia and Montenegro have asserted the formation
of a joint independent state, but this entity has
not been formally recognized as a state by the
United States.

Antarctic Circle

Boundary representation is
not necessarily authoritative

Antarctica

30
60
90
120
150
180

802172 (R00350) 9-93

INDEX

Covered elsewhere: Cases are indexed separately in the "Table of Cases." Treaties, resolutions, and miscellaneous agreements are indexed separately in the "Table of Treaties/Resolutions/Miscellaneous Instruments" (including the ICJ Statute). This index does *not* generally include references to countries.

Names of individuals: The Index includes the names of scholars whose works are referred to in the text (but not footnotes or bibliographies). A name without a parenthetical country designation refers to a classical scholar from another era. Heads of State are listed under the subheading Presidents/Rulers.

Abbreviations used in this Index: ADR—Alternative Dispute Resolution; CSCE—Conference on Security and Cooperation in Europe; ECSC—European Coal and Steel Community; EU—European Union; GATT—General Agreement on Tariffs and Trade; ICAO—International Civil Aviation Organization; ICC—International Chamber of Commerce; ICJ—International Court of Justice; ICSID—International Centre for the Settlement of Investment Disputes between States and Nationals of Other States; IL—International Law; ILC—International Law Commission; NAFTA—North American Free Trade Agreement; NATO—North Atlantic Treaty Organization; NIEO—New International Economic Order; NGO—nongovernmental organizations; OAS—Organization of American States; OAU—Organization of African Unity; PCOA—Permanent Court of Arbitration; PCIJ—Permanent Court of International Justice; PRC—People's Republic of China; UN—United Nations; UNCED—United Nations Conference on Environment and Development; US—United States; WIPO—World Intellectual Property Organization; WTO—World Trade Organization.